routledge international encyclopedia of queer culture

The *Routledge International Encyclopedia of Queer Culture* covers gay, lesbian, bisexual, transgender and queer (glbtq) life and culture post 1945, with a strong international approach to the subject.

The scope of the work is extremely comprehensive, with entries falling into the broad categories of Dance, Education, Film, Health, Homophobia, the Internet, Literature, Music, Performance, and Politics. Slang is also covered. The international contributors are from a wide array of backgrounds: scholars, journalists, artists, doctors, scientists, lawyers, activists, and an enormous range of ideologies and points of view are represented. Major entries provide in-depth information and consider the intellectual and cultural implications of their subjects in a global context. Information is completely up to date, including full coverage and analysis of such current or ongoing issues as same-sex marriage/civil union and the international AIDS epidemic. Additionally, there are important appendices covering international sodomy laws and archival institutions, which will be of great value to researchers. The encyclopedia is fully cross-referenced and many entries carry a bibliography. Where possible World Wide Web references are given. There is a full index.

The combination of its wide scope, determined international coverage and appendices make the *Routledge International Encyclopedia of Queer Culture* a uniquely ambitious work and an extremely rich source of information. It is a priority addition for all libraries serving scholars and students with an interest in glbtq culture, history and politics across the disciplines.

David A. Gerstner is Associate Professor, Department of Media Culture, City University of New York, College of Staten Island, USA.

routledge international encyclopedia of queer culture

edited by
david a. gerstner

Routledge
Taylor & Francis Group

LONDON AND NEW YORK

First published 2006
by Routledge
2 Park Square, Milton Park, Abingdon, Oxon, OX14 4RN

Simultaneously published in the USA and Canada
By Routledge
270 Madison Avenue, New York, NY 10016, USA

Routledge is an imprint of the Taylor and Francis Group, an informa business

© 2006 Routledge

Typeset in Bembo and Helvetica by Taylor & Francis Books
Printed and bound in Great Britain by MPG Books Ltd, Bodmin

British Library Cataloguing in Publication Data
A catalogue record for this book is available from the British Library

Library of Congress Cataloging in Publication Data
A catalog record for this book has been requested

ISBN10: 0-415-30651-5
ISBN13: 978-0-415-30651-5

In Memory of Sarah Pettit and Riyad Wadia

contents

introduction

> All of us failed to match our dreams of
> perfection. So I rate us on the basis of our
> splendid failure to do the impossible.
>
> William Faulkner

William Faulkner, the dandy-author of
Oxford, Mississippi, who was influenced by
a queer *fin de siècle* aestheticism in his youth,
remained particularly fond of 'splendid' or
'magnificent' failures, especially when he
spoke about the fictional worlds he created.
In Yoknapatawpha County, where existence was measured by endurance, Faulkner's characters struggled against fate and
the cultural forces determined to contain
their desires. Yet, Faulkner's declaration of
failure articulates his inability to describe
with any accuracy the entirety that defines
Yoknapatawpha and its residents. What is
truly splendid about this failure, however, is
Faulkner's aesthetic gesture, his hope to
grasp as much as possible the richness of
experience and presence his characters
inhabit. The *Routledge International Encyclopedia of Queer Culture* is a splendid failure as
well, since its richness lies in its hope to
achieve the impossible. What it does
achieve, however, is quite splendid!

When this project on international queer
culture began, Faulkner came to mind as I
and the consultants on this work considered
a patch of land much larger than Yoknapatawpha County. How does one possibly
cover such a wide, diverse, and vast world
of queer cultural production on the inter-

national stage? Is it even worth the effort to
embark on such a venture when the project
is set to fail from the outset? From the
energies and response this collection generated – from consultants to contributors to
editors to colleagues – the answer was
an enthusiastic yes! Whereas Faulkner's
encouragement about failure resonated
throughout the compiling of the encyclopedia, his conclusion that people merely
endure begged some rethinking. Indeed,
though global queers often endure, they
also (as this collection reveals) *do*.

QUEER PRACTICES

The initial and, perhaps, most challenging
question in putting this encyclopedia together was how to address global gay, lesbian,
bisexual, transgender, and queer (glbtq)
cultures, given that the study, politics, and
institutions supporting glbtq practice have
been framed by a North American-Western
European hegemony. One might argue, at
the outset, that since the end of World War
II (the historical divide that serves as the
brief for this collection) and the United
States' cultural-ideological dominance á la
the Marshall Plan, the very concept of a
'contemporary' glbtq culture takes hold as
de facto Western. Such arguments, however,
neglect centuries of global queer practice at
work in non-Western societies, the traces
of which remain significant across cultures,
including so-called 'first world' countries.

ix

To be sure, one can argue, alternatively, that contemporary Western glbtq cultures derive much from 'non-Western' glbtq (and otherwise) cultures. The entries here clearly demonstrate that although an artificial privilege of authority is often assigned to scholars, activists, politicians, and artists in North America and Europe, we do well to consider the historical migration of cultural practices, and forgo assertions of historical firsts determined by national boundaries.

Yet, given the economic, political, and institutional power that North American and European queers wield in glbtq quarters, the question remained prescient, if not over-arching, since the very collection here is produced by a major American-British press. The consultants and contributors were thus extremely instrumental in shaping the coverage of the material to assure that a truly international scope was met. Needless to say, our success at compiling these entries was restricted by the historical timeframe of the project (post-1945), the limitations of space, and identifying writers to take up the job.

The enormity of the project raised another important issue: focus. In what way might we depict the detailed workings of worldwide queer culture while, at the same time, producing an encyclopedia that glossed the larger concepts and ideas that demarcate a global glbt-queer space? As the entry list grew and submissions were submitted what became clear was the *work* of queer people. For many historical reasons, as well as the sheer pleasure of it, queer people produce. We make art, we change the terms of politics, we erotically explore the phenomenon of the body, we challenge systems and authority – quite simply, we don't stop doing. A perusal of the entry list here indicates but a sampling of queer practice that should certainly worry those who wish for the erasure of gays, lesbians, bisexuals, and transgenders from the social and historical radar. Queer culture and desire is indeed everywhere; it is impossible to bind its dynamic force by religious force, political diktat, or other forms of insidious heterosexism and violent homophobia. The collection's focus, therefore, highlights the do-ers and their activities in the many diverse ways queers carve their individual and collective presence. In the sphere of the international 'culture industry' (and I use these terms in the broadest theoretical and historical contexts) queers are quite literally everywhere. (Pardon the cliché: We're here. We're queer. Get used to it.)

QUEER: NOTES ON TERMINOLOGY

With the rise of gay and lesbian studies in academia, especially during the 1990s in North America and England, the historical framework for the homosexual movement as a political entity and cultural force took shape around the Stonewall Riots in New York City. This historic event in 1969 subsequently stood as a marker that delineated a pre- and post-Stonewall era, a divide one might arguably pose as the movement out of the closet and into the public arena. But as many historians demonstrate, this break was never so neat and tidy: the history of non-heterosexual desire and the socio-cultural practices it enabled is longstanding, diverse, and transforms both pre- and post-Stonewall eras. Nonetheless, for the Western gay and lesbian political movements, Stonewall was a – if not *the* – moment of political coming-into-being.

Thus, the authority of this history confirmed the currency of the term 'gay.' Its rise in political and economic value ushered in a significant force in a marketplace economy as well as the halls of local, state, and federal governments. Yet, the privileging of this term – with its presumed focus on the male, the white, the middle-class, and the Western – neglected the broad range of sexual practices that cut across race, class, gender, and nation. Moreover, 'gay' ran the risk of essentializing the heterogeneous composition of sexuality.

Queer theorists in the 1990s took to task the use of such singular labels that defined movements such as 'gay' and 'lesbian'. This critique was vital to a rethinking of who was invited to be included under the umbrella of these categories. In this way, queer studies opened a forum for a more complex discussion of bisexuality and transgenderism. By the turn of the century, 'queer' had not only cemented itself as a cottage industry for academic publishing and the popular media; it also found itself mired in similar critiques of essentialism and political dogmatism. It is no easy thing to claim radical difference and sustain it under the terms of global capitalism.

For the purposes of this collection, however, 'queer' provides *at this historical juncture* a means to view the practices of international culture that have been galvanized around the pleasures and struggles of non-heterocentric sexuality. 'Queer' also recommends sexual identities not necessarily dependent upon the Western assertion of the 'gay' movements in 1969 while, at the same time, signaling the importance of terms such as 'gay', 'lesbian,' 'bisexual', and 'transgender'.

THE ENCYCLOPEDIA

> Revolution is not a one-time event.
>
> Audre Lorde

The aim of this Encyclopedia is to emphasize international queer cultural production. It seeks to foreground queer lives from around the world, the materials they produce, and the socio-political-cultural effects left in their wake. It is not meant to be definitive. Such a brief is, needless to say, impossible. Nonetheless, *over 1000 cross-referenced entries* are included here, along with *three appendices*, providing a look into the splendid doings of queers around the world. Given the ever-growing academicization of glbtq studies and the pop-culture phenomenon of 'queer', the Encyclopedia serves as a significant resource for both professional researchers and the general reader.

It is inevitable, of course, that the question will be asked: 'what about. . .?' In fact, the 'what about' question released an avalanche of possibilities when the consultants set to work in the early stages of this project. Often, for reasons beyond our control (such as writers unable to complete an entry or the difficulty of finding writers to write about queer issues in the first instance), some entries are not included here. Entries on Walt Whitman and Oscar Wilde, however, were consciously omitted since, even though these figures are formidable forces in post-1945 culture, they have significant coverage in multiple sources (most probably in a book standing next to this one on a library shelf).

As far as possible, then, the collection sought to demonstrate the people and issues that generate queer culture as an international phenomenon in the post-World War II era. Though North American and Western European entries are found here, special attention was paid to identify queer practices in places such as India, China, Japan, Poland, Lithuania, Africa, Bolivia, and other global sites that are neglected in Western discourse or, more tellingly, not situated on the same dais. By placing these cultural goings-on in the same venue, it is our hope that the inter-relationships as well as the important differences provide provocative discussions, complex alliances, and opportunities for more work and political activities to be produced beyond a nationalist logocentrism.

The weight given to certain categories in the collection may appear surprising to some. Film, video, poetry, and literature, for example, proved tremendous in the amount of work produced in queer cultures. The reasons for this are many. In recent years film and video, especially, have become popular tools in both the telling of queer stories and political activism. As the technology to record events becomes less expensive and more readily accessible, more and more queers turn to video as a means to explore their experiences. But film and the literary arts have had an outstanding and long relationship in global queer cultures. These art forms have unquestionably played key roles in queer representation, indeed since the end of the Second World War if not before.

Political history and activism is undoubtedly a major scene for queer activity around the world. From local community support and stratagems to international political rallies, queers continually prove extremely savvy and adept at moving agendas on human rights, equality, community empowerment, and, most significantly, AIDS. In the annals of political history, glbtq organizations are/were revolutionary in the directing institutional response to the pandemic. Wrestling with economic and moral barriers, international organizations such as ACT UP changed the face of a disease that would have proven far more devastating without glbtq intervention.

What is most striking about the encyclopedia's collection of materials is the way different forms of cultural production and lives intersect. As the cross-referenced entries indicate, queers connect on many different levels. The history of political activism, for example, finds connection with the art world, media, and technology. From dance to science to the Internet to theatre the stakes in these intersections for queer-everyday lives are high. The significance of the Internet in this light cannot be overestimated, particularly on a global platform. The immediacy of this technology excitingly forges unique inter-relationships between the science and the arts, education and political activism, religion and sexual identity. The encyclopedia clearly demonstrates worldwide queer culture as multifaceted and stirring in its ability to transform lived experience by simultaneously engaging a broad, if not creatively disparate, array of disciplines and institutions. It is the hallmark of queer culture to conceptually and continually engage diverse and what often appear to non-queers as incompatible possibilities to create a revolution. Audre Lorde realized this and held steadfast to its promise: Revolution is not a one-time event.

The Encyclopedia is certainly a splendid failure in that the revolutionary possibilities discovered here are yet to come and do not end with one grand event or categorization. What is absent here is only a reminder that more volumes of encyclopedias will always be needed since queer culture is always a work in progress, with many more revolutions set to occur.

A NOTE ON APPENDICES

The *three appendices* included in this encyclopedia provide the reader with international resources at several different levels: developing research, understanding key areas of the world political and legal climate, and connecting queers with organizations in their region.

The first appendix is *an annotated list of glbtq archives around the world*. A wealth of archival material is readily available across the globe; the appendix should prove most useful for anyone seeking to research the documents of glbtq culture. The second appendix, *a compilation of international sex laws*, serves as a guide with the important caveat that the legalities of queer sexual practice change quickly. Therefore, a link to a web site will ensure the reader's access to up-to-date information. The third appendix is *a selection of international political and community-based organizations* around the world and offers a brief description of their function and activities. Its aim is to indicate the range of organizations available in various regions.

The encyclopedia of information collected in this volume makes one thing very certain: queers (to borrow from contemporary queers) were never 'being boring'.

acknowledgements

This collection has benefited greatly from its consultants and contributors, all of whom were marvellous and dedicated to seeing this project through. I also want to thank John Forde, Mark McLelland, Cynthia Chris, Edward Miller, Dwight McBride, Francisco Soto, Kate Aker, Stephen J. Thompson and especially Sally Milner for stepping up to plate at critical moments. Gerard Greenway approached me what seems decades ago to edit this volume. His support and enthusiasm for this work is very much appreciated. I especially want to thank Kristen Holt for holding the editorial fort and assuring that the Encyclopedia was completed on time. An editor of Kristen's sort is hard to come-by.

DAVID A. GERSTNER

consultant editors

Pedro Albornoz, *Instituto Normal Sedes Sapiente, Bolivia*

Paal Bjorby, *Norway*

Fabio Cleto, *University of Bergamo, Italy*

Laura Doan, *University of Manchester, UK*

Alex Doty, *Lehigh University, USA*

Marc Epprecht, *Queen's University, Canada*

David Foster, *Arizona State University, USA*

Gabriel Gomez, *Chicago State University, USA*

Renée Hoogland, *University of Nijmegen, The Netherlands*

Amit Kama, *Open University of Israel*

Surina Khan, *USA*

Mark McLelland, *University of Queensland, Australia*

Tim Meade, *British Embassy, Russia*

Yasmin Nair, *USA*

Marc Siegel, *Germany*

Michelangelo Signorile, *USA*

Jo Smith, University of Auckland, *New Zealand*

Göran Söderström, *Lund and Stockholm Universities, Sweden*

Venus, *Skindog Productions, USA*

Ken Wong, *University of Hong Kong*

contributors

James N. Agar
University College London

Graeme Aitken
Editor, The Penguin Book of Gay Australian Writing

Pedro Albornoz
Universidad Católica Boliviana and Universidad Privada Boliviana

Jose B. Alvarez IV
University of Georgia

Alessandro Amenta
University of Milan

Eric D. Anderson
State University of New York, Stony Brook

Melissa Anderson
New York

Agnes Andeweg
Centre for Gender and Diversity, Maastricht University

Monia Andreani
University of Urbino

Jeffrey Angles
Western Michigan University

John Aravosis
Washington, DC

Francesca Palazzi Arduini
Essayist

Monica Baroni
Italy

Geoffrey W. Bateman
Center for the Study of Sexual Minorities in the Military

Chris Bell
University of Illinois at Chicago

Alina Bernstein
Tel Aviv University

Jay Blotcher
Journalist, writer and visual artist

Tom Boellstorff
University of California, Irvine

Pamela Booker
New York

Anita Brady
University of Otago

Catherine R. Burke
freelance library researcher and indexer

Kellie Burns
University of Otago

Chris Byrne
Gay City News

Cünyet Çakirlar
Istanbul Bilgi University

Eduardo Alfonso Caro
Arizona State University

David Carter
Writer

Giacomo Cesaretti
Italy

Ta-wei Chi
University of California, Los Angeles

Catherine Clay
Lancaster University

Fabio Cleto
University of Bergamo

H.G. Cocks
Birkbeck College, University of London

Richard Cornwall
Middlebury College (emeritus)

Rachel Cowgill
University of Leeds

Fabio Croce
Writer, publisher and editor

Vicki Crowley
University of South Australia

Kathleen M. Cumiskey
College of Staten Island, City University of New York

Michael DeAngelis
DePaul University

Thomas F. DeFrantz
Massachusetts Institute of Technology

Alex Doty
Lehigh University

Vilius Rudra Dundzila
Harry S Truman College, City Colleges of Chicago

Jeffrey Edwards
Roosevelt University

Alberto Emiletti
Italy

Marc Epprecht
Queen's University, Canada

Serap Erincin
Graduate Center and Baruch College, City University of New York

Brett Farmer
University of Melbourne

Melissa A. Fitch
University of Arizona

Stephanie Foote
University of Illinois at Urbana-Champaign

John Forde
Freelance journalist and writer

David William Foster
Arizona State University

Silvia Francolini
Librarian, Lausanne, Switzerland

Massimo Fusillo
Italy

Gustavo Geirola
Whittier College

David A. Gerstner
College of Staten Island, City University of New York

Shohini Ghosh
India

Keith Goddard
South Africa

Gabriel Gomez
Chicago State University

Sean Griffin
Southern Methodist University

Robin Griffiths
University of Gloucestershire

Aeyal Gross
Tel-Aviv University

Jaime Harker
University of Mississippi

Jarrod Hayes
University of Michigan at Ann Arbor

Peter Hegarty
University of Surrey

Daniel Hendrickson
Berlin

Terrell Scott Herring
Pennsylvania State University

Stephen Hicks
University of Salford

Kristen Holt
New York

Trevor Hope
Bilkent Unviersity

Jim Hubbard
ACT UP Oral History Project

Andy Humm
Gay USA

Michael Hurley
La Trobe University

Mikel Imaz
State University of New York at Plattsburgh

Peter A. Jackson
Australian National University

Rebecca Jennings
University of Manchester

Amit Kama
The Max Stern Academic College of Emek Yezreel

Surina Khan
Women's Foundation of California

Martin Kich
Wright State University, Lake Campus

Travis Kong
Hong Kong Polytechnic University

Matthew Krouse
Mail and Guardian Online, Africa

David Kurnick
Columbia University

Lisa Y.M. Lam
University of Illinois at Urbana-Champaign

Stephanie Lee
University of Hong Kong

Dafna Lemish
Tel Aviv University

Loykie Loÿc Lominé
University of Winchester

Denilson Lopes
University of Brazil

David M. Lugowski
Manhattanville College

Michael Luongo
Freelance journalist, New York

Jan Magnusson
Göteborg University

Anthony Manion
Gay and Lesbian Archives, South Africa

Giora Manor
Israel

Fran Martin
University of Melbourne

William Martin
University of Chicago

Kym Martindale
Falmouth College of Arts

Cris Mayo
University of Illinois at Urbana-Champaign

Mark McLelland
University of Queensland

Maaike Meijer
Maastricht University

Edward Miller
City University of New York

Stephen D. Miller
University of Massachusetts, Amherst

Alida M. Moore
University of Mississippi

Yasmin Nair
Academic and activist

Caryn E. Neumann
The Ohio State University

Jean Bobby Noble
University of Victoria, Canada

Chris Nuzzi
College of Staten Island, City University of New York

J. Todd Ormsbee
San Jose State University

Gilad Padva
Film and TV Department, Tel Aviv University, Israel

Pamela Pattynama
University of Amsterdam

David Pendleton
University of California, Los Angeles Film and Television Archive

Daniel Enrique Pérez
Arizona State University

Michael J. Pinfold
University of Gloucestershire

Gian Piero Piretto
Milan State University

Marco Pustianaz
University of Eastern Piedmont

Michael Quieto

Graeme Reid
University of the Witwatersrand

Lynette Reini-Grandell
Normandale Community College

John Paul Ricco
University of Nevada, Las Vegas

Adrian Rifkin
London

Sasha Roseneil
University of Leeds

Joseph Salvatore
New School University

Bea Sandor
Hungary

Trino Sandoval
Phoenix College

Paul Schindler
Gay City News

Ward Schrijver
Amsterdam

Kanishka Sen
Ohio Northern University

M. M. Serra
Film Co-op, New York

Moshe Shokeid
Tel Aviv University

Wren Sidhe
UK

Carolyn Skelton
University of Auckland

Anneke Smelik
Radboud University Nijmegen

Jo Smith
University of Auckland

Chantal Stoughton
Writer and subeditor, newspapers and magazines, Japan, Hong Kong, and the United Kingdom

Kirsten Moana Thompson
Wayne State University

Geraldine Treacher
Ministry of Education, Aotearoa/New Zealand

Amanda Udis-Kessler
The Colorado College

Ruth Vanita
University of Montana

Venus
Skindog Productions, USA

João Luiz Vieira
UFF-Universidade Federal Fluminense, Brazil

Nina Wakeford
University of Surrey

Robert Wallace
York University

Lee Walzer
Attorney and author

Katherine Watson
Manchester Metropolitan University

Thomas Waugh
Concordia University

Peter Wells
Author and filmmaker

Michael Williams
University of Southampton

Joseph Wlodarz
University of Rochester

Day Wong
The Hong Kong Polytechnic University

Ken Wong
University of Hong Kong

Michael T. Wong
Harvard University

Audrey Yue
The University of Melbourne

Ying Zhu
*College of Staten Island, City University
of New York*

Cui Zi'en
Beijing Film Academy

Ying Zhu
*College of Staten Island, City University
of New York*

Amalia Ziv
Tel Aviv University

thematic list of entries

ACADEMICS AND SCHOLARSHIP

BISEXUALITY

DANCE

ECONOMICS

FINE ARTS

HEALTH: BODY AND MIND

MUSIC

Hinduism
Hope and Unity Metropolitan Community Church
    (HUMCC)
Islam
Isvara
Judaism
Judge, Mychal
Metropolitan Community Church (MCC)
Paganism, queer
Pope, the and Catholicism
Priesthood
Synagogues, gay
Wicca
World Congress of Gay and Lesbian Jewish
    Organizations

SEX INDUSTRY

Bathhouse
Byrd, Robin
Halsted, Fred
Porn star
Pornography, Internet
Sex industry
Shaw, Aiden
Stryker, Jeff

SPORT

Ashe, Arthur
Bean, Billie
Beckham, David
Coaching and homophobia
Didrikson, Babe
Eurogames
Figure skating
Football, American
Galindo, Rudy
Gay Games
Johnson, Magic
King, Billie Jean
Kopay, Dave
Louganis, Greg
Navratilova, Martina
Roberts, Ian
Rugby
Soccer
Sport and glbtq culture
Swimming
Waddell, Tom
Wrestling

TELEVISION AND RADIO

Absolutely Fabulous
Are You Being Served?
Avengers, The
Ball, Alan
Batman
Brideshead Revisited
Buffy the Vampire Slayer
Cable television, gay
Cameron, Rhona
Carry On
Clary, Julian
de Leeuw, Paul
DeGeneres, Ellen
Dosokai
Dynasty
E! Entertainment Television
Early Frost, An
Emery, Dick
Florentine (Israel)
Flowers, Wayland and Madame
Forsyth, Bruce
Grayson, Larry
Herman, Pee Wee
Hudson and Halls
Inman, John
Julian and Sandy
Klafim Ptuhim
L Word, The
La Rue, Danny
Los Beltrán
Mutchnik, Max
Norton, Graham
Number 96
O'Donnell, Rosie
Oranges Are Not the Only Fruit
Queer as Folk
Queer Eye for the Straight Guy
Queer Nation (television
    programme)
Real World, The
Sex and the City
Simpsons, The
Six Feet Under
Smith, Anna Nicole
South Park
Star, Darren
Teletubbies
Television, Gay
Television talk shows
Thailand, television

alphabetical list of entries

A

ABBA

pop group

Comprising two performing and songwriting heterosexual couples from Sweden, the pop rock group ABBA rose to international fame with the single 'Waterloo' in 1974. Their undeniable appeal to the gay community since the era of **disco** has been attributed to the kitsch of their hypersentimental lyrics and excessively orchestrated harmonies. They also present a notable example of a group that did not require decades of historical distance to be perceived as the embodiment of **camp**. Hits such as 'Gimme Gimme Gimme (A Man After Midnight)' and 'Dancing Queen' have attained the status of gay anthems both despite and because of the overt heterosexuality of their lyrical address. The ABBA phenomenon continued into and beyond the 1990s, initiated by the **Erasure** cover release *Abba-esque* and perpetuated by the musical *Mamma Mia!*, which incorporates over a dozen of the group's songs in its loose narrative of heterosexual courtship.

See also: Musicals, theatre

MICHAEL DEANGELIS

ABERCROMBIE & FITCH

leisurewear company

One of America's most recognizable sportswear companies, as well known for its homoerotic photo spreads of adolescent male models as for its merchandise. Founded in 1892 by David T. Abercrombie, the store sold camping, fishing and hunting gear. In 1900 Ezra Fitch bought part of the company and the store name was officially changed to Abercrombie & Fitch in 1904. Abercrombie resigned from the business in 1907, and Fitch evolved the company into the largest sporting goods store in the world, outfitting clients who included Ernest Hemingway, Amelia Earhart, Howard Hughes, the Duke of Windsor and Presidents Taft, Harding and Kennedy. Following the lead of Calvin **Klein**, the company upped the sexual content in its quarterly catalogues and advertising campaigns, featuring homoerotic picture spreads of athletic male models photographed by Herb Ritz and Bruce **Weber**. Unsurprisingly, the strategy attracted a devoted gay following and the company's range of casual wear, fragrances and accessories are now popular with young gay and straight consumers alike.

JOHN FORDE

ABSOLUTELY FABULOUS

TV series

The brainchild of British comedian Jennifer Saunders, *Absolutely Fabulous* (1992–2003) achieved cult status for its witty satire of the fashion industry and the camp excess of its two female leads. The comedy centres on public relations executive Edina Monsoon (played by Saunders), whose relentless search for the latest fashion, lifestyle and diet trends is a continual source of irritation to her sensible, bookish teenage daughter Saffron. Competing for Edina's attentions is her best friend Patsy Stone (Joanna Lumley), an ageing model and party girl whose foul mouth, continual cigarette smoking, and Olympian-level alcohol and drug consumption creates continual chaos – and much of the show's comedy. Playfully satirizing the fickle excesses of the fashion industry and joyfully celebrating Patsy and Edina's uncouth hedonism, the show has attracted a dedicated fan base. Lumley's drag-queen-like performance as Patsy, complete with blonde beehive wig, bondage-inspired couture and a continual volley of bitchy tirades, has won the show gay cult status, including a drag tribute at the Sydney Gay and Lesbian Mardi Gras parade and a tribute techno single by the Pet Shop Boys.

Later episodes have played on the queer appeal of the characters, including flashbacks to Patsy having a sex change and wearing man-drag in 1970s Marrakesh. Another episode sees Edina searching for her estranged gay son in New York and being married to Patsy in a same-sex commitment ceremony. Plans to adapt the show for US television were discontinued, although its influence can be seen in a number of US sitcoms, including *Cybill* and *Will & Grace*.

See also: Camp; *Will & Grace*

JOHN FORDE

ACHMAT, ZACKIE

b. 1962

activist, filmmaker, scholar

Born in Johannesburg, Zackie Achmat is best known for his pivotal role in securing access to treatment at affordable cost to millions of HIV+ South Africans. Aside from being an AIDS activist, Achmat

played a key role in the formation and subsequent campaigns of the National Coalition for Gay and Lesbian Equality that successfully lobbied for the inclusion of sexual orientation in South Africa's constitution. He has also made his mark in gay and lesbian filmmaking and academic writing in South Africa. His documentary *Gay Life is Best* centred on the annual Gay and Lesbian Pride march held in Johannesburg in 1992. In 1999 he directed *Apostles of Civilised Vice, Parts 1 & 2*, a history of same-sex desire that investigates lesbian and gay experience and personalities in South Africa from colonial to contemporary times. *Apostles* expands on a seminal article with the same title published in 1993 that challenged conventional academic wisdom on the study of homosexuality in South Africa.

GRAEME REID

See also: AIDS; HIV

ACHTENBERG, ROBERTA

b. 1950

politician, activist

Roberta Achtenberg, born 20 July 1950 in Los Angeles, California, is a lesbian civil rights activist who became the first openly gay person to be confirmed by the United States Senate in a political post. After developing a successful legal practice, Achtenberg worked on the Anti-Sexism Committee of the National Lawyers Guild, developing a manual to help lawyers represent their gay and lesbian clients; the manual was later published as *Sexual Orientation and the Law* (1985). She was elected to the San Francisco Board of Supervisors in 1989. In 1992, Democrat President-elect Bill Clinton invited her to join his staff as Assistant Secretary of Housing and Urban Development. Her appointment was successful, despite rigorous opposition from conservative Senators, including Jesse Helms, who accused her of leading an 'insane assault on family values'. She left the post in 1995 to run in the primary for the San Francisco mayoralty, which she lost by a narrow margin. She lives and works in San Francisco with her partner and their children.

JOHN FORDE

ACKER, KATHY
b. 1943; d. 1997
writer, performer

In her eclectic cultural production, ranging across many areas (she wrote ten novels, a book of essays, poetry and rock lyrics, a screenplay and an opera libretto, and worked on musical, theatre, music and art performances), Kathy Acker was a bohemian celebrity of New York's Greenwich Village, and a highly influential figure for late twentieth-century metropolitan subcultures. Her punk, renegade, post-feminist work irreverently abuses and debunks tradition, sadistically renovating it in a voracious literary and artistic practice. Her mixture of autobiography, parody and exhibited plagiarism tackles the relations between language, identity, patriarchy and containment, so as to destabilize hierarchies, set values, myths and stereotypes. Wildly pornographic and deliberately disturbing the middle classes in its subject matter (unapologetically addressing in raw language topics such as incest, sadomasochist practices and suicide), and a committed follower of body-building, piercing and tattooing, Acker also explored the tensions between body and writing, enacting the metamorphoses of her own slippery identity and projecting herself in her powerful characterizations. She died in Tijuana in 1997.

FABIO CLETO

ACT UP (AIDS COALITION TO UNLEASH POWER)
activist organization

Despite a colourful street presence and a lasting impact on how the world viewed people with HIV and AIDS, ACT UP remains all but unknown to most beyond the AIDS community. Perhaps an insistence on outsider status fed this virtual anonymity. Perhaps it was its relatively brief lifespan; although a small number of chapters continue to operate, ACT UP commanded its greatest public attention from 1987 to 1994. During those years, scores of chapters across the globe collaborated on street demonstrations, break-ins at pharmaceutical companies and in the hounding of politicians. Nearly two decades after its founding, ACT UP remains an intriguing footnote to the history of the AIDS pandemic.

The creation of ACT UP is the stuff of legend: On 10 March 1987, author Nora Ephron was scheduled to speak at New York City's Lesbian and Gay Community Services Center. She cancelled due to illness, requiring a last-minute replacement. That person was Larry **Kramer**, a playwright, director and, most recently, the co-founder of **Gay Men's Health Crisis (GMHC)**, founded in 1982 as the first social service organization for people suffering from AIDS. Notorious for sparking the internecine fights that preceded his dismissal from GMHC, Kramer had grown weary of what he saw as bureaucratic foot dragging by board members. He felt that GMHC should have broadened its mandate to include reformation of the healthcare system and political structure that had marginalized People with AIDS (PWAs).

More than 41,000 Americans had succumbed to AIDS by 1987. HIV was, for most, a swift and terminal disease. The only drug available was AZT, a virulent compound originally developed to fight cancer. In his speech that evening, Kramer identified the inequities of American life that had served as the petri dish for the epidemic: homophobia, poverty, political conservatism, pharmaceutical industry greed and, not least, the imminent collapse of the overtaxed American healthcare system. If

3

people did not assume a proactive stance, Kramer continued, at least half of the people in that room would die within the decade. Two days later, an ad hoc group gathered for the first time. A week later, it had a name: The AIDS Coalition To Unleash Power (ACT UP). On 24 March 1987, the fledgling organization attracted nearly 200 people to Wall Street to protest the cost of AZT, which Burroughs Wellcome (the pharmaceutical company that produced it) priced at an unprecedented US$10,000 annually.

The dynamics of the first ACT UP demonstration would become a mainstay of the group's repertoire: the presence of people with AIDS front and centre, their Kaposi's sarcoma cancer lesions visible as a symbol of patient empowerment; the focus of dissent on big business, whose emphasis on profits prevented access to drugs by all but the rich; the graphically striking signs, banners and slogans, and the spirited chants; the civil disobedience scenarios, a lively hybrid of Yippie humour, gay camp and civil rights movement piety; and the feeding frenzy by the media, reluctant at the onset of the epidemic to properly cover its ravages, but now eager to record the circus-like chaos caused by these upstarts. News of this unapologetically confrontational new organization raced through the gay and lesbian community and beyond. ACT UP organizations independently sprang up in other cities across America and tackled the issues on their respective home fronts, pledging themselves, like the founding group, to political non-partisanship and non-violence. (A coalition of ACT UP chapters, called ACT NOW – the AIDS Coalition to Network, Organize and Win – was organized and thrived briefly.)

ACT UP was viewed as a gay and lesbian organization because of its origins. However, people of all sexual orientations and backgrounds joined. ACT UP attracted Marxist communists, 1960s anti-war marchers, 1970s feminists, Stonewall-era gay activists –

even wealthy white-collar workers who had recently seroconverted and realized they were now considered second-class citizens in Reagan's America. ACT UP attracted educators, community leaders, politicians and, sometimes, celebrities: Susan Sarandon and Patty Duke both addressed the founding group; artists Keith **Haring** and David **Wojnarowicz** participated in ACT UP/New York demonstrations. ACT UP/New York members included directors Todd **Haynes** and Tom **Kalin**, writers David Leavitt, Sarah **Schulman**, David Feinberg, Michelangelo **Signorile**, Douglas **Crimp** and John Weir.

To onlookers, New York's weekly meetings seemed an exercise in chaos; three-hour sessions offered speeches dense with acronyms and medical terms. Emotions often ran high. But ACT UP meetings were stringently moderated according to Robert's Rules of Order, which required a majority vote for all actions. Subcommittees were formed to address issues of housing for HIV poor, HIV in prison, treatment options and condom distribution in schools. Each week members would be assaulted – and enlightened – by enormous amounts of information. Flyers and medical data were distributed. Members would announce the latest bureaucratic or scientific outrage and the floor would vote on demonstrations. The success of the previous week's demo was gauged and strategies rethought. And, inevitably, members would learn of the death of another comrade who, only a few weeks, was at the barricades with them. Attendance would swell by the early 1990s to several hundreds.

ACT UP's ambitions were outsized from the start. To change the course of the epidemic, members would have to change the very structure of American life. The medical system required an overhaul, as did the economic system. A key target for reform was the United States Food and Drug Administration (FDA) approval system, a labyrinthine process that often took ten years from test tube to shelf. To that end, ACT UP chose the FDA's Rockville, Maryland, headquarters for its first national action. It attracted several hundred people from the fledgling ACT UP chapters nationwide, as well as supporters from more staid healthcare advocacy groups. Before the start of the working day on 11 October 1988, activists surrounded the building and prevented workers from entering. For nine hours, ACT UP maintained its assault, resulting in skirmishes with Maryland police, scores of arrests and, most significantly, national media attention.

However, ACT UP was more than a band of hotheads. Despite the public grandstanding and occasional irreverence, members had become self-educated medical experts. ACT UP's Treatment and Data Committee was eventually invited to sit down with leading AIDS doctors (including Dr Anthony **Fauci**) and pharmaceutical executives and to testify before Congressional panels. With such unprecedented access, major victories were attained quickly: the FDA approval system was expedited; a number of new AIDS drugs were brought to market; the price of AZT was lowered; national laws were passed to outlaw job and housing discrimination against people with HIV; new research began on the opportunistic infections that accompanied HIV; clinical trials of new drugs, which traditionally overlooked women and people of colour, finally enrolled people from these underserved communities; the Center for Disease Control (CDC) definition of AIDS was finally expanded to recognize seroconverted females; pharmaceutical giants were forced to lower prices and make HIV drugs available to sufferers in Africa; and ACT UP tactics were adopted by other patient empowerment groups.

ACT UP's impact on culture in general was equally visible. Many members of the New York chapter wore a popular uniform of bomber jacket or leather jacket, earrings, tight, cuffed jeans and Doc Marten boots.

This standard-issue garb became the new look of the urban homosexual. Within the decade, suburban heterosexuals would co-opt the look. ACT UP posters, t-shirts and buttons, rendered in bold colours and graphics, became a new standard for political art, ultimately bleeding over into mainstream advertising (see **AIDS, arts and**).

ACT UP pledged to break down barriers – sometimes literally – between those in power and those outside the gates of power. On 4 June 1989, for example, members of ACT UP chapters worldwide stormed the opening ceremonies of the International Conference on AIDS in Montreal, protesting the event's exclusion of PWAs. This bold action won ACT UP its first international attention. The next year, the International Conference in San Francisco was officially opened by ACT UP/New York member Peter Staley.

The group had its detractors. Some mainstream gay and AIDS organizations resented ACT UP's impolitic behaviour, feeling it hurt the community's chance for assimilation. Several groups cited ACT UP's autonomy that bordered on arrogance; the New York group did not often alert local mainstream organizations before travelling to protest in another state. Others pointed to the group's meagre participation by African-Americans and Latinos, and accused ACT UP of paying scant attention to those communities. But ACT UP had the Majority Action Committee, devoted to issues of colour. While men outnumbered women in the rank and file, ACT UP subcommittees targeted female issues. More prescient organizations saw ACT UP's arrival as a chance to play out a good cop–bad cop dynamic with the powers that be for advancement of the community agenda.

In 1989, ACT UP launched a protest that would become a landmark event. 'Stop the Church' would take on the mighty Roman Catholic Archdiocese, whose intervention in public policy had negatively affected AIDS education, gay rights and women's reproductive rights. Before the 10 December event, ACT UP allied with WHAM! (Women's Health and Action Mobilization) plus several gay, health, religious and education groups. 'Stop the Church' drew 5,000 protestors to St Patrick's Cathedral in New York City and garnered international media attention, most of it hostile. But ACT UP was now a force to be reckoned with. ACT UP chapters overseas soon displayed increased vigour. These allies faced a greater resistance than their American compatriots on issues such as gay life, intravenous drug use and prostitution. Particularly powerful were ACT UP chapters in Amsterdam, Berlin, Paris and Tokyo.

By the early 1990s volunteer members of ACT UP/New York and other chapters were wooed away to paying jobs with mainstream AIDS organizations. ACT UP/New York itself was becoming increasingly decentralized: subcommittees would spin off and become self-sustaining organizations like Housing Works, Treatment Action Group and Youth Education Life Line (YELL).

ACT UP was committed to non-partisan politics; both Republicans and Democrats were targets of ACT UP's group ire. But among the consistent targets were Presidents Ronald Reagan and George Bush, New York Mayor Ed Koch and North Carolina Senator Jesse Helms. The latter had his home covered in a giant condom by ACT UP members. A Labor Day 1991 march on President Bush's summer home in Kennebunkport, Maine would bring ACT UP its greatest vindication: a testy dismissal by President Bush during a presidential debate. Bush criticized the tactics of the group and emphasized Barbara Bush's time spent with HIV-infected babies.

As a jaded public grew inured both to the epidemic and the demonstrations of ACT UP, the groups accelerated their tactics. ACT UP/New York initiated a series of political funerals, in which the bodies of deceased members were marched through the streets of New York and Washington DC. On 11 October 1992, ACT UP members from all over the country converged on Washington and deposited the ashes of AIDS casualties on the White House lawn. (The renegade ACT UP/San Francisco assaulted a mainstream local AIDS advocate with cat litter and faeces to protest her salary and policies. Since ACT UP was pledged to non-violence, the action was decried by other chapters.)

While ACT UP's agenda grew larger and its subgroups more fractious, a cadre of members, frustrated at an increasing bureaucracy dogging group actions, broke off in early 1990 to dedicate direct-action tactics to issues of homophobia. The group went on to become **Queer Nation**.

Over the years ACT UP groups have withered away from a combination of battle fatigue, fundraising problems, and the misperception that the 1994 protease inhibitors (the so-called 'cocktails' which immediately slowed PWA fatalities in the United States and Western Europe) marked the end of the epidemic. More recently, conservatism has returned to the public AIDS debate, and scientists are wary about seeking government funding for studies involving gay men or sex workers. ACT UP/New York continues its work, albeit on a modest scale, but commanded headlines in the summer of 2004 with a nude protest outside the Republican Convention. However, weekly meetings, which once drew 1,000 people, now attract barely a dozen. ACT UP/DC and ACT UP/San Francisco soldier on in name only. However, ACT UP/Philadelphia continues to stage local demonstrations and promote treatment policy reformation. Housing Works, the spin-off from ACT UP/New York, remains an effective critic of city, state and federal governments.

How will the legacy of ACT UP be viewed? The AIDS activist movement has yet to be immortalized in a mainstream film or TV biopic, the dubious yardstick for American fame. However, the ACT UP

Oral History Project, founded in 2003 by Sarah Schulman and Jim Hubbard, has already filmed testimonials by 60 surviving members. This ongoing archival effort, available on the Internet, will provide generous material for a future scholar seeking to assess the work of this unique organization.

See also: AIDS; HIV

Web sites

http://www.actupny.org
http://www.actuporalhistory.org/

JAY BLOTCHER

ADAIR, PETER

b. 1943; d. 1996

filmmaker

Peter Adair, born 25 November 1943 in Los Angeles, was a documentary filmmaker whose work increased visibility and understanding about homosexuality and AIDS in America. Adair's first film *Holy Ghost People* (1973), which profiled fundamentalist Christians who test their faith by drinking strychnine and handling poisonous snakes, attracted the praise of anthropologist Margaret Mead. He is best known for his documentary *Word Is Out: Stories of Some of Our Lives* (1977). Based on Adair's interviews with 26 gays and lesbians over a period of five years, the film was acclaimed as the first positive portrait of the range and diversity of homosexuality in America. His other documentaries include *Stopping History* (1983), about anti-nuclear activism, *The AIDS Show: Artists Involved with Death and Survival* (1986), co-directed with Rob Epstein, and *Absolutely Positive* (1991), a ground-breaking portrait of 11 Americans living with AIDS. He died of an AIDS-related illness on 27 June 1996.

See also: AIDS

JOHN FORDE

ADDICTION / TWELVE-STEP PROGRAMMES

Beginning in 1935 with Alcoholics Anonymous, they now exist for many addictions, such as drug and nicotine abuse, and sexual compulsion.

MICHAEL PINFOLD

ADLON, PERCY

b. 1935

director

Percy Adlon is an inventive German screenwriter and director who has won international acclaim for his strong female characters and sympathetic depictions of lesbian relationships. Beginning his career as a documentary filmmaker for German television, he graduated to feature films with *Céleste* (1981), a drama about the relationship between gay writer Marcel Proust and his young female housekeeper. He achieved international success with *Bagdad Café* (*Out of Rosenheim*, 1987), starring German actor Marianne Sägebrecht as a tourist stranded at a California roadside diner, and *Rosalie Goes Shopping* (1989), again starring Sägebrecht as a spending-obsessed housewife, and featuring Brad Davis. His 1991 film *Salmonberries*, starred a young kd lang as an androgynous Eskimo who has an (unconsummated) relationship with a woman. Adlon was a contributing director to *Red Hot + Blue* (1990), a film of music videos based on the best-selling album.

JOHN FORDE

ADOPTION / FOSTER PARENTS

During the late twentieth century, lesbian, gay and bisexual (lgb) people began to see foster care or adoption as possible parenting options. Despite many obstacles, they approached childcare agencies, persevered with their applications, and, in many cases, have had children successfully placed in their care. However, this is complicated by law, childcare policy and practice.

In the United Kingdom lgb people are not legally barred from foster care in England or Wales, but in Scotland a couple of the same sex cannot be approved. The Adoption & Children Act 2002 allowed joint adoptions by same-sex couples, as well as continuing to allow individual lgb people to adopt. In the United States, individual states have different laws. Florida prohibits adoption by homosexuals, and restrictions are imposed by Mississippi and Utah. Foster care by lgb people is legal in most states but Arkansas prohibits it.

Pioneering studies in the UK (Skeates and Jabri 1988) and the US (Ricketts 1991) identified that many lgb carers were hidden from view because, at that time, so few were 'out'. These studies also noted that openly lgb people who applied to foster or adopt were subject to much greater scrutiny than their heterosexual counterparts. There was also a tendency to place only the most disabled and 'hard-to-place' children with lgb carers.

During the 1990s greater numbers of lgb people were open about their sexuality when applying to various childcare agencies, as published accounts demonstrate (Hicks and McDermott 1999). In addition, national or local support groups began to spring up. In the UK, the Lesbian and Gay Foster and Adoptive Parents Network (LAGFAPN) established groups based both in **London** (in 1989) and in **Manchester** (in 1994).

In the twenty-first century there is some recognition by agencies that they ought to move beyond treating all foster care and adoption applicants as 'the same', since lgb applicants and carers have concerns specific to their sexuality that need discussion and support. However, despite these attempts to treat lgb applicants fairly, there are still many examples of outright rejection and forms of discrimination, even though stud-

ies demonstrate the secure development of children of lesbian mothers (Tasker and Golombok 1997). There is a need for more support groups for lgb applicants/carers, social work practice guidance, training for childcare agency workers and associated professionals, as well as a baseline of legal equality.

Bibliography

Hicks, S. and McDermott, J. (eds) (1999) *Lesbian and Gay Fostering and Adoption: Extraordinary Yet Ordinary*, London: Jessica Kingsley Publishers. (A collection of personal accounts by lesbians and gay men involved in foster care and adoption, with an extended editorial essay which pulls together key themes as well as issues of research, law, policy and practice.)

Ricketts, W. (1991) *Lesbians and Gay Men as Foster Parents*, Portland: National Child Welfare Resource Center, University of Southern Maine.

Skeates, J. and Jabri, D. (eds) (1988) *Fostering and Adoption by Lesbians and Gay Men*, London: London Strategic Policy Unit.

Tasker, F.L. and Golombok, S. (1997) *Growing up in a Lesbian Family: Effects on Child Development*, New York: Guilford Press.

STEPHEN HICKS

AFRICA, NORTH: FRANCOPHONE LITERATURE

North African literature written in French after the 1950s features an abundance of gender non-conformity and non-normative sexualities. Rare is the widely known Francophone North African author who has not written at least one novel featuring marginal sexualities; several major authors have even made a career from sexual iconoclasm. More recently, openly gay and lesbian writers have also emerged. Representations of homosexuality are so numerous that one must consider whether this praise of sexual diversity has political implications beyond the realm of sexual politics. Whereas nationalist movements often closely guard dirty secrets to enforce political unity, writers from North Africa use sexual dissidence to contest official models of nationality that rely on specifically Islamic family values.

While North African writers wrote in French before the mid-twentieth century, the 1950s are considered foundational by literary historians. As nationalist movements gained momentum, writers revisited the cultural practices of their childhoods and contrasted these with the 'civilization' imposed through French education – and these narratives often include sexual discoveries that are not exclusively heterosexual. The narrator's cousin in *La Colline oubliée* (The Forgotten Hill, 1952), by the Kabyle Algerian writer Mouloud Mammeri, has a homoerotic relationship with a musician/dancer. In his 1953 *La Statue de sel* (*The Pillar of Salt*), the Jewish-Tunisian writer Albert Memmi describes collective play during which one boy performs fellatio on the others. Once a **bottom**, the Moroccan protagonist of Driss Chraïbi's *Le Passé simple* (*The Simple Past*, 1954) has become a **top**. Although criticized for not being political, these childhood narratives can be read as national allegories, in which the story of a not-so-heterosexual individual also recounts the history of a nation redefined in oppositional ways. Although sexual practices considered non-normative in the West may not be subversive when confined to private spaces in North Africa, the representation of such sexualities in a novel brings the most private act into public discourse, readable by insiders and outsiders alike.

Subsequent generations became more explicitly political, either in relation to national struggles or in opposition to oppressive post-independence governments. The best-known writers showcasing marginal sexualities are the Algerian Rachid Boudjedra and the Moroccan Tahar Ben Jelloun. In Boudjedra's often-criticized *La Répudiation* (*The Repudiation*, 1969), Rachid narrates his mother's repudiation to a French nurse/lover whose sexuality he considers abject (like his mother's) even as he desires her. His late brother Zahir, a homosexual, occupies a central place in this story, even if Rachid cannot completely understand Zahir's sexuality or his politics. A scene in which the entire family discovers Zahir having sexual intercourse with a friend on the roof-top terrace is one of the longest and most detailed, explicit and poetic descriptions of male same-sex intercourse in North African literature. Zahir also embodies opposition to a corrupt, patriarchal post-independence elite (personified by the father, Mr Prick). Since *La Répudiation*, Boudjedra has included male homosexual characters in a number of his novels, even after he switched to writing in Arabic: in the 1987 French version of *La Pluie* (Rain), the narrator has a lesbian aunt.

In Ben Jelloun's *La Prière de l'absent* (Prayer for the Departed, 1981), a major character recovers the repressed memory of an adolescent homoerotic friendship/love as the novel's characters return to their national origins to give a new-found baby his roots. *L'enfant de sable* (*The Sand Child*, 1985) and its sequel *La Nuit sacrée* (*The Sacred Night*, 1987) tell the story of Ahmed, a female baby who has been raised as a boy, who eventually marries a woman. After Ahmed later becomes a woman, s/he has erotic encounters with (other) women. The female narrator of *Les Yeux baissés* (Downcast Eyes, 1992) describes as part of her life story a homoerotic encounter with another girl that leads to a more sexual dream, which explicitly reveals sensual pleasure to be a source of feminist resistance.

While most such representations are of male same-sex desire, as Ben Jelloun and Boudjedra demonstrate, female homoeroticism is not totally invisible. In terms much less explicit than those described before, the feminist Algerian writer Assia Djebar stages a number of homoerotic moments within the women's *hammam* in *Ombre sultane* (*A Sister to Scheherazade*, 1987) and in the title story

9

of *Femmes d'Alger dans leur apartement* (*Women of Algiers in Their Apartment*, 1980). Although she would probably deny the label lesbian writer (as she denies those of woman, French or Algerian writer), Nina Bouraoui sets a lesbian love story in a Swiss all-girl boarding school in *La Vie heureuse* (Happy Life, 2002). In her previous *Garçon manqué* (Tomboy, 2000), a female narrator's refusal of a gendered identity parallels her refusal to be pinned down within a double nationality. In the novel *Bab el-Oued* (1995), Merzak Allouache includes a lesbian love affair in a context of women's restricted circulation after the 1988 riots in Algiers led to increased violence.

Allouache's novel was based on his film *Bab el-Oued City* (1994). Although he did not feel able to film this affair during the clandestine production in Algeria, where civil conflict had already escalated into armed struggle, the queeny Didine imitates American soap operas to the delight of semi-cloistered women in both versions. Allouache is thus part of a more recent extension of the political deployment of same-sex eroticism in resistance to fundamentalism. Perhaps no writer testifies to the dangers of such a critique more than Tahar Djaout, a journalist, poet and novelist who was assassinated in 1993. In *L'invention du désert* (The Invention of the Desert, 1987), a historical novel about the rise of the Almohads, the story of dynasty founder Ibn Tumart allegorizes Algerian civil conflict of the 1980s. In Djaout's version, Ibn Tumart consolidates his power by attacking cross-dressing *epheboi*, much to the disappointment of his contemporaries.

After such a rich tradition of supposedly heterosexual representations of queer sexualities, a handful of openly gay writers appeared on the literary scene during the 1990s. Beginning in 1995 with *L'enfant ébloui* (The Dazzled Child), the Moroccan Rachid O. has written four autobiographical novels in which he relates his cross-generational loves as a boy and his affairs with European men as a young man. In *Un 'Poisson' sur le balançoire* ('Fish' on a Swing, 1997) and its sequel *Une Promesse de douleur et de sang* (A Promise of Suffering and Blood, 1998), which are explicit enough to be characterized as erotica, Eyet-Chékib Djaziri recounts the boyhood loves and affairs of a bi-national, French-Tunisian protagonist. Any discussion of North African gay writing must also recognize Jean Sénac, an Algerian poet of European origins. In spite of his open praise for the love of boys, he was a member of the Ben Bella government after independence and, even after being marginalized once Boumédienne took power in 1965, went on to animate a poetry programme on the radio that was as popular as many TV shows. Whereas most Western scholars have emphasized the difference between modern homosexuality and the age- and gender-differentiated models of same-sex behaviours they attribute to Arab-Islamic societies, these gay writings have continued the work of their predecessors in blurring the binary distinctions upon which a constructionist understanding of homosexuality is founded.

Further reading

Hayes, J. (2000) *Queer Nations: Marginal Sexualities in the Maghreb*, Chicago: University of Chicago Press.

JARROD HAYES

AFRICA, SOUTH OF THE SAHARA: FILMMAKING

Gay filmmaking in Africa has been informed by the dual histories of post-colonial cinema on the continent and by post-Stonewall queer cinema production in the so-called developed world. But grass-roots production and documentary film and TV production have also added to the growing body of gay and lesbian film and television in Africa.

Out in Africa, the only dedicated gay and lesbian film festival on the African continent, first appeared in 1993, a year before South Africa's first democratic elections. In 1995 South Africans encountered the work of black filmmakers from the diaspora, when Isaac **Julien** attended the festival with his imagistic study, *Looking for Langston* (1989), revealing the gay aspect of the Harlem Renaissance. That year the festival also screened the road movie, *Days of Pentecost*, with a largely African-American cast directed by Lawrence Elbert, and hosted British, Indian-born filmmaker Pratibha **Parmar**. At the festival Parmar introduced the documentary, *Warrior Marks* (1993) – narrated by black novelist Alice **Walker** – about female genital mutilation in traditional African society. The work was the result of travels they both undertook to Gambia, Burkina Faso and Senegal.

In 2000 the same festival, now named the J&B Rare South African Gay and Lesbian Film Festival, showed Ernest Dickerson's drama, *Blind Faith* (1997), in which the gay son of an African-American policeman stands accused of the murder of a white youth after a homophobic incident. The African diaspora, even as removed as the United States, forms part of a localized African cultural psyche, and Dickerson's work is incorporated since he had functioned as a cinematographer for black filmmaker Spike Lee, who had filmed segments of *Malcolm X* (1996) in Africa.

South Africa's only gay and lesbian film festival has consistently provided a forum for discussion and workshops on gay and lesbian filmmaking in the African context. In 1999 HIV and AIDS activist Zackie **Achmat** and producer Jack Lewis screened their *Apostles of Civilized Vice, Parts 1 & 2* (1999) at the South African Gay and Lesbian Film Festival. This two-part documentary took into account same-sex desire from colonial times to the latter day using dramatic realizations of past-era liaisons. In the same year this documentary

was also aired by the public broadcaster SABC.

Lewis is a prolific documentary filmmaker in South Africa. His collaborations include *Sando to Samantha: Aka the Art of Dikvel* (1998), with Thulanie Phungula, the true story of Sando Willemse, aka Samantha Fox, a black drag queen, HIV+, turned soldier in the South African Defense Force. Another is *Goniwe's Sacrifices* (2004), about homophobia directed against a gay traditional healer. Lewis' most recent collaboration has been with Canadian filmmaker John **Greyson** in the making of the historical *Proteus* (2003), an interracial love story between a Dutch sailor and a black slave set on the Robben Island penal colony early in the eighteenth century.

It is the work of the late Tasmanian-born, Paris-based Philip Brooks (1954–2003) that has broken barriers and shown that the African subject in gay documentary can feature as participant and not objectified alien. His collaboration, *Woubi Chéri* (1998), with partner Laurent Bocahut, is described as the first film to give African homosexuals a chance to describe their world in their own words. Filmed in France and the Ivory Coast, the documentary delves into the lives of Abidjan's gay community, cross-dressing prostitutes and members of the Ivory Coast Transvestites Association.

Brooks also functioned as producer and professional supporter on the groundbreaking grassroots AIDS-awareness documentary series *Steps for the Future*. Included in this series was Beverley Palesa Ditsie's *Simon and I* (2002), about her friendship with activist Simon **Nkoli**. Another on a gay subject in this series is Brian Tilley's *It's My Life* (2001), about the trials and tribulations of AIDS activist Achmat. Brooks' final task was to produce the Brazilian-Portuguese feature film, *Madame Satã* (2002), directed by Karim Ainouz. Although it is set in the African diaspora, its depiction of Brazil's seedy Lada district, home to carnival legend João Francisco dos Santos, points to a growing consciousness around the experiences of the gay underclass in the underdeveloped world.

Guinean Mohamed Camara's *Dakan* (1997), meaning 'destiny', is, however, regarded as the first feature film with a gay plot from sub-Saharan Africa. It deals with the romance between two students in Conakry and begins with what has been described as 'the most sexually explicit opening scene in African cinema'. Public protests attested to this. In South Africa, besides *Proteus*, the feature film has had a cult makeover in the work of Stanimir Stoykov. In the manner of John Waters, his *Pussy* (2003) uses white drags to shock and parody mainstream feature film elements. His other works on similar themes are *Thrush* (2002) and *Leaps Ahead* (2002).

Ultimately it is the documentary that has triumphed as a tool of expression for gay filmmaking in Africa. Perhaps this is because there are greater possibilities in the distribution of works that can be broadcast, used as educational tools and which can be shown at film festivals. The wide range of gay and lesbian subjects includes the African hairdressing salon in Paulo Alberton's and Graeme Reid's *Dark and Lovely, Soft and Free* (2000), gay marriage in the late Mpumelelo Njinge's, *My Son the Bride* (2002) and white, gay, male military conscription under apartheid in Gerald Kraak's *Property of the State: Gay Men in the Apartheid Military* (2003).

One further work, Gretha Schiller's and Mark Gevisser's *The Man Who Drove with Mandela* (1998), elevated the documentary form to new heights by mixing fact and dramatized characterization. In the film, British actor Corin Redgrave plays gay white theatre director Cecil Williams, arrested while driving with Nelson Mandela in 1962. The documentary garnered a number of awards, including the Gay Teddy Bear for Best Documentary as well as Best Documentary at the Berlin International Film Festival.

The outright honesty of these documentaries shows the gay filmmaker as positive role model. This is somewhat undermined by the small, but growing, porn industry in Africa. Yet, even some of these products stand out – e.g., the South African-made *Jocks of the Bushveld* (1998) and French pornographer, Jean Noel Rene Clair's Abidjan-located *Black African Gold* (date unknown).

See also: Brooks, Philip and Laurent Bocahut; Camara, Mohamed; Ditsie, Beverley; Njinje, Mpumi and Paolo Alberton; Steps for the Future

MATTHEW KROUSE

AFRICA, SOUTH OF THE SAHARA: LITERATURE

A cliché of African nationalist discourses holds that homosexuality does not exist in Africa except where imposed by colonialism. Yet the corpus of African novels in French and English is sprinkled with references to just such a condition. Critics such as Daniel Vignal (1983) and Chris Dunton (1989) have argued that African literature most often confirms such clichés. In 'Out in Africa' (1997), however, Gaurav Desai turns the lens of literary study back on itself to demonstrate that this supposed lack of complexity in African novels may be due as much to the limitations of literary criticism as to those of the novels. Desai thus points towards a more complex approach to representations of homosexuality, one that highlights the queerness of African literature itself. More nuanced readings can thus show how African novels often destabilize the very clichés they might seem at first to confirm.

An instructive example is Wole Soyinka's *The Interpreters* (1965), read as homophobic by some yet reclaimed by others. This novel contains the most developed gay character in African literature – Joe Golder, a mixed-race African-American teacher.

Because of the other characters' intolerance, Vignal stresses the inability of Africans to understand Golder's sexual identity, while Dunton describes Soyinka's characterization of Golder as unsympathetic, albeit complex. Like others, Dunton suggests that Golder's homosexuality frustrates his desire to be more authentically black, because homosexuality cannot be truly African. Desai, however, distinguishes between the novel's representation of Golder and its characters' opinions to read Golder as sympathetic and highlight the parallel between both Golder's sexual and racial identities and his refusals to pass as white and straight. Whereas other critics blame the suicide of a Christian convert upon Golder after his attempt to seduce him, Desai points out how these critics are complicit in reproducing the very homophobic assumptions – instilled by Western Christianity – that propel this character to his death. Unlike the vast majority of the novel's critics, Desai also grants Golder the status of an eponymous interpreter – we could also call him a queer reader, for Soyinka provides not only an interesting representation of queerness, but also an allegory for reading, a queer model for interpreting African literature.

Like *The Interpreters*, some novels use an encounter with the West as a catalyst for introducing homosexuality. In Ama Ata Aidoo's *Our Sister Killjoy* (1977), the Ghanaian protagonist Sissie meets a married German woman who comes on to her in Europe. Because Sissie responds that such desires are not natural, some critics have read the novel as reinforcing the notion that homosexuality is a Western aberration. But during the attempted seduction Sissie returns in memory to her native village and remembers a missionary calling sodomy a crime while separating two African girls in bed together. Aidoo thus historicizes Sissie's response by pointing out that colonization actually imposed a specifically Christian homophobia. She also situates the

nationalist cliché that Africans are sexually purer than Europeans within the colonial discourse that characterized Africa as being in a state of nature and, therefore, uncivilized and ripe for the civilizing mission. The colonial associations of such characterizations are explicitly articulated in Camara Laye's 1966 *Dramouss* (*A Dream of Africa*), in which a Guinean protagonist does not understand the advances of a French man. When a French woman points out that he is a 'faggot' and explains what this word means, the horrified protagonist responds that such practices do not exist in Africa. It is the French woman, however, representative of colonial power, who voices the colonial cliché of Africa's sexual purity.

Some justifications of the homophobic cliché have cited a supposed lack of words in African languages to name same-sex desire. Anthropologists have nonetheless uncovered over 70 such terms. Of these, the Wolof *gor-djiguen* (man–woman) has appeared in several Senegalese novels: neighbourhood women in Mariama Bâ's *Un Chant écarlate* (*Scarlet Song*, 1981) gossip about a boy who prefers girls' play to that of boys and say that he will surely become a *gor-djiguen*. The term also occurs in Ken Bugul's *Le Baobab fou* (*The Abandoned Baobab*, n.d.), when the novel's female protagonist befriends a Belgian homosexual. Bugul offers the most direct refutation of the nationalist cliché when the narrator describes homosexuals from her native village who were also referred to as *gor-djiguen*. Bugul's association of Western models of homosexuality and the gender-differentiated model named by *gor-djiguen* challenges a number of binaries upon which constructionist models of a modern Western homosexuality are based: civilized/'primitive', modern/pre-modern, 'egalitarian' homosexuality/role-based same-sex behaviours and desires. She therefore questions the totalizing colonial notion of an African difference from the West, and this with a double-edged critique as she also contradicts the notion of an exclusive European homosexuality when pointing out that *gor-djiguen* were exclusively homosexual whereas her Belgian friend had been married.

As in much Francophone North African literature, sub-Saharan writers sometimes incorporate homosexuality into novelistic political critiques. Works of this sort include Yambo Ouologuem's *Le Devoir de violence* (*Bound to Violence*, 1968), Yulissa Amadu Maddy's *No Past, No Present, No Future* (1973) and Bessie Head's *A Question of Power* (1974), as well as others mentioned above. It would be easy to read these novels as exploiting abject presentations of homosexuality to elicit anti-colonial rage, but often homophobic characters are themselves subject to a political critique, especially when, although they were anti-colonial nationalists before independence, their Western education (which brought them into contact with European homosexuals to begin with) later allows them to join a corrupt elite.

It would be impossible to name here every African novel that mentions homosexuality. Vignal's bibliography contains 23 such works and Dunton's contains at least 32. Readers interested in pursuing further African representations are thus directed to these essays and their bibliographies.

See also: Africa, North: Francophone literature; Aidoo, Ama Ata; Head, Bessie; Ouologuem, Yambo; Soyinka, Wole

Bibliography

Desai, G. (1997) 'Out in Africa', *Genders* 25: 120–43.

Dunton, C. (1989) '"Wheyting Be Dat?" The Treatment of Homosexuality in African Literature', *Research in African Literatures* 20, 3: 422–45.

Vignal, D. (1983) 'L'homophilie dans le roman négro-africain d'expression anglaise et française' (Homophilia in Black African Novels in English and French), *Peuples noirs/peuples africains* 33: 63–81.

JARROD HAYES

AFRICAN QUEER STUDIES

Queer studies in Africa are concentrated in South Africa for political reasons. A glance at the list of clients who have recently made use of the Gay and Lesbian Archives of South Africa, the only academic resource of its kind in Africa, provides evidence of increased scholarly attention paid to same-sex relations in the area. Current research covers a wide range of topics, interrogated from various disciplinary perspectives. The existence of this research resource and the possibility for transparent research on same-sex sexuality is a consequence of South Africa's liberal constitution, adopted in the wake of political transition. South Africa's constitution represented a substantial break with a patriarchal past and provided a vision of a new order of gender equality. For the first time anywhere in the world, it also protected gays and lesbian from discrimination. This ushered in an era in which gay and lesbian communities are much more visible and where sexuality is an accepted topic for public discussion and debate, as well as providing a conducive site for research on homosexuality.

This situation is unique on the African continent. Certainly political leaders of countries bordering South Africa have been particularly vocal in their scathing public attacks on homosexuality as an 'un-African' perversion, something imported from the West. This explains why research in South Africa, while limited, is comparatively well established. The difference between old and new ways of understanding homosexuality in Africa can be characterized as a tension between traditional models that found ways of accommodating homosexuality provided it was concealed in a cloak of silence and discretion, and a modern, 'Western' emphasis on a vocal, rights-based identity politics.

For scholars working in Africa, historical source material on same-sex relations is to be found in the scattered accounts of missionaries, colonial doctors, travellers, explorers and anthropologists. Many of these contributions have been brought together in the edited collection, *Boy Wives and Female Husbands* (1998). Rudi Blys (1996) draws extensively on similar writings from the colonial period to demonstrate how the colonial project's obsession with race classification intersected with the stratification of sexual identities in the West. Blys' book, *The Geography of Perversion* (1996), provides an innovative way of reading colonial texts. Other sources are medical and psychiatric reports, court records and legal documentation. The limited scope and biased nature of source material remains an ongoing challenge for scholars. The fragments that do exist need careful contextual interpretation and a sensitive reading 'against the grain'.

Chris Dunton, in an essay entitled '"Wheyting Be Dat?" The Treatment of Homosexuality in African Literature' (1989), provides a survey of African fiction that deals with the subject of homosexuality pejoratively, as a symptom of the corrupting influence of the West. He also surveys novels dealing more positively with same-sex relations between blacks and whites while showing the conspicuous absence of any texts portraying non-pejorative homosexual relationships between African men or between African women.

Starting in the 1980s, and situated within labour studies, research on homosexualities in South Africa centred on sexual arrangements between men in mining compounds and prisons. This work was based largely on life-story narratives. Subsequently these interpretations were extended by other scholars who emphasized the possibility of same-sex desire beyond the sexual mechanics of deprivation and the absence of women that underpinned many of the 'situational homosexuality' arguments. The experience of women within the migrant labour system has been explored to a lesser extent, in the context of gift-exchange relationships entered into between older and younger women, known as '*mummies and babies*', in rural Lesotho. Research demonstrating the ways in which intimate friendships between women in Lesotho have been constrained by the identity category of 'lesbian' has provided further insight into women's same-sex intimacies.

Given the limited publishing opportunities, research findings are often made available in the grey literature produced by advocacy and activist groups. In this respect the Internet, with its promise of relatively easy access and user anonymity, also provides a useful and popular forum for the dissemination of ideas. **Behind the Mask** (www.mask.org.za), a continent-wide information web site, is used extensively by activists and researchers alike. In South Africa the publication in 1994 of *Defiant Desire* marked an important moment in the development of queer studies in that country, as did the establishment of the Gay and Lesbian Archives at the University of the Witwatersrand, three years later. In 2003 the International Association for the Study of Sexuality, Culture and Society (IASSCS) held its fourth bi-annual conference, 'Sex and Secrecy', for the first time in Africa. The conference provided a forum for academics working in sexuality studies from around the world. Significantly the initial findings of a research project on African women's same-sex experiences were presented at the conference. There are, however, limited opportunities for dissemination of research findings within academic courses in the South African academy and none elsewhere in Africa.

Bibliography

Blys, R.C. (1996) *The Geography of Perversion*, New York and London: Cassell.

Dunton, C. (1989) '"Wheyting Be Dat?" The Treatment of Homosexuality in African Literature', *Research in African Literatures* 20, 3: 422–45.

Gevisser, M. and Cameron, E. (1994) *Defiant Desire*, Johannesburg: Ravan Press.

Murray, S.O. and Roscoe, W. (eds) (1998) *Boy Wives and Female Husbands,* New York: St Martin's Press.

GRAEME REID

AFRIKA, TATAMKHULU ISMAIL

b. 1920; d. 2002

writer

South African poet and novelist Tatamkhulu Ismail Afrika's later works are characterized by an aggressive, ambivalent homophobia/homoeroticism. Afrika grew up in Cape Town where he was classified as a white person. He served in the Second World War, including three years as a prisoner of war. Upon his return to South Africa he became an early, radical anti-apartheid activist. In 1964 he converted to Islam, founded the militant group al-Jihad and spent time in prison, where rough forms of male–male sex were used by the state to intimidate political prisoners. Themes of self-doubt about his sexuality and the need to assert an appropriately heterosexual 'struggle masculinity' imbue his work. Short stories such as 'The Quarry' (in *Tightrope*) involve men who violently deny homosexual attraction yet at the same time voyeuristically and explicitly describe male physiques, genitals and even haemorrhoids. His 2002 novel *Bitter Eden* involves a love triangle between men in a Second World War prisoner of war camp.

MARC EPPRECHT

AGADATI, BARUCH

b. 1895; d. 1976

dancer

Modern dance in Israel came on the scene following the end of the First World War, when, in 1919, the first ship brought pioneers to Yaffo (Tel Aviv), including Baruch Agadati, a dancer with the Odessa Ballet.

Soon after his arrival in then British Mandatory Palestine, Agadati presented solo performances, called 'concerts', in which he danced a series of portraits representing men of contrasting characters from the Jewish Shtettel. Among the solos he choreographed in Israel was that of an Arab, an 'effeminate' dandy from Yaffo, who held a flower in his hand, and who, in spite of his refined airs, urinated on the stage back wall (a cultural habit in the Middle East then). This, of course, affronted the middle classes. He was the first bohemian in modern Israel.

GIORA MANOR

AGUILERA, CHRISTINA

b. 1980

pop singer

Born on Staten Island, New York, and raised in Wexford, Pennsylvania, Christina's ethnic roots are a cross between Ireland and Ecuador. Hers is a 'rags to riches' story of early talent show entries to internationally renowned, Grammy-award-winning singer/songwriter, and all at an extremely young age. The release of *Christina* in 1999 unleashed chart-toppers such as 'Genie in a Bottle' and 'What a Girl Wants', while crossover audiences emerged among Spanish-speaking Americans with the release of *Mi Refleio* (2000). She had a strong gay and lesbian following from the outset. An escape from the confines of 'cute girl singer' was effected with the release of *Stripped* (2002), which asserted an opinionated and up-front female sexuality (particularly with the track *Dirrty*, which interestingly draws upon gay male iconography in its accompanying video performance). Christina has won several awards including Best Female Performer at the MTV Europe Awards in July 2003.

MICHAEL PINFOLD

16

AIDOO, AMA ATA

b. 1942

writer

Ghanaian novelist, short-story writer, poet and playwright, Ama Ata Aidoo's work explores the social tensions in modern African society from an African nationalist and feminist perspective. Her 1977 work *Our Sister Killjoy* is an important contribution to destabilizing the stereotype of a heterosexually pure Africa threatened by a perverse, predatory West. In a first for an African novel, an African woman (Sissie) fantasizes about a sexual relationship with a German lesbian (Marija). Although she quickly expresses horror at the thought, Sissie sustains a decent and sympathetic relationship with Marija.

MARC EPPRECHT

AIDS

In 2003 the world witnessed the twentieth anniversary of the human immunodeficiency virus (HIV) epidemic. In 1995, with the licensing of Saquinavir as the first protease inhibitor and the advent of the 'cocktail', or highly active anti-retroviral therapy (HAART) and subsequent agents, the world recognized that it was possible to control viral replication and restore immunological health to those who were ravaged by HIV. Almost immediately, persons dying from HIV and AIDS treated with HAART were now living with the disease and returning to functional, productive lives. Buoyed up by enthusiasm, the medical community naïvely predicted that HIV could be eradicated from an infected individual following a period of treatment. Not only was this not true, a successful vaccine to protect uninfected persons has yet to be developed.

The implications for global culture are difficult to comprehend; while it is viewed as a 'controllable disease' in industrialized nations, it threatens entire economies in resource-poor nations. Here we will contrast the United States and Western Europe with the more global picture. While this is not expected to be a full chronology of the global HIV pandemic, it should help paint a picture of the complexity of HIV as it affects different cultures within our own regions as well as the world. The approach to controlling HIV and AIDS cannot be left to one individual or one government, but truly must be a concerted, integrated effort. The efforts of one individual cannot be minimized – by ourselves we might prevent a single infection (which might be our own); several may greatly affect local communities; and until we have a true cure, we have to emphasize prevention.

To better understand the numbers, several important concepts must be defined here:

- *Incidence*: refers to the number of times an event occurs in a given time, e.g., the number of new AIDS cases presenting each month or year, or the number of new HIV infections being detected during a specified period of time.
- *Prevalence*: means the total number of specific conditions in existence in a defined population at a precise point in time, e.g., the number of AIDS cases or number of HIV infections which have so far been reported in your own country/region/community.
- *Surveillance*: the systematic collection of facts (data) about disease occurrence is part of surveillance.

While the medical community has yet to successfully eliminate HIV from an infected person, significant and substantial technological and therapeutic advances have occurred over the past 20 years. The earliest and in some ways most important breakthroughs have included the identification of HIV as the cause of AIDS in

1983, and the ability to test for antibodies, and later viral components, in blood and serum. In doing so, the modes of HIV transmission were quickly elucidated, and theoretically we could stop the spread of HIV from person to person. Examples of effective campaigns have included the grassroots approach to safer-sex practices among gay males in San Francisco in the late 1980s (Lemp *et al.* 1997) and among injecting drug users in New York during the early 1990s (Des Jarlais *et al.* 2000); the successes of the AIDS Clinical Trial Group in prevention of mother-to-child transmission (MTCT) of HIV through the use of AZT (Connor *et al.* 1994; Sperling *et al.* 1996), then combination therapies with or without elective caesarean section, which can virtually bring the transmission rate to zero (Mandlebrot *et al.* 1998); the well-integrated national and community approaches to the ABC programme (Abstinence, Be Faithful, Use Condoms), which made substantial changes in the incidence of new-infection rates in Uganda (Mulder *et al.* 1995) and Tanzania (Ng'weshemia 1996); and the clear understanding that HIV can be spread percutaneously through infected blood or body fluids.

However, durable and sustained prevention, and implementation, in many nations have proved to be more elusive than anticipated. What previously was considered a disease of the gay male or injecting drug user population has spread, for example, into all parts of the United States. Approximately 800,000–1,200,000 persons in the US are infected with HIV – or 0.4 per cent of the US population (Centers for Disease Control and Prevention 2004). The number of new HIV infections remains at approximately 40,000 persons per year (Karon *et al.* 1996). The proportion obviously varies greatly by city and exposure risk demographics. For example, by the end of 2002, Washington DC had the highest AIDS rate in the nation at 162.4 per 100,000 population (Karon *et al.* 1996). Yet this

represents only a fraction of those who are HIV+ in that city.

It is estimated that of those infected in the United States, in spite of the availability of information and resources, only one-third are in a treatment programme; one-third are aware of their status but have chosen not to pursue therapy; and remarkably, one-third have yet to be diagnosed, largely because they do not identify themselves as being in an exposure risk group (Hellinger 1998). Additionally, there is an alarming resurgence of risk behaviours among young gay male populations (Dilley *et al.* 2002; MMWR 2004), and a persistent and disproportionate increase in new HIV cases among inner-city populations, persons of colour, women and rural populations. In fact, in some US subpopulations, the HIV/AIDS rates are not significantly different to those reported in developing countries. Such examples include: 1:4 gay men in New York City, Boston, Washington DC, San Francisco and Miami; nearly 2:3 of persons in methadone maintenance programmes in inner-city Baltimore; 1:3 women in Western Massachusetts migrant farm workers.

Worldwide, the number of persons living with HIV continues to expand, and World Health Organization (WHO) estimates now exceed 40 million persons (WHO 2004). These numbers constitute more than the entire population of the state of California as reflected in the 1 July 2003 US census (pop.: 35,484,453; *US Census Bureau Population Statistics 2003*). Approximately 14,000 new infections occur daily, resulting in approximately 5 million newly infected persons in 2003 according to the most recent UNAIDS/WHO AIDS Epidemic Update. Of these figures, between 2.1 and 3 million children under the age of 15 years have been infected with HIV, with 700,000 alone occurring in 2003. This is the equivalent of the combined populations of the cities of Boston (pop.: 589,000; US Census 2002) and Cambridge (pop.: 101,000;

US Census 2002), Massachusetts, becoming infected with HIV in one year. Globally, from 1999–2003, between 2.5 and 3.5 million deaths have been associated with HIV. The enormity of these figures is staggering. As regards those undergoing treatment, WHO estimates reported at the 2004 International AIDS Conference in Thailand indicated that 700,000 or just over 16 per cent of the HIV+ individuals in developing countries now receive anti-retroviral therapy.

Regionally, there are significant differences and commonalities associated with the groups at risk for HIV and its transmission. For example, HIV came later to Asia, and mostly through the drug trade and commercial sex workers. While no HIV infections were reported from the late 1980s to nearly 1990 in Asia, by 1997 HIV was well established across that continent. The countries of Southeast Asia, with the exception of Indonesia, the Philippines and Laos, have been comparatively hard hit, as has India. While the prevalence remains low in China, the total number of HIV+ persons exceeded 1 million as of 2003. Only a few countries in the region have developed sophisticated systems for monitoring the spread of the virus, so HIV estimates in Asia often have been made on the basis of less information than in other regions. Overall, about 6.4 million people are currently believed to be living with HIV in the region – just over 1 in 4 of the world's total estimated HIV+ population.

The picture is fragmented in Latin America, with most infections being in marginalized groups. Stigma around HIV, which is high in developed countries, appears to be even more pronounced in Latin America. Most men who have sex with men do not identify themselves as 'homosexual', while women who are found to be HIV+ are assumed to be involved with the commercial sex trade. The rapid increase in infected women shows that heterosexual transmission is becoming more prominent, with in some areas up to 50 per cent of the HIV+ population comprising women.

In Eastern Europe, a combination of economic policy changes as well as a collapse of the public health infrastructure in the post-Soviet era has resulted in large increases in HIV infections. Until 1994 mass screening of blood samples from people whose behaviour put them at risk for HIV showed extremely low levels of infection. As the Soviet Union dissolved, and former regional socialist economies made transitions to either complete autonomy or developed a free-market economy, HIV infections increased more than sixfold; indeed, by the end of 1997, 190,000 adults were infected, and by 2003 Russian estimates of 240,000 persons HIV+ contrasts with WHO/UNAIDS estimates of 750,000–1,200,000. The most common form of spread is through unsafe drug injecting and to a lesser extent through sex workers (Field 2004). The rise in new cases of STDs may reflect a dramatic increase in unprotected sex, which indicates that the risk of HIV infection is spreading rapidly throughout the general population of Eastern Europe.

Over two-thirds of all the people living with HIV in the world live in sub-Saharan Africa, accounting for more than 80 per cent of the world's AIDS deaths. An even higher proportion of the children living with HIV in the world are in Africa: an estimated close to 90 per cent. Several factors have been identified and are enumerated simplistically for this section. First, more women of childbearing age are HIV-infected in Africa than elsewhere. Second, African women have more children on average than those in other continents, so one infected woman may pass the virus on to a higher than average number of children. Third, nearly all children in Africa are breastfed, which accounts for nearly half of all vertically transmitted (mother-to-child) HIV infections. Finally, new drugs that reduce transmission from mother to child before and around childbirth are far less readily available in developing countries, including those in Africa, than in the industrialized world. In general, West Africa has seen its rates of infection stabilize at much lower levels than East and southern Africa, where the virus is still spreading rapidly, despite already high levels of infection. For example, in Botswana the proportion of the adult population living with HIV has doubled over the last five years, with 43 per cent of pregnant women in a major urban centre testing HIV+ in 1997 (*SAfAIDS News* 1997).

In Western Europe, HIV infection rates and epidemiology appear to be very similar to those in the US and Canada, with regional differences. The majority of new infections are concentrated among infecting drug users in the southern countries, particularly Greece and Portugal; the rest are through sexual exposures. Antiretroviral drug availability and more sophisticated obstetric services have accounted for very low MTCT rates. Although cases of HIV infections continue to rise in the industrialized world, cases of AIDS are falling. This downturn is probably the result of the new anti-retroviral drug therapies which postpone the development of AIDS and prolong the lives of people living with HIV.

The majority of infections outside of the United States and Western Europe are from heterosexual exposures, contaminated blood either by the sharing of needles among injecting drug users, contaminated blood supplies and associated factors, or seemingly innocuous healthcare practices such as the re-use of single-use items such as hypodermic needles and syringes. In the case of children, most infections still occur through MTCT during labour and postpartum; as indicated earlier, as many as 50 per cent of newborns infected with HIV acquire the infection through breastfeeding. It is by understanding these modes of transmission that we may develop prevention

strategies or interventions. One obvious strategy is the testing of the national or regional blood supplies and the utilization of single-use needles and syringes in healthcare settings. Despite this knowledge, failures do occur however. In the early 1990s one such glaring event was the knowing inclusion of contaminated clotting factor into pooled supplies in France. More recently, because of the collision of healthcare practices in central China, almost entire villages became infected with HIV. Reasons included the practice of purchasing serum in China; although the serum was screened for HIV, the blood cells that were separated were not, and were 'pooled' or combined with blood cells of similar blood type; also, the blood was transfused back into the donor so as not to make them overly anaemic from frequent donation (because they were paid for their serum, donors used the practice to supplement their income). The amplification and spread of HIV here is both obvious and astounding. Add to it the practice of using a syringe or needle multiple times without adequate sterilization between individuals and further transmission results. In such instances there are obvious operational interventions that would prevent transmission.

A variety of prevention strategies aimed at behavioural changes nonetheless have had an impact in some areas. For example, the ABC approach, when advocated and programmatically supported from a governmental level and combined with advocates at the grassroots level, has succeeded in decreasing new HIV infection rates among military conscripts in Thailand and young women in Uganda. The success of the programme was the integration of the message of 'abstain from sexual encounters until [you are] involved in a monogamous relationship; be faithful in that monogamous relationship; and if not [abstain or remain faithful], use a condom with encounters'. Unfortunately, some are taking sections of this programme out of context, even linking release of funding for prevention programmes only to specific behaviours such as abstention.

Perhaps the greatest impact has been in the ability to reduce HIV transmission rates in mother-to-child settings during childbirth and the first year of life from 17–35 per cent to less than 1 per cent. Following the impressive results of AIDS Clinical Trial Group (ACTG) 076 (the mother-to-child-transmission or MTCT interruption study utilizing zidovudine [AZT or ZDV, the first drug used to attempt to treat people with HIV in the mid-1980s]) during active labour, further gains have been made that virtually guarantee the prevention of HIV in the newborn child. Prior to delivery of the child, these include improved voluntary counselling and testing during pregnancy, maximizing maternal health through improved nutrition and supplemental vitamins, treating any pre-existing infections, effectively reducing the peripheral HIV viral load to less than 1,000 copies/mL (ideally, viral suppression to undetectable levels using available assessment procedures) and using Caesarean section if necessary. Following delivery, advances include the use of anti-retroviral agents (ARVs) for the newborn child, the substitution of a milk formula for breast milk, and with the MTCT-plus programme that recognizes the child's ultimate survival is based upon the continued health of its mother. However, in highly-endemic areas of the world, HIV testing and counselling is not readily available or performed for pregnant mothers, and access to medications that can be used to prevent MTCT or elective caesarean section are available to fewer than 1 per cent of pregnant women. Indeed, in many parts of the world, simply substituting breast milk for formula can actually increase child mortality rates because of a lack of access to a reliably clean water supply. Clearly, as a global neighbourhood, we should not see 700,000 children being infected with HIV annually.

The effectiveness of prevention activities that are focused on social or individual behaviour changes is variable, as outlined above. A more traditional method of active prevention that sidesteps behaviour is that of vaccination. The first large-scale attempts at vaccination to induce protective immunity were no better than placebo. The US military utilized two different vaccine candidates in healthy HIV+ individuals as well as a group of HIV− persons. The target proteins included the conserved and variable regions of the HIV gp160 transmembrane proteins that are responsible for 'docking' with the CD4 receptor. While antibody responses were demonstrated, there was no increased viral killing, or change in natural history of infection or disease. More recently, large-scale efforts to trial vaccines throughout the world have been put into effect. Because of the differences in the different HIV subtypes from around the world, many are now combination or multivalent vaccines. Measuring outcomes to truly know the effectiveness of these candidates will take years. Thus, this type of work must proceed in parallel with all other existing prevention, testing and counselling, and treatment efforts. Very disturbingly, data from Bruce Walker's group at Harvard Medical School (Altfeld *et al.* 2002) and others (Goulder and Walker 2002) clearly demonstrate not only HIV superinfections in HIV+ persons (i.e., secondary infection by a much more virulent strain of HIV), but also changes in the rates of disease progression induced by the more virulent strain which have raised concerns that even the best possible form of vaccination − i.e., natural infection − did not prevent infection by the second strain or change the course of the disease. This clearly raises questions about the effectiveness of *any* vaccine strategy.

In spite of seemingly obvious prevention strategies, addressing the issues around global AIDS is far more complex than a simple political or funding dilemma. Cultural competency, cultural taboos and long-established cultural beliefs that are behavioural and may not be supported by evidence-driven decision-making are proving to be far more difficult to implement. Similarly, barriers to care further limit effectiveness. Stigma associated with HIV infection remains one of the major roadblocks to testing in most parts of the world, including the United States. Perhaps because the world became aware of HIV through the US and Europe, the world assumes incorrectly that HIV is an infection of marginalized groups – gay men, injecting drug users and prostitutes. Ironically, HIV is in fact very democratic, and infects persons of all walks of life – men, women, gay, straight, black, white, rich, poor. Indeed, as of the beginning of 2004, women accounted for 50 per cent of all HIV infections in the world (WHO 2004). And perhaps because HIV was made a stand-alone infection, it is not included routinely in broader health education or prevention and treatment programmes such as sexual health, mental health, methadone clinics or, more globally, in tuberculosis clinics. In maintaining this single emphasis, rightly or wrongly, the stigma associated with HIV/ AIDS may be inadvertently perpetuated – and thus the advance of the disease may be furthered.

As treatment procedures advance, the reliability of medication streams remains tenuous. Indeed, that stream may be interrupted anywhere, from access to medication either through interruptions in funding or lack of availability and distribution, to self-discontinuation resulting from non-compliance with the medication itself. While, globally, programmatic capacity-building both to maintain supply and distribute ARVs is a daunting issue, such difficulties continue to be experienced in the US. Indeed, competing economic forces pose major problems in the US. Since the late 1990s, fiscal tightening and state and federal budget deficits have developed concurrent

with the rise in the cost of ARVs using newer agents (for example, the fusion inhibitor T-20, or Fuzeon®, costs a staggering US$20,000 per year alone for a single agent). Supplemental programmes such as the AIDS Drug Assistance Program and state Medicare programmes continue to be at risk for wait-listing, restricted formularies or simply not paying for services.

Another major difficulty is that the scale of many programmes may overwhelm the economies of developing countries. If US$30 million was provided for prevention, treatment and testing programmes to countries with an annual Gross National Product of only US$30 million, this could potentially topple the existing infrastructure that spends and tracks finances and therfore invert that nation's budget for health. However, if transmission rates are to change, improving the health of persons infected with and affected by HIV and staving off the exploding epidemic in the process is essential, and this requires that very aggressive and inclusive approaches be taken on all fronts simultaneously. Simply setting a policy without developing the economic, health and healthcare delivery infrastructures is useless. Possessing ARVs but not adequate dispensing programmes, or not understanding the utility of medications in monitoring, and dealing with side effects and adverse responses, or in treating other infections that co-exist alongside HIV (e.g., tuberculosis, diarrhoeal diseases, hepatitis B and C), or those that are regionally endemic such as HTLV-1 and 2, is both irresponsible and extremely dangerous.

Drug availability alone is not sufficient. Ironically, although the US has the greatest access to resources in the world, it also has the worst medication adherence in the world, with over 50 per cent of those taking HIV medications missing at least 10 per cent of their doses (Reynolds et al. 2004). This ultimately poses a public health threat as well as compromising the individual's health and treatment success, as poor adherence is directly associated with the emergence of viral resistance. Compare this to resource-poor areas. Indeed, major pilot programmes in resource-poor settings in Africa have demonstrated near-perfect adherence rates to ARVs. The largest barriers in Africa are availability, and the reliability of both the agent itself and its supply and distribution. In Western society, as noted above, poor adherence is directly associated with the emergence of viral resistance, and also results in treatment failure and the emergence of primary resistance in newly infected persons. For example, in Boston alone, of 120 viral isolates from persons newly diagnosed HIV+, 10 per cent were found to have primary resistance mutations (Hanna *et al.* 2003). This means that a standard three-drug regimen would fail to work for these individuals. A resistant virus is now a public health problem.

The slow emergence of background resistance is only one part of an emerging threat. Resistance is clearly associated with an adherence to medication, and we have already demonstrated that while this is a potential concern in resource-poor areas, adherence rates are far better than those in industrialized nations. In the US, there have been dramatic shifts in risk-taking among gay men. In the late 1980s and early 1990s, grassroots community efforts to control the spread of HIV were undertaken in cities with high prevalency rates such as New York (**55**) and San Francisco. In that era (before HAART was available and when, at best, dual ARVs were used), HIV was the leading cause of death among men aged 19–35 (CDC data). Safe-sex practices, although not embraced immediately when espoused by public health officials, became a matter of course throughout communities. Such practices increased when local community groups, sometimes with the backing of government funding, informed the community about the prevention of HIV. As HAART became increasingly

available, voluntary counselling and testing programmes – mostly anonymous – promoted early diagnosis and were accessed widely. As a direct result of these efforts, transmission rates of not only HIV, but other sexually transmitted diseases such as syphilis and gonorrhoea declined significantly as well (CDC data).

In the past five years, a growth in 'circuit drugs' and public misunderstanding about HAART and HIV superinfections have all led to a marked increase in unsafe or unprotected sexual practices. 'Barebacking', or sex without a condom, has been linked to a lack of inhibitions associated with drugs such as methamphetamine or 'crystal meth'. The availability of erection enhancers such as Viagra®, Levitra® and now Cialis® compound the problem. A recent study by the San Francisco Department of Health clearly demonstrated the direct relationship between the use of methamphetamine and Viagra® and the rise in new HIV infections and sexually transmitted diseases (Wong *et al.* 2004). Perhaps most disturbing on a personal scale is the replacement of the pursuit of emotional companionship by the immediacy of lust, physical contact and availability in this world of immediate gratification. Indeed, the complexity of HIV prevention in this sexually charged culture is so great that a simple message of 'wear a condom' rings hollow. To truly address behavioural changes in these settings requires addressing the needs or desires that drugs such as crystal meth or Ecstasy seem to fill.

From these examples, simply providing information clearly does not translate into behavioural changes. Thus, the challenges in prevention lie not only in truly understanding the cultural context of the individual (a young woman in Ghana versus a young gay man in New York City versus an injecting drug user in Russia), but also a means by which those basic needs that override knowledge and perpetuate risk-taking are also addressed.

An equally daunting challenge is that of balancing patent laws, international trade agreements and medication availability between the developed and developing countries. The monthly cost of a typical ARV regimen in most non-Western nations is equivalent to or exceeds the annual per person healthcare budget. While HIV is a pandemic, and as Laurie Garret (1994) deemed, a 'plague of the 20th century', it does not occur in a medical vacuum. A variety of strategies have been suggested to bridge this gap: (1) industry agreements to provide licensed agents at cost; (2) marketing agreements with local pharmaceutical companies; (3) means by which patents can be 'broken' for the local manufacturing of generic forms of the drug. Obvious problems exist regarding the quality and safety of generic agents (as well as the availability of sham medications). However, more daunting on a global scale are the economic and legal ramifications of patent violations or breaking patents – it seems potentially more substantial a challenge to selectively permit patents to be broken for the better good of humankind. Conversely, should Western nations continue to bear the burden of the higher costs of the medication, in effect subsidizing international distribution efforts of the more well-intentioned pharmaceutical companies? The cost of developing an agent that comes to market was estimated to be at least US$802 million in 2002 (DiMasi, Hansen and Gabowski 2003).

Perhaps on the global scale, the most significant barrier to prevention and care lies in the political arena. The various US presidential administrations have waffled with regards to the importance of HIV for local communities as well as the nation. During the early 1980s, the very period when HIV was being recognized as the cause of AIDS (or that stigmatizing term 'gay-related immune deficiency' or GRID), sitting President Ronald Reagan spent the first three years of the epidemic doing nothing, at a time when over 6,000 individuals were dying from the disease; it was not until the end of his second term that he publicly addressed the situation, at the third International HIV/AIDS Conference. Now, in the twenty-first century, President George W. Bush has proposed US$15 billion in US aid to the world community. However, these funds have been tithed to countries that advocate 'abstinence only' prevention programmes and that do not support abortion, and monies are limited to patent-restricted medications (i.e., *not* generics – the monthly cost of a generic combination regimen is now less than US$30 compared to US$900 plus cost of medications alone in the US). Further politicization has occurred also. The CDC routinely revise HIV prevention guidelines. This is a governmental agency that, with the exception of funding, has been relatively immune from Congressional or administrative agendas. The pending revisions would expand what has been a troubling reality of the last five years – increasing content and administrative constraints on the use of scientifically accurate information and population-specific interventions. Re-stated within the regulations are: an expanding use of condom-efficacy challenges; a reassertion of the primacy of abstinence; and a cavalier use of the obscenity clause from *Miller* v. *California* (US Supreme Court decision: 418 US 915, 1974). All will constrain the development of materials and the decision-making of local review groups. Equally disturbing, the scope of application of the guidance appears to reach well beyond the agency's federally funded projects to their other prevention web site, marketing and communication efforts now supported by states or private individual donors and foundations. These other funding sources have been critical to insure that effective prevention messaging reaches targeted populations when federal sources have restricted certain messages.

Promisingly, global responses to HIV and AIDS have increased dramatically since the late 1990s. It is essential that the world confronts HIV and AIDS on a massive, geopolitical level, and some steps have been taken to do so: (1) monies are now being released or promised to aid those nations with lesser economies; (2) complex trade issues around patent rights are being streamlined or bypassed in order to make available more inexpensive generic forms of ARVs and prophylaxis for opportunistic infections; (3) pharmaceutical companies are negotiating price agreements for some of the more complex-to-manufacture agents; and (4) the WHO and UNAIDS have released jointly a programme referred to as '3 by 5' – an acronym suggesting the institutions hope to get 3 million people in the developing world into treatment by 2005. While admirable, this latter initiative demonstrates the difficulties faced by those attempting to respond to the situation on a global level. It will undoubtedly require the coordinated efforts of non-governmental organizations, academic programmes from countries more experienced in the multiple aspects of HIV interventions, national ministries of health, religious organizations and grassroots programmes. These must be equitable, non-judgemental and able to reach the most marginalized sections of a region's population – often the section that is at the highest risk for all health disparities, notwithstanding HIV.

See also: HIV; AIDS

Bibliography

Altfeld, M., Allen, T.M., Yu, X.G. et al. (2002) 'HIV-1 Superinfection Despite Broad CD8+ T Cell Responses Containing Replication of the Primary Virus', Nature 420: 434–9.

Bush, George W. (2003) State of the Union Address, 2003, available at: http://www.americanrhetoric.com/speeches/stateofunion2003.html.

Centers for Disease Control and Prevention (2004) HIV/AIDS Surveillance Report, 2003, Atlanta: US Department of Health and Human Services, CDC, vol. 15, pp. 1–46; available at: http://www.cdc.gov/hiv/stats.hasrlink.htm

Connor, E.M., Sperling, R.S., Gelber, R. et al. (1994) 'Reduction of Maternal–infant Transmission of Human Immunodeficiency Virus Type 1 with Zidovudine Treatment', New England Journal of Medicine 331: 1173–80.

Des Jarlais, D.C., Perlis, T., Friedman, S.R. et al. (2000) 'Behavioral Risk Reduction in a Declining HIV Epidemic: Injection Drug Users in New York City, 1990–1997', American Journal of Public Health 90: 1112–16.

Dilley, J.W., Woods, W.J., Sabatino, J. et al. (2002) 'Changing Sexual Behavior Among Gay Male Repeat Testers For HIV: a Randomized, Controlled Trial of a Single-session Intervention', Journal of Acquired Immune Deficiency Syndrome 30: 177–86.

DiMasi, J.A., Hansen, R.W. and Gabowski, H.G. (2003) 'The Price of Innovation: New Estimates of Drug Development Costs', Journal of Health Economics 22: 151–85.

Field, M.G. (2004) 'HIV and AIDS in the Former Soviet Bloc', New England Journal of Medicine 351: 117–20.

Garret, L. (1994) The Coming Plague: Newly Emerging Diseases in a World out of Balance, New York: Farrar, Strauss & Giroux.

Goulder, P.J. and Walker, B.D. (2002) 'HIV-1 Superinfection – a Word of Caution', New England Journal of Medicine 347: 756–8.

Hanna, G.J., Balaguera, H.U., Freedberg, K.A. et al. (2003) 'Drug-selected Resistance Mutations and Non-B Subtypes in Antiretroviral-naïve Adults with Established Human Immunodeficiency Virus Infection', Journal of Infectious Diseases 188: 986–91.

Hellinger, F.J. (1998) 'Cost and Financing of Care for Persons with HIV Disease: An Overview', Health Care Financing Review 19 (Spring): 1–14.

Karon, J.M. et al. (1996) 'Prevalence of HIV Infection in the United States, 1984 to 1992', Journal of the American Medical Association 276: 126–31.

Lemp, G.F., Porco, T.C., Hirozawa, A.M. et al. (1997) 'Projected Incidence of AIDS in San Francisco: the Peak and Decline of the Epidemic', Journal of Acquired Immune Deficiency Syndrome Human Retrovirology 16: 182–9.

Mandelbrot, L. et al. (1998) 'Perinatal HIV-1 Transmission: Interaction between Zidovudine Prophylaxis and Mode of Delivery in the French Perinatal Cohort', Journal of the American Medical Association 280: 55–60.

MMWR (2004) 'High-risk Sexual Behavior by HIV-positive Men Who Have Sex With Men – 16 Sites, United States, 2000–2002', Morbidity and Mortality Weekly Report 53: 891–4.

Mulder, D., Nunn, A., Kamali, A. and Ken-geya-Kayondo, J. (1995) 'Decreasing HIV-1 Seroprevalence in Young Adults in a Rural Ugandan Cohort', *British Medical Journal* 311: 833–6.

Ng'weshemia, J.Z., Boerma, J.T., Pool, R. *et al.* (1996) 'Changes in Male Sexual Behaviour in Response to the AIDS Epidemic: Evidence from a Cohort Study in Urban Tanzania', *AIDS* 10: 1415–20.

Reynolds, N.R., Testa, M.A., Marc, L.G. *et al.* (2004) 'Factors Influencing Medication Adherence Beliefs and Self-efficacy in Persons Naïve to Anti-retroviral Therapy: a Multicenter, Cross-Sectional Study', *AIDS Behaviour* 8: 141–50.

SAfAIDS News (1997) 'HIV Seroprevalence Among Pregnant Women in Botswana' 5: 9.

Sperling, R.S., Shapiro, D.E., Coombs, R.W. *et al.* (1996) 'Maternal Viral Load, Zidovudine Treatment and the Risk of Transmission of Human Immunodeficiency Virus Type 1 From Mother to Infant', *New England Journal of Medicine* 335: 1621–9.

US Census Bureau Population Statistics 2003, available at: http://eire.census.gov/popest/data/states/tables/NST-EST2003–01.php).

US Supreme Court decision: 418 US 915 (1974) *Marvin Miller* v. *State of California*, No. 73–1508, Supreme Court of the United States, 25 July.

WHO (2004) *HIV/AIDS Annual Report*, Geneva: World Health Organization, December.

Wong W., Chaw, J., Kent, C., Alpers, L. and Klausner, J. (2004) 'Risk Factors for Early Syphilis Among Men Who Have Sex With Men Seen in an STD Clinic, San Francisco 2002–2003', *National STD Prevention Conference*, Abstract no. C02B.

World Health Organization and UNAIDS Global Initiative to Provide Antiretroviral Therapy to 3 Million People with HIV/AIDS in Developing Countries by the End of 2005, available at: http://www.who.int/3by5/publications/documents/en/3by5StrategyMakingItHappen.pdf

Zhang, L., Chen, Z., Cao, Y. *et al.* (2004) 'Molecular Characterization of Human Immunodeficiency Virus Type 1 and Hepatitis C Virus in Paid Blood Donors and Injection Drug Users in China', *Journal of Virology* 78: 13591–9.

Further reading

Aldhous, P. and Tastemain, C. (1992) 'Three Physicians Convicted in French "blood-supply trial"', *Science* 258: 735.

Barre-Sinoussi, F., Chermann, J.S., Rey, F. *et al.* (1983) 'Isolation of a T-lymphocyte Retrovirus from a Patient at Risk for Acquired Immune Deficiency Syndrome (AIDS)', *Science* 220: 868–71.

Brown, T., Mulhall, B. and Sittitrai, W. (1994) 'Risk Factors for HIV Transmission in Asia and the Pacific', *AIDS* 8, Suppl. 2: S173–82.

Castro, A. and Farmer, P. (2005) 'Understanding and Addressing AIDS-related Stigma: From Anthropological Theory to Clinical Practice in Haiti', *American Journal of Public Health* 95: 53–9.

Celentano, D.D., Bond, K.C., Lyles, C.M. *et al.* (2000) 'Prevention Intervention to Reduce Sexually Transmitted Infections: a Field Trial in the Royal Thai Army', *Archive of Internal Medicine* 160: 535–40.

Chowdhury, S. (1995) 'HIV-control Programme in Thailand', *National Medical Journal of India* 8: 181–2.

Chu, P.L., McFarland, W., Gibson, S. *et al.* (2003) 'Viagra Use in a Community-recruited Sample of Men Who Have Sex with Men, San Francisco', *Journal of Acquired Immune Deficiency Syndrome* 33: 191–3.

Crosby, R. and Declemente, R.J. (2004) 'Use of Recreational Viagra among Men Who Have Sex with Men', *Sexually Transmitted Infections* 80: 466–81.

Crosby, R. and Mettey, A. (2004) 'A Descriptive Analysis of HIV Risk Behavior among Men Having Sex with Men Attending a Large Sex Resort', *Journal of Acquired Immune Deficiency Syndrome* 37: 1496–9.

Darby, S.C., Kan, S.W. and Spooner, R.J. *et al.* (2004) 'The Impact of HIV on Mortality Rates in the Complete UK Haemophilia Population', *AIDS* 18: 525–33.

Department of Health, District of Columbia (2004) *The HIV/AIDS Epidemiologic Profile for the District of Columbia 2004*, pp. 1–52, available at: http://dchealth.dc.gov/about/pdg/epi_profile_2004.shtm.

'France's Blood Scandal', *Nature* (1995) 373: 546.

Frasca, I. (2003) 'Men and Women – Still Far Apart on HIV/AIDS', *Reproductive Health Matters* 11: 12–20.

Gallo, R.C., Salahuddin, S.Z., Popovic, M. *et al.* (1984) 'Frequent Detection and Isolation of Cytopathic Retroviruses (HTLV-III) in Patients with AIDS and at Risk for AIDS' *Science* 4 (May): 500–3.

Gisselquist, D.P. (2002) 'Estimating HIV-1 Transmission Efficiency Through Unsafe

Medical Injections', *International Journal of STDs and AIDS* 13: 152–9.

Goodwin, R., Kozlova, A., Nizharadze, G. and Polyakova, G. (2004) 'RUSSIA/GEORGIA/UKRAINE: High-risk Behaviors and Beliefs and Knowledge about HIV Transmission among School and Shelter Children in Eastern Europe', *Sexually Transmitted Diseases* 31, 11 (November): 670–5.

Guay, L.A., Musoke, P., Fleming, T. *et al.* (1999) 'Intrapartum and Neonatal Single-dose Nevirapine Compared with Zidovudine for Prevention of Mother-to-child Transmission of HIV-1 in Kampala, Uganda: HIVNET 012 Randomized Trial', *Lancet* 354: 796–802.

Hamers, F.F. and Downs, A.M. (2004) 'The Changing Face of the HIV Epidemic in Western Europe: What are the Implications for Public Health Policies?' *Lancet* 364: 83–94.

Harawa, N.T., Greenland, S., Bingham, T.A. *et al.* (2004) 'Associations of Race/Ethnicity with HIV Prevalence and HIV-Related Behaviors among Young Men Who Have Sex with Men in 7 Urban Centers in the United States', *Journal of Acquired Immune Deficiency Syndrome* 35, 5 (15 March): 526–36.

Hirschfield, S., Remien, R.H., Walavalkar, I. and Chaisson, M.A. (2004) 'Crystal Methamphetamine Use Predicts Incident STD Infection among Men Who Have Sex with Men Recruited Online: A Nested Case-Control Study', *Journal of Medical Internet Research* 6: e41.

Ho, D.D. (1996) *XI International AIDS Conference, Vancouver, British Columbia, Canada, 10 July.*

Khromova, Y. (2002) 'High Rates of Sexually Transmitted Diseases (STDs), HIV and Risky Behaviors among Female Detainees in Moscow, Russia', *XIV International AIDS Conference, Barcelona, Spain*, Abstract no. ThPeC7600.

Koblin, B.A., Chesney, M.A. and Husnik, M.J. (2003) 'High-risk Behaviors among Men Who Have Sex with Men in 6 US Cities: Baseline Data from the EXPLORE Study', *American Journal of Public Health* 93, 6 (June): 926–32.

Loughlin *et al.* (2002) *130th Annual Meeting of APHA*, Abstract no. 46575.

Mason, C.J., Markowitz, L.E., Kitsiripornchai,S. *et al.* (1995) 'Declining Prevalence of HIV-1 Infection in Young Thai Men', *AIDS* 9: 1061–5.

Massachusetts Department of Public Health (2005) *HIV/AIDS in Massachusetts: An Epidemiologic Profile FY 2005*, available at http://www.mass.gov/dph/cdc/aids/aidsreports.htm #annual

Minkin, S.F. (1991) 'Iatrogenic AIDS: Unsafe Medical Practices and the HIV Epidemic', *Social Science Medicine* 33: 786–90.

Newell, M.L., Brahmbhatt, H. and Ghys, P.D. (2004) 'Child Mortality and HIV Infection in Africa: a Review', *AIDS* 18, Suppl. 2: S27–S34.

Newell, M.L., Coovadia, H., Cortnia-Borja, M. *et al.* (2004) 'Mortality of Infected and Uninfected Infants Born to HIV-infected Mothers in Africa: a Pooled Analysis', *Lancet* 364: 1236–43.

Opening session, XV International AIDS Conference, Bangkok, Thailand, 2004, available at: http://www.who.int/3by5/mediacentre/news40/en/

Pallela, F.J., Delaney, K.M., Moorman, A.C. *et al.* (1998) 'Declining Morbidity and Mortality Among Patients with Advanced Human Immunodeficiency Virus Infection', *New England Journal of Medicine* 338: 853–60.

Phanuphak, P. (2004) 'Antiretroviral Treatment in Resource-poor Settings: What Can We Learn from the Existing Programmes in Thailand?' *AIDS* 18, Suppl. 3: S33–S38.

Reagan, Ronald (1987) Opening Remarks, 3rd International Conference on HIV/AIDS, Washington DC, 31 May.

Redfield, R.R., Birx, D.L., Ketter, N. *et al.* (1991) 'A Phase I Evaluation of the Safety and Immunogenicity of Vaccination with Recombinant gp160 in Patients with Early Human Immunodeficiency Virus Infection. Military Medical Consortium for Applied Retroviral Research', *New England Journal of Medicine* 324: 1677–84.

Roumelioutout-Karayannis, A., Nestoridou, K., Mandalaki, T., Stefanou, T. and Papaevangelou, G. (1988) 'Heterosexual Transmission of HIV in Greece', *AIDS Research into Human Retroviruses* 4: 233–6.

Ruxrungtham, K., Brown, T. and Phanuphak, P. (2004) 'HIV/AIDS in Asia', *Lancet* 364: 69–82.

Semple, S.J., Patterson, T.L and Grant, I. (2004) 'A Comparison of Injection and Noninjection Methamphetamine Use in HIV+ Men Who Have Sex with Men', *Drug Alcohol Department* 76: 203–12.

Shakarishvili, A. (2002) 'High Rates of Sexually Transmitted Diseases (STDs) and Related Risk Behaviors in Homeless Population in

Moscow, Russia – Potential Impact for HIV Transmission', *XIV International AIDS Conference, Barcelona, Spain*, Abstract no. ThPeC7431.

Stall, R., Mills, T.C., Williamson, J. *et al.* (2003) 'Association of Co-occurring Psychosocial Health Problems and Increased Vulnerability to HIV/AIDS among Men Who Have Sex with Men', *American Journal of Public Health* 93: 939–42.

Steel-Duncan, J.C., Pierre, R., Evans-Gilbert, T. *et al.* (2004) 'Uptake of Interventions, Outcomes and Challenges in Caring for HIV-exposed Infants in Kingston, Jamaica', *West Indian Medical Journal* 53: 308–14.

Torian, L.V., Weisfuse, I.B., Makki, H.A. *et al.* (1996) 'Trends in HIV Seroprevalence in Men Who Have Sex with Men: New York City Department of Health Sexually Transmitted Disease Clinics, 1988–1993', *AIDS* 10: 187–92.

UNAIDS/WHO HIV/AIDS Fact Sheets (2000) Geneva: World Health Organization.

MICHAEL T. WONG

AIDS FILM, AMERICAN

The struggle to use film in America to address the complexities of AIDS has produced some of the most spectacular and heartfelt, as well as some of the more problematic, films the country has produced. In America, two predominant genres of AIDS film have emerged: (1) mainstream narrative; and (2) documentary or avant-garde. Regardless of genre, films about AIDS, ideally, have the potential to disrupt stereotypical and uninformed assumptions about the disease. Generally speaking, the AIDS film prompts individuals to consider the ramifications of HIV and AIDS, galvanizing them to consider how AIDS concerns both them and others.

Since AIDS affects numerous communities and populations, the AIDS film can be located in different genres in an effort to reach specific audiences. Its form is often a direct indication of the level of complexity with which AIDS is presented. Genres include dramas (*Our Sons*, dir. John Erman, 1991; *It's My Party*, Randal Kleiser, 1996);

the adaptation of stage plays (*Love! Valour! Compassion!*, Joe Mantello, 1997; *Angels in America*, Mike Nichols, 2003); musicals (*Jeanne and the Perfect Guy*, Olivier Ducastel and Jacques Martineau, 1998); avant-garde art films (*Tongues Untied*, Marlon **Riggs**, 1989; *SILENCE = DEATH*, Rosa von **Praunheim**, 1989); and documentaries (*Paul Monette: The Brink of Summer's End*, Monte Bramer, 1996). Although the AIDS film appears in such varied forms, similarities exist across the board. For the most part, the AIDS film hopes to achieve a representation of AIDS as a complex cultural, human and political phenomenon. Of course, not all films are successful in addressing these complexities.

Indeed, issues of representation, especially in narrative film, are important to investigate when assessing the AIDS film. In most instances of the AIDS narrative film, the individual with the disease is a gay white man, even though statistics prove that, worldwide, women and people of colour bear the brunt of the disease in considerably larger numbers. When women and/or people of colour *are* represented, the portrayal is often a shallow one. For example, Robin Wright Penn's portrayal of Jenny Curran in *Forrest Gump* (Robert Zemeckis, 1994) is one that sidesteps the significance of the disease by erasing its mere mention. Although the viewer suspects that Jenny is dying from AIDS because of the indirect references she makes to the disease, the word AIDS is never uttered in the film. Instead, the viewer must decode the meaning behind her statement 'I caught a virus', drawing a parallel between 'a virus' and the human immunodeficiency virus, HIV. That Jenny is the promiscuous hippie who catches a 'virus' and Forrest is the hero who manages to emerge unscathed is significant, evidence of a narrative favouring the hero and a putative punishment for the promiscuous individual. Further evidence of the movie's burying of AIDS occurs when the titular character refers to a friend who died of a mysterious disease. Since *Forrest Gump* is set in the early 1980s, the viewer immediately recalls the mystery surrounding AIDS during this time.

To be sure, there is often a vast difference between 'mainstream' films and 'independent' films about AIDS – the former frequently obfuscate issues of race, class and gender see *It's My Party* and *Long-time Companion* Norman René, 1990, while the latter often foreground these very issues (*Tongues Untied*).

Moreover, the AIDS narrative film is often didactic; that is, its humanism over-reaches and defuses the broad array of issues AIDS leaves in its wake. The 1995 film *Boys on the Side* (Herbert Ross) is a good example. In this film, Mary-Louise Parker's character, Robin, reveals her HIV+ status to her two friends, Jane and Holly, played by Whoopi Goldberg and Drew Barrymore respectively. Subsequently, Jane and Holly become Robin's caregivers. Although the support Jane and Holly extend to Robin is admirable, the tone of the narrative takes on a preachy quality that distracts from more significant issues such as the cultural and medical concerns women with AIDS face on a daily basis.

Despite the history of negative stereotypes to which the disease has given rise, the AIDS film has occasionally appealed to American mainstream audiences. One of the first AIDS films, the made-for-TV movie *An Early Frost* (John Erman, 1985) was a critical success, garnering numerous awards, including a Peabody. Tom Hanks earned the first of his two Oscars for *Philadelphia* (Jonathan Demme, 1993), in which he portrays Andrew Beckett, a lawyer fired from his job because of his AIDS status as well as his sexual orientation. By the time Ed Harris received a supporting actor Oscar nomination for his portrayal of an HIV+ individual in *The Hours* (Stephen Daldry, 2002), AIDS was more easily digested by the audience than it was during the early to mid-1990s when, as in *Forrest Gump*, the disease was, for all intents and purposes, unutterable. As these latter plaudits indicate, a growing awareness of HIV+ and AIDS-affected individuals has altered the way in which representation is both produced in film and received by its audience. Yet it is difficult to assess whether viewers of these and other AIDS films identify with the HIV+ person being portrayed or whether they are simply drawn into a narrative guided by award-winning performances.

On another level, however, the American AIDS film has worked as a tool for AIDS prevention as well as for compassion, encouraging the audience to act decisively in terms of support for the everyday necessities of people with the disease, as well as working towards stemming the tide of new HIV infections. Such action can be on a personal level (taking an HIV-antibody test) or take a more overt, political form (participating in an AIDS protest). In these instances, the AIDS film represents the broad range of issues that make up the AIDS epidemic. In either case – as a form of mainstream, narrative entertainment or a call to action – the AIDS film, has proven an important cultural response to the disease.

Further reading

Hart R. Kylo-Patrick (2000) *The AIDS Movie: Representing a Pandemic in Film and Television*, New York: Haworth Press.

CHRIS BELL

AIDS IN THE BLACK AND HISPANIC COMMUNITIES, UNITED STATES

A number of media depictions suggest that a major upswing in incidences of HIV and AIDS has occurred in black and Hispanic communities recently. AIDS activists and prevention workers have decried this proposition, insisting that AIDS has been a concern in these communities for years (see **ACT UP**; **AIDS prevention**).

In 1981, when the virus that causes AIDS first raised alarm bells, many individuals directed blame at the 4Hs: 'Homosexuals', 'Heroin addicts', 'Haemophiliacs', and 'Haitians'. Since most Haitians are black (and many are self-acknowledged black homosexuals), AIDS has always been a concern in black communities, albeit often an unacknowledged one. In the years since general culture and the scientific communities came to a clearer determination of how HIV/AIDS is caused and spread, and recognized that the number of those at risk is larger than initially believed, several high-profile AIDS cases in black communities have transformed perceptions of the disease (take, for example, the AIDS-related deaths of America's first black network news anchor, Max Robinson [1988], singers Sylvester [1988] and Jermaine Stewart [1997], tennis ace Arthur Ashe [1993] and rapper Eazy-E [1995]). Arguably, no single individual generated more AIDS-related discourse in black communities than Earvin 'Magic' **Johnson**, former point guard with the Los Angeles Lakers. When Johnson announced his HIV+ status at a press conference on 7 November 1991, many individuals in black communities finally realized the magnitude of the disease. In the days and weeks following his announcement, testing centres experienced a drastic increase in black individuals requesting HIV-antibody tests. Johnson has since evolved into one of the black communities' most recognizable AIDS activists, sporadically appearing in public service announcements and pharmaceutical advertisements.

The fact that it took nearly ten years for black communities to grasp the threat posed to them by AIDS shows just how far-reaching the stereotype of AIDS as a gay white disease was, and continues to be. Moreover, this stereotype had/has purchase in Hispanic communities, even though Hispanic individuals were infected with HIV and have been dying from AIDS since the early 1980s. Just as Magic Johnson's

HIV diagnosis signalled a change in the conception of AIDS in black communities, the death of Pedro **Zamora** from AIDS in 1994 made a direct impact upon Hispanic communities. Zamora, the Cuban-born member of MTV's *The Real World*, was an outspoken AIDS activist after learning of his HIV diagnosis while attending high school in Miami. Viewers across the nation were touched by his charm and runway model looks and, when the virus began to progress, were riveted by his televised struggle. Realizing the toll HIV and AIDS had taken in their communities, many Hispanic celebrities, perhaps most notably talk show host Cristina Saralegui, took up the cause.

In 2001, the Centers for Disease Control released a statistic that 7 per cent of white gay and bisexual men are HIV+ compared with 15 per cent of Hispanic gay and bisexual men and 30 per cent of black gay and bisexual men. Although this statistic measured individuals in only six urban cities, and only those of a particular sexual orientation, the study demonstrates how drastically different AIDS prevalence is between white communities and communities of colour (read here black and Hispanic). Many AIDS prevention initiatives now specifically target communities of colour, focusing their efforts in churches, community centres and other locales that people of colour frequent.

One of the most notoriously difficult venues to conduct AIDS prevention in is the American prison system. Since the sexes are segregated, prison officials see very little need to educate inmates about AIDS and AIDS prevention. Condoms are also discouraged in many prisons. However, sexual activity does in fact occur in such settings. And since the incarceration system in the US is occupied predominantly by people of colour, blacks and Hispanic, especially men, many contract HIV while in prison. An additional danger is that, should these individuals be paroled, they are released into the general population not having had a test for HIV-antibodies, and thus often unknowingly spread HIV to sexual partners outside prison.

In the United States the politics of race plays a considerable role in addressing AIDS in black and Hispanic communities. Since a number of non-native-born Hispanic individuals struggle with speaking English, linguistic difficulties, along with the lack of availability of AIDS educational materials in Spanish, may preclude many individuals from seeking testing and treatment. A large percentage of both blacks and Hispanics also lack access to the healthcare system, since according to the National Survey of American Families, many are uninsured or underinsured in comparison to the white population. An awareness of cultural differences is vital in stemming the tide of new HIV infections and treating those who are already infected. In addition, the continued deconstruction of the stereotype of AIDS as a gay white male disease is necessary both to ensure compassion towards black and Hispanic men and women with HIV and AIDS and, more significantly, to raise consciousness within these communities to combat the effects of the disease.

Web sites

HIV/AIDS Surveillance, Centers for Disease Control and Prevention, available at: http://www.cdc.gov/hiv/surveillance.htm

National Survey of American Families: Snapshots II – Key Findings by Race and Ethnicity, available at: http://anfdata.urban.org/nsaf/race-ethnicity.html

CHRIS BELL

AIDS PREVENTION

AIDS prevention is a phrase used to describe a multifaceted approach to stopping the spread of HIV and AIDS.

Ever since 1983, when it was determined how HIV is spread, prevention has become a top priority in stemming the tide of new infections. Prevention efforts are plentiful, with virtually every international AIDS service organization having a prevention component. Key national and international organizations involved in prevention include: **American Foundation for AIDS Research (amfAR)**, **Gay Men's Health Crisis (GMHC)**, National Association of People with AIDS (NAPWA), and UNAIDS. AIDS prevention includes the distribution and/or availability of condoms at bars and community events; forums sponsored by AIDS service organizations; and the creation and maintenance of dialogue about AIDS, including the United Nations-sponsored World AIDS Day. Indeed, numerous AIDS service organizations and international governments are urgently devoted to AIDS prevention. Their efforts include monitoring the general population to discern new trends in AIDS incidence and prevalence, as well as informing the population about those trends. Once trends are identified, new prevention efforts are devised and put into practice.

The clear aim of AIDS prevention is to protect individuals from contracting the disease. On one level, prevention is conducted by scientists and researchers who analyse epidemiological data, review statistics and survey methodologies in an effort to identify individuals and communities at risk for HIV **seroconversion** (infection). On another level, activists, including persons with AIDS, play a role in AIDS prevention efforts by working directly in communities most affected by the disease, such as black and Hispanic communities and glbtq communities. Either in collaboration with medical professionals or on their own, these individuals develop and implement effective prevention mechanisms.

Originally, HIV/AIDS was viewed as a disease that affected only certain segments of society, namely gay white men. This position was significantly transformed when the broader impact of the disease was realized. The thrust behind AIDS prevention efforts

31

now targets the specific needs of individual communities or populations. For instance, an AIDS prevention effort designed for youth will be drastically different from one intended for women who want to conceive. Importantly, AIDS prevention efforts prove most effective when provided in languages that are spoken by the targeted population(s).

Since AIDS prevention is complex and cuts across a diverse set of cultures, reinforcement and ongoing reassessment given changes in behaviour and scientific developments is crucial to its success. Many prevention efforts, for example, have opted to integrate a social marketing strategy in their efforts. That is, AIDS prevention announcements directed at an urban audience may appear on a subway train or tube, on a platform or on the side of a bus. Viewers will see the image of a racially indeterminate individual standing on a nondescript streetscape with the words 'I'm glad I know my HIV status' superimposed above this individual. Each repeated viewing is intended to reinforce awareness and prevention, while also providing information about prevention organizations and testing facilities. Other reiterative prevention methods involve the use of television (commercials, themed episodes of TV shows), radio (public service announcements, guest speakers on call-in shows) and newspapers (editorials, advertisements). The advent of the Internet has resulted in a preponderance of AIDS prevention efforts being delivered online, especially in chat rooms and as banner ads (see **Internet and glbtq culture**).

Although AIDS prevention methods have successfully lowered the rate of new infections, opposition to these efforts abound. Barriers include legal sanctions against syringe exchange programmes because many police agencies and government officials do not condone the exchange of needles for clean drug habits, even though syringe exchange programmes have proven efficacy in reducing the spread of HIV/AIDS. Additionally, the reticence of

church and faith-based organizations forestalls prevention activity since these groups advocate 'abstinence-only' initiatives, or choose to take no role at all in disseminating AIDS prevention information. In some schools, colleges and universities, **condoms** are not made available to those seeking them because condoms purportedly promote sexual activity. Moreover, HIV+ speakers who have been invited to share their lived experiences with the disease in school settings are sometimes instructed not to mention condoms or overt sexual activity during their presentations.

Perhaps the most unfortunate blocks to effective AIDS prevention include the lack of consistency that exists among prevention techniques, as well as inadequate funding resources for prevention organizations. In the first instance, the prevention messages often contradict one another. A case in point is when on the one hand, an individual is encouraged to practice **safe sex**, then on the other hand told to avoid sexual activity completely (to abstain). Individual decisions are made even more complex when, for example, the use of recreational drugs is debated as a behavioural activity that potentially contributes to higher infection rates. Lack of funding, however, forces many prevention initiatives to fold before their efficacy can be measured. Although AIDS prevention has received millions of dollars from governments, corporations and private donors since the early 1980s, service organizations often find they must align their prevention methodologies with the mindset of a particular grantor or donor. If prevention efforts are viewed as controversial – as needle exchange is – monies for funding can be difficult to attain.

Since HIV is caused by a virus, and viruses, such as AIDS, are not easy to cure, scientists and researchers devote their time to isolating a vaccine so as to prevent further infections. Until that vaccine is identified for HIV infection and AIDS, prevention remains the most definitive tool in the fight against the disease.

See also: Condoms; Seroconversion

Web site

Centers for Disease Control, Division of AIDS Prevention, available at: http://www.cdc.gov

CHRIS BELL

AIDS, ARTS AND

Since the early years of the AIDS pandemic, artists and activists have responded in ways that attempt to represent and reflect various realities of the disease, as well as to critically intervene in the ongoing and often contested debates and negotiations over what AIDS is, what it means and how it might be addressed and, ultimately, redressed. In these ways artists and AIDS activists have assumed a concerted role in the very ways in which AIDS is understood. To the extent that AIDS has affected every aspect of late twentieth and early-twenty-first century society, it has been addressed by practitioners working in every art form and across various social and cultural identities and communities. The works that have resulted are intended to document, memorialize, galvanize and symbolize the multiple conditions and effects of AIDS. Whether out of a sense of history, loss, rage or the need to educate, one measure of this work's critical achievement is its insistence that AIDS is beyond the scope of, and can never be adequately circumscribed by, any one conceptual framework, representational theme or genre of aesthetic inquiry. The long list of artists who have died from AIDS-related causes – many in the early years of their lives – includes those who also took up AIDS as an issue in their own work, in ways that were often personal and yet were still able to resonate with the experiences of others.

The first public reports of AIDS appeared in 1981, and within three years some of the earliest artistic responses began to appear. Although it is unlikely that one will ever be able to determine the very first works to address AIDS, it was theatre and performance that seem to have taken the lead. This includes Jeff Hagedorn's *One*, at the Chicago Lionheart Theater in 1983; and *The A.I.D.S. Show* at San Francisco's Theater Rhinoceros in 1984. Many of the earliest productions also functioned as fundraising events, setting a precedent that continues up to the present day. In 1984, with the production of William Hoffman's *As Is*, the first play about AIDS to be presented on Broadway, and Larry Kramer's *The Normal Heart*, AIDS achieved recognition in mainstream theatre and the attention of larger audiences.

In 1986 an anonymous group of art activists going by the name SILENCE = DEATH Project created what would quickly become the most recognized logo and motto of the AIDS activist movement: a **pink triangle** accompanied by the galvanizing equation: SILENCE = DEATH. Working with a historical knowledge of the Nazis' use of the pink triangle as a means of symbolically marking and identifying homosexuals in the concentration camps, as well as its subversive appropriation by gay activists in the 1970s as a positive symbol of resistance and liberation, this group printed their design on T-shirts, posters, buttons, crack-and-peel stickers and protest placards. In 1987 the AIDS activist coalition ACT UP was founded, and the pink triangle design was conferred to the group, and they in turn reproduced it widely and greatly expanded its visibility in the public sphere.

Besides the agitprop graphics, videos and demonstrations by AIDS activists, there have been others who have endeavoured to document or narrate the lives, and just as often the deaths, of those affected by the epidemic. For some photographers, such as

Nicholas Nixon and Rosalind Solomon, it was an attempt to 'put a face on' AIDS by producing portraits that were often criticized for being overly sentimental and invasive, or for their obsessive focus on the ravaged bodies of the suffering. By 1990 major film studios were releasing films about AIDS into the mainstream, most notably Norman René's *Long-time Companion* (1990) and, three years later, Jonathan Demme's *Philadelphia*. Other filmmakers have taken a more decidedly radical approach, such as Gregg **Araki** in his queer punk story of two HIV+ men on the run, *The Living End*, and John Greyson in *Zero Patience*, billed as the first AIDS musical.

In 1989 a group of artists and curators in New York created Day without Art, in which art institutions attempted to register the deaths of artists and the effects that AIDS has had on their communities, by, for instance, draping or removing works from public display. The event took place on 1 December: World AIDS Day.

Perhaps in some way provoked by these actions, certain artists have regarded AIDS less as something to document, depict and portray, than as a provocation to confront the difficult and perhaps ultimately impossible task of bearing witness to AIDS in one's art. Two of the most well-known examples of this non-representational approach are installation artist Felix **Gonzalez-Torres**, and filmmaker Derek **Jarman**. In the late 1980s and 1990s, Cuban-born New York artist Gonzalez-Torres' work dealt with issues of absence and loss, including the death of his own boyfriend from AIDS, through a highly minimal and anonymous aesthetic. In gallery installations that amounted to little more than a large pile of individually wrapped candies, or a stack of sheets of paper left there for the taking, these works, instead of thematizing AIDS, materially performed its effects, such as wasting, disappearing and longing. In his 1993 film *Blue*, British filmmaker Derek Jarman created a 73-minute film of mono-

chromatic blue that at once attests to his own loss of sight because of AIDS and, more broadly, to the exhaustion of images – positive or negative – that is one of most elusive yet very real effects of AIDS.

See also: ACT UP; AIDS; Greyson, John; Kramer, Larry

Further reading

Crimp, D. (ed.) (1988) *AIDS: Cultural Analysis, Cultural Activism*, Cambridge and London: MIT Press.

—— (2002) *Melancholia and Moralism: Essays on AIDS and Queer Politics*, Cambridge and London: MIT Press.

Crimp, D. and Rolston, A. (eds) (1990) *AIDS Demographics*, Seattle: Bay Press.

Gott, T. (ed.) (1994) *Don't Leave Me This Way: Art in the Age of AIDS*, Canberra: National Gallery of Australia.

Haver, W. (1996) *The Body of this Death: Historicity and Sociality in the Time of AIDS*, Stanford: Stanford University Press.

JOHN PAUL RICCO

AILEY, ALVIN
b. 1931; d. 1989
dancer, choreographer, artistic director

Alvin Ailey, pre-eminent African-American dancer and choreographer and founder of the Alvin Ailey American Dance Theater, was born into abject poverty on 5 January 1931 in Rogers, Texas. He began his career at Lester Horton's Hollywood dance studio and made his Broadway debut as partner to Carmen De Lavallade in the 1954 Truman Capote musical *House of Flowers*. His multiracial repertory company, formed in 1958, performs Ailey's masterful *Revelations* (1960), danced to spirituals and gospel music, alongside new choreography and revivals of work by important modern dance choreographers. Although closeted throughout his lifetime, Ailey's work consistently encouraged queer spectatorship through depictions of glamorous masculinity, as in the virile working men of *Blues Suite* (1958) and in the sensual, intimate, same-sex partnering of *The River* (1970), an abstract ballet he made for the American Ballet Theater. Ailey made more than fifty ballets for an international roster of companies before he succumbed to AIDS. He died on 1 December 1989 in New York City.

THOMAS F. DEFRANTZ

AKERMAN, CHANTAL

b. 1950

director

Born in Brussels, Belgium, Chantal Akerman is hailed as one of the most important European directors of her generation. Her stylistically avant-garde drama and documentary films deconstruct gender stereotypes and contemporary female and lesbian identity. Her first feature, *je tu il elle* (I... You... He... She, 1974), explores heterosexual romantic myths in a series of erotic vignettes. Her next feature, *Jeanne Dielman, 23, Quai du Commerce, 1080 Bruxelles* (1975), a harrowing tale of a mother and part-time prostitute, was hailed as a feminist classic. *Les Rendez-vous d'Anna* (1978) tells of a young woman's sexual adventures with men and women. Although openly lesbian, Akerman's reluctance to identify as a lesbian director resulted in her withdrawing *je tu il elle* from the New York Gay Film Festival. She is best known to Anglo-American audiences for *Un divan à New York* (A Couch in New York, 1996). Her 2000 feature, *La Captive*, was adapted from Proust's *Remembrance of Things Past*.

JOHN FORDE

ALBEE, EDWARD

b. 1928

playwright

Born 12 March 1928 in Washington DC, the adopted son of Reed and Frances Albee, Edward Albee had an upbringing surrounded by wealth and privilege. And yet, until he was 30, he drifted largely unfocused through life. His first play, *The Zoo Story*, was unanimously rejected in the United States, but it received its first performance on 28 September 1959 in Berlin, on a bill with Samuel Beckett's *Krapp's Last Tape*; Beckett would be one of the major influences on Albee's work, and Albee would go on to create the American absurdist theatre. His major plays include *The Sandbox* (1959), *The American Dream* (1960), *Who's Afraid of Virginia Woolf?* (1962, Tony Award), *A Delicate Balance* (1966, Pulitzer Prize) and *Seascape* (1975, Pulitzer Prize). Although he failed to create a hit in the 1980s, Albee returned to prominence in 1994 with *Three Tall Women* (Pulitzer Prize) and won both the Tony and the Pulitzer for his 2002 play, *The Goat, or Who is Sylvia?*

CHRIS BYRNE

ALBERTON, PAOLO

See: Njinje, Mpumi and Paolo Alberton

ALDRICH, ROBERT

b. 1918; d. 1983

director

American film director and producer noted for a flamboyant, wry style. Working his way up through the studio system, Aldrich trained as a script clerk and an assistant director before branching out in the 1950s as an independent producer–director. With a versatile output encompassing film noir (*Kiss Me Deadly*, 1955), westerns (*Vera Cruz*, 1954) and romance (*Autumn Leaves*, 1956), Aldrich found his greatest success in the 1960s with sensational melodramas such as *Whatever Happened to Baby Jane*, 1962 and *Hush, Hush, Sweet Charlotte*, 1964. Featuring ageing classic female stars in over-the-top performances and characterized by a gothic, camp style, these films proved instant favourites with queer audiences. Aldrich's queer cult status was further confirmed with the lesbian-themed *The Killing of Sister George*, 1968. Although less overtly camp in tenor, Aldrich's later films, such as *The Longest Yard*, 1974 and *Hustle*, 1975, continue his distinctively dark, sensationalist style.

BRETT FARMER

ALFARO, LUIS

b. 1964

writer/performer

Luis Alfaro is an award-winning performance artist, playwright, poet, short-story writer and activist born and raised in the Pico Union district of Los Angeles, California. In 1997 he was awarded a MacArthur Foundation Genius Fellowship. Queer and gender issues are a central theme in his work, which focuses on the lives of members of marginalized groups. His performance art is particularly transgressive for the way he uses his own body to deconstruct notions of gender and race. Moreover, his queer configurations of the body reject gender and racial norms. For example, in his performance piece *Downtown* (1993), Alfaro portrays women without subscribing to traditional notions of femininity. He also rejects stereotypical representations of Chicano gay men by refusing to accept gay norms with regard to physical characteristics and sexual constructs. Queer politicized bodies are also evident in his written texts, where he uses language to reflect the concepts he brings to his work.

DANIEL ENRIQUE PÉREZ

AL-FATIHA FOUNDATION

Founded in 1998 at a glbt Muslim retreat in Boston, Massachusetts, the Al-Fatiha Foundation is an organization that promotes progressive Islamic notions of peace, equality and justice. Since its founding, the organization has grown to include many chapters across the United States and is a member of a larger international network of glbtq Muslim organizations around the world including affiliate organizations in Canada, the United Kingdom and South Africa.

SURINA KHAN

ALL AFRICA RIGHTS INITIATIVE

All Africa Rights Initiative is a coalition of African glbtq organizations whose inaugural annual conference was held in Johannesburg in February 2004 with representatives of 22 groups from 17 African countries. One of its goals is to facilitate cooperation in the struggle for human rights for sexual minorities throughout Africa, including the right to provide honest and effective education for HIV and AIDS awareness. It aims also to assist in the formation of new gay rights associations and networks, and to work for the development of distinctly, proudly African glbtq identities.

MARC EPPRECHT

ALLEN, PETER

b. 1944; d. 1992

singer, songwriter

A consummate showman and comedian, Allen's colourful career and personal life was cut short by his early AIDS-related death. Born in Tenterfield, New South Wales, Australia, he began singing in pubs in Australia, moving to Sydney and forming the popular Allen Brothers band with his friend Chris Ball. While performing in Hong Kong in 1964, he met Judy **Garland**, who hired Allen's group as her supporting tour act. Allen married Garland's daughter Liza **Minnelli** in 1967, whom he divorced in 1970. He also had a relationship with

Mark Herron, Garland's then husband. He pursued a cabaret career in the United States, writing songs for Olivia Newton-John and Helen Reddy, winning an Oscar for his collaboration with Burt Bacharach on 'Arthur's Theme' and penning his signature tune 'I Go to Rio'. He co-wrote the musical *Legs Diamond* with Harvey **Fierstein** in 1988. Undaunted by its failure, Allen resumed his solo shows. His last performance was in Sydney, Australia in 1992. He was diagnosed with HIV the same year and died five months later. His life and music were memorably portrayed in the 2003 Broadway musical *The Boy From Oz*.

JOHN FORDE

ALMODÓVAR, PEDRO

b. 1949

filmmaker

The Spanish filmmaker Pedro Almodóvar emerged from the *movida* – the Madrid-based youth and art movement inspired by the anarchy and style of punk, which developed in late 1970s Spain following the death of Franco. He was born on 24 September 1949, in Calzada de Calatrava, Ciudad Real, Castilla-La Mancha, Spain. Almodóvar gained international prominence with his fourth film *What Have I Done to Deserve This? (¿Qué he hecho yo para merecer esto!!*, 1984) and is today (11 films later) arguably the best-known director not making English-language films. His work presents a serio-comic view of characters driven by sexual desire (often in reaction to a childhood trauma) and at odds with each other and with social convention.

His comedies typically adapt the candy colours and frenetic pace of American comedy from the 1950s and 1960s: the pop comedies of Frank Tashlin and Blake Edwards, the social satire of Billy Wilder and the bedroom farces starring Doris **Day** and Rock **Hudson**. Almodóvar's dramas are inspired by the melo- and psychodramas

of Hollywood from the same period by such directors as **Hitchcock**, **Minnelli** and Sirk, with their virtuoso command of *mise-en-scène* (use of decor, colour and the placement and movement of both the camera and the characters on screen) to depict inner turmoil and interpersonal relationships.

Almodóvar's films can be seen as synthesizing several different strains of gay filmmaking. Only two films from his long and varied career centre on gay male protagonists – *Law of Desire (La Ley del deseo*, 1986) and *Bad Education (La Mala educación*, 2004), but many of his other films contain gay or lesbian characters. Several films feature male-to-female transsexuals (*Law of Desire* [1986]; *All About My Mother* [*Todo sobre mi madre*], 1999) or men who perform in drag (*High Heels* [*Tacones lejanos*], 1991; *Bad Education*). These characters often exemplify Almodóvar's vision of gender and sexuality as a tragicomic source of both pleasure and pain by being figures either of pathos, victimized by a world that insists on a compulsory heterosexuality and a strict division between the sexes, or of wisdom, since they have been able to resist these ideologies.

Many of his films contain a good deal of camp humour, from the 'low', scatological camp of Almodóvar's debut feature, *Luci, Pepi, Bom and the Girls* (1980) – which resembles nothing so much as an early John **Waters** film, with a touch of the Andy Warhol/Paul Morrissey films – to the 'high' camp of the sublime bedroom farce *Women on the Verge of a Nervous Breakdown (Mujeres al borde de un ataque de nervios*, 1987). Since *Women*, most of Almodóvar's subsequent films have been melodramas that centre on shifting gender roles and sexualities. Many of these have female protagonists (*The Flower of My Secret* [*La Flor de mi secreto*], 1995; *All About My Mother*), although his most recent films, *Talk to Her (Hable con ella*, 2002) and *Bad Education*, could rightly be called 'male melodramas'.

His satiric or darkly humorous treatment of sexual violence towards women, particularly in *Tie Me Up, Tie Me Down* (*¡Átame!*, 1990) and *Kika* (1993), have led to his work being labelled misogynist. Almodóvar has also been instrumental in helping to bring international renown to such actors as Carmen Maura, Antonio Banderas, Victoria Abril and Penelope Cruz.

DAVID PENDLETON

ALMOND, MARC AND SOFT CELL

b. 1956

pop singer and band

Marc Almond formed duo electro-pop band, Soft Cell, in 1980 with Dave Ball. The huge international success of their second release, 'Tainted Love', a cover of Gloria Jones' successful single, fashioned a pop genre, marrying the 1970s disco scene with the electronic 1980s. Their songs were an anthem for the pre-AIDS gay British scene, indulging in winking debauchery and decadence, eulogies to self-indulgence and destruction, and Almond established himself as a master queen and a superb torch singer before queer electro-pop took over the charts. After three landmark records with Soft Cell, accompanied by videos that made the most of camp profligate imagination, Almond changed his focus, espousing the theatricality of flamenco guitars and violins (in two superb records he published with the Mambas) and the French decadent poetry and cabaret traditions, while still garnering a number of successful hit singles. In 2002 he rejoined his former Soft Cell partner to stage a comeback.

FABIO CLETO

ALTMAN, DENNIS

b. 1943

writer, advocate

A Professor of Politics at La Trobe University, Melbourne, Dennis Altman has been a front-running participant in gay and sexual politics internationally for over 30 years. His writing has become increasingly diverse since his ground-breaking *Homosexual Oppression and Liberation* first appeared in the United States in 1971 and became a primary text of gay liberation. His work ranges from autobiography – *Defying Gravity* (1997) – and a novel – *The Comfort of Men* (1993) – to the politics and political sociology for which he is best known – e.g., *Global Sex* (2001) and *The Homosexualisation of America* (1982). He writes from within an Australian liberal tradition informed by social democratic values, libertarian sexual politics and secular humanism. He believes that 'social justice is not divisible' and is consistently critical of both 'queer' theory and insular versions of gay community politics.

Altman has been deeply involved with government and community responses to HIV/AIDS in Australia and the Asia Pacific; his writing on such topics includes *AIDS in the Mind of America* (1986) and *Power and Community* (1994). He has also been instrumental in the development of Asian-Pacific infrastructures for HIV, arguing that HIV is a bigger threat to international security than terrorism. Gender is increasingly central to his analyses of social trends in developing countries. Altman argues that the development of international responses to HIV/AIDS forms part of the globalization of human welfare.

MICHAEL HURLEY

AMATEUR PORN

Amateur porn generally comprises pornographic photos, films and (usually) video produced using non-professional performers, usually without the sets, costumes, dialogue and fictional scenarios that characterize the pornography produced by the **porn** industry. While amateur porn has always existed, its prominence ballooned in the late 1990s as home video equipment improved while also becoming cheaper and more readily available. Additionally, the rise of the Internet provided a place for amateur pornographers to display and market their work. Amateur porn typically consists of sex between two or more partners filmed using a single video camera. Two prominent (and overlapping) subgenres are: bareback sex (which is taboo in professional porn); and sex involving straight men (often in the military) having sex with each other or with gay men.

DAVID PENDLETON

AMBIENTE

Spanish slang which refers to the homosexual social scene. A person associated with *ambiente* is not a stranger to the glbtq subculture, may frequent gay events and locations, and have friendships with other homosexuals, but is not necessarily out.

PEDRO ALBORNOZ

AMERICAN CIVIL LIBERTIES UNION (ACLU)

Founded in 1920, the ACLU is the leading national advocate of individual rights in the United States. It has 53 state affiliates across the country. In many states, the ACLU is the only organized voice for civil liberties. The ACLU's Lesbian and Gay Rights Project is a special division of the organization, and has as its goal 'equal treatment and equal dignity for lesbians, gay men and bisexuals'. One role the Project has is to bring 'impact' lawsuits – cases designed to have a significant effect on the lives of lesbians, gay men and bisexuals. Project staff write and promote laws and policies that seek to achieve equality and fairness for gay people. The Project also educates the public, legislators, policy-makers and opinion leaders through books, position papers, articles, lectures and media campaigns. It targets five areas: (1) discrimination; (2)

family and relationships (including same-sex marriage); (3) lesbian and gay teens and young adults; (4) laws that criminalize sexual intimacy; and (5) expression and association.

SURINA KHAN

AMERICAN FOUNDATION FOR AIDS RESEARCH (AMFAR)

Since its inception, amfAR has been, and continues to be, one of the world's leading organizations dedicated to HIV/AIDS prevention, education and advocacy.

In 1983 a group of individuals, including researcher Mathilde Krim and gay activist Sheldon Anderson, working in New York City, grew alarmed by the lack of initiatives to treat and prevent **HIV** and **AIDS**. These individuals decided to counter the city's conservative government, led by Mayor Edward Koch, and to expose the federal government (under the leadership of Ronald Reagan) for its lack of concerted action in fighting the disease. Calling themselves the AIDS Medical Foundation (AMF), the group began raising money for research and public education campaigns. In 1985 AMF merged with the Los Angeles-based National AIDS Research Foundation (NARF) to become amfAR.

amfAR coordinates a Basic Research programme that allocates seed money for new HIV anti-retroviral medicines and innovative prevention strategies. The organization's Clinical Research and Information programme investigates experimental HIV treatments. amfAR's Public and Professional Education initiatives seek to educate the general public about the disease through workshops and national conferences, including the annual National HIV/AIDS Update Conference, a major gathering of researchers, providers, prevention experts and persons living with HIV/AIDS. The group's Public Policy branch works to educate government officials, urging them to work to increase the standard of care for persons living with HIV/AIDS both in the United States and abroad. In total, amfAR has given over US$200 million to more than 2,000 AIDS research and prevention efforts worldwide.

Realizing that critical funding resources would be available in arts and entertainment communities, Elizabeth **Taylor** volunteered as Founding National Chairperson. Taylor, whose efforts were precipitated by the death of her friend, actor Rock **Hudson**, has served in this role for nearly 20 years. Her efforts have inspired a host of other Hollywood luminaries to support amfAR, including Sharon Stone, who has chaired amfAR's Campaign for AIDS Research since 1995.

See also: AIDS; HIV

CHRIS BELL

AMERICAN UNDERGROUND CINEMA

Although lesbian and gay experimental cinema can trace its heritage to the 1895 film *Dickson Experimental Sound Film* (a film of two men waltzing made by W.K.L. Dickson for the Edison Company), there are intriguing precursors such as James Sibley Watson's and Melville Webber's *Lot in Sodom* (1933), Willard Maas' coy and breathtaking *Geography of the Body* (1943) and Alla Nazimova's *Salome* (1923).

The true history of lesbian and gay experimental cinema in the United States, however, begins after the Second World War with Kenneth Anger's *Fireworks* (1947) and Gregory Markopoulos' trilogy *Du sang, de la volupté, et de la mort* (Of Blood, of Pleasure, and of Death, 1947–8). Unlike mainstream filmmakers, experimentalists insisted on forthright lesbian and gay imagery, including graphic depictions of sex. This led to arrests and confiscations throughout the 1960s and into the 1970s, but was a crucial aspect of the opening up of American culture and homosexuality at that time.

Gay filmmakers such as Andy **Warhol** and Jack **Smith** dominated the American underground scene in the 1960s. By the 1970s, however, a new generation of self-consciously gay and lesbian filmmakers had forged a post-Stonewall, openly sexual cinema. During the 1980s filmmakers struggled with ways of dealing with AIDS in a complex manner and a number of important figures in the arena died of the disease. The glbtq scene was revivified in the late 1980s with the creation of the New York Lesbian and Gay Experimental Film Festival (called MIX after 1993). Then, during the 1990s, lesbian and gay experimental cinema transformed in two important ways: first, it exploded with a vast amount of activity because of the availability of inexpensive, high-quality video equipment; and, second, film- and videomakers of colour came onto the scene.

Although in the 1950s **Anger** made the camp *Eaux d'artifice* (1950–3) and the pansensuous *Inauguration of the Pleasure Dome* (1954), James **Broughton** made the homosuggestive *The Pleasure Garden* (1953) and **Markopoulos** contributed two shorts, it wasn't until the 1960s that the gay sensibility burst onto the screen again with Smith's seminal *Flaming Creatures* (1963) and the ever-evolving *Normal Love* (1964). Both displayed an exotic pansexuality that aroused the authorities and influenced innumerable filmmakers and performance artists. Anger's *Scorpio Rising* (1963) defined a hot, rough-and-tumble homosexuality and, through its use of rock 'n' roll songs, insisted on the very centrality of homoeroticism to American popular culture. In one of the great ironies, perhaps the most forthright depiction of gay sex appeared in *Christmas on Earth* (1963), made by Barbara Rubin, a 16-year-old who later embraced Orthodox Judaism, had seven children and died during childbirth.

Warhol's *The Chelsea Girls* (1966), an amphetamine-fuelled, double-projection homosexual epic, explores and explodes lesbian sadomasochism, an accommodating bisexuality, the choice of homosexuality, while it skewers dysfunctional families. The title of Warhol's film *Blow Job* (1964) is a deliberate provocation, but the film is about the ecstatic beauty of the silver screen where the image we see is the face of gorgeous man against the rough silver walls of Warhol's Factory. *My Hustler* (1965) is most likely the first film to depict the gay subculture of **Fire Island**. His later films, *Bike Boy* (1967) and *Lonesome Cowboys* (1968) evoke a homosexual culture and sensibility.

George and Mike Kuchar separately and together churned out their camp classics throughout the 1950s and 1960s and continue to make work today. Tom **Chomont** made dazzling, ethereal films such as *Oblivion* (1969), *Phases of the Moon* (1968), *The Heavens* (1977) and *Earth* (1978). Meanwhile Broughton's work, which since the 1940s has contained elements of homoeroticism and homosensibility, burst into full gay bloom in the late 1970s with his personal and filmic collaboration with Joel Singer. In addition to these films, Roger Jacoby, in Pittsburgh, made his glorious, hand-processed films with **Ondine**, including *L'Amico Fried's Glamorous Friends* (1976), the incomparable *Kunst Life* (1975) and *How to Be a Homosexual* (1980–2).

However, it was not until the next generation that male–male and female–female sex was depicted unashamedly on screen: innovative films include Curt McDowell's *Loads* (1980), Michael Wallin's *The Place Between Our Bodies* (1975) and Barbara Hammer's *Multiple Orgasms* (1975) and *Dyketactics* (1973). Meanwhile, a counter-tradition existed in the lyrical beauty of Nathaniel Dorsky and the desexualized exactitude of Warren Sonbert. Indeed, the late 1980s and early 1990s brought a resurgence of lesbian and gay experimental film. Jerry Tartaglia made his startlingly powerful AIDS trilogy, *A.I.D.S.C.R.E.A.M.* (1988), *Ecce Homo* (1989) and *Final Solutions* (1990). Wallin created the tautly constructed and

resonant *Decodings* (1988) and *Black Sheep Boy* (1995). Jack Waters and Peter Cramer continually re-imagined and presented their extraordinary *Gesamtkunstwerk*, *The Ring, OUR Way* (1987–92), a Super-8, 16-mm, projected video, live performance version of Wagner's *Ring* seen through the prism of American racial politics. The remarkably prolific and hardworking Barbara **Hammer** made the evocative *Optic Nerve* (1985) and *Endangered* (1988) before turning her attention to feature-length experimental documentaries. Su **Friedrich** continued to delight and challenge audiences with her complex and beautiful black-and-white explorations of sex, politics and culture. Lawrence Brose's work became more complex, beautiful and even more experimental, as he successfully combined an intense chemical attack on the image with evermore intricate use of the optical printer.

After two decades of creating lyrical, otherworldly enchantments, Chomont explored the intensities of sadomasochism and found a way to transfer his highly filmic visual style to video in such works as *The Dog Diary* (1996) and *Slash Portrait for Clark* (1994). Marguerite Paris, who filmed the first three Gay Pride marches in New York in Regular-8, continued to make meditative, tough and uncompromisingly lesbian films such as *Burma Road* (1979), *Haitian Initiation* (1989) and *October 1967 Pentagon Peace March* (1991). Among recent filmmakers, Anie Stanley's personal and mysterious Super-8 handiwork stands out.

The most immediate, powerful and innovative work that dealt directly with AIDS was made on video. Because most of the work was documentary and conformed to the half-hour time slots of cable-access TV, it is generally not considered experimental. However, many of the practitioners, including Jean **Carlomusto**, Gregg **Bordowitz** and the collectives, Testing the Limits and DIVA-TV, were knowledgeable students of the history of media. More significantly, out of a sense of urgency and necessity, AIDS video activism pushed and pulled the documentary form to places it had never been before.

Among the most important works about AIDS that appeared on film were Carl George's tender and seminal Super-8 film, *DHPG, Mon Amour* (1989), which influenced numerous filmmakers while giving hope and encouragement to people with AIDS, and Brose's haunting remembrance of his lover, *An Individual Desires Solution* (1985). Some of the more personal and experimental AIDS pieces included Phil Zwickler's and David Wojnarowicz's justifiably bitter *Fear of Disclosure* (1989), Bordowitz's unsentimental and revelatory *Fast Trip, Long Drop* (1993) and Marlon Riggs' incomparable and magnificent *Tongues Untied* (1989). The indefatigable James Wentzy made 150 half-hour cable TV shows almost single-handedly, plus a number of shorter, experimental pieces.

During the 1990s, the large numbers of film- and videomakers of colour brought a renewed vitality to the experimental scene. By 1992 Cheryl **Dunye**, Dawn Suggs and Shari Frilot were making exciting groundbreaking work. Nguyen Tan Hoang made playful, exuberant and smart films such as *maybe never (but I'm counting the days)* (1995) and *Forever Bottom* (1999). Raul Ferrara-Balanquet explored the confluence and conflicts of race, Latino identity and African heritage, while Thomas Allen Harris used his own family to explore the complexities of politics, religion and race. The various manifestations of identity, which seem so singular and fixed in mainstream culture, get a thorough working over in experimental media: Jocelyn Taylor's examination of the female body and Lynne Chan's exploration of popular culture and gender identity resonated with Stuart Gaffney's quiet, surreptitiously insightful work, Ho Tam's elegant constructions of transnational Chinese (male) identity and Charles Lofton's thoughtful, sexy examinations of black (gay) male identity.

The tradition of experimental queer cinema began with a few brave, poetic expressions of homosexuality in the late 1940s. It radically insisted on the legitimacy of full sexual expression in the 1960s and 1970s, dealt unflinchingly with the horrors of the AIDS crisis in the 1980s and then, with the availability of less expensive video equipment and computer-based editing systems, blossomed into a diverse, complex and confident exploration of all aspects of the gay, lesbian, bisexual and transgender communities in the 1990s and into the early years of the twenty-first century.

See also: Bordowitz, Gregg; Kuchar, George and Mike; Riggs, Marlon; Wojnarowicz, David

JIM HUBBARD

AMNESTY INTERNATIONAL

Amnesty International is a 'worldwide movement of people who campaign for internationally recognized human rights'. Its mission is to undertake research and action focused on preventing and ending grave abuses of the rights to physical and mental integrity, freedom of conscience and expression, and freedom from discrimination, within the context of its work to promote all human rights. Until 1991 Amnesty would not interpret its mandate to include human rights abuses against lesbian, gay, bisexual and transgender people. Then, in 1991 Amnesty expanded its mandate to include lesbian and gay people and subsequently formed OUTfront, Amnesty International United States' Program on Human Rights and Sexual Identity. OUTfront is part of an international network of Amnesty activists in more than 20 countries who organize to confront human rights violations and protect the rights of lesbian, gay, bisexual and transgender people.

SURINA KHAN

ANAL SEX

Anal fingering, probing, penetration/intercourse, licking (rimming) or sex-toy insertion by and of male or female participants.

MICHAEL PINFOLD

ANDERSON, ROBERT

b. 1917; d. 1989

playwright

Considered one of the most successful playwrights to capture the mood of mid-twentieth-century America, Anderson's major themes focused on the trials of loneliness and separation engendered by the individual's alienation from culture. His play *Tea and Sympathy* (1953) is considered to be the archetypal expression of a young man's struggle with homosexuality during the more conservative 1950s, when being gay was thought of as aberrant and depraved. The play, set in a boarding school, ends with the young man 'proving' his heterosexuality by losing his virginity to the sympathetic and lonely older wife of a teacher who utters the famous line: 'When you talk about this. And you will. Be kind.'

Anderson's later plays include *All Summer Long* (1954), *Silent Night, Lonely Night* (1959) and *I Never Sang for My Father* (1968). Anderson also wrote for the movies, his works including *The Nun's Story* (1959), *The Sand Pebbles* (1966) and adaptations of his plays.

CHRIS BYRNE

ANDREWS, JULIE

b. 1935

actor

Julie Andrews, British singer and actor, is best known for popular stage and film musicals. A singing child prodigy, Andrews performed from an early age on the British music hall circuit, rising to international prominence playing feisty, headstrong women in hit Broadway shows such as *The Boy Friend*, *My Fair Lady* and *Camelot*. Hollywood stardom followed with a string of phenomenally successful films in the 1960s, including *Mary Poppins* (1964), *The Sound of Music* (1965) and *Thoroughly Modern Millie* (1967). Pigeonholed by the wholesome image of these hits, Andrews ventured into darker roles, often in films made with husband, director Blake Edwards, but few proved popular with audiences. The sophisticated, cross-dressing comedy *Victor/Victoria*, reprised as a smash Broadway musical in 1995, refuelled her career and helped cement her status as a queer icon. However, a botched throat operation in 1998 saw Andrews lose her famous singing voice. She nonetheless continues to perform in non-musical roles.

BRETT FARMER

ANGER, KENNETH

b. 1930

filmmaker, historian

An elusive, legendary experimental filmmaker and Hollywood historian, Kenneth Anger (born Anglemyer) is acknowledged as a leading figure in the American underground and gay filmmaking movements. Born into a Hollywood show-business family, Anger, according to legend, had a cameo role in Max Reinhardt's film *A Midsummer Night's Dream* (1935) at the age of 4. He made his first film, *Who's Been Rocking My Dreamboat*, in his early teens, already demonstrating his precocious talent and penchant for taboo sexual themes. His filmmaking reputation rests on a body of work under three hours in duration, titled *The Magick Lantern Cycle*, which fuses stylistic avant-garde techniques (especially non-linear editing and montage) with explicit homosexual fantasies of rough sex, leather culture and an interest in the occult.

The earliest film in the series, *Fireworks* (1947), was made over a weekend in Anger's family home while his parents were away. A cinematic wet dream involving sexual fantasies of sailors, cowboys and pilots, it features Anger (then aged 19) descending into the night to scour the waterfront looking for rough sex, and culminates in the image of a sailor's erection that ejaculates like a firework. *Fireworks* heralded the beginnings of an explicitly homoerotic American underground cinema, giving visual expression to the repressed homosexual desire of the period, creating, in Anger's words, 'a temporary release from inflammable desires dampened by day under the cold water of consciousness'. The film attracted widespread praise, notably from French gay filmmaker Jean **Cocteau**. Soon after, Anger moved to Paris (financing the move by stealing and selling his family silverware), where he became involved with Cocteau, the writer Anaïs Nin and discovered the writings of the occultist Aleister Crowley, who became a major influence on his later work.

After working with Cocteau on a series of abortive projects, Anger made the experimental shorts *Puce Moment* (1949) and *La Lune des lapins* (Rabbit's Moon, 1950). In *Eaux d'artifice* (1950–3, dedicated to Pavel **Tchelitchev**), he again indulged his cruising and rough trade fantasies, this time counterpoint against a fantasia of fountains, exotic fauna and a Vivaldi soundtrack. Again achieving international notoriety, *Eaux d'artifice* was the subject of a landmark censorship case in 1959, in which the Supreme Court concluded the film could be legally shown in American theatres, despite its explicit homosexual content. Anger's next piece, *Inauguration of the Pleasure Dome* (1954), was based on occult writings by Crowley and starred Nin, who chronicled the making of the film in her diaries.

In 1962 Anger returned to the United States and completed his best-known work,

Scorpio Rising (1963), a homoerotic homage to 'the masculine fascination with the Thing That Goes'. Referencing the fetishized leather aesthetic of Marlon Brando in *The Wild Ones* and James Dean in *Rebel Without a Cause*, the film superimposed 1960s pop tunes over erotic close-ups of naked male torsos, and hunky leather boys polishing and racing their cars and motorcycles. During this period, Anger also started work on *Hollywood Babylon*, an alternative history of **Hollywood** chronicling every major scandal of the pre-Second World War film industry. Written in gleefully purple prose, the work simultaneously glories in the camp spectacle and glamour of Hollywood stardom and voyeuristically dissects scandals of adultery, drug abuse, suicide, orgies and hidden homosexual affairs. Originally published in France, it quickly became an underground best seller, but the controversial, potentially libellous subject matter prevented its US publication until 1975.

After the footage for his next film project was stolen by his star, Manson-Family member Bobby Beausoleil, Anger published his own obituary in *The Village Voice*. After a suitable period of mourning, Anger took his remaining footage and made *Invocation of My Demon Brother* (1969), another homage to Crowley that fused homoerotic, occult and Satanic imagery with concert footage of the Rolling Stones.

The final chapter of the 'Crowley' trilogy, *Lucifer Rising* (1974; 2nd version 1980), took over a decade to complete. A bizarre fusion of occult mythology and B-movie pop culture, it features the Egyptian gods Isis and Osiris being summoned, eventually appearing in pink flying saucers over the Valley of the Kings, and starred Marianne Faithful, with experimental music by Mick Jagger. Anger published *Hollywood Babylon II* in 1985, again exposing celebrity scandals of post-1950s Hollywood, concluding with a lament about 1980s Reaganist economics and moral conservatism. His recent works include the short film, *The Man We Want to Hang* (2002), in which Anger films close-ups of paintings by Crowley. He continues to re-edit and present retrospectives of his works. Anger's legacy of stylistic and narrative innovation has inspired generations of filmmakers as diverse as Andy **Warhol**, Martin Scorsese, David Lynch and Todd **Haynes**. Anger's work is a precursor to Pop Art and New Queer Cinema movements. His life and work was the subject of a 1991 documentary by Nigel **Finch**.

See also: American underground cinema; New Queer Cinema, International

Further reading

Hunter, Jack (ed.) (2001) *Moonchild: The Films of Kenneth Anger* (Persistence of Vision, 1), London: Creation Books.

Landis, Bill (1995) *Anger: The Unauthorized Biography of Kenneth Anger*, New York: HarperCollins.

JOHN FORDE

ANGLICAN CHURCH

The Anglican Church, with its 450–year history, has struggled deeply with issues of human sexuality and is divided in its application of set rules. These are based on the Gospels, interpreting that homosexual genital acts fall short of an ideal and are to be met by a call to repentance. In March 2004 Gene Robinson, who has lived with his male partner for 15 years, was ordained a bishop in the state of New Hampshire, making the issues of ordaining practising gay priests and blessing same-sex unions highly visible and controversial.

MICHAEL PINFOLD

ANIME

Anime is a uniquely Japanese form of animated movies and TV programmes. It is closely related to manga (Japanese comics), and stories that originate as manga often become anime – in fact, a popular manga is almost guaranteed to become an anime, and perhaps also a live-action film or TV programme as well. Manga, in fact, is the great generator of Japanese popular culture, and besides film and television, there are many examples of items as diverse as video games, CDs, toys, clothing, snack foods and more, all able to point to manga as their original source.

One aspect of anime and manga that inevitably attracts the attention of a gay audience is the manner in which characters are drawn. Male characters – especially heroic or sympathetic ones – tend to be drawn in an androgynous manner. This becomes particularly exaggerated in *shojo* (girl's) manga and anime, where the characters are drawn in accordance with the *bishonen* ('beautiful boy') tradition, in which male characters share the willowy proportions, fine features and wispy, often gravity-defying, hairstyles of the female characters. There are even *shojo* manga that take gay male love as their theme, and it is interesting to note that these manga are almost universally written and illustrated by women, for an audience of women. The most popular of these stories make the transition to anime, taking along with them the stylistic tenets of the *bishonen* tradition. These tenets have become ubiquitous, with the result that male characters in boys' (*shonen*) manga and anime can look every bit as much the androgyne as their *shojo* counterparts. Some examples of anime that feature gay male characters are *Fake, Ninja Scroll* and *Kizuna*.

Lesbian relationships are also present in the world of anime and manga, but with much less frequency than gay male relationships. The popular *Sailor Moon*, for example, contained a lesbian couple in its original Japanese version, and although this subplot was deftly excised in the dubbed version shown on American television, it can be seen in the unedited DVD release. For some reason, however, Japanese girls seem to prefer to read and/or watch stories about gay men rather than gay women – a phenomenon surely worthy of sociological inquiry.

Stories involving transgender characters are also quite popular in anime and manga. These take two forms. The first of these involves characters who pretend to be the opposite sex, dressing up and acting the part. The classic example of this is Osamu Tezuka's *Princess Knight*, in which a girl born into a royal family pretends to be a boy so that she can be declared heir to the throne. The other form taken by transgender stories are the more recent tales in which characters actually become the opposite sex, usually by some sort of supernatural means. The most famous of these is *Ranma 1/2*, the story of a young male martial artist who, as the result of falling into a cursed spring, becomes a beautiful girl whenever he is splashed with cold water. The situation is temporary, since he instantly regains his masculinity when doused with hot water, and the entire affair is played for laughs, with Ranma pursued by multiple suitors of both sexes. Another example of this type of story is *Eerie Queerie*, in which a teenaged boy who is a spiritual medium takes on the personalities of the female ghosts he channels. This results in two of his male classmates becoming infatuated with him, leading to a love triangle.

Why do such themes occur so regularly in Japanese popular culture? One probable reason is that the native Japanese Shinto religion contains no prohibitions against gay relationships – in fact, love between men was traditionally viewed as the most pure form of love. Even the warrior samurai believed that physical love between the samurai master and student was desirable, because it forged a bond that could be useful in combat. Modern Japanese society is highly tolerant of gay relationships as

long as they adhere to the same constraints that apply to heterosexual ones: basically, that public displays of affection be limited to holding hands.

CHRIS NUZZI

ANZALDÚA, GLORIA
b. 1942; d. 2004
writer

Lesbian writer, editor and cultural critic whose work helped establish the voice of feminists of colour in the United States. Anzaldúa is best known as the co-editor of Persephone Press's collection of feminist criticism, *This Bridge Called My Back: Writings by Radical Women of Colour* (1981). Acclaimed as a landmark in feminist publishing, the collection critiqued the racism of established Anglo-American feminism, giving full expression to lesbian feminist thinking. Anzaldúa edited a follow-up anthology, *Making Face, Making Soul/ Haciendo Caras: Creative and Critical Perspectives by Women of Colour* (1990), which profiled the complex interactions of gender, class and ethnicity within contemporary feminist identity. Her own writing includes fiction, poetry and essays, including the book *Borderlands/La Frontera: The New Mestiza* (1987), in which she defined 'queer' identity as a subversion of gender norms and a platform for political change in the struggle against racism and homophobia.

JOHN FORDE

AQUENO, FRANK
performance artist, activist

Artist and activist who is best known as the creator and webmaster of the Internet web site Queer By Choice, in which he disputes theories about the genetic determinism of homosexuality and advocates queer identity as a conscious and positive lifestyle choice.

His controversial argument has led to a long-standing public dispute with **Parents, Families and Friends of Lesbians and Gays (PFLAG)**. He explores the complexity of contemporary sexual identity in his plays and performance pieces, including *Queer Pier* (first performed in 1992), *HETERO!transbiLESBOyQUEER* (1993), *Reparations* (1995), *Mom Lies/Dad Lives* (1996), *To Provoke and Offend* (1997) and *The Pursuit of Happiness* (1999). His other writings include *Being Frank: Essays, Interviews and Performances* (1999).

JOHN FORDE

ARAKI, GREGG

b. 1959

filmmaker

American independent filmmaker Gregg Araki is identified with New Queer Cinema. Araki's work is inspired by Jean-Luc Godard's 1960s New Wave Cinema, horror films, documentaries, TV news, road movies and adolescence melodramas. He began his career in 1987 with *Three Bewildered People in the Night*. His significant film, *The Living End* (1992), portrays the anarchistic voyage of an HIV+ gay couple to the seashore, the metaphoric living end. In *Totally Fucked Up* (1993) Araki represents agonized queer adolescents in alienated Los Angeles. One character is thrown out after coming out to his parents, while another falls in love with an unfaithful student and commits suicide. *The Doom Generation* (1995) is a queer version of the serial killer subgenre, a violent journey of two young men and a woman, ending in a gory spectacle of sex and gay-bashing. Araki also directed *Nowhere* (1997) and *Splendor* (1999). His latest film, *Mysterious Skin*, opened in 2005.

See also: New Queer Cinema, International

GILAD PADVA

ARE YOU BEING SERVED?

TV series

This English TV comedy (1972–85) and movie (1977) was in the tradition of the British *Carry On* farces. *Are You Being Served?* followed the antics of a mismatched team of department store assistants. Repressed and sexually perverse Captain Peacock, lewd middle-aged Mrs Slocombe, buxom bimbo Miss Brahms and camp 'bachelor' Mr Humphries (played by John **Inman**) traded a series of innuendoes, notably Inman's sexually loaded catchphrase, 'I'm free!' Enjoying huge popularity in the 1970s, Inman was later criticized for perpetuating effeminate gay stereotypes. *Grace & Favour* (1992–3), a misjudged attempt to reunite the cast and characters, failed following criticism of its outdated humour.

JOHN FORDE

ARGENTINA, FILMMAKING

It would be possible to cull from the enormous inventory of cinema in Argentina an impressive list of films readable from queer perspectives regarding gender identity, structures of desire and non-heteronormative sexuality, or simply a questioning of patriarchal values. Yet, because Argentine society can be characterized as (still) rigidly homophobic, one wonders if such an investigation would yield much of significant interest. An important place to begin would be with the career of Latin America's premier woman director, María Luisa Bemberg (1922–95), as all of her (fewer than a dozen) films are feminist in nature and most reveal important queer dimensions.

There are four Argentine films that are pertinent to any discussion of queer culture, all dating from the period since the return to constitutional democracy in 1983 following almost two decades of neo-fascist tyranny. *Adiós Roberto* (*Goodbye, Roberto*, 1985) by Enrique Dawi recounts the homoerotic affair between two men, one of whom is fleeing a stifling marriage. The film ends ambiguously, with the viewer unclear as to whether he will return to his wife, remain with his lover or enjoy the love of both. But the depiction of his transition from straight to gay is exceptionally eloquent. Much of the film is a projection of the guilty conscience of the married man on furlough from heterosexuality, as he is visited in his imagination by figures of authority such as his dead father, his parish priest, a friend, his mother and even the neighbourhood whore who thought she had convinced him of his heterosexuality. These vignettes are gems of homophobic discourse in Argentina.

Otra historia de amor (*Another Love Story*, 1986) by América Ortiz de Zárate also focuses on homophobia, but in this case how it functions in the workplace. Two men who work together – one married – have an affair. The film closely follows soap opera conventions, although modifying them in strategic ways, and ends happily, when one man at the last moment renounces a career opportunity abroad to remain with his lover.

Bemberg's *Yo la peor de todas* (*I the Worst of All*, 1990) sticks close to the known facts of the life of the seventeenth-century nun poet Sor Juana Inés de la Cruz. There is little material evidence that she ever engaged in lesbian sex, but there are many queer dimensions regarding her close emotional and intellectual relations with other women. This is unquestionably the most famous lesbian-marked film from Latin America.

Marcelo Piñeyro's *Plata quemada* (*Burnt Money*, 2000) underscores the queer dimension of a real-life male criminal duo. Piñeyro is not known for gay-friendly filmmaking, nor are the stars of the film. Yet the way in which a complex homoerotic relationship is related to Genetian criminality is skilfully handled. And although theirs is a classically tragic demise – they die in each other's arms – they do so after burning their ill-gotten gains in a final defiance of capitalism and its version of heteronormativity.

Also worth mentioning, even though it was made in Portuguese in Brazil, is *A intrusa* (*The Intruder,* 1979). Made by an Argentine filmmaker, Carlos Hugo Christiansen, it is a queer interpretation of a short story by Jorge Luis Borges, whose sexuality is one of the great enigmas of Argentine culture.

Dawi, Ortiz de Zárate, Bemberg and Christiansen are now deceased, which may be one reason why there has not been more queer film in Argentina.

DAVID WILLIAM FOSTER

ARGENTINA, LITERATURE

The founding text of Argentine narrative is a short story by Esteban Echeverría, probably written during his Uruguayan exile in the 1830s but not published until 1871. The story concludes with the punitive rape by a mob of an opponent of the regime. Perhaps not strictly homoerotic, the story very clearly figures a male–male genital act, and prefigures a long line of male–male rape scenes in Argentine literature. The most important Argentine literary text of the nineteenth century is José Hernández's two-part poem of Gaucho life, *Martín Fierro* (1871 and 1876), in which homosocial bonding figures as an alternative to heterosexual family life.

Jorge Luis Borges is an Argentine cultural icon. There are many questions regarding his personal life, especially his sexuality. Of importance is the often queer world of his fiction, including the virtual absence of women and the extensive representation of anti-patriarchal configurations of intimacy, friendship and the overall design for living. *A Intrusa*, one of his most curious stories regarding brotherly love; was made into a film that enraged Borges (see **Argentina, filmmaking**).

Buenos Aires is noted for its variegated bohemian culture, symbolized by Alejandra Pizarnik. The daughter of Jewish exiles, an institutionalized psychotic and a lesbian, Pizarnik penned dense accounts of the deepest corners of emotion and desire. Her Genetian meditation on the sixteenth-century Hungarian lesbian tyrant, Erzsebet Bathory, is one of Argentina's most notorious queer texts and challenges a facile 'liberal' understanding of homoerotic desire. Osvaldo Lamborghini is Pizarnik's male bohemian peer. Undoubtedly, Manuel **Puig** is Argentina's most famous queer writer, whose themes of homophobia and violence in same-sex relationships provocatively resist simple notions of 'gay' culture.

Since its return to constitutional democracy in 1983, after almost two decades of neo-fascist – and homophobic – tyranny, Argentina has made enormous advances in the protection of queer life and, consequently, its visibility, including a range of popular culture and even TV soap operas. As a result there has been a strong growth in the field of queer literature, although as yet no one of Puig's importance has emerged. Of note, however, is the sociologist Juan José Sebreli, who has published a history of 100 years of homosexuality and a work on the homoerotic dimensions of soccer. Manuel Mujica Láinez and Ernesto Schoo have both authored a number of novels featuring the gay demi-monde of oligarchic society. Mujica Láinez's 1966 *Bomarzo* is an Argentine classic of (homo)-social otherness. There is also something definitely queer about the narrative world of César Aira, although not so much in terms of homoerotic desire. Reina Roffé writes from abroad, and her novels explore the psychological dimensions of non-patriarchal feminine identities. Osvaldo Soriano publishes mostly in Spain, his themes hypermasculine gays. Sylvia Molloy, who lives in the United States, has written an important lesbian novel, and her literary scholarship has many queer dimensions.

Finally, Osvaldo Bazán explores the hitherto underexamined relationship between the Left and queerness.

One more author worthy of note, even though he mostly wrote in French, is **Copi** (aka Raúl Damonte), who is now recognized as Argentina's most important queer dramatist. Despite his status however, his drag interpretation of Eva Duarte de Perón has never yet been performed in Argentina.

DAVID WILLIAM FOSTER

ARMAH, AYI KWEI

b. 1939

writer

The Ghanaian novelist Ayi Kwei Armah provides sharp critiques of both colonial rule and postcolonial corruption and political oppression that have resulted in his exile in Tanzania. Many of Armah's novels contain sexually explicit scenes charged with heavy symbolism. His *Two Thousand Seasons*, published in 1979, is remarkable for equating the Arab exploitation of Africa during the era of the slave trade to homosexual rape.

See also: Ouologuem, Yambo

MARC EPPRECHT

ARMANI, GIORGIO

b. 1943

fashion designer

A fashion designer born in Piacenza, Italy, Armani began his career in 1964. He created the Giorgio Armani label in 1975, and in 1982 he appeared on the cover of *Time*, putting the final seal of approval on his fame. From his first collections, Armani's style proved to be deeply innovative, the result of a successful blending of comfort and elegance. A worldwide symbol of sophistication and style, many stars and artists choose to wear his designs. Among the many prizes awarded to him, he has won the prestigious Cutty Sark Award for the Best International Men's Wear fashion designer more than once.

ALBERTO EMILETTI

ARTETA, MIGUEL

b. 1965

film director

Born in San Juan, Puerto Rico, and a graduate of Wesleyan University as well as the American Film Institute, Arteta's work explores the eccentric and obsessive underbelly of human sexuality. His debut feature, *Star Maps* (1997), is a dark tale of a Mexican teenage boy and aspiring actor who is pimped by his father as a male prostitute in Los Angeles. He achieved critical acclaim at the Sundance Film Festival with *Chuck & Buck* (2000), a chilling study of male friendship and homoerotic desire, featuring a 27-year-old man who tracks down his former best friend and stalks him, hoping to re-enact their childhood sex games. Arteta's deft touch with bizarre family dynamics proved an ideal match for directing two episodes of the award-winning TV series *Six Feet Under* (2001). Arteta also directed *The Good Girl* (2002), a droll retelling of Flaubert's *Madame Bovary* set in the American Midwest.

JOHN FORDE

ARZNER, DOROTHY

b. 1897; d. 1979

film director

The only female **Hollywood** director to thrive from the 1920s to the 1940s, Dorothy Arzner became a touchstone for feminists in the 1970s and was queerly re-evaluated in the 1990s. Arzner worked as a typist, editor and writer before she directed her first film (*Fashions for Women*, 1927). However, she was soon at the helm of a major 'talkie' (*The Wild Party*) and the novelty of a woman director was used for publicity purposes. Key films included *Christopher Strong* (1933), *Craig's Wife* (1936) and *Dance Girl Dance* (1940). Arzner directed features until 1943; she later worked in television and radio and taught during the 1960s.

Feminist film studies rediscovered Arzner, recognizing women's struggles within patriarchal societies and the irony of their fates as themes in her work. Gays enjoyed her work with Joan Crawford, Lucille Ball, Katharine Hepburn and Rosalind Russell, but only later scholarship analysed the bonds among women and the queer critique of heterosexuality in Arzner's films. Research also revealed her 40-year relationship with dance impresario Marion Morgan.

DAVID M. LUGOWSKI

ASHE, ARTHUR

b. 1943; d. 1993

tennis player, activist, author

Arthur Ashe, born in Richmond, Virginia, was the first prominent black tennis player in history, winning three Grand Slam singles, including the 1975 Wimbledon Cup. As an activist he co-organized Artists and Athletes Against Apartheid, a group whose influence helped create the economic sanctions that ultimately brought an end to apartheid. In 1985 he was honoured in the International Tennis Hall of Fame, and in 1988 he published the three-volume set of the history of the black athlete in the United States, *A Hard Road To Glory*. In 1992 he was celebrated as *Sports Illustrated*'s 'Sportsman of the Year'. Ashe, who was heterosexual, acquired HIV from a blood transfusion in 1983 but kept the knowledge private until 1992. His admittance brought an outpouring of compassion and support. He died on 6 February 1993 in New York City, having raised awareness of AIDS to a level where paranoia and fear were no longer the overriding emotions.

ERIC ANDERSON

ASHLEY, APRIL

b. 1935

model

Born male in England and raised as George Jamieson, Ashley did not go through male puberty but instead developed breasts. At age 14 he began work with the Merchant Navy and at 16 attempted suicide. In 1953 he was treated in Walton Hospital's psychiatric ward with male hormones and electric shock treatment. From 1956 to 1960 George worked as a performer with a Paris female impersonator troupe. During this time a transsexual friend introduced him to Dr Burou, who in 1960 performed a sex-change operation on George in Casablanca. Afterwards he began life anew as April Ashley.

April Ashley worked as one of Britain's top models and in 1963 married Arthur Corbett, a war hero and the son of the Second Lord Rowallan. Corbett himself was also a cross-dresser. Corbett sued for divorce in 1970, and, because Ashley was born male, the English court pronounced her marriage to Corbett as null. This ruling still stands in England today. Following the ruling, Ashley was publicly reviled and fired from her modelling job. In 1986 she moved to the United States, where she now lives.

LYNETTE REINI-GRANDELL
VENUS

ASIA, FILMMAKING

The 1996 controversy over *Fire* by Deepa **Mehta** and the 1997 acclaim for *Happy Together* (*Chun guang zha xie*) by Wong **Kar-wai** have raised the profile of queer Asian films in the West. Although the directors are not gay or lesbian, these films have attained mainstream circulation and global queer subcultural acclamation. A few factors explaining this phenomenon relate to the efficient assimilation of Hong Kong films into **Hollywood**, the globalization of gay and lesbian cultures, and the different institutional specificities of production, distribution, reception and regulation. Hollywood's recent incorporation of Hong Kong film styles and stars has paved the way for the flow of other Asian cinema into the West at the same time that the mainstream multiplex art house has emerged to market a new genre for its increased number of screens, thus creating the opportunity for a global audience for Asian films and a new audience for Asian queer films. The globalization of gay and lesbian cultures, aided by the impact of new media technologies, has also led to an East–West exchange of queer politics, lifestyles and aesthetics, fuelling new desires and audiences among Asia's newly emergent gay and lesbian social movements. Such factors have led to an increased visibility for Asian queer films in the West and a demand for them in Asia: countries such as Japan, Korea, India, Taiwan and China (Hong Kong) are examples of such cultures of circulation compared to others such as Vietnam, Cambodia and Indonesia.

Filmmaking in Asia is driven primarily by commercial demand. India and Hong Kong are the two largest film-producing centres in the world, with outputs in excess of 300 films a year. As successful mainstream commercial industries, they depict queer cultures through genre conventions such as the male buddy Bollywood epic or the transsexual martial arts film. These films, however, may not necessarily support the affirmation politics of sexual minorities. Indeed, the directors of *Fire* and *Happy Together* have refuted the same-sex claims of their films and promoted instead the universal themes of love and oppression. Nonetheless, these films, like many others, have been 'queered' through reception.

Issues of reception relate to different interpretations. Although sexual minorities have always 'read against the grain' to uncover affirming subtexts, hidden histories or marginal representations, these interpretations, and their politicizations, are not necessarily universal. The terms 'queer filmmaking in Asia' and 'queer Asian cinema' are clearly misnomers for a region that encompasses many diverse cinemas, traditions, industries and audiences. Under such a rubric, it is problematic to discuss the representation of homosexuality or the history of gays and lesbians in the cinema from a Western, Stonewall-centred politics; nor is it unproblematic to speak of them in terms of an indigenous essence (see **Indigenous queer identities**). Andrew Grossman (2000: 1) suggests that queer Asian cinema 'both engage[s] and refute[s] "Eastern" and "Western" conceptions of homosexuality and sexual politics'. Queer Asian films negotiate heteronormative and homophobic demands; they are also local products made under specific cultural, political and sexual milieus.

Across Asia, social and religious constraints, the different developments of gay and lesbian movements, and filmmaking environments controlled by censorship, all affect the representation of queer in the cinema. Japan boasts a pre-Second World War modernist film style, a 1960s leftist-inspired New Wave movement and a current popular entertainment industry queered by 'pink' pornography and *hentai* (lesbian) anime. In China and South Korea, state-funded industries have given way to transnationally funded art-house and blockbuster productions that also capitalize on the currently fashionable subculture of homosexuality. In Singapore, despite the demands of a state-controlled film economy, the cinema has engaged creatively with unofficial representations of queer (see **Singapore, filmmaking**). With the exception of period-styled films such as *Farewell My Concubine* (*Ba wang bie ji*, Chen Kaige, 1993), *Swords-man 3: The East is Red* (*Dongfang bubai*, Ching Siu-tung, 1992) and *Gohatto* (*Taboo*, Nagisa Oshima, 1999), the representation of homosexual characters in Asian cinema has been, by and large, influenced by twentieth-century modernity. In particular, the globalization of queer since the 1990s and its effects on Asia have resulted in a few high-profile queer films that show the uniqueness of a region with a complex history of Western colonization and indigenous traditions. These factors contribute to an emerging queer and Asian cinema that showcases diverse aesthetics and histories and creates new 'queerscapes' (Leung 2001) that celebrate and critically engage Asia's new sexual identities.

In Japan films evoke queerness through the representation of alternative sexuality. One of the great masters of Japanese cinema, 'feminist' director Kenji Mizoguchi, used film as a form of social criticism and exposed the social condition of women. His portrayal of single and fallen women as prostitutes, geishas and mistresses in the critically acclaimed *Osaka Elegy* (*Naniwa erejī*, 1936), *Sisters of Gion* (*Gion no shimai*, 1936), *The Life of Oharu* (*Saikaku ichidai onna*, 1952) and *Ugetsu Monogatari* (1953), inspired themes that were further developed by the New Wave cinema of Nagisa Oshima. *In the Realm of the Senses* (*Ai no corrida*, 1976) and *The Empire of Passion* (*Ai no borei*, 1979) engaged issues of sexuality, power and identity while *Merry Christmas Mr Lawrence* (1982) and the more recent *Gohatto* demonstrated the relationship between men in Japanese prison camps and post-Shogun Tokugawa's Meiji samurai culture. Taboos such as incest and child sexuality were also evident in *The Profound Desire of the Gods* (*Kamigami no Fukaki Yokubo*, Shohei Imamura, 1968), *Nanami: First Love* (*Hatsukoi: Jogoku-hen*, Susumu Hani, 1967) and *Emperor of Tomato Ketchup* (*Tomato Ketchup Kotei*, Shuji Terayama, 1970). Other films challenging the status quo include Yasuzo Masumura's *Passion* (*Manji*,

1964), a B-grade satire about a housewife who falls in love with a female model and embarks on a lesbian relationship; Toshio Matsumoto's experimental *Funeral Procession of Roses* (*Bara no soretsu*, 1969), a black comedy about transgenderism; and Kon Ichikawa's *An Actor's Revenge* (*Yukinojo henge*, 1963), a spectacle that celebrates the kabuki career of a nineteenth-century Tokugawa-era *onnagata* (a stage actor of female roles). Kinji Fukasaku's homage to this tradition in the stylish *Black Lizard* (*Kurotokage*, 1968), starring Akihiro Maruyama, Japan's most famous female impersonator, as a jewel thief, is a camp classic.

Also emerging around this radical period of the 1960s and 1970s was the 'pink film genre' (soft-core erotica), which exploited gay sexuality for a predominantly heterosexual audience (Grossman 2000). Notable examples include Nakamura Genji's *Beautiful Mystery* (*Kyokon densetsui: utsukushii nazo*, 1983), *More Love* (Koshi Shimada, 1984), *Muscle* (*Kurutta butokai*, Hisayasu Sato, 1988), *Melody for Buddy Matsumae* (*Matsumae-Kun no senritsu*, Hiroyuki Oki, 1992) and *I Like You, I Like You Very Much* (*Anata-ga suki desu, dai suki desu*, Hiroyuki Oki, 1994). During the 1980s and 1990s queer representations enjoyed mainstream popularity with the rise of manga and anime consumption in everyday Japanese culture. A subgenre of lesbian-themed (*hentai*) and *shonen ai* (boy love) animated erotica flourished (McLelland 2003). Homoeroticism, tomboyism and gay romances were explored in *Here is Greenwood* (*Koko wa Greenwood*, Yukie Nasu, 1991), *The Song of Wind and Trees* (*Kaze to ki no uta*, Keiko Takemiya, 1987), *Homosexual White Paper: A Man's Decision* (Teruo Kigurashi, 1992), *Kizuna* (Kazuma Kodaka, 1995) and *Revolutionary Girl Utena: The Movie* (*Shojo Kakumei Utena*, Kunihiko Ikuhara, 2001), based on the successful TV series showing from 1997 until 1999. Usually written by and produced for a voyeuristic, young and heterosexual audience, these films (and books) have created a new popular cultural form that queers the characters through the appeal of their gender ambiguity. Even adolescent TV cartoons such as *Bubblegum Crisis* (*Baburugamu kuraishisu*) and *Sailor Moon* also feature lesbian superwoman and same-sex desire.

The globalization of queer in Asia from the 1980s onwards has seen the emergence of the generic gay and lesbian film with its politics of visibility. In Japan, *Afternoon Breezes* (*Kaze tachi no gogo*, Hitoshi Yasaki, 1980), *Summer Vacation: 1999* (*1999 – Nen no natsu yasumi*, Shusuke Kaneko, 1988), *Rough Sketch of a Spiral* (*Rasen no sobyo*, Yasushi Kojima, 1990), *Twinkle* (*Kirakira hikaru*, Joji Matsuoka, 1992), *Okoge* (Fag Hag, Takehiro Nakajima, 1992), *800 2 Lap Runners* (Ryuichi Hiroki, 1993), Ryosuke Hashiguchi's *Nagisa no Shindobaddo* (*Like Grains of Sand*, 1995) and *Hush!* (2001) and Kaze Shindo's *Love/Juice* (2000) feature various themes of coming out, repressed lesbianism, teenage homosexuality, urban gay lives and queer parenting. In the experimental *I.K.U.* (2000), Shu Li Cheang parodies science-fiction porn to reclaim lesbian desire and expose the misogyny of Japanese pornography (Jacobs 2003). While some of these films were successful in Japan because they appealed to heterosexual audiences, factors such as visibility politics, male homoeroticism, straight voyeurism and genre conventions also frame other cinemas in the Asia region.

In India a queer film culture has emerged through mainstream subversion and state intervention (see **India, filmmaking**). Bollywood films that have traditionally used the male 'buddy genre' to explore heterosexual romance and family values have been reclaimed by India's gay and lesbian sub-cultures. *Dosti* (Satyen Bose, 1964), *Sholay* (Ramesh Sippy, 1975), *Anurodh* (Shakti Samanta, 1977), *Namak Haram* (Hrishikesh Mukherjee, 1973), *Main Khilari Tu Anari* (Shakti Samanta, 1994) and *Hara Pheri* (Priyadarshan, 2000) are reinvented as same-sex love and homosocial bonding, and heart-throb Akshay Kumar celebrated as a gay icon (Waugh 2001; Ghosh 2002). More recently, queer sensibility has begun to haunt the popular film circuit, with *Ghaav* (Kumar Jay, 2002) and *Samvedna* (Sanjeev Chadha, 2002) portraying openly out gay and lesbian characters. Urban and localized queer identities are more readily explored in India's parallel cinemas. Produced under the state-subsidized industry, *BOMgaY* (Riyad Wadia, 1996), *Bombay Boys* (Kaizad Gustad, 1998), *The Pink Mirror* (Sridhar Rangayan, 2002) and *Mango Souffle* (Mahesh Dattani, 2003) show how metropolitan gays have adopted a globally recognizable cosmopolitan lifestyle and identity. Diasporic films and documentary videos such as *Khush* (Pratibha Parmar, 1991), *Fire* (Mehta, 1996), *Summer in my Veins* (Nish Saran, 1999), *Kalihgat Fetish* (Ashish Avikunthak, 2000), *Bombay Eunuch* (Michelle Gucovsky, 2001) and *My Friend Su* (Neeraj Bhasin, 2001) have also explored themes of coming out, transsexuality, and living with HIV and **AIDS** through negotiating indigenous traditions and imported identities.

In 1997, on the eve of British Hong Kong's return to the motherland China, art-house director Wong Kar-wai was awarded the Palme d'Or at the fiftieth Cannes Film Festival for *Happy Together* (*Chun guang zha xie,* 1997), a road movie about two Chinese gay men travelling and partying in Argentina. *Happy Together* was a landmark film for queer Asian cinema; its critical acclaim on the international festival circuit reflected a global recognition of Asian and queer cinema. Its celebrated status in the mainstream, diasporic and Asian queer communities attested also to the coming of age of a modern Asian queer identity (Yue 2000). The film's gay star, the late Leslie **Cheung**, was hailed as a global queer icon and canonized as Asia's greatest diva superstar. The reunion subtext reflected a cinema and a place that was anxious about its handover to the socialist motherland. Indeed, popular Hong Kong cinema

(see **Hong Kong, filmmaking**) during the 1980s and 1990s was replete with tropes of gender ambiguity and queer sexuality that functioned as a border-crossing device. Transsexual martial artists are commonplace in swordplay epics, as demonstrated by box-office hits such as *Swordsman 3: The East is Red* (*Dongfang bubai*, Ching Siu-tung, 1992), *Fong Sai Yuk* (Corey Yuen Kuei, 1993) and *Eagle Shooting Heroes* (*Donhchengxijiu*, Jeff Lau, 1993). Its famed action cinema features homoerotic male camaraderie, secret 'big brother' love, lesbian assassins and tomboy supercops. Classics here include *The Killer* (*Diexueshuangxiong*, 1989) and *A Better Tomorrow* (*Yingxiongbense*, 1984), both by John Woo, *Pink Force Commando* (1984) and *Golden Queen's Commando* (1984) by Yin-ping Chu, *Naked Killer* (*Chiluo Gaoyang*, Clarence Fok, 1992) and *Jiang Hu: The Triad Zone* (*Jiang Hu Gaoji*, Dante Lam, 2000).

The prolific output of the Hong Kong film industry, together with its extensive deployment of 'queer', allows the cinema to function as a heuristic model for the general rubric of an Asian queer cinema. Such a cinema can be considered a modern cinema that stages an encounter with its indigenous traditions, colonial histories, regional routes and global present. Like the two seminal gay films from China, *Farewell My Concubine* and *East Palace, West Palace* (*Dong gong xi gong*, Zhang Yuan, 1996) that reclaim local gay heritage and display new queer publics, Hong Kong's *Confessions of an Intimate Courtesan* (*Ainu*, Chor Yuen, 1972), *The Twin Bracelets* (*Shuang Zhuo*, Huang Yu-Shan, 1990), *Stage Door* (*Hu Du Men*, Shu Kei, 1995), *A Queer Story* (*Ji Lao Si Shi*, Shu Kei, 1996), *Intimates* (*Zi Shu*, Jacob Cheung, 1997), *Sex and Zen* (*Yuputuanzhi Touqingbaojian*, Michael Mak, 1991), *Hold You Tight* (*Yu Kuaile Yuluoda*, Stanley Kwan, 1997), *Away with Words* (*San Tiao Ren*, Christopher Doyle, 1999) and *Lan Yu* (Kwan, 2001) also incorporate cultural pasts and cultural futures. In China, the homosexual passions of the Beijing Opera and the subterranean gay ghettos of the cityscape in Hong Kong, Cantonese opera, silk sisterhood, sex work, sexual histories, urban gay bars and toilet beats appear in the aforementioned films. These stories disrupt the Western coming-out narrative of leaving 'home' and joining a queer community; rather, they reclaim indigenous gay and lesbian traditions, show how Asian homosexuality is negotiated through the Confucian family, and open up new non-normative and hybrid spaces of queer belonging. The characters in these stories are not defiantly 'out'; they are shown to move between the heterosexual matrix of the Confucian family and the homosexual subculture. By interweaving straight and queer worlds, these characters carve out new hybrid sexual identities and communities. Central to these is a self-conscious reclamation of local heritage (for example, the emphasis on opera and silk sisterhood in *Intimates* and *Farewell My Concubine*) and the emergence of local queerscapes.

This framework for an Asian queer cinema is best exemplified in Taiwan by Ang Lee's award-winning *The Wedding Banquet* (*Xi yan*, 1993), in which a diasporic Taiwanese-Chinese gay identity is negotiated through a convenient marriage to an illegal Chinese migrant woman and a cosmopolitan cross-cultural homosexual Manhattan lifestyle. Like the good son protagonist who yearns for a reunion with his father in *Happy Together*, the good son is a prodigal son who procreates and continues the family's bloodline. Diasporic Chinese gay subjectivity and de facto queer lifestyle are negotiated through Confucian family values; identity is multiply compartmentalized (Berry 1994). This geography of sexual identity is also evident in the films of Tsai **Ming-liang**, Taiwan's most acclaimed arthouse director. The poaching of an unleased apartment for the sublimation of sex in *Vive L'Amour* (*Aiqing wan sui*, 1994), the camp interludes of Grace Chang/Ge Lan,

a 1930s Shanghai pop diva, in *The Hole* (*Dong*, 1998) and the ghostly presence of a gay kung fu gaze in *Goodbye, Dragon Inn* (*Busan Bubai*, 2003) show how queer practices emerge in liminal, spectral and non-normative spaces. In *The Outcasts* (*Niezi: The Outsiders*, Kan-ping Yu, 1986) and *A Cha-Cha for the Fugitive* (*Gai Taowanje de ChaCha*, Tsai-sheng Wang, 1996), for example, these spaces are bars, nightclubs and local punk subcultures; in *Fleeing by Night* (*Ye Ben*, Li-kong Hsu, 2000), *The Peony Pavilion* (*Wo de meili you ai chou*, Kuo-fu Chen, 1995) and *The Silent Thrush* (*Shisheng Huamei*, Sheng-fu Cheng, 1991), the spectres are of history and opera; and in *Where is My Love* (*Qiangpo Puguang*, Jofei Chen, 1995), *Murmur of Youth* (*Meili Zaichang*, Cheng-sheng Lin, 1997) and *Incidental Journey* (*Haijiao Tianya*, Chen, 2001), they are the postmodern vectors of chance encounters and transient desires.

In Korea chance encounters and transient desires inflect new forms of intimacy outside the traditional heterosexual nuclear matrix. *Broken Branches* (*Naeil ui hyahae hurunun kang*, Jeo-ho Park, 1995), the country's first gay film, interrogates this through the narrator's relationship with a married man. In *301–302* (Chul-soo Park, 1995) and *Memento Mori* (*Yeogo Guidam 11*, Tae-yong Kim, 2000), lesbian intimacy is explored through the female friendships between neighbours and classmates. Similar to the unexplained desire between Im-woo and his student in *Bungee Jumping of Their Own* (*Beonjijeonpeureul hada*, Dae-seung Kim, 2000), the flashbacks in *Memento Mori* are attempts to rework the trauma of repressed sexual history. As in *Norang Mori 2* (Yoo-min Kim, 2001), queer protagonists emerge as outcasts and intimate strangers in these films.

Asia's queer film representations and cultures have also been influenced by the metropolitan gay and lesbian social movements in Asia since the 1990s. Most notably, local gay and lesbian film festivals have enabled the global circulation of queer films and inspired local queer film traditions. Japan has been at the forefront of this movement, inaugurating the Tokyo International Gay and Lesbian Film Festival in 1991. Hong Kong (1998), Seoul (1999) and Taiwan (2002) have also showcased annual festivals comprising a mix of imported and local films. Indeed, it is within the global queer film festival circuit that some Asian films have attained international recognition and secured global distribution, for example, Thailand's *Iron Ladies* (Young-yooth Thongkonthun, 2000); the Philippines' *Midnight Dancers* (Sibak, 1994) and *Burlesk King* (2000), both by Mel Chinglo, and Nick Deocampo's *Children of the Regime* (1985), *Revolutions Happen Like Refrains in a Song* (1987) and *Private Wars* (1997); and China's *Fish and Elephant* (*Jinnian Xiatian*, Yu Li, 2001) and *Nan Nan Nu Nu* (Liu Bingjian, 1999). This circuit not only enables the global exchange of queer films; it has also showcased Asian queer filmmakers such as the late Lino **Brocka** (*Manila: In the Claws of Darkness*, 1975; *Macho Dancer*, 1988) and diasporic queer Asian filmmakers such as Canada's Richard Fung (*Chinese Characters*, 1980; *Dirty Laundry*, 1995; *Fighting Chance*, 1990; *Sea in the Blood*, 2000) and Australia's Tony Ayres (*China Dolls*, 1997; *Sadness*, 1999).

Whether they are commercially popular or fiercely independent, queer Asian films have emerged in recent times to engage and disrupt Western, Orientalist and neo-Orientalist models of sexual politics. They celebrate Asian queer identities and carve out new spaces of belonging. By contesting Eastern and Western orthodoxies, they mark the emergence of a queer and Asian modernity that questions the cost of its present condition.

See also: Ayres, Tony; Coming out; Fung, Richard; Kwan, Stanley; Oki, Hiroyuki; Parmar, Pratibha; Yu, Li

Bibliography

Berry, Chris (1994) 'Sexual Dis/Orientations or are Homosexual Rights a Western Issue?', in *A Bit on the Side*, Sydney: EMPress, pp. 65–104.

Ghosh, Shohini (2002) 'Queer Pleasures for Queer People: Film, Television and Queer Sexuality in India', in Ruth Vanita (ed.) *Queering India: Same-sex Love and Eroticism in Indian Culture and Society*, New York: Routledge, pp. 207–21.

Grossman, Andrew (ed.) (2000) '"Beautiful Publicity": An Introduction to Queer Asian Film', in *Queer Asian Cinema: Shadows in the Shade*, New York: Harrington Park Press. *Journal of Homosexuality* 39, 3/4: 1–29.

Jacobs, Katrien (2003) 'Queer Voyeurism and the Pussy-Matrix in Shu Lea Cheang's Japanese Pornography', in Chris Berry, Fran Martin and Audrey Yue (eds) *Mobile Cultures: New Media in Queer Asia*, Durham: Duke University Press, pp. 205–21.

Leung, Helen Hok-sze (2001) 'Queerscapes in Contemporary Hong Kong Cinema', *positions* 9, 2 (Fall): 423–47.

McLelland, Mark (2003) 'Japanese Queerscapes: Global/Local Intersections on the Internet', in Chris Berry, Fran Martin and Audrey Yue (eds) *Mobile Cultures: New Media in Queer Asia*, Durham: Duke University Press, pp. 52–69.

Yue, Audrey (2000) 'What's So Queer About *Happy Together*?: aka Queer (N)Asian: Interface, Mobility, Belonging', *Inter-Asia Cultural Studies Journal* 1, 2 (August): 251–64.

Waugh, Thomas (2001) 'Queer Bollywood, or "I'm the player, you're the naïve one"', in Matthew Tinkcom and Amy Villarejo (eds) *Keyframes: Popular Cinema and Cultural Studies*, New York: Routledge, pp. 280–97.

Further reading

Patal, Geeta (2002) 'On *Fire*: Sexuality and Its Incitements', *Queering India*: 222–33.

AUDREY YUE

ASIA, LITERATURE

Unlike queer Asian film (see **Asia, filmmaking**), which in recent years has been highlighted in venues such as film festivals and promoted online through web sites, queer Asian literature has no such focus as a field of study or inquiry. Comparative literature specialists are still overwhelmingly entrenched in the Western literary tradition, and when comparative studies with Asian literatures do occur, they are confined, for the most part, to China, Japan and India. Queer Asian literature, when it is acknowledged at all, is embedded within the study of national literatures. Recent publications of anthologies, however, have begun to make those queer national histories more available to wider audiences. Vanita and Kidwai's *Same-sex Love in India* (2000) and Miller's *Partings at Dawn* (1996) reach back to the literary histories of India and Japan respectively to reveal a tradition of engagement with gender and same-sex sexuality. While not an anthology, Bret Hinsch's study, *Passions of the Cut Sleeve: The Male Homosexual Tradition in China* (1990), serves a similar purpose for mainland China up to the end of the Qing Dynasty in 1911. Both *Same-sex Love in India* and *Partings at Dawn* contain works by modern and contemporary writers. Fran Martin's anthology, *Angelwings: Contemporary Queer Fiction from Taiwan* (2003), locates a vibrant and active community of queer writers in present-day Taiwan, while *Ladlad: An Anthology of Philippine Gay Writing* (Garcia and Remoto 1994) does the same for the Philippines. There is evidence that similar traditions, past and present, exist in Korea and Thailand. As for Indonesia, Vietnam, Cambodia, Laos, Burma and other countries in South and Southeast Asia, those discoveries have yet to be made.

In the early years after the Second World War, writers such as Kamleshwar and Mohammed Basheer in India, Kawabata Yasunari, Fukanaga Takehiko and Mishima Yukio in Japan, and Por Intharapalit in Thailand, wrote about male transvestites, schoolboy love, sadomasochistic yearnings and homosexual men as members of a sordid underworld. Although not homosexual himself, the Nobel Prize winning author

Ōe Kenzaburō (Japan) wrote two homoerotic works entitled *Shiiku* (*Prize Stock*, 1958) and *Seiteki ningen* (Homo sexualis, 1963). Japanese author Inagaki Taruho, in contrast, was not shy about his orientation and published two non-fiction works, *A-kankaku to V-kankaku* (Anal Feeling and the Vaginal Feeling, 1954) and *Shōnen'ai no bigaku* (The Aesthetics of the Love of Young Men, 1958). During the 1970s there was a resurgence of writing by authors such as Kamala Das (India), Kritsana Asoksin (Thailand), and Takahashi Mutsuo and Aizawa Keizō (both Japan) who were more direct than earlier authors had been about their desires and orientations. In Taiwan, Pai Hsien-yung published an openly gay novel, *Nie zi* (*Crystal Boys*) in 1983 about the men and boys of New Park in Taipei.

It was not until the 1990s, however, that literature on a variety of queer themes started to blossom throughout Asia. Japan's 'gay boom' of the late 1980s and early 1990s saw the publication of a number of novels on topics such as male prostitution (*Yes Yes Yes*, Hiruma Hisao, 1989; *Hatachi no binetsu* [*A Touch of Fever*], Ryosuke Hashiguchi, 1993), the struggle to fit in with society (*Kirakira hikaru* [*Twinkle Twinkle*], Ekuni Kaori, 1991; *Okoge* [*Fag Hag*], Nakajima Takehiro, 1992), the gay bar scene in Tokyo (*Shinjuku Ni-chōme de kimi ni attara* [If I Met You in Shinjuku Ni-chōme], Nishino Koji, 1993; *Tisshu* [Tissue], Nishino Kōji, 1995) and lesbian love (*Shiro bara no fuchi made* [Until the Edge of a White Rose], Nakayama Kaho, 2001). In more recent years, novels such as *Natsu no yakusoku* (A Promise for Summer, 2000) by Fujino Chiya and *Majo no Musuko* (The Witch's Son, 2004) by Fushimi Noriaki have won prominent literary awards that have brought further attention to same-sex relationships in Japan.

Likewise, in Taiwan an efflorescence of **tongzhi** and *ku'er* (neologisms approximating the meaning of the words 'gay and lesbian' and 'queer') literature focus on what

Fran Martin calls (2003) 'transgressive sexuality'. Chu T'ien-wen's 1994 prize-winning novel *Huangren shouji* (*Notes of a Desolate Man*) is a work of introspection in which the main character, Xiao Shao, a gay intellectual, mourns the loss of a close friend from AIDS. It is considered a hall-mark in *tongzhi* literature. Other works by Chu T'ien-hsin ('Chunfeng hudie zhi shi' ['A Story of Spring Butterflies'], 1992), Ling Yan (*Shisheng huamei* [*The Silent Thrush*], 1990), Tsao Li-chuan ('Tongnü zhi wu' ['The Maidens' Dance'], 1990); 'Guanyu tade baifa ji qita' ['Regarding Her White Hair and Other Matters'], 1996) and Du Xiulan (*Ninü* [*Rebel Daughter*], 1996) all investigate the world of female same-sex love using topics as diverse as romance among teenage schoolmates, relationships among actresses in the Taiwanese opera and friendship among older lesbians. Taiwan's best-known lesbian author, Qiu Miaojin, died at her own hands in 1995, the same year her novel *Eyu shouji* (*The Crocodile's Journal*, 1994) won the China Times Hon-orary Novel Prize. Her second novel *Mengmate yishu* (*Montmartre Testament*), an autobiographical narrative, was published posthumously in 1996. Queer (*ku'er*) litera-ture in Taiwan has also been published by the women writers Hong Ling and Chen Xue, while the male authors, Dong Qizhang and Wu Jiwen, have written novels with transgendered characters and themes.

In China, the output of gay/queer lit-erature has been determined in part by the resistance from external political forces. Since 1995 several novels, stories and col-lections have been published that touch either directly or indirectly on same-sex love and desire. Although dealing with homosexuality only tangentially, *Broken Tile* (1997) by Su Tong was the first novel to explore same-sex desire. It opened the way for more explicit novels, for example *Taoshe zhuichun* (*The Peach Colored Lips*, 1997) by Cui **Zi'en** and *Good Man Gelu* (published in Hong Kong, 1997) by Tong

Ge. The same year also saw the publication in Hong Kong of a collection of stories by mainland Chinese authors: *Same Sex Love Stories*. Wang Xiaobo's collection of plays and novellas, published in 1998, led to one of its stories – 'Tender Feelings' – being cinematized as the popular gay film *East Palace, West Palace* (*Dong gong xi gong* 1996). Chen Ran's 1995 novel *Breaking Open* led the way for the publication of more explicit lesbian works such as *The Loving Days* (1999) by Ge Zhi and *The Bygone Days of Shanghai* (2003) by Zhang Haoying.

As Ruth Vanita has noted in her anthol-ogy *Same-sex Love in India* (co-edited with Saleem Kidwai, 2000), it was not until after the 1998 movie *Fire* (dir. Deepa **Mehta**) was released that a nationwide public debate on homosexuality began. In 2003, India held both its first Gay Pride march and its first gay and lesbian film festival in Mumbai (**Bombay**). Since 1997 there have been a growing number of literary works on queer themes in a variety of languages, representing the linguistic and geographic diversity of Indian writers. Vikram Chan-dra, a rising star in India's literary world, was educated in the United States and makes his home in both the US and India. His story – written in English – 'Artha', in the collection *Love and Longing in Bombay* (1997), tells the tale of a Muslim man searching for his Hindu lover. Nisha da Cunha, a female writer, has written a story in English called 'La Loire Noire'. Recounting a man's grief over his lover's death from AIDS, it can be found in her collection *Set My Heart in Aspic* (1997). Both Rajesh Talwar and Mahesh Dattani have written plays with queer themes that have been produced in India (*Inside Gay-land* [2001] and *Seven Steps Around the Fire* [2004]). Other well-known writers include the disabled Parsi writer, Firdaus Kanga, Leslie de Noronha (*Dew Drop Inn*, 1994), R. Raj Rao and P. Parivaraj.

Recent literary works from Thailand that explore queer life include an autobiographical work by Natee Teerarojjanapongs (*Kwa-ja Kao Kham Sen Shi-Khao* [Before I Stepped Across the White Line], 1990) and two gay novels by Wirat Kanokanukhroh (*Sak Dork-mai* [Dying Flowers], 1995–6 and *Dai Si-muang* [The Purple Thread], 2002). Very little of this literature has been translated into English.

There is rich potential for the literature discussed here to be used comparatively by literary critics and scholars who study Asia. So far that potential has not been realized outside of the circle of scholars and translators who have made these works available to the Anglophonic world and written about them within the context of national literatures. The discovery of queer literary histories and contemporary literary trends can have a profound effect on the way we view non-Western queer cultures and queer subjectivity as it is represented in those cultures. It remains to be seen whether those discoveries will lend themselves to broader panoramic views of the Asian world.

See also: China, literature; Hong Kong, literature; India, literature; Philippines, literature; Taiwan, literature

Bibliography

Garcia, J. Neil C. and Remoto, Danton (eds) (1994) *Ladlad: An Anthology of Philippine Gay Writing,* Manila: Anvil.

Hinsch, Bret (1990) *Passions of the Cut Sleeve: The Male Homosexual Tradition in China,* Berkeley and Oxford: University of California Press.

Martin, Fran (ed. and trans.) (2003) *Angelwings: Contemporary Queer Fiction from Taiwan,* Honolulu: University of Hawaii Press.

Miller, Stephen D. (ed.) (1996) *Partings at Dawn: An Anthology of Japanese Gay Literature,* San Francisco: Gay Sunshine Press.

Vanita, Ruth and Kidwai, Saleem (ed.) (2000) *Same-sex Love in India,* New York: Palgrave Press.

STEPHEN D. MILLER

ATHEY, RON

b. 1961

performance artist

Ron Athey was born in Ohio but raised in southern California in a family of Pentecostal religious devotees who proclaimed the young boy a prophet. He began performing at underground galleries in Los Angeles with Rozz Williams in 1981. From these initial performances, he developed a unique style, mixing thematic elements from his religious upbringing with the imagery and practices of queer sadomasochism and body manipulation culture. During the 1990s, he formed a performance group and developed a series of intense performance pieces that featured piercing, cutting, mummification and other sadomasochistic practices. Athey produced a trilogy of works with the group: *Martyrs & Saints* (1992), *4 Scenes in a Harsh Life* (1993), and *Deliverance* (1994). He has often encountered difficulties with censorship and funding, especially within the United States. In 2002 he premiered a multimedia work in Hamburg, Germany, about schizophrenic women and prophecy entitled *Joyce.*

DANIEL HENDRICKSON

AUCKLAND

Auckland (Maori name *Tamaki-makau-ra*) is New Zealand's largest city and accommodates approximately one-third of the country's population. Located at the top half of the North Island, Auckland has the largest glbt population in New Zealand. Also known as 'The Queen City', Auckland hosts the major festival, parade and dance party Hero (which is timed to complement the Sydney, Australia, Mardi Gras). The street parade has been broadcast on mainstream New Zealand television.

JO SMITH

AUDEN, W.H.

b. 1907; d. 1973

poet

Born in York, England, Auden grew up in Birmingham. He was educated at Christ Church, Oxford, a mediocre student, and took a third-class degree in English. However, while at Oxford he met and was influenced by many significant poets including Cecil Day Lewis, Louis Mac-Neice and Stephen Spender. After graduating, Auden spent a year in Berlin (1928–9), joining a bohemian set that included his former schoolfriend and later literary collaborator Christopher **Isherwood**.

Until that point Auden's reading of Freud had convinced him of the 'immature' nature of his homosexuality. The more liberal atmosphere of **Berlin**, however, enabled him to acknowledge his sexuality. Literary success followed his return to England where, in 1930, Faber & Faber published his first commercial volume, *Poems*. Further critical acclaim turned Auden into one of the most influential and controversial poets of the period. At this time he also worked with Benjamin Britten as assistant director of the GPO Film Unit, the pioneer of British documentary film. While never a member of the Communist Party, Auden aligned himself with Leftist causes against fascism and went to Spain in 1937 where he wrote republican propaganda and gave radio broadcasts. In 1939 he moved to the United States to escape the war and met his long-time companion Chester Kallman. As editor of the Yale Series of Younger Poets, Auden was instrumental in launching the careers of Adrienne **Rich**, John Ashbery and several other major poets. In 1972 Auden returned to Oxford where he died the following year.

H.G. COCKS

AUSTRALIA, FILMMAKING

There have been various queer representations in Australian mainstream and alternative films. In the first half of the twentieth century a handful of feature films hinted at stereotypical queerness. The Australian 'renaissance' films of the 1970s (Rayner 2000: 6–7) included a small number of glbt characters and queer subtexts. During the 1980s and 1990s, however, several films featured explicit queer characters and storylines.

During the late 1960s and 1970s – a time of growing awareness of the need for a distinctive and independent Australian identity – some successful Australian films included glbt characters. In 1972 Bruce Beresford's *The Adventures of Barry Mackenzie*, for example, introduced the transgender Edna Everidge. The 1971 *Wake in Fright*, directed by Ted Kotcheff, featured a sinister gay doctor as part of a dystopic critique of Australian masculinity. Not only mainstream cinema introduced glbt storylines and characters. In 1977 Tom Cowan directed a 'feminist' short-feature film, *Journey Among Women*, set in colonial times, which included a lesbian relationship between two escaped women convicts. Although praised by a number of women at the time, the film was critiqued by many as directed towards voyeuristic heterosexual men.

Several Australian films have been set in single-sex schools and explore homosexual incidents and queer subtexts. Fred Schepisi's *The Devil's Playground* (1976) is the story of erotic awakenings among boys within a repressed community. The film draws upon the aesthetic influences of European art cinema and includes scenes of boys awkwardly engaging in mutual sexual exploration. Peter Weir's *Picnic at Hanging Rock* (1975), set in 1901, sensually portrays a romantic relationship, on the one hand, between girls as a prelude to heterosexual awakening while, on the other hand, it presents an unsettling lesbian subtext between the head of the school and a maths teacher. Laura, the main character in Beresford's *The Getting of Wisdom* (1977) develops an intense emotional attachment to an older girl with whom she briefly shares a bed. Although a relatively positive portrayal of lesbian desire, it ends dubiously with the older girl getting married. The *Mad Max* trilogy (1979, 1981, 1985) includes several perversely queer characters. Further, Mel Gibson's leather-clad Max developed a significant fan base of gay males.

Several flamboyant and queerly camp films of the 1990s presented explicitly or subtextually gay and transgendered characters. A few of these films were led by heterosexual stories that had queer appeal because of the way the narrative challenged Australia's gender and sexual conventions. *Strictly Ballroom* (1992), directed by Baz Luhrmann, highlighted the body of a young male dancer while it parodied mainstream conventions and Australian identities. Later, Luhrmann directed the camp *William Shakespeare's Romeo & Juliet* (1996), which portrayed Mercutio as a transvestite.

Stephan Elliott's *Priscilla Queen of the Desert* (1994) followed the adventures of three drag queen performers (one a transsexual) who had tired of the Sydney scene. They travelled through the outback where they regained a more positive sense of their place within the Australian culture and landscape. Although challenging conventions of Australian masculinity and attaining international success in the mainstream cinema, many within Australia criticized it for its misogyny and ethnic stereotypes. *Priscilla* also influenced Hollywood's production of the glbt film *To Wong Foo, Thanks for Everything! Julie Newmar* (1995). *Muriel's Wedding* (1994), a satirically camp comedy, directed by P.J. Hogan, parodied romantic conventions. There is the hint of a lesbian relationship between Muriel and the more sophisticated and attractive Rhonda, who is a catalyst for Muriel's transformation.

Not all 1990s films were extravagantly camp. The 1994 *The Sum of Us*, directed by Geoff Burton and Kevin Dowling, starred Russell Crowe as an out gay man in search of a committed relationship, whose sexuality was supported by his father played by Jack Thompson. The low-budget film, *Love and Other Catastrophes* (1996), directed by Emma-Kate Croghan, was the first successful Australian film to positively and casually portray lesbian characters on equal terms with heterosexual characters. The film played on Hollywood's romantic, screwball comedy genre that informed its sexual confusion and farcical narrative.

The 1994 long short film *Only the Brave* and the 1998 feature *Head On*, both directed by out lesbian Ana Kokkinos, gained something of a cult following. Kokkinos' cinematic style suggests a dystopic and unsettling vision associated with European art films. The films focus on young, queer and Greek-Australian characters who struggle with their queer desire as it is framed through the conflicts occurring through their traditional family conventions, wider Australian youth culture and societal homophobia. The great strength of *Only the Brave* is in the sensitive and sensual portrayal of the intense relationship between the main women characters. Ari, the central character in *Head On* (based on a novel by Christos **Tsiolkas**), was played by the Australian heterosexual sex symbol Alex Dimitriados, whose naked and finely toned body appealed to many gay men. Not oversentimentalized, the film explores Ari's frequent indulging in rough casual sex with older and very ordinary men: as he proclaims at one point in the film, 'I'm a man, I take it up the arse.' His drag queen friend, Toula (played by Paul Capsis), heroically challenges gender, sexual and ethnic conventions. She stands her ground within both the Greek community and with the abusive, racist and sexist Melbourne police.

Increasingly, since the late 1970s, many low-budget, independent short and long films made by or about glbt Australians have been shown in both queer and mainstream film festivals across Australia and overseas. For instance, Queer Screen presents a range of local and international queer-fiction and documentary films at the Sydney Mardi Gras Festival as well as throughout the year. In 2000 Samantha Lang's *The Monkey's Mask* was shown at festivals and released on video. This is an explicitly lesbian film with an interesting edginess that, although received ambivalently by the mainstream public, was given international exposure through the film festival circuit. The film is a curious mixture of poetry and film noir qualities such as a *femme fatale* and detective story narrative.

Bibliography

Rayner, J. (2000) *Contemporary Australian Cinema: An Introduction*, Manchester and New York: Manchester University Press.

Further reading

Hunn, Deborah (2003) 'Australian Film', in *An Encyclopedia of Gay, Lesbian, Bisexual, Transgender and Queer Culture*, available at: http://www.gbltq.com/arts/aus_film.html

CAROLYN SKELTON

AUSTRALIA, LITERATURE

Australian glbt literature grew dynamically from the early 1990s with unprecedented interest from mainstream publishers and a large number of titles and authors published across a range of genres. The origins of this boom lay in significant part with the out gay and lesbian writers and small press publications of the 1970s and 1980s. However, publishers' enthusiasm for this new niche did not endure and a tax on books in July 2000 has since stymied the Australian book industry in general, with a marked decline in the publishing of glbt literature in particular.

Historically, few titles were published throughout the 1950s and 1960s. The most notable were Jon Rose's *At the Cross* (1961), a wide-eyed teenager's introduction to the gay underworld and bohemian nightlife of the Second World War, and Neville Jackson's novel *No End to the Way* (1965) set in Perth. The 1970s saw the publication of Dennis Altman's groundbreaking, *Homosexual Oppression and Liberation* (1971), David Malouf's *Johnno* (1975) and in 1979 Patrick White's most gay-specific novel, *The Twyborn Affair*. In 1975 *All That False Instruction* by Kerryn Higgs, a frank exploration of lesbian love, was published under the pseudonym Elizabeth Riley. Gay and lesbian themes were also tackled by poets (Margaret Bradstock, Don Maynard) and some mainstream writers (Frank Moorhouse, Louis Nowra).

The first anthology of Australian gay and lesbian writing, *Edge City on Two Different Plans*, was published in 1983 and featured the likes of Sasha Soldatow and Gary Dunne. Historian Garry Wotherspoon edited *Being Different* (1986), a collection of short memoirs of Australian gay men from various eras. Margaret Bradstock and Louise Wakeling subsequently edited a lesbian companion volume, *Words from the Same Heart* (1988). Wotherspoon is also notable for the publication of his history of gay Sydney, *City of the Plain* (1991). The 1980s and early 1990s saw a number of lesbian writers emerge, such as Helen Hodgman, Bron Nicholls, Jenny Pausacker, Gillian Mears and Andrea Goldsmith. Especially significant was *Working Hot* (1989) by Kathleen Mary Fallon, a groundbreaking erotic novel. Sumner Locke Elliott, acclaimed for several general novels, published posthumously in 1991 a gay autobiographical novel *Fairyland*.

In 1987 Laurin McKinnon founded BlackWattle Press, Australia's first small gay and lesbian press. He began by publishing the literary journal *Cargo* with poet Jill Jones, followed by anthologies and fiction by the likes of Gary Dunne, John Lonie, Tim Herbert and Kirsty Machon. Black-Wattle was also significant in nurturing fledgling writers who later published with major presses (Christos **Tsiolkas**, Phillip Scott, Graeme Aitken, Con Anemogiannis). However, in 2000, with the new sales tax looming, BlackWattle closed down. In Melbourne Susan Hawthorne established Spinifex Press in 1991, publishing lesbian and feminist titles and authors such as Finola Moorhead. This continues to operate successfully.

In 1993 Robert **Dessaix** edited *Australian Gay and Lesbian Writing: An Anthology* and went on to achieve best-selling status as a literary author in his own right. From the mid-1990s onwards, major Australian publishers began to follow the lead of the American publishing industry and view gay and lesbian books as a significant niche market. They published an unprecedented number of titles, most notably Timothy Conigrave's *Holding the Man* (1995), Tsiolkas' *Loaded* (1995) and Dorothy Porter's *The Monkey's Mask* (1994). Other writers to emerge during this period include Fiona McGregor, Annamarie Jagose, Neal Drinnan and Bruno Bouchet.

The 1990s saw many writers find their subject in HIV and AIDS, documenting their experiences in memoirs such as Eric Michaels' *Unbecoming* (1990) and John Foster's *Take Me to Paris, Johnny* (1993). Conigrave's *Holding the Man*, published posthumously, became an unlikely national best seller and stands today as a popular modern classic of Australian gay literature. Larrikin journalist Peter Blazey's *Screw Loose* (1997) provided a lively, personal history of Australian gay life and history and also chronicled his living with HIV/AIDS. Well-known theatre director Richard Wherrett came out as HIV+ in his intimate family memoir *Desirelines* (1997) and also edited the anthology *Mardi Gras: True Stories* (1999).

Indigenous Australian voices have been rare, the main exceptions being Wayne King's memoir *Black Hours* (1996), the poetry of Lisa Bellear, and playwright Eva Johnson. Non-Anglo voices have been better represented from the mid-1990s by the likes of Tsiolkas, Con Anemogiannis, Tony **Ayres**, William **Yang** and Andy Quan. Transgender literature has also been scarce and generally confined to memoirs such as Katherine Cummings' *Katherine's Diary* (1993), and to biographies like Suzanne Falkiner's *Eugenia: A Man* (1988). In 2003 Tracie O'Keefe and Katrina Fox edited the anthology *Finding the Real Me: True Tales of Sex and Gender Diversity*, which included a significant number of Australian contributors.

The twenty-first century has seen far fewer Australian glbt books published, yet at times the quality has been especially exciting. Independent major publishers Allen & Unwin were responsible for Fiona McGregor's *Chemical Palace* (2002), a queer and stylistically adventurous narrative of dykes and gay men living and partying in inner-city Sydney. Then, in 2003, they published something altogether new – David Menadue's *Positive*, a memoir about living with AIDS, rather than dying from it. Finally, late in 2003, 20-year-old Alasdair Duncan burst onto the literary scene with *Sushi Central*, a debut novel which addressed gay youth as never before. This narrative of 16-year-old schoolboys was no coming-out story – rather it was a provocative, sexy, textually exciting and utterly contemporary tale of boys exploring their sexuality.

See also: Altman, Dennis; Porter, Dorothy Featherstone; White, Patrick

Further reading

Aitken, Graeme (ed.) (2002) *The Penguin Book of Gay Australian Writing*, Melbourne: Penguin Books.

Dessaix, Robert (ed.) (1993) *Australian Gay and Lesbian Writing*, Melbourne: Oxford University Press.

Hurley, M. (1996) *A Guide to Gay and Lesbian Writing in Australia*, Sydney: Allen & Unwin.

GRAEME AITKEN
(ASSISTED BY MICHAEL HURLEY)

AUSTRALIAN CENTRE FOR LESBIAN AND GAY RESEARCH (ACLGR)

Established at the University of Sydney in 1993, the ACLGR supports multidisciplinary research in the areas of gender, sexuality, and gay and lesbian studies. The ACLGR hosts an annual public lecture and a variety of seminars, conferences and forums each year. The Centre also publishes regular newsletters, a large volume of conference papers and a number of books addressing contemporary issues in Australian glbtq communities. The ACLGR is located on Sydney's Darlington Campus and provides affiliation and resources for visiting scholars, glbt community groups and ACLGR members.

KELLIE BURNS

AVENGERS, THE

TV series

Cult British TV series (1961–9) about two government secret agents – the quintessentially English, bowler-hat-wearing John Steed (Patrick MacNee) and a series of assistants, most memorably the vampish, catsuit-wearing agent Emma Peel (Diana Rigg). Episodes focused on Steed's efforts to vanquish enemy spies or mad scientists bent on world domination, usually dispatched effortlessly by Steed with a mixture of witty dialogue and elaborately choreographed fight scenes. The first series paired Steed with physician Dr David Keel (Ian Hendry), followed by two seasons with anthropologist Catherine Gale (Honor Blackman). The eventual pairing of MacNee and Rigg produced one of television's sexiest couples, with the actors frequently writing their own dialogue. The show's exuberant **camp** aesthetic assures its popularity with retro-loving gay audiences. A 1998 film version starring Ralph Fiennes and Uma Thurman was a critical and box-office failure.

JOHN FORDE

AVERSION PROJECT

The a Version Project was established to research stories told to South Africa's Truth and Reconciliation Commission (TRC) about the abuse of homosexuals by health professionals in the South African Defence Force (SADF) during the apartheid era. A report of the project was published in 2000. Between 1967 and 1991 all white males over 16 had to register for military service in the SADF. Conscripts who did not conform to military ideologies were labelled 'deviant' and subject to military discipline; this included those perceived as homosexual. SADF policy during this period stated that homosexuality was a 'behavioural disorder' and recommended that homosexuals be sent for 'treatment'. This included admission to military psychiatric wards for evaluation and treatment and the use of aversion therapy (electric shocks). Drugs, shock and hormonal treatments were also administered without the informed consent of patients. Many 'patients' suffered lasting negative effects and the number of gay-related suicides was high.

ANTHONY MANION

AYRES, TONY

b. 1961

writer, director

Known for his portrayal of gay Asian life in Australia, Ayres was born in Macao and graduated from the Australian Film, Television and Radio School in 1990. A writer as well as a director, Ayres edited an anthology of short stories entitled *String of Pearls: Stories About Cross-dressing* (1996) and *Hard Stories About Gay Men and Sex*

(1997). In 1997 he directed his first film, *China Dolls*. This short documentary mixed autobiographical material with documentary footage to investigate the experiences of gay men of Asian descent living in Australia and the sexual and racial hierarchies of gay male culture. In 1999 Ayres worked with Chinese-Australian gay photographer William **Yang** to transform Yang's theatrical piece *Sadness* into a short film. In 2002 Ayres directed the feature film *Walking on Water*, which depicts a group of friends coping with the death of a friend from AIDS.

JO SMITH

AZT

AZT (also known as Zidovudine) is widely used in the treatment of human immuno-deficiency virus (HIV) infection, usually in combination with other anti-virus drugs. HIV is the virus that causes acquired immune deficiency syndrome (AIDS). AZT cannot cure or prevent HIV infections or AIDS but is used to slow the disease process in patients by preventing HIV from reproducing.

See also: AIDS

KEN WONG

B

BABENCO, HÉCTOR

b. 1946

filmmaker

Babenco is not noted for any particular commitment in his films to queer issues but he did choose to undertake the 1985 filming of *El beso de la mujer araña* (*Kiss of the Spider Woman*), a 1976 novel by Manuel **Puig**. Babenco filmed in English using an international cast, which perhaps meant he perceived a viable market for the film. The film was well received, and William Hurt won an Oscar for his portrayal of the main character, a stereotypical homosexual who has a penchant for recounting B-films with troubled and tragic heroines. Puig deplored Babenco's treatment of his novel, which he considered insufficiently nuanced with regard to the main character.

There are 'dirty realism' elements of homosexuality in two of Babenco's films that denounce grim social conditions and injustices. In his acclaimed *Pixote* (1981), a male–male rape is portrayed as a form of power and dominance. In his most recent film, *Carandiru* (2003), about the notorious eponymous prison in Brazil, the fate of a transvestite is included as one of the twenty-six vignettes that make up the film.

DAVID WILLIAM FOSTER

BABUSCIO, JACK

b. 1937; d. 1990

journalist, activist

Born in New York, Jack Babuscio was a forceful film critic and gay counsellor during the 1970s and 1980s. He regularly wrote on gay culture in *Gay News* and other journals, and is best known today for 'Camp and the Gay Sensibility', a quite influential overview of cinematic camp. While defining camp as a nexus of irony, aestheticism, theatricality and humour, his essay posits it as inherent to a 'gay sensibility', thereafter a most popular formula supporting a positive identity politics. His experiences in counselling are recorded in *We Speak for Ourselves* (1976; 2nd edn, 1988), which gathers together case histories and interview transcripts, and which represents a landmark contribution to gay self-understanding and acceptance. He died in London in 1990.

FABIO CLETO

BACON, FRANCIS

b. 1909; d. 1992

painter

Francis Bacon is recognized as a key British twentieth-century painter. His works feature screaming faces and beaten bodies, explore a preoccupation with pain and violence, and display a fascination with gay male masochism. He was openly gay and refused to censor his art, painting work denoting a radical sexuality, but was lauded by a largely conservative art public. Born in Dublin, he witnessed Ireland's civil war, which he claimed started his fascination with violence. He was sent from the family home for sleeping with his father's horse grooms at the age of 16, eventually settling in London under the tutelage of (and in a relationship with) the painter Roy de Maistre. Throughout the 1960s his lover, George Dyer, was his favourite subject. Bacon was offered a knighthood and the Order of Merit, but refused both. He died in Madrid, in the arms of a Spanish banker with whom he had been having an affair.

MICHAEL PINFOLD

BAD OBJECT CHOICES

reading group

The lesbian and gay theory reading group Bad Object Choices, founded in 1987, organized the conference 'How Do I Look? Queer Film and Video' in New York in 1989, papers from which (by Cindy **Patton**, Stuart **Marshall**, Judith **Mayne**, Richard **Fung**, Kobena **Mercer** and Teresa **De Lauretis**) were published under the same title. The name 'Bad Object Choices' implies a critical appropriation of heterosexist psychoanalytic theory, while the conference title indicates the centrality of visibility to political activism of the time. The anthology combines activist and academic agendas, and its discussions of race and gender in queer visibility remain salient.

See also: Psychoanalysis

TREVOR HOPE

BAKER, GILBERT

b. 1951

artist, activist

Gilbert Baker, an artist and activist born in Chanute, Kansas, created the **rainbow flag**

in San Francisco in 1978 as a symbol of lesbian, gay, bisexual and transgender liberation and diversity. The eight stripes in Baker's original flag stood for sexuality (pink), life (red), healing (orange), nature (green), sunlight (yellow), magic (turquoise), serenity (blue) and spirit (purple). Later versions varied the number of stripes. In 1979 his flag was adopted by Pride parade leaders to show the strength and solidarity of the San Francisco gay community in the wake of the assassination of out gay city Supervisor Harvey **Milk**. He made a mile-long flag for the New York celebration of the twenty-fifth anniversary of **Stonewall**, and a mile-and-a-quarter flag – the longest of any kind ever produced and extending from the Gulf of Mexico to the Atlantic Ocean – for Key West's Gay Pride parade on the twenty-fifth anniversary of the flag itself.

ANDY HUMM

BALDWIN, JAMES

b. 1924; d. 1987

writer

One of the most prominent American postwar novelists and the major literary voice of the civil rights movement, James Baldwin was raised in a strictly religious family in Harlem, New York City. After a career as a teenage preacher, Baldwin lost his religious faith as a young man and moved to New York City's Greenwich Village, where he began publishing book reviews. In 1948 he relocated to Paris to gain distance on the daily racism of American life that would be his most consistent subject as a writer. Publishing essays in journals such as *Partisan Review* and *Commentary*, Baldwin became known as a fierce critic of American fantasies of racial and sexual purity. His essays were characterized by a prose style that combined the oratorical fire of the black church and the stately cadences of Henry James. Among his notable early essays were the 1949 'Everybody's

Protest Novel', an attack on the aesthetic straitjacket of 'protest fiction', and 'Notes of a Native Son', a 1955 meditation on American racism that centres on an account of Baldwin's early family life and the 1943 riots in Harlem. His fiction (particularly *Giovannni's Room* [1956] and *Another Country* [1962]) sparked controversy with their depiction of gay and interracial relationships. Although Baldwin's political writings (notably the searing essay 'The Fire Next Time' [1963]) remained uncompromising in their critique of American racism, Baldwin found himself the target of attacks – at times homophobic – by a younger generation of radical black writers. Baldwin continued to write fiction, plays, and essays until his death in the south of France from stomach cancer.

See also: Black glbtq literature

DAVID KURNICK

BALL, ALAN

b. 1957

screenwriter, director

A highly respected and acclaimed screenwriter and director, Ball, who was born in Atlanta, Georgia, began his scriptwriting career on the TV sitcoms *Grace Under Fire* (1994–5) and *Cybil* (1995–8). He also created *Oh Grow Up* (1999), a semi-autobiographical sitcom about one gay and two straight men sharing a New York apartment. His first produced film screenplay, *American Beauty* (1999), a black comedy about a middle-aged married man who undergoes a mid-life crisis and fantasises about a teenage cheerleader, was filmed by director Sam Mendes. Ball's poignant, multilayered screenplay explored the secret pain of middle-class suburbanites, including a homophobic (and closet gay) army colonel, and won him an Academy Award for Best Original Screenplay. He next wrote and executive-produced the multi-award

winning TV series *Six Feet Under* (2001–2003) for cable network HBO, winning an Emmy for his direction of the pilot episode and a Golden Globe Award for Best Drama Series.

JOHN FORDE

BANANA, CANAAN

b. 1936; d. 2003

politician

Canaan Sodindo Banana was Zimbabwe's first president, elected in 1980. His homosexuality was well known to Zimbabwean glbtq communities but only made public in 1997 when Jefta Dube, Banana's former aide-de-camp, shot dead a man who accused him of being Banana's wife. During the trial, Dube's defence was that he had been forced to have sex with Banana. This, and claims of abuse from others, led to a full-scale investigation and Banana's conviction on multiple accounts of sodomy and sexual assault by the Supreme Court in 2000. He was sentenced to ten years, but pardoned by Robert Mugabe less than a year later. Banana never admitted his homosexuality, and even after conviction described homosexuality as an abomination in the eyes of God. This prompted GALZ (Gays and Lesbians of Zimbabwe) to issue a statement condemning Banana for hypocrisy. Although remembered for his important role in the liberation struggle and influence in bringing peace to Matabeleland, his convictions for sodomy meant that he was not awarded national hero status upon his death.

KEITH GODDARD

BANGKOK

Located at the crossroads of mainland Southeast Asia, Thailand (called Siam until 1939) is a rapidly developing society of 63 million people. Historically, Thailand has not criminalized homosexuality or transgenderism and there is no tradition of state intervention in the private lives of individuals to enforce heterosexual norms. Bangkok, the capital since 1782, is a sprawling metropolis of 10 million and is the unrivalled centre of national economic, political and cultural activity. Highly visible gay, lesbian (*tom-dee*) and transgender/transsexual (*kathoey*) cultures have emerged since the 1960s. The unrivalled centre of Thai queer life, Bangkok is a major destination for queer tourists from Asia and the West, and an international centre of male-to-female sex change operations and cosmetic surgery.

PETER A. JACKSON

BANNON, ANN

b. 1932

writer

Ann Bannon is the pseudonym of Ann Thayer. Thayer earned a PhD in linguistics from Stanford and has been an academic and a dean at Cal State Sacramento. As Ann Bannon, she is the author of five novels about lesbian life in the 1950s and 1960s, all of which centre on roughly the same cast of characters and which are now known as the Beebo Brinker series (1957–62). Bannon's novels were initially published by the pulp house Fawcett/Gold Medal, which published sexually racy, yet conventionally moralistic novels designed to appeal to men. Bannon's novels, because they did not have a formulaic unhappy ending for her lesbian protagonists, are considered pioneering works of lesbian fiction. The Beebo Brinker series has remained a cult favourite, and has been reprinted by a wide variety of queer, and now mainstream, presses. Bannon is much in demand as a lecturer and has been widely cited, interviewed and discussed in academic and popular presses.

STEPHANIE FOOTE

BARRETO, BRUNO

b. 1953

filmmaker

Bruno belongs to the famous Barreto filmmaking clan, although he is not particularly associated with queer culture. Brazilian filmmaking, however, is famous for taking on complex social issues, as in Barreto's 1981 film of Nelson Rodrigues' play *O beijo no asfalto* (Kiss on the Asphalt). *Beijo* concerns an Everyman who engages in a dramatic show of human sympathy by kissing a man who lies dying in the street. Catastrophe ensues, and the man is denounced as a homosexual. Barreto effectively explores the relentless dynamic of homophobia. The protagonist is ultimately shot by his father-in-law, who confesses that he has always loved him; the former dies in the arms of the latter, pietà style.

Além da paixão (Beyond Passion; 1985) involves a relationship between a male prostitute and a transvestite performer, but this is not the principal action of the film. By contrast, the homoeroticism in Fernando Gabeira's memoir of political activism, *O que é isso, companheiro?* (What's This, Comrade?) disappears from Barreto's film adaptation (1997, released in English as *Four Days in September*).

DAVID WILLIAM FOSTER

BARTHES, ROLAND

b. 1915; d. 1980

cultural theorist

Roland Barthes, a French writer, critic and academic, became famous for his contributions to structuralist and post-structuralist philosophies. Homosexual and Protestant, Barthes was a classic social outsider, and his work reflects a fascination with all things marginal. Pioneering a brand of cultural criticism developed from semiotics, Barthes interrogated texts for their repressed subtexts and silences. Through his criticism,

Barthes sought to expose and subvert the ideological operations of culture and to open a space for non-normative meanings. His work is thus often seen as an important intellectual precursor to queer theory.

See also: Theory and theorists, queer

BRETT FARMER

BARTLETT, NEIL

b. 1958

writer, director

Neil Bartlett is an English author and theatre director. His 1988 book, *Who Was That Man? A Present for Mr Oscar Wilde*, pieces together the queer world of Wilde's time from whatever traces he can find, including literature, newspapers and criminal records, interrogating in the meantime what relation this might have to contemporary queer London. The book was followed by two novels, *Ready to Catch Him Should He Fall* and *Mr Clive and Mr Page* (published in the United States as *The House on Brooke Street*) which tackles the importance of space and history in relation to queer lives. Throughout the 1990s, Bartlett became increasingly involved in the theatre, writing and translating plays as well as directing and performing.

DANIEL HENDRICKSON

BASQUIAT, JEAN-MICHEL

b. 1960; d. 1988

artist

Jean-Michel Basquiat, a Haitian-African-American artist born in Brooklyn, achieved almost instantaneous success in the 1980s New York art world, before his early death from a drug overdose. Starting out as a teenage graffiti artist in the streets of SoHo, his bold, colourful, childlike work mixed influences from graffiti art, anatomy textbooks, African iconography and pop culture, winning him the admiration and

friendship of artist Andy **Warhol**, with whom he frequently collaborated. After his first show in 1981, Basquiat rocketed to fame, feverishly promoted (and exploited) by art dealers keen to capitalize on his exotic ethnicity and fashionable street connections. His phenomenal output of work was alternatively fuelled and hampered by a heavy drug habit. Openly bisexual, he had a number of male and female lovers including, famously, Madonna. A film about his life, *Basquiat* (1996), was made by his friend, the artist Julian Schnabel.

JOHN FORDE

BATES, ALAN

b. 1934; d. 2003

actor

A leading British character actor of remarkable versatility, Alan Bates' sensitive interpretations of gay characters have endeared him to audiences worldwide. A graduate of the Royal Academy of Dramatic Art, Bates rose to fame in the lead role of John Osborne's innovative play *Look Back in Anger* (1956), worked with gay director John **Schlesinger** on the films *A Kind of Loving* (1962) and *Far from the Madding Crowd* (1967), and was nominated for an Academy Award for *The Fixer* (1968). He is best known for his performance as a sexually ambiguous schoolteacher in Ken Russell's *Women In Love* (1969), in which he wrestled nude with Oliver Reed. His other gay roles include ballet impresario Sergei Diaghilev in *Nijinsky* (1980) and a bisexual civil servant in love with a young criminal and his dog in *We Think the World of You* (1988).

See also: Russell, Ken

JOHN FORDE

BATHHOUSE

Bathhouses have been a place of resort for men seeking sex with men since before the period of gay liberation, when they were often located in grand hotels or were magnificent Moorish-style establishments such as the Voltaire in **Paris** or the Imperial in **London**. Since then, increasing numbers of 'gay-only' baths have opened in metropolitan and provincial cities (usually with more formica than marble) and are a major deposit of gay-directed entrepreneurial capital. Typically configuring passages and corridors of cabins around a central core of steam room, sauna, and whirl and plunge pools, they resemble a twilight mall of sexual exchange, often with spaces equipped to indulge outdoor fantasies, or rooms for **sadomasochism**, **water sports** and other hardcore activity, while the flickering of porn videos punctuates the space as a whole. Each bathhouse, depending on country, city and prevailing local mores, has its own etiquette regarding **cruising** and sociability. Many promote safer sex, and while large numbers were closed in the United States at the height of the AIDS crisis in the 1980s, in Europe they saw a new golden age. Writers such as Andrew Holleran and Samuel Delany have realized an intense poetic of the bathhouse experience.

ADRIAN RIFKIN

BATMAN

comic, TV series, film

More correctly known as *The Batman*, the fictional superhero first appeared in *Detective Comics #27* in 1939, and was later developed into a leading member of the DC Comics family by creator Bob Kane, inspiring a number of animation spin-offs, novels, radio, TV and film adaptations worldwide. However, the sexual orientation of America's leading 'caped crusader' has been a heated topic of debate for over half a century following the publication of psychiatrist Fredric Wertham's controversial analysis of the character in his book *Seduction of the Innocent* in 1954. Wertham's exposition of the psychosexual daddy-boy or 'Ganymede-Zeus' gay wish-fulfilment relationship between Batman and his loyal 'boy wonder' sidekick Robin proved to be highly embarrassing for the comic industry during such a puritanical period in American culture – a time when homosexuality was still perceived as an illegal and psychopathological illness. The spectre of queerness that haunted post-war cultural perceptions of the character was also exacerbated by the ultra-camp television adaptation of the comic that emerged in the 1960s, complete with its effeminate leotards and cameo appearances by closet queen **Liberace** and gay cultural icon Eartha Kitt. Adam West's portrayal of Batman was far from the macho masculine ideal that one would expect from such a heterosexual standard bearer, and his highly theatrical man-to-man combat style and overall lack of interest in any of the female protagonists he encountered left much to the imagination for the fledgling underground gay community of the time. More recently, gay director Joel Schumacher has been universally applauded by the gay press for re-accentuating the queerness of the character that was so lacking in Tim Burton's decidedly heterocentric incarnation of the comic in 1989, through his overtly camp and fetishistic *mise-en-scène* – a development that is still met with resigned disapproval from more purist factions of the comic fraternity from which the character evolved.

Bibliography

Wertham, Fredric (1954) *Seduction of the Innocent*, New York: Reinhart.

ROBIN GRIFFITHS

BEAN, BILLY

b. 1964

baseball player

In 1999 Billy Bean, born in Santa Ana, California, became the third professional baseball player to publicly come out of the closet after retiring from the sport. His story, featured in a front-page article of *The New York Times*, was striking because he detailed the lengths to which he went to hide his sexuality from his teammates, including marrying a woman whom he later divorced as he slowly grew aware that he was gay. Tragically, his first male lover died the night before a ball game, an event he mourned in silence since his family and team were unaware of his sexuality. During his professional career Bean played for the Detroit Tigers, the Los Angeles Dodgers and the San Diego Padres. His biography, *Going the Other Way: Lessons from a Life in and out of Major-League Baseball*, was published in 2003. Today Bean and his partner run a restaurant in Miami.

ERIC ANDERSON

BEAR

Gays who delight in their body hair, sporting moustaches and/or beards, are referred to as 'bears'. These men self-organize into bear fraternities across the world and have established social networks, via newsletter, the Internet and in gay clubs and bars. They are self-identified, tend to be of the larger build and/or older, with younger members referred to as bear 'cubs'. They are sometimes affiliated with the leather community, motorcycle clubs, sadomasochistic scenes, or 'Girth and Mirth' organizations.

MICHAEL PINFOLD

BEATON, CECIL

b. 1904; d. 1980

photographer, designer

One of the twentieth century's most celebrated photographers and designers, Beaton is best known for his theatrical, flamboyantly posed portraits of celebrities and royalty. Born on 14 January 1904 in London, he began his photography career in 1920s London, and under the patronage of Dame Edith Sitwell, one of his first sitters, became the lead portraitist for the burgeoning modernist movement. He travelled to New York in 1928, photographing a number of Hollywood film actors for *Vanity Fair*, *Vogue*, *Life* and *Harper's Bazaar* magazines. He met Greta **Garbo** in 1932, with whom he developed a lifelong obsession. Despite his self-identified homosexuality, he pursued a sexual relationship with Garbo, chronicled in his *Diaries 1944–1948* (published in 1972). During the late 1930s he made his portrait of Queen Elizabeth, the late Queen Mother, eventually going on to become the British royal family's official photographer. After the Second World War, he branched into stage and costume design, winning awards for his work on stage and film versions of *My Fair Lady* (1957) and *Gigi* (1958). He died on 18 January 1980 in Salisbury, England.

JOHN FORDE

BECHDEL, ALISON

b. 1960

writer

Alison Bechdel attended Oberlin College and currently resides in Vermont. Since 1984 she has been the author of the popular series of comics, *Dykes to Watch out for*. First published by a small gay newspaper in Minnesota, the comic quickly gained a readership and was distributed in a broad array of queer publications. Within the world of 'dykes to watch out for', Bechdel has publicized the struggle of small, alternative cultural venues within a corporate monoculture that seeks to assimilate difference. Many of her comics are set in an independent feminist bookstore or in a cooperative house shared by dyke roommates. Her comics have been released in book form by small, alternative presses Firebrand and now Alyson Press. Noted for the verisimilitude of her drawing, Bechdel is noted also for her sophisticated ability to track out the changing cultural and political strategies of a multiracial, multicultural queer culture within the complex emotional and personal lives of her characters.

STEPHANIE FOOTE

BECKHAM, DAVID

b. 1975

footballer

Ball-bending British footballer David Beckham has become a queer icon for the twenty-first century. An accomplished athlete associated with Manchester United, England and, more recently, Real Madrid, it was the regally trashy **camp** of his 1999 wedding to Spice Girl Victoria Adams, along with good-natured flirtations with gay culture, that made Beckham an international celebrity. As has been widely reported, benders like Beckham. Whether it's the fluid panoply of labels applied to him – new man, gay, straight, narcissist, metrosexual, pansexual, family man, and more recently love-rat – or his ceaseless, and frequently homoerotic, advertising of designer labels, few public figures have so successfully bridged the gay–straight divide. Indeed, for the 2002 hit film *Bend it Like Beckham*, his name was a catalyst for both cross-cultural aspiration and a queer coming-out narrative. This was also the year he fully consolidated his gay icon status by posing for the cover of gay magazine *Attitude* while serving as England captain (with hair bleached especially for the occasion).

Beckham's willingness to don the vestments of gender bending led many to question his sexuality, which is clearly articulated as straight at the same time as he winks to the boys in the crowd with clear joy at his pink kudos. Out-reinventing Madonna, Beckham's sometimes questionable vicissitudes of fashion resonate on the streets. From brunette to blonde, via Mohican and cropped, via sarongs, nail varnish and tattoos, Beckham, dressed and undressed, is a body designed to set gaydars fluttering. His appeal may be skin-deep, but in eschewing football machismo for a queerer homosociality, perhaps it is not so superficial.

MICHAEL WILLIAMS

BEHIND THE MASK

Behind the Mask (www.mask.org.za) is an organization that seeks to support and empower glbtq people in Africa through the gathering and dissemination of well-researched and accurate information. The brainchild of Dutch anti-apartheid activist and journalist Bart Luirink, Behind the Mask launched its web site in 1999. The site has grown exponentially in popularity from 13,000 to 300,000 hits a month in less than five years. From Algeria to Zimbabwe, Zambia to Angola, Behind the Mask's networks of correspondents and informants includes information on 35 African countries, written in English, Portuguese and French. In a continent where homosexuality is hidden and taboo, Behind the Mask supplies important information on contemporary developments while tapping into the possibilities offered by the Internet as a vital and anonymous means of communication. A confidential ListServ facilitated by the site brings together activists across the continent to discuss and respond to issues affecting glbtq people in Africa.

GRAEME REID

BEHR, MARK

b. 1963

writer

Tanzanian-born South African novelist of Afrikaner descent, Mark Behr's first novel, *The Smell of Apples*, won several literary prizes for its depiction of white racism, sexual hypocrisy and abuse from a young boy's perspective during the years of high apartheid (mid-1970s). His second novel, *Embrace* (2000), tells a coming-of-age story of a boy with strong bisexual feelings. In addition to its explicit gay, bisexual and hints of lesbian eroticism, the novel contains graphic scenes of sexual intercourse with animals. Behr has also provoked controversy in South Africa by confessing to having spied for the apartheid regime.

See also: Coming-out novels

MARC EPPRECHT

BELGIUM, FILMMAKING

Since the 1970s Belgium has established a significant queer film presence on the international art-house and festival circuit. Given its tri-lingual identity and, thus, strong co-production links with its European neighbours, Belgium's cinematic presence is inevitably one without a distinct national label to promote itself, being better known for its documentaries and art-house auteurs including Chantal **Akerman**, Harry Kümel and, more recently, Bavo **Defurne**. Seemingly overshadowed by its neighbours, it is precisely Belgium's apparent lack of cultural coherence that makes it a particularly productive context for questioning and exploring sexuality among the other complex facets of identity As Philip Mosley argues: 'the question of identity is at the heart of Belgian life, affecting cinema as much as any other Belgian cultural form' (Mosley 2001: 1). Such self-consciousness is no surprise considering the many social and political upheavals Belgium has endured through the twentieth century and may go some way to explain the somewhat displaced, escapist themes of its queer cinema.

The early 1970s saw something of a queer renaissance in Belgian cinema. Although Kümel's first feature, *Monsieur Hawarden* (1968), was a *fin-de-siècle* cross-dressing murder-mystery, it was his *Le Rouge aux lèvres* (*Daughters of Darkness*, 1970) that won a cult lesbian following. Bringing a queerer twist to the conventions of the lesbian vampire genre, Kümel's film tells the story of young newlyweds who arrive at a bleak Ostend hotel out of season, only to find that they are very much in-season for the ageless Countess Bathory (Delphine Seyrig). From the moment she appears, the camera lingering on her veiled red lips, Seyrig mesmerizes as the 'Scarlet Countess' as she unfurls herself across the film as if part of the decadent fabric of the hotel. But this is no lesbianism for men. The young husband is violent and misogynistic, himself a repressed homosexual; his 'mother' (revealed to be an old-school aesthete) dons a dressing-gown, pastels and face powder in his English orchid-house. Bathory, however (her less-palatable deeds obscured by Dietrich-style glamour), is the film's most engaging character, turning the young woman against her husband through an intoxicating blend of breathy seduction and women's lib.

Seyrig would later work with Akerman, whose breakthrough film *je tu il elle* (I... You... He... She, 1974), presented further innovations in lesbian cinema. Deploying her trademark long, static takes, Akerman's film documents the sexual encounters of a single woman adrift in the modern landscape. The film has been celebrated not only for its frank representation of lesbian sex but, more provocatively, for its work to 'de-aestheticize' women's lovemaking, chiefly through a naturalistic use of sound, thus deconstructing both **Hollywood** and art-house depictions of female sexuality. Akerman's films, Catherine Fowler (1999) argues, are about leaving Belgium, and her relation to place, alienation and non-belonging, and the very 'blankness' of Belgium as a cinematic space. In this film and others, such as *Les Rendez-vous d'Anna* (1978), Akerman explores women's relationships with lovers of both sexes and rejects the ghettoizing labels of gender and sexuality to which she is subjected as a 'lesbian' filmmaker. Akerman's screenwriter on *La Captive* (2000) and *Demain on déménage* (2004) was the renowned Belgian author, critic and filmmaker Eric de Kuyper, who had previously explored his fascination with the male body in a series of homoerotic experimental films in the 1980s including *Naughty Boys* (1983), *A Strange Love Affair* (1985) and *Pink Ulysses* (1990).

Other gay and lesbian-themed films emerged from Belgium through the 1970s and 1980s, including Robbe de Hert's *Maria Danneels of het leven dat we droomden* (Maria Daneels or the life we dreamt, 1982) for Belgian television; Patrick Conrad's *Mascara* (1987), starring Charlotte Rampling in a bizarre thriller based on the Orpheus myth, where a police inspector and his sister are drawn into a murderous tale of opera, incestuous obsession and transsexual nightlife; Gérard Corbiau's *Le Maître de musique* (*The Music Teacher*, 1988); and Fina Torres' lesbian-themed comedy, *Mécaniques célestes* (*Celestial Clockwork*, 1994). Another queer crossover, winning the Best Foreign Language Film category for Belgium at the Golden Globes, was Alain Berliner's first feature, *Ma vie en rose* (1997). Here, a young boy fights to have his transsexuality accepted by his perplexed family, as he daydreams of escaping the archetypal pastel-coloured conservatism of suburbia by flying away to the vibrantly kitsch world of Barbie-esque TV character 'Pam'. Again, the film evokes the dream of challenging the boundaries of 'reality' and convention in favour of a more colourful, albeit plastic, version of home. This is a dream shared by many of the short films of Defurne, Belgium's leading gay filmmaker since the late 1990s, whose work both eulogizes the obsolescence of youth while capturing its brightest dreams.

Bibliography

Fowler, C. (1999) 'All Night Long: the Ambivalent Text of "Belgianicity"', in G.A. Foster, *Identity and Memory: the Films of Chantal Akerman*, Trowbridge: Flicks Books, pp. 77–93.

Mosley, P. (2001) *Split Screen: Belgian Cinema and Cultural Identity*, New York: State University of New York Press.

Further reading

Foster, G.A. (ed.) (1999) *Identity and Memory: the Films of Chantal Akerman*, Trowbridge: Flicks Books.

Weiss, A. (1992) *Vampires and Violets: Lesbians in the Cinema*, London: Jonathan Cape.

Williams, M. (2003) *Ivor Novello: Screen Idol*, London: BFI.

—— (2004) 'The Body Picturesque: The Films of Bavo Defurne', in R. Griffiths (ed.) *Queer Cinema in Europe*, London: Intellect Books.

MICHAEL WILLIAMS

BENETTON, UNITED COLOURS OF

Went into business in the United States in 1980. Famous for its controversial advertising campaigns depicting homosexuals, people with AIDS and death row prisoners. One of the main fashion groups which create mainstream gay advertisements.

KEN WONG
STEPHANIE LEE

BENJAMIN, HARRY

b. 1885; d. 1987

doctor and sex researcher

An influential pioneer in the field of gender studies, Benjamin was born in Berlin,

Germany and moved to the United States in 1913 to study endocrinology at Columbia University.

At the outbreak of the First World War he attempted to return to Germany, but was diverted to England. Eventually allowed to return to New York, he became a US citizen but maintained contact with German sexologist Magnus Hirschfeld and Viennese endocrinologist Eugen Steinach, who conducted the first medical experiments to determine the role of hormones in the production of secondary sex characteristics.

In 1949 Benjamin took a professional interest in helping a transsexual patient, a practice which at that time was viewed in the United States as unacceptable, with doctors refusing to administer hormones or perform genital reconstruction surgery on transgendered people. Benjamin was instrumental in bringing about the acceptance of this practice.

Benjamin published *The Transsexual Phenomenon* in 1966 and developed a set of medical standards and ethics used in the treatment of transsexuals today.

LYNETTE REINI-GRANDELL
VENUS

BENNETT, MICHAEL

b. 1943; d. 1987

dancer, choreographer, director

Born Michael DeFiglia, Michael Bennett began his career as a dancer in movies and on Broadway, which led to his lifelong affection for dancers. His debut as a choreographer was with *Joyful Noise* (1966), followed by *Promises, Promises* (1968). He achieved lasting fame alongside Hal Prince and Stephen **Sondheim** in *Company* (1970) and *Follies* (1971). But it was the show he developed from a series of interviews with dancers that became his greatest legacy: *A*

Chorus Line (1975). The play won the Tony Award, the Pulitzer Prize and for many years held the record for the longest-running show on Broadway. His next project *Ballroom* (1978) was a critical failure, but Bennett returned with the dazzling *Dreamgirls* (1981). Bennett, an active bisexual, was married for a time to actor/dancer Donna McKechnie. When diagnosed with AIDS, he quit directing, abandoned the musical *Chess* (1986), withdrew into seclusion and kept his illness a secret until his death.

CHRIS BYRNE

BENNING, SADIE

b. 1973

videomaker

Sadie Benning is a videomaker and lesbian activist well known in the US queer community of the 1990s. Her first videos were made at the age of 15 using a Fisher Price Pixelvision, a toy camera she continued to use since the artistic look produced suited the intimate atmospheres of her stories. Biographical features and interest in the inner self characterize all her work, with particular reference to themes of identity and sexuality, the discoveries and malaise of adolescence, and the anger, anxiety and frustrations in having to relate to a violent, homophobic society. In her films Benning also uses images from television, the press and popular culture, highlighting the lack of positive and empowering images for lesbians and women to identify with.

Benning has worked on projects in collaboration with other artists and activists, and has performed with the band **Le Tigre**. In 2005 she was the recipient of a Guggenheim fellowship.

MONICA BARONI

BERGER, HELMUT

b. 1944

actor

The strikingly beautiful blond actor Helmut Berger is best known for his collaborations with director Luchino **Visconti**. In Visconti's *La Caduta degli Dei* (*The Damned*, 1969), Berger gave a memorable performance as the gay heir to a doomed manufacturing dynasty in Nazi Germany, whose perversions run to performing in Marlene Dietrich drag, orgies with Nazi soldiers and incest with his mother. He played the title role in *Dorian Gray* (1970), based on Oscar Wilde's novel, and starred in Joseph Losey's *The Romantic Englishwoman* (1975). After Visconti's death in 1976, Berger's career flagged, and he spiralled into alcoholism and drug abuse, exploited to compelling effect in the film *Eroina* (Heroin, 1983). He made a comeback on German and American television in the 1980s, notably as the swarthy villain Peter de Vilbis in **Dynasty** (1983–4), and appeared in *The Godfather Part III* (1990). He has directed two TV films and published an autobiography, *'Ich' Ullstein* (1998).

JOHN FORDE

BERLIN

Germany's capital city has been the centre of the European gay rights movement since the 1890s, and is the home of Magnus Hirschfeld's Scientific-Humanitarian Committee and the Institute for Sexual Research. The sexually experimental and decadent **cabaret** scene of the 1930s was immortalized in writings by Christopher **Isherwood**. Under the Nazi regime, Berlin was the centre of brutal prosecution, imprisonment and the execution of gay and lesbian people. Since reunification in 1990, the city has become one of Europe's gay capitals, with an established leather, **sado-masochism** and fetish scene, and hosts a gay street festival every July.

JOHN FORDE

BERNHARD, SANDRA

b. 1955

comedian, writer, singer, actor

Best described as 'pansexual', Sandra Bernhard is open about past gay relationships (for instance with model Patricia Velazquez, and her erotically charged and very public friendship with **Madonna** during the early 1990s) and has a high profile within queer culture. She performed as a lesbian character in the US sitcom *Roseanne* throughout the 1990s, has made several TV appearances including in **Will & Grace,** and her one-woman shows (*Without You I'm Nothing*, 1988, and *I'm Still Here… Dammit*, 1998) deal with issues of sexuality and are popular with gay audiences. Her allegiance to the women's liberation movement has been public, adding to her forthright persona. The film that established her reputation as an actor came when she appeared with Robert DeNiro and Jerry Lewis in Martin Scorsese's satire *The King of Comedy* (1983).

MICHAEL PINFOLD

BERNSTEIN, LEONARD

b. 1918; d. 1990

composer

One of the world's first celebrity composers and conductors, Bernstein was responsible for some of American musical theatre's enduring classics. Born 25 August 1918 he attended Harvard and the prestigious Curtis Institute. After graduation he attained overnight fame as a last-minute replacement conductor for the New York Philharmonic Orchestra in 1944, later becoming its musical director. He scored another triumph in his debut at Milan's La Scala opera house in 1953, directing Maria **Callas** in *Medea*. He is best known for his musical theatre works *On The Town* (1944), *Wonderful Town* (1953), *Candide* (1956) and *West Side Story* (1957). He also skilfully utilized television to popularize classical music, including his educational series of Young Peoples' Concerts (1958–72). His enthusiastic support of jazz, pop and rock 'n' roll put him at odds with the classical music establishment, as did his controversial association with the Black Panthers.

Bernstein's flamboyant public persona was in contrast to his closeted homosexuality. Although he married in 1951 and had three children, he nonetheless had several gay relationships before his death on 14 October 1990. His final major composition, the opera *A Quiet Place* (1983), features a bisexual male lead character.

JOHN FORDE

BERZON, BETTY

b. 1928; d. 2006

writer, therapist

Psychotherapist and author whose therapeutic work encourages gay and lesbian patients to develop healthy relationships and overcome the negative effects of **homophobia**. She began her career as a journalist, interviewing public figures including Eleanor Roosevelt and Talullah Bankhead. She discovered her lesbianism as a student in California and, after brief residences in **Paris** and **New York**, she returned to California and opened Berzon Books, promoting the works of Anaïs Nin and Edith Sitwell. After hospitalization and treatment for mental illness, she trained as a psychotherapist, concentrating on behavioural therapy. In 1971 she co-founded the Los Angeles Community Services Center and openly embraced her lesbian identity. Her influential self-help gay and lesbian therapeutic guides include *Positively Gay: New Approaches in Gay and Lesbian Life* (1979) and *Permanent Partners: Building Gay and Lesbian Relationships That Last* (1988).

She published her *Surviving Madness: A Therapist's Own Story* in 2002.

JOHN FORDE

BEYALA, CALIXTHE

b. 1961

writer

Cameroonian-French novelist and essayist Calixthe Beyala was born into a poor family in Cameroon but acquired a privileged education that took her to Spain and France where she settled in 1984. Her prolific work is characterized by a bold, feminist sensibility and style that stresses commonalities between Western and African struggles for women's emancipation. Her first two novels, *C'est le soleil qui m'a brûlée* (The Sun Hath Looked Upon Me, 1987) and *Tu t'appelleras Tanga* (Your Name Shall Be Tanga, 1988) have as their protagonists young African women who are oppressed and exploited by their mothers as well as by men. In Tanga's case, a brief sexual relationship with a white woman in prison probably represents the first lesbian scene ever published in a novel by an African woman. *Femme nue femme noire* (Naked Woman Black Woman, 2003) is also remarkable in its explicitly erotic style, the main character enjoying her sexuality in a way that elevates freedom from male sexual domination to a political strategy for African women.

MARC EPPRECHT

BEYER, GEORGINA

b. 1957

actor, politician

Georgina Beyer, formerly George Bertrand, was elected to New Zealand's Parliament in 1999. She is considered to be one of the first transsexuals elected into national office in the world. Of Maori descent, Beyer was initially raised in a farming environment in the North Island of New Zealand. She later shifted between Wellington, Auckland and Sydney, working as a stripper, prostitute and actor. She has appeared in such films as *Jewel's Darl* (1985) by Peter **Wells** and Stewart **Main**, a short film which is structured around a day in the life of a transsexual and a transvestite who have a close but platonic relationship. She has also had small roles on mainstream TV shows such as *Close to Home* and *Shortland Street* (popular New Zealand soap operas). After visiting a friend in a small rural community, Beyer stayed on as a drama tutor and was eventually elected Mayor of Carterton in 1995.

JO SMITH

BIDGOOD, JAMES

b. 1933

photographer, film director

Arriving in New York City in 1951, James Bidgood initially worked as a window-dresser and costume designer. From 1963 until 1967, he worked as a freelance photographer for various physique magazines published by Weider, including *Muscleboy*, *Demi-Gods* and *The Young Physique*. He is most well known for his film *Pink Narcissus* (released in 1971), which he worked on from 1964 until 1970, only for it to be completed (to his dissatisfaction) by the Hollywood studio Sherpix. Still bearing the directorial credit of 'anonymous', the film, based on the myth of Narcissus, is a homoerotic meditation on the beauty and innocence of male youth, cast in romantically surrealist fantasy settings, all of which were actually constructed and filmed in Bidgood's tiny New York apartment. The film has since become a cult classic and its glamour aesthetic is similar to the work of photographers David **LaChapelle** and **Pierre et Gilles**.

JOHN PAUL RICCO

BIRMINGHAM SCHOOL

The name 'Birmingham School' is used as shorthand for the Centre for Contemporary Cultural Studies, founded in 1964 at Birmingham University, and for the scholarship associated with the discipline of British Cultural Studies that the centre virtually defined. The influence of the School has extended along with the international rise of Cultural Studies, the academic field within which glbt studies finds its most important institutional context. Three broad tenets of the School mark its significance for queer studies: culture is a site of struggle in which dominant ideologies are imposed but also resisted; culture is a field of self-expression through which marginalized groups create a sense of identity; the dynamic nature of societies cannot be understood through reference to any single model of conflict (e.g., class struggle or patriarchy and women's resistance), but only by acknowledging that forms of difference and allegiance are mapped onto one another in complex and shifting ways. The rise of cultural studies in the university mirrors the crises of the traditional Left and the renewal of radical thought by social movements organized around race, gender and sexuality. While some scholarship in queer studies has developed subversive approaches to the venerated artefacts of 'high culture', Cultural Studies has also legitimated attention to mass culture and commodities and to the ways in which subcultures appropriate these transgressively for their own purposes. Glbt scholars influenced by the Birmingham School and British Cultural Studies include Sally Munt, Elizabeth Wilson, Kobena **Mercer** and Richard Dyer.

TREVOR HOPE

BISEXUALITY AND THE BISEXUAL MOVEMENT

An activist bisexual movement developed in the United States, beginning in the

1970s. This movement spread to other countries such as the UK, Germany, the Netherlands and Australia, growing in tandem with a cross-national bisexual community. Both the movement and the community have worked to create a bisexual cultural space, in which books could be written, music recorded and performing arts enjoyed.

The term 'bisexuality' is currently most often used either behaviourally (referring to sexual activity with men and women) or to describe a sexual identity that one might have by nature of his/her attractions to, or sexual engagement with, men and women. Bisexual attraction, bisexual behaviour and bisexual identity are not coterminous (e.g., Aggleton 1996; Denizet-Lewis 2003; Esterberg 1997; Firestein 1996; George 2001; Rust 2000, 2002; Stobie 2003; Stokes and Damon 1995; Weinberg *et al.* 1994, 2001; Wishik and Pierce 1995). After clarifying the bisexual behaviour–bisexual identity distinction, this entry will cover the development of the bisexual movement and community; the existence and nature of biphobia; bisexual feminism and lesbian–bisexual relations; and the tension surrounding whether to build up or break down the bisexual identity.

Development of the bisexual movement/community

The current bisexual movement/community in the United States, arguably the largest, has developed in the context of frequently changing social and political situations. These historical changes have, in turn, significantly changed bisexual concerns and priorities (Hutchins and Kaahumanu 1991; Ochs and Highleyman 2000; Tucker 1995; Udis-Kessler 1996b; Weise 1992). In the 1970s the sexual liberation movement led to a publicly marked moment of 'bisexual chic' and provided both a social space and specific sexual free-

dom goals for bisexually identified people, especially in cities such as San Francisco. This period saw the development of a number of local bisexual organizations. During the 1980s bisexual men became targeted as 'AIDS vectors' and 'AIDS bridges' from the gay male community to heterosexual society, even as male bisexual organizers (and some bisexual women) began to die from AIDS complications. Politicized bisexuals became active in AIDS activism and safer sex education over the course of the decade. During the same period, some lesbian feminists were leaving lesbian communities, or struggling to remain within them, after becoming involved with men; these women increasingly turned to bisexual feminist groups in Boston, Seattle and elsewhere. By the beginning of the 1990s bisexuals were focusing on community development, bringing together different strands of political theory and activism, cultural creation, sexual connection and academic concerns. From the late 1980s through much of the 1990s, bisexuals prioritized identity politics, demanding explicit inclusion by name in gay and lesbian organizations and activities. Finally, beginning in the 1990s, academics in such countries as the US, the UK and Australia began to develop bisexual theory, which has largely taken a postmodern and deconstructionist turn. Related trends have occurred in many other countries, with 66 countries currently hosting bisexual or bi-inclusive organizations (Ochs 2001a).

Biphobia

While the bisexual movement began largely as a way to target sex-phobia and its attendant internalized homophobia, the movement has increasingly specified biphobia as its major political concern. Biphobia, the fear and hatred of bisexuals and bisexuality, tends to become manifest as a mixture of bisexual invisibility and the stereotyping of bisexuals and bisexuality. Just as homophobia is linked to heterosexism, biphobia is linked to 'monosexism', a form of inequality in which the highest value is placed on romantically and sexually relating only to one sex (whether one's own or the 'opposite' sex).

Most industrialized countries in which self-identified bisexuals live are ordered by a hierarchical, binary homosexual–heterosexual dualism, in which lesbian and gay individuals and communities permeate heterosexual society. In such a setting, bisexuality and bisexuals tend to be invisible, with both practices and people regularly defined as heterosexual, homosexual, lesbian or gay even when 'bisexual' would be more technically accurate. For example, Blackwood (1986) discusses 'homosexuality' around the world, but most of the practices described are carried out by individuals who also marry, and who are thus, at least, behaviourally bisexual. As another example, Fraser (1999) shows that Simone de Beauvoir's bisexuality was ignored or suppressed by both the media and many of her biographers. Self-identified bisexuals regularly face pressure to define themselves as either heterosexual or lesbian/gay, even when neither label seems to fit 'authentically', and self-identified bisexuals also face disbelief about the accuracy of their self-labelling. Such disbelief leads to stereotypes about bisexuals as experimenting heterosexuals, closeted lesbians/gay men, fence-sitters, cowards, confused or going through a bisexual phase (Colker 1996; Udis-Kessler 1996a).

Bisexuals face additional stereotypes, mostly focusing on sexual practices, politics and AIDS. The most common of these stereotypes posit bisexuals as sexually insatiable, as AIDS vectors and as traitors to the lesbian/gay struggle, who will return to the closet when the going gets rough and who will leave same-sex partners for opposite-sex partners eventually (Hemmings 1994;

Udis-Kessler 1996a). Films, the mainstream media and the lesbian/gay media have contributed to these stereotypes, particularly regarding AIDS (Beemyn and Steinman 2002; Miller 2002; Udis-Kessler 1994). By focusing on bisexual identity rather than unsafe sex practices, the media have contributed to the stigmatizing of bisexual men and failed to show the role of racism, biphobia, and homophobia in the sexually unsafe practices of some men of colour (Colker 1996: 17–18; Denizet-Lewis 2003) (see **AIDS in the black and Hispanic communities**). Some research actually suggests that bisexually identified men are more likely to practice safer sex than behaviourally bisexual men who do not so identify (Aggleton 1996; Kennedy and Doll 2001).

Biphobia is best understood as a kind of 'double discrimination' that can be internalized in the same way as homophobia (Ochs 1996; Ochs and Deihl 1992). The existence of biphobia can lead bisexuals to stay closeted, whether out of fear of others' responses or because they do not experience themselves as fitting the stereotypes. The relatively small number of people who openly and politically identify as bisexual continues the vicious cycle of stereotyping and bisexual invisibility (Ochs 1996, 2001b; Ochs and Deihl 1992).

A number of bisexual and bi-friendly authors have written about biphobia, beyond those listed above. Arnesen (1991) describes biphobia at the hands of the military, Comstock (1996: 113–14) demonstrates the existence of biphobia among lesbians and gay men of faith and Colker (1996) presents legal cases where bisexuality was literally legislated out of existence or specifically targeted for discrimination. Bryant (2001) documents biphobic stereotypes about behaviourally bisexual characters in American films from 1916 to 1999. In addition, some researchers have developed measures to study biphobia and have found evidence of it in lesbian, gay and heterosexual populations (Eliason 2001; Herek 2002; Mohr and Rochlen 1999; Mulick and Wright 2002). Study results suggest that heterosexuals dislike bisexual men more than bisexual women, gay men or lesbians.

Various bisexual activists and theorists have suggested that biphobia is a direct result of 'the threat posed by bisexuality to the comfortable and well-accepted binary perception of straight–gay/lesbian sexual orientation, as well as of gendered reality' (Shokeid 2001: 64). Udis-Kessler (1991), writing on biphobia as a crisis of meaning, pointed out that the hetero/homo binary has served both heterosexuals and lesbians/ gay men well, albeit in different ways. She has noted the need of heterosexual people in a homophobic society to be able to say: 'I am not gay.' The same article considered the need of lesbians and gay men to be able to affirm their homosexuality as real and legitimate, rather than a matter of sexual fluidity, and indicated the challenge of bisexuality to a lesbian/gay 'ethnicity' model. Garber's (1995) work on biphobia continued in this tradition, as has much of the feminist and deconstructionist analysis since the early 1990s.

Bisexual feminism and bisexual–lesbian relations

Of the various communities with which bisexual activists have been in dialogue and tension, few are as important as lesbian-feminist communities. As noted earlier, during the 1980s and 1990s many bisexual women had been involved in separatist lesbian-feminist communities before rediscovering or reacknowledging attractions to men, and feminism strongly informed their approaches to bisexuality when they did become engaged with bisexual communities (Hutchins and Kaahumanu 1991; Orndorff 1999; Rust 1995; Udis-Kessler 1996b; Weise 1992). This historical narra-

tive also helps to explain why so many leading bisexual activists in the 1980s and early 1990s were women. As Steinman (2001) suggests, because gay men did not politicize their biphobia in the same way as did lesbians (see also Ault 1996; Berenson 2002; Faderman 1991: 234–5; Rust 1995), bisexual men had less incentive than bisexual women to develop an oppositional, politicized bisexual community based on a 'valorized' bisexual identity. A widely studied lesbian–bisexual struggle took place over the Northampton (MA) Pride March between 1989 and 1993 (Hemmings 2002; Nathanson 2002). This march became a site of struggle over the meaning of community and coalition, the question of whether bisexuality could be feminist and, more generally, the loss of lesbian-feminist space and resources during a period when bisexuality and 'queerness' were becoming more visible.

Politically, lesbian feminists have charged that bisexuality re-privileges heterosexuality, prioritizes sexual desire over political analysis, depoliticizes sex as a site of oppression and erases radical feminist theories of sexuality (Jeffreys 1999; Wilkinson 1996). Bisexual feminists in turn claim that bisexual feminism challenges the hierarchical dualism at the heart of sexism (Weise 1992). Bisexuality also enables some feminists to use their relationships with men as a location of feminist struggle and challenges compulsory heterosexuality by allowing women who are not exclusively lesbian to relate sexually and romantically to other women (Berenson 2002: 19; Weise 1992).

Theoretically, the most important tension between lesbian-feminist and bisexual-feminist political analyses revolves around whether feminism requires a Marxian notion of false consciousness, in which women who relate to men are always and only deluded or desperate. Bisexual feminists claim that such a model actually silences women and denies their moral agency, rather than affirming and trusting women's choices, experiences and reality. Orndorff (1999: 6), for example, argues that 'asserting our bisexuality is a truly feminist stance, because we are defining ourselves based on our real desires and insisting that these be taken seriously'. Lesbian-feminist analyses of the social construction of patriarchy can lead to a deep suspicion of the bisexual feminist prioritizing of authenticity; what bisexual feminists see as the liberation of speaking their own truth can be seen as hopelessly uncritical by some lesbian feminists.

Lesbian–bisexual tensions have eased considerably since the early 1990s. George (2002) has noted that recent changes in feminism and diversification in the lesbian community have led to a reduction in lesbian discomfort with bisexuality. Wilkinson's (1996) otherwise critical article suggests that bisexuality be put on a radical feminist agenda, rather than simply rejected. At the same time, bisexual feminists (in, e.g., Weise 1992) acknowledge that lesbian biphobia is not identical to societal homophobia and that sexual relationships with men are not sufficient to change sexist social structures more generally.

To build up/to break down: dilemmas in bisexual identity

As the bisexual community has developed, activists have increasingly asked whether their goal is 'to build a strong, coherent movement based on sexual identity, or to break down identity-based distinctions altogether' (Highleyman 1995: 73). Bisexuals experience and express their sexuality and politics in differing ways, and while many activists believe that a solid bisexual identity is necessary for an effective movement, others think that bisexuality in and of itself points to the breakdown of traditional sexual identities and boundaries. An anthology in bisexual politics (Tucker 1995), for example, suggests political strategies that include focusing on bisexual inclusion in lesbian/gay organizations, breaking down sexual classifications entirely, prioritizing sexual liberation, challenging heterosexism and monosexism and drawing connections between different kinds of oppression. Tensions about whether to prioritize the development or the destabilization of bisexual identity may be based on different ways of understanding bisexual politics; on developing a political identity versus simply living a behaviourally bisexual life; or on academic theories of deconstruction over against developing a personal identity along 'ethnic' lines. Finally, some theorists (Garber 1995: 87) believe both that identity politics is necessary and that, for bisexuals, it may not be viable.

For much of their existence, the bisexual community and movement have engaged in identity-building activities and priorities, whatever hesitations individual bisexuals may have had about reifying the bisexual identity. For example, much of the earliest bisexual writing involved personal narratives clearly built around '**coming-out novels**' as a writing genre prioritizing sexual authenticity (e.g., Hutchins and Kaahumanu 1991; Klein and Schwartz 2001; Orndorff 1999; Rose *et al.* 1996; Tucker 1995; Weise 1992). Bisexual activists also focused on challenging stereotypes about bisexuality, and on ending bisexual invisibility (e.g., Udis-Kessler 1996a). Books such as the anthology by Kolodny (2000) of writings by bisexual people of faith, and the 1997 work by Bryant studying behaviourally bisexual characters in film presumed some degree of coherence to bisexuality, even as both books also suggested the variety of bisexualities available for practice and self-identity. Bisexuals have also engaged in 'reclaiming' as 'really' bisexual various historical figures adopted by lesbians and gay men, from Walt Whitman to Shakespeare (e.g., Hutchins and Kaahumanu 1991; Garber 1995). Hutchins (1996: 243) has also claimed that there are specific political issues for bisexuals to focus upon, such as discrimination against bisexuals, the scapegoating of bisexuals with regard to AIDS and the refusal to accept the validity of bisexual experience and reality.

At the same time, bisexual theorists, bisexual activists and other bisexuals view bisexuality as an identity constantly on the edge of destabilization. Many bisexual theorists identify bisexuality with postmodernism (Bi Academic Intervention 1997; Storr 1999) and consider it 'a sign of transgression, ambiguity and mutability' (Däumer 1992: 103). Some bisexual activists seek to move away from a focus on bisexual identity to 'idea-driven' politics (Highleyman 1995) or profess a goal of using bisexuality to bring an end to all sexual identities. Finally, individuals in the bisexual community may view themselves as sexually fluid, may reject the bisexual label as not adequately descriptive of them (Ochs 2001b) or may find the community valuable for friendships and sexual relationships while not engaging in any kind of identity-based political activism.

Developments in bisexual theory

As noted above, bisexual theorists tend to be deconstructionists. Hall and Pramaggiore (1996), for example, offer a collection of writings that treat the fence as an epistemological location for the study of various kinds of cultural texts. For these editors, bisexual epistemologies 'refuse one-to-one correspondences between sex acts and identity [and] between identification and desire' and thus represent a rejection of traditional identity politics (Hall and Pramaggiore 1996: 3).

Bisexual theorists, however, clearly do treat bisexuality itself as a legitimate locus of academic study. For example, most bisexual theorists are troubled that queer theorists have not made explicit and extensive use of bisexuality as a way to develop queer theory further (Bi Academic Intervention

1997; Hall and Pramaggiore 1996; Hemmings 2002; James 1996; Storr 1999). In this sense, however slippery the bisexual identity, bisexuality itself stands for and means something – particularly epistemologically. Moreover, some of the best theoretical writing (e.g., Hemmings 2002) manages the constructionist/deconstructionist tension rather than refusing one of its 'sides'.

Bisexual activists, theorists and others have proposed many directions for activism, community development and academic theory. The basic diversity among bisexuals, and the varied ways of being bisexual, suggests that differences will remain within the bisexual movement, the bisexual community and academic studies of bisexuality. This diversity may be both the greatest strength and the greatest weakness of the bisexual movement, and is likely to proliferate rather than stabilize in times ahead, with the possible exception of the academy (where a modified deconstructionism seems to be holding sway). If the bisexual movement can find ways to capitalize on its diversity without being stymied by it, the movement will continue to do valuable work in the world.

See also: Feminist movement, the

Bibliography

Aggleton, P. (ed.) (1996) *Bisexualities and AIDS*, Bristol, PA: Taylor & Francis.

Arnesen, C. (1991) 'Coming Out to Congress', in L. Hutchins and L. Kaahumanu (eds) *Bi Any Other Name*, Boston: Alyson Publications.

Ault, A. (1996) 'Hegemonic Discourse in an Oppositional Community', in B. Beemyn and M. Eliason (eds) *Queer Studies*, New York: New York University Press.

Beemyn, B. and Steinman, E. (2002) 'Introduction', *Journal of Bisexuality* 2, 1: 1–7.

Berenson, C. (2002) 'What's in a Name?' *Journal of Bisexuality* 4: 9–21.

Bi Academic Intervention (eds) (1997) *The Bisexual Imaginary*, London: Cassell.

Blackwood, E. (ed.) (1986) *The Many Faces of Homosexuality*, New York: Harrington Park Press.

Bryant, W. (1997) *Bisexual Characters in Film*, New York: Harrington Park Press.

—— (2001) 'Stereotyping Bisexual Men in Film', *Journal of Bisexuality* 1, 2/3: 213–19.

Colker, R. (1996) *Hybrid*, New York: New York University Press.

Comstock, G.D. (1996) *Unrepentant, Self-affirming, Practicing*, New York: Continuum.

Däumer, E. (1992) 'Queer Ethics; or the Challenge of Bisexuality to Lesbian Ethics', *Hypatia* 7, 4: 91–105.

Denizet-Lewis, B. (2003) 'Living (and Dying) on the Down Low', *The New York Times Magazine*, 3 August: 28ff.

Eliason, M. (2001) 'Bi Negativity', *Journal of Bisexuality* 1, 2/3: 137–54.

Esterberg, K. (1997) *Lesbian and Bisexual Identities*, Philadelphia: Temple University Press.

Faderman, L. (1991) *Odd Girls and Twilight Lovers: A History of Lesbian Life in Twentieth-Century America*, New York: Columbia University Press.

Firestein, B.A. (ed.) (1996) *Bisexuality*, Thousand Oaks: Sage.

Fraser, M. (1999) *Identity Without Selfhood*, Cambridge: Cambridge University Press.

Garber, M. (1995) *Vice Versa*, New York: Simon & Schuster.

George, S. (2001) 'Making Sense of Bisexual Personal Ads', *Journal of Bisexuality* 1, 4: 33–57.

—— (2002) 'British Bisexual Women', *Journal of Bisexuality* 2, 2/3: 175–91.

Hall, D.H. and Pramaggiore, M. (eds) (1996) *RePresenting Bisexualities*, New York: New York University Press.

Hemmings, C. (1994) 'Locating Bisexual Identities', in D. Bell and G. Valentine (eds) *Mapping Desire: Geographies of Sexualities*, New York: Routledge.

—— (2002) *Bisexual Spaces*, New York: Routledge.

Herek, G.M. (2002) 'Heterosexuals' Attitudes Toward Bisexual Men and Women in the United States', *Journal of Sex Research* 39, 4: 264–74.

Highleyman, L. (1995) 'Identity and Ideas', in N. Tucker (ed.) *Bisexual Politics*, New York: Harrington Park Press.

Hutchins, L. (1996) 'Bisexuality', in B. Firestein (ed.) *Bisexuality*, Thousand Oaks: Sage.

Hutchins, L. and Kaahumanu, L. (1991) *Bi Any Other Name*, Boston: Alyson Publications.

James, C. (1996) 'Denying Complexity', in B. Beemyn and M. Eliason (eds) *Queer Studies*, New York: New York University Press.

Jeffreys, S. (1999) 'Bisexual Politics', *Women's Studies International Forum* 22, 3: 273–85.

Kennedy, M. and Doll, L. (2001) 'Male Bisexuality and HIV Risk', *Journal of Bisexuality* 1, 2/3: 109–35.

Klein, F. and Schwartz, T. (eds) (2001) *Bisexual and Gay Husbands*, New York: Harrington Park Press.

Kolodny, D.R. (ed.) (2000) *Blessed Bi Spirit*, New York: Continuum.

Miller, M. (2002) 'Ethically Questionable?', *Journal of Bisexuality* 2, 1: 93–112.

Mohr, J.J. and Rochlen, A.B. (1999) 'Measuring Attitudes Regarding Bisexuality in Lesbian, Gay Male, and Heterosexual Populations', *Journal of Counseling Psychology* 46, 3: 353–69.

Mulick, P.S. and Wright, L.W. (2002) 'Examining the Existence of Biphobia in the Heterosexual and Homosexual Populations', *Journal of Bisexuality* 2, 4: 45–64.

Nathanson, J. (2002) 'Pride and Politics', *Journal of Bisexuality* 2, 2/3: 143–61.

Ochs, R. (1996) 'Biphobia', in B. Firestein (ed.) *Bisexuality*, Thousand Oaks: Sage.

—— (ed.) (2001a) *Bisexual Resource Guide*, Boston: Bisexual Resource Center.

—— (2001b) 'Uncommon Wisdom', *In the Family* Fall: 5.

Ochs, R. and Deihl, M. (1992) 'Moving Beyond Binary Thinking', in W. Blumenfeld (ed.) *Homophobia*, Boston: Beacon Press.

Ochs, R. and Highleyman, L. (2000) 'Bisexual Movement', in B. Zimmerman (ed.) *Lesbian Histories and Cultures*, New York: Garland.

Orndorff, K. (1999) *Bi Lives*, Tucson: See Sharp Press.

Rose, S. *et al.* (1996) *Bisexual Horizons*, London: Lawrence & Wishart.

Rust, P.C.R. (1995) *Bisexuality and the Challenge to Lesbian Politics*, New York: New York University Press.

—— (ed.) (2000) *Bisexuality in the United States*, New York: Columbia University Press.

—— (2002) 'Bisexuality: the State of the Union', *Annual Review of Sex Research* 13: 180–240.

Shokeid, M. (2001) 'You Don't Eat Indian and Chinese Food at the Same Meal', *Anthropological Quarterly* 75, 1: 63–90.

Steinman, E. (2001) 'Interpreting the Invisibility of Male Bisexuality', *Journal of Bisexuality* 1, 2/3: 15–45.

Stobie, C. (2003) 'Reading Bisexualities from a South African Perspective', *Journal of Bisexuality* 3, 1: 35–52.

Stokes, J. and Damon, W. (1995) 'Counseling and Therapy with Bisexual Men', *Directions in Clinical Psychology* 5: 1–14.

Storr, M. (1999) 'Postmodern Bisexuality', *Sexualities* 2, 3: 309–25.

Tucker, N. (ed.) (1995) *Bisexual Politics*, New York: Harrington Park Press.

Udis-Kessler, A. (1991) 'Present Tense', in L. Hutchins and L. Kaahumanu (eds) *Bi Any Other Name*, Boston: Alyson Publications.

—— (1994) 'Beyond AIDS Vectors, Deluded Closet Cases, and Lugs', in J.T. Sears (ed.) *Bound by Diversity*, Columbia: Sebastian Press.

—— (1996a) 'Challenging the Stereotypes', in S. Rose *et al.* (eds) *Bisexual Horizons*, London: Lawrence & Wishart.

—— (1996b) 'Identity/Politics', in B. Beemyn and M. Eliason (eds) *Queer Studies*, New York: New York University Press.

Weinberg, M.S., Williams, C.J. and Pryor, D. (1994) *Dual Attraction*, New York: Oxford University Press.

—— (2001) 'Bisexuals at Midlife', *Journal of Contemporary Ethnography* 30, 2: 180–208.

Weise, B.R. (ed.) (1992) *Closer to Home: Bisexuality and Feminism*, Seattle: Seal Press.

Wilkinson, S. (1996) 'Bisexuality "A La Mode"', *Women's Studies International Forum* 19, 3: 293–301.

Wishik, H. and Pierce, C. (1995) *Sexual Orientation and Identity,* Laconia: New Dynamics Publications.

AMANDA UDIS-KESSLER

BLACK CAT

The first gay bar in San Francisco. Opened in 1933 in the Barbary Coast area, it gradually became a gay bar after the Second World War. In 1951 the bar's owner won a California Supreme Court decision ruling that bars cannot be closed because they serve gay patrons. The bar gained fame for the performances of hostess Jose T. Sarria, who defiantly led patrons in the anthem 'God Save the Nelly Queens' and ran for city Supervisor in 1961. The bar finally closed in 1963.

ANDY HUMM

BLACK GLBTQ FILMMAKING

Although often marginalized in overviews of lesbian and gay cinema, films by and/or about black queers have long played an important role in the history of queer cinema and independent film in general. Faced with often daunting social, political and economic obstacles – including racism in lesbian/gay communities, homophobia in black communities and the lack of funding opportunities – black queer filmmakers from a variety of locations in the diaspora have nonetheless produced a rich body of work that explores, celebrates and interrogates black queer subjectivities *and* cinematic forms.

Before the late 1980s black queer images were at times visible on screen in mainstream and independent cinema, but they often served merely to signal either deviance or diversity. Many blaxploitation films of the 1970s and early Spike Lee films from the mid-1980s, for instance, use images of black queerness to contrast with and shore up idealized visions of black heterosexuality. Meanwhile, white-directed gay narrative and documentary cinema of the same period (*Boys in the Band, Portrait of Jason, Word is Out, Before Stonewall*) do indeed acknowledge and give voice to black queers, but such films often shut down any detailed examination of race (and racism) in gay culture.

In 1989, however, came the release of two experimental documentaries – *Looking for Langston* by Isaac **Julien** and *Tongues Untied* by Marlon **Riggs** – an event that heralded a new era in queer filmmaking. Although the products of different cultures and taking widely divergent forms, both films introduced the strategies of black and queer representation that would be taken up by a variety of filmmakers during the New Queer Cinema boom of the early 1990s. Challenging the 'burden of representation' whereby black (and queer) cultural production is inevitably seen as *representative* of the community, both Julien's and Riggs' films instead 'signify' on the traditions of black gay representation (Mercer 1994: 225). The films present a multiplicity of voices and images, they blur the lines between fantasy and reality, they stage a dialogic interplay between sound and image and they interrogate both racism and the boundaries of race itself. Both revel in the erotic power of black male bodies, while confronting the objectification of the white gaze. And like many of the black queer films from the period, they explore interracial desire and the crisis of the AIDS epidemic.

Although directed by a white lesbian, the other major black queer film from the early 1990s is the award-winning documentary *Paris is Burning* (Jennie Livingston, 1990) about black (and Latino) gay and transgender performers in the Harlem drag balls of the mid-to-late 1980s. Structured along more conventional documentary lines, which led some to criticize the film's 'ethnographic gaze', *Paris is Burning* still troubles realist documentary traditions through its interrogation of 'realness' and 'authenticity' in relation to both drag and transgender identities. Films about black transgender people have been relatively scarce since *Paris*, but Preeti A.K. Mistry's 2002 short film *Junk Box Warrior*, featuring Trans Slam Poet Marcus Rene Van, and Stephanie Wynne's documentary *The Cookie Project* (2003) about an African–American male-to-female lesbian suggest new directions for this underexplored area of black queer life.

Black lesbian filmmaking has taken place primarily in the documentary and short film genres. Michelle Parkerson's early films were portraits of black female performers and her 1987 short documentary, *Storme: The Lady of the Jewel Box*, explored the life and career of black lesbian male impersonator, Storme DeLarverie. Following on the heels of Parkerson, a number of black lesbians have contributed short films and documentaries to the queer filmmaking boom since the early 1990s, including Dawn Suggs (*I Never Danced the Way Girls Were Supposed To*, 1992), Aarin Burch (*Spin Cycle*, 1991), Jocelyn Taylor (*Bodily Functions*, 1995), Shari Frilot (*Strange & Charmed*, 2003), Jamika Ajalon (*Shades*, 1994), H. Len Keller (*Ife*, 1992), Aishah Shahidah Simmons (*In My Father's House*, 1996), Stephanie Wynne (*Train Station*, 1996), Debra Wilson (*Butch Mystique*, 2003) and, of course, Cheryl **Dunye** (*She Don't Fade*, 1991). Diverse in their styles and approaches, many of these short films grapple with the complexity of screening black lesbianism and questions of difference and desire.

The key elements of Dunye's short film work (intraracial conflict, interracial desire, the filmmaking process) come together in *The Watermelon Woman*, which also explores queer historiography and media analysis – themes that occupy many black queer filmmakers. In the film, Dunye plays a young filmmaker looking for Fae Richards, a fictional 1920s-era black actor known for stereotypical 'mammy' roles. Dunye's search unearths a rich lesbian history that she rescues from oblivion and that mirrors her own lesbian life. Indeed, like Julien's *Langston* and Yvonne Welbon's acclaimed documentary *Living with Pride: Ruth C. Ellis @ 100* (1999) about the oldest living black lesbian, Dunye's exploration of the black queer past enriches and reinflects the black queer present. Historical reenactments (and fantasies of the cultural past) also anchor Rodney Evans' narrative feature *Brother to Brother* (2004), in which a young painter in modern New York tastes queer life in the Harlem Renaissance through a series of encounters with Bruce Nugent. Their moving intergenerational bond not only subverts gay culture's ageism but also queers the process of historical memory itself. A similar interest in familial and communal histories can also be seen in the documentary work of African-American director Thomas Allen Harris (*Vintage: Families of Value*, 1995; *That's My Face*, 2001).

Concerned with the pleasures and pains of media images and the power relations surrounding them, many black queer films cast a critical eye on media representations. Marlon Riggs' *Ethnic Notions* (1986) and *Color Adjustment* (1991) deconstruct black stereotypes in American media and culture, while Isaac Julien's *The Darker Shade of Black* (1993) and *BaadAsssss Cinema* (2002) interrogate the representation of race, gender and sexuality in rap/reggae music and blaxploitation cinema. Short filmmakers have mined similar territory in recent years: Etang Inyang negotiates her complex identification with and desire for Pam Grier in *Badass Supermama* (1997) and Charles Lofton's *O Happy Day* (1996) interweaves voices and images of the Black Panthers, blaxploitation and black gay porn in a gay fantasia on the Black Power era. Cheryl Dunye's narrative feature film *Stranger Inside* (2001) also presents a notable reworking of the women-in-prison genre.

In spite of Dunye's relative success, black queer feature films have been scarce over the past 20 years. Isaac Julien's groundbreaking 1991 film *Young Soul Rebels* presents a vibrant tapestry of music, sexuality and racial politics in late 1970s London. In 1997 came the release of Stephen Winter's gritty and gripping *Chocolate Babies*, about a band of black AIDS activist guerillas. And in 2000, Patrick-Ian Polk's *Punks* presented a glossy take on the romantic trials and tribulations of a group of West Hollywood gay men of colour.

Although most black queer cinema so far has emerged from American and British contexts, a few international filmmakers have begun to address homosexuality in the African diaspora, particularly in relation to notions of tradition, family and community.

Dakan, the controversial 1997 narrative feature film by Mohamed **Camara**, was the first sub-Saharan African film to deal with homosexuality; Sue Maluwa-Bruce's short documentary *Forbidden Fruit* (2000) examines the struggles of two women lovers in Zimbabwe; and Philip Brooks and Laurent Bocahut's documentary *Woubi Chéri* (1998) looks at gay identities and queer activism on the Ivory Coast. Most recently, Karim Ainouz's narrative feature *Madame Satã* (2002) presents the queer life of black Brazilian bandit, street fighter and transvestite performer João Francisco dos Santos.

While numerous barriers still hinder black queer filmmaking internationally, the recent success of filmmakers such as Evans and Dunye in the United States and the expansion of queer filmmaking from the African diaspora suggest that black queer films will persist despite a hostile political climate. The diversity of black queer filmmaking troubles any attempt to quantify and categorize it; in their very multiplicity, these films enact their shared investment in testing the limits of racial, sexual, gendered and national identities. And the success of black queer cinema can surely be measured by the difficulty involved in marking its boundaries or in predicting what new forms it might take in the future.

See also: Brooks, Philip and Laurent Bocahut; New Queer Cinema, International

Bibliography

Mercer, Kobena (1994) *Welcome to the Jungle: New Positions in Black Cultural Studies*, New York: Routledge.

Further reading

Aaron, Michele (ed.) (2004) *New Queer Cinema: A Critical Reader*, New Brunswick: Rutgers University Press.

Gever, Martha, Greyson, John and Parmar, Pratibha (eds) (1993) *Queer Looks: Perspectives on Lesbian and Gay Film and Video*, New York: Routledge.

Van Leer, David (1996) 'Visible Silence: Spectatorship on Black Gay and Lesbian Film', in Valerie Smith (ed.) *Representing Blackness: Issues in Film and Video*, New Brunswick: Rutgers University Press, pp. 157–81.

JOE WLODARZ

BLACK GLBTQ LITERATURE

Black gay and lesbian literature is an important part of the black literary tradition: both began in the Harlem Renaissance period of the 1920s, one of the most crucial moments in African-American intellectual life. The gay and lesbian writers of the Harlem Renaissance were cautious about introducing sexual themes into their novels as black artists had to confront racial and sexual violence. Increased sexual freedom made such expression more acceptable, although the situation was easier for black gay artists than for black lesbians, who also had to fight against black and white machismo using a process of celebration and denial of their sexual preferences.

Richard Bruce Nugent's *Sadhji* (1925) was the first black gay short story published, but his autobiographical text *Smoke, Lilies and Jade* (1926), with its famous celebration of black male beauty, formed the gay manifesto for the Renaissance. Other black bisexual writers who introduced gay themes into their works were Wallace Thurman (*Blacker the Berry*, 1929; *Infants of the Spring* 1933) and Claude McKay (*Home to Harlem*, 1928; *Banjo*, 1929). Langston Hughes' 'Young Sailor' and 'Café: 3 A.M.' were more reticent in alluding to the poet's bisexuality, as were Countee Cullen's 'Black Christ' and 'Song in Spite of Myself', with Hughes and Cullen choosing to use coded language to express their sexual identity.

After the end of the Harlem Renaissance, James **Baldwin** became the symbol of African-American literature and gay American literature. In his stories, Baldwin explores the willingness to express himself as a homosexual, the awareness of this identity and of adolescent sexual discovery. His works include *Outing* (1951), *Go Tell it on the Mountain* (1953) and the gay masterpiece *Giovanni's Room* (1956).

During the 1960s and 1970s the civil rights movement, the feminist movement, black power, the emergence of a black gay and lesbian middle class and the birth of a white gay and lesbian movement helped black gay men and lesbians to develop a new sexual consciousness that affected gay literature. The post-Baldwin gay writers dealt with a great variety of themes: private life, family relationships, love, sex, and political issues such as homophobic fears and racist violence, and the relationship, sometimes conflictual, between the black gay community and the African-American community.

The most important black gay writers since the 1960s have been: Joseph Beam with *In the Life* (1986), Gordon Heat with *Deep are the Roots* (1992), Randall Kenan with *A Visitation of Spirits* (1989), Steven Corbin, Essex **Hemphill**, Melvin Dixon, Samuel **Delany**, Craig Harris, Assoto Saint, Reginald Shepard and Johnnie Ray. Racism continues to be a central issue in every black gay's work but so too are interracial love, the colonized sexual imagination, white gay racism and, at the end of the 1980s, AIDS.

During the Harlem Renaissance, black lesbians existed in an ambivalent state; sexism prevented women of any colour openly expressing a lesbian lifestyle, but in addition, black women had to fight against a highly sexualized cultural image.

African-American lesbian identity remained ill-defined during the Harlem Renaissance, although a number of lesbian and bisexual blues singers such as Bessie **Smith**, Ma Rainey and Ethel Waters attained a level of sexual openness in their music. Nella Larsen,

Alice Dumbar-Nelson, and Angelina Weld Grimké were the primary black lesbian writers of the period. However, these authors did not overtly proclaim a lesbian identity in their work, instead using coded words and deep silences to describe their condition of being black, female and gay.

It was not until the 1960s and the 1970s that black lesbians began publishing works with lesbian themes with an immense variety of stylistic and generic concerns. The first openly black lesbian novel published in the United States was Ann Allen Shokley's *Loving Her* (1974), in which she explores several themes including the awakening of lesbian desire, racism among white lesbians, interracial relationships, sexism in black communities and homophobia. Audre Lorde's *From a Land Where Other People Live* (1973) and Pat Parker's *Movement in Black* (1969) represent the general themes of Afro-American lesbian literature of the 1970s, an intersection of sexuality, gender, race and class.

Gloria Naylor, Ntozake Shange and Alice **Walker** during the 1980s and the 1990s opened the way for a large public to access Afro-American lesbian literature. These years saw a proliferation of black lesbian novels and poetry exploring erotic domains and political issues. Black lesbian writers such as Audre **Lorde**, Cheryl Clarke and Ann Allen Shokley offered a new figure of black woman which gave force to the image of the black women that created and empowered African female tradition. Through their work came a new concept of womanhood and a strong, new identity for black lesbian women. By incorporating specific references to historical and mythical figures into poetry and fiction, the African-based womanist tradition affirmed lesbian identity, black feminism and black womanhood.

See also: Hughes, Langston

SILVIA FRANCOLINI

BLACK LAUNDRY

Black Laundry (Kvisa Shchora in Hebrew) is a direct action group based in Tel Aviv, Israel, which fights for Palestinian freedom and social justice. The purpose of Black Laundry's actions is to stress the connection between different forms of oppression, specifically the repression against glbt people and against Palestinians. During the Tel Aviv Pride parade in July 2002, Black Laundry's activists wore black shirts and carried a banner saying 'No Pride in Occupation'. In 2003 they took part in Queer For Peace, the international peace mission in the West Bank. A Black Laundry group is also present in New York City.

ALBERTO EMILETTI

BLACK QUEER STUDIES

Black queer studies is an emerging field characterized by interdisciplinarity and cultural exploration. One impetus for the development of the field is the white Eurocentrism present in studies of sexuality. Black queer studies, in turn, arises from queer theory's attempt to correct masculinist and monosexual dominance in Eurocentric analysis. A shared methodology within this diverse field is the simultaneous and mutually informing examination of racism and heterosexism.

The most common assumption about black queer studies is that it is the study of persons who are black and queer. Such work within this paradigm includes sociological and survey-based research on the lived experiences of contemporary subjects; historical and archival work to recover black queer historical figures (e.g., civil rights leader Bayard **Rustin** and blues singer Ma Rainey); and an examination of black queer authors within the literary tradition (e.g., James **Baldwin** and Audre **Lorde**). This particular area of investigation addresses contemporary authors in popular genres, such as Samuel **Delaney** and James Earl

Hardy. However, while this is an important area of investigation, black queer studies also incorporates a wide range of other subject matters and practices.

Many scholars also highlight and interpret texts that take blackness and queerness as their subject matter. Such texts are privileged documents for understanding a black queer tradition. This body of work includes writing both by authors who identify as queer and those who do not. Examples include Baldwin's *Giovanni's Room* (1956) and *Another Country* (1962), Alice Walker's *The Color Purple* (1982), Gloria Naylor's *The Women of Brewster Place* (1983), James Earl Hardy's hip-hop novel *B-Boy Blues* (1994) and Delaney's *The Mad Man* (1995), which addresses cruising culture. Other texts studied include poetry by writers such as Melvin **Dixon**, Essex **Hemphill** and, more controversially, Langston **Hughes**.

A key practice in black queer studies is the close reading of texts through a lens that analyses oppression. Queer and race-based readings allow the critic to trace multiple oppressions and identities across race, sex and class divisions. These studies include the reading of texts that are not explicitly 'about' queerness. Two highly influential examples of this type of scholarship are Deborah McDowell's introduction to *Quicksand and Passing* (1986) and Siobhan Somerville's book, *Queering the Color Line: Race and the Invention of Homosexuality in American Culture* (2000). McDowell, for example, performs a reading of Nella Larsen's *Passing* in terms of female same-sex intimacy while Somerville addresses such diverse topics as queerness in early twentieth-century blackface film, and the life and writings of Jean Toomer.

The diverse and emerging body of work in the field of black queer studies is an ongoing and immediate formation raising heretofore underdeveloped questions about the nature and politics of identity, the role of the critic in shaping meaning and the appropriateness of essentialism in the study of race and sexuality. The abiding work of scholars in black queer studies who examine authors, texts and theories of interpretation, as well as the growing interest among academic publishers will continue to expand the understanding of key issues related to race, sex and sexuality.

See also: Walker, Alice

MICHAEL QUIETO

BLACKMAIL

The illegal extortion of money on threat of exposure of a secret, such as closeted homosexuality. It was the subject of the 1961 film *Victim*, starring Dirk **Bogarde**.

ANDY HUMM

BLACKWOOD, CHRISTIAN

b. 1942; d. 1992

filmmaker

Berlin-born documentary director and cinematographer, whose extensive body of work profiles artists and filmmakers. He worked as a child actor before making films in his twenties. He won the 1996 Sundance Film Festival Grand Jury Prize for *Private Conversations* (1986), a behind-the-scenes look at the filming of Arthur Miller's play *Death of a Salesman* starring Dustin Hoffman. *Observations Under the Volcano* (1983) took a similar look at John Huston's film *Under the Volcano*. Other documentaries include *Straight, No Chaser* (1989) about Thelonius Monk; *Zwei Hotels, Nacbard in Nahost* (Two Hotels in our Troubled Middle East, 1988), *Nik and Murray* (1986), *All by Myself* (1982), a profile of Eartha Kitt, *Edith Head* (1979), *Roger Corman: Hollywood's Wild Angel* (1977) and *Signed: Lino Brocka* (1967) about the openly gay Filipino film director.

Blackwood died in New York City, 22 July 1992.

JOHN FORDE

BLAIS, MARIE-CLAIRE

b. 1939

playwright, novelist, short-story writer, poet

Born in Quebec City in 1939, Marie-Claire Blais is an award-winning figure in Canadian literature. She has lived in the United States, China, France and Quebec. Her relationship with sculptor Mary Meigs is the subject of *Lily Briscoe: A Self-Portrait* (1981) and *The Medusa Head* (1983). Blais was a Canada Council Fellow in Paris; a Guggenheim Fellow, sponsored by Edmund Wilson, in the United States; recipient of France's Prix Medicis for *Une saison dans la vie d'Emmanuel* (*A Season in the Life of Emmanuel*, 1965); Canadian Governor General's award winner twice, for *Le sourd dans la ville* (*Deaf to the City,* 1979) and, in 1996, for *Soifs* (*These Festive Nights*); and was made a member of the Order of Canada in 1980. Her most well-known lesbian novel is *Les Nuits de l'Underground* (*Nights in the Underground*, 1978).

See also: Canada, literature

JEAN BOBBY NOBLE

BLAKK, JOAN JETT

b. 1957

performer

Born Terence Smith in Detroit, Blakk is an African-American drag performer, singer and activist who first gained fame as a candidate in a mock attempt to become Mayor of Chicago in 1991. Queer Nation Chicago sponsored the campaign through impromptu political actions and club dates, resulting in a quickly produced video called *Drag'in for Votes* (1991). Heartened by a rush of pub-licity, Blakk and Queer Nation then unofficially entered the 1992 US presidential election, resulting in another video entitled *Lick Bush in '92* (1993). Despite these political efforts, Blakk never gained office but moved to San Francisco where her performing career continued to mix drag and political humour in the talk show *Late Nite with Joan Jett-Blakk* that ran throughout the 1990s. Blakk has since moved back to the American Midwest where he/she leads a much more private life dominated by beliefs formed through a long-standing relationship with the **Radical Faeries**.

See also: Queer Nation

GABRIEL GOMEZ

BLESSED MINORITY CHRISTIAN FELLOWSHIP (BMCF)

The Blessed Minority Christian Fellowship was established in 1992 and is derived from the religious subgroup of the Hong Kong Ten Percent Club. Pronounced *gay yun* in Cantonese, the Fellowship's name has the double meaning of Christ's grace (a literal translation of the term) and Christ's grace towards gays.

In 1996 BMCF registered as a non-profit statutory body in Hong Kong. The group offers regular services such as worship, choir practice, fellowship meetings, recovery group meetings and hospital visits, and also holds irregular events such as study groups for new Christians, retreats, and evangelistic meetings, providing spiritual support for the participants and helping them to construct a positive gay, Christian identity.

TRAVIS KONG

BLUR

pop group

Defined by an extraordinary talent for variety in their production, ranging from pop to gospel, and uncovering the camp treasures of British popular music traditions,

Blur and their lead singer Damon Albarn (b. 1968, London) rapidly reached star status as one of the best British pop bands of the 1990s. In a highly and ironically transgressive attitude, Blur's sound and look sent up the whole imagery of English working-class Laddism, giving birth to BritPop and bringing back the 1960s ambiance, with echoes of the 'Beatles vs Rolling Stones' competition as they were pitted against Oasis in the rivalry for the coolest band of the decade. A talent for catchy refrains joined a sapient provocation in songs such as *There's No Other Way* and *Girls & Boys* (whose refrain paid evident homage to The Kinks' *Lola*), sung as hymns to juvenile rebellion and gender reversals. Add to that the heartbreaking beauty and impishness of Damon Albarn and you have a gay icon.

FABIO CLETO

BODY-BUILDING

Long identified with queer culture, especially since the 1950s, when 'beefcake' magazines first appeared. Sculpting the body in public and the pure desirability of the 'beefy' body is particularly visible in such gay ghettos as Chelsea and Greenwich Village in **New York**, the Marais in **Paris**, Soho in **London** and West Hollywood in **Los Angeles**.

See also: Ghetto, gay

LISA Y.M. LAM

BOGARDE, DIRK

b. 1921; d. 1999

actor

After serving in the Second World War, Dirk Bogarde joined a theatre group, which quickly led to his working in films. He became something of a matinée pop idol, playing heart-throbs and comedy roles throughout the 1950s. During the 1960s he took on more challenging roles, most significantly that of a barrister blackmailed because of homosexuality in the film *Victim* (1961). The film was, at the time, extremely controversial, and today is credited with changing public opinion in favour of the decriminalization of homosexuality in Britain. Bogarde subsequently made several more highly acclaimed films, most notably with Joseph Losey (*The Servant*, 1963; *Modesty Blaise*, 1966; *The Accident*, 1967) and Luchino **Visconti** (*The Damned*, 1969; *Death in Venice*, 1971). During the 1990s, Bogarde semi-retired and began a successful writing career, producing both autobiographical books and novels. He continued to take interesting roles in films, including Liliana Cavani's *The Night Porter* (1974), Fassbinder's *Despair* (1978) and Alain Resnais' *Providence* (1977).

DANIEL HENDRICKSON

BOLAN, MARC

b. 1947; d. 1977

English singer

Born Mark Feld in London, Bolan soon developed a sartorial sense that got him noticed. His group T Rex was feted as darlings of the underground (at one time, David Bowie opened for them). Via TV appearances, Bolan's use of glitter, satin, feathers and silks was copied by fans immediately and adopted as a slant on traditional masculinity by the emerging Gay Liberation Front. 'Hot Love' became the band's first UK no. 1, allowing the single-handed creation of a new musical genre – '**Glam Rock**'. 'Get It On' became the second no. 1, followed by 'Children of the Revolution' and '20th Century Boy'. In 1974 Bolan's marriage to June Child ended and he became partner to his backing singer Gloria Jones, with whom he had a son. 'I Love to Boogie' became a hit in 1976, but 1977 brought the tragedy of Bolan's death in a car crash.

MICHAEL PINFOLD

BOLIVIA, FILMMAKING

Filmmaking in Bolivia is severely limited because of the lack of economic, human and technical resources as well as the population's general disregard for national cinematographic production in favour of commercial **Hollywood** productions. Most of the nation's films have focused on social criticism issues, primarily describing and vindicating the situation of indigenous Andean peoples – usually miners or farmers. Until 2003 the inclusion of queer subjects and themes was practically non-existent, sometimes involuntary and never positive. One of the earliest films with a detectable queer subtext is *La Cruel Martina* (Cruel Martina, 1986), based on a popular tale telling the story of a woman who fiercely rejected any interaction with men, showing affection only to women. The female lead is depicted as the Monstrous Feminine Other whose presence destabilizes androcentric social constructs of a profoundly Catholic, third world, rural country; she must be annihilated to restore the 'natural' social order.

The controversial *Mamá no me lo dijo* (Mother Never Told Me, 2003), a milestone in queer Bolivian cinema, was produced, written and directed by the human rights activist group **Mujeres Creando**. The film's non-linear narrative combines documentary and biographical approaches with a colourful, explicit, poetic visual language to explore and denounce institutionalized sexual and social discrimination against men and women, gay and straight. Rodrigo Bellot's *The Ballad of Sexual Dependency* (2003), awarded the film critics' award at the Locarno Film Festival in Venice, is a coming of age movie depicting the sexual dependencies of five characters in a non-linear, split-screen narrative with strong homoerotic content.

PEDRO ALBORNOZ

BOMBAY (MUMBAI)

Bombay is India's commercial centre and the heart of the 'Bollywood' film industry, creating a relatively tolerant environment for homosexuality. While homosexuality remains illegal in India, and Bombay's gay and lesbian community is closeted by Western standards, they still manage to host a number of gay cultural events and there is a thriving Internet-based community.

JOHN FORDE

BONO, CHASTITY

b. 1969

activist, actor

Born 4 March 1969, the daughter of pop duo Sonny Bono and **Cher**, Chastity Bono achieved gay iconic status in her own right when she came out as a lesbian in 1995. Named after the movie *Chastity* (1969) starring her mother and written by her father, she was a child performer on the TV shows *The Sonny & Cher Comedy Hour* (1971) and *The Sonny & Cher Show* (1976), later graduating from the High School for Performing Arts in New York. In 1990 *Star* magazine outed Bono as a lesbian, which she publicly denied, waiting until 1995, when she came out in *The Advocate*. Consolidating her mother's popularity with gay and lesbian audiences, Bono became one of America's first celebrity lesbians and a committed spokeswoman for the **Gay and Lesbian Alliance Against Defamation (GLAAD)**. She has made cameo appearances with Ellen DeGeneres on *Ellen* (1997) and *The Roseanne Show* (1998) and published a memoir, *Family Outing*, in 1999. She has also starred in the lesbian-themed films *Bar Girls* (1994) and *Fronterz* (2004).

JOHN FORDE

BOOCK, PAULA

b. 1964

writer

Born in Dunedin, New Zealand, novelist, playwright, screenwriter and publisher Paula Boock is known primarily for her novels aimed at teenage readers. In 1998, in what was described as a ground-breaking achievement, Boock won both the prize for young adult fiction and the supreme prize at the *NZ Post* Children's Book Awards (the country's premier awards for children's literature) for her fourth novel *Dare, Truth or Promise*, a story about two teenage girls who fall in love. The judge's decision caused considerable controversy, as right-wing Christian leaders and some mainstream commentators condemned the novel's subject matter as unsuitable for a teenage audience. *Dare, Truth or Promise* also won the Lambda Literary Award for young adult fiction in 2000. In 2003 Boock published the essay, 'On Makeup and Makeover', which, in part, connects childhood experiences about experimentation with her mother's makeup to issues of sexual identity and coming out.

ANITA BRADY

BORDEN, LIZZIE

b. 1958

film director

The daughter of a Detroit stockbroker, bisexual independent filmmaker Lizzie Borden found cult critical success in 1983 with the release of her violent lesbian-feminist, science-fiction documentary *Born in Flames*. She began her career in film after moving to New York City during the 1970s, and her love of Jean-Luc Godard led to her first attempt at filmmaking, the black and white film *Regrouping* in 1976. Borden followed the success of *Born in Flames* with the pseudo-documentary *Working Girls* (1986), a mundane exploration of a day in the life of a lesbian photographer who moonlights as a high-class prostitute. She later went on to direct for cult TV horror show *Monsters* and the Hollywood-made erotic fantasy *Love Crimes* (1991). Today Borden continues to explore the complexities of female sexuality and has contributed to softcore porn producer Playboy Video.

ROBIN GRIFFITHS

BORDOWITZ, GREGG

b. 1964

film- and videomaker

Gregg Bordowitz is a contemporary video and film artist, AIDS activist and theorist, and a co-founder, in the late 1980s, of the video collectives DIVA TV and Testing the Limits. He was also a member of ACT UP. His work draws upon the energy of early AIDS activism, which responded to insufficient funding as well as to the need to provide images and texts about the disease that did not use the pathologizing tropes of mainstream representations. In the years since, AIDS in the United States has become a manageable disease for mostly white gay men with access to new drug cocktails but it remains a deadly and prohibitively expensive global epidemic for others, concentrated in sub-Saharan Africa.

Bordowitz's work records these shifts without falling into the familiar traps of humanism and redemption that often surround the disease. His short film *Some Aspect of a Shared Lifestyle* (1986) responded to the 1983 Bowers and Hardwick case, which designated gay sex as illegal sodomy, as well as to the rise in AIDS. In it he juxtaposes and synthesizes a myriad set of texts and genres: TV news footage, newspaper reports and interviews conducted with a hand-held camera. Such techniques crop up again in his *Fast Trip, Long Drop* (1995), in which we learn that Bordowitz was diagnosed with HIV in 1988 and now lives wondering when he might die. The film never descends into a merely reflective personal narrative about the director's own infection. Instead, in a series of staged talk-show formats where he appears as a 'guest', he angrily dispenses with the easy humanism of 'survivor' discourse and insists that AIDS is as much an onus for the uninfected as the infected. This political perspective emerges yet again in his 2001 film *Habit,* in which Bordowitz is found at a different personal and political juncture, with the privilege of access to the new drug cocktails. Bordowitz turns his attention to the growing numbers of infected bodies in South Africa and their fight to legalize access to cheap generic drugs. The contrast is now between men such as Bordowitz and South African patients who forgo regular checkups because they know they can never have access to drugs.

Gregg Bordowitz is widely published and his work has appeared in anthologies such as *AIDS: Cultural Analysis, Cultural Activism* (Douglas Crimp (ed.) 1988). A collection of his writings, *The AIDS Crisis is Ridiculous,* was published in Autumn 2004. In 2002, *Habit* was released in tandem with his installation *Drive* at the Chicago Museum of Contemporary Art. His work has also been archived as part of the Estate Project at the New York Public Library. His inclusion in the collection testifies to the importance of AIDS work and activism that considers the historical realities of AIDS without nostalgia.

See also: ACT UP

YASMIN NAIR

BOSWELL, JOHN
b. 1947; d. 1994
scholar

In his 1980 work, *Christianity, Social Tolerance, and Homosexuality*, John Boswell argued that the degree of oppression and suppression in a given historical moment marks the degree to which 'gay' communities could be formed and publicly recognized. He further argued that, even in the most tightly regulated social environment without any recognizable sexual category, people who are same-sex attracted can see themselves as being different and separate from society at large, thereby having great impact on their notions of self and identity. Boswell's is a history where same-sex desire, same-sex sexual behaviour, same-sex love and affection, social acceptance or intolerance, subjective identification, situation, frequency of desire and behaviour, cultural meanings of desire and behaviour all go into making a highly differentiated 'homosexuality' at any given time. At the time of its publication, other historians criticized Boswell for re-essentializing gay identity, and to this day he is often dismissed as an essentialist. His later work, *Same-sex Unions in Premodern Europe* (1995), investigated evidence that, according to Boswell, supported the assertion that the early church supported same-sex unions through a same-sex nuptial liturgy. Boswell joined the history faculty of Yale in 1975 and, in 1987, helped organize the Lesbian and Gay Studies Center at Yale. He died from complications of AIDS in 1994.

J. TODD ORMSBEE

BOTHA, KEVIN
b. 1962
activist

Lawyer and founding member of the Gay Association of South Africa (GASA), that country's first national gay rights group, Kevin Botha played a controversial role in 1986 by defending GASA's refusal to aid leading black gay activist Simon **Nkoli** who had been imprisoned for anti–apartheid politics. This tacit support for racial segregation contributed to GASA's collapse in acrimony soon after. Botha, however, went on to play a leading role in rebuilding a gay rights movement that reached across racial, linguistic and other divides. He helped in particular to negotiate and then to secure the adoption of one of the world's first national constitutions to prohibit discrimination on the basis of sexual orientation.

MARC EPPRECHT

BOTTOM

Participation in anal sex as the recipient of penetrative activities, in opposition to the insertive practices of the '**top**'.

MICHAEL PINFOLD

BOWEN, GARY

b. 1961

writer

Openly gay novelist and editor whose work explores homoerotic and sadomasochistic (S&M) themes within the *Diary of a Vampire* (1995), an S&M-themed horror story about Rafael, a gay vampire, which was shortlisted for the Bram Stoker Horror Writing Award. His erotic short-story collections include *Winter of the Soul: Gay Vampire Fiction* (1995) and *Man Hungry* (1995). Bowen has also edited the gay fantasy anthologies *Icarus and Angels* (1996), *Floating Worlds: Oriental Fantasies* (1996), *Western Trails* (1996) and *Queer Destinies: Erotic Science Fiction Stories* (1999).

See also: Sadomasochism

JOHN FORDE

BOWERY, LEIGH

b. 1961; d. 1994

designer, club promoter

Born in Sunshine, Australia, Leigh Bowery moved to London at the age of 19 and quickly became a well-known figure on the club scene due to his outrageous outfits and performances, both alone and with his band, Minty. In 1984 he began a long-time collaboration with the dancer Michael Clark, designing costumes and eventually performing in several of Clark's pieces. In 1985 Bowery started the short-lived but notorious club Taboo, which solidified his place as one of the most intriguing figures on the London club scene. His fantastic costumes often made use of his large body, displaying and distorting it in unexpected ways. In 1990 the painter Lucien Freud saw Bowery in a gallery performance and asked him to pose. Freud presented Bowery's large body completely nude. Bowery continued performing and designing clothes until his death from AIDS-related meningitis in 1994.

DANIEL HENDRICKSON

BOWIE, DAVID

b. 1947

artist and pop performer

Born David Robert Jones, the role David Bowie played in popularizing a glamorous queer identity, and in paving new ways to achieve pop stardom, can hardly be underestimated. The heyday of Bowie's cultural significance was achieved by his otherworldly dandified image, androgynous vocal inflection and eclectic music. Using a number of personae (Ziggy Stardust, Aladdin Sane, the Thin White Duke, etc.), Bowie was the epitome of the 1970s glam artist, indulging in ambiguity, cross-dressing, role play and aristocratic detachment. A master in manipulating the media for self-promotion, he capitalized on what he tagged his own 'ambisexuality': even before his blatant sexuality had ceased to cause sensation, he reinvigorated controversies by means of rather disconcerting statements ('Hitler was the first superstar') and by refusing to give up identity by career moves. The queer science-fiction imagery and dystopianism of the early 1970s were followed by the nihilist minimalism of his 'Berlin years', by the heterosexual dance turn of the 1980s (seen by many as a betrayal of the sexual revolution ethos, as portrayed in Todd Haynes' 1998 film on the glam rock era, *Velvet Goldmine*), and by a return to his underground origins in the late 1990s. Changing roles with the same ease as he adopted new images, he also dedicated himself to cinema, art and music production (e.g., he produced albums by Iggy Pop and Lou Reed). A son of Warhol's Factory, Bowie never ceased experimenting with the borders between art and the market, and cloned himself into the New Romantic legion of his camp followers and imitators. Whatever his merits as an artist, he created a number of songs and images that capture the *Zeitgeist* of the queer 1970s.

FABIO CLETO

BOY GEORGE

b. 1961

musician, DJ

Boy George was born George O'Dowd in Kent, England. In 1982 he formed the internationally renowned group Culture Club with guitarist Roy Hay, bassist Mikey Craig and drummer Jon Moss. The group swept the world with their music, including huge hits such as 'Do You Really Want to Hurt Me' and 'Karma Chameleon', trendsetting the New Romantic movement of the 1980s. The revelation of George's addiction to heroin led to his downfall and ultimately to the dissolution of the group in 1986. A cover version of the 'The Crying Game' (1992), taken from the film of the same name that hinges on the disclosure of a transvestite as a twist of the plot, saw a revival in George's pop career in 1992. Today George is recognized foremost as a leading dance music DJ, a solo artist and for his Broadway musical *Taboo* (2002), produced in New York by Rosie **O'Donnell**.

George's flamboyant cross-dressing style – his braids, elaborate makeup. and eccentric dress – was unique in the 1980s pop scene, and the advent of MTV made him a global cultural icon. Many considered George's 'effeminate' look socially threatening and criticized him as an offending 'she-male', while others were awed by his androgynous persona. For a long time George denied his gayness and declared himself a bisexual; his secret relationship with the bisexual drummer in Culture Club, Moss, was not revealed until 1990. George openly reasserted his bisexuality in 1995 but later on publicly identified himself as a gay man. His expressions of **camp** and **drag** have been an area of inquiry in academia, especially in the ways they problematize the notion of masculinity.

LISA Y.M. LAM

BRACEWELL, CHARLES

performer, filmmaker

Born in New Zealand, Bracewell is an openly gay performer, actor, writer and director, who is best known for his drag alter ego, Miss Ima Starr. A regular on the Australasian drag performance circuit, Ima Starr became one of New Zealand's first recognizable drag personas. He wrote and directed the films *Siren* (1996), *Homecoming Queen* (1999), in which Bracewell, as Ima Starr, visits his home town in rural New Zealand, and *A Spoonful of Desi* (2003), and performed as drag queen Chantal in Peter Wells' and Rex Pilgrim's gay-themed feature film *I'll Make You Happy* (1999). He recently produced the Australian short film *Big Fat Greek Fag* (2005).

See also: Wells, Peter

JOHN FORDE

BRAM, CHRISTOPHER

b. 1952

writer

A prolific novelist and columnist whose work explores the spectrum of gay sexuality in historical and contemporary American society, Bram's early novels were set in New York – *Surprising Myself* (1987) a love story set in 1970s gay New York, *Hold Tight* (1988), of wartime spying and prostitution in 1940s Manhattan and *In Memory of Angel Clare* (1989), a dark tale of the devastation caused by the AIDS crisis. His next two novels explored closeted gay identities in the wider political context of the Vietnam War (*Almost History*, 1992) and contemporary Washington DC (*Gossip*, 1997). His best-known work, *Father of Frankenstein* (1995), is a fictional reimagining of closeted gay Hollywood based on the life of gay film director James **Whale**. It was adapted into an Oscar-winning film by gay writer-director Bill Condon, and starred Ian **McKellen** as Whale (*Gods and Monsters*, 1998). *The Notorious Dr August: His Real Life and Crimes* (2000) chronicles a bisexual interracial love triangle in nineteenth-century America and Europe. Bram's critical writing has also appeared in *Lambda Book Report* and *Christopher Street* magazines.

JOHN FORDE

BRAND, DIONNE

b. 1953

writer, filmmaker

Dionne Brand is an important novelist, poet, essayist and documentary filmmaker. Born in Guayguayare, Trinidad, she moved to Toronto, Canada in 1970. Graduating in 1975 from the University of Toronto, with a BA in 1989, Brand went on to complete an MA in education. She has taught creative writing and has been been writer-in-residence in universities, including the University of Toronto. With six films and twenty books, Brand is a prolific worker.

Multiple displacements through sexuality, race, class and gender are documented across her work in queer and postcolonial languages and forms. *Land to Light on* (1997) won the Canadian Governor General's Award for poetry. Two successful novels have been published in Canada, the United States and the United Kingdom: *In Another Place, Not Here* (1996) and *At the Full and Change of the Moon* (1999). Meanwhile *A Map to the Door of No Return* (2001), part memoir, part postcolonial theory, chronicles the simultaneity of diasporic subjectivities, postcolonial homelands and counter-cultural histories.

JEAN BOBBY NOBLE

BRAZIL, FILMMAKING

In his pioneering book, *The Homosexual Character in Brazilian Cinema* (2001), Antonio Moreno selected 127 films produced between 1923 and 1996 to demonstrate the abyss that separates the plurality of human desire from its representations. These representations have been limited to a repetitive axis of stereotypes that, not surprisingly, points to the endemic social prejudices found in both a sexist as well as an authoritarian Brazilian society. These representations have ranged from alienation to poverty, from the promiscuous to the dangerously marginal, and to the social arriviste, or, on a lighter note, to ridiculed objects of easy, autophagic laughter.

From Luiz de Barros' 1923 comedy *Augusto Anibal quer casar* (Augusto Anibal Wants to Get Married) onwards, mistaken identities based on cross-dressing were a favourite in Brazilian film comedies. Men posing as women can be seen, for example, in silent comedies such as *Fragments of Life* (José Medina, 1929) and all throughout the sound era, with the popularization of the *chanchada* genre of musical comedies linked to radio, circus and vaudeville. Actors such as the famous double act Oscarito and Grande Otelo had some of their best moments in drag, parodying literary or historical characters such as Helen of Troy (Oscarito in *Carnival Atlantida*, 1952) or Shakespeare's Juliet (Otelo in *Carnaval no fogo*, 1949). This successful trope proved to be very durable and can be seen even in the heyday of the *chanchada* genre, such as in Oscarito's incomparable imitation of a Rio socialite in a classic mirror sequence in Carlos Manga's *Os dois ladrões* (The Two Thieves, 1960) or even in a rare example of a Cinema Novo film paying tribute to the popular legacy of the *chanchada*, the tropicalist allegorical *Macunaíma* (1969), where director Joaquim Pedro de Andrade has actor Paulo José perform in drag when he tries to trick a lascivious industrialist. From the late 1960s until the mid-1980s the most visible examples of Brazilian cinema took the form of the spate of vapid erotic comedies – *pornochanchadas* – that were churned out to fill the vacuum left by political censorship and self-exiled filmmakers. Sexist and reactionary, gay characters in those films were, again, objects of ridicule.

Gay and lesbian images changed somewhat during the Cinema Novo phase, whether in the unexpected and very ponderous kiss on the mouth exchanged by the two women in Glauber Rocha's *Black God White Devil* (1964) or the risqué sex scenes between the two women performed at the request of two voyeuristic males in Walter Hugo Khoury's *Noite vazia* (Empty Night, 1964). The more experimental underground phase of modern Brazilian cinema known as *cinema marginal* did little to improve matters. What are today seen as classics, such as Rogerio Sganzerla's *Red Light Bandit* (1968) or Julio Bressane's *The Angel is Born* (1970) and *Killed the Family and Went to the Movies* (1970), the films – besides insisting on stereotypes of comic effeminate men – developed homophobic connotations. The two women lovers of

Killed the Family, for example, end up killing each other. More subtle and poetic instances of female bonding can be seen in David Neves' quietly lyrical *Memoria de Helena* (Memories of Helen, 1969), while two of the best tragic-in-drag **diva** impersonations are the pathetic Carlos Kroeber in Saraceni's *A casa assassinada* (The Murdered House, 1971) and William Hurt's Oscar-winning role as the queen Molina in Héctor Babenco's politically charged adaptation of *Kiss of the Spider Woman* (1985).

However, this bleak panorama changed the moment the authoritarian regime in Brazil stopped restricting the space for social activism. Despite the political eclipse of the Left, the counter-cultural attitudes of the 1960s became socialized and disseminated. The 1970s and 1980s, however, witnessed a veritable explosion of new social movements in the alternative public sphere. Alongside human rights groups, militant labour unions and environmental organizations, gay and lesbian associations started to come out into the open. This period also saw the founding of Brazil's first gay newspaper, *O Lampião* (1978), as well as the appearance of the first articulated grassroots groups such as the pioneering Somos (São Paulo, 1979) and the Grupo Gay da Bahia (Salvador, Bahia, 1980) which, with other groups, cultural critics and intellectuals, have drawn attention to these forms of mediated representations, not only those of sexual conflicts but also of ethnic and minority groups in general. Referring to Latin America generally, Jorge Castañeda sums up the process:

> Changes in life-styles, customs, forms of political engagement, and attitudes towards the 'other' and a major upheaval of cultural mores and production took place across the continent. The young attempted to incorporate political opinions into their everyday life; the cultural realm became politicized and transformed by the alterations around it. In literature,

the arts, the theatre and music, in sexuality and dress codes, through growing up and giving birth, the urban, intellectualized middle classes were undergoing a major transformation. In highly conservative societies, this represented a monumental shakeup.

As larger social movements grew in strength, the production of film and video documentaries echoed, mediated and even advanced this process. The 1980s and 1990s gave rise, as a consequence, to a healthy crop of gay, lesbian and feminist films and videos testifying self-identified social groups with different degrees of a shared gay culture. More recently, questions of racism and black consciousness have appeared alongside gay and lesbian issues, as in *Madame Satã* (dir. Karim Ainouz, 2002), a fictional biography of popular marginal character João Francisco dos Santos, who inhabited the underworld of gay criminality in a bohemian slum district of Rio de Janeiro during the 1930s. Not that these themes were new to Brazilian cinema, of course. Contemporary Brazilian films such as Héctor Babenco's *Pixote* (1980) – where an adolescent and defiant drag queen occupies the lowest rung among a group of street kids – or Bruno Barreto's *Beijo no asfalto* (Kiss in the Asphalt, 1985), Sergio Amon's *Aqueles Dois* (Those Two, 1985), the festival favourite *Vera* (1987) by Sérgio Toledo, or Sérgio Bianchi's *Romance* (1988) – the first feature to address the AIDS pandemic – are only a few examples in which gay themes were the centre of the narrative and, most importantly, broke out of a ghetto category.

Even when the plot is not ostensibly gay, there is an explicit homoerotic aesthetic in the voyeuristic depiction of the male body, as in Luiz Carlos Lacerda's camp post-*chanchada* film, *For All, o trampolim da vitória* (For All, 1997) or Djalma Batista's paean to a fictional soccer player in *Asa Branca, um sonho brasileiro* (Asa Branca, a Brazilian

Dream, 1981), followed by *Brasa adormecida* (Sleeping Ember, 1986) – both films starring a young Edson Celulari at his most handsome – and the more experimental biopic about the eighteenth-century Portuguese Romantic poet, Manuel Bocage, *Bocage, o triunfo do amor* (Bocage, the Triumph of Love, 1997). These feature films echo the more recent explosion of gay and lesbian issues in the short and feature film and video arena, as well as in prime-time television, with the now regular presence of more positive homosexual characters such as a young lesbian couple in TV Globo's prime-time soap opera, *Mulheres apaixonadas* (Women in Love, 2003).

The expansion of the gay market after 1995 also points to a greater interest in Brazilian gay-porn production aimed at national and international audiences. A predictable combination of a mythical tropical landscape, racial mixing and the pitfalls of sexual tourism promoted by the circulation of images of Rio's beach culture, all conspire to create a new set of stereotypes, either recycling the traditional myth of the Latin lover or, on another register, the submissive colonial subject. From a different perspective, Brazil is also currently witnessing an increasing number of short films and videos of an experimental nature created by a younger generation. To name just a few: Aleques Eiterer, Edyala Yglesias, Marcelo de Trói, Wilton Garcia, Juliana Caetano and Rodrigo Gontijo show the greatest promise. Their work includes a range of styles, from (mock) documentary to auteurist principles and to genre transformation, expanding the aesthetic language to simultaneously include social liberation and gay and lesbian visibility. Somehow this new generation of film- and videomakers is upholding a long-standing tradition of transgression against the cultural representations of non-normative sex and desire as associated with sin, sickness, deviation, illegality, submission and, ultimately, death.

101

Also worth noting is the recent rise of Gay, Lesbian, and Transgender Studies in Brazil as an academic area of inquiry, especially since 2002, when the second annual meeting of ABEH (the Brazilian Association of Homocultural Studies) was held in Brasília. Film and other audiovisual media constitute a central focus of the Association's research. Another example that highlights these positive transformations is the annual film and video festival Mix Brasil which enjoyed its thirteenth birthday in 2004. There are, as well, the Gay Pride parades taking place in different Brazilian cities every year, especially São Paulo where the 2004 event brought together the record-breaking figure of more than 1 million participants. The event now forms part of the official tourist calendar of the city.

JOÃO LUIZ VIEIRA

BRAZIL, LITERATURE

It is not an oversimplification to state that the constitution of a homoerotic literature in Brazil only developed slightly during the late nineteenth and early twentieth centuries. Besides isolated short stories and poems, overall a silence about homosexuality remained. When homosexuality does become visible (particularly following the Second World War), it occurs as a stereotype or as an image of impossible or failed homoerotic desire. A few exceptions are worth noting, among them *Grande Sertão: Veredas* (Great Hinterland Trails, 1956) by João Guimarães Rosa (1908–67), a revolutionary work in its sophisticated treatment of the main character's sexual ambiguity; *Crônica da Casa Assassinada* (1959, Chronicle of the Assassinated House) by Lúcio Cardoso (1912–68) explores the emergence of a figure whose homoerotic identity is marked by guilt and strong religious and/or existential anguish. This type of angst-ridden writing has a long ancestry, especially among catholic writers. Beyond the Catholic horizon, but still inside the realm of deep existential anguish and guilt mixed with the anxiety of an out-of-the-ordinary identity, is the work of Polish-born and Jewish writer, Samuel Rawet (1929–84), an author whose work needs to be studied for the way his fiction analyses the foreignness of homosexual identity in the so-called ordinary world.

During the 1960s Brazil's city streets served as a space of visibility for gay characters whose identities took shape in a libertarian fashion in which gays were portrayed in a neo-naturalist way that mixed questions of sexuality with social, economic and political issues. These works emerged against a backdrop of a country in which the shades of an authoritarian regimen took hold following the military coup of 1964. Authors such as Gasparino Damata (1918–82), Luiz Canabrava (1926–), and Aguinaldo Silva (1944–) present a direct, realist narrative to search for an image that is broader than the denial of sexual desire. This literature registers social reality through an intellectual fascination for the outcast. Other significant works in this genre that draw on the association between political and sexual repression are: *Nivaldo e Jerônimo* (1981) by Darcy Penteado (1926–87); *Meu Corpo Daria um Romance: Narrativa Desarmada* (My Body Would Produce a Novel: Unharmed Narrative, 1984) by **AIDS** activist Herbert Daniel (1946–92) with its pungent yet liberating sensuousness; and the less conventional works, *Testamento de Davi deixado a Jonathan* (Jonathan's Last Testament to David, 1976) by João Silvério Trevisan (1944–) and Silviano Santiago (1936–), *Stella Manhattan* (1985). The works by Trevisan and Santiago, however, tend to break from the neo-naturalistic or allegorical mode associated with the earlier authors. But it is under a sentimental and existential gaze rather than a political one that suggests how a 'homotextuality' takes shape from the margins and shifts to the centre of Brazilian contemporary literature, especially in works that present alternative experiences to heteronormative culture.

When the utopian and rebellious energies that had agitated the 1960s and 1970s began to lose strength, a postmodern horizon of homoerotic desires and identities during the 1980s and 1990s fomented in a paradoxical landscape straddled by melancholy and joy. The pleasures of sexual drift countered by the fear of AIDS engaged a search for new types of sexual relations and experiences. It is in this direction that the works of novelists Caio Fernando Abreu (1948–96), Edilberto Coutinho (1933–55), José Carlos Honório (1964–), Jean-Claude Bernardet (1936–), João Gilbert Noll (1946–) and Bernardo Carvalho (1960–); the poetry of Robert Piva (1937–), Glauco Mattoso (1951–), Ana Cristina Cesar (1952–83), Antonio Cícero, Guillermo Zarvos, Valdo Mota (1959–) and Ítalo Moriconi (1953–); as well as the lyrics by **Cazuza** (1958–90) and Renato Russo (1960–6), among others take root.

AIDS, in the 'homotextual' context of Brazilian literature, derives from within a rich body of national work The activist works of Herbert Daniel, Jean-Claude Bernardet's *A Doença – Uma Experiência* (The Illness – an Experience, 1996) and Santiago's *Uma História de Família* (A Family Story, 1992) are worth noting. As these writers view it, AIDS is not only an element of affirmation for the homosexual 'outsider'. Rather, AIDS affectively redefines the drift and fluidity of sexuality and desire.

In more recent writing, once again the streets return, but as something more than a space of furtive meetings. Instead, the streets translate the drift and the instability of desire, from that of a gay stigma to commonplace urban affectivity. The city thus takes its shape through many forms of desire. Perhaps, considering the tensions that occur in sexual and identity drift, the works that resonate most with these destabilizations of desire are those by João Gilberto Noll. His writing during the 1980s

presented the Brazilian version of aesthetics associated with the 'road movie', where emotions are articulated through dry images and concise vocabulary while the characters drift not only through spaces, but through their desires.

Although not as visible as certain English-language gay contemporary fiction, a change in Brazilian literature has occurred in terms of how home and family space are considered no longer as sites of oppression but as places of affectivity and creative cultural production. In this way the work of Abreu is instructive since it does not exclude the loving experiences between men. Abreu renders these relationships as basic to an understanding of contemporary Brazilian history. Moreover, the importance of Abreu's work is that his books, such as *Morangos Mofados* (1982) and *Os Dragões não Conhecem o Paraíso* (1988), confront the post-utopian fatigue extant during an age of simulacra where homosexuality often precariously and dangerously assimilates into heteronormative ideology. Abreu represents a fragile possibility of hope and lightness in a time defined by pain, indifference and loneliness in which narratives are often highly stylized but lack sincere meaning.

DENILSON LOPES

BRESSAN, ARTIE

b. 1943; d. 1987

filmmaker

Bressan established a career as a director of gay pornography, including the popular *Passing Strangers* (1974) and *Pleasure Beach* (1983). He made the documentary *Gay USA* (1978), a panoramic portrait of gay culture across America, partially inspired by Anita Bryant's anti-gay advocacy. His first mainstream narrative film *Abuse* (1983), a gay love story between a filmmaker and a 14-year-old child abuse victim, was based on his own relationship with Thomas

Carroll. Bresson is best known for the drama *Buddies* (1985), the first American film to dramatize the AIDS epidemic. Based on Bressan's personal struggles with the disease, the film chronicles the friendship of a 32-year-old gay man dying of AIDS in a Manhattan hospital and his 25-year-old volunteer counsellor. The film was praised for its honest and unsentimental treatment of AIDS, made more poignant by Bressan's death in 1987.

JOHN FORDE

BRIDESHEAD REVISITED

TV series

A lavish, nostalgic and enduringly popular British TV adaptation of Evelyn Waugh's novel, *Brideshead Revisited* (1980) focuses on the homoerotic friendship of its two male protagonists. The narrator, Charles Ryder (Jeremy Irons) meets the beautiful, charmingly insouciant, Sebastian Flyte (Anthony Andrews) at Oxford University in the 1920s. Charles is drawn into Sebastian's decadent clique, which includes the effeminate Wildean homosexual Anthony Blunt (Nickolas Grace), and develops a 30-year-long obsession with the glamorous but doomed Flyte family. The relationship between Charles and Sebastian, although never consummated, is tenderly portrayed, and Charles later transfers his affections to Sebastian's troubled sister Julia (Diana Quick). John Gielgud stars as Charles' father.

JOHN FORDE

BRIGGS INITIATIVE, CALIFORNIA

A 1970s anti-gay political initiative, placed on the California ballot by Senator John Briggs, which attempted to ban gays and lesbians from working or teaching in public schools and to prohibit any teacher found to be 'advocating, imposing, encouraging or promoting' homosexuality. Inspired by successful anti-gay initiatives in Oklahoma and Arkansas and Anita Bryant's anti-gay 'Save Our Children' campaign, Briggs launched the initiative in San Francisco in 1977. Newly elected city supervisor Harvey **Milk** vigorously opposed the move and mobilized grassroots organizations such as the Concerned Voters of California in support. Mayoral advisor David Mixner conscripted actors, musicians and, crucially, the then California Governor Ronald **Reagan** to oppose the initiative, resulting in its defeat by almost a million votes in 1978. The outcome was hailed as a major victory for the gay rights movement. Three weeks later Milk was killed by Dan White, a fellow city Supervisor who had supported the initiative.

JOHN FORDE

BRIGHT, SUSIE

b. 1958

performance artist, activist

Editor, performer, author, journalist and activist, Susie Bright is one of the United States' most prolific moving forces in the debate on eroticism and sexual politics favouring sexual freedom. Since 1993 she has edited anthologies of erotica and is one of the founders of the iconoclastic magazine *On Our Backs*. She edited *Nothing But the Girl: The Blatant Lesbian Image* (1996), the first portfolio and history ever published of lesbian erotic photographers. Bright is also known as 'Susie Sexpert', advising men and women of varied sexual orientations, and offering performances, classes and public lectures worldwide.

MONICA BARONI

BRIGHTON, SUSSEX (UK)

A seaside resort in Sussex, England, about 50 miles south of London, Brighton rivals London as England's gay capital. It was the unofficial residence of the Prince Regent (later King George IV), who commissioned the spectacular John Nash-designed Royal Pavilion, and became a popular Victorian-era holiday destination, later attracting famous guests Oscar Wilde, Ivor Novello, J.R. Ackerley and Nöel Coward. After a period of decline, it now boasts a large gay and lesbian community, and the annual Brighton Pride festival is one of Europe's most popular gay events.

JOHN FORDE

BRITTEN, BENJAMIN

b. 1913; d. 1976

composer

Benjamin Britten began composing while still a child, attracting the attention of the older composer Frank Bridge. He later studied at the Royal College of Music, but did not complete a degree there. In 1936 he met the tenor Peter Pears, who became his lover and his most important collaborator. The two went to the United States in 1939, following fellow pacifists W.H. **Auden** and Christopher **Isherwood**. On their return trip to England, Britten wrote *Peter Grimes* (1945), the first of several operas, virtually all of which featured Pears in the lead role. Many of the operas, most notably *Billy Budd* (1951, based on Melville) and *Death in Venice* (1973, based on Thomas Mann) have more or less overt homosexual themes. In 1961 Britten wrote perhaps his most well-known non-operatic work, *War Requiem*. The work, again featuring Pears, combined texts from the traditional Latin mass with the anti-war poetry of Wilfred Owen. After a period of serious illness, Britten died in 1976 of heart failure.

See also: Opera

DANIEL HENDRICKSON

BROADWAY CARES / EQUITY FIGHTS AIDS

Founded in 1988 by members of the Producers' Group, the goal of Broadway Cares is to raise money to support AIDS service organizations around the United States. In 1982 the organization merged with Equity Fights AIDS, which had been formed in 1987 by the Council of Actors' Equity Association. The merged organization funds the social service work of the Actor's Fund and awards grants twice a year to AIDS service organizations. By 2001 the organization had donated more than US$40 million to this cause.

Web site

www.broadwaycares.org

CHRIS BYRNE

BROCKA, LINO

b. 1939; d. 1991

actor, film director, activist

Social activist and former missionary Lino Brocka is widely considered the greatest filmmaker in the history of cinema in the Philippines. In a career that spanned 21 years (until his untimely death in a car crash in 1991), Brocka made over 70 films, finally finding international success following the critical acclaim that greeted his 1976 film *Insiang* at the Cannes Film Festival. Openly gay, he was a renowned champion of human rights and anti-censorship causes – themes which were very much evident in his work and led to his temporary imprisonment as a political dissident by the Marcos regime in 1985. Beginning his filmmaking career in 1970, Brocka broke new ground in terms of the representation of homosexuality in Filipino film with the release of *Dipped in Gold* (*Tubog sa Ginto*), a film that was inevitably condemned by the Catholic Church and had limited commercial success. Other notable gay-themed films include *Jaguar* (1979) and the controversially erotic *Macho Dancer* (1988), and his influence as a gay filmmaker is evident in the later works of such Filipino directors as Mel Chionglo (especially his *Midnight Dancers* [1994] and *Burlesk King* [1999]) and Brocka's own Los Angeles-based nephew, Q. Allan Brocka, whose forthcoming feature-length documentary *Uncle Lino* is a moving celebration of the life of the uncle he never met.

ROBIN GRIFFITHS

BRONSKI, MICHAEL

b. 1945

writer

The long-time gay political activist and writer Michael Bronski became active on the Boston gay scene during the 1970s, writing articles for *Fag Rag* and *Gay Community News*. During this time he met his lover, poet Walta Borawski, with whom he lived until Borawski's death from AIDS in 1995. Bronski's first book, *Culture Clash: The Making of a Gay Sensibility* (1984), traced gay culture in literature, theatre, opera and cinema from Walt Whitman to the beginnings of the AIDS crisis. A further collection of his writings on sexual politics, *The Pleasure Principle*, was published in 1998. In addition to his books and journalism, Bronski has edited collections of writings by gay men on various subjects.

DANIEL HENDRICKSON

BRONSKI BEAT

See: Somerville, Jimmy and Bronski Beat

BROOKS, PHILIP AND LAURENT BOCAHUT

Brooks, Philip

b. 1953; d. 2003

filmmaker

Bocahut, Laurent

b. 1964

filmmaker

Born in Tasmania, Philip Brooks began his love affair with Africa at age 13 when he spent a year in Ethiopia. During the apartheid era he began travelling to South Africa where he clandestinely shot films such as *Bussing*, and *Health Under Apartheid*, both powerful indictments of the apartheid system. He settled in **Paris** in 1978. In 1984 he was a founder of the Paris Gay and Lesbian Film Festival and was President of the Festival between 1997 and 2000. In 1990 he met Laurent Bocahut, who became his companion and with whom he created the production company Dominant 7. Through the company he and Laurent have produced several documentaries and feature films, many of them with a gay theme. His enduring interest in Africa is reflected in the award-winning documentary *Woubi Chéri* (1998) on the love lives of gays living in the Ivory Coast.

GRAEME REID

BROPHY, BRIGID

b. 1929; d. 1995

writer

Novelist, essayist and biographer, Brigid Brophy stands out as one of the most challenging and controversial figures in 1960s queer Britain. While married to art historian Michael Levey, she publicly countered monogamy and advocated bisexuality, unconventional relations and flexible family structures, thus making her marriage the subject of great debate in the press. Her sexual and social experimentations found a perfect weapon in her essays (witty and sharp polemics on a variety of social and art issues), in her biographies on Mozart, Ronald Firbank and Aubrey Beardsley, and in her novels, as diverse in genre as they are subversive: comedies of manners, fairy tales and picaresque tales ranging from lesbian finishing schools to imaginary kingdoms and to 'hyperesthetic' hedonism. Her experimentalism peaks in *In Transit* (1969), a baroque avant-garde masterpiece that – after Virginia Woolf's *Orlando* – stages the breakdown, fluidity and contradictoriness of the protagonist's sexual and linguistic identity, appropriately set in an airport terminal and told in a 'bitextual' narrative.

FABIO CLETO

BROSSARD, NICOLE

b. 1943

writer

Born in Montreal, poet, novelist and essayist Nicole Brossard is one of Quebec's most significant avant-garde writers. Co-founder of the cultural journal, *La Barre du jour* (1965), she has published many novels including *Picture Theory* (1982), *Le Desert mauve* (*The Mauve Desert*, 1987), *Baroque at Dawn* (1997) and lesbian 'theory-fiction', *Un livre, Sold-Out* (1980); numerous books of poetry including *Daydream Mechanics* (1980), *Lovhers* (1986), *Installations: avec et sans pronoms* (1987), *Typhon dru* (1997), *Musee de l'os et de l'eau* (1999); and co-directed one film, *Some American Feminists* (1976). Formally experimental, Brossard enacts a Monique Wittig-like project of deconstructing gender imperatives through violent (French and English) textualities. She won the Canadian Governor General's Award twice for poetry (1974, 1984) and Le Grand Prix de Poésie de la Foundation les Forges in 1989 and 1999. In 1991 she was awarded Le Prix Athanase-David for a lifetime of literary achievement. Brossard has

been widely translated and anthologized and frequently collaborates with Daphne **Marlatt**.

See also: Wittig, Monique

JEAN BOBBY NOBLE

BROUGHTON, JAMES

b. 1913; d. 1999

poet, experimental filmmaker

Born in Modesto, California on 10 November 1913, James Broughton was educated at Stanford University and the New School for Social Research. A poet, filmmaker and Dionysian gay sage, Broughton eschewed the labels homosexual, heterosexual and bisexual, describing himself as a 'pansexual androgyne'. Two early films, *The Potted Psalm* (1947), a collaboration with Sidney Peterson, and *Mother's Day* (1948), position Broughton as a pioneer figure of the 'San Francisco School' of experimental film. *A Long Undressing* (1971) and *Special Deliveries* (1990) collect Broughton's ecstatic and visionary poetry, which has been identified with the San Francisco Renaissance. His best-known films include *Song of the Godbody* (1977), in which Broughton explores his own body in close-up, accompanied by the Whitmanesque words, 'This is my body, which speaks for itself . . . This is my body, which sings of itself'; and *Gardener of Eden* (1981), a brief document of his honeymoon with collaborator Joel Singer, whom he married in 1976.

M.M. SERRA

BROWN, RITA MAE

b. 1944

writer

A prolific writer and social activist, Rita Mae Brown is arguably the most successful lesbian author in late twentieth-century America. Born in Pennsylvania, Brown

107

moved to Florida with her adoptive mother and attended the University of Florida until she was expelled for civil rights activism. A graduate of New York University, she was initially active in the women's movement, but left the National Organization of Woman (NOW) in 1970, dismayed at their refusal to address lesbian-feminist concerns. In 1973 Brown catapulted to the forefront of lesbian fiction with the publication of *Rubyfruit Jungle*, a lesbian *Bildungsroman* that remains a cult classic. Brown's famous novel, in which 'Rubyfruit' is a euphemism for female genitalia, queers the familiar trope of the city as jungle, transforming the urban wilderness into a sexual emporium for irrepressible protagonist Molly Bolt. Brown is the author of more than a dozen novels and has received Emmy nominations for the mini-series *The Long Hot Summer* and the variety show *I Love Liberty*.

ALIDA M. MOORE

BROWN, RON

b. 1966

dancer, choreographer, artistic director

Born 18 July 1966 in Brooklyn, New York, Ronald K. Brown studied dance with Mary Anthony, performed with Jennifer Muller and, through inspiration from poet Donald W. Woods, came to explore gay African-American men's histories in dance. He formed his company Evidence in 1985, to perform his subtle choreography in dances about social conditions including gender, class, race, cultural assimilation and the construction of identity. His early work *Dirt Road/Morticia Supreme's Review* (1994) explored brutalities of poverty in non-linear vignettes set to poetry and music by Essex **Hemphill**, Donald Woods, Aretha Franklin, **Sylvester** and Billie Holiday. He often juxtaposes neo-African movements with club dancing and modern dance release techniques, as in his highly successful work *Grace* (1999),

made for the Alvin Ailey American Dance Theater. A vibrant collaborator, Brown often questions the construction of queer African–American male identity in terms of weight, stance and dance motion.

THOMAS F. DEFRANTZ

BRUHN, ERIK

b. 1928; d. 1986

dancer

Bruhn was born 3 October 1928 in Copenhagen, Denmark. The most acclaimed male ballet dancer of the 1950s, Bruhn's flawless technique, athleticism and charisma paved the way for future generations of dancers, including his lover Rudolf **Nureyev**. He studied at the Royal Danish Ballet School, becoming their principal dancer and performing with ballet companies around the world. He achieved international stardom after his 1955 performance as Albrecht in *Giselle* at New York's Metropolitan Opera House, a role with which he became enduringly associated. In 1961 he met Nureyev and the two embarked on a sexual relationship and long-term friendship. In 1971 Bruhn retired because of ill health, but after emergency surgery he returned to dancing in 1974, taking character parts in *Giselle*, *The Moor's Pavane* and *Rasputin*, often alongside Nureyev in the lead. In 1975 he choreographed *Coppelia*, also performing as Dr Coppelius. He was appointed Artistic Director of the National Ballet of Canada in 1983, where he made his home with his partner, dancer Constantin Patsalas. He died, 1 April 1986, in Toronto, Canada.

JOHN FORDE

BRÜNING, JÜRGEN

filmmaker

German filmmaker Jürgen Brüning founded the Kino Eiszeit (Ice Age Cinema) in Berlin in the 1980s. The theatre became an important venue for experimental and independent work by young filmmakers. He then went on to become one of the most ubiquitous figures in the international New Queer Cinema scene, working as filmmaker, curator and producer. His 1994 film *He's Bald and He Is a Racist, He Is Gay and He Is a Fascist* explores the phenomenon of gay men adopting the skinhead look in Germany. In 2002 he released *Saudade*, a gay thriller set in a small village in Brazil. In addition to his own filmmaking, he is very active as a producer, both in the German porn industry and with international filmmakers such as Ela Troyano and Bruce **La Bruce**.

See also: New Queer Cinema, International

DANIEL HENDRICKSON

BRYNNTRUP, MICHAEL

b. 1959

film- and videomaker

The extremely prolific filmmaker Michael Brynntrup studied at the Braunschweig School of Arts with Birgit Hein. He works in several different media, but is still perhaps best known for his work in film and video. His work very often plays with autobiography, but the relation to self and validity is always highly contested. In his film *Loverfilm: eine unkontrollierte Freisetzung von Information* (Loverfilm: An Uncontrolled Dispersion of Information, 1996), for instance, he takes the viewer through a chronological countdown of his previous lovers. Although the information is presented systematically and authoritatively, it soon becomes clear that at least some of the images are found footage from old Super-8 porno films. In other films, this clash between documentary and fantasy is played out in relation to the artist's own body, which is often presented as somehow foreign or unknown. Still other films feature figures from **Berlin** queer life, especially

drag performers, sometimes playing multiple roles.

DANIEL HENDRICKSON

BUCHANAN, PAT

b. 1938

politician

One of America's most high-profile conservative politicians and commentators, Buchanan is a vigorous opponent of homosexuality. Born 2 November 1938 in Washington DC, he trained as a journalist before working on Richard Nixon's 1966 presidential campaign. He also worked as Nixon's advisor and speechwriter in the White House until 1974. He worked briefly for President Gerald Ford, then made a career as a political columnist and TV commentator, on programmes including *The McLaughlin Group* and *Crossfire*. In 1985 he became the White House Communications Director for Ronald Reagan's presidency. He unsuccessfully challenged George W. Bush for the 1992 Republican Party Presidential nomination and finished second behind Bob Dole in 1996. In his books *A Republic, Not an Empire* (1999) and *Where the Right Went Wrong* (2004), he accuses the Republican Party of abandoning its traditional conservative values in favour of neo-conservatism. He is an outspoken critic of gay and lesbian rights and has founded a number of conservative lobby groups.

JOHN FORDE

BUCKLEY, WILLIAM F.

b. 1925

journalist, editor

A conservative journalist and commentator, in 1955 Buckley founded the *National Review*, which soon became the leading journal of conservatism in America, and which he edited until 2004. He began his long-running syndicated column, 'On the Right', in 1962, and began hosting a weekly TV show, *The Firing Line*, in 1966. By 1971 the programme was broadcast nationally on the Public Broadcasting System (PBS), and when it ended in 1999 it was the longest-running TV show in the US featuring the same host. In 1965 he was an unsuccessful candidate for the mayoralty of New York City. He was a presidential appointee to the US Information Agency, the United Nations and the National Security Council under the Reagan and Bush administrations. He has also published fiction and two volumes of biography.

JOHN FORDE

BUDDHISM

Siddhartha Gautama was reputedly a historical person living in northern India about 500 BC who became the Buddha or 'Enlightened One' after a long period of ascetic practice. The Buddha never adopted an 'official' position on homosexual behaviour. Whereas Buddhist monks are expected to be celibate and must refrain from all sexual interaction, lay followers follow a precept 'not to go wrong regarding sexual action'. Differing interpretations have been given to this precept in different Buddhist societies over time, but Buddhism has seldom condemned sexual interactions other than those that involve coercion, violence or deceit.

MARK McLELLAND

BUFFY THE VAMPIRE SLAYER

TV series

Based upon the less than successful 1992 film of the same name, *Buffy the Vampire Slayer* first aired on US television in March 1997, and ran for seven seasons until its untimely demise in 2003. A cult phenomenon worldwide, the show metaphorically paral-

leled its supernatural elements with the more natural anxieties of adolescence and contemporary teenage 'rites of passage' scenarios. During its seven-year run, the series was unique in its approach to teen sexuality and identity, and featured a number of queer characters, both human and inhuman, from closeted gay jocks to lesbian witches and transgender demons. Even Buffy herself spent most of the earlier shows leading a closeted double life, until finally 'coming out' to her shocked mother, whose loaded response was, ironically, 'Have you tried not being a slayer? Why did you *choose* to be this way?'

However, the series reached a major turning point in its fourth season by revealing that one of its central and most popular characters, novice witch Willow (Alyson Hannigan), was in fact a lesbian – the first mainstream teen drama to feature such a character. While the show received some criticism over its subsequent decision to conform to the narrative stereotype that lesbians either die tragically or are inherently evil – Willow embarked on a murderous rampage after the tragic death of her girlfriend, Tara – the show's real accomplishment lies in the fact that it was the first programme to place a loving lesbian relationship on equal footing with the day-to-day relationship problems of its heterosexual teenage counterparts.

ROBIN GRIFFITHS

BURNETT, BRUCE
b. 1954; d. 1985
AIDS activist

An early New Zealand AIDS prevention and support activist, Bruce Burnett played a primary role in initiating the first discussion of and responses to AIDS in New Zealand's gay community. Burnett returned to New Zealand in 1983 from San Francisco suffering from deteriorating health due to AIDS-related conditions. At that time there were few openly HIV+ gay men in New Zealand and no official AIDS-related deaths. After organizing two workshops on ways to deal with HIV-related issues, Burnett established the AIDS Support Network (ASN) in Auckland. He then travelled to New Zealand educating and enthusing gay men about HIV prevention and support. By the time of his death in June 1985, the ASN was receiving some government funding, and by November of that year the organization had branches in most cities and large towns. In 1986 a new HIV outpatient clinic in Auckland was named the Burnett Clinic in his honour.

GERALDINE TREACHER

BURNIER, ANDREAS

b. 1931; d. 2002

writer

Catharina Dessaur, aka Andreas Burnier, was a novelist, essayist and a poet, as well as a feminist and radical lesbian. As a scholar she held a Chair in Criminology at the University of Nijmegen and was, consecutively, a philosopher, then teacher of spiritual traditions and Jewish culture. Burnier's early novels have meant a great deal for the cultural visibility of lesbian identity in the Netherlands, and still make for wonderful reading experiences. Her first novel, *Een tevreden lach* (A Contented Smile, 1965) appeared under the male pseudonym of 'Andreas Burnier', henceforth her *nom de plume*. The book cover showed the author with a moustache and a beard – clearly a lesbian joke. The ruse was quickly unravelled, but Burnier continued to write a series of beautiful and liberating novels. Her most explicitly lesbian works are *Een tevreden lach*, *Het jongensuur* (The Boy's Hour, 1969), *De huilende libertijn* (The Crying Libertine, 1970) and *De literaire salon* (The Literary Salon, 1983). Burnier's work combines feminist rebellion with

philosophy, mysticism and the longing for a masculine or transgendered existence.

MAAIKE MEIJER

BURNS, KENNETH

activist

Kenneth Burns, with Marilyn Rieger and Hall Call, was elected to the leadership of the **Mattachine Society** in Los Angeles after a contentious national convention in 1953. The founders of Mattachine, such as Harry **Hay**, had been American communists and designed the radical but secretive group along the lines of Communist Party cells to avoid exposure. As this was at the height of Joseph McCarthy's purge on Communism and homosexuals, the founders either withdrew to protect the organization from attack or were unseated. Burns and his faction were outspokenly anti-communist and pursued a more moderate path. They also ushered in an era of growth and expansion for Mattachine. They were more likely to conduct the business of the organization under their own names rather than pseudonyms. They broadened the services of the society to include counselling and legal help as well as job referrals, presaging the gay and lesbian social service establishment that would develop during the 1970s.

See also: McCarthy, Joseph and McCarthyism

ANDY HUMM

BURROUGHS, WILLIAM

b. 1914; d. 1997

writer

William Seward Burroughs was born into a privileged home in Saint Louis, Missouri, and given an excellent education, graduating from Harvard. His erudition and his cynical wit impressed beat writers Jack Kerouac and Allen **Ginsberg**, who was studying at Columbia University, New

York. At this time, Burroughs had developed a heroin addiction and was working upon his first (to be published) text, *Junky* (1953). Soon afterwards he wrote *Queer*, a book not published until 1985, exploring his homosexuality. He had a common-law wife, Joan Vollmer Adams, but shot her dead in a practical joke, showing off a 'William Tell' type trick. He claims that his writing career was in atonement, moving to Tangier and composing the fragments that became, at Kerouac's suggestion, his most celebrated work, *Naked Lunch* (1959). His influence has been immense within counter-cultural movements: Kurt Cobain released an album with Burroughs entitled *The Priest They Called Him* (1992) while Gus **Van Sant** starred him in his short film, *Thanksgiving Prayer* (1991).

MICHAEL PINFOLD

BUTCH / FEMME

Lesbian identities based on highly masculinized and feminized gender models. The term is widely associated with British and American lesbian bar culture of the 1950s.

REBECCA JENNINGS

BUTLER, ALEC

b. 1959

playwright

Born in Cape Breton Island, Nova Scotia, Canada, Alec Butler is an established playwright, experimental filmmaker and transsexual artist/activist. Although he continues to be published under his birth name 'Audrey', Butler completed a female-to-male (FTM) gender reassignment in 1999, changed his name to 'Alec' and continues to produce new work that documents this process, including a recent video trilogy called *The MisAdventures of Pussy Boy*. His work is widely published and his plays include: *Cradle Pin: A Play in Two Acts*

(1988), *Claposis* (1990), *Medusa Rising* (1992), which was nominated for two Dora Mavor Moore Awards, and *Black Friday: A One Act Play* (1990), finalist for the Governor General's Award for English Drama. Butler's recent work continues to interrogate intersections between gender, sexuality and class, and has expanded to include transsexual men. Thematics in his work explore tensions between female and transsexual masculinity, the increasing political distance between poor and/or street-involved queers/trans peoples, and lesbian/gay social movements.

JEAN BOBBY NOBLE

BUTLER, JUDITH

b. 1956

philosopher, cultural theorist

Judith Butler's 1990 book *Gender Trouble: Feminism and the Subversion of Identity* became a definitive text in queer theory. She argues that, rather than pursuing a politics grounded in identity, feminism might take as a political priority the subversion of identity categories, which she considers to be a mechanism of power. The way in which gender, understood as the performative repetition of roles with no origin in 'fact', is inflected and even parodied in queer contexts is central to this subversion. Although gender cannot be read as the expression of a 'pre-social' biological sex, Butler insists on the materiality of the body as it is rendered in particular cultural contexts. In accounting for the 'psychic life of power' (the title of her 1997 book), she remains extensively engaged with psychoanalysis, while demonstrating the ways in which it has colluded in making the existence of those who live outside the norms of heterosexual kinship unintelligible and even unlivable.

See also: Psychoanalysis; Theory and theorists, queer

TREVOR HOPE

BUTLER DECISION, 'R. V. BUTLER', CANADA'S OBSCENITY LAW

Named after the 1992 constitutional challenge to then current obscenity laws, the 'Butler Decision' was the outcome of judicial proceedings against Donald Butler, owner of an adult video store. The case sets out three tests for determining whether something is obscene: community standards of tolerance; degrading and dehumanizing materials which harm women; and artistic merit, or that which is 'bad sex', the representation of sex in and of itself ('dirt for dirt's sake'). The decision provides for an 'arbiter' in determining what counts as undue exploitation; hence, the emphasis on 'harm' adjudicated by community standards of tolerance.

The language of the Butler decision is ambiguous, often mixing conservative constructions of sexuality (as inherently dangerous) with the concern of preventing harm to women and society. For instance, its application maps neatly onto pre-existing sexual and political hierarchies. While feminist legal groups applauded the harm-based foundation of the law, 'Butler' led to a series of highly publicized seizures of books and magazines bound for the Toronto women's bookstore Glad Day Bookshop and Vancouver's Little Sisters Art and Book Emporium. 'Butler' is also often criticized for lending credibility to police and Canada Customs' view that gay and lesbian literature and other sexual cultures are always already obscene. Six weeks after the Butler decision was handed down, Toronto police charged Glad Day Bookshop for selling *Bad Attitude*, a lesbian sex magazine whose images of **sadomasochism** were subject to extensive scrutiny at the subsequent 1993 obscenity trial. The outcome of the sex-panicked trial was one that legally constructed sadomasochism practices as unintelligible, indefensible and, therefore, 'bad sex'. An additional Toronto gallery was raided and an exhibition by Eli Langer

was seized under Butler's provisions. Langer's work attempted to draw attention to the prevalence of child sexual abuse but police and Crown prosecutors charged that the art itself was child pornography.

Such biases have been subject to legal challenge. In 1996, Little Sisters launched a constitutional challenge that, while not directly contesting 'Butler', questioned the constitutionality of the censorship practiced by Canada Customs that it authorized. The Supreme Court's answer validated the claim of undue treatment and Canada Customs was warned to act more judiciously.

JEAN BOBBY NOBLE

BUURMAN, GON

b. 1939

photographer

Autodidact Gon Buurman is well known in the Netherlands for her publications and exhibitions in the field of social photography. She made her breakthrough in gay and lesbian circles with her book *Poseuses; Portraits of Women* (1987, text by Pamela Pattynama). The black-and-white pictures of self-aware women visualize a new cultural identity for the Amsterdam lesbian movement in the 1980s. For the first time, Dutch lesbians posed openly as lesbians and thereby replaced the history of invisibility, secrecy and taboos by a proud self-image. The lesbian 'pose', highlighted through Buurman's portraits, projects, on the one hand, a pursuit of lesbian identity for historical reasons. On the other hand, it reveals a postmodern rejection of fixed identity. *Poseuses* visualizes therefore not only lesbian bodies, but also lesbians' manifold, shifting and contradictory identities. Buurman's six other books include *Uit verlangen* (From Desire, 1998) and *Work it out* (1998).

PAMELA PATTYNAMA

BYRD, ROBIN

b. 1957

actor, producer

Actor and dancer who made a career as a TV show host for *The Robin Byrd Show* (1977) and acted in porn classic *Debbie Does Dallas* (1978). Byrd was born on 6 April 1957 in New York City. In 1995, the Time Warner cable network announced its intention to prohibit broadcasts of Byrd's late-night adult entertainment TV show. Byrd and her co-producer Al Goldstein joined with the **American Civil Liberties Union (ACLU)** and successfully argued that Time Warner were infringing the First Amendment. She currently hosts *Access Nation* (2004), dressed in her trademark black crocheted bikini and white lip gloss and nail polish.

JOHN FORDE

C

CABARET

A restaurant or nightclub that serves alcohol and showcases a variety of musical, comic and erotic entertainment, cabaret has famously been a haven for sexual deviancy, providing a community for underground gay, lesbian and transgendered communities, a thriving venue for gay (and frequently commercialized) sex and a platform for some of the twentieth-century's notable queer performers, writers and artists.

The cabaret is thought to have originated in France in the 1880s, as a private club with the audience grouped around a small stage, showing a variety of musical and comic acts, linked together by a master of ceremonies. Performances were frequently sexually provocative, with coarse humour directed against the conventions of polite bourgeois society. The most famous example of French cabaret, the Moulin Rouge nightclub, premiered the sexually suggestive dance the Cancan and attracted writers including Arthur Rimbaud, Paul Verlaine and the painter Toulouse-Lautrec.

Cabaret was established in Berlin around 1900 by Baron Ernst von Wolzogen. The intimate and spontaneous atmosphere of the French cabaret remained, but a controversial brand of social and political satire developed alongside. During the Weimar Republic of the 1920s and 1930s, the Berlin Kabarett, most famously the Kit Kat Klub, was a centre for underground literary and political movements and a discreet but thriving gay community. Performances frequently criticized the rise to power of the Nazi party and were often censored by Nazi militia.

Among the artists active in the cabaret were the playwright Bertolt Brecht and the composer Kurt Weill, whose *Die Dreigroschenoper* (*The Threepenny Opera*, 1928) established their reputations and the stardom of the singer Lotte Lenya. The decadence and political upheaval of the 1930s Berlin cabaret scene was chronicled in Christopher Isherwood's semi-autobiographical *Goodbye to Berlin* (1939) (see **Isherwood**, Christopher), later dramatized as the play *I Am a Camera* (1951, filmed 1955) and as the musical *Cabaret* (1966), later a successful film (1972) starring Liza **Minnelli** and Joel Grey. The cabaret survives in post-Second World War Germany, continuing a tradition of sexual licentiousness, but has lost most of its political relevance. Contemporary singers Ute Lemper and Marianne Faithfull have produced successful revivals of Weimar German cabaret music.

The English cabaret (also called 'music hall') developed from taproom concerts given in city taverns during the eighteenth and nineteenth centuries. The first specialized music hall was built by Charles Morton in London in 1852, and by the end of the nineteenth century the rapid growth of urban populations had increased the demand for such entertainment. Unlike legitimate theatre, music halls allowed alcohol and tobacco sales, and its low humour frequently subverted censorship laws. Shows featured singers, comedians, dancers, acrobats and musicians, and included singers Lillie Langtree, Gracie Fields and Sophie Tucker, actors Sandra Bernhardt, George Alexander and Sir Herbert Beerbohm Tree, and Diaghilev's Ballet Russe. Drag performers were a popular feature of music hall, including stars such as Douglas Byng. The music hall declined with the growth of cinema, radio and television, but the twentieth century saw the growth of nightclub and piano bar cabaret, famously including Noel Coward, Hinge and Bracket, and Danny **La Rue**.

In the United States, cabaret (related to American 'vaudeville') developed in frontier and urban settlements from the mid-eighteenth century, with coarse, frequently obscene, sometimes racist, material aimed towards a heterosexual male audience. The first vaudeville theatre was established in New York by Tony Pastor in 1881, its aim being to 'clean up' the profession. By the 1890s, vaudeville was established as a nationwide chain of theatres, offering non-offensive 'family' entertainment. Undeterred, underground clubs flourished in the metropolitan centres, with venues such as Columbia Hall on the Bowery at Fifth Street in New York regularly showcasing drag performances and providing a centre for gay communities. While vaudeville declined in the 1930s with the growth of cinema, nightclub-based cabaret enjoyed a steady reputation in the 1940s and beyond. Leading exponents included Lenya and Coward, who successfully relocated their careers to the United States, Eartha Kitt, Ethel Merman, **Liberace**, the openly lesbian singer and actor Frances Faye, Judy **Garland** and her daughter, Liza **Minnelli**. Modern revivalists of cabaret include Bette **Midler**, who first performed cabaret in a 1970s San Francisco gay bathhouse, the transsexual Lady **Chablis** and the drag artist **Lypsinka**.

JOHN FORDE

CABLE TELEVISION, GAY

When most TV programmes and movies would not touch gay themes or dealt with them in terms of negative stereotypes, the emergence of cable television provided an outlet for gay people, especially in cities, who used the public and leased access stations to inform people about their lives and activities in an unmediated and mostly uncensored fashion. The first known regular show of this kind in the United States was *The Emerald City*, shown on Manhattan Cable in the early 1970s.

Lou Maletta started the Gay Cable Network in New York in 1982 and continued it until 2001, producing weekly erotica, entertainment and news programming, including ground-breaking gay coverage of national political party conventions from 1984 until 2000. The network also covered the emerging AIDS epidemic when the mainstream press was largely ignoring the issue. Maletta networked his shows around the US, as did Dyke TV out of Brooklyn, New York.

Many have taken advantage of public access opportunities on their local cable systems to produced glbtq-themed programmes, including *Lifestyle Update* and *Gay Talk* in Los Angeles. In 2001 Canada dedicated a national cable digital channel to 'Pridevision', the world's first gay TV network to programme around the clock. Gay themes and characters have proliferated on America's uncensored cable television, from reality shows such as MTV's ***The Real World*** to HBO's ***Six Feet Under*** to Showtime's ***Queer as Folk***, and ***The L-Word***. In 2004 several US media companies announced plans for gay-themed cable networks.

ANDY HUMM

CADMUS, PAUL

b. 1904; d. 1999

artist

Cadmus achieved his greatest success in the 1930s, as one of the most adept satirists of modern American culture and its social norms, especially around issues of masculinity. His social realist paintings (e.g., *The Fleet's In!*) of sailors, circus performers and the 'fairy', although not only openly gay images, are, nevertheless, representations of social types that were imagined to exist outside the confines of normative masculinity. Depicting such locations as New York's Riverside Drive, Greenwich Village and West Side YMCA, Cadmus explored the varying degrees in which erotically charged social relations between men and the places where these took place were rendered visible in the popular imagination. In all of these ways, it can be said that his work as a gay artist amounts to nothing less than a strategic and savvy defiance of the era's codes against the outright depiction of gay male subjects in art.

JOHN PAUL RICCO

CAJA, JEROME

b. 1958; d. 1995

performance artist

The artist and drag performer Jerome Caja studied at the San Francisco Art Institute, where he met the artist Charles Sexton, with whom he would have a long and important relationship. In addition to his work as a painter, he was a ubiquitous presence in the San Francisco queer club scene of the 1980s and 1990s, often appearing as a drag go-go dancer. Although he used a wide variety of objects as surfaces on which to paint (scraps of metal, wood or paper, bottle caps and, most controversially, Sexton's ashes, who died of AIDS in the early 1990s), the material that he used as paint was almost always nail polish. Caja's work,

almost all miniatures, is peopled with a cast of stock characters, including animals, clowns, sailors, saints, transsexuals and drag queens. Deeply influenced by his Catholic upbringing, many of his paintings are religious scenes or make use of religious iconography, often mixing the sacred and the profane.

See also: Drag

DANIEL HENDRICKSON

CALIFIA, PAT

b. 1954

author, activist

Pat Califia, born Patrick, a female-to-male transsexual, radical sex activist and author, has published many books, erotic short stories, poems, articles and essays. Born in Texas in a Mormon family, he came out as a lesbian in 1971. He moved to San Francisco, where he began writing on **butch/femme** sexuality and **sadomasochism**, drawing much critical fire from lesbian separatists. Among his best-known books are *Macho Sluts* (1989) and *Public Sex: The Culture of Radical Sex* (1994). During his prolific career Califia has always spoken up for freedom of sexual expression, defending all sexual minorities and creative sexual practices.

See also: Female-to-male (FTM) transsexual

MONICA BARONI

CALLAS, MARIA

b. 1923; d. 1977

opera singer (soprano)

Cecilia Sophia Anna Maria Kalogeropoulou was born on 2 December 1923 to Greek émigrés newly arrived in New York, her father having opened a pharmacy in Manhattan under the assumed name of Callas. Maria began piano lessons at the age of 5, and when her parents separated in

1937 she moved back to Greece with her mother and began to study singing at the Athens Conservatoire with the Spanish soprano Elvira de Hidalgo. She made her debut in Athens aged 15, in Mascagni's *Cavalleria rusticana* (Rustic Chivalry), and achieved her first real success there in the title role of Puccini's *Tosca*, debuting on 27 August 1942. Hopeful of a professional operatic career she returned to New York three years later and in 1947 was engaged to sing in Ponchielli's *La Gioconda* in Verona under Tullio Serafin. She went on to perform in Venice, Turin and Florence, then Rome, Buenos Aires and Naples in 1949, and Mexico City in 1950. She was feted at La Scala, Milan, in Verdi's *I vespri siciliani* (The Sicilian Vespers) on 7 December 1950, after an initially cool response to her Aida. For the next 15 years Callas would reign supreme as the world's most celebrated opera star, with press coverage of her life both on- and offstage helping to create the Callas legend which has far from diminished in the years since her death.

Although she had no particular connection with the flourishing but secretive gay culture of the 1950s, Callas drew a considerable following of gay male fans as her career unfolded. In many ways her self-transformations fulfilled the ambitions of the closeted individual. As a teenager she had been gawky and overweight, but through strict dieting she recreated herself as a svelte, sophisticated society woman and prominent member of the international jet set of the 1950s and 1960s. Dressed in stylized black, with an elegant coiffure, classical features, pale complexion and long lines of kohl on her eyelids, she carried something of her stage persona over into real life. Her natural singing voice required rigorous discipline: the breaks between registers and inequality of tone were hard to disguise; the middle voice could be harsh, with a muffled, nasal quality; and prolonged high notes acquired a broadening tremolo as the years passed. Yet Callas honed this voice

into an instrument of extraordinary expressive power, agility, colour and emotional range. In the struggle for dramatic truth she often took risks with the voice, leaving herself exposed and vulnerable, as an audio recording of her much admired 1958 Lisbon performance as Violetta in Verdi's *La Traviata* demonstrates. In the final phrases he gave to his dying, consumptive heroine, Verdi had called for a high, sustained note to be uttered as quietly as possible; for security, most sopranos hit this note initially in full voice, but Callas honoured Verdi's directions despite the wavering it produced on the note.

Callas' charismatic stage presence and superb acting abilities held audiences spellbound at a time when opera performers tended to lack dramatic spontaneity. She identified completely with the characters she played, living every moment and bringing a keen musical intelligence to every detail of their emotional journey. While for some this degree of self-involvement signals a camp aesthetic, there was no irony in her intentions and she conceded nothing to the artificialities of performance: 'to sing is an expression of your being', she once said, 'a being which is becoming'.

Callas rapidly acquired a reputation for temperamental, 'queenish' behaviour, but this was mainly because of recurring vocal problems and the exceptionally high standards she imposed on herself. She clashed repeatedly with Rudolph Bing at the New York Met, and she famously walked out of a gala performance of Bellini's *Norma* at Rome on 2 January 1958 rather than continue out of voice, despite the presence of the Italian president. Among her fans' most cherished anecdotes is her performance of the Act I duet with Jason (John Vickers) in Cherubini's *Medea* at La Scala, 11 December 1961. As vocal difficulties began to trouble her, the audience began to hiss, which she ignored until the scene where Medea denounces Jason. Her first 'Crudel!' ('Cruel one!') was aimed at him, but the second she addressed to the audience, and the following 'ho dato tutto a te' ('I gave everything to you') was directed straight at the gallery. The duet ended with an ovation.

Callas' troubled personal life is often seen as being at the root of her professional difficulties. In 1949 she had married Giovanni Battista Meneghini, an Italian businessman 30 years her senior; but in 1959 she announced their separation, having fallen in love with Aristotle Onassis. She became his long-term mistress and secretly bore him a son who died after only a few hours. Despite expectations that they would marry, it was Jackie Kennedy, the widow of John F. Kennedy, who became Onassis' wife on 20 October 1968. Callas never recovered from this public betrayal, and it almost certainly contributed to the gradual physical and vocal decline that took hold in the mid-1960s. A series of vocal crises culminated in her collapse onstage after Act III of *Norma* at the Paris Odéon in May 1965. She gave a final, but brilliant Tosca in Franco Zeffirelli's acclaimed production at Covent Garden, London, on 5 July 1965.

In May 1970 Callas was rushed to hospital having overdosed (probably unintentionally) on barbiturates. She recovered and went on to give master classes at Juilliard and occasional concert performances in the early 1970s, the last of which took place in Sapporo, Japan, 11 November 1974. Thereafter she withdrew to her apartment on the Avenue Georges Mandel in Paris. Onassis' death on 15 March 1975 is believed to have hastened her own demise from a heart attack two years later, on 16 September 1977, aged 53. Her ashes remained at Père Lachaise until spring 1979, when they were returned to Greece and scattered in the Aegean.

Inner fire, passion, and strength of character combined in Callas with an enigmatic remoteness and vulnerability. Her most famous roles were Norma, Medea, Anne Boleyn, Lucia, Verdi's Lady Macbeth and Violetta, and Tosca, and the fates of these tragic women echoed eerily her own.

Footage of her performances is scarce, but she left behind a rich recorded legacy: her Tosca with de Sabata, her Violetta with Franco Ghione, her Butterfly and her Lucia (both with Karajan) are among those still savoured by fans. Of all the great divas, it is without doubt Callas, 'La divina', who is the most beloved by opera queens. Her importance as a gay icon is underlined by the Callas obsession of Mendy in Terrence McNally's 1985 play *The Lisbon Traviata*; and in the film *Philadelphia*, her rendition of 'La mamma morta' – the haunting aria sung by Maddalena, who sacrifices her life for love in Giordano's *Andrea Chénier* – accompanies crucial moments of reflection and disclosure for Tom Hanks' character in his struggle with AIDS.

See also: Diva; Opera

Further reading

Bret, D. (1998) *Maria Callas: the Tigress and the Lamb*, London: Robson.

Koestenbaum, K. (1993) *The Queen's Throat: Opera, Homosexuality, and the Mystery of Desire*, London: GMP Publishers, pp. 134–53.

RACHEL COWGILL

CALLOW, SIMON

b. 1949

actor, director

Simon Phillip Hugh Callow, born in London, an actor, director, author and active supporter of gay and AIDS causes. During the mid-1970s he was open about his gayness as an actor when few others were, joining the **Gay Sweatshop Theatre Company** in 1975. His later autobiography, *Being an Actor* (1984), dealt candidly with his homosexuality. In 1979 he originated the role of Mozart in the National Theatre's *Amadeus*. Other significant roles have included the 'out' character, Gareth, in the 1994 hit film, *Four Weddings and a Funeral* (his was the funeral), a portrayal that went a long way towards helping general audiences see gay people as rounded human beings. He is also featured in such Merchant-Ivory classics as *A Room with a View* (1985), *Maurice* (1987) and *Jefferson in Paris* (1995), and played Tilney, Master of the Revels, in *Shakespeare in Love* (1998). He has starred in one-man stage shows, *The Importance of Being Oscar* (1997), about Oscar Wilde, and *The Mystery of Charles Dickens* (2001), and has written about his passionate friendship with leading London play agent Peggy Ramsay in his memoir, *Love is Where it Falls*.

ANDY HUMM

CAMARA, MOHAMED

b. 1959

film director

Born in the Guinean capital, Conakry, actor Mohamed Camara made *Dakan*, his first feature film, in 1997. This was a film for which Camara was both director and scriptwriter. *Dakan*, the first West African feature to deal with homosexuality, opens with an explicit scene in which two men embrace passionately. The taboo nature of the film meant that it had to be shot clandestinely in Guinea. The film challenges the fallacy that homosexuality is un-African. At the same time, *Dakan* emphasizes that homosexuality is shaped by particular cultural norms that go against the idea of a universal gay culture. These themes have sparked controversial debate at several international film festivals. Camara has stated his intentions behind making the film: 'I made this film to pay tribute to those who express their love in whatever way they feel it, despite society's efforts to repress it.'

GRAEME REID

CAMERON, EDWARD

b. 1953

activist

South African judge and prominent human rights, HIV and AIDS activist, Edward Cameron, in 1993 founded the AIDS Law Project and an umbrella organization of non-government organizations, the national AIDS Consortium. He played an important role in achieving the sexuality clause in South Africa's post-apartheid constitution and helped to draft the Charter of Rights on HIV/AIDS. In 1995 he was the first openly gay man to be appointed as a high court judge, then, in 1999, became the first high public official in South Africa to reveal his HIV+ status. Shortly after this he was appointed to the highest court in the country, the Constitutional Court. Cameron's hard-hitting critiques of his government's foot-dragging and confusion over the provision of anti-retroviral therapy helped radicalize the Treatment Action Campaign. He was also co-editor, with Mark Gevisser, of the first book devoted to gay and lesbian history and identity published in Africa (*Defiant Desire*, 1994).

MARC EPPRECHT

CAMERON, RHONA

b. 1965

comedian

One of Scotland's most popular female comedians, Rhona Cameron began her career on the United Kingdom stand-up circuit, winning the prestigious 'So You Think You're Funny' competition at the 1991 Edinburgh Fringe Festival. She became Britain's first openly lesbian TV presenter on *Gaytime TV* (1988–99) and has interviewed Chastity **Bono**. She co-wrote and starred in a lesbian-themed sitcom, *Rhona* (2000), a tribute to the American sitcom *Rhoda*. She became a national star after her appearance on the reality TV show *I'm a*

Celebrity, Get Me Out of Here! (2002), in which she sparred with other celebrity guests in the Australian outback and delivered a moving impromptu speech about tolerating human differences. She has also hosted TV shows *Russian Roulette* (2002) and *The Luvvies* (2003), and published *1979: A Big Year in a Small Town* (2003), a comic memoir about her childhood in Scotland.

JOHN FORDE

CAMP

The most elusive and protean of cultural categories, frustrating all essentializing and deterministic definitions (for it is no 'thing': it just 'happens'), camp stands out among the major components of – and in many ways, virtually cognate to – twentieth-century queer culture. Camp has been claimed to be the main queer mode of representation and performance, a style (or sensibility) marked by a paradoxical celebratory and derisive relish for frivolity, aestheticism, allusiveness, heterogeneity and internationalism, and favouring indirection and double coding, narcissism and parodic excessiveness.

Unsurprisingly, its very linguistic and factual existence is intangible. Of unknown origins (possibly from the French 'se *camper*'), the word 'camp' itself first appeared in print in early twentieth-century slang dictionaries, in early gay novels such as Charles Ford's and Parker Tyler's *The Young and Evil* (1931), and in reviews of Broadway productions. Such occurrences document its currency value in the lingo of theatricals, café society and the fashion world, in discussions of literary aesthetes Aubrey Beardsley, Max Beerbohm, Ronald Firbank, Noel Coward and Carl Van Vechten, in show business (music hall, ballet, opera and cinema) and in underground city life, especially in the queer demi-monde of theatre, a relatively safe space at the time for illegal sexual identities and practices.

Given the merging of theatricality, male homosexuality and the aesthetic sense can be traced back to Oscar Wilde's 1895 martyrdom and to the clandestine regime it inaugurated, many commentators have framed early twentieth-century camp as a homosexual survival strategy and a form of 'gay labor' (Tinkcom 2002), a humour cementing solidarity among stigmatized subjects, akin to the role soul played in the African-American community. Rather than a properly secret language such as **Polari**, however, camp was an 'openly secret' language, flaunting the very condition of secrecy and enabling the monitoring of social borders; the camp, coded communication enabled recognition because it marginalized straights, who could not understand.

Such marginal circulation gave way to an impressive discursive visibility in postwar years. Camp gained its first lengthy discussion in Christopher Isherwood's novel *The World in the Evening* (1954; see Cleto 1999), which introduces us to the encrypted realm of camp (divided between the Low Camp of **drag** – 'an utterly debased form' – and High Camp, i.e., 'the whole emotional basis of the Ballet, for example, and of course of Baroque art', expressing seriousness 'in terms of fun and artifice and elegance'), camp that could only be apprehended 'esoterically' ('You have to meditate on it and feel it intuitively, like Lao-tze's *Tao*'). Predictably enough, Isherwood's discussion failed to bring camp out of the 'fairy world' (see Isherwood, Christopher).

In the 1960s camp progressed from British upper-class theatres to American pop culture, becoming a mass phenomenon, a move in concert with the 'betrayal' of its exclusiveness inherent to the popularization that Susan Sontag noted in her seminal essay, 'Notes on Camp' (1964; see Cleto 1999). Sontag construed camp as a sensibility that captured the *Zeitgeist* of the naughty 1960s, and her essay catapulted both its subject and author to celebrity status, as magazines and newspapers picked up its statements and began extensively to use camp – now an ironic aesthetic taste for kitschy middle-class pretensions – to describe and promote contemporary pop culture. In describing camp as either a style of performance (deliberately producing camp), or a mode of perception (camp being in the eye of the beholder, either finding naïve camp in the failure of excessive intentions or recognizing deliberate camp as such), Sontag had in fact pinpointed it as an 'apolitical' taste that welcomed hierarchy inversion (in the 'So bad it's good' formula) for the mere fun of it, just as it favoured surface over content, artifice over nature, disguise over authenticity, stylization over intent, detachment over 'serious' commitment, and celebrated 'quotation marks', narcissistic self-parody, life as theatre and self as role-playing.

Camp was no longer cognate to the queer subculture; it now belonged to the pop revolution of the 1960s. In the second half of the twentieth century, as it has been noted in later criticism (most notably in Andrew Ross' 'Uses of Camp' [see Cleto 1999], and in both Booth 1983 and Core 1984), camp – while maintaining its relevance within such former cultural spaces as the 'Low Camp' of the drag underworld and thus progressively reaching a wider visibility, and when coupled with the decriminalization of homosexuality – became a pervasive presence in the entertainment industry, a major marketing strategy and a high-selling product in itself. Camp would still be found in high literate culture: in the writings of W.H. **Auden**, James Merrill, Edward Field, James McCourt and Patrick Gale, the plays of Tony **Kushner**, in Charles Ludlam's Theater of the Ridiculous (see **Ludlam**, Charles) or in the film criticism of Tyler **Parker** and Vito **Russo**. However, literary camp would now also be found everywhere else, thanks to the queer pulp covers and sensationalist novels of the 1960s and 1970s.

In cinema, as censorship loosened its strings, camp would become a major fea-

ture of a growing number of over-the-top or trashy productions (e.g., the films of John **Waters** and Russ **Meyer**) and find its way into mainstream movies (witness the Ken **Russell** extravaganzas). The underground scene was in fact gaining access to an unprecedented popularity: Andy **Warhol**, a supreme queen of pop camp, brought **drag queens** to superstardom, Pop Art moved from the supermarket to highbrow galleries, and camp became the major mode for representing celebrity culture, entering gossip columns and volumes (those cultural spaces hyped and parodied in Kenneth Anger's 1975 'book of revelations', *Hollywood Babylon*).

The campy bricolage of upper-class codes, theatrical transgression and effeminacy was utterly 'democratized' and adopted by working-class youth countercultures, who exhibited a subversive camp relish for forgotten cultural forms such as, in the case of Teds and Mods, Edwardian queer tokens, Victoriana and the Union Jack. But that same bricolage was also being deployed by mainstream identities, who started ransacking flea markets for the camp frisson of acquiring cheap memorabilia. All-American families were lured into the double-coded naughtiness of pop camp by TV programmes such as *Batman*, *Charlie's Angels* and *The Avengers*. Music charts and high streets were flooded with the screaming queens of **glam rock** stars (the New York Dolls, David Bowie, Bryan Ferry, Elton John, etc.) and **disco** music (with Sylvester and Village People, to name a couple), and their wannabes, who would pave the way to the **New Romantic** and electro-pop masquerade of the 1980s, and to the Britpop and neo-glam scene of the 1990s. Overnight, the world seemed to have turned into a queer stage.

And yet, it was a queer stage peopled by very few openly gay characters and virtually no lesbians at all – and especially anyone fighting for the acknowledgment of the gay right to full citizenship. However, in response to the pop camp fad, camp started being discussed as a peculiarly gay formation and language. Esther Newton's 1972 ground-breaking sociological investigation, *Mother Camp* (see Cleto 1999), mapped the uses and functions of camp in the world of stage and street female impersonation, and while suggesting a series of constant stylistic traits 'intimately related to the homosexual situation and strategy' – incongruity, theatricality, humour – she posited camp as survival strategy existing 'in the eye of the homosexual beholder'. Jack Babuscio's 'Camp and the Gay Sensibility' (see Cleto 1999), along with a whole bulk of early gay criticism, followed Newton in charting cinematic camp and in framing it as embedded in the very idea of a 'gay sensibility' and a 'genuine' homosexual culture. The wide currency value camp had gained among heterosexuals during the 1960s was alleged to have been reduced to a style that could be adopted precisely because it effaced its authentic gay origin. Reclaiming camp from pop was in fact part of a complex self-definitional enterprise within the gay community promoting identity politics, one that defined both camp-as-gay-issue and the gay eye/I that could perform/acknowledge it. By reclaiming camp, gay critics were identifying a powerful tool, enabling on the one side a gay history and canon, and on the other side, the gay cultural authority they were willing to represent.

Ironically, camp was severely criticized during the 1970s, not only in its 'degayified' pop form, but also in its queer deployments. As gay rights movements such as the Gay Liberation Front fought for social equality and the gay right to exist, camp was dismissed because it was a pre-**Stonewall** strategy, a self-stigmatizing ghetto that presupposed and reinforced the very subordinating stereotypes (and the capitalistic logic of conspicuous consumption) that it derided.

The legacy of the 1960s 'democratization' of camp, and of the 1970s gay tension between reclaiming and critique, resides in the acknowledgement of camp as a political issue, and as a complex ('queer') political strategy that erodes and subverts dominant categories rather than straightforwardly contesting them. An obvious instance is the camp subversion of gender roles: by enacting femininity as masquerade within gay drag, camp may either reinforce the stigma of homosexual deviance from normality or denaturalize gender as cultural construct, depriving the dominant of its self-ratifying devices, 'nature', 'reality' and 'truth'. In this regard, camp has been praised for endorsing what in the 1980s would be tagged 'second wave feminism'. Just as gay studies and cultural criticism had provided a first framework for the understanding of camp, the historicist framing of gender, or sexual constructionism (paving the road to Judith Butler's queer theory and performativity), turned out a best ally to the critical reappraisal of the politics of camp. The 1990s saliency of the odd twins 'camp' and 'queer' was proved as they were adopted by radical activists, with groups such as **Queer Nation**, **ACT UP** and **Radical Fairies** rejecting 1970s assimilationist gay rights activism in favour of the relentless subversion of cultural hierarchies. Once an accommodating instrument, marginalizing queers as it provided them with a survival space, the sharp wit of camp could be used to its full cutting potential, returning stigma in the face of dominant culture.

Despite recurrent mourning for the 'death of camp' (see Harris 1997), camp itself shows no signs of durable crisis: any lamentations are due largely to its volubility, to its endless metamorphosing – camp finds its value in its ability to just 'happen', to change and refashion itself, to disappear and reappear, just like an Arabian phoenix, and to excite and frustrate taxonomical approaches. Far from vanishing, camp effects may in fact be found in cultural spaces other than the gay (white, middle-class, metropolitan) framework previously taken for 'genuine' camp. As the queer unsettling of gay/het and original/derivative binarisms was fully acknowledged in camp, a previously unaccounted for variety of camps have emerged in recent years: lesbian camp, with the **butch/femme** dynamic duo transgressively reinscripting gender roles and the male gaze (see Sue-Ellen Case's 'Toward a Butch-Femme Aesthetic', in Cleto 1999), bisexual camp and even queer heterosexual ('anti-straight') 'feminist camp', encompassing a whole tradition of same-sex female mimicry – from Mae **West** to Joan **Crawford** to **Madonna** – that Pamela Robertson's 1996 *Guilty Pleasures* unfolds.

As the idea of a gay origin and property of camp was challenged by its queerness, accounting for the complex dialectic between dominant and deviant, the door was opened to camp effects and issues that previously had been silenced in gender-focused understandings of camp, such as ethnicity (from blackface camp comedy to blaxploitation to Latino drag to Joan Jett **Blakk**) and the questioning of the very existence, outside the English-speaking world, of such a nominalist category. While the word 'camp' finds no adequate translation in other languages, there are many camp sites in other national cultures (not only in the drag world, but also in the literate culture of, say, Jean **Cocteau**, Alberto Arbasino, Aldo Busi, Manuel **Puig**, Renaud **Camus**, or in the cinema of Luchino **Visconti**, Pedro **Almodóvar**, Rainer Werner **Fassbinder**). What is at stake is how far such camp tagging may be a mere act of acknowledgement of a camp site, or an effect of the Anglo-American overcoding camp eye, which mirrors itself in other cultures and categories, or again the result of an internationalization of Anglo-American camp, i.e. an instance of globalized US pop culture. Most likely, no definitive answer is in sight, and this may be for the better, as both critics and practitioners will keep on setting up new camps, charting borders and makeup, and then moving on to another site. Camp happens wherever we may find it, and whenever we make it happen, after all, it will continue to elude us; for its ultimate authenticity resides – to mention a famous essay by Richard Dyer (1976; see Cleto 1999) – in its being 'so camp as keeps us going', whatever that 'we' may be.

Bibliography

Booth, Mark (1983) *Camp*, London: Quartet.

Cleto, F. (ed.) (1999) *Camp: Queer Aesthetics and the Performing Subject*, Ann Arbor: University of Michigan Press.

Core, P. (1984) *Camp: The Lie That Tells the Truth*, New York: Delilah.

Harris, D. (1997) *The Rise and Fall of Gay Culture*, New York: Hyperion.

Robertson, P. (1996) *Guilty Pleasures: Feminist Camp from Mae West to Madonna*, Durham: Duke University Press.

Tinkcom, M. (2002) *Working Like a Homosexual: Camp, Capital, Cinema*, Durham: Duke University Press.

Further reading

Bergman, D. (ed.) (1993) *Camp Grounds: Style and Homosexuality*, Amherst: University of Massachusetts Press.

Bronski, M. (1984) *Culture Clash: The Making of Gay Sensibility*, Boston: South End Press.

Meyer, M. (ed.) (1994) *The Politics and Poetics of Camp*, New York: Routledge.

FABIO CLETO

CAMPBELL, COLIN

b. 1942; d. 2001

filmmaker

Canadian video art pioneer Campbell grew up in Manitoba and taught at New Brunswick's Mount Allison University before settling in Toronto, where for 30 years he was a pillar of the art community and influential teacher, first at Ontario College of Art and later the University of Toronto. Author of more than 50 works, Campbell often incorporated his own brilliantly restrained transgender performance (among the best known is the wry 1976 triptych *Woman from Malibu*) and pushed the possibilities of narrative towards unprecedented ambiguity and complexity without ever losing its immediacy and impact. The early *I'm a Voyeur* (1974) epitomized the moment when minimalist conceptual games were becoming increasingly infused with the sexual tensions of voyeurism, performance and identity. Fascinated by soap opera, Campbell obsessively satirized art world denizens and queer rebels alike – the bad, the beautiful and the superficial – and contributed perhaps more than anyone to the consolidation of art video as a queer stronghold. Campbell's anomalous 1991 work in celluloid, *Skin*, dramatized testimonies by women with AIDS and he was awarded the prestigious Bell Canada Award in Video Art in 1996.

THOMAS WAUGH

CAMUS, RENAUD

b. 1946

writer

Renaud Camus is one of the most prolific French writers of recent years, with over 50 *récits*, novels, essays in art criticism, elegies, polemics and travel books to his name. In addition, he coined the word *achrien* as a substitute for unsatisfactory words such as 'homosexual'. His annual diaries are a philosophical and gossipy record of French cultural, social and political mores, a contemporary gay equivalent of those written by the Duc de Saint-Simon during the *ancien régime*. While Camus speaks of himself as a writer rather than as a 'gay writer', his work is a complete expression of gay sexuality as an everyday practice of the self in different activities ranging from sex to worldly socializing. In *Tricks*, exquisitely prefaced by Roland Barthes, ejaculation is the predetermined form of narrative closure,

while in much of Camus' work the labyrinthine structures of his grammar imply cruising as the source of literary form. Both a candidate for the Académie Française and the epicentre of a scandal over his alleged anti-Semitism, Camus no longer lives in Paris but conducts his cultural activity from his château in the Gers. This he has made into a sanctuary of refined avant-garde artistic practices as well as of a neo-conservative political party called In-nocence.

ADRIAN RIFKIN

CANADA, FILMMAKING

Glbtq cinema and video in Canada is surprisingly rich, prolific and diverse, given a country with a population less than that of California, and has built an international reputation beginning in the 1980s. As with Canadian cinemas as a whole, Canadian queer cinemas have a bicephalous structure embodying the country's two official linguistic cultures: French, concentrated mostly in Quebec; and English, concentrated in the other nine provinces and three territories. Canadian glbtq cinemas can also be seen as *tri*cephalous, with three thriving branches based in the distinct queer urban cultures of the largest metropoles, Vancouver, Toronto and Montreal. Significant but less prolific regional scenes have also emerged, especially in the Prairies, centred mostly in Winnipeg, and in the Atlantic region, centred mostly in Halifax. The other fundamental characteristic to which Canadian queer cinemas' conspicuous vitality can be attributed is their roots in public arts funding, both provincial and federal. The latter derives from Ottawa-financed cultural institutions such as the Canada Council for the Arts with its admired peer jury system, the documentary and animation studio of the National Film Board of Canada (NFB), the Canadian Broadcasting Corporation and the feature-funding agency Telefilm Canada, all of which tend to alleviate the flattening of diversity imposed by the marketplace.

Before the decriminalization of most same-sex sexual activities with the Omnibus Bill of 1969, a sprinkling of isolated pioneers had discreetly explored ambiguities of identity and desire, but these explorations pale alongside the forthright avant-gardes of New York and Paris. The famous couple composed of producer Guy Glover and animator Norman **McLaren** reigned at the NFB from 1939 until the 1980s. The latter's films of the 1950s and 1960s can be creatively subtexted, but his only explicit work was his last, the 1983 ballet parable *Narcissus*. Younger pioneers of the postwar generation were somewhat less cautious and McLaren's disciple Claude Jutra burst forth in 1963 with an independent autobiographical feature *À tout prendre* (All Things Considered), but this *nouvelle vague*-influenced exploit was to be his only explicit work. David Secter's feature *Winter Kept Us Warm*, produced at the University of Toronto in 1965, was less brash, a triangular coming-out narrative that surprised not only with its beefcake but also with its unexpected tenderness and cruelty.

The post-Omnibus decade was more fruitful as the Canadian feature industry also began to find its state-subsidized legs. Still, the breakthroughs were sporadic as community infrastructures and audiences crystallized very slowly. Both major Montreal features of the 1970s were set in that city's ebullient tenderloin district: *Il était une fois dans l'est* (Once Upon a Time in the East), André Brassard's raucous 1973 adaptation of theatrical characters by wunderkind Michel **Tremblay**; and Frank Vitale's *Montreal Main*, a discreet intergenerational love story that raised surprisingly few eyebrows in 1974. Toronto's entry into the arena in 1978 was more upbeat: Richard Benner's backstage melodrama *Outrageous!* starring female 'impressionist' Craig Russell doing Judy (Garland), Barbra (Streisand) and Ethel (Merman). A few activist documentaries

also began to circulate, especially in Montreal: independents by community-based Harry Sutherland and the Réseau Vidé-Elle collective, as well as NFB productions by Margaret Wescott, who made the first major Canadian lesbian film in 1978, a documentary symptomatically entitled *Some American Feminists*. Alongside these celluloid efforts, the 1970s also saw strong groundwork laid in video art, especially in the work of pioneers Paul **Wong** (Vancouver) and Colin **Campbell** (Toronto), both offering conceptual, corporeal and corrosive imagery in their own distinctive ways.

The first post-Omnibus generation came to the fore in the 1980s and brought more confidence, continuity and coherence to the queer screen, openly declaring a politics of sexual identity and increasingly depicting a specific glbtq social universe. Auteur feature fiction gradually emerged, although the first major women's features in Toronto and Montreal respectively, Patricia Rozema's 1985 comic box-office hit *I've Heard the Mermaids Singing* and Léa Pool's poetic feminist melodramas, including the queerfest perennial from 1986, *Anne Trister*, all encountered a reception attenuated by the directors' reticence to publicly affirm the sexual identities that were palpable on-screen, a situation that would only be clarified in the 1990s. In contrast men's features were more provocative, both in terms of aesthetics and authorial personae: for example, Fernand Bélanger's *Passiflora* (with Dagmar Guessaz-Teufel), an irreverent 1986 docu-drama that sent up everything from synchronized sound to the Pope and was suppressed by the NFB, and John Greyson's *Urinal*, a 1989 video-inflected narrative that had Sergei Eisenstein and Frida Kahlo discoursing on the politics of toilet sex with Dorian Gray in present-day Toronto.

Greyson had emerged from an effervescent short film, video and documentary scene which continued to be far more productive than the feature film sector throughout the decade. Buoyed up by artists' co-ops and parallel distribution centres in all three metropoles, a lively stream of short narrative, experimental and documentary films and videos became the toast of the international network of queer community film festivals that was then consolidating. Alongside Greyson, Campbell and Wong, the key makers who first made an impact in the 1980s, were the Montrealers Jeanne Crépeau, Michel Langlois, Marc Paradis, Bashar Shbib and the duo Serge Murphy and Charles Guibert; the Torontonians Marusya Bociurkiw, Richard **Fung**, Laurie Lynd, Wrik Mead, Midi Onodera and Margaret Moores, as well as the duo Janis Cole and Holly Dale; and the Vancouverites Lorna Boschman, Sara Diamond and Joe Sarahan. By the end of the decade, the NFB had also climbed on the bandwagon, after years of silence and false starts, and by the mid-2000s had produced almost 50 documentaries and animations about sexual minorities and identities. Of these the most successful was Lynne Fernie and Aerlynn Weissmann's 1992 inventive hybrid feature *Forbidden Love: The Unashamed Stories of Lesbian Lives*, an international hit about pre-Stonewall bar culture, identities and fantasy.

AIDS had an impact on Canadian cinemas similar to that in the United States and Europe. The pandemic launched a tide of activist video in the late 1980s, featuring work by Michael Balser, Anne Golden and Nik Sheehan, as well as by Greyson and Fung. This tide morphed into a stream of personal, more introspective works during the 1990s, including several enduring masterpieces: Greyson's ebullient musical feature *Zero Patience* (1993) and several first-person experimental works by people living with AIDS, most notably Esther Valiquette's 1990 *Récit d'A* (The Story of A) and Mike Hoolboom's trilogy *Frank's Cock* (1993), *Letters from Home* (1996) and *Positiv* (1997).

The 1990s and the 2000s saw not only the awakening of the NFB but also the quantum proliferation of networks of young alternative documentarists and avant-gardists, most born after 1969. This wave was, by and large, post-identity in its consensus, not so much affirming glbtq identities but interrogating their constructed homogeneity and celebrating diversity and contradiction as well as pleasure. In addition to Fung, Onodera and Wong, alternative artists who attracted international attention for their probing of ethno-cultural relativities around sexuality included Dionne **Brand**, Thirza **Cuthand**, Kevin DSouza, Sheila James, Michelle Mohabeer, Atif Siddiqi, b.h.yael, José Torrealba and Wayne Yung. Feature directors such as Deepa **Mehta** and the expatriate Ian Iqbal Rashid were also in step with this energy.

No doubt the most conspicuous queer Canadian filmmakers on the international scene were the new cycle of fiction feature auteurs who met acclaim at international festivals throughout the 1990s and early 2000s. Rozema and Pool staged comebacks with the interracial romance *When Night is Falling* (1995) and the autobiographical coming-of-age tale *Emporte-moi* (*Set Me Free*, 1998) respectively, while Onodera, Crépeau and Montreal's Manon Briand all made their first features. On the male side, Denis Langlois, Michel Langlois, Daniel MacIvor, Jeremy Podeswa and Scott Smith all followed promising first features with strong subsequent work. Greyson scored anew with *Lilies or the Revival of a Romantic Drama* (1996) and Quebec City theatre director-writer Robert **Lepage** shifted his attention to the big screen in 1995 with *Le Confessionnal* (*The Confessional*). Perhaps the most stunning feature debuts of the period came from the hinterlands, rich in landscape and longing: the Acadian Rodrigue Jean's *Full Blast* (1999), the Winnipegger Noam Gonick's *Hey Happy!* (2000) and Thom Fitzgerald's *The Hanging Garden* (1997), which applied a Nova Scotian brand of magic realism to the classic coming-out/coming-of-age formula. Wry, energetic video work by Winnipeg performance artist Shawna **Dempsey** also confirmed that the metropoles did not have monopolies on subversive sexual representation.

Both *Lilies*, an adaptation of Michel Marc Bouchard's tender coming-of-age period melodrama *Les Feluettes*, and *Le Confessionnal*, an adaptation of Lepage's stage work, received the Genie Best Film Award of their respective years from the Canadian Academy. These were not the only theatrical adaptations that met with approval either from the critics or at the box office. Already in the 1970s, alongside Brassard's adaptation of Tremblay, a non-glbtq-directed adaptation of John Herbert's pre-Stonewall stage hit *Fortune and Men's Eyes* (1971) had been undeservedly neglected, and theatre again provided inspiration for feature filmmakers decades later: Émile Gaudreault's comic hit *Mambo Italiano* (2003) was based on the stage hit of the same name by Steve Gallucio; Brad Fraser brought his own play *Poor Super Man* to the screen as *Leaving Metropolis* (2002) and MacIvor and Sky Gilbert were two other theatrical artists who successfully moved into film. Respectful heterosexual-directed adaptations of Fraser and Bouchard, as well as of playwright René-Daniel Dubois' *Being at Home with Claude* (1992), confirmed the potential of theatrical adaptation for feature glbtq filmmakers.

Heterosexual directors sometimes also contributed memorable images to the 1990s surge of queer-oriented fiction, from Anne Wheeler's *Better than Chocolate* (1999), a popular baby-dyke romance with a political edge, to Atom Egoyan's endearingly quirky gay male characterizations in such art-house hits as *Exotica* (1994). Others, from David Cronenberg to Jean-Claude Lauzon, offered compromised and conflicted images of male sexual diversity that fed cultural panics about same-sex desire.

Television increasingly became a player in the queer moving image landscape. Exports from Scott Thompson to *DeGrassi:*

The Next Generation (2001–) attracted international audiences during the queer TV boom in the US and the UK of the 1990s and 2000s. The domestic Anglophone market, lagging far behind its Quebec counterpart, also became increasingly energized by sexual diversity, thanks in part to cable channels such as Showcase, Life and Pride Vision. The Canadian queer documentary heritage received a boost from the small screen, reflected in such successes as Larry Peloso's 2002 *Prom Fight: The Marc Hall Story* and Gerry Rogers' 2000 digicam cancer diary *My Left Breast*. Outside of TV and the NFB, more confrontational and ambitious political work from documentary veterans such as Nancy Nicol also benefited from the new climate.

In general, sexual frankness and iconoclasm were the hallmarks of this generation of short and feature makers, despite the emerging, more conservative agenda of **same-sex marriage** in the Canadian body politic. Cynthia Roberts' *Bubbles Galore* (1996), starring Nina Hartley and Annie Sprinkle and a Canadian supporting cast, was denounced in Parliament in the late 1990s for its state-funded venture into so-called lesbian pornography. But Bruce **LaBruce**, although never publicly funded, epitomized best the risk-taking among his cinematic cohort with his 1990s low-budget, personal features about filmmaking, sexual obsession and marginality, culminating in international art porno productions in the 2000s. Transsexual activist, performance artist and sex worker Mirha-Soleil **Ross** produced a cycle of videotapes at the same time, equally personal manifestos of transsexuality and bodies, as well as political struggles around sex-work.

Some observers, such as Katherine Monk (2001), have wondered whether Canadians have a national propensity for 'kinky, dark, quirky and obsessive sex' caused by their frigid climate. However, rather than an outgrowth of a monolithic national psyche, Canadian glbtq filmmakers' high-profile achievement was the result of several inter-connected elements: the relatively bias-free process of public funding and institutions; the ongoing culture of anti-censorship resistance dating back to the 1960s; the flourishing metropolitan infrastructures of media, culture and nightlife, including thriving community festivals in all major centres that originated as early as the late 1970s; and the dynamic pyramidal base of video and short film production that proved to be the training ground and crucible for the Canadian queer artistic achievements and international profile alike.

Thanks to Hollywood's grip, especially in English Canada, domestic features continued to occupy only 2 per cent of national theatre screens, and few of the breakthrough queer feature films of the 1990s and 2000s showed profit. As the pressure to commercialize the feature film industry increased during the mid-2000s, the purse-strings at Telefilm Canada tightened and there were ominous signs that the Canadian queer success story might be on the verge of sliding back to the lean years of the 1970s. Even as glbtq Canadians celebrated unexpected victories in the courts for same-sex marriage, at the same time warning was served that the audiovisual wedding banquet could not be taken for granted.

Bibliography

Monk, Katherine (2001) *Weird Sex and Snow Shoes and Other Canadian Film Phenomena*, Vancouver: Raincoast Books.

Further reading

Armatage, Kay, Banning, Kass, Longfellow, Brenda and Marchessault, Janine (eds) (1999) *Gendering the Nation: Canadian Women's Cinema*, Toronto: University of Toronto Press. (An anthology situating queer cinemas within the feminist problematic.)

Gittings, Christopher E. (2002) *Canadian National Cinema: Ideology, Difference and Representation*, London and New York:

Routledge. (An alternative history, linking sexual diversity to postcolonial and other ideological perspectives.)

Johnson, Lorraine (1997) *Suggestive Poses: Artists and Critics Respond to Censorship*, Toronto: Toronto Photographers Workshop and The Riverbank Press. (Anthology situating queer anti-censorship struggles within the larger political context.)

Lee, Helen and Sakamoto, Kerri (eds) (2002) *Like Mangoes in July: The Work of Richard Fung*, Toronto: Insomniac Press/Images Festival. (A thorough anthology of critical perspectives.)

Waugh, Thomas (2006) *The Romance of Transgression in Canada: Sexualities, Nations, Moving Images*, Montreal: McGill-Queen's. (Historical and thematic essays on Canadian glbtq cinemas, with a comprehensive critical companion.)

THOMAS WAUGH

CANADA, LITERATURE

Canadian glbtq literature is composed of two separate categories: one in English (Anglo-Canadian) and one in French (Québécois). Emerging from different literary traditions and reflecting different political agendas, they have limited inter-action, although they share some common themes (e.g., AIDS and gender identity) and stimulate and play off of each other.

Anglo-Canadian glbtq literature

Anglo-Canadian glbtq literature began to emerge in the mid-1960s, with landmark texts such as Edward Lacey's 1965 book of gay poetry *Forms of Loss* (heralded as the first openly gay book of Canadian poetry), Jon Herbert's 1964 play *Fortune and Men's Eyes* (set in a prison, and realistically depicting and denouncing the inhuman and violent treatment of homosexuals) and Scott Symons' 1967 novel *Combat Journal for Place d'Armes* (a multilayered journal of autobiography offering a three-fold perspective on homosexuality and the creative process). The list of the most eminent contemporary Anglo-Canadian glbtq authors includes the poets Dionne **Brand** and Douglas LePan, fiction authors Edward Phillips and Jane Rule, playwrights John Palmer and Ann-Marie MacDonald, but establishing a set canon is no easy task. Scholar Peter Dickinson proposed one in his 1999 pioneering study *Here is Queer: Nationalism, Sexualities and the Literature of Canada*. Problematizing the absence of a coherent national identity and the presence of a destabilizing sexual identity, his book is highly regarded, although some critics have noted that its canon might be too narrow because it does not include some authors such as bill bassett and the Native American writer Daniel David Moses. This is emblematic of the key problem of Anglo-Canadian glbtq literature: a problem of definition and delineation. In many respects, Anglo-Canadian glbtq literature struggles to distinguish itself from that of the United States. The cultural border between Canada and the US is fluid, with American expatriates (such as Peter McGehee and Jane Rule) now living and working in Canada, while Canadian-born authors (such as Lauren Wright Douglas) have relocated to the United States. As noted by Douglas Chambers (2002): 'Caught between the traditionally overwhelming influence of British culture and, more recently, the powerful stranglehold of American literature, the Canadian voice (gay or straight) is hard to hear.'

Québécois glbtq literature

Québécois glbtq literature appeared slightly later than its Anglo-Canadian partner, emerging in the 1970s with the works of celebrated pioneers such as Michel **Tremblay** (*Demain matin Montréal m'attend* [Tomorrow Morning, Montreal Will Be Mine] 1970; *Hosanna* 1973) and Marie-Claire **Blais** (*Le Loup* [The Wolf], 1972; *Les nuits de l'underground* [Nights in the Underground: An Exploration of Love],

1978). The literature of the early 1970s reflects the development at that time of the gay and lesbian liberation movement in Québec, the organization of a gay and lesbian community in Montreal, as well as the political success of a liberal piece of legislation passed – in 1977 Quebec became the first jurisdiction in North America to add sexual orientation to its anti-discrimination Human Rights Act. Understanding its political and historical context is paramount to appreciate Québécois glbtq literature, as it developed as part of the so-called 'Révolution Silencieuse' (Quiet Revolution) of the 1970s, when advocates of separatism from Canada became more and more vocal in their campaigns about independence, Québécois identity and Québécois culture. The political dimension of Québécois glbtq literature is a feature of many books, such as Stephen Schecter's 1984 *T'es beau en écoeurant* (You Are Such a Cutie), about the love affair in Montreal between Anglophone Michael and Francophone Richard. In simple terms, glbtq Québécois literature appears as a double form of resistance, about a (sexual) minority in a (linguistic) minority. The literary/identity politics of Québécois glbtq literature operates on two levels – the sexual and the linguistic – which accounts for some of its literary creativity, especially in the work of writers such as Jovette Marchessault, Nicole Brossard, André Roy and Jean-Paul Daoust – all names that predominantly belong to the contemporary canon of Québécois glbtq literature, alongside those of playwrights Michel Marc Bouchard and Marie-Claire Blais.

Beyond these differences of language and political agenda, Canadian glbtq literature addresses typical glbtq themes, from coming-out stories (well illustrated by Will Aitken's 1989 autobiographical *Terre Haute*) to gender identity (for instance Jacques Bélanger, now Brigitte Martel, *Né homme, comment je suis devenu femme*, [Born a Man, How I Became a Woman], 1983) via class issues (a good example being David Type's 1983 play *Just Us Indians* set in downtown Toronto, not to mention the use of *joual* by authors such as Michel Tremblay, *joual* being an idiomatic French spoken by working-class Québécois). In the 1980s and early 1990s Canadian glbtq literature also contributed to the global phenomenon of AIDS literature, with numerous works, most notably Sky Gilbert's 1984 play *The Dressing Gown*, Alain Emmanuel Dreuilhe's 1997 influential diary *Corps à corps: Journal de sida* (Mortal Embrace), Peter McGehee's 1991 *Boys like Us*, and the 1992 anthology edited by James Miller, *Fluid Exchanges: Artists and Critics on the AIDS Crisis*.

Canadian glbtq literature is very dynamic, notably thanks to the vitality of publishing companies all across the country, from Talonbooks in Vancouver (British Columbia) to Gynergy in Charlottetown (Prince Edward Island). It spans all literary genres: fiction and non-fiction, drama and poetry, all very well represented, with a special mention for periodicals as a major source of glbtq writing (the two most famous periodicals being Montreal-based *Le Berdache* and the now defunct *Body Politic* from Toronto, 1971–87). These periodicals show how Canadian glbtq literature, rather than being an elitist phenomenon, is actually anchored in the community it serves and represents. Together with the cultural work of organizations such as the Canadian Gay Archives (Toronto) and the LAMBDA Institute of Gay and Lesbian Studies (Edmonton), and with many web sites, literary prizes and conferences, it contributes to the development of Canadian glbtq culture in general.

See also: Canada, performance and theatre

Bibliography

Chambers, D. (2002) 'Canadian Literature in English', in C.J. Summers (ed.) *Glbtq: An Encyclopedia of Gay, Lesbian, Bisexual, Transgender, and Queer Culture*, Chicago: glbtq, Inc.

Dickinson, P. (1999) *Here Is Queer: Nationalisms, Sexualities, and the Literatures of Canada*, Toronto: University of Toronto Press.

Miller, J. (ed.) (1992) *Fluid Exchanges: Artists and Critics on the AIDS Crisis*, Toronto: University of Toronto Press.

LOYKIE LOÏC LOMINÉ

CANADA, PERFORMANCE AND THEATRE

The years 1967–8, a period highlighted by centennial celebrations across Canada, offer a useful point of origin for Canadian glbtq performance and theatre. Not only does it herald the emergence of two of the country's best-known gay playwrights but, also, it foregrounds the cultural context that shapes queer performance throughout the nation. In 1967 John Herbert, a Toronto playwright, premiered *Fortune and Men's Eyes,* his first play, off-Broadway, to considerable acclaim; since writing the play in 1964, Herbert had laboured in vain to find a Canadian producer willing to gamble on the play's homoeroticism and scatological argot. The following year, Michel **Tremblay**, a Montreal playwright, premiered his first play, *Les Belles-soeurs* (The Sisters-in-Law) using *joual*, a Québécois dialect that was considered equally scandalous. While Herbert waited until 1975 to see his play produced in Toronto, Tremblay saw *Les Belles-soeurs* achieve immediate success in Montreal, so much so that it quickly was translated and produced across Canada. Ironically, both plays dramatize the oppression of people marginalized and abused by social institutions – a consistent trope in Canadian glbtq theatre and performance. Whereas Herbert castigates Canada's judicial and penal systems by depicting the corruption and abuse of four adolescent boys incarcerated in a reformatory, Tremblay focuses on the tribulations of a group of working-class women, to condemn the heteronormativity promulgated by the Roman Catholic Church. The

131

playwrights' choices in these plays index the differing priorities of Canada's two founding cultures that mark Canadian queer culture as, at least, a bifocal site. More importantly, they help to explain why the representation of queer subjects advanced more quickly in Quebec than the rest of the country.

In 1970 Tremblay introduced *La Duchesse de Langeais*, the first in a series of plays that feature transvestite protagonists; by the end of the decade, the success of this series established him as the most important Québécois playwright of his generation – a remarkable feat given his focus on disenfranchised sexual dissidents. Although they received a less enthusiastic response when they were translated and produced outside Quebec, the plays nevertheless attracted more attention than any other queer work produced in Canada at this time – another irony, given that English-Canadian playwrights also had begun to introduce gay, lesbian and queer subjects to the stage. In Toronto, the epicentre of a burgeoning alternative theatre movement, renegade companies welcomed the contributions of openly gay playwrights. Generally, however, the gay plays produced by these companies, typified by John Palmer's *A Touch of God in the Golden Age* (1971) and Larry Fineberg's *Hope* (1972), reinforced pre-Stonewall stereotypes of gay men whose personal dysfunction is more easily attributed to internalized homophobia than social oppression. Unlike Tremblay's queer characters, who share a sense of outraged community, albeit one that allows them to be (simply) interpreted as allegorical representations of French-Canada's marginal status in English-speaking North America, these characters frequently exist in a heterosexual context in which they are adrift, if not doomed.

During the 1970s Montreal and Toronto, along with other large Canadian cities, witnessed the rapid growth of queer communities replete with clubs, bars, bathhouses,

social centres and businesses. Like the parades and public demonstrations that heralded this growth, performances by lesbian and gay musical groups, drag artists, stand-up comics and disc jockeys proliferated inside queer venues, helping to shape and unify these communities from inside queer culture. Craig Russell, a 'female impersonator' who began his career in Toronto during the early 1970s, is perhaps the most famous performer to emerge from a Canadian queer milieu during this period. To impersonate a range of famous divas, Russell combined a three-octave vocal range with detailed characterizations, often achieving remarkable verisimilitude. After performing in numerous drag venues across North America, Russell starred in *Outrageous*, a semi-autobiographical Canadian film directed by Richard Benner in 1977, which led to an international stage career that declined along with the performer's health during the 1980s. By this time, however, other artists and organizations had emerged within Canada's queer communities to further the proliferation of theatre and performance that he had helped initiate.

Of these organizations, the most important is Buddies in Bad Times Theatre which, after renting a number of venues following its inception in 1979, moved to its own space adjacent to Toronto's queer village in 1994. In the mid-1980s, Sky Gilbert, one of the company's co-founders and its first artistic director, refined Buddies' mandate to emphasize gay and lesbian material. Although Gilbert had written and directed gay plays earlier than this, only in 1984, with a play called *The Dressing Gown,* did he position himself as a gay playwright. The sold-out run of *Drag Queens on Trial*, a play that he wrote and produced in 1985, raised both his and Buddies' profile – which achieved even greater heights when the play subsequently toured Canada and the United States. That same year, Gilbert inaugurated *4-Play*, a festival of four new plays, two by lesbians, two by gay men, which, by the end of the decade, had become the centrepiece of *Queer Culture*, a city-wide event integrating social, political and cultural activities sponsored by a range of gay and lesbian organizations.

Besides launching the careers of queer artists such as Sonja Mills, Daniel MacIvor, Audrey Butler and David Demchuk, *4-Play* helped to establish queer theatre and performance as a legitimate source of new Canadian plays. The strength and vibrancy of Buddies not only raised the profile of queer performance in Canada but, in addition, helped theatres in other Canadian cities to champion queer plays in their regions. The publication of work by Gilbert and others associated with the company was foundational to a queer Canadian canon of drama that includes plays from across the country. Two of Vancouver's most important gay writers, Gordon Armstrong and Colin Thomas, have seen their plays produced nationally and published, as have Kent Stetson and Bryden MacDonald, gay playwrights from Canada's East Coast. Brad Fraser, a queer playwright from Alberta, achieved international success with *Poor Super Man* (2001) – a play which, like his earlier *Unidentified Human Remains and the True Nature of Love* (1988), was both published and adapted into a feature film. Ann-Marie MacDonald, a lesbian actor and writer living in Toronto, found similar success with *Goodnight Desdemona* (*Good Morning Juliet* (1988)), as did Tomson Highway, a Cree playwright whose two plays about life on a native reservation, *The Rez Sisters* (1986) and *Dry Lips Oughta Move to Kapuskasing* (1987), garnered international plaudits along with publication. Numerous other queer writers established national reputations by having their work televised as well as published and produced: for example, two plays by Timothy **Findley** (*Elizabeth Rex,* 2000; *The Stillborn Lover,* 1993), as well as plays by Diane Flacks, are now available on video.

The proliferation of queer theatre in Canada finds a small but significant parallel in the work of performance artists for whom video recording and gallery presentations define a different conceptual framework. David Bateman and David Roche, two queer artists based in Toronto, perform in galleries as well as theatres. Working independently and together, these witty performers often cross-dress and utilize camp intertexuality and word play to create presentational pieces that challenge assumptions of gender and sexual stereotyping as well as genre categories. In a similar vein, Shawna **Dempsey** and Lori Millan, lesbian artists living in Winnipeg, parody homosocial institutions such as the Girl Guides and Canadian Park Rangers with performances and installations that they also document on videotape. While other queer artists such as Richard **Fung**, Bruce **La Bruce** and John **Greyson**, after using videotape to begin their careers, turned to film, their continued use of queer actors helps to perpetuate a sense of community among Canada's queer performers.

In 1996 John Greyson directed *Lilies or the Revival of a Romantic Drama*, a film he adapted from a play by Michel Marc Bouchard, a gay Québécois playwright whose politics, if not aesthetics, recall the work of Tremblay. *Lilies* (*Les Feluettes*, 1988), which starred Brent Carver, a gay Canadian actor whose performances have won numerous awards in Canada and the United States, received the Genie Best Film Award (Canada's equivalent of the Oscar), capping the remarkable success of Bouchard's play since its Montreal premiere in 1987. Perhaps because Tremblay 'naturalized' queer characterization earlier in Quebec than his peers in the rest of the country, queer theatre and performance flourishes there more than it does in Canada's other provinces. This became especially evident during the 1980s and early 1990s when a host of Québécois playwrights emerged along with Bouchard to write plays often grouped as *la nouvelle dramaturgie* (the new dramaturgy). The formal innovations of these plays (multiple narratives, protracted monologues, self-referential structures) are no more remarkable than their focus on queer subjects and situations. Plays by Québécois artists as diverse as Marie-Claire **Blais**, Normand Chaurette, René-Daniel Dubois, Robert **Lepage**, Jovette Marchessault and Pol Pelletier illustrate queer theatre and performance at its most original and vibrant. As more of these plays are translated and produced internationally, they provide resources and inspiration not only for Canadian artists but for people around the world.

ROBERT WALLACE

CANDOMBLE

Candomble is a syncretistic Brazilian folk religion that draws upon both African and Christian religious figures, rites and symbolism. It is practiced primarily by the poor and disadvantaged, but in recent years has begun to attract more middle-class followers. Spirit possession by gods of both genders is fundamental to Candomble and many mediums are homosexual or transgendered men. Given Brazil's widespread machismo governing male behaviour, acting as the mediums through which supplicants communicate with the gods is an important way in which homosexual and effeminate men can gain status and acceptance within the community.

MARK McLELLAND

CAPE TOWN

Africa's 'gay capital', Cape Town is known for its spectacular beaches and mountains and possesses an urban ambience that recalls a Mediterranean *dolce vita*. It also has some of the most liberal anti-discrimination laws in the world, earning it an international reputation as a gay-friendly destination, something which city, and even some

church, officials have actively cultivated. A brutal massacre of eight men at a gay massage parlour in January 2003 led to fears of a homophobic backlash but was later found to be a 'normal' organized criminal protection racket.

MARC EPPRECHT

CAPOTE, TRUMAN

b. 1924; d. 1984

writer

Born in New Orleans, Truman Capote's most famous works include: *Other Voices, Other Rooms* (1948), *The Grass Harp* (1951), the novella *Breakfast at Tiffany's* (published 1958, filmed in 1961) and *In Cold Blood* (1966), his six-year-long study of the Clutter family murder case in Kansas. In public he was waspishly gay and outrageous. He offended and insulted people, and remarked that Jack Kerouac's work 'isn't writing at all; it's typing'. A social climber and a back stabber, his behaviour was frequently considered offensive by the friends he cultivated in American high society, but this belied his deep sensitivity as a writer and his commitment to investigating the lives of those who existed on the fringes of the mainstream world. His literary reputation was further enhanced with the posthumous publication in 1987 of his unfinished novel *Answered Prayers*.

MICHAEL PINFOLD

CARLOMUSTO, JEAN

b. 1959

filmmaker

New York-based video artist and media activist whose work combines documentary, experimental and dramatic techniques. In *Doctors, Liars and Women: AIDS Activists Say No to Cosmo* (1988), she and co-director Maria Maggenti profiled the protest by the Women's Committee of

ACT UP against *Cosmopolitan* magazine for publishing an article containing misleading information on the potential risks of heterosexual sex for women. With colleague Gregg **Bordowitz**, she produced the *Living with AIDS* documentary series for the **Gay Men's Health Crisis (GMHC)**, and courted controversy for the programme *Healthcare Not Welfare* (1991), in which AIDS activists criticized the Gulf War and advocated improved public healthcare. Her documentaries include *L Is for the Way You Look* (1991), a playful exploration of lesbian history and role models including Martina Navratilova, Madonna and Simone de Beauvoir, and *To Catch a Glimpse*, an experimental exploration of her family history.

JOHN FORDE

CAROW, HEINER

b. 1929; d. 1997

filmmaker

German filmmaker Heiner Carow is best known for two films made in the German Democratic Republic (GDR). One, *The Legend of Paul and Paula* (1973), is the story of the torrid affair between two disaffected young people in East Berlin. The fantastical, almost surreal elements in the film brought disapproval from the authorities, but made it the most popular film ever in the GDR. The other, *Coming Out* (1989), was East Germany's first and only gay-themed film. The film concerns a young teacher who becomes almost simultaneously involved in two love affairs, one with a female colleague, the other with a young gay man. Carow's ambivalence about his homosexuality is played out in the context of anti-gay violence in East Berlin, as well as racism and other forms of intolerance. It had its premiere on 9 October 1989, the night that the Berlin Wall fell. Carow used the occasion of the film to come out personally.

DANIEL HENDRICKSON

CARROUSEL DE PARIS, LE

Le Carrousel de Paris is a transgender and transsexual cabaret and revue which has been performing in Paris for over 40 years. During the late 1950s the revue provided a platform from which transsexual stars such as Bambi, Capucine and Coccinelle broke into the mainstream, appearing in numerous avant-garde films and becoming international socialites. Le Carrousel also had an important impact upon transgender performance worldwide, especially in Japan where their 1963 tour provided inspiration for local transgender talent.

MARK MCLELLAND

CARRY ON

film series

A British film series of sex farces, produced by writer Talbot Rothwell and director Gerald Thomas, which gained huge popularity for their sexually suggestive humour and slapstick scenarios. The first films in the series, *Carry On Sergeant* (1958), *Carry On Nurse* and *Carry On Teacher* (1959) were box-office successes, and were followed by similarly titled and themed films over the next 20 years. Series regulars included Barbara Windsor (usually playing a buxom sexpot) and Kenneth **Williams**, whose effeminacy and caustic sarcasm became one of the most recognizable depictions of homosexuality in 1960s and 1970s Britain. The series had fallen from favour by the late 1970s, with feminists and gay rights activists accusing the filmmakers of sexist and homophobic stereotyping. A recent attempt to revive the genre, *Carry On Columbus* (1992), starring Julian **Clary** as a Williamsesque character, was a critical and box-office failure.

JOHN FORDE

CARTER, ANGELA

b. 1940; d. 1992

writer

Born in Eastbourne (UK), Angela Olive Carter was the most subversive, empowering literary figure of her generation, acknowledged as such by the establishment she threatened, along and the growing popularity of the feminist and postmodernist theory she promoted. A writer and journalist, authoring novels, essays, poetry, a film script, short stories and radio plays, she produced a iconoclastic mythography, debunking the classic and contemporary myths that enforce subordination. Her surreal, witty and fantastic writing merges high and pop culture, folklore and formula fiction, and stages the intertwining of language and power, assailing both as it liberates the irrational forces of the neo-Gothic and subverts the enlightenment ideas of patriarchal Order and Nature. Carter's magic realism supported the insurgence of a constructionist feminist, lesbian and queer criticism. The protagonist of *The Passion of New Eve* (1977), for instance, travels through an apocalyptic America devastated by a culture war, undergoes a sex change and runs after his/her silver screen idol (who turns out to be a drag queen). Such picaresque journeys and the erosion of identity, typical of Carter's writing, plunge the reader into a chaos that holds the promise of liberation from patriarchy, prefiguring new modes of sexuality identity. She died in London in 1992.

FABIO CLETO

CARTER, CHRIS

b. 1952

politician

After his election as Member of Parliament (MP) for the Te Atutu electorate in 1993, Chris Carter became the first openly gay MP in New Zealand. Following his election for the social democratic New Zealand Labour Party, Carter publicly announced that he was gay. In coming out, Carter hoped to provide a positive role model for young gay men and lesbians, and to encourage acceptance of homosexuality. Carter lost his seat in the 1996 election, but his presence in Parliament opened the way for the election of two more out MPs: gay-identified Tim Barnett and transsexual Georgina **Beyer**. Prior to the 1999 election, Carter was instrumental in the formation of Rainbow Labour, the gay, lesbian and transgender branch of the Labour Party. In 1999 Carter was re-elected and in 2002 he was voted into the Cabinet by the Labour Party Caucus, becoming New Zealand's first openly gay Cabinet Minister.

GERALDINE TREACHER

CASTILLO, ANA

b. 1953

writer

Born, raised and schooled in Chicago, Ana Castillo has become one of the most prolific and renowned Chicana writers. She is a poet, novelist, short-story writer, essayist, artist and self-described Xicanista – a term she created to describe Mestiza women in the United States. Her landmark novel, *The Mixquiahuala Letters* (1986), won the American Book Award from the Before Columbus Foundation and established her as one of the leading Chicana feminist writers. This epistolary novel explores the relationship between two women on a journey to Mexico. In the novel, as in many of her works, Castillo candidly explores Chicana sexuality. Her novel *So Far from God* (1993) has become a staple in many Chicana/o literature courses both in the US and abroad. It is a prime example of the way Castillo creates a female homosocial environment where close bonds of survival are formed between women in a patriarchal society in which they often face male violence.

See also: Chicana/o and Latina/o literature

DANIEL ENRIQUE PÉREZ

CASTLE, TERRY

b. 1953

academic

An American literary and cultural critic, Terry Castle teaches at Stanford University, specializing in eighteenth-century literature and popular culture. She caused controversy in 1995 with her publication of 'Was Jane Austen Gay?' in the *London Review of Books*. This analysed the homoerotic passion evident in letters written between Jane and her sister Cassandra and also showed how the marriages in Austen's novels bring about closeness between the heroine and hero's sister rather than the heterosexual couple. Although never stating that Austen was lesbian, Castle's essay was seen by the Jane Austen Society as a slur. The subsequent homophobic press attacks ignored the subtleties of Castle's arguments and ironically proved Castle's contention, outlined in *The Apparitional Lesbian* (1993), that 'lesbian' is a sign displayed in Western culture in order to be obliterated. Her latest work, *The Literature of Lesbianism* (2003), is an edited anthology of historical writings.

WREN SIDHE

CATHOLICISM

See: Pope, the and Catholicism

CAVANI, LILIANA

b. 1933

filmmaker

Italian filmmaker whose frank depictions of perverse sexuality and power plays within sexual relationships have won her notoriety and praise in equal measure. Born on 12 January 1933 in Carpi, she graduated from the Centro Sperimentale di Cinematografia in Rome, going on to make films and documentaries for RAI, Italy's national TV network. After the success of her first feature film, *Francesco D'Assisi* (1966), she moved into more controversial territory. Her follow-up feature, a biography of Galileo published in 1968, incurred the wrath of the Vatican for its anti-church viewpoint. She is best known for *The Night Porter* (1974), a disturbing portrait of a sadomasochistic love affair between a former Nazi commandant (played by Dirk **Bogarde**) and a woman he raped in a concentration camp. The film's apparent eroticizing of Nazi imagery and brutality shocked audiences, although some critics praised Cavani's insightful analysis of sadomasochism and fascism. Apparently unfazed by the criticism, Cavani explored similar themes in *Beyond Good and Evil* (1977), a biography of Nietzsche, and *Berlin Interior* (1978), a lesbian love story set in Nazi Germany. After several years directing opera, she returned to film with *Il gioco di Ripley* (2001), an adaptation of the Patricia **Highsmith** novel *Ripley's Game*.

JOHN FORDE

CAVEN, INGRID

b. 1938

actor, singer

This German actor and singer first studied psychology before going to Munich to study acting. After deciding to give up on the theatre, she began studies to be a teacher. It was at this time that she met Rainer Werner **Fassbinder** and Peer Raben at their Action Theater. She soon became involved with the group and abandoned the idea of teaching. She was married to Fassbinder between 1970 and 1972. She appeared in several of his films, as well as films by Daniel **Schmid**, Jean Eustache, Werner **Schroeter** and Lothar Lambert. In 1978 she became a successful chanteuse, and very often sang songs with texts by the French writer Jean-Jacques Schuhl set to music by her old friend Raben. In 2000 Schuhl published an experimental novel called *Ingrid Caven*, based on incidents from her life. Caven has lived in Paris since 1977.

DANIEL HENDRICKSON

CAZUZA

b. 1958; d. 1990

singer, composer

After a short trip to San Francisco in 1979, purportedly to study photography, the Brazilian-born Cazuza began doing theatre work in his native Rio de Janeiro. It was at this time that he started developing his career as a musician, first as the lead singer of the rock group Barão Vermelho, and then solo. In 1987, when his solo career was securely established, he learned he was **HIV +**. The following year he spoke to the press about his status, as well as his bisexuality, becoming the first major Brazilian public figure to come out as a person with **AIDS**. He continued his by then very successful music career as much as his health would allow, giving concerts until very late in his life. He took several trips to the United States for treatment, but finally died in Rio in 1990.

DANIEL HENDRICKSON

CELEBRITY CULTURE

When Rudolf Valentino died in 1926, so the story goes, mass hysteria ensued and some distraught female fans even committed suicide. Valentino's phenomenal stardom was created and controlled by the studio system: to be a star was to reach the apex of fame. By the 1970s stars were no longer contracted to studios at fixed rates

and fame had become a more plastic commodity, acquired even by those who might have played secondary roles in national headlines. In 1996 Kato Kaelin, O.J. Simpson's 'houseguest' and a witness in the famous murder trial, was on the cover of *Playgirl*. The star has given way to the celebrity, and celebrities often emerge as accidental by-products of media events. The explosion in celebrity culture can be attributed in part to the Internet, which allows for web sites devoted to the most fleeting public personalities. But celebrity culture is now also inextricably linked to consumption, fashion and product placement, as evident in the popularity of magazines such as *In Style* which teach readers how to dress, eat and shop like their favourite celebrities. Today, the Italian Monica Bellucci is occasionally seen in films but her work as an actor is outshone by her appearances in advertisements as a paid spokesperson for Cartier and Dolce & Gabbana. Contemporary celebrity culture is a star system with logos attached.

Queer celebrity icons have been women such as Judy **Garland**, who struck a chord with gay 'subculture'. Her widely publicized history of alcoholism and depression and her role as Dorothy singing 'Over the Rainbow' in *The Wizard of Oz* provided metaphorical narratives of survival. Performers such as Bette **Midler** and **Madonna** have actively sought or appropriated their gay fan bases through their overt use of queer imagery and style. Queer icons who emerge *as* queer are still relatively rare: **Divine**, John Water's transvestite muse, and Quentin **Crisp** are among the few. This does not prove that celebrity culture is homophobic; instead, it exposes the complex link between the consumption of desire and consumerism, often coded as heterosexual. Both Greg **Louganis**, the gay Olympic diver, and Martina **Navratilova**, the tennis player, came out relatively late in their careers, and they have never been as prominent commercial spokespersons as their heterosexual peers. With the waning of the AIDS activist movement and the mainstreaming of queer culture, queer identity and celebrity have become intensely commodified. The TV programme *Queer Eye For The Straight Guy* features five flamboyantly gay men (now celebrities in their own right) who coach straight men in the rituals of consumerism, coded as crash courses in interior decoration, personal style and the ambiguous entity 'culture'. A spin-off, *Queer Eye For The Straight Girl*, features a heterosexual woman being made over by a team of gay men and a lesbian. As gays and lesbians in the mainstream increasingly seek social and cultural legitimation through same-sex marriage, it is inevitable that queer celebrities should refashion themselves as models of respectability whose wholesale consumption of goods and lifestyles fosters expectations of what a queer should look like: apolitical, hip, affluent, cosmopolitan and able to coordinate colours with impeccable taste.

YASMIN NAIR

CENTER FOR LESBIAN AND GAY STUDIES (CLAGS)

CLAGS was founded in April 1991 under the leadership of Martin Duberman, at the Graduate Center of the City University of New York. The establishment of the first research centre within a university devoted to glbt scholarship represented a major event in the gradual acceptance and institutionalization of glbt studies in the United States in the late 1980s and 1990s. The Center organizes public seminars, the Kessler Lecture Series, reading and discussion groups (some of which are held online) and conferences, has published collections of essays, and awards fellowships and prizes to academic and independent researchers. CLAGS has been genuinely interdisciplinary in orientation, hosting programmes in economics, biology and law, for example, as

well as history, theatre and media. The Center has consistently foregrounded advocacy and public policy and maintained a balance between approaches based in the humanities and social sciences. From its early years, CLAGS has devoted energy to promoting study of the cultural diversity of the manifestations of sexuality, explicitly including the study of sexism, racism and classism in its mission, and the Center is working to develop an International Research Network linking researchers of glbt issues across the world. Transgender studies have become a more consistent focus under Executive Director Paisley Currah. This office has also been held by Jill Dolan and Alisa Solomon. The Board of Directors is diverse by many criteria and includes a number of community and cultural activists as well as full-time university faculty.

TREVOR HOPE

CHABLIS, LADY

b. 1957

cabaret performer

An African-American, transsexual cabaret performer, Lady Chablis became a national celebrity as the star of *Midnight in the Garden of Good and Evil* (1997), gay author John Berendt's non-fiction best seller about a Savannah murder trial. In Berendt's book, Chablis (real name Benjamin Knox) becomes the author's guide to Savannah's social underworld, revealing the town's hidden hypocrisies and vibrant homosexual subculture. In the book's comic centrepiece, Chablis gatecrashes an invitation-only black debutante ball, passing successfully as a woman, and wittily ridicules African-American social pretensions. Chablis scored a further coup by convincing director Clint Eastwood to let her play herself in the 1997 movie adaptation, opposite John Cusack and Kevin Spacey. Although the film was a commercial and critical flop, Chablis' performance was widely praised. She continues to perform in Savannah. Her autobiography *Hiding My Candy* (a reference to her anatomical concealment technique) was published in 1996.

JOHN FORDE

CHAMBERLAIN, RICHARD

b. 1934

actor

A popular romantic lead actor, Richard Chamberlain rose to fame in the TV series *Dr Kildare* (1961–6), where his matinee idol good looks won him a devoted female fan base. His status as 'King of the Mini-Series' was confirmed with romantic leading roles in *Three Musketeers* (1973), *Lady Caroline Lamb* (1973) and *Casanova* (1987). He is best known for *The Thorn Birds* (1983), a TV adaptation of Colleen McCullough's controversial novel, in which he plays an Australian priest who has a lifelong affair and a child with a woman. His film work includes playing gay composer Tchaikovsky in Ken Russell's *The Music Lovers* (1971) and *The Bourne Identity* (1988). In 1992 Chamberlain admitted his homosexuality in an interview with French magazine *Nous Deux*, but the confession was subsequently denied by his American manager. In his 2003 memoir *Shattered Love* he finally acknowledged that he was gay and in a long-term relationship with director Martin Rabbett.

JOHN FORDE

CHANNING, CAROL

b. 1923

actor

American musical theatre performer, Carol Channing, is celebrated for her flamboyant, zany persona and brash singing style. Dropping out of college to pursue an acting career, Channing worked throughout the

1940s on the New York musical revue circuit where she honed her distinctive stage image as the ditzy, wide-eyed blonde with a huge, mega-watt personality and a raspy, belting voice to match. It was an image that found its perfect complement in Channing's breakthrough role as Lorelei in the 1949 Broadway hit *Gentlemen Prefer Blondes*. Fourteen years later, in 1963, Channing got her second defining role as the eponymous star of *Hello, Dolly!*, which she repeated in numerous revivals through into the 1990s. Her larger-than-life character and excessively theatrical style effectively denied Channing the opportunity to reprise either role in the film versions of these shows, but it is arguably what has attracted and sustained much of her strong gay following.

BRETT FARMER

CHENEY, MARY

b. 1969

activist

The openly lesbian daughter of Republican politician and Vice-President Dick Cheney, Mary Cheney is one of America's most high-profile figures in conservative politics. After graduating from university, Cheney worked as a gay community liaison officer for Coors Brewing Company, where she was instrumental in ending a 20-year boycott of the company's products by the gay community. In 2004 she worked with her father on the George W. Bush presidential re-election campaign and served on the advisory board of the Republican Unity Coalition, a gay–straight Republican Party alliance aiming to promote party tolerance towards gays and lesbians. In 2004 Cheney became the target of several gay rights groups who urged her to speak out against the Bush administration's opposition to same-sex marriage. She continues to head her father's campaign team.

JOHN FORDE

CHENG, ANDREW YUSHU

b. 1967

filmmaker

Andrew Cheng is a Shanghai-based digital video maker whose directorial debut *Shanghai Panic* (2001) won him the Dragon and Tigers Award at the Vancouver International Film Festival. The docu-drama style film portrays young Shanghainese grappling with drugs, HIV and homosexuality. Cheng studied film production in Australia and returned to China in 1997 to found his own production company, directing spots for MTV-China. Cheng's second digital drama, *Destination Shanghai* (2003), is a Chinese version of Andy Warhol's *Heat*. The film comprises a series of theatrically staged scenes depicting encounters between members of Shanghai's sexual underworld. Formally and visually daring, Shanghai in *Destination Shanghai* is transformed into a psychedelic city of intense light and colour. The film won Cheng more international recognition, including the recommendation for the Rolex Mentor and Protégé Arts Program in which Cheng will make films under the direct guidance of renowned filmmakers such as Godard and Polanski.

CUI ZI'EN
YING ZHU

CHER

b. 1946

variety show hostess, singer, actor

Cher's career spans five decades. Initially known for her 1960s music and variety show with then husband Sonny Bono, Cher (born Cherilyn Sarkisian) became one of the most internationally recognized (and photographed) singer-actors of the 1970s and 1980s. When her film career stalled during the 1990s, Cher reinvented herself as a flamboyant club diva, endearing herself to North American and British gay male cultures and circuit parties. Her resilient and steely attitude are frequently commented on in popular glossy magazines, while her queer coronation was marked by camp appearances on *Will & Grace*. Cher is the mother of lesbian activist Chastity **Bono**. Her major film performances include *Mask* (1985), *Silkwood* (1983) and *Moonstruck* (1987, Best Actress Academy Award). Signature songs include 'Gypsies, Tramps, and Thieves', 'I Got You, Babe', 'If I Could Turn Back Time', 'Believe' and 'Song for the Lonely'.

TERRELL SCOTT HERRING

CHÉREAU, PATRICE

b. 1944

director

The self-styled 'enfant terrible' of French cinema, Patrice Chéreau made his name as a theatre director before making his first feature film in 1975. Openly gay and frequently controversial, his work showcases a gay aesthetic of baroque excess and an explicit, unsentimental take on sexual politics. He achieved international acclaim for *La Reine Margot* (Queen Margot, 1994), a lavish, violent and sexually explicit melodrama about the sixteenth-century French royal family. His most open exploration of gay sexuality, *Ceux qui m'aiment prendront le train* (*Those Who Love Me Can Take The Train*, 1998), followed a group of gay, transsexual and **HIV+** friends attending the funeral of a gay artist. Chéreau again raised controversy with *Intimité* (*Intimacy*, 2001), an adaptation of Hanif Kureishi's novella about a heterosexual love affair, which featured explicit, unsimulated sex scenes between the actors. *Son Frère* (*His Brother*, 2003) is an intense study of terminal illness, presumably inspired by AIDS.

JOHN FORDE

CHEUNG, LESLIE

b. 1956; d. 2003

actor

Asian cinema's answer to James Dean, Leslie Cheung's brooding charisma and sullen beauty rocketed him to international fame. He emerged as a Cantonese pop star in the 1980s and film success soon followed in *A Better Tomorrow* (*Yinghung boon sik*, 1986) and *He's a Woman, She's a Man* (*Gum gee yum yip*, 1994), a cross-dressing love story. He is best known to Western audiences for his work in *Farewell My Concubine* (*Ba wang bie ji*, Chen Kaige, 1993), where he played a gay Chinese opera singer whose life follows the same tragic path as his most famous cross-dressing stage role. In *Happy Together* (*Chun guang zha xie*, 1997), a gay love story set in Argentina, Cheung's sunglasses, unlit cigarettes and studied arrogant insouciance recalled Hollywood legends such as Dean. He lived an unorthodox personal life, publicly denouncing his father (a major break with Chinese family tradition), and never married, adding to speculation that he was gay. He committed suicide at age 46.

JOHN FORDE

CHICANA/O AND LATINA/O LITERATURE

Glbt subjects have been present in Chicana/o and US Latina/o literature since the genre emerged. In fact, a literary dialogue between Chicanos/Latinos and glbt members began in 1959 when José Antonio Villarreal wrote his landmark novel *Pocho*, where the Chicano protagonist befriends a gay Anglo man. But such dialogues during what is often considered the beginning of Chicana/o literature were highly limited and usually took place between heterosexual Chicanas/os-Latinas/os and gay Anglo men who were often classified as the 'other' or some perverse character who played minor roles in such texts. These dialogues eventually evolved into more complex ones that often included a figure not present in the early stages of Chicana/o and Latina/o literature, that of a Chicana/o and Latina/o protagonist with a distinct gay or lesbian identity. In fact, the queer presence in such texts has since shifted from including only a gay Anglo male in a minor role to including Chicano/Latino gay men and Chicana/Latina lesbians in leading roles.

In tracing the history of Chicano literature, *City of Night* (1963) by John **Rechy** would be the first novel with a gay Chicano leading character, making him the pioneer of gay Chicano writing. Moreover, this novel was only the third US novel to deal openly with a gay theme. However, although Rechy contributed to the establishment of a visible gay identity in the US in the 1960s, he was not acknowledged as a gay Chicano writer until much later, and this despite the phenomenal success of *City of Night*, perhaps the most successful Chicano novel ever. He was rejected in the Chicano literary canon until the late 1970s, when a long and slow process of incorporating him into the canon took place. In order for Rechy to create a discourse on queer Chicano sexuality, he had to remove his main character from the barrio. Even though his early protagonists had a Chicano identity, they occupied spaces outside Chicano culture where experimenting with their sexuality was possible. Homoerotic acts between the Chicano protagonists and other men were also typically limited to sexual encounters with Anglo men. Nevertheless, Rechy must be recognized for his attempt to create a discourse on male Chicano homoeroticism. The publication of *The Sexual Outlaw: A Documentary* (1977) places him at the forefront of a battle against normative sexual behaviour among men. Despite Rechy's continued success and publication of several gay novels, works by and about glbt Chicana/o and Latina/o subjects remained virtually invisible until the 1980s.

In the 1980s a new generation of Chicana/o and Latina/o writers emerged with a new queer voice. Chicana and Latina feminists fought to establish a presence in Chicano/Latino culture and in the Anglo-dominant culture. Cherríe **Moraga**, Gloria **Anzaldúa** and others paved the road for a new discourse on sexuality and made a Chicana/Latina lesbian identity visible with their publication of *This Bridge Called My Back: Writings by Radical Women of Color* (1981). Although not explicitly a lesbian text or exclusively a Chicana/Latina text, it is a landmark anthology that opened the door for such readings. Then, in 1983, Moraga published *Lo que nunca pasó por sus labios* (*Loving in the War Years*), the first Chicana lesbian text in which a Chicana lesbian identity is the central theme.

Despite the presence of the two pioneers, Rechy and Moraga, gay Chicano/Latino and lesbian Chicana/Latina literature during the 1980s was still relatively scarce. Anzaldúa, Ana **Castillo**, Michael **Nava** and Rechy made some significant contributions to this discourse during the 1980s, and Juanita Ramos' *Compañeras* (*Latina Lesbians*, 1987) was also an important contribution. However, the relatively little amount that was created was typically not well received and often not even reviewed by critics. Nevertheless, a dialogue had begun, and Chicanas and Latinas insisted on maintaining an open discussion on female sexuality in general and female homoeroticism in particular. Some of these women made it clear that gay Chicano/Latino men had to be a part of a discourse on homoeroticism in Chicano/Latino culture.

The 1990s gave birth to a plethora of gay- and lesbian-centred texts, both creative and theoretical, especially during the latter half of the decade. For the first time in the history of Chicana/o and US Latina/o literature, both Chicana/Latina lesbians and Chicano/Latino gay men proliferated. Some of the most recognized creative writers were Francisco Alarcón, Emma Pérez, Castillo,

Nava and Rechy. Of the theoretical texts, Moraga's *The Last Generation* (1993), helped to establish the notion of **Queer Aztlán**, and Tomás Almaguer's 'Chicano Men: A Cartography of Homosexual Identity and Behaviour' contributed significantly to a discourse on homoeroticism and Chicano/Latino men. The publication of Jaime Manrique's *Eminent Maricones: Arenas, Lorca, Puig, and Me* (1999) and anthologies such as *Chicana Lesbians: The Girls Our Mothers Warned Us About* (1991), *Bésame Mucho: New Gay Latino Fiction* (1999) and *Virgins, Guerrillas and Locas* (1999) solidified the visibility of glbt Chicana/o and Latina/o writers.

DANIEL ENRIQUE PÉREZ

Further reading

Foster, D.W. (ed.) (1999) *Chicano/Latino Homoerotic Identities*, New York: Garland Publishing. (This anthology includes an essay by Manuel de Jesús Hernández-G. on US Latina/o glbt cultural production.)

CHINA, FILMMAKING

A taboo topic only a few decades ago, homosexuality has become the subject of several important films made not only in Hong Kong and Taiwan, but also in the People's Republic itself. Many of these films are the work of queer filmmakers, but several important examples come from filmmakers who do not identify as queer but who use the figure of the gay man or lesbian as a vehicle not only for registering changing notions of gender and sexuality but for investigating the status of subjectivity and the place of the individual in the contemporary world.

Before the rise of China's Fifth Generation of filmmakers, and the Taiwanese and Hong Kong new waves, all of which emerged during the 1980s, there were no overt depictions of homosexuality in Chinese cinema. However, one of the ways in which pre-revolutionary Chinese cinema explored the modernizing of the nation was by noting changes in traditional gender roles. Sun Yu's *The Highway* (aka *The Big Road*, 1934) heralds the building of a paved highway through the countryside as a harbinger of modernity. The bodies of the men on the road crew are displayed as heroic, in keeping with the film's leftist message, centred on the strength and power of workers and peasants working collectively. Seen today, the film's emphasis on the workers' bodies and musculature can easily seem homoerotic. (Further, the film's two female leads seem as interested in each other as they are in any of their male comrades.) In his documentary *Yang and Yin: Gender in Chinese Cinema* (1996), contemporary Hong Kong filmmaker Stanley **Kwan** finds a homoerotic undercurrent in the physically intimate and emotionally intense male bonding in Wu Yonggang's *Waves Wash the Sand* (1936), an allegorical tale of a banker and a convict shipwrecked on an island while handcuffed to each other.

This intense male bonding found its female counterpart decades later in Xie Jin's melodrama *Two Stage Sisters* (1965), about two opera actresses. Raised together since girlhood, the two title characters are not blood siblings but are inseparable, until circumstances intervene – notably pre-Revolutionary bourgeois decadence. In the wake of the Cultural Revolution, mainland Chinese cinema often used melodrama and its female protagonists to explore the subordination of the individual to the demands of the nation and its economic and social progress.

During the 1980s the filmmakers of the Fifth Generation renovated Chinese cinema by re-examining the status of the individual. For Chen Kaige, the most famous member of this group of filmmakers, this reassertion took the form of a re-examination of Chinese masculinity, beginning with Chen's first film, *Yellow Earth* (1984), about a soldier stationed in a rural town in 1939. Chen's second film, *The Big Parade* (1985), continued this project by taking place in the all-male world of an army squad in training. The tenderness expressed among the soldiers revisits the thematics of intense male bonding seen in earlier eras of Chinese filmmaking and serves to render poignant their submission to regimentation.

Chen expanded his versions of masculinity with *Farewell My Concubine* (*Ba wang bie ji*, 1993). The film tells the epic story of a young man, Dieyi (played by Hong Kong star Leslie **Cheung**), trained as an opera singer specializing in female roles, and his passionate friendship with a fellow performer from the time they bond as boys at an academy for opera performers through turbulent decades of Japanese occupation, war and revolution, until their reunion in 1977. While the film was internationally acclaimed, its portrayal of homosexuality was controversial. On the one hand, such subject matter was (and still is) considered taboo by mainland Chinese censors; the film was funded by a Taiwanese producer. On the other hand, Chen countered that Dieyi was not a homosexual but a victim of his training and his times, and that his affection for his co-star was brotherly affection confused by Dieyi's own gender confusion. It was precisely this reading of the film that in turn caused many queer commentators to label the film homophobic, with its suggestion that Dieyi's sexual ambiguity stems not from within but is imposed upon him by his training and by a series of seductions and/or rapes, including an encounter with a decadent, opium-smoking homosexual. Ultimately, the combination of the film's success and its controversy helped to make homosexuality an important topic for Chinese cinema.

This topic was next taken up in 1996 by prominent filmmaker Zhang Yuan, whose *East Palace, West Palace* (*Dong gong xi gong*) concerns a gay writer, A-Lan, who is arrested for cruising in a Beijing park and then spends a long night in the park's pavilion being interrogated by a badgering policeman, Xiao Shi. In the course of the interrogation, A-Lan makes clear his attraction to the policeman, who is alternately fascinated and repelled by A-Lan's homosexuality, his confession of his attraction, his attempt to seduce his interrogator and his seemingly passive acceptance of his submission to, and humiliation by, the law. In its perversion and decadence, A-Lan's desire seems to represent the masochistic relationship between the citizen and the state in the years after the Tiananmen Square massacre. At the same time, the seductive and unsettling effect of A-Lan's masochism may suggest a subversive side to this kind of perverse subjectivity. With its vivid colour and elaborately formal framing and camera movement, the film's hermetic visual style – combined with the fact that the film was almost entirely shot on studio sets – enhances the film's sense of allegory. As with Chen and *Farewell My Concubine*, Zhang was only able to make *East Palace, West Palace* with the assistance of a foreign producer (in this case French). Although homosexuality has never been illegal in China, it remains enough of a taboo that any film about queer sexuality will most likely not receive any monetary support from any of the government-funded or -subsidized studios or production companies.

However, as the 1990s progressed, the Chinese film industry underwent a restructuring, as government funding decreased, making room for a wave of small independent films, often slice-of-life stories registering changing conditions in Chinese society. This wave included Li Yu's *Fish and Elephant* (*Jinnian Xiatian*, Yu Li, 2001). Often labelled 'China's first lesbian film', *Fish and Elephant* uses non-professional actors: specifically, a lesbian couple who play a pair of lesbians in the film. A more eccentric example of this wave of independent filmmaking is Liu Bongjian's *Men and Women*

(aka *Man Man Woman Woman*, 1999). *Men and Women* employs an offbeat mixture of realism, with its narrative of a young man from the countryside who arrives in Beijing and ends up coming out of the closet, and satiric fantasy, with its parallel episodes detailing the antics of a group of queer activists who employ fanciful guerrilla tactics.

The film was written by Cui **Zi'en**, a well-known figure in the Beijing queer scene. In 2001 Cui organized Beijing's first gay film festival, which included the first People's Republic of China screening of *East Palace, West Palace* before the event was shut down by the authorities. (The second such festival, again involving Cui Zi'en, took place in April 2005 and was forced to change venue at the last minute, when Beijing University withdrew its permission for the festival.) Cui has gone on to make his own films on digital video (DV), as the spread of such new technologies has further broadened China's independent film movement. In the last few years, Cui has become one of China's most prolific and innovative filmmakers, making both features (*The Old Testament*, 2001; *Feeding Boys, Ayaya*, 2003) and shorts.

Another important queer member of China's DV movement is Shanghai-based Andrew Cheng (*Shanghai Panic*, 2001; *Welcome to Destination Shanghai*, 2003). With his recourse to extravagant narrative events that mix melodrama with science fiction or religious allegory, Cui Zi'en cultivates an aesthetic of excess, even while retaining a minimalist simplicity in his visual style. Cheng, in contrast, keeps his films firmly rooted in reality, while imbuing them with the ellipticality typical of the contemporary 'art film', particularly of the punk and DIY variety.

A brief consideration of the 2001 film *Lan Yu* can serve as a conclusion. The film is a hybrid, representative in some ways of the history of Chinese queer cinema to date, while at the same time it suggests possible directions for the future. Directed by the aforementioned Hong Kong film-maker, Stanley Kwan, *Lan Yu* is based on a novel published anonymously on the Internet. It tells the story of an architecture student (the title character), fresh from the country, who resorts to sleeping with a somewhat older, jaded entrepreneur in order to make some money. To the surprise of both men, they fall in love, although their relationship is tested not so much by official repression but by the anything-for-a-buck ethos of the entrepreneur (played by actor Hu Jun, who played the policeman in *East Palace, West Palace*). The film itself is a Hong Kong–China co-production, produced by a mainlander and shot using a mainland cast and crew. Footage shot surreptitiously on video in Beijing was sent to Hong Kong for editing and the finished cut was transferred to film for distribution.

While a queer cinema of, and by, gay men has begun to develop in China, lesbian representations are harder to find, aside from *Fish and Elephant* (and a couple of lesbian characters in *Shanghai Panic*). However, the ever-increasing number of new filmmakers in China now includes women, and one imagines that it is only a matter of time before the emergence of lesbian film and video occurs.

See also: Hong Kong, filmmaking; Taiwan, filmmaking

Further reading

Berry, Chris (1996) 'Sexual DisOrientations: Homosexual Rights, East Asian Films, and Postmodern Postnationalism', in Xiaobing Tang and Stephen Snyder (eds) *In Pursuit of Contemporary East Asian Culture*, Colorado: Westview Press, pp. 157–82.
—— (1998) '*East Palace, West Palace*: Staging Gay Life in China', *Jump Cut* 42: 84–9.
—— (2004) 'The Sacred, the Profane, and the Domestic: Locating the Cinema of Cui Zi'en', *Positions* 12, 1: 195–202.
Reynaud, Bérénice (1999) *Nouvelles Chines, nouveaux cinémas*, Paris, *Cahiers du cinéma*.

DAVID PENDLETON

CHINA, *TONGZHI* LITERATURE

Drawing upon the idea of the kindred spirit, Chinese gay activists have appropriated the term *tongzhi* (comrade) to refer to same-sex lovers, deftly highjacking the class-based narrative and changing it to a gender-based one. A collection of novellas and short stories exploring *tongzhi* relationship debuted in February 1997 in Hong Kong, featuring works from Hong Kong, Taiwan and mainland China. The anthology, *The Same Sex Love Stories* (*Tata tata de gushi*, 1997) brought *tongzhi* writers in the People's Republic of China (PRC) out of the closet for the first time. In May 1997 the PRC's first contemporary queer novel, *The Peach Colored Lips* (*Taoshe zhuichun*), by Cui **Zi'en** debuted in Hong Kong to critical and popular acclaim. Cui's manuscript was rejected by more than 20 mainland publishers. The only mainland literary magazine that dared to publish his groundbreaking work was *Mongyuan*, which selectively published excerpts of the novel in 1999 under the special section titled 'Cui Zi'en's Literary Work'. Cui fastidiously called the excerpt 'the virgin edition (*Jieben*)'. Another gay writer, Tong Ge, saw his gay-themed novel, *Good Man Gelu* (*Haonan Gelu*), appear in Hong Kong the same year and become a popular hit in the local gay community.

The first novel published in the PRC that touched on, albeit in passing, the theme of homosexuality was Su Tong's *Broken Tile* (*Shuiwa*, 1997). Soon after, Wang Xiaobo's collection of plays and novellas *Forever* (*Dijiu Tianchang*, 1998) appeared, with a short story 'Tender Feelings' (*Shishui louqing*) leading the charge in foregrounding the subject of homosexuality. A film based on the same story, *East Palace, West Palace* (*Dong gong xi gong*, Zhang Yuan, 1996) became China's first gay film. The first PRC-published *tongzhi* novels covering sexual and gender 'transgression' in all variations are Cui Zi'en's *Enter the*

Clowns (*Choujiao dengchang*, 1998) and *The Rose Bed* (*Meigui chuangta*, 1998). Droll yet poignant, *Enter the Clowns* contemplates, philosophically and allegorically, the relationship between gender and sexuality, as transsexuality challenges sexual identity and same-sex partnership challenges the traditional notion of the domestic sphere. *The Rose Bed* was aggressively experimental in its narrative structure, attracting attention from Chinese literary circles.

In 1999 came a debut novel explicitly depicting Chinese female same-sex relations, *The Loving Days* (*Miqing de rizhi*, written by the female writer Ge Zhi). It is worth noting that lesbianism emerged as a literary trope in PRC after the mid-1990s, amidst the increased commodification of female gender and sexuality in the mass media in which erotic feelings and sexual 'transgressions' between women were granted visibility in the broader public consciousness. Considered by voyeuristic male readers and critics as, at its worst, self-indulgent and socially irresponsible, yet at its best charming and erotic, the newly emerged subgenre comprises autobiographical and semi-autobiographical works by women writers that articulate the fear of and longing for sisterhood and lesbian relationships. Chen Ran's *Breaking Open* (*Pokai*, 1995), for one, grapples with the question of constructing a social space for female companionship in an urban environment. Yet it was not until the publication of Ge Zhi's *The Loving Days* (1999), that the subject of sex between women received sustained exploration. Another major work exploring intimate relationships between women is Zhang Haoying's *The Bygone Days of Shanghai* (*Shanghai wangshi*, 2003). Initially appearing on the Internet as an online serial novel, the story charts the tale of a fatal encounter between two women who must face the threat of death. The lesbian subgenre enjoys popularity among a diverse spectrum of readers.

With 'comrade' literature continuing to gain momentum in the PRC, the ideolo-gically non-conformative and commercially more adventurous Pearl River Press in southern China launched Cui Zi'en's 'Peach Colored Novel series' in 2003, officially endorsing *tongzhi* literature. The series includes *The Peach Colored Lips* (*Taoshi zhuichun*), debuted in Hong Kong years earlier.

CUI ZI'EN
YING ZHU

CHINESE TONGZHI CONFERENCE

First held in 1996 in Hong Kong, the Chinese Tongzhi Conference was organized by a number of Chinese lesbians, gays, bisexuals and transgendered activists (called *tongzhi*, or 'comrades', for short). The aim of the Conference was to provide an opportunity for Chinese *tongzhi* from around the world to meet up and share their experiences and reflect upon *tongzhi*-related issues in the Chinese context in order to build up a worldwide network of Chinese *tongzhi*.

Issues that are discussed frequently include: coming out; lesbian and bisexual identities; *tongzhi* culture, media and the arts; social services; human rights; AIDS; the institutions of marriage and the family; racism; and religion. Particular attention is paid to identity politics and to questioning the applicability of the model of the les–bi–gay liberation movement in Anglo-Saxon societies to the Chinese *tongzhi* movement.

The manifesto of the Chinese Tongzhi Conference is a clear statement of their beliefs:

(1) same-sex love has always existed;
(2) same-sex lovers are discriminated against;
(3) traditional Chinese society was tolerant towards same-sex love;
(4) hostility and violence against homosexuality is not found in traditional Chinese culture;
(5) increased exchanges among *tongzhi* in Chinese societies are beneficial;

147

(6) the confrontational politics of the West should not be imposed upon Chinese societies;

(7) we should respect each other regardless of sexual orientation.

The Conference has been held four times to date: in 1996 (Hong Kong), 1998 (Hong Kong), 1999 (Hong Kong) and 2001 (Taiwan). Each time an average of 200 participants attended the three-night–four-day conference.

TRAVIS KONG

CHINESE UNDERGROUND FILMMAKING

Chinese underground filmmaking emerged in the early 1990s with a group of new film school graduates circumventing official channels in their effort to obtain overseas financing and distribution. This was a means of survival because the new mavericks' cinematic practice had been relegated to the margins both ideologically and financially. Specifically, the hegemonic official apparatus continued to squash alternative voices while the newly decentralized film market looked to established filmmakers for commercial viability. All these factors left the new brigade with no option but to seek alternative means of capital and distribution. Paradoxically, their international recognition often hinged upon their status as being on the verge of illegality by either dodging or courting censorship. Indeed, an official stamp of sanction proved valuable in ensuring international attention. However, international acknowledgement could only go so far in providing basics and the late 1990s subsequently began to witness the 'surfacing' of many filmmakers previously working 'under ground'. Zhang Yuan, for one, sought government permission and financing to make *Seventeen Years* (1999) and has since opted to work within the system in order to have his films screened domestically.

As the deregulation and decentralization of the Chinese film industry deepens, new forms of collaboration between studios and the private sector in film financing and licensing have made it possible to produce independent films without challenging state regulations. This has granted a legitimate space for the production and distribution of films made by the independent sector. As an example, the ban on Jia Zhangke's film (*Unknown Pleasure*, 2002) was lifted in January 2004. Although never screened publicly in China, Jia's films have garnered many awards in international film circles and attracted much critical attention domestically. In a remarkable turn of events, the Film Bureau lifted the ban, to the delight of the director of the Youth Workshop at the Shanghai Studio, Ma Ning. Ma has been working with Jia closely for the past year to develop new projects geared towards a domestic market.

Notwithstanding their multifaceted approach towards filmmaking, the pioneering Chinese underground filmmakers shared one thing in common: by telling stories from their own perspective, such filmmakers were irreverent towards institutional regulations and defiant of ideological manipulation. The result was a group of films that explored an urban milieu inhabited by marginalized youth, where rock music became the language of expression and isolated apartments provided private spaces in which anguish and loss were savoured and mourned. Melancholy and moody, the early underground films captured vividly the anxiety felt by the filmmakers who found their own generation in the shadow of the established forerunners and hegemonic discourses. Stylistically, the early underground filmmakers attempted to forge either an experimental approach that favoured narrative fragmentation or a *cinéma-vérité* approach that foregrounded documentary-style realism. Experimental films such as *The Days* (Wang Xiaoshuai, 1993), an atmospheric drama about a deteriorating marriage, and *Falling in Love* (Li Xin, 1993), a Wong Kar-wai style elliptic contemplation on relationships, were more reflective of the so-called art cinema narration, which featured goal-bereft protagonists and employed an episodic structure that relied heavily on voice-over narration to piece together a fragmented narrative. Zhang Yuan's *Beijing Bastards* (1993), in contrast, was a semi-documentary film featuring China's famous rock stars. Jia Zhangke's *Rainclouds over Wushan* (1995) exposed the daily boredom of ordinary Chinese people and their sexual yearnings, at an excruciatingly deliberate pace and in a realistic manner.

As Zhang Yuan and Jia Zhangke are poised to co-operate with the regulators in a common fight for the market, new underground filmmakers have emerged in the early 2000s, promising to expand the critical horizon and sharpen the experimental edge of underground films. The recent wave of underground films includes a mix of documentary and features that explore provocative themes such as sexuality, economic disparities, the dismal condition of migrant workers, AIDS, prostitution, drug addiction, crime, and art itself. The new films have moved beyond the confines of the personal and the urban to focus on larger social issues that have fallen through the cracks of mainstream representation.

Stylistically, the new films continue to explore *cinéma-vérité* and avant-garde approaches to differentiate themselves from a commercial cinema. Shot in 16 mm, *Beijing Suburb* (Hu Ze, 2002) is a semi-documentary fiction film in which the protagonists, the residents of an artist's community in a suburb of Beijing, play themselves. The film draws a harrowing picture of the marginalization and harassment experienced by independent artists. The sexual frankness of the dialogue and the excessive nudity in Ying Weiwei's *The Box* (2002) utilized a *cinéma-vérité* style to its core. The uniqueness of *The Box* lies in its ground-breaking effort to

document the intimate relationship between two women. The broach of homosexuality as a cinematic topic can be traced to Zhang Yuan's *East Palace, West Palace* (1996), in which a park policeman entrusted by the authorities to arrest and interrogate sexual transgressors has a homosexual encounter with a subject of his interrogation.

With the subject of homosexuality remaining taboo, the most authentic development in Chinese underground film is that of queer cinema. The first Gay and Lesbian Film Festival was held in Beijing in 2001 but was quickly shut down. One of its organizers was the openly gay literary critic, novelist and screenwriter Cui **Zi'en**. Cui was the chief editor and writer of the column 'Underground Cinema in China' in *Music and Performance* published in Nanjing in 2000, anticipating the arrival of queer DV makers such as Andrew Chen (*Shanghai Panic*, 2001), Li **Yu** (*Fish and Elephant*, 2001), and Cui himself. Cui ventured into directing queer DVs in the early 2000s. Cui's uncompromisingly experimental approach and his flamboyant personality were responsible for putting queer cinema onto the map of Chinese film.

As Chinese underground filmmaking continues to evolve, low-cost digital technology has offered new freedom to filmmakers. Although less polished than its film counterpart, the low-cost circulation of DVDs (some of them illegal) provides better public access. Internet viewing further opens up an alternative screening space. Interestingly, the censor bans the distribution and screening of films without prior approval but not DVDs. So, as small amounts of capital have freed up and technology for filmmaking has become more accessible, young filmmakers have opted to make DVs, not for theatrical distribution but for alternative screening spaces such as privately owned DV salons and clubs.

See also: Kar-wai, Wong

149

Further reading

Shuqin Cui (2001) 'Working from the Margins: Urban Cinema and Independent Directors in Contemporary China' *Post Script* 20, 2/3 (Winter/Spring): 77–92.

Ying Zhu (2003) *Chinese Cinema during the Era of Reform: The Ingenuity of the System*, Westport: Praeger Books.

YING ZHU

CHO, MARGARET

b. 1968

comedian, actor

Korean-American comedian whose work deals frankly with her bisexuality and ethnicity. Cho was born on 5 December 1968 in San Francisco, California. She began performing stand-up comedy aged 16, winning a comedy contest and an opening gig for comedian Jerry Seinfeld. She moved to Los Angeles in the early 1990s to pursue her stand-up career and in 1994 won the American Comedy Award for Female Comedians. In the same year, she developed and starred in the CBS sitcom *All-American Girl*, billed as the first network comedy series about Asian-Americans. Cho's experiences on the short-lived project and her struggles with drug addiction formed the basis for her successful 1999 show 'I'm the One That I Want', which toured the US for two years and was developed into a TV film and best-selling book. Her other successful tours include 2001's 'Notorious C.H.O.' (also filmed), 2003's 'Revolution' and 2004's 'State of Emergency'. She has received awards from the Gay and Lesbian Alliance Against Defamation (GLAAD) and Lambda for her promotions of gay and lesbian rights. Her acting work includes the cult film by Gregg **Araki**, *The Doom Generation* (1995), *Face/Off* (1997) and a cameo on *Sex and the City*. She also scripted the film *Bam Bam and Celeste* (2005).

JOHN FORDE

CHOMONT, TOM

b. 1942

experimental filmmaker

A pioneer of erotic experimental cinema, Tom Chomont's exploration of explicit sexuality, especially sadomasochistic relationships, exposes the passionate intensity of forbidden loves. Chomont earned a graduate degree in Film Studies at Boston University from 1964–6, and in 1966 was in-house manager of the Film-Makers' Cinematheque. Chomont was awarded one of the earliest production grants from the New American Cinema in 1969. Further recognition came with an American Film Institute production grant for *Space Time Studies* (1977). His work was featured in one-person shows in 1975, 1984 and 2002 at the Museum of Modern Art in New York. Scott MacDonald also featured Chomont's work in 'A Critical Cinema'. He was given a retrospective (over 30 films and videos) by MIX: Lesbian and Gay Experimental Film Festival in 2002. His film titles include *Flames* (1965), *Jabbok* (1967), *Love Objects* (1971), *Razor Head* (1984) and *The Dog Diary* (1996). Canadian filmmaker Mike Hoolboom's portrait, *Tom* (2002), refers to Chomont as 'the ultimate outlaw'.

See also: Sadomasochism

M.M. SERRA

CHRYSTOS

b. 1946

poet, activist

Born in San Francisco to a Menominee Indian father and part-Lithuanian/part-French mother, self-described as an 'Urban Indian', Chrystos lives on Bainbridge Island (Washington) and has worked on land and treaty rights issues for various indigenous peoples. She has published four volumes of poetry that detail living with oppression, violence against women and children, racism, poverty and the continued colonization of first nations people's land and culture. She also writes lesbian erotic poetry. *In Her I Am* (1993) celebrates the pleasures of fierce **butch/femme** desire. Her work has appeared in many anthologies, notably the ground-breaking works *This Bridge Called My Back: Writings by Radical Women of Color* (1981) and *Living the Spirit: A Gay American Indian Anthology* (1988). 'Now we are rare and occasionally cherished as Eagles', Chrystos writes in *Dream On* (1991), '[but] Never forget America is our Hitler'.

JEAN BOBBY NOBLE

CIRCLE JERK

A male activity of group masturbation commonly performed either through self-excitation in the company of others or in participation with others; the bodies of the other participants form the physical circle.

MICHAEL PINFOLD

CITRON, MICHELLE

filmmaker

Feminist avant-garde filmmaker, best known for *Daughter Rite* (1979), a dramatic narrative shot in *cinéma-vérité* style about a 28-year-old woman, Maggie, and her difficult relationship with her mother. In still pictures and interviews with herself and her younger sister, Maggie relives her angry childhood and her anger against her mother, seen only in photographs and home movies. Citron's script was based on interviews she conducted with over 40 mothers and daughters. In her next film, *What You Take for Granted* (1984), Citron again created a dramatic narrative about six women working in male-dominated workforces, based on real-life interviews. The film portrays a lesbian relationship between two

of the women. Citron lectures in film production at Northwestern University, Illinois.

JOHN FORDE

CIVIL UNION

See: Same-sex marriage/civil union

CLARKE, SHIRLEY

b. 1919; d. 1997

filmmaker

Shirley Clarke, a central figure in experimental and independent American film, was born and lived in New York City. In *The Connection* (1961) and *The Cool World* (1963) she brought *cinéma-vérité* and documentary conventions to fictional films. This, together with a focus on outsiders, led to *Portrait of Jason* (1967), in which Jason Holiday, a black gay man, speaks directly to the camera. Clarke, who was heterosexual, gave Holiday space to describe his take on society and his hopes for the future, a prospect tempered by fantastic tales from his wide-ranging experiences as a small-time entertainer and hustler who also uses drugs.

GABRIEL GOMEZ

CLARY, JULIAN

b. 1959

comedian

British comedian and TV presenter Julian Clary is famous for his flamboyant costumes and camp, bitchy, sexual humour. He started on the London comedy circuit in drag cabaret as 'Gillian Pie-Face', but gained public attention with his later act, 'The Joan Collins Fan Club', dressed in leather and rubber fetishwear and accompanied by his pet and long-time co-star, Fanny the Wonderdog. He hosted game shows, *Sticky Moments* (1989), *All Rise For Julian Clary* (1996) and starred in the sitcom *Terry and*

Julian, following in the camp comedy tradition of Kenneth **Williams** and John **Inman** but, unlike his predecessors, he openly and unapologetically expressed his homosexuality. In 1993 he drew criticism after making a sexual joke about British politician Norman Lamont on national television; he subsequently left Britain for two years on a world tour. He has appeared in *Carry On Columbus* (1992), the game show *Prickly Heat* (2000) and frequently stars in Christmas pantomimes.

JOHN FORDE

CLIFF, MICHELLE

b. 1946

writer

Poet and writer whose work explores her lesbian and multicultural ethnic identity. Born in the then British colony of Jamaica on 2 November 1946, she was raised in a Caribbean neighbourhood in New York City, and lived between Jamaica and the United States. Her first book, a collection of prose poetry, *Claiming the Identity They Taught Me to Despise* (1980), explores the racial inequalities of colonial rule and the ambiguous advantages of being light-skinned in a racist society – a theme later developed in her novels *Abeng* (1984) and *No Telephone to Heaven* (1987). Her most recent novel, *Free Enterprise* (1993), is an historical drama based on John Brown's raid on Harper's Ferry. Other publications include *The Land of Look Behind: Prose and Poetry* (1985), *Bodies of Water* (1990) and *The Store of a Million Items: Stories* (1998).

JOHN FORDE

CLIFT, MONTGOMERY

b. 1920; d. 1966

actor

An American film actor noted for his good looks and introspective star persona, Montgomery Clift was a pioneering proponent of Method Acting who brought to the screen a new style of male star whose image was rooted in vulnerability and tenderness. An accomplished stage actor who made his Broadway debut at age 14, Clift was lured to Hollywood where he became an overnight sensation with his performance as a gently rebellious cowboy in *Red River* (1948). His popularity with audiences and critical status as an actor of great depth and sensitivity was consolidated further in films such as *The Heiress* (1949), *A Place in the Sun* (1951) and *From Here to Eternity* (1953). Off-screen, Clift's personal life was problematic. Plagued with anxieties, many allegedly pertaining to his queer sexuality, he spent the last few years of his life indulging in increasingly self-destructive behaviour, dying of a heart attack aged just 45.

BRETT FARMER

CLONES

Popular self-styling, prevalent in the 1980s for gay men, appropriating hypermasculine styles of dress, grooming and facial hair, sometimes as a parody of cultural machismo.

MICHAEL PINFOLD

CLOSET

A term used to describe a gay or lesbian person who keeps their sexuality hidden, usually to avoid discrimination or persecution from a homophobic society. Accordingly, the term 'coming out of the closet' refers to a person's public revelation about their homosexuality. Didier Eribon argues that it is possible to occupy closeted and uncloseted identities simultaneously, such as being out to friends but closeted in the workplace. The philosophy of the closet has been discussed by academics including Judith **Butler** and Eve Kosofsky **Sedgwick**. Institutional examples of the closet include the United States military's 'Don't Ask

Don't Tell' policy, under which gays and lesbians must conceal their sexuality if they are to retain their posts.

See also: Coming out

JOHN FORDE

CLUB CULTURE

Club culture refers to the cultural products – particularly music and fashion – and to the practices, rituals and the social and embodied experiences that have developed in relation to the physical spaces of nightclubs. Club culture occupies a central place in contemporary glbtq culture, in terms both of its global ubiquity and its significance to individuals and wider glbtq communities.

To understand the importance of glbtq club culture it is vital to appreciate the meaning of the word 'club', which suggests a degree of exclusivity of membership. Glbtq clubs are spaces that regulate entry and participation according to sexuality and/or gender identification. The policing of clubs by 'door whores' and bouncers, serves to create spaces in which ways of being and forms of intimacy are able to emerge away from the pressures of heteronormativity. Clubs are third spaces, neither home nor work, which are sites of recreation, pleasure and identity formation. Clubs that are either devoted exclusively, or which are positively welcoming, to gays, lesbians, bisexuals and transsexuals, are both psychically and socially important to those who often feel excluded, marginalized or invisible in the heteronormative public spaces of work and of recreation, and in conventional familial contexts. In the liminal space of the club, glbtq people experience a degree of freedom from heterosexual convention and from the acts of self-policing that structure everyday life. Clubs play a vital role for those seeking to explore same-sex desire and non-normative gender performance for the first time, as places in

which identifications with a glbtq community can develop. Clubs are also the site for the formation of sexual/love connections and for the making of friendships and acquaintanceships.

However, although glbtq clubs are by their very nature discriminating in terms of who is admitted, the boundaries between glbtq club culture and mainstream club culture have always been porous. Glbtq clubs serve as cultural trendsetters in music, fashion and drug consumption, pioneering new genres of music (disco, garage and house, most notably) and field-testing new drugs (Roseneil, 2002). The movement of new musical genres and new drugs from glbtq clubs to the mainstream takes place because such clubs tend always to retain a degree of openness, most welcoming heterosexual clubbers whose attitudes are sufficiently queer.

Glbtq club culture is overwhelmingly an urban phenomenon, with trends led by clubs in the global gay cities, particularly **New York**, Chicago, **London** and **Sydney**. Glbtq club culture has its roots in the gay speakeasies and jazz clubs of 1920s and 1930s New York (Buckland 2002). After the ending of prohibition, gay nightlife revolved around bars, which regularly suffered police harassment, until, in the post-**Stonewall**-era gay nightlife began to come out into the open. The first discotheques to become central to glbtq life in New York were The Loft, which was racially and sexually mixed, The Sanctuary and The Gallery, which opened in New York in the early 1970s and gave early prominence to disco music. The mid-1970s saw the establishment of Paradise Garage, a club predominantly frequented by black and Latino gay men. There, gay African-American DJ Larry Levan pioneered a style of music that gradually spread across the world, and which came to be called 'garage'. Characterized by a strong beat, with heavy percussion, and a soaring vocal lead, garage music often has a lyric celebrating pride, community and love. In 1977 DJ Frankie **Knuckles** established The Warehouse in Chicago, where he started experimenting with remixing tracks, adding percussion and producing a heavier, rhythmic style of music, with a repetitive 4/4 beat, between 120 and 140 bpm. This genre came to be known as house music, and by the mid-1990s it dominated club culture, both gay and mainstream, all over the world. In Britain a harder, faster variation of house music, influenced by Detroit techno, developed in the gay after-hours club Trade, which began in 1990 and which broke many of the DJs who came to dominate the international club scene, most notably Tony de Vit.

There is considerable diversity amongst glbtq clubs, both within one city and between cities and countries, in terms of the spaces that clubs occupy, the clientele they cater for (in terms of gender, sexuality, age, race/ethnicity, class and the degree of mixing of these categories) and the music played. But clubs everywhere are places which exist for socializing, dancing and the consumption of intoxicating stimulants (alcohol and drugs). The consumption of drugs has long been a widespread feature of glbtq club culture (see **Ecstasy**), and serves to heighten the experience of the music and the sociality of the club, to both relax and reduce inhibitions and to stimulate clubbers to dance and stay awake through the night.

The ethos of club culture is fundamentally participatory. While a DJ is a central figure in any club, and his or her skills in mixing records and engaging with, and responding to, the dance floor are key to the success of any club, club culture is *made* by clubbers on the dance floor. The energy, excitement and joy of the embodied, sensory experience of dancing in a club, and the passing, intense, transitory sociality of encounters with fellow clubbers constitutes the essence of club culture.

Bibliography

Buckland, F. (2002) *Impossible Dance: Club Culture and Queer World-Making*, Middletown: Wesleyan University Press.
Roseneil, S. (2002) 'The Heterosexual/ Homosexual Binary: Past, Present and Future', in D. Richardson and S. Seidman (eds) *The Lesbian and Gay Studies Handbook*, London: Sage, pp. 27–44.

Further reading

Amory, D.P. (1996) 'Club Q: Dancing with (a) Difference', in E. Lewin (ed.) *Inventing Lesbian Cultures in America*, Boston: Beacon Press.
Currid, B. (1995) '"We are Family": House Music and Queer Performativity', in Sue-Ellen Case, Philip Brett and Susan Leigh Foster (eds) *Cruising the Performative: Interventions into the Representation of Ethnicity, Nationality and Sexuality*, Bloomington and Indianapolis: Indiana University Press, pp. 165–96.
Rietveld, H. (1998) *This is our House: House Music, Cultural Spaces and Technologies*, Aldershot: Ashgate.

SASHA ROSENEIL

COACHING AND HOMOPHOBIA

Contemporary sports were largely founded in Western culture based, in part, on the early twentieth-century premise that sport served to prevent male youths from becoming effeminized or 'becoming' homosexual. Because coaches believed that sexuality was constructed by the presence of role models, and because homosexuality was equated with effeminacy, they maintained that degrading homosexuals engendered a more masculine male youth. Thus, **homophobia** has been embedded within sport since the beginning of organized play. Sport remains one of Western culture's most homophobic institutions because of the 'closed-loop system' in which coaches are obtained and trained. This closed-loop system occurs because of the highly competitive nature of athletics, which structurally limits those who can excel in a sport. Those who do (in addition to being naturally talented) must also adhere to the narrow worldviews of the athletic system and often develop identities around being an athlete. When their careers end, these athletes then have difficulty disengaging from sport and frequently seek coaching as a way to stay within the institution. Thus, coaches are obtained from a self-selected minority of athletes who are likely to remain committed to the values of their institution. Because most coaching positions require no formal education, coaches learn their trade by emulating other coaches and therefore tend to reproduce themselves. Without intervention from an outside agency, or formal education, there is little impetus to change the homophobic nature of sports.

ERIC ANDERSON

COCTEAU, JEAN

b. 1889; d. 1963

writer, artist, filmmaker

Born 5 July 1889 in Maisons-Lafitte, Yvelines, Île-de-France, Jean Cocteau was a prolific writer, critic, artist and filmmaker, Cocteau's unapologetic expression of his homosexuality inspired generations of gay artists. Born to a middle-class family, he ran away from private school to Marseilles, finding an alternative education in the bohemian world of cafés, theatres and salons. A talented writer and artist, he worked with Vaslav Nijinsky, Sergei Diaghilev, Pablo Picasso, Igor Stravinsky, Amedeo Modigliani, Eric Satie and André Gide. His novels *The Great Split* and *The Imposter* (1923) became classics of French postwar literature. His recurring themes – the magical power of childhood, the anarchic spirit of humanity and the pleasures of homosexual desire, featured in his novel *Children of the Game*, (*Les Enfants terribles* 1929, also a play and film), his journal *Opium* (1930) and *The White Paper* (1931). In 1937 he met actor Jean **Marais**, who became his lover, cinematic muse and the

star of films *La Belle et la bête* (Beauty and the Beast, 1946) and *Orphée* (Orpheus, 1950). Cocteau championed the work of gay writer Jean **Genet**, securing his release from prison and helping publish his early works. He died on the same day as his favourite singer Edith Piaf, only hours after recording a radio tribute to her. He is best remembered for his films, which are hailed as masterpieces of cinematic poetry. Cocteau died on 11 October 1963, in Milly, Île-de-France.

JOHN FORDE

COHN, ROY

b. 1927; d. 1986

lawyer

Lawyer and right-wing activist Roy Marcus Cohn, who never publicly admitted his homosexual orientation, died of AIDS. Cohn became infamous for assisting in the prosecution of Julius and Ethel Rosenberg as 'atom spies' in 1951 and engaging in illegal *ex parte* communication with the judge who sentenced them to death. He served as Senator Joseph McCarthy's right-hand man in ferreting out alleged communists and homosexuals from government and entertainment jobs (what became known as 'blacklisting' in Hollywood).

As a private lawyer, Cohn was famous for drawing upon 'the favor bank', a system of political backscratching, in order to help his clients, who included socialites and organized crime figures. He was disbarred just before his death for unprofessional conduct. He denied having AIDS when confronted by the US TV news programme, *Sixty Minutes*. Cohn worked with the Catholic Archdiocese of New York to keep New York City's lesbian and gay rights bill from being passed until 1986. He was portrayed as a major character in Tony Kushner's epic play about AIDS, *Angels in America* (1990).

See also: McCarthy, Joseph and McCarthyism

ANDY HUMM

COLMAN, ROBERT

b. 1959

actor, director, teacher

Robert Colman was born in Johannesburg, South Africa, and trained as a performer at the University of Cape Town. He has appeared in numerous theatre, film, and TV productions and has won awards for his work. Colman often works collaboratively, devising and directing theatre productions, with both experienced and 'non' actors, spanning community theatre, mainstream and fringe. His work deals largely with gay and lesbian issues, such as HIV and AIDS and South African politics. *After Nines!* (1998), Colman's community theatre production about aspects of South African gay and lesbian life and history, is a landmark of queer post-apartheid theatre, and gave black lesbians and gays the opportunity to tell their stories on stage for the first time in South Africa. Colman followed this production with *Your Loving Simon* (2003), a play based on the prison letters of gay activist Simon **Nkoli**.

ANTHONY MANION

COLOMBIA, FILMMAKING

Since the problem of violence has affected Colombian cultural production for nearly 50 years, filmmakers and writers have grappled with this dominant theme in their work. However, in recent years, Colombian filmmakers have focused on gay, lesbian, bisexual and transgender cultures, which are explicitly shown, or suggested, in various manners through the language of film. Some salient examples include *La mansión de Araucaima* (1986), directed by Carlos Mayolo, and based on the novel *La mansión de Araucaima; relato gótico de tierra caliente* (1973) by Alvaro Mutis. *La mansión* is transgressive in the sense that it not only portrays nude female and male bodies (except for the genitals), but also presents both heterosexual and homosexual prac-

tices that go beyond what a conservative patriarchal society such as Colombia expects.

Ilona llega con la lluvia (Ilona Arrives With the Rain, 1996) – based on Mutis' 1988 novel of the same title – is directed by Sergio Cabrera. Abdul, Maqroll and Ilona are the main characters in a love triangle, where suggestive images of heterosexual, bisexual and homosexual practices are intimately explored by the filmmaker through the cinematic play of light. Nonetheless, by the film's end, the lesbian subtext that surfaces in the film does not survive while the gay male liaison does.

La vendedora de rosas (The Rose Seller, 1998), directed by Víctor Gaviria, portrays the depressing and cruel reality of youth from a low socio-economic stratum who, as a result of socio-political violence, drug trafficking and corruption, are victims of poverty, drugs, sex and death in the violent streets of Medellín. A salient feature of this film is the use of non-professional actors; they perform within the context of their own lived-world stories. Although there does not seem to be any explicit queer dimension here, it could be argued that a homosocial pact (which could imply homoerotic bonds) exists among both female and male groups since only same-sex groups live and survive together.

La Virgen de los Sicarios (Our Lady of the Assassins, 2000), directed by Barbet Schroeder, is based on Fernando Vallejo's 1994 novel of the same title. *La Virgen* was made in Spanish and filmed exclusively in Colombia with Colombian actors. The openly gay Vallejo is the main character, played by Germán Jaramillo. The focus is Medellín and its precipitous decline in everyday life during the reign of the Medellín cartel. Throughout the story, Vallejo witnesses killings by *sicarios* (hired assassins), who usually kill people for the most insignificant reasons, many of which are totally shocking to the viewer. Interestingly enough, through this representation of violence, the film also portrays the loving homosexual relationship between Fernando – the older wealthy man who has recently returned to his hometown – and two young *sicarios*, Alexcis and Wilmar. Schroeder's transgressive and discreet filmmaking allows us to see both explicit and suggested homoerotic exchanges between these male characters.

EDUARDO ALFONSO CARO

COLOMBIA, LITERATURE

Over the last 50 years, the problem of violence has affected Colombian society and its cultural production. As a result, violence has been one of the main concerns in narrative, poetry, theatre and film. There has not really been a tradition of queer literature. However, in recent years, some authors have begun to shift their focus to gay, lesbian, bisexual and transgender cultures. Albalucía Angel is a writer, journalist, art critic and professor. Her first work, *Los girasoles en invierno* (Sunflowers in Winter, 1968), analyses women's reality and their violent inscription into gender roles. *Misiá señora* (1982) focuses on the homosexual identity of the protagonist and the homosexual desires with which she experimented in her childhood. In *Las Andariegas* (1984) – inspired by *Les Guerrillères* (The Women Warriors, 1969), a classic of lesbian literature by Monique **Wittig** – and the play *Siete lunas y un espejo* (1991), Angel subverts the patriarchal proposal of man/woman as the only possible gender categories. In *Misiá señora* she breaks with the traditional and canonical style of the novel and turns it into poetic prose; she further proposes feminine solidarity among women to resist masculine domination. Most of Angel's works postulate gay liberation and sexual dissidence as true alternatives for women to establish their own identity and to break with centuries of masculine hegemony.

Gustavo Alvarez Gardeazábal is both writer and politician. In his literary works, connections between reading, writing and sexuality are detailed. In some of his texts, the gay individual is used as a scapegoat to examine either social marginality or the politics and economics of social regimes; the construction of a gay identity is bound up with the notion of the marginal, the subaltern, and questions of social power. Both the homoerotic and homosocial dimensions appear in his fiction as a way to liberate the individual from the heterosexual/homosexual binarism imposed by patriarchal culture. His most recent works are *Los sordos ya no hablan* (1991), *Las letras de la paz: Manifiesto de Caicedonia* (2001), and *Comandante Paraíso* (2002).

Fernando Vallejo is a writer, biologist and film producer whose fiction is mostly autobiographical and forthrightly transgressive. In *El fuego secreto* (1987), for example, Vallejo narrates the generational story of drugs and homosexuality in Bogotá and Medellín. *La Virgen de los Sicarios* (Our Lady of the Assassins, 1994, later made as a film by Barbet Schroeder in 2000) portrays the cruel violence that scourged Medellín during the reign of the Medellín cartel, and the love relationship of a middle-aged homosexual with two young *sicarios* (serial killers). His recent works include *Almas en pena, chapolas negras* (1995), *El río del tiempo* (2000), *El desbarrancadero* (2001) and *La rambla paralela* (2002).

Ana María Reyes has a degree in Education from Universidad Pedagógica Nacional de Bogotá. Her work, *Entre el cielo y el infierno: historias de gays y lesbianas* (Between Heaven and Hell: Stories of Gays and Lesbians, 2003), contains 12 gay and lesbian short stories, each with very suggestive titles, some of which are 'Entre el cielo y el infierno' ('Between Heaven and Hell'), 'Bajo la sotana' ('Underneath the Soutane'), '¿Quieres casarte conmigo?' ('Do You Want To Marry Me?'), 'El pariente más cercano' ('The Closest Relative'), 'El huequito' ('The Little Hole') and 'Una fiesta inolvidable' ('An Unforgettable Party').

Alonso Sánchez Baute, with a law degree from Universidad Externado de Colombia in Bogotá, began writing in his spare time and developed a passion for literature. He has published three novels and a compilation of short stories. His most recent work is *Al diablo la maldita primavera* (2003), in which the main character – a drag queen – becomes a stunning woman; his/her accounts offer us a visit to the hidden, frivolous, spectacular but also marginal Bogotá: the gay Bogotá. This novel led him to win the Premio Nacional de Novela Ciudad de Bogotá in 2002.

Finally, Jaime Manrique, a poet, novelist, essayist and translator, is considered by many critics as the most accomplished gay Latino writer of his generation; critics call him a *pícaro* (a rogue), prone to shock his readers by pushing the moral standards of the time. He has published the novels *Colombian Gold* (1983), *Latin Moon in Manhattan* (1992) and *Twilight at the Equator* (1997), as well as *My Night with Federico García Lorca* (1995, revised in 1997). In 1999 he completed *Eminent Maricones: Arenas, Lorca, Puig, and Me*, a book about well-known gay authors Federico García Lorca, Reinaldo Arenas and Manuel Puig.

See also: Puig, Manuel

Further reading

Correa, Fabio E. (1997) 'Identidad gay, homo-socialismo, homoerotismo: hacia una lectura Queer de la novelística de Gustavo Alvarez Garedeazábal', dissertation, Arizona State University.
Foster, David W. (1991) *Gay and Lesbian Themes in Latin American Writing*, Austin: University of Texas Press.

EDUARDO ALFONSO CARO

COMING OUT

Also called 'coming out of the closet'. A term used to describe a gay or lesbian person's public revelation of their sexuality, particularly to family members.

JOHN FORDE

COMING-OUT NOVELS

Texts detailing sexual confessions have a long history within the Western tradition, going back at least as far as the *Confessions* by Saint Augustine (AD 397). However, the 'coming-out' novel, which hinges on the first-person narrator's growing awareness and eventual declaration of his or her homosexual identity, as opposed to his or her desire for homosexual acts, is a characteristically modern genre. Classics of the genre include novels by Edmund **White** and Felice **Picano**. Many lesbian and gay readers have welcomed these stories, which they perceive as offering truthful and ultimately liberating narratives of homosexual identity formation. However, others, including many queer theorists, see the genre as confining, because it reduces the complexities of human desire to a developmental sequence, the final 'climax' of which is the narrator's emergence as a fully formed 'lesbian' or 'gay'.

MARK McLELLAND

COMMUNITY HEALTH CENTRES

The 1970s saw homosexuality stigmatized and pathologized by many in the mainstream medical establishment. Glbtq individuals desired places where they could receive comprehensive healthcare in an environment that would welcome, not ostracize, them. Community health centres, such as Whitman Walker in Washington DC and Howard Brown in Chicago, were established to meet this need.

In the 1980s many community health centres concentrated on proactive responses to the HIV and AIDS crises. In the mid-1990s, with AIDS being viewed as a chronically manageable disease by many, the centres expanded their scope to address the syndemic or total health needs of the individual. Presently, many community health centres have dedicated a measurable component of their efforts to addressing the specific health concerns of women.

By providing a safe space for glbtq individuals to discuss and act upon critical issues of well-being, community health centres have dramatically improved the health options for such individuals.

CHRIS BELL

CONDOMS

The male condom is a thin shield worn on the penis during sexual intercourse. The female condom is inserted into the vagina prior to sexual activity. The most effective condoms are made out of latex or polyurethane (plastic). Condoms may be used with a water-based lubricating agent; for example, KY Jelly. Condoms do not require a prescription and are often provided at no charge at health clinics, community centres and bars. They are also available for over-the-counter purchase. When used consistently and correctly, condoms are an effective barrier against HIV and AIDS, certain sexually transmitted diseases (STDs) and pregnancy.

See also: AIDS; HIV

CHRIS BELL

CONSOLI, MASSIMO

b. 1945

writer, activist

Writer, journalist, translator and gay activist Massimo Consoli is looked upon as one of the key Gay Movement leaders. In the 1960s he was one of several who promoted gay groups in Rome and, in 1973, he created a social minorities studies centre. In 1975 he became a journalist and founded the association, Movimento Politico Omosessuale (MPO) and its organ, the *O-mpo* magazine. Since the 1970s he has continued to promote cultural activities and write books. He opened a gay centre in Rome and set up one of the biggest European archives of gay history, the Archivio. In 1990 the archive was declared culturally meaningful by the Italian Ministry of Culture and became part of the Central State Archive. In 1988 Consoli discovered the grave of Karl Heinrich Ulrich in the cemetery in L'Aquila and now, each year, he organizes a ceremony to commemorate him as the father of Italy's modern gay movement.

ALBERTO EMILETTI

CONVERSION OR REPARATIVE THERAPY

It has been customary within the field of psychiatry to consider homosexuality a mental illness treatable with some form of conversion or reparative therapy. Members of the American Psychiatric Association (APA), up until 1973, believed that homosexuality was something that could be 'cured' through therapy and that the individual seeking treatment would eventually be able to lead a 'normal', heterosexual lifestyle. In the past, a person with homosexual desires or feelings of attraction towards members of the same sex was treated with intensive therapy, electric shocks, mind-altering drugs, lobotomies and institutionalization.

After 1973 clinicians within the APA were encouraged to respect the dignity of their homosexual patients and to treat homosexuality as just another aspect of a person's social identity. Homosexuality is now considered by most practitioners to be a normal expression of one's sexual orientation. However, there is still a small minority of professionals within APA (less than 1 per cent of the total membership) who believe homosexuality can be 'cured' through conversion or reparative therapy.

The process of conversion or reparative therapy requires the patient to accept the belief that their homoerotic feelings are caused by environmental factors and that

159

once the root of these feelings are better understood, they can be cured of their homosexuality. This type of therapy has been aimed primarily at men. As a result, many of the treatment options and activities involve the male patient reconnecting with his manhood and sense of masculinity. The majority of therapists engaged in this work are also men. In his 2000 book *Growth Into Manhood*, Alan Medinger argues that homosexuality is not a single issue, but a complex set of problems that unite to produce homosexual desires. Each overlapping issue must be dealt with if one is to reduce or eliminate homosexual feelings. From resolution, the heterosexual desires needed to develop required life changes will emerge. The complex issues that produce homosexual desires fall into four categories: masculinity; authenticity; need-fulfilment; and surrender. It is believed by those who practice and participate in reparative therapies that gay men's 'authentic' (read: heterosexual) self will emerge once they have the courage to surrender to their craving for the masculine by developing 'healthy' ways of fulfilling their need to be close with other men. This is often done via weekend retreats, week-long seminars and many ex-gay ministry events. Gay men who undergo the conversion process establish close supportive bonds with other men who understand their experience. They are encouraged to engage in platonic physical connection with men through physical activities, therapeutic massage or by asking for and receiving non-sexual hugging, holding or other 'appropriate' forms of touch from heterosexual male friends, mentors and family members. Not unlike Alcoholics Anonymous, successful ex-gays form strong communities of support for those who are just starting out and support new ex-gays in their times of need.

The APA opposes conversion or reparative therapies as well as any psychiatric treatment that is based on the assumption that homosexuality is a mental disorder. In December of 1998 the Association issued a statement warning clinicians that there is no published scientific evidence supporting the effectiveness of conversion or reparative therapy aimed at changing one's sexual orientation: 'The potential risks of reparative therapy are great; including depression, anxiety, and self destructive behaviour since therapist alignment with societal prejudices against homosexuality may reinforce self-hatred already experienced by the patient' (APA Position Statement on 'Reparative' Therapies 1998). Despite this warning from the largest professional organization of practicing clinicians and academics, a few psychiatrists and psychologists persist in their support of these types of treatment, namely, the National Association for Research and Therapy of Homosexuality (NARTH), a professional organization of conversion and reparative therapists. Their web site (http://www.narth.com) is a clearing house for all literature related to the malleability of sexual orientation, the prevention of homosexuality and the treatment of homosexuality as a mental disorder. The professionals within this organization have come under fire because there has been no evidence supporting the success of these therapies. In fact, of the limited studies that have been conducted, the success rate of these therapies has been listed at very close to zero per cent.

KATHLEEN M. CUMISKEY

COOPER, DENNIS

b. 1953

writer

An American writer now based in Los Angeles, Cooper was born in Pasadena, California. Although he has written poetry and criticism (primarily of art and popular music), he is best known for his novels, which typically centre on confused adolescent boys and adult men who are drawn to these boys by the desire to protect them, victimize them, or both. Cooper's writing bears the influence of the French *nouveau roman* of the 1950s, with its ellipticality and ambiguity, emphasizing description as much as narrative. At the same time, Cooper also bears the influence of Hollywood genre films (particularly youth films and horror films, and most specifically, their confluence in the slasher film) and of the punk subculture in Los Angeles. Cooper himself has named as his two earliest influences the Marquis de Sade, for his conflation of sex and violence as a ruthless critique of morality, shot through with pitch-dark humour, and Arthur Rimbaud, for his creation of a poetic voice situated in isolation from the society around it, expressing itself with dark poetry featuring startling imagery. Cooper's novels centre on the confluence of sex and violence. The novels, all relatively brief, are written in a spare style that mixes a deliberate inarticulacy with precise, carefully chosen imagery, as well as deadpan, often extremely dark, humour.

DAVID PENDLETON

COPI

b. 1939; d. 1987

cartoonist

Born in Buenos Aires as Raúl Taborda Damonte, Copi went to Paris in 1962, where he lived for the remainder of his life. In 1965 he published a cartoon strip, 'La Femme assise' (The Seated Woman), in *Le Nouvel Observateur*. The strip, in which a woman, seated and always viewed from the side, has conversations with other people and a vast array of animals, made Copi one of the most popular cartoonists in France. Subsequently, he published several novels and play-scripts, often himself appearing in drag in his plays. Both the novels and the plays are full of the extraordinary adventures of rats, snakes and other animals, as well as drag queens and transsexuals. Copi was actively involved in, albeit critical of, the gay

political movement in Paris, often using his extravagant characters to criticize the normal gay male participants in the movement.

DANIEL HENDRICKSON

COPLAND, AARON

b. 1900; d. 1990

composer

Prolific American composer whose works are credited with the creation of a uniquely American and modernist musical form and the celebration of America's diverse cultural influences. Copland was born on 14 November 1900 in Brooklyn, New York. After studying music in France in the 1920s, he returned to the city, achieving success with his 'Symphony for Organ and Orchestra'. His work embraces jazz, folk, Hispanic, and country and western influences, while thematically exploring American legends and history, notably *El Salon Mexico* (1936), *A Lincoln Portrait* (1942), *The Tender Land* (1954) and *Fanfare for the Common Land* (1943). His ballet suites *Billy The Kid* (1938), *Rodeo* (1942) and *Appalachian Spring* (1944) draw heavily on American western and cowboy themes. He has also composed scores for *Of Mice and Men* (1939), *Our Town* (1940), *The Red Pony* (1948) and *The Heiress* (1949). Openly gay from an early age, he pursued a number of relationships throughout his life, including with his protégé Leonard **Bernstein**. He died on 2 December 1990 in New York.

JOHN FORDE

COTTAGING

Practice of soliciting for sexual contact between men in public conveniences, known in gay slang terms as 'cottages'. It is often dangerous and has been criminalized as indecency.

MICHAEL PINFOLD

CRAWFORD, JOAN

b. 1904; d. 1977

actor

Perhaps the definitive Hollywood screen **diva**, Crawford, born in Texas, is as famous for her tormented private life as for her acting career. After a brief stint as a model in lesbian pornography, she was signed by MGM in 1925. She achieved overnight success with *Our Dancing Daughters* (1928), becoming one of their most bankable stars. After being dropped by MGM, she made *Mildred Pierce* (1945) for rival studio Warner Bros., winning an Academy Award for her performance. Her infamous public rivalry with fellow diva Bette **Davis** was immortalized in *Whatever Happened to Baby Jane?* (1962), a camp-Gothic melodrama about two rival actor-sisters. Crawford's reputation was gruesomely resuscitated after her death with her stepdaughter Christina's memoir *Mommie Dearest* (1978), which revealed Crawford to be a violent alcoholic who beat her children with wire coathangers. Memorably portrayed by Faye Dunaway in a 1981 film of the same title, Crawford now epitomizes the queer iconography of a life of self-hatred masked by glamour.

JOHN FORDE

CRIMP, DOUGLAS

b. 1944

art historian, cultural theorist

Douglas Crimp's importance to queer theory and activism lies in two connected spheres: his legitimizing of art history or visual studies beyond the traditional institutions of high culture, and his refusal to erase the erotic in both political activism and the academy. His anthology, *AIDS: Cultural Analysis/Cultural Activism* (1988), placed both of these concerns at the centre of queer theory, while *Melancholia and Moralism* (2002) emphasizes the continuing significance of AIDS, attacking what he reads as the rise of a gay conservative politics (represented, for example, by Michelangelo **Signorile** and Andrew **Sullivan**) committed to a deathly moralism. Crimp was a member of Bad Object Choices and ACT UP.

See also: ACT UP; Bad Object Choices

TREVOR HOPE

CRISP, QUENTIN

b. 1908; d. 1999

performer

Born Denis Charles Pratt in Sutton (Surrey, England), Quentin Crisp is the epitome of the complexity and contradictoriness of homosexual history during the twentieth century. He led a varied and lengthy life, in his early years as a commercial artist, prostitute, tap-dancing teacher and nude model at an art school – a role he was assigned for his blatant homosexuality, as a result of exemption from military service – while in his old age he became a media celebrity in the United States. Even during pre-Second World War years, Crisp was a perfect instance of the outrageously camp queer: effeminate, witty, flamboyantly dressed and heavily made up. Designed to defy stuffed shirts as much as it was a form of self-protection, turning scorn into laughter, Crisp's ambiguous stance is echoed in the politics of his old age: while condemning the injustice he had suffered, he never became a spokesperson for gay rights politics, nor did he refute self-derision and the pathologizing of the homosexual. A year after the decriminalization of homosexual practices in Great Britain, the publication of his outstanding *The Naked Civil Servant* (1968), a frank account of his growing up as 'not merely a self-confessed homosexual, but a self-evident one', made him famous. International stardom followed, with the TV dramatization of his autobiography in the US in 1976. Celebrated as, in his own words, 'one of the stately homos of England', Crisp became an appreciated writer, actor, performance artist and arbiter of taste and style, progressing to the status of queer institution and master queen in the 1980s and 1990s – he was crowned Queen Elizabeth I in Sally Potter's film *Orlando* (1992), based on Virginia Woolf's classic story of time and gender pilgrimage. He died in Manchester in 1999.

FABIO CLETO

CRUISE

A popular form of leisure travel for predominantly middle- and upper-middle-class North American and Western European gay men and women. During the 1990s companies such as Atlantis offered all-gay cruises to regions such as the Bahamas, the Mediterranean, Mexico, Australia and Kenya. These ships function as floating resorts which package sociability, athletic activity and sightseeing. Promotions often focus on 'exotic islands' and tend to be globalizing and Eurocentrist.

TERRELL SCOTT HERRING

CRUISING

To search (in public places) for sexual partners. Can be done in bars, public toilets, parks and other public places where gay men meet in order to have sexual intercourse.

KEN WONG

CRYSTAL METH

Crystal methamphetamine, a stimulant once popular in the 1960s and 1970s, has begun to be widely used by gay men in recent years. Crystal meth is a white crystalline powder that is similar to amphetamine in its chemical composition. The drug can be injected intravenously, snorted or smoked. It is referred to as 'speed' or 'crank'. Smokeable varieties are called 'ice' or 'glass'.

Crystal meth is an addictive drug that wears off quickly, encouraging the user to get high again. It causes the central nervous system to release dopamine into the body. A small dose can have deleterious effects including tremors, diminished appetite, and increased heart rate and body temperature. High doses are often followed by mood swings and euphoric feelings.

Popular at circuit parties, clubs and bathhouses, and sometimes combined with Viagra for marathon sexual sessions, crystal meth usage can lead to a greater risk of contracting HIV and other sexually transmitted diseases. Community health centres are working to combat these risks through aggressive harm reduction.

CHRIS BELL

CUBA, FILMMAKING

Cubans who previously enjoyed access to a wide range of cinematographic productions found themselves in the realm of Marxist–Leninist ideological consumerism after the triumph of the Cuban Revolution in 1959. The newly formed government created the Cuban Art and Cinematographic Industry Institute (ICAIC), with the objective of supporting the dissemination of a national filmic history. Proponents of the Revolution understood the importance of cinematographic communication and the propagandist-ideological effect it would have on the individual and the collective consciousness of the Cuban people. By creating a network of mobile theatres, the ICAIC brought productions to remote areas, thus breaking the elitist metropolitan monopoly that the middle class had consolidated. With great mastery, the government of Fidel Castro used cinema to disseminate its plans and to exalt the successes of the Revolution. In all formative and cultural productions, the central theme addresses the Revolution and the propagation of its ideology. All Hollywood films were replaced by Soviet and other productions that asserted the basis of the new state ideology and promoted Marxist-Leninist thought.

Cuban filmmakers initially assumed a supportive role, seeking parallel growth with the revolutionary process. The first films produced addressed marginalized classes and attempted to encourage unified public support of the changes promoted and implemented by the new government. The ICAIC filmic production during the second half of the 1960s concentrated on the search for identity by 'the Cuban' or the idealized Cuban revolutionary, motivated in great part by the euphoria of the Revolution and the centennial of the Ten Year War (1868–78). However, observation of film production during the 1970s reveals a series of controversial elements, due in large part to the direction of Alfredo Guevara (b. 1926), who brought several like-minded intellectuals together under the auspices of the ICAIC. Cultural production diminished considerably during the 1980s and 1990s with the fall of the socialist block, motivating the ICAIC to execute films with more controversial elements and to rely on co-productions with foreign companies. The expression of dissidence in Cuba has often resulted in the closing of newspapers, indiscriminate firings, rejection of publications and jail. Nevertheless, the Cuban experience has demonstrated that screenwriters and directors who do not affiliate with the regime make it possible to integrate into the body of a work a subtext that lends itself to a contestatory reading without being open, unbridled or illogically critical.

From its inception, Cuban revolutionary ideology has categorically rejected any dissident expression that does not adhere to its precepts. Cuban gays have thus found themselves at the epicentre of iron-fisted persecution, repression and ridicule for more than two decades. The official position taken by Castro and the regime against the sexual dissident during the 1960s endures today, as the 'homosexual condition' is still considered an impediment for the revolutionary citizen and membership in the exclusive Cuban Communist Party is explicitly prohibited for gays. However, more recent attempts at filmic expression concerning gays in Cuba, such as the cinematographic representation of Reinaldo Arenas' autobiography, *Antes que anochezca* (Before Night Falls, 1992), and the screenplay *Fresa y Chocolate* (Strawberry and Chocolate, 1993), have received international acclaim.

JOSE B. ALVAREZ IV

CUBA, LITERATURE

The Cuban Revolution had a positive influence on Latin American political consciousness and on the cultural thought of the entire third world during the 1960s. A few months after the guerrilla triumph of 1959, Haydée Santamaría, under governmental auspices (la Casa de las Américas), founded a cultural centre that provided space to Latin American writers who previously had lacked access to publishing houses because of economic or political reasons. In literary circles there was an almost instant flourishing of journals and literary supplements as well as a great dissemination of young poets, narrators and essayists. The cultural mechanisms and institutions from the island under the state budget catapulted to an international sphere a large number of writers from different generations or groups who were considered loyal to the ideology of the Revolution. Over the last four decades, narrators and poets such as Nicolás Guillén, Roberto Fernández Retamar, Miguel Barnet, Mirta Aguirre, Nancy Morejón, Lisandro Otero, Jesús Díaz, Abel Prieto, Senel Paz, Raúl Hernández Novás, Jorge Luis Hernández, Arturo Arango, and Leonardo Padura Fuentes, have taken advantage of an educational, cultural, and editorial policy that has never been within reach of the majority of writers from other Latin American countries.

Nevertheless, there exists a group of writers who were marginalized at the national level, and therefore at the international level, who, for many years, did not have the opportunity to publish in Cuba. Their works have seen few, if any, Cuban editions and lack the appropriate and necessary public exposure. One of the explicit goals of the new government was to inculcate in all of its subjects new systems of thought, action and response at the cognitive level. The government decreed from the outset what it meant to be a *good revolutionary*, a concept to which all Cuban citizens would adhere in order to avoid alienation or repression. Cuban cultural production of the 1960s conformed to such parameters, with the majority of Cuban writers and filmmakers, along with others throughout the world, caught in the revolutionary fervour that inundated the island. For such reasons the control, dogmatism and official censorship of the new regime were not felt strongly, at least until the beginning of the 1970s when a dissident line was adopted by several writers, most notably Anton Arrufat (b. 1925), Reinaldo Arenas (1943–90) and Heberto Padilla (b. 1932). The Cuban cultural community soon recognized that the party politics of Marxism-Leninism and the spontaneity of cultural creation inevitably represented conflicting interests and could not coexist. Initial experiences proved that coerced harmony brought about imminent shock, accounting for the diminishing innovative quality of Cuban cultural production during the 1970s, a period regarded (appropriately) by Cuban intellectuals and scholars as the 'Black Decennium'.

In a general sense, the persecution of gays coincides with the persecution of the dissident: a homosexual is a dissident when compared to the bourgeois norm of conjugal life. Historically, in Cuba, as in the rest of Latin America, direct repression of gays has been openly practiced, along with the rejection of social and artistic attempts at expressing sexual deviance. In the case of Cuba in particular – whose socialist society has perpetuated bourgeois relations among heterosexuals – official responses to such attempts, while many, in the1960s normally took the form of indiscriminate arrests and subsequent transfers of citizens (all men suspected of being homosexual) to the camps of the Military Units for the Aid of Production (UMAP). Lamentably, many Cuban intellectuals suffered imprisonment in these work camps the most renowned of which include writer Reinaldo Arenas; poet and director of the publishing house El Puente, José Mario; and poet Jorge Ronet.

JOSE B. ALVAREZ IV

CUKOR, GEORGE
b. 1899; d. 1983
director

An enormously successful American film director, George Cukor's career spanned over five decades and he was the man behind many of Hollywood's greatest classics. Although his popular designation as a 'woman's director' was possibly a coded reference to his homosexuality, Cukor worked productively with many leading female stars, for example Norma Shearer, Greta **Garbo** and Katharine **Hepburn**, and provided them with some of the best films of their careers. An accomplished theatre director in New York before migrating to Hollywood at the beginning of the sound era, Cukor garnered a reputation for quality filmmaking across diverse genres, including comedy (*The Philadelphia Story*, 1940), drama (*Camille*, 1937) and musicals (*My Fair Lady*, 1964). While many of his films might be seen to evince a queer sensibility, he is most widely celebrated in gay cultures for his work on the camp classic *The Women* (1939) and Judy Garland's 1954 comeback vehicle, *A Star is Born*.

BRETT FARMER

CUNNINGHAM, MICHAEL

b. 1952

writer

Born in Ohio, Cunningham was raised in southern California, a suburban existence that serves as the inspiration for his first, hard-to-find novel *Golden States* (1984). Since the success of his first mature novel, *A Home At the End of the World* (1990), Cunningham's work has grown increasingly ambitious. *Flesh and Blood* (1995) tells the sprawling story of a Greek-American family over three generations. His breakthrough novel, *The Hours* (1998), was his most experimental to date; drawing inspiration from Virginia Woolf's *Mrs Dalloway*, the book interweaves the stories of three women (Woolf herself, and two fictional creations) as they wrestle with the constraints of domesticity, codes of sexual propriety and their own artistic ambitions. Like Cunningham's earlier books, *The Hours* is notable for its frank treatment of the AIDS epidemic and the creation of queer families as central aspects of life in the late twentieth century. The novel won the Pulitzer Prize in 1999.

DAVID KURNICK

CURRY, TIM

b. 1946

actor

A British comic actor, Tim Curry achieved instant fame and enduring cult status as Frank N' Furter, the transvestite star of *The Rocky Horror Picture Show* (1975), a gender-bending horror-film parody based on Richard O'Brien's stage musical. Dressed in high heels, fishnet stockings and garishly over-applied makeup, Curry's gleefully perverse performance as a mad scientist who invents a boy-toy monster and sexually corrupts two clean-cut teenagers epitomized the sexually adventurous spirit of the 1970s, while his sultry renditions of songs 'I'm Just A Sweet Transvestite', '(Let's Do The) Timewarp' and 'Don't Fight It, Feel It' still inspire imitations from fans at midnight 'Rocky Horror' screenings worldwide. His subsequent career juggles stage work – notably as Mozart in *Amadeus* on Broadway and Macheath in *The Threepenny Opera* for the English National Theatre – with an amusing array of comic villains in films such as *Annie* (1982), *The Three Musketeers* (1993) and *Charlie's Angels* (2000).

JOHN FORDE

CUTHAND, THIRZA

b. 1978

video artist

Born in Saskatchewan of Cree and Scots descent, Cuthand broke into international queer festivals with the self-reflexive *Lessons in Baby Dyke Theory* (1995), even before graduating from Vancouver's Emily Carr Institute of Art and Design. Her prize-winning work is raw, intimate, ironic, sexy and taboo-shattering, as in the sado-masochistically charged *Helpless Maiden Makes an 'I' Statement* (1999) or *Untouchable* (1998), an autobiographical reflection on inter-generational eroticism. Often exhibited in aboriginal as well as queer and women's arts events, Cuthand's allegorical pageant *Through the Looking Glass* (1999) explicitly confronts the identity and cultural conflicts entailed by her native heritage. With her 2001 tape *Anhedonia* (inability to experience pleasure), Cuthand entered new territory, dealing with characteristic frankness with her own bipolar condition and assembling a tough iconography of corporal and psychic abjection.

THOMAS WAUGH

D

DALDRY, STEPHEN

b. 1960

director

One of Britain's most celebrated directors, Stephen Daldry began his craft at the Crucible and Gate Theatres, before being appointed Artistic Director of London's Royal Court Theatre (1992–5). He went on to direct the long-running, Tony Award-winning revival of J.B. Priestley's *An Inspector Calls* and David Hare's *Via Dolorosa*. His second feature, *Billy Elliot* (2000), was a moving, multi-award-winning drama about an 11-year-old boy's struggle to become a ballet dancer, against the wishes of his conservative working-class family. Billy's emerging sexuality is sensitively portrayed. Daldry's second film, an adaptation of Michael Cunningham's novel *The Hours* (2002), told the interlocking stories of three women, including bisexual author Virginia Woolf, and commented on lesbian experience in three generations. Openly gay for most of his career, Daldry surprised many by marrying dancer Lucy Sexton in 2001 and fathering a child in 2003.

See also: Cunningham, Michael

JOHN FORDE

DALL'ORTO, GIOVANNI

b. 1958

writer, activist

Giovanni Dall'Orto is one of the most renowned gay journalists in Italy. As a wri-ter and activist, he has done much to promote the importance of a gay community, through its own press, its sense of history and its specific culture. With *Leggere omosessuale* (Reading Homosexuality, 1983) he provided Italian readers with the first bibliography of gay literature, while his historical studies led to his collaboration with Wayne Dynes on *The Encyclopaedia of Homosexuality* and with Robert Aldrich and Garry Wotherspoon on *Who's Who in Gay and Lesbian History*. As a journalist and editor of the gay monthly *Babilonia* (1997–8) and of *Pride* (2000–) he has published a wealth of articles dealing with politics, gay culture and history. With his mother Paola he wrote *Figli diversi* (Different Sons, 1991) to help young gays come out to their families. *Manuale per coppie diverse* (Handbook for Different Couples, 1994) addresses gay couples with advice about handling relationships and the problems of daily life. Strenuously opposed to new deconstructive trends of queer theory, Dall'Orto is very active online, with a well-maintained web site, *La gaya scienza* (http://digilander.libero.it/giovannidallorto/)

MARCO PUSTIANAZ

DALLESANDRO, JOE

b. 1948

actor, model

Born Joseph Angelo D'Alessandro III in Pensacola, Florida, but raised in New York

City, Joe Dallesandro was the most successful 'superstar' of the underground film movement of the 1960s and 1970s. A former teen hustler and soft-porn gay model, Dallesandro was 'discovered' on the street by Warhol collaborator Paul Morrissey in 1967, and made his film debut half-naked in *The Loves of Ondine* at the age of 18, before rising to notoriety as a cast member of Morrissey's controversial first feature-length film for Warhol, *Lonesome Cowboys* (1968). His status as leading sex icon of the Warhol Factory was firmly established when he was cast as the central protagonist of Morrissey's acclaimed underground classic trilogy *Flesh* (1968), *Trash* (1970) and *Heat* (1972); with its full frontal nudity, drug-taking and transvestism, the trilogy broke new ground in its uncompromising objectification of male sexuality on the screen. Later immortalized in Lou Reed's tribute to the Factory days *Walk on the Wild Side*, Dallesandro relocated to Europe in the mid-1970s to pursue a more 'mainstream' career and appeared in such European arthouse classics as Serge Gainsbourg's *Je t'aime moi non plus* (I Love You No More, 1975) and Louis Malle's *Black Moon* (1975). And since his return to the United States in 1980, he has made numerous appearances in films as diverse as Francis Coppola's *The Cotton Club* (1984) to John Water's ultra-camp musical *Cry-Baby* (1990). Although consistently cast in more supporting roles in recent years, Dallesandro remains a unique and enigmatic icon of underground cinema.

ROBIN GRIFFITHS

DANCE

For queer people, dance in all idioms represents an ideal combination of physicality, aesthetic possibility and social occasion. In dance, queer artists and audiences gather to witness excellence of form, share in narrative stories of queer life and imagine physical expression unbound by socially proscribed limits of sexuality. More than in other art forms, dance allows the exploration of queer corporeality through the medium of the body – the physical foundation of a queer ontology. Dance has inspired a large and ever-expanding queer expertise among its practitioners, in no small part because it has embraced queer presence at every historical juncture.

Because dance practice is ubiquitous among humans, an overview of queer presence in dance will extend to all corners of the globe and all historical eras. As a realm, dance includes theatrical dance and social dance, its two most prevalent idioms in the West. Queer presence in theatrical dance includes, for example, the extravagant spectacle of Balthasar de Beaujoyeulx's 1581 Balet Comique de la Royne as well as the twentieth-century Broadway presentations of Michael **Bennett** and Tommy Tune. Dance also allows spiritual exploration, and some queer artists have turned to dance as a way to access worship, notably in Alvin Ailey's landmark work *Revelations*.

In ballet, the exuberant assemblage of spectacle and the body in luminously detailed motion have always spawned queer vistas of possibility. From 1909–29 Serge Diaghilev capitalized on the sizeable desire of queer people to assemble and witness dance, and his company the Ballet Russe created a series of masterworks that celebrated queer dance icons, including Vaslav Nijinsky (1889–1950), who performed the hypersensual leading role in his own *L'Après-midi d'un Faune* (1912), and his sister, choreographer Bronislava Nijinska (1891–1972), who performed the central role of a resistant sacrificial maiden in Nijinsky's *Le Sacre du Printemps* (1913). Other ballet companies followed in Diaghilev's wake as preferred sites for queer cosmopolitan identity, including Swedish impresario Rolf de Maré's company, Les Ballets Suédois (in existence from 1920–5), to which featured his lover, Jean Borlin

(1893–1930) as premier danseur and choreographer.

The list of queer ballet artists includes the form's greatest celebrities from all parts of the world: Sir Frederick Ashton (1906–88) of the Royal Ballet; French-born Maurice Béjart (1927–), whose splashing and radical theatricality attracted huge crowds to ballet shows; American partners Robert Joffrey and Gerald Arpino, who created the Joffrey Ballet in 1953; Rudi Van Dantzig (b. 1933), director of the Dutch National Ballet; American Lar Lubovitch, who choreographed an exquisite male duet to Mozart's *Concerto 622*; British-born Matthew Bourne, who created in 1995 a *Swan Lake* with all-male swans; and dancer Erik **Bruhn** (1928–86), who served as Director of the Royal Swedish Ballet and the National Ballet of Canada. Bruhn was a lover of Rudolph Nureyev (1938–93), probably the most famous queer ballet star of the twentieth century. Besides artists and devoted audience members, every ballet company attracts queer presence among its affiliated designers, composers, librettists, photographers, patrons and directors.

Modern dance, a form brought into being by a number of strong-willed, independent women, some of whom were themselves queer, emerged as a twentieth-century response to the codified strictures of ballet. The idiom had as its goal to broaden stage representations of women and allow for personalized movement in theatrical settings. Americans Ruth Saint Denis (1877–1968), Isadora Duncan (1879–1927), and German-born Mary Wigman (1886–1973) number among the most important generative artists, along with lesbian American Loie Fuller (1862–1928) who created patents for her lighting innovations. These women supported their gay male colleagues and allowed modern dance to become a refuge for artists to engage physical creativity without fear of sexual or identity recriminations, Saint Denis married the gay dancer Ted Shawn (1891–1972) in 1914, and the ambitious duo created a dynasty in Denishawn, a network of schools and touring dance productions that became a centre for creativity, training scores of artists including Martha Graham (1894–1991), bisexual choreographer Doris Humphrey (1895–1958) and queer dancer and choreographer Charles Weidman (1901–75). Shawn later created Ted Shawn and his Male Dancers at his Massachusetts retreat Jacob's Pillow. The company established a serious place for homosocial male stage presence in modern dance. Isadora Duncan, who enjoyed affairs with both men and women, and was briefly married to queer Russian poet Sergei Esenin, freed the bourgeoise woman's body from its corsets to dance barefoot in loose, Greek-inspired gowns.

An ever-expanding string of queer couples follow in the innovative steps of these artists. Life partners Alwin Nikolais (1910–93) and Murray Louis (b. 1926) formed a company that experimented with light and full-body masks that obscured gender. Master choreographer Merce Cunningham (b. 1919), who danced with Graham before forming his own company in 1953, remained involved with composer John Cage (1912–92) for most of his adult life. The two were at the forefront of postmodern stage innovation, working with dance techniques to generate unexpected performance scores for dancers and musicians. Among contemporary artists, Bill T. Jones (b. 1952), who began his career with his partner Arnie Zane (1948–88) emerged as an internationally renowned queer artist known for his highly provocative works that address xenophobia and racism, including the evening-length *Still/Here* (1994), which explored terminal illnesses including cancer and AIDS.

Other important queer artists of the postwar era include celebrity choreographer Paul Taylor (b. 1930), whose work rarely addresses sexuality; choreographer and filmmaker Yvonne **Rainer** (b. 1934), who began to explore lesbian identity in films during the 1990s; Mark **Morris** (b. 1956), who in 1989 made a dance version of Purcell's *Dido and Aeneas* (1989) in which he played the dual female roles of Dido and the Sorceress; Joe **Goode** (b. 1951), whose signature work *29 Effeminate Gestures* (1987) catalogues various 'inappropriately feminine' gestures; Krissy Keefer (b. 1953), who founded the San Francisco-based Bay Area Dance Brigade to create multicultural feminist work; Australian-born Lloyd Newson, whose London-based company DV8 (formed in 1986) has produced a series of physical theatre works that explore queer masculinity, sexism and abuse.

Queer dance around the globe continues to expand its horizons. Feminist choreographer Chandralekha, based in Madras, experiments with depictions of sexuality and intimacy in same-sex choreography, while Chinese-born Wen Wei Wang, based in Vancouver, recently formed Wei Wang Dance to explore the queer immigrant experience. In more restrictive societies, long-standing carnival celebrations celebrate queer corporeality, as in the Reyog masked dance festival in Ponorogo, Java, derived from homosocial male mythologies involving elaborately decorated young men and their older male protectors. And burgeoning Pride festivals in Brazil, South Africa, Australia and China continue to enhance representations of queer bodies in motion. In all, queer presence in dance on stage, in social settings, in religious rituals or as part of state-sponsored events continues to propagate, inspiring audiences to consider the basic humanity of queer physicality in motion.

See also: Ailey, Alvin; Jones, Bill T. and Arnie Zane

Further reading

Cohen, Selma Jeanne (ed.) (1998) *International Encyclopedia of Dance*, 6 vols, New York: Oxford University Press.

Daly, Ann (2002) *Done Into Dance: Isadora Duncan in America*, Middletown: Wesleyan University Press.

DeFrantz, Thomas (2004) *Dancing Revelations: Alvin Ailey's Embodiment of African American Culture*, New York: Oxford University Press.

Desmond, Jane (2001) *Dancing Desires: Choreographing Sexualities On and Off the Stage*, Madison: University of Wisconsin Press.

Garafola, Lynn (1992) *Diaghilev's Ballets Russes*, New York: Oxford University Press.

Greskovic, Robert (1998) *Ballet 101: A Complete Guide to Learning and Loving the Ballet*, New York: Hyperion.

Jonas, Gerald (1992) *Dancing: Pleasure, Power and Art of Movement*, New York: Harry Abrams.

Kopelson, Kevin (1997) *The Queer Afterlife of Vaslav Nijinsky*, Palo Alto: Stanford University Press.

Nikolais, Alwin and Louis, Murray (2005) *The Nikolais/Louis Dance Technique: A Philosophy And Method Of Modern Dance*, New York: Routledge.

Reynolds, Nancy and McCormick, Malcolm (2003) *No Fixed Points: Dance in the Twentieth Century*, New Haven, Yale University Press.

THOMAS F. DEFRANTZ

DANILOWITZ, JONATHAN

b. 1945

activist

Jonathan Danilowitz was one of the first activists for the Society for the Protection of Personal Rights, its subsequent chairperson, founder of Israel's chapter of **PFLAG (Parents, Families and Friends of Lesbians and Gays)** and Israel's first representative at the **Gay Games**. Danilowitz achieved international recognition as the flight attendant who sued his employer, El Al Israel Airlines, for equal same-sex spousal benefits – including flight privileges – available to mixed-sex spouses. He fought and won all the way to the Israeli Supreme Court, which ruled in his favour in 1994, based on a prohibition on sexual orientation discrimination in the equal employment law. His case serves as the legal landmark for gay rights in Israel. The ruling was later cited by the House of Lords in the United Kingdom and in South Africa's Constitutional Court as a precedent. Danilowitz's struggle with the airline served as a focal point for the coming out of gay people, and politics and civil rights in Israel during the 1990s.

AEYAL GROSS

DAUGHTERS OF BILITIS

The first lesbian organization established in the United States, Daughters of Bilitis (DOB), was founded in 1955 in San Francisco by four lesbian couples. The name comes from a poem by Pierre Louÿs about a fictional contemporary of Sappho, and the deliberate indirectness of it as a reference to lesbianism reflects the importance of secrecy to the organization's members in the conservative moral climate of the 1950s. DOB was initially established as a secret social club that would offer an alternative to lesbian bars. However, its direction quickly shifted to more politicized concerns and the organization became a key part of the homophile movement that preceded gay liberation. Chapters were established in a number of cities, and in 1956 DOB began publishing a monthly magazine, The Ladder. Nonetheless, the perceived risks of association with a lesbian organization meant initial membership numbers were small, and later perceptions of it as politically conservative ensured they remained so. DOB's early political stance was firmly integrationist, and its continued association with this relative conservatism saw it increasingly rejected by lesbians as gay liberation pursued more radical agendas. The disbanding of the national organization in the early 1970s and the cessation of The Ladder's publication in 1972 signalled DOB's effective end, although some chapters have remained periodically active.

DOB's origin as an alternative to the bars was a result of increasing levels of police harassment and the prevalence of a butch/ femme culture that made some members feel uncomfortable. The organization's move towards a more politicized concern at professional and public attitudes towards lesbianism resulted in a split within membership that saw the working-class members, who wanted the organization to remain more closely aligned to its 'social club' origins, leave DOB. In part as a consequence of this split, DOB became permanently identified as a predominantly middle-class organization. Under the leadership of Phyllis Lyon and Del Martin (see **Martin, Del and Phyllis Lyon**), DOB began to work closely with the **Mattachine Society** in the emerging **homophile movement**, participating in conferences, social events and the early politicizing of gay concerns. In a movement overwhelmingly dominated by men, DOB also sought to address specific issues facing lesbians, and was repeatedly required at Mattachine conferences to articulate those concerns in defence of its women-only membership.

In its address to lesbians, however, DOB would later attract considerable criticism for its conservative, assimilationist politics. This conservatism clearly inflects the Statement of Purpose printed at the front of each issue of The Ladder. Proclaiming Daughters of Bilitis 'A Women's Organization for the Purpose of Promoting the Integration of the Homosexual into Society', the statement outlined education of 'the variant' (the word 'lesbian' is never used) as among its key roles. Within this education strategy, DOB counselled its members to dress and behave according to prevailing norms of femininity and to pursue acceptance and respectability in mainstream society. Further, while DOB also sought to educate the public, and to disestablish certain taboos attached to lesbianism, its meetings were at times addressed by outside speakers openly hostile to any such efforts. The organization seemed willing to listen to, and at times adopt, a framework of identity that would become unacceptable as the gay liberation movement gained momentum.

While DOB ultimately did adopt a political stance more in keeping with the organizations that emerged in the wake of Stonewall and the beginnings of lesbian feminism, the perception of it as accommodationist (and middle class), along with divisions over the extent to which it would adopt the newer radicalism, ultimately forced its demise. Nonetheless, DOB, like Mattachine, played a key role in establishing the legitimacy of homosexuality as a distinct minority, and thus contributed to the political consciousness that would enable the emergence of more radical movements. The very fact of its existence in the climate of institutionalized hostility towards and harassment of lesbians that characterized the 1950s can be considered a remarkable achievement.

Further reading

D'Emilio, J. (1983) *Sexual Politics, Sexual Communities: the Making of a Homosexual Minority in the United States, 1940–1970*, Chicago: University of Chicago Press.

Faderman, L. (1991) "'Not a Public Relations Movement": Lesbian Revolutions in the 1960s through '70s', in *Odd Girls and Twilight Lovers: A History of Lesbian Life in Twentieth-Century America*, New York: Columbia University Press.

ANITA BRADY

DAVIES, TERENCE

b. 1945

filmmaker

British filmmaker whose poetic and highly autobiographical works explore sexual and religious guilt through a gay sensibility. Davies was born on 10 November 1945 in Liverpool, England. He studied at Coventry Drama School, where he wrote *Children* (1976), the first in a loosely based trilogy of short films about a gay man's struggle with family, religion and homosexuality, completed with *Madonna and Child* (1980) and *Death and Transfiguration* (1983). His first feature, *Distant Voices, Still Lives* (1988) was a poetic evocation of his working-class childhood, characterized by lingering imagery and the use of 1950s music to provide narrative links, and won Davies the Cannes Film Festival's International Critics' Prize. His follow-up feature, *The Long Day Closes* (1992), also set in 1950s Liverpool, focused on the young gay protagonist's relationship with his mother. His next film, *The Neon Bible* (1995), told the story of a boy's childhood in the American South. *The House of Mirth* (2000) was a masterful adaptation of Edith Wharton's novel about the social annihilation of an outsider in nineteenth-century New York society.

JOHN FORDE

DAVIS, ANGELA

b. 1944

activist, teacher

Angela Yvonne Davis was born on 26 January 1944 in Alabama. She has cultivated a philosophy based on radical black politics and activism. In 1967 she joined the black liberation struggle, joining the Student Nonviolent Coordinating Committee (SNCC) and the Black Panther Party. She gained notoriety after her arrest for suspected involvement in the attempt to free George Jackson from a courtroom in 1970. Eventually acquitted, she was nevertheless briefly on the FBI's most wanted list for fleeing arrest.

Davis is internationally known for her ongoing work to combat all forms of oppression in the United States and abroad. She has consistently advocated the rights of black women, who face the dual problems of sexism and racism.

As an academic Davis has studied the relationship between gender, racism and Marxism. She radicalized feminism through a class and anti-racist vision and promulgated a new form of black female identity and politics. She is a tenured professor in the History of Consciousness Department at the University of California, Santa Cruz.

Further reading

Davis, A. (1974) *Angela Davis, An Autobiography*, New York: Random House.
—— (1982) *Women, Race and Class*, New York: Random House.
—— (1988) *Women, Culture, and Politics*, New York: Random House.
—— (1998) *Blues Legacies and Black Feminism: Gertrude 'Ma' Rainey, Bessie Smith and Billie Holiday*, New York: Pantheon Books
—— (2003) *Are Prisons Obsolete?* New York: Seven Stories Press.

SILVIA FRANCOLINI

DAVIS, BETTE

b. 1908; d. 1989

actor

As melodrama diva, camp queen and tough-and-tender dame, Bette Davis has been loved, admired and imitated by lesbians, gay men, bisexuals and all types of queers. Her flamboyant gestures (often with a cigarette), large, flashing eyes, insistent, staccato speech, keen intelligence and emotional intensity were best served by a series of 'women's pictures' made in Hollywood between the mid-1930s and mid-1940s. For many lesbians, Davis' strong on-screen relationships with women and girls in films such as *Marked Woman* (1937), *The Old Maid* (1939) and *Now, Voyager* (1942) offer pleasurable, sometimes erotic, frissons. Gay men tend to prefer the tragic or bitchy Bette of *Of Human Bondage* (1934), *The Little Foxes* (1941) and *Whatever Happened to Baby Jane?* (1962). Her long-time rivalry with *Baby Jane* co-star Joan **Crawford** is a source of endless fascination for gay men. Where gays, lesbians and other queer fans come together is on *All About Eve* (1950), in which she plays a Broadway star who

mentors a younger woman, 'woman-bonds' *and* flings bitchy quips while being adored by both women and men.

ALEX DOTY

DAVIS, VAGINAL

b. 1969

performer

Vaginal 'Creme' Davis was born and raised in the Watts district of Los Angeles. She named herself after her idol, revolutionary activist Angela **Davis**. She first started performing on the punk scene in LA during the 1980s, often with a group she had formed called the Afro Sisters. She later published a fanzine named after one of the group's other members, 'Fertile La Toyah Jackson'. She has formed three different bands: black fag; Pedro, Muriel & Esther (PME); and íCholita!, the female Menudo, in which she appears as Graciela, a teenaged Chicana. PME released a CD in 1996 entitled *The White to be Angry*.

Davis has hosted in a number of important performance and music clubs in Los Angeles, including Sucker, G.I.M.P. (with Ron **Athey**) and Bricktops, a 1920s-themed club. She has also developed performance pieces outside the club scene with which she has toured the United States and Europe. In addition to her live performance work, Davis has made a number of videotapes, including *That Fertile Feeling* (again with Fertile La Toyah Jackson) and *Voodoo Williamson: The Dona of Dance*, in which she plays a charismatic Caribbean modern dance instructor who works with troubled youth. In 1999 she made *The White to be Angry*, a video about a young white skinhead who cannot seem to escape effeminate gay men and black people. The video features three short narrative segments, homages to Woody Allen, Clive Barker and Bruce **La Bruce**.

DANIEL HENDRICKSON

DAY, DORIS

b. 1924

actor

An enduring cinematic and musical icon, Doris Day's trademark brand of fresh-faced optimism and chaste flirtatiousness earned her the title 'America's Sweetheart', and she continues to attract analysis from contemporary queer theorists. Beginning her career as a big band singer, Day made her first movie with Warner Bros in 1948, soon becoming one of their most bankable stars. Often typecast as a bright-eyed virgin, she broke the mould with her feisty performance as a Wild West tomboy in *Calamity Jane* (1953); her rendition of the film's theme song 'Secret Love' has subsequently been adopted as a lesbian anthem. She is best known for her comic collaborations with Rock **Hudson**, with whom she made *Pillow Talk* (1959), *Lover Come Back* (1961) and *Send Me No Flowers* (1964) – the pair's infectious on-screen chemistry given ironic resonance following the revelation of Hudson's homosexuality. Her prolific recording career includes the hit song 'Que Sera Sera'.

JOHN FORDE

DAYAN, YA'EL

b. 1938

journalist, politician

Author of eight books, veteran journalist and recipient of the Bruno Kreisky Human Rights Award (1991) and the Olof Palme Award for Peace (1998), Dayan served as a Labour Party Member of the Knesset (the Israeli Parliament) for three consecutive terms between 1992 and 2003. Early in her term, she formed a parliamentary subcommittee for the prevention of discrimination on the basis of sexual orientation and served as its chair until its demise when she left the Knesset. On 2 February 1993 the subcommittee had its first meeting, which proved to be one of the most crucial defining moments in the Israeli–glbtq community history, for it sparked a political chain reaction in various aspects of the public domain. The very existence of this formal body proved to have far-reaching legal, social and psychological effects. A heterosexual woman, Dayan remains one of the most steadfast and committed advocates of glbtq rights in Israel.

AMIT KAMA

DE LA IGLESIA, ELOY

b. 1944

filmmaker

Born in Zarautz, in the Basque region of Spain, Eloy de la Iglesia was one of the first Spanish filmmakers to deal openly with questions regarding homoerotic desire. His film career includes *Los placeres ocultos* (*Hidden Pleasures*, 1976), which may be the first openly gay movie made in Spain. De la Iglesia's films often depict the problematic existence of marginalized segments of Spanish society in the immediate aftermath of Francisco Franco's long dictatorship: prostitution, political violence, youth gang culture, homoerotic desire and drug addiction being the most salient topics. It can be said that Eloy de la Iglesia's filmmaking takes into account the years of the Spanish *transición* or the transition from the Franco dictatorship to a democratic society in Spain during the late 1970s and the early 1980s as it is viewed in his 1978 film *El diputado* (The Deputy). During the 1980s De la Iglesia went on to direct box-office success films such as *El pico* (*The Shoot Up*, 1983) and the most recent, *La estanquera de Vallecas* (*The Lady in the Vallecas Kiosk*, 1987).

MIKEL IMAZ

DE LAURETIS, TERESA

scholar, author

A professor in the History of Consciousness graduate programme at the University of California, Santa Cruz, Teresa De Lauretis is an internationally recognized feminist theoretician. Born in Italy, she moved to the United States upon completion of her doctoral work in Milan. She has taught in various American universities. Following an interdisciplinary approach combining semiotics, psychoanalysis, film theory, literary theory and queer theory, De Lauretis has made original, authoritative contributions to the foundations and development of gay and lesbian studies, in particular her study of lesbian sexuality from a psychoanalytic perspective, including her important 1994 book, *The Practice of Love: Lesbian Sexuality and Perverse Desire*.

MONICA BARONI

DE LEEUW, PAUL

b. 1962

performer, TV host, singer, writer

Having started his career in Dutch cabaret, de Leeuw soon won national fame with his revolutionary TV shows. A performer with a unique style of his own, his shows are a combination of everyday life and show business, featuring both straightforward and unorthodox interviews. He does not shy away from controversial topics, such as AIDS, deafness or mental disabilities. The shows granted him great acclaim as well as a number of prizes (e.g., the Bronze Rose in Montreux in 1993, an Emmy in 1997 and an Academy Award in 1998). De Leeuw does not present his homosexual lifestyle as a special topic in his shows, but rather treats it as a matter of course. His marriage to his partner Stephen Nugter in 2000, and the adoption of two infant sons in 2001 and 2002, have rendered him a role-model,

even evoking a response from the Dutch parliament.

In the field of theatre de Leeuw has starred in musicals (*Les Miserables* and his own production of *Foxtrot*), as well as in plays (*Torch Song Trilogy*).

WARD SCHRIJVER

DE SIMONE, TITTI

b. 1970

politician, activist

Titti de Simone was the first self-proclaimed lesbian elected to the Italian parliament in the general election of 2001. It was a significant event for Italy's political history and the glbtq movement, and was accompanied by the election of Franco Grillini, Arcigay honorary president. De Simone belongs to Rifondazione Comunista, the most radical of Italy's left-wing parties, and at the time of her election was Arcilesbica president. Her fight against all forms of discrimination includes battles for the legal recognition of gay couples and the rights of lesbians, gays and transsexuals to adopt, and for access to medically assisted procreation.

MONICA BARONI

DEAKIN, DESTINY

b. 1957

artist

Destiny Deakin is an indigenous artist who lives in Melbourne. She is of Ku'a Ku'a/ Erub/Mer peoples from the Maryborough region and the Torres Strait Islands off the far northeast tip of Australia. Her vibrant imagery fearlessly combines black humour with searing critique of orthodoxies that belie the diverse and often contradictory worlds of Aboriginal and Torres Strait Islander experience. Best known for her use of Polaroid camera snapshots, bubble jet ink and laser prints on paper and vinyl,

Deakin works with text, kitsch artefacts and tourist paraphernalia, black and white dollies, contemporary urban settings and fragments of life lived on the edges of towns and cities. Also working with video and installations, her approach has been described as a combination of the Kafkaesque and Sapphic, with subject matter ranging from a critique of contemporary Aboriginal male ideation and abuse of Aboriginal women to the gestures of white feminism unable to grasp with any great depth the workings of racism and its appropriations. The wordplays, juxtapositions and laughter niggle at insecurities that so often precipitate strong assertion. Her work defies any singular definition of what it means to be Aboriginal and woman in Australia. Deakin has exhibited widely, venues including the Museum of Modern Art, New York, the Watershed Media Centre in Bristol and the Museum of New Zealand, with works included in *Africus*, as well as the inaugural Johannesburg Biennale, the *Quinta Bienal de la Habana* (the Fifth Havana Biennial) and the Second Asia Pacific Triennial of Contemporary Art at the Art Gallery in Brisbane.

VICKI CROWLEY

DEAN, JAMES

b. 1931; d. 1955

actor

An American cultural and screen icon, James Dean's melancholy beauty, explosive talent and early death attract enduring glbt adulation. Dean studied acting in Los Angeles, moving to New York in 1952, where he attended classes at the Actors Studio. He made a spectacular Broadway debut as a gay Arab in a stage version of André Gide's *The Immoralists*, before starring in three films that cemented his fame – *East of Eden* (1955), *Rebel Without A Cause* (1955) and *Giant* (1956). His compelling combination of bravado, sensitivity and

frustrated desire for intimacy with distant father figures (echoing his difficult relationship with his own father) resonated with glbt and straight audiences. Desired on- and off-screen by both men and women, Dean allegedly pursued a number of gay relationships, notably with Clifton Webb and Bill Bast, and was known to frequent leather and S&M (sadomasochism) bars in Los Angeles before his death in a car accident, aged 23.

JOHN FORDE

DEFURNE, BAVO

b. 1971

film director, producer

Bavor Defurne's exquisitely photographed short films, populated by impossibly beautiful young men, are Belgium's biggest gay cinematic export, with a loyal international following on the festival circuit. Honing his skills at Saint Lukas Art School in Brussels, Defurne worked as a set decorator for Peter Greenaway and Vincent Ball, but is best known for his short films, beginning with *Particularly Now, In Spring* (1995), which eulogizes the youth of a group of athletes. Next, under the aegis of his new production company, Laika Films, came *Saint* (1996), a haunting treatment of the martyrdom of Saint Sebastian. *Sailor* (1998) foregrounded Defurne's kitsch borrowing from popular culture, but his highest profile film is the prize-winning tale of a scout's coming out, *Campfire* (2000), swiftly adopted by the Belgian government for school education. He is currently preparing his first full-length feature, *Secretly Inside*, and, with Laika Films producer Yves Verbraeken, is overseeing work by newcomers Kim Wyns (*Happy Together*, 2004) and Alex van Stratum (*Fast Forward*, 2004).

MICHAEL WILLIAMS

DEGENERES, ELLEN

b. 1958

actor

Born in New Orleans, Louisiana, Ellen DeGeneres earned the accolade 'The funniest person in America' after winning state and then national competitions for comedians. She made several appearances on national TV shows, including the *Tonight Show* (1986), where she earned the distinction of being the only female comic to be invited by Johnny Carson to sit on the couch on a first appearance. She received a Cable ACE Award nomination for her HBO one-woman show *Command Performance: One Night Stand*.

Her career in network television began with a role as office oddball, Margo Van Meter, on *Open House* (1989–90) and, later, as nurse Nancy MacIntyre, in *Laurie Hill* (1992). In 1993 Ellen started work on a successful spring replacement show originally entitled *These Friends of Mine*, which eventually ran as *Ellen* for the 1994–5 season. *Ellen* ran for four successful seasons and aired its controversial hour-long 'coming-out' episode on 30 April 1997 to an audience of over 42 million. This episode confirmed the open secret that, on- and off-screen, Ellen DeGeneres/Ellen Morgan was lesbian. ABC cancelled the show in 1998 after much negative campaigning by conservative religious groups in the United States.

Ellen has written one book, *My Point and I Do Have One* (1995), has starred in several feature-length movies, most notably with Sharon Stone in *If These Walls Could Talk, 2* (2000, produced by her one-time girlfriend, Anne Heche) and has released a CD of comedy. She currently hosts a popular TV talk show, *The Ellen DeGeneres Show* (2003).

JEAN BOBBY NOBLE

DELANOË, BERNARD

b. 1950

politician

Elected in 2001 as the Mayor of Paris, Delanoë is the city's first socialist mayor since 1871 and Paris' most high-profile openly gay public official. He was born on 30 May 1950 in Tunis and raised in the French colony of Tunisia, finishing his education in Toulouse. He became secretary of the Socialist Federation of Aveyron and was mentored by François Mitterand, the future French president. He became a Paris city councillor, then deputy to the National Assembly in 1981, and in 1983 became the head of the national Socialist Party Federation. He rose to prominence in the 1990s as a critic of Jacques Chirac's 18-year tenure as Mayor of Paris and his corruption-rife administration, which paved the way for Delanoë's successful election in 2001. His open admission of his homosexuality proved to be a non-issue for voters and confirmed Paris' status as a gay-friendly European capital. In 2003 he survived an attempted assassination.

JOHN FORDE

DELANY, SAMUEL R.

b. 1942

writer, academic

Born in New York City, the most authoritative account of Samuel Delany's life and work remains his autobiography, *The Motion of Light on Water* (1988). From his earliest science-fiction novels, such as *The Jewels of Aptor* (1962) and *Babel-17* (1967), his writing has been charged with a polymorphous, queer sensuality and sexual charge. It realizes the human body as produced and re-made in the density of sexual acts that are spread through a space and time vast enough to enable them to unfold in all their potential complexity. In his *Nevèryon* series, sexuality and Marxist political

177

economy merge to form a compelling novelistic refiguring of human social history on a scale comparable to the epic masterpieces of William Morris or Doris Lessing. His work has become increasingly bold and open as his status has grown and as social mores have changed, so that it remains, even now, on the very margins of the acceptable and normative queer comportment, by turns still sexually and socially challenging (see especially *The Mad Man* [1994]).

ADRIAN RIFKIN

DELARIA, LEA

b. 1958

actor

Lea DeLaria is a stand-up comic, musician, actor and singer. DeLaria was the first openly gay comic on national television (1993, *The Arsenio Hall Show*) and was host of Comedy Central's all-gay special *Out There*. DeLaria has performed extensively throughout Australia, New Zealand and North America. Her career as a comic led her into acting and she has made appearances on television via *Matlock* (1986), *The John Larroquette Show* (1993), *Saved By the Bell* (1993), *Friends* (1994), and *The Drew Carey Show* (1995). Her films include: *Rescuing Desire* (1996), *Plump Fiction* (1997) and the very successful *First Wives Club* (1996). An accomplished singer, Lea appeared as Hildy in the New York Shakespeare-in-the-Park's 1997 production of *On the Town*. She has released a CD of jazz cover tunes titled *Play It Cool* (2001).

JEAN BOBBY NOBLE

DEMENT, LINDA

b. 1959

artist

Linda Dement is a pioneer of computer-generated interactive art in Australia. Variously referred to as a cyber-feminist and as working with the 'monstrous female', her work navigates the interior surreal, the psyche, blood lust, depression, memory and pain, fantasy, sexualities, bodies, flesh, scar and wound. Perhaps best known for *Typhoid Mary* and for her subsequent CD-ROMs *In My Gash*, *Cyberfish Girlmonster* and *Euridice*, Dement weaves together text, object, flesh and montage, and works between the ideational and affective of cultural experience. While she has used stills, primarily she allows the viewer to move almost blindly through her work, touching the screen which takes you here and there. Unafraid of madness, sexual and psychic violence, her works are sensuous, seductive and lush in colour. Dement's work is visually tactile, sometimes harsh and humorous, and through her precision and clinical attention to detail she provides the viewer with an intense experience of the murkiness of the unspoken and the macabre. So seemingly provocative are her images that, at one point, access to her work within an exhibition in Australia was only through a guard and password. Dement began exhibiting in 1984 and has since exhibited widely in Australia and elsewhere. She is also a published author of short stories and notes; writing and stories are often the starting point of her work. As a noted lesbian artist she describes her work as a corporeal and highly personal exploration of desire, repression, abuse and violence.

VICKI CROWLEY

DEMPSEY, SHAWNA

b. 1963

video and performance artist

Canadian video and performance artist, Dempsey first attracted attention in 1990 with *We're Talking Vulva*, a rap music film about female genitalia (co-director Tracy Treager), which as part of Canada's National Film Board's *Five Feminist Minutes* reached an unprecedented worldwide audience.

Featuring a giant plastic pudenda outfit, *Vulva* set its lesbian references within a feminist diversity agenda, but such cunt-in-your-face subversiveness left no one guessing. Based in artist-run spaces in her native Winnipeg, the prolific and zany Dempsey followed up with a prize-winning roll of more lesbian-explicit tapes, often in collaboration with Lorri Millan. These usually featured the hyperactive Dempsey in such get-ups as a day-glo fright wig (*Medusa Raw*, 1992) and a 1950s cut-out housedress (*Good Citizen Betty Baker*, 1996). Throughout, the pastiche of trash narrative forms such as nature documentary satirizes the foibles – as well as the pleasures – of queer community and essentialism.

THOMAS WAUGH

DENEUVE, CATHERINE

b. 1943

actor

French film actor noted for her extraordinary beauty and elegance, Catherine Deneuve rose to fame during the 1960s in a series of landmark films including *Les Parapluies de Cherbourg* (*The Umbrellas of Cherbourg*, 1964) and *Belle de Jour* (1967). In a long and prolific career that has seen her work with many of Europe's most famous directors, Deneuve has developed a reputation as a consummate screen actor of great depth and intelligence. A veritable institution in her native France, she has attracted a strong international queer following, particularly among lesbians, due in equal parts to her smouldering eroticism, inscrutable cool persona, and starring presence in queer cult favourites such as *The Hunger* (1983) and *8 Femmes* (*8 Women*, dir. François Ozon, 2002). In 1996 she risked controversy when she filed a lawsuit against the San Francisco-based lesbian magazine, *Deneuve*, forcing a

change of name; this has not had negative impact on her queer popularity however.

BRETT FARMER

DENTAL DAM

A small sheet of latex, originally used during dental surgery, promoted in the 1980s as a form of 'safer sex' protection to be used as a barrier during oral sex.

KATHERINE WATSON

DEPARTMENT STORES

The rise of department stores parallels the emergence of identities challenging gender norms and the anchoring of desire to reproduction within the bourgeois family. Ironically, the rise of shopping as a leisure activity, originally rooted in the strictly gendered middle-class division of labour, has located women as agents as well as objects of desire, and the perceived threat was registered in cultural texts as early as Émile Zola's *The Ladies' Paradise* (1883). The camp *double entendre* in John Inman's frequent announcement, 'I'm free' in the British 1970s situation comedy *Are You Being Served?* thus continues a long tradition in which department stores and commodity culture are seen as sites of deviance and sexual opportunity.

See also: *Are You Being Served?*; Inman, John

TREVOR HOPE

DEPATHOLOGIZING OF HOMOSEXUALITY

The depathologizing of homosexuality began with the foundational research of Alfred **Kinsey** in 1947 and Evelyn **Hooker** in 1957. Kinsey, through his research on men's sexual lives, reported extensive variability in human sexual expression, beyond exclusive heterosexuality. His research demonstrated that homosexual experiences were more common amongst men than previously had been assumed. Since the beginning of the practice of psychotherapy, clients who expressed homosexual desires have been considered mentally ill. Homosexuality was considered a condition that was both treatable and preventable. Hooker, in her research, critiqued the validity of psychology's link between homosexuality and mental illness. She determined, through testing, a group of psychotherapists, that diagnosing homosexual clients as mentally ill could not be supported by empirical evidence. Her findings led to the conclusion that diagnosing homosexuality as a mental disorder was arbitrary and based primarily on society's bias against homosexuals.

During the 1970s a group of activists and scientists, in a series of radical actions, demanded that the American Psychiatric Association (APA) remove homosexuality from the Diagnostic and Statistical Manual (DSM). The DSM is a manual that was created by a board of APA psychiatrists to promote the systematic diagnosis of mental illnesses. Homosexuality was included in the first edition of the manual as a mental disorder. The fight for its removal intensified at the beginning of 1970, when a group of gay rights activists attended the annual APA convention in San Francisco. These activists disrupted sessions conducted by leading psychologists who specialized in the 'treatment' of homosexuals.

The disruption at the 1970 APA convention resulted in the APA granting a group of gay activists, psychiatrists and research psychologists the opportunity to conduct their own panel at the 1971 convention in Washington DC. The panellists argued for the removal of homosexuality from the DSM and for the liberation of all homosexuals who were being abused and confined under the guise of 'psychotherapy'. In 1972, at the annual APA convention held in Dallas, Dr John E. Fryer

(1938–2003), wearing an oversized tuxedo, rubber mask, huge wig, and using a microphone to distort his voice and the pseudonym, Dr H. Anonymous, addressed a crowd of over 100 with the words, 'I am a homosexual, I am a psychiatrist.' Frank Kameny, a Harvard astronomer who had been fired from his job with the US Army Maps Service because he was gay, appeared with Fryer on stage. In his address, Fryer implored fellow psychiatrists to end the pathologizing of their homosexual patients, warning them that it would be risky, but adding: 'We are taking an even bigger risk, however, not accepting fully our own humanity, with all the lessons it has to teach all the other humans around us and ourselves. This is the greatest loss: our honest humanity'. Barbara Gittings, a gay rights activist who had convinced Fryer to speak at the convention, said that he had helped to bring about the change: 'His speech shook up psychiatry. He was the right person at the right time.' Fryer, understanding the risks to his career, did not officially reveal that he was 'Dr Anonymous' until the APA annual convention in Philadelphia in 1994 – 22 years later.

In December 1973, after more protests, debate and the incredible advocacy and scientific rigour of Dr Judd Marmor (1910–2003), the APA board of trustees voted to remove homosexuality from its list of mental disorders and to urge that 'homosexuals be given all protections now guaranteed other citizens'. The members ratified the decision in April 1974. In 1975 the APA issued a resolution to affirm that homosexuality, as behavioural practice and lifestyle, causes no significant impairment to daily functioning. Professional psychologists were urged to promote the removal of the stigma of being mentally ill from individuals labelled as homosexual. The APA created a gay and lesbian taskforce in 1978 and a group called the Association of Gay and Lesbian Psychiatrists was established. In 1984, Division 44, the Society for the Psychological Study of Gay and Lesbian Issues, was created within the APA. Homosexuality was removed completely from the DSM in the mid-1980s.

See also: Kinsey Report, The

KATHLEEN M. CUMISKEY

DESSAIX, ROBERT

b. 1944

novelist, broadcaster

Long respected in Australia as a literary commentator on ABC radio, Robert Dessaix has established a strong critical reputation as a writer and editor, producing eight books in nine years. He began by editing *Australian Gay and Lesbian Writing. An Anthology* (1994), the first work from a major Australian publisher to tackle such issues, and co-editing *Picador New Writing* (1993). He followed these with the acclaimed memoir, *A Mother's Disgrace* (1994), a best-selling novel, *Night Letters* (1996), an edited collection of his radio interviews, *Speaking Their Minds: Intellectuals and the Public Culture in Australia* (1998), a collection of his essays titled *And So Forth* (1998), *Secrets* (1997, co-written with Drusilla Modjeska and Amanda Lohrey) and *Corfu* (2001). He is widely anthologized, appearing in both *The Penguin Book of Gay Australian Writing* and *The Best Australian Essays 1999*. Dessaix was made a Chevalier dans l'Ordre des Arts et des Lettres in 2002, for services to French culture.

MICHAEL HURLEY

DI MASSA, DIANE

b. 1961

comic book writer

Diane Di Massa is the creator of *Hothead Paisan: Adventures of a Homocidal Lesbian Terrorist*, a raw series of comic zines begun in 1991. Di Massa's work focuses on a radical lesbian confronted by entrenched heterosexism invisible to everyone but herself. Her frenetic, energetic and often apocalyptically violent comics have carved out a space in the world of graphic arts and comics in which lesbians and women are visible as more than sidekicks or curvaceous super villains. *Hothead Paisan*'s violent use of oversized, parodically depicted guns and knives, combined with the ordinariness of her life with her cat and her friends, offers an alternative to the assimilationist trend of contemporary rights-based glbt politics. Di Massa's depiction of Hothead's exuberantly violent responses to sexism and oppression have kept the anarchic radicalism of early queer and feminist groups in the eye of a queer reading public.

STEPHANIE FOOTE

DIANA, PRINCESS OF WALES

b. 1961; d. 1997

Diana Spencer was born on 1 July 1961 at the Queen's Estate in Sandringham (UK). Her wedding to Charles, Prince of Wales, in 1981 was watched by approximately 750 million people on television worldwide, catapulting her into the international limelight for the rest of her life. Their unhappy marriage, during which she suffered from bulimia and depression, ended in divorce in 1996. Especially popular with the gay community for combining a love of fashion and partying with hard work for charitable causes, her involvement with HIV/AIDS was credited with transforming attitudes to those suffering from the disease. Unprecedented global mourning followed her death in a car crash on 31 August 1997, and her funeral, which was watched by over 2.5 billion people, was accompanied by a song sung in her honour by Elton John.

SASHA ROSENEIL

DIDRIKSON, BABE

b. 1914; d. 1956

athlete

Perhaps the greatest all-around athlete ever, Mildred Didrikson Zaharias was nicknamed 'Babe' because she once hit five home runs in a baseball game. Although accomplished at baseball, basketball, diving and bowling, she found initial fame in track and field events. In the 1932 Olympics she won two gold and one silver medal, and owned or co-owned three world records. In 1938, in an attempt to end rumours that she was male, Didrikson married a professional wrestler and adopted a more traditional feminine image. In 1940 she won her first golf tournament; between 1946 and 1947 she won 17 amateur tournaments, including the 1946 US Women's Amateur and the 1947 British Amateur. She was a founding member of the Ladies Professional Golf Association (LPGA) and, in 1951, one of the first four inductees into the LPGA Hall of Fame.

ERIC ANDERSON

DIETRICH, MARLENE

b. 1901; d. 1992

actor

Nurtured by the sexual openness of 1920s Weimar Germany, Marlene Dietrich became an international star with the film *Der blaue Engel* (*The Blue Angel*, 1929), playing vibrantly tawdry cabaret singer Lola-Lola. During the 1930s she and director Josef von Sternberg went on to make six films in Hollywood, establishing the knowingly ironic, bisexual and gender-troubling image that secured Dietrich's place in the pantheon of queer stars. Two films from this period, *Morocco* (1930) and *Blonde Venus* (1932), offer particularly queer readings. The queerness of her films was reinforced by her public appearances, for which she wore everything from trousers to haute-couture gowns; meanwhile stories about her bisexual escapades abounded. During the 1960s and 1970s Dietrich performed in cabarets and concerts, maintaining her lesbian, gay and bisexual following. As Baroness von Semering, the pimp for David Bowie's gigolo, in *Just a Gigolo* (*Schöner Gigolo*, 1978), Dietrich ended her film career on a queer note. Her daughter Maria Riva's autobiography, *Marlene Dietrich* (1993), confirmed her mother's bisexuality, with an honest account of Dietrich's many male and female lovers.

ALEX DOTY

DIFRANCO, ANI

b. 1970

musician

A singer-songwriter, Ani DiFranco's politicized contemporary rock–folk music and lyrical explorations of her feminism and bisexuality have won her a dedicated queer fan base. She began performing at the age of 9, quickly cultivating an identity on the independent music scene with her bohemian appearance (piercings, shaved or dreadlocked hair) and her highly individual, charismatic live performance style. After being rejected by major recording companies, she founded her own label, Righteous Babe Records, in 1990, and continues to release her work independently. Her politicized lyrics and accomplished guitar playing have brought frequent comparisons to Bob Dylan, whom she supported in a 2003 world tour. Openly bisexual, many of her song lyrics explore her relationships with women and modern gender politics. A prolific recording artist, her albums include *Evolve* (2003), *Revelling Reckoning* (2001), *Up Up Up Up Up Up* (1999), *Dilate* (1996), and *Not a Pretty Girl* (1995).

JOHN FORDE

DIGNITY

Dignity is an independent, non-profit, national organization based in Washington DC that 'works for respect and justice for all gay, lesbian, bisexual, and transgender persons in the Catholic Church and the world', as declared in the organization's mission statement. Established in 1969 in San Diego under the leadership of Patrick Nidorf, first as a counselling group, then as a support group in Los Angeles, Dignity USA has been a national organization since 1973, with chapters located throughout the United States. In local chapters Dignity members worship with other glbtq and supportive Catholics, socialize, share personal and spiritual concerns, and work together on educational and justice issues.

MONICA BARONI

DISCO

The term 'disco' relates to two connected phenomena: (1) a musical form arising from 1970s soul and funk, and later associated more exclusively with dance music; and (2) the bar and club settings where this music was played and danced to. The significance of these combined phenomena to post-Stonewall gay culture is inestimable.

Disco music assumed various forms from the mid-1970s to the early 1980s, but it was consistent in delivering a danceable beat marked by rhythmic bass patterns and thumping percussion. Especially in its earliest manifestations, the eroticism emanating from disco demanded the talents of strong and soulful vocalists such as Donna **Summer**, Gloria Gaynor, **Sylvester** and others equipped to work with the sexual and emotional dimensions of the music. The prominently love-themed song lyrics enhanced the power of the musical performance through frequent repetition of the chorus and refrains.

Repetition became more strategic with the introduction of the extended play (EP) dance record in the mid-1970s, when elaborately orchestrated dance mixes also emerged. EPs and mixes provided a showcase for DJ talent, resulting in uninterrupted music and a seamless experience for dancers on the dance floor.

With its soul and funk roots, disco was originally associated with marginalized American cultures, originating as it had in black – and black, gay – clubs. At first, the popular press highlighted the racial and sexual origins of the phenomenon, and disco was considered to reflect new racial and sexual attitudes that had arisen from the progressive social movements of the 1960s. The proliferation of new dance clubs that not only tolerated homosexuality but defined themselves as same-sex establishments was aligned with such progressive attitudes, marking the monumental advancement of a culture that, less than a decade earlier, had feared raids and arrests whenever its members dared to congregate in drinking establishments.

In addition to offering a safe space, disco offered the definitive example of the customer-driven commodity in an increasingly visible, trend-setting gay market that was wielding considerable consumer clout within the culture industries of the 1970s. As the dance floor became the primary testing ground for the success or failure of musical pieces and artists, the gay community experienced a unique form of power in the regulation and advancement of popular musical tastes.

When disco's popularity began to skyrocket, however, strategic marketing agencies were soon commissioned to facilitate a profitable gay-to-straight crossover. The fact that disco was never inherently 'gay' originally made the crossover much easier to effect and manage. Some aspects of this move supported a progressive agenda, promoting a 'universalization' of the dance experience and a place where people could relate and mix irrespective of gender, race or sexuality. In due time, however, the mainstream popularity of disco effected an insidious form of dominant cultural masking, whereby the gay roots of the phenomenon were largely disavowed. This erasure of homosexuality was already in place by the time of the release of *Saturday Night Fever* (1977), a disco film that attempts to return homosexuality to the margins of public culture. The 'Disco Sucks' backlash of 1979 offered the most blatant and heavily publicized attempt to contain the productions of a re-marginalized culture, in this case by mass destruction of the artefacts themselves.

The crossover potential of disco was certainly augmented by the genre's development as a cultural hybrid even before straight culture accepted it, making disco a prime candidate for mainstream marketing amalgamation. Disco's hybridity arose from the ways in which the musical form highlighted its own sense of derivation. Its beats and rhythms were not difficult to replicate, and by the late 1970s disco had begun to rely upon the musical instrument best suited to hybridity – the synthesizer. Disco was also used for cover versions of classics that originated from disparate musical genres and artists, from Gordon Lightfoot to Moussorgsky.

Before disco as genre and place was transformed by the ravages of the AIDS epidemic during the early 1980s, the phenomenon made an indelible mark as a creative testament to gay culture's influence upon a mainstream culture that longed for something different.

See also: Stonewall, Club culture

Further reading

Kornbluth, Jesse (1979) 'Merchandising Disco for the Masses', *The New York Times*, 18 February, Sunday Magazine section: 18, 21–4, 44–5. (This article details crossover strategies that secured disco's mainstream popularity.)
Lombardi, John (1975) 'Selling Gay to the Masses', *Village Voice*, 30 June: 10–11. (This

piece discusses the masking of gay cultural roots in mainstream cultural promotion.)

MICHAEL DEANGELIS

DITSIE, BEVERLY

b. 1972

activist, filmmaker

Beverly Ditsie was born and educated in Soweto, Johannesburg. In 1989 she became a founding member of the multiracial Gay and Lesbian Organization of the Witwatersrand (GLOW), and in 1990 helped to organize South Africa's first Gay and Lesbian Pride March. During the 1990s Ditsie often appeared on local television to speak on lesbian issues, inspiring other black lesbians by her example. She was threatened repeatedly with violence as a result of her media presence. In 1995 Ditsie addressed the United Nations on lesbian issues at the Fourth World Conference on women in Beijing, and in 1998 spoke at the UN Global Women's Tribunal in New York. In 1996 she left GLOW, feeling that the leadership did not take lesbian issues seriously, and formed a short-lived black lesbian organization called Nkateko. Her life and sometimes fraught relationship with Simon **Nkoli** are recounted in her documentary, *Simon and I* (2002).

ANTHONY MANION

DIVA

Deriving from the Latin for goddess, the term 'diva' originally referred to the 'prima donna' or principal female star of opera. Today, its use has broadened to denote any powerful female figure, usually in the performing arts and media, but sometimes even in non-artistic fields. Queer cultures have had a long and rich association with divas. Diva worship – the celebration or fandom of divas – has been a staple of both gay and lesbian cultures since at least the late nineteenth century. Divas that have been feted by gays and lesbians over the years include: operatic singers such as Maria **Callas**; film stars such as Judy **Garland**, Bette **Davis** and Catherine **Deneuve**; musical theatre performers such as Julie **Andrews** and Carol **Channing**; popular singers such as Barbra **Streisand**, Diana **Ross**, Dusty **Springfield** and **Madonna**; and many others. Drag and transgender cultures have equally strong traditions of celebrating the diva as a privileged figure of queer investment. Indeed, it is not uncommon for members of transgender communities to refer to each other as divas.

The reasons for this intense association between queers and divas are complex and varied. In large part it stems from the desire – if not the fundamental need – for queer-identity role models. Unlike other social minorities, queers generally grow up in isolation from others who share their desires and identities, and thus they don't have the benefit of communal structures such as family, religion or school through which to establish and consolidate their queer sense of self. Divas have arguably been deployed by queer cultures to help meet this need and to perform vital identity-building work.

One thing about divas that makes them receptive to such processes of queer identity-building is that they are figures of transformation, empowerment and survival. Both in general biographical terms, and in more specific terms of individual performance and style, divas transform themselves from something ordinary into something extraordinary, often surmounting major obstacles to do so and acquiring in the process heightened powers of personal agency and authority. Such a scenario has strong and immediate appeal for a social group such as queers that has traditionally had to struggle to gain acceptance and respect.

To the extent that they frequently unsettle conventional forms of gender and sexuality, divas themselves can also be apprehended as figures of queerness. The very definition of the diva as a strong, authoritative woman is fundamentally transgressive of traditional, patriarchal notions of femininity. This is why divas are so often demonized or ridiculed in mainstream contexts – because they challenge orthodox hierarchies of gendered power. Many divas extend this subversion by actively incorporating queer elements such as cross-dressing into their persona and work.

While these multiple points of affinity suggest how and why divas function as identification figures for queers, it should not be forgotten that they equally function as objects of desire, especially, although not exclusively, for lesbians. Magnetizing in their glamour and power, divas are patently sexual, and queer cultures have responded enthusiastically to their erotic charms and pleasures.

Further reading

Koestenbaum, Wayne (1993) *The Queen's Throat: Opera, Homosexuality and the Mystery of Desire*, New York: Poseidon.

BRETT FARMER

DIVINE

b. 1945; d. 1988

actor, nightclub singer, drag queen

Harris Glenn Milstead, born in Towson, Maryland, knew stigmatization when growing up as an overweight, effeminate boy in the Baltimore suburbs. By the early 1970s he had become a sleazy, obese, drag superstar, the muse of trash auteur John **Waters**, who both gave him his art name and drag persona Divine and made him famous, in a camped up, queer version of the Sternberg–Dietrich partnership. As such, Divine's outrageous, debasing, and nonetheless sexy, star image epitomizes the queening of America's celebrity culture.

A star in Waters' underground classics such as *Mondo Trasho* (1969), *Multiple Maniacs* (1970), *Pink Flamingos* (1972) and *Female Trouble* (1975), Divine was the ultimate queen of filth and debauchery. The outrageous, upside-down world of Waters' films, which owed much to Andy Warhol, Kenneth Anger and Russ Meyer, staged the clash between social degradation and all-American values, giving vent to what the American way of life negates – queers, drugs, nymphomaniacs, murderers, theft and deception, abortion, etc. Waters' queer world provided Divine with an extraordinary setting for his impersonations of hyped-up femininity, embodying aggressively made up, utterly vulgar and ruthless figures that would do anything to get famous, or simply to cope with the craziest of environments. Significantly, Divine found fame thanks to his role in *Pink Flamingos*, a film staging the contest to achieve 'filthiest' primacy between two families: in a most (ill) famed film ending, Divine eats a poodle's fresh faeces and proclaims herself 'the filthiest person alive'.

While acting in Waters' films, during the 1970s Divine started pursuing an independent career. In 1973 he worked with The Cockettes, a San Francisco drag stage troupe; in 1976–7 he appeared onstage in New York and London in a parody of prison movies, Tom Eyen's *Women Behind Bars*. The following year he was guest of honour at the Alternative Miss World Contest that was filmed by Andrew Logan as *I Wanna Be a Beauty Queen*, and in 1979 he appeared in *Tally Brown* by Rosa von **Praunheim**, a documentary on the eponymous underground superstar. By the 1980s he had become an international disco diva, an appreciated nightclub singer and performer, making the most of his raunchy and bitchy talent for provoking audiences, often appearing as a guest in TV talk shows and entering the hit charts with singles such as *Shoot Your Shot* (1982) and *You Think You're a Man* (1984).

When Waters moved from cheap underground movies to counterculture Hollywood black comedies, as with the first 'odorama' movie ever made (*Polyester*, 1981), he made a decisive contribution to Divine's cult stardom. And yet, Divine wished to be acknowledged for his talent as a character actor, and occasionally give up drag. In the 1980s he won some non-drag film roles, playing a gangster in Alan Rudolph's film *Trouble in Mind* (1985), an LA detective in Michael Schroeder's *Out of the Dark* (1988) and doubling himself into two roles in his last film for Waters, *Hairspray* (1988), one a tamed housewife, the other a nasty male segregationist who runs a TV station.

Shortly after the release of *Hairspray*, network television Fox booked him for a regular part as 'Uncle Otto' in the TV programme *Married with Children*. Before he could take up the role, he died in his hotel suite from sleep apnoea

Labelled by *People* magazine as 'the Drag Queen of the Century' and celebrated in Steve Yeager's documentary *Divine Trash* (1998), Divine's role in queer counterculture is significant: it is appropriate that the spot where he actually ate poodle's faeces became a 'museum' signalled by an inscription on the sidewalk ('This place designated a museum: Divine! *c.* 1969'), a reminder of his amazing deeds and a landmark in the history of American culture.

Further reading

Jay, B. (1993) *Not Simply Divine*, New York: Simon & Schuster.

Milstead, F., Heffernan, K. and Yeager, S. (2001) *My Son Divine*, Los Angeles: Alyson.

Moon, M. and Sedgwick, E.K. (1993) 'Divinity: A Dossier – A Performance Piece – A Little-Understood Emotion', in E.K. Sedgwick, *Tendencies*, Durham: Duke University Press.

Pela, R. (2002) *Filthy: The Weird World of John Waters*, Los Angeles: Alyson.

Waters, J. (1981) *Shock Value: A Tasteful Book About Bad Taste*, New York: Dell.

FABIO CLETO

DIXON, MELVIN

b. 1950; d. 1992

writer

Openly gay African-American poet, novelist and translator, whose works continued the legacy of novelist James **Baldwin** in their exploration of the experiences of black gay masculinity, Dixon was born in Stamford, Connecticut in 1950. His first book of poetry, *Change of Territory* (1983), compared and contrasted the history of American slavery and the northward migration of African-Americans from the Southern states with the contemporary cultural alienation of African-Americans. His novels *Trouble the Water* (1989) and *Vanishing Rooms* (1991) explored homophobia and racism in contemporary New York, and reflect the influences of Baldwin, Ralph Ellison and Zora Neale Hurston. He lectured in English literature at Williams College and Queens College, and published a volume of criticism, *Ride Out The Wilderness* (1987). His final book of poems, *Love's Instruments* (1995), was published posthumously after his death from AIDS in 1992.

JOHN FORDE

DOLCE & GABBANA

Dolce, Domenico

b. 1958

fashion designer

Gabbana, Stefano

b. 1962

fashion designer

Created by the Italian designers Domenico Dolce, born in Palermo, and Stefano Gab-bana, born in Milan, the Dolce & Gabbana label is a worldwide synonym for elegance and transgression. Its style represents a distinctive combination of sensuality and tradition, mixing together male and female clothing detail, conventional fashion elements and innovative ingredients. Openly gay, Dolce & Gabbana design stage outfits for many gay icons, for example, Whitney Houston and Kylie Minogue, as well as for their favourite, Madonna. It is for these reasons that today they are much-loved fashion designers for gay people all over the world.

Dolce & Gabbana were romantically involved for 19 years; however, in 2005 they announced that this was no longer the case, although they would continue to collaborate professionally.

ALBERTO EMILETTI

DONIS, ALEX

b. 1964

artist

Alex Donis was born in Chicago and raised in Los Angeles. He studied graphic design at Long Beach State University where he developed his art. His work centres on issues of gender, sexuality, race and cultural fantasy in which homoerotic images abound. In one of his most controversial exhibitions, titled *My Cathedral* (1997), Donis included fictionalized same-sex images of renowned political, religious and pop icons embracing and kissing, among them César Chávez and Che Guevara. The exhibition opened at Galería de la Raza in San Francisco but was vandalized twice and two paintings destroyed. Donis' transgressive images of same-sex couples continue to play an integral role in his artwork. His installation *WAR* (2001) depicts members of the LA Police Department dancing with gang members. The scenarios are both humorous and erotically charged. They present two hypermasculine groups commonly associated

187

with violence in a positive, romantic and erotic forum. In much of his work, the macho male figure is commonly feminized to deconstruct stereotypical gender identities.

DANIEL ENRIQUE PÉREZ

DONOGHUE, EMMA

b. 1969

Award-winning Irish novelist, short-story writer, dramatist and literary historian who has had a significant impact upon Ireland's literary landscape with her representations of lesbian identity and existence. Born in Dublin and living (since 1998) in Ontario, Canada, Donoghue gained a PhD from the University of Cambridge, England, where she wrote her first novel, *Stir-Fry* (1994). Set in contemporary Dublin, this lesbian **coming-out novel** represents an important contribution to the genre for young Irish lesbian readers. Her second novel, *Hood* (1995), also set in Dublin, explores the experience of bereavement and mourning for someone who has still not come out, a familiar topic in gay men's writing but unusual in lesbian fiction. Both novels hold a mirror to the homophobia still pervasive in contemporary Irish society (in particular its institutionalization by the Roman Catholic Church) while their humanist appeal has brought the Irish lesbian novel into the mainstream.

CATHERINE CLAY

DONOVAN, MARTIN

b. 1957

actor

A handsome, quietly charismatic heterosexual actor born in Reseda, California, Donovan has impressed gay audiences with his willingness to tackle gay film roles. A graduate of the American Theater of Arts in Los Angeles, he is best known for his work with independent director Hal Hartley, with whom he has made six features, including *Simple Men* (1992), *Amateur* (1994) and *The Book of Life* (1998). In Angela Pope's *Hollow Reed* (1996) he plays a gay doctor fighting for legal custody of his 9-year-old son, after he suspects his ex-wife's boyfriend has been physically abusing the child. The film's pro-gay parenting perspective garnered praise, as did Donovan's passionate love-making scenes with his co-star Ian Hart. In Don Roos' black comedy *The Opposite of Sex* (1998), Donovan played a soft-spoken gay teacher who overcomes a manipulative half-sister, homophobic abuse and accusations of sexual abuse to end the film happily partnered and raising a baby.

JOHN FORDE

DORADO, ALEJANDRA

b. 1963

multimedia artist

Alejandra Dorado reveals, under a false veneer of humour and naïveté, a gender-bending, iconoclastic, campy and ironic work that denaturalizes conventional gender representation schemes. Portraying herself in the nude, Dorado appropriates and subverts stable heterocentric gender archetypes and stereotypes, such as the Roman matron Lucretia (who preferred death to dishonour after being raped) and Saint Sebastian (a gay cultural icon who also happens to be the patron saint of Dorado's native city, Cochabamba). Dorado intentionally misrepresents and exposes these figures as artificial and ideologically normalized social constructions. In other works, such as *Por tu culpa* (Mixed Media, 2003), she strips a soldier of the emblems that stabilize gender representation as well as exalt the physical and moral values of male heterosexuality (weapons and medals that stand for aggressiveness and physical accomplishment). Moreover, the soldier's head in this work is superimposed on the body of a half-naked woman in an affected pose. The lower half of the work, done in lavender, depicts clothing associated with the gay clone – an ultra-virile fantasy of gay male culture. Thus, Dorado plays with male anxieties of inadequacy (gay and straight) to deconstruct the military hero by stripping him of his symbolic virility, exposing him as his greatest fear – a gay male transvestite.

Dorado celebrates, exhibits and sanctifies her narcissism. Her work is calculated: she chooses a particular media for its functional material and semantic possibilities. The computer photo-manipulation in her work allows for a complex interplay with the concepts of image, icon, representation, falsification and authenticity. Her installations are recognized for their theatrical nature and, indeed, her work refers to theatricality and performance. The collage effect of her work raises the possibilities of decontextualization and re-signification.

PEDRO ALBORNOZ

DOSOKAI

TV programme

Dosokai (Alumni Reunion, 1993) was a pioneering TV drama dealing with homosexual issues that was aired during prime time on Japan's commercial NTV network. The series was part of the 'gay boom' that swept Japanese media during the early 1990s and which featured movies, magazine reports and novels centring on (predominantly male) homosexuality. The ten-part drama drew top ratings, being well written and produced, featuring an all-star cast and accompanied by a hit soundtrack. NTV's second gay-themed series, Romance, which aired in 1999, portrayed a considerably bleaker picture of gay life than its predecessor.

MARK MCLELLAND

DOTY, MARK

b. 1953

poet

Mark Doty was born in Maryville, Tennessee. His first book of poems, Turtle, Swan was published in 1987, and his second, Bethlehem in Broad Daylight, in 1991. His third collection of poems, My Alexandria (1993), won the National Book Critics Circle Award and Britain's T.S. Eliot Prize, and was also a National Book Award finalist. Doty received a Lamda Literary Award for his fourth collection, Atlantis (1995). Doty's homosexuality plays a key role in his poetic enterprise. Several of the poems in My Alexandria deal with the aftermath of learning that his partner is HIV+. His memoir, Heaven's Coast (1996), is a prose account of life during the AIDS era, and of watching his lover die. Doty's poems also reference gay bars and drag queens, while consistently maintaining an interest in aesthetic concerns and beauty. Doty's other recent works include the poetry collections Sweet Machine (1998) and Source (2001), and the autobiography Firebird (1999). In 2002 Doty published Still Life with Oysters and Lemon, a brief philosophical meditation on art, memory and time. Doty has been the recipient of fellowships from the Guggenheim Foundation and the National Endowment for the Arts. He lives in Houston, Texas, where he teaches at the University of Houston, and Provincetown, Massachusetts.

KRISTEN HOLT

DOUDART DE LA GRÉE, MARIE LOUISE

b. 1909; d. 1981

writer

Doudart de la Grée is the author of two lesbian novels, *Vae Solis* (*Wee de Eenzamen/Woe the Lonely Ones*) and *Zondaressen* (*Female Sinners*). *Vae Solis,* written in 1943 and published in 1946, shares some similarities with Radclyffe Hall's *The Well of Loneliness.* A very sentimental story, in which the protagonist, Anne, finally conquers her shame and accepts her lesbianism, meanwhile having had several brief affairs with women who all turn out to be not 'like that', the novel ends with her a disappointed woman. *Zondaressen* centres on female friendships in a nunnery. Doudart de la Grée was married and had a son, but led a stormy love life, including many women lovers. A beautiful woman, she specialized more in life itself as a work of art than in serious writing. In 1948 she had an affair with the famous Dutch lesbian writer Anna Blaman, who was about the same age. The couple's letters were published in 1990.

MAAIKE MEIJER

DOUGHERTY, CECILIA

filmmaker

Experimental filmmaker and writer whose works explore family interactions and the representation of lesbians in popular culture. Dougherty has independently produced over 25 videotapes for film festivals and exhibitions, including *Gay Tape: Butch and Femme* (1985), an exploration of attitudes towards gender roles within lesbian communities; the series *Claudia* (1987), *Kathy* (1988) and *Grapefruit* (1989), which explore the representation of lesbian sexuality; an experimental family narrative *Coal Miner's Granddaughter* (1991); *Joe-Joe* (1993), an adaptation of gay playwright Joe Orton's sexually explicit diaries; and *My Failure to Assimilate* (1995), which explores the politics of social exclusion. She teaches video production and criticism at the New School for Social Research and Bard College, and lives in New York and Dublin, where she was involved in protests against the exclusion of lesbian and gay men from the annual St Patrick's Day Parade.

JOHN FORDE

DOVE, ULYSSES

b. 1947; d. 1996

dancer, choreographer

Dove began dance study while a pre-med student at Howard University and graduated with a dance degree in 1970 from Bennington College. In New York he danced with the Merce Cunningham Company, Mary Anthony, Pearl Lang and Anna Sokolow. In 1973 he joined the Alvin Ailey American Dance Theater, where he quickly rose to the rank of principal dancer, acclaimed for his commanding presence, clarity of movement and truthful dramatic intensity. He turned to choreography at Ailey's urging and created the 1980 solo 'Inside' for star dancer Judith Jamison. He left the Ailey company that year to begin a significant freelance career choreographing dances, marked by relentless speed, violent force and daring eroticism, for the Basel Ballet, Swedish Cullberg Ballet, Dutch National Ballet, London Festival Ballet, American Ballet Theater, New York City Ballet and Groupe de Recherche Choréographique de l'Opéra de Paris, where he spent three years as assistant director. Dove's death from AIDS placed him among the most prominent of publicly discussed gay, male, black dance artists.

See also: Ailey, Alvin

THOMAS F. DEFRANTZ

DOWN LOW

Originating in hip-hop culture to imply secrecy, the down low is now invoked as an identifier for black and Hispanic men who engage in sexual activity with other men but who do not identify as gay. Health experts view men on the down low as responsible for recklessly spreading HIV to their partners.

CHRIS BELL

DRAG

Usually applied to ostentatiously exaggerated transvestitism, ironically playing up imitations of the opposite sex, drag is a complex, diversified phenomenon that defies a single, all-encompassing definition. The origin of the term is uncertain: it seems to date back to the Elizabethan age in England, where it was used for male actors playing women's roles in theatres where transvestism was the rule.

Examples of male-to-female and female-to-male drag are to be seen in all ages, but it is above all the MTF figures we find in literature, the theatre, and cinema. In glbtq culture drag is often associated with performance and parody by drag queens, usually – but not always – gay men or transgender women bewigged and dressed weirdly and wonderfully: often they imitate female stars of the world of entertainment, performing in drag shows, clubs or in Gay Pride events and parades.

It was during the 1920s that Paris, London, Berlin and New York saw a characteristic 'transvestite style' taking off in a big way. Particularly famous are the performances by singers such as Judy **Garland** and Marlene **Dietrich**, who popularized male dress for women and to some extent set the style – the type of clothing, strikingly short hair, dinner jacket, monocle and cigar – to be seen in so many lesbian nightclubs and bars of the time. Although arising from a common tradition, gay and lesbian drag parted ways to develop along different paths. It was eventually the connection between gay culture and drag that was consolidated with the emergence of the drag queen. In evidence as early as the interwar years, it made its greatest impact in the 1960s, when drag took on political connotations. Indeed, drag entered the major annals of history with the **Stonewall** rebellion of 1969, which was led by transvestites and drag queens and is considered the real beginning of the modern gay liberation movement. As for female-to-male drag, it was not until the mid-1980s that a lesbian drag king subculture emerged, albeit not simply as a reflection of drag queen culture.

Although drag is often associated with cross-dressing, transvestitism, transsexualism and transgender, it is not synonymous with any of these terms. Drag is essentially action, not identity: it shakes up all rigid definitions for gender and sexuality, parodying the stereotypes of femininity and masculinity. In this connection we find expressions such as gender-fuck or gender bending being used. In a sense, drag cuts across the other categories, which may enact drag situations. At the same time, however, it retains its own peculiar character as masquerade, as theatrical action – flaunted, spectacular and camp.

Between the 1980s and 1990s, and thanks to the creativity and performances of drag stars such as **Divine** and **RuPaul**, drag found a place in popular culture and ever more room outside the queer and glbt communities – in art, cinema and the fashion system – attesting to a veritable 'drag renaissance' both in mainstream and media culture.

MONICA BARONI

DRAG BALL

Drag balls originated in Harlem, the site where African-American and Latino cross-dressing men displayed their refashioning of both clothing and gender. Through various talent categories, participants competed over their performative 'realness'. The film *Paris Is Burning* and **voguing**, a dance craze, were two popular cultural offshoots of these events.

GABRIEL GOMEZ

DRAG KING

By definition, drag kings are women who dress in men's attire and perform in a masculine manner that underscores masculinity's malleability as a social construct. There is no historical timeline of drag king culture per se. However, since the early 1990s drag king popularity has steadily become a central feature in queer clubs around the world. Scholar Judith **Halberstam** differentiates the contemporary drag king phenomenon from the traditions of male impersonation that stretched over 200 years. Where drag kings draw attention to the theatrical nature of masculinity itself, the male impersonator attempts to convince the audience of his maleness. Likewise, the drag king is dissimilar to the drag butch lesbian, who does not simply put on or take off her masculinity for theatrical effect. While these differences help to clarify the specifics of drag king culture, the culture itself is a continually changing phenomenon and many drag king activities blur the lines between these differentiations. For instance, many self-identified butch lesbians perform drag in a manner that focuses less on theatrics and more on perfecting their likeness to men. Some lesbian femmes utilize exaggerated drag costumes to highlight the very falseness of their attempt to pass as men. There are even drag queens who dress as kings and kings who perform gay maleness. Although the drag king receives far less attention in mainstream popular culture than his drag queen counterpart, there are a variety of web sites, books, photographic exhibitions and documentaries that highlight the artistic and political pleasures of the drag king genre.

KELLIE BURNS

DRAG QUEEN

A male dressed as a female, often elaborately, and displaying mock feminized gestures and expressions, often in conjunction with others in a drag show.

MICHAEL PINFOLD

DRAG SHOW

Performance in which men parade and entertain while elaborately dressed as women. A gross mimicry of feminine behaviour and female style, it is usually humorous and parodic.

MICHAEL PINFOLD

DU PLESSIS, JEAN

b. 1945

psychologist, author

Born in Uitenhage, South Africa, on 27 June 1945, Jean Du Plessis is a psychologist and counsellor, whose work has focused on research about, and care of, those suffering from cerebral palsy and other neurological conditions, and therapeutic support on sexual orientation issues. He has worked extensively with gay and lesbian patients and aims to encourage gay people to live meaningful lives and fight homophobia by educating the general public about homosexuality. His book, *Oor Gay Wees* (1999), based on his research in clinical practice, is a self-help manual for gay people, and their family and friends.

JOHN FORDE

DUBOWSKI, SANDI SIMCHA

b. 1971

filmmaker

Sandi Simcha Dubowski is an American Jewish documentary filmmaker. His first short documentary video work, *Tomboychik*, won a Golden Gate Award at the 1994 San Francisco International Film Festival. His film *Trembling Before G-d* (2001), a recipient of 12 international awards, explores the lives of Jewish orthodox gays and lesbians whose tradition prohibits homosexual intercourse. Michele, for example, born in Brooklyn and thrown out after coming out to her parents, revisits her neighbourhood after seven years; Mark, an orthodox man from London, is sent to Israel following his Rabbi's declaration that no gay men exist in the Holy Land; and a married woman with children speaks (her face in shadow) about her depression caused by her inability to fulfil her lesbian identification. Dubowski, an openly gay artist born into a secular Jewish family in New York, became newly religious himself during the six years it took to make this film.

GILAD PADVA

DUCASTEL, OLIVIER AND JACQUES MARTINEAU

Ducastel, Olivier

b. 1962

director

Martineau, Jacques

b. 1963

director

French filmmakers and domestic partners, Ducastel and Martineau have attracted considerable critical praise and commercial success with a series of innovative, queer, coming-of-age films. Ducastel, who originally trained and worked as an editor, and Martineau, a college professor, met and fell in love in 1998 while working on their first feature film, the quirky, queer-themed musical, *Jeanne et le Garçon Formidable* (*Jeanne and the Perfect Guy*). Centring on the story of a promiscuous young woman who becomes infatuated with an HIV+ man, the film established the pair's characteristic style: an adventurous formalism wedded to a thematic concern with young social and sexual misfits trying to find their place in the world. Follow-up films include the charming road movie *Drôle de Félix* (*Adventures of Félix*, 2000) and *Ma Vraie Vie à Rouen* (*The True Story of My Life in Rouen*, 2002), an intimate auto-portrait of a gay teenager, shot entirely on digital video.

BRETT FARMER

DUFFY, CAROL ANN

b. 1955

poet

Glaswegian, prize-winning poet Duffy is also a playwright, poetry editor and critic, and writes for children, but she is best known for her poetry. Her work ranges from gritty and harsh (as in 'Psychopath' [*Selling Manhattan*] and 'Standing Female Nude' [*Standing Female Nude*]) to the elegiac ('Moments of Grace' [*Mean Time*]) and fiercely or gently sensual ('Valentine' and 'Warming Her Pearls' respectively). Duffy offers witty and provocative social perspectives via unexpected voices: in 'Psychopath', the speaker is the psychopath himself, whose extreme misogyny is a chilling comment on gender ideologies; in the futuristic 'Descendants' (*The Other Country*), the speaker's 'nuked' environment is a warning; in *The World's Wife* and *Feminine Gospels*, women's voices undermine patriarchy's sense of its own importance and history.

KYM MARTINDALE

DUFFY, MAUREEN

b. 1933

writer

British novelist, poet and playwright, and activist in the gay rights movement since the 1960s. Honorary president of the Gay and Lesbian Humanist Association since 1979 and a leading figure in the Arts Lobby Against Section 28, Duffy has consistently placed themes of social and sexual oppression at the centre of her work. Her first explicitly lesbian novel, *The Microcosm* (1966), examines lesbian subcultures, weaving real-life stories around the fictionalized clientele of a London lesbian bar. Criticized by some lesbian readers for its application of Freudian psychology and its apparent championing of the butch, this novel was radical in its rejection of congenitalist theories of homosexuality dominant in England at this time, and in its assertion of all the varieties of queerness. Duffy has continued to represent marginalized sexualities in subsequent fiction and dramatic writings, while lesbian eroticism is explored most fully in her poetry.

See also: Section 28

CATHERINE CLAY

DUIKER, SELLO

b. 1974

writer

Black South African novelist Sello Duiker grew up in a relatively privileged Soweto home then trained as a journalist at the historically elite, predominantly white Rhodes University. His first book, *Thirteen Cents* (2000), won the Commonwealth Writers' Prize for Best First Novel, Africa region. It follows a mixed-race street child through life in gang-dominated Cape Town, including graphic scenes of sexual violence. His second book, *The Quiet Violence of Dreams* (2001), focuses on Tsepho, a young black man who struggles with mental illness, an addiction to drugs, an abusive father and his own confused sexuality. Tsepho is brutally gang-raped but eventually becomes an accomplished and much-desired rent boy. While many of the clients and male prostitutes depicted in the novel are white, homosexuality is portrayed as natural or traditional to Africa. Duiker's female characters also forcefully challenge stereotypes about African women's sexuality.

MARC EPPRECHT

DUNYE, CHERYL

b. 1966

filmmaker, director

Born in Liberia, Cheryl Dunye grew up in Philadelphia and was educated at Temple and Rutgers Universities. She is best known for *The Watermelon Woman* (1996), the first African-American lesbian feature film, a fictional story about a young filmmaker who seeks to uncover the truth behind another character, an elusive black actor from the 1930s. This film uses the tropes of documentary to create fiction for a style Dunye has called 'Dunyementary', an approach that often leads to a humorous look at race, class, gender and sexual orientation. *The Watermelon Woman* was widely influential and even included in the 1997 Whitney Biennial. Dunye has received many such distinctions, including a 1998 Rockefeller Foundation fellowship, while her works have been screened throughout the world. Her subsequent feature, *Stranger Inside* (2001), won the Audience Award at the San Francisco International Film Festival.

GABRIEL GOMEZ

DURBAN (MKHUMBANE)

South Africa's third largest city, noted by Mary Renault for its relative tolerance of gays and lesbians among whites as early as the 1950s. The African township of Mkhumbane also became renowned during those years for its celebration of male–male marriages among blacks. The site of Africa's first (albeit short-lived) Gay Liberation Movement at the University of Natal–Durban in 1972, the city and province is now served by KwaZulu–Natal Provincial Coalition for Gay and Lesbian Equality.

MARC EPPRECHT

DUSTAN, GUILLAUME

b. 1965; d. 2005

writer

Guillaume Dustan exploded onto the French literary scene in 1996 with his first novel *Dans ma chambre* (In My Room). The novel's raw, first-person description of queer life in Paris and its frank depiction of drug use and the struggles of gay men with safe sex quickly became the focal point of debates within the gay community. Dustan followed this novel with the short narrative, *Je sors ce soir* (I'm Going Out Tonight, 1997), a blow-by-blow account of a single night out in a Parisian gay club. These and his later books are unabashedly and sometimes unflatteringly autobiographical and are written from a decidedly gay perspective. Since 1999 he has been the editor of the book series, Rayon gai, which publishes both French lesbian and gay authors as well as translations. His novel *Nicolas Pages* (1999) won France's prestigious Prix de Flore.

DANIEL HENDRICKSON

DUVERT, TONY

b. 1945

writer

French novelist and essayist Tony Duvert is loosely associated with the nouveau roman school of writers, but of a somewhat younger generation. Very little is known about his personal life, giving rise to occasional outlandish speculation. He has published several books that are stylistically varied. Some are more or less standard narratives (*When Jonathan Died* [*Quand mourut Jonathan*], 1978), others intensely experimental fiction (*Strange Landscape* [*Paysage de fantaisie*], 1972), still others straightforward essays. Almost all of his work deals with inter-generational homosexual relationships. He has published two collections of essays on sexual politics: *Le Bon sexe illustré* (1974) is a scathing critique of sex education in France; *L'Enfant au masculin* (1980) is a collection of essays on a wide variety of topics and remains one of the most radical and significant French theoretical books on sexual politics to date.

DANIEL HENDRICKSON

DYKE ACTION MACHINE (DAM!)

DAM! is a New York-based public art collaboration founded in 1991 by Carrie Moyer and Sue Schaffner. The purpose DAM! sets itself is to highlight and criticize the prejudices and stereotypes that exist about lesbians in mainstream culture. To this end special posters are produced, alluding to and imitating advertisements familiar to all but displaying lesbian images and situations that offer a parody of mainstream images. As in the comparable public art projects of Barbara Kruger and the **Guerrilla Girls**, DAM! reappropriates public spaces in an ironic key, challenging the viewer's heterocentric outlook. So far, DAM! has organized annual 5,000-piece poster campaigns for the streets of New York, displaying its own posters side by side with mainstream outdoor advertising. Disguised as advertising, DAM!'s public art project is wider and more varied than the art found in museums and art galleries.

MONICA BARONI

195

DYKES ON BIKES

A contingent of lesbian motorcyclists whose traditional leading of the San Francisco Lesbian, Gay, Bisexual and Transgender Pride Parade has become as traditional as the parade itself. The group began in 1976 with a small contingent of women riding in the San Francisco Pride Parade and calling themselves 'Dykes On Bikes'. Their presence was an instant success, and eventually the group became the Parade's leaders. As membership increased, L.B. Gunn, Kalin Elliott-Arns, Christine Elliott-Arns and Mel formed the Women's Motorcycle Contingent (WMC) in the late 1980s as a non-profit organization. The group changed its name to Women's Motorcycle Contingent Dykes On Bikes to be inclusive of all women who rode motorcycles and wished to participate in the Parade. Affiliate groups exist throughout the United States, with similar groups leading Pride parades in New York, London and Sydney.

JOHN FORDE

DYNASTY

Cult American TV drama (1981–9), produced by Aaron Spelling, *Dynasty* is about the lives and loves of a wealthy oil-mining family and attracted a devoted gay following for its ground-breaking gay characters and the camp bitchiness of its star, Joan Collins. The convoluted sex-and-scheming narrative revolved around a love triangle between oil tycoon Blake Carrington (John Forsyth), his bitter, ambitious ex-wife Alexis (Collins) and his former secretary and new wife, Krystle (Linda Evans). Entertainingly and accurately portraying the greed, glamour and excess of 1980s America, the programme established Collins as a Bette Davis-like gay icon. Steven, Blake and Alexis' bisexual son (played by Al Corley in 1981–2 and Jack Coleman 1983–9), presented a yo-yo-ing sexuality that reflected the producers' ambivalent attitudes towards positive presentations of homosexuality – gay in series 1 (1981) and married with a child by series 2 (1982), Steven's relationship with men eventually found fulfilment with Bart Fullmont (Kevin Conroy).

JOHN FORDE

E

E! ENTERTAINMENT TELEVISION

A 24-hour cable network in the United States with programming dedicated to the world of entertainment, style and fashion. Launched in 1996 together with the web site *E! Online*, the network's content includes the popular *E! True Hollywood Stories* that irreverently profiles stars of film, entertainment and music struggling with fading careers, broken marriages, and alcohol and drug addiction. Also popular are behind-the-scenes profiles of notable film successes and flops. Highlights of the network are gay gossip columnist Ted Casablanca's show, *The Awful Truth*, comedian Joan Rivers' fashion show with daughter Melissa and reality TV series *The Anna Nicole Smith Show*.

See also: Smith, Anna Nicole

JOHN FORDE

EARLY FROST, AN

Made-for-television film

Screened in the US on 11 November 1985, *An Early Frost*, directed by John Erman, was the first prime time made-for-TV film to deal sympathetically with the subject of AIDS. Set in a wealthy Chicago middle-class suburb, the film tells the story of Michael, a young, successful gay lawyer (played by Aidan Quinn) who discovers that he is HIV+, and returns home to con-

front his family about both his homosexuality and impending illness. Although criticized by some for the rather clichéd depiction of the relationship between a repressed, 'straight-acting' Michael and his 'out' and therefore unfaithful lover Peter, the film became the prototypical AIDS narrative and played a crucial role in both educating people about the disease and de-mythologizing perceptions of homosexuality and AIDS.

ROBIN GRIFFITHS

ECONOMIC THEORY AND GLBTQ CULTURE

In a global economy, glbtq cultures/identities are subject to lingual diffusion as illustrated by the international financial success of straight director Ang Lee's film, *The Wedding Banquet* (*Xi Yan*, 1993). That is to say, markets both instantiate and eviscerate queer identities by, on the one hand, shaping products and jobs to appeal especially to glbtq customers and workers and, on the other hand, by seeking to increase profits by expanding hitherto queer product niches to include straights.

Can one capture the economic impact of queer culture on the circular flow of national output/consumption by measuring how many units of currency per year of queer culture are bought and sold? Does one count only sales of new glbtq books, art, movies, television, radio, theatre, receipts at gyms, sex clubs and bars? Does one include the shows deriving from glbtq cultures but aiming at mainstream culture, such as *Queer Eye for the Straight Guy*? How should one account for clothing designs by glbtq people or sales by stores catering to glbtq consumers but also selling to straight people?

Conventional thinking in economics might lead one to consider measuring the share of queer culture in a nation's Gross Domestic Product. Yet this standard approach fails because boundaries for glbtq cultures do not exist, and this conventional thinking is now being challenged by the new field of queer political economy (Cornwall 1997), which posits that, as we grow up, we each develop neural pathways used to perceive, to 'think', and to verbally articulate ideas leading to an interdependence between: (1) language-based cognitive codes physically encoded in neural networks, and (2) markets connecting profit-driven sellers and novelty-seeking buyers. In short, part of each person's cognitive code is a social map that we use to try to place ourselves and each other into social identities.

To look at how markets interact with glbtq identities at the start of the twenty-first century, we must understand why globalization is increasingly guiding the activities of more and more humans around the world and is also increasingly linking international markets to one other. This happens first for capital markets, whose per-unit transaction costs are relatively low, but it is spreading ever more widely to include markets for manufacturers, agriculture and even services, as transaction costs for communicating, searching, enforcing/adapting and shipping between 'national' markets continue to fall.

This process of globalization contributes to the evolution of cultures around the world because markets seduce their participants to adopt a common mental code for evaluating the items traded on these mar-kets. This interaction between markets and cultures consists, first, of transforming the language-based cognitive codes that people use to think. For example, historically, a key by-product of the spread of wage labour was to enable people to think of being economically independent from their kin and from agricultural activities. This allowed glbtq individuals to move to urban areas and to meet each other and to dis-cover their often hidden (from themselves) same-sex erotic interests as they participated as customers of boarding houses, molly houses, bathhouses, coffee shops and cruis-ing spots in, for example, England in the eighteenth century. Somewhat similarly, although changed by the filter imposed by gender in Western cultures, lesbians emerged as a self-aware and socially dis-tinguished group in the nineteenth and twentieth centuries (see Cornwall 1997 for references).

This process appears to be replicating in other cultures as the role of agriculture shrinks and that of wage labour spreads. It leads to people generally investing height-ened importance in categories we now label glbtq, but which had often hitherto seemed not worthy of much public notice. Thus, newly positioned enunciators of norms of respectability (especially doctors and, later, psychologists) not only attached the label 'homosexual identities' to people for whom same-sex erotic interaction was of some importance, but they invested these iden-tities with the connotation of being the most abominable, most unthinkable human trait (even as they came to be thought of much more than previously); homo-sexuality was created as an extreme exemplar of 'Other' (Laqueur 2003). This 'queering' of certain behaviours and individuals, labelling them egregious transgressors of respectability, led those so labelled to react by adhering more strongly to each other as a distinct group, even flaunting the con-demned behaviour. Thus, the queer impre-cations were 'queered' by being embraced by their targets in newly evolving niches in labour, housing and entertainment markets.

A response by profit-seeking business to the emergence of distinct glbtq people was to aim products (for example, club clothes, bars and clubs, books and periodicals) at them. This formation of queer market niches gave such businesses a degree of brand-name distinctness and hence market power through which they could earn monopoly profits. Of course, this evolution of markets reinforces the social cohesion of self-identifying participants in queered markets, but it can also seduce non-queer, self-imagined non-homophobic people ('metrosexuals') as well as not-gay-self-identified glbtq people who discover a certain pleasure (perhaps of tweaking norms of respectability) when consuming these newly queered goods (for example, by attending glbtq dance clubs). This evolution suggests to marketers–producers that they can increase profits by aiming at self-conceived 'sophisticated' heterosexuals.

Thus, we might argue that glbtq identities get doubly queered by globalization: markets serve as a social blender, mixing and matching body–costume–identity parts across whatever social identities currently exist, both reifying (for example, queering previously straight products such as music/dance venues) and also dissolving these cultural boundaries (queering hitherto queer product niches by seducing non-glbtq people to join glbtq people with the result the product is made less queer). Queering seems to be like negation: double queering results in un-queering.

But globalizing queerness is not a simple process. The spread of the term 'gay' is very problematic: it suggests the Western notion of 'gayness' is spreading to non-Western societies, but it may mean very different things in other cultures, where social names/categories and practices have long existed for various types of same-sex relations. Simply assigning 'gay' or 'queer' to an international market may blind us to distinct cultural patterns and evolutions (Murray and Roscoe 1997: 34, 314; Vanita and Kidwai 2000: xxiii)

The erasure of national boundaries by markets leads us to inquire what globalization does to national identities/nationalisms. This question is important because the rise of contemporary notions of sexual orientation coincided with the rise of the modern European state, which in turn is closely tied to the creation and reification of the Other, a bourgeois-self-justifying social process tied to that inventing the label 'homosexual'. One recent example can be found in the United States, following the Second World War, when the terms traitor, 'Red' and pervert were conflated in McCarthyism and in the many laws and policies that came out of it.

Indeed, the political usefulness of arguing that homosexuality is a 'threat' to national security, and doing this in order to re-enforce national identity, has been observed in many nations following the end of the Second World War. But we can see here how international markets can also work to weaken identities and so to eviscerate nationalism and homophobia. For example, in recent years Singapore has become especially welcoming to gay visitors by encouraging circuit parties, even though gross indecency, in public or private, between two male persons is, at least at the start of 2004, punishable by two years in prison. Such events may also serve, as in Ang Lee's film, to divert attention from class and ethnic inequality. Thus global markets *are* the wedding banquet that marries and blends middle-class, capitalist social identities in a paradoxical feast of transnational, intercultural consumption, production, marketing, and politics.

See also: *Queer Eye For The Straight Guy*

Bibliography

Cornwall, Richard (1997) 'Deconstructing Silence: the Queer Political Economy of the Social Articulation of Desire', *Review of*

Radical Political Economics 29, 1 (March): 1–130.

Laqueur, Thomas W. (2003) *Solitary Sex: A Cultural History of Masturbation*, New York: Zone.

Murray, Stephen O. and Roscoe, William (1997) *Islamic Homosexualities: Culture, History, and Literature*, New York: New York University.

Vanita, Ruth and Kidwai, Saleem (ed.) (2000) *Same-sex Love in India*, New York: Palgrave Press.

RICHARD CORNWALL

ECSTASY

Class A drug (MDMA, 3,4 methylene-dioxymethamphetamine), widely used in glbtq club culture. Induces feelings of euphoria, psychedelic states and well-being, and energizes users to dance for long periods.

SASHA ROSENEIL

EDKINS, DON

b. 1953

filmmaker

A South Africa-based documentary filmmaker, Don Edkins' *Goldwidows* (1991) takes an intimate, sympathetic look at the hard life of Basotho women who have been left behind in Lesotho by husbands who migrate to work in South Africa. He subsequently co-produced (with Mike Schlomer) *The Color of Gold* (1992), which tells the men's side of the story. Following a group of Basotho miners through their day at work, it includes remarkably frank discussion of male–male sexuality in the mine compounds as well as striking expressions of disbelief towards HIV and AIDS education. Edkins then founded **Steps for the Future** to present issues of sexuality, HIV/AIDS and human rights to African audiences. His film *Simon and I*, notably, sheds light on the political tensions between black gays and lesbians in South Africa

through Beverly Ditsie's reminiscences of her fellow gay rights activist, Simon Nkoli.

See also: Ditsie, Beverly; Nkoli, Simon

MARC EPPRECHT

EHRENSTEIN, DAVID

b. 1947

writer

Writer and journalist whose work concentrates on world film history and gay filmmaking. Ehrenstein was born on 18 February 1947 in New York City. He started his writing career in 1966 by interviewing Andy Warhol for *Film Culture* magazine, and also contributed articles to *Village Voice*. He moved to Los Angeles with his partner Bill Reed in 1976 and worked as a film critic. He and Reed collaborated on the book *Rock on Film* (1982) and wrote a history of homosexuality in Hollywood, *Open Secret: Gay Hollywood 1928–1998* (1998). Ehrenstein was a consultant and researcher on *The Celluloid Closet* (1995), Rob Epstein and Jeffrey Friedman's documentary about Hollywood film representations of homosexuality. He has appeared in a number of TV documentaries about Hollywood history, including *Anthony Perkins: The E! True Hollywood Story* (1998), an exposé on the actor's closeted homosexuality.

JOHN FORDE

EICHELBERGER, ETHYL

b. 1945; d. 1990

performer

Drag queen and performance artist who was one of the leading lights of New York's East Village drag performance scene. Born James Eichelberger on 17 July 1945 in Pekin, Illinois, Eichelberger studied at the American Academy of Dramatic Arts in New York City. He acted professionally for several years before joining Charles Ludlam's Ridiculous Theatrical Company, where he developed his drag alter ego, Ethyl. He wrote and performed in over 40 drag-themed comic plays, usually satirizing famous historical women such as Jocasta, Medea, Clytemnestra, Lola Montez, Nefertiti and Lucrezia Borgia (for which he won an Obie Award in 1982). His comedy combined historical satire with pop culture references, accordion-accompanied songs, fire eating and acrobatics, playfully equating the tortured lives of his divas with the struggles of gay men. He toured many of his shows in Europe and Australia, and appeared in Broadway productions of *The Comedy of Errors* and *The Threepenny Opera*. After living with AIDS for several years, he committed suicide on 12 August 1990 in New York City.

JOHN FORDE

EISENSTEIN, SERGEI

b. 1898; d. 1948

filmmaker

Soviet filmmaker, remembered today not only for his films but also his drawings and his writings on film aesthetics. After beginning his career as a stage director and making a remarkable film debut with *Strike* (1924), he became internationally famous with his second film, *Battleship Potemkin* (1925). He made two more films (*October* [1927] and *The General Line*, also known as *The Old and the New* [1929]) before embarking on a long trip through Europe and on to **Hollywood**, officially to research the sound technologies revolutionizing the film industry, but also as a goodwill ambassador from the Soviet Union. Upon reaching Hollywood in 1930, Eisenstein actually signed a contract to make films for Paramount, but his rejection of melodrama and realism, in favour of experimentation with form, made him an ill fit for the Hollywood studio system. Unable to get

any films made within the system, Eisenstein found a wealthy and powerful patron in Upton Sinclair, the best-selling author active in leftist politics. Sinclair agreed to fund Eisenstein's *Qué Viva México!*, which was to be a five-part portrait of that country's peoples and history.

Eisenstein and his team went to Mexico in December 1930 for what was to be a six-month-long shoot, but which stretched on for a year, until Sinclair finally recalled the group in January 1932. When he returned to Moscow, Eisenstein found the Soviet Union a different place. The state-controlled film industry was now conforming to the Stalinist dogma of 'socialist realism' and the kind of formal experimentation that fuelled Eisenstein's filmmaking was no longer sanctioned. Eisenstein began shooting a film entitled *Bezhin Meadow* in 1935, but filming was interrupted by official demands for changes, until finally, in early 1937, the unfinished film was shut down and shelved. In fact, during the last two decades of his life, Eisenstein was only allowed to finish and release two films: *Alexander Nevsky* (1938) and *Ivan the Terrible, Part I* (1945), the first of a projected trilogy.

When not making films, Eisenstein kept himself busy reading voraciously, drawing, teaching and writing lectures and essays on film aesthetics and techniques, as well as memoirs; he also directed a production of Wagner's *Die Walküre* in 1940. He completed *Ivan the Terrible, Part II* in 1946, only to see the film banned. Despite this setback and his failing health, he continued with plans for the third part of the Ivan trilogy, until his death from a heart attack.

The exact nature of Eisenstein's sexuality is difficult to define, as it was for Eisenstein himself, in part because it may not have fit any of the usual definitions and in part because of the puritanical nature of the early Soviet Union, particularly under Stalin. Other than a handful of youthful attempts and a string of mild infatuations,

Eisenstein seems to have been incapable of romantic or sexual relations with women. However, according to his friend and first biographer Marie Seton, he was reluctant to consider himself a homosexual. Instead, he subscribed to the notion that sublimating his sexuality in his work would help him become a greater artist. He was supported in this view by Sigmund Freud's analysis of Leonardo da Vinci, one of Eisenstein's personal heroes. Spurred by Eisenstein's lack of interest in women and his status as an aesthete, gossip about his sexuality seems to have circulated in Soviet film circles during the 1920s.

There has been a great deal of speculation that Eisenstein may have had an unrequited affection for Grigori Alexandrov, the tall, handsome, athletic (and heterosexual) young man whom Eisenstein met early in his career. For over a decade, Alexandrov was Eisenstein's main collaborator, working as an actor, co-writer and assistant director. During his visits to Berlin in 1926 and 1929, Eisenstein visited lesbian and gay bars there and visited Magnus Hirschfeld. His first, and perhaps only, homosexual experience seems to have taken place in Mexico. In a 1931 letter to his friend Pera Atasheva, Eisenstein confesses to a brief sexual relationship with Jorge Palomino y Cañedo, a historian from a wealthy aristocratic family. It was rumours from Mexico about Eisenstein's sexual conduct that seem to have played a part in convincing Sinclair to pull the plug on *Qué Viva México!*, and as if to add insult to injury, Eisenstein was briefly detained crossing the border back into the States at Laredo, when US Customs discovered a trunk full of his erotic drawings, dubbed 'pornographic' for their mixture of religious and (homo)sexual imagery.

Upon his return to the Soviet Union, Eisenstein would have had grounds to fear persecution from the authorities, both for his aesthetics as well as his sexuality. In 1934 Soviet authorities (as part of a Stalinist campaign for a return to 'family values') outlawed homosexuality, which had been decriminalized after the Revolution.

Eight months later Eisenstein married Atasheva. By all accounts the relationship between the two, while affectionate, was not sexual. The two never lived together and had no children.

DAVID PENDLETON

ELECTROSHOCK THERAPY

Also known as 'electro-convulsive therapy' (ECT), this is a controversial medical practice of exposing patients to a brief, high-voltage electric shock or drugs to induce an epileptic seizure. It was used extensively in the twentieth century to 'cure' patients of their professed homosexuality. The procedure was developed as a treatment for schizophrenia in 1938 by Italian psychiatrists Ugo Cerletti and Lucino Bini. They theorized that as epilepsy and schizophrenia have opposite chemical effects on the brain, inducing epilepsy could offer some relief from mental illness. After apparent successes, their theories were published and adopted internationally, becoming standard psychiatric practice from the 1930s through to the 1960s. ECT was used extensively as one of a number of 'therapies' to cure patients of homosexuality, particularly in Mormon and other anti-gay religious communities. Hundreds of thousands of gay and lesbian people including singer Lou Reed were subjected to the treatment, often during adolescence. Variations included 'aversion therapy', where patients were given electric shocks to discourage their sexual responses to homosexual stimuli, and lobotomies or chemical castration. ECT and aversion therapies were widely discredited in the 1960s, culminating in the American Psychiatric Association removing homosexuality from its list of mental disorders in 1973. ECT is still used to treat psychiatric disorders.

JOHN FORDE

ELLIS, PERRY

b. 1940; d. 1986

fashion designer

Born on 3 March 1940 in Portsmouth, Virginia, Ellis made his name as a designer of women's sportswear and developed a highly lucrative fashion empire. Ellis started his career as women's sportswear buyer for Miller & Rhoads department store and later for John Meyer. In 1976 the Vera Companies conglomerate invited Ellis to design his first sportswear line, called Portfolio. His comfortable, casual 'slouch' look, with oversized jackets, mohair sweaters and baggy pants, using natural fabrics, was an instant success with both critics and consumers. He opened his own company, Perry Ellis International, in 1978. His runway fashion shows demonstrated his flair for showmanship, ending with Ellis' trademark skip down the runway. His fashion empire expanded into menswear, shoes, furs, linens and fragrances, aided by his legal counsel and long-term partner Laughlin Barker. In 1984 he joined with Levi Strauss & Co. to produce the Perry Ellis America sportswear brand, and conceived a daughter with his long-time friend Barbara Gallagher. He died of an AIDS-related illness on 30 May 1986 in New York, days after the showing of his celebrated fall collection.

JOHN FORDE

EMERY, DICK

b. 1917; d. 1983

entertainer

Dick Emery's impersonations of social stereotypes became famous in Britain during the 1960s and 1970s with the screening of the *Dick Emery Show* by the BBC. It is ironic that during these decades of enormous change in gender boundaries that his overly camp personification of a gay man ('Clarence') and a sex-starved single woman ('Mandy') became the mainstays of his act.

He had flirted with a camp persona in 1960 with the character Chubby Catchpole in *The Army Game*, but his lasting impression is perhaps synonymous with his catchphrase – 'Oooh, you are awful, but I like you!'

MICHAEL PINFOLD

EMINEM

b. 1972

rapper

Eminem, a white rapper from Detroit, Michigan, was born Marshall Mathers in 1972. He achieved national prominence in 1999 with the release of his first album, *The Slim Shady LP*, produced by Los Angeles rapper turned hip-hop impresario Dr Dre (who has produced all of Eminem's albums to date). But Eminem reached superstardom with his second album, 2000's *The Marshall Mathers LP*. His lyrics are marked by inventive wordplay and an anarchic worldview, expressed as violent anger directed equally at authority figures, bullies from his schooldays, himself and, especially, women, including his mother and his wife. The controversy caused by the misogyny of Eminem's lyrics was exceeded by that caused by their homophobia.

For queer hip-hop fans, such lyrics represented a conundrum: how to reconcile the pleasure of listening to Eminem with these verbal assaults? Some argued that Eminem's homophobia was merely a report from the front, an honest accounting of the homophobia of both hip-hop culture and the white underclass. Others chalked it up to the all-consuming rage that courses throughout Eminem's lyrics, and which he turns periodically even on himself. For many, of course, the answer was to reject the star. While Eminem himself has never backed down from these lyrics, he has worked in subtle ways to mitigate his reputation as a homophobe. As signalled by the proliferation of alter egos, Eminem is as shrewd a manager of his own image as Madonna, and this canniness proved valuable in seeking to mend relations with his gay fans. One example occurs in the film *8 Mile* (2002), a semi-autobiographical vehicle that portrayed the rapper as a talented, if confused, young man from the wrong side of the tracks. In the film, Eminem's character Rabbit comes to the defence of a gay co-worker who is being verbally harassed during a cigarette break.

More controversially, Eminem performed his hit 'Stan' at the Grammys with Elton John, a fan of the rapper. While this move was largely seen as a shrewd gesture of reconciliation towards the gay community, many remained adamant in their condemnation of Eminem and aghast at John's defense of him.

Eminem's two most recent albums (*The Eminem Show*, 2002; *Encore*, 2004) demonstrate the rapper's continued popularity, although neither matched the sales of *The Marshall Mathers LP*. These albums have seen an abating of violent imagery in the lyrics and a concomitant decrease in their homophobia.

DAVID PENDLETON

ERASURE

pop music duo

After leaving Depeche Mode in 1980 and Yaz four years later, songwriter and instrumentalist Vince Clarke teamed up with singer Andy Bell to form the British duo Erasure. Mixing pop with danceable rhythms, the duo produced a number of club hits such as 'Chains of Love' and 'A Little Respect'. Despite Vince Clarke's admitted straightness, Bell's onstage theatrics and lyrical ambiguities have secured Erasure's identity as a gay group. Although few of the group's passionate pop ballads feature male-to-male address, Erasure queers straight pop culture by reworking assumedly straight classics alongside already gay co-opted ABBA hits, in a camp celebration

that rarely resorts to irony and never to cynicism. Strengthening the camp strain are the group's elaborate visual orchestrations in music videos and outrageous costume choices in their concerts (during one of which Bell sang 'Que sera, sera' dressed in a diaper on a swing seat).

MICHAEL DEANGELIS

ESHED, NOGA

b. 1951

stage artist and author

Israeli-born Eshed is a singer, composer, playwright and writer. She has written and performed music for the theatre, and participated in a number of all-women plays. Among these was the first lesbian play in Hebrew, *Skin* (1986), which she co-authored with playwright Enulla Shamir. The two collaborated again in 1989 on the cross-gendered play *What Do You Remember, Jonathan, Jonathan*. Most notably, Eshed has published the first collection of lesbian short stories in Israeli literature, *Queen-Bee's Nectar* (1998). The stories, which depict a broad spectrum of lesbian life, mostly set outside the urban gay subculture of Tel Aviv, convey the specificities of lesbian existence in Israel; they feature lesbians in kibbutzim and in small towns, lesbians in the military, married lesbians and even orthodox lesbians. The lesbian existence they represent, which predates the recent flourishing of gay life in Israel, is both ubiquitous and largely invisible.

AMALIA ZIV

ESTRO

Estro is a publishing house run by women for women that operated in Italy between 1985 and the early 1990s. It published fourteen books in a women's studies series, a series of translations of important texts of lesbian thought and some narrative works.

The intention of the women who set up Estro was to circulate theoretical and cultural reflections on women's thought, and more specifically on lesbianism. Among the most important texts published were: Saffo's *Poesie* (Poetry), with an innovative translation by Iolanda Insana; Adrienne Rich's *Lo spacco alla radice – Sources* (1985); Rosanna Fiocchetto's *L'amante celeste. La distruzione scientifica della lesbica* (1987); and Teresa De Lauretis' *Differenza e indifferenza sessuale. Per l'elaborazione di un pensiero lesbico* (1989).

See also: De Lauretis, Teresa; Rich, Adrienne

MONIA ANDREANI

ETHERIDGE, MELISSA

b. 1961

rock musician

Rock singer and songwriter Melissa Etheridge delighted millions of lesbian fans by coming out in 1993, becoming one of the music industry's first openly lesbian artists. Born in Kansas, she began writing and performing in her early teens, moved to California in 1982 and played music in women's bars before signing a record contract. A self-titled debut album was released in 1988, scoring a hit with 'Bring Me Some Water' and establishing her trademark husky-voiced rock–country sound. She scored further success with the Grammy-winning album *Never Enough* (1992). A long-time supporter of gay rights, her public coming out was followed by the pointedly titled album, *Yes I Am* (1993). The singles 'Nowhere To Go' and 'I Wanna Come Over' from her 1995 album, *Your Little Secret* (1995), describe a clandestine lesbian relationship. Her high-profile four-year relationship with Julie Cypher (with whom she had two children) made her a national spokesperson for the legal recognition of same-sex relationships. In February 2005 Etheridge performed at the Grammy Awards,

her first performance since being diagnosed with breast cancer. Her impassioned performance in a Janis Joplin tribute, her hair having fallen out as a result of chemotherapy, was lauded by advocates for breast cancer patients and research as an inspiring message to others suffering from the disease.

JOHN FORDE

EUROGAMES

The Eurogames are an annual sporting competition in which the central objective is to highlight and address issues of homophobia in mainstream sporting cultures. The European Gay and Lesbian Sporting Federation oversees the Eurogames and encourages the growth of gay community sporting teams and organizations across Europe. The first two Eurogames were held in The Hague, the Netherlands, in 1992 and 1993, with successive host cities including Frankfurt, Berlin, Paris, Zurich, Hanover, Copenhagen and Munich. Although a yearly event, the Eurogames are not held in **Gay Games** years so as to ensure maximum participation. The Eurogames welcome athletes regardless of their sexual/gender orientation or country of origin.

KELLIE BURNS

EUROVISION SONG CONTEST

The European Song Contest (ESC), a popular media event attracting roughly 1 billion viewers worldwide each year, has been appropriated by gay men who turned it, through social practices and interpretive strategies, into an empowering celebration. For gay men, watching the ESC serves the fantasy of 'getting away' from everyday heterosexual reality to a fantasy world 'out there' demarcated as gay-territory. Experiencing the ESC goes well beyond the music's lyrics, rhythms and melody. It is additionally the performer, the act of performance itself and the stage (both literally and metaphorically) that constitute the site of gay-identity construction, a sounding board against which to examine oneself in relation to others. Engagement with the ESC is associated with early intimate experiences with love, sex and identity as well as the yearning for sexual desire. ESC music and performance is a social phenomenon that has developed an attachment to camp sensibilities while it creates community through its broadcasts to parties and in-house competitions. Gay men, through ESC, exchange experiences, opinions, feelings and sexual desire via the Internet. In 1998 Dana International (an Israeli male-to-female transsexual) won the 1998 ESC Award for her song *Diva*. She has since assumed a spokesperson role for this cultural event. The significance and multiplicity of meanings elicited through this form of popular music initially designed for a general audience goes beyond national, cultural and linguistic borders because it provides a site wherein the terms of identity and desire are no longer fixed.

See also: International, Dana.

DAFNA LEMISH

EVANS-PRITCHARD, EDWARD EVAN

b. 1902; d. 1973

anthropologist

Edward Evan Evans-Pritchard was an English anthropologist whose fieldwork in southern Sudan during the 1930s led to his highly influential book *Witchcraft among the Azande*, in which an apparently irrational belief system is explained to a Western audience in structural and functional terms. Evans-Pritchard discovered at this time the widespread practice of homosexual relations among both Azande men and women. Male warriors, notably, customarily took a young boy as a servant/lover known as *badiya ngbonga*. The effects of colonial rule

and homophobic Christian propaganda largely attenuated the custom. Evans-Pritchard did not publish this remarkable finding until just before his death, a revealing instance of homophobic self-censorship among the first generation of Africanist scholars.

MARC EPPRECHT

EVEN, UZI

b. 1940

scholar, politician

Although already an established scientist and chair of the Department of Chemistry at Tel-Aviv University, Uzi Even came to public light when he appeared at the first conference on gay rights held in the Israeli Parliament (Knesset) in 1993. At this event he told of his dismissal from his military reserve job due to his homosexuality. What followed was not only a reform that abolished discrimination against gay soldiers in the Israeli army, but also a coming out of gay issues from the political closet. Even was the first establishment figure to publicly come out in Israel, and the effect of his Knesset appearance was overwhelming. Since then he has remained one of the foremost spokespersons for the Israeli gay community, and in 2002 was elected to the Knesset as part of the Meretz party as Israel's first openly gay lawmaker. In 1996 Even and his partner, Amit Kama, set a precedent by becoming foster parents to a gay teenager who had been forced to leave his family home. In 2004 the pair married in Canada and started a battle to have the marriage registered in Israel.

AEYAL GROSS

EVERETT, RUPERT

b. 1959

actor

Rupert Everett, a British actor, rose to fame in the stage play *Another Country* (filmed in 1984), a story of gay love and homophobia based on the life of gay British spy Guy Burgess. Despite his matinee–idol good looks and cheery ease with his homosexuality, Everett's career waned after a brief, unsuccessful attempt at pop stardom and a series of film flops (notably, as the victim of sadomasochistic desire in *The Comfort of Strangers* [1990]). He made a welcome return as Julia Roberts' gay friend in *My Best Friend's Wedding* (1997). Preview audiences were so impressed with Everett's performance that the script was rewritten to increase his time on screen. He was praised for his role as a gay father in *The Next Best Thing* (2000) alongside Madonna and scored international success in film adaptations of Wilde's *An Ideal Husband* (1999) and *The Importance of Being Earnest* (2002). He has published three comic novels, including *Hello Darling, Are You Working?* (1994).

JOHN FORDE

EX-GAY

'Ex-gay' is an identity label used to describe an individual who has undergone some form of conversion or reparative therapy. As a result of therapy and/or spiritual intervention, ex-gays believe they are no longer gay or lesbian. The process of becoming an ex-gay is often sponsored by faith-based organizations with an agenda of excluding glbtq people from society. Many ex-gays, and those seeking 'conversion', attend workshops, conferences and church services where they give testimony about the trials of homosexuality and the successes of conversion. This testimony is laced with fundamentalist religious undertones, because most ex-gays belong to ex-gay ministries. Ex-gays believe that homosexuality can be 'cured'. Therapists who specialize in 'sexual reorientation therapy' consider homosexuality to be a mental disorder and reject the depathologizing of homosexuality by the American Psychiatric Association (APA). 'Successful' ex-gays accept that sexual orientation is rooted in biological functioning and either lead a heterosexual lifestyle or are abstinent.

See also: Conversion or reparative therapy; Depathologizing of homosexuality

KATHLEEN M. CUMISKEY

EXIT

Exit is South Africa's longest running lesbian and gay publication. It was launched in 1985 (replacing *Link/Skakel*) with the purpose of providing news and information and fostering a sense of community. The newspaper is published monthly in English and Afrikaans and has a circulation of 20,000. It is distributed nationally, as well as in neighbouring Namibia, Botswana and Swaziland. In addition to the club round-ups, hunk pictorials, camp humour and personal advertisements that remain its stock in trade, *Exit* has also increased its coverage of social issues, **HIV** and **AIDS**, politics and gay liberation since it came under new ownership during the 1990s.

ANTHONY MANION

F

FAG HAG

Perceived by some as a pejorative term, denotes a female friend of a gay man, often in an intense and emotional relationship, privately nurtured but put on public display in gay bars and social venues.

MICHAEL PINFOLD

FALWELL, JERRY
b. 1933
clergyman

Baptist minister and TV evangelist Falwell, born 11 August 1933 in Lynchburg, Virginia, is best known for founding the conservative Christian lobby group The Moral Majority and for his vitriolic public condemnations of homosexuality. An active supporter of racial segregation during the 1950s, he rose to national fame in the 1960s with his televised religious services *The Old-Time Gospel Hour.* He founded The Moral Majority in 1979 to promote his conservative beliefs and support like-minded political candidates. In 1983, he sued pornographer Larry Flynt for libel and emotional distress over a satirical cartoon portraying Falwell committing incest with his mother, but lost the case on appeal to the Supreme Court. Throughout the 1980s, The Moral Majority supported anti-gay rights legislation, advocating a ban on gay and lesbian teachers. Falwell's homophobic comments include 'outing'

Tinky Winky (a character in the children's TV show *Teletubbies*) as gay. He was widely criticized in the press for blaming the 11 September 2001 terrorist attacks in the United States on gays and non-Christians.

JOHN FORDE

FAN SITES

An almost perfect network to readily disseminate images, gossip and news, the Internet has spawned hundreds of unofficial fan sites devoted to glbtq celebrities, icons, TV shows and films. Many are 'homage' sites and primarily provide image galleries and biographical information. Others function more as communities and include active message boards and chat rooms where rumours, plot developments and sightings are discussed extensively. These sites, in particular, often serve wider cultural and political ends. Numerous participants on *Bad Girls* fan sites, for example, saw the site, with its readily available queer support network, as a safe space in which to come out. Other sites are devoted to 'proving' an allegedly closeted celebrity's queer inclinations. Fan sites can also attempt to persuade a show's producers of the importance of its queer fan base. The significant online presence of lesbian *Xena, Warrior Princess* fans, for example, is widely credited with influencing the deliberately ambiguous relationship of the show's main characters.

See also: Slash fiction

ANITA BRADY

FANON, FRANTZ

b. 1925; d. 1961

writer

Martinique-born French psychiatrist Frantz Fanon's work had a profound influence on the emergence of revolutionary black consciousness during the 1950s. In his *Black Skin White Masks* (1952), he characterized white racism against blacks as fundamentally rooted in sexual rivalry, including repressed homosexual desire of white men for black men. This book also gave credence in black nationalist circles to the prejudice that black men were not prone to so-called 'neurotic homosexuality' (homosexual desire or orientation). Rather, if they engaged in passive sodomy or cross-dressed, it was out of economic need created by a system of racial oppression. Fanon's work in Algeria during the years of French repression led him to write *The Wretched of the Earth* (1961), in which he advocated violence as a legitimate, ennobling response to the violence and humiliations of colonial racism, implicitly including putative sexual humiliations such as homosexuality.

MARC EPPRECHT

FARR, GARETH

b. 1968

composer, percussionist, drag artist

Farr has revitalized the New Zealand classical music community while also performing a polished drag act for the New Zealand public. Born in Wellington, New Zealand, Farr studied composition, orchestration, and electronic music at Auckland University before attending Eastman School in Rochester, New York, where he graduated with a Master of Music degree. Aged 25 he became Chamber Music New Zealand's youngest composer-in-residence. The New Zealand Symphony Orchestra and the Auckland Philharmonia have performed his works. He scored Douglas Wright's ballet *Buried Venus* (1996). His music is heavily influenced by his extensive study of percussion, both Western and non-Western (including the Balinese gamelan and Pacific Rim percussion). While Farr has achieved mainstream success within a predominately conservative creative industry, his time in New York led to the development of an alter ego called 'Lilith Lacroix' (born in 1994 in Club Marcella in Rochester). Lilith features in Farr's show, *Drumdrag* (1997).

See also: Wright, Douglas

JO SMITH

FASSBINDER, RAINER WERNER

b. 1945; d. 1982

filmmaker

Rainer Werner Fassbinder grew up in Munich, where he lived most of his life. His parents divorced when he was 6 and the boy's father moved away to Cologne. He began writing poems, stories and plays while still quite young. He attended the Fridl Leonhard drama school where he met his future collaborators, Hanna Schygulla and Irm Hermann. It was also at this time that he made his first 8-mm films, all of which are now lost. In 1966 he applied to study film in Berlin but failed the entrance exams. In the process, however, he met another candidate, Daniel **Schmid**, who later became an important friend and collaborator.

In 1967 Fassbinder made his first extant short film, *The Little Chaos*, and had his first contacts with the Action Theater in Munich, where he met Ursula Strätz and Peer Raben. After a second failed attempt to enter film school, he joined the Action Theater where he began to direct and write plays. In 1969 his foray into feature-length films began, four in that year alone. He was to keep up this frenetic rate of production throughout his life, often working with the same stock cast and crew. During this time he met and began a short relationship with the Bavarian black actor Günther Kaufmann, who remained a staple actor in his films until the director's death.

In 1970 he married the actor Ingrid **Caven**, who also appeared in many of his films. Fassbinder continued to have relationships with men, even during their two-year marriage. Caven once said: 'Rainer was a homosexual who also needed a woman. It's that simple, and that complex.' His most important relationship during this time, however, was with El Hedi ben Salem, who starred as the immigrant worker who becomes involved with an older German woman in *Ali: Fear Eats the Soul* (*Ali: Angst essen Seele auf*, 1974). With this film Fassbinder gained a wider international reputation while developing a personal cinematic style that merged Hollywood melodrama (*à la* Douglas Sirk) with Brechtian political punch.

One of Fassbinder's most significant relationships started in 1974 when he met a young waiter named Armin Meier. Meier, who had been raised in a Catholic orphanage, was classically good-looking but illiterate. Fassbinder's relationship with him was rocky and continually plagued by their social differences. Many critics have cited similarities in their relationship with Fassbinder's 1975 film, *Fox and his Friends* (*Faustrecht der Freiheit*), which tells the story of a young working-class man who has a destructive relationship with a man from a rich family. It was also during this time that he penned his last stage play, *Garbage, the City, and Death*, which unleashed a storm of controversy over whether or not the play's representation of a Jewish real estate agent was anti-Semitic. Schmid made a film version of the play the following year enti-

tled *Shadow of Angels*, starring Fassbinder as one of the leads.

By the mid-1970s Fassbinder's international reputation was solidified, as evidenced by a retrospective at the New York Film Festival – many more would follow. In 1977 Germany was in crisis due to internal terrorism that culminated in the Mogadishu hijacking. Fassbinder, not one to neglect contemporary politics, contributed an episode to the film, *Germany in Autumn* in which he is seen arguing with both his mother and Armin Meier about the politics of the day. Meier died a year later from an overdose.

In the late 1970s and early 1980s Fassbinder made what were to be some of his most well-known films. *The Marriage of Maria Braun* (*Die Ehe der Maria Braun*, 1978) is an allegory of postwar Germany embodied in the figure of a woman (Schygulla), while *In a Year with Thirteen Moons* (1978) features a brilliant performance by Volker Spengler as the transsexual, Elvira. He also completed a pet project: the filming of Alfred Döblin's novel of pre-Second World War Germany, *Berlin Alexanderplatz*. Made for TV with 13 parts and an epilogue, it is undoubtedly Fassbinder's most ambitious project. His final film, *Querelle* (1982), is based on the novel by Jean **Genet**, *Querelle de Brest*, and featured an internationally famous cast including Jeanne Moreau and Brad Davis.

The frenetic pace of his life coupled with a decidedly unhealthy lifestyle took its toll when Fassbinder died in 1982 at the age of 37. He had made more than 40 films.

DANIEL HENDRICKSON

FASSIE, BRENDA
b. 1964; d. 2004

singer

Brenda Fassie was a black South African pop star who became an iconic figure to gays and lesbians in the region in part because of her open bisexuality. Fassie grew up in the impoverished Cape Town township of Langa. Promoted by her mother, she began performing at the age of 5 and at 16 started singing professionally. Her first hit came with 'Weekend Special' in 1983. With this she rocketed to international fame, and over the course of her career she won numerous awards, including Best Selling Release for four straight years in a row (1998–2001). Her ability to win audiences across the deep racial divides in South Africa led the ruling African National Congress to adopt one of her songs for its election campaign in 1999.

Fassie was married in 1989 and bore a son soon afterwards in line with traditional expectations for young black South African women. That marriage quickly fell apart, however, and Fassie subsequently came out with a lesbian relationship – among the very first public figures in Africa to do so. She also flaunted a lifestyle in the 1990s that was fuelled by cocaine and alcohol addiction. One lover, Poppie Sihlahla, died beside her in bed from an apparent overdose. Despite seeking drug rehabilitation, Fassie's personal life continued to create scandal as she moved between boyfriends and girlfriends, sometimes accompanied by accusations of physical abuse and criminal intent. In December 2002 she 'married' another female lover, Sindiswe Khambule, although this too broke apart in public acrimony.

Fassie died following a cardiac arrest at the age of 39. She was at the height of a resurgent career.

MARC EPPRECHT

FAUCI, ANTHONY

b. 1940

scientist, researcher

Dr Anthony Stephen Fauci is known for his efforts in researching HIV/AIDS, primarily through his role as Director of the National Institute for Allergy and Infectious Diseases (NIAID), an organization within the National Institutes of Health (NIH).

Fauci was born on 24 December 1940 in Brooklyn, New York. He received his medical degree from Cornell University in 1966. He arrived at NIAID in 1968, advancing to the director's position in 1984. In this role he supervises numerous research protocols that examine responses to and preventative measures for autoimmune disorders, including HIV/AIDS. Fauci lectures widely and is a frequent media interviewee. He has over 1,000 scientific articles in print. As a measure of his stature and influence, *Scientific American* magazine recently named him the thirteenth most-cited scientist in the world for the period 1983–2002. Since a considerable amount of Fauci's work is devoted to HIV/AIDS prevention, research and treatment, it is telling that this timeframe encompasses much of the AIDS pandemic to date.

CHRIS BELL

FEAST

The Adelaide Lesbian and Gay Cultural Festival was begun in 1998 by a collective of four community cultural workers. Held in November, this significant annual three-week festival showcases local gay, lesbian, bisexual, transgender and intersex visual, performing arts, music, film, literary events, forums, community events and tourism. Feast is an established leader in the circuit of glbt cultural festivals in Australia and promotes a vibrant, edgy and engaged sense of community, diverse identities, pride and celebration as well as being intentionally political and responsive. Feast begins with a huge Opening Night Party and culminates with a public event, Picnic in the Park.

VICKI CROWLEY

FEINBERG, LESLIE

b. 1949

writer, political activist

Leslie Feinberg is a leader in the American transgender rights movement. Feinberg's first novel, *Stone Butch Blues* (1990), put transgender movements on the map, relating the story of Jess(e), a young female-to-male transgendered person who lives between existing gender categories. The novel enjoyed unprecedented popularity and Feinberg, along with other writers such as Joan Nestle, Dorothy Allison, and Jewell Gomez, became associated with a **butch/ femme** renaissance in the 1980s and 1990s. Feinberg, along with partner Minnie Bruce Pratt (poet and author of *S/HE* [1995]), has since become a highly sought-after speaker who articulates the necessity of a broad-based, multi-issue coalition among social justice movements and activisms (including sexuality, anti-poverty, gender, labour, native self-determination and treaty rights, anti-war and anti-racist). Feinberg is also the author of *Transgender Warriors: Making History from Joan of Arc to Dennis Rodman* (1996) and *Trans-Liberation: Beyond Pink or Blue* (1998).

JEAN BOBBY NOBLE

FEINSTEIN, MICHAEL

b. 1956

pianist, vocalist

A native of Columbus, Ohio, Michael Feinstein has become one of the most celebrated American vocalist-pianists. Ira Gershwin hired him as an archivist during the 1980s and Feinstein also performed at the lyricist's parties in Hollywood. Through such exposure he developed contacts with Hollywood celebrities (among them, Liza Minnelli) who promoted his talent. Feinstein has released over 18 albums since 1988; in the most famous of these he performs the music of Gershwin and Cole

Porter. Openly gay, Feinstein belongs to the **Human Rights Campaign (USA)** and performed at the 'Equality Rocks' concert on the eve of the Millennium March in 2000. He prefers being categorized as 'queer' rather than 'gay', and in the context of a long-term openness about his sexual identity he expressed disappointment with the gay magazine, *The Advocate*, for the redundant act of outing him.

MICHAEL DEANGELIS

FEMALE-TO-MALE (FTM) TRANSSEXUAL

Describes the process of transformation, through hormones, surgeries or other non-medical means, so as to change one's gender assignment from female to male.

JEAN BOBBY NOBLE

FEMINIST MOVEMENT, THE

One of the most influential and far-reaching movements of the last 150 years, the feminist movement has had an incalculable effect on glbt debates and action. Key feminist ideas have underpinned many glbt issues, including the cultural myths of marriage, family and romance (see the work of Shulamith Firestone and Audre **Lorde**) and the cultural construction of gender and sexuality (e.g., Simone de Beauvoir; Judith **Butler**; Adrienne **Rich**). Feminist activists have also consistently campaigned around key issues affecting glbt communities.

Although a hugely contested term, feminism has its roots in nineteenth-century activism when women organized around 'equal rights'. Between 1915 and 1920, the activity of the women's movement resulted in the attainment of suffrage (the vote) for women in more than 25 countries worldwide. A 'second wave' of feminism during the 1970s shifted the emphasis to 'women's liberation', hinging on the idea that private as well as public domains were areas of male power and therefore were political. Issues such as the role of women in the home and reproduction therefore became subject to critique. By the end of the 1970s, the feminist movement as a coherent group with unified goals had started to be heavily critiqued, with many calling for a recognition of diversity among women. This resulted in an explosion of writing and campaigning around issues of ethnicity and nationality, class, sexuality, disability and age, reflecting the huge diversity of women's experience. Some have argued that the 1980s saw the beginnings of a 'third wave' of 'postfeminism', reflecting this fragmentation of the movement.

Regardless of the inherent tensions of the movement, feminism continues to be a defining feature of glbt theory and action.

KATHERINE WATSON

FERNIE, LYNNE

b. 1946

filmmaker

A versatile member of the Toronto arts scene, Fernie's first film became the National Film Board (NFB) of Canada's most important queer title and one of the biggest international lesbian hits of the 1990s: *Forbidden Love: The Unashamed Stories of Lesbian Lives* (1992). Fernie and her co-director, soundperson Aerlyn Weissman, injected fresh postmodern aesthetics, politics and erotics into feminist documentary. Two seemingly disparate historical topics – lesbian-themed pulp novels imported from the USA in the postwar era and the emerging lesbian bars in Canadian metropoles – come together to stir up the abject aura of the pre-Stonewall 'underground'. An insightful line-up of dyke seniors preside, linked by a fictional narrative of a country girl who ends up in the arms of a butch urban brunette. Fernie and

Weissman went on to prize-winning independent documentaries on the elderly lesbian writer Jane Rule before Fernie came back to the NFB for two innovative shorts aimed at anti-homophobia work in schools.

THOMAS WAUGH

FERRY, BRYAN AND ROXY MUSIC

b. 1945

pop singer and group

When he formed Roxy Music with Brian Eno in 1971, dandy singer Bryan Ferry fashioned something altogether new on the music scene – upper-class camp rock, a reaction against 1960s art-rock. Rather than ostensibly playing on homosexual innuendoes and on gender bending, as would become common in the age of glam and glitter, Roxy Music displayed a queer sophistication, mixing high culture and kitsch. This was accomplished through bizarre costuming and luscious record covers drawing on the rhetoric of fashion (*Country Life*'s cover starred two models in see-through lingerie), the glamour of cinema and the avant-garde. As an experimentation in style, Roxy Music represent a seminal instance of glam and new wave queerdom.

FABIO CLETO

FICHTE, HUBERT

b. 1935; d. 1986

writer

Hubert Fichte's Jewish father fled Germany before his birth. He was raised mostly in Hamburg, but in order to avoid Nazi persecution, his Protestant mother hid him at a Catholic orphanage for a year (1942) in Bavaria. He was one of the first postwar German authors to introduce the subject of homosexuality directly into his work, but his perspective on sexuality was never disconnected from other social issues.

213

His sometimes semi-autobiographical novels are set in an underworld inhabited by hustlers, drug users and other socially liminal characters. His knowledge of foreign languages and extensive travelling also gave him a perspective on other marginalized people in the world, including racial and ethnic minorities. He published two volumes of essays called *Homosexualität und Literatur: Polemiken* (Homosexuality and Literature: A Polemics, 1987/8). His most substantial work is a series of novels, experimental in form, grouped under the title *The History of Sensitivity*, which he left unfinished at the time of his death from AIDS in 1986.

DANIEL HENDRICKSON

FIERCE PUSSY FESTIVAL

The Fierce Pussy Festival took place on 28 August 1993 in New York City's Tompkins Square Park. The East Village event comprised female musicians, poets, performance artists, sideshow entertainers, interactive installations, visual artists and political action groups. Although the event was organized by a small group of female activists squatting on the Lower East Side, it was not intended to be solely political in nature. Rather, the intention was to present a cultural event that would raise awareness of women's issues by attracting a more general audience. However, on that day, Tompkins Square Park – its trees and pathways strewn with papier-mâché apples and snakes – was also the site of many groups representing women's political, health and social issues. Information tables were set up, where groups passed out their literature; sold zines, pins and stickers; and even offered plastic speculums with instructions on how to conduct one's own vaginal exam.

JOSEPH SALVATORE

FIERSTEIN, HARVEY

b. 1953

actor, playwright

Harvey Forbes Fierstein is a playwright, actor, performer and former drag queen, born in Brooklyn, New York. Fierstein, who often criticizes hostility towards sissies and cross-dressers, won Tony Awards for both Best Play and Best Actor in Paul Bogart's adaptation of the Broadway success *Torch Song Trilogy* (1982), a semi auto-biography of Fierstein. The play represents his romantic affairs, his complex relationship with his typically Jewish mother and the daily hardships of an ageing drag performer. Fierstein won another Tony Award in 1983 for Best Book of a Musical for the controversial *La Cage aux folles*. He wrote and performed *Spookhouse* (1984) off-Broadway, *Safe Sex* (1987) on Broadway and co-authored *Legs Diamond* (1989) with Charles Suppon. Fierstein has acted in several films including *Mrs Doubtfire* (1993), *Bullets Over Broadway* (1994), the queer subversive *Dr Jekyll and Ms Hyde* (1995), *Independence Day* (1996) and *Common Ground* (2000). In 2004 he appeared on Broadway as Tevye in *Fiddler on the Roof*.

GILAD PADVA

FIGURE SKATING

In Western cultures, athletic teams are ranked by the level of violence and teamwork they are required to utilize to order to perform. For example, sports that hold violent masculinity and group interaction as the norm (such as American football) occupy the top rank while artistic sports (or sports considered 'feminine') are positioned at the bottom (see **Coaching and homophobia**). Figure skating exemplifies the bottom ranking since it is both an individual and aesthetic sport. Male skaters, socialized into the sport young, find themselves in a complex social space, because all skaters, regardless of sexuality, are suspected to be homosexual. Heterosexual male skaters thus spend a great deal of energy defending their heterosexuality. Indeed, research shows that a great number of heterosexual skaters flee the sport in an attempt to escape the social stigma. The presumption of homosexuality, however, creates a semi-tolerant environment for those who are in fact gay. Several openly gay skaters have emerged from the closet, the most notable being national champion Rudy **Galindo**. But heterosexual athletes are often resentful of this openness because, as they see it, they themselves are guilty-by-association. As a result, all male skaters, gay and straight, find themselves bearing the brunt of homophobia. Making matters more complex, male figure skaters literally share the same space (locker rooms) with hockey players who often display a violent, homophobic, form of hypermasculinity. Naturally, this arena of suspicion regarding male homosexuality does not translate to female skaters, who are culturally perceived as heterosexual.

ERIC ANDERSON

FILIPIAK, IZABELA

b. 1961

writer

Poland's first openly lesbian writer, Izabela Filipiak has opened doors for others through her diverse published work (novels, short stories, plays, poetry, articles). Her fiction, which troubles the autobiographical tendency of much contemporary Polish writing with a grotesque or fantastic descriptiveness, deals with experiences of exile and return (she lived in New York from the mid-1980s until 1996), with growing up as a woman in Poland and with relationships between women. Her 1997 novel *Niebieska menażeria* (Blue Menagerie) combines all these elements in rewriting a critical moment in

Poland's recent history (the Solidarity movement of the late 1970s and early 1980s) from the perspective of a newly returned émigrée. Filipiak's 2004 dissertation on the early twentieth-century transgender poet Maria Komornicka likewise reconstructs Polish literary history from a queer perspective, and like her 2003 collection of newspaper articles *Kultura obrażonych* (Culture of the Insulted) has upset many of Polish culture's more vocal homophobes.

WILLIAM MARTIN

FILM FESTIVALS, QUEER

Queer film festivals have gradually become well established and a part of contemporary culture in the Western world over the course of the last 20 years. Although most of these festivals are still regarded as independent and marginal events, some of them have become part of mainstream culture.

Queer film festivals are titled in a few different ways; in 2005 only a few of the festivals that can be examined within this group were called 'queer'. A great percentage of festivals that focus on queer films are called 'lesbian and gay', or 'gay and lesbian' film or film and video festivals. The word 'lesbian' started becoming a part of the title of such festivals during the early 1980s, and then in the late 1990s festival producers started integrating the words 'bi' and 'trans' into their programmes and titles. Most queer festivals, even if they are smaller scale events, have three main categories: feature, documentary and shorts. In 2005 queer film festivals are still a considered a cultural product of the Western world, although queer film festivals in take place on all continents – Asia, Australia, Africa, Europe, North America and South America.

A remarkable percentage of queer film festivals take place in North America. Especially in the United States, there are queer film festivals in most states. In California alone there are more than ten queer film and video festivals and some of these are big enough to include specialist subcategories. One of the most widely recognized of these events is The Outfest: The Los Angeles Gay and Lesbian Film Festival. The Outfest was founded in 1982, and in its first 20 years has presented around 4,000 films and videos from around the world. The festival takes place in July and lasts more than ten days. Over the last few years different programmes such as the screenwriting lab have been integrated into the festival. Other highlights from California include OUT/Rageous in Santa Barbara, Queer Filmistan: The South Asian LGBT International Film Festival, East Bay Gay: The Annual Gay Asian Film Festival, and most importantly, one of the oldest queer events, Frameline:The San Fransisco International Lesbian and Gay Film Festival. San Francisco has hosted Frameline, a major event for the queer film industry with its awards and cash prizes, since 1977. Some of the other major queer film festivals in the US include The Tampa International, The Miami Annual, Out Far! Phoenix International, Atlanta's Out on Film and the Philadelphia International Gay and Lesbian Film Festival. New York, the cultural capital of the United States, hosts MIX: The New York Lesbian and Gay Experimental Video and Film Festival, which has started as an alternative to the New York Gay Film Festival and is one of the first of its kind to introduce interactive multimedia.

The most established Canadian queer film festival, Inside Out – Toronto Lesbian and Gay Film and Video Festival, has an international significance; the smaller image+nation festival takes place in Montreal. Like many other film festivals around the world it begins in mid-September and extends into October, the month acknowledged as the glbt history month.

On the other side of the Atlantic, England hosts the London Lesbian and Gay Film Festival that lasts nearly two weeks with an extended programme and an audience of over 20,000. Further northwest is yet a more exciting event in Manchester: the Queer Up North festival, which started as a small gathering in 1992 and is now one of the largest of its kind. In Scotland Glasgow hosts one of UK's largest arts festivals, the Glasgay festival. In Ireland, the Dublin Gay and Lesbian Film Festival (renamed Outlook in 2004) keeps expanding its programme. A similar growth can be observed in most queer film festivals of the late 1990s. Other major festivals in English-speaking countries include the Australian Melbourne Queer Film Festival and the Sydney Mardi Gras Film Festival, huge events with cash prizes and worldwide recognition. New Zealand also hosts a major festival that tours the country, The Out Takes Lesbian and Gay Film Festival. Out in Africa is the queer film festival of South Africa.

Northern and Western Europe, like Northern America, host a significant number of well-established festivals. Austria's Identities Queer Film Festival in Vienna, Belgium's Gay and Lesbian Film Festival of Brussels and the new Pink Screens Alternative Gender Film Festival, Amsterdam Pink Filmdays in the Netherlands, Finland's Vinokino Lesbian and Gay Film Festival that starts in Turku, then moves on to Helsinki and places greater emphasis on documentaries than feature films, Norway's Skeive Filmer in Oslo, Denmark's Copenhagen, Portugal's Lisbon and France's Gay and Lesbian Film Festival in Grenoble, and one of the major worldwide queer film festivals Paris Gay and Lesbian Film Festival, Germany's Verzaubert Queer Film Festival in four cities (Berlin, Munich, Cologne and Frankfurt), Italy's three major festivals Turin International, Milan's Gay and Lesbian Film Festival and Rome's Gay Village, and Spain's Barcelona and Madrid

Gay and Lesbian film festivals are the highlights.

In Eastern Europe The Czech Republic has hosted a major event since 1996, the Mezipatra Gay and Lesbian Film Festival that is held in both Prague and Brno. The festival, attended by around 20,000 visitors, has become a popular event and is supported by influential public institutions such as Czech national television and radio. The small but intense programme of the Hungarian Gaypride Gay and Lesbian Film Festival also started in 1996 and hosts a number of social events as well as films. One of the world's oldest queer festivals is in Slovenia, the Ljubljana Gay and Lesbian Film Festival, which began in 1984. In other countries in Eastern Europe there are some festivals with an extended section devoted to queer films, for example the !f Istanbul Independent Film Festival. The alternative festival started in 2001 and has a section called Rainbow Films.

In South America, Brazil and Mexico host the most significant queer film festivals, the Mix Brasil, and the Mix Mexico: Sexual Diversity Film/Video Festival. In Southeast Asia and the Far East, India had its first queer film festival in 2003, the Larzish International Film Festival of Sexuality and Gender Plurality. When the festival started homosexuality was still a crime in the country. Larzish is organized by two lesbian support groups – OLAVA and Humjinsi – and the India Centre for Human Rights and Law. Other noteworthy events in the area are The Hong Kong Lesbian and Gay Film and Video Festival, The Tokyo International Lesbian and Gay Film Festival in Japan, Seoul International Queer Film and Video Festival in Korea, The Bangkok Pride Gay and Lesbian International Film and Video Festival, and The Q! Film Festival of Jakarta, in Indonesia.

SERAP ERINCIN

FINCH, NIGEL
b. 1949; d. 1995
filmmaker

A gifted filmmaker, Nigel Finch's career spearheaded the growing confidence and openness of British gay cinema, before his untimely death from AIDS in 1995. He rose to prominence with the documentary *Chelsea Hotel* (1981), which profiled the famed New York hotel and its legacy of famous gay guests, including Oscar Wilde, Tennessee Williams, William Burroughs, Quentin Crisp and Andy Warhol. His documentary subjects include artist Robert Mapplethorpe (1988) and filmmaker Kenneth Anger (1991). He achieved international acclaim for his direction for television of *The Lost Language of Cranes* (1992), an adaptation of David Leavitt's novel about a father and son both coming to terms with their homosexuality. His only feature film, *Stonewall* (1995), completed after his death, was an uplifting musical biopic about a group of drag queens who led the 1969 **Stonewall Riots** in New York.

JOHN FORDE

FINDLEY, TIMOTHY
b. 1930; d. 2002
writer, filmmaker

Born in Toronto, Timothy Findley was a monumental figure in the Canadian literary landscape until his death in June 2002. The recipient of numerous awards, including the Canadian Authors Association Award, the Order of Ontario, the Ontario Trillium Award, he was also appointed an Officer of the Order of Canada. Findley's third novel, *The Wars* (1977), established his place as a major Canadian writer and won him the Governor General's Literary Award. Findley has produced scripts for the stage, television, radio and film, in particular, *The National Dream* (1974), co-written with his life partner William Whitehead. The film received an Alliance of Canadian Cinema Television and Radio Artist (ACTRA) Award. *The Wars* was followed by seven novels, two collections of short stories and several collections of non-fiction. Findley's work has been widely translated and has achieved international acclaim. 'It can be said of Findley', one critic noted, '...that he has written only masterpieces'.

JEAN BOBBY NOBLE

FINLEY, KAREN

b. 1964

artist

New York-based performance artist, visual artist, writer, director and actor, Karen Finley was born in Chicago and earned her Master of Fine Arts degree from the San Francisco Art Institute. Despite being raised in a socially conscious household Finley suffered physical and psychological abuse from her father, who committed suicide when she was still a young girl. As a young woman, Finley worked for social programmes such as 'Operation PUSH' and 'Punks for Peace'. Much of Finley's work deals with the issues of violence against women, family dysfunction, sexuality, gender, homophobia, abortion and suicide.

Finley's performance piece that continues to create the most controversy is 'The Chocolate-Smeared Woman', in which a nude Finley smears chocolate syrup (as a metaphor for excrement) all over her body. The piece commented not only on the treatment of women but also on New York's Tawana Brawley case, in which a 16-year-old girl was found covered with faeces. Finley reached a level of national notoriety when Jesse Helms, having never witnessed the performance, condemned its contents as indecent, resulting in the National Endowment for the Arts' censorship of Finley's work by refusing to grant funding. Congress ruled that if a work of art is to be federally funded then that work of art must meet a standard of decency. In 1998 Finley challenged this mandate in Supreme Court. She lost her case, but after the court ruled against her, Finley responded by creating a performance that confronted Helms, entitled 'Revenge of the Chocolate-Smeared Woman'.

JOSEPH SALVATORE

FIRE ISLAND

An Arcadian retreat for urban Americans, Fire Island Pines and Cherry Grove are considered New York's pre-eminent gay and lesbian resorts. They boast pristine sand beaches (sometimes used for cruising), a vibrant nightlife, striking scenery and one of the oldest gay and lesbian communities in the United States, stretching back a century. As a result there is extreme positivity in both the reception and promotion of sexual minorities. A shifting population of homeowners, home renters, hotel guests and casual lodgers form the principal nucleus of social activity, and there are plenty of bars and clubs to welcome them all.

Fire Island's roots go back to 1653, when Isaac Stratford constructed a whaling station and named it Whalehouse Point. There are 17 separate communities, with the two mentioned above (Cherry Grove and 'the Pines') being loyally queer-affirmative. The island itself is a 32-mile-long sand bar south of Long Island, 50 miles east of New York City. It faces into the Atlantic, with an ancient maritime sunken forest and an historic lighthouse (constructed by the Federal Government in 1825, it is an important landmark for ships coming into New York Harbour – for many European immigrants the lighthouse was the first sight of land upon arrival in America). The Fire Island Association brings together the communities to ensure that the conservation of the coastline remains the top priority – a public law passed in 1964 deemed it an area of unspoiled natural beauty. Several hundred residents remain during the winter months and that number swells to around 40,000 in the summer. It is free of all but essential vehicle travel (no private cars are allowed) and almost all visits are by ferry or private boats.

An international and diverse gay community is evident in the gay resorts, and an atmosphere of sexual abandon, late-night parties and drink- and drug-fuelled excess pervades. Since the devastation that the gay community experienced in the 1980s with the onset of AIDS, there has been some tempering of this lifestyle, and more caution practised in sexual liaisons; the community is keen for it to be known via advertisements and holiday brochures that while there is fun to be had, that fun is safe. Popular cruising grounds in the island's forest, jokingly referred to as 'The Judy Garland Memorial' or 'The Meat Rack', continue to attract more reckless sexual thrill-seekers, and as such Fire Island remains symbolic of a pre-AIDS bohemian paradise, steeped in its own self-reflexive nostalgic vision.

Cherry Grove has about 300 homes and is slightly more 'downmarket', with a 'village' atmosphere where the predominance of different facets of the queer community is very evident; 'the Pines' offers roughly 700 homes as retreats for the rich, famous and creative of New York – it is less brash and more stylish, very fashion- and body-conscious and has some of the Island's most luxurious homes. Fire Island may not have the same cachet for New Yorkers as the Hamptons, but in its casual acceptance it is seen as one of the best places to experience the holidaying gay lifestyle in America.

Further reading

Newton, Esther (1993) *Cherry Grove, Fire Island: Sixty Years In America's First Gay And Lesbian Town*, Boston: Beacon Press.

Nichols, Jack (1976) *Welcome To Fire Island: Visions of Cherry Grove and the Pines*, New York: St Martin's Press.

MICHAEL PINFOLD

FISTING

Also known as fist-fucking. The practice involves penetrating the vagina or anus with all or much of the hand and forms part of heterosexual, gay male, and lesbian sexual relationships.

KELLIE BURNS

FITZGERALD, THOM
b. 1968
filmmaker

A Canadian filmmaker, New York-bred Fitzgerald made his first feature while studying at Nova Scotia College of Art and Design, but catapulted to international attention with his second work, the prize-winning *The Hanging Garden* (1997). This *Bildungsroman* of a scarred and fat queer boy in a dysfunctional Nova Scotia family reanimated almost every formula of gay narrative: return of the native, law of the father, compulsory heterosexuality, sibling complicity, the homosocial triangle, the bush garden (seashore mode), wedding explosions, the (queer) reconstitution of the family, and flowers. Subsequent features are underrated: *Beefcake* (1999), a hybrid essay narrative on the pre-Stonewall golden era of physique eroticism, complete with jiving muscle studs; the Romania-set *Wild Dogs* (2002), a melodrama of messed up Canadians abroad, foiled against ethnographic performances by local dog-catchers, beggars and beefcake; and *The Event* (2003), a meandering 'assisted suicide' AIDS drama set in post-9/11 Manhattan. Despite a cooling in his critical reception, Fitzgerald's reputation as the most prolific and unpredictable director of his generation in Canada remains.

THOMAS WAUGH

FLINZER, JOCHEN

b. 1956

artist

Jochen Flinzer is a Hamburg artist who has pioneered an art that combines classic, random, modernist techniques of chance, such as the throwing of dice or other pre-determined systems of decision, to figure an intense series of identifications with the images and social-sexual strategies of contemporary gay life. For example, in delicately stitching around the outlines of the figures kissing or fucking in one of Tom of Finland's *Kake* stories, Flinzer endows the original drawings with the sensuousness of a new and uncanny form of attention. In another work, his plotting of a map of Amsterdam with his sites of sexual encounter wittily defaces the tourist aspects of the city. But by displaying the criss-crossing of the red or black thread on the reverse of these works, he also shows the viewer something like a Russian constructivist composition. Flinzer has thus found a forceful visual form that articulates the particularities of gay subjectivity with great traditions of the making of the modern art object, bringing together both identification and distance within each work.

ADRIAN RIFKIN

FLORENTINE

TV programme

An award-winning, popular Israeli TV drama series, *Florentine* (also spelled *Florentene*) was transmitted on Israel's commercial channel, Channel 2, between 1997 and 2001. Named after and set in a Tel Aviv neighbourhood, it tells the story of a group of friends in their twenties, some of whom have been close since high school and throughout their compulsory military service. The series, comprising 39 episodes, was co-created and directed (during the first two seasons) by Eytan **Fox**, and had gay men as leading characters, a first for Israeli television. Like much of Fox's other work, *Florentine* explores the intersection of the private and the political.

ALINA BERNSTEIN

FLOWERS, WAYLAND AND MADAME

b. 1939; d. 1988

ventriloquist/puppeteer

Born in Dawson, Georgia, Wayland Flowers always appeared with Madame, an aged but chicly thin puppet sporting outrageous makeup and a turban. In the United States, the pair performed in nightclubs and on television, where Flowers' use of an outspoken, feather boa-clad alter ego, allowed him to openly express humour with a queer bent. Together they appeared on the TV shows *Laugh-in*, *Solid Gold* and *Hollywood Squares* from the 1960s through the 1980s, until Madam *appeared* to leave Flowers for her own sitcom, *Madame's Place* (1982). Despite this brief separation, when Flowers died of AIDS, Madam and he were interred together.

GABRIEL GOMEZ

FOOTBALL, AMERICAN

American football was popularized in the early part of the twentieth century, although its roots can be traced back to a number of ancient European games with the similar object of moving a ball across a goal line. American football is deeply ingrained within American culture, at a number of levels. High school and college football teams are thought to build community cohesion as a town rallies around 'our' team to beat another team. This is particularly evident in small towns. Professional football (the National Football League) is a highly discussed sport among men, and it has become tradition for families and friends to gather to watch both the 'Rose Bowl' and the 'Super Bowl'. But football is also a central element to the lives of many boys and men who attempt to gain masculine worth by proving themselves physically superior to others on the football field. Characterized by hard tackles and extremely high rates of injury, the physical violence of the game enables those who play it to be considered the most masculine of American athletes because violence against other men and risk-taking are considered desirable masculine traits in contemporary American culture. But in addition to football being a hypermasculine arena, the homosocial nature of football provides for the formation of an intimate bond among football players. This bonding, combined with protective gear that exaggerates the physical form, also makes football a homoerotic arena. Severe **homophobia** thus presents itself as a way to mitigate the homoeroticism of the sport.

ERIC ANDERSON

FOOTBALL

See: Soccer

FORD, CHARLES HENRI

b. 1913; d. 2002

poet, novelist

Charles Henri Ford's artistic career spanned eight decades and encompassed many of North America and Western Europe's major artistic movements. He published 15 books of poetry and presented prints, paintings, drawings, sculptures and photographs, as well as one film, *Johnny Minotaur* (1971), at international and national exhibitions. Ford served as editor of the art magazine *View*

(1940–7) that was known for its cutting-edge production values, promotion of expatriate European artists in America (such as Marcel Duchamp, Max Ernst and Ford's long-time lover, painter Pavel **Tchelitchev**) and its publication of surrealist verse by André Breton. Ford is remembered by cultural historians of modernism for scripting one of the more explicitly homosexual novels of 1930s bohemian life. Co-authored with friend Parker **Tyler**, *The Young and Evil* (1933), was banned in both America and England upon publication but currently has been 'revived' by queer literary academics.

TERRELL SCOTT HERRING

FORD, TOM

b. 1962

fashion designer

The openly gay designer Tom Ford revived the Gucci label in the 1990s, thus turning himself into one of the biggest names in fashion. A former model, Ford worked at Chloe and Perry Ellis before being appointed as Gucci's womenswear designer in 1994, transforming the stagnant label into a sexy hedonistic line coveted by celebrity clients who included Madonna. In 1995 he was appointed as Gucci's creative director, and with chief executive Domenico de Sole, embarked on a major expansion programme, turning the Gucci Group into a powerful fashion and luxury goods conglomerate. Hailed as an innovative architect of modern fashion, Ford revitalized the Yves St Laurent label and headhunted new designing talent including Stella McCartney and Alexander McQueen. Ford's rugged good looks – accented with his trademark white pressed shirt open to the chest, dark blazer and jeans – made him a style icon who appealed to both men and women. He resigned from Gucci in 2004.

JOHN FORDE

FOREST TOWN

Affluent Johannesburg suburb that, in 1966, became 'South Africa's Stonewall' following a massive police raid on a private party involving hundreds of gay men. Subsequent scandal led to a parliamentary inquiry, an attempt by the state to criminalize homosexuality and the first gay rights political lobby in Africa.

MARC EPPRECHT

FORREST, KATHARINE V.

b. 1939

writer

A prolific novelist and editor, Katharine Forrest was born in Canada and now lives in the United States. She has produced some of the most influential work in lesbian fiction of the last 40 years, traversing the genres of romance, science fiction and mystery. In her early work, *Curious Wine* (1983), she crafted what many critics believe to be the definitive coming-out romance for lesbians, and in her Kate Delafield mystery series, which currently numbers seven novels, Forrest has achieved cross-over popularity and has changed the boundaries of mass-market genre fiction by chronicling the professional and personal life of a no-nonsense and out lesbian homicide detective. The winner of numerous awards from the Lambda Literary Foundation, Forrest has also contributed to the world of glbt arts and letters by teaching classes in creative writing and by acting as Senior Fiction editor at Naiad Press from 1984 until 1994.

See also: Coming-out novels

STEPHANIE FOOTE

FORSTER, E.M.

b. 1879; d. 1970

writer

British novelist whose life and work was deeply affected by his repressed homosexuality. Forster was born on 1 January 1879 in London, England. In his first two novels, *Where Angels Fear To Tread* (1905) and *A Room With A View* (1908), he wittily satirized the prudery of English society, allowing his female protagonists to find emotional and sexual fulfilment in the sensuous Italian landscape. In *A Passage To India* (1924), he examined the (suggestively homoerotic) friendship between an Englishman and an Indian man, which is strained by the injustices of British colonialism. Influenced by the Whitmanesque ideal of comradeship and the writings of Edward Carpenter and John Addington Symonds, Forster believed that homosexuality could bridge the barriers between working- and upper-class men. This fantasy was realized in his novel *Maurice*, begun in 1913, in which the upper-class hero finds love with a gamekeeper. The manuscript was circulated privately, and, at Forster's request, published after his death in 1971. He collaborated with Eric Crozier on the libretto for Benjamin Britten's opera *Billy Budd*, and publicly defended the works of D.H. Lawrence and Radclyffe Hall. His work received a major boost in popularity in the 1980s and 1990s with several successful film adaptations of his novels, directed by gay filmmaker James Ivory. Forster died on 7 June 1970, in Coventry, England.

JOHN FORDE

FORSYTH, BRUCE

b. 1928

comedian

One of Britain's most enduring stage and TV personalities, Bruce Forsyth's humour combines masculine bravado with camp self-awareness and innuendo-laden humour. A full-time entertainer from the age of 14, he rose to fame in the late 1950s as the host of TV variety show, *Sunday Night at the Palladium*. His status as king of light entertainment was confirmed with his successes in *The Bruce Forsyth Show* (1966), *Play Your Cards Right* (1979) and *The Price Is Right* (1995). He made a triumphant comeback in 2000 as the host of the revived *Sunday Night At The London Palladium*. An avowed heterosexual, with a penchant for marrying his younger female co-hosts, Forsyth's career nonetheless exists within a tradition of camp British comedy, which has influenced his successors, TV game show hosts Julian **Clary** and Graham **Norton**.

JOHN FORDE

FORTUYN, PIM

b. 1948; d. 2002

politician

Pim Fortuyn was born on 19 February 1948 in Velsen, the Netherlands. As well known for his flamboyant dress sense and open homosexuality as his hard-line nationalist and anti-immigration policies, Fortuyn was one of Europe's most controversial political figures before his assassination in 2002. He studied at the University of Amsterdam, becoming involved in the student communist movement and later pursuing an academic career in sociology. Shedding his communist ideals, he became a media commentator, attracting national attention for his anti-Islamic immigration stance. In his book *Against The Islamicisation of our Culture* (1987), he singled out fundamentalist Islam as a threat to gay and women's rights, sexual freedom and casual drug use. Elected head of the right-wing Leefbaar Nederland party in 2001, he was sacked after he called for an end to Islamic immigration and a repeal of the Dutch constitution's anti-discrimination provisions. Undaunted, he formed his own party, Lijst Fortuyn, instantly overtaking his old party in the polls and taking almost 40 per cent of the vote in Rotterdam's 2002 city elections. He courted controversy by speaking publicly about homosexuality, including the pleasures of backrooms and the taste of semen. He was assassinated on 6 May 2002 in Hilversum, three months before the Dutch national elections, in which it was predicted his party would take 20 per cent of the vote.

JOHN FORDE

FOSTER, JODIE

b. 1962

actor, film director

Jodie Foster, Yale graduate, is one of America's most highly respected actors and directors whose allure is fuelled by rumours of her lesbianism. After a series of mature child performances in *Alice Doesn't Live Here Anymore* (1974), *Bugsy Malone* (1976) and *Taxi Driver* (1976), the adult Foster won two Academy Awards for her gritty performances as a rape victim in *The Accused* (1988) and an FBI agent in *Silence of the Lambs* (1991). Foster's on- and off-screen persona fuses intelligence with a potent, yet highly controlled sexuality. Famously outed as a lesbian by *The Advocate* magazine in 1991, Foster has never publicly confirmed or denied her sexuality. Her directorial efforts include *Little Man Tate* (1991), *Home For the Holidays* (1995) and *Flora Plum* (2004).

JOHN FORDE

FOUCAULT, MICHEL

b. 1926; d. 1984

philosopher

Born in Poitiers, French philosopher and intellectual figure Michel Foucault is known for producing a 'critical history of thought'. Foucault worked in various universities, became Professor of the History of Systems of Thought at the Collège de France in 1970 and was involved in several social protest movements. His work focuses on 'discourse', meaning a group of statements with internal rules that produces the object of which it speaks. For example, a 'discourse of sexuality' delimits what can and cannot be said or known about our sexual lives. In *La Volonté de Savoir* (*The History of Sexuality, Volume 1*, 1976), Foucault argued that 'the homosexual' emerged as a specific type only in nineteenth-century bio-medical discourses. One effect of this was a 'reverse discourse', in which homosexuality began to speak out on its own behalf. Foucault's work has had a major impact upon lesbian and gay studies, and especially queer theory. He died in Paris of an AIDS-related illness in 1984.

See also: Theory and theorists, queer

STEPHEN HICKS

FOX, EYTAN

b. 1964

filmmaker

Eytan Fox is an Israeli mainstream filmmaker. His debut film, *After* (1990), portrays unfulfilled desire between a closeted gay officer and his cadet. Following *Song of the Siren* (1994), he directed the first season of the Israeli TV series *Florentine* (1997), scripted by his partner Gal Uchovsky, who also wrote Fox's romantic TV musical *Gotta Have Heart* (1997). His film *Yossi & Jagger* (2002) focuses on the relationship of a closeted officer, Yossi (Ohad Knoler), and his handsome deputy, Jagger (Yehuda Levy) in a remote army base. In a memorable scene Yossi and Jagger dance and have sex in the snow to the sounds of pop star Rita's 'Let's Remove the Foggy Curtain!' Yossi keeps the affair secret however, even after Jagger is killed in a military action. Fox's new film, *To Walk on Water* (2003), deals with the relationship between an Israeli Mossad agent and a German brother and sister whose grandfather was an infamous Nazi officer.

GILAD PADVA

FRANCE, FILMMAKING

France has a long and rich cinematic legacy and has developed one of the world's most successful and respected film industries. More artistically oriented and less commercially driven than its **Hollywood** counterpart, French cinema is marked by an aesthetic, moral and political flexibility that has afforded considerable scope for the representation and exploration of queer issues.

Many of the central hallmarks of French cinema, including its celebrated, if occasionally lampooned, 'tradition of quality' and its cult-of-the-director-as-artist, were established throughout the so-called golden age of the 1930s through to the 1950s. Happily devoid of the sort of puritanical censorship that regulated Hollywood under the **Production Code**, French cinema of this era was often characterized by a proportionate liberalism, particularly in matters of sexuality, which helped to give it an enduring reputation for risqué content. In part, the permissiveness of French cinema was a genuine reflection of social attitudes. True to its foundational ideals of libertarian individualism, modern France has generally been very tolerant of variant sexualities, albeit with the proviso that they remain private and discreet. In equal part, however, the cultivation of a cinematic permissiveness under the cloak of artistic expression was a strategic way for the French film industry to forge a distinctive profile and market niche in the face of Hollywood's global domination.

Although few classical French films focused exclusively or even primarily on queer issues, many contained elements of queerness as a way of endorsing their claims to artistic urbanity and/or pitching for commercial sensationalism. Key examples here would include representations of lesbianism in films such as the 1936 and 1957 versions of *La Garçonne* (The Bachelorette); the 1947 thriller, *Quai des Orfèvres*; and, perhaps most famously, the 1950 cult classic

Olivia, which was substantially cut for its US release and given the tabloid title *The Pit of Loneliness*. Correlative depictions of male homosexuality can be found in many other notable French films of this period such as Jean Vigo's 1933 classic, *Zéro de conduite* (*Zero for Conduct*) and several works of the acclaimed golden age director Marcel Carné, including *Hôtel du Nord* (1938), *Les Enfants du paradis* (*Children of Paradise*, 1945) and *L'Air de Paris* (*Air of Paris*, 1954).

Indeed, Carné was one of a handful of queer filmmakers who was able to use classical French cinema's penchant for moral liberalism and artistic freedom to make films with decided, if carefully coded, queer dynamics. He was joined by others such as Jacqueline Audry, the proto-feminist director behind such queer-inflected classics as the aforementioned *Olivia*, the adaptation of Sartre's *Huis Clos* (1954) and the charming gender-bending comedy *Le Secret du chevalier d'Eon* (*The Secret of the Knight of Eon*, 1959); and perhaps most famous of all, Jean **Cocteau**, whose films of the 1940s and 1950s, with their surreal, dreamlike visuals and striking homoeroticism, exerted a profound influence on French filmmaking that can still be evidenced today.

For all its iconoclastic pretensions, the celebrated New Wave that emerged in French cinema during the late 1950s and 1960s, garnering international attention and renown, was surprisingly straight. Few of the movement's luminaries showed much interest in queer issues and some, such as François Truffaut, were openly homophobic. Nevertheless, queer elements surface in certain films of the New Wave, such as the male and female homoeroticism of Truffaut's *Jules et Jim* (1962) and Godard's *Masculin–Féminin* (1966), and the recurrent use – some might say, exploitation – of lesbianism as transgressive motif in the films of Claude Chabrol such as *Les Biches* (*Bad Girls*, 1968).

More queer supportive were the films made by women directors who emerged in the wake of second-wave feminism, for example Agnès Varda, Coline Serreau and the Belgian-born but largely French-resident, Chantal **Akerman**. Inspired by liberationist politics and buoyed up by the increasing opportunities made available to women filmmakers through events such as the annual International Women's Film Festival at Créteil, these directors embarked on a rich cinematic exploration of female-centred narratives and desires. Of particular note are films such as Akerman's experimental meditation on sexual fluidity, *Je, tu, il, elle* (*I...You...He...She*, 1974) and Serreau's comic tale of a bisexual ménage à trois, *Pourquoi Pas!* (*Why Not!*, 1977).

Representations of queerness were not limited to the more artistic elements of French cinema but were equally evident in its popular mainstream. Comedy has long been a staple of popular French cinema and queerness has proved a rich source for its humour whether in the comedic transvestism of classic screen clowns such as Fernandel and Louis de Funès, or the more overtly queer scenarios of later films such as *La Cage aux folles* (1978) and others by comic *auteur* Francis Veber. Melodrama has offered another rich context for queer explorations in popular French film, with such notable examples as the classic, *Les Amitiés particulières* (*This Special Friendship*, 1964); Jacques Rivette's controversial adaptation of Diderot's *La Réligieuse* (*The Nun*, 1969); and Vallois' wartime psychodrama, *Nous étions un seul homme* (*We Were One Man*, 1979).

A different but equally commercial context for queer representations was the strain of mainstream pornography that emerged as an increasingly visible element of French cinema following the government's 1967 abolition of state censorship. Fuelled by the international success of sexually explicit arthouse fare such as *Last Tango in Paris* (1972), French cinema turned out a series of enormously popular soft-core porn films in the 1970s including *Emmanuelle*, the highest grossing film of 1974, and *Bilitis* (1977). Although not queer in any conventionally political sense, these films invariably offered images of lesbianism, albeit cast through the lens of heterosexual male fantasy.

Since the 1980s French cinema has produced increasingly overt and serious representations of queer sexualities. Two films released in 1983 are often regarded as breakthroughs in this respect: *L'Homme blessé* (*The Wounded Man*), a blisteringly graphic portrayal of a teenage hustler's obsessive love for an older man by Patrice **Chéreau**, and *Coup de foudre* (*Entre Nous/At First Sight*, 1983), Diane Kurys' poignant portrait of a lesbian love affair in 1950s provincial France. The critical and commercial success of these films arguably paved the way for subsequent queer-themed films such as the 1986 comedy hit, *Tenue de soirée* (*Evening Dress*); Cyrill Collard's controversial semi-autobiographical portrait of bisexuality in the age of AIDS, *Les Nuits fauves* (*Savage Nights*, 1992); the lyrical ode to adolescent homoeroticism, *Les Roseaux sauvages* (*Wild Reeds*, 1994), by Andre **Téchiné**; Alain Berliner's delightful exploration of juvenile transgenderism in the French-Belgian co-production, *Ma Vie en rose* (*My Life in Pink*, 1997); and Claire Denis' cinematic poem on the sensuality of the male body and repressed desire in *Beau Travail* (1999).

As the disparate nature of these films might suggest, contemporary French cinema is not generally marked by the sort of thematically coherent or even readily identifiable strain of queer filmmaking that has typified movements such as the New Queer Cinema in the United States. In part, this is caused by the relative absence of US-style identity politics in French queer cultures. Following France's long-standing traditions of liberal individualism alluded to earlier, many French queers consider their sexuality an aspect of privatized individuality

rather than a communitarian or minority identity. There are signs of change in this respect, with the rise of increasingly identity-based forms of queer culture, but these remain controversial and are often critiqued as a form of creeping Americanization.

The work of young contemporary French queer filmmakers such as François **Ozon**, Sébastien Lifshitz, Sylvie Ballyot, Anne-Sophie Birot, Olivier **Ducastel** and Jacques Martineau is revealing in this context. All are openly gay and all use their films to articulate and explore explicitly queer issues, but none lay claim to a specifically gay classification and there is little sense of overtly communitarian gayness in their work. More often than not, queer sexuality features in their films as simply one axis of individuation among many.

See also: New Queer Cinema, International

BRETT FARMER

FRANCE, LITERATURE

Despite the fact that canonical French literature of the first half of the twentieth century is marked by major figures associated with homosexuality (Proust, Gide, Cocteau, Colette, Yourcenar), post-Second World War French literature is not as clearly marked with a visible or obviously homogenous strand of gay and lesbian writing, let alone contemporary queer theory and culture, as is the case in the United States or the United Kingdom. While major gay male and lesbian writers did emerge from the 1950s through to the 1970s, notably Jean **Genet** and Monique **Wittig**, much gay and lesbian literary activity remained fairly marginal from 1945, through the 'intellectual revolution' of 1968, central to which was the fight for sexual liberation, until the dual political and cultural watersheds that were Mitterrand's victory in 1981 and the then imminent, albeit unexpected, AIDS crisis.

From the mid-1940s until his death in 1986, Jean Genet consistently attempted to construct an image of his self as an outlaw. His provocative and incantatory, almost mystically lyrical, prose links erotic depictions of sexuality to violence, treachery and theft. Although he was much admired by important intellectual figures (especially Sartre and Cocteau), Genet constantly coveted marginality, and he celebrates this in his written works (indeed, finds such marginality in and through writing). From the 1950s onwards, when the French novel was renewing itself through the formalized experimentation of the *nouveau roman*, Genet moved more to dramatic works that engage in a play of illusion and reality in relation to political structures of domination. In terms of sexuality, Genet positively celebrates the perceived threat that his own outlaw status bestows on him. His texts aim to use the literary domain to construct a (sexual) self that is a constant threat to well-mannered society.

Wittig, likewise, uses violence and provocation to attack the patriarchal order which shores up sexual stasis and gender inequality. Her texts (such as *The Oppoponax* [*L'Opoponax*] and *Les Guérillères* [The Warriors]) aim to explode patriarchal forms of language and structure and to reconstruct them from a lesbian perspective. A radical lesbian separatist, Wittig longs for a genderless society wherein freedom from the taxonomic labelling of identity politics might be realized. While Genet takes refuge in being cast, and casting himself, as the marginal, Wittig wishes to move beyond a time and culture in which language has such a power to place, name and control. Both writers are shockingly provocative, emotionally difficult and formally inventive.

For much of the 1960s and 1970s homosexual/gay and women's movements engaged in intellectual and political fights for freedom. While much lesbian creativity was subsumed within the wider women's movement and perhaps overly dominated by ultimately futile attempts to define, describe, produce and critique a specifically 'women's writing' (*écriture féminine*), the promise of sexual freedom which seemed to be realized in the historical moment of 1968 ultimately came to nought. The major thrusts of gay writing of the 1970s continue some of the trends of Genet's own approach – the gay man as outsider – albeit in less obviously visible ways because many of the other main gay writers were not as successful or acclaimed as Genet. Works by Pierre Guyotat, Julien Green and Tony **Duvert** pose questions as to the links between gay sexuality and voyeurism, domination and violence in often provocative and unsettling ways. There is also a concerted effort to represent in, and through, writing a decensored depiction of the gay male body and of gay male sexual activity. If in 1970s France it remained 'impolite' to foreground in any sort of public discourse issues that belonged in private, issues related to sexuality and identity, these writers confront and defy this societal injunction, and yet the relatively marginal positioning of them and their works also demonstrates the successful functioning of a society that attempts to silence them.

If 1968 failed to deliver the freedoms which were so desired, 1981 came to be seen as another such watershed. Subsequent to important legal changes after Mitterrand's victory (the repeal of homophobic laws introduced under the Vichy regime) and given important intellectual impetus by the later works of crucial theoretical thinkers such as Roland **Barthes** and Michel **Foucault** (especially *Barthes* by Barthes [1974], *A Lover's Discourse: Fragments* [1978], *Incidents* [1987] and the monumental three-volume *History of Sexuality* [1976–1984] respectively) gay writing and ideas central to gay politics and activism began to assert a more clearly visible presence through the 1980s. This visibility and its literary representation was tragically concretized by the AIDS crisis and key writers, especially Hervé **Guibert** and Cyril Collard, who adopted AIDS as a major trope of their literary works.

Guibert's work, in particular, reached a reasonably wide popular audience both in France and abroad and has been the subject of continuing critical attention. Guibert's initial notoriety stemmed from the reception of *To The Friend Who Did Not Save My Life* (1990) and its thinly veiled portrayal of the death of Foucault (the character Muzil in Guibert's autobiographical novel), an event (June 1984) that Guibert had previously fictionalized in a less well-known short story 'The Secrets of a Man' (in *Mauve la vierge* [Mauve the Virgin], 1988). The controversy surrounded the supposed revelation that Foucault/Muzil had been an admirer of sadomasochism. Guibert's treachery, as some saw it, was the springboard to a frenetic outpouring of writing in the last few years of his life, most of which reached a far wider audience than did his numerous works before *To The Friend*. While in no sense an activist or militant gay political writer, he was much criticized by ACT UP/Paris for his supposed individualizing dramatization of AIDS. Guibert's later works, from 1990 onwards (he died in late 1991), continue his interest in the literary transcription of the decaying/dying body and the effects of this on (gay) desire and notions of identity. His preference for a mode of writing best termed *autofiction* (the playful (re)creation of selfhood in and through fiction) links his work with that of Genet while also prefiguring the mixing of autobiography, fiction and erotic gay desire present in French gay writing of the late 1990s.

Reacting against the individualized heroic depiction of AIDS found in Guibert and Collard, writers such as Vincent Borel and Guillaume **Dustan** have radically resocialized AIDS and its links to sexuality (identity and activity) and other aspects of culture (such as drugs and nightclubs, music and the rave scene in Borel) in their polemical and stylized writings. Dustan, the *nouveau poète maudit* of the twenty-first century, has been strongly criticized by ACT UP/Paris for his 'autopornographic' texts (such as *Dans ma chambre* [In My Room], 1996) and their shame-free, stylized celebration of promiscuous gay sex. Dustan's radicalized depiction of the gay male desiring (and desired) body recalls, in what is rhetorically almost a post-AIDS world (a 'reality' also featured strongly at the end of Borel's *Un Ruban noir* [A Black Ribbon, 1995]), some of the simplistic force that Barthes so admired in *Tricks* (1977), the famous cruising text by Renaud **Camus**. Dustan continues and modifies an emergent tradition of French gay writing which encompasses the work of both Genet and Guibert; all three in different ways are interested in how literary forms can be used to give expression to a fluid and shifting sense of the sexualized self: Genet's homosexual persona becomes Guibert's mobile gay self (an attempt to escape the taxonomic rationale of medical and AIDS discourse), which in turn Dustan modifies to an ironically self-questioning queer stereotype that, 'though portrayed consistently at the level of the individual, is anchored in a (questioning of a) collective sense of queer community'.

This emergent visibility of what might be called specifically 'gay writing' in France is predominantly a male centred phenomenon. With the major exception of Wittig, lesbian writing in postwar France has been even more lacking in visibility than gay male writing. This is explained in part by the lack of sustained lesbian separatism in the various women's and feminist movements of the 1970s, by the fact that most depictions of lesbian desire have historically been in male authored texts and, more latterly, by the initial male-centredness of the literary reaction to, and appropriation of, AIDS. Despite these factors, the depiction of lesbian desire in the 1970s works of Wittig, Leduc and Rochefort can be seen to form a textual prehistory to the subsequent work of writers such as, in the 1980s, Jocelyne François and Mireille Best and, in the 1990s, Hélène de Monferrand (Cairns 2002).

Although still marginal and hotly debated, since they are arguably at odds with the Republican universalism of the French tradition (Martel 1996), queer cultures and queer studies are slowly beginning to assert a presence within France (Eribon 1998), even if their long-term survival and flourishing there are yet to be secured. Despite the precariousness of their visibility in France itself, the burgeoning of publishing and academic interest in matters queer returns readers and researchers time and again, thanks largely to Foucault, to the complex and problematic interaction of gender, sexuality and French culture.

Bibliography

Cairns, L. (2002) *Lesbian Desire in Post-1968 French Literature*, New York: Edwin Mellen Press.

Eribon, D. (ed.) (1998) *Les Études gays et lesbiennes*, Paris: Éditions du Centre Pompidou (Gay and Lesbian Studies).

Martel, F. (1996) *Le Rose et le noir. Les Homosexuels en France depuis 1968*, Paris: Seuil; trans. Jane Marie Todd, *The Pink and the Black. Homosexuals in France since 1968*, Stanford: Stanford University Press, 1999.

Further reading

Cairns, L. (ed.) (2002) *Gay and Lesbian Cultures in France*, Bern: Peter Lang.

Eribon, D. (ed.) (2003) *Dictionnaire des cultures Gays et Lesbiennes*, Paris: Larousse.

Heathcore, O., Hughes, A. and Williams, J. (eds) (1998) *Gay Signatures: Gay and Lesbian Theory, Fiction and Film in France, 1945–1995*, Oxford: Berg.

Robinson, C. (1995) *Scandal in the Ink. Male and Female Homosexuality in Twentieth-century French Literature*, London: Cassell.

Schehr, L.R. (1995) *Alcibiades at the Door: Gay Discourses in French Literature*, Stanford: Stanford University Press.

JAMES N. AGAR

FRANK, BARNEY

b. 1940

politician

Barney Frank, one of the most prominent openly gay politicians in the United States, has represented the Fourth Congressional District of Massachusetts since he was elected to the House of Representatives in 1980. He is the Senior Democrat on the Financial Services Committee and is also a member of the Select Committee on Homeland Security. Previously, he served as Massachusetts State Representative and an assistant to the Mayor of Boston. In 1987 he became the first openly gay Member of Congress in the US. Frank is a prominent figure in the liberal wing of the Democratic Party and has been outspoken on many human rights issues, as well as on issues of glbtq rights. He said in a 1996 interview: 'I'm used to being in the minority. I'm a left-handed gay Jew. I've never felt, automatically, a member of any majority.' Like other Jewish Democrats, he is a strong supporter of Israel.

SURINA KHAN

FRANKIE GOES TO HOLLYWOOD

pop music group

The rise and fall of Frankie Goes to Hollywood, a Liverpool band fronted by singers Holly Johnson (b. 1960) and Paul Rutherford (b. 1959) – unprecedentedly gay and proud pop stars – took place overnight. Their first single, 'Relax', an unabashed look at gay sex, was released in 1984, the first in a sequence of three UK chart-topping singles (the other two being 'Two Tribes' and 'The Power of Love'). All three were dance tracks marked by throbbing rhythms, powerful guitar riffs, a distinctively robust voice and controversial lyrics sung in an epic, vibrant style. A combination of the ban imposed on 'Relax' by the BBC, spectacular music videos and shrewd marketing made them reach sudden star status with their first album, *Welcome to the Pleasuredome*, followed by a less successful album and by their split in 1987. Johnson and Rutherford both undertook solo careers after the band broke up. In the early 1990s Johnson was diagnosed with AIDS; he has since retired from the music business.

FGTH represent the epitome of the early 1980s gay pop music scene – amazingly popular, short-lived, cunningly marketed and controversial.

FABIO CLETO

FRASER, BRAD

b. 1959

playwright

Born on 28 June 1959 in Edmonton, Alberta, Canadian Brad Fraser is an openly gay playwright whose witty and violent works explore sexual ambiguity, urban isolation and AIDS. He is best known for the award-winning *Unidentified Human Remains and the True Nature of Love*, a dark comedy about sexually ambiguous characters living in states of ironic detachment in a menacing urban landscape threatened by AIDS and serial killers. Courting praise and controversy for its violence and sexual explicitness, it was later filmed as *Love and Human Remains* (1993), with a screenplay by Fraser. The play *Poor Super Man*, a love story between a gay and a straight man, was made into a film with Fraser adapting and directing, was retitled *Leaving Metropolis* (2002). *The Ugly Man*, a violent reworking Thomas Middleton's revenge tragedy *The Changeling*, featured explicit depictions of gay sex and sexual urination. His other works include *Snake In Fridge*, *Martin Yesterday* and screenplays for the US TV series **Queer As Folk**.

JOHN FORDE

FREARS, STEPHEN

b. 1941

director, screenwriter

Renowned for tackling controversial and sexually explicit subject matter, Frears rose to fame with two low-budget, gay-themed TV films, *My Beautiful Laundrette* (1985) and *Prick up Your Ears* (1987). The former, an upbeat portrait of a young Pakistani man falling in love with a Cockney skinhead, was widely praised as one of the best British films of the 1980s. *Prick Up Your Ears* dealt was a darkly comic biopic of gay playwright Joe **Orton** and his abusive relationship with his lover (and murderer) Kenneth Halliwell. In a controversial first for British television, Frears filmed sexually explicit scenes of Orton's sexual exploits in men's toilets. Frears has continued to produce dark psychological dramas of sexual manipulation and betrayal, notably in *Dangerous Liaisons* (1988) and *The Grifters* (1990). His characteristically non-judgemental perspective on human sexuality, in all its complexities and dysfunctions, has won him respect from gay audiences worldwide.

JOHN FORDE

FREED UNIT

film production organization

The Freed Unit was a specialist film production unit at MGM studios that made musicals under the supervision of producer Arthur Freed (1894–1973). An accomplished songwriter, Freed's greatest skill lay in his ability to assemble the best available talent into a tight-knit team and to inspire them to maximum creativity. Together, the

Freed Unit was responsible for many of the most popular and highly regarded Hollywood musicals, including *Meet Me in St Louis* (1944), *Singin' in the Rain* (1952) and *An American in Paris* (1951).

The significance of the Freed Unit for queer culture lies not only in its authorship of avowed gay cult classics such as *The Pirate* (1947), but in its central employ of many queer and/or queer-significant artists, so much so that the Unit was sometimes disparagingly referred to as 'Freed's Fairies'. Associate producer, Roger Edens; directors, Vincente **Minnelli** and Charles Walters; stars, Judy **Garland** and Judy Holliday; prop master, Edwin Willis; and choreographer, Jack Cole, worked at various times in the Freed Unit and their contributions helped cement the Unit's marked tendencies towards camp and other queer aesthetics.

BRETT FARMER

FRIEDKIN, WILLIAM

b. 1935

director

The heterosexual film director William Friedkin has won both acclaim and derision from gay audiences for his controversial depictions of homosexuality. His film *The Boys in the Band* (1970), a comedy–drama about eight gay friends who celebrate a birthday party, was hailed as a breakthrough for Hollywood's portrayal of homosexuality. The film divided gay audiences with its camaraderie and witty, bitchy dialogue and the characters' evident self-loathing. After commercial and critical success with *The French Connection* (1971) and *The Exorcist* (1973), Friedkin then destroyed his goodwill with the gay community with the film *Cruising* (1980), a lurid thriller about a closeted policeman investigating a murder in the world of gay leather and S&M (sadomasochism) bars. Despite a disclaimer stating that *Cruising* did not represent the whole gay community,

gay audiences were outraged, boycotting and protesting at screenings; the film was a commercial failure. Friedkin's subsequent films have seldom involved homosexuality.

JOHN FORDE

FRIEDRICH, SU

b. 1954

experimental filmmaker

A resident of New York since 1976, Su Friedrich was born in New Haven, Connecticut. A graduate of Oberlin College with a background in Art and Art History, Friedrich's films express a complex feminist, lesbian analysis of social and cultural structures. Her 12 film works include *Gently Down the Stream* (1981), *The Ties That Bind* (1984), *Sink or Swim* (1990), *Hide and Seek* (1996) and *The Odds of Recovery* (2000). Her numerous fellowships include: Rockefeller Foundation (1990); Guggenheim (1989); a DAAD grant as artist-in-residence in Berlin (1984); and grants from The New York State Council on the Arts (1993, 1992, 1989, 1986, 1982); The New York Foundation for the Arts (1993, 1989); and the Jerome Foundation (1992, 1989, 1986). Friedrich's work is discussed in *Vampires and Violets: Lesbians in the Cinema* (1992) by Andrea Weiss, *Screen Writings* (1994) and *Avant-Garde Film: Motion Studies* (1993) by Scott MacDonald. Friedrich is a Professor at Princeton University.

M.M. SERRA

FRY, STEPHEN

b. 1957

actor, director

A witty and accomplished writer, comedian, actor and TV presenter, Stephen Fry began his career with the 'Footlighters' troupe at Cambridge University. Openly gay since his teens, he achieved success in the TV comedy series *A Bit of Fry and*

231

Laurie (1987–95), co-written with fellow Cambridge comic Hugh Laurie. He appeared in the cult TV comedy *Blackadder* (1986–9) and as the scheming butler Jeeves in *Jeeves & Wooster* (1990), again alongside Laurie. In the film *Peter's Friends* (1992), Fry starred as a bisexual aristocrat revealing his HIV+ status to his friends. He scored a career high in the film *Wilde* (1997), with a sensitive portrayal of disgraced gay writer Oscar Wilde (with whom he is often compared). He has written several comic novels, a volume of autobiography, *Moab Is My Washpot* (1997), and made his film directorial debut in 2003 with *Bright Young Things* (2003).

JOHN FORDE

FUCK BUDDIES

Popular term for two or more persons whose relationship consists of frequent sexual couplings, independent of emotional or material attachments.

TERRELL SCOTT HERRING

FUNG, RICHARD

b. 1954

writer, filmmaker

Richard Fung is a Trinidadian-Chinese man based in Toronto whose video projects and writing explore the complex interconnections between sexuality, race, diaspora and history, making his an influential voice in both queer and postcolonial studies. *Dirty Laundry* (1996) weaves historical reportage with a modern love story in an attempt to discover links between same-sex eroticism among Canada's contemporary Chinese community and their ancestors. The haunting video *Sea in the Blood* (2000) describes Fung's sister's long illness and death interspersed with scenes taken from his life with his HIV+ partner. His 2002 video *Islands* looks at race, sexuality and homophobia, and was voted Best Experimental Work at the Worldwide Short Film Festival. Fung is the author of many seminal essays and is much in demand as a speaker. He is the recipient of many prestigious awards including the Bell Canada Award for Lifetime Achievement in Video Art.

MARK MCLELLAND

FUSHIMI, NORIAKI

b. 1963

writer

Noriaki Fushimi is one of Japan's most prolific gay writers and activists. He came to prominence in 1991 with the publication of his book *Private Gay Life*, which helped fuel the 'gay boom' that swept Japanese media at the beginning of the 1990s. He later served as editor of important collections such as *Queer Studies 96* and *Queer Studies 97*. In 1999 he founded the journal *Queer Japan* which, unlike previous gay magazines, contains no pornography but focuses on lifestyle and identity issues. In 2001 Fushimi became involved in the public debate between Ken **Togo** and Satoru **Ito** over the value of foreign versus indigenous identity categories, organizing a roundtable discussion and publishing the results in *Okama wa Sabetsu ka?* (*Is Okama Discriminatory?*). His magnum opus *'Gei' to iu Keiken* (*The Experience Called 'Gay'*), published in 2002, contains the most extensive history of recent Japanese queer life.

MARK MCLELLAND

G

GABRIEL, JUAN

b. 1950

singer

One of the most famous Mexican popular singers and composers, Juan (Alberto Aguilera) Gabriel is very well known in his country and all over Latin America. His songs – 'Querida' (Darling), 'Se me olvidó otra vez' (I Forgot it Again), 'Luisa María' and 'Noa Noa' – have been recorded by many singers in Latin America, Spain and the United States. Although never out of the closet, Gabriel's persona and feminine mannerisms – at least for some critics – defy Mexico's dominant machismo. Due to the fact that his most popular songs lack specific gender endings, common to the Spanish language, they express universal feelings of love without jeopardizing middle-class sensibilities. His lyrics continue the tradition of the troubadours (*amour courtois*) while, at the same time, subverting it by erasing its masculine/feminine opposition. Consequently, the conformist themes of the old traditions became asexual and available to a wider, global audience regardless of his or her gender and, significantly, regardless of the suspicions attending Juan Gabriel's sexuality.

GUSTAVO GEIROLA

GALAS, DIAMANDA

b. 1952

vocalist

The internationally renowned vocalist, avant-garde composer, pianist, poet and AIDS activist Diamanda Galas was born in San Diego, California. She was raised in a strict Greek Orthodox family, where she was encouraged to pursue her gift for music. Mastering classical piano lessons, she became, age 14, a member of the Symphonic Orchestra of San Diego. Soon, however, she abandoned the piano to study voice.

Galas' famous three-and-a-half-octave-ranged voice has been said to defy description. A devoted fan of Baudelaire and Poe, Galas obsesses over the themes of isolation, claustrophobia, rape, genocide, imprisonment, disease, torture, insanity, Satanism, vampirism and death. Her controversial *Plague Mass* (1991) is a trilogy, denouncing those who consider AIDS a 'divine retribution' for the act of homosexuality. In 1989 Galas, along with members of ACT UP, was arrested at St Patrick's Cathedral after staging what she terms a 'Die-In', a peaceful demonstration protesting Cardinal O'Connor's negative position on AIDS.

JOSEPH SALVATORE

233

GALGUT, DAMON

b. 1963

writer

Gay South African novelist and poet Damon Galgut's first novel, *A Sinless Season* (1989), is set in a boys' reformatory school. The story includes two graphic scenes of male gang rape which suggest that violent homophobia is an organic outgrowth of patriarchy in white South African society. The theme is also developed in relation to racial conflict in *The Beautiful Screaming of Pigs* (1992), in which a spontaneous male rape takes place after the trauma of battle against Namibian freedom fighters.

MARC EPPRECHT

GALINDO, RUDY

b. 1969

figure skater

Born and raised in California, Rudy Galindo became the United States men's **figure skating** national champion in 1996, which was a first in three distinct ways. He was the first Mexican-American, openly gay and HIV+ national champion. Before this triumph, Galindo had been widely known for successfully skating with Kristi Yamaguchi. Together they won the US National Championships in 1989 and 1990, but hopes for a win at the 1992 Olympics dissolved when Yamaguchi decided to compete alone. Galindo took this setback hard, and soon faced other challenges. His brother George contracted AIDS in 1992, and while Rudy was caring for him, his father Jess suffered a heart attack and died. George succumbed soon after, and within months another key person in Rudy's life, his longtime coach, Rick Inglesi, also died of AIDS. Despite this series of difficulties and a modest background, Rudy 'Val' Galindo's courage to be himself has made him a hero to figure-skating fans everywhere.

GABRIEL GOMEZ

GANATRA, NISHA

b. 1974

filmmaker

Lesbian filmmaker whose work explores the interplay between her Indian cultural heritage and contemporary lesbian culture. Ganatra was born in Vancouver, Canada, on 25 June 1974. An habitué of Canada's 1990s grunge scene, she was a drummer in Brooklyn garage band The Flying Guacamoles, before studying filmmaking at New York University film school, and making two short films *Junky Punky Girlz* (1996) and *Drown Soda* (1997). Her self-scripted feature film debut, *Chutney Popcorn* (1999), was a comedy about Reena, a lesbian living in New York with her girlfriend, who decides to become a surrogate mother for her infertile sister. The film, which played on the comic clashes between Reena's traditionalist Indian family and urban lesbian grunge, was a hit on the international gay film festival circuit. Her subsequent work continues to explore Indian immigrant experience in a romantic comedy genre, including *Cosmopolitan* (2003), *Fast Food High* (2003) and *Cake* (2005).

JOHN FORDE

GARBER, MARJORIE

scholar

Marjorie Garber is Professor of English and director of the Humanities Center in the Faculty of Arts and Sciences at Harvard University. In her books she addresses various themes of interest for queer culture, including the links between gender and visual art and culture, cross-dressing, bisexuality and desire. In one of her most famous and indeed internationally acclaimed books, *Vested Interests: Cross-Dressing and Cultural Anxiety* (1992), Garber explores the theme of drag appeal in history, photography, literature and pop culture, from

Shakespeare to Madonna, observing the deep-reaching connections between clothing, gender representation, sexuality and social organization.

MONICA BARONI

GARBO, GRETA

b. 1905; d. 1990

actor

A Hollywood icon, the aloof, beautiful Garbo was one of the relatively few stars with equal appeal for gays and lesbians. An acting student and model discovered by the great filmmaker Mauritz Stiller (believed to be gay), Garbo joined him when he was invited to Hollywood. She quickly became a star, typically cast in vehicles where romance turns tragic, often because Garbo is revealed to the hero as a sexually 'experienced' woman. Gays enjoyed her melodramas of failed romance, intense acting and sexual ambiguity. Her strong features, swept-back hair and deep voice enhanced her male drag in *Queen Christina* (1933), a biopic of the bisexual seventeenth-century monarch. Other films helmed by gay directors include *Flesh and the Devil* (1927); a rare comedy, Ernst Lubitsch's witty *Ninotchka* (1939); and George Cukor's tender *Camille* (1936), among those films.

Queer fans were titillated by the fact that Garbo never married and by tales of romance with women (writer Mercedes de Acosta, for example) and men alike. Although her last film, the unsuccessful *Two-Faced Woman*, was made in 1941, Garbo played a role in postwar culture, her absence only enhancing her air of mystery. Generations of queers followed rumours of never-realized comebacks and lovers of every persuasion; those based in New York enjoyed spotting the reclusive diva on her shopping rounds.

DAVID M. LUGOWSKI

GARLAND, JUDY

b. 1922; d. 1969

actor

It is claimed that when the American film star and singer Judy Garland died of a barbiturate overdose in June 1969, the resulting grief in the New York gay community was so intense that it helped spark the **Stonewall Riots**. Although possibly apocryphal, this story highlights Garland's status as a privileged icon of queer cultures, particularly during the mid-twentieth century but, residually, through to the present day.

There are many reasons for Garland's extraordinary queer iconicity. A major star who rose to fame as the quintessential girl next door in a string of sunny MGM musicals, Garland's image underwent a profound shift during the 1950s when news of chronic problems in her personal life, including depression and substance abuse, became public. The resulting sense of fracture between her public and private personae resonated deeply for queers of the time and their experiences of closeted life. The raw emotionalism of Garland's singing and her projection of a survivalist spirit became a beacon for queers of the 1950s and 1960s who associated Garland's search for happiness 'over the rainbow' with their own struggles for social tolerance and equity. In addition, Garland seemed to gravitate towards queers in her personal life, marrying at least two men, including director Vincente **Minnelli**, whose queer sexuality has been widely suggested.

The passing of time has inevitably diminished the intensity of queer identifications with Garland but she remains a beloved and historically important icon for 'friends of Dorothy' everywhere.

BRETT FARMER

235

GAULTIER, JEAN-PAUL

b. 1952

fashion designer

Hailed as the 'enfant terrible' of fashion, Jean-Paul Gaultier's sexually flamboyant fashion and cheerfully perverse public persona has made him one of gay culture's most admired personalities. He began his career working for couture house Pierre Cardin, and launched his first solo collection in 1975, with the help of his long-time partner Francis Menuge. His bold designs fused his love of corsetry and Catholic iconography with punk, Gothic and bondage wear, he repopularized tartan and – somewhat controversially – introduced skirts for men. His appearances on the camp British TV show *Eurotrash*, sporting his trademark tartan kilt and platinum blond hair, further added to his cult appeal. He was given international exposure as costume designer for Madonna's 1990 'Blonde Ambition' tour, creating her now-iconic pointed basque and bra. He has also designed costumes for filmmakers Luc Besson, Peter Greenaway and Pedro Almodóvar. In 2003 he became chief designer for the Hermés label.

JOHN FORDE

GAY GAMES

The idea of a gay international sporting competition began in 1981 when the San Francisco Arts and Athletics (SFAA) established and organized the first Gay Olympics. SFAA founder Tom **Waddell** saw the event as an opportunity to provide an alternative sporting space that emphasized personal best over winning and challenged the heteronormativity of mainstream sporting cultures. Scheduled for September 1982, the United States Olympic Committee, in August of that year, obtained a restraining order barring the SFAA from using the word 'Olympics' in association with their event. This ironic legacy prompted the renaming of the Gay Olympic Games as, simply, the Gay Games. Held in San Francisco, Gay Games I: *Challenge '82* attracted 1,350 athletes from 12 nations who competed in 11 sporting events. Its successor, Gay Games II: *Triumph in '86*, was once again held in San Francisco, this time welcoming 3,500 participants in 17 sports and a large number of artists participating in the newly integrated Gay Games cultural programme. In 1987 Gay Games founder and mentor Waddell died of AIDS and soon after the SFAA became the Federation of Gay Games. Vancouver, Canada hosted Gay Games III: *Celebration '90*, which attracted 7,500 athletes competing in the 23 sports along with an additional 1,200 participants partaking of the cultural festivities. Gay Games IV: *Unity '94* were held in New York City to commemorate the twenty-fifth anniversary of the Stonewall Riots. Leading up to the Games the Federation successfully lobbied the government to ensure a waiver be signed allowing competitors living with HIV to enter the United States without special visa provisions. *Unity '94* attracted 11,000 athletes from 45 countries competing in 35 sports and over 1,500 cultural participants.

Much in keeping with the model of the Olympic Games in 1993, the Federation introduced a bidding process for the selection of successive host cities. The first to be selected was Amsterdam, the Netherlands, and Gay Games V: *Friendship '98* marked the globalization of the Gay Games. Amsterdam welcomed 14,500 athletes to compete in 29 official and 4 demonstration sports. Four years later the Games went 'down under' to Sydney, Australia, where Gay Games VI: *Under New Skies 2002* attracted more than 12,000 athletes from more than 70 countries competing in 31 sporting events. The breadth of the cultural festival at Sydney 2002 attracted performers and artists from around the world. Montreal, Canada, was selected the host city for the Gay Games VII: *Rendez-vous in 2006*.

With the Gay Games now firmly established as a quadrennial sporting and cultural festival, opportunities arise to situate the event within contemporary discussions concerning the politics of identity and the relationship between gay and lesbian communities and the **pink dollar**. The Gay Games allow us to critique the political effectiveness of an event with growing budgetary demands and obvious reliance upon commercial and capital investment against broader discussions around both the mainstreaming and Americanization of gay and lesbian culture and those concerning queer, bisexual, transgendered and intersex politics.

KELLIE BURNS

GAY AND LESBIAN ALLIANCE AGAINST DEFAMATION (GLAAD)

Formed in New York in 1985 to protest the *New York Post*'s grossly defamatory and sensationalized AIDS coverage, GLAAD works to promote and ensure 'fair, accurate and inclusive representation of people and events in the media as a means of eliminating homophobia and discrimination based on gender identity and sexual orientation'. After its founding in New York, GLAAD's work quickly spread to Los Angeles, where it began to educate Hollywood's entertainment industry on the importance of more accurate and realistic portrayals of gay people and people living with AIDS in film. As GLAAD's work grew and evolved over time, the organization moved from a chapter-based to a national organization, with offices in New York City and Los Angeles. To serve regional and local media interests, GLAAD's Regional Media Program grew to serve local communities and media outlets across the country via directed 'monitor and mobilize' campaigns, calls to action, media trainings and on-the-ground community and media support.

GLAAD has cultivated relationships with media professionals across two decades and was influential in pressing *The New York Times* to change its editorial policy to use the word 'gay'. Since then GLAAD's 'Announcing Equality' project has resulted in more than 140 other newspapers across the country – *The New York Times* included – including same-sex union announcements alongside other wedding listings. GLAAD has reached media insiders, as well as impacted millions through newspapers, magazines, motion pictures, TV and visibility campaigns. It has focused media attention on the hate-motivated murders of Matthew Shepard, Arthur 'J.R.' Warren, Brandon Teena, Fred Martinez, Gwen Araujo and others; the anti-gay advocacy of 'Dr Laura' Schlessinger; Eminem's hate lyrics; the openly gay heroes and victims of 9/11; the anti-gay right's fraudulent 'ex-gay' ads; and attempts by Catholic Church officials to scapegoat gay priests.

SURINA KHAN

GAY, LESBIAN, AND STRAIGHT EDUCATION NETWORK

The organization was founded in 1990 with a conference of 70 gay and lesbian educators as the Gay and Lesbian Independent School Teachers Network (GLISTN). In 1994 the Gay, Lesbian, and Straight Teachers Network (GLSTN) became a national organization when it incorporated as a 501 c (3). Since then it has worked to ensure safe and effective schools for all students and played a crucial role in encouraging the formation of the Massachusetts Governor's Commission on Gay and Lesbian Youth which eventually recommended passage of the first statewide law to protect gay and lesbian youth in public schools. GLSTN changed its name to the Gay, Lesbian, Straight, Education Network (GLSEN) in an effort to reach out to new allies. GLSEN's three focus areas are: 'make anti-LGBT bullying, harassment and name calling unacceptable in America's schools; engage and empower educators as partners in creating schools where every student can fully participate in school life; and ensure that the national agenda to create effective schools includes LGBT issues'.

SURINA KHAN

GAY LIBERATION FRONT (GLF)

GLF was a lesbian, gay and bisexual (lgb) liberation movement established following the **Stonewall Riots** of 1969. It was formed in New York, with chapters subsequently springing up across parts of the United States and Europe. In 1970 the New York group held a protest march in June, and GLF held its first UK meeting at the London School of Economics in October.

GLF rejected the assimilationist tendencies of other lgb groups, instead urging lgb people to challenge oppression, have pride in themselves, 'come out everywhere' and declare their sexuality openly. GLF also said that being gay or lesbian was a political choice potentially open to all. Indeed GLF suggested that, in a liberated society, the narrow categories of 'homo/hetero-sexuality' would disappear altogether (Power 1996).

GLF was involved in a range of activist events, including challenging the American Psychiatric Association to remove homosexuality from its list of mental disorders (which it did in 1973) and opposing lesbian oppression within the women's liberation movement. There were many problems within GLF, and lesbians, who argued that some gay men were sexist, walked out en masse in 1972. GLF was largely defunct as an organization by the mid-1970s but many of its ideas are still very influential.

STEPHEN HICKS

GAY LO

A derogatory term for a gay man or gay men.

KEN WONG

GAY MALE S/M ACTIVISTS (GMSMA)

The oldest, largest organization dedicated to the support, socialization, education and political activism of gay men involved in leather, bondage, fetish and sadomasochistic (S&M) communities, GMSMA was founded in New York in 1980. In 1983 members coined an expression – 'safe, sane, consensual' – now widely used in fighting stereotypes and characterizing the healthy activities promoted by the organization. Although membership is international, GMSMA, which inspired similar gay and lesbian groups worldwide, remained based in **New York**. It holds social events and bi-weekly sessions on topics from bondage, mummification and flogging techniques to sadomasochism and the law, spirituality, boot fetishism and proper fisting. In-depth seminars developed, as did 'dungeon demos', in which men could watch tops and bottoms perform their specialties. GMSMA works actively with the Anti-Violence Project and various gay, women's and AIDS organizations, and became a key supporter of New York's annual 'Pride' march. A sponsor of Leather Pride Night, in 1997 GMSMA initiated Folsom Street East, a fundraising block party.

See also: Sadomasochism

DAVID M. LUGOWSKI

GAY MEN'S HEALTH CRISIS (GMHC)

GMHC was established in 1982 in response to the growing incidence of HIV infection amongst gay men. Since the response of the local New York governing bodies to these infections was lax, a group of eight gay men, including authors Larry **Kramer** and Edmund **White**, decided to organize a group that would provide information about HIV to gay men in New York.

GMHC is now considered an information clearing house, disseminating sound advice on HIV and AIDS prevention, education and treatment. The organization offers case management and client advocacy, and also engages in public policy issues. Additionally, the organization responds to non-HIV and AIDS-related health concerns, for example, combating the recent rise in syphilis infections among gay men.

GMHC retains its sensitivity towards its core constituency (the titular gay men), although the organization has offered services to men, women and children since the mid-1980s. All services are provided free of charge.

CHRIS BELL

GAY–STRAIGHT ALLIANCES

Gay–straight alliances (GSAs) meet in over 2,000 schools in the United States. The Equal Access Act of 1984 provides legal support for GSAs (and other after-school programmes), enabling sexual minority youth and allies to find space in public schools for queer issues often ignored by official curricula. A number of districts have attempted to ban GSAs, arguing that alliances are disruptive because they are contrary to local norms. Thanks to the assistance of Lambda Legal Defense, those challenges have so far been unsuccessful. The Gay, Lesbian, and Straight Educators Network (*www.glsen.org*) provides information on organizing and maintaining GSAs.

See also: Lambda Legal

CRIS MAYO

GAY SWEATSHOP THEATRE COMPANY

Founded in 1975, following a successful season of lunchtime gay plays staged at the Almost Free Theatre in London, Gay Sweatshop was Britain's landmark first openly gay theatre company. The intention of founding members Drew Griffiths, Alan Pope, Roger Baker and Philip Osment was to counteract mainstream perceptions and prejudices concerning homosexuality, and in its early years the company was proactively involved with the political work of both the **Gay Liberation Front (GLF)** and the Campaign for Homosexual Equality (CHE) with its ground-breaking touring productions of *Mister X* (1975) and Jill Posener's *Any Woman Can* (1976). However, despite this initial success, the company was plagued with financial difficulties throughout the 1980s, following the suspension of grant support by the Arts Council of Great Britain, and experienced a cycle of closure and revival while simultaneously defending itself against critical indifference and artistic uncertainty. Despite this, the company produced such notable successes as Andy Kirby's moving AIDS drama *Compromised Immunity* (1986) and Jackie Kay's acclaimed *Twice Over* (1987); and under the artistic direction of James Neale-Kennerley and Split Britches' Lois Weaver had renewed success in the 1990s with such plays as *Fucking Martin* (1994), *Lust and Comfort* (1995) and *The Hand* (1995). The company finally closed in 1997 following the withdrawal of Arts Council funding yet again, and its failure to secure alternative sponsorship because of the nature of its productions.

ROBIN GRIFFITHS

GAYDAR

(1) An expression for a gay man's supposed ability to detect whether or not another man is gay; (2) an Internet web site created by QSoft Limited as an online chat site for gay men, where members can communicate in chat rooms, advertise personal profiles and photographs and look for sexual partners. Currently the most popular web

site of its kind, Gaydar also provides pornography for its fee-paying members.

JOHN FORDE

GAYLE

An argot spoken by white and coloured (mixed-race) gays in South Africa since the 1990s. Deriving from moffietaal and international gay culture, it offers a means to communicate sexual desire and identity without attracting homophobic attention.

MARC EPPRECHT

GAYZIM

magazine

gayZIM is a free online magazine for anyone interested in Zimbabwean glbt issues and events. Launched in 1999 by Evan Tsouroulis and Christopher Hunt, it serves as the organ of GALZ (Gays and Lesbians of Zimbabwe). It advocates full and equal civil human rights for glbt Zimbabweans, the promotion of true democracy in Zimbabwe and freedom from censorship.

See also: Goddard, Keith

KEITH GODDARD

GEFFEN, DAVID

b. 1943

record producer

Arguably the most powerful openly gay man in the entertainment industry, David Geffen began his career in the mailroom of the William Morris Agency, later moving into management. As an agent in 1968 he represented Joni Mitchell, Neil Young, and Crosby, Stills and Nash. He founded Asylum Records in 1971, signing Mitchell, Bob Dylan and The Eagles, before selling to Warner Bros and branching into film production. In 1973 he opened the Roxy nightclub in Los Angeles, where he met friend (and one-

time fiancée) Cher. He founded Geffen Records in 1980, signing Donna Summer, Elton John and Guns 'n Roses. He scored producing successes with *Cats* and *Dreamgirls* on Broadway, and the queer-themed films *Personal Best* (1982) and *Interview With the Vampire* (1994). In 1994 he co-founded Dreamworks SKG studio with Steven Spielberg and Jeffrey Katzenberg. After years of pressure from gay activists, Geffen came out publicly in 1992. He is a prominent contributor to gay health initiatives.

JOHN FORDE

GENDERFUCK

Generally refers to gender-crossing play, often by presenting 'opposite' gender attributes on one's body, as a way to challenge dominant perceptions about sex, gender and sexuality.

LISA Y.M. LAM

GENDER PUBLIC ADVOCACY COALITION (GENDERPAC)

GenderPAC works to end discrimination and violence against gender stereotypes by changing public attitudes, educating elected officials and expanding legal rights. Its primary concern is promoting understanding of the connection between discrimination based on gender stereotypes and sex, sexual orientation, age, race and class. GenderPAC works with corporations, lawmakers and the general public on breaking down myths related to gender stereotyping by providing language, statistics, legal background and training.

SURINA KHAN

GENET, JEAN

b. 1910; d. 1986

writer

Shortly after his birth in Paris, Jean Genet was abandoned to the care of public authorities and placed with foster parents. At 13 he ran away from a residential school for gifted children where he had been placed. At 15 he ran away again, this time from a hostel for troubled youth. He would continue running away from various institutions until he landed in the penal colony of Mettray, a place that would haunt his work and imagination for years to come. Enlisted in the army at 18, he travelled to the Middle East and northern Africa. On a trip to Paris he met André Gide, his first contact with the literary world. He deserted from the army in 1936 and travelled under false papers throughout Western and Eastern Europe. A year later he was again in Paris where he committed a series of misdemeanours, landing him in jail for increasingly long periods. For a short period of time he worked as a *bouquiniste*, one of the booksellers who worked from stalls lining the river Seine. He was in and out of prison over the next few years. While in prison he began to write, first poetry, then his novel, *Notre Dame des Fleurs* (*Our Lady of the Flowers*, 1943). At this time he met Jean **Cocteau**, who became a strong supporter, helping to get his novel published.

The mid-1940s were a feverishly productive period for Genet; he wrote virtually all of his novels during this period. *Miracle de la rose* (*Miracle of the Rose*, 1946), *Pompes funèbres* (*Funeral Rites*, 1947) and *Le journal du voleur* (*The Thief's Journal*, 1949) were all, more or less, autobiographical, whereas his novel *Querelle de Brest* (1947) told the story of a wayward sailor as mythical hero. All of the novels are set in an underworld where homosexuality, criminality and betrayal blend into a poetical and romantic whole. Perhaps the greatest success of the novels is their creation of an entire world, as real as it is specific only to Genet's texts.

In 1946 he was again condemned to prison, which sparked a defence campaign on the part of Cocteau, Jean-Paul Sartre and others. In 1949 Genet received a presidential pardon and was released. Shortly thereafter, still with the support of Cocteau, he made his only film, *Un Chant d'amour* (1950). The film is set in a prison and poetically presents the romantic and sexual fantasies of the inmates. The film was subject to censure, both in France and abroad, for many years, but it remains a masterpiece of experimental cinema.

Genet underwent a period of creative block until the mid-to-late 1950s when he wrote two plays, *Le Balcon* (*The Balcony*, 1958), set in a brothel, and *Les Nègres* (*The Blacks*, 1958). Both works took up explicit political themes in a provocative and unexpected manner. In particular, *The Blacks* attested to a sophisticated understanding of the politics of race and racism in France, a theme that Genet would continue to develop throughout the rest of his life.

After completing these works, Genet travelled to southern Europe, mostly Greece. His fame, especially as a playwright, was expanding throughout the world. He then wrote *Les Paravents* (*The Screens*, 1961), his final play, about the war in Algeria, continuing his exploration of politics and racism. During the late 1960s he became increasingly active in political causes, first with the students at the Sorbonne, then later with the Black Panthers and the Palestinians, travelling at their request both to the United States and the Middle East. He started work on a second film project in 1976, *La Nuit venue*, but abandoned it after two years. His later output is almost entirely political in nature. He wrote articles on the rights of immigrants in France, on Palestinian women and, most notoriously, the essay, 'Four Hours at Shatila', a first-person account of what he had seen immediately following an Israeli attack on two Lebanese villages in 1982. He also published interviews with the German writer Hubert **Fichte**, with the black American activist Angela **Davis**, and with the Moroccan writer Tahar Ben Jelloun. A few years before his death in 1986, he wrote his last book, *Prisoner of Love*, an account of his time with the Panthers and especially the Palestinians. The book is in many ways a culmination of his life and thought, both aesthetic and political. At his request his body was buried in Morocco.

DANIEL HENDRICKSON

GENTRIFICATION

Gentrification is the remaking of urban working-class residential neighbourhoods and commercial areas for higher-income, usually white newcomers from the professional middle class. It was once a sporadic phenomenon irrelevant to larger patterns of urban life, and a term used almost exclusively by academic and urban planning specialists. However, by the 1980s gentrification was at the cutting edge of change in urban areas, becoming so pervasive by the turn of the century that it is now a cultural and political keyword.

Contemporary gentrification is linked in the public imagination with gay men, and to a lesser extent lesbians, who are presumed to constitute a crucial 'cutting edge' of neighbourhood change. This linkage has to do with assumptions about gay and lesbian disposable income (namely, that there is a lot of it), as well as about gay and lesbian aesthetic sensibilities (that is, that they cry out against middle-class suburban blandness and déclassé urban squalor alike [see Florida 2002]). It also has to do with the fact that gay neighbourhood-building in fact proceeded, often in a highly visible fashion, in otherwise declining city-centre areas in the 1970s, just prior to the takeoff of gentrification as a widespread and systematic process (Castells 1983). These enclaves typically became anchors for broader urban change in subsequent decades.

In cultures dominated by the white professional middle class, this presumed linkage between gays and lesbians and gentrification has produced a widely welcomed 'recognition' in the mass media of 'positive achievements' – indeed the 'civilizing' work – of gay and lesbian communities in the urban environment. At the same time, given that gentrification on the ground level is a process generating a substantial amount of conflict, gay men and lesbians have become particularly conspicuous outsiders in rapidly changing neighbourhoods – enemies, in fact, in the eyes of many long-time residents facing the prospect of displacement (Bryant and Poitras 2003; Queer to the Left 2004). What is more, all of this 'attention' has further deepened the class and race inflections of 'gay' and 'lesbian' identities in the culture that made the gay and lesbian gentrification narrative possible in the first place (Knopp 1998).

Geographers, who have produced nearly all the extant research on gentrification, debate whether and how different cultural groupings (e.g., gays and lesbians, artists, 'yuppies', 'the creative class') factor into gentrification processes in different places. They have found, however, that fundamental to the timing of gentrification as widespread and systematic, as well as to the geographical specificity of the phenomenon in cities, are not the housing choices of specific social groups, nor consumer demand more broadly, but the restructuring of late twentieth-century capitalism – a nexus of finance capital, the housing industry and local state institutions. As Neil Smith puts it: 'Gentrification is a back-to-the-city movement all right, but a back-to-the-city movement by capital rather than people' (Smith 1996: 70) More specifically, three powerful forces emerged and interlocked in the face of the global capitalist crisis of the 1970s: (1) the declining rate of profit in the industrial sector sent investors looking for investment alternatives in the real estate sector; (2) a growing 'rent gap', whereby the market value of city-centre properties had fallen so low over time, relative to property values in their respective metropolitan hinterlands, that the purchase and redevelopment of city-centre properties was enticing for their especially high possible rates of return; and (3) central-government cutbacks in social expenditures and revenue sharing forced city centre political regimes into greater 'entrepreneurialism', subsidizing and otherwise luring and protecting private investment in upscale residential and retail developments as a means of fiscal survival (Smith 1996).

None of this necessarily disputes the notion that gays and lesbians might somehow be among a 'first wave' of neighbourhood newcomers, but other research and analysis does. Lawrence Knopp has produced the most detailed and sustained analysis of the relationship of gays and lesbians to gentrification and finds generalizations difficult to make (see his bibliography in Knopp 1998). Efforts to identify a relationship between lesbian and gay residential concentration and housing vacancy rates on a national scale in the United States have produced no statistically significant findings, except in seven cities where gay and lesbian concentration positively correlates with housing vacancies at a statistically significant level, indicating that gay and lesbian in-migration in neighbourhoods in these cities is about replacing others who have left, not displacing others by outbidding them (Bailey 1999).

Other research and analysis complicates the dominant gay–lesbian-gentrification narrative in other ways: gay men in the US on average earn less than straight men, and women, on average, whether straight or gay, earn less than men, making gays and lesbians disproportionately vulnerable to residential displacement (Badgett 2001); the shrinkage of affordable housing is now the most pressing health issue facing people with AIDS (PWAs) in many cities, and PWAs, most on low and fixed incomes, tend to be concentrated in areas now being targeted by developers for gentrification (Queer to the Left 2004); queer bars, sex clubs, and public cruising and gathering spaces in many cities have come under attack by developers, neighbourhood newcomers and city officials eager to promote ever more upscale development (Delany 1999; Warner 1999).

Bibliography

Badgett, M.V. and Lee (2001) *Money, Myths, and Change – The Economic Lives of Lesbians and Gay Men*, Chicago: University of Chicago Press.

Bailey, Robert W. (1999) *Gay Politics, Urban Politics – Identity and Economics in the Urban Setting*, New York: Columbia University Press.

Bryant, Linda Goode and Poitras, Laura (2003) *Flag Wars: A Cautionary Tale*, Zula Pearl Films.

Castells, Manuel (1983) 'Cultural Identity, Sexual Liberation and Urban Structure: The Gay Community in San Francisco', in *The City and the Grassroots – A Cross-Cultural Theory of Urban Social Movements*, Berkeley: University of California Press.

Delany, Samuel R. (1999) *Times Square Red, Times Square Blue*, New York: New York University Press.

Florida, Richard (2002) *The Rise of the Creative Class – And How It's Transforming Work, Leisure, Community, and Everyday Life*, New York: Basic Books.

Knopp, Lawrence (1998) 'Sexuality and Urban Space – Gay Male Identity Politics in the United States, The United Kingdom, and Australia', in Ruth Fincher and Jane M. Jacobs (eds) *Cities of Difference*, New York: Guilford Press.

Queer to the Left (2004) *Gentrification Keywords*, Chicago: Queer to the Left.

Smith, Neil (1996) *The New Urban Frontier – Gentrification and the Revanchist City*, London and New York: Routledge.

Warner, Michael (1999) 'Zoning Out Sex', in *The Trouble with Normal – Sex, Politics, and the Ethics of Queer Life*, London: The Free Press.

JEFFREY EDWARDS

GERMANY, FILMMAKING

The rich period of Weimar cinema (1919–33) had a major international influence on queer cinema of the 1980s and 1990s, from its innovative portraits of same-sex love in *Mädchen in Uniform* (Girls in Uniform, Leontine Sagan, 1931), and *Pandora's Box* (*Die Büchse Der Pandora*, G.W. Pabst, 1929), to the androgynous cross-dressing films of Asta Nielsen (*Hamlet*, 1921), Curt Bois and Mona Maris (*Der Fürst von Pappenheim/The Masked Mannequin*, 1927), Elizabeth Bergner (*Der Geiger von Florenz/ Impetuous Love*, 1926) and Rheinhold Schünzel (*Viktor und Viktoria*, 1933).

The German gay liberation movement began in 1897 with the founding of the Scientific-Humanitarian Committee by Dr Magnus Hirschfeld (1868–1935), whose work on the 'third sex' attempted to overturn the 1871 criminalization of sodomy in the notorious Paragraph 175 (which was not ultimately abolished until 1969).

In 1919 the first international gay film appeared: *Anders als die Andern* (*Different from the Others*, Richard Oswald). During the Third Reich (1933–45), the Nazi campaign to imprison and exterminate homosexuals began with the burning of Hirschfeld's Institute for Sexology in 1933. The pink triangle that homosexuals were forced to wear in concentration camps would become the international symbol for queer culture in the postwar era.

After the Second World War there was a lull in queer filmmaking, but with the arrival of das Neue Kino (the New German Cinema) in the late 1960s, questions of sexual, psychological or national identity became prominently intertwined in the work of three contemporary filmmakers: Rainer Werner **Fassbinder** (1945–82), Werner **Schroeter** (1945–) and Rosa von **Praunheim** (1942). Before his premature death, Fassbinder's prolific direction of 44 films was extraordinarily diverse, with his most explicitly homosexual films including *Faustrecht der Freiheit* (*Fox and His Friends*, 1975), *In einem Jahr mit dreizehn Monden* (*In A Year with 13 Moons*, 1979) and *Querelle* (1982). One important thread can be traced through the transgender appeal of Nazi film

star and iconic diva Zarah Leander, whose career was echoed in Fassbinder's explorations of femininity as masquerade, in *Die bitteren Tränen der Petra von Kant* (*The Bitter Tears of Petra von Kant*, 1972), *Lili Marlene* (1980) and *Die Sehnsucht der Veronika Voss* (*Veronika Voss*, 1982).

Similarly, Werner Schroeter's work as a director of theatre and opera, as well in as film, underscores his fascination with camp spectacle, whether of the sadistic male body in *Der Rosenkönig* (*The Rose King*, 1986) or the eroticized female face and voice in his lesbian trilogy *Der Tod der Maria Malibran* (*The Death of Maria Malibran*, 1972), *Willow Springs* (1973) and *Flocons d'or/Goldflocken* (1976).

Rosa von Praunheim, through his prominent AIDS activism, provocative interventions in the public sphere and hyperbolic gender performances in his films, forms a link to younger filmmakers of queer German cinema in the 1990s. Director of over 40 films, including *Nicht die Homosexuelle is pervers, sondern die Situation, in der er lebt* (*It is not the homosexual who is perverse but the situation in which he finds himself*, 1970) and *Ein Virus kennt keine Moral* (*A Virus has no Morals*, 1985), Praunheim is perhaps the most prominent gay filmmaker after Fassbinder.

Queer German cinema is allegorical, fetishistic and spectacular, and questions essentialist notions of identity, including non-heterosexual sexualities, by exploring crossgender identification and transgendered bodies. Questioning the boundaries of sexuality and desire through formal experimentation with the language of cinema is typified by the work of Schroeter, Ulrike **Ottinger**, Monika **Treut** and a younger generation of filmmakers, including Mathias **Müller**, Michael **Bryntrup**, Hans Scheirl and Ursula Pürrer. Like Fassbinder in *Querelle* and Schroeter in *Der Rosenkönig*, Treut explores sadomasochism in *Verführung; die grausame Frau* (*Seduction: the Cruel Woman*, 1985) and *Die Jungfrauenmaschine*

(*The Virgin Machine*, 1988). Like Praunheim's films with American settings (*Uberleben in New York/Survival in New York*, 1989), Treut's *My Father is Coming* (1991) dramatizes nationality, whether American or German, as drag.

Formally stylish, postmodern and allegorical, Ottinger's fantasy narratives feature lush costumes and sets, and frequently follow the structure of the medieval morality play: *Superbia-der Stolz/Superbia-Pride* (1986) and *Freak Orlando* (1981), or the episodic quest: *Madame X: eine absolute Herrscherin* (*Madame X: an Absolute Ruler*, 1978), *Bildnis einer Trinkerin* (*Ticket of no Return*, 1979), and *Johanna d'Arc of Mongolia* (1989). Alongside the experimental aesthetics of queer German cinema is a continuing tradition of narrative realism, which includes stories of homophobia and coming out, biographies of prominent gays and lesbians, and documentaries of political activism and AIDS: examples include Wolfgang Petersen's *Die Konsequenz* (*The Consequence*, 1977); Frank Ripploh's *Taxi Zum Klo* (*Taxi to the John*, 1981), Alexandra von Grote's *Novembermond* (*November Moon*, 1985); Wieland Speck's *Westler* (1985); Percy Adlon's *Salmonberries* (1991); and Stefan Hayn's *Tuntenfilm* (*Film of Queens*, 1989–90).

Stories of the persecution of Jews, homosexuals, transvestites and others form a continuing theme, from Max Färberböck's 1999 *Eine Liebe größer als der Tod* (*Aimée and Jaguar*) to the 1992 ensemble production *Verzaubert* (*Enchanted*), about gays and lesbians who survived the Third Reich. Similarly, Praunheim's *Ich bin meine eigene Frau* (*I am my own Woman*, 1992), starring well-known Berlin entertainer Tima die Göttliche, tells the colourful story of Charlotte von Mahlsdorf, born Lothar Berflede, a transvestite who survived both the Holocaust and the Communist period in East Berlin. In 1989 Heiner Carow's *Coming Out* was the first East German film to deal with oppression against homosexuals in the DDR (Deutsche Demokratische Republik). During the 1990s queer films exploring transsexuality included Treut's *Gendernauts* (1999), Hans Scheirl's *Dandy Dust* (1998) and Praunheim's *Vor Transsexuellen wird gewarnt* (*Transsexual Menace*, 1996).

In addition to the work of Treut, Ottinger and Elfi Mikesch, important developments in lesbian filmmaking have included the bar scene subgenre, e.g., Katrin Barben's *Bar Jeder Frau* (*The Bad Girl Bar*, 1992), Birgit Durbahn's *Mit den besten Wünschen* (*With Best Wishes*, 1982) and dyke noir animation by Berliner lesbians Nathalie Percillier, Claudia Schillinger, Lilly Besiller, Claudia Zoller and Stefanie Jordan. The visual Expressionist style of Heidi Küll's animated *Geliebte Mörderin: Ein Film Noir* (*Beloved Murderer*, 1991) and other shorts by the Berlin group brings us back full circle to the extraordinary aesthetic influence of the Weimar period in Queer German Cinema.

Further reading

Kuzniar, Alice (2000) *The Queer German Cinema*, California: Stanford University Press.

KIRSTEN MOANA THOMPSON

GERMANY, LITERATURE

Given the broad acceptance of homosexuals in German society today, one might expect queer literature to be equally integrated into the German book market and in the public imagination – this is not the case however. While contemporary German gay and lesbian writing is hardly different thematically or stylistically from that of other traditions, its reception is.

On the one hand, major publishers are resistant to acquiring gay- or lesbian-themed titles; when they do, they rarely promote them as such because of the perception that doing so will limit sales. This purportedly stems from experience. Rowohlt Verlag took on a number of prominent foreign books during the late 1980s and early 1990s, expecting the burgeoning gay/lesbian literary market in the UK and the United States to reproduce itself in Germany, but its translations of David Leavitt and Hervé **Guibert** never made it past a first print run, and this in a country where foreign authors frequently sell better than native writers. Suhrkamp Verlag has published novels by Joachim Helfer (b. 1964), but eschews mentioning their queer content in jacket or publicity copy. DTV has published three novels by Antje Rávic Strubel (b. 1975), including *Offene Blende* (Open Aperture, 2001) and reputedly is expanding its list of queer writers, although so far its web site features only heterosexually-oriented 'Women's Literature' and 'Men's Literature'. Fischer Verlag ventured a single German print run of Jeanette Winterson's *Written on the Body* in 1993 and has since published all of two books by gay writer Andreas Steinhöfel (b. 1962), while letting its paperback edition of Verena Stefan's (b. 1947) ground-breaking novel *Häutungen* (Shedding, 2001; Frauenoffensive 1977) go back out of print. Aufbau Verlag has admirably kept *Es ist spät, ich kann nicht atmen* (It's late, I can't breathe), a seminal first-person AIDS narrative by Mario Wirz (b. 1956), in print since 1992, and has published posthumously three books by Detlev Meyer (1950–99), including a reprint of his important 'Biography of Consternation' trilogy: *Im Dampfbad greift nach mir ein Engel* (An Angel reaches for me in the Steamroom, 2001; original edn, Eremiten-Presse, 1985). But despite these notable exceptions, mainstream houses are at best ambivalent towards queer writing.

In response, a strong network of gay and lesbian publishers and an energetic consortium of bookstores have evolved. This coalition began during the late 1970s with Verlag rosa Winkel and Prinz Eisenherz bookstores in West Berlin, and by the mid-1990s included a host of other institutions:

in Hamburg, the gay publisher and bookstore MännerschwarmSkript Verlag; in Berlin, lesbian publishers Frauenoffensive and Krug & Schadenberg, the gay publisher Bruno Gmünder Verlag, and the lesbian and gay publisher quer Verlag; and in Munich, the gay Max & Milian bookstore. The publishers put out anywhere from six to sixteen new titles a year in print runs averaging 2,500, ranging from hack erotica to timely non-fiction, light novels, literary fiction and poetry. Of the latter, novels such as *Benjamins Tagebuch* (Benjamin's Diary, 2000) by Michael Sollorz (b. 1962) and *Bilder von Ihr* (Her Pictures, 1996) by Karen-Susan Fessel (b. 1964) continue to sell in high numbers. All of these houses are committed to maintaining robust backlists and promoting promising new talents such as Peter Hofmann (b. 1965), Peter Rehberg (b. 1965), Corinna Waffender (b. 1965) and Antje Wagner (b. 1971). The bookstores, for their part, serve as resources for both publishers and local communities. It is largely as a result of their enterprise that a mainstream paperback publisher such as Piper Verlag can reissue titles such as Marcus Brühl's (b. 1975) cheeky coming-out novel *Henningstadt* (2005; original edn, MännerschwarmSkript in 2001) or Stephan Niederwieser's (b. c.1965) popular *An einem Mittwoch in September* (One Wednesday in September, 2005; original edn, quer Verlag, 1998). In 1992 the consortium established a bi-annual literary award that includes publication of nominees in accompanying 'best of' anthologies; and it publishes a quarterly catalogue and website (*www.gaybooks.de*) providing mini-reviews of new books.

The autonomous publicity is necessary as mainstream media systematically ignore queer publishers; and writers who publish with them are occasionally denounced, even in left-oriented media, as 'career gays'. Perlentaucher.de, a highly regarded online digest of book reviews from major newspapers, founded in 2000, so far covers only three non-fiction titles from quer Verlag, one German fiction title from MännerscharmSkript and one translated novel from Krug & Schadenberg. As the gay publisher Detlef Grumbach correctly points out, had Helfer's novel *Cohn & König* (1998), for example, been publicized as queer or published by a queer house, it never would have received the reviews it did. A number of local and online queer magazines do regularly review new books; and critics such as Axel Schock (b. 1965) have helped to define the contours of contemporary queer literature in Germany.

The only gay German writer to have household-name status is Ralf König; but as a comic book author he remains outside the traditional literary canon. While Arnold Stadler (b. 1954) was awarded the prestigious Büchner Prize in 1999, of his novels only *Sehnsucht* (Desire), published three years afterwards, deals with gay subjects, and that only peripherally and to mixed reviews. Classic (and long-dead) gay novelists Hubert **Fichte** (1935–86) and Hans Henny Jahnn (1894–1959) are widely appreciated for their literary value; and Michael Roes (b. 1960), with his epic postmodernist novel *Rub' Al-Khali* (1997), may be considered a successor to Fichte. But representing homosexual experience in German literature is still viewed generally and insidiously as incompatible with good writing. As Christoph Geiser (b. 1949), a Swiss novelist who publishes in the mainstream, remarked in an interview following a 1999 reading: 'Any author who deals with gay themes runs the risk of being shunted into the "pink corner"... People tell me again and again: "Better not read those passages, otherwise the audience will just close up and you'll get labelled"'.

Further reading

Bubeck, Ilona (ed.) (2005) *Sappho küsst die Sterne. Neue deutschsprachige Literatur von Lesben*, Berlin: quer Verlag.

Jones, James W. (2002) 'German and Austrian Literature: Nineteenth and Twentieth Centuries', available at: http://www.glbtq.com/literature/german_aus-trian_lit2_19c_20c,7.html.
Ott, Thomas (ed.) (2005) *Im Paradies. Beiträge zum Literaturpreis der Schwulen Buchläden*, Hamburg: MännerschwarmSkript.
Schock, Axel (1995) 'Männertreu, Prinz Eisenherz & Co.', *Börsenblatt des deutschen Buchhandels*, 3, 10 (January): 6ff.
—— (1997) 'Das Coming-Out der Seejungfrau', *Spiegel-Spezial* (October), TK–TK.

WILLIAM MARTIN

GEVER, MARTHA

writer, editor

Writer and academic whose work focuses on gay and lesbian representation in film and popular culture. Gever co-edited *Queer Looks: Perspectives on Lesbian and Gay Film and Video* (1993) with John **Greyson** and Pratibha **Parmar**, an influential study on lesbian and gay filmmaking. She is the author of *Entertaining Lesbians: Celebrity, Sexuality and Self Invention* (2003), a study of lesbianism in popular culture in which she argues that the acceptance of 'celebrity' lesbians Martina Navratilova, kd lang, Melissa Etheridge and Rosie O'Donnell is a result of their innovative and courageous self-invention as positive role models, rather than a pre-existing climate of cultural liberalism. Her other works include *Out There: Marginalisation and Contemporary Culture* (2002, co-edited with Russell Ferguson, Trinh T. Minh-Ha and Cornel West).

JOHN FORDE

GHETTO, GAY

A neighbourhood where relatively large numbers of gays and/or lesbians have residences, visibly occupy public space, participate in gay-/lesbian-specific community institutions, and otherwise participate in social networks to some degree of isolation from straight worlds (Levine 1979). Unlike 'gay/lesbian neighbourhood', 'gay/lesbian enclave' or even 'gay/lesbian liberated zone', the ghetto metaphor speaks to the power dynamics between dominant and subordinate cultures, as well as to the psychic fears members of dominant groups have about subordinate 'others'. More specifically it speaks to the simultaneous instantiation and reproduction of dynamics of power and fear in and through the urban built environment: ghettos simultaneously contain, protect and display subordinate groups and cultures. Further, the ghetto metaphor speaks to the relationship of public space to cultural and political citizenship: ghetto dwellers are not part of 'the general public' (Bronski 1998).

Unlike Jewish and black ghettos, however, gay/lesbian ghettos, which are almost exclusively post-Second World War American phenomena, are largely the products of the subordinate group (gays and lesbians) itself, deliberate strategies of community-building, social change, profit-making and political empowerment, even if they are at the same time the product of exclusion (Castells 1983). While in almost all cases dominated by middle-class white men (but see Boyd 2003, Gates and Ost 2004 and Rothenberg 1995 on lesbian enclaves and ghettos), these spaces have been central to making queerness visible. However complicated this visibility may be, it has advertised and continues to advertise new sexual possibilities and ways of relating to others that have influenced all kinds of people and enabled many kinds of glbtq people to be more open about their lives and to find lovers and friends in an otherwise hostile and violent world. Also, in a political system in which electoral representation is geographically based, residential concentration has facilitated the building of political power. By the 1970s gay/lesbian ghettos had helped

to fashion a sexual citizenship modelled along the lines of traditional (in the US context) 'ethnic' urban inclusion – at the expense of long-standing dominant conceptions of homosexuality as pathological in one way or another – epitomized by the 1977 election of Harvey Milk to San Francisco's Board of Supervisors (city council) from that city's Castro neighbourhood (Epstein 1999; Epstein and Schmiechen 1984).

Bibliography

Boyd, Nan Alamilla (2003) 'Lesbian Space, Lesbian Territory', in *Wide Open Town – A History of Queer San Francisco to 1965*, Berkeley: University of California Press.

Bronski, Michael (1998) 'The Gay Ghetto and the Creation of Culture', in *The Pleasure Principle – Sex, Backlash, and the Struggle for Gay Freedom*, New York: St Martin's Press.

Castells, Manuel (1983) 'Cultural Identity, Sexual Liberation and Urban Structure: The Gay Community in San Francisco', in *The City and the Grassroots – A Cross-Cultural Theory of Urban Social Movements*, Berkeley: University of California Press.

Epstein, Robert and Schmiechen, Richard (1984) *The Times of Harvey Milk*, Black Sand Productions.

Epstein, Steven (1999) 'Gay and Lesbian Movements in the United States – Dilemmas of Identity, Diversity, and Political Strategy', in Barry D. Adam, Jan Willem Duyvendakm and Andre Krouwel (eds) *The Global Emergence of Gay and Lesbian Politics – National Imprints of a Worldwide Movement*, Philadelphia: Temple University Press.

Gates, Gary and Ost, Jason (2004) *The Gay and Lesbian Atlas*, Washington DC: Urban Institute.

Levine, Martin P. (1979) 'Gay Ghetto', from *Gay Men: The Sociology of Male Homosexuality*, London Harper & Row.

Rothenberg, Tamar (1995) '"And She Told Two Friends": Lesbians Creating Urban Social Space', in David Bell and Gill Valentine (eds) *Mapping Desire – Geographies of Sexualities*, London and New York: Routledge.

JEFFREY EDWARDS

GIBSON, KENTE

b. 1933

playwright

South African playwright Kente Gibson is known as the father of black theatre in that country. Among his other achievements is the play *Too Late*. Written and performed in 1963, it broke a taboo in black South African society with its frank depiction of sexual relationships between black men in prison. Kente broke another deep taboo in 2003 when he became one of the first high-profile artists in South Africa to publicly admit his HIV+ status.

MARC EPPRECHT

GIELGUD, JOHN

b. 1904; d. 2000

actor

An undisputed star of the twentieth-century English stage, Sir John Gielgud was born into a theatrical family (his great-aunt was the actor Ellen Terry) and trained at the Royal Academy of Dramatic Arts. His celebrated stage performances include Shakespeare's Romeo, Hamlet and Macbeth. He won unexpected international popularity and an Academy Award for his role as an English butler in the comedy *Arthur* (1981). Other notable work includes the film *Prospero's Books* (1991) and *Brideshead Revisited* (1981) for television. He was knighted for services to acting in 1953 – the same year he was arrested for attempting to solicit gay sex in public. Intensely guarded about his personal life, he never publicly acknowledged his homosexuality, but was a generous private contributor to gay rights organizations. He published an autobiography, *An Actor and His Time*, in 1979. Martin Hensler, his partner of 30 years, died in 1999. Gielgud himself died on 21 May 2000.

JOHN FORDE

GILBERT AND GEORGE

Proesch, Gilbert

b. 1943

artist

Passmore, George

b. 1942

artist

The two artists met in 1967 while attending St Martin's School of Art in London (Gilbert was born in Italy, George in England), and soon embarked on a collaborative artistic practice that they have maintained ever since. Dropping their surnames and dressing in nearly identical business suits, their work primarily consists of large-scale black-and-white photo collages structured in a grid formation and often partially tinted with primary colours. These works focus primarily on young males, religious symbolism and the artists themselves as a couple (and often some combination of these subjects). In addition to this work, they have also presented themselves as 'living sculptures', as in their performance piece 'Singing Sculpture', in which their faces are covered with metallic paint, they move as though automatons and continuously lip-synch the words to a recording of the English song 'Underneath the Arches'.

JOHN PAUL RICCO

GINGRICH, CANDACE

b. 1966

activist

The openly lesbian half-sister of conservative Republican politician Newt Gingrich, Candace has used her public profile to promote gay and lesbian rights and critique the Republican party's anti-gay political agenda. Gingrich was born on 2 June 1966 in Baltimore. She acknowledged her lesbianism as a college student and came out publicly in 1994, shortly after her brother became Speaker of the House of Representatives; the announcement received national attention. She has been openly critical of the Republican party's policies on gay rights and same-sex marriage, and particularly anti-gay comments made by Senator Jesse Helms. In 1995 she became the national spokesperson for the Human Rights Campaign's National Coming Out Project and lobbied Congress to secure HIV/AIDS funding. In 1996 she cemented her celebrity status by playing a minister who presides over a same-sex wedding on the TV sitcom *Friends* and published her autobiography, *The Accidental Activist*.

JOHN FORDE

GINSBERG, ALLEN

b. 1926; d. 1997

poet

Allen Ginsberg's importance for glbtq culture is hard to overestimate for three reasons: first, he is arguably *the* ur-gay culture figure of the modern American era; second, because his career is highly varied and complex; and third, because his influence on gay culture is pervasive, even if often indirectly (for example, see the literary innovations with which the Beats paved the way for the social, artistic and political upheavals of the 1960s).

Much of Ginsberg's creative power comes from his conscious determination to fulfil gay poet Walt Whitman's call for future poets to speak with 'candor'. Ginsberg's refusal to censor himself not only meant that he wrote about homosexual desires and acts but that he led his life as an openly gay man, never hiding nor apologizing for his sexuality, which included an openness regarding his relationship with his lover Peter Orlovsky.

Born in Newark, New Jersey, Ginsberg found his artistic mentors when he met William S. **Burroughs** and Jack Kerouac

during his freshman year at Columbia University. Later, other key members of the circle appeared, such as Neal Cassady and Gregory Corso. All these men were either homosexual or bisexual; besides being close friends with them, Ginsberg had sex with all of them. It was through their close friendships that they noted the difference between the way they spoke to each other and the way social reality was portrayed in literature. Feeling the oppressiveness of the conformity demanded by society after the Second World War, Ginsberg and his friends sought to challenge such conformity, and did so, largely by writing frankly about their own experiences.

The refusal to conform exacted a price, as the Beats' work was often condemned as being 'barbaric' and unliterary, and such criticism was often directed at their frank sexuality (including homosexuality) and their depiction of drug use. Ginsberg's breakthrough composition, *Howl* (1956), was censored, primarily because of its candid portrayal of and celebration of homosexuality. After the police seized *Howl* and put its publisher on trial, Judge Clayton Horn ruled the book was not obscene.

Although he became famous during the 1950s and celebrated in the 1960s with the rise of the counter-culture he had helped create, Ginsberg's openness about his homosexuality continued to cause state opposition: he was thrown out of both Cuba and Czechoslovakia and arrested while in Italy. Ginsberg fulfilled the role of poet as prophet, as he continued to advocate a turn away from the violence and materialism that permeates modern society. He championed higher consciousness through his support of alternative media, innovative musicians, politically progressive movements, the legalization of drugs, ecological movements and sexual freedom. In the 1960s he worked with Timothy Leary to promote psychedelic drugs, helped popularize the chanting of Hindu mantras, originated the concept of the 'Be-In' and worked with anti-war activists to oppose the war in Vietnam. He became a Buddhist in the 1970s. To advance the goal of a society that was not destructive and repressive, he travelled the world reading poetry, often in collaboration with musicians, while continually espousing political, artistic and sexual freedom.

Further reading

Ginsberg, Allen (2001) *Spontaneous Mind: Selected Interviews 1958–1996,* ed. David Carter, New York: HarperCollins.

DAVID CARTER

GLAM ROCK

A largely British phenomenon that rapidly gained popularity in the United Sates, glam (or glitter) rock was the queer offspring of the late 1960s adolescent-driven disaffection for progressive rock, with its epic sound and institutional value. Glam was – in John Lennon's derogatory words – 'rock and roll with lipstick on', a subversion and perversion of the music establishment, at once a return to sound basics and the set-up of an outrageous show.

During the early 1970s the music scene and the high streets of the UK were flooded with platform boots, flamboyant outfits, high pitched vocals, eerie makeup and outlandish hairdos. Drawing from the historic nexus of music and sexuality, from the Mod and Ted subcultures and from the gender bending of early Mick **Jagger**, the ebullient sex icons of the glam era – Gary Glitter, Alvin Stardust, Marc **Bolan** and T-Rex, Slade, Alice Cooper, Suzi Quatro, **Jobriath**, Electric Light Orchestra, Mud, Wizard, Sweet, the **New York Dolls** and Roxy Music (possibly the epitome of glam rock, thanks to androgynous Brian Eno and charismatic frontman Bryan **Ferry**) – turned into the superstars of a new, bright, glittering age. Master chameleon David

Bowie, who performed at popular TV programme *Top of the Pops* in gaudily coloured knitted bodystockings in July 1972, led such alien invasion of theatrical style to its peak of mass diffusion.

Glam was not just music, albeit at once androgynous and hypersexed. It encompassed fashion, attitude and self-irony: it was a whole camp way of life, abhorring anything natural, authentic and true, replacing bourgeois values with hype, drugs and decadence, hedonism and self-indulgence, and promising joyous, glowing decadence, fun and freedom to the children of the (sexual) revolution. Glam was embedded in the history and codes of effeminacy, investing the theatrical and the counterfeit on the body surfaces so as to stage a makeup contest of masculinity and femininity. It was a world in which boys would be girls and girls would be boys, a 'mixed up muddled up shook up world' (as The Kinks would say) in which heterosexuality faced sexual otherness and found sheer pleasure in doing so.

The age of glitter would soon fade, and in 1975 – shortly after Bowie's killing of Ziggy Stardust – glam was no longer the big issue in pop music. Still, its influence in that half-decade was impressive, touching upon popular icons such as Elton **John**, Lou **Reed** (who came from the twinkling world of Warhol's Factory and who, on his Bowie-produced *Transformer*, abandoned his tough leather outfit in favour of glam, inviting us all for a walk on the wild side), **Iggy Pop** and the Stooges, Rod Stewart, Kiss and Queen. Echoes of the glam revolution in later years would be found in punk, in the 1980s new romantic drag show and in the 1990s neo-glam, all wild guitar riffs and humour, as best represented by Suede, the Darkness, the Ark and Placebo.

As much of queer show business, glam was both socially subversive and wildly entertaining, so as to end up being politically ambivalent, and not just for the dubious character of its fashionable state-ment of homo-, bi- or pan-sexuality (largely meant to gain market visibility). Glam queered the heterosexual world, involving both heterosexuals and gay people in a seduction game, and the game was played to different ends. As best staged in Todd Haynes' epic film *Velvet Goldmine* (1998), while glam indeed served its practitioners as a tool of subcultural recognition and iden-tity definition, it did so by fully inscribing subcultures within bloodthirsty capitalistic strategies that incorporate and contain sub-version in the very same gesture of moving and transgressing borders – art/fashion, male/female, gay/heterosexual – of legiti-macy by setting up a bourgeois freak show of mass consumption.

Further reading

Cagle, V.M. (1995) *Reconstructing Pop/Subculture: Art, Rock, and Andy Warhol*, New York: Sage.

Frith, S. (1981) *Sound Effects: Youth Leisure, and the Politics of Rock'n'Roll*, New York: Pan-theon.

Gill, J. (1995) *Queer Noises: Male and Female Homosexuality in Twentieth-Century Music*, London: Cassell.

Hoskyns, B. (1998) *Glam! Bowie, Bolan and the Glitter Revolution*, New York: Faber & Faber.

FABIO CLETO

GLORY HOLE

Hole cut into the partition separating the stalls in public men's rooms, created to facil-itate oral sex. Also, by extension, similar holes are constructed in commercial sex venues.

DANIEL HENDRICKSON

GODDARD, KEITH

b. 1960

musician

The musician and composer Keith Anthony Goddard joined the Gays and Lesbians of Zimbabwe (GALZ) in 1992. He helped guide the association through its public confrontations with the country's president, Robert Mugabe, resulting in the recognition of homosexuality as a human rights issue in Zimbabwe and elsewhere in Africa. Goddard played a key role in GALZ's transformation from a relatively elite, primarily white association to one that reflected the African majority population and the democratic ideals of the gay rights movement. In 1997 he took up the post of GALZ Director. Goddard also played a founding role in the **All Africa Rights Initiative**.

MARC EPPRECHT

GOMEZ, MARGA

b. ?1956

performance artist

Marga Gomez was born in Harlem, New York to a Cuban father and a Puerto Rican mother. Both parents were in show busi-ness; her childhood became the basis for two of her most famous theatrical mono-logues, *Memory Tricks* (1991) about her mother, and, *A Line Around the Block* (1996), about her father. Gomez moved to San Francisco in the 1980s and became a regular at the Valencia Rose Cabaret, a venue dedicated to gay comedians. Gomez also founded the Latino comedy group, Culture Clash and, in 1988, was voted Entertainer of the Year by the San Fran-cisco Council on Entertainment. During the 1990s Gomez performed theatrical works that include, *Marga Gomez is Pretty, Witty and Gay* and *Marga Gomez's Intimate Details*. In 1997 she released her first comedy recording *Hung Like A Fly*. Her stand-up career was highlighted in the 2003 documentary *Laughing Matters*. Other film and TV credits include HBO's *Tracey Takes On* and the feature film *Sphere* (1998). She has contributed to three anthologies, *Out, Loud and Laughing* (1995), *Contemporary*

Plays by American Women of Color (1996) and *Out of Character* (1996). Her work *Los Big Names* premiered in 2004 in Washington DC

MELISSA FITCH

GÓMEZ-PEÑA, GUILLERMO

b. 1955

performance artist, writer

Guillermo Gómez-Peña was raised in Mexico City and arrived in the United States in 1978. Gómez-Peña's performance art and writings revolve around border culture and identity. His work, while clearly manifesting a queer aesthetic, is not particularly gay- or lesbian-themed. From 1984 to 1990 Gómez-Peña was a founding member and performer of the Border Arts Workshop. He has also contributed to the national radio show, *Crossroad*, and serves as an editor for various theatre journals. Gómez-Peña was granted a MacArthur Foundation Fellowship in 1991 and received the American Book Award in 1997 for his 1996 text *The New World Border*. His performance art has been presented in the US, Canada, Mexico, Europe, Australia, the Soviet Union, Colombia, Puerto Rico, Cuba, Brazil and Argentina. His most recent books include *Dangerous Border Crossers* (2000) and *Codex Spangliensis* (2000).

MELISSA FITCH

GONZALEZ-TORRES, FELIX

b. 1957; d. 1996

artist

From the late 1980s until his death from AIDS in 1996, Cuban-born New York artist Felix Gonzalez-Torres created moving yet formally spare works of art in order to address the personal and communal loss and death experienced as a result of the AIDS pandemic. At a time of political moralizing in and on the arts in the US on the political Left and Right, and censorious campaigns against non-mainstream art, Gonzalez-Torres' work strategically eschewed these debates by creating works that, in their reinvention of minimal and conceptual art forms, made it nearly impossible for them to be reduced to a single ideological statement. In gallery installations, generic objects such as wall clocks, stacks of paper and piles or 'spills' of individually wrapped candies, all functioned as elegiac evocations of time shared (i.e. 'Perfect Lovers' [1991], two identical clocks set side by side and originally set to the same time) or lost (i.e. the stacks and spills were left there for visitors to take). He died in 1996 in New York City.

JOHN PAUL RICCO

GOODE, JOE

b. 1951

dancer, choreographer

Born 13 March 1951 in Presque Isle, Maine and raised in Hampton, Virginia, Goode earned a degree in Drama from Virginia Commonwealth University. He then moved briefly to New York and studied with Merce Cunningham and Finis Jhung, but settled in San Francisco where he danced with Margaret Jenkins.

In 1980 he began to make works for himself and in 1985 formed the Joe Goode Performance Group. Known for working with theatrical gesture in dance, and the incorporation of spoken word and simple songs to serve his finicky theatrical sensibility, the Group achieved international recognition during the 1990s. Tall and lanky, Goode's work often portrays ironic, humorous autobiography, as in the 1984 solo *I'm Sorry*, in which he voiced ironic apologies for being a homosexual artist concerned with feminist issues as he danced. He frequently addresses HIV and AIDS in his stage work, as in the prize-winning *Deeply*

253

There (Stories of a Neighbourhood) (1998) which depicts the impact of AIDS in the queer-centred Castro District of San Francisco. His mixed-gender company is also concerned with family tensions and dependent relationships between queer and straight people.

THOMAS F. DEFRANTZ

GORRIS, MARLEEN

b. 1948

filmmaker

One of the world's most acclaimed lesbian directors, Gorris' work celebrates the power of female and lesbian communities in her work and makes a sustained critique of heterosexual patriarchy.

Gorris was born on 9 December 1948 in Roermond, Limburg, the Netherlands. After training as an actor at Amsterdam University, she created a furore with her first feature *De Stilte rond Christine M.* (*A Question of Silence*, 1982) in which three women brutally murder a male shopkeeper, citing their motives as frustration about the abuse of women in a male-dominated society. She followed this with *Gebroken spiegels* (*Broken Mirrors*, 1984) and *The Last Island* (1990), a grim examination of male brutality among a group of plane-crash survivors. *Antonia's Line* (1995), a comic drama about a woman who raises a child in an all-female community, was a surprise international hit, winning Best Foreign Language Film Oscar. Her work has been criticized for invariably portraying men only as idiots or potential rapists. Gorris' first English-language feature, *Mrs Dalloway* (1997), based on Virginia Woolf's novel, emphasizes the lesbian relationship between two female characters. Other work includes *The Luzhin Defence* (2000) and *Carolina* (2003).

JOHN FORDE

GOYTISOLO, JUAN

b. 1931

writer

The Spanish novelist Juan Goytisolo has lived most of his life in Paris. He began writing shortly after arriving in France, quickly gaining renown in both his native and adopted countries. His early work takes the form of more or less traditional narratives, but beginning with the trilogy *Marks of Identity* (1966), *Count Julian* (1970) and *Juan the Landless* (1975), he took on an increasingly experimental style, using unconventional punctuation and elements from languages other than Spanish. Most of his novels are deeply marked by the Moorish influence in Spain and Arab culture in general. During the mid-1980s he wrote a pair of autobiographical books, *Forbidden Territory* and *Realms of Strife*, in which he recounts very frankly the development of his sexual life, both in terms of his homosexuality and in relation to his female life companion. These personal matters are presented not simply as biographical details, but rather as integral parts of his intellectual and political engagement.

DANIEL HENDRICKSON

GRAN FURY

art activist organization

Gran Fury was one of the most recognized AIDS activist art groups in the United States during the late 1980s and early 1990s. They formed as a group in 1988, although their roots go back two years earlier when, as an ad hoc group of activists, they created what would soon become the main emblem of the AIDS activist movement: a pink triangle on a field of black with the words 'SILENCE = DEATH' printed below. Originally designed as a poster to be pasted all over the streets of lower Manhattan, two years later the graphic was transformed into a neon sign as part of a street-level window display at the New Museum of Contemporary Art on lower Broadway in Manhattan, entitled, 'Let the Record Show'. With an enlarged photo of the Nuremberg trials as backdrop, the display foregrounded six public figures who had expressed homophobic and AIDS phobic views in the media (e.g., Jerry Falwell, William F. Buckley). That same year, 1987, ACT UP was founded, and in collaboration with Gran Fury used the SILENCE = DEATH logo as their own, reproducing it on T-shirts, baseball caps and crack-and-peel stickers. Working closely with ACT UP although retaining autonomy throughout, Gran Fury went on to produce agit-prop, guerrilla AIDS activist graphics for public spaces in American cities, until their disbanding in 1994. Typically, their work mimicked the graphic design of consumer advertising in a strategic attempt to insinuate their anti-capital,-Catholic Church,-Federal government,-news media messages into a mainstream public mediascape.

See also: ACT UP

JOHN PAUL RICCO

GRANT, CARY

b. 1904; d. 1986

actor

Cary Grant, a British-born, suave leading man with a memorable sardonic voice, began his film career appearing with women dear to queer audiences: Mae **West**, Tallulah Bankhead and Marlene **Dietrich**. His bi-gender (some would argue, bisexual) aura, however, met its match in Katharine Hepburn's **butch-femme** persona. In *Sylvia Scarlett* (1936), for example, Grant's character is marked as bisexual since he is attracted to both a countess and Hepburn's drag persona, 'Sylvester' Scarlett. In *Bringing up Baby* (1938), Grant dons a frilly chiffon dressing gown and exclaims 'Because I just went gay all of a sudden!' During the 1930s Grant's rumoured

bisexuality appeared to be confirmed when he moved in with actor Randolph Scott. Two of his later films stand out in particular for their queer connections: *Night and Day* (1946), in which he plays bisexual songwriter Cole **Porter**, and *I Was a Male War Bride* (1949), in which he dresses in drag as an American Army officer's French 'war bride'.

ALEX DOTY

GRAY, STEPHEN

b. 1941

writer, scholar

Stephen Gray is a South African novelist, poet, playwright and professor of English literature. Two of his eight novels explore homosexual themes as they intersect with different layers of oppression under apartheid. *Time of Our Darkness* (1988) has at its heart an affair between a gay white teacher and one of his black pupils. As well as sensationally erotic depictions of paedophilia and male prostitution, the novel questioned the stereotype of a rigid homo/hetero dichotomy using a comic bisexual interlude. The next year saw *Born of Man*, in which a gay man becomes pregnant, providing a vehicle to mock the hypocrisy and prejudice inherent in South African attitudes towards sexuality. A self-identified bisexual, Gray was also a critic of South African gay theatre and contributed articles to the gay press during the 1970s.

MARC EPPRECHT

GRAYSON, LARRY

b. 1923; d. 1995

comedian, TV presenter

Born William White in England, Grayson worked for three decades as a drag act in music halls under the name of Billy Breen. TV work was slow in coming, until the independent ATV hired him, bringing his

255

catchphrases – 'Seems like a nice boy' and 'What a gay day' – to a mass audience. But it was his transition to the BBC to host *The Generation Game* in 1978 that made him famous. His was a self-mocking, camp humour beloved by a broad public, although throughout his life he remained closeted and at odds with the gay liberation movement.

MICHAEL PINFOLD

GREENHAM COMMON WOMEN'S PEACE CAMP

The Greenham Common Women's Peace Camp was a long-running (1981–94) women-only protest camp situated outside the United States Air Force Greenham Common base in the UK. It was established to oppose NATO nuclear cruise missiles. Catalyzing a global upsurge in peace activism by women, the camp drew tens of thousands of women to take part in non-violent direct action, many of whom were arrested and imprisoned. The camp developed a queer, anti-militarist feminism (Roseneil 2000) which radically challenged conventional politics, and was a space in which women explored their identities and sexualities. Many Greenham women were lesbians, or became lesbians, during their time there, and Greenham played a central role in the development of lesbian visibility in 1980s Britain.

Bibliography

Roseneil, S. (2000) *Common Women, Uncommon Practices: The Queer Feminisms of Greenham*, London: Cassell.

SASHA ROSENEIL

GREYSON, JOHN

b. 1960

filmmaker

The Canadian film and videomaker John Greyson was born in British Columbia but grew up primarily in London, Ontario. In 1980 he moved to Toronto and began writing for *The Body Politic* and other local publications. At the same time he began making his first videos, taking on current queer political issues such as race and racism, police harassment and, most especially, AIDS. *A Moffie Called Simon* (1986) is a short drama about the jailed South African black gay activist Simon **Nkoli**. *The ADS Epidemic* (1987) retells the story of Thomas Mann's *Death in Venice* (by way of Visconti's film version) as a music video, denouncing the new epidemic, the Acquired Dread of Sex (ADS). *Urinal* (1988) mixes documentary and drama elements to comment on the policing of washrooms. In 1991 Greyson made another experimental documentary, *The Making of Monsters*, about the culture of anti-gay violence. The film includes famous songs by Bertolt Brecht and Kurt Weill set to new words. The film's banning by the Kurt Weill estate would prompt Greyson to explore issues of censorship, copyright and **homophobia** in his later work, especially in *Uncut* (1997). In 1993 Greyson released a feature-length musical comedy, *Zero Patience*, about Patient Zero, the French-Canadian flight attendant who had been accused of bringing AIDS to North America. Greyson's greatest mainstream success came with the film *Lilies* (1996), based on a play by the Quebec playwright Michel Marc Bouchard. The film received four Genie Awards from the Academy of Canadian Cinema and Television, including one for Best Picture.

See also: Visconti, Luchino

DANIEL HENDRICKSON

GUERRILLA GIRLS

art activists

The Guerrilla Girls are a New York-based group of feminist artists and activists formed in 1985. Unhappy with the almost total absence of women on America's art and culture scene, the Guerrilla Girls set about inundating the art world and the public in general with posters, books, workshops, performances and actions that revealed the sexism and racism of cultural ideology and the arts in America. To focus attention more directly on the content of their platform rather than on themselves, they chose to remain anonymous, adopting as pseudonyms the names of dead female artists such as Violette LeDuc, Georgia O'Keeffe and Frida Kahlo. They made public appearances in schools, museums and organizations of all types while dressed as gorillas as a challenge to the traditional stereotypes of female beauty (and in a neat pun on the name of the group itself). Many of their posters are dedicated to lesbian and gay issues. They support lesbian and gay rights, and some members of the group define themselves as queer.

MONICA BARONI

GUIBERT, HERVÉ

b. 1955; d. 1991

writer

Hervé Guibert attracted attention in literary circles in France while he was still quite young, thanks to his experimental novels which blended fictional and autobiographical elements. In 1983 he co-wrote the screenplay for Patrice Chéreau's film *L'Homme blessé*, the story of a young man's involvement with an older hustler. After writing a very frank, semi-autobiographical novel about his experiences living with HIV (*To the Friend Who Did Not Save My Life*, 1990) and making a notorious appearance on a French literary TV show, Guibert became one of the most well-known

writers in France, and certainly the most famous person with AIDS. In addition to his work as a writer, he also worked as a photographer and made a video. The video *Le Pudeur et l'impudeur* (Modesty and Immodesty, 1990) chronicles his daily life with his illness. He continued to write, further exploring the boundaries between fiction and autobiography, until his death in 1991.

See also: Chéreau, Patrice

DANIEL HENDRICKSON

GUTTMAN, AMOS

b. 1954; d. 1993

filmmaker

Amos Guttman is an Israeli filmmaker of Jewish-Hungarian origins whose films are distinguished by spectacular aesthetics and melancholic atmospheres inspired by the films of Murnau, **Visconti**, Fellini, **Pasolini** and **Fassbinder**. His films often focus on marginalized young gay men who cannot accept their sexuality. Guttman pioneered gay Israeli filmmaking, which began with his student films *Recurring Premiers* (1977) and *A Safe Place* (1979). His features include *Afflicted* (1983), the story of Rubi (Jonathan Segal), a frustrated young filmmaker in Tel Aviv; *Bar 51 – Sister of Love* (1985), the tragic love story of a brother and sister in a queer nightclub; *Himmo, King of Jerusalem* (1987), a queer perspective on Israel's 1948 war of independence. His significant *Amazing Grace* (1992) is the story of unfulfilled love between a boy and an older man who is HIV+. Guttman died of AIDS at the age of 39.

See also: Israel, filmmaking

GILAD PADVA

H

HAINES, WILLIAM

b. 1900; d. 1973

actor, director, interior decorator

Along with fellow silent star Ramon Novarro, William Haines represents part of an early gay Hollywood culture. Starting out in films in 1922, he was playing leads by 1925 and starred in popular MGM films (*Brown of Harvard*, 1926; *Show People*, 1928). Typically cast as a boyish smart-aleck, Haines continued into talkies but his career slowed as the Jazz Age ended. An ageing look and persona used in routine vehicles coupled with the growing homophobia of Depression culture ended his career by 1934.

Haines' role in queer culture continued through later fame as a decorator, but also via his friendship with Joan **Crawford**, who referred to Haines and his partner of 50 years, Jimmie Shields, as the 'happiest married couple in Hollywood'. Gossip about his Hollywood exploits also contributed to his niche in the overlapping cultures of film buffs and gays. Rock Hudson's death increased interest in other gay stars; a 1998 biography and the increased availability of Haines' work further fuelled popular and scholarly attention.

DAVID M. LUGOWSKI

HALBERSTAM, JUDITH

gender theorist

An associate professor of Literary and Cultural Studies at the University of California, San Diego, and renowned film critic, Judith 'Jack' Halberstam is one of North America's leading gender theorists. Specializing in queer theory and visual culture, Halberstam is known as the author of *Female Masculinity*, the first full-length study of the subject, which proffers a distinctive alternative to male masculinity in its exploration of the fluid diversity of gender from lesbian **butch/femme** role play, to transgender 'dykes' and '**drag king**' performances. Building upon Judith Butler's ground-breaking 1990 book *Gender Trouble*, Halberstam quickly established herself as a leading scholar at the cutting edge of contemporary queer studies.

See also: Butler, Judith; Theory and theorists, queer

ROBIN GRIFFITHS

HALFORD, ROB

b. 1951

rock singer, writer, producer

By announcing his homosexuality during a spontaneous moment in a 1998 MTV

258

interview, Rob Halford became the first openly gay artist in heavy metal, a music genre known for its predominately heterosexual fan base. Significantly, his career suffered no backlash. He shattered a stereotype and reinforced the truth that glbt persons are involved in every profession.

Best known as lead singer for the archetypal heavy metal band Judas Priest, Halford joined the band in 1973 and created a unique persona with his powerful voice, short cropped hair and leather stage wardrobe. He left in 1992 to pursue other projects including *Fight*, *Two* and *Halford*, as well as contributing to the soundtrack of the film *Buffy the Vampire Slayer*. He also produced *A Small Deadly Space*, an album about AIDS and received an Outstanding Music Award nomination from the **Gay and Lesbian Alliance Against Defamation (GLAAD)** for his album *Crucible*.

CATHERINE R. BURKE

HALSTED, FRED

b. 1941; d. 1989

actor, director

Actor and director of gay pornographic films, Fred Halsted is best known as the director of *LA Plays Itself* (1972), which is now hailed as a classic of gay pornography. He was born on 17 July 1941 in Long Beach, California. His film appearances include *A Night at Halsted's* (1981) and *El Paso Wrecking Corp.* (1978). He directed *Sex Garage* (1972), *Truck It* (1973) and *Sextool* (1975), which are credited with introducing BDSM (bondage and discipline, dominance and submission, and sadomasochism) sex play into mainstream American gay pornography. After the death of his lover, fellow porn star Joey Yale, he committed suicide on 9 May 1989, in Dana Point, California. *LA Plays Itself* is now

held in the Museum of Modern Art's film collection.

JOHN FORDE

HAMMER, BARBARA

b. 1939

filmmaker, activist, artist

Since 1972 Barbara Hammer has created over 80 experimental shorts, feature-length films and videos. She is the most prolific lesbian feminist film artist in the history of cinema.

Hammer was born in Hollywood on 15 May 1939. She studied psychology, art and English literature at the University of California, Los Angeles, and at San Francisco State University.

Recognition of her work began with the debut of her sexually explicit 1974, three-minute experimental film, *Dyketactics*, regarded as the first film celebrating lesbian love made by a lesbian. Hammer sought to construct a political and erotic lesbian gaze in her 'alternative autobiographies'. She is featured in most of her work, from the early 1970s in such films as *I Was/I Am* (1973), where she appears in both motorcycle drag and a gown, to the later, experimental documentaries such as *Tender Fictions* (1995), the goal of which is to reassert the presence of the lesbian in cinema.

Hammer received the prestigious Frameline Award for her contribution to lesbian and gay cinema. Her trilogy of experimental documentaries on lesbian and gay histories are considered classics (see *Nitrate Kisses*, 1992; *Tender Fictions*, 1995; *History Lessons*, 2001). In 2002 Hammer was made a Fellow at the Radcliffe Institute of Advanced Study for her 16-mm feature documentary film called *Resisting Paradise*. Shot in the Mediterranean fishing village of Cassis, the film contrasts the histories of French Resistance fighters with those of the painters Bonnard and Matisse, who continued to produce landscapes, portraits and still lifes in this land of light and beauty even as the Nazis occupied France.

In *The Exploding Eye, A Re-Visionary History of 1960s American Experimental Cinema* (1997), Wheeler Winston Dixon writes: 'Hammer's intense productivity places her on the scale of Brakhage or Warhol as a major force in the independent cinema; Hammer neatly inverts the patriarchal forces implicitly and often "invisibly" at work in independent cinema practice'.

M.M. SERRA

HANDKERCHIEF CODES

Handkerchief codes are more commonly known as 'hanky codes'. The emergence of a system of coloured handkerchiefs worn by gay men in the back pockets of their trousers to signify their sexual interests is hard to date, but the practice was fully in place by the 1960s and 1970s. Casual-sex seekers and those interested in sadomasochism could signify desires discreetly yet publicly by placing hankies in their left pockets to indicate they were tops/active/ dominant, while bottoms signified their status by placing handkerchiefs in their right pockets. A light blue-coloured handkerchief indicated a desire for oral sex; while navy blue signified anal sex. Extensive lists, with variations among them, covered many practices (for example, a red-and-white-striped handkerchief indicates a desire for an erotic shaving scene). The practice declined due to the threat of AIDS and the rise of Internet dating, as well as an increased openness regarding homosexuality in general. However, handkerchief coding is still widely practiced in leather/BDSM (bondage and discipline, dominance and submission, and sadomasochism) communities (for example, grey signifies bondage, fuchsia indicates spanking, while yellow advertises an interest in water sports).

See also: Leather; Sadomasochism

DAVID M. LUGOWSKI

HARING, KEITH

b. 1958; d. 1990

artist

American artist Keith Haring was inspired by popular graphics such as graffiti, cartoons and comics. His work integrates urban street culture, homage to classic artworks and pop art imagery. Born 4 May 1958 in Kutztown, Pennsylvania, Haring moved to New York City in 1978. During the 1980s his unique style was recognized by critics and Haring soon exhibited his art around the world. Themes and images in his paintings include club subculture, grotesque animals, dancing angels, crawling babies, sexual encounters and gay romance. His works are characterized by humour, irony, reflexivity and sensuality. Haring, who started his career as an underground artist painting in subway tunnels, combined political slogans in his later artwork, including: 'Silence = Death', 'Ignorance = Fear', 'Crack Is Wack', and 'ACT UP!' As a political activist, he donated frescos to children's hospitals and promoted campaigns for HIV prevention. Haring died of AIDS-related complications at the age of 31.

See also: ACT UP

GILAD PADVA

HARRIS, E. LYNN

b. 1955

writer

Born on 20 June 1955 in Flint, Michigan, E. Lynn Harris is an African-American novelist whose works focus on middle-class African-American experiences and deal frankly with black male homosexuality. He financed the publication of his first novel, *Invisible Life* (1991), after failing to find a publisher. Eventually acquired by Anchor Books, the tale of Raymond Tyler, a bisexual black man torn between loving a woman and another man, became a national best seller. Harris continued Tyler's story in *Just As I Am* (1996) and *Abide With Me* (1999). His novel *And This Too Shall Pass* (1996) won the James Baldwin Award for Literary Excellence. In his memoir *What Becomes of the Brokenhearted* (2003), Harris revealed his childhood anxiety about his homosexuality and the prejudices experienced by black gay males. In *If This World Were Mine* and *Diaries of a Light-skinned Colored Boy*, he addresses issues of racial prejudice and the search for a healthy, black, gay male identity. He also co-edited *Gumbo: A Celebration of African American Writing* (2002).

JOHN FORDE

HARRISON, HUGH

filmmaker

Screenwriter whose work deals with sexual obsession within the phone sex industry. Harrison wrote *Dream Man* (1991), a dark drama about a gay phone sex operator struggling with loneliness and failed personal relationships. *Jerker* (1991), based on Robert Chesley's play, revolves around two gay men who meet on a phone sex line and develop an obsessive online relationship.

JOHN FORDE

HARVEY MILK INSTITUTE

The Harvey Milk Institute (HMI), named for the openly gay San Francisco politician,

opened in 1978, offering school courses through a youth services agency for students unable to attend regular high school because they experienced anti-glbt harassment. Although HMI has received public monies since its founding, in 2003 it received substantially more funding and has reorganized into a public high school. Students include racially and ethnically diverse glbt youth, youth perceived to be and harassed as glbt, and children of glbt parents. With a graduation rate of 95 per cent and a college acceptance rate of 60 per cent, HMI is more academically successful than most other New York City public high schools.

See also: Milk, Harvey

CRIS MAYO

HASHIGUCHI, RYOSUKE

b. 1962

filmmaker

Ryosuke Hashiguchi is Japan's most high-profile gay film director. His complex movies have also attracted a mainstream audience. His first feature, the 1993 *Hatachi no Binetsu* (*A Touch of Fever*), about a young gay hustler, was screened in Berlin and became a surprise success in Japan, contributing to the 'gay boom' that swept the media during the early 1990s. This was followed by *Nagisa no Shindobaddo* (*Like Grains of Sand*) in 1995, which chronicles the complicated relationship between two gay men and a female rape victim. After a six-year break from directing, Hashiguchi returned with *Hush!*, a ménage à trois between a gay couple and the woman who wants one of them to father her child. *Hush!* was a box-office success in Japan and was the first of Hashiguchi's films to be released in the United States.

MARK MCLELLAND

HASS, SHARON

b. 1965

poet

Sharon Hass is a poet writing in Hebrew. She is the author of *The Mountain Mother is Gone* (1997), *The Stranger and Everyday Woman* (2001) and *Subjects of the Sun* (2005). Hass' poetry is condensed, at times nearly hermetic, highly figurative and draws on a wide array of mythological sources, always endowing individual experience with rich cultural reverberations. Some of the themes it addresses are the eroticism and ambivalence of the mother–daughter tie, and the ways these are reproduced in love relationships between women, and the gendered plurality and multivocity of the self. Hass' poetry forges a new language for female sexuality, avoiding the confessional and appropriating a broad variety of cultural narratives and idioms.

Some of her poems have appeared in English, e.g., in *The Defiant Muse* (1999), a collection of Hebrew feminist poetry.

AMALIA ZIV

HAVANA

Cuba's vibrant capital often finds its population enjoying daily public interaction in the community, filling city streets and sidewalks with life at all hours. Since the 1990s, gay culture has been increasingly visible and accepted in Havana. Gay hangouts have varied throughout the years; nevertheless, consistent gay sites include the ice cream parlour Coppelia and the adjacent La Rampa (the end of Calle 23. finishing at the famous Malecón).

JOSE B. ALVAREZ IV

HAY, HARRY

b. 1912; d. 2002

activist

English-born Harry Hay was an instrumental founder of the gay movement in the United States and a Communist activist during the 1930s. He married a woman but maintained liaisons with men including actor Will Geer, who portrayed 'Grandpa' on the TV programme *The Waltons*. Hay organized the gay group 'Bachelors for Wallace' to support Henry Wallace, the leftist candidate, for president in 1948. With Bob Hull, Dale Jennings, Chuck Rowland and Rudi Gernreich, Hay organized the **Mattachine Society** in 1950, the first of the **homophile movement** groups. It evolved from a discussion group to a national organization of over 4,000 members in California with many national chapters.

Hay left the Communist Party as a response to its anti-gay policies and resigned from Mattachine in 1953. He devoted himself to gay studies, especially in Native American culture. During the 1960s he organized the Los Angeles Committee to Fight the Exclusion of Homosexuals from the Armed Forces. He was the first co-chair of the southern California Gay Liberation Front. When the Stonewall Riots erupted in New York in 1969 he said, 'The East Coast is finally catching up'.

In 1979 Hay founded the **Radical Faeries** in Arizona. Throughout his life he maintained his controversial political positions, as when he supported **NAMBLA (North American Man/Boy Love Association)** when it was excluded from Gay Pride parades. Hay envisioned the key role of gay people in society as that of educators, bringing opposites together. He died on 24 October 2002.

ANDY HUMM

HAYNES, TODD

b. 1961

director

A leading figure of the New Queer Cinema movement of the 1980s, Todd Haynes has subsequently moved into mainstream film production and is considered one of the most influential queer filmmakers in contemporary US cinema.

Graduating in the mid-1980s from Brown University with an Honours degree in Art and Semiotics, Haynes moved to New York City, where he helped found Apparatus Productions, an organization for the promotion of independent cinema, while also becoming actively involved in AIDS activism. Haynes' first major film, *Superstar* (1987), reflects this dynamic intersection of interests in avant-garde cinema, critical theory and sexual politics. A boldly innovative work that makes striking use of animated puppetry to narrate the story of pop star Karen Carpenter's unsuccessful battle with eating disorders, *Superstar* presents a trenchant critique of the social commodification of femininity and its role in fostering body-image psychopathologies such as anorexia. A hit on the festival and underground circuits, *Superstar* became embroiled in controversy when the Carpenter estate filed a lawsuit for copyright infringement, forcing the film's withdrawal from public exhibition.

Haynes' next endeavour, *Poison* (1991) thrust him even more spectacularly into the limelight of public controversy. Weaving three highly stylized stories around interrelated themes of sexual difference and social intolerance, *Poison* is a metaphoric exploration of social attitudes to AIDS that was feted by critics upon its release in 1991 and awarded the Grand Jury Prize at the prestigious Sundance Film Festival. Funded partly by the National Endowment for the Arts, the film became a major cause célèbre when singled out by conservative moral commentators Senator Jesse Helms and Reverend Donald Wildmon during their crusade against the use of taxpayers' dollars for 'obscene' art. Ironically, the resulting furore gave both the film and Haynes extraordinary exposure, while also consolidating the emergence of New Queer Cinema by focusing critical and popular attention upon the work of young gay and lesbian filmmakers.

Haynes soon moved into major feature-film production, issuing a string of increasingly accomplished and successful works: *Safe* (1995), *Velvet Goldmine* (1998) and *Far from Heaven* (2002). Despite the presence of bigger budgets and high-profile stars, these films continue to bear Haynes' trademark investment in innovative aesthetics and social critique. All three films focus on various outsiders struggling to find a place in a seemingly hostile environment. In *Safe*, the first of Haynes' collaborations with actor Julianne Moore, a middle-class housewife develops a mysterious illness that launches her on a journey of self-discovery. *Velvet Goldmine*, Haynes' ode to the era of **glam rock**, focuses on a flamboyant, David Bowie-esque rock star and his entourage of social and sexual dissidents. *Far from Heaven* resurrects the formal style of Hollywood melodrama to explore the costs exacted by 1950s suburban normativity from an archetypal 'happy homemaker' whose world unravels when her husband's homosexuality is revealed. A fiercely personal and original filmmaker, Haynes' commitment to cinema as a politically informed artistic practice is set to continue with his next project, an experimental biopic of the singer-songwriter Bob Dylan.

See also: New Queer Cinema, International

BRETT FARMER

HEAD, BESSIE

b. 1937; d. 1986

writer

South African-Botswanan teacher, journalist and novelist, Bessie Head grew up as a coloured (mixed-race) person in apartheid South Africa before exiling herself to Botswana in 1964. Her writing is characterized by strong feminist and anti-racist themes. In *A Question of Power* (1974) Head allows the coloured protagonist of the novel (Elizabeth) to recognize the injustice of homophobia while reading about Oscar Wilde. Yet Head's treatment of the topic also contributed to a long-standing stereotype when Elizabeth dreams of 'weak', 'disease[d]' and dying coloured homosexuals who embody racial humiliation at the hands of whites. As a coloured woman she is tormented by the shame that *moffies* cause her and the way they divide coloureds politically from unambiguously heterosexual black Africans in the struggle against apartheid.

See also: *Moffie*

MARC EPPRECHT

HELMS, JESSE

b. 1921

politician

Born on 18 October 1921 in Monroe, North Carolina, the five-term Republican Senator for North Carolina (1972–2003) and a long-time spokesperson for the conservative religious right, Helms is infamous for his anti-gay opinions. He served in the Navy during the Second World War and worked as a journalist and as assistant to Senator Willis Smith before being elected to the Senate in 1972. Dubbed 'Senator No' for his opposition to liberal and gay rights initiatives, Helms advocated compulsory prayer in schools and an aggressive anti-communist foreign policy. He made

sustained criticism of the National Endowment for the Arts' support of gay artists such as Robert **Mapplethorpe**, Marlon **Riggs** and Andres Serrano. In 1988 he destroyed a Mapplethorpe exhibition catalogue on the floor of the Senate, sparking a national debate which led to the cancellation of the Washington DC leg of the exhibition. He also blocked the promotion of California governor William Weld and lesbian Clinton appointee Roberta **Achtenberg**. He retired from politics in 2003.

JOHN FORDE

HEMPHILL, ESSEX

b. 1957; d. 1995

writer

Openly gay writer, poet and editor who became one of the leading voices in African-American poetry and drew attention to black gay masculinity in contemporary American culture. Hemphill was born on 16 April 1957 in Chicago, Illinois. He began writing poetry at age 14, partially to redress the absence of a gay sensibility in African-American literature. He studied in Washington DC, where he founded the *Nethula Journal of Contemporary Literature* in 1978, and began performing his poetry in coffee houses and gay venues. In 1983 he co-founded Cinque, a performance poetry group, which gained fame after appearing in Marlon Riggs' documentaries *Tongues Untied* (1989) and *Black Is...Black Ain't* (1995). He self-published his first two poetry collections, *Earth Life* (1985) and *Conditions* (1986), and contributed to a number of black gay anthologies, including his friend Joseph Beam's *In The Life: A Black Gay Anthology* (1986). After Beam's death from AIDS in 1988, Hemphill finished the editorship of the award-winning anthology *Brother to Brother: New Writings By Black Gay Men* (1991). His 1992 collection, *Ceremonies: Prose and Poetry,* received widespread acclaim. He died from AIDS-related illnesses on 4 November 1995 in Philadelphia, Pennsylvania.

JOHN FORDE

HENSZELMAN, STEFAN CHRISTIAN

b. 1960; d. 1991

filmmaker

Gay film director, best known for *Venner for altid* (Friends Forever) (1987) a comic drama about Kristian, a 16-year-old boy struggling to accept his homosexuality, who discovers that his thuggish friend Patrick is gay and having an affair with the school soccer team captain. The film won Henszelman the Audience Award at the 1988 San Francisco International Gay and Lesbian Film Festival. His last film was *Dagens Donna* (1990).

JOHN FORDE

HEPBURN, KATHARINE

b. 1907; d. 2003

actor

It was once reported that Hepburn said she did not know what a homosexual was when she filmed Tennessee Williams' *Suddenly Last Summer* (1959). This is notable if for no other reason than that she was a close friend of gay director George **Cukor**, with whom she made three films: *Little Women* (1933), *Sylvia Scarlett* (1936) and *Pat and Mike* (1952). In *Sylvia Scarlett* Hepburn dressed as 'Sylvester' Scarlett, was kissed by a woman and was addressed by a man who says, 'I know what it is that gives me a queer feeling when I look at you'. Hepburn also worked with lesbian director Dorothy **Arzner** in *Christopher Strong* (1933), in which she played flying ace Cynthia Darrington. Hepburn's combination of athletic spunk, wit and classiness ensured her appeal to a wide range of queer men and women. Later in her career, her spinsters (*The African Queen*, 1951) and tra-

gic mothers (*Long Day's Journey into Night*, 1962; *The Lion in Winter*, 1968) were especially appreciated by her lesbian and gay fans.

ALEX DOTY

HERMAN, JERRY

b. 1931

composer

The openly gay American lyricist and composer Jerry Herman has penned a string of enormously popular Broadway musicals. Best known for his 1960s mega-hits, *Hello, Dolly!* (1963) and *Mame* (1964), Herman's work is characterized by strong female leads, popular melodies and feel-good optimism. Cultivating a large gay following with his brand of unabashedly adoring diva musicals, Herman brought the queerness of both the genre and its audiences centre stage in 1983 with Broadway's first, overtly gay mainstream musical comedy, *La Cage aux Folles* (1978), which introduced the anthemic queer standard, 'I Am What I Am'. Diagnosed that same year with HIV and subsequently losing his partner to AIDS in 1992, Herman has devoted much of his time in later years to AIDS education and support. He still writes the occasional work however, such as the 1996 TV musical *Mrs Claus* and the 2002 concept show, *Miss Spectacular*.

BRETT FARMER

HERMAN, PEE WEE

b. 1952

actor

During the 1970s Paul Reubens worked in comedy clubs and on TV game shows. While a member of the Los Angeles-based Groundlings Comedy troupe, he developed his Pee Wee Herman character. Pee Wee, an androgynous, sexually ambiguous geek, was first seen on an HBO special, *The Pee*

Wee Herman Show, in 1981. Reubens'/Pee Wee's big break, however, came with the film *Pee Wee's Big Adventure* (1985). The film's success led to a follow-up, *Big Top Pee Wee* (1988), which did less well. In between films, Reubens created the children's show *Pee Wee's Playhouse* (1986–90), which attracted a large adult audience for its campy humour; queer double entendres and its cast of hunky cowboys, a queeny genie and lesbian-coded characters. The show ended when Reubens was arrested in a 1991 police sting of a porn theatre. During the 1990s Reubens played queerly inflected supporting roles in films such as *Batman Returns* (1992), *Buffy the Vampire Slayer* (1992) and on television in *Murphy Brown*.

ALEX DOTY

HERO, FREEDOM AND DEVOTION PARTIES

Three dance parties held in urban centres in New Zealand. Hero (Auckland) is the largest. Devotion occurs in Wellington and Freedom is based in Christchurch.

JO SMITH

HETEROSEXUALITY

Since Western society coined the term 'homosexuality', it has often been shaped by its perceived opposite, heterosexuality. The dominance of heterosexuality in culture often works to make it seem simultaneously omnipresent and invisible. Many, for example, implicitly regard strangers on the street as heterosexual unless something specific (or stereotypical) suggests otherwise. This presumption keeps heterosexuality empowered by making it appear natural and inevitable – unlike forms of non-heterosexuality which are regularly deemed unnatural or abnormal. Yet, definitions of heterosexuality have shifted across the second half of the twentieth

century, supporting arguments that sexual orientations are socially constructed rather than biologically essential. Furthermore, changes in concepts of heterosexuality and of homosexuality continually affect each other.

Prior to the Second World War, homosexuality was linked strongly to gender roles. The medical community and society at large thought that gay men had the souls of women and lesbians conversely desired to be men. Therefore, 'effeminate' men and 'masculine' women that felt same-sex desire were labelled homosexual. However, conventionally masculine men who played the aggressive role in homosexual sex, or traditionally feminine women who played the passive, receptive role, often considered themselves (and were considered by others) as heterosexual. (Such conceptions still hold in certain societies around the world to this day.)

Gendered models of sexuality gave way after the war, particularly with the publication of the Kinsey Report in 1948. Kinsey's research indicated that about 10 per cent of the American male population considered themselves homosexual, and that 37 per cent had participated in homosexual sex at least once. The American public was shocked by the statistics: there simply were not that many effeminate men walking the streets. Realizing that some homosexuals did not fit the gender-inversion stereotype, the categories of heterosexuality and homosexuality were realigned. It was recognized that one could no longer simply enact conventional gender behaviour to be heterosexual; she or he also had to only have relations with the opposite sex.

Upholding traditions of heterosexuality was considered paramount during the Cold War. American strength was linked directly to its morality. As such, women were laid off from jobs they held during the war and encouraged to adopt the roles of housewife and mother. The enormous birth rate increase in the United States after the war (the 'Baby Boom') indicates how much traditional heterosexuality was being practiced.

Yet, the boundaries of 'acceptable' heterosexuality began to broaden as well. Unlike the first half of the century, when it was improper to even mention it in public company, the topic of sex became more and more prevalent in popular culture. In the wake of military films on venereal disease and 'cheesecake' posters during the war, heterosexual sex was increasingly acknowledged in motion pictures (particularly from various European countries, but increasingly in America also), in literature and theatre, in the new music of rock 'n' roll, and in new magazines such as *Playboy* and *Cosmopolitan*. As censorship and obscenity regulations were relaxed, heterosexual sex was no longer displayed as being only for wedded couples; rather, it was increasingly regarded as a source of pleasure both in and out of marriage. Such developments continued throughout the 1960s, becoming what commentators began calling a 'sexual revolution'. Divorce rates went up. Heterosexual couples decided to live together rather than marry. Contraceptives allowed heterosexuals greater freedom from worries of pregnancy. The end of various laws barring interracial marriage (or miscegenation) in the US also opened up another type of heterosexual expression.

While many saw the sexual revolution as merely an opportunity to have more heterosexual intercourse, the era also often challenged conceptions of sexuality. The second wave of the feminist movement attempted to liberate women from limiting roles enforced by a male-dominated heterosexual culture. The counter-culture also played with gender images, as women went without makeup, men grew long hair and both wore similar types of clothing. Feminism's championing of female-centred sexual desire and the counter-culture's celebration of free love created an atmosphere for the modern gay rights movement to

emerge at the end of the 1960s. In these radical environments, the barriers between heterosexuality and homosexuality were not always set in stone. Many hippies and feminists experimented sexually as part of the revolution.

While the sexual revolution continued into the 1970s, gay rights activism often worked to segment the population more thoroughly into either homosexual or heterosexual (and the growth of lesbian separatism during this period shows boundaries being drawn even within the homosexual communities). Similarly, many feminist groups attempted to distance themselves from lesbianism. Consequently, heterosexual experimentation extended into spouse-swapping or mainstream interest in straight pornographic films such as *Deep Throat* (1972) but not into other orientations.

Most social historians consider the start of the 1980s as the end of the sexual revolution. The popular press began giving large coverage to the rise in various sexually transmitted diseases (STDs), such as the spread of herpes. Herpes ended up as a relatively minor concern as people grew more aware of AIDS, particularly when the press announced that AIDS was not 'just a homosexual disease' and that straight people could be infected also. Concomitant with new concerns about STDs was a social shift to the right, as conservative and religious fundamentalist groups gained strength. Such movements had enormous effects on homosexual communities, but also strongly impacted notions of heterosexuality. Just as 1950s America stressed traditional patriarchal heterosexuality in battling the Cold War, so too did 1980s America (as well as Great Britain and West Germany, among others), with its attempts to return to what were called 'family values' in order to restore national pride. Simultaneously, a backlash against feminism and a celebration of hypermasculine iconography (including movie stars Arnold Schwarzenegger and

Sylvester Stallone, and former cowboy-actor-turned-president Ronald Reagan) tried to reverse the achievements of the sexual revolution for both homosexuals and heterosexuals.

By the end of the 1980s gay rights activism had been re-energized. Radical groups such as ACT UP and **Queer Nation** demanded a better response to the AIDS crisis and better acceptance of sexual difference. Reappropriating the word 'queer', activists and academics examined sexual desire as polymorphous and complex rather than a simplistic binary of either 'hetero' or 'homo'. In doing so, queer theory interrogated the social construction of sexuality itself. While most of Queer Studies focused on marginalized sexualities, authors such as Michel **Foucault**, Judith **Butler** and Eve Kosofsky **Sedgwick** implicated the dominant heterosexual paradigm as well. Some activists and academics even identified as 'straight queers': people who had heterosexual desires but felt limited or marginalized by normative definitions of heterosexuality. Activists specifically worked to bring these disparate communities together as queers to fight for a shared cause or against a shared oppression.

Heterosexuality has shifted in multiple directions in the wake of queer theory. The 'men's movement' of the 1990s showed various heterosexual males redefining their gender roles – upholding some form of masculinity, but one that allowed greater sensitivity. Third-wave feminism has attempted to support women's equality while regarding all gender roles for women as equally performative. Marketers also tapped into queerness in order to create new products and customers, as evidenced by the cable TV series *Queer Eye for the Straight Guy* and the creation of a new target group, the 'metrosexual': a heterosexual man whose shopping habits mimic those of an ideal urban gay male consumer. Appositely, growing acceptance of queers

made others more rabid in policing the boundaries of heterosexual power. Heterosexuality in the US once defined itself as the only federally legal form of sexual behaviour. In 2003 the Supreme Court erased that distinction by striking down so-called 'sodomy laws'. Lawmakers, religious groups and others in the US and other countries desperately tried to withstand attempts to eradicate another significant part of heterosexuality's definition: marriage. The US government passed the Defense of Marriage Act in 1996 and a constitutional amendment was proposed to ban same-sex marriage. As history indicates, the reassessment and redefinition of heterosexuality will continue for the foreseeable future.

See also: ACT UP; Kinsey Report, The; Same-sex marriage/civil union

Further reading

D'Emilio, J. and Freedman, E.B. (1988) *Intimate Matters: A History of Sexuality in America*, New York: Harper & Row.

Foucault, M. (1978) *The History of Sexuality, Vol. I: An Introduction*, trans. R. Hurley, New York: Pantheon.

Katz, J.N. (1995) *The Invention of Heterosexuality*, New York: Dutton.

Wittig, M. (1992) *The Straight Mind and Other Essays*, Boston: Beacon Press.

SEAN GRIFFIN

HIACYNT

Hiacynt (Hyacinth) is the code name for a campaign initiated by the Polish police on 15 November 1985 in Warsaw, upon request of the then internal affairs minister General Czesław Kiszczak. Its aim was to intimidate, arrest and register people suspected of being homosexual. Continuing until 1988, it led to the compilation of the *Różowe kartotek'* (pink catalogues) containing information about the sexual orientation of more than 11,000 people. Ostensibly justified under a law about the control of venereal diseases, the campaign actually intended to damage democratic environments and to hinder the constitution of associations that might have opposed the government. Notwithstanding anti-discriminatory laws, the catalogues have not yet been destroyed.

ALESSANDRO AMENTA

HICK, JOCHEN

b. 1960

filmmaker

German filmmaker Jochen Hick has directed both documentaries and narrative features. He studied filmmaking in Hamburg and Bologna and, in addition to directing, he has worked as a journalist as well as a TV and film producer. His films include *Via Appia* (1990), shot in Brazil, and the documentaries *Menmaniacs: The Legacy of Leather* (1995) and *Sex/Life in L.A.* (1998). In 2000 he made a thriller, *No One Sleeps*, shot in San Francisco, about a young German gay man who comes to the United States to continue his deceased father's research into the possibility that HIV was an American government experiment gone awry. In 2002 he returned to documentary with *Ich kenn keinen – Allein unter Heteros* (*Talk Straight: The World of Rural Queers*), about gay men living in small towns in Swabia, Germany. The film received the Teddy Award for Best Documentary at the Berlin International Film Festival. Hick currently lives in Hamburg.

DANIEL HENDRICKSON

HIGHSMITH, PATRICIA

b. 1921; d. 1995

novelist

American mystery writer most famous for her creation of the bisexual criminal Tom Ripley, a character who has inspired several films (including *The Talented Mr Ripley*, Anthony Minghella, 1999) and has made the Ripley novels cult classics among gay male readers. Highsmith's only lesbian novel, *Carol*, was first published in 1952 as *The Price of Salt* and under a pseudonym, and its story of the love of two women placed under the surveillance of a private detective may be read as a critique of the 'witch hunts' which defined the McCarthy era. The novel was equally bold in its renunciation of insanity and suicide which complemented lesbianism in most 1950s popular fiction, offering instead a homosexual love story with a happy ending. In life Highsmith distanced herself from Cold War blacklisting efforts in the less oppressive climates of England, France and Switzerland, leaving the United States permanently in 1963.

CATHERINE CLAY

HIJRAS

The *Hijras* of India comprise the most well-known community of eunuchs in the world. Much of the scholarship and popular discourse around them has unproblematically appropriated *hijras* as queer or transgendered subjects that fall outside Western binaries of sex and gender. The truth is both more elusive and complex.

Hijras are men who voluntarily and ritualistically castrate themselves. They are sometimes males with ambiguous genitalia who fall outside normative concepts of masculinity and virility and need a community. *Hijras* generate many of the cultural myths about themselves and operate within complex social structures. They trace their mythological origins to ancient Hindu texts but are not always Hindu; many are in fact Muslims. They earn their living by showing up unannounced at weddings and births to sing and dance, demanding money for the entertainment in exchange for their blessings: It is widely believed that turning them away leads to infertility or bad luck. *Hijras* often engage in sex work also. The eunuchs are treated with a mixture of reverence and fear as long as they remain on the margins of society, and they rarely travel outside their social groups. They live in households governed by central authority figures who define the groups' interactions with the outside world. *Hijras* protect themselves by keeping alive a widespread belief in their symbolic powers, powers that go to the heart of central cultural tropes of sex, gender and sexuality. In recent years some *hijras* have emerged as political leaders, demanding greater political representation in mainstream society.

YASMIN NAIR

HINDUISM

A polytheistic religion which evolved from the Vedic religion of ancient India, now the dominant religion of India. Hindu attitudes towards homosexuality vary in degrees of tolerance. The Laws of Manu state that men who participate in anal intercourse lose caste and that men who shed semen in another man must perform penance. These rules were adopted by the ruling British to justify punishment of homosexuality during colonial rule in India. By comparison, Vatsyayana's third-century text *Kama Sutra* refers positively to same-sex male and female behaviour. *Hijras*, a 'third sex' of men – many of them transgendered or eunuchs – who dress as women are believed to have the power to render others potent or impotent with their curses and blessings; they perform ceremonial functions at Hindu weddings and birth ceremonies.

JOHN FORDE

HITCHCOCK, ALFRED

b. 1899; d. 1980

film director

Alfred Joseph Hitchcock was born in London and became a US citizen in 1955. In a career spanning just over 50 years, Hitchcock completed 53 feature films, 23 during his 'British period' (*c.*1925–40) and 30 during his work in Hollywood (1940–76), where he earned the title 'Master of Suspense' for his expertly crafted thrillers. Hitchcock films have long been a fertile site of contestation for structuralists, psychoanalysts, feminists and queer theorists, especially in his representations of gender and sexuality, which are said to underscore the narratives of fear and suspense in his works.

The implicit or explicit association between non-heterosexuals, perversity and fascism has been widely noted in many Hitchcock antagonists, such as the transvestite killers in *Murder!* (1930) and *Psycho* (1960); the notorious female villain Mrs Danvers (Judith Anderson) who has an overt fixation on her former mistress in the murder mystery *Rebecca* (1940); the psychopathic killers, Brandon and Phillip, who strongly register as homosexuals in *Rope* (1948); and the queerly paired duo, Bruno Anthony (Robert Walker) and Guy Haines (Farley Granger) in *Strangers on a Train* (1951). Many criticize such coding as homophobic representations that stigmatize and demonize lesbians, gays and transvestites by equating them with moral depravity and pathological derangement. Hitchcock's films are thus often seen as ideological texts that reinforce the dominant sexual ideology that sexual 'others' are social deviants posing much fear and threat to the stability of the patriarchal heterosexual society at large.

The rise of queer studies, however, has opened more possibilities in the reading and study of Hitchcock's films. One example is Lucretia Knapp's re-reading of *Marnie* (1964) through a lesbian position of spectatorship, in which Knapp unearths the queer voices in the film and redirects our attention to the underexplored issue of lesbianism in the works of Hitchcock. Another significant input of Queer Studies has been its emphasis upon the possible heterogeneous and polymorphous sexuality and desires circulating in the texts. Scholars such as Tania Modleski, Lee Edelman, Alexandra Doty and D.A. Miller, through analyses of the queer representation in, or queer reading of, Hitchcock's films, have pointed out how the disturbing elements in Hitchcock characters rest not so much on their being homosexuals, but more on their defiance of simple categorization. For example, the sexual ambiguity, as exemplified in the much-discussed film *Psycho* and the character of Norman Bates (Anthony Perkins), complicates the question of gender and sexuality. Many see the cross-dressing murderer Bates, for example, as a pejorative portrayal of transvestites as dreadful schizophrenics, while for others, Bates presents an expression of bisexual desire through the simultaneous embodiment of 'mother' and 'son' in Norman. Queer theorists, alternatively, point to a queer Norman who, with his gender and sexual elusiveness, defies and interrogates the traditional and seemingly stable identities of male, female, heterosexual, homosexual and bisexual.

It has also been remarked, unlike earlier studies, how queer narratives in Hitchcock's films may serve less to support, but indeed challenge and disrupt, their own heterosexualizing ideology. Edelman's queer analysis of *The Birds* (1963), for example, demonstrates how the killing birds' predilection for children can be read, in terms of sexuality, as a future-negating force that dislocates the promise of heterosexual romance and its reproductive futurity.

LISA Y.M. LAM

HIV

Drs Luc Montaigner and Robert Gallo coined the term HIV – Human Immunodeficiency Virus – in 1983. HIV damages or kills cells in the human body's immune system, preventing the body from fighting infections. HIV is spread through unprotected sexual contact, the sharing of non-sterile drug paraphernalia and from mother to child during the birthing process and/or breastfeeding. An individual who has contracted HIV is said to be HIV+. Individuals can learn their HIV status through a test for HIV antibodies (disease-fighting proteins) in the bloodstream. There is no cure or vaccine for HIV. In the majority of cases HIV leads to AIDS.

See also: AIDS

CHRIS BELL

HLOBONGA

Zulu word that originally connoted intra-thigh sex between unmarried boys and girls, a custom widely practiced in African societies as a form of safe-sex play and learning. Also known as *gangisa* among the Tsonga and *ukumetsha* among the Xhosa, it became notorious during the early twentieth century after migrant labourers in the mines of South Africa and Rhodesia adapted it to male–male sexual practice.

MARC EPPRECHT

HOCKNEY, DAVID

b. 1937

artist

As a student at the Royal College of Art in London during the early 1960s, Hockney had already received acclaim as a member of the British pop art movement, producing paintings that unabashedly represented gay male subjects in everyday domestic settings. In 1963 he visited Los Angeles for the first time, drawn there by the homo-erotic photographs in gay nudist and phy-sique magazines being published in the city. He immediately fell in love with the sun-light of southern California, and in paint-ings that depicted beautifully tanned young male bodies in and around the private swimming pools of the Hollywood Hills, Hockney created some of the most stun-ning images of West Coast American cul-ture. The 1974 film *A Bigger Splash,* directed by Jack Hazon, is virtually unmat-ched in its frank portrayal of Hockney as a gay man and creator of gay-themed works.

JOHN PAUL RICCO

HOCQUENGHEM, GUY

b. 1944; d. 1988

writer, activist

Although influenced by the Lacanian psy-chology of his time, Guy Hocquenghem laid aside the analytic category of 'homo-sexual desire' in favour of an important tautology: that desire, simply, is desire. In other words, there is no fundamental dif-ference in the quality of desire that can be attributed to its object – rather, desire simply 'is'.

Born in the suburbs of Paris, Hocquen-ghem studied at the Ecole Normale Supér-ieure. He took part in the 1968 student revolts when he joined the Communist Party and, like many others, was expelled because of his homosexuality. Soon after, he became an early member of the Front Homosexuel d'Action Révolutionnaire. His work includes the books *Le Désir homosexuelle* (Homosexual Desire, 1972), *L'Après-Mai des faunes* (The AfterMay of Fauns, 1974), *Le Dérive homosexuelle* (Homosexual Drift, 1977) and a doc-umentary film he wrote and produced, *Race d'Ep! Un siècle d'image de l'homosexualité* (1988). He died from AIDS in 1988. The English-speaking world has touched only

marginally upon his research and theories of sexuality.

J. TODD ORMSBEE

HOLLIBAUGH, AMBER

b. 1946

activist, writer, videomaker

Amber L. Hollibaugh's tenure as a political activist and lesbian sex radical spans 30 years to date. Early essays (especially 'What We're Rollin' around in Bed With') were anthologized in classic feminist texts such as *Powers of Desire: The Politics of Sexuality* (1983) and *Heresies: The Sex Issue* (1981). Her early work theorizes **butch/femme** sexual erotics, lesbian sadomasochism, racism, sex work and classism in second-wave feminism.

From 1990 to 1998 Hollibaugh was director of the Lesbian AIDS Project at **Gay Men's Health Crisis (GMHC)** in New York City. Her growing profile as a community lesbian HIV and AIDS activist and educator led to an appointment as a video producer with the AIDS Dis-crimination Unit of the Human Rights Commission of the City of New York. Subsequent work includes the video *The Heart of the Matter* (winner of the Freedom of Expression Award at the Sundance Film Festival) and an important collection of essays, *My Dangerous Desires* (2000).

JEAN BOBBY NOBLE

HOLLINGHURST, ALAN

b. 1954

writer

Alan Hollinghurst, a novelist, translator, editor and staff member of the *Times Lit-erary Supplement* between 1982 and 1995, was born in Stroud, Gloucestershire, UK, in 1954. In his work, he has consistently presented gay sex and sexuality as the most polished and refined of arts. The publication of *The Swimming Pool Library* (1988), a passionate elegy to the pre-AIDS era in gay London, brought international acclaim to its author. Hollinghurst staged a Nabokovian teacher–pupil passion in *The Folding Star* (1994) and a comedy of gay manners in *The Spell* (1998), set in the English countryside and in the London club scene.

The 1980s are also the setting of his 2004 novel, *The Line of Beauty*, which centres on Nick Guest, a recent Oxford graduate and gay man, who has taken up residence with the family of a good friend, a family headed by the Conservative Member of Parliament Gerald Fedden. *The Line of Beauty* was awarded the Man Booker Prize.

Hollinghurst's writing is marked by a sapient intertwining of explicit, straightforward representations of gay life and sexuality with a mastery of characterization, vivid description, and linguistic and psychological nuances of almost poetry-like distinction, placing him in the 'line of beauty' continuing from early twentieth-century stylists such as Ronald Firbank, E.M. Forster and Henry James.

FABIO CLETO

HOLLYWOOD

As the single most successful and widely distributed of all world cinemas, Hollywood exerts enormous influence, peddling commodified entertainment – and with it, social and political ideas and values – to audiences around the world.

Queer cultures have had a significant, if frequently fraught, relationship to Hollywood. Historically, queers have played a privileged role in Hollywood at the levels of both production (as valued labourers in the industry) and consumption (as particularly devoted audience constituencies). For its part, however, Hollywood has often shown a persistent reluctance to engage queer sexualities in an explicit or continuingly significant fashion.

Some critics claim, not without grounds, that Hollywood cinema is marked centrally by twin logics of heterosexism and **homophobia**. For much of its history, Hollywood was governed by the infamous Production Code, which explicitly forbade the representation of homosexualities and other 'sex perversions', while mandating the maintenance of the 'sanctity of the institution of marriage and the home'. The result on-screen was an exclusive, and artificially glamorized, heterosexual world in which queers were seldom seen. In the rare instances that a queer character might appear, s/he was invariably cast negatively as either something to be ridiculed, such as the mincing sissy or lumpish tomboy of Hollywood comedy, or something to be feared, as in the long line of queer killers that have haunted the Hollywood thriller. This heterocentric logic is arguably so entrenched that, even following the demise of the Production Code in the 1960s and the subsequent removal of official sanctions against queer representations, Hollywood has continued to promote an ideological worldview in which heterosexuality is cast as the idealized norm and queer sexualities are still relegated to positions of subordinate, and often vilified, marginality.

To represent the sexual politics of Hollywood cinema in such stark terms is, however, to simplify what is in reality a complex and multilevelled set of issues, while at the same time diminishing the significance of Hollywood to queer cultures and audiences. Although there can be little doubt that Hollywood has been, and still is, marked by strong currents of heterocentrism, it has been equally marked by competing, even countervailing, trends that complicate easy assessments of it as exclusively or unproblematically straight.

The key to any critical understanding of Hollywood is to recognize its primary status as a commercial enterprise. It may be many other things besides – an art, an entertainment form, a cultural practice –

but Hollywood, first and foremost, is a business and, like any business, its driving force is the maximization of profit. This defining pursuit of profit has certainly helped to strengthen Hollywood's conservative bent. Loath to risk anything that might alienate potential consumers, Hollywood films tend to uphold the status quo and work within broadly mainstream social frames. Yet, it has also inspired an opportunistically pluralist mode of filmmaking wherein multiple features and modes of address are combined to ensure the broadest possible audience appeal. Far from the closed homogeneity claimed for it by some, the typical Hollywood movie is perhaps best understood as a dynamic ensemble of diverse voices and elements – stardom and genre, narrative and spectacle, romance and action, special effects and performance – that are held together in relative balance in a strategic bid to, quite literally, 'offer something for everyone'.

Hollywood's heterocentric discourses may function as an obvious, even primary, lure for straight audiences but there are many other discourses circulating in Hollywood cinema that operate as points of appeal and engagement – intentionally or otherwise – for queer spectators. Popular Hollywood genres such as the musical and the melodrama, for example, readily invite queer investment and interpretation with their emphasis upon sexual spectacle and stylistic excess. Similarly, the exploration of otherness and social deviancy in horror and science-fiction films signal important points of symbolic queer address. Even the **macho** hegemonies of the western seem remarkably homosexual, as opposed to merely homosocial, if read from a pertinently queer perspective. Although these genres often seek to impose a socially sanctioned image of heterosexual supremacy at the film's end, this doesn't eradicate their strong queer dynamics and appeal.

An understanding of Hollywood cinema as a polyvocal complex offers an interesting context in which to consider the question of Hollywood's many queer personnel. From its earliest period, Hollywood attracted a steady stream of queer workers who found employ in almost every facet of the industry, from screenwriting (Christopher **Isherwood**, DeWitt Bodeen) and costume design (Adrian, Miles White) to directing (Dorothy **Arzner**, George **Cukor**, Vincente **Minnelli**) and editing (William Reynolds). Given the collaborative nature of film production, it is difficult to ascertain the precise effect of these individual queer workers on final film products, but their presence nevertheless signals the important contributions of queer artists to Hollywood filmmaking. Moreover, there is evidence to suggest that studio bosses strategically pursued queer employees, especially in the design professions, as a way of giving their film products a distinctive style and profile in the marketplace. The **Freed Unit** at MGM, for example, was widely noted, both in its employment practices and visual style, for a decidedly queer bent.

Two things should be noted about Hollywood's queer workers: most of them were men, reflecting the masculinism that dominated the industry for much of its history and that still persists today, and nearly all worked behind the camera. Although there have been many queer performers whose faces have graced the Hollywood screen, few if any have had the privilege of being open about their sexuality. Most have remained either coyly ambivalent, as in the case of stars such as Greta **Garbo** and Marlene **Dietrich**, or fiercely closeted behind an artificial straight veneer, such as Rock **Hudson**. Those stars who have ventured public disclosure of their queer sexuality, like William **Haines**, often faced rejection and unemployment. Even today, other than a handful of relatively minor film actors, no major Hollywood star has yet come out as queer, although many remain the subject of speculation and gossip.

While certainly regrettable, the reluctance of stars to disclose their queer sexuality is another symptom of Hollywood's commercial cast. Stars are vital to Hollywood's economic operations and they function as one of its principal points of appeal. Should a star come out as queer, the fear is that this could limit the scope of his/her audience marketability. The received economic wisdom suggests it is preferable to keep open the question of a queer star's sexuality, thereby accommodating both straight and queer audiences. In fact, some contemporary Hollywood stars actively cultivate an ambiguous sexual persona precisely in order to court queer audiences while not alienating their straight fan base.

The continuing closetedness of queer stars notwithstanding, Hollywood cinema has undergone significant changes in its relations to queerness throughout the contemporary era. Two things are paramount here. First, the demise of the Production Code and the increasing liberalization of censorship and social attitudes have enabled contemporary Hollywood to explore queer material in ever-more explicit ways. A series of landmark films in the late 1960s with overt queer content, such as *The Killing of Sister George* (1968), *Midnight Cowboy* (1969) and *The Fox* (1967) broke the ice and helped pave the way for the subsequent exploration in mainstream Hollywood film of varied forms of queerness, from lesbianism (*Personal Best*, 1982; *The Color Purple*, 1985) and male homosexuality (*Philadelphia*, 1993; *In and Out*, 1997) to transvestism and transgenderism (*Victor/Victoria*, 1982; *To Wong Foo, Thanks for Everything! Julie Newmar*, 1995; *Flawless*, 1999). If Hollywood has yet to produce an overtly queer blockbuster to rival 'straight' classics such as *Gone With the Wind* (1939) or *Titanic* (1997), it at least has made important, if frequently hesitant, steps in the right direction.

The second significant development is that, following the collapse of the studio system and the subsequent fragmentation of its production and exhibition practices, Hollywood has largely transformed from a centralized industry geared towards a singular, mass audience into a multiform complex that services varied markets. Mainstream, mass entertainment arguably remains its economic backbone, but contemporary Hollywood has sought increasingly to diversify its output and, by so doing, to capture medium-scale, niche markets. An obvious sign of this shift is the incorporation of 'independent' film companies that deal with 'specialist' or non-mainstream film fare as integral subsidiaries of most major Hollywood corporations. Within such a context, queer audiences are emerging as an important niche group for Hollywood cinema with studio-based 'independents' producing and/or distributing films explicitly geared to a queer market. It is a curious, although not altogether unwelcome, development that has seen the 'independent' subsidiaries of contemporary Hollywood studios produce overtly queer-themed films such as *Velvet Goldmine* (1998), *The Talented Mister Ripley* (1999), *Boys Don't Cry* (1999) and *Far From Heaven* (2002). Such production and marketing has also enabled the entry into 'mainstream' filmmaking of openly, and sometimes even radically, queer filmmakers such as Todd **Haynes**, Rose **Troche** and John **Waters**, thus ensuring the continued presence of queer artists at the heart of the Hollywood enterprise. And, indeed, Ang Lee's *Brokeback Mountain* (2005) continues this queer presence.

See also: Musicals, film; Production Code, The (Hollywood)

Further reading

Barrios, R. (2002) *Screened Out: Playing Gay in Hollywood from Edison to Stonewall*, London and New York: Routledge.

Hanson, E. (ed.) (1999) *Out Takes: Essays on Queer Theory and Film*, Durham: Duke University Press.

Mann, William J. (2002) *Behind the Screen: How Gays and Lesbians Shaped Hollywood, 1910–1969*, New York: Penguin.

BRETT FARMER

HOMBRE

In Bolivia, a Spanish slang word that means, literally, 'man'. It is used in *ambiente* to refer to straight-acting homosexual men and sometimes to butch lesbians.

PEDRO ALBORNOZ

HOMO LO

A commonly used Cantonese slang word which means gay man or gay men.

KEN WONG

HOMOPHILE MOVEMENT

The homophile movement is the name given to the early, pre-**Stonewall**, gay and lesbian rights movement in the United States that emerged during the 1950s. It began with the formation of the **Mattachine Society** in Los Angeles in 1950 led by Harry **Hay**, the lesbian organization **Daughters of Bilitis**, founded in 1955 in San Francisco by Phyllis Lyon and Del Martin, and ONE, Inc., established in Los Angeles under the leadership of Dorr Legg, who had split from Mattachine. Hay said he preferred homophile ('an implication of spiritual love') to homosexual ('a legal term relating to people who commit specific sexual acts').

Although radical for its time in bringing gay men and lesbians together, as well as in insisting on the end of societal persecution of gay people, some of the movement's approaches appear accommodationist and conservative by post-Stonewall standards – even though the gay and lesbian rights movement's emphasis on radical transformation versus accommodation has been an ongoing debate within the movement since Stonewall. But just as integrationist leaders of the African-American civil rights movement of the 1950s and 1960s such as Martin Luther King eventually had to share the stage with black nationalists such as Malcolm X and Black Power advocates such as Stokely Carmichael, many of the homophile movement leaders were eclipsed – at least for a time – by more militant groups and other cultural movements following Stonewall (for example, the **Gay Liberation Front**, the Gay Activists Alliance, the Lesbian Feminists Liberation, women's liberation, anti-Vietnam War activity and the Black Power movement).

In the 1950s the homophile movement operated, for the most part, under the radar and outside the glare of the media, although they were occasionally attacked in the press as 'subversive' organizations during the time of the McCarthy witch hunts. This was also a time when homosexual people were often committed to mental institutions and lobotomized, excluded from many forms of employment and socially ostracized. The major focus of the early homophile groups was community-building and conducting limited public education on the humanity of gay people.

The East Coast Homophile Organizations was formed in 1963, consisting of Mattachine of Florida, Washington, Philadelphia and New York, with annual conferences leading to a national meeting in 1966 in Kansas City, Missouri, where the North American Conference of Homophile Organization was founded with 20 groups. In 1968 the Conference adopted Washington DC activist Franklin Kameny's 'Gay is good' slogan. After Stonewall, the movement had grown to between 50 and 60 groups. One year after Stonewall, approximately 1,500 homophile groups were established. And by 1971, 2,500 organizations had been formed – a truly national gay rights movement.

Among the homophile groups that emerged in San Francisco in the early 1960s were: the Council on Religion and the Homosexual (CRH), the League for Civic Education, the Tavern Guild, the Imperial Court, and the Society for Individual Rights. Although proper permits were in order, a New Year's benefit for the CRH was raided by police and prominent attendees were arrested. It was a police tactic that ultimately backfired and served as a precursor to Stonewall.

Homophile movement leaders organized the first public demonstrations for lesbian and gay rights in US history, beginning with 10 people in April 1965 at the White House, another there in May, followed by a demonstration at Philadelphia's Independence Hall on 4 July. Other demonstrations were held in Washington at the Pentagon, Civil Service Commission, and the State Department. By October the homophile movement had managed to gather 65 demonstrators at the White House – an extraordinary number for the time. The demonstrators wore conservative business attire so as not to appear offensive and carried placards declaring equal rights for homosexuals. Columbia University was the first to house a campus gay group in the country, the Student Homophile League. This was founded in 1967 by Bob Martin, a disciple of Kameny. Martin set up chapters at Rutgers and Cornell also.

Although there were several short-lived gay groups in the US during the 1920s, 1930s and 1940s, the national Mattachine Society lasted from 1950 and dissolved in 1961, although some local chapters remained in existence and maintained their names. The activism of Hay, Lyon, Del Martin and Kameny endured into the twenty-first century, as they never abandoned their core mission of ending anti-gay discrimination. Lyon and Martin were the first same-sex couple to be married by San Francisco Mayor Gavin Newsom in 2004 when he issued licenses to 4,000 couples despite a state law that forbade it.

See also: Martin, Del and Phyllis Lyon

Further reading

D'Emilio, John (1998) *Sexual Politics, Sexual Communities: The Making of a Homosexual Minority in the United States, 1940–1970*, 2nd edn, Chicago: University of Chicago Press.
Tobin, Kay and Wicker, Randy (1972) *The Gay Crusaders*, New Hampshire: Ayer Company Publishers.

ANDY HUMM

HOMOPHOBIA

A term used to describe the fear or hatred of homosexuality. Homophobia is based upon the assumption that homosexuality is unnatural or inferior to heterosexuality, a contention confirmed by some influential religious beliefs and historical precedent. Psychologists have argued that some homophobic behaviour may be based on a secret fear of the aggressor's own repressed homosexuality or the perceived unstabilizing influence of homosexuality on 'normal' sexuality.

The pressures of homophobia cause gay and lesbian people to conceal or deny their sexuality and to live closeted or semi-closeted lives. Homophobia is thought to contribute towards mental health problems, social isolation and disproportionately high suicide rates among gay and lesbian people.

Although homophobia is largely manifested by heterosexual aggressors, it also exists among gay and lesbian people themselves. Commonly described as 'internalized homophobia', it is caused by gay and lesbian people absorbing negative attitudes about homosexuality within a homophobic society, leading to denial or self-hatred about their sexuality.

The term was first coined by American psychotherapists George Weinberg and K.T. Smith. As a medical student, Weinberg noted that many of his teachers and colleagues were so 'phobic' about homosexuality that they judged it reasonable to administer electric shock treatment to gay patients in the belief that it would cure them. In his book *Society and the Healthy Homosexual* (1972), he defined homophobia as a 'dread of being in close quarters with homosexuals'. Smith's article 'Homophobia: A Tentative Personality Profile' (1971) reached similar conclusions. Weinberg's and Smith's arguments were instrumental in challenging homophobic prejudices, resulting in the American Psychological Association's removal of homosexuality from its list of mental disorders in 1973. The term was adopted by the gay community to describe fear, hatred or violence against gay and lesbian people.

Historically, homophobia can be traced as far back as the history of homosexuality itself, although it has varied through time. Ancient Greco-Roman culture was accepting of homosexuality, but state-approved homophobia increased with the rise of Judeo-Christian religious teaching, which categorizes male homosexuality as sinful. The Catholic Church vigorously persecuted homosexuality, with the torture and execution of 'sodomites' dating from 1292. Homophobia was prevalent in European law until the French Revolution in 1791, when the French government decriminalized all consenting sexual activity. Most countries in Napoleonic Europe adopted this policy of tolerance, with the exception of the German states and Great Britain, which criminalized homosexuality in 1885, and subsequently introduced the law throughout the British Empire. Hitler's government in Nazi Germany demonstrated virulent homophobia, leading to the imprisonment and execution of thousands of gay men. Homophobia was present in American society from the Pilgrim settlers onwards, and followed the English law prohibiting homosexuality. Homophobia intensified in post-Second World War

America, as Senator Joseph McCarthy led a nationwide witch hunt against homosexuals, branding them 'anti-American' subversives.

Sex researcher Alfred Kinsey's *Sexual Behaviour in the Human Male* (1948) radically influenced acceptance of homosexuality and the rethinking of homophobic attitudes. The subsequent gay rights movement of the 1960s and 1970s bolstered anti-homophobic initiatives. The pervasive influence of homophobia has inspired many gay and lesbian people to demand an end to discrimination and unfair treatment. The high-profile killing of gay student Matthew **Shepard** in Wyoming focused international attention upon the brutality of homophobia.

See also: Closet; Homosexual panic; Kinsey Institute; Kinsey Report, The; McCarthy, Joseph and McCarthyism; Paragraph 175

JOHN FORDE

HOMOSEXUAL LAW REFORM ACT, NEW ZEALAND

The Homosexual Law Reform Act, New Zealand, passed on 11 July 1986, legalized consensual sex between males over the age of 16. Previously, 'indecent' acts between men were punishable with imprisonment, as was the renting of property to male homosexuals. The Act followed almost two decades of lobbying by different organizations, an unsuccessful Private Member's Bill, and several failed attempts to present bills to parliament. The Law Reform Bill, introduced by Labour Member of Parliament (MP) Fran Wilde, originally comprised two parts: one decriminalizing homosexual acts between consenting adult men and one prohibiting discrimination on the grounds of sexual orientation. The latter was dropped from the Bill but achieved as part of the Human Rights Act 1993.

Wilde, who collaborated on the Bill with specifically formed regional Gay Task Force groups, urged the Bill be kept secret until its introduction into Parliament on 8 March 1985. However, within a week both National and Labour Party MPs had mobilized opposition. A petition was launched with the Salvation Army collecting signatures, culminating in a ceremonious presentation on the steps of Parliament of a document with an alleged 835,000 signatures.

Lesbian and gay groups opposed the petition by disrupting meetings, circulating educational pamphlets and organizing marches. Influenced by American gay liberation and feminist activism, they utilized ideas of pride, visibility and public education. AIDS became an important topic on both sides of the debate, including within Parliament: it was argued that decriminalization would lead to the spread of HIV and that safer-sex campaigns were impossible while male homosexual acts were illegal.

GERALDINE TREACHER

HOMOSEXUAL PANIC

A form of male psychological anxiety when confronted with homosexuality, 'homosexual panic' has been controversially employed as a partial defence to acts of homophobic violence in the United States and elsewhere since the mid-1960s.

'Homosexual panic' was first defined as a psychological disorder in 1920 by American clinical psychiatrist Edward J. Kempf, based on his case studies of 19 World War One veterans who experienced non-violent anxiety in response to their own latent homosexuality. Kempf's findings were subsequently used (and misapplied) in American criminal assault and homicide cases from the mid-1960s onwards, as an attempt to provide psychological justification for violent homophobic attacks. The first recorded American case successfully employing homosexual panic was *People* v. *Rodriguez* (1967, California, US), where the

defendant killed an older man in an alley, arguing that his actions were the result of acute homosexual panic brought about by the victim trying to have sex with him. The defendant's conviction was reduced to second-degree murder.

Despite the clear distortion of Kempf's findings, which related only to non-violent anxiety in response to a sexual identity crisis, 'homosexual panic' came into usage as a partial or complete defence in gay-bashing cases in the United States, Great Britain, Australia and New Zealand. In most cases the crime was disproportionately violent in response to a real or perceived non-violent sexual advance. Critics of the defence, including Gary Comstock, argued that homosexual panic was based on homophobic assumptions that gay male sexuality is so repugnant as to justify violent attacks and led to gay victims being unfairly blamed for provoking violence. The popularity of the defence effectively kept gay men silent, fearful of expressing their sexuality openly, and exposed them as easy targets for robbery and violence without legal protection.

The defence came under widespread criticism during the 1990s, after a series of high-profile murder trials. In the Australian cases *R* v. *McKinnon* and *R* v. *Bonner*, the defendants were acquitted of murder after violently beating and killing their older gay victims in response to alleged homosexual advances. In the Californian case *People* v. *Schmitz* (1995), the defendant murdered Scott Amedure three days after Amedure confessed a secret attraction to him on the *Jenny Jones* TV talk show. The defendant was found guilty of a lesser charge of second-degree murder after a jury accepted his argument that he was humiliated by Amedure's homosexual interest. In 1998 Matthew **Shepard**, a gay 21-year-old student from Laramie, Wyoming, was brutally beaten and left to die by Aaron McKinney and Russell Henderson, who later claimed that the assault was in response to Shepard making sexual advances towards them in a bar. The brutality of Shepard's murder caused international outrage, leading to widespread condemnation of violence against gay people. McKinney's attempts to plead the defence were met with widespread criticism from politicians and gay activists, and he was subsequently found guilty of first-degree murder. Galvanized by the Shepard case, many legislatures have since passed anti-hate crime laws. In New South Wales, Australia, homosexual panic defence has been banned as a defence in assault and murder cases.

JOHN FORDE

HONG KONG, FILMMAKING

A large number of mainstream films from Hong Kong feature same-sex desire, with no commitment to gender politics. Since the 1990s however, there have been some mainstream films incorporating topics related to homosexual and bisexual relationships. Many of these represent homo-/ bisexual affections in the form of cross-gendered performance, for example, *Xiao ao jiang hu zhi dong fang bu bai* (*Swordsman II*, 1991) produced by Tsui Hark, *Gum gee yuk yip* (*He's a Woman, She's a Man*, 1994), directed by Peter Chan and Lee Chi, and *Shen tan mo lu* (*I Wanna Be Your Man*, 1994), directed by Cheung Chi-sing. These films achieved tremendous commercial success. Yet film critics commented that the representations of **tongzhi** (lit. 'comrades' but now a synonym for gays and lesbians and other sexual minorities) were greatly distorted. Queerness is stereotypically delineated in such ways as gay characters being effeminized and lesbian characters mostly depicted as masculine tomboys. In *He's a Woman, She's a Man*, gay couples were nicknamed 'Auntie', their existence primarily to be the butt of jokes. Homo-/bisexuals were represented as 'the Other', opposite to the privileged and

legitimate heterosexual institution, exposing filmmakers' negative attitudes towards any sexual orientation other than the heterosexual model. As some local film critics and spokespersons of queer groups claim, mainstream filmmakers have long manipulated homophobia in mainstream culture and produced comedic queer characters in order to make a steady financial return in filmmaking.

Lesbian characters suffer from the same stereotyping/discrimination. Those lesbians who do feature in mainstream films are often there merely to provide an erotic display of female bodies. As early as 1972, Chu Yuan directed *Ai nu* (*Intimate Confessions of a Chinese Courtesan*), in which lesbian love focused upon love scenes between two women. In 1984's *Tong chiu ho fong nui* (*An Amorous Woman Of Tang Dynasty*), directed by Eddie Fong Ling-Ching, the major female character, although depicted as bisexual, was only so because she was a failure with heterosexual relationships. Later films continued to approach homosexual issues using the same logic. In these, queers eventually switched their sexual orientation to provide the requisite 'happy ending'. *Ya Fei yu Ya Ji* (*The Days of Being Dumb*, 1992), directed by Ko Sau-leung, depicted Anita Yuen's identity of lesbian as the result of a disappointment with men and heterosexual relationships, and she finally fell in love with a straight man. *Jie mei qing shen* (*He and She*, 1994), directed by Lawrence Cheng, was no exception, relating the story of a man 'switching' from straight to gay and then 'back to normal' again. Sometimes queers simply appear in films as a symbol of 'modern lifestyle', as in *San tung gui shut doi* (*The New Age of Living Together*, 1994), directed by Sylvia Chang.

This celebration of heterosexuality revealed that most Hong Kong filmmakers did not really aim to produce queer films. Marketability has long been the primary preoccupation of filmmakers, and queer themes are viewed as something either to be appropriated or assimilated into the mainstream. Little effort has been made to comprehend and present the social situation of homo-/bisexuals in Hong Kong, nor has there been any exploration of queer identities in relations to politics, society and culture. As most discussions among circles of queer groups, academics and film critics suggest, genuine queer film did not exist in Hong Kong before the end of the twentieth century. Then, in 2004, a series of Stanley Kwan and Yonfan productions were well received by the critics, particularly Kwan's *Lan Yu*, which featured gay men's relationships in great depth.

Hong Kong cinema's independent productions permit a more open discussion of queer issues. However, these productions most often lack backing and thus suffer from limited distribution and exhibition. Since the independent queer filmmakers lack financial resources and industrial credibility, they have weak bargaining power when negotiating a distribution deal. Distributors are also risk-aversive, considering such productions non-marketable.

Yau Ching's independent film *Ho yuk* (*Let's Love Hong Kong*, 2002), which illustrates a lesbian's sexual desire, hosted several fundraising screenings to raise money to subsidize production costs. Yau's film was produced in 2002 and is set in an economically and spiritually depressed Hong Kong. The three major female characters are depicted with far more sophistication than is usual in mainstream films. These lesbians are; a cyber sex worker, an unemployed stalker and a middle-class professional engaged in restless homosexual desires, playing endless games of chasing, rejecting and seducing.

Julian Lee Chi-Chiu is another key figure in the arena of independent video and film. Previously a photographer and erotic novelist, Lee began his collaboration with director Stanley Kwan to bring his novel,

Sam yuen yi ma (*The Accident*), to the screen. '[S]ix Hearts wander at the alley of loneliness. Secret Passion unleashed on the highway of erotic desire', *The Accident* (1999) is a story that opens with a gay man from the mainland getting into a taxi and immediately being attracted to the driver. Homosexual desires are explored and further complicated by interactions with other relationships. In 2003 Lee produced another feature, *Yao ye hui lang* (*Night Corridor*). Like a number of other independent queer films, this was an official selection of Hong Kong International Film Festival. In the film, Lee portrays a series of exploitative relationships, combining repressed homosexuality, paedophilic abuse, the Oedipus complex and primal cruelty, all brought crashing down upon the head of a gay artist.

It is noticeable that within Hong Kong's independent video and filmmaking circle, there is a wider spectrum of creative works. The new filmmakers do not need to label their productions to fit in with existing genres and do not create only queer films. The third film from Yan Yan Mak, former film student and independent filmmaker, is *Hu die* (*Butterfly* 2004), the story of a 30-something teacher in Hong Kong who has to choose between her family and her new lesbian love while in parallel another couple of young women fights against the persistent prejudices which make their relationship difficult. Yan Yan Mak also produced the docu-style feature *GeGe* (*Brother*) in 2001, while her debut dealt with the topic of teenage suicide. She states that *Butterfly* 'is a love story about homosexuality. It is also a story about honesty, about honesty to oneself!'

Some film critics have suspected that among mainstream Hong Kong films, buried within the genre of action and martial arts, are homoerotic aesthetics subtly embodied in the portrayals of masculine images and male friendships. Named as 'Godfather of the Kung-fu Film', Chang

Cheh's films, produced from the 1960s to the 1980s, and including works such as *One-armed Swordsman* Trilogy, initiated a whole era of masculine martial arts films in which male dominance and affection outweighed heterosexual love. Chang's style, and the success of the genre, has greatly influenced other male directors; one of his followers, John Woo, has included ambivalent homoerotics in his films since 1980s, starting with his major success *Yinghung boon sik* (*A Better Tomorrow*, 1986). Both Chang's and Woo's male characters (Wang Yu, Chow Yun-Fat) portray violent aesthetics in the context of male affection. Despite the characters not being defined as homosexual, and denials by the the directors that they are intentionally celebrating male–male eros, this unique genre has become an arguable space of debate in Hong Kong queer cinema.

KEN WONG

HONG KONG, LITERATURE

It is essential to read Hong Kong literature on glbt topics in light of the political and historical context of the country. In 1984 the United Kingdom agreed to allow Hong Kong, once a British colony, to become a special region of China, beginning in 1997. Since 1984, with the not entirely welcome prospect of reunion with China, numerous writers have registered anxiety for the future of Hong Kong. Such anxiety is observable in the literature depicting desire.

Among the most noteworthy of such works are the popular novels by Lilian Lee (Bihua Li), which respond explicitly to the decision on Hong Kong's future made by two superpowers, the United Kingdom and China. Lee's novels portray lesbian, gay and transgender characters, which are allegorical of the uncertain identity of Hong Kong. *Green Snake* retells a lesbian version of the age-old Chinese tale about two snake genies, *Farewell My Concubine* focuses on a

man-loving Peking Opera female impersonator and *Kawashima Yoshiko* (the heroine's Japanese name) depicts a transgender Manchurian princess who is strikingly similar to Hong Kong for oscillating between China and another superpower (Imperial Japan). All these novels have been adapted into films. However, the movie *Farewell My Concubine* (*Ba wang bie ji*, 1993) contradicts Lee's novel by omitting the Hong Kong point of view, which is pronounced in the original novel. The film adaptation concludes in Beijing, but the original novel ends in Hong Kong in the ominous 1984. The female impersonator dies in the movie but does not in the novel.

The urge to reconsider history and the hope of reconfiguring desire coexist in *Betrayal* by Hong Ngai (Ni Kuang). The most popular science-fiction writer among Chinese readers for decades, the prolific Ngai habitually glorifies heterosexual manhood. Nonetheless, *Betrayal* features three man-loving military officers, one of whom eventually opts for sex-reassignment surgery and becomes a woman. *Betrayal* centres on a mid-twentieth-century battle in China, the disastrous outcome of which resulted from a mysterious relationship among men. The sexually alternative characters correspond to non-normative understandings of history. Ngai is also a supporter of lesbian literature, strongly advocating the genre when he sat on the jury of a literary award in Taiwan.

Other writers who exhibit an interest in the conjunction of history with desire, although they are not necessarily as cynical as Lee or as playful as Ngai include Bikwan Wong (Biyun Huang), one of the most accomplished writers in Hong Kong. Her works depict nostalgia for a lesbian-like affinity between two college girl students in her 'She's a Young Woman and So Am I'. This story is categorically different from most of Wong's writings, which are better known for their being macabre and grotesque rather than being mellow. Although her other works are not as bona fide lesbian as the aforesaid story, they are generally preoccupied with various prickly relationships among women.

More nostalgic of spent youth is 'The Central and South Bays: The Forbidden Love of the Beautiful Boys' by Yonfan (Fan Yang), who is known for his camp films. Yonfan adapted this story into his cult film *Bishonen* (1998), whose Japanese title literally means 'beautiful boys'. The story and the film portray a homoerotic melodrama depicting affairs between male prostitutes and a policeman who undresses himself to please voyeuristic old men. Yonfan's story and film are based upon not only an outspoken infatuation with the police in uniform or naked, but on a real-life controversy, when Hong Kong policemen were arrested for undressing themselves in front of rich patrons.

Since the publishing industry and the book market in Taiwan are relatively larger than those in Hong Kong, numerous Hong Kong writers have their works published and reputations established in Taiwan. A remarkable example is Kaicheung Tung (Qizhang Dong), who won major awards for fiction in Taiwan. In his award-winning novella *Androgyny*, a married woman finds her potential for lesbianism while investigating androgynous lizards. The novella is admired for its portrayal of the heroine's mentality, and the critics reportedly find it incredulous that the author is a man rather than a woman. In his novel *Doubled Corporeality*, a man in Japan wakes up to find himself transformed into a woman. Although these works by Tung seem concerned less with Hong Kong politics than with gender theory imported from the West, Tung's lesbian and transgender fantasies reveal a utopian impulse to transcend mundane life. Exactly at the time Tung was developing his utopian fantasies, many Hong Kong citizens hurriedly left for such utopian countries as Canada, fearing the looming reunion with China.

Although some Hong Kong writers and intellectuals resist China's influence, others attempt to reconcile with it from a perspective that prioritizes sexualities over the antagonisms among Chinese regimes. An exemplar is John Loo (Jiangxiong Lu), who founded Worldson Publication, a publishing house in Hong Kong devoted to glbt writings. Loo has attempted to bring together writers among the politically separated Chinese communities, namely, Hong Kong, Taiwan and China. He edited *His–His Her–Her Stories: Short Stories by Authors of China, Taiwan, and Hong Kong*, which gives equal cover to lesbian and gay stories as well as to writers from under different governments. He has also edited *A New Reader on Chinese Tongzhi: Essays and Conference Proceedings*, which resulted from an unprecedented convention of Chinese glbt people from Hong Kong, China, Taiwan and other countries. Held in 1998, post-handover, this conference is less illustrative of China's relaxed attitude towards glbt people than the determination of people in Hong Kong to defend human rights, glbt rights included.

Such concern with human rights can be attributed to the tradition of activism in Hong Kong. While activists in Taiwan and China garner most of the attention, it should be acknowledged that they are preceded and helped by their Hong Kong forerunners, many of whom are writers. A veteran activist, Xiaomingxiong (Samshasha) published the comprehensive *History of Homosexuality in China* as early as 1984; Edward Lam (Yihua Lin), a versatile theatre artist, publishes essays that are explicitly queer; Wah-shan Chou (Huashan Zhou), a sociologist, publishes oral histories from his interviews with queer people. The lesbian and bisexual activists may seem less visible, but they also are devoted to publishing pamphlets.

See also: Taiwan, literature

TA-WEI CHI

HOOKER, EVELYN

b. 1907; d. 1996

psychologist

Born into poverty in Nebraska, Evelyn Gentry won a scholarship to the University of Colorado where she received both a BA and MA in Psychology (1924–30). She received her PhD from Johns Hopkins University in 1932. Hooker befriended a gay student – Sam From – who, in 1943, introduced her to gay male subculture. In 1953 the National Institute of Mental Health (NIMH) funded Hooker's proposal to study 'non-patient' male homosexuals. Through personal friends, the **Mattachine Society**, and ONE Incorporated, Hooker recruited 30 male homosexuals, matched them with 30 male heterosexuals and administered several projective personality tests to them all. Psychological experts who read participants' responses could not discern each man's sexual orientation. The two groups were deemed equivalently 'well-adjusted', thus questioning prevailing notions about distinct homosexual types in clinical psychology. Hooker subsequently studied gay communities ethnographically and helped coordinate the NIMH Task Force on Homosexuality whose 1969 report argued that homosexuality should be considered neither psychopathological nor criminal.

PETER HEGARTY

HOOKS, BELL

b. 1952

feminist thinker, writer

Born Gloria Watkins in Hopkinsville, Kentucky, hooks' use of a penname is meant to honour both her grandmother (whose name she took) and her mother, and to provide her with a separate voice from the person Gloria Watkins. Her writings cover a broad range of topics on gen-

der, race, teaching and the significance of the mass media, with her first book, *Ain't I A Woman; Black Women and Feminism* (1981), establishing her as a radical feminist. She is most interested in the interconnectedness of power structures, or what she calls, 'White Supremacist Capitalist Patriarchy'. But she also turns attention to the agency of being, as opposed to the passivity of receiving culture. She calls, for instance, for 'enlightened witnesses', and engagement with mediated representations. She is a leading public intellectual with a distinguished academic career and has published extensively in the academic press.

MICHAEL PINFOLD

HOOVER, J. EDGAR

b. 1895; d. 1972

government official

The head of the Federal Bureau of Investigation (FBI) for the US government for over five decades, Hoover's systematic persecution of homosexuals, communists and other perceived political enemies made his name synonymous with the Orwellian police state. Hoover was born in Washington DC on 1 January 1895. He started his career as a clerk for the Justice Department in 1971, gaining promotion quickly for his vigorous prosecution of communists. In 1934 he was appointed head of the Bureau of Investigation (later renamed the FBI in 1935), a position he held until his death. Under his leadership, the Bureau became one of the most efficient – and ruthless – police agencies in the world, frequently using illegal methods to gather private information about political leaders and suspected political dissidents. He vigorously participated in the prosecution of communists and homosexuals during the McCarthy witch hunts of the 1950s and led harassment campaigns of gay rights groups including the

Mattachine Society. He spent much of his career quashing rumours that he was gay and that his second-in-command, Clyde Tolson, was his lover. Photographs of both men in drag were discovered after Hoover's death, on 2 May 1972.

See also: McCarthy, Joseph and McCarthyism

JOHN FORDE

HOPE AND UNITY METROPOLITAN COMMUNITY CHURCH (HUMCC)

The HUMCC, based in South Africa, held its first service in 1994, the same year in which South Africa's first democratic elections took place. The late Reverend Tsietsi Thandekiso (1948–97) was its founding pastor. The church grew out of an informal prayer group catering to the needs of gay Christians who felt alienated from their religious congregations and uncomfortable with the secular politics of other gay and lesbian organizations. Initially, the church met in the Harrison Reef Hotel in Hillbrow, home to the oldest surviving gay bar in Johannesburg, the Skyline. The HUMCC continues to enjoy the support of a young African congregation and now meets in an Anglican church in Johannesburg. A young woman preacher, Nokthula Dhladhla, and founder member Paul Mokgethi are the leaders of this unique congregation that serves to integrate (against popular wisdom) African, Christian and glbtq identities.

GRAEME REID

HOTLANTA

Nickname for the major US city of Atlanta, Georgia, a cosmopolitan haven for southern and international queers.

TERRELL SCOTT HERRING

HOUSING WORKS

See: ACT UP

HSIEN-YUNG, PAI

b. 1937

writer

Taiwanese Pai Hsien-Yung is a prominent short-story writer and novelist, and one of the founders of the magazine *Hsien Tai Wen Hsueh* (Modern Literature). Many of Pai's works touch upon gay issues, but his first and only novel to date, the 1983 work *Nie-zi* (*Crystal Boys*) remains the most significant of all. The novel relates the struggles of a group of Taiwanese gay boys and the dark kingdom of these 'exiled sons'. Heralded as the first gay novel of modern Taiwanese literature, *Crystal Boys* has since generated much controversy. Many consider it influential in the construction of queer subjectivity of the Taiwan *tongzhi* community, especially in its outing of the New Park (now renamed 228 Memorial Peace Park) as a queer, urban space. *Crystal Boys* was made into a feature film in 1986, and the premiere of the TV drama of the same name appeared in 2003. Like the novel, the TV programme sparked another round of fierce discussion in Taiwan.

LISA Y.M. LAM

HUBBARD, JIM

b. 1951

experimental filmmaker

A native New Yorker, Jim Hubbard's films combine the radiant beauty of self-processed film with a political/social investigation of gay life. Hubbard believes that experimental film can communicate more honestly the lesbian/gay experience than homosexual-themed narrative films. He co-founded MIX: The New York Lesbian and Gay Experimental Film Festival with

Sarah **Schulman** to promote experimental film and to provide visibility for gay and lesbian film/video artists. His acclaimed works include *Elegy in the Streets* (1989), an exquisitely hand-processed remembrance of Roger Jacoby, a filmmaker who died of AIDS, whose dedication to forming a mass response to AIDS infuses the memorial not with nostalgia but activism; and *Two Marches* (1991), a hymn to the AIDS crisis that was broadcast on the Sundance Channel in 2000. Hubbard's 19 films are a series of personal visual essays of intertwined loss and liberation. *Memento Mori* (1995), a 16-mm cinemascope hand-processed meditation on death, was awarded the Hamburg Lesbian and Gay Film Festival Short Film Jury Ursula Award. His works have screened at numerous festivals including Berlin, London, Toyko and Los Angeles. In 2003 Hubbard, with Schulman, launched the ACT UP Oral History project, a series of in-depth interviews with AIDS activists.

M.M. SERRA

HUDSON AND HALLS

Hudson, Peter

b. NA; d. 1992

chef

Halls, David

b. NA; d. 1994

chef

The Australian Peter Hudson and the Englishman David Halls met, fell in love and set up house together in Auckland during the 1960s. Between 1975 and 1986 'Hudson and Halls' were extremely popular, camp and flamboyantly entertaining chefs on Television New Zealand. Although never explicitly out, they were presumed to be a couple. In the late 1980s their entertaining kitchen antics were shown successful on BBC television and throughout

Europe. Hudson died in 1992 of cancer. Halls committed suicide in London fourteen months later.

CAROLYN SKELTON

HUDSON, ROCK

b. 1925; d. 1985

actor

Rock Hudson was an American film actor whose popular screen persona as the all-American, heterosexual everyman was shattered in the mid-1980s by his highly publicized death from AIDS and the consequent revelation of his homosexuality.

Born Roy Scherer, Hudson's was an entirely fabricated star image. He was placed under contract to Universal in the early 1950s where his name was changed, his teeth capped and he underwent a gruelling schedule of physical and social grooming. Tall, muscular and dazzlingly handsome, Hudson was pitched as a clean-cut matinee idol. The fact of his homosexuality was rigorously concealed by the studio, aided by an orchestrated, if brief, marriage of convenience.

Hudson shot to major fame during the mid-1950s with a series of popular romantic melodramas, including *Magnificent Obsession* (1954) and *All That Heaven Allows* (1955). The image of the romantic playboy set in these films was extended and refined in a number of hit sex comedies that Hudson made later, often with Doris **Day** (*Pillow Talk* (1959) and *Lover Come Back* (1961)). The popularity of these films was such that Hudson became the iconic embodiment of a normative American heterosexuality for an entire generation. When news of his homosexuality and terminal struggle with AIDS was made public in 1984, the result was an initial media frenzy and backlash against the star that had 'lived a lie'. A certain public equilibrium was restored and eventually Hudson won widespread sympathy, playing his last and possibly most influential role as the celebrity face of AIDS.

BRETT FARMER

HUGHES, HOLLY

b. 1955

performer, writer

Performance artist, playwright and writer whose work deals humorously with her lesbian identity, Hughes was born on 10 March 1955 in Saginaw, Michigan. She began her career as an abstract painter and moved to New York in 1979, becoming involved with WOW Cafe, a lesbian experimental theatre group. Her early works 'The Well of Horniness' (1983), 'The Lady Dick' (1984) and 'Dress Suit for Hire' (1988) were satiric explorations of lesbian butch/femme stereotypes. In 'World Without End' (1989), she used the starting point of her mother's death to explore the relationships between mothers and lesbian daughters. In her Obie-winning 'Clit Notes' (1990, later published as a book), she shocked her audiences by revealing her sexual attraction to her father and to butch lesbians who reminded her of him. In 1990 she and three other artists received national attention when their National Endowment for the Arts (NEA) grants were cancelled on the basis that their work breached the NEA's decency policies. Known as the NEA Four, they successfully sued the NEA for reinstatement of the grants but were unable to revoke the decency clause.

JOHN FORDE

HUGHES, LANGSTON

b. 1902; d. 1967

writer

One of the most prominent American poets of the twentieth century, Langston Hughes, born in Joplin, Missouri, was raised in the Midwest and settled in New York during the 1920s. With the publication of his first book of poetry, *Weary Blues* (1926), Hughes established himself as the most prominent voice of the African-American cultural movement known as the Harlem Renaissance. With Countee Cullen, Zora Neale Hurston, Wallace Thurman, Alain Locke, Nella Larsen and Bruce Nugent, Hughes unapologetically explored the realities of black American life. Like other modernists, the Harlem writers were frank in their depiction of urban queer cultures. In a four-decade long career incorporating drama, fiction and essays, Hughes infused his work with the rhythms of African-American speech and music, particularly the blues and jazz. Among his better-known works are the 1935 play *Mulatto*, which ran for over a year on Broadway, and the poetic cycle *Montage of a Dream Deferred* (1951).

See also: Black glbtq literature; Racism

DAVID KURNICK

HUMAN RIGHTS CAMPAIGN (USA)

Founded in 1980, the Human Rights Campaign (HRC) claims to be the largest gay and lesbian organization in the United States, with more than 500,000 members. HRC is a bipartisan organization that 'works to advance equality based on sexual orientation and gender expression and identity, to ensure that gay, lesbian, bisexual and transgender Americans can be open, honest and safe at home, at work and in the community'. It lobbies Congress; mobilizes grassroots action; invests to elect pro-glbt Congress members; and increases public understanding through education and communication strategies on a number of topics affecting glbt Americans, including workplace, family, discrimination and health issues. The HRC Foundation, an HRC-affiliated organization, engages in research and provides education and programming. HRC

287

has often been criticized by progressive grass-roots activists, particularly those of colour, for its single-issue focus on glbt rights, which fails to recognize the interconnections between sexuality, gender, race and class.

SURINA KHAN

HUMAN RIGHTS LEGISLATION, NEW ZEALAND

The Human Rights Act 1993 consolidated and amended existing legislation to outlaw discrimination on the grounds of sexual orientation, disability and 'the presence of disease organisms in the body' in New Zealand. The proposed legal protection of homosexuals and those with HIV met with moral and religious opposition in parliament and in public debates. However, the opposition did not equal the furore surrounding the **Homosexual Law Reform Act**, indicating a growing public tolerance of homosexuality.

GERALDINE TREACHER

HUMSAFAR TRUST

Initiated by three self-identified gay men in Mumbai, the Humsafar Trust coordinates support and health options for men who have sex with men in India. The Trust operates the Humsafar Centre, a safe space for gay men. The Centre's resource library offers texts about gay life in India, as well as multilingual, culturally sensitive sexual health materials. HIV and STI counselling and testing are conducted in its clinic. The Trust's work includes AIDS prevention and education, with condoms and safe-sex information being distributed at parks, beaches and other cruising areas in Mumbai. A member of the International Gay and Lesbian Human Rights Commission, the Trust has challenged Section 377 of the Indian Penal Code, which criminalizes homosexuality. The Trust organizes work-

shops for academics, activists, politicians and clients on human rights issues. The Trust also collaborates with like-minded organizations, including the **Naz Foundation**. Although headquartered in the large metropolitan area of Mumbai, the Trust's reach encompasses smaller cities and rural areas throughout India.

CHRIS BELL

HUNGARY, LITERATURE

Approaching the topic of queer literature in Hungary is relatively simple, in that there are comparatively few queer-identified writers. It is also problematic however, because of precisely this lack of emphatically queer writers. Glbtq writers have been closeted, or unable to find a language to address the queer subject within Hungary. Indeed, it was almost impossible to write about queer subjects in the decades following 1945.

This difficulty was definitely present for Erzsébet Galgóczi (1930–89), the first Hungarian author to write about a lesbian character, in her novel entitled *Within the Law* (1980). (Its title is *Another Love* [1991] in the English translation while the film based on this novel and Galgóczi's short stories directed by Károly Makk is called *Egymásra nézve* [*Another Way*, 1982].) The tension caused by being closeted surfaces in many of Galgóczi's loosely auto-biographical short stories. Not to conflate Galgóczi with her narrators, the events and experiences of her life still very much define even her third-person narratives. Coming from a peasant family, she wanted to find her place in Budapest as a young intellectual in the 1950s and was convinced that as a writer she had a social duty: to help create a more just society. Her characters do not find a place for themselves however; they do not want to be peasants, and they are sick of the lies and false promises of the communist system. Galgóczi's position between classes, and her search for truthful speech in an era defined by lies, would have created enough tension on their own, but a deeper tension exists within many of her female characters.

In *Within the Law*, a relatively late novel, she introduced a lesbian protagonist, Éva Szalánczky, a journalist. Surrounded by rigidly structured gender roles, Szalánczky cannot find her place among either men or submissive women. After facing failure both in her work life, where she is censored for being a politically provocative reporter, and in her love life, where her relationship with a married woman culminates in violent tragedy, she commits suicide – not by her own hand directly, but the system's (she dies trying to cross the Yugoslavian border). With her determined move away from her peasant upbringing, her political activities and honesty within a system based on lies and her lesbianism, Éva Szalánczky's character is an exemplary intersection of the elements that held Galgóczi and her texts in constant tension.

Péter Nádas (1942–) is one of the most respected and translated contemporary Hungarian writers. Politics and relationships are at the centre of his works, wherein the workings of society reveal themselves in bodily relationships. In his intricately woven novel, *A Book of Memories* (originally published in 1986, in English in 1997), liberty is considered in relation to sexuality, love and the body. One narrative occurs during the late nineteenth and early twentieth centuries, and the narrator of this thread is also the protagonist of the second and third narratives in the novel: he also tells of his childhood in 1950s Budapest (and the multivalent affections he felt, especially towards a boy), and about his time in East Berlin in the mid-1970s, including a love triangle between himself, a man and a woman. These plots constantly focus on questions of individual knowledge in society, how politics affect bodies and bodily relationships, and on how these themes can be conveyed: 'what we can narrate about our own lives' – often through the relationships between bodies. In Nádas' work, every aspect of personal life is entangled with ideology and history.

In 1997 a lesbian novel was published by Agáta Gordon (1963–) called *Kecskerúzs* (*Goat Rouge*), which narrates the story of a few women in long, floating, unpunctuated sentences. There is a common thread running through Galgóczi's and Gordon's novels, in that their protagonists use an immense number of quotations. They both seem to be on a constant quest for representations, images and found words that would express their experience in a culture built upon silencing them. The structure of Gordon's novel is based upon a set of poems that the narrator finds in the hospital she is taken to, while waiting for her psychiatrist. She recognizes herself and her life in the lines, and each chapter opens with a poem from this book. Both the poems and the prose text contain several references that are based on the metaphor of the machine. The narrator is emphatically not an individual, she does not have concrete distinctive features, a body or a name – she is perceived and presented as a historical and, most of all, linguistic-textual construction. Rigid gender categories continually dissolve, as masculinity and femininity are permanently contested concepts, their interchangeability blurring the boundaries between them.

Ádám Nádasdy (1947–), a poet and professor of linguistics, has published several volumes of fine poems addressing his gay identity openly. His poems are usually built upon recollections; he writes extensively on relationships and on communication – both verbal dialogues and the dialogue his body engages in with other bodies. Everyday speech finds its way into sonnets and intricate rhymes, or finely structured free verse in his prosody. His most recent volume, *The Orderliness I Am Creating* (2002) contains many poems about mourning –

reflecting on the story and afterlife of a love that lasted for 20 years and ended with the death of his partner. Nádasdy again stands in dialogue with his memories, his pangs of guilt and his love. After painful, excruciating episodes there is always reflection, and the beauty of discovery and understanding. Nádasdy has also begun to publish short stories featuring gay characters.

András Gerevich (1976–) is a younger poet. Some of his poetry touches on the subject of gay relationships. His starting points are often memories of relationships, a need of the other or partings. Sometimes a simile unfolds into a larger, surrealistic image in his poems. His volume *Men* was published in 2005.

There are also initiatives to encourage queer writers in Hungary. The Labrisz Lesbian Association has edited a volume of short stories and poems, some of them written by Hungarians (*Headwind*, 2001), and a volume of lesbian autobiographical writings (*Self-Portraits Developed*, 2003). The gay magazine *Mások* (1991–) has been publishing gay literature since its inception. Its editors also published a collection of autobiographical stories by László L. Ladányi (1931–), a Hungarian gay man who was born in Romania and lives in Germany.

BEA SANDOR

HUSTLING

Term used to describe the activity of soliciting for sex by young participants for payment and/or personal advantage. The mark of a good hustler is an absence of sex while getting paid. The perfect 'trick' (event), or 'john' (client), is walked away from with money after no or little sexual contact. As opposed to prostitution proper, hustling's ultimate goal is to profit financially, not to trade – it is a 'con'.

MICHAEL PINFOLD

I

IBIZA

One of the Balearic Islands off the southeast coast of Spain, Ibiza's international reputation as a party destination also embraces an energetic and fully integrated gay scene. The island features numerous gay nightclubs and is a mandatory venue of the international gay dance party circuit. The Figuertes and Es Cavallet beaches are popular with gay tourists.

JOHN FORDE

IDOL PICTURES

Idol Pictures was founded in 1993 by Jack Lewis and Zackie **Achmat**. Idol Pictures have produced several ground-breaking films on South African gay and lesbian history and identity, using a characteristic docu-drama technique. Films include *A Normal Daughter* (1998) and *The Life and Times of Kewpie of District Six* (1998), which recovers ignored memories of gay life in District Six, one of the sites of apartheid's notorious forced removals. *Sando to Samantha: aka The Art of Dikvel* (1998) is a raunchy reconstruction of the experiences of Sando Willemse, aka Samantha Fox, a drag queen from Bonteheuwel in Cape Town turned soldier in the South African Defence Force in 1991. *Apostles of Civilised Vice, Parts 1 & 2* (1999) reveals lesbian and gay life in South Africa from colonialism to the twentieth century. Most recently,

Idol Pictures collaborated with John **Greyson** on the feature film *Proteus*, set in early eighteenth-century Cape Town. The film tells the story of the ill-fated relationship between a young Khoi herder Claas Blank, and Dutch sailor, Rijkhaart Jacobsz.

GRAEME REID

IGGY POP
b. 1947
singer

Born James Newell Osterberg, Iggy Pop, the 'Godfather of Punk', dropped out of the University of Michigan to pursue a career in music. His heroin addiction and consequent behaviour became problematic for his back-up band, the Stooges, so that their line-up underwent changes and they disbanded in 1974 as a live group. In 1977 David Bowie, with whom Iggy had relocated to Berlin, produced two studio albums – *The Idiot* and *Lust For Life*, from which comes Iggy's most well-known track, 'The Passenger'. His influence within the subcultural movement of punk rock was evident in the latter's musical attitude and appropriations, but also in terms of performance. Iggy's live performances have been legendary, sexually provocative and ambivalent, shocking audiences to such an extent that the British TV show,

291

So It Goes (1976), was pulled after his slot and never aired again.

MICHAEL PINFOLD

IHIMAERA, WITI

b. 1944

writer

In 1995, after more than two decades as one of New Zealand's most celebrated writers, Witi Ihimaera came out publicly with the publication of his novel, *Nights in the Gardens of Spain*. The novel concerns a university lecturer coming to terms with his homosexuality. It remained on the New Zealand best-seller lists for over six months. While not autobiographical as such, *Nights in the Gardens of Spain* echoes important aspects of Ihimaera's own life. In interviews he often discusses his experiences of being both gay and Maori, a subject he addresses further in *The Uncle's Story*. Within this novel, Ihimaera condemns what he sees as the homophobia of Maoridom and the colonizing impetus of a Pakeha (white)-centred gay culture. In 2003 Ihimaera's novel *The Whale Rider* was adapted into the successful film, *Whale Rider*.

ANITA BRADY

IL DITO E LA LUNA

publishing company

Il Dito e La Luna is an Italian publishing house established in 1995 in Milan, Italy, aiming to promote the circulation of Italian books on lesbian and gay topics. The founders and women now collaborating on it are active in the Italian lesbian movement; for years they have been contributing to the dissemination of lesbian culture and rights for homosexual people. The Il Dito e la Luna publications include studies and novels by Italian and other writers, as well as the magazine *Towanda!*, a quarterly covering lesbian culture and politics. Each issue contains a special feature on one particular topic and columns on cinema, books, Italian and foreign current affairs and comics. *Towanda!* is the first lesbian magazine to be retailed in bookshops. It sees the collaboration of important Italian theorists and writers such as Liana Borghi and Margherita Giacobino.

MONICA BARONI

IN THE LIFE

Originally this phrase was used to describe gay or lesbian African-Americans without conspicuously calling them homosexual. Like many African-American phrases, the meaning of these words has expanded. *In the Life* is also the name of an influential anthology of gay black writings, the organization that sponsors the Atlanta Black Pride celebration and even a PBS TV news series on gay events. Consequently, another similar phrase has developed, but with a distinct difference. Someone 'on the down low' is not visibly gay, despite engaging in homosexual sex, and this has led some overtly masculine, black men to define themselves as on the down low in order to differentiate themselves from more open, gay black men.

See also: down low

GABRIEL GOMEZ

INACZEJ

Inaczej (In a Different Manner) was one of the most serious and important Polish glbt magazines (alongside *Filo*, *Gejzer* and the feminist *Zadra*, open to glbt concerns). Its pages hosted many interviews with writers, activists and politicians, in addition to debates, investigations and democratic discussions about glbt culture in Poland. The first issue was published in June 1990 with the name: *Inaczej: Pismo Mniejszości Seksualnych* (In a Different Manner: Magazine of the Sexual Minorities). The magazine was discontinued in June 2002.

ALESSANDRO AMENTA

INDIA, FILMMAKING

India has the largest film industry in the world, releasing approximately 1,000 films a year to an international audience of 3.6 billion. Since the mid-1980s India has also seen the emergence of a politicized independent documentary movement that distributes its films through non-state networks and videotape circulation. However, it was only in 1996 that *BomGay,* the first gay identified film, made its appearance. *BomGay,* by Riyad Vinci **Wadia**, is a highly stylized avant-garde film structured around six poems by the gay poet R. Raj Rao. The film was circulated widely in glbt circles and at international film festivals. Wadia's next film, *A Mermaid Called Aida,* is a feature-length documentary on well-known transsexual Aida Banaji. During the late 1990s queer films and filmmakers started to become increasingly visible.

The urban Indian mediascape underwent dramatic changes during the 1990s. In 1991 the Congress government initiated economic restructuring with globalization as its main imperative. This was accompanied by an open sky policy that resulted in the proliferation of satellite TV channels, thereby dismantling the government's monopoly over television. These two developments ran parallel to the rise of the Hindu Right, led by its political front, the BJP (Bhartiya Janata Party or the Indian National Party).

The rapid spread of new media and telecommunications technologies radically transformed the cultural practices of the urban middle class. As newer images flowed into people's homes, viewers responded with both anxiety and enthusiasm. As a result of its reach, popularity and psychological presence, television came to haunt the public imagination as an ominous and uncontrolled force causing deviant behaviour and corroding 'Indian cultural values'. This led to widespread demands for stringent legislation, greater censorship and even a ban on private TV channels. The anxieties emerged as a direct result of the increasing popularity of TV and the expanding space being devoted to the expression of sex and sexuality. Throughout the 1990s the Hindu Right made targeted attacks on the more transgressive representations of women's bodies and sexualities. The moral panic, however, was not restricted only to the Hindu Right but was shared by various groups, including feminist organizations.

Despite public anxieties, there was growth of sexual speech. Queer spaces emerged in both the electronic and print media. Newscasts, talk shows, sitcoms and a variety of TV shows challenged conventional family values and sexual normativity. Sitcoms featured characters who were unmistakably queer and who challenged heterosexual assumptions. A number of mainstream feature films, such as *Daayra* (The Square Hole), *Darmiyaan* (In Between) and *Tamanna* (Desire), explored glbt sexualities in India.

The paradox of the times climaxed in 1998 with the controversy around the feature film *Fire* by Deepa **Mehta**, starring well-known actresses Shabana Azmi and Nandita Das. *Fire* is a love story about two married sisters-in-law who fall in love with each other and have a relationship. Since *Fire* was released on the commercial circuit, the film publicity put into circulation an unprecedented volume of speech and representation around glbt issues. The posters, created through special photo sessions, showed the two women occupying the same diegetic space that had conventionally belonged to heterosexual lovers. The film is particularly subversive because the relationship grows within a Hindu, middle-class family; the kind that is usually believed to embody traditional family values. Moreover, the film ends with the lovers happily united.

Two weeks after the film was released extremists of the Hindu Right in Mumbai and Delhi attacked and vandalized theatres showing the film. The BJP government defended the actions of its allies, claiming that the film went against 'Indian culture'. A petition submitted by the groups that led the attack on *Fire* argued that if women's 'physical needs' were 'fulfilled through lesbian acts' then the institution of marriage would collapse and the reproduction of human beings would stop. The attack on *Fire* met with strong opposition from glbt, human rights, feminist and cultural groups. On 6 December 1998, 32 organizations and concerned citizens held a peaceful protest in front of Delhi's Regal cinema. This allowed for nationwide visibility of sexual politics in India. Most of the national newspapers reported the event prominently and affirmatively. The film was eventually re-released and enjoyed a successful commercial run.

The late 1990s and early 2000s saw the emergence of films and videos that addressed glbt issues directly. In 1998 Nishit Saran's debut documentary *Summer in My Veins* forcefully foregrounded the existence of glbt presence and politics. Made as a student film at Harvard University in the United States, this autobiographical 'coming-out' video received both popular attention and critical appreciation. Naveen Kishore's *Performing the Goddess* is a testimony about the life of veteran female impersonator Chapal Bhaduri who, for many decades, played the roles of women and goddesses in Bengali folk theatre.

Film and TV narratives were displacing heteronormative assumptions. *ETV Bangla* (a regional channel in the Bengali language) broke new ground with the made-for-TV film *Ushno Taar Jonno* ('For the Sake of Warmth' or 'Warm for Her') directed by Kaushik Ganguly. Same-sex relationships are central to the plot and the cast includes

Chapal Bhaduri and two of Bengal's top actresses, Rupa Ganguly and Choorni Ganguly. The film was telecast for a series titled 'Tales of Domesticity'. Mainstream films such as *Rules: Pyar Ka Superhit Formula* (Rules: For the Success of Love) and *Kal Ho Na Ho* (If Tomorrow Never Comes) feature queer characters as normative and not as 'funny' or 'deviant'. Queer subcultures have always been attracted to Bombay popular cinema. Despite the absence of explicit homosexuality, the film narratives are frequently about intense homosocial relationships in which the boundaries of love and friendship constantly overlap.

Over the years international film festivals, theatrical releases and non-commercial public screenings have brought international glbt films to the attention of the Indian public, thereby influencing queer cinephiles and filmmakers. In October 2003 glbt groups in Mumbai held the First International Film Festival of Sexuality and Gender Pluralities, showcasing a number of independent films produced by the glbt community and marking an important moment in the history of queer film culture in India.

Further reading

Ghosh, Shohini (2002) 'Queer Pleasures for Queer People: Film, Television and Queer Sexuality in India', in Ruth Vanita (ed.) *Queering India: Same-sex Love and Eroticism in Indian Culture and Society*, New York: Routledge.

SHOHINI GHOSH

INDIA, LITERATURE

Homosexual relationships have been represented and discussed in Indian literature for more than two millennia. After British colonial rulers criminalized homosexuality in 1860 and systematically inculcated **homophobia** among educated Indians, homophobia, formerly muted, became dominant in Indian literature. Genres such as the *ghazal* (Urdu love lyric) that had conventionally celebrated male–male love, were heterosexualized, while new genres such as the novel tended to depict male homosexuality as sordid and diseased, and female homosexuality as a premarital phase or the resort of women deprived of men. Older traditions persisted in the positive representation of intensely emotional and romantic friendships. Typical of the portrayal of male homosexuality as embedded in a perverted underworld are Mohammad Basheer's 1947 Malayalam novel *Shabdangal* (*Voices*) and Kamleshwar's 1956 Hindi novel *Ek Sadak Sattavan Galiyan* (*The Street with Fifty-Seven Lanes*).

Ismat Chughtai's Urdu novel *The Crooked Line* sympathetically depicts the intensity of schoolgirl romances as a premarital phase in women's lives. This type of depiction, sometimes framed in the nostalgic memory of an unhappy wife, continues to appear in later fiction by women, such as Shobhana Siddique's passionate and explicit Hindi story *Lab ba Lab* (*Full to the Brim*), and with a twist in Kamala Das' lyrical Malayalam novelette *Chandana Marangal* (*The Sandal Trees*). In 1976 Kamala Das shocked the literary world with her depiction of sex, including lesbian sex, in her fictionalized autobiography in English, *My Story*. Some of her poems also discuss homosexuality.

From the 1940s to the 1970s Aubrey Menen, himself gay, wrote several extravagantly imaginative English novels with homoerotic themes and characters. From the 1960s onward, the Writers' Workshop, based in Calcutta, published homosexual poems in collections by several little-known writers, some of whom went on to become famous. Among them are Vikram Seth, Inez Vere Dullas, Suniti Namjoshi and Hoshang Merchant. Other poets in English include Adil Jussawala, S. Anand, Ian Iqbal Rashid, Owais Khan and Ruth Vanita. Many homosexual love lyrics, published in magazines and anthologies, conceal gender by using the 'I–you' format.

Namjoshi is among the earliest and most gifted Indian lesbian writers. Her *Feminist Fables* and *Blue Donkey Fables* are now classics; her novels *Mothers of Maya Diip* and *Conversations of Cow*, her numerous poems and her recent *Goja: An Autobiographical Myth* constitute, among other things, an ongoing meditation on what it means to be an Indian lesbian. Vikram Seth's tour de force, *The Golden Gate*, and his later novels *A Suitable Boy* and *An English Music* all have gay characters and subplots.

Both male and female authors nonetheless continue to publish homophobic novels and short stories. Most of these focus on women, and conclude with the lesbian's conversion to heterosexuality through rape or marriage or with her violent death. While Shobha De wrote a series of potboilers in English, most of which contain sympathetic portraits of gay men, she also has a virulent depiction of the lesbian as psychopath in *Strange Obsession*.

The Indian tradition of apparently heterosexual writers producing sensitive depictions of same-sex love also continues. In 1989 Vijay Dan Detha's brilliant Rajasthani story, *Dohri Joon* (*A Double Life*), was published in Hindi, and shortly thereafter performed as a play in Delhi. The story adapts premodern Indian tropes such as the mistaken marriage and the miraculous sex change to envision a utopian lesbian future. Later fictions in this category include Vikram Chandra's long story in English, "Artha" in his *Love and Longing in Bombay*, Manju Kapur's English novel *A Married Woman*, short stories in English by Nisha da Cunha and in Tamil by Ambai, and V.T. Nandakumar's Malayalam novel, *Randu Penkuttikal* (*Two Girls*).

Trikone, founded in 1986 in California by two Indian men, India's oldest gay magazine *Bombay Dost*, founded in 1990, and many other newsletters and magazines in

Indian cities began to publish the new lesbian and gay writing that exploded onto the literary scene in the 1990s. During this decade, the rapid growth of lesbian, gay and anti-AIDS organizations in urban India created a new demand for openly lesbian and gay writing. These movements also spawned plenty of literature with a propagandistic intent. For example, after the AIDS Bhedbhav Virodhi Andolan (AIDS Anti-Discrimination Movement or ABVA) filed a writ petition in 1994, challenging the constitutionality of the anti-sodomy law (the petition was heard in 2003 by the Indian Supreme Court), lawyer Rajesh Talwar wrote an English play, *Inside Gayland*, that satirically depicted an Indian heterosexual man's visit to a planet where heterosexuality is criminalized as immoral and unnatural.

Also in the 1990s, it became increasingly futile to try to distinguish Indian writers from writers of Indian origin who live abroad, as many writers now spend time and publish both in India and abroad or migrate to the West, while others are of mixed Indian and foreign origin. The celebrated painter Bhupen Khakhar came out late in life and writes highly acclaimed short stories in Gujarati; Mahesh Dattani has written a series of award-winning plays in English, several on gay themes, that play to packed houses in Indian cities; Marathi Namdeo Dhasal and Madhav G. Gawankar explore male homosexual experience in the urban streets; and in a series of autobiographical novels in English, Parsi writer Firdaus Kanaga explores the sorrows and joys of being both gay and disabled. One of the earliest in the plethora of gay novels in English in the 1990s was Leslie de Noronha's *Dew Drop Inn*; other gay writers in English include R. Raj Rao and P. Parivaraj.

A number of these writers have received national and international awards and other types of recognition, and have contributed to the new wave of interest in Indian literature worldwide.

Further reading

Merchant, Hoshang (ed.) (1999) *Yaraana: Gay Writing from India*, Delhi: Penguin.

Sukthankar, Ashwini (ed.) (1999) *Facing the Mirror: Lesbian Writing in India*, Delhi: Penguin.

Vanita, Ruth (ed.) (2002) *Queering India: Same-sex Love and Eroticism in Indian Culture and Society*, New York: Routledge.

Vanita, Ruth and Kidwai, Saleem (ed.) (2000) *Same-sex Love in India*, New York: Palgrave Press.

RUTH VANITA

INDIANA, GARY

b. 1952

writer, critic

Born Gary Hoisington in New Hampshire, Indiana the writer came into existence with a name change and a move to Los Angeles, where he wrote for zines spawned by a nascent punk movement. By the 1980s, and now based in New York, Indiana was writing, acting and directing plays, which together with appearances for the Wooster Group, the Mudd Club, a band called the Boners and some small European films, placed him firmly as part of the city's downtown scene. He has written for *Artforum* and *Art in America,* and from 1985–8 was art critic at *Village Voice*. Indiana's fiction mines his past, a place where bohemia meets celebrity for sex, drugs and other pursuits. If his first novel, *Horse Crazy* (1988), tracks an ordinary but attractive junkie/hustler, notoriety dominates the three later novels that feature famous killers; the Menendez brothers in *Resentment: A Comedy* (1997), *Three Month Fever: The Andrew Cunanan Story* (1999) and Sante and Kenneth Kimes in *Depraved Indifference* (2002).

GABRIEL GOMEZ

INDIGENOUS QUEER IDENTITIES

In recent decades a major revolution has taken place in how homosexuality is conceptualized in the modern world. First emerging in the United States, but soon spreading to other Western nations, was a new mode of homosexual subjectivity enabled by the forces of modernization, particularly the mobility encouraged by wage-based capitalism. Young, upwardly mobile gay men and lesbians were developing a sense of shared identity and lifestyle, not just behaviour. Mainstream society acknowledged this shift by catering to a gay and lesbian market. Suddenly, being gay or lesbian was as much about what clothes one chose to wear, where one took holidays, how often one worked out at the gym and which area of town (or which cities or even countries) one chose to live in, as it was about choice of sexual acts or partners. Then, towards the end of the twentieth century, gay and lesbian lifestyles and identities became increasingly apparent in metropolitan areas throughout other parts of the globe. In the 1990s it was possible to discover gay discos in Shanghai, gym bunnies in Manila, dyke bars in Taipei and gay fashion designers in Tokyo. This process was described by Dennis Altman (1996) as 'global queering'.

Despite the fact that homosexual behaviour has been observed throughout all the world's cultures over time, the manner in which it has been structured, conceptualized and expressed has differed considerably. Modern Western homosexual relationships are often characterized as 'egalitarian' in that they take place between two equal partners; but in most cultures homosexuality has been expressed in transgender relationships, where one partner takes on the role or identity 'opposite' to their birth sex, or intergenerational relationships where an adult is involved with a partner who has not yet achieved adult status.

While international conventions on child sex have impacted upon the prevalence of intergenerational relationships, transgender homosexual identities are still very apparent in the world today and include Thai *kathoey*, Philippine *bakla* and Samoan *fa'afafine*. Rather than being eclipsed by the encroachment of Western lesbian and gay identities, it can be argued that the processes of modernization are actually helping to increase the visibility of these traditional minorities. For instance, Thai media have seen a boom in interest in *kathoey* or male-to-female transsexuals. Many of Thailand's most popular TV dramas feature at least one *kathoey* character. International tourism, too, has seen a massive growth in the number of cabarets and bars featuring *kathoey* who perform for foreign visitors in the nightlife districts of Pattaya and Bangkok.

In the Philippines, *bakla*, another category of transgendered males, has taken over the beauty industry, with many *bakla* running hair and makeup salons. *Bakla* thus often provide much needed income for their extended family and, as they generally do not have children of their own, are able to offer support to the children of their siblings. Samoan *fa'afafine*, too, play a similar role in their extended families. Since they remain unmarried, they are able to care for their parents in old age and supervise children while other members of the family are at work. The family-based social systems in their respective societies mean that these traditional identities and roles continue to be of significance and importance whereas the individualism implicit in Western gay or lesbian identities makes them more difficult to reconcile with local structures.

The transgender identities described above are generally most apparent among poor and disadvantaged groups and, although homophobia may not be entirely absent, transgender individuals can achieve positions of authority and respect within their extended families because of the income and services they provide. In contrast, Western gay and lesbian identities, are often criticized for being implicated in specifically middle-class lifestyles and concerns. As Michael Tan (1996) points out, the trouble with the notion of 'global queering' is that: '[A]n elite "gay" culture is held up as the norm, with hopes that eventually we'll have "gay and lesbian rights" defined mainly as gay marriages; to bring home Steve to mom and dad for Thanksgiving dinner; to be able to adopt and raise children and to claim frequent flyer miles for a same-sex partner to fly to Sydney for the Mardi Gras'.

The signifiers of acceptance and success mentioned by Tan are largely relevant for white, middle-class gay men and may have little relevance to poor white men, women of colour, indigenous minorities or inhabitants of the developing world. Given the fact that many 'developing' nations have only recently emerged from the experience of having their cultures overrun by the forces of Western colonialism, it is not surprising to find some members of sexual minorities outside the West expressing scepticism about the liberatory potential of typically Western models of lesbian and gay identity.

Does, then, the process of 'global queering' imply that specific, local, indigenous sexual identities and practices are being undermined by a kind of gay imperialism, yet another colonial encroachment from the West? Not really, since this model, which views globalization as a unilateral movement 'from the West to the Rest', fails to take into consideration the regional flows, intercultural borrowings and hybridity that are also part of globalization. This process is often referred to as 'glocalization', that is, practices, narratives, lifestyles or identities that may have a certain 'global' currency are given very particular meanings or expressions when they are adopted in distinct 'local' environments.

When considering how these local borrowings work, it is important not to arbitrarily divide the world into two opposing 'developed' and 'developing' camps. For example, many theorists from rich societies such as Taiwan and Hong Kong have begun to advance local models of sexual identity that differ markedly from narrowly defined categories such as lesbian and gay. Instances include, during the 1990s, the emergence of the term *tongzhi* as a preferred designation for many same-sex desiring Chinese. The word originated as a Chinese translation for the Soviet communist term 'comrade' and was originally used by Hong Kong gay activists who wanted to employ an inclusive indigenous term for same-sex eroticism in association with the First Lesbian and Gay Film Festival in Hong Kong in 1989. Unlike lesbian and gay, which denote specifically sexual identities and which have negative connotations for some, *tongzhi* is a positive term, denoting inclusiveness, and has become widely used in Hong Kong and Taiwan to connote a range of queer identities.

Another problem with Western notions of queer identity and activism is that 'queer' is very much implicated in contemporary Western systems of 'normality' and 'difference' that do not necessarily map onto the way in which normality has been constructed in other societies or historical periods. For instance, it is common knowledge that during the classical era of Greek civilization heteronormativity, as we currently understand it, was not considered 'normal', at least for elite male citizens. At this time it was considered perfectly acceptable for adult male citizens to court, seduce and engage in sexual relationships with male youths – public gymnasiums (where young men exercised naked) being a popular site for such trysts.

A more recent example of local practice that confounds current notions of normality occurs among the Sambia, a tribe of more than 2,000 people who live in the highlands of Papua New Guinea. The Sambia have strongly essentialist views about the differing nature of men and women. While girls are thought to progress unproblematically through the process of puberty on their way to becoming adult women, boys are thought to need the intervention of adult men in order to facilitate this process. One of the ways in which adult men pass on the essence of their masculinity is through oral intercourse during which boys ingest adult male semen. In Sambian society all adolescent males ingest semen from adult males until the age of about 15 when they themselves begin to inseminate younger boys and then go on to get married. Therefore both homosexual and heterosexual practices are considered 'normal' and, indeed, necessary at different stages of a male's life. This does not make Sambian men 'bisexual' in the Western sense, however, since sexual behaviour is dictated by ritual concerns and not personal preference.

Even within some societies, particularly those of Latin America, which are nominally 'Western', heteronormativity does not operate in quite the same manner as in North European or Anglo-Saxon cultures. In many Latin American societies even today, it is sexual *role* and not sexual *identity* that is important in sexual encounters. So long as adult men act in a 'macho' manner, which involves being the penetrating partner in association with women or other (usually younger or effeminate) males, their masculinity is not compromised. A man who is *activo* (active) in sexual interactions with other men is not stigmatized as homosexual, only those men who are *pasivo* (passive), allowing themselves to be penetrated, are looked down on. The notion that two adult men might engage in a reciprocal affair and be alternately *activo* and *pasivo* is considered queer in the terms of this system. Intriguingly, the Mexican term for 'gay' men who engage in such reciprocal relationships is *internacionale* (internationals), signifying that this practice is not considered indigenous to Mexico but a result rather of the influence of global queering.

The emphasis upon gender performance in Latin American societies has enabled the emergence of sexual identities that do not fit easily into the Anglo-Saxon paradigm that operates in terms of a hetero–homo binary. For instance, in Brazil, the *travesti* are a group of male-to-female transgender sex workers who offer services to gender-normative males. *Travesti* not only cross-dress but also employ medical procedures such as hormone therapy and silicone injections to produce a more female (and therefore desirable) body for their clients, but they are neither transvestites nor transsexuals in the commonly understood sense of these terms. Importantly, since *travesti* are understood to play the 'female' role in sexual interactions, male clients can engage in sex with them without themselves being labelled homosexual or deviant. *Travesti* claim to be appalled by the idea that two gender-normative men might have sex with each other and, although they do sometimes agree to penetrate their clients, charge more for this service, which they claim contradicts their gender role. Rather than being undermined by globalization, 'local' identities such as *travesti* are themselves being exported to other societies. Brazilian *travesti* who can afford the fare often travel to European cities such as Paris and Milan where they receive much higher rates of pay for their services than in Brazil.

It is clear that human societies are so diverse that behaviours which would be considered queer, or downright unethical or illegal in the contemporary West, might, in their indigenous settings, be considered quite normal. Similarly, identity categories that may appear quite self-evident and unobjectionable to Westerners may be unintelligible to people of other societies and time periods; notions of what is or is not 'queer' are still very much embedded in the particular conventions of North American and Northern European societies. While evidence of the diffusion of typically Western notions of lesbian and gay identity and lifestyle certainly exists, a model that assumes a unilateral movement from a Western centre to a 'developing' periphery is clearly inadequate. Equally problematic is a model that fixes local, indigenous identities in some kind of unchanging 'traditional' past which is under constant threat of erosion. Rather, globalization means that everything is in flux, including the identity categories of both the West *and* the rest.

Bibliography

Altman, Dennis (1996) 'On Global Queering', *Australian Humanities Review*, July, available online at: http://www.lib.latrobe.edu.au/AHR/archive/Issue-July-1996/altman.html (accessed 4 June 2003).

Tan, Michael (1996) 'A Response to Dennis Altman from Michael Tan in the Philippines', *Australian Humanities Review*, available online at: http://www.lib.latrobe.edu.au/AHR/emuse/Globalqueering/tan.html (accessed 4 June 2003).

Further reading

Berry, C., Martin, F. and Yue, A. (eds) (2003) *Mobile Cultures: New Media in Queer Asia*, Durham: Duke University Press.

Herdt, G. (1997) *Same Sex Different Cultures: Exploring Lesbian and Gay Lives,* Boulder: Westview Press.

MARK MCLELLAND

INDONESIA, SEXUAL CULTURES

While still poorly understood by most Westerners, Indonesia is geopolitically significant. Stretching a distance greater than that from California to New York, Indonesia is the world's largest archipelago, with over 3,000 inhabited islands and over 600 spoken languages. With over 200 million citizens it is the fourth most populous nation (after China, India and the United States). Since nearly 90 per cent of Indonesians are Muslim, it is also home to more Muslims than any other country.

Indonesia's glbtq sexual cultures can be placed into three general categories:

Ritual transgenderisms and homosexualities

Transgenderisms and homosexualities linked to ritual or performance have existed in many (but not all) parts of the archipelago as far back as written and oral texts permit us to speculate. These are typically only for men, for only part of the life span, and do not release the persons who take them up from heterosexual marriage. Perhaps the best-known case involves ritual specialists known as *bissu*. Bissu were usually men who guarded sacred objects in the Bugis royal courts and who would for certain purposes dress in a manner combining male and female clothing. Like many ritual transgender practices, it does not appear that the *bissu* profession was identified with a sexual culture and sexual restraint was often seen as a way for *bissus* to increase their mystical powers. Some ritual transgenderisms and homosexualities, including *bissu*, persist now; others have been discontinued because of the influences of colonialism and religions such as Islam and Christianity, and are known only through historical texts.

Warias

Warias (better known to the Indonesian public as *banci* or *béncong*, terms most *warias* consider derogatory) are persons seen to be born as men who, usually in childhood, come to believe that they have the souls of women, or souls that are both male and female. They dress in a feminine style, usually all day long, although rarely do they try to pass as women. While the historical record is still incomplete, it appears that *warias* first appeared in the Indonesian archipelago during the nineteenth century. From the beginning *warias* were associated not with ritual but with the developing market culture of colonial-era cities; they appear to have made their living as performers in popular theatre, in small-scale trading and through sewing and sex work. In contemporary Indonesia *warias* are visible in daily life to a degree that surprises tourists and other visitors. They are particularly associated with salons and other situations where body transformation is called for, such as bridal makeup. They appear on TV advertisements and shows, and perform for public events, including political rallies. Despite this social recognition, *warias* also face discrimination; sometimes from their families of origin, sometimes from passers-by on the street. *Warias* rarely marry women or have sex with each other; their ideal sexual and romantic partner is a 'normal' man. Often it is expected that this man will eventually leave their *waria* partner for a wife, but it is also common for a man to continue a relationship with a *waria* after marriage, with or without his wife's knowledge.

In contemporary Indonesia *warias* live not just in urban areas but in rural environments also, although the best-known *waria* organizations and events take place in cities. *Warias* are found across the Indonesian nation and are not seen as being exclusive to any particular ethnic group. As the reference to political rallies above indicates, they are increasingly present in the public sphere.

'Gay', 'lesbi', and 'tomboi' Indonesians

From the available data it appears that some Indonesians began to use the terms *gay* and *lesbi* during the 1970s, with an acknowledged national social network taking form in the 1980s. Unlike ritual transgenderisms and homosexualities or the '*waria*' identity, Indonesians do not usually learn about 'gay' identity from their community. Most 'gay' men say they first learned they could be 'gay' from fragmentary coverage in the mass media. Once seeing themselves as

'gay', these men are often able to meet other 'gay' men in parks and shopping centres or by 'playing eyes' with a man who they hope might be 'gay'.

On the surface of things, 'gay' men might appear similar to gay men in the West, particularly since the Indonesian term 'gay' is clearly derived from the English 'gay'. However 'gay' men have transformed the concept gay in unexpected ways. Since most 'gay' men (like most Indonesians) do not travel outside Indonesia or speak English, their links to Western homosexualities are fractured. Almost none, for instance, know the significance of things such as **Stonewall** or the **rainbow flag**. Significantly, most 'gay' men marry women and assume that Western gay men do the same. This state of affairs reflects not only 'gay' men's incomplete knowledge of Western homosexualities, but the importance of heterosexual marriage in contemporary Indonesian society. This is not just the product of 'traditional' sexual cultures but is shaped by the Indonesian nation-state's emphasis upon marriage and the nuclear family as core elements of national society.

Since the term 'gay' is still not well understood by Indonesian society (many think it is English for *waria*), 'gay' men rarely face overt discrimination. This is particularly the case because few 'gay' men reveal themselves as gay to family, co-workers or friends who are not gay themselves. Since Indonesia was a Dutch colony and its penal code is based upon Napoleonic law, which was relatively uninterested in homosexuality, legal action against 'gay' men is rare. However, some openly 'gay' men have experienced discrimination, as in the case of Dédé **Oetomo**. In a number of cities 'gay' men have created organizations and even published small magazines.

The term 'lesbi' appears to have existed as long as 'gay' ('lesbian' is also found but is less common, probably because −*an* is a suffix in the Indonesian language). Like 'gay' men, most 'lesbi' women learn about the concept lesbi through mass media and then meet other 'lesbi' women. However, since it is more difficult for women to move about unaccompanied than men, 'lesbi' women face particular barriers in forming a community; they must largely do so in more policed environments such as at home or school. Nonetheless, 'lesbi' women have formed communities and even organizations in a number of Indonesian cities. Like 'gay' men, many 'lesbi' women marry heterosexually, for reasons that often include both personal desire (for children, for social acceptance, for God's favour) and social pressure.

One of the most important differences between 'gay' and 'lesbi' Indonesians is that while the *waria* identity has existed for some time, there has been no similarly recognized identity for female-to-male transgendered or transvestite persons. Such persons in Indonesia go by a variety of names, the best known of which is *tomboi* (sometimes spelled 'tomboy' or 'thomboy'). The fact that the 'lesbi' and *tomboi* identities have come into being at around the same time (rather than decades apart as in the case of 'gay' and *waria*) has important consequences. For instance, while 'gay' men rarely have sex with *waria*, 'lesbi' and *tomboi* persons are often ideal sexual partners. Additionally, while *waria* is understood as a uniquely Indonesian identity, the *tomboi* identity seems to reflect the existence of tomboy identities across Southeast Asia.

Further reading

Blackwood, Evelyn (1998) 'Tombois in West Sumatra: Constructing Masculinity and Erotic Desire', *Cultural Anthropology* 13, 4: 491–521.
Boellstorff, Tom (2003) 'Dubbing Culture: Indonesian Gay and Lesbi Subjectivities and Ethnography in an Already Globalized World', *American Ethnologist* 30, 2: 225–42.
—— (2004) 'Playing Back the Nation: *Waria*, Indonesian Transvestites', *Cultural Anthropology* 19, 2: 159–95.
Graham, Sharyn (2001) 'Negotiating Gender: Calalai' in Bugis Society', *Intersections: Gender, History, and Culture in the Asian Context*, issue 6, available at: http://wwwsshe.-murdoch.edu.au/intersections/issue6/graham.html (accessed 23 September, 2001).
Oetomo, Dédé (1996) 'Gender and Sexual Orientation in Indonesia' in Laurie Sears (ed.) *Fantasizing the Feminine in Indonesia*, Durham: Duke University Press, pp. 259–69.

TOM BOELLSTORFF

INGE, WILLIAM

b. 1913; d. 1973

playwright

In the work of American playwright William Inge, searing dramas of life in small-town America reveal a keen critique of social and sexual repressiveness. A drama college graduate, Inge held a variety of teaching and journalist positions before being inspired to try scriptwriting through a chance meeting and subsequent friendship with Tennessee **Williams**. An auspicious debut with *Farther Off from Heaven* (1947) was followed by a series of highly successful plays throughout the 1950s, including *Come Back Little Sheba, Bus Stop, The Dark at the Top of the Stairs* and the Pulitzer Prize-winning *Picnic*. Hailed by critics as a major new talent for his exposés of stifling provincialism in the American heartland, Inge's career faltered badly in the 1960s when he experienced a string of flops. Strictly closeted, Inge struggled with his homosexuality and in later life became increasingly prone to bouts of severe depression and alcoholism, eventually committing suicide at age 60.

BRETT FARMER

INMAN, JOHN

b. 1935

comic actor, mime

John Inman is best known for his camp performance as Mr. Humphries, the flamboyant sales associate he portrayed for ten seasons on the British TV series *Are You*

Being Served? Primarily a homosexual comedy stereotype, the character of Mr. Humphries pouted, postured, and squealed 'I'm free' as he scurried to measure an inside leg. He was drawn to both men and women and sometimes exhibited tendencies towards bisexuality. Initially the portrayal received criticism from gay groups but, by the end of the series, both actor and character became something of a gay icon.

CATHERINE R. BURKE

INTERNATIONAL LESBIAN AND GAY ASSOCIATION (ILGA)

ILGA is an international federation of national and local groups dedicated to achieving equal rights for lesbians, gay men, bisexuals and transgender people around the world. Founded in 1978, it has more than 400 member organizations, including members from every continent and approximately 90 countries. ILGA member groups range from small collectives to national groups and, in some cases, entire cities. The organization focuses public and government attention on cases of discrimination against glbtq people by supporting programmes and protest actions, asserting diplomatic pressure, providing information and working with international organizations and the international media. The hallmark of the organization is its world conferences, held in different parts of the world every one to two years, which bring together hundreds of activists from many countries and play an important networking role for international glbtq activists and organizations.

The ILGA World Conference is the highest decision-making body of the organization regarding legislation, approval of new members, and internal and external priorities. Each member organization expresses its opinions and concerns and votes on conference matters. The ILGA Executive Board consists of two Secretaries General (one female and one male), a Women's Secretariat, and two representatives (one female and one male) from each of the six ILGA regions: Africa; Asia; Australia, New Zealand and the Pacific Islands; Europe; Latin America and the Caribbean; and North America. During the 1990s ILGA was embroiled in controversy when it applied for consultative status with the United Nations and Jesse **Helms**, then a right-wing Senator from North Carolina, opposed the application by attacking the organization for including the **North American Man/Boy Love Association** (NAMBLA) as a member.

SURINA KHAN

INTERNATIONAL, DANA

b. 1971

singer

Dana International is a popular Israeli singer, a male-to-female transsexual and the winner of the 1998 **Eurovision Song Contest** (ESC) with her song *Diva*. The ESC Award garnered her international celebrity. Born in Tel Aviv as a boy named Yaron Cohen to a religious Jewish family of Yemenite origin, Dana made her musical debut during her teen years. Her drag queen performances at the age of 19, as well as her rumoured sex-change operation at the age of 22, positioned her as a politically committed cultural leader of the gay and transgender community in Israel. Through her choice of music and lyrics (often written by her), she addresses border crossing of many kinds. Her songs are often multilingual (including Hebrew, English, Arabic, Italian and French) and mix popular Western and Middle-Eastern music.

DAFNA LEMISH

INTERNET AND GLBTQ CULTURE

Internet services for lesbian, gay, bisexual and transgender communities developed

303

during the 1980s, as the first newsgroups and online networks were forming. Despite some hostility amongst mainstream Internet groups, online services with non-heterosexual content have flourished, first run by hobbyists and activist groups, and more recently by corporations such as PlanetOut.com and Gay.com. Early research on the queer Internet focused on issues of identity and the problems and opportunities of 'virtual' community. More recent research has analysed the impact of corporate control of glbtq portals. The constant evolution of Internet technologies and services means that most aspects of glbt life have some related content online. However studies of new technologies tend not to be integrated into mainstream queer theory in the same way as other forms of cultural production such as films.

One of the first Internet services to be developed in 1983 was the newsgroup net.motss (motss stood for 'members of the same sex'). This group grew out of a singles newsgroup net.singles, and was forced to use the motss acronym following objections to using the word gay in the group name. soc.motss was a public forum, constrained by the rules and attitude of other newsgroup users. Meanwhile individual gay men and lesbians were also developing independent and experimental queer Internet services. One such was the Lesbian Cafe Bulletin Board Service, which ran in Midwest America during the early 1990s. A computer user logging on to the Lesbian Cafe would be greeted with textual descriptions of a cafe-bar setting, including a 'bisexual futon'. Online conversations were conducted around the conceit that participants were together in a cafe-bar, including being bought a drink or chatting to others near the fireplace.

The proliferation of queer online services during the early 1990s was led by hobbyists and those who could maintain email mailing lists at their workplaces. At this time many email mailing lists were dominated by those working in the computer industry or studying in universities in the United States. Certain lists attracted hundreds of users, such as the Sappho list, which has been used widely in studies of the Internet glbtq phenomenon (e.g. Hall, 1996). Email distribution lists required relatively low technical know-how and by the late 1990s there was a list for every possible queer subculture, from gay male bear cultures, to transgender support groups, to lesbians with horses. Articles in the popular media at this time suggested that the Internet was becoming increasingly important for those isolated from urban queer scenes. However local lists for those living in large cities also proliferated, suggesting that Internet services supplemented other meeting places and face-to-face groups.

Hobbyists were also responsible for the earliest queer web sites, and for registering domain names such as lesbian.org (Amy Goodloe in 1994). Many web pages were gateways into chat rooms or mailing list archives. However they also were portals for information about queer life in regions of the world outside the United States. The Queer Resources Directory was set up by pioneer Ron Buckmire in 1991 as an electronic archive for **Queer Nation** and maintained a vast inventory of information about lists, web pages and resources. Nevertheless, most online content focused on the United States. Buckmire's survey of the mailing list QueerPlanet in 1995 showed that 42 per cent of the 319 subscribers were participating using email addresses from US educational institutions (.edu), with a further 28 per cent from commercial or non-profit domains within this territory.

The experience of soc.motss founders was not an isolated incident in the establishment of queer online services. Many online services faced disruption as a result of invasion by homophobic participants and developed both informal and formal mechanisms to try and avert this. Mailing lists often required screening of potential new members by the mailing list organizer. Some chat rooms adopted names that were not obviously queer-related. The development of filtering software, supposedly for the purpose of protecting children from unsuitable content, was a concern for those developing services for young queer people. This worry was not without grounds. In 1988 some gay forums were included in a ban of unsuitable content by a service provider in Germany. Goodloe responded to homophobic or salacious emails about her web site by posting them unedited on her web pages.

Since the late 1990s most of the larger queer Internet services have been run commercially. PlanetOut.com began as Microsoft forum in 1995 and quickly established itself on America OnLine (AOL) and then the wider Internet. Such portals were free to use, and so depended largely on advertising revenue. They reinforced the view amongst some companies in the United States that glbtq communities constituted a promising market segment, and also that they could be reached via the web. The increasing conglomeration of such services has been noted, and doubts raised about the way in which this is beneficial for the diversity of glbtq communities (Gamson, 2003). Some online portals, such as QueerCompany in the UK, were launched with extensive advertising campaigns, only to be disbanded a couple of years later when revenues did not materialize. The most frequently used online services run by commercial organizations are those that facilitate chat rooms, dating services or pornography. Chat spaces have been particularly significant for gay men's sexual practices (Campbell, 2004). Sites such as gaydar.co.uk also provide crossovers into other media such as a gaydar digital radio station.

Researchers who have investigated queer cultures online have tended to focus on issues of identity, and in particularly the ways in which different groups within glbtq cultures have been excluded by others (Wakeford, 1998). Early lesbian lists such as Sappho had ongoing debates about the inclusion of transgendered people within its forum. Much was written about the ways in which Internet services could provide support and networks for the queer community, particularly for those who could not be open about their sexuality elsewhere in their lives. Implicit in much of this work is that online communication was an adequate substitute for face-to-face participation in clubs, bars and public encounters. A psychological study suggested that participation in a virtual group was 'a crucial part of the demarginalisation process' (McKenna and Bargh, 1998). The authors of this study claim that 37 per cent of users 'came out' as a direct result of news group participation.

Bibliography

Campbell, John Edward (2004) *Getting It On Online: Cyberspace, Gay Male Sexuality, and Embodied Identity*, New York: Harrington Park Press.

Gamson, Joshua (2003) 'Gay Media, Inc.: Media Structures, the New Gay Conglomerates, and Collective Sexual Identities', in Martha McCaughey and Michael D. Ayers (eds) *Cyberactivism: Online Activism in Theory and Practice*, New York: Routledge, pp. 255–78.

Hall, Kira (1996) 'Cyberfeminism', in Susan Herring (ed.) *Computer-Mediated Communication: Linguistic, Social and Cross-Cultural Perspectives*, Amsterdam: John Benjamins, pp. 147–70.

McKenna, Katelyn and Bargh, John (1998) 'Coming Out in the Age of the Internet: Identity "Demarginalization" through Virtual Group Participation', *Journal of Personality and Social Psychology* 75, 3 (September): 681–94.

Wakeford, Nina (1998) 'Urban Culture for Virtual Bodies: Comments on Lesbian "Identity" and "Community" in San Francisco Bay Area Cyberspace', in Rosa Ainley (ed.) *New Frontiers of Space, Bodies and Gender*, London: Routledge.

NINA WAKEFORD

INTERNET: POLITICS AND ACTIVISM

Gays and lesbians discovered early the potential of the Internet for online community building and political activism. Interestingly, it has been individuals rather than established gay rights groups who have been most inspired, and thus have had the most notable successes, in using the online medium.

The earliest significant use of the Internet for gay community-building can be credited to an organization called Digital Queers in 1992. With cries of 'We're here, we're queer, we have email!' Digital Queers founders Tom Rielly and Karen Wickre were two of the first gay and lesbian activists to recognize the potential of the Internet, and technology more generally, for organizing and networking the gay community. Among other activities, Digital Queers raised money and donated computer equipment to help gay rights groups become more tech. savvy. Digital Queers eventually merged with the **Gay and Lesbian Alliance Against Defamation (GLAAD)**.

Two years later, in 1994, gay journalist Rex Wockner launched one of the first and most powerful gay news email lists in America – a list that continues to this day. Wockner's daily updates – comprised of links to daily stories of interest to a politically motivated and gay-friendly readership – are emailed to several hundred influential editors, activists and acquaintances. While simple in its approach, Wockner's list instantly gives a story a stamp of credibility and gravitas that separates it from the myriad gay news on any given day.

During the same year as Wockner started his list, Gay.com's Mark Elderkin found inspiration in serendipity. One day in 1994, he decided, on a whim, to see if he could register the web address Gay.com. It was available, so he bought it, and launched Gay.com, a simple web page devoted to his dog. Suddenly, Elderkin found his page visited by a growing audience of gay people looking for anything they could find about gays online. Responding to the obvious interest, Elderkin relaunched Gay.com in 1996 as a gay chat service. By 1999 Gay.com was drawing more than 1 million visitors each month. Over the years, Gay.com's popularity continued to grow.

Gay.com's chief competitor, PlanetOut.com, was founded in 1995 by Digital Queers' Tom Rielly, with the goal of becoming the premiere web site for gay content. Through its parent company, PlanetOut Corp, the enterprise served gay programming on MSN, Yahoo! and America OnLine (AOL). PlanetOut and Gay.com's parent company, Online Partners, merged in 2001 to become PlanetOut Partners, and ultimately, PlanetOut Inc.

In 1996 a Nebraska couple named Jean Mayberry and Aleta Fenceroy launched the 'Fenceberry' email list. Similar to Rex Wockner's news list, while Wockner opted for quality (perhaps five stories a day), Fenceberry went for quantity. On a typical day the Fenceberrys, as they quickly became known to their fans, would send up to 35 gay-related news stories to their subscribers. Begun at a time when most newspapers were yet to have web sites, the Fenceberrys provided an invaluable service for disseminating gay news across the country, particularly articles from smaller, more obscure papers that might otherwise be overlooked. The Fenceberrys signed off in 2004, noting that 'the service just doesn't feel as indispensable as it did a few years ago'.

GLAAD became one of the first, if not the first, national gay rights groups to use the Internet in an innovative and especially effective way in 1996 with their GLAAD lines, an email news update and action alert. GLAADlines quickly became an indispensable must-read for online activists of the era. The short, succinct updates included the gay news of the day and often a quick call to action, commending a reporter for a particularly well-done story or chastising a company for some sin against the community.

One of the first important uses of the Internet for individual gay advocacy came in early 1998. At the time, Timothy McVeigh (no relation to the Oklahoma City bomber) was being kicked out of the US Navy for violating the 'Don't Ask Don't Tell' policy – even though McVeigh had not actually admitted to being homosexual. The Navy found out McVeigh was gay by asking America Online if a certain AOL 'screen name' belonged to Timothy McVeigh of Honolulu, Hawaii. The online giant, violating its own privacy policy and possibly federal law, confirmed that the account was that of McVeigh. Online activists John Aravosis and Barbara Bode issued email updates, action alerts and press releases on McVeigh's behalf, suddenly catapulting the once-obscure sailor to status as one of the top stories in the country. With the subsequent help of a legal team, McVeigh successfully sued the Department of Defense, retired from the Navy and settled with America Online for an undisclosed sum.

In late 1998 came a second defining event for the gay and lesbian community, the nation, and for the history of gay online advocacy. In early October the US was shocked to learn that Matthew **Shepard**, a young gay college student, had been found badly beaten and tied to a fencepost in Laramie, Wyoming. In an effort to make it easier for gays and lesbians and their allies to find out information about Shepard's case, online activist John Aravosis launched Matthew Shepard Online Resources. The frequently updated site (that nowadays would be called a web log) quickly became the central online resource for updates on Shepard's condition, the overwhelming public response to the crime and the year-long trial against his now-convicted murderers. The site's bulletin board was used to organize over 70 candlelight vigils across the country, and until 2004, when the board was taken down, still elicited condolences from around the world.

Two years after the Shepard tragedy, one of the most effective online advocacy campaigns ever carried out took place. On 1 March 2000, StopDrLaura.com was launched to force the cancellation of Dr Laura Schlessinger's planned TV show. Schlessinger had called gays a 'biological error', among other slurs, and friends John Aravosis, Joel Lawson, Robin Tyler, Alan Klein and William Waybourn decided to fight back with what would become the first-ever successful boycott of a TV show. Within days of its launch, StopDrLaura quickly became an unstoppable juggernaut. In its first few weeks of operation, the site generated over 17,000 emails to Paramount. Shortly thereafter, StopDrLaura organized protests at Paramount and then 34 cities around the US and Canada (coordinated by local StopDrLaura groups in each locale). By the end of the nine-month campaign, funded mostly by the online sale of T-shirts, StopDrLaura.com's 3 million visitors forced over 170 advertisers in the US and Canada to drop the TV show. Shortly thereafter, Dr Laura's show was cancelled.

Not long after the launch of StopDrLaura.com, gay conservative writer and pundit Andrew **Sullivan** became one of the first, and certainly the most prominent, gay American to start blogging. AndrewSullivan.com's witty and biting commentary quickly became a popular bookmark for conservatives of every orientation, and even for a few of Sullivan's liberal fans and detractors. Since that time, Sullivan has been joined by other high-profile gay bloggers from the Left, including Jim Capozzola of Rittenhouse Review and John Aravosis of AMERICAblog.com, all of whom blog to this day.

One of the most effective online campaigns to target the White House was also a gay-run and-inspired campaign. DearMary.com was launched in February, 2004 by activist John Aravosis in order to pressure the openly gay daughter of Vice-President Dick Cheney, Mary **Cheney**, to speak out against President

Bush's anticipated support for a federal constitutional amendment banning gay marriage. While Ms Cheney never came forward, the site generated a firestorm of publicity and controversy, making Mary Cheney's lesbianism a household fact and, more importantly, lifting the taboo on the media's coverage of her homosexuality. Ultimately, Mary's mother, Lynne Cheney, spoke out in opposition to the amendment, and Mary was mentioned during the Presidential and Vice-Presidential debate that year. DearMary.com shares some of the credit for both.

In 2005 straight and gay bloggers joined together on a story that seemed to involve everything – national security, gay rights, sex and politics – when bloggers from a wide variety of sites, including Eschaton, DailyKos.com and AMERICAblog.com, worked with progressive non-profit Media Matters to unmask White House reporter Jeff Gannon as a gay male prostitute named James D. Guckert.

Web sites

http://www.AMERICAblog.com
http://AMERICAblog.blogspot.com/2005/02/man-called-jeff.html
http://www.AndrewSullivan
http://atrios.blogspot.com
http://www.DailyKos.com
http://www.DearMary.com
http://www.Gay.com
http://www.GLAAD.org
http://www.PlanetOut.com
http://Rittenhouse.blogspot.com
http://www.StopDrLaura.com
http://www.wiredstrategies.com/mcveigh.htm
http://www.wiredstrategies.com/shepardx.html

JOHN ARAVOSIS

INTERNET PROVIDERS, GAY

The growth in the 1990s of web portals as access points to the Internet included sites that targeted gay users. The two largest of these were Gay.com and PlanetOut.com who, by 2001, were each claiming over one million members. Both sites raised levels of venture capital unprecedented for gay businesses due to a combination of traffic figures, **pink dollar** rhetoric and the cited advantages of the Internet for reaching gay consumers. In 2000 the companies merged to become PlanetOut Partners, Inc., with both sites continuing to provide news, advice, consumer opportunities, chat facilities and a rapidly expanding personals service. The PlanetOut Partners' sites are not the only gay portals, and other sites offer alternative facilities. However such is the size of the PlanetOut Partners' market share that a number of gay commentators question the political desirability of their quasi-monopoly status as online providers of gay information and interaction.

ANITA BRADY

INTERSEX

Intersex is an umbrella term used to describe a variety of anomalies within an individual's chromosomes, genitals or internal reproductive organs. Intersex infants unsettle the narrowly inscribed gender roles of boy/girl and are therefore labelled 'psychosocial emergencies' by the medical world. Immediate gender reassignment surger(ies) are routinely encouraged by doctors *treating* intersexuality. Intersex activists argue that the real crisis lies with the manner in which infants and their parents are stigmatized and traumatized by the shame and pathologies attached to the intersex body. Informed support is offered by organizations such as the Intersex Society of New Zealand and the Intersex Society of North America.

KELLIE BURNS

INTERSEX TRUST AOTEAROA NEW ZEALAND (ITANZ)

ITANZ was founded in 1997 by Mani Bruce Mitchell. It is a non-profit charitable trust that provides education, advocacy and liaison services to intersexuals, their families and friends. Through its work, ITANZ challenges the binarized system of sexual identity that requires each person to be recognizable as male or female, and the consequent designation of **intersex** as an abnormality that can be cured through medical intervention.

ANITA BRADY

IRIGARAY, LUCE

b. 1930

philosopher

One of the most influential contemporary French feminist philosophers, Luce Irigaray is an interdisciplinary thinker whose work ranges from philosophy, through psycho-analysis to linguistics. Among her most important works, translated into many languages, is *Speculum de l'autre femme* (*Speculum of the Other Woman*, 1974), an acute critical study of the way in which Western thought, impregnated with phallogocentrism, cannot accept sexual difference and the existence of a different female subjectivity. In the work that is most interesting for lesbian culture, *Ce sexe qui n'en est pas un* (*This Sex Which Is Not One*, 1977), Irigaray challenges the cultural image of the female body as a commodity of exchange. Effectively, if the body has meaning and expresses meaning because it is solid and evident like the male organ (the reference is to Lacan's phallus), then the woman's body and the sexuality-language of women is something that is subtracted from the masculinist economy of quantity and space. The body of the woman is fluid, however, and not invisible or empty, as masculinist discourse would have it. Instead, the body of the woman is composed of another matter that cannot be represented within patriarchal culture. This body highlights the unsaid of an original erotic female economy, which is expressed in the dialogue

and contact of the lips – hence, the metaphor for sex and language, the site of the creation of relation, of pleasure and of expression, and of female and different meaning.

MONIA ANDREANI

ISHERWOOD, CHRISTOPHER

b. 1904; d. 1986

writer

Born on 26 August 1904 in Cheshire, England, Isherwood is the Anglo–American novelist whose frank and unapologetic writings about homosexuality made him a pioneer of the gay liberation movement. He was educated at Cambridge University, and with his friend and lover W.H. **Auden** and Stephen Spender, became a rising star of the 1930s English literary scene. His stories *Goodbye To Berlin* (1939), based on his three-year residence in that city, provided a vivid portrait of the sexual decadence of 1930s Germany. In 1939 he emigrated to the United States, settling in Los Angeles, where he began writing screenplays and converted to Hinduism. His novels *The Memorial* (1932), *The Last of Mr Norris* (1935), *The World in the Evening* (1954) and *A Single Man* (1964) highlight the pain and loneliness of gay men living in a homophobic society and advocate greater acceptance of homosexuality. He wrote candidly about his sexuality in his autobiographies *Kathleen & Frank* (1971) and *Christopher and His Kind* (1976). His work received renewed attention with the musical *Cabaret* (1966, filmed by Bob Fosse in 1972), based on his Berlin stories. He died on 4 January 1986 in Los Angeles, California.

JOHN FORDE

ISINQUMO

Zulu-based argot that developed among gay African mine workers to conceal their homosexual desires and intentions from the majority non-gay men in South Africa who had sex with men.

MARC EPPRECHT

ISLAM

A monotheistic religion which believes that Mohammed conveyed the words of Allah in writing the Qu'ran, which details proper conduct for believers (Muslims). Without a central leadership figure, various interpretations of the Qu'ran co-exist, although homosexuality is explicitly referenced as sinful. The Qu'ran 4.16 defines 'liwat' (male homosexuality) as an aggravated form of adultery, which is punishable, but grants leniency if the participants repent and cease their behaviour. Dominant interpretations of the law order the execution or whipping of Muslim males engaged in same-sex relations.

JOHN FORDE

ISLAMIC WORLD, THE

Discussions of glbt culture, issues, identity and history in the Islamic world are so highly stigmatized as to constrain an accurate assessment of these phenomena. One reason for this dilemma is the ongoing Islamization and growth of Islamist movements that narrow the agenda for research and define topics considered illicit in Islam. Islamic legal and moral attitudes towards same-sex relations, the patriarchal social system and the residual strength of family and clan ties have discouraged openly practiced homosexuality and corresponding organizations. Moreover, the concept of sexual rights as human rights is not yet in place.

Islamic legal experts classify all individuals, even transgenders, as males or females based on set physical criteria. Islamic law penalizes homosexual acts with some variations according to madhhab (legal schools of Islamic law). Most contemporary states have adopted civil laws strongly influenced by Western codes but Islamic law remains paramount in countries such as Saudi Arabia, or where reinstated, as in Iran. Under Islamic law, all sexual acts except those in a contracted marriage are illicit. The crime of zina (fornication and adultery) includes homosexual acts. But since the parentage of children is not at issue, violations can be ignored or excused under jurists' claims of 'doubt'. Socially, homosexuality is also tolerated, with some exceptions. In Oman the presence of a large number of homosexuals who could have been stigmatized as male prostitutes was instead considered a reasonable outlet for male sexual urges.

Qu'ranic condemnation of homosexuality is found in surah VII: 80–1, a reference to Lot, and in surah XXVI: 165–6 and IV: 16, which imply the natural condition of heterosexuality, yet mention no specific punishments. Various hadith, a secondary source of Islamic law, refer to the Prophet's abhorrence of homosexual acts. Medieval literary texts mention lesbians and homosexuals and suggest that women and men resorted to same-sex acts to avoid pregnancy and/or parental responsibilities (Musallem, 1983). Literary and historical sources also describe traditions of pederasty or homoeroticism along with bisexuality. As long as men eventually married and fathered children, their other proclivities did not actually constitute an alternate sexual identity. Yet there was another variety of person, referred to as a mukhannath (comparable to the modern Omani khanith), who were considered unlike 'normal men' because they continued to prefer the passive homosexual role even as adults; such individuals were regarded as a third sex. The ideals of courtly love that glorified unrequited and unconsummated love during the medieval period may also have been a factor. Most modern casual observers still attribute homosexual behaviour to the socially imposed separation of the sexes.

310

Nineteenth-century laws restricted public female performers and encouraged males or boys in what were called *khawal* performances or in dramatic or dance troupes. An argot specific to homosexuals related to the secret language of entertainers is still employed in Egypt. A tradition of male–female transvestism and homosexuality existed in Turkish dance, classical vocal music and later in TV and film dramas. Disapproval of transvestism is indicated in four Prophetic *hadith* – one of which states: 'Cursed are those men who wear women's clothing and those women who wear men's clothing'. Nevertheless, a female transvestite tradition in Iraq, as well as various historic 'warrior women' and the interesting 'sworn virgins' of the Balkans, have been documented along with other transvestite traditions in Ottoman-controlled lands.

A world-class singer, the late Zeki Muren was accustomed to appearing on stage in women's clothing. Bulent Ersoy, a highly admired vocalist, underwent transgender surgery and was therefore banned from certain performances in Turkey. Dana **International** is another transsexual performer. Muslims have received variant official opinions on transsexual surgery. Modern laws in the region either treat homosexuality as an offence against society and public morality while not explicitly forbidding it for adults, or classify it as a crime with set penalties. In the Islamic Republic of Iran, sodomy has been categorized as a *qisas* crime, the secondary category of offenses, punishable by death, or if confessed less than four times, by flogging. Lesbianism is punishable by 100 lashes under Article 129 of the Islamic Penal Code and a lesbian act is vaguely defined as two unrelated women who 'stand naked under one cover without necessity' (Vahme-Sabz 2000). In Turkey, homosexuality falls under 'indecency and offenses against public morality', covered by Articles 419, 547 and 576; transsexuals are defined and regulated in law also. In Iraq, until 2003, homosexuality between consenting adults was not penalized, only acts with minors. In Syria, sodomy with males, females or animals may be punishable with a one year prison sentence. In Morocco, the penal code punishes same-sex acts with a prison sentence of between six months and three years with an additional fine. It should be mentioned that Morocco and Tunisia attract a substantial gay tourist trade that has increased the exploitation of all parties. In Algeria, the family law code as well as the penal code carries a sentence for homosexual acts. Bahrain's strict punishments of sodomy derived from the Indian penal code and were revised in 1956 to include corporal punishment and imprisonment for up to ten years.

Police brutality is an issue for male homosexuals in the region. In Egypt 52 men were arrested on 11 May 2001 on the Queen houseboat/nightclub moored on the Nile bank of the island of Zamalak. They were held and put on trial on charges of 'obscene behaviour' with 'contempt for religion' by the Emergency State Security Court for Misdemeanors. The charge of obscene behaviour allows for a sentence from three months to three years, while 'contempt for religion' falls under Article 98(f) of the Penal Code and carries a prison sentence from six months to five years. Only two of the defendants faced the second crime, and 23 were sentenced. Increased gay Internet activities and the Islamist impact on public attitudes concerning homosexuality and Western influence probably led to this incident. Egyptian authorities rebuffed communications from gay rights and human rights organizations on behalf of the plaintiffs.

Judges in Saudi Arabia may issue their own interpretations or follow the guidelines of the Judicial Board influenced by the Hanbali jurist, al-Maqdisi (d. 1033/1624), who wrote that sodomy must be punished as fornication. There are numerous reports of beheadings, including those in July 2000 of three Yemeni men found guilty of homosexual acts and molesting young boys and Saudi men. They were executed in Abha in the same month. As elsewhere in the Gulf, foreign nationals have been accused of homosexuality. Locals argue that homosexuality is often tolerated but that certain severe or serious cases are pursued.

Homosexuals were targeted in Iran after the Islamic Revolution in 1979 and by the Taliban, even though homosexuality was present in the *madrasas* (religious schools) of Pakistan from which the Taliban emerged and the Afghani refugee camps. Elsewhere, some lesbians and gay men have been killed in honour crimes, or experienced beatings by family members; they lack legal protection from such assaults.

Gays frequent certain locations in larger Middle Eastern cities, and organizations and web sites have been established to protect their rights or enhance networking, although more of these exist in expatriate communities. Many gay groups operate clandestinely because homosexuality – as an identity – is construed as a Western import, or even a Zionist plot. Figures such as Irshad Manji, a Canadian-Muslim lesbian progressive have come under strong attack.

The isolation and individual limitations that gays experience may be even more significant than legal restrictions. HIV infection and AIDS is increasing in Muslim countries. Medical authorities assert that inaccurate statistics, treatment policies that restrict care to married individuals or those accompanied by their parents, and reliance on 'Islamic medicine' (in Pakistan, for example) are specific local conditions to be faced.

Bibliography

Musallem, B.F. (1983) *Sex and Society in Islam: Birth Control before the Nineteenth Century*, Cambridge: Cambridge University Press.

Vahme-Sabz (2000) 'Violence Against Lesbians in Iran', in Pinar Ilkkaracan (ed.) *Women and Sexuality in Muslim Societies*, Istanbul: WWHR/KIHP.

Further reading

Bellamy, James (1979) 'Sex and Society in Islamic Popular Literature', in Afaf Lutfi al-Sayyid Marsot (ed.) *Society and the Sexes in Medieval Islam*, Malibu: Undena.

Duran, Khalid (1993) 'Homosexuality and Islam', in Arlene Swidler (ed.) *Homosexuality and World Religions*, Valley Forge: Trinity Press International.

Ilkkaracan, Pinar (ed.) (2000) *Women and Sexuality in Muslim Societies*, Istanbul: WWHR/KIHP.

Menicucci, Garay (1998) 'Unlocking the Arab Celluloid Closet Homosexuality in Egyptian Film', *MERIP* (Spring), posted at: http://www.merip.org/mer/mer206/egyfilm.htm

Murray, Stephen O. and Roscoe, William (1997) *Islamic Homosexualities: Culture, History, and Literature*, New York: New York University Press.

Sanders, Paula (1991) 'Gendering the Ungendered Body: Hermaphrodites in Medieval Islamic Law', in Nikki R. Keddie and Beth Baron (eds) *Women in Middle Eastern History*, New Haven and London: Yale University Press.

Schmitt, Arno and Sofer, Jehoeda (eds) (1992) *Sexuality and Eroticism Among Males in Moslem Societies*, New York, London and Norwood, Australia: Haworth Press.

Stokes, Martin (2003) 'The Tearful Public Sphere: Turkey's Sun of Art, Zeki Muren', in Tullia Magrini (ed.) *Music and Gender: Perspectives from the Mediterranean*, Chicago: University of Chicago Press.

Swedenburg, Ted (1997) 'Saida Sultan/Dana International: Transgender Pop and the Polysemiotics of Sex, Nation, and Ethnicity on the Israeli–Egyptian Border', *Musical Quarterly* 81, 1: 81–108.

Unni Wikan (1993) *Behind the Veil in Arabia: Women in Oman*, Chicago: University of Chicago Press.

Zuhur, Sherifa (2004) *Criminal Law, Women and Sexuality in the Islamic World*, Istanbul: WWHR/KIHP.

ANONYMOUS

ISRAEL, FILMMAKING

Until the mid-1960s, most Israeli films glorified the heroic Sabra (native Israeli) male body inspired by Hollywood westerns and war films. Such a figure represented a stronger, healthier and more hetero-masculine individual than the Jew of the diaspora. A homoerotic subtext emerged, however, including images of the shapely muscles of Zionist farmers, builders, soldiers and their male bonding and close friendships. In contrast, the Palestinian (Arab) body, whether female or male, evoked both anxiety and passion among Jewish characters, as shown in Alexander Ford's *Sabra* (1933) and in later radical films such as Dan Volman's *Hide and Seek* (1980), the tragic love story of a handsome Jewish teacher and his Arab male lover in Jerusalem during the 1940s; Daniel Wachsman's *Eastern Wind* (1982), in which the Jewish farmer secretly lusts after his Arab male worker; and Amos Guttman's film *Afflicted* (1983), in which the male protagonist is penetrated by a Palestinian fugitive.

The popular *Bourekas* melodramas and comedies of the 1970s and 1980s included negative gay images such as Ze'ev Revah's *Hairstylist for Women* (1984), which features twins of Jewish-Moroccan origin (both acted by the director): Victor is a toilet cleaner who lives in a poor neighbourhood, while Michel is a successful hairstylist ridiculed as a sissy for deviating from his 'authentic' oriental masculinity. In contrast, Israeli political films have challenged traditional masculinities. Judd Ne'eman's *Paratroopers* (1977), for example, portrays a company of recruits who mistreat their weak comrade until he commits suicide.

During the late 1970s Guttman made his first gay films. In 1983 Ron Assulin's *Another Shadow*, about coming out, was banned by Israeli Television. Significantly, in 1986 Ayelet Menahemi directed *Crows*, depicting a group of marginalized gay youth, and Nirit Yaron-Grunich made *Big Girl* about two female high school students. The New Israeli Queer Cinema first appeared, however, in the 1990s with the films of Eytan **Fox** and other young filmmakers. Erez Laufer's *Don't Cry For Me Edinburgh* (1996), for example, documented

an Israeli gay show at the Edinburgh Festival. David Levy's *Blocks* (1997) told the story of a boy who desired his male neighbour, and was winner of the Second Jerusalem Gay & Lesbian Film Festival in 2000. Ran Kotzer has made several documentaries, including: *Positive Story* (1996), *Amos Guttman, Filmmaker* (1997), *The Gay Games* (1999) and *Cause of Death: Homophobia* (2003). Tomer Heymann's popular film *Tomer ve'ha'srutim* (*It Kinda Scares Me*, 2001) recounts his coming out to rough kids for whom he was a counsellor, while Ronit Fox and Tamar Barkai's *Yellow Peppers* (2001) documents a developing romance of lesbian owners of a Jerusalem soup restaurant.

More recently, Itzik Cohen and Jonathan Koniak presented the camp TV sitcom *Mommy Queerest – Johnny* (2002–3). Cohen, a former member of the drag group Pessia's Daughters, and Koniak, who has played gay characters in several TV series, created an anarchistic and carnivalesque comedy based on Doris, a flamboyant drama queen of Jewish-Iraqi origins, and her gay son Johnny. Although this prime-time sitcom is based on ethnic, ageist, gender and sexual stereotypes, it consistently confronts homophobia and celebrates the semi-naked male body, focusing on Yakov, Johhny's muscular boyfriend.

GILAD PADVA

ISRAEL, LITERATURE

In her 2004 essay, 'Dancing on the Needle's Edge: Gay Lingo in an Israeli Disco', Liora Moriel surveys slang in the work of several gay Israeli poets and notes that although such poets initially borrowed urbane and contemporary American slang to convey the degree to which traditional Jewish culture and the Hebrew language failed to accommodate the realities of gay life, they have gradually returned to Hebrew, investing gender-related diction with gay-related meanings. Moreover, in '*Inniut* and *Kooliut*: Trends in Israeli Narrative Literature, 1995–1999', Miri Kubovy argues that once the survival of the Israeli state was no longer so desperately at issue, there was room culturally for a literature that offered alternatives to the 'supremacy of the white patriarchy, heroism, and machismo' (2000: 252).

A gay landmark in Tel Aviv, Café Theo, is a combination bookshop and coffee shop. Named in honour of Theo Meints, a long-time leading voice in the Israeli gay community, the café is owned by Ilan Sheinfeld, who founded the first gay Hebrew publishing firm, Shufra for Fine Literature, Ltd. The café hosts poetry readings, stage shows and art exhibits by gay Israelis and is popular with residents and tourists, despite recurring legal difficulties created by some in its neighbourhood who would like to see it closed. The publishing company is responsible for such titles as *The Dyke and the Dibbuk* by Allen Galford, *Dream Boy* by Jim Grimsley, *AKA* by Ruthann Robson and *The Joy of Gay Sex* by Charles Silverstein.

Café Theo has provided a venue to promote the work of many young gay writers. Both a poet and a photographer, Yossi Berg wrote *The Life Theater*, a collection of poems published under the pseudonym Zipore Dror, which is Hebrew for 'free bird'. To promote his poetry collection, he created 'poetry cards' which pair photographs and artwork with excerpts from the poems. Other gay poets associated with Café Theo have include Zvi Mermelstein and Rafi Vanzani. A lesbian poet who uses the pen name Shez has focused on issues related to child abuse and lesbian relationships.

Rauda Morcos has emerged as a singular figure in contemporary Israeli literature. A lesbian Palestinian poet, she emphasizes a connection between the Israeli oppression of both gays and Palestinians, but she is critical of the Israeli gay rights movement for largely ignoring that connection.

Earlier gay and politically radical, the American poet and translator Robert Friend emigrated to Israeli when the House Un-American Activities Committee seemed ready to revoke his passport.

But, of late, by far the most notorious gay Israeli poet has been Golan Cipel, who was identified as the secret lover of New Jersey governor James E. McGreevey. The men met when McGreevey visited Israel, and he arranged for Cipel to emigrate to the United States, subsequently naming him his 'homeland security adviser'. The extra-marital affair came to public notice after McGreevey contacted law enforcement, claiming that Cipel had tried to extort millions of dollars from him by threatening to sue him for sexual harassment.

Gradually, gay issues have entered the mainstream of contemporary Israeli fiction. Ronit Matalon's *Bliss* (2003) contains two stories told in alternating chapters and linked by a single character, Ofra, an Israeli woman who witnesses the ruination of two Jewish families, one in Israel and the other in France. Ofra travels to France to attend the memorial services for a cousin, a good-natured young man named Michel who, much to his family's distress, was gay and had contracted AIDS. Michel's father, who is Ofra's uncle, is a survivor of the concentration camps who has ostensibly made his peace with the past, building a successful career with the German airline Lufthansa. But the memories that continue to haunt him become a corollary to his attitudes towards his son's homosexuality, attitudes which he can no longer avoid confronting. As the family prepares for the memorial services, simply making the arrangements requires admissions and compromises: as requested, Michel's remains have been cremated following his death, and his father has some difficulty locating a rabbi who will conduct the services without a corpse present.

Benny Ziffer has written two metafictional postmodern novels in which he appears both as author-narrator and as a distinct character – in fact, as several distinct characters, both male and female. These novels, *Ziffer and His Kind* and *The Literary Editor's Progress* (2005), range freely and even wildly in their settings, subjects, moods and themes. They offer a view of gay life in Israel that manages to be both local and cosmopolitan.

Gay issues have been addressed also in contemporary Israeli drama. *Salam Shalom* (2003), a work by a playwright who goes simply by the name Saleem, treats the sorts of issues that Rauda Morcos would like to see more widely addressed. Focusing on the relationship between a gay Israeli and a gay Palestinian, the play explores through the microcosm of the strains on their relationship the linkages between the Israeli marginalizations of its Palestinian and gay populations.

The title of the play *1 Ahad Ha'am* (2003) derives from a Jewish politician who achieved prominence during the period preceding Israeli statehood and whose name has become one of the most common street names in Israeli towns and cities. The action of the play takes place in an apartment building along such a street, and through the residents, a broad range of aspects of contemporary Jewish life are pointedly satirized, including gay life and culture. Two elderly women, who turn out to be men in drag, discuss the sexual peccadilloes of prominent politicians, most of whom are now long retired or dead.

A transgendered playwright, Ronnie Almog is the author of *Somewhere in Between* (2003), a play about a very feminine Israeli young woman who gradually confronts her secret desire to be a man – to become a female-to-male transgender individual. Initially staged in Tel Aviv, the play has been staged in other venues throughout Israel.

Several notable novels written by non-Israelis have featured gay Israeli characters. American novelist Melvin Jules Bukiet has written extensively about Israeli issues. His

Strange Fire (2001) is a contemporary thriller with serious intentions. The novel's protagonist, Nathan Kazakov, is a speechwriter for the Israeli prime minister who loses much of one ear to an assassin's bullet intended for his boss. A Russian emigré, Kazakov is also blind and gay. As he tries to unravel the conspiracy behind the shooting, he confronts many of the paradoxical tensions that lie just under the surface of contemporary Israeli life. Bukiet's postmodern millennial novel, *Signs and Wonders* (1999), has been described by reviewer Elizabeth Hand (1999) as a cross between Salman Rushdie's *The Satanic Verses* and Stanley Kubrick's *Dr Strangelove*, an apt comparison given its anarchic density and its wildly ironic verve.

Alice Bloch's *The Law of Return* (1983) focuses on an American woman who travels to Israel and comes to a deeper understanding of both her Jewishness and her lesbianism. An American novelist who spent much of her formative years in Israel and has family still living there, Judith Frank is a lesbian who has addressed gender issues in Israel in her novel *Crybaby Butch* (2004). She is currently working on a second novel, *Noah's Ark* (2005), which has a similar thematic focus.

In the essay collection *Journeys and Arrivals: On Being Gay and Jewish* (1995), the novelist Lev Raphael includes pieces on representations of gay Jews in Holocaust literature ('Empty Memory? Gays in Holocaust Literature') and on being gay in contemporary Israel ('Letter from Israel, I' and 'Letter from Israel, II').

Bibliography

Kubovy, Miri (2000) '*Innuit* and *Kooliut*: Trends in Israeli Narrative Literature, 1995–1999', *Israel Studies* 5, 1(Spring): 244–65.

Hand, Elizabeth (1999) 'The Fire This Time', a review of *Signs and Wonders*, *Washington Post Book World*, 28 March, p. 4.

Moriel, Liora (2004) 'Dancing on the Needle's Edge: Gay Lingo in an Israeli Disco', in

William Leap and Tom Boellstorff (eds) *Speaking in Queer Tongues: Globalization and Gay Language*, Urbana: University of Illinois Press.

Further reading

Eder, Richard (2003) 'Occupational Hazards', a review of Ronit Matalon's *Bliss*, *The New York Times Book Review*, 10 August, p. 5.

Fischel, Marion (2003) 'New Local Satire Bites', *Jerusalem Post*, 22 August, p. 16.

MARTIN KICH

ISVARA

Formed in 1994 by Julian Chan, a chairman of the Ten Percent Club, Isvara (Zi Zai She) is the first gay Buddhist organization in Hong Kong. Its aim is to enhance communication between gay and non-gay Buddhists. The word '*zi zai*', both in Sanskrit and Chinese, means freedom and comfort. The group has been inactive since the late 1990s.

TRAVIS KONG

ITALY, FILMMAKING

Any analysis of the relationship between homosexuality and cinema in Italy must first distinguish between films made *for* gays and lesbians, as opposed to films made *by* gays and lesbians. From the 1960s onwards films intended for a gay audience have been quite conspicuous. The same cannot be said, however, of gay Italian filmmakers. Therefore, for the most part, this entry focuses on films made for gay audiences, on gay-themed subjects.

The presence of homosexuality in Italian cinematic imagery dates to the end of the 1940s, often marked by homophobic representation. The characters, for example, of the Nazi lesbian and paedophile educator whom Roberto Rossellini portrayed in *Roma città aperta* (*Open City*, 1945)

and *Germania Anno Zero* (*Germany Year Zero*, 1948), respectively, are key early representations of homosexuality in Italian film. A decade later, Federico Fellini's *La dolce vita* (The Sweet Life) presented a young, effeminate man and two transvestites, partly subverting the sullen tones of neo-realism with a more palatable, yet perverse, vision of the homosexual experience.

Beginning in the 1960s, gays and lesbians were visible in Italian film, if generally in subordinate roles and subsidiary functions. A key work during this time is the documentary *Comizi d'amore* (*Love Meetings*, 1964), in which Pier Paolo **Pasolini** asks people from different classes and cultures, from the poet Giuseppe Ungaretti to a southern Italian farmer, their thoughts on the topics of sex and love. Homosexuality is discussed, as are the role and status of women, divorce and prostitution. The interviews overall make it clear that Italian society at the time was generally conservative and conformist. Additionally, representations of gay men were seen in Franco Rossi's 'Scandaloso' (Outrageous), a segment of *Altà infedeltà* (*High Infidelity*, 1963), and in Marcello Fondato's *Certo, certissimo, anzi...probabile* (*Certain, very certain, as a matter of fact... probable*, 1969). Both of these films are comedies, comedy allowing the first honest portrayal of gay characters, especially as they are seen as a potential threat to heterosexual relationships. Comedies reached wide audiences, thus exposing more people to representations of homosexuality.

Often, homosexuals found themselves destined for sombre locales and tragic plots. *La commare secca* (*The Grim Reaper*, 1962), Bernardo Bertolucci's debut, and Franco Brusati's *Il disordine* (*Disorder*), are two telling examples where homosexuality is rendered as dark, pathetic and deviant. Curiously, suburban spaces and bourgeois sensibility provided the forum for diverse representations of homosexuality. In such portrayals, homosexuals were rendered part of the cinematic landscape, provided they kept to their social fringes. Despite a few cases, which included Helmut Berger exhausting the Nazi–fascist model of homosexuality in *La caduta degli dei* (*The Damned*, 1969) by Luchino **Visconti**, a more complicated picture emerged in Italian cinema around images of homosexuality.

Part of the reason for this is that during the 1960s an increase in literary adaptations dealt with issues of homosexuality. Among the most compelling works were Damiano Damiani's *L'isola di Arturo* (*Arturo's Island*, 1962), from Elsa Morante's homonymous work, and Fellini's very loose version of Petronius' *Satyricon* (1969). In 1967, a rather unusual contribution to Italian gay film was found in Paolo and Vittorio Taviani's *Sovversivi* (*The Subversives*). The movie pointed to the ideological crisis suffered by a group of militant communists. The film supplemented the fictional narrative with documentary material; importantly, it marked the first attempt in Italian cinema to discuss homosexuality within a political context through the subplot of a lesbian in love with the wife of a party official.

The presence of lesbians had been rare in Italian film. At the end of the 1960s, however, the lesbian became a *leitmotif* of soft-core pornography. Focusing exclusively on lesbian sex and on a calculated trade of morbidities, this popular genre increased greatly in popularity. Actually, its long apogee, lasting throughout the 1970s, restored, in some measure, the traditional homophobic conception of the homosexual as deviant. This trope of deviancy was promptly extended to other genres, such as the thriller, through images of gay and lesbian psychopaths.

During the 1970s a noticeable change took place with respect to the past and in regard to the breadth of representation and centrality of gay and lesbian characters in film. This is not to say the 'negative' representation of homosexuals disappeared:

although films began to centre around gay characters, works such as Bertolucci's *Il conformista* (*The Conformist*, 1970) and Brusati's *Dimenticare Venezia* (*To forget Venice*, 1979), continued to portray a deviant image of homosexuality.

Bertolucci's work, along with Ettore Scola's *Una giornata particolare* (*A Special Day*, 1977), occupies an important place in the canon of gay filmmaking. Both are set in fascist Italy during the Second World War. Although their portrayal of characters is different and certainly more complex than in earlier Italian cinema, both films condemn the fascist regime. The link, however, between homosexuality and fascism resonates throughout, especially in *The Conformist*. Another film that exhibits complex homosexual characters, is Salvatore Piscicelli's *Immacolata e Concetta* (*Immacolata and Concetta: The Other Jealousy*, 1979), about a lesbian affair in working-class southern Italy.

A famous and scandalous Italian film-maker-poet, Pasolini's works such as *Trilogia della Vita* (Trilogy of Life, 1971–4) and *Salò o Le 120 giornate di Sodoma* (*Salò: 120 Days of Sodom*, 1975) confront sexuality and its confines of bourgeois culture, particularly following the Second World War. Films such as *Teorema* (*Theorem*, 1968) and *Salò*, drawn from de Sade's novel *Les 120 journées de Sodome*, confront sexuality within the context of restrictive bourgeois culture. Another adaptation, Salvatore Samperi's *Ernesto* (Ernest, 1979), from the work by poet Umberto Saba, is notable for its tender and erotic portrayal of homosexuality.

Adaptations of biographies that deal with queer sexualities include the sumptuous *Ludwig* (1973), Visconti's portrayal of Ludwig II of Bavaria, and Liliana Cavani's *Al di là del bene e del male* (*Beyond Good and Evil*, 1977), which looks at the life of Nietzsche (see **Cavani**, Liliana). Both films featured a psychological and historical depth of characters not seen until then in Italian cinema.

During the 1980s independent film-makers employed a number of diverse approaches to homosexuality in film, to the point where any single trend is difficult to distinguish. Indeed, by that time homosexuality had been increasingly assimilated into mainstream Italian culture. *Quartetto Basileus* (*Basileus Quartet*, 1982) and *Il sapore del grano* (*The Taste of Corn*, 1986), for example, explore homosexuality through the filter of more character-driven narratives that place less of a burden on the 'homosexual' as a marginalized deviant.

The first occasion of the Turin International Gay and Lesbian Film Festival, in 1986, was marked by a general tendency towards the new and original, both as a channel for foreign productions and as a record of experimentation. In this context, even a theme such as transgenderism was considered far less taboo than it once had been. Marco Risi's *Mery per sempre* (*Forever Mary*, 1989), for example, is about Mary, a young transgender held in a juvenile jail. The film contains a scene showing a kiss between Mary and the jail's teacher. One might argue that contemporary gay filmmaking finds its best results when it follows the tendencies displayed during the 1980s, when a homosexual self-awareness, devoid of hypocrisy and stereotype, flourished.

The genre of comedy also embraced this more complex tendency. In the ten years that separate Duccio Camerini's *Nottataccia* (*What A Night!*, 1992) from Cristina Comencini's *Il più bel giorno della mia vita* (*The Best Day Of My Life*, 2002), titles embracing and reflecting the glbtq community have increased in number and quality. In a different area, Marco Tullio Giordana's film based on Pasolini's murder, *Pasolini. Un delitto italiano* (*Pasolini, An Italian Crime*, 1995), and Matteo Garrone's *L'imbalsamatore* (*The Taxidermist*, 2001), incorporated fiction with vibrant aspects of the historical real.

Among filmmakers in the 2000s, Pappi Corsicato and Ferzan **Özpetek**, the latter Turkish by birth, are two of the few directors whose works deal directly with homosexuality as a rich and varied topic. Öztepek is particularly interested in complicated questions about modernity, nation and homosexuality. Although not the first filmmakers to address homosexuality (Visconti, Cavani, Piscicelli, for instance, preceded them), these two have succeeded in defining a personal style that, appreciated by the critics and crowned by important awards, is slowly but increasingly exerting its influence within Italian filmmaking.

Further reading

Bertelli, P. (2002) *Cinegay. L'omosessualità nella lanterna magica*, Rome: Croce.
Da Sodoma a Hollywood (1996), Catalogo, XI Festival Internazionale di Film con Tematiche Omosessuali, Turin, 15–21 April 1996, pp. 197–232 (with English translation).

GIACOMO CESARETTI

ITALY, LITERATURE

For some time in Italy, active homosexual writers have not portrayed gay-related stories in their works. Nonetheless, if one reads their works one can note a predisposition towards 'feminizing' situations and persons that are part of behavioural dynamics typical of gays in their times. Such is the case in Aldo Palazzeschi's (1885–1974) novel *Sorelle Materassi* (The Materassi Sisters, 1934) which deals with female characters who have been interpreted by critics in a manner suggesting that they were actually gay males. Other examples include: Giovanni Comisso (1895–1969), whose works *Mio sodalizio con De Pisis* (My Bond with De Pisis, 1954) and *Le mie stagioni* (My Seasons, 1960) pay particular attention to the notion of manly beauty; Umberto Saba (1883–1957), whose works are charged with homoerotic desire, most notably *Ernesto* (Ernest, 1953), a book published only in 1975 lest the homosexuality of the author should become public knowledge; and Sandro Penna (1906–76), writing in verse an explicit panegyric to homosexual love. All of Penna's works, such as *Tutte le poesie* (Complete Collection of Poems, 1979), are still considered today icons of the Italian gay community.

Explicit representation of homosexuality, without moralizing elements, can be found in the narrative works of Piero Santi (b. 1912–89). Santi's novels have perhaps suffered negative commercial consequences due to the coming out of the author himself, effected with the autobiographical work *Diario* (Diary, 1950), republished in 1969 as *La sfida dei giorni* (The Challenge of the Days). The moralizing elements not present in Santi's work can be found in those of Carlo Coccioli (1920–2003), who tried to reconcile religious faith and homosexuality, as can be seen in his first novel *Il migliore e l'ultimo* (The Best and the Last, 1946), in which the protagonist is a gay Italian partisan. Seeking also to reconcile traditional morality and homosexuality was Giovanni Testori (1923–93), in whose work concepts such as torment and sacrilege play a role. Allusions to gay love in his works are frequent but remain nonetheless marginal (often embodied in an obscure character). Worthy of mention is his most explicit theatrical work, *L'Arialda* (1960).

Giuseppe Patroni Griffi (1921), renowned director of film and stage, has portrayed love in a daring manner, as in *Scende giù per Toledo* (Coming Down from Toledo, 1975). More traditional romantic elements are present in his work as well, such as the quintessential cult novel of the Italian gay community, *La morte della bellezza* (The Death of Beauty, 1987).

Regarded as an anti-clerical Catholic, Furio Monicelli's 1929 novel *Il gesuita perfetto* (The Perfect Jesuit, 1929) clearly defines his ideology, but it is perhaps with the works of Pier Paolo **Pasolini** (1922–75) that Italian gay social and political ideolo-

gies found their maximum expression. Through cinema, media, poetry, essays and narrative, Pasolini displayed an immense genius which has led him to be considered by many as the greatest Italian intellectual of postwar times. It is mainly as a result of his work that the many socio-cultural interpretations of the 1950s and 1960s emerged. His homosexuality became the interpretative key of the future reality of a nation in its full social development. He died a victim of prejudice, murdered by one or more of the boys whom he used to see during the nights. Of fundamental importance are his first neo-realistic novel *Ragazzi di vita* (Boys from Real Life, 1955), his essays in *Scritti corsari* (Pirate Essays, 1975), for their absolutely modern socio-political position, and the theatrical work *Affabulazione* (1979).

The unscrupulous elitism of some authors of the 1960s is personified in Alberto Arbasino (b. 1930). Nostalgic for a world he perceived as lost, Arbasino broke the stylistic and formal boundaries of writing with *L'anonimo lombardo* (The Anonymous Lombard, 1959) and *Super Eliogabalo* (1969).

The post-1968 sexual liberation gave birth to a group of young talents who had the courage to write about homosexuality with pride, if not ostentation. Texts by Dario Bellezza (1944–96), *Lettere da Sodoma* (Letters from Sodom, 1972) and *Il carnefice* (The Executioner, 1973), are exemplary of this new-found liberation.

Continuing this tradition, and seeking to further debunk contemporary mores, was Mario Mieli (1952–68) – queer, base, visionary, vice-laden – who in his *Elementi di critica omosessuale* (Elements of Homosexual Critique, 1977) gave voice to the social and political activism of the glbtq community. The same period saw the birth of the grand narrative experience of Pier Vittorio Tondelli, mainly through the works *Altri libertini* (Other Libertines, 1980), wildly written and stylistically innovative, and *Camere separate* (Separate Rooms,

1989), which set a milestone in Italy for its recognition of gay couples.

A laudable historical contribution is provided by Massimo Consoli (b. 1945), with his collection of poems *Viva l'omo-sessualità* (Viva Homosexuality, 1976) and several historical essays, including *Homo-caust – il nazismo e la persecuzione degli omosessuali* ('Homocaust' – Nazism and the Persecution of Homosexuals, 1991). The anthology *Amicizia amorosa* (Loving Friendship, 1980), edited by the poet Antonio Veneziani (b. 1952), presented the poems of the greatest Italian homosexual authors, while his contemporary Riccardo Reim (b. 1953), a stage director, published *Lettere libertine* (Libertine Letters, 1982).

In recent times the new generation of gay writers has been laying the foundation for an authentic gay literature in Italy. The unique formal syllogistic prowess of Aldo Busi (b. 1948) is notable, both for its craft as well as for the fact that – along with Paso-lini, Testori and Tondelli – it did not escape the ire of the censor. His works *Sodomie in corpo 11* (Sodomies in Body 11, 1988) and *Seminario sulla gioventù* (Seminar on Youth, 1984) are remembered as two realistic and unscrupulous masterpieces of the turn-of-the-millennium literary scene.

Contemporary authors continue to be beacons in Italian gay literature: Alessandro Golinelli (b. 1963), symbol of the cynicism and rejection of traditional morality of contemporary youth, as is portrayed in the novel *Basta che paghino* (As Long as They Pay, 1992); Matteo B. Bianchi (b. 1967), whose *Generations of Love* (1999) is a novel high in symbolic value for gay Italian youth; Mario Fortunato (b. 1958), who always includes homosexual characters in his novels, as in *Luoghi naturali* (Natural Environments, 1988); Gianni Farinetti (b. 1953), whose novels also include gay char-acters, albeit portrayed in a more elitist vein; Stefano Benaglia (b. 1965), whose works seek to portray gay characters in

realistic and accessible ways, living with the struggles and transgressions of daily life in familial, work and urban settings, as in *Uccelli di pineta* (Pine-Wood Birds, 2003); Walter Siti (b. 1947), who, with his *Scuola di nudo* (School for Nudism, 1994) and *Un dolore normale* (A Normal Pain, 1999), strives to portray homosexual love in a more ordinary manner; and Gianni Vat-timo (b. 1936), internationally acclaimed philosopher and essayist, whose political contributions have been significant.

The development of publishing houses which are openly glbtq (Edizioni Libreria Croce, Zoe, Il Dito e la Luna, Playground) in Rome, Milan and other cities, is a testimony that gay literature can now take its rightful place in the world of Italian literature.

FABIO CROCE

ITO, SATORU
b. 1953
activist, writer

Satoru Ito is a gay activist, educator and writer who came to prominence in 1991 with a book describing his coming-out story and the difficulties of setting up a household as a same-sex couple in Japan. Despite sympathetic press reports, Ito and his partner were also lampooned in the media as Japan's most visible 'gay couple'. Ito went on to write several more books (two of which have been translated into English) and has become one of the most prominent spokespersons for Japan's gay community. However, he has been criti-cized by some for relying too much on Western models of gay identity and activism and for criticizing those from Japan's queer community who identify with indigenous transgender models that he feels are discriminatory. In 2000 he became embroiled in a very public dis-agreement over this issue with veteran campaigner Ken **Togo** which led to a debate in the Japanese media over identity categories.

See also: Coming-out novels

MARK MCLELLAND

IWASZKIEWICZ, JAROSLAW

b. 1894; d. 1980

poet, writer

The Polish poet, novelist and short-story writer, Jaroslaw Iwaszkiewicz, was born into an aristocratic family. As a young man he fell perfectly into the role of the dashing, artistic dandy. He began his career as a poet and continued to work in this area all his life. His early poetry was stylish and ironic, while his more mature work was marked by a great sensitivity to colour and nature. Despite his lifelong attachment to poetry, his reputation as one of Poland's most important twentieth-century writers rests on his prose work. Several of his novels and short stories continue to be among the most popular in Poland, and quite a few of them have served as the basis for successful films by such directors as Andrzej Wajda and Jerzy Kawalerowicz. Iwaszkiewicz also wrote for the theatre, most notably the libretto for the opera *King Roger*, set to music by his cousin, the composer Karol Szymanowski.

DANIEL HENDRICKSON

IZZARD, EDDIE

b. 1962

actor, comedian

Born in Yemen, but raised in Northern Ireland and Wales, Eddie Izzard has emerged as one of Britain's most original comedy entertainers. Referred to as 'the funniest man in England' by John Cleese, 'male lesbian' Izzard officially 'came out' as a transvestite during his early twenties, a factor which was successfully incorporated into his stand-up comedy act in the 1990s with little negative public response. He has since gone on to accumulate a number of prestigious comedy awards for his work in both the UK and North America, and made his West End acting debut in the world premiere of David Mamet's play *The Cryptogram* in 1994. More recently, Izzard made his first big screen appearances in period crime drama *The Secret Agent* (1996) and ultra-camp box office flop *The Avengers* (1998), before receiving critical acclaim for his role as sexually ambiguous manager Jerry Devine in Todd Haynes' glam rock homage *Velvet Goldmine* (1998). In 2003 he made his Broadway debut in *A Day in the Death of Joe Egg*, for which he was nominated for a Tony Award. He is currently working on a forthcoming autobiographical documentary with the working title of *Diva 51*.

ROBIN GRIFFITHS

J

JACOBI, DEREK

b. 1938

actor

One of Britain's most highly respected actors, Jacobi has developed a distinguished stage career alongside leading roles in experimental gay cinema. He began acting at Cambridge University and trained with the Birmingham Repertory Company. He is best known for his leading role as the eponymous Roman emperor in the TV series *I, Claudius* (1976). Although reluctant to discuss his personal life or his sexuality, Jacobi has tackled a number of gay stage and screen roles. He played gay mathematician Alan Turing in TV drama *Breaking the Code* (1996) and gave a career-best performance as tormented gay painter Francis **Bacon** in the film *Love Is the Devil* (1998), an unflinching examination of Bacon's sadomasochistic relationship with George Dyer. He had an amusing cameo as a gay dilettante in *Up At The Villa* (2000) and provided narration for *The Diaries of Vaslav Nijinksy* (2001).

JOHN FORDE

JACOBS, MARC

b. 1963

fashion designer

Jacobs' designs, which pair retro-inspired prints with contemporary cuts and edgy accessories, place him at the forefront of American fashion. Born on 9 April 1963 in New York City, after graduating from Parson's School of Design, he debuted his Marc Jacobs label in 1986. In 1989 his mentor Perry **Ellis** appointed him vice-president of his womenswear label. In 1992 Jacobs launched his now trademark grunge design look, sending models down the catwalk wearing floral dresses and army boots, but he lost his post at Perry Ellis after disappointing sales. He relaunched his label in 1994 with the support of supermodels Linda Evangelista and Naomi Campbell, later developing mens- and womenswear lines, shoes, handbags and fragrances. In 1997 he developed Louis Vuitton's first ready-to-wear line and was later appointed artistic director for the label.

JOHN FORDE

JAGGER, MICK AND THE ROLLING STONES

b. 1943

rock singer and group

Mick Jagger is the lead singer of the rock group the Rolling Stones, one of the most popular and influential bands in the history of rock 'n' roll. He was born Michael Philip Jagger on 26 July 1943 in Dartford, England, and he and his childhood friend, guitarist Keith Richards, formed the group in 1960, merging rock 'n' roll and blues influences to create a popular and endlessly imitated style. Their first self-titled album (in 1964) was followed by two no. 1 hits, 'The Last Time' and '(I Can't Get No) Satisfaction' (1965). By the late 1960s, the Stones rivalled The Beatles as the world's most popular rock band, going on to produce some of rock's most enduring albums, including *Beggar's Banquet* (1968), *Let It Bleed* (1969) and *Exile On Main Street* (1972), with hit songs including 'Let's Spend The Night Together', 'Sympathy For the Devil', 'Honky Tonk Woman' and 'Hot Stuff'. Jagger's androgynous, flirtatiously sexual stage persona, celebrity girlfriends (Bianca Jagger, Marianne Faithfull, Jerry Hall) and playboy lifestyle added much to the band's popular appeal. Rumours about Jagger's bisexuality were intensified by David Bowie's ex-wife Angela, who claimed to have found the two in bed together. After an acrimonious split with Richards, Jagger launched a solo career with the successful album *She's The Boss* (1985), but they reunited to record *Steel Wheels* (1989), *Voodoo Lounge* (1994) and *Bridges to Babylon* (1997). Jagger continues to release solo albums and has made a second career in film, with roles in *Performance* (1970), *Ned Kelly* (1970) and as a transvestite cabaret singer in *Bent* (1997).

JOHN FORDE

JAPAN, FILMMAKING

Tokyo and other major cities in Japan have enjoyed large and successful queer film and video festivals since 1992 and, unlike similar festivals in Western cities, they appeal to a more general audience. When invited to the first such event in Tokyo, lesbian critic Sarah Schulman (1994) was surprised to find it staged in a major department store with audiences made up of housewives. Indeed, Western movies with queer (particularly gay male) themes and characters have long proven popular with Japanese viewers. The 1980 release of *Cruising* (dir. William **Friedkin**), for instance, sparked widespread media coverage of the American 'hard gay' scene and resulted in a penchant for leatherwear and chains in Tokyo's nightclubs. Other queer hits in Japan have included *La Cage aux Folles* (dir. Edouard Molinaro), *Another Country* (dir. Marek Kanievska) and *Maurice* (Merchant-Ivory productions).

It is not only foreign films with a queer touch that have proven popular in Japan but many indigenous products also entertain queer themes and characters or are susceptible to queer readings. Unlike Western queer media, which tend to be produced by or targeted at self-defining queer communities, queer content is less segregated in Japanese media and can crop up in unexpected places, even in programmes aimed at children, particularly **anime** (animation). The popular children's series *Ranma 1/2*, for instance, features a hero(ine) who changes sex when exposed to water and *Sailor Moon*, a series aimed at young girls, includes heroines with lesbian interests (although these scenes were edited out when the series was broadcast on US television). Japanese kids' programmes contain scenarios unthinkable in the US context – as when the precociously self-aware Shin Chan encounters a transvestite in a public toilet in the *Crayon Shin Chan* movie. Such scenes are possible because, unlike societies in the West, where male homosexuality (in particular) was constructed as morally reprehensible by the church and as criminal and deviant by lawmakers and the state, Japan has largely ignored private homosexual practice and has accorded transvestism an honourable place in the entertainment industry (McLelland 2005).

Like many East Asian nations, Japan has had a long tradition of male transvestite performance and the 'actresses' who appeared in Japan's first homemade feature films prior to 1920 were actually *onnagata*, that is, female-role specialists from the all-male kabuki theatre. Actors in Japan's early cinema continued to appear somewhat feminine, especially those known as *nimaime*, a term deriving from kabuki and meaning secondary or subsidiary star. The most famous of these early stars was Hasegawa Kazuo (1908–84), who played the role of an *onnagata* in the film *An Actor's Revenge* (dir. Kon Ichikawa), originally screened in 1935 and later remade in 1962. Other more recent movies which have featured transvestite stars include the 1968 *Black Lizard* (dir. Kinji Fukusaku), starring Japan's premier transgender diva Miwa Akihiro, and the 1968 *Funeral Parade of Roses* (Toshio Matsumoto), a vehicle for emerging transgender star 'Peter'. Transgender actors have continued to appear in Japanese film, most notably the original 'newhalf' (a term designating an intermediate sex) star Rumiko Matsubara, who was featured in the 1981 movie *In the Storehouse* (dir. Seishi Yokomizu). However, unlike other regional film cultures, such as Hong Kong, Japan did not develop a tradition of portraying transvestite productions on screen, although the all-woman *Takarazuka* review has produced film versions of its most famous stage musicals, which are sometimes shown on television and satellite channels.

Films containing clearly identifiable 'gay' characters date from the early 1990s, when Japanese popular culture underwent a 'gay boom'. At this time mainstream, particularly women's, media were saturated with reports about gay men (less so lesbians) and both local and international gay culture. This led to a spate of movies starring gay male characters, including *Okoge* (Takehiro Nakajima, 1992), *Twinkle* (Joji Matsuoka, 1992) and *Hatachi no binetsu* (*A Touch of Fever*, Ryosuke **Hashiguchi**, 1993). Television, too, featured documentaries and dramas about gay life, including *Dosokai* (*Alumni Reunion*), a ten-part series featuring

the most graphic representations of male homosexual sex so far seen on Japanese television and anticipating the similarly graphic *Queer as Folk* by several years. Yet none of these productions challenged the status quo or set forth an agenda on gay rights; instead they reinscribed gay men in the family system by representing them as 'women's best friends and ideal partners' (McLelland, 2000). This theme has proven enduring. Ryosuke Hashiguchi's *Hush* (2001), for instance, describing a ménage à trois between a gay couple and an isolated young woman who wants them to father her child, was a major critical success in Japan.

Directors whose work features queer themes are often not queer-identified themselves. Nagisa Oshima, for instance, who is best known in the West for his graphic depiction of heterosexual obsession in *Ai No Corrida* (*In the Realm of the Senses*, 1976), has also explored homosexual desire in *Merry Christmas Mr. Lawrence* (1982) and *Taboo* (1999). Japan does, however, have numerous queer-identified directors such as Hiroyuki **Oki**, whose work is screened in art-house cinemas and at queer film festivals both domestically and abroad. Oki's best-known work is the 1994 short film *I Like You. I Like You Very Much*. However, despite the popularity of movies by foreign gay directors such as Derek **Jarman**, Japanese films featuring queer characters and scenarios tend not to emphasize social critique. This is largely because of Japanese society's more muted homophobia – politicians and religious and cultural authorities tend not to launch media campaigns against sexual minorities, homosexual acts are not illegal and there is technically no age for consent for male or female same-sex acts. Hence the obvious inequalities that much Western queer cinema seeks to highlight and challenge are not such pressing concerns for Japanese gay men and lesbians. In this environment, where homosexuality and other queer forms of sex and gender expression are not seen as a threat, it is possible for seemingly queer characters and scenarios to be enjoyed by a more general public.

See also: Hong Kong, filmmaking

Bibliography

McLelland, Mark (2000) *Male Homosexuality in Modern Japan: Cultural Myths and Social Realities*, Richmond, Surrey: Curzon Press.
—— (2005) *Queer Japan from the Pacific War to the Internet Age*, Boulder: Rowman & Littlefield.
Schulman, Sarah (1994) *My American History: Lesbian and Gay Life during the Reagan and Bush Years*, London: Cassell.

MARK MCLELLAND

JAPAN, LITERATURE

Both before and during the Pacific War, Japanese primary schools were segregated by gender. In this environment, passionate, even homoerotic, relationships were not uncommon, and not surprisingly numerous contemporary authors wrote about same-sex relationships. *Shōnen* (Adolescents, 1948–52) by the Nobel Prize-winning novelist Kawabata Yasunari and the humorous *Nanshoku monogatari* (A Tale of Male Love, 1952) by Tachibana Sotō are two examples of semi-autobiographical novels that draw inspiration from the authors' own crushes on attractive male classmates. Fukunaga Takehiko's best-selling novel *Kusa no hana* (Flowers Among the Grass, 1954), which is set before and during the war, describes schoolboy desire as a prelude to adult heterosexuality, but it also suggests that schoolboy relationships are as emotionally intense as those between men and women. Meanwhile, in the 1950s, Inagaki Taruho, a modernist writer who had experienced boyish adolescent desire before the war, began writing non-fictional monographs, including *A-kankaku to V-kankaku* (The Anal Feeling and the Vaginal Feeling, 1954) and *Shōnen'ai no bigaku* (The Aesthetics of the Love of Young Men, 1958), which describe the metaphysical ramifications of the love of beautiful boys.

The next few decades saw the emergence of a generation of writers who wrote boldly about male homoerotic desire. Their works often depict male homoeroticism in terms of a rebellion against social strictures, a quest for new moral directions or an attempt to overcome solitary existence. Playing a central role was Mishima Yukio, who published several works about same-sex desire, including *Kamen no kokuhaku* (*Confessions of a Mask*, 1949), about a boy's discovery of his erotic interest in suffering and dying men, *Kinjiki* (*Forbidden Colors*, 1951) and *Nikutai no gakkō* (The School of the Flesh, 1963), both of which depict men who frequent the underground world of gay bars but who also engage in relationships with women. Another member of Mishima's circle was Takahashi Mutsuo, who often describes men trying to overcome their solitude through orgiastic homoerotic activity. Many of his early works, including the long poem *Homeuta* (*Ode*, 1971), the novella *Seisho densetsu* (Legend of a Holy Place, 1972) and the novel *Zen no henreki* (*Zen's Pilgrimage*, 1974), blur the boundaries between pornography and high literature by using the rhetoric of religion to describe sexual activity. Similarly, *Niku no hasami* (Scissors of the Flesh, 1966) and *Ochi yo shōnen* (Fall, Young Men!, 1974) by the poet Aizawa Keizōō explore the psychology of longing and the relationship between self and other during the sexual act. Several early works by Nobel Prize winner Ōe Kenzaburō, including *Shiiku* (*Prize Stock*, 1958) and *Seiteki ningen* (Homo sexualis, 1963) depict experiments with male homoeroticism as a means of overcoming perceived social difference or as a way to reinvigorate dull lives.

The early 1970s saw the publication of numerous novels about the lives of queer men and the gay districts of Tokyo, including Shinjuku Ni-chōme, the site of many gay bars and cruising spots. Some of these novels emerged – either in fact or in style – from Japan's many glossy semi-pornographic magazines. Minami Shinji's *Otoko no jojōshi* (A Lyric Poem of Man, 1972), Mamiya Hiroshi's *Shinjuku no bishō-nen-tachi* (The Beautiful Young Boys of Shinjuku, 1975) and Ichinose Naoyuki's *Gei bōi* (Gay Boy, 1974) are but a few such examples.

Japan's so-called 'gay boom' of the late 1980s and early 1990s saw the publication of numerous novels, many of which describe queer life in realistic terms. Novels such as Nishino Kōji's *Shinjuku Ni-chōme de kimi ni attara* (If I Met You in Shinjuku Ni-chōme, 1993) and *Tisshu* (Tissue, 1995) describe the protagonists' searches for sexual and romantic encounters in the gay bars of Tokyo. Written in a breezy style similar to that of an entertainment magazine, both describe characters looking for love within a world where one-night stands prevail. Mishima Yukio's paramour, Fukushima Jirō, has written two novels – *Chō no katami* (The Butterfly's Keepsake, 1998) and *Basu-taoru* (Bath Towel, 1996) – but he remains better known for a non-fictional tell-all, *Mishima Yukio: Ken to kankō* (Mishima Yukio: Swords and Winter Red, 1998), about his liaison with the well-known writer. (Immediately after its publication, the Mishima estate successfully sued to have the book withdrawn from circulation.)

The last decade has seen several important films on gay themes turned into novels and vice versa. Nakajima Takehiro's *Okoge* (Fag Hag, 1992), Ekuni Kaori's *Kirakira hikaru* (*Twinkle Twinkle*, 1991) and Hashi-guchi's *Shōsetsu hasshu!* (Hush!, 2002), all deal with being gay and single in a society that demands marriage of all citizens. Each work depicts a new kind of family in which the principal female character serves as an asexual partner to her gay husband or friends.

Recent years have seen the publication of numerous novels about men who exist on the margins of gay society. *Hatachi no binetsu* (*A Touch of Fever*, 1993) by Ryosuke Hashiguchi and the award-winning *Yes Yes Yes* (1989) by Hiruma Hisao both depict young hustlers in Tokyo. The former concerns a desultory college student who, while hustling, develops feelings for a fellow hustler. The latter describes the inner reflections of the protagonist as a variety of customers purchase his services. Fujino Chiya's *Natsu no yakusoku* (A Promise for Summer, 2000) won the Akutagawa Prize, Japan's most coveted literary award, for a simple, readable work about two overweight gay men and their transgendered friend. Fushimi Noriaki's *Majo no musuko* (The Witch's Son, 2004), winner of the Bungei Literary Award, is the story of a middle-aged man living with his mother as he struggles to overcome his depressive inertia and find romance in a world of deadly viruses and terrorist acts. While engaging in occasional trysts in bathhouses and sex clubs, he becomes attracted to someone quite unlike himself and finally opts to pursue a relationship.

Before the Second World War, several important female writers, including Hiratsuka Raichō, Yoshiya Nobuko, Tamura Toshiko, Osaki Midori, wrote about 'passionate sisterhood' between schoolgirls and socially progressive women. The last few decades have seen a resurgence of interest in their work, prompting several works about them and their circle, including *Nyonin Yoshiya Nobuko* (Yoshiya Nobuko, The Woman, 1982) by Yoshitake Teruko and *Yuriko dasuvidānya* (Dasvidanya, Yuriko, 1990) by Sawabe Hitomi.

In the postwar period, several prominent male authors wrote important works about love between women, including 'Kajitsu' (Fruit, 1950) by Mishima Yukio, *Nureta kokoro* (*Damp Heart*, 1958) by Takigawa Kyō, *Utsukushisa to kanashimi to* (*Beauty and Sadness*, 1961) by Kawabata Yasunari and *Supuutoniku no koibito* (*Sputnik Sweetheart*,

1999) by Murakami Haruki. However, until the last decade or so, little writing by women about female–female desire has achieved equal prominence. Notable exceptions include *Warui natsu* (The Bad Summer, 1970) and 'Kōkan' (Fraternization, 1989) by Kurahashi Yumiko and *Kari no jikoku* (Hunting Time, 1970) by the popular mystery novelist Togawa Masako.

Matsumura Rieko is one of the most prominent female writers to emerge in recent years. Her novel *Sebasuchan* (Sebastian, 1981) and the collection of novellas *Nachuraru ūan* (Natural Woman, 1987) explore the complicated dynamics of power in lesbian relationships. Her surreal novel *Oyayubi P no shugyō jidai* (My Period of Education with a Penis as a Toe, 1991–93) tells of a woman whose toe mysteriously turns into a phallus, prompting her friends to question her gender identity and causing her to rethink established categories of gender and sexual identification as well as the entire notion of phallocentrism.

Further reading

Kakinuma, E. and Kurihara, C. (eds) (1993) *Tanbi shōsetsu gei bungaku bukkugaido*, Tokyo: Byakuya Shobō.

Miller, Stephen D. (ed.) (1996) *Partings at Dawn: An Anthology of Japanese Gay Literature*, San Francisco: Gay Sunshine Press.

JEFFREY ANGLES
STEPHEN D. MILLER

JAPANESE TRANSGENDER PERFORMERS

Japan has a long tradition of transgender entertainment. In the Tokugawa period (1600–1867), the all-male kabuki theatre featured *onnagata*, professional female-role players who acted as women on stage. During the Taisho period (1912–26), an all-female revue known as the Takarazuka was founded in which *otokoyaku*, or male-role players, proved a sensation with fans – both remain popular today.

After the Second World War, new kinds of transgender entertainment began to emerge. During the 1950s effeminate male singers known as 'sister boys', and later as 'gay boys', broke into the mainstream. The most famous of these was Miwa Akihiro, whose 1957 hit single 'Meke Meke' led to a 'gay boom' in Japan. Unlike Western societies at this time, homosexuality was not illegal in Japan, and numerous 'gay bars' provided floorshows catering to a straight clientele sprung up in major cities all over the country – reports about them were featured in entertainment magazines.

The early 1960s saw a further boom in transgender entertainment, with the tour of Japan by the French transsexual cabaret Le **Carrousel de Paris**, which included singers such as Carrousel Maki who underwent sex reassignment surgery. Because the stigma of homosexuality was considerably less severe in Japan than in most Western societies, the transition from the bar world to mainstream entertainer proved easy for many.

The 1980s saw a boom in the popularity of boy bands managed by 'Johnny' Kitagawa. Known as 'Johnnies', groups such as Hikaru Genji and later, SMAP, were made up of extremely beautiful, often effeminate youths who were nevertheless extremely popular with women.

During the 1990s transgender performance took on a new twist with the emergence of 'Japanese image bands', where the 'image' of the performers was an important part of their act. Like the 'Johnnies' these bands were made up of beautiful young men, but they went one step further and frequently cross-dressed. Shazna guitarist Izam passed so well as a woman that for a time he was used in Shiseido cosmetics advertisements, whereas Gakt of Malice Mizer is more androgynous. Probably the most famous image-band member of all was Hide of X-Japan. His death by suicide in 1997 was greeted with scenes of mass hysteria not witnessed at the passing of a music star since the war. While the earlier generation of transgender performers was closely associated with the homosexual bar world, the image bands maintain heterosexual lifestyles (in public at least), sometimes referring to Buddhist ideas of rebirth when explaining their transgender leanings.

MARK MCLELLAND

JARMAN, DEREK

b. 1942; d. 1994

filmmaker

Avant-garde British filmmaker Derek Jarman was trained in the fine arts; his work is characterized more by the use of striking imagery and sound than by character development or narrative drive. Jarman studied at the Slade School of Art in London and brought to his films a painterly regard for composition and colour. This is obvious in all his work but is particularly notable in *Caravaggio* (1986), in which he recreates as tableaux several works by the Renaissance painter, and in *Blue* (1993), which bears witness to his admiration for Yves Klein (who created pieces in the powerful International Klein Blue).

Jarman continued to paint and exhibit during his film career. After the Slade Jarman worked as a costume and set designer for ballet, opera and film. It was while working for Ken **Russell** on *The Devils* (1971) and *Savage Messiah* (1972) that Jarman began experimenting with film. He admired the work of Kenneth Anger, Bruce Baillie and Stan Brakhage among others. Common elements in Jarman's films are violence, homoeroticism, aspects of gay representation and nostalgia for a lost innocence/England. He was fascinated by both history and contemporary culture, producing works that are revisionist and often joyfully anachronistic. His *Jubilee* (1977), in which Elizabeth I visits an anarchic future England, is a classic of the punk era. *The Tempest* (1979) meanders between rich beauty and high camp. His interest in

suppressed gay history is most evident in the films *Sebastiane* (1975), *Caravaggio, Edward II* (1991) and *Wittgenstein* (1993). *The Garden* (1990) parallels Christ's torments with those of a persecuted pair of gay lovers.

From the making of *Caravaggio* until his death, Jarman enjoyed a fruitful working relationship with the actor Tilda **Swinton**. In the 1990s Jarman became deeply involved in queer and AIDS issues. His experience of having AIDS is incorporated into his work, especially *The Garden* and *Blue*. Towards the end of his life Jarman, who had always loved gardens, created an unusual and much-imitated one at his cottage in Dungeness in southeast England. He died of AIDS in 1994.

CHANTAL STOUGHTON

JARUS-HAKAK, TAL AND AVITAL

Jarus-Hakak, Tal

b. 1958

activist

Jarus-Hakak, Avital

b. 1960

activist

This lesbian couple were active in CLAF (Community of Lesbian Feminists) since its founding in 1988. Tal, who was among CLAF's founders, served on its board for many years, while Avital was its first paid coordinator. Together, they founded *Claf Hazak*, Israel's first lesbian feminist magazine; Tal also founded a lesbian theatre group. Both were active in many lesbian and feminist activities in Israel. In 1996 Tal sued the Israeli Ministry of Health against its regulations that required non-married women to undergo a psychiatric evaluation before receiving a sperm donation. Following this, the Ministry cancelled this discriminatory practice. A lesbian baby boom thus followed, and the Jarus-Hakaks became the leaders of the battle for recognition of lesbian parenthood and second-parent adoption. In 2005 they won a landmark case in the Israeli Supreme Court which ruled that second-parent adoption is in principal possible under Israel's adoption law. In 1998 Tal was awarded the Felipa de Souza Award from the IGLHRC (International Gay and Lesbian Human Rights Commission) for recognition of her achievements for lesbian rights in Israel. Tal is a lecturer in occupational therapy, and was also part of the Israeli delegation to the **Gay Games** in 1998; Avital is an epidemiologist. Together they have raised three children. They formally changed their family name by combining their respective previous family names.

AEYAL GROSS

JOBRIATH

b. 1946; d. 1983

musician

Jobriath, a glam-era rock musician, was born Bruce Campbell in Pennsylvania. After a stint in the army, he moved to California, creating the name 'Jobriath' from 'Job' and 'Goliath'. He played the part of Woof in the Aquarius Theatre production of 'Hair', then joined the rock band Pidgeon. Pidgeon's album artwork won a Grammy Award, but Jobriath's gender-neutral presentation did not sell so Decca dropped the band.

During the 1970s Jerry Brandt signed Jobriath to Elektra. In 1973 Elektra mounted an unprecedented publicity push to promote Jobriath, the first openly gay rock performer. In press interviews Jobriath stated that he was 'a true fairy'.

The debut single, 'Jobriath', received positive reviews, but the label's initial investment ran out. Six months later 'Creatures Of The Street' was released to unenthusiastic reviews. Jobriath and The Creatures started on their only tour. Half-way through, Elektra dropped the band, leaving them to finish without support. Despite a positive audience reaction, the group disbanded.

Jobriath retired from music and lived in the Chelsea Hotel in New York City until his death in 1983 from an AIDS-related illness.

See also: Glam rock

LYNETTE REINI-GRANDELL
VENUS

JOHANNESBURG

Johannesburg is South Africa's largest city and a microcosm of the nation. Lesbians and gays have been part of the fabric of the city since its establishment as a mining camp in 1886. Johannesburg was a racially segregated city until apartheid was dismantled during the early 1990s. While there have been dramatic changes since then, the city's lesbians and gays remain largely divided along race and class lines. However, well-developed social networks exist and there are many gay public spaces.

ANTHONY MANION

JOHN, ELTON

b. 1947

pop singer

Born Reginald Kenneth Dwight in Pinner, Middlesex, England, Elton John is one of most successful pop stars and one of the richest men in Great Britain. He first entered into the limelight in 1970, with the first in a series of million-selling albums. He then reached superstar status thanks to his outrageous performances – camp extravaganzas accompanied by an unparalleled set of over-the-top wardrobe items and accessories and a huge collection of hats, shoes and glasses. John also appeared as the Pinball Wizard in Ken Russell's film *Tommy*.

During the 1980s his controversial image and extreme visibility made him a favourite target of the tabloid press, which made allegations about his private life that his marriage in 1984 could not silence. Elton John resorted to lawsuits, and to openly confessing his bisexual practices, drug addiction and anxieties about baldness and weight.

His memorable performance at the funeral of gay icon Princess Diana in 1997 completed the picture of a drag superqueen turned living legend.

FABIO CLETO

JOHNS, JASPER

b. 1930

artist

Jasper Johns' artistic career began in the early 1950s, in large part through the prompting of artist Robert **Rauschenberg**, his lover and studio mate for six years (1955–61). Johns is best known for paintings of ready-made images and symbols such as the American flag, maps of the USA, targets and stencilled numbers and letters, most of which include coded references to gay subject matter, including allusions to earlier American gay poets, writers and artists (i.e. Frank **O'Hara**, Walt **Whitman**). Many of his early works allude to his relationship with Rauschenberg (i.e., *Target with Plaster Casts*), including its commemoration following their break-up. Johns' work parodied the rhetoric of mid-century abstract painting in America and its emphasis on masculinity, as in his 1961, *Painting with Two Balls*. Johns' work is increasingly recognized as an important moment in the history of emergent gay-identified art practices.

JOHN PAUL RICCO

JOHNSON, MAGIC

b. 1959

basketball player, AIDS activist

Born in Lansing, Michigan, Earvin Johnson Jr was nicknamed 'Magic' because of the extreme grace with which he moved on the basketball court. He is considered one of the greatest basketball players of all time. During his 13-year career, all of which was spent with the Los Angeles Lakers, he was a member of five championship teams. He was a twelve-time All-Star and a nine-time member of the All-National Basketball Association First Team. Before the 1991–2 season, however, Johnson stunned the world with the announcement that he had tested positive for the HIV virus. His proclamation and defensiveness about his heterosexuality advanced the discourse that AIDS was not only a homosexual disease. Following his announcement, he won a gold medal as part of the United States Olympic Basketball Team. He continued to play and coach with the Lakers for several years after his announcement and has been an active AIDS activist ever since.

ERIC ANDERSON

JONES, BILL T. AND ARNIE ZANE

Jones, Bill T.

b. 1952

dancer, choreographer

Zane, Arnie

b. 1948; d. 1988

dancer, choreographer

Bill T. Jones met Arnie Zane, a Bronx native of Italian-Jewish ancestry, while they were both attending Binghamton University in 1971. The romantic and artistic union formed by these men from disparate backgrounds (Jones is African-American and was born in upstate New York) was central to the 1982 founding of a multicultural troupe, the Bill T. Jones/Arnie Zane Dance Company.

Throughout the 1970s they performed as an openly gay couple, but it was this new company's inaugural work, *Intuitive Momentum* (1982), that first drew widespread attention. Direct engagement with issues such as racism, gay love, sex and AIDS, along with the use of dance and theatrical traditions, a sure visual sense, various media, a collaborative process and dancers of diverse physical appearances, are all hallmarks of the company's work. *Still/Here* (1994) characteristically relied on collaboration, in this case, with participants from the Survival Workshops.

The resulting focus on health, illness and dying brought a refusal from critic Arlene Croce to review or even to see work. Such reactions have not stopped the troupe from earning many awards however, and Jones himself has won a MacArthur Fellowship and a designation as one of America's Irreplaceable Dance Treasures. He has also been commissioned to create dances across the United States and Europe, while the troupe's collaborators include such figures as the writer Toni Morrison, the singer Jesse Norman, the painter Keith Haring and the fashion designer Willi Smith.

Zane is best known for his work with, and continuing influence on, the troupe. However he has also published (posthumously) a book, *The Photography of Arnie Zane* (MIT Press, 1999).

GABRIEL GOMEZ

JONES, GRACE

b. 1948

singer

Starting as a cover model for *Vogue* and *Elle* during the early 1970s, Jamaican-born Grace Jones developed a hard-edged excess in body image, fashion and performance that has resonated among gay males since the disco and new wave eras. As a vocalist and stage performer, Jones was less androgynous than performatively hypermasculine. With chiselled, angular features, she combined sleek hardness with deep, resonant vocals, challenging gender-based codes in look and sound. Through her transformative rendering of

such male-authored erotic narratives as 'Love is the Drug' and 'Warm Leatherette' she emerged as a dominant and empowered entity unimpeded by traditional notions of gender. Jones' musical art is eclectic, reworking disco and new wave while experimenting with reggae, funk and jazz. She extended her gender-bending powers as an actor in such films as *Conan the Barbarian* (1981) and *A View to a Kill* (1985).

MICHAEL DEANGELIS

JOURNAL OF HOMOSEXUALITY

The *Journal of Homosexuality*, published by The Haworth Press, Inc., is a scholarly journal devoted to publishing academic research on homosexuality, sexual behaviour, gender roles and the social contexts of glbt and queer people. This journal serves an interdisciplinary academic audience. Articles are based in fields such as psychology, sociology, law, literature and philosophy. The journal's mission is to confront homophobia through the publication of sound research. The first issue was published in June 1974. It is a landmark journal because it was not until December 1973 that the American Psychiatric Association (APA) removed homosexuality from the Diagnostic and Statistical Manual of Mental Disorders.

The 46 published volumes, since that first issue, serve as an historical archive of the study of sexuality and sexual orientation in that latter half of the twentieth century and beyond. Topics range from the development of a sexual identity (during the 1970s), to the effects of stigma on gay people (during the 1980s), to the debate around paedophilia (during the 1990s), to embracing queer theory's impact on gay and lesbian psychology (during the 2000s), indicating the importance the editorial board places on the significance of the study of the lives of glbtq people.

Each issue is uniquely divided into three sections. The first contains articles organized around a particular theme related to sexual orientation or sexual behaviour. The second section provides a comprehensive review of important new books in the study of sexuality. The third section is an annotated bibliography.

KATHLEEN M. CUMISKEY

JUDAISM

All Jewish denominations have engaged in the examination of the Levitican injunction: 'You shall not lie with a man as one lies with a woman; it is an abomination [to'evah]... they shall be put to death and the fault is theirs alone' (18:22, 20:13). The more traditional branches (the Orthodox movements in Israel, the United States, and other countries) reject open homosexuality, except for its toleration as a disease that deserves compassion. However, in 1982 the Reform movement, the largest brand of American Judaism, declared the acceptance of gays and lesbians as full members, and, in 1990, declared the eligibility of gays and lesbians as candidates in its rabbinical school. The movement has also admitted several gay synagogues to membership.

The Conservative movement, almost as large as the Reform, has, since 1990, offered full and equal membership to individual gay and lesbian congregants, but has not yet openly admitted gay and lesbian candidates to its rabbinical school. The Reconstructionist movement (the smallest and least traditional) officially endorsed, in 1993, full membership of openly gay and lesbian congregants, rabbis and congregations.

MOSHE SHOKEID

JUDGE, MYCHAL

b. 1933; d. 2001

chaplain

Openly gay Catholic priest and former chaplain of the New York City Fire Department, who became the first recorded fatality following the 11 September 2001 terrorist attacks on the World Trade Center. Judge was born on 11 May 1933 in Brooklyn, New York. He joined the Franciscans in 1954 and was ordained a Catholic priest in 1961. He began working in Manhattan in 1986, devoting special attention to gay and lesbian people and AIDS patients, and worked as a chaplain for fire fighters from 1992 onwards. A long-time member of Dignity, a New York gay Catholic support group, Judge regularly participated in Gay Pride marches, and was out to his work colleagues, including Fire Commissioner Tom Von Essen. He died in the World Trade Center while giving assistance to a critically injured fire fighter. New York's Catholic community is currently campaigning for Father Judge's canonization as a saint.

JOHN FORDE

JULIAN AND SANDY

Characters on the BBC radio programme *Round the Horn*, played by Kenneth **Williams** and Hugh Paddick respectively. They are notable for being two gay characters in mass entertainment at a time when homosexuality was still illegal in the United Kingdom, and for their use of **Polari**, or palare, in the sketches, an underground gay language which allowed them to communicate a homosexual undertone to a largely unaware British public. The show was one of the most influential comedy programmes of the time and was transmitted in four series of weekly episodes from 1965 until 1968.

MICHAEL PINFOLD

JULIEN, ISAAC

b. 1960

film- and videomaker

Isaac Julien was born in London to parents from St Lucia. He studied painting and film at St Martin's School of Art, where he made his first film, *Who Killed Colin Roach?* (1983). The film, ostensibly a documentary about the suspicious death of a young black man, already indicates several of what would become Julien's trademark features, especially a resistance to objectivity and an investigation of the politics of representation. His next films were made with Sankofa, the black film and video collective which he co-founded.

He made his first gay-themed film in 1987, *This Is Not an AIDS Advertisement*. The film, shot in a music-video style, counters the anti-sex rhetoric of the period at the same time that it presents a more racially diversified picture of gay men.

In 1989 he made what is still perhaps his best-known film, *Looking for Langston*. The film is in part a celebration of the black American gay poet, Langston **Hughes**, and in part a joyful and seductive portrait of the black male body and black homosexuality. Hughes' estate refused permission to use any of the poet's texts in the film, which Julien turned to his advantage, giving the film a deliberately haunting quality of absence.

Julien's next film, *Young Soul Rebels* (1991), was a narrative feature about two black men, one gay and one straight, who run a soul radio station in London during the late 1970s. In 1993 Julien established a production company called Normal Films, along with singer Jimmy **Sommerville**, fellow filmmaker Steve McLean and producer Mark Nash. The company produced Julien's short films, *The Attendant* (1993) and *A Darker Side of Black* (1994).

Throughout his career, Julien has been attentive to contemporary theoretical concerns, writing texts alone and in collaboration with black academics such as Kobena **Mercer** and bell **hooks**. In 1996 he took the life of the seminal black theorist Frantz **Fanon** as the subject of a film, *Frantz Fanon: Black Skin, White Mask*. Once again, Julien mixes documentary and fictional styles to comment not only on Fanon's life and work, but also on the representational politics of our time.

Starting in the late 1990s Julien has increasingly worked with the format of gallery installation and split- and triptych-screens. In 2000 he collaborated with Venezuelan choreographer Javier de Frutos to create the installation *The Long Road to Mazatlán*. The video footage, shot in and around San Antonio, Texas, mixes the classic iconography of the American Old West with more contemporary and homo-erotic imagery, giving an unsettling quality to both. The free play with stereotypes serves to unlock their restrictive power, opening up a way to use stereotypes for pleasure.

DANIEL HENDRICKSON

K

KAKEFUDA, HIROKO

b. 1964

writer

Hiroko Kakefuda is a writer and intellectual who came to prominence in 1992 after the publication of her pioneering book '*Rezubian' de aru to iu koto* (*On Being* '*Lesbian*'). Prior to this, the term *rezubian* was associated with woman–woman scenes in male pornography; Kakefuda was instrumental in reclaiming the loanword as an identity category for same-sex desiring women. Also in 1992, she founded *Labrys*, an influential (albeit short-lived) lesbian community magazine. Kakefuda was very active as a spokeswoman for lesbian issues during the 'gay boom' of the early 1990s. However, since few other women followed her lead in coming out in front of the media, she soon tired of being the public face of lesbianism in Japan and stepped aside to take a more background role in lesbian and feminist activism. Nevertheless her book represents a milestone in Japanese lesbian visibility.

MARK MCLELLAND

KALIN, TOM

b. 1962

filmmaker

The film- and videomaker Tom Kalin was part of the New York AIDS activist art collective **Gran Fury** in the late 1980s. During this time he also made some of the better known AIDS activist videos. He went on to make the film *Swoon* (1992), which tells the story of Nathan Leopold and Richard Loeb, the lovers who had systematically and unemotionally killed a young boy. The true story had already been the subject of at least two films, most famously Alfred Hitchcock's *Rope* (1948). Kalin's version mixes period and contemporary details to comment not only on the story, but also on the then current debate in the gay community over the question of positive images of gays and lesbians.

DANIEL HENDRICKSON

KAMENY, FRANKLIN

b. 1925

activist

An indefatigable gay rights pioneer, New York-born Franklin Edward Kameny turned to activism after being fired for being gay by the Army Map Service where he was a civilian astronomer. He sued all the way to Supreme Court in the United States, which refused to hear his case in 1961. Since then he has fought to end the denial of security clearances to gay people (which gradually disappeared), the exclusion of gays from the civil service (which took until 1975) and against the ban on gays in the military – still contested in the United States.

In 1961 Kameny organized the **Mattachine Society** of Washington DC, and led the first gay protest at the White House in 1965. In 1968, he coined the slogan, 'Gay is Good' and founded the Gay Activists Alliance in Washington after his run as the first out candidate for Congress in 1971. He worked as a key player in the campaigns to remove homosexuality from the American Psychiatric Association's *Diagnostic and Statistical Manual of Mental Disorders* in 1973 and led a 30-year campaign to repeal Washington's sodomy law, finally prevailing in 1993. He was a co-founder of the National Gay Task Force and the National Gay Rights Lobby (later the **Human Rights Campaign (USA)**). Kameny was the first out appointee to the federal government, named Human Rights Commissioner in 1975.

See also: National Gay and Lesbian Task Force

ANDY HUMM

KAMPANIA PRZECIW HOMOPHOBII

Kampania Przeciw Homophobii (Campaign against Homophobia) has been one of Poland's major glbt organizations since 2001. Led by Robert Biedroń, an activist for SLD (Alliance of the Democratic Left), the campaign, which is not affiliated with any political party, fights stereotypes, prejudice and discrimination, pursuing tolerance and equality of rights for gays, lesbians and transsexuals. It operates through numerous public events (petitions, open letters, exhibitions, film and theatre festivals), legislative projects (institution of same-sex unions), conferences and seminars. In association with ILGA Europe and Lambda Warsaw (active since 1997), it compiles the yearly *Raport o Dyskryminacji* (Report on Discrimination) about the condition of Poland's glbt minority.

See also: International Lesbian and Gay Association (ILGA); Niech Nas Zobacza

ALESSANDRO AMENTA

KARMON, YONATAN

choreographer

During the 1940s – both before and after the foundation of the state of Israel in 1948 – a new phenomenon of Israeli folk dance became popular. This was not the traditional ancient folk dancing gleaned from Jewish (Chassidic or Yemenite) or Arabic indigenous sources. Rather, a new set of modern choreographers emerged who felt that the contemporary Jewish population needed a means of expression for festive and social occasions. One of the leading creators and stage directors of this new tradition was Yonatan Karmon, whose Lehakat Karmon company toured the world and made Israel folk dancing well known everywhere. His company offered a rare opportunity for queer dancers to perform as dancers, on a semi-professional basis, without having to fear discrimination.

GIORA MANOR

KAR-WAI, WONG

b. 1958

filmmaker

Hailed as a postmodern auteur, Wong Kar-wai is one of the best-known of the second New Wave Hong Kong filmmakers. Wong studied graphic design in the late 1970s and became involved in producing TV drama series in the 1980s. After establishing himself as a seasoned scriptwriter for television and films, Wong made his directorial debut with *Wong gok ka moon* (*As Tears Go By*, 1988), a film that marked the emergence of his unique visual style, which has provoked cult-like devotion from critics and fans alike ever since. Among his much-celebrated oeuvre, *Cheun gwong tsa sit* (*Happy Together*, 1997) stands out. The film features two displaced Hong Kong gay men living in Buenos Aires who are struggling to attend to their bruised relationship. Strictly speaking the film is not part of contemporary gay cinema since it ignores homosexuality in explicit social or ideological terms. The film premiered at the Cannes Film Festival where it garnered a Best Director Award for Wong.

CUI ZI'EN
YING ZHU

KAUFMAN, MOISÉS

playwright

A native of Venezuela, Moisés Kaufman is the founder of the Tectonic Theater Project based in New York City. A director, choreographer and playwright, Kaufman achieved notoriety as a member of the experimental theatre company Thespis. He became a force in international theatre with his play for Tectonic, *Gross Indecency: The Three Trials of Oscar Wilde* (1998). The play ran for more than 600 performances in New York and has been performed worldwide. Kaufman followed *Gross Indecency* with *The Laramie Project* (2001), a series of monologues based on the events surrounding the gay-bashing murder of Matthew **Shephard** in Laramie, Wyoming. The play was turned into a film for HBO, which he also directed. His most recently play, *I am My Own Wife* (2003), written by Douglas Wright, tells the story of Charlotte von Mahlsdorf, a German transvestite, as she lives under Nazi occupation. It won 2004 Tony Awards for Best Play and Best Actor, and 2004 Obie Awards for Performance, Direction and Set Design.

CHRIS BYRNE

KAY, JACKIE

b. 1961

writer

Kay grew up a black child adopted into a white Scottish family. Her race and sexu-

ality are integral to Kay's highly acclaimed poetry, fiction and drama, which are often concerned with those who must construct identities from the margins. For example, the 1998 novel *Trumpet* relates the story of a female black jazz trumpeter who lived as a man. Kay's poetry variously explores the problem of identity without clear provenance. *The Adoption Papers* (1992) prompts searching questions about roots, motherhood and loss, while *Other Lovers* (1993) and *Off Colour* (1998) both, although differently, explore being 'someone else'. For Kay, identity is neither rigid nor singular and, she has argued, categories such as gender and race merely protect our prejudices. Consequently, it is the fluidity and arbitrariness of identity as well as the possible reinvents of self in her work that are explored, even promoted.

KYM MARTINDALE

KEENAN, JOE

novelist, screenwriter

Openly gay American writer who achieved success as a comic novelist before pursuing a successful career as a film and TV script writer. His first novel, *Blue Heaven* (1988), a witty farce about gay New Yorkers embroiled in a marriage scam, attracted praise for its upbeat satire of gay nouveau-riche society. It was followed by *Putting on the Ritz* (1991), a similarly themed comedy about two struggling gay songwriters. He co-scripted the film *Sleep With Me* (1994), a romantic comedy in six sequences, including a comic discussion of the homoerotic subtext of the Tom Cruise film *Top Gun*. He was chief writer and executive producer of the multi Emmy-winning comedy *Frasier*, a spin-off of the Frasier Crane character from sitcom *Cheers*. He left after Series Seven but returned to co-script the 2004 season. He also co-scripted the short-lived TV series for CBS *Bram and Alice* (2002).

JOHN FORDE

KEESEY, PAM

b. 1964

writer

Novelist and editor who explores feminist and lesbian themes within the horror genre in cinema and literature. She is the editor of two anthologies on lesbian vampire fiction: *Daughters of Darkness* (1993), *Dark Angels: Lesbian Vampire Stories* (1995), the feminist werewolf anthology, *Women Who Run with the Werewolves* (1996), and (2000), co-edited with Forrest Acherman. She is the author of *Vamps: An Illustrated History of the Femme Fatale* (1997) and founded and edits Monsterzine.com, an online horror movie magazine.

JOHN FORDE

KELLENDONK, FRANS

b. 1951; d. 1990

novelist, essayist

Frans Kellendonk, alongside others such as Doeschka **Meijsing**, is one of the most important innovators of the Dutch novel from the 1980s. His oeuvre remains limited to four novels, a collection of stories and a number of essays, a consequence of his untimely death from AIDS at the age of 39. Inside as well as outside his fictional work, homosexuality is an uneasy theme. Kellendonk, himself a 'passionate homosexual' as one critic described him, showed a profound ambivalence to some expressions of the gay subculture and the political struggle for gay emancipation. His literary style, however, which can be characterized as highly ironical and non–realistic, renders it impossible to easily condemn his work as homophobic, as some literary critics did after the publication of what was to be his

last, most famous and most controversial novel *Mystiek Lichaam* (Mystical Body, 1986). This novel, a family saga, places in opposition the death-drive of a gay man, infected with a 'bizarre letter word', to the procreational powers of his heterosexual sister.

During the 1980s Kellendonk expressed a growing longing for 'the ideal of an organic society', which he saw as symbolized in the community of the Catholic Church. But, ambivalent as ever, at the same time he was very much aware of his own position as an outsider and his attachment to an individualistic lifestyle.

Further reading

Hekma, Gert (1992) 'The Mystical Body: Frans Kellendonk and the Dutch Literary Response to AIDS', in Emmanuel Nelson (ed.) *AIDS: The Literary Response*, New York: Twayne Publishers, pp. 88–94.

AGNES ANDEWEG

KEMP, LINDSAY

b. 1940

performance artist

Once seen, Larry Kemp's work is rarely forgotten. It achieves a wordless, resonant fusion of physical and visual elements that assert the importance of his homosexuality to his performance ethic. Kemp was born in South Shields in the north of England to a mother who encouraged his dramatic interests. He applied for admission to the Royal Ballet, but was rejected; he later studied with Dame Marie Rambert and Marcel Marceau. In 1968 he formed his own company, concentrating on work that reflected gay culture, such as *Flowers* (referencing Genet) in 1974, Oscar Wilde's *Salome* (1976), *Nijinsky* (1970) and *Cruel Garden*, based on the life of Federico Garcia Lorca (1977). His influence on David Bowie (directing him in his Rainbow rock theatre of 1972), Kate Bush, Leigh Bowery and Michael Clark was immense. Film director Derek Jarman used Kemp's company for the Roman orgy scene that begins *Sebastiane* (1976).

MICHAEL PINFOLD

KENTE, GILBERT

b. 1933

playwright, musician

South African playwright and musician, Gilbert Kente pioneered drama that reflected township life for working-class Africans. Among his other achievements, he wrote and produced the first play to broach male–male sex among Africans in prison. *Too Late* was performed in Johannesburg in 1963 then banned by apartheid censors until the homosexual scenes were changed. In 2003 he became one of the first public figures in South Africa to come out with his HIV+ status. Since then he has played a leading role in countering AIDS stigma in that country.

MARC EPPRECHT

KERN, PETER

b. 1949

actor, filmmaker

After having been a member of the Vienna Boys Choir as a child, Peter Kern went on to study acting and shortly thereafter became involved with the group of artists who gathered around Rainer Werner **Fassbinder**. As an actor, he is known for several small roles in the films of Fassbinder, Monika **Treut** and Ulrike **Ottinger**, but more notably for lead roles in films by Daniel **Schmid** (*La Paloma*, 1974; *Heute Nacht oder nie* [Tonight or Never], 1972) and Peer Raben (*Heute spielen wir den Boss*, 1981). During the late 1980s he directed his own films, often treating themes rarely taken up by other gay directors. His 1991 *Streetkid* (*Gossen-*

kind) tells the story of a young hustler. In 1992 he made *Fat Movie* (*Ein fetter Film*), an autobiographical film about being fat and gay. *Kiss, Cuddle and Celebrate* (*Knutschen, Kuscheln, Jubilieren*), made in 1997, is a realistic depiction of the lives of six older gay men who regularly meet in a bar in Dusseldorf.

DANIEL HENDRICKSON

KEYES, ALAN

b. 1950

politician

Conservative African-American politician and vocal opponent of homosexuality. Keyes was born on 7 August 1950 in New York City. He served in the US Foreign Service before being appointed as Ronald Reagan's ambassador to the United Nations General Assembly. He ran unsuccessfully for the Senate in Maryland in 1988 and 1992, and in Illinois in 2004, and for the US presidency in 1996 and 2000. An outspoken moral conservative, he advocated his opposition to abortion and homosexuality on his syndicated radio show 'America's Wake-Up Call' and a TV show *Alan Keyes is Making Sense*. During his Illinois campaign, he attacked Mary **Cheney**, calling her a 'selfish hedonist' and declaring that he would disown his daughter if she were a lesbian. His words proved prophetic: in 2005 Keyes' daughter Maya publicly announced that her father had disowned her after discovering her lesbianism.

JOHN FORDE

KIDRON, BEEBAN

b. 1961

filmmaker

British feminist filmmaker whose work explores the complexities of female relationships. She studied film at the National Film and Television School, and started directing films for the BBC, including *Carry Greenham Home*, a documentary about the women's peace camp. She scored a major success with **Oranges Are Not the Only Fruit** (1990), a TV adaptation of Jeanette Winterson's novel about a young lesbian discovering her sexuality. She made a respectable Hollywood debut with *Used People* (1992) and the self-explanatory documentary *Hookers Hustlers Pimps and Their Johns*. She scored a financial hit with the drag queen comedy *To Wong Foo, Thanks for Everything! Julie Newmar* (1995). Her last film, *Bridget Jones: The Edge of Reason* (2004), featured a lesbian subplot.

JOHN FORDE

KIGHT, MORRIS

b. 1919; d. 2003

activist, archivist

Veteran gay activist Morris Kight was inspired by Eleanor Roosevelt's progressive politics and repelled by the racial discrimination he witnessed growing up in rural Texas. He founded the Gay and Lesbian Resistance in Los Angeles in 1957, and in October 1963, co-founded the West Coast **Gay Liberation Front (GLF)**, 'a cadre of people ready to be out', he said. He was also a founding member of the Stonewall Democratic Club, which was said to have invented a great deal of what is thought of as the gay community in existence in southern California. Locally, Kight made Barney's Beanery restaurant in West Hollywood remove its homophobic sign: 'Fagots (sic) Stay Out'. In 1971 he was also a key founder of the Los Angeles Gay and Lesbian Community Services Center, now the world's largest as well as the principle organizer of 1970 'Christopher Street West', the first West Coast lesbian and Gay Pride parade.

Kight maintained a significant archive of glbtq historical material. The Morris Kight Collection is archived at the University of California at Los Angeles while the Morris Kight Art Collection is held at the ONE Institute and Archives.

ANDY HUMM

KIKI AND HERB

Bond, Justin

b. 1960

Mellman, Kenny

b. 1956

cabaret act

The creation of New York-based performers Justin Bond and Kenny Mellman, Kiki and Herb are an off-kilter musical duo and cabaret act who perform pop songs in an aggressive, deliberately off-tune style, interspersed with politically incorrect humour and soap opera-esque memoirs about their de-escalating show business careers. Bond, a classically trained actor, and Mellman, a pianist, met in San Francisco during the late 1980s, and began performing in cabarets together. Kiki and Herb emerged after a performance at 1993's Gay Pride weekend, based on a prototype drag creation of Bond. The pair perform deliberately miscalculated retakes on pop standards, including medleys of Christmas carols crossed with the Velvet Underground's 'Heroin' and Nirvana's 'Smells Like Teen Spirit'. Kiki, a self described 'boozy chanteuse', channels punk rock intensity with camp excess and erratically diva-like behaviour. The pair's histories includes their meeting in an asylum during the Great Depression, Herb's childhood abuse, Kiki's love affairs with a number of celebrities including Aristotle Onassis and black presidential candidate Dick Gregory, the pair's performances for Princess Grace and the accidental death of Kiki's illegitimate child. They became fixtures at New York cabaret venues, infamously performing for Madonna's birthday party, and developed their act in CD recordings and theatre performances, including *Kiki & Herb: Coup de Théatre* (2003). After touring with the Scissor Sisters in 2004, they performed their (dubiously intentioned) 'farewell shows' at Carnegie Hall in New York, later released as the CD *Kiki & Herb Will Die For You*.

JOHN FORDE

KING, BILLIE JEAN

b. 1943

tennis player

Billie Jean King won 39 Grand Slam titles and helped to make modern women's tennis the sport it is today. She dominated the women's game during the 1960s and early 1970s, winning 20 Wimbledon titles including six singles. She also won the US Open four times and the Australian and French Opens once each. She was world No. 1 five times between 1966 and 1972. King became a feminist figurehead, although not always enthusiastically. In 1973 she convincingly won the 'Battle of the Sexes', a challenge match against ageing ex-pro and male chauvinist icon Bobby Riggs, who boasted he could beat any of the leading women. In 1973 she established the Women's Tennis Association, boosting prize money for women. A palimony suit by her former secretary and lover Marilyn Barnett led to King's outing as a lesbian. She acts as an adviser to the tennis player Serena Williams.

H.G. COCKS

KINSEY INSTITUTE FOR RESEARCH IN SEX, GENDER AND REPRODUCTION

Founded in 1947 by Alfred Kinsey (1894–1956), the Institute is located in Bloomington, Indiana. Despite this Mid-Western location and its affiliation with Indiana University, the institution has faced con-

stant surveillance and vilification by the conservative Right. The Institute was founded in part to provide a research arena for the Kinsey Reports on human sexual behaviour. It currently supports and sponsors analytic and empirical studies on sexuality and reproduction and academic conferences. It is also an important archive of materials that range from sex videos and short films to collections of sexology and fetish items. The Institute thus provides a vital record of sexual life in its complex configurations by considering both the trivia and the methodology of sexuality. The collection and the Institute, in collecting, analysing and recording sexual experience and its texts, challenge any easy distinctions we might make between private and public sex.

YASMIN NAIR

KINSEY REPORT, THE

In 1948 Alfred Kinsey (1894–1956) and his research associates published *Sexual Behaviour of the Human Male*, followed in 1953 by *Sexual Behaviour of the Human Female*. By the time of the second volume, both Kinsey and the Kinsey Institute (named after him) had come under fire from conservatives who declared such studies immoral. In later years 'the Report', as the volumes are collectively known, would be critiqued for its narrow focus: most of the subjects interviewed were white and middle-class. But the Report did attempt taxonomically to document sexual acts without passing any moral judgement: 'This is first of all a report on what people do, which raises no question of what they should do, or what kinds of people do it' (*Human Male*, p. 7). With sections titled 'Nocturnal Sex Dreams' and 'Animal Contact', the books offered surprising revelations about what people do when they are on their own. Kinsey's most famous finding was that a large number of men engaged in homosexual acts. However, there seemed to be no explicit link between acts and identity and categories such as 'homosexual' and 'heterosexual'. In later years the findings were summarized as the '10 per cent rule' and used by Harry **Hay** to found the **Mattachine Society**. The Kinsey Report was followed by the popular and sensationalistic work of sex therapists such as Masters and Johnson, but it remains important for proving that sex does not occur on an easy continuum of normal/ abnormal, straight/gay – and that it is the most quotidian of experiences.

YASMIN NAIR

KIRKUP, JAMES

b. 1918

writer

James Kirkup is a British translator, short-story and travel writer, dramatist, novelist, autobiographer, essayist and poet who published many poems in the BBC's Arts magazine *The Listener* from 1949 to 1965. He became a good friend with its editor J.R. Ackerly. However, the sexual, homo-erotic and scatological overtones of his poems made him a controversial and unpopular figure in Britain's postwar literary and academic worlds. He abandoned the UK for lengthy periods, travelling abroad to Sweden, Spain and Japan. The poem which continues to create most controversy is 'The Love that Dares to Speak its Name', which suggests that Jesus experienced homosexual feelings. Its publication in issue 96 of *Gay News* in 1976 resulted in a campaign led by moral advocate Mary Whitehouse which saw the newspaper's editor successfully prosecuted for blasphemy. It remains illegal to either publish or circulate the poem in the UK today.

MARK MCLELLAND

KIRKWOOD, JAMES

b. 1924; d. 1989

writer, playwright

James Kirkwood was an American librettist, actor, author and playwright whose co-authored Broadway musical, *A Chorus Line* (1975), became the longest-running musical in Broadway history – it ran for 15 years and held the record until 1997, when it was surpassed by *Cats*. Kirkwood was born in Los Angeles to silent film stars James Kirkwood Sr and Lila Lee. However, by the time son James Jr was a teenager, his parents were divorced, their careers in decline and money was tight. In his fiction, Kirkwood revisits his difficult childhood and his lean early years as a stand-up comedian and an actor on daytime television. He is the author of seven novels, two of which became motion pictures: *Some Kind of Hero* (1982), about a disenfranchised Vietnam prisoner of war and, *P.S. Your Cat is Dead* (2002), about an unlucky New Yorker who, after a typically bad day, ties up a gay burglar in his kitchen.

ALIDA M. MOORE

KIRSTEIN, LINCOLN

b. 1907; d. 1996

author, American dance executive

Born on 4 May 1907 in Rochester, New York and raised in Boston, Kirstein enjoyed an affluent childhood that included a strong aesthetic education in the visual and performing arts. While an undergraduate at Harvard, he founded the respected literary magazine *Hound and Horn* and discovered classical dance, of which he became an avid spectator.

He quickly became the most influential proponent of ballet in the United States of the twentieth century, taking up positions as co-founder of the School of the American Ballet (1934), Ballet Caravan (1936), Ballet Society (1946) and the New York City Ballet (1948), the last of which survived as the pre-eminent exemplar of a distinctively American neo-classical style developed by choreographer George Balanchine.

Kirstein achieved success as a poet, art critic, historian and novelist, and published a wide range of seminal essays that detailed his many interests, including monographs on the works of queer artists Jared French, Pavel **Tchelitchev** and his brother-in-law by marriage, Paul **Cadmus**. Bisexual, but closeted for much of his adulthood, in later years Kirstein frankly detailed the many sexual affairs of his lifetime. He died on 5 January 1996 in New York City.

THOMAS F. DEFRANTZ

KLAFIM PTUHIM

TV talk show

In 1997 *Klafim Ptuchim* (Open Cards), a talk show for youth broadcast on Israeli Educational Television, planned to feature an episode on gay youth. Before the screening however, the Minister of Education, Zevulun Hammer of the National Religious Party, instructed Educational TV not to broadcast the episode, citing the argument that the programme was not 'balanced'. The Society for the Protection of Personal Rights, Community of Lesbian Feminists (CLAF) and the Association for Civil Rights in Israel jointly sued, arguing that the decision violated equal protection and freedom of speech. The Supreme Court held for the petitioners, finding that the Minister of Education had no justification to ban the show and emphasizing the need for tolerance towards gay people. However, the Court's reasoning that those who oppose homosexuality should merely tolerate it, but not necessarily respect it, attracted criticism since it did not give due recognition to the equality gays deserve. Nevertheless, the judgement's outcome was a victory for gay Israelis.

AEYAL GROSS

KLEIN, CALVIN
b. 1942
fashion designer

Calvin Klein was born on 19 November 1942 in the Bronx. He is one of America's leading fashion designers, who has become as famous for his provocative, homoerotic advertising campaigns as for his trademark minimalist clothing lines.

After graduating from New York's Institute of Technology in 1968, Klein opened his own business, making women's coats and later branching into sportswear. He became a fixture on the New York club scene, including Studio 54.

His designer jeans line was launched with a Richard Avedon advertisement featuring a young Brooke Shields. His designs were modern, simple and sophisticated, combining comfort and practicality with elegance and sexiness. In 1982 he launched his first underwear line, causing a sensation with an overtly sexual advertising campaign featuring erotic photography by Bruce **Weber** and Herb Ritts of near-naked muscular male models. The campaign heralded a new era in advertising that sexualized the male body as a hairless muscular object of desire, with product lines marketed specifically at gay men. Unsurprisingly, Calvin Klein underwear became a staple of gay couture by the end of the 1980s.

During the 1990s Klein's design concept explored images of androgyny and bisexuality, epitomized by the launch of cK One, his unisex designer fragrance, in 1993. His campaigns increased in sexual explicitness through the 1990s, including rap star Marky Mark (who now acts under his birth name, Mark Wahlberg) provocatively peering into his underwear, and a controversial 1995 campaign for cK jeans which was quickly withdrawn after accusations of child pornography.

Despite two marriages and fathering a child, Klein is widely rumoured to be gay or bisexual. He has never commented publicly about his sexuality.

JOHN FORDE

KNUCKLES, FRANKIE

b. 1955

DJ, composer

Considered the godfather of house music, openly gay DJ Frankie Knuckles is a leading an innovative presence in dance music culture. He was born in New York City on 18 January 1955. He started DJing in the New York gay disco club Better Days in 1972, and worked with his friend Larry Levan at the Continental Baths until 1976, where he won fame for his innovative fusion of disco with soul and rhythm and blues tracks. From 1977 until 1982 he was DJ in residence at the Warehouse in Chicago, playing for a predominantly black gay clientele. At the Warehouse, he developed the hugely popular fusion of electronica, disco, funk and soul which became known as 'house', creating an innovative new sound by mixing songs with blends of pre-recorded rhythm tracks and using drum machines to emphasize the beats. He opened the Power Plant in 1982, cementing his reputation as the creator of Chicago house, before returning to New York in 1987 and signing with Def Mix Productions. His albums include *Beyond the Mix* and *Welcome to the Real World*, and he has remixed tracks for Michael Jackson, Diana Ross and Chaka Khan. In 1997 he received the inaugural Grammy Award for Remixer of the Year. He has also spoken critically about the rise of homophobic lyrics in rap music.

JOHN FORDE

KOCH, EDWARD

b. 1924

politician

Edward I. Koch was mayor of New York City from 1978 until 1989 – tumultuous years for the lesbian and gay movement as well as the period of the emerging AIDS crisis. His courting of the gay vote in 1977 helped distinguish him in a crowded field. The 'bachelor' candidate also campaigned with former Miss America, Bess Myerson (later his Consumer Affairs Commissioner) on his arm to dispel rumours of his homosexuality. Koch accused his runoff opponent, Mario Cuomo, of posting signs that said 'Vote for Cuomo, Not the Homo'. Koch moved to the centre-right as mayor and did not pass the city's gay rights bill (conceived in 1971 by the Gay Activists Alliance) until 1986, after a 10-year campaign by the Coalition for Lesbian and Gay Rights.

Koch was denied a fourth term as mayor in 1989 because of corruption and his inattention to the AIDS crisis, triggering the vociferous opposition of the AIDS activist group, ACT UP, founded in 1987 by Larry Kramer.

ANDY HUMM

KÖNIG, RALF

b. 1960

comic book artist

Germany's best-known comic book artist began publishing in underground gay magazines in West Germany when he was 19; his first collection of those comic strips, *SchwulComix*, appeared in 1981. By the end of the 1980s he had developed his hallmark style, depicting quirky, caricatured figures with exaggerated blobs for noses, as well as his reputation for capturing precisely the loveable, laughable and raunchy splendour of everyday gay life. König launched himself and that splendour into his country's hetero mainstream, once in 1987, when his comic novel *Der Bewegte Mann* (Pretty Baby) appeared with a large commercial publisher, and again in 1994 when it was turned into a hit film (directed by Sönke Wortmann and distributed in English as *Maybe...Maybe Not*). In the novel the domestic harmony of two gay roommates is thrown off-kilter when a straight man moves in with them (curiously,

Wortmann's film foregrounds the straight man's story). Two of König's other 20 or so books have also been adapted for the cinema: *Lysistrata* (1987), which gives Aristophanes' comedy a homosexual peripeteia, was produced as a film in Catalonia in 2002; and *Kondom des Grauens* (*Killer Condom*, 1987, 1988; film adaptation, 1997), has a giant castrating condom terrorizing New York City. König's popularity has been a double-edged sword for the artist (according to interviews), but it raises interesting questions about the reception of work such as his. Few artists have conveyed gay culture to the mainstream as successfully; however straight readers often miss König's irony, finding instead stereotypes affirmed, while gay readers tend to see through the caricatures.

WILLIAM MARTIN

KOPAY, DAVID

b. 1942

athlete

In 1964 David Kopay was co-captain of the University of Washington's Rose Bowl American football team. He then signed with the San Francisco 49ers and played with them for several years. His career as running back continued until 1972, during which time he also played for the Washington Redskins, New Orleans Saints, and Green Bay Packers. After reading a story about an anonymous gay athlete in the *Washington Star*, Kopay contacted the paper and arranged for an article to be written on him. The article was published in December 1975, and in it Kopay came out publicly. He was the first American team sport athlete to do so. In 1977 the American Library Association chose *The David Kopay Story* as a recommended book for all students. It was also on *The New York Times* best-seller list.

ERIC ANDERSON

KRAMER, LARRY

b. 1935

activist, writer

Born in Connecticut, Larry Kramer is one of America's highest profile gay men and is well known as an activist, polemicist, essayist, playwright, novelist, film producer, scriptwriter and, since 1988, as a person living with HIV. Throughout the 1980s Kramer was one of the best-known public advocates of individual, community based and governmental responses to the national emergency posed by the AIDS epidemic. He voiced the urgency of this need and led the way in creating organizational superstructures of unprecedented importance. In 1981 he organized the founding of **Gay Men's Health Crisis (GMHC)**, and in 1987 he catalysed the creation of ACT UP, of which he remained a leader for several years. Kramer began his writing career with a screen adaptation of D.H. Lawrence's *Women in Love* (1969), which received a Golden Globe Award and was nominated for an Oscar; his novel *Faggots* (1978) remains in print; and he is the author of several dramas about AIDS, including *The Normal Heart* (1985), which has been seen in close to 1,000 productions worldwide, and *The Destiny of Me* (1993), for which he received an Obie Award. Many of his essays and speeches have been published in his book of nonfiction: *Reports from the Holocaust: The Story of an AIDS Activist* (1994). He is a recipient of the Award in Literature from the American Academy of Arts and Letters and is also the first creative artist and the first openly gay person to be honoured by a Public Service Award from Common Cause.

See also: ACT UP

SURINA KHAN

KRAUS, BILL

activist

Gay activist who took a leading role in the gay community's response to the AIDS epidemic in the 1980s. His work was documented by journalist Randy Shilts in his account of AIDS research and campaigning in 1980s America. He was memorably portrayed by Ian **McKellen** in Roger Spottiswoode's 1993 film version of Shilts' book *And the Band Played On* (1987). Kraus appeared in *The Times of Harvey Milk* (1984), a documentary about openly gay San Francisco City Councillor Harvey **Milk**. He died of an AIDS-related illness.

JOHN FORDE

KRAUS, GERTRUD

dancer

In 1932 the Viennese-born dancer Gertrud Kraus arrived in Tel-Aviv and finally settled in Israel in 1936. She soon became the doyenne of modern dance in a land where hardly any classical ballet tradition existed. In Israel she lived with her intimate friend, Else Scharff, who was responsible for running the practical and economic side of Kraus' studio. Kraus had great influence on the development of artistic dance in Israel. In 1963 she was awarded the prestigious Israel Prize. Her dances carefully avoided erotic themes yet her popular company had no male dancers. Indeed, when the dramatic material demanded male roles, the taller girls danced the male roles *en travestie*.

GIORA MANOR

KROUSE, MATTHEW

b. 1961

writer, actor, filmmaker

Matthew Krouse raised the ire of the South African security establishment in the 1980s through theatre and film productions that denigrated the holy cows of the apartheid state. During this period, several of his works were banned by state censors and were the subject of right-wing public protests. In the early 1980s he was conscripted into the South African Defence Force during the political state of emergency. His experience as a gay man in the military was featured in a 2003 documentary titled *Property of the State* (dir. Gerald Kraak). His writing has appeared in a number of anthologies, both at home and abroad. In 1995 he edited the first gay and lesbian literary collection to appear on the African continent, *The Invisible Ghetto*. The book enjoyed international co-publication and distribution through Gay Men's Press. Since 1998 he has been the editor of the award-winning arts section of the independent weekly newspaper, *Mail & Guardian*.

GRAEME REID

KUCHAR, GEORGE AND MIKE

b. 1942

filmmakers

Twin brothers George and Mike Kuchar started making films immediately after their twelfth birthday, when they were given an 8-mm home movie camera. Their first films were fashioned after the epics they had seen in the local Bronx cinemas. They enlisted their friends as the cast and fashioned sets and costumes from whatever was handy, a practice they have kept up ever since. The films were very often improvised, with plots developing during the shooting. In 1963, at the prompting of one of their actor-friends, they took some of their films downtown to one of the informal screenings organized by filmmaker Ken Jacobs in his loft. From then on the Kuchar brothers would be an indispensable part of the America underground cinema in New York.

In 1965 the brothers began to make films separately, although each continued to work on the other's projects. Mike soon made what was to remain his best-known film, *Sins of the Fleshapoids*, a futuristic science-fiction film where colour is at least as important as plot or character. George made his first film alone shortly thereafter: *Hold Me While I'm Naked* (1966), a ten-minute meditation on the problems of low-budget filmmaking. In 1971 George was invited to teach at the San Francisco Art Institute as a visiting artist. His first student was the filmmaker Curt **McDowell**, who would become an important collaborator. After McDowell circulated a student petition, George was hired permanently at the Institute. Mike also began spending time in San Francisco and making films there, although he maintains his ties with New York, working at the Millennium Film Workshop. Both of the brothers started working with video during in the 1980s, a medium that has proven to be incredibly productive, especially for George, who has well over 100 video titles to his credit as well as over 60 films.

See also: American underground cinema

DANIEL HENDRICKSON

KUREISHI, HANIF

b. 1954

writer

The son of a white British mother and a Pakistani immigrant, Hanif Kureishi came of age in the London of the 1970s and early 1980s – a world he would memorialize in his work as a place of multiracial tension, polysexual excitement and stifling political conservatism. Kureishi achieved notoriety with his script for the film *My Beautiful Laundrette* (1985), which centres on a gay love affair between an upwardly mobile Pakistani-British entrepreneur and an erst-

while neo-Nazi. Kureishi's first novel, *The Buddha of Suburbia* (1990), is an irreverent, wistful account of the promises and dangers of assimilation set in Thatcherite Britain. In subsequent work, notably the novel *Intimacy* (1999), about a man on the verge of deserting his wife and children, and *My Son the Fanatic* (1997), a film about a London taxi driver's tensions with his zealously religious Muslim son, Kureishi continues to court controversy and to explore the class, racial and sexual divides of contemporary London.

DAVID KURNICK

KUSENGA

The Shona (Zimbabwean) word for the customary practice of adolescent girls to manually lengthen their labia. Usually done alone, but sometimes with a friend, the custom was thought to make a woman more sexually attractive to a future husband. It is practiced widely throughout southern Africa, particularly among Basotho women whose 'traps' became notorious for ensnaring South African men in adulterous relationships.

MARC EPPRECHT

KUSHNER, TONY

b. 1956

playwright, activist

Born on 16 July 1956 in New York City, Kushner is best known for his prize-winning play *Angels in America: A Gay Fantasia on National Themes*. Commissioned by the Eureka Theatre in San Francisco, Part One, entitled *Millennium Approaches*, premiered in 1991, and Part Two, *Perestroika*, in 1992. A sprawling multi-layered epic, it combines a sustained critique of the homophobic policies of 1980s Reaganite America and the devastation wreaked by the AIDS epidemic with intense lyricism and magic realism. Kushner contrasts the lives of two closeted gay men – Roy Cohn, the real-life conservative politician who died of AIDS in 1986, and his fictional protégé Joseph Pitt, a married Mormon lawyer – with two out gay men, Prior, who is dying of AIDS, and his despairing lover Louis. Kushner compares the denial of homosexuality within the Mormon faith with the invisibility of gays in the Reagan administration, and eloquently articulates the anger and pain of a generation of gay men. Hope is offered through the character of Prior, a postmodern prophet who receives visions from an angel, his friend the black drag queen Belize, and Joseph's mother-in-law Hannah, who puts aside her homophobic prejudices to become Prior's nurse. Drawing from an extraordinarily wide range of literary and cultural references, including the Bible, the Torah, Shakespeare and Bertolt Brecht, *Angels* received unanimous international acclaim, including the Pulitzer Prize for drama and was filmed for television by Mike Nichols in 2003.

Kushner's other works include *A Bright Room Called Day* (1994), *Slavs!* (1994) and *Only We Who Guard the Mystery Shall Be Unhappy* (2004), a satire of the Bush administration.

Kushner is a committed spokesperson for gay rights. In 2003 he legally formalized his relationship with his long-term partner Mark Harris.

JOHN FORDE

KWAN, STANLEY

b. 1957

film director

Kwan is one of the most acclaimed Hong Kong directors making queer movies. Born in Hong Kong, he received his undergraduate training in communication studies and, soon after his graduation, joined Hong Kong Television Broadcast Limited (HKTVB) as a trainee actor. He first entered the film industry during the early 1980s, working as assistant director on a number of Hong Kong New Wave movies. His directorial debut came in 1985 with *Nu ren xin* (*Women*), starring Chow Yun-Fat; the film displayed Kwan's sensitivity and empathetic attitude towards females. *Yin ji kau* (*Rouge*, 1987), starring Anita Mui and Leslie Cheung, was a big box-office success as well as a critically acclaimed work. Kwan followed this with *Ren zai Niu Yue* (*Full Moon in New York*) in 1989, *Yuen Ling-Yuk* (*The Actress*) in 1992 and *Hong meigui, bai meigui* (*Red Rose, White Rose*) in 1994. His first attempt at homosexual exploration was the documentary *Yang & Yin: Gender in Chinese Cinema*, in 1996 and he was the first director in Hong Kong to integrate queer readership into Chinese cinema. As attitudes towards gay culture developed through the 1990s, Kwan directed *Yue kuai le, yue duo luo* (*Hold You Tight*, 1997), a drama about a married gay man. In his award-winning movie, *Lan Yu* (2001), Kwan told a love story set in modern Beijing considered to be an honest portrayal of male–male relationships.

JOHN FORDE

L

L WORD, THE

TV series

Lesbian-themed American TV drama series, developed by cable network Showtime, in part to provide a lesbian counterpart to the network's successful gay-themed series **Queer as Folk**. Premiering in January 2004, the pilot episode caused an immediate sensation with its explicit depictions of lesbian sex and a controversial subplot involving blasphemous religious art. The series follows Jenny (Mia Kirshner), who moves to Los Angeles and becomes friends with a group of lesbians, including long-term couple Bette (Jennifer Beals) and Tina (Laurel Hollomon), and sexual predator Shane (Katherine Moenning). Critical opinion on the show's merits has been divided. Lesbian audiences have welcomed the show's exclusive focus on lesbian characters, whereas others argue that the narrative emphasis on sex and the cast of supermodel-thin 'lipstick lesbian' characters is based more on pornographic fantasy than the reality and diversity of lesbian experience. A second season screened in 2005.

JOHN FORDE

LA BRUCE, BRUCE

b. 1964

filmmaker

While producing the legendary 'zine *J.D.* during the late 1980s, Bruce La Bruce also made short Super-8 films. This period culminated with the production of his first feature-length film, *No Skin Off My Ass* (1991), also shot on Super-8. The film features La Bruce as a prissy hairdresser obsessed with skinheads ('the only haircut that makes sense anymore'). This was followed by *Super-8 1/2* (1993), a pseudo-autobiographical pseudo-documentary, and *Hustler White* (1996, made with photographer Rick Castro), which featured Tony Ward as a cheap Santa Monica Boulevard hustler. Alongside their extensive references to other films, all of La Bruce's films contain explicit images of sex that challenge the conventional distinctions between pornography and non-pornography. In 1999 he made *Skin Flick*, the story of a gang of multinational skinheads in London. This was followed in 2004 by *The Raspberry Reich*, a film about a gang of ineffectual would-be left-wing terrorists led by a dynamic, sexy woman.

DANIEL HENDRICKSON

LA RUE, DANNY

b. 1927

entertainer

Once described by Bob Hope as 'the most glamorous woman in the world', La Rue's drag cabaret and stage performances made him one of Britain's most celebrated and enduring entertainers. Irish-born, he began his career performing in shows while serving a term in the Royal Navy, progressing to regional theatre and cabaret, including a long-running partnership with *Carry On* movie star Barbara Windsor at Winston's Club in London. His Hanover Square nightclub, opened in 1964, attracted celebrity patrons Judy Garland, Noel Coward, Elizabeth Taylor and Princess Margaret. He enjoyed success with his shows *Come Spy With Me* and *Queen Passionella*. As Dolly in the 1984 production of *Hello Dolly*, he made history as the first man to play a female role in a West End musical. La Rue's cheery, epicine persona provided an acceptable face for homosexuality in post-war Britain, paving the way for the sexually bolder comic antics of Julian **Clary** and Graham **Norton**.

JOHN FORDE

LACHAPELLE, DAVID

b. 1969

photographer, film- and videomaker

Arriving in New York in the 1980s as a young art student, LaChapelle took his first job working as a photographer for Andy Warhol's fashion/celebrity magazine *Interview*, and began what has since become one of the most successful and award-winning careers in photography, film and video. LaChapelle's signature style – a mix of surrealist juxtaposition, pop art icons, intensely saturated colour and an unabashed presentation of sexually charged tableaux populated with scantily clad male and female bodies – has appeared on the covers of fashion magazines, on album covers, commercial advertisements and music videos; and his portrait photography has captured the personae of a long list of celebrities. A veritable polymath of the visually spectacular, in 2003 he directed *Krumped*, the critically acclaimed documentary on the hip-hop movement, and in 2004 stage-directed Elton John's Las Vegas show, *The Red Piano*. The book

Hotel LaChapelle (1999) is a collection of his work as a photographer.

JOHN PAUL RICCO

LAM, EDWARD

b. 1959

theatre director, film festival organizer

Born in Hong Kong, Edward Yik Wah (Lin Yihua) Lam's creative career began at the age of 14 when he started writing scripts for TV series. A founder of Zuni Icosahedron, an independent cultural collective established in 1982, Lam established his own Edward Lam Dance Theatre in 1991. He came out as a gay man during the 1980s, when homosexuality was still a crime. He produced theatre works that addressed directly discrimination against gay men and celebrated homosexual love (*How to Love a Man Who Doesn't Love Me*, 1989; *Scenes from a Man's Changing Room*, 1991).

As the curator of the first Hong Kong Gay and Lesbian Film Festival (1989), Lam publicly appropriated the term *tongzhi* as a synonym for gays and lesbians and other sexual minorities. Thereafter, the festival was called Hong Kong Comrades (a.k.a., Tongzhi) Film Festival. Lam writes columns and reviews of films, books and the performing arts. Works include *A Man who Sleeps Around* (1994), *Too Many Men, Too Little Time* (1996), *Edward Lam on Love* (2002) and *Edward Lam on Cinema* (2002).

TRAVIS KONG

LAM, MICHAEL

writer

Born in Singapore, brought up in Hong Kong and the United States and now settled in Paris, Michael (Maike) Lam is a writer, film critic and translator of subtitles whose articles appear in numerous magazines and newspapers. As one of the editors of the Hong Kong International Film Festival for several years, Lam has established his own unique style of gay writing through his highly camp but witty analyses of gay films as well as his subversive 'queer reading' and 'twisting' of straight films. Lam is believed to have been the first to reappropriate the term *tongzhi* as a term for gay people in Hong Kong.

His publications include: *Ying Yin Ben* (Photocopies, 1993), *Jia Xing Jing* (Fake Sexual Politics, 1993), *Nan Jie* (The Male Boundary, 1994), *Sex Text* (2000) and *Single-Minded, Double-Entendre* (2003).

TRAVIS KONG

LAMBDA LEGAL

Lambda Legal is a US-based organization committed to 'achieving full recognition of the civil rights of lesbians, gay men, bisexuals, the transgendered, and people with HIV or AIDS through impact litigation, education, and public policy work'. It carries out its legal work principally through test cases selected for their likelihood of success in establishing positive legal precedents for those groups listed above. It pursues litigation in all parts of the country, in every area of the law that affects glbtq communities, such as discrimination in employment, housing, public accommodation and the military; HIV/AIDS-related discrimination and public policy issues; parenting and relationship issues; equal marriage rights; equal employment and domestic partnership benefits; 'sodomy' law challenges; immigration issues; anti-gay initiatives; and free speech and equal protection rights. Its staff of attorneys works on a wide range of cases and its docket averages over 50 cases at any given time.

Incorporated in 1973, after nearly two years of legal battles, New York's highest court finally allowed Lambda Legal to exist as a non-profit organization. At that time there were no US-based groups whose principal mission was to fight for gay rights in the nation's courts and glbtq people had few clearly established legal rights. Throughout the 1970s, Lambda Legal fought – and won – some of the nation's first cases on behalf of gay parents and gay couples. It successfully fought for gay student groups and gay employees who faced blatant discrimination from state-funded universities; challenged the federal government for penalizing gay people and gay groups through discriminatory FBI and IRS practices; and prompted the government to stop barring gay immigrants from entering the country.

During the 1980s Lambda Legal stepped up its efforts against government discrimination while also focusing more on anti-gay bias in corporations and established community institutions. Several major companies led the way in adopting or strengthening anti-discrimination policies in response to lawsuits by Lambda Legal in the 1980s, and some began offering benefits to same-sex partners of employees. Lambda Legal used litigation to pressure the federal government to stop giving gay service members 'dishonourable discharges', their success allowing such individuals to keep their housing and GI benefits. Lambda Legal also won a number of important victories for increasingly visible glbtq communities to hold pride parades, list gay community services in phone books and receive gay publications in prison. Finally, it convinced New York's courts to strike down the state's sodomy law, which was used unfairly against glbtq people.

During the 1990s Lambda Legal led efforts to keep anti-gay initiatives off ballots in a number of cities and states and played a key role in persuading the US Supreme Court to strike down a voter-enacted amendment to Colorado's Constitution that prohibited gay rights laws. Also in the 1990s, Lambda Legal won victories for glbtq youth, who were coming out at younger and younger ages. It won a historic legal precedent, holding schools responsible for harassment and violence against glbtq students and successfully defended the right of **gay–straight alliances** to exist in schools, even in conservative areas such as Salt Lake City, Utah, and Orange County, California.

In 2003 Lambda was successful in its US Supreme Court challenge to Texas' sodomy law, the Supreme Court voting 5 to 3 that Texas' 'Homosexual Conduct' law was unconstitutional. The ruling effectively struck down the sodomy laws in every state that still had them. The decision also overturned the Supreme Court's 1986 ruling in *Bowers* v. *Hardwick*. In that decision – which has been used against gay people in most civil rights cases ever since – the court upheld Georgia's sodomy law in a case brought by a man who was arrested while having consensual sex in his home with another man.

Lambda Legal has offices in New York, Los Angeles, Chicago, Atlanta and Dallas. It also maintains a national network of volunteer Cooperating Attorneys, which widens the scope of its legal work and allows attorneys, legal workers and law students to become involved in its programme by working with Lambda's legal staff.

SURINA KHAN

LAMBERT, LOTHAR

b. 1944

filmmaker

Berlin-based underground filmmaker Lothar Lambert has made over 20 films since the 1970s. All of the films were produced on minimal budgets, with Lambert himself often serving not only as director but also as screenwriter, cameraman, actor and editor. The cast of the films consists of a loyal group of friends – the so-called Lambert Family – most notably the actor Ulrike S. This group portrays various kinds of sexuality, often bringing their own life stories to the screen. The films are almost invariably set in Berlin, where Lambert has lived since early childhood. Beginning in the 1980s, the films achieved international recognition, mostly on the film festival circuit, although not without some degree of controversy because of their representation of gay men and transvestites.

DANIEL HENDRICKSON

LANE, NATHAN

b. 1956

actor

Born Joseph Lane in Jersey City, New Jersey, Lane took the name 'Nathan' after the character Nathan Detroit in *Guys and Dolls*. Growing up with an alcoholic father and manic-depressive mother (what Lane coined a 'bad Eugene O'Neill childhood'), he escaped to New York immediately after high school and pursued acting there and in Los Angeles. He teamed up with playwright Terrence **McNally** on *The Lisbon Traviata* (1989), *Bad Habits* (1990), *Lips Together, Teeth Apart* (1991) and *Love! Valour! Compassion!* (1994). In films, Lane played gay roles in *Jeffrey* (1995) and *The Birdcage* (1996). He also appeared in Kenneth Branagh's *Love's Labors Lost* (2000) and *Nicholas Nickleby* (2002). Back on Broadway, Lane received a Tony nomination for the revival of *Guys and Dolls* (1992) and won the Tony for *A Funny Thing Happened on the Way to the Forum* (1996) and *The Producers* (2001).

CHRIS BYRNE

LANG, KD

b. 1961

singer, songwriter

Raised in the small farming community of Consort, Alberta, Canada, Kathryn Dawn Lang studied music at Red Deer College.

Finding the curriculum restrictive she drifted into performance art and discovered the music of Patsy Cline when asked to imitate her in a 1950s-style musical, *Country Chorale*, in 1982. Later, Lang experimented with a mix of new- and old-style country, new wave rock, blues, jazz and western swing. She developed a zany stage persona, sporting cropped hair, winged glasses, flared skirts and cut-off cowboy boots, and attracted a cult following with high-energy performances and an engaging humour influenced by Minnie Pearl and the Beverly Hillbillies. Her debut album, *A Truly Western Experience*, was released in 1984, and after a gig at The Bottom Line in New York, she was signed by Sire Records, who teamed her up with Welsh producer Dave Edmunds for *Angel with a Lariat* (1987). With the first track on this album, the infectious square dance 'Turn Me Round', Lang reached an international audience in the closing ceremony of the 1988 Winter Olympics.

In 1988 Lang won her first Grammy for 'Crying', a duet with Roy Orbison, and made a bid for recognition from Nashville with *Shadowlands*, a searing collection of jazz, blues and country standards produced by Owen Bradley, who had worked with Cline. This showed a more reflective side to Lang, who by now had swapped glasses and flared skirts for rhinestone jackets and a svelte, androgynous elegance. But this was far from Nashville's idea of femininity, and suspicions that her treatment of country was not entirely respectful, her work garnered little airplay. With *Absolute Torch and Twang* (1989) she moved into a more 'progressive country' sound, blending torch ballads, hillbilly twang, cowboy imagery and fresh input from newfound song-writing partner Ben Mink.

Lang ventured into acting during the early 1990s, inviting the German film director Percy **Adlon** to direct the video for 'So in Love', her contribution to the 1990 **AIDS** benefit album of Cole Porter songs *Red Hot + Blue*. Adlon reciprocated with *Salmonberries* (1991), a feature film starring Lang as a young Eskimo loner drawn into a lesbian relationship with a German émigré. Shot in Alaska, the film featured the song 'Barefoot', which evokes the glacial wilderness as a metaphor of the soul and is one of Lang's eeriest, most finely crafted performances. Deep, unrequited love inspired the painfully introspective album *Ingénue* (1992), which fuelled increasing press speculation over Lang's sexuality. Previously she had preferred to remain 'cryptic', so as 'not to eliminate possibilities for people', but she came out in an interview with *The Advocate* (2 June 1992) to a reaction that was 'totally positive' and which strengthened her flirtatious rapport with a broadening fan base. With the single 'Constant Craving', she crossed over decisively into mainstream pop and found herself at the forefront of a new 'lesbian chic' in nineties culture, appearing in a classic butch/femme pose with Cindy Crawford on the cover of *Vanity Fair* in 1993. Lang has continued to appeal to the popular mainstream with singles from her soundtrack for Gus Van Sant's 1993 film *Even Cowgirls Get the Blues,* as well as *All You Can Eat* (1994) and *Invincible Summer* (2000).

Further reading

Starr, Victoria (1994) *All You Get is Me,* New York: St Martin's Press.

RACHEL COWGILL

LATIN AMERICA, FILMMAKING

Regarding gender, most Latin American films concentrate, in general, on power and masculinity, traditional family and heterosexuality. For most films the narrative focus is often about male bonding and leadership, and the victimization of women, children, blacks and indigenous people. Although the film industry started very early in Latin America – immediately after the exhibition made by Lumière at the end of the nineteenth century – it was only after the international impact of feminism and the gay cultural and political agenda around the mid-1980s that a handful of filmmakers directed their attention to queer issues and glbt characters as protagonists. Getting to this point, however, was a path riddled with homophobia and machismo.

In early comedies – especially those produced during Latin America's golden age of cinema of the mid-twentieth century, in which filmmakers left behind rural themes and started exploring urban topics – cross-dressing was part of a typical narrative plot and genre convention. Much later, cross-dressing and transvestism reappear in many comic films starring the Argentine TV comedians Alberto Olmedo and Jorge Porcel. Curiously, most of these films were produced under the Argentine dictatorship (1976–83). From these performers' extensive filmography – which has not yet undergone academic study – it is worth mentioning *Mi novia Él* (He, My Fiancée, 1975), whose original title was *Mi novia travesti* (My Fiancée is a Travesty) and *Atracción Peculiar* (Peculiar Attraction, 1988), produced immediately before and after the military tyranny respectively.

Many essays have been written about patriarchy in Latin American culture. Doubtless patriarchy is a subject explored by films dealing with rural and urban themes. However, prominent films also demonstrate that matriarchy is no less important than patriarchy. Indeed, it is possible to argue that patriarchy and machismo are a response to the 'silent' powerful matriarchy in which 'traditional' women – mainly inspired by Catholicism – defend patriarchal values and promote male bonding. In this context, two Mexican films are paradigmatic of Latin American queer cinema. They deserve a more detailed commentary because they systematically display the traditional cultural themes that deal with (national) masculinity and homoeroticism and, at the same time, explore the way matriarchy works in Latin American culture. The first of these is *Doña Herlinda y su hijo* (*Doña Herlinda and Her Son*, 1984), a Mexican movie directed by Jaime Humberto Hermosillo. The film tells the story of Doña Herlinda (Guadalupe Del Toro), whose son Rodolfo (Marco Antonio Treviño), a paediatrician, happens to be gay or bisexual. In order to preserve middle-class decency, Herlinda persuades her son to marry and have children while, at the same time, inviting his son's lover – Ramón (Arturo Meza) – to stay at home as part of an extended family. The end of the film is not tragic (as might be expected from this period) and provides a positive narrative resolution from a gay perspective. However, Herlinda's efforts to maintain the status quo (patriarchal values) can also be read as a very conservative strategy. Rodolfo becomes a father and Ramón assumes the traditional, feminine domestic role at home, taking care of the baby (even though he sometimes appears to top Rodolfo). Additionally, although Olga (Letícia Lupercio) – Rodolfo's wife – is a successful professional, she remains unaware of her husband's real sexual orientation. The story is thus completely under the mother's – Herlinda's – control. As a phallic woman, she defies the Mexican – *and* Latin American – tradition of the representation of the mother as submissive and saint. Obviously, the macho's power, masculinity and even patriarchy become a masquerade under this maternal manipulation. Hermosillo's film might be interpreted as an oblique national allegory in which Herlinda serves as a matriarchal symbol of the Nation – as happens in most traditional films – that perversely supports patriarchy while at the same time releases, controls and protects homoeroticism among men.

The second film, one that has recently attracted the interest of North American audiences – despite its controversial critical reception – was *Y tu mamá también* (And Your Mother Too, 2001), a Mexican road movie directed by Alfonso Cuarón. In this film two teenagers – Tenoch (Diego Luna) and Julio (Gael Garcia Bernal) – from different class and cultural backgrounds travel through Mexico and sexually compete for the favours of Luisa (Maribel Verdú), a married woman who, at the end, reveals to them the real object of their desire: their mutual sexual attraction. In this sense, with superb and almost baroque language, Cuarón's film unveils the dark side of homosocial behaviour among men in patriarchal societies. That is, for men to be aware of this 'dark side' is to disrupt any possibility of friendship, male bonding and masculine supremacy. As in *Doña Herlinda*, there is, yet again, a sympathetic woman (Luisa) who understands the 'secret' of men's desire and arranges for them to achieve their mutual satisfaction in a private space. Unlike Hermosillo's film, *Y tu mamá también* provides a melancholic end: the teens have no possibility of continuing their friendship once their desire is revealed and the woman is victimized, as so often happens to female characters who dare to transgress norms of decency. She dies, ravaged by cancer.

Withstanding the famous documentary *Conducta impropia* (Reprehensible Behaviour, 1984), directed by Néstor Almendros and dealing with the repression of homosexuals in Cuba, most films representing homoeroticism and gays are taken from Latin American literature. Key adaptations include: *Un lugar sin límites* (The Place Without Limits, 1977), a Mexican movie directed by Arturo Ripstein and based on a Chilean novel by José Donoso; *El juguete rabioso* (The Rabid Toy, 1984), an Argentine movie directed by José María Paolantonio and based on Roberto Arlt's novel; *La ciudad y los perros* (The City and the Dogs, 1985), a Peruvian film directed by Francisco J. Lombardi and based on the novel by Mario Vargas Llosa. Four films from Latin America have received international acclaim: *El beso de la mujer araña* (*Kiss of the Spider Woman*, 1985), nominated for several Oscars, directed by Héctor Babenco and based on Manuel Puig's novel; *Fresa y chocolate* (*Strawberry and Chocolate*, 1993), a Cuban film directed by Tomás Gutiérrez Alea and Juan Carlos Tabío, based on a short story by Senel Paz; the Argentine film *Plata quemada* (*Burnt Money*, 2000), directed by Marcelo Piñeyro and based on Ricardo Piglia's novel; and, finally, *Antes que amanezca* (*Before Night Falls*, 2000), directed by painter Julian Schnabel and based on the last autobiographical novel by the Cuban author Reinaldo Arenas.

Several films dealing with homosexuality derive from original screenplays. For example, *Señora de nadie* (Nobody's Wife, 1982), directed by María Luisa Bemberg, takes an interesting approach to redefining masculinity in a patriarchal society. The film – surprisingly produced during the dictatorship in Argentina – explores gay-bashing and focuses on the relationship between a gay man and a married woman. Following the military tyranny in Argentina, two films about coming out of the closet were made: *Adios, Roberto* (Goodbye, Robert, 1985), directed by Enrique Dawi, and Américo Ortiz de Zárate's *Otra historia de amor* (Another Love Story, 1986). Another film dealing with a young man's story of coming out, *No se la digas a nadie* (Don't Tell Anyone, 1998), was the first Peruvian movie to focus on a gay character. The film was directed by Francisco J. Lobardi, who uses upper-class hypocritical decency, machismo and homophobia in Lima as the framework through which gay identity is experienced.

More recently, Latin American films have moved beyond melodrama and coming-out narratives. In Barbet Schroeder's *La Virgen de los Sicarios* (Our Lady of the

Assassins, 2001), a gay love story between an older man and a young boy takes place against the backdrop of a disturbed Medellín where drug dealers rule (see **Colombia, filmmaking**). *Mariposas en el andamio* (Butterflies on the Scaffold, 1996), a Cuban film directed by Margaret Gilpin and Luis Bernaza, tells of a group of drag queens who search for respect and, consequently, do their best in order to become part of their neighbourhood.

Few films deal with lesbianism in Latin America. The early and controversial film *Cuando tejen las arañas* (When Spiders Weave, 1977) – with a screenplay by the famous Mexican playwright and novelist Vicente Leñero – is an exception. In this film spiders are lesbians who patiently weave their web and wait for high-class young women – particularly those tired of men and bored and frustrated in their domestic marriages – to become their prey. Lesbianism is portrayed also in *Yo, la peor de todas* (I, The Worst of All, 1990), by the Argentine director María Luisa Bemberg and based on the Mexican biography *Sor Juana, or The Traps of Faith* by Octavio Paz. The Mexican film *Perfume de violetas, nadie te oye* (The Scent of Violets, Nobody is Listening To You, 2001), directed by Marysa Sistach, remains ambiguous about its queer perspective – the entirety of the film suggests a loving relationship between two schoolgirls but, at the end, when one of them kills the other and takes her place, the spectator has to redefine the terms of this dangerous liaison. Infused with magic realism, *Mecánicas celestes* (Celestial Clockwork, 1994), Fina Torres' Venezuelan film is a fascinating picaresque journey of a woman who finally discovers her lesbianism. Finally, the Argentine film *Tan de repente* (Suddenly, 2002), directed by Diego Lerman, deals with lesbianism and other 5w>queer issues through the genre of the road movie, with a dyke duo taking a straight girl on a trip full of surprises and dark humour.

To date, Latin American films portray gays and lesbians in very individualistic and domestic ways. For example, few serious films about AIDS exist – as Mexican director, Victor Saca's *En el paraíso no existe el dolor* (There Is No Pain in Paradise, 1995) makes clear; nor are there films about the gay and lesbian struggle for human rights. Undoubtedly, many national archives remain to be critically scrutinized by scholars before an adequate panorama of, and discussion about, the representation of glbtq issues in Latin American cinema are fully considered. In order to avoid limiting the scope of the issue, however, researchers must explore materials beyond representation of gays and lesbians, transvestites and cross-dressing, beyond international success and avant-gardism. Many movies, such as the classic *Doña Bárbara* (dir. Fernando de Fuentes, 1943) or the entire filmography of Armando Bo, require an urgent queer reading.

Further reading

Martin, Michael T. (1997) *New Latin American Cinema*, 2 vols. Detroit: Wayne State University Press.

GUSTAVO GEIROLA

LATIN AMERICA, LITERATURE

During the twentieth century, representation of homosexual characters in Latin American fiction and poetry progressively intensified after the Second World War. According to two significant essays, one on the history of the homosexual movement in Argentina (Rapisardi and Modarelli 2001) and one on lesbian organizations in Mexico (Mogrovejo 2000) – often overlapping with the history of feminist movements in the region – many factors existed that promoted these developments. Besides the multiple homoerotic and homosocial expressions that can be identified in Latin American literature since the colonial period, literature from the second half of the twentieth century demonstrates a radical transformation in the representation of homosexuality.

First, there is change in the early view of the male homosexual from the traditional *marica* (also called *joto* or **maricón**), a term designating a man who emulates the woman's stereotypical passive role, to a more international – foreign or modern – and versatile model of the 'gay', in which the categories of **bottom** or **top** do not jeopardize the masculine status of the men involved in sexual intercourse. Second, representation of lesbians, which in the popular imagination deals with the *marimacho* (a woman who emulates the macho figure), is linked more closely to feminine eroticism than sex and is more interested in the increasing awareness of women's social situation. Consequently, the representation of the lesbian – undoubtedly scarcer than male homosexuals – is related to the exploration of feminine identity and the deconstruction of the masculine and/in patriarchal society.

Further, there is a difference between early texts that represent male or female homosexuals as characters in a stereotypical way or from an external perspective and recent texts, whether in narrative or in 5w>poetry, in which homosexuals find a voice, their own voice, capable of categorizing, from their particular sexual orientation, the world and reality they live and experience.

In general terms, and also at a risk of being schematic, it is possible to suggest four trends or phases in Latin American narrative and poetry from 1945 to the present. Undoubtedly there are authors whose works cut across these trends and phases. However, some texts are paradigmatic of one trend and, consequently, characterize the phase. Owing to censorship and other repressive factors or national circumstances, some texts were written during one phase but published later, for example, *El diario de*

Jose Toledo (Jose Toledo's Diary) by the Mexican writer Miguel Barbachano Ponce (b. 1930), which was written in 1964 but not published until 1988. Of course, regarding this schematic periodization, some works are precursors of the trend while others follow. It is worth mentioning the situation of authors who, because of their political activities and/or their sexual orientation, went into exile, especially to Spain and the United States where they wrote their works. This is the case, for example, of the Cuban Reinaldo Arenas (1943–90) and many writers from Puerto Rico.

Another important issue to bear in mind is that from the end of the nineteenth century until 1970, Latin American queer authors were strongly influenced by European writers (Oscar Wilde, Marcel Proust, André Gide, Gabriel García Lorca, James Joyce and Jean Genet) and the American, Walt Whitman. However, after 1970 texts written in Latin America began to show a notable cultural and political impact derived from the gay movement in the United States. Furthermore, authors who moved to the US began writing in English, even though their plots focus on Latin America, as happened with Jaime Manrique Ardila, who was born in Colombia but is currently living in New York, and whose works include *Twilight at the Equator* (1990) and *Eminent Maricones: Arenas, Lorca, Puig and Me* (1999), a collection of essays about three paradigmatic homosexual authors. Works written in English by authors born in Latin America are arguably read as belonging to the Latin American or Latino canon. Certainly, the queer canon in Spanish has been expanded significantly since the mid-1990s thanks to the development of Gender and Queer Studies in US academia. Many early works have been scrutinized retrospectively and many textual references linked to homosexuality have been reclaimed, for example, the poems and plays of Sor Juana Inés de la

Cruz (1651–95); the foundational Argentine short story *El matadero* (Slaughter House, 1840) by Esteban Echeverría (1805–51) and *El juguete rabioso* (The Rabid Toy, 1926) by Roberto Arlt (1900–42), considered the first modern novel in Argentina to include the first explicit representation of a homosexual character.

During the first half of the twentieth century, the representation of homosexuals, especially male characters, displayed the sufferings, fears, and tribulations typically related to a life in the closet, with its secret ceremonies and transgressions, with its hopelessness and desperation. Novels and poems refer to furtive encounters, shared clandestine codes and oppressive families. In general, there is remarkable ambiguity at the moment in which homosexual desire is depicted within a homophobic society. Consequently, these coded texts are strongly allegorical. Later, authors explored homosexuality in more open and explicit terms.

The first trend or phase in Latin America discussed here runs from 1945 until the early 1960s. In Argentina, on one hand, some texts – such as *Siranger* (Stranger, written in 1955 but published in 1957) by Renato Pellegrini (b. 193?), 'La narración de la historia' (The Narration of History, 1959), a short story by Carlos Correas (b. 1931) and *Ay de mí, Jonathan* (Woe Is Me, Jonathan, 1976) – explicitly focus on homosexual behaviour and acts – masturbation, anal penetration, rimming, frottage – rituals and urban spaces for sexual intercourse between men. They also denounce hypocrisy and middle-class decency both during and after Perónism. On the other hand, short stories and poems by Jorge Luis Borges (1899–1986) – especially 'La intrusa' (The Intruder) and his view of the tango culture and the *compadrito*; Manuel Mujica Lainez (1910–84) – mainly *La casa* (The House, 1954), *El retrato amarillo* (The Yellow Portrait, 1956), *El unicornio* (The Unicorn, 1965) and *Sergio*

(1976) – and Alejandra Pizarnik's (1936–72) *La condesa sangrienta* (The Bloody Countess, 1965) allegorically elaborate homoerotic content by alluding to distinctive plots and distinct textual strategies.

In Chile, notwithstanding the early works by Augusto D'Halmar (1882–1950), republished during the 1960s, the major figure is the poet Gabriela Mistral (1889–1957). Nobel Prize winner for literature in 1945, canonized Madonna-like teacher–mother figure and Chilean representative for many countries in Europe, Latin and North America, Mistral is a controversial writer who has promoted a passionate critical debate over many years because of her suspected lesbianism. *Amasijo* (Mixture, 1962), written by Marta Brunet (1897–1967), is an early novel that deals with male homosexuality. Its protagonists are from different social classes and their relationship reproduces heterosexual conventions of loving and, as so happens with many feminine characters who transgress social norms, at the end they die.

The first phase in Peru is exemplified by César Moro, who was born in Lima but lived most of his life in Paris and wrote mostly in French, with the exception of his surrealist *La tortuga ecuestre* (The Equestrian Turtle), published posthumously in 1957. Inspired by his Mexican lover Antonio, who also encouraged him to write in Spanish, Moro's beautiful poems focus on passionate and sublime love.

Tentatively, the second phase begins in the crucial year 1968 – the year of the Parisian political revolt and the massacre of Mexican students in Tlatelolco, Mexico City – and continues until 1977, when military dictatorships were established in most Latin American countries, especially those of the Southern Cone. Obviously, after some moments of euphoria, it was a difficult time for political and sexual dissidents. Repression and censorship were rife and affected social life and cultural production. It was also the moment when the Cuban

Revolution demonstrated how the social and political transformation achieved since 1959 had impacted Latin American cultural production. In this sense, it is a historical moment for the political Left to emphasize the revolutionary ethics and decency in Latin America by means of reinforcing social bonds – especially conceived as male bonds in guerrilla warfare and factories – and a straight agenda based in family values. Consequently, homosexuality is strongly scrutinized and homosexuals – as Reinaldo Arenas' novels, especially his autobiography *Antes que anochezca* (*Before Night Falls*, 1992), testify – are persecuted, especially in Cuba. Regarding themes and literary forms, this phase is transitional. On the one hand, homosexual characters – particularly males – are represented in a more detailed way, far from the external mannerisms and the stereotypes. The homosexual assumes his place as the main character and his actions destabilize the feminine/masculine, active/passive dichotomies. By doing so, he also corrodes the double-standard codes of middle-class decency. On the other hand, the texts show a character or a voice definitively in search of his/her sexual liberation. Individual experience and identity are the main issues concerning queer literature in this phase. Diaspora and exile allow writers to confront other cultures (even subcultures in their own environments), other cities and other sexual perspectives and practices. As Isaac Chocrón's Mickey in *Pájaro de mar por tierra* (Bleached Seagull; 1972) and Luis Zapata's Adonis García in *Adonis García, el vampiro de la colonia Roma* (Adonis García: A Picaresque Novel, 1979), characters are open to explore their sexuality and sexual fantasies, whether gay or bisexual, to meet many people and to search for many places, new experiences and extreme pleasures. In both cases – the Venezuelan novel by Chocrón (b. 1930) and the Mexican classic by Zapata (b. 1951) – readers know about the protagonist's adventures by means of interviews recon-

structed by the authors, characters' negotiations with their bodies and, beyond eventual tribulations and fears, their search for sexual exuberance and definition of their identity.

In Argentina novels such as *Las tumbas* (The Tombs, 1971) and *Perros de la noche* (1978, Dogs of the Night) by Enrique Medina (b. 1937) show the furious macho violence, even the ferocity of repressive and homophobic systems (family, prison, school, remand home), especially over women. This violence grows when men are not allowed to express their homosexual desire and when social marginalization and poverty induce young people to crime.

Three major Cuban writers – Jose Lezama Lima (1912–76) and Severo Sarduy (1937–93) – deal with homosexuality. Lezama Lima's *Paradiso* (1966) is not only a *Bildungsroman* that chronicles the experiences of José Cemí from his childhood to the end of his adolescence, but also a summary of all of his ideas and themes displayed in his poetry and essays: language, creativity, androgyny, literature. Many characters in this novel deal with sexuality in many ways: heterosexual intercourse, sodomy, voyeurism, sadomasochism. Many critics have discussed the controversial status of homosexuality in Lezama Lima's texts, from social acceptance to total damnation. In Sarduy's *Gestos* (Gestures, 1963) and *Cobra* (1972), androgyny, homosexuality and transvestism are linked to a search for an exotic, multicultural, parodic and neobaroque body meticulously built and decorated in order to fulfil personal needs and desires.

José Donoso (1925–96), a Chilean writer, whose works were reviewed by critics after his death, focused on homosexuality in many of his texts, whether in a direct or oblique way. In *El lugar sin límites* (Hell Has No Limits, 1966/71), Donoso explicitly includes Manuela, a homosexual drag queen who runs a brothel, dominated by the caudillo (chief) of the town and victimized by men, particularly one who wants 'her' but who cannot admit his desire because of the homophobic 'familiar' environment. Allegorically, Donoso represents oppressive social relationships in a very vertical system of power that characterizes Latin American politics since Spanish colonialism.

Texts during the third phase represent homosexuals committed to movements of radical or revolutionary movements of liberation, whether social, political or sexual. This is a period when many Latin American countries suffered the effects of dictatorships but, at the same time, fought for democracy. Many people, especially workers, union leaders and intellectuals were tortured, others disappeared and many others were expelled into exile. Although a 'gay' identity is not yet available, authors design their homosexual characters as heroes; that is, they promote a 'positive' image of homosexuals as individuals more concerned with social and political issues than with sexual satisfaction. In this sense, characters participate in an agenda linked to liberation of women, indigenous people, blacks and workers. Political commitment, particularly one supported by the revolutionary Left, recycles in its own fashion several Christian values, such as sacrifice, solidarity and immolation, as the iconic status of Che Guevara exemplifies. On the one hand, homosexual characters are viewed positively as participating in the social transformation of the society and, on the other hand, they are brutally victimized and eliminated from the social scene. Undoubtedly, the best and paradigmatic example is Molina in *El beso de la mujer araña* (*Kiss of the Spider Woman*, 1976) by Manuel Puig (1932–90). In Argentina, there are three important novelists who were born in the provinces and wrote about homosexuality: Hugo Foguet (1923–85) and Juan José Hernández (1932) from Tucumán, and Héctor Hermes Villordo (1928–94) from Chaco.

Regarding feminine sexuality, Griselda Gambaro's *Lo impenetrable* (The Impenetrable Madame X, 1984) parodies the importance of the penis and the practice of penetration as providers of sexual pleasure. Madame X continuously goes from her frustration with Jonathan's penis to lesbian satisfaction with her maid Marie, although she always thinks that satisfaction has to be achieved by means of the penis and that something is lacking in lesbian intercourse. Gambaro (b. 1928) also deals with homosexuality in many of her dramatic texts. In Argentina, another relevant author who deals with homosexuality is Néstor Perlongher (1949–92). Perlongher's poems from *Austria-Hungría* (1980) to *Parque Lezama* (1990) give voice to a new pain, to a perverse view and to a new being as they emerge from a marginal subculture.

It is not surprising that many writers focus on homosexuality in this phase. A proliferation of novels and poetry can be found all over Latin America. In Chile, Pedro Lemebel's *Tengo miedo torero* (The Fearful Bullfighter), although published in 2002, is a novel which, in a neo-baroque and kitschy tone, follows Puig's vision revealed in *Kiss of the Spider Woman*, not only regarding the heroism of the queer main character, but also its permanent mixture of avant-gardism and popular culture.

In Puerto Rico, work by Luis Rafael Sanchez (b. 1936) (the scandalous *La guaracha del Macho Camacho* [Macho Camacho's Beat], 1976) and the poetry of Abniel Marat (b. 1958) (*Poemas de un homosexual revolucionario* [Poems by a Revolutionary Homosexual], 1985) are concerned primarily with the double standards of Puerto Rican decency, sexism, racism and homophobia, and the controversial status of Puerto Rico in relation to the United States.

In Mexico, in addition to Luis Zapata, it is worth mentioning novels by Jose Joaquín Blanco (b. 1951) – *Las púberes canéforas* (The

Pubescent Maidens, 1983) – and José Rafael Calva (b. 1953) – *Utopía gay* (1983). Albalucía Angel (b. 1939) is a Colombian writer whose experimental novels, particularly *Estaba la pájara pinta sentada en el verde limón* (The Spotted Bird Was Sitting on the Lemon Tree, 1979) and *Misiá Señora* (Miz Madame, 1982), deal with female sexuality and lesbianism. Cristina Peri Rossi, born in Uruguay in 1941, has been awarded for her fiction, poetry and essays. In her novel *La nave de los locos* (Ship of Fools, 1984) and the anthology, *Cuentos eróticos* (Erotic Short Stories, 1988) she explores lesbianism and the ways in which it differs from masculine homosexuality.

During the 1990s and 2000s, influenced by American gay culture, feminism, gay and lesbian studies, and a more flexible communication among gay movements all over the world, queer literature finally found a voice capable of articulating its search for a homosexual identity and gay social and political rights. AIDS is a global phenomenon that strongly impacts all gay cultural production. *POESIDA* (POETAIDS, 1995), edited by Carlos A. Rodríguez Matos, is a collection of texts written by many authors from Latin America, Spain and the United States. *Ojos que no ven* (Eyes That Do Not See, 1997) by Leyla Bartet, *La misteriosa metáfora de tu cuerpo* (The Mysterious Metaphor of Your Body, 1993) by Doris Moromisato Miasato (b. 1962, a Peruvian author with Japanese ancestors) and short stories by Mariella Sala, also from Peru, deal with exile, violence, virtual and real memory, eroticism, lesbianism and death.

In Mexico *Dos mujeres* (The Two Women, 1990) by Sara Levi Calderon (b. 1942) explores the controversial relationship between Jewish women, lesbianism and upper-class decency. Undoubtedly, Carlos Monsiváis (b. 1938) is a crucial figure in Mexican literature. From a gay and critical perspective, he has written many essays, chronicles and fiction on Mexican

culture and politics. Luis Montaño (1954–85) wrote *Brenda Berenice o el diario de una loca* (Brenda Berenice or the Diary of a Queen, 1985), a novel conceived as a festival or a carnival of language. Every group and character produces a particular slang and argot in order to resist the impositions of the dominant class and to define a cultural identity.

Puerto Rico is very well represented by *Buenos días, tio Sergio* (Happy Days, Uncle Sergio, 1986) by Magali García Ramis (b. 1946), a novel about a girl, Lidia, and her uncle Sergio, a 'different' man – 'most probably a homosexual' as Lidia thinks – who returns from New York and disturbs the fixed masculine and feminine roles and the racial prejudices supported by Lidia's traditional family. Puerto Rican lesbian writer Carmen de Monteflores (1933) also explores how sexism, racism and classism impact her writing and three generations of women in her bilingual novel *Singing Softly/Cantando bajito* (1989), while Puerto Rican poets Nemir Matos Cintrón (b. 1949) – who wrote the first two Puerto Rican books of lesbian poems – Moisés Agosto (b. 1965) and Frances Negrón Muntaner (b. 1966) are activists and scholars concerned with the effect of AIDS on the Latino community, sexism, racism, homosexuality and Puerto Rican emigration to the United States. Finally, it is worth mentioning Cuban writer Mayra Montero (b. 1952), author of *La última noche que pasé contigo* (The Last Night I Spent with You, 1991), in which she explores lesbian relationships among three women.

Bibliography

Mogrovejo, Norma (2000) *Un amor que se atrevió a decir su nombre. La lucha de las lesbianas y su relación con los movimientos homosexual y feminista en América Latina,* Mexico: Plaza y Valdez.

Rapisardi, Flavio and Modarelli, Alejandro (2001) *Fiestas, baños y exilios. Los gays porteños en la última dictadura*, Buenos Aires: Editorial Sudamericana.

Rodríguez Matos, Carlos A. (ed.) (1995) *POE-SIDA*, New York: Ollantay Press.

Further reading

Balutet, Nicolas (2003) *Représentations homosexuelles dans la culture hispanophone. Cet obscure objet du désir*, Paris: L'Harmattan.

Foster, David W. (ed.) (1994) *Latin American Writers on Gay and Lesbian Themes. A Bio-Critical Sourcebook,* Westport: Greenwood Press.

GUSTAVO GEIROLA

LAUBSCHER, B.J.F.

b. 1897

psychiatrist

Chief psychiatrist at the Queenstown Mental Hospital in South Africa, Barend Jacob Frederick Laubscher was an influential interpreter of Freudian psychology to posit a distinct black African sexuality. His *Sex, Custom and Psychopathology: A Study of South African Pagan Natives* (1938) gave scientific gravitas to long-standing colonial stereotypes of voracious, guiltless African sexual appetites. Where Laubscher broke new ground was in noting and attempting to analyse homosexual relations and masturbation among his African patients.

MARC EPPRECHT

LAVENDER HILL MOB

A group formed in 1986 primarily to oppose government inaction in finding treatments for people with AIDS. Co-founders and former Gay Activists Alliance (GAA) members Marty Robinson and Bill Bahlman brought the zap – a media-savvy political confrontation Robinson had perfected in GAA – and civil disobedience tactics to this new organization, whose activism eventually led to the creation of ACT UP, which was co-founded by members of the Lavender Hill Mob.

See also: ACT UP

DAVID CARTER

LE TIGRE

Le Tigre is a post riot-grrrl band founded in New York in 1998. The original members comprised Kathleen Hanna (of the seminal riot grrrl band Bikini Kill), Johanna Fateman and Sadie Benning. The latter was subsequently replaced by J.D. Samson, co-founder of Dykes Can Dance, after Le Tigre's debut album, *Self Titled* (1999). The sounds produced by the band can be considered feminist punk electronic music, blending irony with political commitment, with a joyous assertion of differences and condemnation of prejudice. The members of the band identify themselves as feminists, challenging misogyny, racism, homophobia, classism and imperialism. Le Tigre has become a strong reference point on the musical scene and within international queer culture and communities. Live performances are real shows in every sense, a sort of political electro-pop dance party, with video material, sampled tracks and live instrumentation.

MONICA BARONI

LEATHER

A term used to describe an array of sexual behaviours and identities relating to exploring dominant and submissive sexual roles, fetishism and **sadomasochism**. Leather culture originated in the burgeoning gay scene in American and European port cities during and after the Second World War. Eschewing the stereotypes of effeminate homosexuality, leather culture celebrates the homoerotic appeal of military codes and aesthetics, including the wearing of leather clothing and boots and the giving and receiving of physically painful or dominating stimuli. Leather behaviour and imagery was given definitive expression in Tom of Finland's erotic drawings, Larry Townsend's how-to sex manual *Leatherman's Handbook* (1972) and the photographs of Robert **Mapplethorpe**.

See also: Tom of Finland

JOHN FORDE

LEE, JULIAN

b. 1961

multimedia artist

Julian Chi Chiu (Li Zhi Chao) Lee is a multimedia artist with experience in broadcasting, print media, film directing and dot.com production. He started his career as a researcher and scriptwriter in television, became a photographer and editor of a magazine and then art director and scriptwriter in the film industry in the mid-1980s. He later studied in England (1988) and launched his career as a photographer and video-maker in London, where his pieces have been shown in many exhibitions. Lee's works borrow heavily from the Euro-American liberal arts tradition and touch upon and even celebrate ideas and practices of homosexuality, sadomasochism, meat joy, bestiality and incest. Most of his writings are collected in the 13 books he has published, including seven novels. Since 1997 Lee has turned two of his novels – *The Accident* (*Sam yuen yi ma*, 1999) and *Night Corridor* (*Yao ye hui lang*, 2003) – into feature films.

TRAVIS KONG

LENNOX, ANNIE

b. 1954

singer

From her association with British duo Eurythmics in the 1980s through her more recent solo work, Annie Lennox, born in Scotland, has remained a self-styled musical artist who resists all popular press attempts to define her image. Her appeal to the gay community has been linked to her free play with drag and androgyny. Lennox engages these attributes in ambiguous gender identification, most evident in the controversial music video for her release 'Who's That Girl', in which an Elvis Presley-styled male version of Lennox seduces him-/herself as a woman. Her association with gay-produced projects includes a performance as a singer in Derek Jarman's 1991 film *Edward II* (1991). She acknowledges her popularity among gay audiences at the same time that she dismisses sexual labels. Although her first solo release was entitled *Diva* (1992), Lennox has demonstrated herself to be charitable, philanthropic and indifferent to popular trends.

MICHAEL DEANGELIS

LEPAGE, ROBERT

b. 1957

director

Multidisciplinary stage wunderkind, Lepage is perhaps the least *politically* queer of Quebec's major gay artists. Emerging from the Quebec City theatre world in the 1970s and becoming an international star in the 1980s, Lepage has adapted four of his stage marathons of intercultural time travel as arthouse features. The prize-winning *Le Confessionnal* (1995) remains his greatest hit, with its Hitchcockian intertext and turbulent tapestry of family secrets and suicides, not to mention its queer subplot and monumental sauna set piece. *Le Polygraphe* (1996) and *Nô* (*No, No, Yes!*, 1998) followed, respectively turgid and frothy, more committed to their jibes at Quebec nationalism than their oblique queer undercurrents. Lepage's fifth feature, *La Face cachée de la lune* (*The Far Side of the Moon*, 2003) was his comeback adaptation and is the most autobiographical of his films. The director himself played both of two brother protagonists, one an asexual space geek and the other a pompous guppy whose lover is a tattooed and pierced body-builder as well as a provincial civil servant. Local satire aside, Lepage's universe of shifting historical times and transcultural spaces have spawned some of the more weighty enigmas of the international queer canon.

THOMAS WAUGH

LESBIAN AVENGERS

direct action group

The purpose of Lesbian Avengers is to promote lesbian issues and perspectives that challenge heterosexism, classism, racism and sexism. The first Lesbian Avengers chapter was founded in New York in 1992 by ACT UP activist Sarah **Schulman**. There are now about 55 Lesbian Avengers chapters. There is no national organization or structure. Each chapter undertakes its own direct actions through street theatre, protest and cultural commentary but works in collaboration on major and national events.

MONICA BARONI

LESKLY, HEZY

b. 1952; d. 1994

poet, choreographer, dance critic

Hezy Leskly was the author of four books of poetry: *Ha-Etsba'* (*The Finger*, 1986), *Hibur ve-hisu* (*Plus and Minus*, 1988), *Ha-'Akhbarim ve-Le'ah Goldberg* (*The Mice and Le'ah Goldberg*, 1992) and *Sotim yekarim* (*Dear Perverts*, 1994). Although he created three works of dance, he is known mostly for his poetry, and has been posthumously recognized as one of Israel's important poets of the 1980s and 1990s. The reception of his later work was coloured by his illness and untimely death from AIDS.

Leskly's poetry is characterized by its innovative postmodernist poetics that questions the relation between language and the world and its concern with the artistic goals of poetry. It combines aesthetic longings with poetic procedures such as metaphoric arbitrariness and a predilection towards paradox and absurdity that persistently undermine any promise of beauty and meaning. Leskly's work is humorous and provocative, yet nevertheless accompanied by an underlying tragic sense.

AMALIA ZIV

LEVAY, SIMON

neurobiologist

Born in Dulwich, England, Simon LeVay studied neurobiology at the University of Göttingen in Germany and has taught at Harvard medical school and at the Salk institute in San Diego. In 1992 he co-founded the West Hollywood Institute for Gay and Lesbian Education in Los Angeles. Although prolific as an author on many topics, he is best known for his scientific research on 'the gay brain'. His controversial publications, especially, *Queer Science: The Use and Abuse of Research into Homosexuality* (1996), put forward the argument that biology plays a role in the determination of sexual orientation, a view supported by other gay scientists such as Dean Hamer. LeVay's research concluded that the group of cells involved in the generation of the 'male-typical' sexual drive was twice as big in heterosexual men as in gay men which, he suggests, proves that homosexuality has a neurobiological basis. LeVay has been criticized widely for supporting reductionist versions of homosexuality and for basing his conclusions on small samples from men who died of AIDS-related illnesses.

KATHERINE WATSON

LIBERACE

b. 1919; d. 1987

entertainer

Born Wladzui (Walter) Valentino Liberace in West Allis, Wisconsin, he learned the piano by ear at age 4. His show-business career was built upon his ability to mix a classical and popular style of piano playing that appealed to mass audiences, as showcased on *The Liberace Show* (1952–6). Liberace's flamboyant stage shows became legendary in Las Vegas, and he was the highest paid entertainer on the circuit in 1955 when he opened at the Riviera Hotel on a weekly salary of $50,000. His style was excessively camp and he became known as 'Mr Showmanship', with his trademark candelabra positioned on his grand piano.

His immense popularity prompted speculation about his private life – his fey mannerisms had been noted. He never publicly acknowledged his homosexuality and brought a public libel action against the *Daily Mirror* (UK) for inferring that he was gay. He was finally outed in 1982 when his lover and chauffeur Scott Thorsen (who endured plastic surgery paid for by Liberace to make him look more like his employer) sued him for $113,000,000 in palimony; the case was settled out of court for $98,000.

His death was AIDS-related, as was the death in 1997 of his last young lover Cary James. Liberace bequeathed his estate to the Liberace Foundation for the Performing and Creative Arts. His private museum, opened in 1979 in Las Vegas, features 18 of his 39 pianos, costumes, jewellery and his custom-built cars.

MICHAEL PINFOLD

LIDDICOAT, RENÉE

b. ?1920; d. ?1985

psychologist

South African psychologist Renée Liddicoat pioneered a modern, non-stigmatizing understanding of homosexuality in South Africa. A lesbian herself, her 1956 doctoral dissertation and subsequent articles vindicated the humanity of gays and lesbians. Her submission to the 1968 Select Committee on the Immorality Amendment Bill buttressed other liberal voices such as Mary **Renault** and the Law Reform Movement and played an important role in thwarting the apartheid regime's proposed criminalization of homosexuality.

MARC EPPRECHT

LINK/SKAKEL

Link/Skakel was an early gay publication in South Africa. Launched in 1982, it began as a monthly newsletter distributed nationally to dues-paying members of the Gay Association of South Africa (GASA). Its content reflected the white, male demographics of GASA and focused on club round-ups, community news and hunk pictorials. It had a peak circulation of 5,000. GASA attempted to open sales to the public in 1984, but after the state banned the first two issues – complaining that it 'promoted homosexuality' – distribution was again restricted. In 1985 GASA disbanded *Link/ Skakel* because of high production costs.

See also: Exit

ANTHONY MANION

LIPSTICK LESBIANS

Critiqued as devoid of a queer political sensibility, yet vociferously defended in the same context, lipstick lesbians are lesbians who wear clothing and makeup that is culturally coded as feminine. The term is sometimes used interchangeably with 'femme'. Representations of, and references to, lipstick lesbians were widely circulated in the context of the so-called 'lesbian chic' media phenomenon of the 1990s, which (arguably) rendered the lipstick lesbian fashionable, desirable and, consequently, acceptable to the mainstream.

ANITA BRADY

LITHUANIA, LITERATURE

Lithuanian literature and culture suffered under the Soviet occupation that lasted from the end of the Second World War until independence in 1990/1. One allegedly lesbian author, Janina Degutytė, wrote many volumes of poetry and children's books. Writers from Lithuania but living outside were free from censorship, however, and could address queer themes. John Kertzer penned a coming-out novella about a Lithuanian character. Vytautas Pliura wrote several gay plays and poetry collections, the newest of which was translated into Russian as an example of queer Lithuanian literature. Since independence, Lithuanian cultural and religious attitudes have remained homophobic. Several authors who do not identify themselves as queer have composed works with queer themes, and a pre-war novella was republished. Lithuanian queer literature is a developing genre.

The poet Janina Degutytė (1928–90) became the most popular Lithuanian woman author of the Soviet occupation. It is still virtually impossible to verify her sexual orientation. Her intensely personal poetry evolves the Lithuanian lyric tradition, combining simple vocabulary with musicality in deep layers of symbolic meanings. Its figurative language voices the conscience of a stifled nation. The author's dedication of 1994 poem 'Vakariniai maratonai' ('Evening Marathons') to a woman named Vanda suggests a possible lesbian reading: the complex poetic language describes an intentional, but secretive, meeting of two friends in the dark shadows of night, where they can reveal themselves in a vision of a bright abyss.

In the Lithuanian diaspora, John Ketzer's (1944–) English-language novella *My First Year Out* (1984) relates the narrator's coming out in 1968 Detroit, the year before Stonewall. Just as the author uses a pseudonym to hide his gayness from the Lithuanian community, the protagonist calls himself 'Al', short for 'Algird[a]', hiding his own Lithuanian identity from the gay world. The author moved to Lithuania after independence.

The English-speaking Vytautas Pliura (1951–) has written three staged plays, *Conspiracy of Feelings* (1982), *Dangerous Comedy* (1988), *Don't Let the Bed Bugs Bite, Norma Jean* (1990), and two books of poetry, *Skating on the Dark Side of the Moon* (1995) and *Tenderness in Hell* (2001, republished 2003). Several long production runs of the first play as well as awards for it brought the author notoriety early in his career. It is about racism and homophobia in Los Angeles. Pliura's poetry searches for self as well as social acceptance. The 2003 Russian translation casts Pliura as an example of gay Lithuanian lyricism. Pliura is also noted as a Vietnam War veteran. In the poem 'In the Hands of the Enemy', he relates the inhuman atrocity of grotesque sexual perversion he experienced as a gay prisoner of war. 'Tenderness in Hell' connects the author to his Lithuanian father who was imprisoned in a Nazi concentration camp. Pliura is pursuing a Lithuanian translation of his poetry.

Since independence, several hetero authors have written about queer issues in Lithuania. Edmundas Malūkas' (1945–) 1996 (republished 2000) best-selling soap-opera novel *Juodieji želmenys* (Dark Desires) propagates negative stereotypes of gays, lesbians, and bisexuals. Ruthless gay Satanists control the Lithuanian crime syndicate. They establish a gay restaurant with lesbian nights and a back room for anonymous sex. The novel confuses gays and lesbians with bisexuals, claims homosexuality is a biological threat to national survival, and reflects the homophobia of Lithuanian society.

Jonas Marcinkevičius' (1990–53) 1931 novella *Ties bedugne* (Toward the Abyss) was republished in 2000, with the sensationalist, but false claim of being the first Lithuanian bisexual fiction. Actually, it is a third-party memoir about the heterosexual development of a teenager. He displays no bisexual tendencies at all and rebukes the sole homosexual advance in the book.

Laura Sintija Černiauskaitė's (1976–) 2003 play *Liuče čiuožia* (Lucy is Skating) suggests lesbian relationships. One female character recommends asking another woman, who is looking for casual sex with a man, if she is a lesbian. Later, the two key women of the drama, Liuče and Tania, find a common bond asexually, in contrast to the men in their lives. The play won the Grand Prix at the 2004 Istanbul Theatre Festival in 2004 and has been translated into German.

Some Lithuanian gays and lesbian have published their poetry and short stories anonymously on the web site *www.gayline.lt*. The poetry is about love and longing, while the short stories discuss relationships.

VILIUS RUDRA DUNDZILA

LIU, CATHERINE

b. 1964

writer

Novelist and critic whose works explore the conflicting influences of her Chinese-American cultural heritage and lesbian sexuality. Born in Taipei and raised in New York by a Chinese immigrant family, Liu studied English literature at Yale and earned a PhD in French Literature at the City University of New York. Her first novel, *Oriental Girls Desire Romance* (1987), written while she was a graduate student, is an autobiographical coming-of-age narrative of an unnamed female in 1980s Manhattan who struggles with her ambitions as

an author and her burgeoning sexual identity. Her second novel, *Suicide of an Assistant Professor*, is a comic novel set in the world of academia. Liu has also produced translations of Gerard Pommier's *Erotic Anger: A User's Manual* (2001) and Victor Hugo's *The Hunchback of Notre Dame* (2002). Other works include *Copying Machines: Taking Notes for the Automaton* (2000).

JOHN FORDE

LOG CABIN REPUBLICANS

An organization comprising American gays who identify politically as members of the Republican Party. The first chapter was formed in 1978 to fight California's Proposition 6, a ballot initiative that would have banned gay and lesbian schoolteachers. The group successfully convinced then Governor Ronald Reagan to oppose the measure. Despite Reagan's support for the group, conservative Party members attempted – unsuccessfully – to oust the Log Cabin Group at the National Convention in 1987.

The chapters merged to form a national organization in 1995, working to moderate anti-gay views and promote gay-friendly policies. As the Republican Party's moral conservatism increased under the leadership of George H. W. Bush in the 1990s, many gay and lesbian politicians switched their allegiances to Democrat-elect Bill Clinton. In 2002 President George W. Bush invited the group to an official White House briefing to acknowledge their support of his 2000 campaign. Despite this gesture, Bush has opposed gay civil union and marriage.

JOHN FORDE

LONDON

The capital city of Great Britain, London was founded by the Romans in AD 43.

London's same-sex culture dates back to antiquity, but did not become visible until the eighteenth century. In the eighteenth and nineteenth centuries Soho, Covent Garden, the West End – especially Piccadilly – the City and the Royal Parks neighbourhoods were notorious centres of male homosexual activity. The West End, around Old Compton Street, is now the heart of commercial gay culture.

H.G. COCKS

LONG YANG CHUN

Meaning literally 'dragon male gentleman', the term refers to a legendary male homosexual in ancient China believed to be a male favourite of the King of Wei during the Warring States period (403–221 BC). Using this euphemism, Long Yang Club is a well-known international social group that caters primarily to gay Southeast Asian men hoping to meet Caucasian gay men in major Western cities.

TRAVIS KONG

LÓPEZ, JOSEFINA

b. 1969

writer

María Josefina López was born in Cerritos, San Luís Potosí, México and raised in Los Angeles. She has written and published several plays that centre on the lives of Chicana/Latina women. López is particularly interested in destabilizing the norms that maintain these women in repressive social and sexual roles. For example, her award-winning play *Simply María, or the American Dream* (1992) includes a young Chicana protagonist who defies all of the traditional mores her Mexican family tries to instil in her. In *Real Women Have Curves* (1992), López also addresses these issues while she tackles the pressure women

experience to conform to ideal body images. To do this, she presents a homosocial environment devoid of men where women form intimate bonds and display their bodies. In other plays, López includes gay and lesbian characters who also assist her with her mission to destabilize gender and sexual norms.

DANIEL ENRIQUE PÉREZ

LÓPEZ, YOLANDA

b. 1942

artist

Yolanda López is a visual artist born in San Diego, California and raised in Logan Heights. After moving to San Francisco, she began her career by working as a community artist in the Mission District. She earned an MFA from the University of California, San Diego in 1978. From the beginning of her artistic career, López used her art as a tool for social and political change, working diligently to combat stereotypical images of Chicano/as and Latino/as in public art. She was especially interested in taking a feminist and deconstructionist approach to dispel traditional images of Chicanas and Latinas. In her most celebrated installation, the *Virgin of Guadalupe* series (1978), López takes this most popular and highly revered female icon of Chicano and Mexican culture and revises it to make a statement about female empowerment through mobility. Her most famous work, *Portrait of the Artist as the Virgin of Guadalupe* (1978), is a portrait of the artist jogging in tennis shoes in a pink dress that reveals most of her bare legs. Through the use of such imagery, López provides alternative ways of seeing women, as active agents with full control of their surroundings. Many of López's paintings are devoid of men. She chooses instead to focus on the female experience, especially as it is related to Chicanas and Latinas. Her images are equally transgressive in the way they depict the female body in alternate cultural contexts while exploring the physical and intellectual risks that women take in fighting for social and political change.

See also: Virgin of Guadalupe

DANIEL ENRIQUE PÉREZ

LORDE, AUDRE

b. 1934; d. 1992

poet, activist

Born in Harlem, New York City, to Caribbean immigrants, Audrey Geraldine Lorde graduated from Hunter College and Columbia University, where she received her MA in library studies. Later, she held the position of Chair of Literature at Hunter. She was the recipient of a multitude of awards, including that of New York State's Poet Laureate (1991–3). As a young girl she dropped the 'y' from her first name, signalling the centrality of identity and individuality about which she would later so passionately write. Lorde characterized her identity as 'Black lesbian, mother, warrior, poet'. Indeed, with great eloquence, Lorde managed all these positions, working as a teacher, writer and activist while raising two children after a failed marriage.

During crucial periods such as the civil rights movement in the United States, Lorde taught at Tougaloo College in Jackson, Mississippi. Internationally, Lorde was instrumental in the formation of the Support Sisters in South Africa and often involved herself in relief efforts in areas overseas devastated by natural disasters. Most significantly, Lorde maintained her insistent and lyrical voice against inequality, heterosexism and homophobia.

In 1982 Lorde penned her key lesbian text, *Zami: A New Spelling of My Name*. Her emphasis upon both the emotional and sexual connectedness between women transformed and extended the range of meaning for lesbianism, especially for black women. Lorde called this work a 'biomythography', since it centred on her relationships with women as well as ancestral African mothers. Her identity as a black lesbian remained at the heart of her life projects. She has published more than a dozen books on poetry and six books in prose.

For 14 years Lorde battled cancer, finally succumbing to the disease in 1992. Her work – her revolution – continues to resonate in the struggles over racism and homophobia. As she always reminded us: 'The revolution is not a one-time event'.

DAVID A. GERSTNER

LOS ANGELES

The second-largest city in the United States, Los Angeles arguably ranks third in the queer atlas of US cities, after **New York** and San Francisco, perhaps because the gay community in Los Angeles is not as large or powerful (relative to the city that contains it) as San Francisco's. Nevertheless, Los Angeles has been the site of several important developments in queer history, the most prominent being the **Mattachine Society**. Just as the homosexual subculture of New York has influenced the theatre, art and publishing worlds based there, so has the homosexual subculture of Los Angeles influenced Hollywood and the TV industry.

DAVID PENDLETON

LOS BELTRÁN

TV series

Los Beltrán is a Spanish-language comedy series developed in the United States that first aired in 1999 on Telemundo. It marked the first ongoing, positive portrayal of a gay character in a Spanish programme. Openly bisexual actor Gabriel Romero plays the role of Fernando, a gay doctor who lives with his partner, Kevin. In one episode the couple partake in their own civil union in Vermont, making them the first 'married' gay couple in any programme in the US. Besides making history by presenting these series of firsts, *Los Beltrán* brings to the forefront various glbt issues in a Latino cultural context.

DANIEL ENRIQUE PÉREZ

LOUGANIS, GREG

b. 1960

swimmer

Greg Louganis became famous at the Seoul Olympics in 1988 for winning two gold medals despite having hit his head against the diving board during a practice session. He came out as gay at the 1994 **Gay Games**. In 1995 he revealed that he had been HIV+ at the Olympics. The revelation caused a flurry of public speculation that he might wilfully have exposed fellow divers to the virus but such fears were quickly shown to be untrue. Louganis is one of the few out queer athletes, and his account of his early life as an unhappy biracial adopted child who never felt like he fit anywhere has particularly endeared him to queer fans. He has retired from diving, and currently breeds show dogs. Like Martina **Navratilova** and Rudy **Galindo**, Louganis was rarely granted public endorsement packages, exemplifying the ambiguous position of queer sports stars bound by the underlying heteronormativity of sports discourse.

YASMIN NAIR

LUDLAM, CHARLES

b. 1943; d. 1987

actor

Charles Ludlam moved to New York City in 1965 and quickly became involved with the group of theatre artists associated with the so-called Theater of the Ridiculous. After working with Ronald **Tavel** and John **Vaccaro**, he formed a separate group called the Ridiculous Theatrical Company and began writing his own plays. The group's plays were frequently camp reworkings of stage classics (*Hamlet, Bluebeard, The Ring of the Niebelung*), that mixed in elements drawn from old Hollywood movies. Although the group started performing in bars and other venues on virtually no money, they eventually secured a theatre of their own. Their plays were often popular and critical successes, garnering Obie Awards and other honours. In 1975 Ludlam met Everett Quinton, who became his lover and colleague. The two starred in the most famous of Ludlam's plays, *The Mystery of Irma Vep*, a spoof of Gothic horror films. Ludlam died of AIDS in 1987.

DANIEL HENDRICKSON

LUPE, LA

b. 1938; d. 1992

performer

Guadalupe Victoria Yoli or 'La Lupe', originally from Santiago, Cuba, was a pioneer in queering mainstream Caribbean musical performance styles. Lupe invested her songs with erotic empowerment, peppering her singing with emotive strategies such as high-pitched moaning, epileptic fits and passionate remarks directed towards her orchestra and public. She preferred to express herself in terms of extremes: extreme lamentation, extreme jubilation or extremely sexualized interpretations of music. Frequently her loud, and often sharp – in the sense that she never modulated modest, melodious notes – voice exuded a certain queerness that threatened 'normalcy' while introducing nasal orgiastic cries of 'ay-na-má'. Lupe thrived on irreverence and fought boycotts from the mainstream music industry during her later years in New York. She sang and performed for three decades all the while contesting heterosexist morality with visceral defiance.

KANISHKA SEN

LYNES, GEORGE PLATT

b. 1907; d. 1955

photographer

Openly gay photographer who is best known for his homoerotic portraits of male nudes. Lynes was born on 15 April 1907 in East Orange, New Jersey. He travelled in France during the 1920s, meeting Jean Cocteau and Gertrude Stein, and two Americans, art curator Monroe Wheeler and writer Glenway Westcott, both of whom were later to become his lovers and patrons. His photographic subjects included Stein and Alice B. Toklas, E.M. Forster, Colette, Dorothy Parker, Tennessee Williams, Christopher Isherwood, Aldous Huxley, W. Somerset Maugham and others. He returned to New York in the 1930s, holding his first solo exhibition at the Wheeler Gallery in 1932 and working for *Vogue* and *Harper's Bazaar* magazines. In 1934 Lincoln Kirstein and George Balanchine invited him to photograph the dancers and productions of the American Ballet (later the New York City Ballet), a project he continued until his death. Throughout his career, he photographed a number of male nudes, initially modelled after Greek art but becoming more explicit and openly homoerotic over time. In 1949 he became an intimate friend of sexologist Alfred **Kinsey**, who bought over 600 prints and negatives of his nude studies. Lynes destroyed much of his work before his death in New York City in 1955.

JOHN FORDE

LYON, PHYLLIS

See: Martin, Del and Phyllis Lyon

LYPSINKA

b. 1955

drag artist

The alter ego of John Epperson, Lypsinka is one of America's most celebrated **drag** entertainers. Lypsinka's theatrical career was launched in 1982 with the off-Broadway show *If I Could Go On Lip-Synching!*, a slickly produced medley of lip-synched Broadway show tunes and satirical imitations of Hollywood screen divas including Joan Crawford, Bette Davis and Elizabeth Taylor. Subsequent shows included *The Fabulous Lypsinka Show, Lypsinka! A Day In The Life, As I Lay Lip-Synching, Lypsinka Must Be Destroyed*, the award-winning *Lypsinka! The Boxed Set*, and *John Epperson: Show Trash*. Lypsinka's film work includes *Vampire's Kiss* (1989), *The Witch hunt* (1994) and *Son of Trog* (1999), a satirical sequel to Joan Crawford's film *Trog* (1970). She also appears in the documentary *Wigstock* (1995), the TV specials *Dragtime* and *Sandra After Dark* with Sandra Bernhard, and as a model for The Gap, Valentino and Thierry Mugler.

See also: Drag queen

JOHN FORDE

M

MACDONALD, HEATHER

filmmaker

New York-based lesbian filmmaker who is best known for her award-winning documentary *Ballot Measure 9* (1995). Filmed over eight months, MacDonald followed both sides of a debate over Ballot Measure 9, an anti-gay initiative proposed by the Oregon Citizen's Alliance to amend the state constitution's laws protecting gays and lesbians from discrimination. Combining portions of anti-gay videos produced by the Citizen's Alliance as well as news clips and interviews with the activists who successfully fought Measure 9, the film documents the increase in gay hate crimes in Oregon during the debate and underlines the strength of grassroots gay activism. The film won the Audience Award at the 1995 Sundance Film Festival, and the 1996 GLAAD Media Award for Outstanding Documentary. MacDonald's other works include *Kiev Blue* (1992), a documentary short about nine gays and lesbians living in Russia.

JOHN FORDE

MACHO

Refers to a specific type of gay identity that involves a rejection of conventional effeminacy and an adoption of 'hyper-masculine' attributes.

KEN WONG

MACLENNAN, JOHN

b. 1951; d. 1980

police inspector

Scottish expatriate and Hong Kong police inspector whose involvement in a gay scandal followed by his mysterious death prompted Hong Kong's modern gay rights movement. Born in Scotland, MacLennan moved to Hong Kong and became an inspector with the Royal Police Force. In August 1979, Hong Kong's Attorney General instructed the police Special Investigation Unit to investigate and prosecute homosexuality (then illegal in Hong Kong) within the police force, judiciary and legal profession. The resulting investigations implicated a number of high-profile British expatriate civil servants, causing embarrassment to the government. On 15 January 1980, MacLennan was found dead with five bullet wounds to his chest; he was discovered by a group of fellow officers who had come to arrest him on six charges of being involved in homosexual activities. The police force suggested that MacLennan had killed himself, but the coroner's inquiry returned an 'open' verdict on the cause of his death, leading to widespread media speculation that he had been murdered to prevent him from publicizing the names of high-ranking police officers also under investigation for homosexuality. In November 2001, a judicial inquiry was formed to investigate police handling of the case and to consider whether there were valid grounds for accepting that MacLennan's death was other than suicide. The inquiry report, published in September 1981, criticized the police's handling of the case, but concluded that MacLennan had committed suicide. The decision created a national outcry, prompting many gay and lesbian people to come out publicly in order to protest the MacLennan case and demand equal treatment under the law. In 1991 the Hong Kong government decriminalized homosexuality between consenting adults in private.

JOHN FORDE

MADIKIZELA-MANDELA, WINNIE

b. 1936

politician

Winnie Madikizela-Mandela is a South African politician whose outspoken opposition to apartheid brought her international accolades during the 1980s. She is the ex-wife of former South African president Nelson Mandela. In 1991 she was charged with complicity in the kidnapping, torture and murder of a young boy, Stompie Moeketsi. Her defence argued that the boy had been rescued from a white Methodist Minister who allegedly had been homosexually abusing African boys. Madikizela-Mandela thus became one of the first prominent African leaders to exploit fears and denial about homosexuality among blacks and to link homophobia positively to anti-racism struggles. The trial strengthened the emerging gay rights movement in South Africa and to helped persuade her political party (African National Congress) to formally recognize the contributions of gay rights activists to the liberation of South Africa. Madikizela-Mandela subsequently made a public gesture of condolence for the families of gay men murdered in a criminal attack on a Cape Town massage parlour in 2001.

MARC EPPRECHT

MADONNA

b. 1958

pop star

The ultimate postmodern pop star and gay icon, Madonna has crafted and reshaped her body, attire, persona and career a number of times, and by so doing has found her primal significance in queer culture. Born Louise Veronica Ciccone in Bay City, Michigan, she is a modest singer, musician and actor when compared to the smart businesswoman and stage performer she has revealed herself to be. She gained some popularity during the early 1980s on the New York gay dance club scene but found instant success with her 1983 self-titled debut album, which marked a move into mainstream pop and an erotically charged stage persona. This was to be the first in a striking series of chart-topping records and songs that would project her as one of the most commercially successful artists in the history of popular music. Her extraordinarily powerful video personality was fully staged in *Like a Virgin* (1984), and was enhanced by the newly born MTV network, the best of possible allies in making her an international star and a controversial media celebrity.

Madonna's first stage persona was a rather tacky, sexy, bleached blonde youngster, sporting lace gloves and lingerie, and cross-shaped jewellery, so as to subversively evoke her Italian–American Catholic background. Within a few months she had reinvented herself in *Material Girl* as a platinum blonde, a stylish, glamorous Marilyn Monroe for the 1990s, an event that marked the blooming of her love affair with gay culture which would culminate in the video for *Vogue* (1991). Introducing the mainstream to 'voguing', a dance popular in gay clubs, the move also highlighted a worship for old Hollywood, a tendency associated with gays. Later she compounded her gay-friendly image by joining gay actor Rupert Everett in the video for

American Pie (2000) in a mildly ironic celebration of alleged American tolerance, inclusiveness and democracy.

Over the course of her career, the platinum blonde would become the 'girl-with-a-past' (due to the revelation of her early nude photographs), the mistreated wife (of riotous actor Sean Penn), the dark-haired lascivious woman making love to a black saint (in the video for *Like a Prayer* [1989]) and the person responsible for staging the intertwining of eroticism and religion that characterized the very choice of her stage name. She would later become Marlene Dietrich, an art deco diva; the porn star offering the soundtrack, image, lyrics and manifesto for an aesthetics of unchained desire; a mystic and esoteric queen giving up Catholicism in favour of Kabbalah; the wife of filmmaker Guy Ritchie, mother of two children and author of fairy tales; the cowgirl and disco party-girl; and the censor of American life.

Her versatility in creating new characters was, at least in part, reinforced by her performances on-screen, although these were less successful – according to many critics she managed to perform adequately only in those roles closely resembling her own (pop) self, e.g., the protagonist of *Desperately Seeking Susan* (1987), the demanding vamp of *Dick Tracy* (1990) and the fame-obsessed actor and later national icon of *Evita* (1996).

Madonna has shown a unique flair for marketing, an unrivalled talent both in perceiving trends and fashions, adopting marginal identities (gay, lesbian, sadomasochism/bondage) and cannibalizing them, and in outraging orthodox society – the Christian Right condemned her early performances, the Vatican accused her of making blasphemous videos, the uproar surrounding her 'sexual years' – all were turned into unwilling weapons of advertisement and publicity. From her early photo sessions to the exhibition of the star's intimacy in *Truth or Dare* (1991), a documentary film that chronicled the behind-the-scenes and sensual choreographies, dance and religious imagery of her 1990 Blond Ambition Tour, to the unapologetic portrayal of female sexuality in the 1992 *Sex* book (which exposed her in luscious poses, depicting sadomasochism, lesbianism, and interracial and anal sex), to the *Erotica* video (also 1992), which was banned for years by MTV and VH1, Madonna's explorations of desire have proven the most effective market strategy.

A veritable cross-dresser and style vulture à la David Bowie, Madonna's feminist and camp posturing has also proven to be her best token of queer performativity – a hypererotic female image whose spectacle steadily refuses to be framed by the heterosexist gaze, and retains full control on the frame and on her career. Madonna has become a guardian figure and role model of sorts for younger would-be pop stars (e.g., Christina Aguilera and Britney Spears, whom she crowned with a kiss at the 2003 MTV Video Music Awards) and the ultimate icon for generations of wannabes and for queers worldwide. The complexity of issues raised by such iconicity, staging the tensions and complicity between queer subversiveness and capitalistic vampirism, assure an outstanding presence not only on video networks, in tabloids, in music charts and on-screen, but also in academic syllabi.

Further reading

Frank, L. and Smith, P. (eds) (1993) *Madonnarama: Essays on Sex and Popular Culture*, San Francisco: Cleis Press.

Lloyd, F. (ed.) (1993) *Deconstructing Madonna*, London: Batsford.

Robertson, P. (1996) *Guilty Pleasures: Feminist Camp from Mae West to Madonna*, Durham: Duke University Press.

Schwichtenberg, C. (ed.) (1993) *The Madonna Connection: Representational Politics, Subcultural Identities, and Cultural Theory*, Boulder: Westview.

FABIO CLETO

MAGAZINES AND THE GLBTQ PRESS

Use of the newly coined term homosexuality in late nineteenth-century Europe emerged in tandem with the view that same-gender sexual desire and behaviour constituted a distinct sexual orientation. Scientists, social thinkers and lawmakers increasingly scrutinized the phenomenon of homosexuality, but homosexuals themselves responded slowly to this public discussion.

When Prussia united the disparate German territories into a single state in 1871, Paragraph 175 of its new penal code outlawed homosexual behaviour. Britain, with its Criminal Law Amendment of 1885, also took specific aim at homosexual sodomy. A decade later, Edward Carpenter, a minister, pacifist and Christian socialist who revealed his homosexuality in 1880, published the pamphlet *Homogenic Love and Its Place in a Free Society*, perhaps the earliest printed defence of gay life. Its publication in January 1895 came just months before Oscar Wilde's first criminal trial, and given the resulting popular press outcry against sodomy, Carpenter did not return to his sexual freedom campaign for more than a decade.

In Germany in 1896 Adolph Brand, an anarchist, began publishing *Der Eigene* (One's Own), that nation's first known homosexual periodical. Brand's politics were reactionary and would seem foreign to twentieth-century gay liberationists. Resentful of what he saw as the emasculated state of German society, Brand preached a return to patriarchy, inculcated in young males by older male lovers. His publication spawned an organization dedicated to overturning criminal sodomy penalties.

In 1897 Magnus Hirschfeld established his Scientific Humanitarian Committee, also aimed at repealing Paragraph 175 but based on a progressive worldview emphasizing women's emancipation and democratic reform. A physician and pioneering sexologist, in 1899 Hirschfeld launched two periodicals that combined scientific and cultural reporting and persisted for decades – the *Scientific Humanitarian Committee Newsletter* and the *Yearbook for Sexual Intermediate Types*, the latter title reflecting Hirschfeld's view of gay people as a third sex. During the early 1920s he suffered a public beating for his visibility as a homosexual rights proponent and the Nazis a decade later stripped him of his citizenship.

As the worldwide movement for women's rights gathered steam in the early twentieth century, lesbian periodicals appeared in Europe. The most famous of these, *Die Freundin* (*Girlfriend*), emerged during Germany's Weimar era and was published monthly from 1924 until 1933.

A Bavarian immigrant, Henry Gerber, who learned about the German homosexual rights movement while serving in the US Army there after the First World War, published the first gay periodical in America, *Friendship and Freedom*, in Chicago in 1925; the magazine ran for several months. He was soon arrested on morals charges, of which he was acquitted but not before being ruined financially.

Gay and lesbian Americans of Gerber's era, if they saw anything of their lives in the press, were far more likely do so in the sex digests and confessional magazines in vogue during the 1920s as staples at drugstore counters. Primarily a response to the emergence of birth control and women's greater sexual freedom, these publications had a scandal-tinged, pulp character that cast occasional glances at sexual behaviour considered decidedly exotic.

Nazi persecution stamped out much of the nascent queer culture in Germany and later throughout Europe, although one of the world's longest-lived gay publications got its start in Zurich in 1932 and persisted until 1967. Begun as *Friendship Banner*, the publication, marketed to gay men by subscription only, was renamed *Der Kreis* (*The Circle*) in 1942 and contained cultural and political commentary.

The end of the Second World War unleashed a global era of liberation movements –

anti-colonial in the developing world and on behalf of African-Americans and women in the US – and a press that reflected growing gay and lesbian visibility also took root.

In 1947 a young secretary at RKO Studios in Los Angeles began a small newsletter, *Vice Versa*, under the pseudonym Lisa Ben, an anagram for lesbian. She was only able to produce a small number of copies using mimeograph paper and continued her effort for just one year, but her publication, focused on both politics and culture, was influential, with California lesbians enthusiastically circulating each new issue amongst themselves.

Harry **Hay** led a small group of southern California men in 1950 in forming an early male homophile organization, the **Mattachine Society**, named for the medieval European masked troubadours. In 1953 Dale Jennings and others from that group launched *ONE*, a publication sold by subscription and on newsstands that at its height reached more than 10,000 readers. The Los Angeles postmaster twice seized copies of *ONE*, invoking the 1873 Comstock Act that banned the mailing of obscene materials. After losing in the lower federal courts, *ONE* achieved an astonishing unanimous victory in the US Supreme Court in 1958. The ruling not only paved the way for the growth of the gay press, but also struck down an enforcement tool increasingly used to persecute gay men receiving erotic material by mail.

Two years after *ONE*'s launch, the San Francisco Mattachine chapter started the *Mattachine Review*, more scholarly in its attention to history and culture and more moderate in its politics. It was published for more than a decade.

The 1955 founding by Phyllis Lyon and Del Martin of the San Francisco-based **Daughters of Bilitis**, named for a fictional contemporary of Sappho, led the following year to the launch of *The Ladder*, a lesbian publication that originally focused on culture and was mailed to 200 Bay Area women. During its 16-year life, *The Ladder* became increasingly political, eventually taking on a radical feminist voice.

Another early gay press milestone was the 1953 launch of Bob Mizer's *Physique Pictorial*, the first nationally distributed magazine featuring male erotic photography and illustrations. Sold on newsstands, the magazine by 1957 introduced **Tom of Finland** to American gay men.

By the 1960s homosexuality was receiving mainstream press attention, with a *Life* magazine cover story in 1964, the appearance by West Village gay activist Randall Wicker the same year on Les Crane's national TV talk show and a largely negative CBS Reports special in 1967.

Drum, originally published in 1964 as the newsletter of Philadelphia's gay Janus Society, became the first magazine to combine serious news reporting with a clear erotic component, including full frontal male nudity, and a comic strip, *The Man from A.U.N.T.I.E.*, as well. Faced with federal obscenity indictment in 1969, Clarke Polak, *Drum*'s driving force, agreed to cease publication.

Gay periodicals also began to emerge outside the US in the years leading up to the 1969 Stonewall Riots in New York. The first homosexual publication in Canada, *Two* (named in clear homage to the California Mattachine publication of a decade earlier), was started in Toronto in 1964. The first lesbian publication in Britain, *Arena Three*, was launched the same year.

A local gay rights group in California launched the *Los Angeles Advocate* in 1967, in a print run of 500. By 1975, when the *Wall Street Journal* noted that the bi-weekly magazine had a circulation of 50,000, *The Advocate* was national in scope and had professionalized its operation. A decade later, the magazine brought in high-end national advertisers with its decision to segregate its sexually explicit personals pages, eventually creating an entirely separate publication.

In the several years after *The Advocate*'s launch, there was considerable ferment, especially in New York, and after the June 1969 Stonewall Riots there, in other cities as well. Craig Rodwell, who founded the Oscar Wilde Memorial Bookshop in Greenwich Village in 1967, launched *The Hymnal*, a gay newspaper, the following year. Jack Nichols, who years later began the web site GayToday.com, and his lover Lige Clark, with the help of *Screw* publisher Al Goldstein, founded *Gay*, which became a weekly, in 1969.

In September of that year, *Gay Power*, claiming to be 'New York's First Homosexual Newspaper', came into being, followed in November by *Come Out!*, published by the Gay Liberation Front that grew out of Stonewall. Another post-Stonewall New York faction, the Gay Activists Alliance, launched *Out–The Gay Perspective* several years later, and in 1977, *Gaysweek* arrived on the scene.

Elsewhere, *The Body Politic*, launched in Toronto, did battle with Canada's strict obscenity laws well into the 1980s; Winston Leyland mixed hippie sensibility, literary sophistication and radicalism in founding *Gay Sunshine* in Berkeley; and *Fag Rag* was one radical Boston collective's response to Stonewall. By 1971 *Spectre*, a lesbian newspaper in Ann Arbor, Michigan, was publishing articles about feminist separatism.

Gay publications also began proliferating outside of North America. In 1971 the first magazine for Japanese gay men, *Barazoku* (*Rose Tribe*), was launched, with the words from the Simon and Garfunkel hit 'Bridge Over Troubled Waters' printed in English on the cover. *Lampiano*, the first gay publication in Brazil, first appeared in 1978. *Gay Pied*, a magazine that proved influential among gay men in France, began publishing in Paris in 1979.

Two of the most enduring post-Stonewall publications emerged in Washington and Boston. *The Gay Blade* began publishing in the nation's capital in October 1969, out of the apartment of its first editor, Nancy Tucker, a volunteer, in a newsletter format and a print run of 500. Between 1973 and 1977 the weekly publication, by then biweekly, moved to newsprint, hired its first paid employees and barred the use of pseudonyms by its writers.

In 1973 an activist collective in Boston began publishing *Gay Community News*, a hard-hitting weekly with a decidedly leftist bent eventually distributed nationwide by the tens of thousands. Although it did not survive the 1990s it provided a training ground for some of the nation's leading queer activists, including Urvashi **Vaid**, who went on to run the National Gay and Lesbian Task Force; Kevin Cathcart, who still leads **Lambda Legal**; Richard Burns, who for two decades has headed up New York's gay community centre; and the novelist Sarah **Schulman**.

New York's Charles Ortleb, who published *TheaterWeek*, also founded two important queer publications, *Christopher Street*, a literary magazine, in 1976, and *The Native*, a newsweekly, in 1980. *Christopher Street* brought together some of the leading lights in gay letters, including editor Michael Denneny and authors Edmund **White**, Andrew Holleran and Quentin **Crisp**. African-American publications such as *BLK* and *Brother to Brother* came out of California while the *Zami Newsletter* was published in Toronto.

The Native pioneered AIDS reporting with early 1981 dispatches from Dr Lawrence Mass months before the story hit *The New York Times*. Larry **Kramer** picked up the torch from Mass in early 1983, writing his famous '1,112 and Counting' jeremiad and demanding action by gay men and the government. *Ortleb*'s growing fascination in the late 1980s with AIDS denial and conspiracy theories led to a long decline for both publications, which folded by 1997.

The Native's pre-eminence in New York was already eclipsed in 1989 by *Outweek*, a brash news magazine that captured the anger also animating ACT UP at the height of the AIDS crisis. The magazine, founded by phone sex entrepreneur Kendall Morrison and edited by Gabriel Rotello, a former party promoter, made its name through Michelangelo Signorile's crusading efforts to spotlight the hypocrisy of powerful but closeted gay men who remained silent as other gay men died. In 1990 **Signorile** reported on the secret homosexuality of Malcolm Forbes, shortly after his death, and the following year, in the wake of *Time* magazine coining the term 'outing', exposed the gay life of Pete Williams, the Gulf War spokesman for the Pentagon, which barred military service by openly gay and lesbian soldiers.

By 1991 *Outweek*'s finances were in shambles and it folded. But the success it and high-paying advertisers led gay publishers to raise the stakes. *Out* magazine, originally edited by Michael Goff and Sarah **Pettit**, was introduced in 1992 as a glossy, national gay and lesbian monthly covering politics, culture and lifestyle issues. By the end of the decade, however, particularly after being purchased by *The Advocate*, *Out* focused increasingly on the lifestyle and fashion concerns of affluent gay men, and spawned competition, including *Genre* and, for women, *Curve*.

Supported by what for years was substantial pharmaceutical advertising, *Poz* and *A & U* magazines were launched in the 1990s as glossy monthlies serving people living with AIDS, many of them gay men. A decline in pharmaceutical spending by the end of the century, however, hurt the AIDS magazines and the gay press generally. The emergence of glossy bar zines, such as *HX* and *Next* in New York and *Planet Homo* in Los Angeles also sapped the financial prowess of more traditional gay newspapers in certain markets, as has competition in the delivery of timely news by both the Internet and mainstream dailies.

Despite these obstacles, vital weekly newspapers – among the most prominent of which are Boston's *Bay Windows*, New York's *Gay City News*, *Philadelphia Gay News*, the *Washington Blade*, the *Windy City Times* in Chicago, the *Bay Area Reporter* in San Francisco and *Frontiers* news magazine in Los Angeles – very much remain a part of the gay press scene in America.

Queer publications, both newsprint and glossy, can now be found across the globe. *Pink Ink* is a monthly magazine in Thailand. *QX* is the largest gay and lesbian magazine in Sweden. *Sergay* is Mexico's monthly gay magazine. In February 2005, *Pink Paper*, Britain's long-standing national queer newspaper, was relaunched, promising a return to the serious journalism that many of its readers felt it had abandoned. *Queer* is the largest gay newspaper in Germany, a nation that also supports a lesbian monthly, *Lespress*. The *Sydney Star Observer* is a newspaper that serves Australia's largest queer community. *Tetu* is a glossy French monthly that typically offers cover shots of hunky, shirtless young men.

Where the cultural or legal climate does not support gay print products, web resources have emerged to fill the gap. *www.Gaychile.com* is a lively online site with news, entertainment lists and chat rooms. *Behind the Mask,* at *www.mask.org.za*, serves a similar function across Africa. *www.Gayarab.org*, which bills itself as 'an oasis for the Arab gay', offers chat rooms and links to other sites, including *www.Gayegypt.com*, which calls itself 'the voice of gay freedom inside Egypt'.

PAUL SCHINDLER

MAIN, STEWART

b. 1956

director

Main has contributed much to gay New Zealand filmmaking both through his partnership with writer/director Peter **Wells** and through individual projects. In 1986, the same year that the New Zealand Homosexual Law Reform Act was passed, Main directed the TV drama *My First Suit*, which detailed the sexual fantasies of a 14-year-old boy taken by his mother to buy his first suit. His later work, *Twilight of the Gods* (1994), remains one of the few cinematic explorations of same-sex desire between colonizer and colonized subjects. Set during the New Zealand Land Wars, the film combines homosexual desire with Maori mythology to explore the relationship between a Maori warrior and a British soldier. His short, *One of Them* (1997), explores male teenage sexuality, while *God, Sreenu and Me* (2000) documents Main's journeys in India, his relationship with his Indian assistant Sreenu and the desire of New Zealand tourists for spiritual enlightenment.

JO SMITH

MAKI, CARROUSEL

b. 1942

performer

Carrousel Maki, born Tetsuo Hirahara, is Japan's most high-profile transsexual entertainer. She started her career at age 15, performing as a 'gay boy' in a club in the northern city of Sapporo. In 1962 she was working at the Osaka cabaret Carrousel, named in tribute to the French transsexual performers of Le Carrousel de Paris. At this time she changed her name to Carrousel and underwent a castration operation, the first stage in her sex-change surgery (completed in Morocco in 1972). Maki's career has spanned both stage and screen but today she is known primarily as a singer. In 2000 she was detained on a charge of drug possession, and because her family register still recorded her sex as male, she was remanded in a male prison for one month, high-

lighting the need for the reform of Japan's laws relating to sex change.

See also: Carrousel de Paris, Le

MARK MCLELLAND

MALE-TO-FEMALE (MTF) TRANSSEXUAL

Describes the process of transformation, through hormones, surgeries or other non-medical means, so as to change one's gender assignment from male to female.

JEAN BOBBY NOBLE

MANCHESTER (UK)

Situated in the northwest of England, Manchester is an industrial city that has undergone major regeneration. It has one of the highest concentrations of lesbian/gay people in the UK. The 'gay village' has many clubs and bars, some of which date back to the nineteenth century. Manchester saw publication of Edward Carpenter's *Homogenic Love* in 1894, the Pankhurst sisters' campaigns for women's suffrage and was home to Morrissey of the The Smiths and the TV programme *Queer as Folk*.

See also: Morrissey and The Smiths

STEPHEN HICKS

MANSFIELD, JAYNE

b. 1933; d. 1967

actor

Nicknamed 'the poor man's Marilyn Monroe', Mansfield was a popular actor and sexual icon of the 1950s and 1960s, famous for her trademark high-pitched squeal, platinum blonde hair and cartoonishly ample bust. Mansfield was born on 19 April 1933 in Bryn Mawr, Pennsylvania. She first appeared in a small but sexually provocative role in the film *Pete Kelly's Blues* (1955), followed by breakout roles in *The Burglar* (1957) and scantily-clad appearances in the Broadway play *Will Success Spoil Rock Hunter?* (1957) and *Too Hot to Handle* (1959). Despite her aspirations to a serious acting career, she was typecast in dumb blonde or sex-kitten roles. Her career declined in the 1960s, supplemented by nightclub acts and nude pictorials in *Playboy* magazine, before her early death in a car accident on 29 June 1967 in New Orleans. Her camp appeal has ensured her an enduring fan base and her legacy is continued in the careers of Loni Anderson (who played Mansfield in a 1980 TV movie), Pamela Anderson and Anna Nicole Smith.

JOHN FORDE

MANSON, MARILYN

b. 1969

musician

A provocative rock star, Marilyn Manson's intimidating, theatrical brand of post-punk rock music has been hailed variously as dangerous, anti-social and courageously pro-liberal. Born plain Brian Warner, he formed the band 'Marilyn Manson & the Spooky Kids' in 1989, taking his stage name from movie star Marilyn Monroe and Satanist serial killer Charles Manson.

Deliberately courting controversy, Manson seeks to test the limits of censorship with his alarming gothic appearance, grotesque concert and music video performances and references to perverse sexuality, violence, drug abuse and Satanism. While Manson's confrontational style alienates many would-be liberals, his adoption of bisexual and androgynous personae, eloquent defence of free speech (notably in Michael Moore's film *Bowling for Columbine* [2000]) and playful claim that Jesus was 'the first gay rock star' has won him support from gay audiences. Rumours abound about his backstage orgies with fans and band members.

JOHN FORDE

MAPPLETHORPE, ROBERT

b. 1947; d. 1989

photographer

Following study at the Pratt Institute in Brooklyn, New York (1963–9), Mapplethorpe came onto the scene as an art photographer in the early years of gay liberation in New York City. Correspondingly his work reflected gay male sexual pleasures and the kinds of images that were being increasingly promoted and publicized as part of a new, more open, urban gay lifestyle. However, although the social and political climate was changing, at that time, and again a number of times throughout his career, he had difficulty securing exhibitions of his work because of its explicit homoerotic content. This culminated, in a sense, in the exhibition *The Perfect Moment*, a retrospective of his work, being cancelled by the Corcoran Gallery of Art in Washington DC in 1989, under pressure from the conservative right, including Senator Jesse Helms and the American Family Association. This led to debates in the US Senate based upon accusations that the federal government, through the National Endowment for the Arts and that agency's funding of several of the arts institutions scheduled to present the Mapplethorpe exhibit, were effectively supporting and promoting the public exhibition of pornography. This ultimately led to the passage of the Helms Amendment, which has severely curtailed the kinds of arts projects funded by the National Endowment for the Arts.

The subjects of Mapplethorpe's largely black-and-white photographs were diverse, and all were treated in a rather classically modern style of formal composition and visual clarity. Over the years these subjects included: portraits of New York's demi-monde society; the idealized, muscular nude male body (especially, from the late 1980s, the black male body); floral studies (from 1979); and gay sadomasochistic practitioners and

379

practices (1977–9). The last three subjects came to constitute the contents of three portfolios: 'X': S&M; 'Y': floral; and 'Z': black nudes. Consistently stressing the formal aspects and affinities of these photographs and their groupings, Mapplethorpe intended for all three portfolios to be exhibited not only together but also alongside each other. It was undoubtedly the photos of the 'X' Portfolio that caught the eye and enraged the censors; it portrayed various aspects of a gay sadomasochistic subculture, including leather daddies and their 'boys', bondage rituals, water sports and fisting. Although nearly all of these subjects were set up and photographed in his art studio, Mapplethorpe nevertheless always stressed the very real connections between his professional and sexual lives, and distinguished his documentation of gay sadomasochism based upon his own personal experience in the leather and sadomasochistic subcultures of New York and San Francisco. In other words, Mapplethorpe was not an anthropological voyeur fulfilling a desire to record social 'others'. Rather, he self-identified as one of those others, and in his photographs translated such relatively marginal positions into highly aesthetic icons.

A year before he died of AIDS-related causes in 1989 (and just three months before the Corcoran's cancellation of his retrospective), Mapplethorpe established a foundation that continues to provide financial support for AIDS research and for the development of art exhibitions and the publication of exhibition catalogues that might otherwise go without funding.

JOHN PAUL RICCO

MARAIS, JEAN

b. 1913; d. 1998

actor

French film actor Jean Marais emerged as a major star and heart throb in a series of

landmark films made in the 1940s and 1950s by his lover and mentor Jean **Cocteau**: examples include *La Belle et la Bête* (Beauty and the Beast, 1946) and *Orphée* (Orpheus, 1950). Combining Marais' extraordinary physical beauty with mystical eroticism and emotional vulnerability, these films created an unconventional image for the star that allowed him to find subsequent success in such diverse genres as swashbucklers (*Le Capitaine Fracasse* [Captain Fracasse], 1960), melodramas (*Le Château de Verre* [The Glass Castle], 1950) and detective films (the *Fantômas* series), while also imbuing his work with marked queer resonances.

BRETT FARMER

MARICÓN

A once-derogatory Spanish word for a gay man implying sexual passivity. It has become less inflammatory because of greater openness.

GABRIEL GOMEZ

MARKOPOULOS, GREGORY

b. 1928; d. 1992

filmmaker

Avant-garde American filmmaker whose experimental short films were highly influenced by French modernism, especially the works of Jean Cocteau and Jean Genet. He was born 12 March 1928, in Toledo, Ohio. His first films, a triptych of shorts entitled *Psyche*, *Lysis* and *Charmides* (1948) and *Flowers of Asphalt* (1949) were heavily influenced by Greek myth and Genet's novel *Our Lady of the Flowers*. He continued to make and self-finance films throughout his life, usually acting as writer, director, cinematographer, editor and actor, and editing the films entirely in camera. His work is characterized by a vivid use of colour and the use of montage and music to develop narrative. He is best known for *Twice A Man* (1964), a poetic drama about a young man torn between the attentions of his male lover and his mother, and *Sorrows* (1969), a portrait of the house King Ludwig II of Bavaria bought for composer Richard Wagner. He taught filmmaking at Chicago's School of the Art Institute in 1966 and relocated to Europe permanently in 1968, removing his films from United States distribution soon after. Markopoulos died on 12 November 1992, in Freiburg, Baden-Württemberg, Germany.

JOHN FORDE

MARLATT, DAPHNE

b. 1942

writer

Born in Australia, Daphne Marlatt emigrated with her family to Canada in 1951. While the West Coast of Canada remains her home, she spent several years as a 'writer in residence' at many Canadian universities. A prolific writer/thinker, Marlatt is a major figure in the Canadian literary landscape. After publishing over 14 books of poetry, including *Frames of a Story* (1968); *Leafs/leafs* (1969); *Rings* (1971); *Vancouver Poems* (1972); *Steveston* (1974); *Net work: Selected Writing* (1980); *How Hug a Stone* (1983); *Touch to My Tongue* (1984); and *Salvage* (1991), she published two critically acclaimed novels/'fiction-theory', *Ana Historic* (1988) and *Taken* (1996), as well as numerous critical articles on, among other things, lesbian poetics. As an editor with the feminist literary journal *Tessera*, Marlatt collaborates with writers such as (her then lover) Betsy Warland (*Double Negative*, 1988; *Two Women in a Birth*, 1994). She currently lives in Victoria, British Columbia.

JEAN BOBBY NOBLE

MARRONE, NILA

b. 1939

activist

Bolivian-born activist Nila Marrone resides in the United States. She currently presides over **Parents, Families and Friends of Gays and Lesbians**, New York (PFLAG NYC), is Director of Latin PFLAG NYC and is a member of other organizations that promote the rights of glbtq populations. She publicly advocates and lectures for support for sexual minorities throughout the US and Latin America, by means of letters to legislators and leaders who influence policies regarding sexual rights. On her regular visits to Bolivia she contacts the existing local glbtq groups to provide education and coordinate connections with like-minded institutions abroad.

PEDRO ALBORNOZ

MARSHALL, STUART

b. 1949; d. 1993

filmmaker

A documentary filmmaker, Stuart Marshall spearheaded the 1990s British movement of openly gay artists committed to chronicling gay culture. His documentary *Bright Eyes* (1984), first screened on British television, is one of the earliest examinations of the emerging AIDS epidemic, and highlighted numerous examples of media homophobia and misreporting about the disease. *Comrades In Arms* (1990) is an uplifting profile of six gay and lesbian Second World War veterans relating their same-sex experiences during armed service. *Desire* (1989) chronicled the history of Germany's gay and lesbian movement, profiling the ground-breaking work of German sexologist Magnus Hirschfeld and examining the Nazi persecution of gay men. *Over Our Dead Bodies* (1991) examined the rise of gay lobby groups such as ACT UP, Queer Nation and OutRage!, and critiqued British and American governments and health organizations for their slow response to the epidemic. Marshall died of an AIDS-related illness in 1993.

JOHN FORDE

MARS-JONES, ADAM

b. 1954

writer

Born into an upper-middle class London family, Adam Mars-Jones was educated at Westminster School and Cambridge University. His debut collection of experimental stories, *Lantern Lecture*, earned him recognition by Granta as one of the 'Best Young British Novelists' in 1982. The darkly satirical tone of this early work was replaced by a more sombre, realistic narrative approach in the stories he wrote for *The Darker Proof: Stories from a Crisis* (co-authored with Edmund **White** in 1987) and *Monopolies of Loss*, both collections concerned with the effect of the AIDS epidemic on gay communities and relationships. He is the author of one novel, *The Waters of Thirst* (1993), and a collection of essays, *Blind Bitter Happiness* (1993). Mars-Jones worked continually during the late 1980s and 1990s as a film reviewer for the British newspapers *The Independent* and *The Times*; his reviews are noted for their elegance and their acerbic, sometimes bitchy, wit.

DAVID KURNICK

MARTIN, DEL AND PHYLLIS LYON

Martin, Del

b. 1921

activist

Lyon, Phyllis

b. 1921

activist

Del Martin and Phyllis Lyon are significant figures in US lesbian history. In 1955 they co-founded the **Daughters of Bilitis** (DOB), the first national organization for lesbians in the US. DOB soon opened chapters in main cities and even Melbourne, Australia. Its first national convention, in San Francisco in 1960, was well attended, despite unwanted publicity. The DOB provided lesbians with a meeting place and a forum for political activism. The group put out a national newsletter for their members, with Lyon as the editor, called *The Ladder*. The organization represented the beginning of the ongoing battles lesbians would confront in their determination to be classified as 'legitimate couples'.

Lovers since 1952, Martin and Lyon have become a driving force in the lesbian movement. Co-authors of *Lesbian/Woman* (1972), they document the history of the lesbian movement up to its publication date. Martin also wrote a later book on domestic violence, *Battered Women* (1976). Today Martin and Lyon are still politically active in issues such as social security, Medicare and the Older Americans Act. Both were appointed delegates to the 1995 White House Conference on Aging. The San Francisco-based, Lyon–Martin Women's Health Services Center (which they co-founded in 1979), recently overcame financial difficulties and continues to serve the needs of lesbians and other women. Although Lyon and Martin each spoke in her own voice, they also spoke in one collaborative voice. Their histories as activists have been recorded in the recent documentary: *No Secret Anymore: The Times of Del Martin and Phyllis Lyon*, directed and written by Joan E. Biren. In *Lesbian/Woman*, Martin and Lyon's definition of a lesbian remains significant to their politics: 'a woman whose primary erotic, psychological, emotional and social interest is in a member of her own sex, even though that interest might not be overtly expressed'.

JEAN BOBBY NOBLE

MARTIN, RICKY

b. 1971

pop singer

A hugely successful pop singer from Puerto Rico, Ricky Martin spearheaded the Latino music craze of the late 1990s. Formerly a member of Latino boy band Menudo, Martin starred in Mexican and American soap operas and achieved moderate success with his first two music albums. His third effort, *A Medio Vivir* (1995), introduced rock stylings with a Latino mix, including the international hit single 'Maria'. He won a Grammy Award for Best Latin Pop Performance in 1999, his sexy, charismatic performance at the awards ceremony hurtling him to stardom. His next singles, 'Living La Vida Loca' and 'She Bangs', both topped the US music charts, cementing his international success. Despite persistent rumours that he was concealing his homosexuality so as not to alienate his female fan base, Martin has refused to comment on his sexuality.

JOHN FORDE

MASHOGA

A Swahili (Kenya) term for effeminate, passive male homosexual or transvestite, also known in Zanzibar (Tanzania) as *makhanith* (from a Persian root).

MARC EPPRECHT

MATAGROSSO, NEY

b. 1941

musician

Ney Matogrosso began his career as a singer with the short-lived but extremely successful rock group Secos e molhados. After the group broke up in 1975, Matogrosso launched a solo career, quickly gaining fame both for his unusually high voice and the outlandish costumes and set designs for his shows. These factors have also made him one of Brazil's most conspicuously queer celebrities, a status that he has never shied away from, despite occasional controversy. He has consistently balanced a sense of showmanship with a love of music, recording albums in homage to the singer Angela Maria as well as composers Tom Jobim, Heitor Villa-Lobos and Chico Buarque.

DANIEL HENDRICKSON

MATHABANE, MARK

b. 1960

writer

South African author Mark Mathabane's novel, *Kaffir Boy: The True Story of a Black Youth's Coming of Age in Apartheid South Africa* (1998), is an account of growing up in Johannesburg's main black township, Soweto. It includes a lurid scene that brought attention to the issue of sexual relationships among men in the mine compounds and the danger of men's sexual predation upon young township boys. His other works include *African Women: Three Generations* (1994) and *Miriam's Song: A Memoir* (2001).

MARC EPPRECHT

MATTACHINE SOCIETY

The first major gay group in the United States, founded on 11 November 1950 in Los Angles by Harry **Hay**, an English-born American communist, with Dale Jennings, Chuck Rowland, Rudi Gernreich and Bob Hull. Mattachine initially used a Communist Party secretive 'cell' structure to insulate subgroups from each other as a way to avoid a mass round up of members by government authorities.

The organization was first called the 'Society of Fools' but after partners Konrad Stevens and James Gruber joined, it was renamed the Mattachine Society, an homage to the Societé Mattachine (a French troupe in the Middle Ages who performed in masks to make social commentary) and the Mattachinos (little fools) (Italian court jesters who hid behind masks to tell the truth). The group established a Statement of Purpose in 1951 with the intent to unify gay people while educating both gays and the public about homosexuality and eliminating discriminatory laws. Mattachine conducted discussion groups as a key part of their early meetings to facilitate their agenda.

When Jennings was arrested for 'lewd and dissolute' conduct in 1952, the group initiated a 'Citizens Committee to Outlaw Entrapment', a cause that continues to be an issue into the twenty-first century. Jennings, while not denying being gay, pleaded innocent and the charges against him were dropped when the jury could not reach a verdict. Following this event, Mattachine went through significant changes against the backdrop of an anti-gay crackdown nationally.

In 1953, the year President Dwight Eisenhower issued an executive order excluding those guilty of 'sexual perversion' from employment with the federal government, leading to the firing of more than 600 such employees, the group itself was attacked in the Los Angeles press as a 'subversive' organization. It was also during this period that the US explicitly barred people 'afflicted with psychopathic personality' from entering the country. Under threat of the McCarthy-era purge, the Mattachine founders withdrew or were unseated in elections and new leadership emerged that has been characterized as more conservative and accommodationist, albeit more realistic when working with, for example, the psychiatric profession to educate them about gay people.

Indeed, the contentious national conventions in 1953 led to the ascendance of what is generally characterized as the more moderate Mattachine leadership of Kenneth Burns, Hall Call and Marilyn Rieger, who were anti-Communists. Others argue that the Mattachine founders sought bourgeois respectability, hid their identities and engaged in the kind of secretiveness that hindered their ability to combat anti-gay laws and stereotypes. The 1953 group was elected under their own names, produced an early gay newspaper, *Town Talk*, and began offering legal help, counselling, medical referrals and job placement. The Mattachine Society also published the *Mattachine Review* from 1955 to 1965. In 1958 Mattachine handled 300 cases in these areas. In 1957, the national organization officially moved to San Francisco where education became the organization's top priority. By 1964, the San Francisco chapter alone was handling 3,000 referrals for services a year. As chapters of Mattachine sprang up throughout the US several of its former members created ONE magazine in 1953 with Jennings as its editor. The group organized as 'ONE, Inc'. in Los Angeles with Dorr Legg as its leader. The group won the right to send gay literature through the mail at the US Supreme Court in 1958.

Although the Mattachine Society formally dissolved as a national group in 1961, it continued its work in San Francisco. Groups named Mattachine were established in New York, Washington, Philadelphia and Florida into the late 1960s and early 1970s. The Washington group, founded by Frank **Kameny** in 1961, continues. Mattachine of New York, led by Dick Leitsch, organized a rally one month after the Stonewall Riots, attracting more than 300 demonstrators to Washington Square Park in Greenwich Village. In general, however, Mattachine was rendered irrelevant by the post-Stonewall boom in gay activism.

ANDY HUMM

MAUGHAM, W. SOMERSET

b. 1874; d. 1965

writer

English playwright, novelist and short-story writer whose prolific body of work contains no explicit references to his homosexuality. William Somerset Maugham was born on 25 January 1874 in Paris, France. He trained as a doctor, but became a full-time writer after the success of his first novel, *Liza of Lambeth* (1897). He had great success as a playwright, with four of his plays running simultaneously in London in 1904. He is best known for his novel *Of Human Bondage* (1915), a semi-autobiographical tale about a disabled Englishman's doomed affair with a working-class waitress. He had a child with and married Syrie Wellcome in 1916, but lived apart from her for many years before their divorce in 1927. He is thought to have had a sexual relationship with his long-time friend and secretary Gerard Haxton. He settled permanently in France in 1928, producing spy thrillers, based on his wartime experiences as a British intelligence agent, including *Ashenden; or the British Agent* (1928), and satirical comic novels, notably *Cakes and Ale* (1930). Maugham died on 16 December 1965 in Nice, France.

JOHN FORDE

MAUPIN, ARMISTEAD

b. 1944

writer

Maupin is best known for his novel *Tales of The City* (1978), based on his column in the *San Francisco Chronicle*. A vibrant snapshot of 1970s San Francisco, *Tales* revolves around the residents of 28 Barbary Lane: small-town girl Mary Ann Singleton; eternally romantic gay waiter Michael 'Mouse' Tolliver; disillusioned hippie Mona Ramsey; and pot-smoking transsexual landlady Anna Madrigal. Maupin followed with *More Tales of the City* (1980), *Further Tales of*

the *City* (1982), *Babycakes* (1984), *Significant Others* (1987) and *Sure of You* (1989), perceptively chronicling the changing social climate of the 1980s and the AIDS epidemic. The novels were successfully adapted for television (1993–2003). A tireless spokesperson for gay rights, Maupin appeared in and co-scripted the documentary *The Celluloid Closet* (1995).

JOHN FORDE

MAYBURY, JOHN

b. 1958

filmmaker

After studying at North East London Polytechnic, John Maybury worked with Super-8 film and video. He worked on several of Derek Jarman's films, including doing set designs for *Jubilee* (1977) and video work for *War Requiem* (1989). In the 1980s he joined with a group of artists in London including dancer Michael Clark and designer Leigh **Bowery**. He has had a successful career making music videos for Neneh Cherry, Boy George, Sinead O'Connor and others. His experimental films include *Read Only Memory* (1998), *Genetron* (1996), *Man to Man* (1992) and *Remembrance of Things Fast: True Stories, Visual Lies* (1994), featuring Tilda Swinton, Rupert Everett and the English porn actor Aiden Shaw. In 1997 he made his first narrative film, *Love Is the Devil,* a fictionalized and highly aestheticized biopic of the artist Francis **Bacon**, starring Derek **Jacobi** in the lead role.

See also: Jarman, Derek

DANIEL HENDRICKSON

MAYNE, JUDITH

b. 1948

film scholar

Born in Pennsylvania, Judith Mayne is currently a Distinguished Professor of

French and Women's Studies at Ohio State University. Since the 1990 publication of *Women at the Keyhole: Feminism and Women's Cinema*, Mayne has been one of the leading figures in English-language feminist film studies. She added to this reputation with articles and books written from a distinctively lesbian perspective, particularly, 'A Parallax View of Lesbian Authorship' (1991), *Directed by Dorothy Arzner* (1994) and *Framed: Lesbians, Feminists, and Media Culture* (2000). With a chapter in *Women at the Keyhole*, numerous articles and the full-length book study, Mayne is the undisputed academic expert on **Arzner**, the only woman (and lesbian) director under contract within the Hollywood studio system from the late 1920s until the early 1940s. Mayne's other books include *Kino and the Woman Question* (1989), *Cinema and Spectatorship* (1993) and a study of French director Claire Denis (2004).

ALEX DOTY

MBEKI, THABO

b. 1942

President of South Africa

The second democratically elected President of South Africa, Thabo Mbeki played a key role in preparing the political landscape for entrenching sexual orientation as a human right in that country, one of the first in the world to achieve such a goal.

Mbeki joined the anti-apartheid African National Congress (ANC) when still a teenager, then attended university in England (1962–70). Like many ANC exiles, while there he came into close contact with the vibrant gay element in the European Left and in the anti-apartheid struggle in particular.

Back in southern Africa in 1987, he became the first ANC leader publicly to support the principle of protecting gay

rights and to disavow homophobic views expressed by other leaders in the movement for national liberation. He subsequently (1990–6) helped preserve the equality clause in the proposed new constitution against homophobic attacks and opportunism by other political parties.

Mbeki's reputation as pro-gay took a beating after 1999 however, when as President he questioned the link between HIV and AIDS and obstructed efforts to secure antiretroviral therapy for South Africans infected with HIV. Mbeki belatedly conceded to the scientific consensus and to pressure from the Treatment Action Campaign. However he also drew sharp criticism from gay rights activists in Africa for his tacit support for outspoken homophobe, the Zimbabwean president Robert **Mugabe**.

MARC EPPRECHT

McCARTHY, JOSEPH AND McCARTHYISM

b. 1908; d. 1957

politician

Joseph P. McCarthy was a conservative US Senator from Wisconsin who, during the early 1950s, led Senate hearings dedicated to ridding the government of alleged communists and homosexuals. His system of browbeating witnesses and use of guilt-by-association techniques became known as 'McCarthyism' – an eponym used to this day, especially when people are excluded from employment because of their political sympathies. In the 1950s hundreds of lives were ruined as anti-communist groups persuaded entertainment executives to 'blacklist' persons suspected of 'red' or 'pink' sympathies.

In 1952 Hank Greenspun of the *Las Vegas Sun* wrote, 'It is common talk among homosexuals in Milwaukee who rendezvous in the White Horse Inn that Senator Joe McCarthy has often engaged in homosexual activities'. His Senate aide, attorney Roy **Cohn**, was also a closeted homosexual who eventually died of AIDS in 1986. McCarthy was married in 1954, in part in an attempt to dispel rumours about his homosexuality. McCarthy was also close to Federal Bureau of Investigation Director J. Edgar **Hoover**, another closeted homosexual.

In his heyday McCarthy struck fear into the hearts of many, often yelling at those on trial: 'Are you now or have you ever been a member of the Communist Party?' Even President Dwight Eisenhower was afraid to challenge the Senator from Wisconsin. CBS Newsman Edward R. Murrow finally did in his *See it Now* TV news programme in 1954. In the same year Joseph Welch, an attorney appearing before the Army–McCarthy hearings, famously asked the Senator: 'At long last, have you left no sense of decency?' McCarthy was then censured by the Senate. He died of cirrhosis of the liver in 1957.

ANDY HUMM

McDONALD, BOYD

b. 1925; d. 1993

writer

Editor, film critic and self-proclaimed historian, Boyd McDonald is perhaps best known as editor of the journal *Straight to Hell: The Manhattan Review of Unnatural Acts*, a publication of the true homosexual experiences sent to him by his readers, occasionally intercut with McDonald's own pithy commentary on sex-related news stories. The writings from the journal were later collected in several books, published in the early 1980s, all with provocative one-word titles (*Meat, Stud, Cum*). Although primarily marketed and sold as pornography, McDonald saw his work more as a kind of history of homosexual experience. A Harvard graduate, McDonald compared his work favourably to that of the great sex researchers, saying, 'Compared to Meat,

Kinsey is just Spam'. McDonald was also a well-known classic film buff, and wrote many articles about the films he watched at home on television. These were collected in his book, *Cruising the Movies: A Sexual Guide to 'Oldies' on TV* (1985).

DANIEL HENDRICKSON

McDOWELL, CURT

b. 1945; d. 1987

filmmaker

Curt McDowell moved from Indiana to California in the 1960s, having received a painting scholarship to the San Francisco Art Institute. He soon became interested in film and switched fields of study. He studied with George Kuchar, a visiting professor at the institute, who became McDowell's influential collaborator. McDowell's films usually have a strong sexual element, quite often including depictions of explicit sex. In 1971 he made *Confessions*, a hilarious on-camera confession to his parents about all the sordid details of his sex life. He starred in Kuchar's *The Devil's Cleavage* (1973), with Kuchar returning the favour shortly thereafter by working on McDowell's *Thundercrack* (1975), an underground porno–horror movie. His other films include *Boggy Depot (A Musical for the Whole Family)* (1974) and *Loads* (1980), a film in which McDowell lures men to his apartment and films them masturbating. McDowell died from AIDS in 1987.

See also: Kuchar, George and Mike

DANIEL HENDRICKSON

McINTOSH, MARY

b. 1936

sociologist

In her 1968 article, 'The Homosexual Role', Mary McIntosh argued against the

387

dominant view of homosexuality as a psychiatric 'condition' and instead posited it as a social category. McIntosh argued that distinguishing between social categories and desires problematizes an oversimplification of sexual categories. The split among sexual desire, acts and sexual identity are the hallmark of research into gay and lesbian lives after 1968.

McIntosh taught the sociology of deviance at several universities across the UK and North America during her career, most notably at the University of Essex, where she taught from 1980 to 1996 and served as the Head of Sociology for a number of years. Her publications span the range of deviance studies, including most notably her numerous journal articles and several edited volumes, which focused primarily on feminist and gay and lesbian politics; she has also been also active as a public intellectual, publishing numerous articles in the popular feminist and gay and lesbian press in the UK.

J. TODD ORMSBEE

McKELLEN, IAN

b. 1939

actor, activist

Acknowledged as the leading stage actor of his generation, Sir Ian McKellen, born in Lancashire, England, started acting while still at secondary school. He continued to do so through university, before moving into repertory theatre. His most celebrated stage roles include Marlowe's *Edward II* (1969), *Macbeth* (1976–7) and Martin Sherman's *Bent* (1979; revived 1989–90). He received Academy Award nominations for his portrayal of gay filmmaker James **Whale** in *Gods and Monsters* (1998) and as the wizard Gandalf in *The Lord of the Rings: The Fellowship of the Ring* (2001). Other notable roles include AIDS activist Bill **Kraus** in the TV movie *And The Band Played On* (1993) and the film

version of *Bent* (1997). An autobiographical one-man show *A Knight Out* (1994) has played to rave reviews worldwide. McKellen publicly came out in 1988 in protest at the British government's anti-gay **Section 28** law and co-founded gay activist group Stonewall. He was knighted in 1990 for services to acting.

JOHN FORDE

McLAREN, NORMAN

b. 1914; d. 1987

animator

Scots-born Canadian animator, star employee of the National Film Board (NFB) of Canada, who crowned his 60-film, 43-year career with the Oscar and the Palme D'or. Famous for innovating a distinctive artisanal abstraction, McLaren was not as brash as contemporaries in the metropolitan avant-gardes, but was a queer pioneer in his own way. Recruited in 1939, McLaren stunned the NFB with his un-Disneyesque daubs and scratches right on the celluloid, interpreting wartime propaganda, Quebec folklore, Cold War peace activism and contemporary minimalism. During the mid-1960s, McLaren turned to processed cinematography to celebrate the human body: *Pas de Deux* (1967) and *Ballet Adagio* (1971) used ballet to evoke the inherent eroticism of movement, gesture, and flesh. McLaren returned to ballet in 1983 with *Narcissus*, the classical myth retold as his only explicitly queer film, with its dreamy self-absorption, luscious male–male pas de deux and lonely denouement. McLaren's disciples included Claude Jutra, with whom he made a pixillated parable of non-gendered relationships that might be considered the first Canadian queer film, *A Chairy Tale* (1957).

THOMAS WAUGH

McNAB, CLAIRE

b. 1940

novelist

Australian lesbian crime novelist whose debut novel, *Lessons In Murder* (1988), attracted a devoted international lesbian readership. The first of 14 novels featuring lesbian Detective Inspector Carol Ashton, other titles in the series include *Fatal Reunion* (1989) and *Death Down Under* (1990). She has written four novels featuring undercover agent Denise Cleever, including *Murder Undercover* (2000; short-listed for a Lambda Literary Award), *Out of Sight* (2001) and *Death By Death* (2003). McNab developed a comic sensibility in her Kylie Kendall mystery series, with works including *The Wombat Strategy* (2004) and *Kookaburra Gambit* (2005; nominated for a Lambda Literary Award). She has also written children's fiction under the pseudonym Claire Carmichael and co-edited *The Loving Lesbian* (1997), a guide to relationships, with Sharon Gedan. She currently lives in Los Angeles.

JOHN FORDE

McNALLY, TERRENCE

b. 1939

playwright

Terrence McNally's first play was produced in 1964 when he was considered a major Off-Off-Broadway writer. He established himself with such comedies as *Next* (1969) and scored a huge popular success with *The Ritz* (1975), a comedy set in a gay bathhouse. McNally has consistently addressed gay issues in his writing. *Lips Together, Teeth Apart* (1991) studies the irrational fears people have about AIDS. *Love! Valour! Compassion!* (1994) tells of the relationship among eight gay men. A devoted opera fan, McNally, skewered 'operamania' in *The Lisbon Traviata* (1985) and examined the life of Maria **Callas** in *Master Class* (1995). His 1997 play *Corpus Christi* retells the Christ story and suggests that the Apostles were homosexual. The New York production was cancelled because of the obvious controversy. In musical theatre, McNally wrote the books for *Kiss of the Spider Woman* (1992), *Ragtime* (1997) and *Titanic* (1999).

CHRIS BYRNE

MEHTA, DEEPA

b. 1950

filmmaker

Born in India, Deepa Mehta migrated to Canada in 1973 where she began her career in professional filmmaking. Mehta is best known as the director of *Fire* (1997), about the lesbian relationship between two married sisters-in-law in a middle-class Hindu family. Protesting against the lesbian storyline as being 'anti Hindu' and against 'Indian culture', Hindu fanatics of the Right vandalized theatres and disrupted screenings in India. Support from glbt, human rights and feminist groups eventually ensured the commercial re-release of the film. The controversy was almost single-handedly responsible for giving glbt Indian filmmaking and politics nationwide media coverage. In 1999 Deepa Mehta began shooting *Water*, the final segment of her Elements trilogy, in the city of Varanasi. Hindu Right extremists struck again and refused to let the shooting proceed, resulting in the abandonment of the project. Her other films include *Sam & Me* (1991), *Camilla* (1994), *1947 Earth* (1998) and *Bollywood/Hollywood* (2002).

SHOHINI GHOSH

MEIJSING, DOESCHKA

b. 1947

novelist

In addition to writing, Doeschka Meijsing has worked as a teacher, a scholar, and a

389

literary critic for the progressive weekly *Vrij Nederland*. In 1974 her first collection of stories, *De hanen en andere verhalen* (The Cocks and Other Stories) received an enthusiastic reception. *Robinson*, the novel that followed two years later, could in many respects be considered a classic coming-of-age novel, in which a 17-year-old girl, Robinson, falls in love with one of her teachers. The ending is not happy – not because it is in any way felt to be problematic that the teacher is also a woman, as in earlier literature, but because Robinson has to compete with her father for the affections of the teacher.

This unproblematic presentation of same-sex desire is typical of Meijsing's work. In later novels such as *Tijger tijger* (*Tiger, Tiger*, 1980) and *Utopia* (1982), relations between women are a self-evident, even coincidental aspect of life. In the 1990s the topic of homosexuality almost disappears from her work.

Meijsing is part of a generation of novelists, which includes Frans **Kellendonk**, who scorned the many realistic novels of the 1970s. A lucid style, and a postmodern doubt of the accessibility of reality, is typical of their work. Another important theme in Meijsing's work is how people cope with the lack of a clear identity. Her 'suspicion' of so-called identity politics is therefore only to be expected, although Meijsing did write some essays on the issue of women writers early in her career.

AGNES ANDEWEG

MELBOURNE

Reputedly described by Mark Twain as the wife to Sydney's mistress, with its tree-lined streets, trams and Victorian-era architecture, Melbourne is one of Australia's most multicultural cities, with a thriving theatre, arts and restaurant scene. The city supports a large gay and lesbian community, based around St Kilda, Prahan, South Yarra and

Collingwood. The age of consent is 16 and state legislation outlaws discrimination on the basis of sexuality. Melbourne's annual gay and lesbian festival, Midsumma, takes place in January and February.

See also: Sydney

JOHN FORDE

MERCER, KOBENA

b. 1960

theorist, cultural activist

Kobena Mercer is a queer theorist and key figure in black British Cultural Studies, drawing on psychoanalysis and a tradition of anti-colonial critique, such as that propagated by Frantz **Fanon**, to investigate sexuality as a site of political and psychic investment. In his attention to the role of popular cultural styles in the fashioning of complex identities, he shares the concerns of the **Birmingham School**. His self-critical re-evaluation (in 1989) of his earlier essay on racial fetishism in the photography of Robert **Mapplethorpe** (both of which can be found in his 1994 *Welcome to the Jungle*) questions politics based categorically on identity in favour of the recognition of the centrality of ambivalent identifications to radical democratic struggle.

See also: Theory and theorists, queer

TREVOR HOPE

MERCURY, FREDDY

b. 1946; d. 1991

rock singer

Tanzanian-born Farrokh Bulsara – more commonly known as Freddie Mercury – was lead singer of one of Britain's most popular rock acts, Queen. He and the group combined stirring rock anthems with sexually subversive lyrics and flamboyant onstage performances to achieve huge international success before Mercury's high-profile death from AIDS. Formed in 1970, Queen fused a Bowie-esque glam-rock aesthetic with a hard rock sound inspired by the burgeoning punk scene. They achieved international success with the stirring rock-operatic, 'Bohemian Rhapsody' (1975). The band provided soundtrack music to several action movies, including the hit 'Who Wants To Live Forever' for *Highlander* (1986). Enjoying crossover gay and straight appeal, Queen's lyrics – and even their title – carried subversive clues for gay audiences.

On- and offstage, Mercury adopted and parodied a hypermasculine image, growing a handlebar moustache and dressing in leather and fetishwear, only to subvert his macho image with camp theatricality, such as his appearance in drag for the music video of 'I Want To Break Free' (1984). Famously ambivalent about his sexuality, Mercury had affairs with both men and women and enthusiastically embraced a rock-star lifestyle of heavy drug use and wild parties.

Mercury became ill with AIDS during the early 1990s and shocked audiences with his emaciated appearance in music videos for 'Barcelona' (1991) and his swansong, 'These Are The Days Of Our Lives'. His death provoked international awareness about the disease. In 1992 the remaining members of Queen played a tribute concert to Mercury in London, with benefits going to an AIDS charity.

JOHN FORDE

METROPOLITAN COMMUNITY CHURCH (MCC)

The MCC is an international church founded in 1968 by Reverend Troy D. Perry in Los Angeles. The church's mission is to meet 'the spiritual needs of the lesbian, gay, bisexual, and transgendered community around the world'. With its 'World Center'

based in Los Angeles, another 300 satellite churches are located in Mexico, Australia, Brazil, the Philippines, Nigeria, England and the United States. As a Christian church the MCC follows the principles of the Apostles, the Nicene Creed and the teachings of Jesus Christ, believing that a 'proactive reading' of the Bible offers 'new life' for the glbt community.

DAVID A. GERSTNER

MEULENBELT, ANJA

b. 1945

activist, writer

Anja Meulenbelt has helped to sustain the Dutch feminist movement since 1970. She is famous as a feminist, publisher, prolific literary writer, essayist on political and women's health issues and as a political organizer. Her first novel, *De Schaamte voorbij* (The Shame is Over, 1976), took the country by storm and was widely translated. It became one of the early second-wave feminist novels that changed people's lives, comparable to Erica Jong's *Fear of Flying* (1973), Kate Millett's *Flying* (1974), Marilyn French's *The Women's Room* (1977), and (in Germany) Verena Stefan's *Häutungen* (Shedding, 1975). *De Schaamte voorbij* deals with the escape of protagonist Anja from an unhappy marriage and her social and spiritual self-discovery in the context of both feminism and abundant sexual experimentation, in which the lesbian option is explored in detail. Meulenbelt's second novel, *Alba* (1984), again features lesbian love, but ends on a heterosexual note, a fact sorely regretted by Meulenbelt's avid lesbian readers.

MAAIKE MEIJER

MEXICO, FILMMAKING

Mexican cinema during its golden years (1941–5) does not include a significant number of productions with implicit or explicit gay, lesbian, bisexual or transsexual themes. Even though numerous Mexican films dealing directly with these issues were produced at the end of the millennium, films such as *Distinto Amanecer* (A Different Dawn, Julio Bracho, 1943) and *El monje blanco* (The White Monk, Julio Bracho, 1945), films to which Xavier Villaurrutia contributed as a screenwriter, contained variances of such themes. Villaurrutia's contribution to Mexican cinema, although it did not include overtly glbt themes, reveals – through a queer reading – dialogue representative of hypermasculine Mexican characters and latent homosexuality in the pseudo-machista dynamics of the Mexican Charro singers who were a staple of Mexican films during that era.

Circa 1970, the focus of Mexican films shifted from rural to urban settings. In 1970 two Mexican films depicted the topic of homosexuality: *La primavera de los escorpiones* (The Spring of the Scorpions), directed by Francisco del Villar, deals directly with a gay theme; while Carlos Enrique Taboada touches on a lesbian theme in *El deseo en otoño* (Desire in Autumn). Two other films with homosexual themes from the 1970s include Jaime Humberto Hermosillo's *Matinee* (1976) and Arturo Ripstein's *El lugar sin límites* (Hell Without Limits, 1977). In Hermosillo's case, *Matinee* marks the beginning of his preoccupation with male homosexuality. Ripstein's commercial and critical success with *El lugar sin límites*, where actor Roberto Cobo unleashes the passion and violence of Mexican machismo in his role as a drag queen, not only revealed the public's tolerance of films dealing openly with gay themes but also brilliantly defies the heterosexist and hypocritical notions of machismo in Mexican society.

The 1980s saw an increase in conventionally homophobic films, in which homosexuality was mocked by their treatment of feminine gay characters and trans-vestites. However, in 1984 Hermosillo directed *Doña Herlinda y su hijo* (*Doña Herlinda and Her Son*) and Paul Leduc directed *Frida, naturaleza muerta* (Frida, Still Life). *Doña Herlinda* is perhaps the most celebrated and important openly gay Mexican film of all time. The film demonstrates how subverting the Mexican patriarchy may legitimize Mexican gay culture. In Leduc's case the portrayal of Mexican painter Frida Kahlo and her homoerotic desires are treated with great sensitivity and respect. At the end, Leduc's film represents a surreal vision and a vivid artistry that skilfully mirrored Kahlo's remarkable life. Later, in 1987 Guadalupe Olvera San Miguel directed *Y sigue la marcha andando!* (*And the March Continues!*), in which she combines documentary and narrative forms to present a history of the lesbian movement in Mexico from its origins to the present day (2005).

The 1990s proved to be a significant decade with regard to cinematic productions that focused on glbt issues in Mexico. María Novaro directed *Danzón* (1991), Gabriel Retes *Bienvendio* (*Welcome*, 1993), Arturo Ripstein *La reina de la noche* (Queen of the night, 1994), Oscar Blancarte *Dulces compañías* (*Sweet Companions*, 1994). In these films, there is a noticeable effort to portray a wide range of homosexual characters presented in a humanistic fashion that validates and vindicates their existence.

The turn of the millennium saw several films such as *Corazones rotos* (*Broken Hearts*, 2001) by Rafael Montero, Alan Coton's *Sofía* (2002), Jaime Humberto Hermosillo's *Exxxorcismos* (2002), Julián Hernández's *Mil nubes de paz cercan el cielo, amor jamás acabarás de ser amor* (*A Thousand Peace Clouds Encircle the Sky, Love, You Will Never Stop Being Love*, 2002), Leopoldo Laborde's *Sin Destino* (*No Fate*, 2002) and Feranando Sariñana's *Ciudades Oscuras* (Dark Cities, 2002). The politics of representation in these films suggest the reification of the glbt experience in Mexican cinema and its inclusion in a space historically marginalized by a homophobic and exclusive film industry plagued by the imperatives of heteronormativity. Hernández's film, for example, brings to light the feelings of passion and loneliness from a broken relationship where a gay male couple is the central theme. In the films by Montero and Sariñana glbt themes may not be at the centre. However, each film includes glbt characters in supporting roles that fit naturally into the plot. Coton's film does not directly include a lesbian theme either, but it does pay homage to Mexican feminist poet Sor Juana Inés de la Cruz.

In the first years of the new millennium Mexican cinematic production that includes glbt issues has proliferated exponentially. The marginalization and exclusion of queer culture has diminished significantly in recent years. Films produced from the year 2000 to the present (2005) seem to suggest a reification of queer culture in mainstream Mexican film where the representation of glbt characters have flourished.

Further reading

Garcia Riera, Emilio (1997) *Breve historia del cine Mexicano: primer siglo, 1897–1997*, Mexico City: Ediciones Mapa.

TRINO SANDOVAL

MEXICO, LITERATURE

The year 1901 may be considered the reference point at which gay visibility in urban Mexican society comes to light. It was then that a group of 41 individuals were harassed by Mexico City police who raided the private ball attended by revellers, many of whom were dressed as women. Consequently, this event is documented in the 1906 novel *Los 41* (Those Forty One) by Eduardo Castrejón, who elaborates a picaresque-style novel with queer characters who are ridiculed and condemned. The number 41 has since forever been tainted. Castrejón's novel further established a tradition of sensationalist humour in Mexican literature that effectively defines 'deviant' masculinities by a society that professes a long history of masculinist homosocial bonds. Ultimately, male writers have dominated the literary scene for several decades, and in spite of early literary icons such as Sor Juana Inés de la Cruz (1651–95), or cultural icons such as Nellie Campobello (1909/19–) and Antonieta Rivas Mercado (1900–31), a persistent chauvinism has afflicted the national literary institutions.

National identity in Mexico has thus been predominantly linked to the tough masculine macho who is purportedly *fuerte*, *feo* and *formal* (strong, ugly and formal). Following this line, homosexuality in Mexico has been interpreted as a concept in direct opposition to national interests, and this is reinforced by the fact that 'proper' masculinity has always been the basis of an idealistic Mexican nation. Octavio Paz (1914–98) has used the terms '*rajarse*' (to crack) and '*chingar*' (multifaceted word that connotes the imposition of violence upon another individual) to describe masculinity in Mexican society. Indeed, violence – both physically and discursively – is perceived as the only way to legitimize the precarious sense of masculinity in Mexican society. Yet, words such as those suggested by Paz generate aggression against women, timid or 'deviant' men, '*maricóns*' (faggots), '*jotos*' (effeminate gays), or '*putos*' (term indicating a degenerate gay man, often used to refer to hustlers). It is common between Mexican men to transform violence from being strictly physical into more symbolic discourses including jokes, humour, cursing and contests of wits employing double entendres ('*albur*'), the sole objective being to ridicule another or 'penetrate' him. Consequently, this symbolic penetration reduces the other to a lesser individual, or, in the case of a man, a '*mariquita*' (effeminate variation of '*maricón*').

It is rather problematic to trace descriptions of gay identity in male characters in Mexican literature, because the sexual act between two men is always defined in terms of the dominant (one who penetrates) and the submissive (one who receives); and only the submissive is defined as homosexual. At the same time, historically, some literary genres, such as Mexican theatre, often showcased gay characters in *teatro frívolo* (frivolous theatre, frivolous here, referring to the camp character of such plays), and *Carpa* (popular theatrical groups that toured rural areas all over Mexico) to provide comic relief for the spectators. While a conspicuous homoeroticism is evident in the colonial literature of nineteenth-century Mexico, by the twentieth century effeminacy in men is linked to homosexuality and considered a threat to the nation-building process. Similarly, and at the same time, a carnivalesque element is also attributed to the identity of the male homosexual in the literary tradition. **Homophobia** is hence more evident in twentieth-century Mexican literature, where a series of conflicting ideas are generated around masculinity and nationhood is put under surveillance. Additionally, at certain historical moments in the twentieth century, the lower social classes are categorized as barbaric, bestial and prone towards degeneracy, such as homosexuality. At the other extreme, upper-class educated men have also been rejected as effeminate snobs, unpatriotic and likely to lead 'ambiguous' lifestyles.

During the twentieth century, the *Contemporáneos* (Contemporaries; 1928–31) have been considered the most influential literary generation of playwrights, poets and essayists, chroniclers who challenged concepts of gender in Mexican society. Significantly, and for the first time, many of the male artists professed an openly gay lifestyle. Salvador Novo (1904–74), Xavier Villaurrutia (1903–50), and Elías Nandino (1903–93) were prominent gay intellectuals

from this generation. Novo is particularly relevant because he spoke openly about homoerotic desire in one of his plays, *El Tercer Fausto* (The Third Faust, 1934). Villaurrutia used metaphors of night and death in his poetry and theatrical works such as *Invitación a la muerte* (Invitation to Death, 1940) to express his anguish as a closeted gay man.

Some of the most prominent Mexican novels to incorporate male homoerotic desire include: Paolo Po's *41, o un muchacho que soñaba en fantasmas* (Forty One, or a Boy who Dreamt of Ghosts, 1963), Miguel Barbachano Ponce's *El diario de José Toledo* (The Diary of José Toledo, 1964), Alberto X. Teruel's *Los inestables* (The Unstables, 1968), José Ceballos Maldonado's *Después de todo* (After All That, 1969), Luis Zapata's *Las aventuras, desventuras y sueños de Adonis García, el vampiro de la colonia Roma* (The Adventures, Misadventures, and Dreams of Adonis García, the Vampire in Colonial Rome, 1979). These novels contextualize homoerotic desire with conflicting images of fear, homophobia, satire and social marginalization. Moreover, they provide insight into the traditional interpretations of roles and sexual identities in Mexico, as well as into the identities adopted by many gay men. Many of these characters dominate a sexual relationship and are capable of maintaining a non-stigmatized identity while others assume a 'feminine' role and are stigmatized for their effeminate demeanour.

Zapata (b. 1951–) is probably the most well-known Mexican novelist. He published four novels between 1975 and 1990, all of which develop through characters that are either openly gay or demonstrate homoerotic sensibility. One of the most significant elements of Zapata's novels is the fact that he incorporates intelligent humour and satire to provide social commentary on popular culture, especially cinema. His characters are identified through specific linguistic patterns, where the discourse is shaped through camp that culminates in provocative explicitness. The melodramatic element of Mexican film also finds its way into his novels to generate a romantic sensibility around the characters.

Key works written by Mexican women include: *Amora* (1989) by Rosemaría Roffiel (b. 1945–); *Dos mujeres* (Two Women, 1991) by Sara Levi Calderón (b. 1942–); and *Amante de lo ajeno* (Distant Lover, 1997) and *El suplicio del placer* (The Suffering of Pleasure, 1994), both by Sabina Berman (b. 1956–). These texts invest in creating characters that challenge heterosexist gender roles as well as embark on openly lesbian relationships. *Amora* describes the relationship between Guadalupe, and Claudia (besides incorporating other peripheral storylines) through fragmented narrative and is considered the first lesbian novel in Mexico. Roffiel has also successfully employed poetry as a medium to legitimize lesbian eroticism. *Corramos libre ahora* (Let Us Run Free Now, 1986) is her first poetry collection that prioritizes lesbian pride within a larger framework of female bonding. One of her more recent collections of 12 short stories titled *El para siempre dura una noche* (The Everlasting Lasts Only For A Night, 1999) encompasses a wide range of marginalized characters including lesbians, a man suffering from **AIDS**, a rape victim and a transgender character.

Sara Levi Calderón has received critical acclaim for contesting class expectations, religious sentiments and conventional middle-class gender roles. Valeria, the principal character in her novel *Dos mujeres*, not only searches her own identity by defying her 'proper' roles as a mother, a wife and a daughter, but also challenges heterosexual eroticism when she decides to join her lover/girlfriend, Genovesa.

Sabina Berman has established her reputation as one of the most prominent female playwrights in Mexico City. Her literary production revolves around issues that are both conceptually as well as personally vital to her. These include feminism, lesbian identity and Jewish identity within Mexican culture. Trained formally in psychology as well as theatre, Berman employs biting humour to question conventional attitudes in both male and female characters. While *Amante de lo ajeno* evokes the psychological trauma that two male characters experience before investing a homoerotic relationship, *El suplicio del placer* establishes dialogues in bisexuality, androgyny and cross-dressing.

KANISHKA SEN

MEYER, RUSS

b. 1922; d. 2004

filmmaker

Born Russel Albion Meyer in Oakland, California, American cult filmmaker Russ Meyer is a superb cinematic counterpart to the 1960s queer pulp fiction revolution and an underground protagonist of the age of *Playboy*, beefcake magazines and the porn industry. Trained as a photographer of glamour nudie magazines, he moved into softporn films, titillating the heterosexual audience and relentlessly courting obscenity charges while sending up both sets of conventions. Cheaply produced and loosely plotted, Meyer's films are all trashy, women-centred feasts of parody. His stars are cheesecake pin-ups, the queens of topless bars, excessive, huge-breasted, hypersexed playthings, staging signs of femininity to their very limit of plausibility. However politically ambivalent in its representation of women, Meyer's cinema is a splendid instance of the extent to which liberation from the restraints of gender and sexuality took place, at least in part, by means of some sexploitation, and an irreverent laughter at heterosexual male fantasies and imagery of oppression.

FABIO CLETO

395

MIAOJIN, QIU

b. 1969; d. 1995

writer

Qiu Miaojin is Taiwan's best-known lesbian author. Qiu studied psychology at Taiwan University before moving to Paris for further study, where she committed suicide at the age of just 26. Qiu's literary style is avant-garde, mixing quasi-surrealist description with first-person psychological confessional. Qiu's earliest queer-themed stories appear in her 1991 collection, *The Revelry of Ghosts* (*Guide kuanghuan*), but she is best remembered for her prize-winning novel of 1994, *The Crocodile's Journal*, which has been interpreted as an allegorical critique of homophobia. Qiu's second novel, *Montmartre Testament* (1996) centres on her own difficult life as a student in Paris just prior to her suicide. Qiu's fiction has sometimes been accused of being unduly 'negative' about lesbian experience; however, her status as a public lesbian and intellectual and the emotional honesty and intensity of her writing make her a figure of enduring significance for lesbian readers of Chinese everywhere.

FRAN MARTIN

MICHAEL, GEORGE

b. 1963

pop singer

George Michael first came to prominence during the early 1980s as one half of the pop duo Wham! He and partner Andrew Ridgeley racked up a handful of hits before separating in 1986. Michael then began his very successful solo career, increasingly abandoning his teenybopper image for a more mature style. This led to the release in 1996 of *Older*, an album in which Michael reflects upon many changes in his personal life, most significantly the death of his lover, Anselmo Feleppa, from AIDS in 1993. In 1998, following his arrest for 'lewd behaviour' in a public toilet in Beverly Hills, Michael took centre stage during the media frenzy about homosexuality, coming out and public sex. Michael responded to the events with two songs and a video in which he criticizes the actions of the police as well as the double standard applied to issues of public homosexual sex.

DANIEL HENDRICKSON

MICHALS, DUANE

b. 1932

photographer

Born in McKeesport, Pennsylvania to working-class parents, Michals' path to photography was via art courses at the University of Denver and the Parsons School of Design. Successful commercial work in *Vogue* and *Life* is counterpoised with representations of same-sex love, desire and spirituality, concentrated upon classically inspired representations of the male nude. His work is strongly homo-erotic, drawing upon an influence from the surrealist Magritte in a quest to reveal emotional feeling behind the image of a subject. In 1970 he plotted the psychic terrain of urban gay life with his series *Chance Meeting*. In *The Unfortunate Man* (1978), he allegorizes the effects of gay criminalization, combining photographic image and coarsely handwritten text in what would become his distinctive style. Two books of photographic homage to iconic gay authors: *Homage to Cavafy* (1978) and *Salute, Walt Whitman* (1996) have followed.

MICHAEL PINFOLD

MIDLER, BETTE

b. 1945

singer, actor

An iconoclastic singer, actor and comedian, Bette Midler started her career as cabaret singer, 'The Divine Miss M', in the Continental Baths, a gay sauna in San Francisco. Cheerily and raucously self-parodying her Jewish heritage and her unconventional appearance, Midler successfully reinvented the torch song for the sexually liberated 1970s, establishing a loyal gay fan base. She gave a fearless performance in *The Rose* (1979), a film based on the turbulent life of singer Janis Joplin. After a series of film flops, she scored success with *Down And Out in Beverly Hills* (1986) (in which she made a much-criticized AIDS joke) and in *Beaches* (1988), a sentimental drama about two lifelong female friends. 'Wind Beneath My Wings', a ballad she co-wrote and performed for *Beaches*, became an international hit and was adopted as a Gay Pride anthem. Her TV sitcom *Bette* (2000–1), a misguided attempt at camp self-worship, was a ratings failure.

JOHN FORDE

MIELI, MARIO

b. 1952; d. 1983

activist, theorist

Mario Mieli is the leading thinker and radical activist born out of the 1970s gay liberation movement in Italy. After his experiences in England (1971–4), Mieli was an originator of FUORI, the first gay liberation group formed in Italy in 1972. He then formed COM (Collettivi Omosessuali Milanesi), breaking free from traditional notions of politics through performance, transvestism and gender-fuck situationism. He was active in the performance group Nostra Signora dei Fiori and wrote, with others, *La Traviata Norma* (The Bent Norm, 1976). His 1977 essay *Elementi di critica omosessuale* (reissued in 2002 with an afterword by Teresa De Lauretis) combines Marxism and psychoanalysis (the alienation of Labour and sexuality in capitalist societies; the 'polymorphous perverse' culled from Freud), but subverts them with queer

abandon. The key notion of 'transsexuality' points to the repressed polymorphous and non-differentiated erotic disposition, a transformative potential showing Mieli's resistance against concepts of identity that do not pursue a radical project of alterity. Mieli's critique puts gender and sexuality under the same critical scrutiny by refusing to submit to obligatory identifications. Consequently, gay subjectivity is pursued as an ongoing experiment, never to be stabilized.

His theory is evident in the novel *Il risveglio dei Faraoni* (The Awakening of the Pharaohs), an autobiography in which the identity of the protagonist is dissolved, in order to embrace 'transsexuality' and schizophrenia (pirated version 1994). The later writings of *Oro, eros e armonia* (Gold, Eros, Harmony, 2002) show his interest in mysticism, alchemy and coprophagy. Mieli committed suicide in 1983. His sister, Paola Mieli is planning an edition of his writings. Even though Mieli's life and writings should be placed in the context of a decade that saw the emergence of the New Left and the genuine faith in the revolutionary potential of new subjectivities, his example is still held up by queers who are unwilling to limit gay liberation to a question of civil rights.

MARCO PUSTIANAZ

MIKA

b. 1963

cabaret artist

Formerly an aerobics instructor, Mika developed a sophisticated stage act of song, dance and humour that tours internationally. Mika was born Neil Gudsell, raised in Timaru, New Zealand, and is of Kai Tahu Kati Mamoe and Nga Puhi descent (tribal identities of Maori indigenous to Aotearoa/New Zealand). Mika performed with the Maori Theatre in Education Company before embarking upon a solo career. His first single 'I Have Loved Me a Man' was released in 1989. Since then he has developed shows such as *Mika Haka* and *Tribal Hollywood*. Mika's work can be characterized as a fusion of ancient Maori traditions with new urban styles that include hip-hop, movie theme tunes and big show classics. A significant *takataapui* artist (the Maori term used to denote homosexuality), Mika is committed to the cultural revitalization of his indigenous heritage using the global marketplace as his setting and global popular culture as his material.

JO SMITH

MILITARY, GAYS IN THE (INTERNATIONAL)

In 1974 the Dutch military lifted its ban on gay and lesbian service members and became the first country in the world to officially allow homosexual personnel to serve openly. Since this watershed event, 24 other countries have also instituted policies that protect the rights of gay men and lesbian military personnel, including the United Kingdom, Germany, Canada, Australia, Israel and South Africa.

Still, attitudes and policies towards homosexuality continue to be ambivalent at best in countries such as Russia and Colombia, where gays are subject to contradictory policies that both allow them to serve and to be dismissed for their homosexuality. In the United States, homosexuality remains grounds for dismissal if gay and lesbian personnel disclose their sexual orientation, a policy that has been in place since 1993, when 'Don't Ask, Don't Tell' came into effect. Countries such as Greece, Turkey and Italy also explicitly prohibit service by homosexuals. These countries justify banning gay and lesbian service personnel by arguing that gays undermine unit cohesion, threaten privacy, are psychologically ill and unfit for military service and pose security risks.

Generally speaking, Canada, Australia and many northern European countries are most tolerant of homosexuality in both civilian and military cultures. Along with the Netherlands, countries such as Norway and Denmark were among the first to allow gays and lesbians to serve. Other European countries such as Belgium and France do not officially ban homosexual personnel, but they do not expressly protect their rights to serve. In these countries homosexuality is acceptable but can be a reason for sanction.

In the late 1960s many Western cultures grew increasingly accepting of homosexuality, with the Netherlands leading the way in integrating gay men and lesbians into its society through legal protections, which include standardizing age of consent laws and incorporating anti-discrimination language for sexual orientation in its constitution. Over the years the Dutch military has followed suit and created institutional mechanisms to ensure that homosexuals were integrated as fully as possible into its military culture. To this end it created a trade union called the Homosexuality and Armed Forces Foundation to represent gay and lesbian personnel with the Dutch Ministry of Defense (Anderson-Boers and van der Meulen 1994).

During the early 1990s a number of countries either lifted bans on homosexual personnel or attempted to. In October 1992 the Canadian military lifted its ban after federal courts ruled that the military's policy violated Canada's Charter of Rights and Freedoms. A month later, when Australia adopted a number of international human rights conventions, it also ended its ban. In June 1993 Israel lifted its ban after hearings on gays in the military in the Knesset resulted in public protest against state-sanctioned discrimination. During this time, under the new administration of President Bill Clinton, the United States also considered lifting its ban, but political pressure from conservatives and military officials resulted in the reformulation of policy and a new federal law, known as 'Don't Ask, Don't Tell', which allowed gays and lesbians to serve only if they remained closeted. Britain, a country whose military experts have long been considered hostile to homosexuality, finally changed its discriminatory policy in 2000, after the European Court of Human Rights ordered it to do so in 1999 (Belkin, 2003).

Despite the example of the United States, these cases illustrate a trend in Western democratic industrial nations of increasing military integration of both women and sexual minorities. Countries that are more inclusive of women in the military are more tolerant of homosexuality. As these countries become more accepting of homosexuality and continue to move towards voluntary military forces, they suggest it is not unreasonable to expect 'increasing diversity in the armed forces of Western industrial democracies' (Segal, Segal and Booth, 1999: 236).

In non-Western countries, the issue is not so clear. For many Asian or Latin cultures, the system of sexuality does not depend on such rigid distinctions between homosexual and heterosexual identity. For example, in Singapore there are no laws that pertain to sexual orientation, much less eligibility for military service. All male citizens must serve in national service for roughly two years at the age of 18, and the law does not recognize the distinction between gay and straight. Yet, an administrative policy does exist that requires medical screening of all recruits, which allows doctors to identify effeminate men as sexual inverts and place them in non-combat positions. Given that many self-identified gay men do not appear effeminate, their homosexuality, if discovered, seems to pose little problem for their success in the military.

Ultimately, in a number of different cultural contexts, research shows that, with effective leadership and equal opportunity programmes, allowing gays and lesbians to serve in the military has no negative impact upon morale, unit cohesion or military effectiveness.

Bibliography

Anderson-Boers, M. and van der Meulen, J. (1994) 'Homosexuality and the Armed Forces in the Netherlands', in W.J. Scott and S.C. Stanley (eds) *Gays and Lesbians in the Military*, New York: Aldine de Gruyter.

Belkin, A. (2003) 'Don't Ask, Don't Tell: Is the Gay Ban Based on Military Necessity?', *Parameters* 33: 108–19.

Segal, D.R., Segal, M.W. and Booth, B. (1999) 'Gender and Sexual Orientation Diversity in Modern Military Forces', in M.F. Katzenstein and J. Reppy (eds) *Beyond Zero Tolerance*, Lanham: Rowman & Littlefield.

Further reading

Belkin, A. and Bateman, G. (ed.) (2003) *Don't Ask, Don't Tell: Debating the Gay Ban in the Military*, Boulder: Lynne Rienner.

Belkin, A. and Levitt, M. (2001) 'Homosexuality and the Israeli Defense Forces: Did Lifting the Gay Ban Undermine Military Performance?' *Armed Forces & Society* 27, 4: 541–66.

GEOFFREY W. BATEMAN

MILK, HARVEY

b. 1930; d. 1978

politician

Harvey Milk, born on Long Island, was an openly gay politician, civil rights leader and martyr. He ran a camera shop in San Francisco's gay district, the Castro, that became an unofficial gay community centre. After three unsuccessful runs for public office, and with strong ties to labour and the emerging gay community, he was elected Supervisor in 1977, the first out gay person to do so. He became a hero to gay people around the country as a result. Milk passed a city gay rights bill and became co-chair of the successful 1978 statewide campaign to defeat 'Proposition 6' (also known as the Brigg's Initiative) that would have banned lesbian and gay teachers and those who supported them from public schools. On 27 November 1978, Dan White, a disgruntled former Supervisor who had just killed Mayor George Moscone, assassinated Milk in City Hall. Milk became an international gay martyr. He was the subject of a biography, *The Mayor of Castro Street* (1982), by Randy Shilts and an Oscar-winning documentary, *The Times of Harvey Milk* (1984), by Rob Epstein and Richard Schmiech, narrated by Harvey Fierstein.

See also: Harvey Milk Institute

ANDY HUMM

MILLER, TIM

b. 1958

writer, performance artist

Born in Pasadena, California, Tim Miller is a writer and performance artist whose work on the 'body politics' of contemporary gay identity has been acclaimed internationally from North America to Europe. A cofounder of the prestigious Performance Space 122 in Manhattan and the Highways Performance Space in Santa Monica, Miller received worldwide critical attention in 1990 as one of the infamous 'NEA 4' (National Endowment of the Arts 4) when, along with artists Karen **Finley**, John Fleck and Holly Hughes, they successfully sued the federal government for de-funding their quintessentially queer work on the blatantly homophobic grounds that it failed to uphold 'standards of decency'. More recently, Miller has taught performance at UCLA, and a number of his solo works have been published in the anthologies *Sharing the Delirium* (1994), *O Solo Homo* (1998) and *Body Blows* (2002). Now based in Venice Beach, California, he continues to push the boundaries of queer identity

and performance well into the new millennium.

ROBIN GRIFFITHS

MILLETT, KATE

b. 1934

author, activist, artist

American writer whose book *Sexual Politics* (1970), a comprehensive critique of patriarchy in Western culture and literature, became an immediate best seller and one of the cornerstone texts of the feminist movement. Millett indicted the sexism of novelists D.H. Lawrence, Henry Miller and Norman Mailer, arguing that these supposed champions of sexual freedom were misogynists who promoted and fetishized the sexual subordination and humiliation of their female characters. Millett's disclosure of her bisexuality ignited widespread debate about the (lack of) recognition of lesbian rights within the mainstream feminist movement. Millett's other works include *Flying* (1974), chronicling her coming-out process, *Sita* (1977), a memoir about her affair with a married woman, *The Loony-Bin Trip* (1990), chronicling her treatment for mental illness, and *A. D.: A Memoir* (1995), describing her aunt's disapproval of her lesbian identity. She also founded the Women's Ant Colony Farm, a community of female artists and writers.

JOHN FORDE

MINA

b. 1941

singer

Born in Cremona, Italy, Mina is an icon for Italian gay men. Her debut album, which appeared in the late 1950s, radically altered the predominant melodic style in popular music with extraordinary expressionist vocality centred on body and gesture. Her performances are often compared by musicologists to those of Maria **Callas**. Banned from television because of an extramarital pregnancy, Mina maintained an ambivalent relationship to her immense popularity, refusing international offers to perform with the likes of Frank Sinatra, Louis Armstrong and Federico Fellini. In 1978 she retired from a public career, increasing her mythic stature and remaining influential even among younger generations. Her recordings in multiple languages sustain Mina's continued international popularity. Her contradictory images, at once maternal and passionately transgressive, arouse identification in every kind of queer scene.

MASSIMO FUSILLO

MINAMI, TEISHIRO

b. 1931

activist

Teishiro Minami is a Japanese gay activist instrumental in founding JILGA (the Japanese branch of the **International Lesbian and Gay Association**) in 1984. Like the veteran gay campaigner Ken **Togo**, Minami also founded a gay magazine, *Adon* (1974–96), which became a vehicle for his views. However, his decision to stop publishing pornography in the magazine in 1995 in order to present a more 'serious' side to homosexuality proved fatal to its circulation; it ceased publication the following year. Minami was also an important figure in establishing annual lesbian and gay parades in Tokyo from 1994. However, his autocratic leadership style and preoccupation with presenting a decent, sanitized version of gay life to the public led to widespread criticism from Japan's queer community and a particularly poor parade turnout in 1997. In 2000 the parade was relaunched with a more inclusive policy.

MARK MCLELLAND

MINEO, SAL

b. 1939; d. 1976

actor

Actor Sal Mineo came to national attention at the age of 16 with his sensitive portrayal of Plato, a lonely middle-class teenager who befriends James Dean in *Rebel Without a Cause* (1955). His portrayal won him his first Oscar nomination. In the late 1950s he started a career as a singer, which met with moderate success. In 1961 he won his second Oscar nomination for his work in the film *Exodus*. He subsequently made many more films in Hollywood, but his career suffered from his being typecast as a troubled, slightly tough teenager, a role for which he was now too old. Additionally, his refusal to cooperate in downplaying his homosexuality hurt his career. He began directing theatre, staging successful productions of *Fortune and Men's Eyes* (1969) in both New York and Los Angeles. In 1976, when returning from a rehearsal in Los Angeles, he was attacked and stabbed to death.

DANIEL HENDRICKSON

MING-LIANG, TSAI

b. 1957

filmmaker

Taiwan-based Tsai Ming-liang is famous for the deliberate pace of his films, which cut together long takes, often of static medium and long shots. Tsai is also known for casting his love interest, Lee Kang-sheng, in all his films. Tsai's feature debut, *Ch'ing shaonien na cha* (*Rebels of the Neon God*, 1992), narrates the story of a disenchanted youth who drops out of school after becoming obsessed with a local petty criminal. The hinted sexual tension between the two men is rekindled in *Aiqing wansui* (*Vive L'amour*, 1994), where the same actors return as street vendors who are drawn together by a vacant, upscale apartment. In

401

the penultimate scene, one crawls into bed with the sleeping other and eventually works up his nerve to lean over and kiss his love interest. The smouldering tension takes the most transgressive turn in *He liu* (*The River*, 1997), in which Lee plays a son who accidentally takes his father as his sex partner.

CUI ZI'EN
YING ZHU

MINK STOLE

actor

Nancy Stoll, was born in Baltimore, Maryland and began acting under the name Mink Stole in the 1970s alongside another Baltimore native, filmmaker John **Waters**. She has played several significant roles in his films, most notably as the villainous Connie Marbles in *Pink Flamingos* (1972) and as the obnoxious Taffy Davenport in *Female Trouble* (1974). In addition to her film work with Waters and others, Stole has worked on the stage, including a period as a member of Charles Ludlam's Ridiculous Theatrical Company. She also writes an advice column for a Baltimore newspaper entitled 'Think Mink'.

DANIEL HENDRICKSON

MINNELLI, LIZA

b. 1946

singer, actor

Liza Minnelli, daughter of queer icon Judy **Garland** and rumoured bisexual director Vincente **Minnelli**, captured a queer audience – mostly gay men – with a singing style marked by an emotional openness and vulnerability. Minnelli later married a gay (or possibly bisexual) man (Peter **Allen**), whom she reportedly found in bed with her mother's gay husband (Mark Herron). Unlike her mother, Minnelli's early starring roles in films were serio-comic ones: the kooky 'Pookie' Adams in *The Sterile Cuckoo*

(1969) and the facially scarred title character of *Tell Me That You Love Me, Junie Moon* (1970). These offbeat, outsider characters, rather than her musical talents, initially drew queer fans to Minnelli. But it was her performances in *Cabaret* (1972) and the TV special *Liza with a 'Z'* (1972) that confirmed her queer stardom. Since then, like her mother, Minnelli has suffered physical, emotional and career setbacks, but (also like her mother) has made comebacks, including her 2002 tour, *Liza's Back* (2002).

ALEX DOTY

MINNELLI, VINCENTE

b. 1903; d. 1986

film director

Born in Delaware, Ohio, Lester Anthony Minnelli moved, as a teenager, to Chicago where he became involved in photography, theatre design, painting and acting. His creative energies were first put into service designing window displays for Marshall Fields Department Store. Minnelli's interest in Impressionism, Fauvism and Surrealism brought provocative uses of colour to his displays. His innovative technique and ability to draw upon an eclectic cultural palette won him favour with critics and entertainment-industry producers. In 1931 he moved to New York City, where he soon joined the modernist urbane circles of *Vanity Fair* and 'the smart set'. At his salon, 'The Minnellium', Minnelli hosted queer-artistic coteries with George Platt-Lynes, Pavel Tchelitchev and W. Somerset Maugham in attendance. The Minnellium witnessed principles of 'high art' (painting, literature) commingling with 'low art' (popular music, movies), facilitating a camp aesthetic that Minnelli carried with him to Hollywood.

By the 1940s Minnelli was working at MGM Studios with the popular **Freed Unit**. He arrived dressed in flamboyant clothing and, according to some, wearing mascara. In keeping with its family image, MGM announced the marriage of Minnelli and Judy **Garland** following the success of *Meet Me in St Louis* (1944). The marriage lasted three years, and produced both Liza **Minnelli** and the now camp-classic film *The Pirate* (1948).

Although never identifying himself as a 'homosexual', Minnelli's aesthetic developed along queer-modernist sensibilities. Minnelli's Hollywood films (especially the homosexual-themed *Tea and Sympathy* [1953]) remain cornerstones for queer academics and filmmakers.

Bibliography

Gerstner, David A. (2000) 'Queer Modernism: The Cinematic Aesthetic of Vincente Minnelli', *Modernity*, 2, available at: http://www.eiu.edu/~modernity/modernity.html.

DAVID A. GERSTNER

MINORITIES RESEARCH GROUP (MRG)

A British lesbian organization, established in 1963 by five women: Esme Langley, Diana Chapman, Cynthia Reid, Julie Switsur and Patricia Dunkley. The group was the first of its kind in the United Kingdom and provided a focus for lesbian socializing and a source of information for the increasing media interest in lesbianism of the 1960s.

The group's stated aims were to conduct and collaborate on research about homosexuality, especially in women, and to disseminate information and items of interest to researchers and other interested professionals. This remained an important part of its work; MRG was involved in nine research projects during the 1960s. The studies varied in scale and focus, but were predominantly conducted by psychiatrists or psychologists.

The group's regular and most significant work was the production of the magazine, *Arena Three*. Launched in January 1964, the magazine was distributed monthly to postal subscribers. These were primarily lesbians, but also included homosexual men, married couples and those with a professional interest. The magazine's circulation was modest, totalling between 400 and 450 in the mid-1960s and reaching approximately 600 by 1971. Early issues were written almost entirely by the founder members, but as the number of subscribers grew, the magazine was increasingly filled with contributions from readers. Regular features included reviews of books, plays and films with lesbian content; biographical accounts of historical figures associated with same-sex desire; and short stories. The content and style of the magazine, however, varied considerably between issues. A large letters section allowed readers to respond to the articles and debate aspects of lesbian identity and experience.

In response to readers' requests, MRG also organized social events. These took place once a month and, by March 1964, had proved so popular that a pub function room had to be hired for the event. Members took part in debates, heard visiting speakers and watched film screenings. Smaller local groups also started up in different areas of London and across the country. Disagreement over the attendance of 'butch' lesbians at meetings prompted a debate in 1964 to discuss whether masculine dress drew unwanted and negative attention to the group. While the debate was settled in favour of butch lesbians being allowed to attend, the issue remained a source of resentment and the MRG was criticized by some for being too middle-class and overly concerned with promoting a 'respectable' image, to the exclusion of many, more visible, lesbians. Further disagreements over whether priority should be given to the production of the magazine or to social activities precipitated a split, and in September 1965 a group of London members, including the social organizer Cynthia Reid and her partner, Julie Switsur, broke away from MRG to form a new social group, Kenric. MRG social events continued at the Gateways nightclub until the resignation of Esme Langley as director led to the group's demise in 1971.

Further reading

Hamer, E. (1996) *Britannia's Glory: A History of Twentieth-Century Lesbians*, London: Cassell.

REBECCA JENNINGS

MIRANDA, CARMEN

b. 1909; d. 1955

actor

The so-called 'Brazilian Bombshell' began her career recording samba in Brazil during the 1930s. She was discovered and invited to New York by Lee Shubert in 1939. From Broadway she went to Hollywood where her singing and dancing style captivated audiences and fit Hollywood's wartime interest in establishing closer ties with Latin America. After a brief return to Brazil, where middle-class audiences snubbed her for becoming 'Americanized', she returned to Hollywood. Although she almost never played a lead role, she was for a time the highest-paid woman in the United States. After the war Hollywood's interest in both her and Latin America declined, although she continued to be very popular with audiences. She died of heart failure after a performance on the Jimmy Durante TV show. She remains a much-loved figure in both Brazil and the US, and her extravagant 'Baiana' look has spawned more than one generation of drag queens.

DANIEL HENDRICKSON

MITCHELL, ARTHUR

b. 1934

dancer, choreographer, artistic director

Born Arthur Adams Mitchell Jr on 27 March 1934 in New York City, he began tap-

dance lessons at the age of 10, sang in the glee club and attended the High School of Performing Arts, where he progressed quickly through a modern dance major. He began ballet study at George Balanchine's School of American Ballet in 1952 and performed in several Broadway musicals and with the Donald McKayle Company, Sophie Maslow and the New Dance Group, Louis Johnson and Anna Sokolow. He joined the New York City Ballet (NYCB) in November 1955 and became its first permanent African-American principal dancer, noted for his supple control and precise partnering skills. In 1968 he formed the school that became the Dance Theatre of Harlem (DTH), a premier neo-classical dance company that features ballet dancers of African descent, and of which he was artistic director. Although closed-mouthed about his personal life, Mitchell's efforts allowed many queer ballet artists performance opportunities denied in all other circumstances.

THOMAS F. DEFRANTZ

MITCHELL, JOHN CAMERON

b. 1963

actor, writer, film director

Born in El Paso, Texas, the son of a US Army General, John Cameron Mitchell has emerged as one of the most promising queer film directors and performers working in Hollywood today. After a steady career in the 1980s and 1990s as a bit part actor in a number of American TV sitcoms and films, Mitchell achieved cult success in 1994 with the outrageous off-Broadway musical, *Hedwig and the Angry Inch*, about a German transsexual and her rock 'n' roll band, which he co-wrote with musician Stephen Trask. The film adaptation in 2001 finally earned him mainstream success, including a Best Director Award at the Sundance Film Festival and Best Feature Prizes at the Berlin and San Francisco Lesbian and Gay Film

Festivals. Mitchell is set to push the boundaries of contemporary queer cinema once again with his tantalisingly titled next feature, *The Sex Film Project*, which, in his words, explores a 'pansexual bohemian environment where gender, sexuality, art, music and politics are fluid and volatile'.

ROBIN GRIFFITHS

MIZRAHI, ISAAC

b. 1961

fashion designer

A one-time darling of the fashion world, Brooklyn-native Isaac Mizrahi's flamboyant designs and exuberant campy wit has made him one of America's most recognizable gay personalities. He studied as an actor before switching to fashion design and soon won plaudits in the late 1980s with his bold use of colour and inventive reworking of sportswear, parkas and t-shirts. Drawing heavily on Hollywood film and popular culture to create and promote his work, he combines influences as diverse as *The Mary Tyler Moore Show*, film diva Bette **Davis** and the 1922 silent film *Nanook of the North*, from which he derived the inspiration for his famous 'Eskimo chic' look. Mizrahi's preparations for his 1994 Fall collection were chronicled in the documentary *Unzipped* (1995), showcasing his witty, neurotic commentary. His contract with Chanel was terminated in the late 1990s following disappointing revenues. He has since written and starred in the one-man show *Les Mizrahi* (2000) and hosted *The Isaac Mizrahi Show* (2001–) for television. He has also designed a clothing line for the retail chain Target.

JOHN FORDE

MOFFIE

South African slang term for effeminate male homosexuals, originally with a strong derogatory meaning but often defiantly co-opted by gay rights activists.

MARC EPPRECHT

MOFFIETAAL

Argot among white and coloured (mixed-race) South African gay men dating from the 1950s. It aimed to hide their sexuality in a homophobic society and as an entry code into a shared community. Examples include 'Ada' (buttocks), 'Sally' (to suck off) and 'Tilly' (to masturbate).

MARC EPPRECHT

MONETTE, PAUL

b. 1945; d. 1995

writer

A poet and novelist, whose memoirs about his struggles with AIDS made him one of the most compelling voices in contemporary gay literature. He produced two much-admired collections, *The Carpenter at the Asylum* (1975) and *No Witnesses* (1981), and garnered international attention for his gay-themed debut novel, *Taking Care of Mrs Carroll* (1978). In the early 1980s, he and his lover Roger Horwitz were both diagnosed with HIV. His subsequent struggles with the disease and Horwitz's death in 1986 were chronicled in the memoir *On Borrowed Time* (1988) and in *Love Alone: 18 Elegies for Rog* (1988), a collection of poems. In his autobiography, *Becoming A Man: Half A Life Story* (1992), Monette frankly addressed his early life as a closeted gay man in homophobic post-Second World War America; the book won the National Book Award. A documentary of his life, *Paul Monette: The Brink of Summer's End*, was made in 1997.

JOHN FORDE

MONEY, JOHN

b. 1921

sexologist

From the early 1950s, New Zealand-born sexologist John Money's research at John Hopkins University heavily influenced the 'treatment' of **intersex** children, and transsexuality. Key to Money's research was his belief that gender identity (a phrase he coined) is produced through early childhood experiences and that infants could therefore be assigned either gender irrespective of other sex indicators. A famous case under Money's counsel was that of John Thiessen, an infant raised as a girl following the accidental destruction of his penis. The case was celebrated as proof of Money's thesis until a teenage Thiessen reclaimed a male identity. Nonetheless, Money's research continues to influence the protocol of medical intervention to ensure intersex-born children have a single gender identity, despite criticism from intersex activists. John Money's seemingly radical assertion that gender is environmentally and culturally constructed would later be echoed in feminist and queer theories.

ANITA BRADY

MONROE, MARILYN

b. 1926; d. 1962

actor

Marilyn Monroe's work in films such as *Gentlemen Prefer Blondes* (1953) displayed an on-screen persona that combined sexual knowledge and intellectual naïveté. Monroe's widely known personal history, many details of which she provided to the public, is of a lonely foster child who achieved stardom only to die a sudden and mysterious death. This has made her popular in queer culture where her story symbolizes both survival and tragic doom. Today, Monroe is an instantly recogniz-

able and infinitely reproducible icon, evoked in a visual shorthand of pieces that signify the whole: a blonde wig, a white halter dress, a breathlessly childish voice that somehow evokes a forbidden sexual register. This assemblage of easily recognizable parts has made her a popular drag evocation. In her multiple manifestations, Marilyn Monroe is simultaneously a product of plastic modernity and a unique signifier of late twentieth-century postmodernity.

YASMIN NAIR

MONROE, VLADISLAV MAMYSHEV

b. 1969

artist

Russian-born artist Vladislav Mamushev Monroe works in several media, including as a performance artist. During his military service in 1987, he made his first photographs of himself dressed as Marilyn Monroe, from whom he took his name. He became known in Western Europe during the 1990s when his work was shown in several important exhibitions of young Russian and Eastern European artists. He continues to produce photographs of himself in various drag personalities, playing off gender stereotypes to comment on political and social issues. He lives and works in Moscow and St Petersburg.

DANIEL HENDRICKSON

MONTEZ, MARIA

b. 1912; d. 1951

actor

Film actor, born in the Dominican Republic, Maria Montez's ambition and skill at self-promotion (she started her own fan club and wrote most of the fan letters herself) landed her a contract in Hollywood, playing exotic roles in some of the blockbuster, escapist adventure films of the early 1940s such as *Arabian Nights* (1942) and *Cobra Woman* (1944). She moved to France with her husband, Jean-Pierre Aumont and continued to make films, both in France and Italy, although she never achieved the kind of success she had experienced in Hollywood. She drowned in her bath in Paris in 1951. During the 1960s, largely forgotten, she gained a cult following centred around a group of artists involved in the queer New York and American underground film scene, most notably Jack **Smith**, Ronald **Tavel** and the drag queen Mario **Montez**, whose name is an obvious homage to the star.

See also: American underground cinema

DANIEL HENDRICKSON

MONTEZ, MARIO

actor

Puerto Rican-American drag queen and actor in the New York and American underground film scene of the 1960s and 1970s, Mario Montez began his career as 'the Spanish lady' in Jack Smith's film *Flaming Creatures* (1963), credited then under the name Dolores Flores. Shortly thereafter he took the name Mario Montez and went on to star in Smith's *Normal Love* (1964). He subsequently made several films with Andy **Warhol**, often in conjunction with scriptwriter Ronald **Tavel**. The most well known of these films include *Mario Banana* (1964), *More Milk Yvette* (1966) and *Screentest #2* (1965), in which he plays a would-be starlet undergoing a gruelling screen test for an important role in *The Hunchback of Notre Dame*. Unlike many of Warhol's superstars, very little is known about his previous or subsequent life.

See also: American underground cinema; Smith, Jack

DANIEL HENDRICKSON

MOOREHEAD, AGNES

b. 1900; d. 1974

actor

An American stage and film actor whose classical training and versatility allowed her to emerge as one of Hollywood's all-time great character players. Best known for supporting roles in film classics such as *Citizen Kane* (1941), *Jane Eyre* (1944), *Johnny Belinda* (1948) and *Magnificent Obsession* (1954), Moorehead unexpectedly found late career popularity – and queer icon status – with the part of Endora, the flamboyant and scathingly witty mother-in-law on the long-running 1960s sitcom *Bewitched*. Married and divorced twice, Moorehead is widely rumoured to have been a lesbian and long sported the nickname 'The Lavender Lady'.

BRETT FARMER

MOPELI-PAULUS, ATWELL SIDWELL

b. 1913; d. 1960

writer

Basotho poet and novelist Atwell Sidwell Mopeli-Paulus lived most of his life in South Africa. He co-wrote *Blanket Boy's Moon* with journalist Peter Lanham in 1953. This tells the story of a naïve country bumpkin who migrates to Johannesburg, where he is shocked to witness male–male sex in prison. Later, under the influence of marijuana, he becomes sexually infatuated with a young male prostitute-like character. *Blanket Boy's Moon* is the first novel by an African to depict homosexuality among black men, and is all the more remarkable for the ambivalent way it treats the topic. It includes the suggestion that male–male sex or intimate physical contact was known in rural settings and thus was not a purely urban, modern phenomenon as often claimed. Mopeli-Paulus' memoir was serialized in the popular magazine *Drum* in 1955, where homosexual rape in prison is denounced in straightforward terms.

MARC EPPRECHT

MORAGA, CHERRÍE

b. 1952

writer

Cherríe Moraga was born in Whittier, California. She is an essayist, poet, short-story writer and playwright. She is also the co-founder of Kitchen Table/Women of Color Press (1981) and co-editor of *This Bridge Called My Back: Writings by Radical Women of Color* (1981), which placed her among the most influential Chicana lesbian feminist writers. Moraga's writing centres on the Chicana lesbian feminist experience while addressing issues related to ethnicity, immigrant rights, domestic violence and female sexuality in general. Her book, *Loving in the War Years* (1983), made Chicana lesbianism visible in Chicano popular culture. Her most revered plays, *Giving Up the Ghost* (1986), *Shadow of a Man* (1992) and *Heroes and Saints* (1993), have Chicana leading characters who explore issues of sexuality while fighting against oppression from Chicano/Mexican machismo culture and Anglo patriarchy. Throughout her career, Moraga has been instrumental in politicizing Chicana lesbian identities. During the early 1990s she developed the notion of **Queer Aztlán**.

See also: Chicana/o and Latina/o literature

DANIEL ENRIQUE PÉREZ

MORDDEN, ETHAN

b. 1947

writer

Best known for his four volumes of 'Buddies' stories about gay life in 1960s and 1970s New York City, Mordden's prolific literary output includes novels, journalism and critical studies of musicals, theatre and film. He was born on 27 January 1947 in Pennsylvania. His long-running column, 'Is There A Book In This?', which appeared in *Christopher Street* magazine and was a fictionalized account of his life in New York narrated by his literary alter ego Bud, was later published as *I've a Feeling We're Not In Kansas Anymore: Tales from Gay Manhattan* (1985). This was followed by *Buddies* (1986), *Everybody Loves You: Further Adventures of Gay Manhattan* (1988) and *Some Men Are Lookers* (1997). His novels include *One Last Waltz* (1986), *How Long Has This Been Going On?* (1995) and *The Venice Adriana* (1998). He published a collection of 11 heterosexually-themed short stories, *A Bad Man Is Easy to Find* (1991) under the pseudonym M.J. Verlaine. He has edited numerous anthologies of gay fiction and studies of opera, American musical theatre and film.

JOHN FORDE

MORNING PARTY

A dance party held annually on **Fire Island** in New York, which is one of the main events in the international gay 'circuit' of dance parties. Attracting around 5,000 gay men every year, a share of the profits are donated to the **Gay Men's Health Crisis**.

JOHN FORDE

MORRIS, MARK

b. 1956

dancer, choreographer

Born in Seattle in 1956, Mark Morris became the leading American choreographer of the 1990s and continues to create dance pieces with his company, the Mark Morris Dance Group, located in Brooklyn, New York. Openly gay and often controversial, his works are known for their inventiveness and musicality as well as for Morris' eagerness to please audiences with spectacle, humour and grace.

Beginning his career by studying Balkan folk dance, flamenco and ballet, Morris went on to dance with modern dance pioneers Eliot Feld, Lar Lubovitch and Laura Dean. He started his own company in 1980 and has since created over 100 works with his company as well as creating dances for American Ballet Theater and other prominent companies. Also a remarkable dancer, Morris insists on using live music and often collaborates with other high-profile artists, for example, director Peter Sellars and composer John Adams on the opera *Nixon in China* (1987). One of his most loved works for gay audiences is *The Hard Nut* (1991), a reworking of *The Nutcracker*, which features cross-gendered casting and a 1960s-themed party set in suburbia.

ED MILLER

MORRISSEY, PAUL

b. 1938

film director, producer, screenwriter

Born in New York City in 1938, Paul Morrissey rose to prominence as a cult figure in the American underground film scene of the 1960s, when he was asked to contribute to the artistic development of artist Andy Warhol's early experiments with film. After successfully writing, producing and directing *Lonesome Cowboys* (1968), Morrissey assumed total directorial control of all film produced by Warhol's iconic Film Factory, and produced such cult art-house successes as his 'Flesh Trilogy' – *Flesh* (1968), *Trash* (1970) and *Heat* (1972) – and the 'Eurotrash' classics *Flesh for Frankenstein* (1974) and *Blood for Dracula* (1974). When Warhol lost interest in film in the mid-1970s, Morrissey continued to forge a career as an independent filmmaker, producing offbeat works such as *Forty Deuce* (1982) about teenage hustlers and the gritty

crime thriller about drug pushers *Mixed Blood* (1984). However, he never really achieved the same level of success as his earlier Warhol period and, disillusioned with the burgeoning 'indie' scene, sadly gave up filmmaking in the late 1980s.

See also: American underground cinema; Warhol, Andy

ROBIN GRIFFITHS

MORRISSEY AND THE SMITHS

b. 1959

rock singer and group

Alongside Johnny Marr (b. John Maher, 1963, Manchester, England), Morrissey (b. Steven Patrick Morrissey, Davyhulme, Manchester, England) created one of the most influential and popular British alternative rock band of the 1980s, The Smiths, marking a turning point from the electro-pop of earlier years. Their traditional line-up and sound was boosted by Marr's inspired guitar and Morrissey's charismatic dandy figure. Sneering at middle-class values in a queer mingling of the British upper-class camp tradition with Welfare State tokens, Morrissey paid constant homage to Oscar Wilde in his lyrics and performances, donning a hearing aid and National Health Service spectacles and brandishing a bunch of gladioli. Morrissey's many oblique references to gay culture (witness the cover of The Smiths' first album, a frame from Warhol's 1964 film *Blow Job*), along with his posing and theatrical crooning about social degradation, made him the target of tabloid sensationalism regarding his sexuality, which was only enforced by his controversial social commentary on domestic and school violence, animal rights, royalty, socialism and ethnic stereotypes. Morrissey's sharp wit and passion for unpredictable, cynical statements never failed to ridicule lesser understandings, as he refused to allow his own celibate, effeminate, self-absorbed persona be pinned down. When in 1987, after releasing four landmark records of amazing diversity, ranging from epic grandeur to bitter irony to sheer romanticism, the group split up, Johnny Marr went on to stand out as a highly regarded guitar player, while Morrissey's unique, charismatic image made him an even bigger star in the US, a star that won't lose his spell despite frequent clashes with the press, former Smith's members and record labels.

FABIO CLETO

MOYLE AFFAIR, THE

In 1975 Colin Moyle, a Cabinet Minister in the New Zealand Labour government, was questioned by police after being spotted late at night outside a gay cruising area. In 1976 the Labour party was voted out of office and new conservative Prime Minister Robert Muldoon accused Moyle in Parliament of having been 'picked up for homosexual practices' – at that time still a criminal offence. The resulting inquiry led to Moyle's resignation from Parliament, although he was re-elected in 1981.

JOHN FORDE

MUGABE, ROBERT

b. 1904

President of Zimbabwe

In 1980 Robert Mugabe led the Zimbabwe Liberation Army against Rhodesia, resulting in the birth of Zimbabwe under his ZANU-PF government. All Zimbabweans, including the glbt population, believed this new freedom applied to everyone. Although ZANU-PF made great strides in education and health, challenges to ZANU-PF authority were not tolerated. The 1980s were characterized by brutal massacres of thousands of Ndebele in the south of Zimbabwe. With the dissolution

of the Soviet Union in the 1990s, Mugabe felt threatened by Western calls for multi-party democracy. South Africa's liberation from apartheid meant Mugabe no longer had external enemies to blame for Zimbabwe's economic problems. He turned to the traditional enemy, Britain, and accused glbt people of misusing human rights and democracy, of corrupting Zimbabwean youth and of destroying Zimbabwean culture. Mugabe has issued a series of tirades against glbt persons, calling them 'worse than dogs and pigs' and not deserving of any rights. His outbursts highlight the dictatorial tendencies of his regime and the difficulties that glbt communities face throughout Africa.

KEITH GODDARD

MUIR, MADELINE

filmmaker

Documentary filmmaker, best known for *West Coast Crones: A Glimpse Into the Lives of Nine Old Lesbians* (1990), a documentary in which nine lesbians aged from 61 to 76 tell their stories. As expressed by one of the interview subjects: 'We are old Lesbians inventing ways to live out our aging...We are political Old Lesbians. One of the ways we practice our politics is by sharing with each other the stories of who we are'. Muir's film intercuts interviews with footage of Senior events in the **Gay Games** and of Gay and Lesbian Pride marches.

JOHN FORDE

MUJERES CREANDO

A controversial Bolivian feminist-anarchist activist group, Mujeres Creando advocates for civil rights of social, economic and sexual minorities, as well as victims of political persecution. María Galindo is co-founder and an outspoken lesbian activist. To disseminate information the organization uses strategies ranging from provocative graffiti painted on walls all over the country, TV talk shows, publications, street perfor- mances and filmmaking. The group describes itself as a 'collective of affects and defects, much creativity and proposals... born with the intent of being a transform- ing movement... [and] a space of culture, art and social change, where we can paint, tell stories... subvert orders, patriarchal orders'.

PEDRO ALBORNOZ

MÜLLER, MATTHIAS

b. 1961

filmmaker

After completing his initial studies in Ger- man and Fine Arts, Matthias Müller entered the Braunschweig School of Arts, where he studied film with the well-known German experimental filmmaker Birgit Hein. After returning to his hometown of Bielefeld, he co-founded the film co-operative Alte Kinder (Old Children). He quickly became an important figure in the international experimental film scene with his lyrical and often melancholic works. He frequently uses manipulated film stock (scratched, tin- ted, bleached) and double projection. He has also worked with found footage, most famously in his film *Home Stories* (1990), a tour de force of assemblage consisting solely of clips from 1950s melodramas. In it, var- ious Hollywood leading ladies (Lana Turner, Grace Kelly and others) produce and reproduce everyday gestures inside the home – turning on and off lights, going to the window, opening the door.

DANIEL HENDRICKSON

MUMMIES AND BABIES, AMACHICKEN

Colloquial terms used in southern Africa to describe lesbian-like relationships between African girls and young women modelled on traditional marriage forms. According to anthropologist Judith Gay, they emerged in boarding schools during the 1950s.

MARC EPPRECHT

MUNCH, CHRISTOPHER

b. 1962

filmmaker

A self-taught filmmaker, Munch is best known for *The Hours and Times* (1991), an intriguing fictionalized account of the rela- tionship between John Lennon and Brian Epstein, The Beatles' openly gay manager. Based on a real-life event in 1963, when Lennon and Epstein holidayed alone toge- ther in Barcelona, Munch's film portrays Epstein's unrequited sexual crush on Len- non and the sexual tension between the two men. The film garnered Munch wide acclaim and 1992 Sundance Film Festival's Jury Prize. His follow-up film, *Color of a Brisk and Leaping Day* (1996), examines the treatment of Chinese immigrants in 1940s America, with an eclectic cast including singer Michael **Stipe**. His other work includes *The Sleepy Time Gal* (2001), a drama about a dying woman being reunited with her estranged daughter, and *Harry and Max* (2004), a black comedy about two pop-star brothers.

JOHN FORDE

MUNGOSHI, CHARLES

b. 1947

writer, actor

Zimbabwean novelist, poet, short-story writer, writer of children's stories, actor and screenwriter working in both English and Shona, Charles Mungoshi's prolific oeuvre focuses on growing up in a society torn between traditional and modern Western values. 'A Marriage of Convenience' is a noteworthy intervention in debates around homosexuality. Published in a popular magazine (*Horizon*, August 1996) and subsequently in a prize-winning collection of short stories ('Of Lovers and Wives' in *Walking Still*, 1997), it depicts a young married Shona man who prefers a sexual relationship with his male friend over his wife. Sympathetic to the wife's anguish, the story helps to explain homophobia among African women and how it was exploited for political advantage by President Robert **Mugabe** and other African leaders.

MARC EPPRECHT

MURRAY, STEPHEN O. AND WILLIAM ROSCOE

Murray, Stephen O.

b. 1950

anthropologist

Roscoe, Will

b. 1955

anthropologist

American anthropologists Stuart O. Murray and Will Roscoe's prolific work has contributed to understanding diverse non-Western expressions of same-sex sexual desire, ritual and identity. They have edited several collections, addressing the role that modern Western constructions of homosexuality have had in giving rise to homophobia in non-Western nationalist politics. *Boy-Wives and Female Husbands* (1998), for example, contains essays ranging from seventeenth-century travel stories to contemporary scholarly analysis. It undermines the argument of men such as Robert Mugabe that same-sex sexuality is not indigenous to Africa. Likewise, *Islamic Homosexualities* (1997) stands as a powerful rebuke to the homophobic anti-Western politics of leaders such as Mohammed Mahathir.

MARC EPPRECHT

MUSIAŁ, GRZEGORZ

b. 1952

writer

Of those authors of the latter part of the twentieth century whose writing focused on homoerotic themes and motifs, Polish-born Grzegorz Musiał is probably the most interesting. Strongly influenced by the style and language of Witold Gombrowicz, Musiał's novels are characterized by an open, hybrid and autobiographical structure, a combination of diary, original prose, poetry and digressions. His first works, such as *Stan płynny* (Fluid State) and *Czeska biżuteria* (Czech Jewellery, 1983), deal rather timidly with the homosexual condition. In later novels, such as *W ptaszarni* (In the Aviary, 1989), *Al fine* (In the End, 1997), *Dziennik z Iowa* (Diary from Iowa, 2000) and in his volume of poems *Kraj wzbronionej miłości* (The Country of Forbidden Love), Musiał delves deeper into the relation between homosexuality, society and Catholicism, and examines the theme of transvestism along with the issue of body and sexuality as prison and cage of the individual.

ALESSANDRO AMENTA

MUSICALS, FILM

A form of cinematic entertainment that uses popular song, and sometimes dance, as a mode of storytelling, the musical is a cultural form that has long and enduring associations with queer culture.

Many queers have played an influential role in the historical constitution of the film musical. Composers such as Cole **Porter**, Jerry **Herman**, Leonard **Bernstein** and Stephen **Sondheim**; lyricists such as Lorenz Hart; choreographers Jerome Robbins and Jack Cole; producers such as Roger Edens; and directors such as Vincente **Minnelli** have ensured that the musical's creative economy is marked with a strong queer presence.

There has been an even stronger queer participation in the musical at the level of reception, where queers comprised one of the genre's most significant and loyal audiences. The image of the gay musical fan is a veritable stereotype of queer representation. While the male coding of that image might suggest that gay men have been the musical's primary queer constituency, many lesbians have forged equally, if less visibly, vital investments in the genre.

There are multiple, diverse reasons for the musical's queer appeal. In part, queers are drawn to the genre's fabled utopianism. There is an irrepressible optimism to the musical, in which problems and obstacles are effortlessly surmounted through the transformative power of music. The principal textual drive of most musicals consist in bringing people together – whether as a couple, family or whole community – into the blissful union of song and dance. For many queers who have suffered the isolation of social marginality, the lure of such a utopian scenario can be very powerful. Indeed, many of the musical's most rousing utopian numbers, such as *The Wizard of Oz*'s 'Over The Rainbow', *Carousel*'s 'You'll Never Walk Alone' and *West Side Story*'s 'Somewhere', have become veritable queer anthems.

Musicals are also marked indelibly with strong currents of queer desire. Although its principal storylines are almost always heterosexual, the musical contains a wide variety of erotic configurations, particularly in its more spectacular numbers. One of the claims made for the musical is that it routinely uses its non-mimetic elements of music and dance to articulate, in displaced or metaphoric form, material that would or could not be otherwise presented. This is possibly why the musical was such a consistently popular genre throughout the classical Hollywood era: it accommodated symbolic representations of erotic material prohibited under the Production Code.

A brief list of some of the musical's queer metaphorics would include things such as the gendered inversions of musicals like *Calamity Jane* (1953) and *Annie Get Your Gun* (1950); or the overt display of cross-dressing and transvestism in *Victor/Victoria* (1982) and *The Rocky Horror Picture Show* (1975). One could also cite the homoerotic duos and trios of musicals such as *On the Town* (1949), *Take Me Out to the Ballgame* (1949) and *Gentlemen Prefer Blondes* (1953); or the extravagant erotic fetishism of almost any MGM musical number that one cares to mention.

The musical is also one of the few forms of contemporary popular culture that has consistently placed women in positions of textual agency and authority. Women largely dominate the musical, assuming centre stage, singing the biggest numbers, and, more often than not, functioning as engines of narrative progression. This is particularly the case in **diva** musicals such as *Gypsy* (1962), *Hello, Dolly!* (1969) and *Evita* (1996), where the central female protagonists literally run the show. The empowered female figure of the musical speaks equally, if variously, to lesbians and gay men, and many musical stars including Julie **Andrews**, Carol **Channing**, Judy **Garland**, Liza **Minnelli** and Barbra **Streisand** have become important queer icons.

A popular staple throughout the mid-twentieth century, the musical today has lost a good deal of its cultural currency and, by extension, some of its queer popularity. Nevertheless, the genre continues to enjoy a privileged position in contemporary queer cultures. Repertory screenings and gay video stores ensure that older traditions of queer musical reception continue, while recent musicals such as *Moulin Rouge* (2001) and *Chicago* (2002) have gone on to become new cult favourites. There is even evidence to suggest that the musical itself is becoming increasingly overt in its address to queer audiences – and, by so doing, is explicating its historical queer moorings –

with openly 'gay musicals' such as *La Cage aux Folles* (1978) and *Hedwig and the Angry Inch* (1994).

See also: Production Code, the (Hollywood)

Further reading

Clum, John M. (1999) *Something for the Boys: Musical Theatre and Gay Culture*, New York: St Martin's Press.

Wolf, Stacy (2002) *A Problem Like Maria: Gender and Sexuality in the American Musical*, Ann Arbor: University of Michigan Press.

BRETT FARMER

MUSICALS, THEATRE

Originating in the early twentieth century and born out of competing traditions of operetta and vaudeville, musical theatre is a stage-based entertainment that mixes music, dance and comic narrative. Often dubbed 'the Broadway musical' after New York's famed theatre district, it developed as a distinctively American theatrical genre and, with its central emphasis on ordinary people pursuing happiness and realizing their dreams through the uplifting agency of popular music and dance, musical theatre is often seen to enshrine defining American cultural values such as individualism, democratic libertarianism and populism. The musical also has close and enduring affiliations with queer cultures, leading some to suggest that it is in equal measure a characteristically queer theatrical genre.

Many queer artists have been integral to the historical development and popularization of musical theatre. The canon of queer musical luminaries includes such influential figures as: composers and lyricists Cole **Porter**, Lorenz Hart, Marc Blitzstein, Robert Wright and George 'Chet' Forrest, Jerry **Herman**, Leonard **Bernstein**, John Kander and Fred Ebb, and Stephen **Sondheim**; librettists Arthur Laurents and George C. Wolfe; choreographers Jerome Robbins, Tommy Tune and Michael Bennett; producers and directors John C. Wilson, Vincente **Minnelli** and John Dexter; and a long line of performers from Ivor **Novello** and Noel Coward to Harvey **Fierstein**, Nathan **Lane** and Lea **DeLaria**, to say nothing of the innumerable 'gypsies' – the chorus boys and girls – who have been a legendary source of queer presence on the musical stage. The intensely collaborative nature of theatrical production and the vexed question of authorial sexuality and its effects make it difficult to know, let alone assess, the impact of so many queer artists on the constitution of the Broadway musical. Nevertheless, some critics claim a discernible queer sensibility at the heart of musical theatre, pointing to core elements of the form, such as camp aestheticism, homoeroticism, ambiguous sexuality and diva worship, which, they suggest, are at least partially attributable to queer artistic influence.

Discussions of the relations between musical theatre and queer cultures are on less contentious grounds with questions of reception. The persistent appeal of the musical for queer audiences is widely acknowledged, with the image of the show queen serving as an enduring staple of both queer and mainstream folklore. Historically, that appeal was strongest in the mid-twentieth century when the Broadway musical was at its height as a popular cultural form and spoke in powerful, albeit complex, ways to pre-Stonewall queer cultures. Most commentators suggest that gay and, to a lesser extent, lesbian audiences of the time latched on to the musical's ethos of sunny utopianism and community renewal as a metaphoric form of queer empowerment. In an era when (ignoring positive) even open representations of queerness were few and far between, the musical's central message of climbing mountains, fording streams and finding dreams was a potent lure for gay men and women forced to contend on a daily basis with oppression and homophobia.

Much of the queer enthusiasm for musical theatre has focused in particular around the female stars or divas that dominate the genre. It has been argued that one of the unique aspects of the Broadway musical – and one of its chief queer pleasures – is the extent to which it foregrounds female performers, offering an expansive catalogue of bold and brassy female characters who actively express and pursue their desires in full-throated belter style without suffering the standard 'punishments' of death or social containment routinely meted out to agential women in other narrative forms. The sexual dissidence of the powerful Broadway diva has obvious appeal for queer audiences and undoubtedly informs the enduring gay cult followings of musical theatre stars such as Ethel Merman, Mary Martin, Julie **Andrews**, Carol **Channing** and Bernadette Peters.

Although not as popular today as during the 'golden age' of the 1940s through to the 1960s, the Broadway musical continues as a notable site of queer cultural investment and taste formations. The comparative liberalism of contemporary social attitudes has enabled a more overt articulation of the musical's queer dynamics in terms of both production and reception. In 2004, for example, Broadway's annual Tony Awards ceremony was popularly dubbed 'the gay Tonys' because many of the major categories were won by openly queer productions or performers.

Further reading

Clum, John M. (1999) *Something for the Boys: Musical Theatre and Gay Culture*, New York: St Martin's Press.

Miller, D.A. (1998) *Place for Us: Essay on the Broadway Musical*, Cambridge: Harvard University Press.

Wolf, Stacy (2002) *A Problem Like Maria: Gender and Sexuality in the American Musical*, Ann Arbor: University of Michigan Press.

BRETT FARMER

MUSTO, MICHAEL

columnist

Openly gay journalist and writer, best known for his long-running gossip column 'La Vita Musto' in the New York newspaper *Village Voice*. He began his career as a screenwriter, penning the indie film *Single Room Furnished* (1968). He began writing for the *Village Voice* in 1984, where his cheerfully camp sensibility, caustic wit and encyclopaedic knowledge of Hollywood lore made him one of America's most recognizable newspaper columnists. He has acted in the independent films *Operation Midnight Climax* (2002) and *Night Owl* (1993) and made numerous TV and film appearances as himself, notably in the documentaries *Party Monster* (1998) and *Resident Alien* (1990), as well as appearing on numerous Hollywood-themed programmes for the E! entertainment network.

JOHN FORDE

MUTCHNIK, MAX

b. 1965

TV producer, writer

Openly gay TV writer and producer, Max Mutchnik, with long-term friend and writing partner David Kohan, achieved international success with the ground-breaking gay-themed comedy **Will & Grace** (1998–). He began his TV career as a writer on the coming-of-age drama series *The Wonder Years* (1988), followed by moderate successes with *Dream On* (1990–6), *Boston Common* (1996–7, for which he was also executive producer) and *Good Morning, Miami* (2002). In 1998 he and Kohan created *Will & Grace*, a sitcom about a gay man and a straight woman living together (modelled on Mutchnik's own long-term friendship with a female friend). The series proved a critical and commercial success, winning Mutchnik an Emmy for

Outstanding Television Comedy and three GLAAD Media Awards for its break-through presentation of gay characters. It was syndicated to NBC until 2005 for an estimated US$300 million.

JOHN FORDE

MYKONOS

An island lying off the southeast coast of Greece. Mykonos' combination of tranquil beaches and thriving nightlife has made it one of the world's most popular gay resorts, especially for the annual gay Festival of the Twelve Gods. The island's three main beaches – Paradise, Super Paradise and Elia – each have gay and nude sections. Although relatively unspoiled by commerce, the island hosts many gay bars and boutique clothing stores. The nearby island of Delos, with the ruins of Dionysus' Temple and phallic sculptures, provide a reminder of Greece's gay history.

JOHN FORDE

N

NATIONAL GAY AND LESBIAN CONFERENCE (1972, NEW ZEALAND)

The first National Gay and Lesbian Conference was held in Auckland in 1972, part of the flourishing gay liberation movement that simultaneously emerged in Auckland, Wellington, Hamilton and Christchurch that year. It was organized by Gay Liberation Auckland and was attended by liberation groups from both Wellington and Christchurch. The conference reflected the main concerns of the Auckland delegation: 'consciousness raising', increasing public awareness of homosexuality and providing counselling for lesbians and gay men in the face of oppressive societal values. Many people involved in the early stages of the gay liberation movement were university students; the conferences in the following years were held at student union facilities in Christchurch and then Wellington. The 1973 and 1974 conferences had increasing attendance and participation from the growing number of gay liberation groups being established at that time in New Zealand's cities and larger towns. Increased attendance was also reflected in the creation of the newsletter *Gay Lib News* in late 1972, which was succeeded by *The Gay Liberator* in early 1973: both advertised and reported the conferences as part of gay liberation activism. The annual conferences continued to focus on societal issues and came to have far more structure than the first conference. Tensions soon arose however, both at the conferences and within participating organizations, based around the sexism that lesbians felt they experienced within the gay liberation movement. This led to the formation of lesbian-only groups, some of which continued to participate in the conferences. With the exception of 1983, the conferences were held annually until 1989.

GERALDINE TREACHER

NATIONAL GAY AND LESBIAN TASK FORCE (NGLTF)

The NGLTF is a leading progressive civil rights organization that has supported grassroots organizing and advocacy for lesbian and gay communities since 1973. It works 'for the civil rights of gay, lesbian, bisexual and transgender people, with the vision and commitment to building a powerful political movement'. Its programme areas include training, organizing and coalition-building, while its Policy Institute provides research, analysis and strategy development for activists and organizers. During the 1970s the Task Force's efforts were critical in the campaign to eliminate the sickness classification of homosexuality. It also worked to lift the prohibition on federal civil service employment for gays and lesbians and to make the Democratic Party responsive to the gay community. During the 1980s it took the lead in organizing nationally against homophobic violence, and as AIDS began to devastate gay male communities, the Task Force shaped the first serious efforts in Washington DC to address the epidemic.

SURINA KHAN

NATIONAL INSTITUTES OF HEALTH (NIH)

Originating in 1887 as a one-room hygiene laboratory at the Marine Hospital on Staten Island, New York, the NIH is widely considered one of the world's pre-eminent medical and behavioural health research centres. A branch of the federal Department of Health and Human Services, the NIH is one of the eight health agencies within the Public Health Service. It is the focal point for health research in the United States.

The NIH comprises 27 separate Institutes and Centers devoted to specific health concerns. The Office of the Director coordinates the aims, agendas and responsibilities for all 27 of these. The Office also manages a collective of issue-oriented programme offices, including the Office of AIDS Research.

The NIH safeguards the nation's health and acts as a deterrent against those threats – biological and human-derived – that seek to compromise this health. The organization accomplishes this through a comprehensive network of research initiatives proposed and carried out by scientists across the globe. This corps of scientists develops and tests new research protocols in an effort to prevent disease. Disease, by NIH definitions, includes outbreaks of unknown genetic pathogens as well as recognized infections such as the common cold.

For well over two decades, the NIH has sponsored cutting-edge research on **HIV** and **AIDS**. Recently, NIH scientists have managed to complete the genome sequence of cryptosporidium, a waterborne parasite that lives in the intestines of infected people. For individuals with immune systems weakened by AIDS, the presence of cryptosporidium can be life-threatening. It is hoped that the new genome sequence will bring about new knowledge with regard to the treatment and eventual eradication of this disease. In the last few years, NIH scientists have also identified a protein agent that stops HIV replication in monkey cells. Since humans and monkeys share biological characteristics, scientists are actively studying this protein to see if its human counterpart will have as much efficacy in stemming the tide of replication. This work could have drastic effects upon future HIV therapy and treatment.

The efforts of the NIH are wide-ranging, from researching the causes of and potential cures and treatments for human diseases, to investigating the causal agents underscoring human development, to acting as a knowledge centre and archival resource for medical information. NIH scientists, as well as scientists and researchers working under the auspices of support from the organization at otherwise non-NIH facilities e.g., hospitals and universities, have made numerous medical breakthroughs. In recognition of this, over 100 NIH-affiliated scientists have been named Nobel Laureates in the sciences, the first in 1939, the most recent in 2004.

With a staff of more than 18,000 on its main campus in Bethesda, Maryland and at satellite sites across the country and abroad, and with government funding topping US$27,066,782,000 in US Congressional appropriations for the fiscal year 2003, the NIH is a powerhouse; its efforts to uncover knowledge about disease prevention and treatment virtually unrivalled.

CHRIS BELL

NAVA, MICHAEL

b. 1954

writer

Michael Nava was born in Stockton, California and raised in Sacramento. He obtained a law degree from Stanford University in 1981. After only a few years in private practice, he began writing a series of detective fiction novels that feature a Chicano gay lawyer, Henry Rios, as the leading character. The series spans a 15-year period and comprises seven novels. It began with the publication of *The Little Death* (1986) and ended with *Rag and Bone* (2001). Throughout the series, Rios evolves from a San Francisco public defender to a Los Angeles defence lawyer. His character struggles with alcoholism, failed relationships, the death of a lover to AIDS and the reality of living in a racist and homophobic society. Of particular interest is the way in which Nava uses his legal background to create stories that highlight the injustices experienced by gay men and lesbians. Gay rights are also at the centre of much of his non-fiction.

DANIEL ENRIQUE PÉREZ

NAVRATILOVA, MARTINA

b. 1956

athlete

Born in Czechoslovakia, Martina Navratilova amassed 57 Grand Slam tennis titles in a career spanning 30 years. Just as Billie Jean **King** dominated 1970s tennis, Navratilova was the player of the 1980s, in part by attaining then revolutionary levels of fitness. She won 9 Wimbledon singles titles, 4 US Opens, 3 Australian and 2 French, including a non-calendar Grand Slam in 1983–4. She holds the record for the highest number of career titles (167), including 38 Grand Slam doubles titles.

Navratilova defected to the United States in 1975 and became a US citizen in 1981. Her relationship with writer Rita Mae **Brown**, which began in 1978, led to her outing and forced her to resign as head of the Women's Tennis Association. Although it placed lucrative endorsements in jeopardy, she subsequently spoke out on gay and lesbian issues, addressed gay rights' marches and took a public stand against homophobic legislation in the US.

H.G. COCKS

NAZ FOUNDATION

Established in 1994, the Naz Foundation is a non-governmental organization that disseminates culturally sensitive sexual health information to stigmatized, socio-economically disenfranchised men who have sex with other men in South Asia. The organization works to stem the tide of HIV and other sexually transmitted infections, and to address the human rights issues at the heart of health policy, issues often ignored by local governments, media and mainstream health agencies. The organization brings together and empowers individuals and community-based organizations through capacity building. In 1998 the organization started an HIV/AIDS clinic, the first of its kind in the region, offering counselling and treatment services. Although administrative work is managed through its London office, the organization maintains two offices in India that coordinate client advocacy and programming. Because of its focus on providing a safe, confidential environment for marginalized populations to receive accurate health information, and an attendant dedication to self-advocacy, the Naz Foundation's work is unprecedented in this region of the world.

CHRIS BELL

NDEGÉOCELLO, ME'SHELL

b. 1969

singer

Singer and bassist Me'shell NdegéOcello first achieved fame with her single, 'If That's Your Boyfriend (He Wasn't Last Night)', from her 1994 album, *Plantation*

Lullabies, a mixture of funk and hip-hop which resists easy classification. As a black lesbian with a son, her personal life is equally hard to categorize and has led to conflict with the groups who would both claim her and reject her. She has often reflected on this problem in her music, taking on racism, sexism and homophobia wherever it crops up. Her second album, *Peace Beyond Passion* (1996), contains songs criticizing organized religion's contempt for both blacks and queers, including the song 'Leviticus: Faggot' about a young, black, gay man's rejection by his Christian family. Her third album, *Bitter* (1999), was more personal, exploring sentiments of love and disillusionment in relationships. She returned to the explicitly political with her 2002 album *Cookie: The Anthropological Mixtape*, which features songs about black and lesbian experiences in America and 'the plight of the revolutionary soul singer'.

DANIEL HENDRICKSON

NELL WARREN, PATRICIA
b. 1936
author

Patricia Nell Warren is one of the most popular and respected authors of gay literature in the world. With eight novels to her credit and an estimated readership of over 20 million people worldwide, her books are considered by many to be an intrinsic part of a gay rites of passage as well as a literary synthesis of the gay life experience. Her most celebrated novel, *The Front Runner*, was first published by William Morrow in 1974, and has become the most popular gay love story of all time. This landmark classic about the relationship between an ex-Marine track coach and his Olympic athlete has sold an estimated 10 million copies worldwide and been translated into ten languages. In more recent years, Nell Warren has worked as a distinguished

investigative journalist, columnist and advocate for glbtq youth issues.

ERIC ANDERSON

NESTLE, JOAN
b. 1940
writer, activist

Lesbian writer, academic and activist whose works explore and celebrate lesbian identities. Nestle was born on 12 May 1940 in New York City. She was heavily involved in the gay and civil rights movements of the 1950s and 1960s, and in the wake of the 1969 Stonewall protests she joined the Gay Alliance Union and lobbied for the rights of gay and lesbian teachers, students and workers. In 1973 she and Deborah Edel co-founded the Lesbian Herstory Archive, now one of the world's largest resources of lesbian history. In her first short-story collection, *A Restricted Country* (1987), she wrote frankly about lesbian erotica. Her writings include the Women on Women series (1990, 1992 and 1996), *The Persistent Desire: A Femme–Butch Reader* (1992), a critical analysis of lesbian cultural politics and gender roles within lesbian relationships, a lesbian studies volume (*A Fragile Union,* 1998) and a queer studies reader, *Sister and Brother* (1994), co-edited with John Preston. An early champion of transgender movements, she edited *Genderqueer: Voices from beyond the Binary* (2002), a critical study of transgendered sexual identity.

JOHN FORDE

NETHERLANDS, THE, FILMMAKING AND TELEVISION

Considering a climate of relative tolerance and a thriving gay and lesbian subculture there are surprisingly few gay and lesbian Dutch films. This paradox may be explained by the initial absence of a national cinema and the successful integration of issues of homosexuality into mainstream culture.

After the Film and Television Academy was established in 1958, it took decades for Dutch cinema to professionalize. The first trained Dutch filmmakers began making fiction films during the 1960s – the years of a heady sexual revolution that shook Dutch society very deeply. The favoured film genre of the late 1960s and early 1970s was pre-feminist sex comedies, which often border on pornography by showing full-frontal nudity of both women and men as well as explicit sex scenes. It must be noted that these films are strictly heterosexual.

From the late 1970s onwards, Dutch films included a male gay character or couple among an otherwise straight cast (for example, *Camping* [1978] and the detective film, *Grijpstra & de Gier* [1979]). This mainstreaming of male homosexuality became rather commonplace throughout the 1980s and 1990s, as with films such as *Pervola* (*Tracks in the Snow,* 1985), *De kleine blonde dood* (Little Blonde Dead, 1993), *All Stars* (1997), *Respect* (1998) and *fl. 19.99* (1998). Some films during this period (including *Duinzicht Boven* [View From A Dune Above, 1999] or *Het negende uur* [The Ninth Hour, 2000]) were made by well-known gay playwrights or theatre directors.

The first film to thematize male homosexuality was *Lieve Jongens* (Dear Boys) in 1980. Based on several novels by a famous Dutch novelist Gerard **Reve**, the film explores gay desire and complicated gay relationships. In the same year, Paul **Verhoeven** made a violent, sexually explicit film about teenagers called *Spetters* (Stunners), featuring a relentless female character who may be seen as a precursor of Catherine Tramell in *Basic Instinct* (1992). *Spetters* shows one of the main male characters discovering he is gay after he has been gang-raped. Because of this hackneyed treatment of homosexuality and its gay-bashing scenes, *Spetters* has been accused of being anti-gay. A few years later Verhoeven made a thriller based on another novel by Reve, *De vierde man* (*The Fourth Man*, 1983), about a gay writer who tries to seduce the lover of the femme fatale with whom he has sex by imagining she is a boy (yes, it is a complicated plot). Like *Spetters*, *De vierde man* includes graphic violence, gay sex and blasphemous scenes. Verhoeven's films show a tendency in Dutch cinema to treat male homosexuality as part and parcel of a liberated and permissive society. Nevertheless, within this framework male homosexuality is still stereotypically represented as promiscuous and associated with violence.

One of the few films to treat male homosexuality with sensitivity is *Voor een verloren soldaat* (*For a Lost Soldier*, 1992), based on the autobiographical story of one of Holland's most famous dancers and choreographers, Rudy van Dantzig. The film narrates his relationship as a young boy with a Canadian soldier during the war. *Voor een verloren soldaat* points to an important characteristic of Dutch gay films: they maintain only a very loose link to activism, relying rather on 'high' culture to make an impact by involving famous gay men (novelists, playwrights, actors, dancers, TV hosts). A cultural elite makes gay issues acceptable to a straight audience.

The same situation occurs on public television, where, in the 1990s, famous gay talk show hosts such as Jos Brink, Jan Lenferink and Paul **de Leeuw** not only mainstream male homosexuality, but also display campy aspects of gay subculture. Brink has become famous for kissing the Dutch Queen on her cheek when he hosted her birthday party on television. The gay actor Arjan Ederveen familiarizes Dutch TV audiences with camp and pastiche in his famous mockumentary series *30 Minutes*, which parodies medical documentaries on transsexuality. In 2003 the wildly popular de Leeuw featured a parody of a reality show, *PaPaul*, inviting guests to his own home where he lives with his husband and adopted children.

Lesbian filmmaking was much more connected to feminist activism, the exception being *Twee vrouwen* (*Twice a Woman*, 1979), a typically straight male film production about two women falling in love. The story is based on a novel by yet another famous Dutch novelist, Harry Mulisch. In the same year the feminist film *Een vrouw als Eva* (A Woman Like Eve) was directed by the first Dutch woman filmmaker, Nouchka van Brakel. The film explores a lesbian relationship in the context of the women's liberation movement, featuring Maria Schneider (known from *Last Tango in Paris*, 1972). The film was at the time attacked by feminists for its 'exploitation' of lesbian issues, but is now renowned for documenting the vibrancy of the feminist movement in Amsterdam during the late 1970s. It is to date (2005) the only feature film that takes lesbianism as its theme.

A few years later Marleen **Gorris** made *De Stilte rond Christine M.* (*A Question of Silence*, 1982), the feminist movie about three women who kill a man; it won many international prizes. As in her later movies, *Gebroken Spiegels* (*Broken Mirrors*, 1984), *Antonia* (*Antonia's Line*, 1995) and *Mrs Dalloway* (1997), Gorris always includes intense female friendships (Smelik 1998). Except for *Antonia* (which received the Academy Award for Best Foreign Film in 1995), she seems reluctant to make such friendships explicitly lesbian. The female 'buddy film' is popular with women filmmakers (for example, *Krokodillen in Amsterdam* [Crocodiles in Amsterdam, 1990] by Annette Apon and *Belle* [1993] by Irma Achten). During the early years of the twenty-first century this genre has begun to investigate multicultural friendships between a Dutch and a Muslim immigrant woman, as in such films as *Roos & Rana* (2001) by Meral Uslu or the TV series *Dunya & Desie* (2002) by Dana Nechustan.

The short film *You 2* (2001) by Jenny Mijnhijmer explores lesbianism within a Caribbean-Dutch community. The issue of male homosexuality is still a vexed issue in black and Muslim communities in the Netherlands, and so far has not been addressed in feature films, only in documentaries. On Dutch television lesbianism has also featured as a more campy issue in soap series such as *Medisch Centrum West* (about a hospital) and *Hertenkamp* (Deer Park).

Bibliography

Smelik, A. (1998) *And the Mirror Cracked. Feminist Cinema and Film Theory*, Basingstoke: Palgrave.

ANNEKE SMELIK

NETHERLANDS, THE, LITERATURE

The Dutch glbtq literary landscape after the Second World War is quite diverse. Due to the liberalizing movements of the 1960s, clear tendencies towards more explicitness and acceptance of homosexuality have become visible.

In 1995 Xandra Schutte, editor of *Damesliefde* (Ladies' Love), one of the few anthologies of Dutch lesbian literature, declared that homosexuality was no longer an exciting theme in literature, because the gay and lesbian emancipation had been completed. She did not regret this, unlike the gay writer Gerrit Komrij, who was of the opinion that 'the epidemic acceptance of homosexuality', as he called it, had brought respectability and dullness, which he thought disastrous for literature.

It is true that the social and legal emancipation of homosexuality in the Netherlands has made great progress since 1945. Important moments, in terms of legislation, were the abolition of clause 248bis in 1971, which had rendered illegal same-sex contacts under the age of 21; the adoption of the Equal Treatment Act in 1993, which outlawed discrimination based on sexuality; and the opening up of marriage for gay and lesbian couples in 2001.

Regarding the influence of this emancipation process on literature, the critics quoted above may be right: it could well be argued that the successful emancipation of gays and lesbians in the Netherlands has led to the decline of homosexuality as a literary theme in itself. In contrast, this opinion rests on a questionable concept of literature, which says that the literary value of a work is largely determined by its power to shock its audience. The position of literature has changed also; no longer does it function as the moral standard of the cultural elite.

Of course, there still are glbtq writers in the Netherlands, and glbtq themes do still occur in their work. But for most of them sexual identity is not an (problematic) issue; it is not always an important theme in their work, and it is rarely an issue for the reception of their work.

This was in contrast to earlier decades. Since 1945 several gay and lesbian authors were involved in lawsuits or publicity scandals because of the nature of their work. In 1948 Anna Blaman refused a literary prize for her novel *Eenzaam avontuur* (Lonely Adventure) because of the moralistic tone of the jury report, and in 1966 Gerard **Reve**, by that time the most renowned gay author of the Netherlands, was charged with blasphemy because he had described his desire to have sex with Christ. He was acquitted of the charges on appeal.

The poems and novels written during the 1940s and 1950s and which deal with the theme of same-sex love are still very much dominated by fear and secrecy. Authors such as Nel **Noordzij**, Josepha Mendels, Dola de Jong and Maps **Valk** could not yet imagine the fulfilment of homosexual desire, or only as a romantic longing for something unreachable, as in the poems of Hans Lodeizen.

Only when Andreas **Burnier** and Gerard Reve entered the literary scene did things change drastically. Burnier's novels are peopled by cheerful, bold and humorous lesbians; Reve explicitly and enthusiastically described sex between men. Both Burnier and Reve have received wide acclaim, and both authors have been extremely important for the acceptance and emancipation of homosexuality, not only through their work, but also as public figures in the Netherlands. Other authors of the 1960s and 1970s, such as Jaap Harten and Hans Warren, have undoubtedly profited from the growing openness.

The coming-of-age-novel remained an important subgenre in gay literature throughout the years, as in the work of Rudi van Dantzig, Adriaan van Dis and the Flemish writers Eric de Kuyper and Tom Lanoye. Homoerotic themes can also be found in the work of heterosexual authors such as Simon Vestdijk's *Een alpenroman* (An Alp novel, 1961), Harry Mulisch's *Twee vrouwen* (Two women, 1975) or Renate Dorrestein's *Vreemde Streken* (Strange Regions, 1984).

The feminist movement was an important context for lesbian literature during the 1970s. Anja Meulenbelt's novel *De schaamte voorbij* (Shame is Over, 1976) can be read as a literary rendering of political lesbianism. In the novels of Hannes Meinkema and, in a more ironical manner, Sjuul Deckwitz, feminism and lesbianism are closely connected also. Astrid Roemer and Joanna Werners, both of Surinamese descent, also wrote lesbian novels, but in the 1980s, while poet Elly de Waard brought the classic butch/femme couple to life again.

For Doeschka **Meijsing** and Frans **Kellendonk**, two authors who contributed considerably to the renewal of the novel in the 1980s by opposing realism, homosexuality forms part of their work but not as a political issue. Outside his novels, Kellendonk, who died of AIDS, expressed ambivalence about the gay emancipation movement. He was accused of homo-phobia and anti-Semitism when his novel *Mystiek lichaam* (Mystical Body) appeared in 1986, but his (highly artificial and ironical) work cannot be condemned in any easy way.

A new generation of writers in the 1990s marked the diversity of the Dutch gay and lesbian literary landscape. One has the dandy-esque novels of Willem Melchior, sadomasochistic poetry by Theo van Os or the more introverted coming-of-age novels of Erwin Mortier, *Marcel* (1999) and *Mijn tweede huid* (*My Fellow Skin,* 2000). Karin Spaink, who has also been very active in the glbtq movement, has written about bisexuality and chronic illness. *Een jas vol stenen* (A Coat Full of Stones, 1999) by Renate Stoute is one of the few Dutch novels that deals with the issue of trans-sexualism. Ted van Lieshout, poet and visual artist, was the first to explicitly and subtly write about the relationship between a 12-year-old boy and an older man, from the perspective of the child. Other writers of youth literature who incorporate gay and lesbian themes include Imme Dros, Edward van de Vendel and Diet Verschoor. Lesbian literature in the 1990s also appears in many forms. Novels from authors such as Pauline Slot, Minke Douwesz and Nicolien Mizee have given lesbian literature a multifaceted character. Last but not least, several lesbian pulp novels, often in the form of parodies of existing literature, have been published.

AGNES ANDEWEG

NEW QUEER CINEMA, INTERNATIONAL

First coined in 1992 by *Village Voice* writer and academic B. Ruby Rich, 'New Queer Cinema' has emerged as one of the most hotly contested subjects in queer critical circles in the United States. Generally deployed to describe a seemingly short-lived 'movement' of newly radicalized lesbian and gay filmmaking in America during the early 1990s, brought on by the social and political aftermath of the 1980s AIDS crisis, it was a landmark period for lesbian and gay cinema. The key films and film-makers that comprise the period, namely Jennie Livingston's *Paris Is Burning* (1990), Todd Haynes' *Poison* (1991), Tom Kalin's *Swoon* (1992) and Gregg Araki's *The Living End* (1992), among a number of others, broke new revisionist ground in their ongoing struggle for queer representation in film. And characterized by an irreverent and defiant attitude that deliberately eschewed any necessity for positive gay imagery or a 'hetero-friendly' *mises-en-scène*, these lauded *enfants terribles* were 'cutting edge' in terms of cinematic innovation and stylistic experimentation, significantly influencing the narrative and aesthetic inventiveness of the burgeoning 'straight' American 'indie' scene that captured the imagination of contemporary filmmaking in the 1990s.

Yet as soon as critics began to attempt to define exactly what New Queer Cinema was – a very difficult task given its lack of any discernable manifesto or definitive canon in terms of an interrelated com-monality of technique and/or ideology – it had already seemingly ceased to exist. Its demise was blamed, in part, on its success – it accumulated a plethora of awards and critical acclaim worldwide, from Sundance to Cannes. The desperate need for queer representation at any cost that underpinned the movement, in the face of bitter attack from the religious and political right, and its interconnected 'outlaw' currency as part of the trendy independent film explosion, led to a rapid expansion of mainstream gay-themed filmmaking that was determined to cash in on this evolving queer niche market – irrespective of the quality of the films being produced. The flood of films that suddenly jumped on the queer bandwagon in the mid-1990s led to a loss of the urgency that had motivated new queer filmmakers in the US, and a detrimental process of 'dumbing down' occurred as the mainstream began to churn out its poor imitations or put a queer spin on a well-trodden generic formula. But while critics such as new queer champion B. Ruby Rich began publicly lamenting the rapid death of the movement in the gay press, no real attempt was made to take a step back and look at the much bigger picture, so to speak, or to question whether or not New Queer Cinema was really an exclusively American phenomenon in the first place. The movement may have risen to prominence and classification in the US in the early years of the 1990s, but it was already, and continues to be, an approach to filmmaking on a much wider global scale.

The international underpinnings of the movement were very much evident from the beginning. Rich herself acknowledged the stylistic influences and revered intertextual references that many of the new queer filmmakers had for the earlier quintessentially queer oeuvre of European cinematic deviants **Fassbinder**, **Pasolini**, **Genet**, **Treut** and **Jarman**, or the guerrilla aesthetic and political urgency of the sexually dissident filmmakers of contemporary Asian and Third Cinema. And whereas critical attention selectively foregrounded the achievements of the North American works that made up the New Queer Cinema 'canon', the wider international context of the movement also included a number of key films of non-American origin that were of equal importance to the innovative impact of the new queer milieu: examples include Derek Jarman's *Edward II* (UK, 1991), Isaac Julien's *Young Soul Rebels* (UK, 1991), Pratibha Parmar's *Khush* (India/UK, 1991), Cyril Collard's *Les Nuits fauves* (Savage Nights, France, 1992), Andre Téchiné's *J'Embrasse pas* (*I Don't Kiss*) (France, 1991), Pedro Almodóvar's *¡Átame!* (*Tie Me Up, Tie Me Down*, Spain, 1990), Roeland Kerbosch's *Voor een verloren soldaat* (*For A Lost Soldier*, the Netherlands, 1992),

Tomás Gutiérrez Alea's and Juan Carlos Tabío's *Fresa y Chocolate* (*Strawberry and Chocolate*, Cuba, 1993), Takahiro Nakajima's *Okoge* (Fag Hag, Japan, 1992), Nakamura Genji's *Kyokon densetsui: utsukushii nazo* (*Beautiful Mystery*, Japan, 1993), Tsai Ming-liang's *Qingshaonian Nuozha* (*Rebels of the Neon God*, Taiwan, 1992), or the numerous short films and videos by such underrated filmmakers as Argentina's Lucrecia Martel or Mexico's Ximena Cuevas.

The apparent mainstream co-optation and political dissolution of the American new queer contingent during the mid-1990s may seemingly have ended the movement there – although the uncompromising edginess of films such as Todd Verow's *Frisk* (1995), Gregg Araki's *The Doom Generation* (1995), Everett Lewis' *Skin and Bone* (1995), Scott Silver's *Johns* (1996), Lisa Cholodenko's *High Art* (1998) and the gloriously perverse films of Bruce **LaBruce**, illustrate otherwise – this was not the case internationally. The remainder of the 1990s and early years of the new millennium have witnessed an expansion of the thematic controversy and stylistic innovation that was so central to the formative years of the American works, yet from within a much more diverse ethical, cultural and socio-political context. Films such as François Ozon's *Sitcom* (France, 1998), *Criminal Lovers* and *Waterdrops on Burning Rocks* (France, 1999), Monika Treut's *Gendernaughts* (Germany, 1999), Ferzan Özpetek's *Hamam* (*Steam*, Turkey/Italy, 1997), Wong Kar-wai's *Happy Together* (*Chun guang zha xie*, 1997), Marcelo Piñeyro's *Plata quemada* (*Burnt Money*, Argentina, 2000), Stanley Kwan's *Lan Yu* (Hong Kong, 2001), Zhang Yuan's *East Palace, West Palace* (*Dong gong xi gong*, China, 1996), Mohamed Camara's *Dakan* (Africa/France, 1997), Ana Kokkinos' *Head On* (Australia, 1998) or the queer shorts of Germany's Hans Schierl and Belgian filmmaker Bavo Defurne, to name but a few, are, in comparative terms, of equal seminal importance to the continued evolution of contemporary queer filmmaking as the early years of North American New Queer Cinema, and are just as commercially viable.

Like the United States during the 1990s, queer filmmaking across the globe has evolved, albeit in multifarious ways, in response to both the AIDS crisis and the oppressive transcultural social and representational regimes of a restrictively policed, mainstream, right-wing heteronormativity. But rather than become absorbed into the cinematic cultural *Zeitgeist* of pre-millennial late capitalism, as did the likes of Todd Haynes, Gus Van Sant *et al.*, international queer cinema has maintained its commitment to explore national and cultural specificity in its negotiations of queerness that resist both the universalist narrative of gay liberation/ cultural assimilation and the commodification of a transnational queer culture, aesthetic and politics. Its emergence from a diverse range of socio-cultural locales, with their concomitantly divergent viewing practices that resist the homogenization of queer experience, consequently positions 'International New Queer Cinema' in a much stronger place to really begin to aspire to the radical promise that has so far eluded the 'American New Queer Cinema'.

See also: Araki, Gregg; Haynes, Todd; Kalin, Tom; Van Sant, Gus

Further reading

Aaron, M. (ed.) (2004) *New Queer Cinema: A Critical Reader*, Edinburgh: Edinburgh University Press.

Foster, D.W. (2003) *Queer Issues in Contemporary Latin American Cinema*, Austin: University of Texas Press.

Griffiths, R. (ed.) (2005) *Queer Cinema in Europe*, Bristol: Intellect.

Grossman, A. (ed.) (2000) *Queer Asian Cinema: Shadows in the Shade*, New York: Harrington Park Press.

Kuzniar, A.A. (2000) *The Queer German Cinema*, Stanford: Stanford University Press.

ROBIN GRIFFITHS

NEW ROMANTICS

A British-based music scene that emerged as a backlash against the extreme austerity of punk, New Romanticism represented a style, an era and a collection of disparate popular bands all of whom adhered to a certain mode of presentation. It was a movement of ostentatious glamour, often reviving historical costume, and was associated with a youthful, hedonistic approach to life, centred in clubs such as London's *Blitz*. Men wore makeup and experimented with extreme hairstyles, such as members of the pop groups A Flock of Seagulls, Duran Duran and Spandau Ballet. The music video was the significant instrument of promotion, and the electronic synthesizer superseded the electric guitar. The groups Soft Cell and Culture Club had gay front men (Marc Almond and Boy George, respectively), but the movement attracted a predominance of straight men who flirted with effeminate presentation and so went some way to questioning accepted masculinity.

See also: Almond, Marc and Soft Cell; Boy George

MICHAEL PINFOLD

NEW YORK

Recognized as the start-point of gay and lesbian liberation in 1969 with the **Stonewall Riots**, New York is the site of a diverse glbtq culture. Although the year 1969 and Manhattan (where the riots began) are definitive markers of the gay movement, New York's queer history is long in the making and is shared with its other four boroughs (the Bronx, Queens,

Brooklyn and Staten Island). Manhattan, however, is the centre, where the city's glbtq political, creative and intellectual communities come together. From the New York City Ballet to ACT UP, queers carry considerable cultural clout.

As many historians have shown, the city's glbtq culture reaches back well into the mid- to late nineteenth century. Indeed, a wide range of sexual cultures played a significant role in the city's social and political development. Although these urban sexual cultures were found all around town, Greenwich Village became the focal point for gay and lesbian culture, especially after 1969 but certainly as early as the early 1900s. Now noted for its restaurants, boutiques and early-New York architecture (and number of prams), the Village laid claim to a rich history of sexual and creative experiment. As the face of the Village became more heterosexual, during the late 1980s and early 1990s the especially white gay male community made their way north and gentrified the area called Chelsea. While many identify Chelsea as the gay centre, the entire city is home to an endless array of queer cultural practice that intermingles many races, classes and genders.

DAVID A. GERSTNER

NEW YORK DOLLS

rock group

As a proto-punk rock group, the New York Dolls were a highly influential, albeit short-lived, phenomenon of the mid-1970s. A traditionally rock line up led by vocalist David Johansen was boosted to significance by performances in drag and well publicized drug-taking. Blatant cross-dressing, lipstick and back-combed hairdos made the New York Dolls – whose two records, released in 1973 and 1974, never achieved major sales – a cult band in rock history, being an ideal bridge between the 1960s rough rock productions and gender

bending, the luscious androgyny of early 1970s **glam rock** and the legions of both punks and heavy metal queens – all leather wigs and grimaces – that were to follow.

FABIO CLETO

NEW ZEALAND, FILMMAKING

New Zealand films are funded in part by the government through the New Zealand Film Commission (NZFC, established in 1978). Television New Zealand (TVNZ), a state-owned broadcaster, screens much of the film product funded by this body. Given the small national population (almost 4 million in 2003) and the selective international art-house market, New Zealand funding bodies tend to support projects that have the potential to reach a wide audience. Given these conditions of production, it is perhaps not surprising that while the NZFC has supported many queer short film initiatives, only a very few explicitly queer-themed feature films have emerged from this country since it was established. The most well-known New Zealand queer film is *Desperate Remedies*, made in 1993 by Peter **Wells** and Stewart **Main**, a period drama that derives its aesthetic from the European art-house cinema of Rainer Werner Fassbinder, Hollywood melodrama via Douglas Sirk and the high-blown qualities of the camp aesthetic. Wells and Main are the most influential gay filmmakers in New Zealand, although there also exists a more subterranean queer film culture.

At a time when mainstream New Zealand filmmakers were creating films set in a rural or small town environment (*Sleeping Dogs* [1977] being the most prominent example), Richard Turner's *Squeeze* (1980) was the first New Zealand feature film to have a predominately urban setting. The film focuses on the gay urban community of Auckland's pub and club culture. The Queen Elizabeth II Arts Council gave Turner script development money in 1978 but the NZFC was blocked from making a production grant due to a public campaign waged by moral majority spokesperson Patricia Bartlett (New Zealand's equivalent to the UK's Mary **Whitehouse**). While Turner finally completed the film in 1980 through private funds, Bartlett's campaign resulted in the government adding a new clause to NZFC regulations that addressed the issue of 'public decency'. Accordingly, *Squeeze* must be considered in light of the Homosexual Law Reform Bill (see **Homosexual Law Reform Act, New Zealand**) that sought to legalize sexual acts between consenting male adults, an issue that polarized New Zealand society and informed much of the queer product produced at this time.

The years of struggle surrounding the Homosexual Law Reform Act witnessed an increase in queer art activity and the emergence of a number of gay filmmakers. Wells made his first short film, *Foolish Things* (1981), in reaction to *Squeeze* and it acts as an experimental antidote to what he saw as an aesthetic conservatism in Turner's film. Other filmmakers of this period include Garth Maxwell and his feature film *Beyond Gravity* (1988), which tells of a romance between a New Zealand man obsessed with the solar system and an Italian petty thief. Mark Summerville's short film *Singing Seas* was produced in the same year and depicts gay tribal life in the South Pacific.

In terms of lesbian filmmaking activities in the 1980s, not much is known, although heterosexual filmmaker Judy Rymer directed the lesbian science-fiction drama *Just Passing Through* in 1986 from a script written by Sandi Hall. The 1990s saw the emergence of a formal and experimental form of short films from May Trubuhovich and Katherine Fry. Trubuhovich's *The Assumption* (1992) is an animated film that rewrites the story of Adam and Eve while Fry's *Fine Amour* (1995) is a medieval lesbian love story of conflict between a mystic

and a troubairitz (female troubadour). Her other work, *The Pink* (1993), is a feminist-lesbian fairy tale. While these works are of a formal and abstract nature, Christine Parker's *Peach* (1993) is a more conventionally narrated short film that depicts a encounter between a woman tow-truck driver (played by Lucy Lawless prior to her involvement in *Xena, Warrior Princess*) and the girlfriend of one of the other tow-truck drivers.

Two notable feature films of the 1990s also make reference to lesbian themes. Alison MacLean's *Crush* (1992) contains elements that suggest a love triangle between an American femme-fatale figure, her female best friend, and a young girl, while Fran Walsh's and Peter Jackson's *Heavenly Creatures* (1994) is based upon the **Parker and Hulme Case** of 1954. In 1998 Garth Maxwell directed the feature film *When Love Comes*, which revolves around a trilogy of love stories (one gay, one lesbian, one heterosexual). In this same year, Charles **Bracewell** produced the short documentary *Homecoming Queen*, which details the experiences of a queer boy growing up in small-town New Zealand and features his drag alter ego, Miz Ima Starr. *Georgie Girl* (2002), directed by Annie Goldson and Peter Wells, is the most recent New Zealand export and gives an account of the life of transsexual Maori Member of Parliament Georgina **Beyer**.

Further reading

Carbutt, John (1989) 'Gay Film-making in New Zealand', *Sites* 19 (Spring): 96–100.
Dennis, Jonathan and Bieringa, Jan (eds) (1996) *Film in Aotearoa New Zealand*, 2nd edn, Wellington: Victoria University Press.

JO SMITH

NEW ZEALAND, LITERATURE

In his introduction to *Best Mates* (1997), New Zealand's first anthology of gay male writing, Peter **Wells** celebrates the 'imaginary ancestors' of the country's contemporary queer male fiction. His discussion of that ancestry highlights the importance of a deliberately masculinist literary culture in concealing the queer narratives in New Zealand's literature, while at the same time revealing the importance of gay writing in the creation of that ongoing cultural record. The presence and absence of 'the homosexual' has shaded New Zealand literature from the outset. And that literature's overwhelmingly masculinist discourse has ensured that the 'ancestral imaginings' of lesbian writers require even greater acts of concentration and labour.

During the 1930s the early proponents of a New Zealand national literature sought to cultivate a sparsely rendered realist tradition that would stand in firm contrast to the perceived 'effeteness' of an ornate English literary heritage. Both the style and the substance associated with this embryonic 'national' literary culture made a crucial contribution to the founding myths of New Zealand's 'national identity' as a rugged, hard earned masculinity in which the importance of the bonds of 'mate'-ship is only ever taciturnly acknowledged.

It is ironic then, but perhaps unsurprising, that among the most celebrated of New Zealand's early writers are gay men. While the strict heterosexuality of pre- and post-Second World War New Zealand precluded any direct acknowledgement of gayness, male relationships predominate in most of the country's literature. This celebration of male homosociality enabled a cacophonous subtext in some writing that is difficult to imagine in a literary tradition in which women were held in higher esteem.

Thus, a writer such as Frank **Sargeson**, lauded for his stark, masculine realism, could, in his novella 'That Summer', inflect the bonds of mateship with references to Vaseline, anal penetration, prison sex and naked romping at a well-known Wellington beat. The novelist James Courage was even clearer in his 1959 novel *A Way of Life*, which tells of an affair between a younger and older man. Alongside Courage and Sargeson, Wells adds the poet Charles Brasch as a key definer of 'what it meant to be a New Zealander' in postwar New Zealand.

Yet, in the *Best Mates* anthology, where editors Wells and Rex Pilgrim sought to connect these key figures to more contemporary exponents of gay literature and to create a record of New Zealand's 'gay writing', the executors of the Brasch and Courage estates refused the inclusion of those writers' work because of the anthology's homosexual identification. As Wells' introduction suggests, it seems that a wilfully homophobic blindness continues to render absent the important queer narratives in New Zealand's literary heritage. Nonetheless, a 'conversation' clearly exists. The decadent queer artifice of the Wells and Main film *Desperate Remedies* (1993), for example, stands in such antithetical contrast to the work of Sargeson that it reveals the very artifice of Sargeson's purported homosocial realism. The 1990s saw a marked increase in the publication of gay men's writing. Robert Leek, Noel Virtue, Witi **Ihimaera**, Peter Wells and Graeme Aitken all published significant and often award-winning works.

In contrast to (and almost certainly as a consequence of) this, at times thwarted but nonetheless significant, gay literary continuum, New Zealand's lesbian literature had little of a founding national ancestry to attach itself to. It was primarily the rise of lesbian feminism, and a collective-based impulse to share and record stories that enabled the production of lesbian writing collections. These were often photocopied and stapled sheets compiled by local collectives, such as Dunedin's *Against All Odds* (produced periodically since the 1980s) or publications by lesbian publishing collectives such as Papers, Inc., which produced

The Lavender Annual in 1989. These collections were the forerunners of later anthologies such as *The Exploding Frangipani* (1990) and *Car Maintenance, Explosives and Love* (1997). Within such collections, short stories and poetry predominate, and it was here that many readers often first encountered writers such as Miriam **Saphira** and Ngahuia **Te Awekotuku**. Anthologies remain an important tool in the dissemination of lesbian narratives. Just as gay men's writing has gained in publishing strength, so too has New Zealand's lesbian literature come to include renowned writers and texts. In addition to Saphira and Te Awekotuku, Cathy Dunsford, **Renée**, Beryl Fletcher, Nancy Stone, Julie Glamuzina, Aorewa McLeod and Paula **Boock** are among those who have made important contributions to New Zealand's queer literature.

Further reading

Jones, Lawrence (2003) *Picking Up the Traces: The Making of a New Zealand Literary Culture, 1932–1945*, Wellington: Victoria University Press.

Newton, John (2000) 'Homophobia and the Social Pattern: Sargeson's Queer Nation', *Landfall* 199: 91–107.

Wells, Peter and Pilgrim, Rex (eds) (1997) *Best Mates: Gay Writing in Aotearoa New Zealand*, Auckland: Reed.

ANITA BRADY

NEWTON, ESTHER

b. 1940

scholar

A monumental figure in the field of glbtq scholarship, Esther Newton's 1972 study *Mother Camp: Female Impersonators in America*, and her essay on Radclyffe Hall, 'The Mythic Mannish Lesbian' (1984) forged new ground in both anthropological and glbtq studies. Appearing decades before Judith Butler's *Gender Trouble* (1990) and Judith Halberstam's *Female Masculinity*

(1998), Newton's insights into **butch/femme** dynamics, **drag**, **camp** and gender impersonation introduced many problematics that later queer theorists developed. More recent works, such as *Cherry Grove, Fire Island* (1993), continue to document gay subcultures. Newton's collection of essays, *Margaret Mead Made Me Gay* (2000), is a testament to her importance and significance in twentieth-century glbtq scholarship.

See also: Butler, Judith; Halberstam, Judith

JEAN BOBBY NOBLE

NGAI, JIMMY

b. 1955

writer

Born in Hong Kong, Jimmy Siu Yan (Wei Shao'en) Ngai has worked as a magazine editor, radio producer and advertising copywriter. He is now a freelance film critic, novelist and columnist. In 1996 Ngai published a gay pornographic novel, *I Love Turtle Doves*. He works closely with two major Hong Kong directors, Wong **Kar-wai** and Stanley **Kwan**. He has contributed to a book on Wong Kar-wai called *Four Movies from Wong Kar-Wai (Plus 4 1/3 movies)* (2004) and has written screenplays for Stanley Kwan's *Yue kuai le, yue duo luo* (*Hold You Tight*, 1997), *You shi tiaowu* (*The Island Tales*, 1999) and *Lan Yu* (2001).

TRAVIS KONG

NGUYEN, TAN HOANG

b. 1971

videomaker, writer

Prolific Vietnamese American videomaker, Tan Hoang Nguyen's short videos playfully interrogate desire and queer-Asian male identities. His many videos have been screened at film festivals in both the United States and internationally. His award-winning video, *Forever Bottom!* (1999), takes on the stereotype of Asian men as sexually passive – not to refute it, rather, to aggressively and unapologetically embrace it. In *Pirated!* (2000) Nguyen uses found footage from mainstream films and Vietnamese karaoke videos to retell the story of his family's 1978 escape from Vietnam and his early experiences with two mainstays of masculinity: the pirate and the sailor. *Cover Girl: A Gift from God* (2000) uses the incredible story of a blonde-haired, blue-eyed American woman, who is also a Vietnamese American pop star, to comment on the pressures of assimilation and the preservation of memory for Vietnamese people living in America.

DANIEL HENDRICKSON

NIECH NAS ZOBACZA

Niech Nas Zobacza (Let Them See Us) is Poland's first campaign to raise awareness of sexual minorities. During Spring 2003, 30 photographs by Karolina Berguła, portraying gay and lesbian couples holding hands, were displayed in an itinerant show in Poland's main cities. The exhibition provoked outrage not so much for the subject matter, rather for daring to display homosexual couples in public in the first place. As a rejoinder, a public statement against homophobia was issued, signed by many celebrities from the world of culture, and a project to exhibit the pictures on billboards and at bus stops was developed. The organizer of the project is **Kampania Przeciw Homofobii** (Campaign Against Homophobia).

ALESSANDRO AMENTA

NIELSEN, LASSE

filmmaker

Openly gay Danish filmmaker whose gay-themed feature films explore gay sexuality with ground-breaking candour. His first feature film, *La' os vaere* (Leave Us Alone, 1975), co-directed with Ernst Johansen, was nominated for the Golden Bear at the 1975 Berlin Film Festival. He also wrote the screenplay for Morten Arnfred's film *Maske ku' vi* (Could We Maybe, 1976). He is best known for *Du er ikke alene* (You Are Not Alone, 1978), which tells the story of a 12-year-old boy who falls in love with his 15-year-old friend at boarding school. The film ends happily, with the boys coming out to their family and schoolfriends and showing a sexually explicit film about their relationship.

JOHN FORDE

NIJHOLT, WILLEM

b. 1934

actor, singer

Well-known Dutch actor/entertainer, who has often played homosexual characters on stage. Nijholt's performance in the musical *Foxtrot* (1977) influenced an entire generation.

In 1957 Nijholt enrolled at the theatre school in Amsterdam. His career includes leading roles in *The Elephant Man*, *Children of a Lesser God* and various plays by Noel Coward. He also starred in several TV productions and films.

Nijholt is best known for his performances in cabaret and musical theatre. He played the leading role in two musicals by Annie M.G. Schmidt and Harry Bannink: *Wat een Planeet* (What a Planet) and *Foxtrot*. His role in the latter was modelled after his own life and character. The song 'Sorry dat ik besta' (Apology for my Existence) deals with the lack of traditions in relation to and of parental support for a gay love-affair; often the audience were outraged. In his later years Nijholt performed in the musicals *Cabaret*, *Miss Saigon* and *Oliver*.

WARD SCHRIJVER

NJINJE, MPUMI AND ALBERTON, PAOLO

Njinge, Mpumelelo
b. 1966; d. 2002
filmmaker

Alberton, Paulo
b. 1976
filmmaker

Mpumelelo Njinge was involved in a range of creative arts from clothing design to theatre and, in the latter part of his short life, in filmmaking. He acted in *After Nines!* a play on the history of black gay life in South Africa that performed in South Africa and at the **Gay Games** in Amsterdam (1998) and Sydney (2002). He completed two documentaries, *My Son The Bride* and *Everything Must Come to Light,* on the eve of his untimely death from AIDS-related causes in October 2002. *My Son The Bride* was an acclaimed documentary on Hompi, a young gay man living in a squatter camp, who realized his dreams of marrying the man in his life. Njinge also worked together with Paulo Alberton on the documentary *Everything Must Come to Light*, the story of a lesbian traditional healer in Soweto.

Alberton, a Brazilian filmmaker, was also co-director of an eclectic road movie on networks of gay hairstylists working in small towns and rural areas of South Africa entitled *Dark and Lovely, Soft and Free* (2000).

GRAEME REID

NKOLI, SIMON

b. 1957; d. 1998
activist

Simon Tseko Nkoli's human rights activism was rooted in the youth struggle against apartheid. In 1984 he was arrested for political activities and faced the death penalty for treason along with 21 others in the Delmas trial. Nkoli came out as homosexual while imprisoned, and in so doing helped change the African National Congress' attitude towards gay rights. After his acquittal in 1988, Nkoli formed the Gay and Lesbian Organization of the Witwatersrand and became the public face of the South African fight for gay equality. In 1990 Nkoli established Soweto's Township AIDS Project and became the first African gay man to disclose publicly his HIV status.

ANTHONY MANION

NOORDZIJ, NEL

b. 1923; d. 2003
writer

Between 1954 and 1964, Nel Noordzij, who was trained as a psychologist, wrote a total of 13 books: five books of poetry, collections of short stories and essays, as well as several novels. Noordzij belonged to the Dutch literary avant-garde, the 'angry young (wo)men' of the times. Her work can be characterized as streetwise, explicit on sexual matters and highly critical of the established gender prescriptions. Her novels and stories usually constitute intricate psychological case histories, often portraying recalcitrant women facing difficult dilemmas or finding themselves in crisis. Lesbianism and homosexuality are never thematically distant from her texts, but Noordzij's most explicitly lesbian novel is *Het kan me niet schelen* (I Don't Care, 1955). The story concerns a 30-year-old woman doctor Renée Geluk-van Tricht, who experiences herself as profoundly unreal. Challenging bourgeois propriety, she tries to liberate herself from the masks a corrupt society has imposed upon her. She entertains a troubled relationship with her lesbian friend Jenny, who, in many ways, figures as her double. In 1964 Noordzij withdrew from literary life.

MAAIKE MEIJER

NORTH AMERICAN MAN/ BOY LOVE ASSOCIATION (NAMBLA)

NAMBLA was founded in Boston in December 1978. It grew out of a successful campaign by members of the Boston gay community to fight against a police and media witch-hunt of homosexual men, and specifically against those involved in intergenerational relationships. In 1979 the group made its first public appearance at a national gay and lesbian march on Washington DC. Since then it has gone on to become the most visible defender of man/boy love relationships in the United States, a fact that has also made it an object of attack whenever controversy arises over this issue.

Although the group has been met with harassment and condemnation since its beginnings, these were stepped up during the early 1980s, both from the outside and from within the lesbian and gay community. In 1982 the police and the FBI arrested and otherwise harassed several of the group's members, claiming that the group was responsible for a well-known unsolved missing person case in Boston. After giving rise to a great deal of media hysteria, this claim proved to be unfounded. In October of that same year, some members of Philadelphia's lesbian and gay community openly opposed the use of the local community centre for the group's national conference. Although the group was eventually allowed to hold its conference, it has not fared so well in later conflicts. The group has been refused permission to take part in several lesbian and gay marches due to opposition within the community.

The group describes itself as a political and educational organization, dedicated to promoting support and understanding for relationships between older and younger people. The group is a strong advocate of the sexual rights of youth and a strong opponent of age-of-consent laws. It publishes a regular periodical, *NAMBLA Bulletin*, and occasional other publications.

The issues of youth sexuality and inter-generational relationships are complex and controversial, and the response of the lesbian and gay community to the issue and to NAMBLA has been equally complex. Although there has been a certain degree of support for the organization, including among some prominent figures, there has also been a great deal of opposition. The opposition's stance, however, is also complex, consisting of genuinely ideological opponents of man/boy love relationships *per se* as well as those who simply wish to avoid such a controversial issue.

DANIEL HENDRICKSON

NORTON, GRAHAM

b. 1963

comedian

One of the UK's and Ireland's most popular TV comedians, Graham Norton began his career on the stand-up circuit, making his breakthrough by winning the prestigious Perrier Comedy Award at the 1997 Edinburgh Festival. A stint presenting on *The Jack Docherty Show* (1997) spawned his own TV comedy talk shows *So Graham Norton* (1998–2000) and *V Graham Norton* (2002–4). While his barbed, innuendo-laden wit and penchant for embarrassing his audience recalls fellow camp comics Julian **Clary** and Bruce **Forsyth**, Norton's unapologetic and exuberantly expressed homosexuality has broken new ground for mainstream acceptance of gays in British and Irish television.

In 2004 *The Graham Norton Effect* began airing on the US cable channel Comedy Central.

JOHN FORDE

NOVELLO, IVOR

b. 1893; d. 1951

actor, composer, playwright

Born David Ivor Davies in Cardiff, Wales, Ivor Novello was first celebrated as the

433

composer of the World War One anthem 'Keep the Home Fires Burning', and then for his handsome profile as Britain's premier film and stage star of the 1920s. From 1934 he wrote, produced and starred in lavish West End musicals such as *Glamorous Night* (1935), *Perchance to Dream* (1945) and, appropriately enough, *Gay's the Word* (1951). Like friend and rival Noel Coward, Novello's homosexuality was not entirely closeted, precipitating his incarceration by an apparently homophobic judge for wartime petrol coupon offences, an event inspiring Paul Webb's 2001 play *The Lodger*. This, along with camp tributes from British drag act Hinge and Bracket, and persistent rumours about sex with Winston Churchill, indicates Novello's lasting impact on British queer culture. Novello was also portrayed in Robert Altman's *Gosford Park* (2001), his magnetic appeal suitably acting as a queer dramatic catalyst for all classes and sexualities.

MICHAEL WILLIAMS

NTHUNYA, MPHO' M'ATESPO

b. 1930

writer

'Peasant farmer', domestic servant and author, M'atespo Mpho' Nthunya was born in Lesotho but for many years was resident in the black townships of South Africa. Her 1996 memoir *Singing Away the Hunger*, co-written with American scholar K. Limakatso Kendall, describes terrible poverty, domestic violence and racist police. It also recounts intensely intimate female–female and male–male friendships known as *setsualle*. While these formerly existed in traditional Sesotho culture, Nthunya is nostalgic that they have largely disappeared due to Westernization.

MARC EPPRECHT

NUMBER 96

TV series

Number 96, a trailblazing Australian TV serial, won widespread popularity in the 1970s and subsequently earned cult status for its heady mix of soap opera, sensationalism and camp comedy. Created by David Sale, *Number 96* revolved around 'the lives, loves and emotions' of a group of tenants in a small Sydney apartment complex. During its six-year run from 1972 until 1977, the serial broke new ground with its candid exploration of taboo social issues, many pertaining to queer sexualities. It featured Australian television's first major queer character in the form of the handsome and openly gay lawyer Don Finlayson (Joe Hasham) and broadcast what was allegedly the first same-sex kiss on prime-time TV anywhere in the world. Other queer storylines explored lesbianism, bisexuality and transvestism. Denigrated by both highbrow critics and moral commentators, the serial shot to the top of the Australian ratings, becoming a genuine cultural phenomenon of its time.

BRETT FARMER

NUÑEZ DEL PRADO, MARINA

b. 1910; d. 1955

artist

Bolivian sculptor of international renown, Marina Núñez del Prado's preferred subject matter was the feminine body. Her style evolved from realism, in her initial stages, to elegantly stylized and sensuous abstract shapes. Although Bolivian art critics, social researchers and historical analysts still maintain a rigid silence on the private lives of historically important people, the fact remains that Marina Núñez del Prado's circle of friends was composed mainly of gay artists and celebrities from the Bolivian and international art scene. Childless, she constantly referred to her sculptures as 'my women', a statement scholars interpret strictly as an expression of the artist's sublimated motherhood, refusing other more dangerous possibilities of interpretation and arguing that Núñez was a married woman. However, the constant recurrence of the female nude – frequently veiled under female Andean mythological themes – and the sensuality of her work open the way for homoerotic readings and perceptions.

Núñez del Prado received many international awards during her lifetime, including first place at the Berlin International Exhibit (1936); first place at the 54th Annual Exhibit of the National Association of Women Artists of New York (the first foreign woman to be honoured with this award); and first place in Sculpture at the Hispanoamerican Art Biennial, Madrid (1951). She was a pioneer who successfully carved out a place in art history for herself by appropriating artistic codes in an art scene dominated by men at a time when sculpture was thought of as too heavy and unseemly for women.

PEDRO ALBORNOZ

NUREYEV, RUDOLPH
b. 1938; d. 1993
dancer

A legend of twentieth-century ballet, Nureyev trained at the Leningrad Choreographic School in Russia and joined the Kirov Ballet as a soloist and later as principal dancer. After a hugely successful tour of *Sleeping Beauty* in Paris, Nureyev claimed political asylum in 1961, and remained living and working in the West until his death from AIDS in 1993. An artist of dazzling virtuosity, beauty and sexual charisma, he was hailed as the greatest male ballet dancer since Nijinsky, with whom he was often compared. He created several new roles with leading choreographers, including George Balanchine. An accomplished choreographer, he was artistic director of the Paris Opera from 1983 until 1989. His film work includes *Nijinksy* (1970) and *Valentino* (1977). He also featured in the autobiographical film, *I Am A Dancer* (1971). Openly gay and famously promiscuous, his lovers included the dancer Erik **Bruhn**.

See also: Russell, Ken

JOHN FORDE

O

O'BRIEN, RICHARD

b. 1942

actor, writer

Born Richard Smith in Cheltenham, Gloucestershire, England, Richard O'Brien was a stuntman, actor and writer who took part in many successful movies and musicals and presented the first four years of TV series *The Crystal Maze*. His main contribution to queer culture was his authorship of the epoch-making musical *The Rocky Horror Show* in 1973. Its adaptation for the screen in 1975 brought him worldwide fame as the creator of the ultimate cult film, starring a 'sweet transvestite from Transsexual, Transylvania', an uber-camp vampire hosting and perverting, with the assistance of a drag horde, a young all-American couple in his castle.

FABIO CLETO

OCCUR

OCCUR is the English name used by Japan's most prominent lesbian and gay movement (Ugoku Gei to Rezubian no Kai), which broke away from the Japan branch of the **International Lesbian and Gay Association** (JILGA) in 1986 because of disagreements over the latter's authoritarian management style. OCCUR has waged a number of successful campaigns, such as the reform of Japanese dictionary definitions of

homosexuality so as to remove derogatory nuances and, in 1994, it launched and won a court case against the Tokyo Metropolitan Government which had denied the group access to overnight youth facilities. However, OCCUR has also been criticized for its narrow focus. Lesbian author and activist Sarah **Schulman**, for instance, was accused of 'serious crimes' by members of the organization during a trip to Tokyo in 1992 because she supported a lesbian and gay film festival the sponsors of which OCCUR disapproved.

MARK McLELLAND

OCHS, ROBYN

b. 1958

activist, public educator, writer

Robyn Ochs is among a handful of activists in the United States who have most influenced the development of bisexual communities, and thus bisexual culture, around the world. An activist since 1982, Ochs leads workshops and teaches college classes on bisexuality and biphobia; serves frequently as a spokesperson for the bisexual movement; and publishes the Bisexual Resource Guide (which includes among its resources a list of bisexual and bi-inclusive organizations around the world). She co-founded the Boston Bisexual Women's Network and the (Boston) Bisexual Resource Center. Ochs has written introductory and theoretically advanced essays on bisexuality and biphobia, and has also written on bisexuality and feminism, the history of the bisexual community, bisexual identity and labelling, teaching about bisexuality, and etiquette for working with lesbians and gay men. Ochs stresses coalition-building as a means to more productive social justice work.

AMANDA UDIS-KESSLER

O'DONNELL, ROSIE

b. 1962

actor, comedian

This famously straight-talking comedian began her career on the Long Island stand-up comedy circuit, where she developed her trademark self-deprecating feminist banter. She made her TV debut on *Star Search* in 1984, winning the show's comedy competition five times, and went on to star in the sitcom *Gimme A Break* (1981–7). She also produced and hosted *Stand Up Spotlight* (1988). She made an impressive film debut as a tomboyish, tough-talking baseball player in *A League of Their Own* (1992), opposite her friend Madonna. In 1996 she hosted and executive-produced *The Rosie O'Donnell Show*, which became a ratings success and a Daytime Emmy winner. After years of speculation about her sexuality, O'Donnell publicly admitted her homosexuality in 2002, in the hope of drawing attention to legal inequalities faced by lesbian parents. She raises four adoptive children with her partner, TV executive Kelli Carpenter. She also produced the Boy George stage musical *Taboo* (2003).

JOHN FORDE

OETOMO, DÉDÉ

b. 1953

activist, linguist, anthropologist

Dédé Oetomo, born in Pasuruan, Indonesia, has been the most publicly visible acti-vist for gay/lesbian rights in Indonesia. Oetomo distinguished himself academically from a young age and in 1978 went to Cornell University to pursue a PhD in linguistics. Back in Indonesia he participated in the 1982 founding of the country's first gay organization, Lambda Indonesia. The same year Oetomo also worked on the publication of Indonesia's first gay magazine (*G: Gaya Hidup Ceria*) and since 1987 has helped publish *GAYa Nusantara*, Indonesia's largest and longest-running gay or lesbian magazine. Since 1981 he has been out to the Indonesian mass media, discussing issues based around homosexuality, HIV and AIDS. In 1999 and 2004 Oetomo ran for the national parliament, providing further opportunities to argue that gay and lesbian persons deserve full inclusion in Indonesian society. He has been active with many HIV prevention and gay/lesbian rights organizations at local, national and international levels.

TOM BOELLSTORFF

O'HARA, FRANK

b. 1926; d. 1966

poet

Frank O'Hara was born in Baltimore, but his family moved shortly thereafter to Massachusetts, where he grew up. After serving two years in the US Navy, he entered Harvard in 1946, initially as a music student, although he soon changed his field of study to English. He then went to the University of Michigan where he did his graduate studies. It was here that he began writing seriously, both plays and poems, for which he won the prestigious Hopwood Award in Creative Writing. He moved to New York and began working at the Museum of Modern Art, becoming actively involved in the New York art world and meeting many of its major figures. O'Hara worked as an editor of *Art News* during the early 1950s, but returned to the Museum of Modern Art in 1955. He became increasingly well known both as an art critic and a poet during this time, and his two careers were often interwoven. He published a study of Jackson Pollock in 1959, as well as pieces on David Smith and Robert Motherwell. He also worked in collaboration with artists Larry Rivers, Mike Goldberg and Joe Brainard.

In 1964 City Lights Books published his *Lunch Poems*, so called presumably because the poems were written during lunch breaks from his day job. O'Hara's poems are marked by a deliberate juxtaposition of high and low cultures, mixing allusions to serious art and classical music with queeny references to movie stars and popular singers. He died in November 1966 after being struck by a dune buggy on Fire Island.

DANIEL HENDRICKSON

OKI, HIROYUKI

b. 1964

filmmaker

Hiroyuki Oki is a pioneering Japanese gay film director whose work has been screened at international festivals all over the world. His most acclaimed work is the 1994 *Anata-ga suki desu dai suki desu* (*I Like You: I Like You Very Much*), which chronicles the tension caused between a gay couple when one partner falls for a stranger he sees at a railway station.

MARK McLELLAND

OLAF, ERWIN

b. 1959

photographer

Dutch photographic artist, born Erwin Olaf Springsveld in Hilversum. Olaf studied at the Amsterdam School of Journalism and quickly established himself as a commercial photographer. Major campaigns for Diesel, Carling beer, Tio Pepe sherry, Silk Cut

cigarettes, Nokia – all reveal a distinctive view of the world, taking the human subject as an oblique object of desire, queering the vision of the onlooker. His non-commercial work has resulted in a series of books and exhibitions that explore gender restrictions and provoke consideration of a multifaceted sexuality: examples include *Joy, Chessmen,* and *Mind of their Own.* His work often courts controversy and enters a queer frame of reference not only through his personal visual style, but through association with a broader gay culture – one which considers the dressing up and performance of sexuality.

MICHAEL PINFOLD

OLDHAM, TODD

b. 1962

fashion designer

One of America's leading designers, Todd Oldham is renowned for his signature casual, upbeat styles and improvisatory approach to fashion. He designed his first dress at age 15 out of old K-Mart pillowcases, then relocated to New York in 1998, where he found success with his range of casual- and sportswear, notable for their cheerful use of colour and relaxed styles. During the early 1990s he presented 'Todd Time', a light-hearted DIY fashion advice show for MTV's *House of Style* programme, encouraging viewers to dye their hair with Kool-Aid and wallpaper their bedrooms with wood-grained contact paper or Xeroxed pictures. As well as his clothing line, Oldham has launched a jeans line, a fragrance, a collection of sneakers for Keds and a leopard-skin-clad Barbie doll. In 1994 he was signed as a consultant for German design house Escada.

JOHN FORDE

OLIVIA RECORDS

Opened in 1971, Olivia Records is the first record label created by and run entirely by women. It produced and recorded a range of popular 1970s feminist and lesbian artists, including Holly Near. Co-founded by members of a Washington DC music collective, including lesbian musician Cris Williamson, the label debuted with a split single featuring Meg Christian's 'Lady' and Williamson's 'If It Wasn't for the Music'. Later in the year the label produced its first full-length album recording, Christian's 'I Know You Know'. Williamson's album *The Changer and the Changed* (1975) sold over 100,000 copies within a year, becoming one of the best-selling independent albums of the decade. In 1977 rumours circulated that Sandy **Stone**, a recording engineer for the company, was a transsexual. Faced with threats of a boycott by lesbian separatists, the company asked Stone to resign. In 1982 Williamson collaborated with Tret Fure on *Lumiere*, a children's album, unexpectedly winning a 1982 Parents' Choice Award. The pair continued to record on the label until 1995, when Olivia stopped music production and became a women's travel company. Williamson and Fure subsequently opened another label, Wolf Moon, in 1996.

JOHN FORDE

ONDINE, SUPERSTAR

b. 1935; d. 1989

performer

Robert Olivio, better know as Ondine, or sometimes as Pope Ondine, was one of the most notorious of Andy Warhol's group of superstars and a central figure of the 1960s New York Underground. One of the most flamboyant of the many gay personalities involved in the scene, he is best remembered for his sharp wit, his volatile temper and his unflagging adoration of Maria **Callas**. He is featured in several of Warhol's films, including *Vinyl* (1965), *Chelsea Girls* (1966) and *The Loves of Ondine* (1967). He was also the main force behind War-

hol's book *A: a novel* (1978), which consists entirely of transcribed telephone conversations with Ondine. He later worked with his lover, filmmaker Roger Jacoby, on several films, including *Aged in Wood* (1975), in which Ondine and two friends watch and comment on the Hollywood classic, *All About Eve* (1950).

See also: Warhol, Andy

DANIEL HENDRICKSON

ONODERA, MIDI

b. 1961

film- and videomaker

One of Canada's most internationally recognized, prolific and versatile lesbian film- and videomakers, Onodera was trained at Ontario College of Art and Design, where she established her base in the Toronto arts community. Onodera's first major film, *Ten Cents a Dance (Parallax)* (1985), an ambiguous experimental narrative triptych about sex, games and money, attracted controversy internationally even at the height of the 1980s porn wars: a lesbian courtship scene shifts to an overhead view of a gay male toilet sex scene, and then a heterosexual telephone sex-work encounter. *The Displaced View* (1988) was a more chaste but still innovative documentary on the interface of Japanese-Canadian genealogy with history, memory, gender and sexual identity, themes that recur in the subsequent experimental shorts. Onodera's one feature film, *Skin Deep* (1995), met with a mixed response, despite its intriguing narrative of an Asian-Canadian filmmaker afloat in a maelstrom of artistic, corporal and gender crises. Subsequent experiments have been increasingly digital, interactive and performance-based, continuing to flout expectations of neatly packaged identities.

THOMAS WAUGH

OPERA

There has always been something decidedly queer about opera. Both fans and detractors, for good or for bad, can agree on this point, but no one seems to be able to explain it very well. Exactly what makes opera so queer remains elusive and speculative, and attempts to pin it down have usually been rather unconvincing. But perhaps this phenomenon is due not to flimsy evidence and unconvincing arguments, but rather to the fact that there is so much that is queer about opera, so many queer perspectives to approach it from, that it can quickly become overwhelming. The perspectives are not only varied by time, place and the different experiences of gays and lesbians, they can sometimes even be contradictory, ending with an impression that any explanation for the queer appeal of opera is somehow obviously lacking.

The arguments for opera's queerness can be broken down into three basic categories. Opera is queer because the people who make it or like it are queer, because the contents are queer or because the style is queer.

The sexual non-conformity of composers, singers, patrons and fans has been a consistent theme since the inception of opera. The members of a mostly anonymous group of opera patrons in seventeenth-century Venice, who are perhaps most responsible for establishing the new form, were suspected of being homosexual. This was corroborated by a frequent use of cross-gender casting and by the employment of the so-called *castrati*. During the eighteenth century, boys with promising voices were sometimes castrated to retain their high registers. Although this was never completely legal, the practice was continued until the early nineteenth century. Many of these *castrati* became extremely famous because of their beautiful voices. George Frederic Handel (1685–1759) wrote extensively for the *castrati*, as did Christoph Willibald Glück (1714–87). The

presence of these singers as well as cross-gender casting solidified the sexual ambiguity of early opera.

As opera developed, its creators and patrons continued to be hounded by the perceived presence of homosexuality. In some cases (most famously that of King Ludwig II of Bavaria who was Richard Wagner's most staunch supporter) there was some truth in the matter. In other cases, ungrounded accusations of homosexuality were launched for political reasons or by other critics of opera and its composers.

During the early twentieth century, a significant subculture of lesbian diva worship developed in the United States, centred around such singers as Geraldine Ferrar and Kathleen Ferrier. Later in the century, the phenomenon of the opera queen arose. A vivid, and sometimes vitriolic, subculture of gay male fans was established, mostly in New York and San Francisco, and usually focused on the careers and lives of famous divas. Most well-known divas of the later twentieth century have had their own base of opera queen fans, most notably Maria **Callas** (1923–77). This phenomenon has produced a small subculture of its own, including a special issue of the magazine *Christopher Street* on the subject, writings by gay critics such as Michael Bronski and Lawrence Mass, and Terrence McNally's play *The Lisbon Traviata* (1985).

The first openly gay or lesbian character in opera did not appear until 1937. Alban Berg's *Lulu*, based on the work of Franz Wedekind, features a clearly lesbian supporting character, the Countess Geschwitz. But the opera had long had more than subtle lesbian undercurrents due to the practice of cross-gender casting. During the nineteenth century, when the practice of castrating young boy singers finally fell out of fashion, the roles previously sung by them, in most cases, had to be taken over by mezzo-sopranos. The already familiar practice of writing men's roles for women's voices became quite common. The roles, called *travesti* or trouser roles, were usually those of young heroes, and they very often gave cause for the representation of extremely thinly veiled lesbian romance. The most famous, and perhaps most explicitly erotic, examples are the role of Cherubino in Mozart's *Le nozze di Figaro* (*The Marriage of Figaro*, 1786) and later, that of Octavian in Richard Strauss' *Der Rosenkavalier* (The Knight of the Rose, 1911). Other trouser roles appear in operas by Charles Gounod, Johann Strauss and Bellini. Trouser roles are so frequent in the work of Giaocchino Rossini (1792–1868) that it prompted the American mezzo-soprano Marilyn Horne, a well-known Rossini specialist, to comment: 'I'm either the girl who doesn't get the guy, or I *am* the guy, and that's fine with me'.

Later in the twentieth century, other gay or lesbian characters appeared in opera, including in Benjamin Britten's *Death in Venice* (1973), based on the novel by Thomas Mann, and Hans Werner Henze's *Das verratene Meer* (The Betrayed Sea, 1986–9), based on Yukio Mishima's novel, *The Sailor Who Fell from Grace with the Sea*.

In addition to these cases of explicitly gay or lesbian characters or sexually ambiguous representations, many have argued that the frequent depiction of difficult, socially stigmatized, or even impossible love in opera is a crucial part of its queer appeal. It has often been suggested that gay men in particular identify with female characters who are prevented from realizing their love relationships with men because of social strictures, a common trope in tragic operas.

Perhaps the most elusive argument for the queer value of opera is that of its style. Opera, in which every word is sung rather than spoken in a grand mixture of theatre and music, is intrinsically an art of excess and artificiality. This has been augmented by a tendency towards histrionics and extreme emotional situations in many libretti as well as sometimes dazzlingly virtuoso singing styles. The argument that all of this is somehow queer necessarily assumes a wider argument that links nonnormative sexualities with excess and artifice. Nonetheless, the idea that the very form of opera is queer is compelling, a fact which is attested to in the numerous writings on the subject by gay men and lesbians.

See also: Callas, Maria; McNally, Terrence

DANIEL HENDRICKSON

OPERA QUEEN

'Opera queen' is a gay male identity defined by an obsession with the world of opera and a passionate devotion to the idealized figure of the prima donna. This diva worship inspires zealous opera-going, the exhaustive accumulation of recordings, performance data and memorabilia, fierce partisanship and subjective, rhetorical debate. For some gay men this identity has emerged artificially from texts such as Terrence McNally's 1985 play *The Lisbon Traviata*, and heterosexual male opera fans often resent the implied connection between opera and homosexuality. But for closeted gay men, particularly before Stonewall, immersion in opera served both as a retreat from a hostile environment and a discreet signifier of sexual preference. Freddie Mercury's friendship and collaboration with Spanish diva Montserrat Caballé can be seen as an outcome of the apparent gay male predilection for opera.

See also: Callas, Maria; McNally, Terrence; Mercury, Freddie

Further reading

Koestenbaum, K. (1993) *The Queen's Throat: Opera, Homosexuality, and the Mystery of Desire*, London: GMP Publishers.
Morris, M. (1993) 'Reading as an Opera Queen', in R.A. Solie (ed.) *Musicology and Difference: Gender and Sexuality in Music Scholarship*,

Berkeley: University of California Press, pp. 184–200.

RACHEL COWGILL

OPERA: WOMEN *EN TRAVESTI*

Conventions of female cross-dressing in Western opera open up queer space in a genre where gender representations can otherwise seem stereotypical. Composers expressly call for a male character to be played by a woman in what is variously termed a trouser, breeches or pants role. Mozart, for example, conceived the role of the amorous page Cherubino for a female mezzo-soprano in *Le nozze di Figaro* (*The Marriage of Figaro*, 1786); and after a thinly veiled orchestral depiction of vigorous lovemaking in Richard Strauss' *Der Rosenkavalier* (The Knight of the Rose, 1911), the curtain rises on the Marschallin in bed with her young lover Octavian (played by a cross-dressed woman). Octavian's rapt Act 2 duet with his emerging love interest Sophie is among the most beautiful love music composed for two female voices in Western opera. A form of double travesty adds an extra dimension of erotic gender play in both operas, when romantic intrigue requires the cross-dressed page to don female clothing. The trouser role predates the principal boy in English pantomime – other examples are by Monteverdi (Telemachus), Handel (Radamisto), Bellini (Romeo) and Rossini (Tancredi). The heroine of Beethoven's *Fidelio* (1805) is no trouser role, but she disguises herself as a man almost throughout, fending off the advances of another woman.

Often also played by women are the heroic male roles originally written for the *castrato*, the high male voice produced by castration which went out of fashion during the nineteenth century. Ann Murray, for example, has drawn a considerable lesbian following as Handel's Xerxes, Ariodante and Julius Caesar. Lending themselves to queer reading are Wagner's self-sufficient sisterhoods, the Valkyries and the Rhine maidens; but Berg's portrayal of Wedekind's quasi-masculine Countess Geschwitz in his opera *Lulu* (1937) was the first appearance of an explicitly lesbian character on the operatic stage. More recently, in *Patience and Sarah* (1998), based on the novel by Alma Routsong (alias Isabel Miller), Paula Kimper and Wende Person express lesbian love directly in operatic terms, without the filters of gender masquerade.

Further reading

Blackmer, C.E. and Smith, P.J. (eds) (1995) *En travesti: Women, Gender Subversion, Opera*, New York: Columbia University Press.

RACHEL COWGILL

OPIE, CATHERINE
b. 1961
photographer

American photographer, born in Sandusky, Ohio, Catherine Opie first came to prominence during the early 1990s with a number of photographs of both herself and other figures from the **Los Angeles** and San Francisco queer underground. She made formal portraits of figures rarely photographed: leather dykes, drag queens, transgendered people and other queers. She then turned to taking landscape and architectural photographs, a long-time interest. Her pictures of freeways and mini-malls, taken at dawn and mostly in Los Angeles and southern California, are completely empty of people, giving the photographs a haunting, open quality that both underscores and undermines their pristine formalism. Following this, Opie worked on a series of photographs of lesbian domestic scenes throughout the United States. She is also active as a art teacher.

DANIEL HENDRICKSON

ORANGES ARE NOT THE ONLY FRUIT

TV series

A multi-award winning British TV series of 1990, *Oranges are Not the Only Fruit,* was adapted by lesbian writer Jeanette Winterson from her highly successful novel. Based on Winterson's childhood, *Oranges* is the coming-of-age story of Jess (Charlotte Coleman), an impulsive redhead whose lesbian identity puts her at odds with her adoptive mother, a fervent fundamentalist Christian (Geraldine McEwan). The brutality of Christian homophobia is unflinchingly portrayed, including a scene where teenage Jess is tied up and imprisoned to 'cure' her lesbianism. But Beeban Kidron's buoyant direction and fine performances faithfully render the comedy, optimism and romantic spirit of Winterson's novel.

See also: Kidron, Beeban

JOHN FORDE

ORTON, JOE

b. 1933; d. 1967

playwright

The rise and fall of Joe Orton as the most promising (and wildly gay) of British playwrights of the 1960s represents the epitome of the queer 1960s, voraciously creating and consuming icons, ephemerally and irreverently challenging established hierarchies and values. He was born John Kingsley Orton in Leicester, England. Up until 1963 Orton's only achievement a jail sentence for six months for defacing library books, then came the London production of his first play, which brought him immediate awards, controversy, fame and success, along with a revolutionary impact on the London theatre scene. Hailed as a welfare state Oscar Wilde, he had created a new style in the tradition of British high farce, a style – the 'Ortonesque' – at once obscene, witty and sophisticated, a twisted and quite gay pastiche of modish and everyday language that celebrates a sexual and linguistic polymorphous perversity and debunks the absurdity inherent to social conventions. Within four years, and four outrageously successful plays later, Orton was the biggest name in London. His tragic end in 1967 in London, murdered by long-standing partner Kenneth Halliwell, only added to his reputation as an unsurpassed gay icon whose life has become the subject of various biographies and theatre pieces.

FABIO CLETO

OTTINGER, ULRIKE

b. 1942

filmmaker

Born on 6 June 1942 in Konstanz, Baden-Württemberg, Germany, Ulrike Ottinger is an avant-garde lesbian filmmaker whose work creates lushly erotic fantasy worlds and explores androgynous and marginalized sexuality. She studied painting and photography at the Munich Academy of Arts and made her first film *Laokoon und Sohne* (Laocoon and Sons, 1973) with her then lover, Tabea Blumenschein. The two collaborated again on *Madame X: eine absolute Herrscherin* (Madame X: An Absolute Ruler, 1977), a baroque lesbian-themed fantasy in which six women vie for the affections of Madame X, a whip-wielding dominatrix and pirate. In *Freak Orlando* (1981), a loose adaptation of the novel by Virginia **Woolf** *Orlando* (1928), Ottinger explored the position of society's 'outsiders' by filming midgets, giants, transvestites, obese and limbless people. Her other films include *Dorian Gray im Spiegel der Boulevardpresse* (The Image of Dorian Gray in the Yellow Press, 1984), a lesbian reworking of the novel by **Wilde**; *Johanna d'Arc of Mongolia* (Joan of Arc of Mongolia, 1988), a fantasy about a matriarchal tribe of Mongolian warriors; and *Zwölf Stühle* (2004). Her documentaries explore marginalized

443

world cultures, and include *Taiga* (1992), *China: Die Künste – der Alltag* (China: The Arts, the Everyday, 1985), *Exile Shanghai* (1986) and *Countdown* (1991), a portrait of minorities in Berlin.

JOHN FORDE

OUOLOGUEM, YAMBO

b. 1940

writer

The Malian novelist and poet Yambo Ouologuem was the first African to win a major literary prize in France (le Prix Renaudot). *Le Devoir de violence* (1968), published in English as *Bound to Violence* in 1971, offers a sweeping, scathing critique of Arab and indigenous African oppression of Africa. Similar to Ayi Kwei **Armah**, Ouologuem begins with a depiction of pederasty among corrupt, exogenous elites as a device to evoke repugnance in the reader. The vile and abusive homosexuality of the 'Arabs' is particularly controversial when contrasted with a tender, loving homosexual relationship between the African protagonist and a European man, respectfully and tastefully described later in the novel. So jarring is this section that some have speculated that it is an emulation of black American gay literature, and indeed *Devoir* was found to have been significantly plagiarized from European authors. During the 1990s Ouologuem withdrew from the literary world to directly engage 'Arab' racism and oppression in Mauritania.

MARC EPPRECHT

OUTING

The process of outing has come into being as homosexuals have felt the need either to declare their own sexuality publicly or, more contentiously, to make known the homosexuality of others. In origin it is related to the phrase 'coming out of the closet' to denote a blatant assertion of sexual orientation. At times the practice has been adopted maliciously by the press (as in the coverage of George Michael's arrest), but when used by the gay community as a positive message of self-worth it allows ownership of personal information in the public arena. This was certainly the case when in 1997 Ellen **DeGeneres** famously made known her sexuality under the guise of her TV sitcom character Ellen Morgan; she became the (rather short-lived) first openly gay leading character on networks in the United States, forcing recognition of lesbian subjectivity upon American audiences.

The political dynamics of outing have been used to bring issues of gay rights to the attention of both church and state, as in Sebastian Sandys' naming of three closeted gay bishops at an Anglican church debate in England, which led to the naming of seven other high-ranking church officials as gay, forcing the church to re-examine its policy on homosexuality and on institutionalized homophobia. It is argued by those active as 'outers', such as Michelangelo **Signorile**, that queer homophobes are hypocrites and that their hypocrisy deserves to be exposed, thus discrediting them as perpetrators of discrimination. Signorile also argues that 'outing' is in effect an equalizing principle in journalistic practices (that is, it is not considered 'outing' since the heterosexuality of public figures is discussed openly). A more benign approach to outing targets no one but the self.

See also: Michael, George

MICHAEL PINFOLD

OUTRAGE!

direct action group

Established in May 1990, the British-based OutRage! is the world's longest surviving, non-violent, queer rights direct action group. Employing methods of civil disobedience and outing, it has prompted a significant response from established authorities to the issues raised. Stunts include the Queer Valentine's Carnival and Kiss-In in London, the hijacking of religious services at Westminster Cathedral to protest at the Pope's support of homophobic discrimination in 1992 and the outing of ten Church of England bishops in 1994, which resulted in that church's condemnation of homophobia. It holds a critical attitude towards the institutions, laws and values of straight society, claiming that equal rights on straight terms are not equal at all; its agenda is radical in its approach to sexuality and it rejects the conformist politics of mainstream gay rights movements. The Unmarried Partners Act it promotes includes all unwed couples, gay or straight, along with an Equal Rights Act that protects all against harassment. It also targets schools in promoting sexually related issues that local councils may be averse to include. The policy of direct action has been particularly effective in bringing about changes in police procedures regarding minor sexual 'crimes', so that between 1990 and 1994 the number of men prosecuted for consenting gay behaviour fell by two-thirds; it also shifted police attention to queer-bashers rather than queers. Internationally, OutRage! has exposed oppression in Zimbabwe, Romania and Iran, and in South Africa it has helped to draft anti-discrimination proposals included in the post-apartheid constitution.

See also: Peter Tatchell

MICHAEL PINFOLD

OXENBERG, JAN

writer, director

An American lesbian filmmaker whose work humorously explores lesbian identity and challenges sexual stereotypes. She is best known for her satirical short film *Home Movie* (1972), which chronicles her adolescence and her burgeoning lesbian identity. The film juxtaposes her family's home movie footage (including her performances as a high school cheerleader) ironically with a voiceover commentary and footage of contemporary lesbian feminist cultural events. In *I'm Not One of Them* (1974) and *A Comedy In Six Unnatural Acts* (1975), Oxenberg uses humour to interrogate and celebrate lesbian stereotypes. She featured in Rob Epstein's and Jeffrey Friedman's documentary *The Celluloid Closet* (1995), proving to be a humorous and insightful cultural commentator. She has worked extensively as a TV scriptwriter, including for shows such as *Chicago Hope* (1994), *Once and Again* (1999), *Roswell* (1999) and *Robbery Homicide Division* (2002) and wrote a film screenplay for *My Dark Places* (2005).

JOHN FORDE

OZON, FRANÇOIS

b. 1967

director

Openly gay French film director François Ozon has achieved international recognition for his quirky blend of dark eroticism and humour. Following studies for a Masters degree in Cinema, Ozon gained entry into France's prestigious national film school, La FEMIS, where he turned out a series of short films that garnered immediate attention for their arresting visual style and frank explorations of sexual diversity. Ozon's first feature film, *Sitcom* (1998), continued his thematic fascination with unconventional eroticism and, along with *Les Amants criminals* (*Criminal Lovers*) the following year, earned him a reputation as French cinema's newest *enfant terrible*. International and commercial success followed with films such as *Sous le Sable* (*Under the Sand*, 2000), *8 Femmes* (*8 Women*, 2002) and *Swimming Pool* (2003).

Frequently compared to cinematic masters such as **Hitchcock**, Chabrol and **Fassbinder**, Ozon is an intelligent and skilful filmmaker whose work marries traditional elements of narrative cinema such as character identification and suspense with a sexually subversive edge.

BRETT FARMER

ÖZPETEK, FERZAN

b. 1959

filmmaker

Ferzan Özpetek was born in Istanbul but came to Rome in 1977 to study film history. After working in theatre, including for Julian Beck's Living Theater, he worked as an assistant director. His first feature film, *Hamam* (*Steam / Il bagno turco*), was presented at Cannes in 1997 and enjoyed both critical and popular success. It tells the story of a married, middle-class Italian man who travels to Istanbul and discovers a number of secrets, including his own homosexuality. In 1999 his period piece *Harem Suare* also premiered at Cannes. *His Secret Life* (*Le fate ignoranti*, 2001) is the story of a middle-class woman who discovers, after her husband's death, that he had a male lover for several years. In 2003 Özpetek released his most successful film to date, *Facing Window* (*La finestre di fronte*), the story of a couple whose lives are transformed by the appearance of a strange older man, played by Massimo Girotti in his final role.

DANIEL HENDRICKSON

P

PAGANISM, QUEER

The 'queer' in queer paganism refers both to the form of paganism practiced and to its practitioners. Paganism is a form of spirituality based on a reverence for the natural world and includes an environmental consciousness alongside a radical non-hierarchical politics. While straight pagans might imagine nature as heterosexual and plan their rituals accordingly, queer pagans recognize the profound queerness in a complex natural system that includes such things as male frogs giving birth through their mouths. Nature is not seen to guarantee heterosexuality or to provide recourse for arguments that view homosexuality as unnatural.

Queer paganism in part was born of the Faerie Movement when Harry **Hay** called the first meeting in Arizona in 1979. His goal was to provide an alternative to the capitalistic gay scene, which denied any spirituality, and to explore a possible link between *berdache* (from the French term *bardache*) native people and gay men to see whether gay men might be considered as forming a spiritual tribe in themselves. Interest in queer paganism increased when AIDS triggered a search for a spirituality that could make sense of the deaths while providing a safe and non-judgemental place to mourn and be joyous in a community under attack. Lesbians from the Goddess movement joined together with transgendered peoples, cross-dressers, celibates, drag queens and drag kings to become, as the British Queer Pagan Camp say about their practice, deviant shape-shifters who stir the cauldron of gender in magical work.

See also: Radical Faeries

WREN SIDHE

PARADJANOV, SERGEI
b. 1924; d. 1990
filmmaker

Sergei Paradjanov was born an ethnic Armenian in a multicultural, multilingual area of the Soviet Republic of Georgia. Initially he studied to be a singer, but he quickly became interested in filmmaking. After finishing his studies at the Moscow Film Institute, he made a series of films in the Ukranian language, more or less conforming to the Social Realist standards of the time, before making his 1964 film *Tini zabutykh predkiv* (*Shadows of Forgotten Ancestors*). It was this film that both won him international attention and began his troubles with the Soviet cultural authorities. He was imprisoned throughout most of the 1970s on various charges, including homosexuality and trafficking in art objects and foreign currency. He saw his masterpiece, *Sayat Nova* (*The Color of Pomegranates*, 1968), severely censored. He was allowed to make only two more films before his death in 1990, both making use of folkloric subject matter and lush Georgian locales.

DANIEL HENDRICKSON

PARAGRAPH 175

Paragraph 175 is the section of the German penal code prohibiting sex between men; it was in force from 1871 until 1994. Before 1871 many German states did not prohibit homosexuality. However, in that year, Prussian Emperor Wilhelm I created a single federal state, imposing a Prussian-based criminal code. Paragraph 175 stated that 'any unnatural sex act committed between persons of the same sex' was punishable by imprisonment or loss of civil rights. The post-First World War Weimar Republic practiced relative tolerance towards homosexuality. With the Nazi Party's rise to power in 1933, Hitler invoked Paragraph 175 to justify the execution of the SA. (Stürm Abteilung), Ernst Röhm's paramilitary group. Paragraph 175 was extended in 1935 to punish 'lewd and lascivious behaviour' between men, leading to the imprisonment, torture and execution of 15,000 gay men in concentration camps. The law was not repealed until after the reunification of West and East Germany.

JOHN FORDE

PARENTS, FAMILIES AND FRIENDS OF LESBIANS AND GAYS (PFLAG)

support organization

PFLAG, an international non-profit organization operating out of Washington DC, works to support lesbian, gay, bisexual and transgendered people and their families and friends. The group was set up by Jeanne and Jules Manford in 1972, after they saw their son Morton being attacked at a gay rights rally. About 20 parents attended the first meeting, with similar groups meeting throughout the country. The groups met in Washington DC in 1979 at the First National March for Lesbian and Gay Rights and became an incorporated non-profit organization in 1982. PFLAG's work includes educational programmes, political advocacy and fundraising for college scholarships for gay students.

JOHN FORDE

PARIS

A haven for homosexuality since the French Revolution, when all consenting homosexual acts were legalized, Paris remains one of the world's most gay-friendly cities. The city's cafes and nightlife have hosted gay writers and artists including Arthur Rimbaud, Gertrude Stein, Jean Cocteau, Jean Genet and Simone de Beauvoir. The Marais district boasts a thriving gay community and the annual Gay Pride festival in July is one of Europe's largest gay events. In 2001 the city voted Bertrand **Delanoë** as the city's first openly gay mayor.

JOHN FORDE

PARKER AND HULME CASE (NEW ZEALAND, 1954)

Juliet Parker and Pauline Hulme, both aged 15, were convicted of the murder of Pauline's mother, Honora Hulme, on 22 June 1954, in Christchurch, New Zealand. Hulme's diary, used as evidence during the trial, shows that the pair had a passionate relationship and sometimes enacted heterosexual love scenes. Much was made of their supposed lesbian relationship during the sensationalized trial, contributing to the equation of 'lesbian' with 'mad' and 'killer' in 1950s New Zealand.

The 1994 film *Heavenly Creatures* was an account of the girls' friendship and crime.

GERALDINE TREACHER

PARMAR, PRATIBHA

b. 1977

filmmaker

Born in Nairobi, Parmar arrived in England in 1967. Before making films, she was a youth worker in the Asian community. Her postgraduate study was at the influential Centre for Cultural Studies at Birmingham University, UK. She travelled to India in 1975 and worked on rural development projects, spending three months in Calcutta with Mother Teresa. During the 1980s she was responsible for publishing work by Asian and African women writers for the Sheba Feminist Press. Her film work deals with the culturally and sexually marginalized: examples include *Flesh and Paper* (1990), a celebration of Indian lesbian poet Suniti Barnioshi, *Khush* (1991), an exploration of Asian gay sexuality, *Double the Trouble, Twice the Fun* (1992), examining disability and homosexuality, and *Wavelengths* (1997), set in the sterile world of Internet dating. She has negotiated the mainstream more directly with *Jodie: An Icon* (1996), examining the effects of Jodie Foster as lesbian icon.

MICHAEL PINFOLD

PARMENTER, MICHAEL

b. 1954

dancer, choreographer

Parmenter was raised during the 1960s in a rural New Zealand town where he spent his youth immersed in rugby culture and Brethren fundamentalism. When commenting on his autobiographical work *A Long Undressing* (1995; winner of the New Zealand AIDS Media Award), Parmenter acknowledged that dance was one way to reconcile the two duelling forces of his Christian and gay identities. In the 1980s dance took him to New York and Japan to develop his skills. In 1989 Parmenter was diagnosed as HIV+ and as a response formed, one year later, his own dance company,

Commotion. Significant works from this period include *The Race* (1992) and the dance/opera *Jerusalem* (1999). In 1998 Parmenter was awarded the Member of the New Zealand Order of Merit (MNZM) for his contribution to dance. He speaks publicly on AIDS-related issues and, along with fellow choreographer, Douglas **Wright**, criticizes arts-funding processes in New Zealand.

JO SMITH

PARRY, LORAE

b. 1955

actor, director, playwright

A New Zealand lesbian playwright, Parry was born in Sydney, Australia; she moved to Aotearoa/New Zealand at the age of 15 and later trained at Toi Whakaari (the New Zealand Drama School). In 1993 the newly established The Women's Play Press (a press dedicated to supporting plays featuring strong roles for women) published Parry's second play, *Frontwoman*, a play with a coming-out narrative involving a married suburban housewife and a closeted TV presenter. The play, loosely based on events in 1976 involving a partially closeted lesbian Member of Parliament, Marilyn **Waring**, is considered to be the first lesbian play performed in New Zealand. Parry's 1996 play *Eugenia* was inspired in part by Australasian history as well as by the Brandon **Teena** story. The play focuses on the life of a female Italian migrant who married a woman in the 1910s.

JO SMITH

PASIVO / ACTIVO

Latino counterpart to the **top** and **bottom** dichotomy. Reflecting male heterosexual dominance models and prejudice, the *pasivo* position is considered effeminate, while the *activo* position is coded as virile and manly.

PEDRO ALBORNOZ

PASOLINI, PIER PAOLO

b. 1922; d. 1975

writer, filmmaker

Pier Paolo Pasolini was born and educated in Bologna but spent a great deal of time, including most of the Second World War, in his mother's native area of Friuli. At the age of 20 he published his first book of poetry, written in the Friulian dialect. He would maintain an interest in the various Italian dialects throughout his life. During the Second World War his older brother became a member of the resistance; he was shot in 1945.

Pasolini worked as a teacher after the war and became politically active, serving as secretary of the local division of the Italian Communist Party. In 1949, however, following allegations of sexual misconduct with local boys, he was expelled from the Party. He moved to Rome where he became involved with a group of writers that included Alberto Moravia and Elsa Morante. He worked as a screenwriter, collaborating with Federico Fellini and Bernardo Bertolucci among others. His first novel, *Ragazzi di vita* (Boys from Real Life), was published in 1955. All of the dialogue of this and his later novel *Una vita violenta* (*A Violent Life*, 1959) was written in the Roman dialect. He continued to write poetry, winning an important prize for his collection *Ceneri di Gramsci* (*The Ashes of Gramsci*, 1954).

His career as a filmmaker began in 1961 when he made the film *Accatone!*. He continued to produce films at a rate of one a year, including *Mamma Roma* (1962), featuring Anna Magnani, *Teorema* (*Theorem*, 1968), with Terence Stamp, and *Medea* (1969) starring Maria Callas in a non-singing role. He continued to write, especially poetry and criticism. In the early 1970s he published a regular column on political issues in the newspaper *Il corriere della sera*. These essays were collected into two books; he also published a collection of his theoretical writings on film, *Empirismo eretico* (*Heretical Empiricism*, 1972).

Pasolini made many enemies, especially political ones, and underwent several trials because of his films and writings, usually under the pretext of their obscenity. During the 1970s he made the so-called Trilogy of Life, three films based on classic texts, *The Decameron* (1971) based on Boccaccio, *Canterbury Tales* (1972) based on Chaucer, and *Arabian Nights* (1974) based on the stories of *1001 Arabian Nights*. Although Pasolini himself would famously abjure the project publicly, they remain some of his most popular films.

Pasolini was brutally murdered at Ostia, near Rome, in 1975. The murder is deemed to be the violent reaction of a sole young man (a hustler?) that Pasolini picked up in Rome, but the exact circumstances of his death remain unclear.

Two important posthumous works appeared. His final film, *Salò o le 120 giornate di Sodoma* (*Salò, or the 120 Days of Sodom*, 1975), is a reworking of the Marquis de Sade text, set in fascist Italy. It was conceived at least in part as a corrective to what Pasolini saw as the problems with his Trilogy of Life. His final novel, *Petrolio*, unfinished at the time of his death and published in 1992, is a long series of notes. The main character in the book is the oil executive, Carlo, who not only has two distinct manifestations, but can also become a woman. Both of the works caused a firestorm of controversy and censure.

DANIEL HENDRICKSON

PATTON, CINDY

author

American academic and health researcher whose work has chronicled the history and cultural politics of the AIDS epidemic in America. In her best-known book, *Inventing AIDS* (1991), she argues that AIDS education cannot be politically neutral and that effective AIDS prevention programmes must overcome social prejudices towards sex and homosexuality. She also chronicled the shift in 1980s AIDS activism from gay liberation-inspired resistance to an assimilated AIDS service industry. In *Fatal Advice: How Safe-Sex Education Went Wrong* (1996), a polemic about America's failure to respond to the AIDS epidemic, she argues that US anxieties about pre-marital sex and reluctance to acknowledge homosexuality played into inadequate national education and disease prevention programmes. In *Globalizing AIDS* (2002), she considers the worldwide implications of AIDS treatment and research, and critiques the scientific credibility of American public health policy. Her other works include *Sex & Germs: The Politics of AIDS* (1986) and *Making It: A Woman's Guide to Sex in the Age of AIDS* (1987).

JOHN FORDE

PAU, ELLEN

b. 1961

video artist

Born in Hong Kong, Ellen Pau is a self-taught artist who works as an MTV director, cinematographer, video artist, curator, educator and arts administrator. She is the co-founder and artistic director for a multimedia art collective in Hong Kong, Videotage (founded in 1985). In 1993 Pau made a video called *Songs of the Goddess,* featuring the famous Cantonese opera duo and alleged lesbian couple Yam Kim-Fai and Baak Suet Sin. The video has since been screened at many festivals overseas as a major lesbian work of Hong Kong's independent video scene. Pau has also contributed videos to international art collections, including the forty-ninth International Art Exhibition in the Venice Biennale. Her works (especially *Pledges Series [1993–2001], Drained Series [1989–96]* and *Recycling Cinema [1999–2000]*), usually characterized by strong aesthetic and rhythmical forms, are always polysemic, full of politically charged critiques of post-colonial urban Hong Kong, and intertwined with personal explorations of hybridized cultural and sexual identities.

TRAVIS KONG

PET SHOP BOYS

pop music duo

The Pet Shop Boys are a British pop duo formed in 1981 by Neil Tennant (b. 1954) and Chris Lowe (b. 1959). They scored a hit with their first single, 'West End Girls', in 1985. The song's literate lyrics are both witty and heartfelt. Songs about consumer capitalism, the cult of celebrity and the fall of the Soviet Union – as well as that staple of the pop song, unrequited love – are set to catchy dance music throughout their oeuvre. Although it is easy to read even the earliest Pet Shop Boys' songs as queer, given their bittersweet wit and their sometimes campy excess, the queer content of the songs became more pronounced once Neil Tennant publicly came out in the mid-1990s, around the time of the release of *Very* (1993). (While Chris Lowe has declined to define his sexuality publicly, stating simply that such definitions are not important to an understanding of his music, neither has he distanced himself from the gay content of the music or lyrics.) Although they never again reached the level of popularity in the US that greeted their first hits, they have retained a loyal fan base in the UK and are fixtures on the pop music scene in Britain. Later songs addressed gay culture directly, tackling such topics as AIDS, casual sex and coming out. Indeed, it is possible to see the albums *Very, Bilingual* (1996) and *Nightlife* (1999) as a trilogy about the joys and discontents of life as a sophisticated, cosmopolitan gay man at the end of the 1990s.

DAVID PENDLETON

PETTIT, SARAH

b. 1966; d. 2003

journalist

One of the leading lights of American journalism, the Amsterdam-born Pettit's commitment to lesbian and gay issues challenged how the mainstream press viewed and reported gay culture. In 1989 she became an editor at *OutWeek*, a new gay and lesbian paper, alongside journalist Michelangelo **Signorile**. Under their leadership, *OutWeek* grabbed attention with its coverage of advocacy group ACT UP and its editorial endorsement of outing public figures. The magazine folded in 1991 and in 1992 she and Michael Goff founded *OUT* magazine; she became its editor-in-chief in 1997. As editor she brought lesbian and gay issues into the mainstream media, championed gay rights initiatives and courted high-profile community figures, famously persuading comedian Ellen **DeGeneres** to come out in the magazine's May 1997 issue. She worked at *Newsweek* as a senior arts and entertainment editor from 1998 until her death from cancer at the age of 36 in New York City.

See also: ACT UP

JOHN FORDE

PHARMACEUTICAL COMPANIES

Pharmaceutical companies are licensed by governments to develop, advertise and distribute drugs and medicine to the populace. Because these companies support themselves through proceeds culled from sick persons – individuals who often have limited access to funds – many individuals, for example AIDS activists, are critical of the companies' routine policy of denying life-saving drugs to the lower classes and the indigent.

Pharmaceutical companies develop new drugs and medications through a series of clinical trials. These trials tend to be costly and can take years to complete. Pharmaceutical companies tout their products as the best available on the market. Doing so is one way of recouping the money spent on research and development. A series of recent high-profile cases have underscored how some pharmaceutical companies exaggerate the care-giving properties of a particular drug in order to attract large numbers of consumers. Additionally, since competition between them is often intense, pharmaceutical companies are known for offering perks to doctors and pharmacists for aggressively advertising their products. Such actions have had deleterious effects on the public image of the companies, causing many individuals to view them critically.

Since pharmaceutical companies are capitalist entities, profit is the bottom line. This reality has raised the ire of many AIDS activists over the years who have accused the companies of profiting from human sickness and suffering. In 2001 a group of AIDS activists, led by the Treatment Action Campaign (TAC), worked to combat the money-making guiding principle of pharmaceutical companies in South Africa. The TAC succeeded in encouraging the South African government to import shipments of generic (read: less expensive) AIDS anti-retrovirals, an action that violated patents issued to the pharmaceutical companies. The South African government continued this action for a period of some months, sparking lawsuits by a collective of 41 pharmaceutical companies. In defending its actions, the South African government illuminated its position as a cash-poor country with millions of AIDS-infected individuals. Humanitarian support and attention came from all corners of the world, showing the pharmaceutical companies in a negative light. The 41 pharmaceutical companies eventually dropped their lawsuits and agreed to relax their policies on patents.

Some pharmaceutical companies have made attempts to change their image as being solely cash-driven forces. They have even embarked on endeavours that position them supporting their critics. An example of this is described in the recent essay collection *The AIDS Crisis Is Ridiculous* (2004) by AIDS activist Gregg **Bordowitz**, wherein Bordowitz describes the support given to him by pharmaceutical company Abbott Laboratories for his 2002 art installation at the Museum of Contemporary Art in Chicago. Bordowitz's exhibit, titled *Drive*, features a race car in the shape of a pill emblazoned with pharmaceutical company logos. His commentary is meant to draw light to the expense of AIDS drugs. In addition to the fact that Abbott extended financial support for the exhibit – underwriting the entire show – the organization implied institutional support for the artistic endeavour in that it did not attempt to censor Bordowitz's negative characterization of the company.

Bibliography

Bordowitz, Gregg (2004) *The AIDS Crisis is Ridiculous and Other Writings, 1986–2003*, Cambridge and London: MIT Press.

CHRIS BELL

PHILIPPINES, LITERATURE

In the Philippines, queer literature appeared relatively late by Western terms. It emerged during the 1960s but has only flourished since the 1990s. The Philippines is one of the leading Asian producers of queer literature.

While Filipinos are more tolerant of gays and lesbians than most Asians, the Philippines remains a strongly Catholic and patriarchal society. Many families also possess Chinese heritage. As Filipino-Chinese gays have reported, Chinese families regard homosexuality as an unspeakable topic. These conservative traditions have slowed the development of a strong queer community and hampered the production of queer literature. This oppression and silence has meant that queer works are produced almost exclusively in urban areas for urban audiences.

A long-time colony of Spain, the Philippine Islands became an American territory in 1898 and only gained independence following the Second World War. This historical background and a Filipino diaspora have shaped the literature of the Philippines. Many Filipino writers have studied and lived in the United States, blurring the line between Filipino and Filipino-American literature. Queer authors produce works in both Tagalog and English. Relatively few Tagalog writings have been translated into English.

The first writings by gays challenged the conservative macho culture of the Philippines. Playwright Orlando Nadres shows the formation of an alliance between out and closeted gay men in *Hanggang Dito na Lamang at Maraming Salamat* (Until Then, Thank You Very Much, 1974). The story revolves around the character of Fidel, a middle-aged man whose respectability is threatened by his homosexuality. Nadres was the first widely performed playwright to address the class conflict between obviously effeminate gay men (*bakla*) and masculine-looking and-acting men. The gays who were marked as *bakla* were, for many years, the only ones who publicly identified as queer. In a serialized *komik-novel* published in 1975, Elena Padron also challenged gender identity by telling the story of a post-op male-to-female transsexual seeking revenge on the man who had wronged her before the operation.

More recent queer writers focus on self-affirmation. Danton Remoto and J. Neil C. Garcia, both noted poets and newspaper columnists, are among the best-known and most prolific of the gay authors. Remoto's *Skin, Voices, Faces* (1991) and Garcia's *Closet Quivers* (1992) both reached wide audiences. Along with their edited collections,

Ladlad (1994) and Ladlad 2 (1996), these writings were produced with the stated aim of helping gays and lesbians achieve a sense of pride within the queer community.

Philippine literature is notable for rich characterizations and an emphasis upon substance. Tony Perez's book, *Cubao 1980 at Iba Pang mga Katha* (1992) is an anthology comprising a novella, poems, short stories, letters and a play. Perez controversially argues that opposition to *bakla* culture will strengthen the Philippine gay community. Other notable works include Aida Santos' and Ginay Villar's *Woman to Woman: A Collection of Lesbian Reflections* (1975), R. Zamora Linmark's *Rolling the R's* (1990); Jessica Hagedorn's *Dogeaters* (1990) and Cecilia Manguerra Brainard's anthology *Contemporary Fiction by Filipinos in America* (1997).

Bibliography

Brainard, Cecilia Manguerra (ed.) (1997) *Contemporary Fiction by Filipinos in America,* Pasig City, Philippines: Anvil.

Garcia, J. Neil C. and Remoto, Danton (eds) (1994) *Ladlad: An Anthology of Philippine Gay Writing,* Manila: Anvil.

—— (eds) (1996) *Ladlad 2: An Anthology of Philippine Gay Writing*, Pasig City, Philippines: Anvil.

Further reading

Garcia, J. Neil C. (1998) *Slip/pages: Essays on Gay Criticism*, Manila: De La Salle University Press.

CARYN E. NEUMANN

PHONE SEX

The practice of talking oneself or others into sexual excitation/orgasm via the telephone; undertaken in relationships or, more anonymously, through sex-business phone lines.

MICHAEL PINFOLD

PICANO, FELICE

b. 1944

writer

One of the most celebrated gay writers of his generation, Felice Picano's semi-autobiographical novels and other writings have defined post-Second World War American gay sensibility. He received acclaim for *Late in the Season* (1981), a drama set on Fire Island, and *Ambidextrous: The Secret Lives of Children* (1985), the first of an autobiographical trilogy of novels completed by *Men Who Loved Me* (1989) and *A House on the Ocean, A House on the Bay* (1997). He is best known for the work *Like People In History* (1996), which chronicles 40 years of gay history as experienced by narrator, Roger Sansarc, and for *The Book Of Lies* (2000), a satire of gay academia. He co-edited *The New Joy of Gay Sex* (1992) with Charles Silverstein. He also co-founded Sea Horse Press, one of America's first gay publishing houses, and the gay writers' group The Violet Quill Club alongside Edmund **White** and Andrew Holleran.

JOHN FORDE

PIERRE ET GILLES

Blanchard, Gilles

b. 1953

artist

Commoy, Pierre

b. 1949

artist

Gilles Blanchard and Pierre Commoy are French male artists who have worked together in Paris ever since they fell in love in 1976. Their extravagant photographs, combined with collage and painting, refer to classical, fine and pop art as well as popular culture and camp. Their work is inspired by kitsch memorabilia, Southeast Asian postcards and homoerotic magazines. Pierre and Gilles present celebrities such as Marc Almond, Nina Hagen, Prince, Jean-Paul Gaultier, Michael Jackson, Madonna and Boy George as modern idols and goddesses. They homoeroticize Christian iconography and Greek, Hindu and Egyptian mythologies. Muscular male models are often shown semi-naked or fully exposed in vulnerable positions – bleeding, crying or covered with semen. Some of the photographs integrate the imageries of hardcore pornography, urban violence and martyrdom. They express a unique queer perspective on ancient and modern cults, body worship and sexual subcultures such as sadomasochism, fetishism and cross-dressing.

GILAD PADVA

PINK DOLLAR

The terms pink dollar, pink pound and pink economy are widely circulated in discussions around the growing interdependency between queer communities and the marketplace. Gay men, and to a lesser extent lesbian women, have been identified as a niche market of untapped disposable capital, and mainstream commercial involvement in gay and lesbian communities has intensified accordingly. Gay and lesbian print culture and gay ghettos have become increasingly gentrified and queer community events more dependent upon large-scale corporate funding. Critical discussions of the pink dollar have warned that the radicalism of gay and lesbian politics has been lost to the mainstreaming efforts of gay and lesbian organizations attempting to secure monies from conservative sponsors. Further, the myth of the pink dollar negates the fact that many lesbians and gay men still live in poverty and are unable to access the services offered in commercialized gay ghettos and community events.

See also: Ghetto, gay

KELLIE BURNS

PINK TRIANGLE

In the concentration camps of Nazi Germany, gay men convicted under Paragraphs 174, 175 and 176 of the Reich penal code were forced to wear a pink triangle made of cloth. During the late 1980s, ACT UP (AIDS Coalition to Unleash Power) inverted the pink triangle, reclaiming it as a symbol of gay pride and political activism.

CHRIS BELL

PODESWA, JEREMY
b. 1962
filmmaker

An essential figure on the New Queer Toronto Wave of the 1990s, Jeremy Podeswa trained at Ryerson University and the American Film Institute and toiled on the short-film and queer festival circuit before commanding attention with his first feature *Eclipse* (1994), an artful, trilingual, pansexual carousel of horny but alienated Torontonians caught in a solar eclipse. His prize-winning second feature, *The Five Senses* (1999), followed a similar vein with interwoven narratives, multisexual labyrinths (and beefcake), high-powered acting and evocative urban symbolism. After bread-and-butter exercises in TV movies and cable, Podeswa then stunned everyone with a brilliant short fiction about the masochistic eroticism of an abused and sequestered teenager, *Touch* (2001). No one disagreed with the Toronto International Film Festival programmer who compared the film to Genet: 'Raw, beautiful and haunting, it may be Podeswa's best work'.

THOMAS WAUGH

455

POLAND, LITERATURE

Polish bookstores do not have 'Gay and Lesbian Literature' sections and only recently has the notion of gay, lesbian or queer literature been broached publicly there. But ask some Polish readers about homosexual writers or books and one is sure to hear a list of names and titles that in the Anglo–American context would have long constituted a queer canon.

Witold Gombrowicz (1904–69) usually heads this list with his *Dziennik* (*Diaries*, 1953–66) and the novel *Transatlantyk* (*TransAtlantic*, 1953), which, written during exile in Buenos Aires, presents the protagonist's dilemma of association between a camp gay Argentine and the reserved Polish émigré community. The intense friendship of authoresses Maria Dąbrowska (1889–1965) and Anna Kowalska (1903–69) has long been grist for literary rumour mills. The homosexual-motif-studded oeuvre of Jarosław Iwaszkiewicz (1894–1980) includes his autobiographical novel *Ogrody* (Gardens, 1974) and the 1936 story *Zygfryd* (Siegfried), which depicts a friendship between a rich arts patron and a circus acrobat, and was adapted for the screen in 1987. Julian Stryjkowski (1905–96) engages his homosexual and Jewish identities in the 1983 novel *Milczenie* (Silence). Jerzy Andrzejewski (1909–83) presents homosexuality in a more cheerful light in his novel *Idzie skacząc po górach* (*A Sitter For a Satyr*, 1963), among others. And Miron Białoszewski (1922–83) follows the figure of Le, his real-life partner, through a number of books of reportage-like short prose; his linguistically inventive poetry may also one day prove fertile ground for queer interpretation.

All of these early works, however, were written in what critic Błażej Warkocki (2002) calls a 'poetic of inexpressible desire', and homosexuality figures in them as only one of a cluster of themes. An important exception to this is the 1986 novel *Rudolf* by Marian Pankowski

(b. 1919), which deals exclusively and value-neutrally with a sexual relationship between two men. Pankowski, who has lived in Belgian exile since liberation from a concentration camp in 1945, was the subject of a critical reappraisal in a 2004 issue of the magazine *Ha!Art*, and may be considered a point of departure for current and future gay Polish writing.

The 1990s saw the publication in Poland of a handful of books dealing with homosexuality, but in what several critics have called a 'pre-emancipatory' mode. In his novels *W ptaszarni* (In the Aviary, 1989) and *Al fine* (1996), a memoir, and several volumes of poetry, Grzegorz Musiał (b. 1952) presents homosexual figures at odds with the moral decrepitude of the world. Marek Nowakowski (b. 1935) portrays the homosexual as outsider in his novel *Grecki bożek* (Greek God, 1993). And Marzena Broda (b. 1966) gives voice to the alienation of lesbians in Polish society in her 1994 volume of poetry *Cudzoziemszczyzna* (Land of Foreigners). The late 1990s, according to writer Izabela **Filipiak**, was a time of development for gay and lesbian consciousness and of increased public visibility; Filipiak's own work, which integrates a lesbian perspective throughout, has played a prominent role in this. Books by writers such as Jeanette **Winterson**, Alan **Hollinghurst** and Jean **Genet** have also been made available in translation to Polish readers since the 1990s. And largely through contact with the work of queer thinkers ranging from Foucault to Fuss, gay and lesbian criticism has made strides in the academy, with the production of symposia and scholarship dealing with homosexual identity in Poland.

With homosexuals' increased visibility has come a wave of homophobic discourse and acts over the last few years (e.g., violent attacks by skinheads during the first gay rights parade in Kraków in May 2004). This has prompted Filipiak to compare the defamation of gays and lesbians nowadays to that of Jews and women a century ago, and Błazej Warkocki and Zbyszek Sypniewski to address the situation in their 2004 edited volume *Homofobia po polsku* (Homophobia Polish-Style). The meaning of these circumstances for the future of queer Polish literature is unclear. But a new generation of writers is clearly emerging, one aware of its own literary traditions and searching for an authentic language for newly expressible desires. This search can be seen in the poems of *Dolna Wilda* (The Lower Wilda, 2002) by Edward Pasewicz (b. 1971) and the stories of *Lustro* (Mirror, 2001) by Ewa Schilling (b. 1971). An important watershed is the novel *Lubiewo* (2005) by Michał Witkowski (b. 1975), which explores the rather squalid world of 'two old queens' and the homosexual cultures of Socialist versus post-Socialist Poland. A 'final clearing of accounts with pre-emancipatory Poland', as critic Alessandro Amenta (2004) describes it, it was the most enthusiastically reviewed and talked-about book in Poland of the first half of 2005, inaugurating a new and refreshingly positive awareness of queer writers and culture among the literary mainstream.

Bibliography

Amenta, Alessandro (2004) 'Polish Literature', available at: http://www.glbtq.com/literature/polish_lit.html.

Warkocki, Błażej (2002) 'Otwieranie toalety. Czy w polsce istnieją geje?', *Res Publica Nowa* 168: 9, 52–57.

Further reading

Cuber, Marta (2003) 'Les-Silent-Story. O polskie prozie lesbijskiej', *Ha!Art* 14: 1.

Ostolski, Adam (2005) 'Żydżi, geje i wojna cywilizacji', *Ha!Art* 23: 16–17.

Śmieja, Wojciech (2005) 'Była, jest, będzie? Polska literatura homoseksualna i gejowska. Próba zarysu', *Pogranicza* 54: 1, 31–40.

WILLIAM MARTIN

POLARI

British gay slang, popularized during the 1940s and 1950s as part of the underground gay scene. It was used by comedian Kenneth **Williams** during his 1960s *Round the Horne* radio sketches.

JOHN FORDE

POMO AFRO HOMOS

performance group

Founded by Djola Branner, Brian Freeman and Eric Gupton, the Pomo Afro Homos (Post-Modern African-American Homosexuals) emerged onto the San Francisco area performance scene in 1991. Marvin K. White later joined the ensemble following Gupton's untimely illness from AIDS complications. Known for recasting the traditional forms, omissions and stereotypes of black gay male culture/identity in their seminal stagings *Fierce Love* and *Dark Fruit*, the company attracted critical and popular acclaim through a performance style that fused storytelling and preaching with excellent comic timing. Viewed alongside precursors such as poet/playwright Ntozake Shange and Danitra Vance (the first African-American woman to be a regular cast member on the TV show *Saturday Night Live*), the Pomos served to redefine stage representation and ethic through a new, hard-driving force of form, style and voice in works that merged a distinct textual lyricism in the examination of public/private scripts–boldly and without apology.

PAMELA BOOKER

POPE, THE AND CATHOLICISM

The Pope, or Bishop of Rome, is considered the 'shepherd of the flock', the leader with full power over the entire Catholic Church and the bishops. The Church estimates that 17 per cent of the world population is Catholic, having received the sacrament of baptism, a ritual usually performed shortly after birth and signifying that the individual belongs to the Church.

The election of the Pope is indicative of the political moods and power games within the Church at that time. Under Pope John XXIII, and through the Second Vatican Council (1962–5), a more profound understanding of the basic requirements and expectations of the Church was developed, however the election of Pope John Paul II (1978–2005) signalled a sharp turn away from all democratic experiments, reviving instead the old alliance with the economic potentates to which the Church historically has been allied. The Vatican, the minuscule state that is the Papal 'Holy See' in Rome, is in fact connected with economic and political interests in which the Institute for Religious Works/Marcinkus financial scandal of 1982 highlighted the presence of the international political right. Another organization with great influence over papal political decisions is the Opus Dei.

The Vatican City retains the right to vote in the United Nations and leads alliances to influence, at international levels, decisions relating to the prevention of AIDS (John Paul II notoriously was opposed to the use of condoms), family and demographic policies and women's rights. A striking example of this was the Vatican boycott of birth control at the 1994 Cairo Conference on Population and Development.

A crucial role is also played by the Congregation for the Doctrine of the Faith, a Vatican organ aimed at the doctrinal control of the Church which, as far back as 1986, in a document dealing with the 'pastoral care of homosexual persons', reiterated the doctrine of the sin committed by homosexual persons at the moment in which they accept their sexuality. This concept was reconfirmed in 2003 in the 'Considerations Regarding Proposals to Give Legal Recognition to Unions Between Homosexual Persons'. This document recommends that Catholic politicians take all possible measures to oppose proposed legislation recognizing the rights of gay and lesbian couples.

During the papacy of John Paul II, the Pope assumed a remarkable mass media role. Through declarations, mass audiences and official releases, the Pope tends to represent the figure of the benevolent father–patriarch, a point of reference for those who feel the need for a strong moral authority of a traditional kind and those who see in the Church a refuge from the evils of modern life and wars. This consistently positive image has been belied by some Papal acts and positions, including the famous salute from the balcony of General Pinochet (1987) and the ambiguous role played by the Pope at the time of the war in the former Yugoslavia, with the pre-emptive recognition of the state of Croatia (1992), supported by an extremist Catholic right wing and marked by both homophobic and xenophobic attitudes.

Following Pope Jean Paul's death in 2005, Cardinal Joseph Ratzinger was voted in as the new Pope Benedict XVI. His strict dogmatic approach to homosexuality does not bode well for the relationship between glbts and the Catholic Church.

FRANCESCA PALAZZI ARDUINI

PORN STAR

In stark contrast to the heterosexual adult film industry, gay male pornography, and gay porn stars in particular, hold a rather privileged position in postwar gay culture. Free of the stigma and marginalization of their 'straight' counterparts, gay porn has played an invaluable political role in both affirming gay male sexuality and simultaneously making visible that which for so long had either been suppressed or denied. The gay porn star has therefore risen to the iconic status of celebrity royalty in contemporary gay culture, proactively participating in public Gay Pride parades and sex education debates, and is revered, albeit contentiously, as the acceptable erotic ideal to which all contemporary queers should aspire.

The origins of the gay porn star can be traced back to the American underground film classics of Kenneth **Anger** and James **Bidgood**, to the physique magazines of such companies as the Athletic Model Guild of the 1950s and 1960s, which launched the careers of such pseudo-porn stars as Joe **Dallesandro** and Bobby Kendall. But it wasn't until the landmark release in 1971 of the first 'official' and commercially successful gay porn film, Wakefield Poole's *The Boys in the Sand*, that a gay porn icon was born – the golden 'boy-next-door', Casey Donovan (1943–87). Born John Calvin Culver, aspiring actor and fashion model, Donovan quickly became the positive face of the emergent post-Stonewall gay movement of the time, and remained an idol for gay men worldwide until his AIDS-related death in 1987. However, his success was swiftly overshadowed by the arrival of the hypermasculine Al Parker (1952–92) in 1976, whose contrasting dark rugged looks and butch 'clone' appearance epitomized a hedonistic new generation of liberated gay men exploring their sexuality in the pre-AIDS promiscuous milieu of the late 1970s.

Whereas the burgeoning gay porn industry had expanded quite considerably throughout the 1970s, the advent of home video in the 1980s heralded a major turning point for the adult film industry, both gay and straight. The decline of the porn theatre and the potential for wider distribution and commercial success that the new video market promised led to a major expansion and diversification of the industry, and subsequently a whole new 'stable' of performers emerged. But in contrast to the openly gay-identified personas of Donovan and Parker, the 1980s witnessed a new obsession in gay culture with straight men in 'gay-for-pay' porn. Ironically, it was the straight performer, such as 'powertool' Jeff **Stryker** and his rival Ryan Idol, who was to epitomize gay male sexuality throughout the 1980s and early 1990s, exclusively performing the active or 'top' sexual role to the passive, gay-identified 'bottom' – the most famous of these was Joey Stefano, who would go on to die of a drug overdose in 1994. Problematically, however, the heterosexuality of these stars was often overemphasized, marketing promoting them as somehow more sexually desirable than their gay-identified counterparts, possibly as a means by which to circumvent the stigma of AIDS by shifting focus to the 'untainted tool' of the heterosexual male.

The versatility and accessibility of video also enabled greater ethnic diversity in the industry than previously had been possible, and by the 1990s gay porn began to experiment more freely with the age, ethnicity and body type of performer featured. The young, 'pumped up', white Californians that had so dominated the 1980s scene thus gave way to a multitude of erotic 'types', from the South American and Australasian 'exotica' of Kristen Bjorn to the urban 'blatino' youths of New York.

The successful exportation of internationally produced pornography in the 1990s, particularly from Europe, also posed a real challenge to the racially segregated dominance held by North American producers. The global success of iconic French producer Jean Daniel Cadinot, and the explosion of production in Eastern Europe, particularly in Budapest and Prague by such companies as Bel Ami, led to the rise of Czech porn stars Lukas Ridgeston and Johan Paulik, and a new shift of erotic focus to much younger, 'barely legal' performers, or 'twinks'.

This diversification of the industry has achieved even greater expansion at the turn of the new millennium with the impact of the World Wide Web and online Internet pornography. The surprise success of home-made **amateur porn** has enabled a space for new types and definitions of 'porn star', such as the gay-man-on-the-street opportunistic 'gonzo' productions that bestow instant porn stardom on the everyday queer. As a community that is defined by its sexual activity, gay culture often views pornography as a vital means for affirming gay sexuality in an ever-changing climate of intolerance or indifference. The gay porn star, in his many guises, is therefore not only a mirror to the changing face of gay style and identity throughout the years, but a measure of the highly complex and shifting nature of gay sexuality beyond the heteronormative.

ROBIN GRIFFITHS

PORNOGRAPHY, INTERNET

Since the World Wide Web emerged during the mid-1990s, pornographic material has been one of its chief outputs. Pornography was the first e-commerce sector to post real profits from online transactions, and it has been the first to incur the scrutiny of lawmakers. This has resulted in a host of legal frameworks emerging, particularly in the United States, aimed at protecting children from exploitation via or on the web. The Child Online Protection Act (COPA), the Children's Internet Protection Act (CIPA), the Communications Decency Act (CDA), to name but three, aim to prevent the consumption of imagery by, or the appearance in imagery of, the vulnerable. The proliferation of gay-related pornographic material has enhanced a burgeoning sex-toy and video/DVD market, has promoted the careers of a number of gay performers and, more positively, has allowed free (or subscription payment) access to the homosexually inclined and curious.

MICHAEL PINFOLD

PORTER, COLE

b. 1891; d. 1964

composer

One of the twentieth century's most frequently recorded and performed popular composers, Cole Porter's prodigious output includes songs, musicals and film soundtracks. After an Ivy League education, he made a tour of duty in France during the First World War, marrying his friend Linda Lee Thomas in 1919. Although never revealed publicly, his homosexuality was an open secret in his social circle and he pursued a number of relationships with men (largely tolerated by Thomas). He wrote music for several Broadway plays and films, including *Anything Goes* (1934; filmed 1936), *Rosalie* (1937), *Broadway Melody* (1940), *Kiss Me Kate* (1948; filmed 1953) and *High Society* (1956). In 1945 Warner Bros released *Night and Day*, a sanitized biopic about the Porters' marriage, starring Cary **Grant** as a heterosexual Cole.

Porter's homosexuality, largely closeted during his personal life, was expressed in his lyrics. His work provides a musical study of the closet, be it the bold, sexually explicit 'It's Too Darn Hot' or 'I Get A Kick Out of You', his melancholy torch song 'Every Time We Say Goodbye' or his cynical portrait of sex as a commercial transaction in 'Love for Sale'. This queer sensibility was explored to huge success in *Red Hot + Blue* (1990), a selection of Porter's songs reinterpreted by artists including U2, Annie Lennox, Neneh Cherry, Jimmy Somerville and Iggy Pop, with profits going to AIDS research and relief. The Red Hot Organization cited Porter as a pioneer in the struggle for sexual tolerance, acknowledging his musical and lyrical experimentation.

JOHN FORDE

PORTER, DOROTHY FEATHERSTONE

b. 1954

poet

Porter is a critically acclaimed Australian poet, best known for her popular verse novels: works include *The Monkey's Mask* (1994), *What a Piece of Work* (1999), *Akhenaten*

(1992) and *Wild Surmise* (2002). The lesbian crime romance *The Monkey's Mask* was one of Australia's fastest selling books of poetry and the work was both published internationally and turned into a film. Other works include *Other Worlds: Poems 1997–2001* (2001), *Crete* (1996) and two performed opera librettos with composer Jonathan Mills, *The Ghost Wife (1999)* and *The Eternity Man* (2002).

Porter's poetry is often narrative-based, lyrical, sardonic and passionate, with much lesbian and male homosexual content. It is best defined by the knowingness of its poetics, sensuality of metaphor and wide-ranging subject matter; she covers areas as diverse as ancient Egypt and astrobiology. Porter says that while 'the sexual metaphor [is] the most potent language we have', it is 'also the most frustratingly limited'.

MICHAEL HURLEY

PORTILLO, LOURDES

b. 1944

filmmaker

Lourdes Portillo was born in Chihuahua, Mexico. She is a self-identified Chicana filmmaker. As a co-founder of Cine Acción in San Francisco, she has contributed to the organizational efforts aimed at the role of Chicana/Latina women in film production of the 1980s and the 1990s. Portillo explores women's issues in documentaries such as *Las madres de la Plaza de Mayo* (*The Mothers of the Plaza de Mayo* [1985], co-directed with Sonia Muñoz), depicting the resistance of a group of women against the Argentine dictatorship of the 1980s. The response of Hispanic youth to the celebrity of Texan superstar Selena is the theme of *Corpus: A Home Movie for Selena* (1999). *Señorita extraviada* (*Missing Young Woman*, 2002) documents the mysterious killings and disappearances of young women in Ciudad Juárez, Chihuahua. In *La ofrenda* (*The Days of the Dead*, 1989) Portillo connects the celebration of the dead in Oaxaca, Mexico and the Mission District in San Francisco with issues of AIDS, gender switching and sexual orientation.

TRINO SANDOVAL

POSTCOLONIALISM AND GLBTQ CULTURE

Initially a term derived from literary studies and the examination of British Commonwealth literature, definitions of postcolonialism are the subject of heated debate. Nonetheless, broadly defined, postcolonialism refers to the cultural, social and political experiences of a formerly colonized nation. Key concerns for scholars in the field of postcolonial studies revolve around questions of territorial conquests by imperialist powers (both historical and contemporary), the aftermath and continued effects of colonization on the identities of contemporary communities and the differing responses of colonized subjects to colonial invasion. A central problem of postcolonialism is the issue of how the formerly colonized can express agency, sovereignty and national identity within the institutional and juridical frameworks inherited from the former colonial powers from which they seek to assert independence. As such, literature in the field of postcolonial studies has often privileged issues of national identity over the more personal issue of sexual identity.

One of the writers most influential in postcolonial theory is Frantz **Fanon**, who in his book *Black Skin White Masks* (1967) associated homosexuality with white racism and argued that no indigenous homosexuality existed in Africa. The relationship between postcolonialism and glbtq culture is thus a fraught one, given that Fanon's nationalism represents a common view that considers homosexuality as a leftover of colonization and as the impure side effects of contact with a decadent and immoral

461

Western civilization. While a critique of the importation of Western constructs of sexuality and gender are important, such a stringent denial of activities that fall outside a heterosexual model also functions to reinscribe homophobia. Alternately, the arguably ingrained homophobia that can be found in some postcolonial discourse meets its essentializing counter-image in the glbtq cultural privileging of Euro/American frameworks for discussing sexual identity and the subsequent privileging of sexual categories over issues of national, ethnic and racial specificities.

A newly emergent area of study, 'Postcolonial Queer', attempts to speak across the perceived divide between postcolonialism and glbtq issues. A key focus of some arguments concerns the relatively recent Western privileging of a hetero-/homosexual divide that emerged in the United States during the mid-twentieth century. Such a structuring logic, when applied to questions of sexuality and gender identity in Asia and the Pacific (for example), effectively obliterates the local specificities of such cultures, where the model of 'third gender' operates. In such an approach, the national specificities of indigenous queer identities such as the Indonesian *warias*, Thai *kathoey*, Filipino *bayot* or the Polynesian *fa'fafine* are erased. Thus the concept of 'Postcolonial Queer' functions to address homosexual and queer identity from a transnational perspective by studying how national and ethnic specificities intersect with issues of sexuality and gender. Given the diverse models for understanding sex and gender practices generated by a transnational analysis, one might also consider how such an approach can aid the examination of Western and globalized forms of homosexual and queer subjectivities. Thus, while the study of glbtq cultures can benefit from attention paid to the postcolonial condition, postcolonial scholars have much to learn from glbtq studies.

Given the apparent internationalization of homosexual and queer identities (both Western and otherwise), one could argue that queer culture parallels and indeed dramatizes the social and economic factors of globalization. Postcolonial studies not only examine the heritage of colonial invasion, it also examines how contemporary power formations (from the United States, Japan, Australia, China) continue the networks of colonization established in earlier centuries. Discussions of globalization suggest that nation-states are in decline and that the saliencies of these frameworks for understanding cultural identity are waning. Yet these events are occurring within a postcolonial context in which indigenous sovereignty and postcolonial nationalism are of paramount concern to those individuals and groups formerly colonized. The political desire to assert indigenous nationalism and to defend the nationalist cause at times comes at the cost of suppressing internal differences (Fanon's homophobia being a case in point). Glbtq culture not only exists across the boundaries demarcating national identity (with media products and Internet technologies as prime materials for the construction of this collective and global imaginary), glbtq transnational cultural formations also demonstrate how postcolonial subjectivity is equally transnational and globalized (witness the effect of hip-hop culture upon indigenous movements in the South Pacific or the internationalization of Fourth World arts and media). The study of 'Postcolonial Queer' is thus a study of the relationship between historical and contemporary social, cultural and economic forces wherein issues of nationality, ethnicity and race intersect with issues of gender and sexuality.

See also: Indigenous queer identities

Further reading

Cruz, Arnaldo and Manalansan, Martin (eds) (2002) *Queer Globalizations: Citizenship and the Afterlife of Colonialism*, New York: New York University Press.

Hawley, John C. (ed.) (2001) *Postcolonial, Queer: Theoretical Intersections*, Albany: State University of New York.

JO SMITH

POST-GAY

A term coined in the late 1990s and used (somewhat controversially) within the gay community to describe a gay sensibility in which sexual orientation is no longer a defining criterion of personal identity. The term was used by writer Edmund **White** in 1994 to describe gay authors who were frank about their sexuality but who did not feel limited to writing solely about gay subject matter, and was adopted and expanded upon by British-born editor James Collard as part of his short-lived tenure as editor-in-chief of *Out* magazine. In a 1998 interview Collard argued that advances in gay rights and social tolerance towards homosexuality meant that gay culture could progress beyond the struggle for equal rights and rigid or separatist identity politics. Critics countered that post-gay privileged a largely white, middle-class, gay demographic and ignored the prejudice suffered by many gay and lesbian people. Collard was accused of alienating the queer community, and following a drop in *Out*'s readership, resigned as editor. The murder of Matthew **Shepard** in late 1998 focused international attention upon the prevalence of **homophobia** in American society, effectively negating post-gay theory.

JOHN FORDE

POTATO QUEEN

An Asian man who is predominantly sexually interested in Western or Caucasian men.

TRAVIS KONG

POWER, TYRONE

b. 1913; d. 1958

actor

An American film actor, Tyrone Power emerged as a leading Hollywood star in such popular classics as *The Rains Came* (1939), *The Mask of Zorro* (1940) and *The Razor's Edge* (1946). Part of an acting dynasty, Power was noted less for his thespian talents than his good looks and brooding screen presence. Married three times, Power is widely rumoured to have been bisexual and has been portrayed in several posthumous biographies as an unhappy man who sought to hide his homosexual tendencies, succumbing to alcoholism and dying prematurely of a heart attack at age 45.

BRETT FARMER

PRAUNHEIM, ROSA VON

b. 1942

filmmaker

Born Holger Mischnitzky in Riga, Rosa von Praunheim is one of Germany's leading gay activists. His films provoke self-examination by gay people and advance gay rights. In the early 1960s he took his name from 'rosa Winkel', a reference to the pink triangle of the Nazi era, 'von', from German nobility and Praunheim from the Frankfurt suburb of his childhood. His first gay film, *Nicht die Homosexuelle is pervers, sondern die Situation, in der er lebt* (*It Is Not the Homosexual Who is Perverse But the Situation in Which He Finds Himself*, 1970), caused controversy by portraying irresponsible sexual behaviour. Committed to activism, he courts notoriety, for instance in *Armee der Liebenden oder Revolte der Perversen* (*Army of Lovers or Revolt of the Perverts*, 1972–6), he filmed his students filming a gay porn star performing fellatio on himself. Some of his films document international queer activism; *SILENCE = DEATH*

(*Schweigen = Tod*, 1990), captures the voice of AIDS activist Larry **Kramer**. The autobiographical *Neurosia* (1995) mocks his detractors and reconfigures his own accomplishments.

MICHAEL PINFOLD

PRIESTHOOD

Despite the Catholic Church's disapproval of homosexuality, the establishment of a celibate male clergy has undoubtedly created an environment for secretive same-sex activity. Although priests are expected to observe celibacy, it is estimated that up to 30 per cent of the American priesthood have a gay or bisexual orientation. Under the leadership of Pope John Paul II, church hierarchy was vigilant in punishing priests who advocate or practice homosexuality. The Church's negative attitude towards sex and insistence on the sublimation of sexual desire within religious devotion has created significant problems such as the sexual abuse of children by priests. The Church has been embarrassed by several high-profile lawsuits brought by victims of abuse by priests, resulting in significant compensation being paid. Despite widespread criticism of the Church's anti-gay standpoint, the Church's strict hierarchy and conservatism smothers most possibilities of clergy reform.

JOHN FORDE

PRODUCTION CODE, THE (HOLLYWOOD)

The Production Code refers both to the policy document for standards of decency in film production and to the Office that administered it. The Code governed the moral content of **Hollywood** cinema from the 1930s to the 1960s. Containing a specific injunction against 'sexual perversion or any inference to it', the Code effectively precluded the explicit representation of queer sexualities on screen but, by so doing, it fostered a rich legacy of subtextual queerness in classic Hollywood films.

Throughout its earliest decades, American cinema struggled to obtain social respectability. Widely viewed as morally suspect, even licentious (especially given the rash of high profile scandals that rocked Hollywood at the time), its public reputation reached a nadir in the late 1920s with a social conservative backlash by the likes of the Catholic Church and the Legion of Decency. Facing a public outcry against the perceived immorality of its films, including calls for a boycott from religious leaders and threats of government intervention, the Motion Picture Producers and Distributors Association took it upon itself to develop and adopt a uniform Code of Decency with which to regulate the moral content of Hollywood films.

Drafted in 1930 under the direction of retired Postmaster-General Will Hays and administered from 1934 by arch-conservative Joseph Breen, the Production Code contained restrictions of such sensitive issues as profanity, sacrilege and the glorification of crime. Not surprisingly, many of its most stringent prohibitions pertained to sex, with itemized proscriptions of nudity, adultery, prostitution and sexual perversions. The latter had a particularly devastating impact on queer representations and effectively mandated the creation in Hollywood film of an exclusively heterosexual world in which queers were all but invisible. Or at least in explicit terms – although the Code's strictures were undoubtedly censorious, they produced less an absolute erasure of queer content than its covert displacement.

Unable to signify queerness and other prohibited issues overtly, Hollywood filmmakers became adept at intimating such things through coded or subtextual means. A character's queerness might be suggested through the use of subtle cues such as the aristocratic effeteness of Waldo Lydecker

(Clifton Webb) in *Laura* (1944), or the cool aloofness of Amy North (Lauren Bacall) in *Young Man With a Horn* (1950). At a more abstract level, queerness could be signalled through non-mimetic representational means such as music and gesture, which is arguably why the musical was such a fecund source of queer signification throughout this era. Gay and lesbian audiences were especially attentive to these instances of covert queerness and would use them as the basis for resistant-reading practices.

The hold of the Production Code was irrevocably weakened with the collapse of the studio system in the 1950s. In addition, many filmmakers, inspired by the rise of cinematic neo-realism and its preference for 'adult themes', openly defied the Code's injunctions by making movies with increasingly explicit sexual and violent content. By the 1960s the Code was all but defunct and was abandoned in 1968 for the MPAA rating system that governs motion picture content to this day.

Further reading

Leff, Leonard J. and Simmons, Jerold L. (2001) *The Dame in the Kimono: Hollywood, Censorship and the Production Code,* Lexington: University of Kentucky Press.

BRETT FARMER

PROSSER, JAY

b. 1966

writer

Academic whose work examines gender theory and transgendered identity. Prosser was born on 11 January 1966 in Devizes, Wiltshire, UK. He gained a PhD from the City University of New York and is currently a lecturer in English and American Studies at the University of Leeds, England. He is best known for his critical study *Second Skins: The Body Narratives of Transsexu-*

ality (1998). Combining post-structuralist theory with biographical accounts from transgendered people, Prosser's argument challenged feminist and queer theories about transsexual identity, positing that the reality of a transgendered body carries more weight in transgendered people's view of their identities than do words, texts and abstract discourses. He co-edited with Laura Doan *Palatable Poison: Critical Perspectives on 'The Well of Loneliness'* (2002), a series of critical essays on Radclyffe Hall's ground-breaking lesbian novel. His forthcoming projects include a family memoir involving Chinese and Jewish diasporas and a project on Buddhism in American literature.

See also: Hall, Radclyffe

JOHN FORDE

PSYCHOANALYSIS AND ACADEMIC SCHOLARSHIP

Insisting on the centrality of sexuality to psychic and social structures, queer theorists draw heavily on the work of Sigmund Freud and Jacques Lacan. Since psychoanalysis privileges the relationship between sexuality and gender, most significant psychoanalytic contributions to queer theory (especially those by Judith **Butler**, Teresa **De Lauretis** and Kaja Silverman) are equally interventions in feminist theory, drawing on the work of earlier feminist projects such as those of Luce **Irigaray** and Juliet Mitchell.

Psychoanalysis permits queer theory to explain how operations of power, including norms of gender, become psychically entrenched, and eschews reductive psychologism to demonstrate how individual subjectivity is always produced within a larger symbolic universe. Careful readings of Freud's *Three Essays on the Theory of Sexuality* (1949), notably that by De Lauretis in her *The Practice of Love* (1994), reveal that if heterosexuality is to be read as

465

the 'normal' end of individual development, this norm is both fragile and contingent, rather than 'natural', and ultimately takes as its components the very 'perversions' that conservative psychoanalytic clinical practice has demonized. According to Freud, all human beings have made an unconscious homosexual object choice, and queer theory, rather than seeing homosexuality as the property of a distinct group, has thus posited the significance of homosexuality for entire social structures. One problem in the queer appropriation of psychoanalysis is the status of concepts such as castration and penis envy, especially as these imply the centrality of the symbolic penis ('phallocentrism') to a degree that appears problematic for lesbian sexuality. Another difficulty is the degree to which the Oedipus complex, as a mechanism for articulating the subject within structures of kinship, is valid across cultures.

See also: Theory and theorists, queer

TREVOR HOPE

PSYCHOLOGY AND GLBTQ CULTURE

The relationship between the field of psychology and the lives of gay, lesbian, bisexual, transgendered and queer people has been historically dysfunctional. The American Psychiatric Association (APA), a professional organization of psychiatrists, developed a Diagnostic and Statistical Manual of Mental Disorders (DSM) in 1952. This manual was developed by clinicians in an effort to make the diagnosis of mental disorders more systematic. Homosexuality was included as a disorder in the first and second versions. As a result, many queer people were pathologized and sometimes even institutionalized for being homosexual. The radicalization of gay identity in the 1970s resulted in a full-blown attack on the field of psychiatry by activists and scholars, with the result that homosexuality was removed from the

DSM in 1973 and homosexuality was depathologized. Today, queer people continue to challenge psychological professionals who, although homosexuality is not considered a bona fide mental disorder in adults, still treat homosexual activity in children and variations in gender identity and gender expression as a 'disorder'.

What is not commonly known is that research within psychology has yielded the field of lesbian and gay psychology. The work of many glbt scholars has established homosexuality as a viable sexual orientation; as one aspect of an individual's social identity. There is now one academic journal focused on research on homosexuality, the *Journal of Homosexuality*. Many psychologists have conducted research in support of glbt issues within major academic institutions and in private practice. They have examined the impact of homophobia on the lives of gay people and the process by which one develops into a productive gay or lesbian individual. Venturing to create gay identity development models within the field of psychology has been a brave social scientific and at times political, endeavour. The APA has a division within its professional organization aimed at the psychological study of lesbian, gay and bisexual issues, also known as Division 44. Division 44 was founded in 1985 to promote the understanding of issues related to sexual orientation within the larger organization and beyond. The Division serves as a resource for students looking for graduate programmes in psychology that promote the lives of glbt and queer people. Members of Division 44, through their research and consultation, advocate the rights of gay people from a professional psychologist's position.

The creation of gay identity development models has had an especially profound impact on the lives of gay adolescents. Groups such as the **Gay, Lesbian and Straight Education Network** (GLSEN) and **Parents, Families and**

Friends of Lesbians and Gays (PFLAG) have utilized the research developed by gay and lesbian psychologists to support their curriculum and organizational activities. These groups work with queer youth and their adult allies in educating people on homophobia and what it means to grow up gay.

In recent years the advancements of lesbian and gay psychologists have been challenged by groups of psychologists who continue to believe that homosexuality is a mental disorder. Proponents of conversion therapy and religious fundamentalists have created organized venues for converting homosexuals into heterosexuals. While in the minority, professionals who practice this brand of therapy threaten any progress that has been made within the field towards ensuring that queer people do not suffer from discrimination and violence in their everyday lives.

See also: Conversion or reparative therapy; Depathologizing of homosexuality; *Journal of Homosexuality*

KATHLEEN M. CUMISKEY

PUIG, MANUEL

b. 1932; d. 1990

writer

Puig is Argentina's most famous queer writer. He identified himself as a woman and evoked the parameters of pre-liberation homosexuality. Puig deplored the concept of a gay culture and its influence in Latin America, and he promoted the feminization of the biological male in interaction with hypermasculine partners of desire. This is evident in his autobiographical work *La traición de Rita Hayworth* (*Betrayed by Rita Hayworth*, 1967). Although *The Buenos Aires Affair* (1973) involves a heterosexual couple, their relationship can be read in same-sex terms because of the implicated internal homophobia and violence running through Puig's work.

Puig disrupted this theme in his 1976 novel *El beso de la mujer araña* (*Kiss of the Spider Woman*), which became known internationally through the English-language film version by director Héctor **Babenco** and the Broadway-musical book by Terrence **McNally.** The novel intersects queer identity with political activism; the homosexual as aesthetic phenomenon transforms into gender-bending queerness as an act of revolutionary politics.

Puig's last novel, *Sangre de amor correspondido* (*Blood of Requited Love*, 1982) mitigates the violence of sexual relations through a utopian relationship between a writer and a common labourer. During the last decade of his life, Puig made important contributions to queer theatre.

DAVID WILLIAM FOSTER

PULP FICTION, GAY

Gay pulp fiction is today the object of collector interest, repackaged as camp memorabilia. Gay-themed paperbacks share with other areas of queer pulp fiction (i.e. lesbian, transsexual, drag and fetish pulps) formulaic characterization, plotting and setting of a bleak underworld of drug use and crime. They are generally published with sensational, lurid covers, marked by shocking tag lines, vivid images and bright colours. Significantly, they also shared troubled authorship: while most lesbian-themed pulps were written by heterosexual men, gay pulps were written in some cases by women (witness the novels of Mary **Renault** set in ancient Greece) or by gay authors whose writing was often shrouded in pseudonyms. This was coupled with the 'polishing' of editors who helped keep the narrative within legal standards. Despite such mixture of secrecy and sensationalism, what made such novels gay-specific was the deployment of classic, elegiac themes in male homosexual writing: the discovery of one's sexual orientation; facing a hostile environment; **coming out**, straying into the underworld; fighting for a passionate relationship; and meeting one's doom.

Pulps were also in large part the result of the historical climate of the postwar years, which comprised paranoid McCarthyite culture and the threats to American identity denounced by the 1948 **Kinsey Report**, the struggles of early **homophile societies** and the sexual turmoil of the 1960s, culminating in the 1969 **Stonewall Riots**. Between late 1940s and 1950s, early gay pulps and landmark novels by Gore **Vidal**, Truman **Capote**, Jay Little, James **Baldwin** and William **Burroughs** were focused on what Richard Dyer tags the 'sad young man' pattern – the impossibility of a gay identity, which makes it both fated and desirable. During the 1960s the outpouring became a flood, as the best-selling exposé by John **Rechy**, *City of Night* (1963) introduced the queer underworld of hustlers and drag queens to the public with a success that is testimony to the furtive titillation that the reign of neon-lighted queer obscurity exerted upon both queers and heterosexuals. While early pulps exploited erotic realism (pathological or situational homosexuality, Kinsey-flavoured bisexuality, the transsexual as scientific frontier, etc.), providing a safe ground in which to represent heterodox sexualities under the aegis of the 'public benefit', by 1965 the door was opened to gay pulps needing less pseudo-scientific justification to 'unveil' queer desire.

The resultant flood of gay pulp novels cannot be reduced to the 1960s sexual revolution, camp mania and mass androgyny in fashion and music however: it was both material and legal. On the one hand, it was enhanced by the new system of news-stand distribution that Pocket Books had adopted since the 1940s and which made pulp novels available to those who could look at the right-back racks for lesbian adventures and 'single-handed'

readings. On the other hand, given the 'inherently' obscene nature of gay-themed writing, the history of gay pulp is also the history of legal restrictions on pornography which obliged publishers to tone sexual content down or boost it up as soon as courts started dropping charges. A key precedent was the acquittal in 1961 of H. Lynn Womack, who would go on to create Guild Press (1962) and build a mail-order porn empire. An increasing number of presses on both the East and West coasts (Guild Press, Greenleaf Classics, Pyramid Books, Paperback Library, Brandon House) were ready to co-opt writers for the new field of soft-core (by today's standards) gay writing. Outstanding selling rates were achieved by authors such as Richard Amory (who authored the Loon Trilogy), James Cain, Chris Davidson, Ed Wood and Victor J. Banis, who within 10 years, and under a number of *noms de plume* (either personal pseudonyms, or house names such as 'Don Holliday'), published more than 100 paperbacks, including the popular series The Man from C.A.M.P. that spoofed the James Bond craze by featuring gay spy and superhero Jackie Holmes. A whole new market for gay fantasies (including gay westerns, thrillers and detective stories, war stories, etc.) was thus made available. As gay pulp fiction became more unabashedly explicit in its sexual content, the birth of gay activism following the Stonewall Riots, and the increasing legitimacy of a gay identity, decreed the end of gay pulps. Its pornographic nature was split from its socio-literary justification: gay porn acquired its own right to exist and the possibility of gay writing of literary value and upbeat self-representation was envisioned.

The heritage of gay pulp fiction is thus ambivalent: while pulps – with a few remarkable exceptions – demonstrated both political and literary limits as they enforced stigmatized stereotypes and the doomed destiny of queer identities. Recent critical assessments have stressed the key role such novels played in queer history. Despite the industrial quality of their writing, pulps supplied a voice for those excluded from the dominant picture. The complex, multifaceted and shadowy world they depicted enabled many gay people – and, to some extent, the straight world – to come (literally) to terms with their own understanding. More, pulps are key texts in challenging the myth of Stonewall as a self-generated event. First, because they unveil a scenario of pre-1970s activism in the early homophile societies, in their magazines and in the novels that first offered the very possibility of self-recognition. Second, because they remind us that the definition of a gay identity was part of a negotiation between representation, self-image, market strategies and the industry of culture. As such, gay pulps share with their queer siblings a primary value in US history, invoking new narratives of cultural production that may account for both social and emotional histories.

See also: Pulp fiction, lesbian

Further reading

Bergman, David (1999) 'The Cultural Work of Gay Pulp Fiction', in Patricia Juliana Smith (ed.) *The Queer Sixties*, New York: Routledge.

Bronski, Michael (1984) *Culture Clash: The Making of Gay Sensibility*, Boston: South End Press.

—— (ed.) (2003) *Pulp Friction: Uncovering the Golden Age of Gay Male Pulps*, New York: St Martin's Press.

Dyer, Richard (1993) 'Coming Out as Going In: The Image of the Homosexual as a Sad Young Man', in *The Matter of Images: Essay on Representations*, New York: Routledge.

Nealon, Christopher (2001) *Foundlings: Lesbian and Gay Historical Emotion Before Stonewall*, Durham: Duke University Press.

Stryker, Susan (2001) *Queer Pulp: Perverted Passions from the Golden Age of the Paperback*, San Francisco: Chronicle Books.

FABIO CLETO

PULP FICTION, LESBIAN

Lesbian pulp fiction refers to paperbacks published during the 1950s and 1960s in cheap, mass-produced editions and which featured explicitly sexual lesbian encounters. Pulp fiction emerged as part of an explosion in the publication of paperback novels in the United States during and after the Second World War. During wartime, government-issued paperbacks, known as Armed Forces Editions, created a market for detective stories, westerns and adventure novels in a paperback format. The realist tendencies of these works had increasing appeal, not only for GIs, but also for the large number of independent, working women drawn to cities by the war effort. Although wartime censorship restricted the themes of these early paperbacks, the revolutionary counter-culture of the Beat generation, following the aftermath of war, encouraged a greater focus on deviant behaviour. Novels explored themes such as drug addiction, crime and sexual deviance. In 1950 the publishing house Fawcett, under its new imprint Gold Medal Books, published the first of many lesbian-themed pulp novels, Tereska Torres' *Women's Barracks*. A number of other publishers followed suit, and lesbian pulp fiction became an established genre. During the 1950s and 1960s American pulp fiction also flooded the British market, as publishers sought to evade the influence of US censors.

The target audience of these novels were heterosexual male readers rather than lesbians, and this was reflected in the cover art, which depicted lesbian characters as highly feminine. Nevertheless, while the majority of pulp fiction authors were men, a number of well-known female authors also wrote for a distinct lesbian readership. Prolific writers included Ann Aldrich, March Hastings, Ann **Bannon**, Peggy Swenson and Valerie Taylor.

The novels were often highly formulaic, following a number of established themes.

Many were set in women-only institutions, such as schools, sorority houses, nursing colleges and women's prisons, implying that such environments fostered lesbian relationships. Characters were frequently highly sexualized and the novels were unusually frank in their explicit accounts of lesbian sex. Sexual contact often occurred between an older, experienced woman and a younger, more impressionable girl, for whom the encounter represented a sexual awakening. Physical characteristics were often shorthand for power differences, both on the covers and within the text, with dark-haired or taller women dominating blond, impressionable girls.

Drawing on postwar notions of the origins of lesbianism, lesbian characters were frequently portrayed as coming from unstable family backgrounds, having poor relationships with their parents and having a family history of alcoholism or mental instability. The large number of novels set in women's prisons or reform schools, such as Joan Henry's *Women in Prison* (1953) and Ray Morrison's *Reformatory Girls* (1960), implied a clear link between lesbianism and criminality. The 'otherness' of these characters was clear from titles such as *Odd Girl Out* (1957), *Strange Sisters* (1954), *Women in the Shadows* (1959) and *Twilight Lovers* (1964). The city represented a further common backdrop, drawing on fears of urban moral decay. In Bannon's Beebo Brinker series (1957–62), Beebo's physical expedition from the rural Wisconsin of her childhood to the metropolitan setting of Greenwich Village implied a personal journey of sexual discovery.

Lesbian pulp fiction represented a new departure from the limited number of scientific texts and highbrow literature that previously had dealt with this theme. Pulp fiction was both cheap and readily available, being sold in drug stores, newsagents, and at news-stands. The highly sexualized cover art, featuring women gazing at each other or touching, usually in a state of par-

tial undress, gave the novels an easily recognizable lesbian theme. For women, the act of taking these paperbacks to the counter to make a purchase has been claimed as an act of political courage in the era of McCarthyism. It has been argued that the genre enabled many women to identify themselves as lesbians and build up an awareness of a lesbian community. By the 1970s sales of lesbian pulp fiction began to decline in the face of the Women's Liberation Movement and the growth of lesbian literature, but a recent renewal of interest has prompted Naiad press to revive Bannon's classic Beebo Brinker novels.

See also: Bannon, Ann

Further reading

Faderman, L. (1991) *Odd Girls and Twilight Lovers*, New York: Columbia University Press.

Foster, J.H. (1985) *Sex Variant Women in Literature: A History and Quantitative Survey*, Tallahassee: Naiad.

Zimet, J. (1999) *Strange Sisters: The Art of Lesbian Pulp Fiction 1949–1969*, London: Penguin.

REBECCA JENNINGS

PUNK

Punk was both an offspring of the spectacular body of British **glam rock**, and the progeny of Andy Warhol's groupies and superstars, including the Velvet Underground and Nico, Iggy Pop and the Stooges. While a number of performers, including the Ramones, the Clash, Blondie and Siouxsie Sue, may claim a primary role in shaping punk music both in the UK and the US, punk exploded as a mass phenomenon in 1976 with the international success of the Sex Pistols, who made self-destruction into an anarchistic manifesto, voicing the teenage angst that, in the recession of the 1970s, envisioned 'no future'. Warhol's Factory of serialized iconicity, however, constitutes a key to the whole punk phenomenon, for the Pistols themselves were in fact the result of the cunning manufacturing of producer Malcolm McLaren – in earlier years McLaren had experimented with market strategies with the **New York Dolls** – and later of gay icon Vivienne Westwood, who fashioned the Pistols' image. Between the two they shaped a sly marketing strategy that made shocking spectacle into publicity.

As Dick Hebdige suggests in his groundbreaking 1979 study *Subculture*, punk should be framed in the context of the spectacular youth subcultures of post-Second World War years such as Teds and Mods, distorting, deforming and decontextualizing codes of bourgeois authenticity and naturalness. Just as punk music scorned harmony and order in favour of noise and untalented improvisation, punk style – tattoos and piercings, spiked and wildly coloured hair, torn clothes, safety pins worn as jewellery, swastikas – set the body as the anarchistic stage of excessive consumption, and the 'evil' embodiment of the dominant culture's ghosts. Anarchy, nihilism, seedy sex with groupies, drug abuse and overdoses, the rupture of body surface – all offered a disturbing parody of bourgeois conformity.

The relation of punk to queer culture is complex in nature, and not only because punk was from the beginning a redeployment of historical queer coding and decoding strategies, and a queering of the body, ripped and torn in its gender signs. In concert with the mainstreaming of queer styles in the 1980s, punk had an important impact on mass pop culture, significantly renovating the music scene and fashion styles. However, the vanishing of mass-marketed punk in the 1980s made the movement available to both gays and lesbians, i.e. to those who had been marginalized during the Sex Pistols years (for that punk, albeit in many respects gender bending, was imbued with working-class homophobia).

Punk thus reclaimed its underground and aggressive momentum, offering a community and political feeling for queers that refused club culture and the 'dancing queen' stereotype. Gay bands such as Pansy Division, Team Dresch and God Is My Co-Pilot played 'queercore', finding a niche in the hardcore music scene that enabled them to shout queer desire at the face of prejudice. Queer punk was born, fostered by fanzines such as *Homocore*, *JD's* and *Chainsaw* and by the queer activism of ACT UP, Queer Nation and the Radical Fairies.

Queercore helped to establish an alliance between gay punks and 'riot grrrls', whose punk reframed the female body as a contestation of the male gaze, their icons stars such as Vaginal 'Cream' **Davis** and bands like Fifth Column, the Butchies, Tribe 8 and **Le Tigre**.

Bibliography

Hebdige, D. (1979) *Subculture: The Meaning of Style*, New York: Routledge.

Further reading

Henry, T. (1989) *Break All Rules! Punk Rock and the Making of a Style*, Ann Arbor: UMI Research Press.

Laing, D. (1985) *One Chord Wonders: Power and Meaning in Punk Rock*, Buckingham: Open University Press.

McNeil, L. and McCain, G. (1997) *Please Kill Me: The Uncensored Oral History of Punk*, New York: Penguin.

FABIO CLETO

PURDY, JAMES

b. 1932

writer

Born in Ohio and known primarily as a novelist, although he has also written essays, plays, short stories and poems, and exhibited drawings, Purdy moved to Chicago when he was 16. Although he began to write early in life, Purdy was not able to secure a publisher until he was 33. His work focused on obsessive – albeit unspoken – love between men, distilling an everyday American speech that delved into the disorder that lurks beneath the veneer of civilized small-town life. His later work often ridicules the deliberate shallowness of urban sophisticates, as in *Out With the Stars* (1993).

Purdy has published over 40 books; *Malcolm* (1959) brought him some critical acclaim and support from other gay writers, such as Marianne Moore and Gore **Vidal**, although he has always lived on the margins of literary life and has never succeeded in gaining either fame or fortune. Still refusing Manhattan, he has recently published *Moe's Villa and Other Stories* (2004) and continues to reside in Brooklyn.

ED MILLER

PUSSY PALACE

Organized in 1998 by an ad hoc Women's Bathhouse Committee (members include Chanelle Gallant and Loralee Gillis) and held at rotating men's bathhouses, Pussy Palace in Toronto is a women's sex- and trans-positive space/movement for women interested in casual, kinky and public sex. Held bi-yearly, Pussy Palace is a unique combination of feminist policies, including trans-positive practices, with pro-sex and sex worker practices, including porn rooms, dancers and massage. Staffed by volunteers, from the DJs to the food and drink servers to the cleaning staff and dancers, the club provides access to pools, saunas, hot tubs, showers, a dance space and dozens of small rooms with a bed and locker – all for the purposes of sex. On 12 September 2000 seven officers from the Toronto Police services raided the bathhouse and brought liquor-license violation charges against the club's organizers (the charges were dismissed two years later).

Pussy Palace is significant for a number of reasons. The raid on the bathhouse galvanized the women's, trans and queer communities to change women's sexual culture in Toronto. Privileging women's sexual pleasure, the existence of a bathhouse for women challenged the ways that female sexualities have been conceptualized both inside and outside of queer communities. As a trans-positive space, the Women's Bathhouse Committee was one of the first feminist organizations to include both transsexual men and women. Finally, Pussy Palace created new possibilities for the ways in which women's pleasure is conceived, organized and politically mobilized against increasingly sex-negative legal and moral regulations.

JEAN BOBBY NOBLE

Q

QUEER AS FOLK

TV series

A ground-breaking drama about a group of gay men, originally made for Britain's Channel Four (1999–2000), later remade for American cable network Showtime (2000–4). The UK version, written by gay screenwriter Russell T. Davies, was hailed as a breakthrough for gay visibility on British television, with its almost exclusively gay character base and its honest and confrontational depiction of contemporary gay life. The series (screened on national free-to-air television) pilots with Vince, a 29-year-old working-class supermarket worker and his best friend Stuart, a charming but manipulative sexual legend. Through a long drug-and-booze fuelled evening, ending with Stuart having sex with Nathan, a 15-year-old virgin. This explicitly filmed sex scene, which included British television's first reference to rimming, caused nationwide controversy, with critics arguing that the episode condoned underage sex and stereotyped gay men as drug-addicted sexual predators.

Attractively filmed and wittily scripted, QAF celebrated the exuberance of Manchester's gay scene and the cosmetic glamour of the gay nouveau riche. Largely uninterested in political issues such as same-sex marriage or AIDS, Davies' writing explored how gay men deal (or do not) with growing older in a youth-worshipping and largely commitment-free culture. Teenage Nathan's explosive coming out and desire to embrace adult gay life is contrasted with Vince's and Stuart's arrested adolescence. Vince faces a choice between a new relationship with an Australian boyfriend and the comfort of his unrequited love for Stuart, who faces his own demands from a lesbian couple with whom he has fathered a baby boy. Davies' scripting is impressively non-judgemental, but acknowledges the darker side of the characters' lives, including Phil, an overweight gay man who dies after an accidental drug overdose, and ultra-camp Alexander, who is ostracized by his middle-class parents. Series 2 (2000) concludes the story in two one-hour episodes, with Vince and Stuart finally getting together and leaving Manchester, giving the now proudly out Nathan the keys to the kingdom.

The US version of Queer As Folk was developed for television by Ron Cowan and Daniel Lipman, with creative input by Davies. The action was relocated to Pittsburgh, and storylines and characters considerably extended, with Series One forming 22 one-hour episodes. Considered too sexually explicit for screening on mainstream American TV networks, the series screened on cable channel Showtime. The first three episodes follow the British episodes virtually line for line. Vince is now Michael, an Italian-American supermarket worker, and Stuart becomes Brian, a charming, sluttish PR executive. Nathan becomes Justin, who is made older (17), but still younger than the local age of homosexual consent. The trio play out the same dynamic of Brian seducing Justin while Michael struggles between his unrequited love for Brian and a budding relationship with an attractive doctor. Rounding out the gay cast are Emmett, based on a character in the British series, Alexander, and Ted, a geekish accountant. Like Phil in the British series, Ted suffers a drug overdose after an encounter with a trick but survives and attempts a relationship with his dealer.

In an attempt to redress the male-dominated focus of the British series, female characters are given more screentime in the American version. In one of the show's most interesting variations from the British series (where the lesbian couple are a harmonious and monogamous counterpoint to the promiscuous gay scene), American couple Lindsay and Melanie argue, flirt with infidelity and have a trial separation. *Cagney and Lacey* actor Sharon Gless gives a spirited performance as Debbie, Michael's proudly PLFAG-waving working-class mother. Although the physical attractiveness and physique of its leads are significantly enhanced, the American version maintains (and in some cases, embellishes) the sexual explicitness of the original, including Ted's initiation into BDSM (bondage and discipline, dominance and submission, and sadomasochism) sex.

Storylines are reshaped and given stronger political focus to reflect the American gay experience. Emmett attempts to 'cure' his homosexuality by attending a fundamentalist Christian 'exit' group. Michael's HIV+ uncle, Vic, struggles with homophobic health insurance policies and is unfairly prosecuted for indecent exposure after being cruised by an undercover cop. Series One ends with Justin being brutally gay-bashed after taking Brian to his high school prom. Series Two and Three moves away from the central love triangle, with Brian and Justin negotiating a difficult open relationship and Michael entering a relationship with an HIV+ man. Political themes canvassed include Lindsay and Melanie's relationship commitment ceremony, the investigation of the murder of a young HIV+ hustler and difficulties caused by Brian's involvement with a homophobic politician. A resounding favourite with American glbt audiences and heterosexual women, the show won the 2001 GLAAD Media Award for Outstanding Drama Series.

JOHN FORDE

QUEER AZTLÁN

'Queer Aztlán' is a term coined by Chicana feminist lesbian writer Cherríe **Moraga** during the early 1990s. She formally developed the concept in her seminal manifesto 'Queer Aztlán: The Re-formation of the Chicano Tribe', published in her book *The Last Generation* (1993). After examining the limitations that **Queer Nation** presented for glbt people of colour and those that Chicano nationalism placed on Chicana lesbians and Chicano gay men, Moraga conceptualized a 'Queer Aztlán', based on the notion of Aztlán as the mystic homeland of Chicanas/os. In Moraga's new space, a queer Chicana/o identity is constructed by a radical reconceptualization of identity politics with regards to race and sexuality. In such a space, Moraga envisioned Chicana lesbians and Chicano gay men learning how to deal with issues related to homophobia, gender roles, and sexuality in Chicano and mainstream culture. They would also learn how to deal with racism and discrimination and form a new nation or 'tribe' with close ties to their indigenous past. Queer Aztlán proposes the rise of a new Chicano movement, one that is free of discrimination, violence and homophobia – a safe space and a free world for all Chicana/o glbt members who have traditionally been marginalized from Chicano and Anglo heterosexist patriarchal orders. In this way Chicana lesbians and Chicano gay men would be at the centre of this new nation. Since its conceptualization, a new generation of queer Chicana/o artists 5 Chicana/o and US Latina/o cultural production, thereby shaping new identities for glbt people of colour.

DANIEL ENRIQUE PÉREZ

QUEER EYE FOR THE STRAIGHT GUY

TV series

Ground-breaking, controversial reality/makeover series, first screened on the NBC-owned Bravo channel in 2003 (later screened on NBC's main channel). The programme features five gay fashion and style experts (Ted Allen, food and wine; Kyan Douglas, hair and grooming; Thom Filicia, interior design; Carson Kressley, fashion; and Jai Rodriguez, culture) with a weekly mission to transform an unkempt single or married straight man. The show's mix of style tips and acerbic humour (notably from Carson Kressley, the show's flirtatious, razor-tongued fashion consultant) resulted in record-breaking cable ratings and a devoted audience following. Commentators are divided on *Queer Eye*'s merits. Critics accuse the show's stars of perpetuating stereotypes of gay men as materialistic, bitchy control freaks, while supporters (including the gay rights organization GLAAD [Gay and Lesbian Alliance Against Defamation]) commend the show for promoting positive relationships between gay and straight men and for acknowledging the contribution of gays to fashion and popular culture. Together with the sitcom *Will & Grace*, *Queer Eye* demonstrates the increasing acceptance of gays in twenty-first-century American mainstream entertainment.

JOHN FORDE

QUEER NATION

activist organization

Queer Nation was formed in March 1990 for reasons more pragmatic than idealistic, despite the speculation of queer theorists. The group was created to tackle issues that ACT UP/New York could not. Once small in size and flexible, ACT UP's founding chapter was now three years old and growing quickly. Its weekly meetings were drawing several hundreds of people and the agenda was expanding. New members were demanding the group tackle HIV in prisons, infection among women and needle exchange. The occasional request for a 'gay rights' protest now faced resistance.

Four long-time ACT UP members – Alan Klein, his lover Karl Soehnlein, writer Michelangelo **Signorile** and Tom Blewitt – were concerned about this deadlock and began meeting privately. They felt a number of problems germane to gays and lesbians were going unchallenged: a sharp increase in gay-bashing incidents in New York City as well as nationally, a rash of homophobic rap lyrics by hip-hop singers and, most recently, a *60 Minutes* TV commentary by commentator Andy Rooney explaining, without apology, how gay people made him feel uneasy. The four veteran activists felt that tackling these issues required ACT UP direct action tactics. But clearly a new group was needed.

On 20 March 1990, 60 people attended a meeting at the New York City Gay and Lesbian Community Services Center, the birthplace of ACT UP. (Many who showed up were ACT UP veterans who had burned out, but were now enthused by the prospect of a new organization.) Mindful of the bureaucracy now dogging ACT UP, many demanded that the new group be free from the restriction of majority votes or consensus. Although some even disdained giving the group a name, within two weeks 'Queer Nation'

475

was born. Its mandate: a commitment to queer visibility.

By mid–April Queer Nation had a battery of tactics: 'Nights Out' involved 'invasions' of straight hangouts and the 'Queer Shopping Network' distributed pro-gay pamphlets at exurban malls. This edgy mix of politics and camp humour was reminiscent of the early days of ACT UP/ New York. Queer Nation's main focus, however, was on gay-bashing. The group was galvanized in its first month when a pipe bomb exploded in Uncle Charlie's Downtown, a West Village gay bar, injuring three people. The next evening Queer Nation had mobilized 1,000 street protestors who marched to demand a full police investigation. (Years later, it was determined that the blast had been committed by a faction of the group that brought down the World Trade Center towers in 2001.)

Queer Nation commanded extensive media attention from the start, especially from reporters who had initially ignored ACT UP. Reporters jumped on the group's provocative name, a co-opting of the old epithet that nonetheless still rankled with both gays and straights. By summer 1990 Queer Nation chapters were thriving in Boston, Los Angeles and San Francisco. Queer Nation's shock troops popularized the postmodern-homo aesthetic that began in ACT UP. Masculine gay boys, femme lesbians and punkish, tattooed hybrids of each commandeered the new urban gay look. Queer Nation spun off two contingents: the **Lesbian Avengers** and The Pink Panthers, the latter of which patrolled gay neighbourhoods nightly to discourage bias attacks.

Queer Nation's greatest accomplishment came in its first summer, after the murder of a Queens man named Julio Rivera. Working with the New York City Lesbian and Gay Anti-Violence Project (helmed by Matt Foreman, who would head the National Gay and Lesbian Task Force in 2004), Queer Nation forced a police investigation that resulted in the convictions of three men for the murder.

By the middle of 1991, however, Queer Nation was faltering. The four founders were no longer as directly active in the organization and numbers were dropping. Queer Nation groups in other cities also reported battle fatigue. By 1993 the founding organization had morphed into a weekly encounter group for transvestites and transsexuals. It finally disbanded in the same year.

In 1990 the Queer Nation rallying cry was, 'We're here. We're queer. Get used to it!' Angry and in-your-face, it commanded attention. But by the mid-1990s, with gay-friendly Bill Clinton in the White House, queer politics had become a mainstream matter. Already marginalized, Queer Nation had no place in a new era where organizations such as the **Human Rights Campaign** had become political power brokers. The subsequent community focus on gays in the military and same-sex marriage vividly reflects the conservative turn of the movement. Indeed, popular culture will remember the short-lived legend of Queer Nation only as a slogan. On a segment of *The Simpsons*, a Gay Pride parade glides through the streets of Springfield led by a group of men shouting 'We're here. We're queer. Get used to it!' An unruffled Lisa Simpson calls after them: 'But we are used to it; you do the same thing every year'.

JAY BLOTCHER

QUEER NATION

TV programme

Beginning in 1997, *Queer Nation* is a weekly, late-night, TV programme airing on New Zealand's TV2. The programme began in 1996 under the name *Express Report*, with the purpose of supplying news and information to gays and lesbians. It was the first New Zealand programme by and about homosexual people. In 1999 Livingstone Productions took over production and created 40, hour-and-a-half episodes each year. Each episode presents short feature stories about glbt people and culture. Features in 2003 included a Maori lesbian who wrote her own myths deriving from both a queer perspective and traditional Maori stories; a report on hip-hop and **homophobia**, including interviews with local hip-hop group Nesian Mystic and their lesbian manager; and an Indian lesbian discussing Indian culture and her work in New Zealand theatre.

In 1999, the programme won two AIDS Foundation Media Awards and was a finalist in the TV Guide Television Awards.

CAROLYN SKELTON

R

RACISM

Queer communities are not immune to the racisms of their dominant cultures. As such, queer people often face multiple oppressions because of homophobia within families and communities of origin as well as racism within glbtq communities. Such race-oppression is doubled because it occurs simultaneously in a culture of white hegemony.

Racism in queer communities frequently takes two forms. The more traditionally conceived racism-as-hatred leads to experiences ranging from social aversion and lack of sexual interest to employment discrimination, outright hostility and violence. Another insidious form of racism within queer communities is the fetishization of racial otherness. Mythologies of African virility and penile endowment, Asian submissiveness and other stereotypes bear the marks of racist exoticism. An example of the objectifying function of fetish-based racism is the discourse surrounding the ethnic queen. 'Dinge queen', '**rice queen**', 'bean queen' and other terms, for example, often work to fetishize the race of the body. This is racist to the extent that the subject of desire becomes a racialized object. This racialized fetishism is often coupled with class- and caste-based ideologies.

MICHAEL QUIETO

RADICAL FAERIES

activist organization

Group originating at a national gathering called by Harry **Hay** (previously ousted as leader of the **Mattachine Society** for his communist beliefs), Mitch Walker and Don Kilfhefner in 1979 at Benson, Arizona. Radical Faeries are a network of rural and urban dwellers who see gays/lesbians as a distinct people, with their own culture and spirituality. There are no leaders, and no dogma, but common visions are shared: the sacredness of nature; the interconnectedness of spirit, sex, politics; a commitment to group consensus; an exploration of what being gay/lesbian means. The dualities of either/or, minority/majority thinking are superseded by a 'we are each other' philosophy. The *Radical Faerie Digest* (RFD) is published as a source/contact journal. Generally, the eight pagan holidays of the year (the equinoxes, solstices and quarter-days) are celebrated, although some of the biggest events have been large-scale urban interventions such as the Faerie Action Gathering and the Stonewall 25 celebrations.

MICHAEL J. PINFOLD

RAINBOW COALITION

Rainbow Coalition was the term used by the Reverend Jesse Jackson for the myriad groups supporting his run for the Demo-cratic nomination for President of the United States in 1984. Jackson openly included lesbians and gay men in his litany of America's 'rejected and despised', the first major presidential hopeful to do so (although his party has addressed gay rights as part of its platform since 1972). It later became the name of a civil rights group Jackson headed after the 1984 campaign.

ANDY HUMM

RAINBOW FLAG

Rainbow flags comprise different coloured stripes. The original flag was created by Gilbert **Baker** in 1978 in San Francisco, but it is now an international symbol of lesbian, gay, bisexual and transgender pride and unity. The eight colours symbolize the diversity of the community in terms of sexuality, race and culture. Mile-long rain-bow flags were featured at the Stonewall 25 march in New York and in Key West on the twenty-fifth anniversary of the flag's creation. A large version of the flag flies in the Castro district's Harvey Milk Plaza in **San Francisco**.

See also: Milk, Harvey

ANDY HUMM

RAINER, YVONNE

b. 1934

dancer, choreographer, film director

Born in San Francisco in 1934, Yvonne Rainer has emerged as one of the most prolific choreographers and experimental filmmakers in the history of the American avant-garde. She began her dance training with Martha Graham in New York in 1957 and became a driving force in modern dance throughout the 1960s and 1970s after founding the Judson Dance Theater in 1962. However, from 1968 onwards she became fascinated with the idea of inte-grating short films into her live perfor-mances, finally making a complete transition to filmmaking in the early 1970s with the release of her first feature-length film, *Lives of Performers* (1972), followed by the experimental classic *Film About a Woman Who...* (1974). Continually ana-lysed from within a feminist and/or avant-garde framework, her works have con-sistently sought to redefine the relationship between the spectacle and the spectator, receiving critical acclaim worldwide. In 1997 a simultaneous retrospective of Rain-er's complete oeuvre to date was mounted by the Museum of Modern Art in San Francisco and the Film Society of the Lin-coln Center in New York to coincide with the release of her latest work, a meditation on middle-aged lesbian sexuality entitled *MURDER and murder*.

ROBIN GRIFFITHS

RAKOFF, DAVID

b. 1964

writer, performer

Openly gay New York-based writer, broadcaster and actor, Rakoff has won a dedicated fan base with his insightful, witty and bitchy observations of American con-temporary culture. He is a longtime friend and collaborator of author David Sedaris, to whom he is often compared. He is a regular contributor to American Public Radio International's *This American Life*. His essay collections include *Fraud* (2001), a humor-ous fusion of commentary and journalism covering his tongue-in-cheek investigations into elf populations in Iceland, his imper-sonation of Sigmund Freud in a Manhattan department store or attending a New Age retreat hosted by action-movie star Steven Seagal. *Don't Get Too Comfortable* (2005) is a collection of satirical essays on greed and consumerism in contemporary America. He also works in theatre and film, and directed David and Amy Sedaris in their semi-autobiographical comic play *Stitches* (1994).

See also: Sedaris, David

JOHN FORDE

RAPPAPORT, MARK

b. 1941

filmmaker

Avant-garde filmmaker whose documentaries explore the secret gay subtexts of **Hollywood** cinema. He financed three short films before his first full-length feature, *Casual Relations* (1973). He is best known for *Rock Hudson's Home Movies* (1992), a subversive reinterpretation of the films of closeted gay actor Rock **Hudson**. Inspired by the revelations of Hudson's secret gay life and death from AIDS, the film scans footage of Hudson's films for a homosexual subtext, especially between his male co-stars, and considers the ironies of scenes in *Pillow Talk* (1959) when Hudson's heterosexual leading man pretends to be gay to attract his co-star Doris Day. Another film, *From The Journals of Jean Seberg* (1995), explores the controversial life of the French actor, mixing archival footage and film clips with dramatizations. *The Silver Screen: Cover Me Lavender* (1997) argues for a homosexual subtext in actor Walter Brennan's on-screen relationships with John Wayne and Gary Cooper.

JOHN FORDE

RATTIGAN, TERENCE

b. 1911; d. 1977

playwright

One of Britain's major playwrights between the World Wars, Terence Mervyn Rattigan's first popular success was *French Without Tears* (1936). However, he became determined to write more serious plays and became particularly impassioned about the British elite's failure to prevent the Second World War. *After the Dance* (1939), intended as a satirical criticism of this issue, ironically closed by the outbreak of war. Subsequently, Rattigan produced some of the best-known plays of the period: *The Winslow Boy* (1946) and *Separate Tables* (1954). The rise of the 'angry young man', largely the result of John Osborne's *Look Back in Anger* (1956), rendered Rattigan's 'well-made plays' obsolete. Nevertheless he continued to write some of his best work, including *Ross* (1960). Displeased with England's swinging 1960s, he lived in exile in Bermuda, returning to England to be knighted in 1971.

CHRIS BYRNE

RAUSCHENBERG, ROBERT

b. 1925

artist

Born in Port Arthur, Texas, Robert Rauschenberg spent much of his twenties in New York City, spending his summers at the former Black Mountain College in North Carolina. There he met and collaborated with the composer John Cage and Cage's lover, choreographer Merce Cunningham; the three went on to maintain lifelong friendships and important artistic collaborations. It was also at Black Mountain that Rauschenberg met the artist Cy Twombly, who became his first male lover and studio mate. Following this, he spent nearly six years with the artist Jasper **Johns**, working and living together as a couple. Several of Rauschenberg's works made during his time with Johns, including the assemblages of painting, pre-printed materials and other found objects that he referred to as 'combines', such as *Short Circuit*, and most famously *Bed* (both 1955), allude to their relationship and to the social-cultural codes of mid-century American gay culture.

JOHN PAUL RICCO

REAGAN, RONALD

b. 1911; d. 2004

actor, US president

Born on 6 February 1911 in Tampico, Illinois, Ronald Reagan was the fortieth President of the United States. His name became synonymous with the economic expansion and moral conservatism of 1980s America. After a steady but unremarkable career as a film actor, he joined the Republican Party in 1962, holding the post of Governor of California from 1967 until 1975. He won the US Presidency for two successive terms (1980–9), creating economic growth through deregulation, tax cuts and reductions in state welfare and education spending. He was criticized for his failure to respond to the escalating AIDS epidemic (his first public mentioning of the disease did not occur until 1985) and his consistent underfunding of AIDS-related research and healthcare initiatives. His sympathies towards fundamentalist Christianity created a pervading climate of homophobia, impeding gay civil rights initiatives. His anti-gay policies prompted widespread protests by ACT UP and other advocacy groups. Notable artistic satires include photographer Oliviero Toscanis, whose computer-generated image of Reagan covered with AIDS-related skin lesions made the cover of Benetton's 1994 *Colors* magazine, and Tony Kushner's play *Angels in America* (1991/2). Reagan died on 5 June 2004 in Los Angeles, after suffering from Alzheimer's disease.

JOHN FORDE

REAL WORLD, THE

TV programme

Inspired by *An American Family*, MTV's first reality TV show features seven 20-somethings that the network selects to live in a shared home in the hopes of fomenting interpersonal conflict and spicy video confessions. Many gay and lesbian household members have been included during the 15 seasons, which started in 1992. Some credit the show with encouraging a greater acceptance of gays and lesbians among Generation X viewers. In the third season, set in San Francisco, Pedro **Zamora**, a very photogenic AIDS educator who was born in Cuba, became one of the first TV personalities to discuss what it was like living with HIV. Zamora died from AIDS-related causes mere hours after the broadcast of the season finale of *The Real World*.

ED MILLER

RECHY, JOHN

b. 1934

writer

The author of twelve novels, along with plays and non-fiction volumes, a regular contributor to many prominent journals and an acclaimed university lecturer, John Francisco Rechy stands out as a prominent figure in contemporary American literature and a veritable icon in gay history and culture. His first novel, *City of Night* (1963), was a classic of underground life the subject matter of which was presented in a rigorous, unsentimental, forthright and all but morbid manner. It was a controversial book and an international best seller, imparting to its author an immediate notoriety. His following works – most notably *Numbers* (1967) and *The Sexual Outlaw: A Documentary* (1977) – continued to explore the complexities, rituals and spaces of life on the fringes of American society, stretching the linguistic potential of literature to empower the dispossessed and the disregarded. At once erotic, passionate, ironic and enraged, Rechy's works are of literary distinction for both gays and straights, for they show a distinguished talent in manipulating and mixing narrative styles and voices, in deploying cinematic techniques and in the intermingling of history and fiction, accounting and moral peroration.

FABIO CLETO

RED RIBBON

The Red Ribbon Project – originally a loop of red silk ribbon fastened onto a lapel or pinned to a shirt – was designed by the Visual AIDS Artists' Caucus during the late 1980s, as a symbol of commitment to people living with AIDS. Sponsored by the group **Broadway Cares/Equity Fights AIDS**, the Red Ribbon debuted at the televised 1991 Tony Awards. It is now an internationally recognized symbol of solidarity.

JOHN FORDE

REED, LOU AND THE VELVET UNDERGROUND

b. 1942

rock musician and group

Taking their name from a sociological pulp paperback devoted to BDSM (bondage and discipline, dominance and submission, and sadomasochism) practices, the Velvet Underground were formed in 1965 by Lou Reed and experimental musician John Cale. It was Andy **Warhol** who brought them to join the Exploding Plastic Inevitable show he was producing, added singer Nico to their performances and styled their first record's cover (the famous banana). The band thus became the source of the soundtrack to Warhol's Factory and to the pop art world, and among the most influential bands in rock history. In the years 1966–70, when Lou Reed left the band after releasing four records marked by epochal tracks such as 'Heroin', 'Walk on the Wild Side' and 'Venus in Furs', they paid open homage to the gay underworld of drugs, transvestism and social stigma: a task Lou Reed also brought to splendid accomplishment in his solo debut, *Transformer*. They thus offered a

powerful image of the darker side of the 1960s, holding their epic of metropolitan decadence in opposition to the libertarian rhetoric of West Coast counter-cultures.

FABIO CLETO

REID, GRAEME CHARLES

b. 1965

scholar, activist

Born in Johannesburg, South Africa, Graeme Charles Reid was educated at the University of the Witwatersrand. He founded the South African Gay and Lesbian Archives in 1997, which he ran until 2001. Reid is the author of a number of scholarly articles on homosexuality in South Africa, and in 2000 co-directed the documentary film *Dark and Lovely, Soft and Free*, which focused on gay life outside metropolitan areas in South Africa. Reid's recent work has focused on the social and cultural constructions of sexuality in contemporary South Africa. He holds a research position at the Wits Institute for Social and Economic Research and teaches in the University of the Witwatersrand's postgraduate programme. In addition, Reid has long been involved in gay activism, including acting as secretary and treasurer of the Gay and Lesbian Organization of the Witwatersrand from 1993 to 1995.

ANTHONY MANION

REINKE, STEVE

b. 1963

video artist

Canadian video artist, trained at the Nova Scotia College of Art and Design. Reinke's legendary *One Hundred Videos* (1989–96), whereby he committed to producing 100 short videos before the millennium, is his demented masterpiece. Rescuing scraps from the stock-shot dumpster is a principal strategy behind this agglomeration of miniatures, but they also demonstrate dexterous video-graphic interactivity and observation. Reinke's recurrent voiceover is not literally autobiographical but his personal sensibility shines through this self-reflexive encyclopedia about the artistic process and our image-bank unconscious; about the body, the self and identity; about childhood and regression; about narrative and humour; about same-sex obsession, transgression, fetishism and, above all, voyeurism. Titles such as *Eighty Prominent Dermatologists* (1992) speak for themselves. Since the completion of this serial epic, Reinke continued his prolific output, offering longer, more complex works that often extend his traditional themes and obsessions.

THOMAS WAUGH

RENAULT, MARY

b. 1905; d. 1983

writer

Mary Renault was born Eileen Mary Challans in London, England but used a *nom de plume*. She graduated from St Hugh's College, Oxford in 1928, the same year as the prosecution of Radclyffe Hall's novel *The Well of Loneliness*. Her first few novels, such as *Purposes of Love* (1939) and *The Friendly Young Ladies* (1944), included lesbian and gay characters with medical experience and were informed by her nursing background. Moving to South Africa with her partner Julie Mullard in 1948, a new focus appeared in her writing. She turned to the classical world to explore the complexities of sexuality, unhampered by threats of prosecution for obscenity which the use of contemporary characters in a modern world might have brought. Renault wrote of Alexander the Great's love affairs with men in novels such as *The Persian Boy* (1972) but used few lesbian characters in later writings.

WREN SIDHE

RENÉE

b. 1929

writer

Born in Napier, New Zealand, playwright and author Renée has described herself as a 'lesbian feminist with socialist working-class ideals'. Her extensive body of work largely reflects this ideological and cultural perspective, and is known for its straight-forward, realist style.

Renée's career as a playwright began at age 50. Among her most acclaimed work is a trilogy, beginning with 1985's *Wednesday to Come*, which focuses on women's experiences at different stages in New Zealand's social history. It was in her first novel, *Willy Nilly* (1990) that lesbian narratives began to feature significantly in her texts. *Willy Nilly* centres on the chaos and revelation surrounding a lesbian and her daughter on the latter's wedding day. In 1993 Renée published *Daisy and Lily*, a story of childhood lovers separated by the conventions of heterosexuality who return to each other 40 years later.

ANITA BRADY

RENO

b. 1956

performance artist

Reno is a Latina and lesbian performance artist, political satirist, actor and producer. Reno's stream of consciousness style is frantic and frenetic. Her biting, deeply analytical comedy takes jabs at American politics and everyday life. Eight weeks after 11 September 2001, Reno boldly took the stage in her show entitled: 'Rebel without a Pause'. She burst onto the scene in 1989 with her show 'Reno: In Rage and Rehab', about her methamphetamine addiction. Lily Tomlin, a patron of Reno's work, supported her first feature film, made for HBO and titled *Reno Finds Her Mom*, a brutally honest depiction about the performer's search for her birth mother. Reno's performances, highlighted by fragmented speech and pacing, are truly queer. In revealing the funny, brutal life of a New York lesbian with Attention Deficit Disorder, Reno embraces the many fractures of identity and makes it powerful to be a misfit.

KATHLEEN M. CUMISKEY

REPARATIVE THERAPY

See: Conversion or reparative therapy

REVE, GERARD

b. 1923

writer

Gerard Reve's first novel, *De Avonden* (*The Evenings*), published in 1947, established him as a significant albeit controversial writer. After running into trouble with the Dutch government over charges that his work was pornographic, he left the Netherlands for England. For a brief period he wrote in English, resulting in *The Acrobat and Other Stories* (1956). He returned to the Netherlands after the publication of that book. The controversy over Reve continued throughout the 1960s when he began to write openly about homosexuality. In the wake of a very public conversion to Catholicism, he was officially charged with blasphemy in 1967, but the case was later dismissed. He has since written many novels, but is perhaps best known in the English-speaking world for the film *The Fourth Man* (1983), which was based on his novel of the same name.

DANIEL HENDRICKSON

RICE QUEEN

A Western or Caucasian man who is predominantly sexually interested in Asian men.

TRAVIS KONG

RICH, ADRIENNE

b. 1929

poet, writer

Adrienne Rich is one of the most eloquent, provocative voices in the field of sexuality, race, language, power and women's culture. Rich criticizes the self-censure of female writing by elaborating a project of destructuring language that links the feminine experience to anti-feminist patriarchal ideology. Rich approaches poetry as experience, rather than as a description of experience. In her work Rich addresses the question of female identity in a political sense, criticizing the rigid identification forms of certain types of feminism. For her, the lesbian-feminist entity is in movement, deconstructible, flexible and open to continuous transformations. According to Rich, in order to relaunch a lesbian-feminist ethic we need to valorize what she calls the 'lesbian continuum'; that is, the specifically female continuum of solidarity and creativity which has touched, and in some cases filled, the lives of women. Her numerous works, translated into many languages, include: *Of Woman Born: Motherhood as Experience and Institution* (1976); *The Dream of a Common Language: Poems, 1974–1977* (1978); and *What Is Found There: Notebooks on Poetry and Politics* (1993).

MONIA ANDREANI

RIGGS, MARLON

b. 1957; d. 1994

filmmaker

A leading African-American filmmaker whose films provide an articulate and passionate critique of racism and explore the complexities of black gay male identity. Riggs was born on 3 February 1957 in Fort Worth, Texas. He was raised in Germany and Texas, where he experienced first-hand the racism endemic in the racially segregated South. He was educated at Harvard and Berkeley's Graduate School of Journalism, where he later taught documentary filmmaking. His documentary *Ethnic Notions* (1987), which explored racial stereotypes, garnered Riggs critical acclaim and an Emmy.

A recurring theme in Riggs' work is the competing and conflicting facets of gender, ethnicity and sexuality in constructing black gay male identity. In his films and writing, he criticized not only the racism of the culturally dominant white gay community, but the homophobia also existing within African-American communities. He focused on the relative prejudice experienced by the 'sissy' gay black man, as opposed to the respect accorded to the conventionally masculine, heterosexual, black man. As a self-professed sissy himself, Riggs used filmmaking to express his anger about his status as a pariah and to demand respect for homosexual masculinity in the African-American community.

His most famous film, *Tongues Untied* (1989), was a ground-breaking exploration of black male sexuality, incorporating interviews, poetry, performance art and rap to expose the homophobia and racism experienced by many black gay men. Riggs made the film after almost dying of kidney failure, which was later revealed to be AIDS-related. The film was shown at the Cannes and Berlin Film Festivals to considerable international acclaim. His other films include *Color Adjustment: Blacks In Prime Time* (1991), a scathing critique of the limited representation of black people on television, and *No Regrets* (*No, Je Ne Regrette Rien*, 1993), which features interviews with HIV+ black men.

Riggs was as passionately committed to fighting for freedom of expression as he was to gay rights issues. His essays and criticism were published in *Black American Literature Forum*, *Art Journal* and *High Performance*, as well as in the anthology *Brother To Brother* (1991). He also served on the Public Broadcasting Service's policy committee and the National Endowment for the Arts.

Riggs died of AIDS-related complications in 1994, shortly before the completion of his final film, *Black Is...Black Ain't* (1995), a documentary examination of the diversity of black identity, using music, historical reference and personal testimony.

JOHN FORDE

RIMMING

The practice of stimulating the anus and the outer sphincter muscle with the tongue during sex. Although not exclusively a gay sexual practice, rimming is commonly associated with gay sex, especially as a way of relaxing a partner's anus before attempting penetration or to promote anal orgasm.

JOHN FORDE

ROBBINS, JEROME
b. 1918; d. 1998
dancer, choreographer, stage director

Born Jerome Rabinowitz on 11 October 1918 in New York, Robbins studied music and dance as a child and quit college to study ballet and modern dance. He joined the American Ballet Theater in 1940, and in 1944 choreographed the breakthrough ballet *Fancy Free*, set to a commissioned score by Leonard **Bernstein**, which later that year became the hit Broadway musical *On The Town*. His exceptional Broadway work achieved an extravagant integration of dance, music and character development, and encompassed the majority of the most important musicals of the twentieth century, including *The King and I* (1951), *West Side Story* (1957) and *Fiddler on the Roof* (1964). His numerous significant ballets, the majority of which were made for the New York City Ballet, include *Age of Anxiety* (1950), *The Cage* (1951), *Dances at a Gathering* (1969), *Watermill* (1972) and *Glass Pieces* (1983). Firmly closeted, and deeply ambivalent about his sexuality, Robbins testified before the House Un-American Activities Committee in 1953, naming names of Communist Party members to avoid public disclosure of his homosexuality. He died on 29 July 1998 in New York.

THOMAS F. DEFRANTZ

ROBERTS, IAN

b. 1965

rugby player

Australian Rugby League player Ian Roberts made headline news in 1995 when he publicly came out as gay. Widely regarded as one of the best front-rowers in rugby history, Roberts made his professional debut playing for the Sydney Souths team in 1986. Quickly developing a reputation as a skilful on-field tactician with a fearless streak, he transferred to Manly in 1991 in a deal that reputedly made him the most highly paid rugby player in the world. Roberts challenged the traditional macho stereotypes of his sport when he came out in 1995, the first professional footballer of any code to do so. While there was some negative commentary, the response from both media and fans was surprisingly supportive and Roberts emerged as an important symbol of gay pride. Following his retirement from football in 2000, Roberts started a new career as an actor, gaining entry to Australia's prestigious drama school, NIDA.

BRETT FARMER

ROBINSON, TOM

b. 1950

musician

Tom Robinson is a gay British rock 'n' roll musician born in 1950. Robinson emerged as a singer-songwriter in 1977 during the heyday of the punk scene, although his earliest recordings are not themselves punk but rather straight-ahead rock 'n' roll, with exhortatory lyrics attacking racism, class inequity and homophobia. His best-known recording is the sardonic sing-along 'Glad to be Gay' (1978), an ironic updating of the tradition of the popular British music-hall song. In the 1980s Robinson's music evolved towards moody atmospherics somewhat akin to Peter Gabriel and late 1970s David Bowie, with the songwriting becoming more autobiographical. In the 1980s, Robinson married a woman, although he continues to define himself as a gay man. His later recordings are dominated by confessional anthems that continue to revolve around Robinson's leftist politics and his experiences as a gay man. The mood in these later recordings is neither defiant nor melancholic but more often rueful and mellow.

DAVID PENDLETON

RODRGUEZ CASAS, FERNANDO

b. 1946

artist

Bolivian-born artist Fernando Rodríguez Casas' earliest work explores the multiple possibilities, limits and meanings of perspective, allowing for diverse levels of interpretation from philosophic points of view. Rodríguez Casas is influenced by the philosophy of Michel **Foucault** and Ludwig Wittgenstein. He caused a stir with the 1999 exhibit, *Diez figuras y una crucifixion* (Ten Figures and a Crucifixion), in which he used the male nude to complete his philosophical quest for meaning, expanding his previous oeuvre and approach, overtly including reflections upon homosexuality and the historical silence surrounding it. In this work he also included quotes from Francis **Bacon** and Leonardo da Vinci while appropriating art-movement languages generally centred on male heterosexual desire, such as Cubism, Dadaism and Impressionism, in order to re-signify them and incorporate homosexual desire. How-ever, to label his work as simply homo-erotic or gay would be reductive given the wide diversity of cultural, theoretical and material resources with which they are imbued. An outspoken activist for human civil and sexual rights, Rodríguez Casas currently teaches at Rice University in the United States.

PEDRO ALBORNOZ

ROLLING STONES

See: Jagger, Mick and the Rolling Stones

ROME

The strong presence of the Catholic Church, meant the Italian capital never witnessed a gay community until the 1970s when the first political groups appeared. The Circle Mario Mieli is an active political organiza-tion that has put together the yearly gay parade since 1991. World Pride 2000 ran concurrently with the Catholic Jubilee celebrations and was epoch-making. The Roman glbt community thus gained a stronger visibility, a City Counsellor for gay rights, a bookshop and a large number of bars including the Leather Club Roma.

MASSIMO FUSILLO

ROREM, NED

b. 1923

composer, writer

One of America's most celebrated compo-sers, Rorem's prolific output spans sym-phonies, operas, orchestral works, art songs, theatre and ballet music, as well as critical writings and memoirs. He was born on 23 October 1923 in Richmond, Indiana. After graduating from the prestigious Curtis Institute and Juilliard, where his early compositions attracted much acclaim, Rorem moved to France, where he lived

and worked until 1959. His life in the artistic and social world of postwar Europe is eruditely described in *The Paris Diary of Ned Rorem*, in which he also candidly details his gay sexual experiences. This was followed by his highly successful *New York Diaries*. Among his best-known composi-tions are adaptations of work by W.H. Auden, Jean Cocteau and Walt Whitman; his suite 'Air Music' (1975), which won the Pulitzer Prize; and 'More Than A Day' (2000), based on gay love poems by his friend Jack Larson. 'Another Sleep' (2002), a song cycle based on texts by Shakespeare and Sappho, was dedicated to Rorem's lover Jim Holmes, who died in 1999.

JOHN FORDE

ROSS, DIANA

b. 1944

singer

Diana Ross is an African-American singer whose soulful voice, confident sensuality and flexible pop styling made her the best-selling female artist of the 1960s and 1970s, as well as an icon for that era's black and gay communities.

Born in Detroit, Ross became a leading proponent of the Motown sound, shooting to stardom as lead vocalist of the phenom-enally successful 'girl group' The Supremes. Launching a solo career in 1970, Ross' star continued to rise as she successfully rode shifting waves of musical fashion embracing soul, disco and even synth-pop. During this period, select forays into acting furnished Ross with a series of high-profile film roles including her Oscar-nominated perfor-mance as Billie Holiday in *Lady Sings the Blues* (1972). Noted for her steely ambition and occasionally fiery temperament, Ross has been celebrated in gay cultures as a diva, an iconic symbol of empowered black femininity and resilience.

BRETT FARMER

ROSS, MIRHA-SOLEIL

b. 1969

performance artist

Canadian performance artist, videomaker, transsexual activist, curator and sex worker. Transplanted Québécois Ross is Toronto's most visible and prolific transgender cultural voice. Star of the National Film Board's well-intentioned documentary *In the Flesh* (Gordon McLennan, 2000), Ross' 16 or so own video productions had much more raw artistic energy and political bite – 'gut-busting, ass-erupting and immoderately whorish', as she entitles her compilation of video excerpts. The tapes, often made in collaboration with Xanthra MacKay and Mark Karbusicky, blur boundaries between document, demonstration, performance, narrative, autobiography, representation . . . and provocation. Ranging across her own personal body, history and experience to the political fields of reproductive technology and animal rights, Ross covers a broad landscape of politics and desire. *Yapping Out Loud: Contagious Althoughts from an Unrepentant Whore*, an epic 2002 document of a bravado theatrical performance, may be her most momentous work. Ross founded Toronto's 'Counting Past Two' trans-arts festival in 1998.

THOMAS WAUGH

ROUGH TRADE

A slang term for non-gay men (usually working class or in the military) available for sex with other men, often in exchange for money. The term predates the Gay Liberation Movement that began in the 1960s and is no longer widely used, as the model of choosing straight men as sexual partners has become stigmatized in the gay community.

DAVID PENDLETON

ROUND THE HORN

See: Julian and Sandy

ROXY MUSIC

See: Ferry, Bryan and Roxy Music

ROZEMA, PATRICIA

b. 1958

filmmaker

One of the world's most renowned lesbian filmmakers, Patricia Rozema's scriptwriting and direction wittily portrays women struggling to express their lesbian sexuality in the face of social disapproval. Born in Canada and raised in a strict Dutch Calvinist family, her highly acclaimed first feature, *I've Heard The Mermaids Singing* (1987), is a bittersweet comedy about a scatterbrained secretary falling in love with her lesbian art curator boss. *When Night Is Falling* (1995), a drama about a female Calvinist academic who must choose between her devoted boyfriend and a free-spirited lesbian circus performer, won international praise for its intelligent, passionate exploration of the conflicts between religious faith and sexual desire and for its beautifully filmed lesbian love scenes. Rozema aroused controversy with her next project, a bold reworking of Jane Austen's *Mansfield Park* (1999), rewriting Fanny Price as a forthright feminist and suggesting a lesbian *frisson* between Fanny and Mary Crawford.

JOHN FORDE

RUDNICK, PAUL

b. 1957

writer

Openly gay American playwright, screenwriter and novelist Paul Rudnick is noted for his biting wit and high camp humour. With a drama degree from Yale, Rudnick started his career writing occasional pieces for popular magazines and quickly gained a reputation as a mordant satirist. Major success came in the early 1990s with *Jeffrey*, a comical play about a young gay man with a crippling AIDS phobia. The show's combination of sensitive social issues and black comedy – a Rudnick hallmark – proved popular with critics and audiences alike, and, in 1994, Rudnick – who had already cut his screenwriting teeth on films such as *Sister Act* (1992, writing under a *nom de plume*) and *Addam's Family Values* (1993) – adapted the play into a successful film. Further screenwriting projects to bear the Rudnick stamp of camp humour include the mainstream gay comedy, *In and Out* (1997); a satirical biopic of Jacqueline Susann, *Isn't She Great* (2000); and the 2004 remake of *The Stepford Wives*.

BRETT FARMER

RUGBY

It is widely believed that rugby was born in 1823 when a player with a disregard for the rules of football took the ball in his arms and ran with it, thus originating the distinctive feature of the rugby game. Rugby was founded as, and remains, a deeply homosocial activity among men. It normalizes violent masculinity because the game is characterized by hard tackling, even though the players wear very little protective gear. The immense physical violence of rugby enables players to be considered the most masculine of men in many European cultures, because they epitomize standards of Western masculinity that value physical aggression and risk-taking. But, paradoxically, the homosocial nature of the sport also allows for contact between ostensibly heterosexual players in a fashion normally prohibited in other arenas. Thus, rugby may also be described as a rather intimate and homoerotic sport, where men are in constant contact with each other's bodies, as Peter Wells' 1990 film, *A Taste of Kiwi*, explores (see **Wells**, Peter).

It is perhaps the presence of homoeroticism in the nature of the sport that brings about a great deal of homophobia from the players; indeed, rugby is often regarded as a deeply homophobic sport. Not only does homophobia occur through name-calling and the stigmatizing of others as gay, but is evident in songs and rituals performed by players in an attempt to validate a sense of heterosexual masculinity. Nonetheless, gay players have existed within the sport (e.g., Ian **Roberts**), and all-gay rugby teams can be found among amateur heterosexual rugby leagues.

ERIC ANDERSON

RUPAUL

b. 1960

drag performer, singer, composer, actor

Sometimes known as Andre Charles, RuPaul was born in San Diego and moved to Atlanta as a teenager. There he found notoriety with nightclub stars Mona Foot and Lady Bunny. During the 1980s he moved to New York, where he often appeared as Star Booty, until his experience as a club kid and drag performer finally coalesced into the persona RuPaul. This 6' 7" creation, including high heels and hair, soon made an impression with the album *Supermodel to the World* (1993). It included three no. 1 Billboard maxi-single chart hits for the dance music single, 'Supermodel (You Better Work)' and the two songs 'Back to My Roots' and 'House of Love'.

Before long this exponent of love was bringing a mix of glamour, nightlife savvy and a camp but sincere updated sense of black pride to diverse venues. RuPaul even sang a version of 'Don't Go Breaking My Heart' (1993) with Elton John on his *Duets* album. Soon there were numerous appearances in films such as *Crooklyn* (1994), *To Wong Foo, Thanks for Everything! Julie Newmar* (1995) and *The Brady Bunch Movie* (1995), as well as an endorsement for MAC lipstick. Television appearances followed on such shows as *Port Charles, Veronica's Closet, Nash Bridges, Walker, Texas Ranger* and *Sabrina, the Teenage Witch*. From 1996 until 1998, the talk show *The RuPaul Show* ran three times per day, six days a week, on VH1. For the complete story, consult RuPaul's autobiography, *Lettin' It All Hang Out* (Hyperion, 1995).

GABRIEL GOMEZ

RUSSELL, KEN

b. 1927

filmmaker

A flamboyant and controversial filmmaker whose baroque visual style, heightened, melodramatic storylines and sexually explicit themes challenged the puritanism of British cinema. Happily married with children, Russell has attracted admiration from gay audiences for his frank depictions of gay and lesbian relationships, and his aesthetic of **camp** excess. His third feature, a sexually explicit adaptation of D.H. Lawrence's *Women In Love* (1969), brought him international acclaim and a Best Director Academy Award nomination. Scripted by Larry **Kramer**, the film starred Alan **Bates** as a sexually ambiguous schoolteacher who seeks physical relationships with men and women, and includes a highly erotic scene in which Bates and Oliver Reed wrestle nude. Russell returned to Lawrence with *The Rainbow* (1988), featuring a lesbian relationship between Ursula (Sammi Davis) and her gym instructor Winifred (memorably played by Amanda Donohoe). His other gay-themed dramas include *The Music Lovers* (1971), starring Richard **Chamberlain** as the composer Tchaikovsky, and *Valentino* (1977), starring dancer Rudolph **Nureyev**. He achieved commercial success with *The Boy Friend* (1971), an *homage* to 1930s Busby Berkeley film musicals, and the rock opera *Tommy* (1975). His films *The Devils* (1971), featur-

ing set design by Derek Jarman, and *The Lair of the White Worm* (1988), playfully fuse horror and camp aesthetics. *Salomé's Last Dance* (1988) sets Wilde's play *Salomé* in a nineteenth-century male brothel, with Wilde as a sexually playful spectator. An enthusiastic writer and commentator on film, Russell's legacy has influenced many gay filmmakers, including Jarman and Pedro **Almodóvar**.

JOHN FORDE

RUSSIA, FILMMAKING IN

The first Russian movies concerned with gay themes occurred during the 1990s, after the collapse of the Soviet Union. Since gay Russian literature as well as glbtq life could only exist underground, gay Russian cinema similarly could neither be realized nor circulated before this time. In 1933 homosexuality was criminalized and subsequently led to official deportations from the country. A gay Russian film director did however work in the Soviet Union during these years and deserves mention, even if his movies were not openly dedicated to gay themes. Sergei Paradzhanov (originally Paradzhanian, 1924–90) was born in Soviet Georgia of Armenian origins. He became a human rights activist in the late 1960s (a politically troubling time for the filmmaker), during which time he completed *Sayat Nova* (1969), the story of an ancient martyred Armenian monk, poet and hero. Unfortunately, it was not released outside Armenia for several years because Paradzhanov refused to let the Soviet government edit it. In 1977 a bootleg copy of the original was smuggled out and shown in Paris. When shown in New York, his film was heralded as the best Soviet film of the postwar period by many critics. By that time Paradzhanov had already endured many years of public humiliation in his homeland, including five years in prison. In 1978 he was released following protests from several Western luminaries but was not allowed to make films. He was arrested again in 1982 but saved by the French government's intervention. When Brezhnev's regime ended, he returned to filmmaking and continued to do so until he died of lung cancer in 1990.

Sotvorenie Adama (The Creation of Adam, 1993) is directed by Yurii Pavlov and is considered to be the first openly gay Russian film. In the film a guardian angel falls in love with his 'guardee', breaks all angelic regulations, comes down to Earth, lures him into his bed, cheats on his boy(-angel)-friend, and goes back to heaven, leaving the man with an expectant wife. The movie is at the same time romantic, innocent, explicit and funny. It was, ironically, reviewed as being too Russian for the gay international audience and too gay for Russian spectators.

In *Mania Zhizeli* (Giselle's Mania, dir. Aleksei Uchitel', 1995), Olga Spesivtseva, a classical ballerina of the early twentieth century, falls in love with the gay dancer Serge Lifar. Their love is impossible and sends Olga into madness and death. For the first time in Russian cinema, the homosexuality of male dancers is confronted directly, even if only to demonstrate that such revelations have tragic consequences, especially for women.

Soviet director Kira Muratova explores homosexuality in the 1997 film, *Tri istorii* (Three Stories), based on murder and a crime that goes unpunished. The role of the homosexual character (a young gay man forced to hustle to pay back his debts) is honestly and correctly depicted but it is a far from positive portrayal. In the film gay people are seen as unnatural or ill since, according to Muratova's symbolic world image, every human being in her movie, in spite of sexual tastes, is connected with crime and obsessed by murder. A fascinating and ambiguous movie of the mid-1990s, *Serp i molot* (Hammer and Sickle), directed by Sergei Livnev, takes us back to

the 1930s when Stalin's regime directed experiments on the nature of humans. Also during this time, since the army needed males, several women were transformed into men. One of the transsexuals becomes a well-known engineer, but she never manages to adapt to her new condition and to the nightmarish world in which she must live. Livnev's film about this subject was never released, albeit more because of bureaucratic problems than issues of censorship.

In 2000 a film dedicated to the life of Russian writer Ivan Bunin was released. *Dnevnik ego zheny* (His Wife's Diary) was directed by Aleksei Uchitel', in which love triangles and lesbianism of the intelligentsia circles during the first decades of the century are rendered. Similarly, in *Mest' shuta* (The Clown's Revenge, 1993), directed by Boris Blank and starring Boris Moiseev (the camp Russian actor), Rigoletto, Gilda and the Duke of Mantua indulge in sexual entertainments through a spirit of generous kitsch and camp sensibilities.

Two documentary films consider the political and social problems of glbtq cultures in Russia. Both films deal with issues of coming out, life in prison, homophobia and gay and lesbian organizations. The first film, *Moim podruzhkam* (To My Women Friends) specifically explores lesbian culture and was realized in 1993 by Natalia Sharandak. The second, *Moskovskie golubye* (Moscow Fags, 1995) is directed by Yakov Posel'sky and studies his relationship with Slava Mogutin, his boyfriend. The film concentrates on this well-known gay couple, responsible for many provocative and brave actions in Moscow that led to the (traumatic) emigration to the United States of Mogutin (and his American partner). The couple were known for their openly gay interviews, publications in Russian magazines and the attempt to register their wedding in Moscow in 1994.

Russian director Pavel Longuine now works in France, but his films remain devoted to Russia and Russian socio-political concerns. In his *Luna Park* (1992), for example, a young man involved in fascistic ethnic purges against Jews and gays, discovers that his father is a Jew and that he has had a love affair with a young female friend of his. Longuine's film is indicative of the confusion, violence and curiosity of the early 1990s in post-Soviet Russia with regard to new issues such as freedom of thought, action, speech and sexuality. New subjects, characters and problems, connected with glbtq themes will most likely develop as a result and interest broader audiences. However this will only happen following the Russian way – slowly and with caution.

GIAN PIERO PIRETTO

RUSSIA, LITERATURE IN

With the criminalization of homosexuality under Stalin in 1933, Soviet society became more and more puritanical and homophobic. Nikita Krushchev, after Stalin's death and during the so-called 'thaw', attacked young abstract painters with the worst possible insult: *pidarasy* (pederasts). During the 1970s several non-conformist and resistance movements emerged, but most underground literature and culture was more concerned with social and political issues than with private life and sexuality. Even within *samizdat* (an underground publication) and dissident circles, homosexuality was considered an embarrassment and not worthy of attention. Indeed, Russian literary language at this time was extremely puritanical; every attempt to break with traditional approaches was regarded with suspicion and diffidence. It was not until 1979, far away from the Soviet homeland, that a young Russian émigré published a provocative novel in the United States that hinted at bisexuality and homosexuality. Eduard Limonov (born Eduard Savenko in 1943) described his

own New York experiences in *Eto ia, Edichka* (*It's Me Eddie*). When, after the collapse of the Soviet Union, the book, along with other novels, was published in Russian in Russia, the author claimed he was embarrassed for his work's explicit and frank language.

The publication of Limonov's writings in Russia is connected to Aleksandr Shatalov, a poet himself and publisher of a gay magazine, *Glagol* (Verb), that is devoted to the rediscovery of alternative Russian literary works. The magazine combines forgotten avant-garde forms and 'unofficial' sexualities in its selections. It was the first to publish Limonov in Russia.

Within the Soviet Union the most popular gay writer and, indeed, the most original gay personality was Yevgeny Kharitonov (1941–81). Unfortunately he died of a heart attack before *perestroika* allowed him to publish his works and lead a secure life. A writer and choreographer, openly gay in life and literature, Kharitonov was an example of how 'gayness' existed but was tolerated by authorities only if it were not *too* explicit and flamboyant. Kharitonov was convinced that homosexuality was a gift from God and that it could positively affect his genius. His literary works (poetry, short stories, plays and essays) were never published during his lifetime, but his professional life as a theatre specialist was celebrated. He was interrogated by the KGB in 1979 about the murder of a gay man as well as his participation in a dissident literary collection, *Katalog*. His best-known work is *Dukhovka* (The Oven), the diary of a gay man falling in love with a straight boy. The first publication of his works, once again thanks to Shatalov's *Glagol*, was in Moscow in 1993, twelve years after his death.

Another interesting example of the interrelationship between gay life and literature during the Soviet era is that of Gennady Trifonov. Born in Leningrad in 1945, he worked as the literary secretary of a well-known conformist Soviet writer, Vera Panova, whose husband, also a writer, was gay. After Panova's death the KGB inquired about Trifonov's activities, both literary and private. His request to emigrate in 1975 led to his imprisonment a year later. His case became famous in the West, thanks to glbtq periodicals and friends who lived abroad. Only under *perestroika* was Trifonov allowed to travel and visit foreign countries. He is the founder, with Olga Zhuk, of the Russian literary journal *Gay Slaviane!* (Gay Slavs!) and is now a Professor of Literature and English in a St Petersburg private school.

Nikolai Kolyada (b. 1957) is a representative of the Soviet province of Kazakhstan, where he worked as an actor in the Sverdlovsk (now Ekaterinburg) Academic Theatre. He wrote his first play in 1986. As a son of *perestroika*, he became famous the world over. The staging of his *Rogatka* (The Slingshot) in 1989 by Roman Viktiuk (a leading Russian gay theatre director) in San Diego, California, led to several performances in different foreign countries. In 1993 the play finally opened in Moscow. In the play, the student Anton accidentally prevents Il'ya, a cripple and a drunkard, from committing suicide. An unusual feeling of homosexual desire and affection arises. The strange and impossible feelings that they experience under the Soviet regime lead Il'ya finally to commit suicide. Kolyada was often accused of melodramatics and oversentiment. After the Moscow premiere of his play, including the play's gay sex scene, President Yeltsin halted discrimination against homosexuality, and decriminalized it. Viktiuk (b. 1936), the play's director, was born in the Ukraine. He studied at the Moscow Theatre Institute and, as a gay man, combined personal and political intolerance for the conservative and prudish world of Soviet culture. His work was first presented in the most liberal territories of the Soviet Union, the Baltic Republics. Only after *perestroika* did he manage to come out to the theatre world. Arguably, he is the first Russian director to understand and make use of a camp sensibility.

Yaroslav (Slava) Mogutin (b. 1974) is one of the most eccentric figures of the contemporary Russian gay literary world. He became famous during the early 1990s, when his essays and poetry appeared regularly in Russian periodicals, both underground and mainstream. He was the editor of Kharitonov's works and has translated both James Baldwin and William Burroughs. A gay journalist and poet, his words so provoked the post-Soviet establishment that at the age of 21 he left the country to escape numerous death threats. After landing in New York in 1995, he applied for political asylum. Thanks in part to a campaign mounted on his behalf by PEN and Amnesty International, he became the first Russian granted US sanctuary from persecution for sexual orientation.

In 2002 a leading Russian writer, Vladimir Sorokin (1955), referenced gay culture with his novel (whose title was a clear postmodernist quotation) *Goluboe salo* (Blue Lard). *Goluboi* (blue) is the Russian slang expression for gay. Sorokin's story implied a homosexual relationship between Stalin and Khrushchev. The author was indicted for pornography by the conservative Russian puritans, but the trial garnered substantial publicity as, consequently, did the book. The most complete anthology of contemporary gay, Russian literature in English translation remains *Out of the Blue* (1997), edited by Kevin Moss for the Gay Sunshine Press. The best-known gay, Russian literary journal is *Mitin Zhurnal* (Mitia's Magazine; Mitia stands for Dmitrii Volchek, the editor). A reliable web site is *www.gay.ru*, where the book section offers online reviews and a subscription to receive by email updates about new gay Russian literary productions.

GIAN PIERO PIRETTO

493

RUSSO, VITO

b. 1946; d. 1990

film critic, historian

The outstanding role played by Vito Russo in contemporary queer culture is largely due to his seminal book, *The Celluloid Closet*, turned down by 18 publishers and eventually published by Harper & Row in 1981. Spurred on by his involvement in early gay activism, his writings for the gay press and his work in the film department at the Museum of Modern Art in New York in the early 1970s, and thanks to extensive research in a number of institutions throughout the US and in London, *The Celluloid Closet* was the first book (with the exception of Parker Tyler's 1972 *Screening the Sexes*) to chart gay and lesbian imagery in cinema. It was not a gossip book outing famous actors, but rather an extraordinarily in-depth documented historical research devoted to how male and female cinematic homosexuality emerged through silence and indirection, lifting the veil of censorship on coded references and uncovering homoerotic subtexts in popular cinema. It was a look into the representation of sexual otherness, into the modes by which normality relegates difference to the fringes of visibility. In an analysis that encompasses over 300 movies – ranging from rare footage of homoerotic couplings in the early twentieth century, to Hollywood films showing Laurel and Hardy cuddling each other in bed, or Marlene Dietrich and Jack Lemmon in drag, to the Hollywood Motion Picture Production Code censorship that prohibited representation of 'sex perversion' – a thronged gallery of sissies, lesbian butch-haircut vampires and screaming queens introduce the reader to manhood and womanhood as defined by gender role mythology. As he wrote in his introduction, 'we have cooperated for a very long time in the maintenance of our own invisibility. And now the party is over.' The very possibility of a cultural counter-history, both exhilarating and disturbing, was opened.

Vito's was a pioneering book for its subject (the gay and lesbian culture heritage) and methodology (employing historical reviews and commentary to illuminate the historically coded implications of what people perceived in pictures at the time). But it was also a landmark book in defining the very possibility of a gay spectatorship: accessible, witty and enjoyable, so as to end up being highly marketable (and to prefigure a gay criticism market). The book was written by a gay man, which paved the way for a generation of politically committed gay filmmakers and critics.

By the late 1980s Vito had become a beloved figure (his book being reissued in a second, enlarged edition in 1987), intensely lecturing throughout the US, when he died of complications from AIDS. His dream of making a movie out of *The Celluloid Closet* was made reality thanks to the efforts of Robert Epstein and Jeffrey Friedman, who used the screenplay Russo had crafted in 1986 and, in 1995, released the same-titled film. The film version was welcomed by critical acclaim and internationally released, bringing Russo's legacy to an even wider audience. It tasted like both a treasure of knowledge, and a tribute to its witty, knowledgeable researcher, a pioneer whose seminal role is dutifully acknowledged by the Vito Russo Center Library in New York City, and the Vito Russo Award for Filmmaking.

Further reading

Dyer, R. (1990) *Now You See It: Studies on Lesbian and Gay Film*, New York: Routledge.

Ehrestein, D. (1998) *Open Secret: Gay Hollywood, 1928–1998*, New York: William Morrow.

Walters, S.D. (2001) *All the Rage: The Story of Gay Visibility in America*, Chicago: University of Chicago Press

FABIO CLETO

RUST, PAULA

b. 1959

sociologist

Paula Rust has studied bisexuality extensively, focusing on lesbian biphobia and lesbian–bisexual relations; bisexual identity development; bisexuals' experiences and perceptions; the history of social science research on bisexuality; and the history of the concept of bisexuality. Rust demonstrated that lesbian characterizations of bisexual women secured boundaries between the two groups by defining clearly who was and was not a 'real' lesbian. She studied bisexual identity development, creating a flexible model that rejects sexual essentialism. Rust compiled the first social science anthology on bisexuality, which includes coverage of bisexuality in HIV research, demographic findings about bisexuality among other topics. More recently, Rust has posited that the conditions of the development of bisexuality as a concept – the hetero-/homosexual divide of the late nineteenth century – were also the conditions for the social suppression of bisexuality, and thus for biphobia.

AMANDA UDIS-KESSLER

RUSTIN, BAYARD

b. 1912; d. 1987

activist

A tireless political strategist and activist, Rustin's central role in the American civil rights movements was frequently overshadowed because of prejudice he faced as an openly gay man. He was born on 17 March 1912 in West Chester, Pennsylvania. Raised a Quaker, he moved to New York in 1937, where he became involved with the Young Communist League (although he later disavowed communism), black trade unions and the Fellowship of Reconciliation. He was imprisoned for three years as a conscientious objector during the Second World War. Shortly after his release, he organized the 'Journey of Reconciliation', in which protesters deliberately violated the segregated seating patterns on buses and trains in the Southern states. Regularly beaten and arrested, Rustin served 22 days on a chain gang in North Carolina. His account of the experience, serialized in the *New York Post*, prompted the abolition of chain gangs in this state.

In 1963, Rustin worked with Dr Martin Luther King Jr on the Montgomery Bus Boycott, persuading King to adopt a nonviolent protest stance. He organized the 1963 March on Washington for Jobs and Freedom, then the largest demonstration in American history, at which King gave his historic 'I Have A Dream' speech. Senator Strom Thurmond denounced the march, calling attention to Rustin's homosexuality, but Rustin was publicly defended by King.

Openly gay, Rustin experienced frequent discrimination and lack of recognition because of his sexuality, and spoke openly about homophobia within American society. In his later years he became an active campaigner for gay civil rights, labour law reform, nuclear disarmament and the treatment of refugees. His published essays include *Down The Line* (1971) and *Strategies for Freedom: The Changing Patterns of Black Protest* (1976). The documentary *Brother Outsider: The Life of Bayard Rustin* (2003), did much to redress public ignorance about Rustin's work.

Rustin died on 24 August 1987 in New York City.

JOHN FORDE

S

SADOMASOCHISM (S&M)

Sexual practices in which the play of domination and submission extends from the difficult psychology of the mindfuck to the use of elaborate and expensive equipment for restraint, enclosure, penetrations and the giving of both the broad palette and microtechnologies of pain. Essentially a consensual and intellectual relation in our period, it has little to do with the eponymous Sade and Sacher-Masoch, whose linking was rather an outcome of nineteenth-century sexology. It is common to heterosexuality, bisexuality and homosexuality, and has a vast pornographic literature.

ADRIAN RIFKIN

SAFE SEX

Although sporadically encouraged prior to 1981, 'safe sex' became a mantra in response to HIV/AIDS. Safe sex is defined by taking precautions to prevent the transmission of **HIV** and other sexually transmitted diseases (STDs). These precautions include proper and consistent use of a condom and dialogue between sexual partners. Safe sex is a predominant component of most HIV/AIDS/STD education and prevention efforts, although some conservative factions encourage outright abstinence. Since abstinence is not a viable option for many of the world's populations, safe sex

has given millions of people an effective strategy for remaining healthy.

CHRIS BELL

SALZGEBER, MANFRED
b. 1943; d. 1994
film producer

Manfred Salzgeber was born in Lodz, in present-day Poland, but grew up in Stuttgart. He moved to Berlin and was involved in gay and lesbian film from very early on, appearing in Rosa von Praunheim's 1970 film *Nicht die Homosexuelle is pervers, sondern die Situation, in der er lebt* (*It Is Not the Homosexual Who is Perverse But the Situation in Which He Finds Himself*). From that time on, he was one of the most engaged and active figures in gay German filmmaking, first with his Bali Cinema and then later with his own distribution firm, Salzgeber Editions, which specialized in AIDS-related films. He was also for many years director of the Panorama section of the Berlin International Film Festival and was the main force in ensuring the significant place of gay and lesbian film in that important festival. He died from AIDS in 1994.

DANIEL HENDRICKSON

SAME-SEX MARRIAGE / CIVIL UNION

Gay and lesbian people have been attempting to have their relationships recognised

496

officially by the state since the beginnings of organized society. John Boswell's definitive text, *Same-Sex Unions in Premodern Europe* (1994), reveals a long history of same-sex unions in pre-modern Europe, although he notes that because of widespread religious and cultural disapproval of homosexuality, most ceremonies were conducted in private and without orthodox legal or religious sanction.

With the rise of gay and lesbian civil rights movements during the 1960s and 1970s, some activists argued for the legal recognition of same-sex relationships, but the issue was shelved while the gay and lesbian community concentrated on the repeal of anti-sodomy laws.

Opinion is divided within the gay and lesbian community as to whether same-sex relationships should be recognized. Some activists argue for the right to marry in the same manner as heterosexual couples. Others view marriage as a heterosexist and repressive religious institution and argue that allowing same-sex couples to marry represents an undesirable assimilation of gay culture into the heterosexual mainstream.

Many activists and writers argue for an alternative form of civil union that affords partners the same rights and responsibilities as legal marriage, thus avoiding the historical connotations of marriage. Many politicians argue that civil unions are the most expedient strategy for gaining recognition for same-sex couples, so as to avoid opposition from critics wishing to maintain marriage as an exclusively heterosexual institution. Many activists, however, argue that same-sex relationships should exist outside of the law, with no formal legal recognition.

In 1989 Denmark became the first country to grant legal recognition of same-sex relationships, with a civil partnerships registration system granting registered same-sex couples the same rights and responsibilities as married couples, except for the right to adopt children.

In the United States, the same-sex unions argument has met with fierce and sustained opposition from the conservative religious right. The first same-sex marriage case, *Baker* v. *Nelson*, was heard in Minnesota in 1970, but was dismissed in the State and Supreme Courts. Subsequent cases in Kentucky (*Jones* v. *Hallahan*, 1973) and Washington State (*Singer* v. *Hara*, 1974) met with similar failures. The same-sex marriage movement received a boost with the Hawaiian Supreme Court's 1993 decision in *Baehr* v. *Lewin*, which argued that denying same-sex marriage violated Hawaii's Equal Rights Amendment, and referred the case to a trial court. In 1996, the trial court reached the same decision, but the case was referred to the Hawaiian Supreme Court. The Court reserved its decision for over two years, giving the Hawaiian legislature time to pass a law restricting marriage to opposite-sex partners. A similar process followed in the state of Alaska in 1998.

The movement suffered a major setback in 1996 when the federal government passed the Defence of Marriage Act, which defined marriage as a relationship between a man and a woman and released individual states from the obligation to recognize other states' same-sex relationship legislation. Despite this setback, in the 1999 case of *Baker* v. *State*, the Vermont Supreme Court found in favour of six same-sex couples seeking the right to marry. The court stopped short of requiring the state to issue marriage licences, but directed the Vermont legislature to adopt an alternative legal arrangement for marriage between same-sex couples. In 2000 Vermont passed America's first civil union system for same-sex couples, and has since attracted thousands of couples from throughout the United States and other countries.

In 2001 the Netherlands became the first country to allow same-sex couples to marry and adopt children. Belgium and the Canadian state of Ontario followed suit in 2003, and Taiwan in 2004, with Spain set to adopt similar laws in 2006.

To date, the argument for civil partnership has had more success than same-sex marriage, with civil partnership legislation enacted in the American states of New York, New Jersey, Indiana and Arizona, and in countries including Australia (the states of New South Wales, Australian Capital Territory, Queensland, Tasmania and Victoria), Argentina, Brazil, Canada, Chile, the United Kingdom, Finland, France, Germany, Greenland, Hungary, Iceland, Ireland, Luxembourg, New Zealand, Norway, Portugal and Sweden.

JOHN FORDE

SANTORUM, RICK

b. 1958

politician

Conservative US Senator who is known for his opposition to homosexuality and efforts to block gay rights initiatives. Santorum was born on 10 May 1958 in Winchester, Virginia. He worked on Senator John Heinz's re-election campaign while still an undergraduate and, after graduation, worked for Pennsylvania Senator J. Doyle Corman from 1981 to 1986. After a four-year tenure as an attorney, he was elected to Congress for Pennsylvania's 18th District in 1990. Advocating fiscally and morally conservative policies, he cut state spending on welfare, healthcare and education, and drafted a reform programme requiring welfare recipients to work for their benefits. He was elected to the Senate in 1994, where he raised controversy by sponsoring a law restricting abortion procedures. A vocal opponent of homosexuality, which he has compared to incest, he criticized the Supreme Court's decision to strike down anti-sodomy laws in *Lawrence* v. *Texas* (2004) and has actively campaigned against same-sex marriage initiatives.

JOHN FORDE

SAPHIRA, MIRIAM

b. 1941

artist, psychologist, writer

As an author, poet, researcher, bibliographer, publisher, artist, activist and psychologist, Miriam Saphira is ubiquitous in New Zealand lesbian culture. Her work is often concerned with ensuring that narratives and experiences (especially those likely to remain untold) are collected and made public. In 1984 Saphira's *Amazon Mothers* became the first lesbian non-fiction book to be published in New Zealand. She has published three collections of poetry, as well as the autobiographical *A Man's Man: A Daughter's Story* (1997), about her father's hitherto unknown gay life. In addition to her own work, Saphira has compiled a number of collections of lesbian writing and bibliographies about lesbian literature. Her art exhibitions, such as 1997's *Taking the 'His' Out of History*, are particularly concerned with issues of lesbian visibility. Saphira has a PhD in psychology and has published several books on child abuse.

See also: New Zealand, literature

ANITA BRADY

SARGESON, FRANK

b. 1903; d. 1982

writer

An iconic literary figure, Frank Sargeson is often described as the 'father' of New Zealand literature. Born Norris Davey, Sargeson changed his name when, in 1929, he and another man were caught masturbating each other and convicted for 'indecent assault'. The incident remained a secret until after the writer's death. Publicly, Sargeson only ever referred obliquely to his homosexuality, and his autobiographies reveal little about his 40-year relationship with Harry Doyle. Most famous for his short fiction, Sargeson's early writing is celebrated as a starkly realist account of the inarticulate world of working-class men. Yet, in works such as 'The Hole that Jack Dug' (1945) and 'That Summer' (late 1930s), Sargeson knowingly blurred the line between homosocial mateship and homosexual desire in a way that suggests a simmering puritanical violence which prevents the expression of desire. The more ornate style of his later work retained the key theme of a dark and conformist New Zealand.

See also: New Zealand, literature

ANITA BRADY

SCANDINAVIA, LITERATURE OF

Scandinavia lies in the northern region of Europe. It comprises Sweden, Denmark, Norway, Finland and Iceland. Historically, Denmark and Norway have been in union, as have Sweden and Finland, and Sweden and Norway. Iceland was developed by Norwegian settlers. The languages spoken in all the Scandinavian countries are related, with the exception of Finnish. Scandinavia's common history has produced a shared view on domestic affairs. Laws adopted in one country are often adopted in other Scandinavian countries also.

After the Second World War, the Soviet Union and the United States dominated international affairs. Both scientific research and popular culture were imported to Scandinavia from the US and were often translated into the Nordic languages. When considering post-Second World War Scandinavian gay and lesbian literature, one must bear in mind translations of books from Europe and the US. After the defeat of the Third Reich, homosexuals and communists proved to be the new threat to a stable society – in the view of ruling American leaders. The witch hunt of Senator McCarthy exerted its influence on Scandinavia as well. When the Cold War ended in 1989, new enemies superseded the old ones.

The 1950s

American sexologist Alfred C. Kinsey (1894–1956) produced what came to be the starting point for the organization of homosexual groups and movements in Scandinavia with his statistical surveys *Sexual Behaviour in the Human Male* (1948) and *Sexual Behaviour in the Human Female* (1953) (see **Kinsey Report, The**). A disengaged view of homosexuality was presented in these works, and a surprisingly high number of men and women were shown to have had same-sex experiences.

As a direct result of Kinsey's report on male sexuality, the organization Forbundet af 1948 (The Association of 1948) was founded in Denmark. In 1950 an offshoot of the organization was founded in Norway as 'Det Norske Forbundet af 1948' (The Norwegian Association of 1948), and later that same year Sweden saw its own group come together under the name RFSL (The Swedish Federation for Lesbian, Gay, Bisexual and Transgender Rights). To become a member one had to be recommended by other members. The strategy was to conform to heterosexual society. Anonymity was prescribed and the use of pseudonyms flourished. These organizations came to be the leading instigators of change and reform for homosexual men and women in the Nordic countries.

Nevertheless, pre-war views on homosexuality as a third sex prevailed. Renowned Danish journalist Christian Houmark (1869–1950) published two memoirs after his death in 1950. *Naar jeg er død: et Selvportræt* (When I'm Dead: a Self Portrait) focuses on the tragic destiny of the male homosexual. The Danish writer Herman Bang's (1857–1912) *Breve til Fritz* (Letters to Fritz, 1951) was published posthumously.

Forbundet af 1948 produced a membership magazine called *Vennen* (1949–74). It was confiscated during a police raid in 1955 during the so-called 'Store pornografiaffære' (Great Porno Affair), leading to a number of arrests, but was re-established in 1956 with the journalist and author Martin Elmer (b. 1930) as a leading force. Elmer has written a number of books, novels and articles, as well as the script for the TV programme *Et foragtet mindretal* (A Despised Minority) in 1968. The Store pornografiaffære was a serious blow to gays and lesbians and led to many homosexuals taking their lives. In 1956 *Pan* was established as a membership paper; it continues to be published today and is the longest-running gay and lesbian publication in the world.

Sweden had its own scandals during the early 1950s. The so-called Haijby and Kejne affairs exposed public panic after the decriminalization of male homosexuality in 1944. Haijby was a presumed lover of King Gustav V and was paid considerable amounts of money to keep quiet about their affair. Kejne was a priest who thought he had stumbled on a homosexual conspiracy involving the highest ranks of society. The affair led to an investigation that proved nothing substantial but forced the resignation of a minister.

The literary climate was hence very oppressive, yet Swedish teacher and author Nils Hallbeck (1907–97) published novels on homosexual desire. *Grabb på glid* (Boy Astray, 1949) and *Blodet begär* (Craving Blood, 1951) could be mentioned among a great number of such books. Gösta Carlberg (1909–73) placed his novels in antiquity and received good reviews. *Den sparade ynglingen* (Young Man Saved, 1954) and *Offerynglingen* (Young Man Sacrificed, 1954) both told the story of ancient Thebes.

One of the few lesbian characters of the time, Viveka, appears in the crime story by Maria Lang (1914–91) *Mördaren ljuger inte ensam* (The Murderer Doesn't Lie Alone, 1949), in which jealousy leads to murder. The murderer is the lesbian character, upholding a tradition of murderous lesbians in popular culture. After having described her confusion when she discovered her strange attraction, she eventually finds it natural and pleasing to her – only to die in the same instant she has told her story to the others.

The 1960s

All these negative conceptions of sexuality gradually changed during the 1960s, when sexual liberalism swept through Scandinavia. The change was the result of a liberalization of the law. Sexual information was provided by educational films and comedies. *Kaerlighedens ABZ* (ABC of Love, 1961) by Inge and Sten Hegeler in Denmark and *De erotiska minoriteterna* (The Erotic Minorities, 1964) by Lars Ullerstam in Sweden, were examples of informational literature that created a new atmosphere for homosexual men and women. The long series of short stories called *Kärlek 1–14* (Love 1–14, 1965–70) was a success. One of its authors, Annakarin Svedberg (b. 1934) also wrote two lesbian novels, *Vingklippta* (Clipped Wings, 1962), a dark but graphic portrait of gay life in Stockholm during the early 1960s, and *Din egen* (Yours Truly, 1966), a song of praise to sexuality and love as life's main forces. In parallel with this, however, in Denmark *Den grimme lov* (The Ugly Law) reigned between 1961 and 1965. This criminalized a partner in a sexual encounter, where a pack of cigarettes could be seen as payment for sex and caused much harm within the male homosexual community.

In Norway Jens Bjørneboe (1920–76) was bisexual and wrote of his experiences with men. The poem 'Elegi for en hengt sopar' (Elegy to a Hanged Bugger, 1965) depicts the tragic death of a gay man. His pornographic novel *Uten en tråd* (Without a Thread, 1966) was banned. Bjørneboe pleads for a humanitarian respect of all kinds of love. His follow up, *Uden en trævl II* (Without a Thread II, published in Denmark in 1968) was even harsher in its criticism of society's homophobia. The main character, Lillian, has many hetero-sexual experiences, only to find true happiness in a lesbian relationship with the prostitute Renate. Bjørneboe found a young disciple in Gudmund Vindland (b. 1949). His coming-out novel *Villskudd: sangen till Jens* (Wild Shot: The Song For Jens, 1979) was a huge success and was commemorated in 2004 with a party at Soho in Oslo arranged by the Pink Pen and the gay and lesbian book club Kursiv. His follow-up, *Stjerneskudd* (Star Shot, 1989), told the rest of the story of Yngve Vilde, who had fled into alcohol and drugs upon discovering that his love was in contra-diction to society's norms. Odd Klippenvåg (b. 1951) treats the same subject in *Otto, Otto* (1983). Per Knutsen (f. 1951) writes novels for the young such as *Svart cayal* (Black Eyeliner, 1988), about the 14-year-old Johnny, who loves makeup.

The Swedish author Bengt Martin (b. 1933) wrote the coming-out story *Sodomsäpplet* (Apple of Sodoma, 1968) and *Nejlik-musslan* (Carnation Clam, 1969). The books are also called *The Story of Joakim*. Joakim Mander lives with his single mother. His father has died, and to make money they let a room to Verner. Joakim takes a fancy to Verner and, upon realizing his true feelings, looks up the word homosexual in an ency-clopaedia. The heteronormative description makes Joakim understand his homosexuality as a sickness and abnormality and he attempts suicide. In the second novel he finds refuge in the world of the theatre. Bengt Martin became a national gay repre-sentative in Sweden when he appeared in a televised Storforum (Big Forum, 1968) together with his partner Hans.

Many fictional characters wrestle with their belief in God. Eva, who has fallen in love with Claudia, is such a character. The Swedish author and translator Eva Alex-anderson (1911–94) has created an impressive treatment of carnal love, true faith and religious devotion in her novel *Kontradans* (Counterdance, 1969).

The United States' domination of world affairs has displayed itself in the influx of trends, movies and literature, as well as through the student rebellion of the 1960s. The **Stonewall Riots**, which took place in New York in 1969, were followed by demonstrations in commemoration of the event in Copenhagen in 1971, in Sweden in 1971 (Örebro) and in Norway in 1973. Marxism and left-wing radicalism inspired the revolt. There was a strong belief in the need to come out of the closet.

The Danish writer, Christian Kampmann (1939–98), radicalized by these events, joined up with the Gay Liberation Front. He wrote the so-called 'bøssetrilogin' (The Gay Trilogy) consisting of *Fornemmelser* (Sensations, 1977), *Videre trods alt* (Go On In Spite Of It All, 1979) and *I glimt* (In Glimpse, 1980). These books were a high-light in the so-called confessional literature trend, where the general idea was to show the universal by depicting the very perso-nal. Kampmann was killed by his compa-nion and lover, the author Jens Michael Schau (b. 1948), when they both tried to write a follow-up to the popular TV series *Matador*. Schau later wrote about the events in his novel *Katarsis* (Catharsis, 2000).

The radicalized feminist movement of the 1960s and 1970s put forward lesbians as a driving force, though they were much opposed by the heterosexual feminists. The Danish writer Bente Clod (b. 1946) gives a good example of a woman, Bente, breaking away from her suburban villa quarters and sharing a new way of life with her female lover Jeanette in her novel *Brud* (Breaking Up, 1977). The question is not why are they homosexual but why they are not allowed to live openly and without recri-mination as homosexuals.

The same ideas permeate the magazine *Stina Line* (with various other names 1983–8), a lesbian-feminist paper from the Swedish town of Gothenburg. There was a world of history to be researched and cul-ture to present. Openness was the goal.

Norwegian Gerd Brantenberg (b. 1941) published a novel called *Opp alle jordens homofile!* (Homosexuals of the World Unite!, 1973), which appeared one year after homosexuality was decriminalized in Norway. It depicts the life of a woman who refuses to regard her homosexuality as a problem or a sickness. The book circulated in Oslo's gay community and made Brantenberg well known when her next book *Egalias døtre* (Egalia's Daughters, 1977) appeared. It became an international success. Like her lesbian sisters in Scandinavia, Brantenberg set out to find the cultural heritage of the women doubly suppressed – by male chauvinist society and also by gay men. She and four others put together a bibliography with commentaries, *På sporet af den tabte lyst* (On the Track of Lost Desire, 1986). It represents four and a half years of research into Nordic literature to discover novels that depict love between women.

Sweden

Radical in his will to oppose the pressure of Swedish society, Jonas Gardell (b. 1963) made his debut with *Passionsspelet* (The Passion Play, 1985) about the boys Hampus and Johan, who are suggested as doubles for Jesus Christ and Judas. From his debut religious matters have been central to Gardell, as in his collection of essays, *Oskuld* (Virgin, 2000) and *Om Gud* (On God, 2003). Gardell and his partner Mark Levengood are a popular and public gay couple, often spoken about in the press. Gardell is also an acclaimed stand-up comedian and probably the most influential gay person in Sweden.

During the 1950s Swedish author Birgitta Stenberg (b. 1932) lived a bohemian life in France, Italy and other places around the Mediterranean. In 1981 she printed a novelistic tale of her escapades in the literary world during her youth. Her lesbian lovers are portrayed and described in the

dichotomy butch/femme and how the different roles felt to the ever-experimenting Birgitta. *Kärlek i Europa* (Love in Europe, 1981) sold well as did her sequels *Apelsinmannen* (The Orange Man, 1983), about the Kejne affair and a gay poet in Stockholm, *Spanska Trappan* (Spanish Stairs, 1987), about sex, drugs, poetry and the role they played during her time in Rome, and *Alla vilda* (All Wild, 2004), about life in Mallorca in the 1950s. Radclyffe Hall was an inspiration for her first novel. *The Well of Loneliness* (trans. 1932) has been very influential in lesbian circles in Sweden. The translation was republished in 2004 as the first item by the newly founded lesbian and gay publishing house, Normal, in Stockholm.

Finland

Among the Nordic countries, Finland is the most homogenous, but also the most homophobic country. Immigration is scarce and homosexuals were treated as sick deviants for a long time. Influences from Sweden and other Nordic countries are influential in Finnish social development. In 1974 the Finnish liberation movement SETA was founded, SETA comprising the first four letters in the phrase 'sexual equality' in Finnish. The President of the Finnish Republic, Tarja Halonen, was chairwoman of SETA from 1980 to 1981.

The Swedish-language Finnish writer Christer Kihlman (b. 1930) wrote a number of books depicting his own life and love of men. *Människan som skalv* (The Man Who Collapsed, 1971), an autobiographical novel on alcoholism, homosexuality and a troubled marriage, created a public discussion on homosexuality. The subject of homosexuality was not new to him. *Den blå modern* (The Blue Mother, 1963) contained a homosexual main character. *Alla mina söner* (All My Sons, 1980) tells of two Latin American boys, José and Juan, and the love Kihlman felt for the latter. It is a novel about geographical and economical differences. *Gert Bladhs undergång* (The Fall of Gert Bladh, 1987) portrays the head of a department store in Helsinki whose erotic adventures with boys abroad are used by his opponents in the fight for control over the business.

The best-known Finnish author is probably Tove Jansson (1914–2001), the creator of the Moomintrolls, which have enchanted children around the world. Tove Jansson also wrote books for adults however, such as *Rent spel* (Fair Play, 1989), in which two elderly ladies share a life together, just as Jansson did with her life-long love, Tuulikki Pietilä, a graphic artist.

The popular and well-liked Finnish author Pirkko Saisio (b. 1949) has written a lesbian novel of note, *Kainin tytär* (The Daughters of Kain, 1984). She shares her life with filmmaker Pirjo Honkasalo. Saisio published a trilogy under a pseudonym, Jukka Larsson, creating a stir when she revealed her identity.

Ystävän muotokuva (Portrait of a Friend, 1998) by Pentti Holappa (b. 1927) is a sad, romantic and at the same time happy portrait of the author's longtime love affair with painter Asser Vaho. Art and artists, love between men, as well as love between men and women, are central themes.

Iceland

The Icelandic language contains quite coarse expressions directed towards homosexuals, reflecting a long-held homophobia. Not until 1978 was the first liberation movement formed. Samtökin '78 started with twenty members; it now has 400 (the total population of Iceland is approximately 270,000).

During the 1990s several Icelandic authors dealt with same-sex love, includig Guóbergur Bergsson, Kristín Ómarsdóttir (b. 1962) and Vigdís Grímsdóttir (b. 1953). The descriptions have a flavour of lived experience. Grímsdóttir's novel *Z: ástarsaga*

(Z: A Love Story, 1996) tells the tale of Z, who lives with the dying Anna. Her novels have been translated into many languages.

Queer theory in Scandinavia

Another wave of influence from the United States was felt in the 1990s. Queer theory made a mark mostly in university research (see **Theory and theorists, queer**). Assistant professor Tiina Rosenberg (b. 1958), in Stockholm, explored gender transgression in trouser roles in **opera** and theatre in her work *Byxbegär* (Trouser Desire, 2000). In *Queerfeministisk agenda* (Queer Feminist Agenda, 2002) she studies political action as it relates to postmodernism, finding that they thrive well together. Assistant professor Jens Rydström (b. 1955) produced a dissertation on sodomy, sexual intercourse with animals and the historical development of the homosexual (published by Chicago University Press as *Sinners and Citizens: Bestiality and Homosexuality in Sweden, 1880–1950* [2003]). The work won the John Boswell prize two years later. Assistant professor Nils Axel Nissen (b. 1967), in Oslo, produced an award-winning thesis in 1996, *Prince and Pauper: the Life and Literary Career of Bret Harte*. Finnish Lasse Kekki (b. 1964) defended his doctoral dissertation *From Gay to Queer: Gay Male Identity in Selected Fiction by David Leavitt and in Tony Kushner's play 'Angels in America I–II'* in 2003. Assistant professor Dag Heede (b. 1962), in Odense, writes about queer novels by the Danish author Karen Blixen (1885–1962) in *Det umenneskelige* (The Unhuman, 2001) and about the hidden queerness of H.C. Andersen (1805–75) and his lifelong love of men in *Hjertebrødre: krigen om H. C. Andersens seksualitet* (Brothers of the Heart: the War on H. C. Andersen's Sexuality, 2005).

Heede has made some progress in his attempt to queer the Danish literary canon. The queer view of identity as a societal construct has been influential in recent intellectual debates in Scandinavia. In these debates it is posited that gays and lesbians are marginalized by society, not as an expression of an 'inner' loss but as a result of heteronormative structural violence. Verbal expressions are actions. As a result of such academic work, a number of non-heteronormative sexualities are now taken into account. For example, in Sweden an ombudsman for homosexual affairs was founded as HomO in 1999.

Contemporary developments

The glossy free monthly magazine QX (Queer Extra, 1995–) is edited by Jon Voss (b. 1959), who has finally succeeded in producing an informative and influential paper that reflects events and developments in the queer community after failures with *Magazine Gay* (1984–5) and *Reporter* (1986–95). QX also constitutes the largest Nordic glbtq community on the net (*www.qx.se*).

The Norwegian author Anne Holt (b. 1958) is a good example of the popularity gained by some lesbians in recent years. The lives of Holt, her partner and their children are followed by monthly magazines. She has written a series of crime fiction with Hanne Wilhelmssen as lead character, including *Død joker* (Dead Joker, 2000). In addition to solving murder mysteries, Hanne has a private life with Cecilie, who has cancer. Hanne feels she has worked too much and loved her partner too little. Holt however refuses to classify her novels as gay and lesbian literature.

The AIDS plague exerted a huge influence upon gay culture of the 1980s. *Onans bok* (The Book of Onan, 1999), by the Swedish writer Ola Klingberg (b. 1965), describes the fear a medical student, Peter, feels throughout the decade. When he finds his lover in a waiting room in Huddinge hospital, he asks himself if sex is possible without being infected. Klingberg's second novel, *Ringen i New York* (The Ring in New York, 2004), is about opera lovers

and how they meet at the Met in New York during a performance of Wagner's *Ring*. The main theme of the book concerns artistry and the questioning of what a story is.

Coming-out stories have been printed from the 1960s up to the present. *Duktig pojke* (Brave Boy, 1977), by the Swedish author Inger Edelfeldt (b. 1956), and *Spelar roll* (Plays a Role, 1993), by Hans Olsson (b. 1962), are both good examples. In *Spelar roll*, Johan has found himself an historic role model in Alexander the Great. Other novels of importance are: *En av dem* (One of Those, 2000) by Ingrid Sandhagen (b. 1970), about a young boy who falls instantly in love with his classmate, and *I väntan på liv* (Waiting for Life, 1999) by Erika Kolterjahn (b. 1974), about young Marta's coming to terms with her homosexual feelings.

The lesbian novel in Sweden has seen considerable growth remarkably since the 1960s. Works include those by Lotta Lundberg (b. 1961), who wrote *Låta sig hända* (Let Oneself Happen, 1998) about the relationship between a teacher and a pupil, and Eva Lejonsommar (b. 1962), *En av oss* (One of Us, 1998), about the need for openness in the lesbian community.

Swedish author Louise Boije af Gennäs (b. 1961) produced a realistic and entertaining novel on lesbian love, *Stjärnor utan svindel* (Stars Without Dizziness, 1996), in which the upper-class woman Sophie, modelled on the author herself, falls recklessly in love with Kaja, a radical lesbian feminist. Class differences and the gap between the heterosexual and the homosexual move the plot forward. Lesbian life in contemporary Stockholm is vividly depicted. Kaija is modelled on the journalist Mian Lodalen (b. 1962), who later published a hilarious and realistically brutal novel on lesbian life in the capital of Sweden, *Smulklubbens skamlösa systrar* (The Shameless Sisters of the Club of Crumpets, 2003). Her follow-up *Trekant* (Threesome,

2005) continues to trace the life of the protagonist My and her friends Mackan and Hedda.

Further reading

Brantenberg, Gerd *et al.* (1986) *På sporet av den tapte lyst: Kjærlighet mellom kvinner som litterært motiv*, Oslo: Aschehoug.

Gatland, Jan Olav (1990) *Mellom linjene: Homofile tema i norsk litteratur*, Oslo: Aschehoug.

—— (1996) *Skeive skrifter: Bibliografi over homofile tema i norsk litteratur*, Oslo: Biblioteksentralen.

Homosexuella och samhället: Betänkande av utredningen om homosexuellas situation i samhället (Homosexuals and Society. Report from the Official Investigation of the Situation of Homosexuals in Society), Stockholm: Liber/ Allmänna förlaget, 1984.

Kekki, Lasse (2000) 'Kihlman, Christer', in Robert Aldrich and Garry Wotherspoon (eds) *Who's Who in Gay and Lesbian Culture: 1945 to Today*, London: Routledge, pp. 227–8.

—— (2003) *From Gay to Queer: Gay Male Identity in Selected Fiction by David Leavitt and in Tony Kushner's play 'Angels in America I–II'*, Bern and New York: P. Lang.

Kekki, Lasse and Ilmonen, Kaisa (eds) (2004) *Pervot pidot: homo-, lesbo-ja queer-näkökulmia kirjallisuudentutkimukseen*, Helsinki: Like.

Löfström, Jan (ed.) (1998) *Scandinavian Homosexualities: Essays on Gay and Lesbian Studies*, New York: Harrington Park Press.

Magnusson, Jan (2000) 'Från tragiskt öde till fritt vald livsstil. Bögar och lesbiska i det sena nittonhundratalets svenska litteratur', in Martin Andreasson (ed.) *Homo i folkhemmet: Homo-och bisexuella i Sverige 1950–2000*, Göteborg: Anamma, pp. 59–75.

Pakkanen, Johanna (1996) 'Hänen ruusuiset käsivartensa-missä Suomen lesbokirjallisuuden rajat?' *Uusin silmin: Lesbinen katse kulttuuriin*' ('Her Rosy Arms – Where are the Limits of Finnish Lesbian Literature?' With New Eyes: A Lesbian Gaze at Culture) Pia Livia Hekanaho *et al.* (eds) Helsinki: Helsinki University Press, pp. 38–65.

Rosenberg, Tiina (2000) *Byxbegär*, Göteborg: Anamma.

Söderström, Göran (ed.) (1999) *Sympatiens hemlighetsfulla makt: Stockholms homosexuella 1860–1960* (The Secret Power of Sympathy: Male Homosexuals in Stockholm 1860–1960), Stockholm: Stockholmia.

Söderström, Göran and Magnusson, Jan (eds) (2003) *Farväl heteronormativitet: papers presented at the conference Farewell to Heteronormativity, University of Gothenburg, May 23rd through 25th, 2002*, Stockholm: Lambda nordica.

JAN MAGNUSSON

SCHLAFLY, PHYLLIS

writer, activist

Dubbed the queen mother of America's religious right movement, writer and broadcaster Schlafly is a vocal opponent of feminist and gay rights initiatives. She founded The Eagle Forum in 1972, a pro-Republican organization that promotes conservative 'family values' and lobbies against abortion, and feminist and gay rights movements. During the 1970s she led the successful fight against the Equal Rights Amendment, partly by claiming that it would allow constitutional protection for gay and lesbian people. Her books include *A Choice Not An Echo* (1964), setting out her arguments against abortion, and her anti-feminist polemic *Feminist Fantasies* (2003). She served on President Reagan's Commission on the Bicentennial of the US Constitution from 1985 to 1991, and her monthly newsletter, 'The Phyllis Schafly Report', newspaper columns and radio commentaries are nationally syndicated. She was forced to tone down her anti-gay vitriol after her eldest son John was outed as gay by *QueerWorld* magazine.

JOHN FORDE

SCHLESINGER, JOHN

b. 1926; d. 2003

director, screenwriter

One of the leading lights of the British 'New Wave' social realist film movement, Schlesinger's early films – *A Kind of Loving* (1962), *Billy Liar* (1963) and *Darling* (1965) – were fresh, daring explorations of 1960s 'Swinging London'. He won an Academy

Award for Best Director for *Midnight Cowboy* (1969), a gritty portrait of male hustlers in New York. He scripted and directed *Sunday Bloody Sunday* (1971), a semi-autobiographical drama about a middle-aged man (Peter Finch) and woman who are in love with the same young man (Murray Head). The film broke new ground with its honest and sympathetic portrayal of homosexuality, including a passionate kiss between the male lovers, and marked Schlesinger's coming out as a gay director. He directed two TV plays, *The Englishman Abroad* (1983) and *A Question of Attribution* (1992) about gay spies Guy Burgess and Anthony Blunt. His last film, *The Next Best Thing* (2000), starred Rupert Everett as a gay man raising a child with his female best friend (played by Madonna).

JOHN FORDE

SCHMID, DANIEL

b. 1941

filmmaker

Filmmaker Daniel Schmid was born in Switzerland and grew up in the grand Hotel Schweizerhof, owned by Schmid's family for generations. He studied filmmaking in Berlin, where he met Rainer Werner **Fassbinder**. The two collaborated frequently, most significantly on the film, *Schatten der Engel* (*Shadow of Angels*, 1976), which Schmid directed. The film was based on a notorious play by Fassbinder, who also played one of the lead roles, and featured Ingrid **Caven** in the lead role as a beautifully fragile prostitute. Caven played in several of Schmid's earlier films, most significantly *Heute nacht oder nie* (*Tonight or Never*, 1972) and *La Paloma* (1974). During these early years Schmid met his partner and collaborator, Raúl Gimenez, who works as art director and occasional actor on many of Schmid's films. Schmid has made films about Japanese kabuki theatre

and **opera**. In the 1980s he began to work as an opera director, which comprises a significant part of his artistic output.

DANIEL HENDRICKSON

SCHOLARSHIP AND ACADEMIC STUDY, GLBTQ

The current academic literature on gay and lesbian life, experience, politics and identities falls roughly into three academic disciplines, each with its own theoretical starting point and research methods: the sociology of sexuality, gay and lesbian history and queer theory/studies. Although work in these three disciplines covers similar issues and time periods, they are often at odds with each other as to the interpretation and, therefore, what they see as the significance of glbtq studies. A brief history of the development of these three disciplinary approaches to queer sexuality highlights the sometimes invisible connections between them, especially how emergent understandings of identity and desire have shaped the disciplinary boundaries surrounding the study of homosexuality.

The current academic inquiry into homosexuality took root in the late 1960s as a sociological critique of the psychiatric models that had dominated knowledge about sexualities since the nineteenth century. With its focus on historical-social formations of sexualities, this late 1960s work gave rise both to the specific sub-discipline of gay and lesbian history and to a rethinking of deviance within sociology. By the mid-1980s, queer theory had emerged as a third approach, influenced by postmodern philosophy and feminist theory and critique of gender and sexual categories.

Debates continue to rage among these three disciplines on how to conceptualize homosexuality accurately, not only academically but also in politically productive ways. Historians and sociologists criticize queer theorists (who primarily have backgrounds in the humanities) for their 'textualism and "underdeveloped" conception of the social' (Seidman 1996: 13). For their part, queer theorists criticize historians and sociologists for reproducing sexual binaries, heteronormativity and unitary identity categories. Additionally, sociologists and historians come under fire for systematizing sexuality in totalizing terms while ignoring the ruptures in categories and for failing to see the influence of the cultural on the material. Sociologists meanwhile criticize historians for failing to see the social structures that organize sexualities, while historians criticize sociologists for not historicizing social structures, thereby rendering them static and unchanging. Ironically, all claim to get to the heart of the same phenomenon, something that might be called a 'gay experience' (although queer theorists simultaneously undermine the category 'experience' even as they lay claim to it).

Foundations

Prior to 1968, the bulk of scholarly work carried out on people who were same-sex attracted or who engaged in same-sex sexual behaviour treated homosexuality in terms of pathology and deviance, diagnosis and treatment in the traditions of sexology, psychiatry, and, with a few notable exceptions, psychology. The social context of the late 1960s, however, enabled new ways of thinking about sex and sexuality within the social sciences and humanities (see D'Emilio 1992). Rejecting the psychiatric model, British sociologist Mary **McIntosh** originated new lines of inquiry with her 1968 social theorization of the category 'homosexual'. Offering one of the first rigorous academic arguments describing the social construction of sexuality, McIntosh argued that homosexuality was a social category describing a social role, not a type of human being or a mental condition. Also in

1968, French lesbians had formed Le Front Homosexuel d'Action, demanding abortion rights, homosexual rights and the sexual rights of minors. One early member, Guy **Hocquenghem**, saw in the group's thinking the possibility not only for gay liberation but for the radical restructuring of sexuality altogether (see Hocquenghem 1993). From his background in Lacanian theory, Hocquenghem refused to differentiate desire based on object, insisted that there was something threatening about homosexuality to contemporary regimes of sexual and social powers and located the fear of homosexuality in the paranoia of a phallic society and its refusal to legitimate the pleasure of the anus. His analysis has remained an underexplored resource in the interpretation of twentieth-century gay and lesbian history, sociology and queer studies.

For sociologists, there began a 30-year legacy of mapping out the contextual specificity of homosexual identities in time and place. Through the early 1970s, sociologists in England laid the groundwork for what may be called the 'constructionist' point of view, which would eventually clarify the notion of historical construction and set the terms of the debates in both history and sociology. For example, Jeffrey **Weeks** and the Gay Left Collective carried McIntosh's argument to its logical conclusions: namely, that identity is itself historical. Weeks argued that same-sex desire was only intelligible in social contexts, so there could be no one-to-one relationship between society and the individual's sense of self. Most influential, however, was the social theorist Michel **Foucault**, who dramatically reshaped the direction of historical, social and cultural inquiry into homosexuality with his 1978 work, *History of Sexuality*. Famously, Foucault declared that the sodomite had died in the mid-nineteenth century and that in his place the 'homosexual' was born. Specifically, Foucault described the cultural processes whereby the sexual subject was compelled to speak, where sexuality was called forth and positively invoked by the Victorian discourses that appeared to suppress it. From there, Foucault theorized culture as a matrix of systems of knowledge which act upon bodies to shape them and regulate their behaviour, thereby producing sexuality.

Historians had the difficult task of demonstrating that there even was such a thing as a history of sexuality. In the United States, a significant intellectual movement to give a history to gay and lesbian people was underway. Jonathan D. Katz's watershed 1976 work *Gay American History* was the first attempt to demonstrate that such a thing as a history of homosexuality did indeed exist in the United States. Katz's approach waffled back and forth between insisting on the historical specificity of something that could be called 'homosexual behaviour' and speaking of gays and lesbians as a 'people' that could be studied across time and place. As the 1970s wore on, historians found their footing, following Weeks' and Foucault's lead. By 1980 the consensus in gay and lesbian history was the social constructionist – i.e., a radically historicized – model of homosexuality.

One important scholar who sought to engage seriously with the assumptions of historical construction was John **Boswell**, whose 1980 work *Christianity, Social Tolerance, and Homosexuality* on early Christian Western Europe stands as a critical engagement with the assumptions of constructionism in historiography. Boswell, however, has become emblematic of the problems of sexual presentism. For Boswell, the degree to which social acceptance or suppression operates determined the degree to which same-sex identities could be made public. Homosexuality was thus highly differentiated not because cultures were so strong in constructing sexuality. Rather, as Boswell saw it, same-sex attracted individuals, who see themselves as different in any given social context, are able to form identities and communities that fit into their given societies. Boswell was criticized for re-essentializing gay identity, and his work has had limited effect on the direction of gay and lesbian history as a whole.

David Halperin, a classicist, is one of the most outspoken critics of Boswell (Halperin 1989). Halperin's own work is more emblematic of the historical consensus that the notion of sexuality as an aspect of the subject, a part of the personality, is a relatively new cultural phenomenon, arising out of the historical conditions of late modernity.

Queer theorists arrived on the scene during the 1980s, most of them strongly influenced by Foucault's work, but moving in increasingly critical directions. Social factors of the late 1970s and the 1980s were pushing gay and lesbian scholarship in different directions. Steven Seidman has pointed to the emergence of the far right in the late 1970s (e.g., the Moral Majority), battles within the feminist movement over definitions of 'gender' and 'woman' as categories of analysis, as well as the beginning of the AIDS crisis in the Western gay male population as the social forces driving a new level of critique within gay communities and academic gay studies. The result was what Seidman calls 'a radical politics of difference', or what came to be called 'queer theory' (Seidman 1996: 11). Taking their cues from poststructuralism and Lacanian psychology, queer theorists began where the scholars of the 1970s left off, assuming the radical historicization of homosexual desire and identity, but taking the next step to undermine the 'homosexual subject' itself and to critique the regulatory effects of a reified homosexuality. Early queer theory rejected the homosexual subject as a social actor because, they argued, to see it as such reproduces the heterosexual/homosexual binary, thereby continuing the process of the heterosexualization of society. An additional strand of queer theory took up Foucault's argument that sexuality as a category of analysis was part of a sexual system of knowledge that structures Western societies, and so focused its attention on the institutional practices and discourses that produce knowledge about sexuality (Seidman 1996: 12–13).

History

Since 1980 the field of gay and lesbian history has greatly expanded and now encompasses an ever-growing body of work. A handful of key works stand at the core of these inquiries and dominate the historical conception of sexual difference. D'Emilio, for example, has traced works of gay history produced between 1978 and 1990 in terms of two broad themes: the emergence of gay identities and subcultures and the histories of persecutions and resistances. Other works focusing on identity and subculture seem to challenge any possibility of a transhistorical subject that could be called 'gay'. Works about classical antiquity and Europe throughout the early modern period, for example, undermine Boswell's conclusions, showing a sexuality organized not by identity but by class position, age, gender hierarchy and morality. Little evidence suggests the formation of subcultures, according to these works, until the eighteenth century. Interestingly, however, all of these works point, like Boswell, to differing levels of social tolerance towards same-sex sexual practices; and despite the relative absence of sexual communities, none of them disprove the formation of identities. Much of this pre-modern history rests on histories of ideology and social control, being limited as it is to official court and magisterial documents as well as church and religious writings.

The most common historical method for researching contemporary gay and lesbian history has been, and remains to this day, oral history. For example, in his famous re-examination of the Stonewall Riots of 1969, Martin Duberman (1993) used oral history methods not only to expand the knowledge of those fateful and symbolically central summer nights, but also to explore the variation in gay and lesbian experiences and perspectives of the events that have come to be called the birth of gay liberation. Elizabeth Kennedy and Madeleine B. Davis (1993) concluded from their ground-breaking research on pre-Stonewall working class and black lesbians in Buffalo, New York, that the interplay of subjectivity, memory and meaning evident in storytelling highlights the multiplicity of queer identities. They documented the provisional nature of adopting a 'lesbian' identity depending on space and circumstance, how black and white women defined lesbian in different ways and how 'outness' was inextricably tied to class position.

In archival history, the struggles concerning the definitions of sexual identities, desires, their manifestations in the past and how to treat them in the present are more central. For example, Jonathan Katz's second book, *The Gay/Lesbian Almanac*, relies on a problematic historical framework, based on a misunderstanding of Foucault, that split homosexuality into the 'pre-identity period', during which homosexuality was seen as an act, and the 'identity period', when homosexuality was seen as intrinsic to the person. D'Emilio's ground-breaking 1983 work, *Sexual Politics, Sexual Communities*, sees the medical discourses of homosexuality as a result rather than a cause of the formation of homosexually identified individuals and communities at the end of the nineteenth century. Both Allan Bérubé (1990) and D'Emilio locate the contemporary, institutionalized gay identity in the post-Second World War era.

At the forefront of lesbian cultural history, Lillian Faderman (1991) has demonstrated her resourcefulness in collecting historical evidence ranging from newspapers and official documents to works of popular culture. In the process, Faderman was able to reconstruct a cultural history of lesbians. Her work has come under close scrutiny, however, as her narrative tends to privilege the 'real lesbian' over others, and to privilege the 1970s notions of lesbian women over older, class-based, butch/femme models of lesbian life.

In 1994 another ground-breaking work in US gay history, *Gay New York* by George Chauncey Jr, challenged key assumptions in gay and lesbian history about how homosexuality was regulated through enforceable secrecy, or in contemporary terms, the '**closet**'. From his research on the pre-World War One and interwar gay community of New York City, George Chauncey argued that there have built up in gay history several historical myths that must be debunked. First, the myth of *isolation* holds that gay men lived separate from each other because of the hostility of the dominant culture. To demonstrate the contrary, Chauncey shows that there were communities based on homosexual identities as early as the 1890s in New York City. Second, the myth of *invisibility* holds that whatever gay world might have existed, it was hidden and therefore difficult for isolated individuals to find. Chauncey showed instead a gay subculture that was widely known to exist and accessible as part of the 'spectacle' of New York. At the same time Chauncy admitted that degrees of secrecy were necessary, but insisted that this precipitated the invention of a gay subcultural language allowing gay men to find and communicate with each other safely. The third historiographical myth is that of *internalization*, which argues that homosexuals uncritically internalized the homophobia of their period. Instead, Chauncey showed a powerful gay community in New York with the resources to support individuals in their rejection of the dominant views of homosexuality as perversion, sickness and criminality.

Although the works of D'Emilio, Faderman and Chauncey are examples of rigorous scholarship, they point to several problems in contemporary gay history as it now stands – primarily its reliance on identity constructionism. As D'Emilio's work focused on the institutional movement, national in scale, it problematically ignores race and gives only cursory nods to class and gender as important factors in the organization of sexual communities. More problematically, D'Emilio's history tends to reify gay identity, ignoring the incredible diversity of 'gayness' that existed between the Second World War and 1980. For her part, Faderman leaves unexamined the notion of 'lesbian' itself, presuming the salience and self-evidence of an 'authentic' lesbian. Chauncey's work goes far to counter these tendencies by noting that homosexual men in the early twentieth century had many different ways to identify themselves and each other that were structured by gender and class. But all three leave out some important aspects of sexual identity formation, namely the complex relationship between desire, identification and community. So while historical method has shed great light on the differences between sexualities over time, it has so far left open important questions about those sexualities that perhaps cannot be met under the current frameworks.

Queer theory

Queer theory begins where gay and lesbian history leaves off, by levelling a radical critique at the assumptions of the project of history itself. As most overviews of queer theory argue, queer theory tends to be a catch-all phrase for the critical inquiry into the meaning and power of representations of sexuality, especially non- or counter-normative sexualities and their performances (Jagose 1996, Sullivan 2003, and Turner 2000). Lisa Duggan (1992) explains that, first, queer theory critiques the humanist position which assumes there is a self to begin with and that it should be at the centre of a historical narrative. Second, it criticizes the empiricist method that claims to know a gay experience and subjectivity of the past. And third, it critiques the tendency to treat the categories of identity as stable and unitary in the past. This third critique lies at the heart of a queer perspective on culture, society and history. Queer theory seeks to point out the multiplicity and instability of all identity categories in general, and by extension, the slippage in the practices involved in claiming identities, where the performance of the category inevitably fails to reproduce the category, thereby destabilizing it at its subjective core. Judith **Butler** (1993) has offered the most salient and well-known articulation of this critique of categories. Queer theory, then, isn't about identities, but about the critique of identities. For her part, Eve Kosovsky **Sedgwick** problematizes a binary conception of sexual desire, arguing that it actually facilitates homophobia through its unspoken privileging of heterosexual desire and practice and by eliding other differences in desire and practice.

Michael **Warner** has also sought to define queer theory and its relation to sociology and history. Addressing one major critique levelled against queer theory, Warner argued that in modern societies, sexual identity formation is intricately connected to other regimes of power and, more to the point, is thus necessarily contingent in its adoption. For Warner (1993), gay and lesbian identities are both ascribed and chosen by subjects, defining a political interest group unique in modern society. Warner goes on to argue that queer is fundamentally an undermining of *normal* as a social category. So, because its focus is upon interrogating normative sexualities, queer theory leaves open the possibility of maintaining a focus on the deeply personal (desires and sex acts) while at the same time not 'acceding to the pressure to clean up personal identities by enforcing rigid identity boundaries'. One hopeful end of queer theory, then, might be to acknowledge both the liberating *and* the limiting power of identity categories and, further, to open

up the normative regimes of sexuality to enable and expand the realm of possible desires and practices.

There remains a general distrust between queer theorists and gay and lesbian historians, despite their broad overlap in theory and method. Speaking generally, queer theorists and critics tend to ignore lesbian and gay historical texts altogether, or at best to treat to them with critical condescension. Duggan (1995) argues, for example, that gay and lesbian historians will always occupy an intellectual backwater until they engage in the theoretical debates with queer theory and agree to interrogate their assumptions about evidence and documentation. For their part, gay and lesbian historians have tended largely to ignore the implications of the critique of queer theorists of their work. Nonetheless, some scholars have begun to bridge the gaps between the disciplines. Henry Abelove (1995) has suggested that queer perspectives in history can bring gay and lesbian subjects out of obscurity, insisting on their centrality; that queer critiques of subjectivity and of the ability of individuals to have agentive, original, authentic action would change the way that historians approached their topics; and finally, because queer theory seeks constantly to destabilize identity throughout the past and present, and because the performance of that destabilization is always primary, that writing history itself may be a queer act.

Conversely, historical perspectives may have much to offer a queer theory. Escoffier *et al.* (1995) posed a series of questions to queer theorists, in an effort to historicize the notion of queer itself and to see the possible material effects that such an intellectual project may have. Specifically, they worried that queer, as a historical category itself, would have the same kinds of effects as all categories of analysis, namely, to elide the difference and variety of other kinds of sexualities. Donna Penn (1995) has argued that by shifting attention away from the material practices and cultural meanings whereby individuals create identities in history, and onto theoretical notions of multiplicity and performativity, 'queer' may elide as much as it illuminates. Such questions point to the beginning of a dialogue between the two disciplines, where queer itself, both as a theory and a practice, must be aware of its own location in history and social context.

Sociology

The most biting critique of queer theory comes from sociologists and social theorists, as social theorists see queer theory as a regulating discourse in itself that serves to structure social relationships and hierarchies, both within and without academia. Sociologists were the first to insist on the contextualization of behaviour and social meanings of same-sex desire and sexual behaviour, beginning with McIntosh in 1968, and their focus on social deviance and social movement theory when treating gay and lesbian subjects has gradually expanded since then. Sociologists drew upon their disciplinary heritage to formulate social-structural theories of homosexuality that relate sexual desires, practices and politics to larger social formations such as the institutional structures of capitalism and liberal democracy; these social-structural approaches argue for the enabling of subculture and identity formation in relation to other social institutions and formations.

Recently, Max Kirsch (2000) has argued that queer theory's insistence on a multiplicity of identities has unintentionally reproduced the alienation produced by the atomization of social subjects necessary for the capitalist and nationalist social organizations of modernity. He argues that 'queer' itself is a cultural discourse, and therefore ideological in its circulation, reproducing the structures of capitalism by rendering identities unintelligible (or at best meaningless) and communities ineffectual. Although queer theorists lay claim to sweeping social implications for their critique, linking queer issues to the larger social-structural systems, Kirsch undermines queer theory's critique of social power by highlighting its own effect within the very system it purports to critique. Yet the queer critique is not easily dismissed within sociology. Echoing queer theoretical assumptions, Seidman, Warner and Ki Namaste, agree in their assertions that grand sociological theories inevitably reproduce the dominant normatives of the society from which the originate. Namaste (1994) is particularly pressing in his corrective on sociology. He demands that sociology interrogate all sexual categories, desires and practices, not only homosexual ones. Otherwise, sociology will itself reproduce a heteronormativity as it leaves unexamined the homosexual/heterosexual binary.

In his own work, Seidman posed the question of how queers are able to identify with each other, to recognize themselves in others like them. He argues for the existence of a common set of experiences, but not in the usual sense. Rather than seeing object choice or desire as the commonality driving queer community formation, Seidman argued that queer be seen as a social episteme. This queer epistemology would then be one which would foreground the *experiences of being queer* (i.e., sexually different) in a particular society, 'categories of secrecy and disclosure, knowledge and ignorance, the private and the public, double selves, constructed identities and perspectives emphasizing the social organization of bodies, desires, and sexualities' (1994: 171). In yet another work, Seidman offered the sociological remedies to the political weaknesses of queer theory. It would be the social perspective combined with the queer episteme that re-enables a queer politic and renders queer theory useful to sociological inquiry. Here subjectivity, self and identity would all be conceived as being, this moves towards 'social positioning, as marking social juncture in the institutional, administrative, juridical organization of society, and as an axis of social stratification' (1993: 136). Locating identity in a multi-dimensional social space features its macro-social significance; we are compelled to relate the politics of representation to institutional dynamics. Thus, Seidman has woven together the queer critique of identity with the social institutions that make it operational within society.

Disciplinary problems

During the 1990s interdisciplinary studies led to pointed criticism of the types of knowledge that can be produced from within the confines of academic disciplines. Escoffier, for example, distinguished between community scholars and academics. He argued that academics, ensconced as they are in institutionally sanctioned disciplines, have other primary concerns, namely the maintenance of disciplinary boundaries – which has material impact on funding, programme and course availability, and jobs – and achieving career goals by accumulating prestige and getting tenure. For Escoffier, the disciplinary distinctions between history, sociology and queer studies separate academics from the people they purport to represent – gay men, lesbians, transgenders and bisexuals (see Escoffier 1998). Thus, flowing through the disciplinary boundaries are three conflicting values, which push and pull against the production of knowledge about gay men, lesbians, transgenders and bisexuals. First, the majority of queer scholars are themselves queer, which puts them into often uncomfortable relationships with their respective sexual communities. Second, multiple and competing political and economic exigencies drive the production of scholarship, undergirded by the hope that the knowledge produced within the academy has political and social impact. And finally, because scholars need to position themselves within academia, prestige and tenure are inextricably linked to the kinds of knowledge they produce. Academia privileges and rewards certain kinds of inquiries, languages and knowledges while it punishes and ignores others.

More problematic, as academic discourses of sexuality gained institutional legitimation during the 1980s and 1990s, certain ideas became received knowledge within, often to the detriment of rigorous analysis. The prime example of this has been the misapprehension of Foucault's thesis in *History of Sexuality*. Foucault's work became almost canonical in its effect on the academic conversation about sexuality, lending a kind of authority to the invocation of his name. Problematically, much of this invocation is based on a false understanding of his fundamental argument. Halperin (1998) has recently sought to correct the misappropriation of Foucault. To historians, Halperin points out that Foucault himself spoke of sexual identities existing before the medicalization period of the nineteenth century. Thus, he could not have meant that sexual identities themselves were historically new phenomena. Furthermore, to queer theorists, Halperin shows that in fact Foucault offers a theory of *discourse*, of which sexuality is one *effect,* in order to undermine any sort of theory of sexuality. Foucault's argument was *not* that sexual identity itself was a new social phenomenon. Rather, Foucault's project was to trace the history of a shift in the *regulatory* discourses, namely, from the discourses of sodomy and deviant action to the internalization of a pathological sexuality in the medicalization of sexual desire during the late nineteenth century. For Foucault, these represented two radically different social regimes of controlling bodies and channelling desires in particular directions as they related to and reproduced other dominant social structures (e.g., the nuclear family). Foucault acknowledged various kinds of sexual morphologies (bodily manifestations) and sexual identities (psychological orientations) through history;

and he maintained the crucial distinction between sexual acts and sexual identities. This misapprehension of Foucault is but one of the problems encountered since such research was institutionalized, and Halperin's corrective, although important, does not directly engage the primary assumptions of social contructionism in sociology and history, nor the anti-subjectivity of queer theory, nor the kind of knowledge these assumptions produce.

The disciplinary boundaries produced in history, sociology and queer studies, coupled with the institutionalization of the production of knowledge, may in fact be hemming in and holding back progress of the field, broadly defined. Meanwhile, as these conflicting value systems tear at individual scholars studying queer issues, the knowledge they produce seems to be stuck on issues of identity and its social construction. Political analyses rely on identity; analyses of homophobia rely on identity; historical inquiry circulates around who is and who isn't 'gay'; sociology reproduces identity categories necessarily as it seeks to study social phenomena. The future of queer studies may yet lie in shifting academia's attention away from theories of identity towards a method that would focus on the multiplicity of desires and their consummation. As fields of inquiry, gay and lesbian history, the sociology of sexuality and queer studies could reconceive of identity as one possible *way* that queers organize their lives and rid themselves of the cumbersome assumption that an organized, socially recognizable category is necessary for individuals to *identify* themselves as being sexual. It would further free up scholars to see sexually different individuals and groups as having similarities based on their experiences within normatizing social structures rather than as sharing objects of desire. A focus on desire and its consummation would not erase identity and social construction; rather it would reduce them to their proper place in the study of sexuality, allowing us to move, perhaps, towards a vision of queer values and ethics, where desires are enabled and multiplied rather than foreclosed.

Bibliography

Abelove, Henry (1995) 'The Queering of Lesbian/Gay History', *Radical History Review* Spring: 46–55.

Bérubé, Allan (1990) *Coming Out Under Fire: The History of Gay Men and Women in World War Two*, New York: Plume.

Boswell, John (1980) *Christianity, Social Tolerance, and Homosexuality: Gay People in Western Europe from the Beginning of the Christian Era to the Fourteenth Century*, Chicago: Chicago University Press.

Butler, Judith (1993a) *Bodies That Matter: On the Discursive Limits of 'Sex'*, New York: Routledge.

—— (1993b) 'Imitation and Gender Insubordination', in Henry Abelove, Michele Aina Barale and David M. Halperin (eds) *The Lesbian and Gay Studies*, New York: Routledge.

Chauncey, George Jr (1994) *Gay New York: Gender, Urban Culture, and the Making of the Gay World, 1890–1940*, New York: Basic Books.

D'Emilio, John (1983) *Sexual Politics, Sexual Communities*, Chicago: Chicago University Press.

—— (1989) 'Gay Politics and Community in San Francisco Since World War II', in Martin Duberman, Martha Vicinus and George Chauncy Jr (eds) *Hidden from History: Reclaiming the Gay and Lesbian Past*, New York: New American Library.

—— (1992) *Making Trouble: Essays on Gay History, Politics, and the University*, New York: Routledge.

Duberman, Martin (1993) *Stonewall*, New York: Plume.

Duggan, Lisa (1992) 'Making It Perfectly Queer', *Socialist Review* 22: 11–31.

—— (1995) 'The Discipline Problem: Queer Theory Meets Lesbian and Gay History', *GLQ: A Journal of Lesbian and Gay Studies* 2, 3: 179–91.

Escoffier, Jeffrey (1998) *American Homo: Community and Perversity*, Berkeley: California University Press.

Escoffier, Jeffery, Kunzel, Regina and McGarr Molly (eds) (1995) *Radical History Review* Spring.

Faderman, Lillian (1991) *Odd Girls and Twilight Lovers: A History of Lesbian Life in Twentieth-century America*, New York: Penguin.

Foucault, Michele (1990 [1978]). *The History of Sexuality, Vol. 1, An Introduction*, New York: Vintage.

Gay Left Collective, The (ed.) (1980) *Homosexuality: Power and Politics*, London and New York: Allison & Busby.

Halperin, David M. (1989) *One Hundred Years of Homosexuality: And Other Essays on Greek Love*, New York: Routledge.

—— (1993) 'Is There a History of Sexuality', in Henry Abelove, Michele Aina Barale and David M. Halperin (eds) *The Lesbian and Gay Studies Reader*, New York: Routledge.

—— (1998) 'Forgetting Foucault: Acts, Identities, and the History of Sexuality', *Representations* 63: 93–120.

Hocquenghem, Guy (1993 [1972]) *Homosexual Desire*, Durham: Duke University Press.

Jagose, Annamarie (1996) *Queer Theory: An Introduction*, New York: New York University Press.

Katz, Jonathan (1992 [1976]) *Gay American History*, rev. edn, New York: Plume.

Kennedy, Elizabeth Lapovsky (1997) 'Telling Tales: Oral History and the Construction of Pre-Stonewall Lesbian History', in Martin Duberman (ed.) *A Queer World: The Center for Gay and Lesbian Studies Reader*, New York: New York University Press.

Kennedy, Elizabeth Lapovsky and Davis, Madeline D. (1993) *Boots of Leather, Slippers of Gold: The History of a Lesbian Community*, New York: Routledge.

Kirsch, Max H. (2000) *Queer Theory and Social Change*, New York: Routledge.

McIntosh, Mary (1968) 'The Homosexual Role', *Social Problems* 16, 2: 182–92.

Namaste, Ki (1994) 'The Politics of Inside/Out: Queer Theory, Poststructuralism, and a Sociological Approach to Sexuality', in Steven Seidman (ed.) *Queer Theory/Sociology*, Cambridge: Blackwell Press.

Penn, Donna (1995) 'Queer: Theorizing Politics and History', *Radical History Review* Spring: 24–42.

Seidman, Steven S. (1993) 'Identity and Politics in a "Postmodern" Gay Culture: Some Historical and Conceptual Notes', in Michael Warner (ed.) *Fear of a Queer Planet: Queer Politics and Social Theory*, Minneapolis: Minnesota University Press.

—— (1994) 'Queer Pedagogy/Queer-Ing Sociology', *Critical Sociology* 20: 169–76.

—— (ed.) (1996) *Queer Theory/ Sociology*, Cambridge: Blackwell Press.

Sullivan, Nikke (2003) *A Critical Introduction to Queer Theory*, New York: New York University Press.

Turner, William B. (2000) *A Genealogy of Queer Theory*, Philadelphia: Temple University Press.

Warner, Michael (1993) 'Introduction', in *Fear of a Queer Planet: Queer Politics and Social Theory*, Minneapolis: Minnesota University Press.

Weeks, Jeffrey (1980) 'Capitalism and the Organization of Sex', in the Gay Left Collective (ed.) *Homosexuality: Power and Politics*, London and New York: Allison & Busby.

—— (1993 [1991]) 'Sexual Identification Is a Strange Thing', in C. Lemert (ed.) *Social Theory: The Multicultural and Classic Readings*, Boulder: Westview Press.

J. TODD ORMSBEE

SCHROETER, WERNER
b. 1945
filmmaker

Werner Schroeter began making 8-mm films in the late 1960s, influenced by **opera** and **American underground cinema**, especially that from New York. Throughout the 1970s his films consisted of loosely connected or episodic narrative fragments, steeped in histrionics and with a passion for gesture. He also collaborated with and worked alongside other German gay and lesbian directors of his generation, using the same actors and technical personnel as **Fassbinder**, Monika **Treut**, Daniel **Schmid** and Rosa von **Praunheim**. In 1986 he made *Der Rosenkavalier* (The Knight of the Rose), starring his old friend Magdalena Montezuma in her final role before her death from cancer, and in 1990 he made *Malina*, based on the novel by Ingeborg Bachmann and starring Isabelle Huppert. Throughout the 1990s he turned his attentions frequently to the stage, directing both theatre and opera, although he did make two feature-length documentary films. In 2002 he returned to narrative filmmaking with *Deux* (Two), once again starring Huppert.

DANIEL HENDRICKSON

515

SCHULMAN, SARAH

b. 1958

writer, activist

Born in New York City, Sarah Schulman is both a major figure in and prolific contributor to – across media – the glbtq cultural/political scene. Her early fiction, almost always set in Manhattan, deconstructs lesbian identities. Her work often combines fiction with political issues and is situated at the multiple, intersecting points of identity/identification. These conflicting intersections, juxtaposed against the backdrop of the inner city, fuse an often anti-realist aesthetic with sharp political critique. Her novels include: *The Sophie Horowitz Story* (1984), *After Delores* (1988), *People in Trouble* (1990), *Empathy* (1992), *Rat Bohemia* (1995), *Shimmer* (1998) and *Girls, Visions, and Everything* (1999). She has also penned many plays (*The Child*, 2000; *Freud Was My Co-Pilot, Heaven and Hell (On Earth)*, 2001) and has written political/cultural theory (*My American History: Lesbian and Gay Life During the Reagan Years*, 1994; *Stagestruck: Theatre, AIDS and the Marketing of Gay America*, 1998).

Schulman is the recipient of many awards, including a Guggenheim Fellowship in 2001 for playwriting, the American Library Association Gay/Lesbian Book Award (1999), the Gustavus Meyers Book Award on the Study of Human Rights (1994), the New York Foundation for the Arts Fiction Fellow in 1987 and 1991 and she received the Gregory Kolovakos Memorial Prize for AIDS Fiction in 1990. She recently completed work on a video-archive project documenting ACT UP and the AIDS political movement, a continuation of her long-standing activist involvement with organizations such as **Lesbian Avengers**.

JEAN BOBBY NOBLE

SCISSOR SISTERS

pop band

Dubbed 'the best pop band in the world' by U2's Bono, the New York-based band's fusion of anthemic pop and flamboyant performances made them one of 2004's biggest musical successes. Emerging from Manhattan's 1990s electroclash scene, the band was formed by gay songwriter and lead singer Jake Shears (born Jason Sellards) and his songwriting partner and producer Babydaddy (Scot Hoffman). Later joined by vocalist Ana Matronic (Ana Lynch), drummer Paddy Boom (Patrick Seacor) and guitarist Del Marquis (Derek Gruen), their self-titled debut album combined disco, pop, rock and electroclash influences, including a dazzling Bee Gees-esque cover of Pink Floyd's 'Comfortably Numb'. Their lyrics discuss coming out ('Take Your Mama Out'), gay cruising ('Lovers In the Backseat') and crystal meth addiction in New York's gay scene ('Return to Oz'). Their glam-rock inspired dress sense, queer sensibility (all but Boom are queer-identified) and high-energy stage performances have won them cult status in Europe and America. Their public profile was bolstered by a 2004 supporting tour with Elton John.

See also: Glam rock

JOHN FORDE

SECTION 28

An infamously homophobic piece of British legislation, 'Section 28' was the common name for Section 2a of the Local Government Act 1986, passed by the conservative Thatcher government, which prohibited local authorities in England and Wales from 'promoting' homosexuality and labelled gay family relationships as 'pretend'. In practice, the law prevented teachers from helping students seek information about homosexuality and safe sex, and local authorities from providing services for gays and lesbians.

After a prolonged campaign by gay rights organization Stonewall, prominent gay figures (including Sir Ian McKellen) and educators, the law was finally repealed in 2003.

JOHN FORDE

SEDARIS, DAVID

b. 1956

writer

An openly gay author, writer of memoirs, broadcaster and raconteur, whose witty reminiscences of his childhood and cosmopolitan career history have won him a dedicated gay and straight fan base. Sedaris was discovered performing stand-up comedy in Chicago, and first drew national attention with a stint on National Public Radio in 1996, where he recounted his experience as a Christmas elf at Macy's department store, later published as a play, *The Santaland Diaries* (1988). His work has also appeared in *Esquire* and *New Yorker* magazines and has included scriptwriting for television's *Seinfeld*. His books include *Barrel Fever* (1994), *Naked* (1997), *Holidays on Ice* (1997) and the international best seller and Lambda Literary Award-winning *Me Talk Pretty One Day* (2000), in which he wittily recounts his childhood in North Carolina, his treatment for a childhood lisp, a failed career as a performance artist, a speed addiction and his relocation to France with his partner Hugh Hamrick.

JOHN FORDE

SEDGWICK, EVE KOSOFSKY

b. 1950

literary critic

Eve Kosofsky Sedgwick explores the paradox of 'homosocial desire' in *Between Men* (1985), a book that assisted in the emergence of queer theory largely by raising still-unresolved questions about the relationship between gender and sexuality. At the centre of her work is the concept 'homosociality' through which she refers to forms of same-sex solidarity that, among men, come to appear radically incompatible with homosexual desire. Homophobia is almost a structural inevitability in homosocial contexts since male bonding must be distinguished from – and yet, in the intimacies it fosters remains contiguous with – the erotic. In *Epistemology of the Closet* (1990), Sedgwick emphasizes the structural significance of the homosexual/heterosexual divide, arguing that both homophobic and anti-homophobic perspectives vacillate between 'minoritizing' and 'universalizing' views; a distinction that displaced what had become a rather timeworn dispute between essentialists and social constructivists. Elsewhere, and often with moving autobiographical explicitness, she addresses 'cross-identification': identification, that is, with a group or groups of which one is not a member in the fashioning of one's fraught sense of self-identity. In light of such commonplace transgressions of identity categories, she cautions that critical taxonomies such as race, class, and sexuality fail to capture the complexities of human difference.

See also: Scholarship and academic study, glbtq; Theory and theorists, queer

TREVOR HOPE

SEROCONVERSION

The introduction of pathogen-fighting antibodies into the bloodstream. In the case of HIV, seroconversion is detected when HIV antibodies show up during testing.

CHRIS BELL

SEWING CIRCLE, THE (HOLLYWOOD)

The name given to a group of Hollywood actresses who were thought to have been lesbian or bisexual. The term was first used by Marlene **Dietrich**, one of the most famous rumoured members of the group, who referred to a group of Hollywood women as her 'sewing circle'. The group included scenarist Mercedes de Acosta, who had affairs with Dietrich, Greta **Garbo** and Isadora Duncan. Other members included Tallulah Bankhead, Barbara Stanwyck, Joan **Crawford**, Hattie McDaniel, Dolores Del Rio, Dorothy **Arzner**, Judy **Garland** and costume designer Edith Head. In his book *The Sewing Circle: Female Stars Who Loved Other Women*, Axel Madsen argues that the Circle provided essential emotional support for the members, who were required to cultivate glamorous (and closeted) public images or enter into marriages of convenience to protect their Hollywood careers. Many members came under investigation in the 1950s by Joseph McCarthy's Un-American Activities Committee (see **McCarthy**, Joseph and McCarthyism).

JOHN FORDE

SEX AND THE CITY

TV programme

One of the definitive TV series of the late twentieth century, airing from 1998 to 2004, *Sex and the City* was produced for cable channel HBO by gay *Melrose Place* creator Darren **Star**. Based on the newspaper column-turned-novel by Candace Bushnell, the show followed four single 30-something women negotiating sex and the single life in New York City, led by sex columnist Carrie Bradshaw (played by Sarah Jessica Parker, who also executive-produced the show). Episodes followed the quartet's sexual adventures as they attempted balancing feminist independence with the search for a fairytale Mr Right. The show's combination of witty dialogue, fashion-friendly feminism and no-holds-barred sexual frankness defined a generational *Zeitgeist* for single women. The show also attracted a devoted gay following, especially for the sexual antics and camp

excess of man-eater Samantha Jones (Kim Cattrall). The other two main characters were the cynical workaholic lawyer Miranda (Cynthia Nixon) and the Park Avenue WASP Charlotte (Kristin Davis). The characters' discussions of anal sex, fuck buddies, rimming and 'straight gay men' arguably reflect the influence of gay culture upon modern heterosexuality.

JOHN FORDE

SEX INDUSTRY

Same-sex prostitution has been in existence since homosexuality itself. Ancient Greek and Japanese art depicts scenes of young male prostitutes having sex with (and being paid by) male clients. Before legalization of homosexuality, the sex industry was a recognized – albeit frequently unsafe – space for the expression of same-sex desire. Clients who otherwise define themselves as heterosexual may use the services of male prostitutes to fulfil a perceived socially unacceptable desire. Prostitution has frequently been a source of income for gay and lesbian people, especially young people who have been ostracised by their family or community, or for transgendered people as a means of financing sex reassignment surgery. Same-sex prostitutes are frequently socially marginalized, subject to criminal conviction or exposure to HIV/AIDS.

JOHN FORDE

SEX PANIC!

activist group

A 1990s American sex-activist group which made a brief but controversial critique of perceived moral conservatism within the gay community. The group, whose members included historian Alan Berube, gathered at the 1997 National Gay and Lesbian Task Force's annual 'Creating Change' conference to organize against a 'sex panic' within gay culture. Unofficially titled the National Sex Panic Summit, Berube and other speakers denounced gay authors Larry **Kramer**, Gabriel Rotello and Michelangelo **Signorile**, whose writings criticized drug use and barebacking within the gay scene, accusing them of promoting an anti-sex initiative in the guise of AIDS activism. The summit participants produced a 'Declaration of Sexual Rights', demanding an end to the 'scapegoating' of sexually active people and prohibitions on public sex. Kramer responded by accusing the group of advocating and romanticizing unsafe sex and HIV+ status. Rotello and Signorile denied the accusations of neo-conservatism but reiterated their safe-sex argument.

JOHN FORDE

SEXUAL MINORITIES

An umbrella term for people who have been marginalized as the sexual 'other' in heteronormative culture because of their alternate sexual preferences.

LISA Y.M. LAM

SHAW, AIDEN

b. 1966

porn star, writer

An actor in gay pornographic films, Shaw is also a published poet and novelist. Shaw was born on 22 February 1966 in Harrow, England. He worked as a prostitute while studying theatre and visual arts in England. He moved to Los Angeles in the early 1990s, where he met porn director Chi Chi La Rue and began acting in gay pornographic films. He made over 50 hard-core films with the Falcon, Catalina and Studio 2000 studios, including *Grand Prize* (1992), *Grease Guns* (1993), *The Backroom* (1995) and *Forced Entry* (1996). In 1995 he was photographed by **Pierre et Gilles** for the work *Midnight Cowboy*. He was diagnosed as HIV+ in 1997. He bran-

ched into mainstream film acting in *Kiss Kiss Bang Bang* (2000), also composing the score, and continues to make occasional appearances in pornographic movies. His first novel *Brutal* (1996) was a semi-auto-biographical account of male prostitution and drug addiction. He has also published *Boundaries* (1999), *Wasted* (2001), a memoir *My Undoing* (2004) and a volume of poetry.

JOHN FORDE

SHAW, FIONA

b. 1958

actor

Hailed as one of Britain's leading stage actresses, Fiona Shaw, born in Ireland, trained at the Royal Academy of Dramatic Arts in London and has worked with the National Theatre and the Royal Shakespeare Company. Renowned for tackling difficult roles and for her physically and emotionally taxing stage performances, she is best known for her collaborations with her partner, director Deborah **Warner**. The pair achieved widespread acclaim for a production of Shakespeare's *Richard II* (1995), with Shaw playing the doomed king. Other collaborations include *The Prime of Miss Jean Brodie* (1998), *The Waste Land* (1995), *Medea* (2002), which transferred to Broadway (winning Shaw a New York Critics' Award and a Tony nomination) and *The Powerbook* (2002), based on Jeanette Winterson's novel. Her film work includes *Triumph of Love* (2001), in which her character falls in love with a cross-dressing Mira Sorvino, and a recurring role as shrewish Aunt Petunia in the *Harry Potter* films.

JOHN FORDE

SHAW, PEGGY AND LOIS WEAVER

writers and performers

More widely known as the artistic directors and central performers of US lesbian-feminist performance group Split Britches, Peggy Shaw and Lois Weaver first met in Berlin in 1977. Former founding members of male drag group Hot Peaches and feminist theatre group Spiderwoman respectively, they found success as a duo at the Women's One World (WOW) Festival in New York, and formed Split Britches with scriptwriter Deb Margolin in 1981. They have since toured internationally, and won critical acclaim and numerous awards for both their solo and collaborative works that typically explore themes of gender, sexuality and lesbian identity, notably *Dress Suits for Hire* (in collaboration with Holly Hughes, 1987), *Belle Reprieve* (with Bloolips Drag Theatre Troupe, 1991) and *Lust and Comfort* (with the **Gay Sweatshop Theatre Company**, 1995). Since 1997 Weaver has taught contemporary performance at Queen Mary, University of London, and a published collection of Split Britches scripts, edited by Sue Ellen Case, won the Lambda Literary Award for Drama in 1996.

ROBIN GRIFFITHS

SHEPARD, MATTHEW

b. 1976; d. 1998

Matthew Wayne Shepard, born in Casper, Wyoming, is best known as the University of Wyoming college student murdered because of his sexual orientation. On 6 October 1998 Shepard went to a bar where he met two men, Russell Henderson and Aaron McKinney. Henderson and McKinney decided to lure Shepard out of the bar, intending to rob him. According to police reports, Shepard was targeted because he was gay. The three men drove to a rural location outside of Laramie, where Shepard was lashed to a split-rail fence, pistol-whipped and left for dead. He was hit with such force his skull was fractured six times. The brutal nature of Shepard's death became a rallying cry for glbtq people worldwide. His name is now

synonymous with equal rights and the criminalization and cessation of anti-gay violence. Shepard's story was retold in the multiple award-winning *The Matthew Shepard Story* (2002) and Moises Kaufmann's film and play, *The Laramie Project* (2002).

CHRIS BELL

SHER, ANTHONY

b. 1949

actor, writer

A native of South Africa (born on 14 June 1949 in Cape Town), Sir Anthony Sher studied acting in London from 1969 until 1971 and has since based his film, theatre and TV career in England. He worked for the **Gay Sweatshop Theatre Company** in the 1970s and joined the Royal Shakespeare Company in 1982. His title role in *Richard III* (1985) won him rave reviews and an Olivier Theatre Award. He achieved fame for his role as a predatory gay lecturer in *The History Man* (1981) for British television. His film work includes *The Young Poisoner's Handbook* (1995), *Indian Summer* (aka *Alive and Kicking*) (1996), in which he starred as the lover of a young HIV+ man, and *Mrs Brown* (1997). He came out publicly in his book of poetry and drawings, *Characters Paintings, Drawings and Sketches* (1989). He has also published novels, theatre journals, plays and an autobiography, *Beside Myself* (2002). He was knighted in 2000.

JOHN FORDE

SHERWOOD, BILL

b. 1952; d. 1990

filmmaker

Born on 14 June 1952 in Washington DC, Bill Sherwood was an openly gay filmmaker whose only feature-length film, *Parting Glances* (1986), was one of the most highly acclaimed gay-themed movies of the 1980s.

The film was a comic but deeply moving portrait of gay life in 1980s New York, focused around Michael, a gay book editor, his lover Robert and Michael's former lover Nick, who is dying of AIDS. As one of the first cinematic attempts to deal with the AIDS epidemic, the film received considerable acclaim. Sherwood's promise as a filmmaker was tragically cut short by his own death from an AIDS-related illness, at the age of 37, in New York City on 10 February 1990.

JOHN FORDE

SHOW QUEENS

Idiomatic term, generally affectionate in nature, used to refer to gay male fans of musical theatre. Originally coined as part of gay subcultural argot, the term has passed into mainstream consciousness and use. Show queens are stereotypically characterized by their detailed knowledge of Broadway musicals; expansive collection of original cast recordings; and passionate devotion to musical divas such as Julie **Andrews**, Carol **Channing**, Ethel Merman, Liza **Minnelli** and Barbra **Streisand**.

BRETT FARMER

SIGNORILE, MICHELANGELO

b. 1960

writer, radio host, activist

Born in Staten Island, New York City, with a degree in journalism from Syracuse University, AIDS activism propelled Michelangelo Signorile, an entertainment industry publicist, to set up in 1989 (with Gabriel Rotello) New York's *Outweek* magazine. He used this to write about powerful, closeted gay men and women who remained silent about the crisis, including the late Malcolm Forbes and Pete Williams, the 1991 Gulf War spokesman for the anti-gay Pentagon. *Time* magazine dismissed his

reporting as 'outing' and Signorile earned the enmity of many gay leaders – but he also earned a huge audience. The author of several best sellers, including *Queer in America* (1993) and *Life Outside* (1997), he has also written for *The Advocate*, *The New York Times*, *Newsday* and the *New York Press*. A satellite radio pioneer, Signorile hosts a daily talk show on Sirius Radio and continues to work as an activist and columnist.

PAUL SCHINDLER

SILVERA, MAKEDA

b. 1955

writer, activist

Born in Jamaica but living in Canada for over 30 years, Makeda Silvera co-founded Sister Vision Press: Black Women and Women of Color Press in 1985. Sister Vision published more than 50 collections, giving voice to Caribbean, Asian, First Nations, African and mixed-race women on many issues including the intersections of sexuality and race. Makeda has written three books, *Silenced: Conversations with Domestic Workers in Canada* (1989), *Remembering G and Other Stories* (1991) and *Her Head a Village and Other Stories* (1994). Her editorial work includes: *Piece of My Heart: A Lesbian of Colour Anthology* (1991), *Pearls of Passion: A Treasury of Lesbian Erotica* (1995) and, more recently, *Ma-ka, Diasporic Juks: Contemporary Writing by Queers of African Descent* (1997). Her first novel, *The Heart Does Not Bend*, was published to great success in 2002.

JEAN BOBBY NOBLE

SIMPSON, MARK

b. 1965

journalist, author

Dubbed 'the gay Anti-Christ' and 'a skinhead Oscar Wilde', Mark Simpson's provocative brand of cultural commentary and defiantly disreputable appearance as a shaven-haired tattooed muscle boy has made him the *enfant terrible* of British gay journalism. In his long-running column for British style magazine *Attitude*, he established a witty critique of Gay Pride movements and gay consumerist culture, cheerfully setting himself at odds with *Attitude*'s urban gay readership. He pioneered the term 'metrosexual' to describe the crisis in modern masculine identity as heterosexual men absorb the narcissism and status anxiety of gay culture. An avowed nostalgist for the closeted gay past, his writings frequently focus on the military and other bastions of homosocial bonding. His articles have also appeared in the *Independent on Sunday* and *Salon.com*. Book collations of his writings include: *It's A Queer World* (1995), *Anti Gay* (1996), *Sex Terror* (2002) and *Saint Morrissey* (2003), an affectionate commentary on British pop singer Morrissey.

JOHN FORDE

SIMPSONS, THE

TV programme

The Simpsons began as an animated segment on *The Tracey Ullman Show* in 1987. It was expanded into a half-hour animated sitcom in 1989. Created by cartoonist Matt Groening, the show is about a middle-class family living in the fictional town of Springfield. The Father, Homer, is an incompetent nuclear power plant employee and Marge a stay-at-home wife and mother with a beehive of blue hair. Their three children, Bart, Lisa and Maggie complete the brood. So what's queer about *The Simpsons*?

To begin, Homer has had tender encounters with a gay male secretary (voiced by Harvey **Fierstein**), mooned over good-looking men and sung a version of 'Mandy' called 'Andy' in front of a bathroom mirror. Homer's jealousy-induced tiffs with Bart occurred most memorably when Bart adopted a foster father mentor. It came as a surprise when,

in 'Homer's Phobia' (16 February 1997), Homer's homophobia surfaced because of his concerns that hanging out with a gay man (voiced by John **Waters**) would make his son gay. But Bart had already shown his queerness when he and best friend, Millhouse, dressed in women's clothes, bounce up and down on a bed and sing, 'Sisters are Doin' It for Themselves'.

Waylon Smithers is the semi-closeted assistant to nuclear power plant owner, C. Montgomery Burns. Smithers' unrequited love for his boss frequently seems masochistic in light of the imperious and sadistic Mr Burns. Smithers focuses his energies on his Malibu Stacy (read: Barbie) collection about which he has written and performed a musical. Yet, although Smithers enjoys himself in all-gay settings, he remains painfully in the closet to those in Springfield and the show's loyal queer viewers.

Although Marge's sister Selma has married several times, Patty (Selma's twin), has dated only one man (fussy principal Seymour Skinner) and on one episode was seen as the only woman leaving a bordello. In 2005, after much speculation, it was revealed that Patty is indeed gay.

ALEX DOTY

SINGAPORE

Despite homosexuality being illegal and state censorship of Internet content, a gay and lesbian social movement has emerged through AIDS organizations, gay and lesbian activism and queer lifestyle consumption. Since 2000 Singapore has staged annual gay and lesbian dance parties bigger than Australia's Mardi Gras parades. With more male saunas and lesbian nightclubs than **Sydney**, it has eclipsed the Antipodean city as the gay and lesbian capital in the Asia-Pacific region.

AUDREY YUE

SINGAPORE, FILMMAKING

Bugis Street (*Yaojie huang hou*, Yonfan, 1994) was the first film to be made in Singapore in 1994 when the Singapore Film Commission board was established. A country renowned for its draconian media censorship laws and Victorian prohibition of homosexuality, *Bugis Street*, a mainstream and international festival hit dealing with the fate of transsexual sex workers in the city during the 1960s, set the standard for how gay and lesbian film content can thrive in a governed film industry. The star of *Bugis Street* is not the teenage transvestite prostitute but the eponymous street, notorious in colonial Singapore for its deviant Asian hookers and Anglo-European clients. Queer content was ignored because the film memorialized the street as an icon that had disappeared as a result of the country's rapid urban development. Almost all subsequent films that were produced officially however – be they melodrama, romance or comedy – readily embraced queer content and followed in this tradition.

While overtly queer topics are banned, queer content is tolerated, and may even be encouraged through the staging of other plots. Award-winning *Mee Pok Man* (Eric Khoo, 1995), *Army Daze* (Ong Keng San, 1996), *12 Storeys* (Khoo, 1997), *Money No Enough* (*Qian bu gou yong*, Y.L. Tay, 1998), *Forever Fever* (Glen Goei, 1998), *Talking Cock* (Colin Goh, 2002) and *I Not Stupid* (*Xiaohai bu ben*, Jack Neo, 2002) celebrate drag queens, coming-out themes and same-sex friendships. The digital handi-cam revolution has also enabled the emergence of an underground and independent short-film genre. MTV-style *15* (Royston Tan, 2003), banned in Singapore because it showed group masturbation and male genitalia, was a global jury hit. Part of the Singapore diaspora, US-based Madelaine Lim's critically acclaimed documentary, *Sambal Belacan in San Francisco* (1997), showcases overseas Singapore lesbian identity inter-sected by migration, family values and queer community in San Francisco.

Further reading

Udhe, Jan and Udhe, Yvonne Ng (2000) *Latent Images: Film in Singapore*, Singapore: Oxford University Press.

Yue, Audrey (2003), 'Paging "New Asia": Sambal Is a Feedback Loop, Coconut is a Code, Rice Is a System', in Chris Berry, Fran Martin and Audrey Yue (eds) *Mobile Cultures: New Media in Queer Asia*, Durham: Duke University Press, pp. 245–66.

AUDREY YUE

SISSY

'Effeminate' male, stigmatized as suffering from gender identity disorder. In heteronormative culture, 'effeminate' men are often considered homosexuals. Some macho gay men also express sissy-phobic feelings.

GILAD PADVA

SISTER NAMIBIA

human rights organization

Based in Namibia, Sister Namibia is an autonomous non-governmental women's human rights organization that was established in July 1989, on the eve of Namibia's independence, with the purpose of working for women's rights and gender equality. It aims to 'increase awareness among women, men and young people of the ways in which political, social, cultural, legal and economic systems of power control girls and women; to promote the full recognition and protection of the human rights of girls and women; and to oppose and challenge sexism, racism, homophobia and other discourses and practices that oppress and divide people'. Sister Namibia works in the fields of media, education, research, advocacy and cultural activities in order to promote gender equality and to work against violence, discrimination and oppression. Areas in which it is involved include Media, Sexuality Research and Education, Women in Politics, and a Women's Human Rights and Leadership Training Programme. It also runs a Resource Centre, which collects local, regional and international materials on women and gender issues.

SURINA KHAN

SIX FEET UNDER

TV programme

The multiple Emmy-winning black comedy created for American cable network HBO in 2002 by Alan **Ball** is about a family of undertakers in suburban California. Like Ball's screenplay for *American Beauty*, *Six Feet Under* reveals the perversities lying beneath respectable middle-class life. Patriarch Nathaniel Fisher's sudden death in the pilot episode unleashes a chain of secrets and self-discoveries, including the gradual coming out of conservative son David (Michael C. Hall) and his troubled relationship with Keith (Mathew St Patrick), an African-American policeman. The show's mordant wit and complex, non-judgemental characterizations won it a devoted gay fan base. GLAAD (**Gay and Lesbian Alliance Against Defamation**) gave it an award it for its sensitive, complex portrayal of gay characters. The series premiered in 2001 and ended its run in 2005.

JOHN FORDE

SKESANA

A derogatory slang term used in southern Africa to refer to the passive, effeminate partner in male–male sex. Derives from a late nineteenth-century neologism meaning 'mine marriage' or 'boy wife'. Since the mid-1990s it has been co-opted by Zimbabwean activists to mean homosexuality in the broadest sense (*hungochani* in Shona).

MARC EPPRECHT

SLASH FICTION

Although its exact parameters are debated, it is generally agreed that slash fiction refers to fan-written fiction that describes and develops same-sex relationships between media characters. The term 'slash' derives from the convention of employing a stroke or slash ('/') to connect characters and their newly scripted relationship (so Kirk/Spock from *Star Trek*, Buffy/Willow from **Buffy the Vampire Slayer** or Xena/Gabrielle from **Xena, Warrior Princess**, in three of the genre's most popular pairings).

Slash fiction first appeared during the late 1960s or early 1970s in *Star Trek* fanzines that intermittently featured stories that posited a sexual relationship between Mr Spock and Captain Kirk (the majority of which were written by women). The genre saw a marked increase in production during the 1990s with the growth of the Internet, a medium that provides an almost ideal forum to disseminate slash fiction texts. This growth was accompanied by the utilization of an ever-expanding pool of slash fiction characters. Although the genre conventionally featured characters from TV texts with strong fantasy elements, slash fiction increasingly encompasses a wide ranging media culture and now includes members of various 'boy bands' and *Harry Potter*'s teenage wizards. Initially almost exclusively male/male, slash fiction increasingly includes female/female pairings that draw particularly on texts highlighting 'strong', queer or sexually ambiguous female characters.

From the outset, the 'appropriateness' of slash fiction has been hotly debated within fan communities and remains a subject of intense discussion in many online forums. Proponents of the medium often use the stories and the discussions they engender to challenge assumptions of heterosexuality that usually accompany mainstream readings of a character's sexuality.

ANITA BRADY

SMITH, ANNA NICOLE

b. 1967

model, reality TV star

A modern-day example of camp excess and disposable celebrity, Anna Nicole Smith, a Texan model and *Playboy* centrefold, became a tabloid star in 1994 when she married J. Howard Marshall, an 89-year-old millionaire whom she met while working as a stripper in a Houston nightclub. After Marshall's death, Smith faced a legal battle from his family over his US$1.6 billion estate, eventually being awarded $88 million. Smith's drag queen-like persona and trademark peroxide-blonde hair and surgically enhanced breasts were further popularized in the E! Network's reality TV show, *The Anna Nicole Smith Show* (2002–3).

JOHN FORDE

SMITH, BESSIE

b. 1894; d. 1937

singer

Known as the 'Empress of the Blues', Smith rose from severe poverty to become one of America's most enduring musical legends. Smith was born on 15 April 1894 in Chattanooga, Tennessee. She worked as a street corner singer from the age of 9, and as a teenager joined blues singer 'Ma' Rainey in the Moses Stokes Travelling Show. She made her first recordings in 1923, including 'Down Hearted Blues', which sold 780,000 copies in less than six months, garnering her financial security and an enduring fan base. She had relationships with both men and women, including a volatile affair with singer Lillian Simpson. Her composition 'Foolish Man Blues' refers to 'a mannish actin' woman and a skippin', twistin' woman acting man'. She died on 26 September 1937 in Clarksdale, Mississippi, as a result of injuries sustained in a car accident. Edward Albee's play, *The Death of Bessie Smith*, perpetuated the myth that Smith was denied medical assistance because she was black. Her grave remained unmarked until 1970, when a gravestone was erected, partially funded by singer Janis Joplin.

JOHN FORDE

SMITH, JACK

b. 1932; d. 1989

filmmaker, performance artist

Jack Smith was born into a working-class family in Columbus, Ohio, but the family moved around quite a bit in search of work. At the age of 19 he moved to Chicago where he worked as an usher in a cinema, gaining much of his encyclopedic knowledge of Hollywood B-movies. He came to New York in 1953, where he would spend the remainder of his life. While taking film classes at City College of New York, he met the aspiring filmmakers Bob Fleischner and Ken Jacobs. He began working with them and later with Ron Rice. In 1962 Smith finally had the opportunity to make his own film, based extremely loosely on the wartime escapist films of Maria **Montez**. The film, *Flaming Creatures* (1963), was shot on the roof of a theatre in New York, and is composed of several segments involving drag queens, starlets, pseudo-Oriental figures, vampires and other creatures, including an early performance by the drag queen Mario **Montez**, here called Dolores Flores. The film is highly sexual, but not in any way reducible to individual sexualities or specific sexual relationships. There are frequent close ups of body parts, both of men and women, both genital and non-genital, which give the film an undefined but clearly non-normative sexuality. It was shot on outdated black-and-white film stock that gives the film an unspecific exotic quality.

Later that year, Jonas Mekas arranged for Smith to publish an article in *Film Culture*, the periodical that was in many ways the voice of the burgeoning American underground cinema. The article, 'The Perfect Filmic Appositeness of Maria Montez', is ostensibly about the largely forgotten Hollywood starlet, but in a wider sense it is a brilliant manifesto about a specifically queer appreciation of film in general and of Hollywood film in particular. At this time, Smith also began working seriously with photography. His work as a photographer, although never as well known as his films, would remain a central part of his artistic output throughout his life.

After premiering in New York, *Flaming Creatures* was taken to an experimental film festival in Belgium, where it was promptly banned by the Belgian Ministry of Culture. In 1964 New York police seized *Flaming Creatures* on grounds of obscenity and arrested the organizers of the screening and the projectionist. Confiscation and censorship would hound the film for many years to come. A week after the *Flaming Creatures* debacle, the same fate befell Jean Genet's *Un Chant d'amour*. These two events sparked a debate over censorship and homosexuality that made *Flaming Creatures* the most famous underground film in America. Smith's film was found to be obscene by the New York Criminal Court and was almost impossible to see for many years thereafter.

Following the *Flaming Creatures* scandal, Smith began working on a film that, in a tongue-in-cheek rebuttal to his critics, he called *Normal Love* (1964); once again it featured Mario Montez. Smith also appeared in the films of many of the filmmakers working in the New York underground, including Andy **Warhol**, Ron Rice, Gregory **Markopoulos** and Piero Heliczer. He also worked with the Theater of the Ridiculous (see **Ludlam**, Charles), both as costume designer and actor and, in 1969, he appeared as the Walrus in Robert Wilson's *Life and Times of Sigmund Freud*.

Throughout the 1970s he created his own plays and now legendary multimedia performances, usually performed in his loft to a small audience. He continued to make short films, as well as cutting and re-editing his older films, particularly *Normal Love*, for use in the performances. He travelled within the United States, Germany and Italy, giving performances and lectures at museums, universities and art schools. In the 1980s he continued to work and perform, although his health was deteriorating badly because of AIDS. He died in 1989.

DANIEL HENDRICKSON

SOCCER

There is no one original source of the modern game of soccer. Soccer history can be traced back to a number of games in a great number of cultures. In contemporary culture it has grown to be extremely popular with lesbians and is also considered a safer sport for gay men. Because of the occasional, but intense, contact involved between athletes (who wear only shin guards for protection), and because of the highly coordinated team effort involved, one might expect athletes in soccer to exemplify the same high degree of homophobia as do athletes in similar sports such as baseball, basketball and, perhaps, ice hockey. Soccer, however, is unique compared to these other team sports. Although it would be hard to describe it as 'gay friendly', it could be described as providing a safer space for gay and lesbian athletes than other team sports. Soccer players tend to exhibit a broader, larger worldview when it comes to issues of sexuality. The reason for the variance may be attributable to the European origins of the sport: whereas baseball, basketball and hockey are inventions of North America. European countries have been found to be considerably more progressive on issues of homosexuality than the United States. Soccer, in the United States, may also be less homophobic than sports of American origin because it was introduced to the country in the 1970s and did not start from the same cultural standpoint – to engender masculinity – as did early American sports.

See also: Beckham, David; Coaching and homophobia

ERIC ANDERSON

SOFT CELL

See: Almond, Marc and Soft Cell

SOLEDAD

See: Zamudio, Adela

SOLONDZ, TODD

b. 1959

director, screenwriter

The *enfant terrible* of 1990s independent filmmaking, Solondz's unrelenting, unsentimental portraits of human misery and cruelty have won him critical plaudits and controversy. A graduate of Yale and New York University's Tisch School of the Arts, his first feature, *Welcome to the Dollhouse* (1995), a harrowing examination of a nerdy pre-teen girl's hellish existence in New Jersey, was awarded the Sundance Grand Jury Prize. *Happiness* (1998) caused international scandal with its sympathetic portrayals of a stalker, a predatory child rapist and an obese serial killer, but won Solondz the Cannes Festival Screenwriting Award. His follow-up feature, *Storytelling* (2001), featured an African-American lecturer who coerces his female student to yell racist abuse while he anally rapes her. Although none of his characters are specifically gay, Solondz's unsentimental perspective, persistent identification with social outcasts and non-judgemental take on sexual perversions informs a queer aesthetic.

JOHN FORDE

SOMERVILLE, JIMMY AND BRONSKI BEAT

b. 1961

pop singer and group

Band formed in 1983 by minute, soprano-voiced Jimmy Somerville, keyboard player Steve Bronski and Larry Steinbachek, in gay London, just as British electro-pop went political: openly gay, committed, and with an impact. Their debut single, 'Smalltown Boy', was released in the same year to immediate international acclaim. It was soon followed by memorable songs such as 'Why' and a cover of George Gerswin's 'It Ain't Necessarily So'. The political devotion of Bronski Beat was made even clearer in their first album (released in 1984), which was titled *The Age of Consent* and featured a pink triangle on the front cover, pointing to a troublesome parallelism in discrimination between Nazi prosecution and the current legislation of Great Britain. The entertainment of indirection, tongue-in-cheek, double-coded understanding of the late 1970s disco and early 1980s pop scenes thus gave way to campaigning for gay visibility and civil rights. After leaving Bronski Beat in 1985, Jimmy Somerville maintained his noteworthy hits record with the Communards, a duo he formed with Richard Coles, fashioning hallmark songs such as 'You Are My World'. Jimmy's distinguished vocal style and a remarkable series of successful disco revivals (Harold Melvin's 'Don't Leave Me This Way', Donna Summer's 'I Feel Love', Gloria Gaynor's 'Never Can Say Goodbye' and Sylvester's 'You Make Me Feel'), made him one of the outstanding queens of international pop music, offering a bridge between historical, falsetto queerdom and contemporary gay politics.

FABIO CLETO

SONDHEIM, STEPHEN

b. 1930

composer

American composer and librettist, whose works explore a comic queer sensibility and extend compassionate understanding towards society's misfits and outsiders. When only 26, he was invited to write the lyrics for the musical *West Side Story* (1956) by Leonard **Bernstein**, a retelling of Shakespeare's *Romeo and Juliet* set among New York street gangs, and the following year, the songs for *Gypsy* (1957), a musical about stripper Gypsy Rose Lee and her ferociously ambitious mother. Both musicals were critical and popular successes, winning him numerous accolades. His first score as composer-lyricist was the farce *A Funny Thing Happened on the Way to the Forum* (1962). His cosmopolitan body of work includes *A Little Night Music* (1973), based on the Ingmar Bergman film; *Pacific Overtures* (1976), a satire about nineteenth-century American imperialism in Japan; *Sweeney Todd* (1979), about a nineteenth-century English serial killer; and *Into The Woods* (1987), a macabre reworking of the Grimm Brothers fairy tales.

JOHN FORDE

SOUKAZ, LIONEL

b. 1955

filmmaker

French film- and videomaker Lionel Soukaz became involved in the experimental film scene in France during the early 1970s, serving as projectionist for film festivals and working with collectives that arranged screenings of new work. He became

involved with the burgeoning homosexual movement that grew out of the group F.H.A.R. (Front Homosexuel d'Action Révolutionnaire). It was out of this involvement that he met and collaborated with Guy **Hocquenghem** to make *Race d'Ep!* (1979), an experimental documentary on the history of homosexuality in Europe. The film was only released after a petition appeared, signed by several prominent cultural and political figures. Soukaz went on to make other films, including *Ixe* (1980), an aggressively provocative film containing images of gay sex and drug use.

DANIEL HENDRICKSON

SOUTH PARK

TV programme

Premiering on Comedy Central in 1997, *South Park* has emerged as one of the most controversial animated series in TV history. Created by Matt Stone and Trey Parker, the series follows the decidedly surreal adventures of a group of 8-year-old boys living in the town of South Park, Colorado. A social satire on many aspects of American culture and society, the show is renowned for 'pushing the envelope' in its irreverent and characteristically blunt exploration of society's greatest taboos. And as one of these many taboos, its rather ambivalent exploration of homosexuality has received a fairly mixed response from the gay community, from condemnation to acclaim. In addition to much speculation over the sexuality of both Stone and Parker, the show has featured a number of 'out' and 'closeted' gay characters, from the über-camp Big Gay Al, who takes in Stan's gay dog Sparky at his 'Big Gay Animal Sanctuary' and educates the children on the history of homosexuality via his 'Big Gay Boat Ride'; to the repressed and self-loathing teacher Mr Garrison, who proclaims that 'Gay people are evil' when challenged about his own sexuality. Notable episodes have included a 'Getting Gay with Kids' choir tour of Central America, and a recent storyline in which the whole town's male population receives a 'Queer Eye for the Straight Guy' makeover and become brainwashed 'metrosexuals' that straight-bash anyone who isn't gay. But the town's womenfolk finally save the day and the men are 'de-gayed' and return to their 'normal' lives.

ROBIN GRIFFITHS

SOYINKA, WOLE

b. 1934

writer

One of Africa's most prominent artist-intellectuals, Wole Soyinka was raised in the Anglican Church and educated in Nigeria and Britain. He worked at the Royal Court Theatre in London as a dramaturgist before returning to Nigeria in 1960 to study African drama. Soyinka writes in English, but his dramatic work is profoundly syncretic, incorporating the influences of Irish theatre, Greek drama and, especially, the cosmology of his own Yoruba people. In addition to volumes of poetry, autobiography and literary criticism, Soyinka has written two novels, one of which (*The Interpreters*, 1965) features a gay, African-American historian who poses uncomfortable questions to his Nigerian acquaintances about the homoerotic practices indigenous to West African culture. An outspoken proponent of democracy and peace, Soyinka has been jailed repeatedly by successive military regimes in Nigeria; since 1994 he has lived in exile, mainly in the United States. He was awarded the Nobel Prize for literature in 1986.

See also: Indigenous queer identities

DAVID KURNICK

SPAIN, FILMMAKING

Spanish filmmakers began to deal openly with queer issues during the 1970s – a trend that has consolidated remarkably during the subsequent decades. Even though it is Pedro **Almodóvar** whose name stands out in discussions about Spanish filmmaking as a whole, one must bear in mind work by the likes of Basque film director Eloy **De la Iglesia**, who has directed gay-related films since the mid- and late 1970s.

Yet, queer filmmaking in Spain may have tradition stretching back earlier than the effervescent years of post-Franco Spain. Luis Buñuel's 1928 film *Un Chien Andalou* (An Andalusian Dog), for example, is a highly controversial and provocative surrealistic film that can be read in queer terms not only for its erotic references and avant-garde aesthetics, but also because the film was conceived in reference to gay Spanish poet Federico García Lorca, who befriended Buñuel and Eugenio Salvador Dalí during his university years in Madrid. The decades that followed Franco's victory in the Spanish Civil War (1936–9) and Lorca's death were marked by a profound conservatism in sexual matters. Family, state and religion were the three key ideological concerns of Spanish society for almost 40 years and homosexuality in culture, let alone film, was unacceptable. During the late 1970s and early 1980s, however, a number of film directors started to deal in an open and unapologetic manner with queer issues. De la Iglesia and his 1976 film, *Los placeres ocultos* (Hidden Pleasures), is the first instalment of a gay male-themed trilogy followed by *El diputado* (The Deputy, 1978) and *Galopa y corta el viento* (Running Against the Wind), where homoeroticism and politics are intertwined. Another Basque film director, Imanol Uribe, made the film *La muerte de Mikel* (Mikel's Death) in 1984 where the protagonist, played by Imanol Arias, tries to come to terms with political oppression and sexual repression in the Basque country. Yet another Basque director, Pedro Olea, directed *Un hombre llamado 'Flor de Otoño'* (A Man Named 'Autumn Flower') in 1978. Set in Barcelona during the 1920s, the film depicts the assassination attempt upon dictator Primo de Rivera by a group of anarchists led by a gay transvestite.

Whether or not Almodóvar took into account these previous examples of gay related films, his name has become synonymous with the new Spanish queer cinema over the last two decades. No other Spanish film director has enjoyed such international success and recognition as he has an Oscar nomination for *Mujeres al borde de un ataque de nervios* (*Women on the Verge of a Nervous Breakdown*, 1988); an Oscar for the Best Foreign Language Movie *Todo sobre mi madre* (*All About My Mother*, 1999); and an Oscar for the Best Adapted Script, *Hable con ella* (*Talk to Her*, 2002). In a sense, Almodóvar breaks down the 'serious' tradition set by earlier filmmakers in dealing with sexuality, gender and pop culture. The first openly gay movie made by Almodóvar was the 1986 film *La ley del deseo* (The Law of Desire), starring Antonio Banderas, Eusebio Poncela and Carmen Maura.

Another Oscar-winning Spanish movie, Fernando Trueba's *Belle Epoque* (1992), has interesting queer dimensions regarding cross-dressing and lesbian representations. The character played by Ariadna Gil can be interpreted as lesbian. Even though the representation of lesbians is much smaller and scant compared to the presence of their gay male counterparts, there is a growing number of lesbian-themed films in Spain. Almodóvar's films, especially *Tacones lejanos* (*High Heels*, 1991) and *All About My Mother*, have an important lesbian presence. But perhaps the first openly lesbian movie ever made in Spain is *Costa Brava* (1996) by directors Marta Balletbó-Coll and Ana Simón Cerezo. Besides the Spanish film industry's international recognition of queer films at the hands of Almodóvar, first-rate Spanish actors such as Antonio Banderas and Javier Bardem have played gay characters in both Spain and in the United States. Noteworthy is Bardem's lead role in Reinaldo Arena's *Antes que anochezca* (*Before Night Falls*, 2000), which was adapted to film and directed by Julian Schnabel and for which he received an Oscar nomination for Best Actor.

Because the status of gay and lesbian people in Spanish society has improved dramatically since the end of the Franco regime, this change has been reflected in Spanish cultural production. Filmmaking is no exception. Worth mentioning in this context is the proliferation of gay- and lesbian-related film festivals throughout Spain, those held in Madrid and Barcelona being the most salient. Once a taboo subject, prone to ridicule and outrage, gay and lesbian themes and characters are gaining respect and acceptance within the Spanish film industry. This is particularly the case for independent features such as *Costa Brava* and Gerardo Vera's *Segunda piel* (Second Skin, 2000) starring Ariadna Gil, Cecilia Roth and Javier Bardem.

Further reading

Kinder, Marsha (1993) *Blood Cinema, The Reconstruction of National Identity in Spain*, Berkeley and Los Angeles: University of California Press.

MIKEL IMAZ

SPAIN, LITERATURE

Spain may have one of the longest and most respected literary traditions in the Western world, but this preeminent position has not resulted in an extensive treatment of homoerotic and queer themes. Even though we are able to find references to sexual activity between individuals of the same sex (particularly male–male sexual intercourse) in relatively early periods of Spanish literature – notably King Alfonso X 'El Sabio' ('The Wise') and his thirteenth-century code of law, known as *Las siete partidas* (The Seven Laws) as acts of sinful nature, and in texts such as *El libro de Buen Amor* (The Book of Good Love) by Juan Ruiz Arcipreste de Hita (written around 1330–43) and *El lazarillo de Tormes* (The Blind Man's Guide from Tormes, 1554) – it is not until the twentieth century that we find extensive depictions of homoerotic characters and themes. It is important to bear in mind that in a discussion about homoerotic dimensions in Spanish literature we understand the cultural perceptions surrounding a homoerotic individual.

As part of Mediterranean/Hispanic culture, homoerotic desire traditionally has been viewed differently in Spain compared to Anglo-American culture. This difference has to do with the sexual roles that the individuals (specifically male individuals – female homoeroticism presents a different perception) perform during the sexual act; that is, the active or macho figure, who purportedly does not lose an iota of his masculinity, and the passive or 'feminine' figure who is perceived as queer (see **Pasivo/ Activo**). This perception is the case in most Latin American societies that present a Hispanic/Mediterranean tradition inherited from the Spanish Conquest and subsequent colonization and remains embedded into the twentieth and twenty-first centuries.

One of the most salient and important literary and artistic movements in early twentieth-century Spain is the so-called Generación del '27. This group of poets and artists of the 1920s and early 1930s created an avant-garde poetic language. One of the most prominent authors from this group was the Andalusian poet Federico García Lorca (1898–1936), one of Spain's greatest poets of all times and an important gay cultural figure. References to homoerotic desire are common in Lorca's work. Of particular interest is his *Poeta en Nueva York* (Poet in New York, 1929–30), a book of poems published after his visit to New York, Cuba and Argentina in the late 1920s. His 'Oda a Walt Whitman' is one of the most significant poems in the

book since it is in recognition of the American poet's work and the influence he had upon Lorca. Lorca witnessed the artistically vibrant cultural manifestations of New York, such as the Harlem Renaissance, the jazz clubs and the eroticism of sailors and street workers that feature in his poems. The poet also became increasingly open about his sexuality: his last written work, the play *El público* (The Public, 1930), is considered an eminently homoerotic work. Lorca was an important public figure and a cultural icon for many queer-identified people, especially in contemporary Spanish society. His murder in August 1936 by the Franco-allied Spanish Guardia Civil set the tone of a brutal and repressive dictatorship that ruled Spain until the mid-1970s.

Another important author involved with the Generación del '27 is Luis Cernuda (1902?–1963). Cernuda's poetry reveals an important homoerotic element, particularly two of his poetic texts, 'Los placeres prohibidos' (Prohibited Pleasures, 1931) and 'La realidad y el deseo' (Reality and Desire, 1936). Cernuda's perception of an oppressed sexuality regarding homoerotic desire, explicitly noted in the titles of the aforementioned texts, along with his support for the Republican cause, forced him into exile before the end of the Spanish Civil War (1936–9). His openly homoerotic poetry, an openness that could bring revolutionary consequences for the human individual in terms of social liberation and freedom of expression, brought disapproval and censorship by the Spanish literary establishment under the Franco regime. Cernuda's work would not receive full recognition until several decades later. He died in Mexico in 1963.

Indeed, not until the 1960s, with the rare exception of an essay by Juan Gil-Albert, 'Heraclés: sobre una manera de ser' ('Heraclés: About a Way of Being', written in 1955 but published 20 years later), an homage to the Ancient Greek world and a defence of the virile homoeroticism versus the 'effeminate' one, did Spanish literature deal openly with homoerotic themes. One of the greatest Spanish writers of the twentieth century, if not the most well known, Juan **Goytisolo** (1931–) caused a stir with his 1966 novel *Señas de identidad* (*Marks of Identity*), a critical denunciation of Spain's repressive dictatorship and the injustices suffered by many under the Franco regime. Goytisolo not only attacked the culturally barren Spain that came to be under so many years of dictatorship, but in later novels *Reivindicación del Conde Don Julián* (*Count Don Julian's Vindication*, 1970) and *Juan sin tierra* (*John the Landless*, 1975), he denounces the sacred cultural traditions of *la España eterna* (Traditional Spain), where sex customs, particularly homoerotic desire and sexuality among men, are condemned. In later years, when he chose Morocco as his home after years of exile in Paris, Goytisolo chastised the culture of racism in Spanish society, especially towards Arabs. He has also written extensively about the ravages of AIDS in *Las virtudes del pájaro solitario* (*Virtues of the Solitary Bird*, 1988).

Terenci Moix (1943–2003) and Eduardo Mendicutti (1948–) are two of the most recent and dynamic contemporary gay novelists in Spain. In the case of Moix, his novels deal in great part with contemporary Spanish popular culture, even though in novels such as *Mundo macho* (Macho World, 1998), the author recreates the civilization of Ancient Egypt. Mendicutti published *Una mala noche la tiene cualquiera* (Anyone Has a Bad Night, 1982), a lucid recreation from the perspective of a transvestite of the 23 February 1982 attempted *coup d'état*, and *El palomo cojo* (The Lame Pigeon, 1991), later adapted into a film. Luis Antonio de Villena (1951–) has written an extensive body of poetry, among other genres. With considerable media coverage in Spain, de Villena's gay subjects remain an important aspect of his work.

Lesbian literature, although less visible than gay male literature, has had an increasing presence in Spain during the last four decades.

Among the authors who have written about lesbian dimensions of sexuality, friendship among women and heterosexual deception, are Esther Tusquets (1936–) with her first novel *El mismo mar de todos los veranos* (*The Same Sea as Every Summer*, 1978); Carmen Riera (1948–) *Palabra de mujer* (A Woman's Word, 1980); and Lola Van Guardia *Con pedigree* (With Pedigree, 2000).

Further reading

Bergman, Emilie L. and Smith, Paul Julian (eds) (1995) *¿Entiendes?: Queer Readings, Hispanic Writings,* Durham: Duke University Press.

Foster, David William (ed.) (1999) *Spanish Writers on Gay and Lesbian Themes: A Bio-Critical Sourcebook,* Westport: Greenwood Press.

Manrique, Jaime (1999) *Eminent Maricones: Arenas, Lorca, Puig, and Me,* Madison: University of Wisconsin Press.

Perriam, Chris (1995) *Desire and Dissent. An Introduction to Luis Antonio de Villena,* Oxford: Berg.

MIKEL IMAZ

SPANDAU BALLET

pop band

Originating from the Islington area of London in the late 1970s, Spandau Ballet emerged as a key player in the New Romantics popular music movement that challenged the rough-edged utilitarian punk movement with synthesized electro-pop sounds. With dandified hairdos, kilts and flamboyant, frilly dress, the group's stylistic disruptions of conventional masculinity echoed the strategies of glam-rock artists of the early 1970s. Early elaborate music videos adopted the lighting conventions of the German Expressionists. Quite experimental in synthesized musical orchestration in their first release *Journeys to Glory* (1981), by the mid-1980s the group was producing more elaborately orchestrated pieces, epitomized by their 1983 release *True* and its successful title track.

The group had disbanded by the end of the decade. After taking the lead roles in the 1986 gangster film *The Krays* (1990), twin brothers, guitarist/songrwriter Gary and bassist Martin Kemp continued careers as screen and TV actors.

See also: New Romantics

MICHAEL DEANGELIS

SPECK, WIELAND

filmmaker

Openly gay German filmmaker whose work chronicles the changing nature of Berlin's gay communities. He is best known for *Westler* (1985), an auto-biographical drama about two gay lovers who are separated by the Berlin Wall, based on Speck's own love affair with an East German man. Speck cast his lover in the film, in the hope that this public outing would prompt the East German authorities to repatriate him to the West. The plan was successful, and Speck was reunited with his lover, completing the film using another actor. In 1989 he directed six gay-themed short films for the German AIDS Foundation. His short film series *Among Men* (2001) portrayed the West German gay scene through the hedonistic 1980s, the rise of the AIDS epidemic, and East–West reunification. In the documentary *Die Erika und Klaus Mann Story* (2000), co-directed with Andrea Weiss, he dramatized scenes from the life of Thomas Mann's (queer) children.

JOHN FORDE

SPELLMAN, CARDINAL FRANCIS JOSEPH

b. 1889; d. 1967

Catholic Archbishop

Roman Catholic Archbishop of New York from 1939 until his death in 1967,

Francis Spellman was a flagrantly active homosexual who was protected from exposure by a pre-Stonewall code among gay people and a journalistic reluctance to discuss such matters. Sometimes referred to as 'The American Pope', his chancery was called 'The Powerhouse' at a time when the Cardinal of New York had considerable political influence, especially in promoting a conservative social agenda that included crackdowns on gay establishments.

Spellman was appointed by Pope Pius XII, the Catholic pontiff faulted for not speaking out against the atrocities of Hitler and Mussolini during the Second World War. Spellman was a close ally of such fellow right-wing closeted individuals as Roy Cohn, J. Edgar Hoover and Senator Joseph P. McCarthy during the 1950s and 1960s. His rival was Bishop Fulton J. Sheen, also closeted, one of the most popular TV personalities in the 1950s.

ANDY HUMM

SPORT AND GLBTQ CULTURE

Sport, in Western culture, has been described as one of the most homophobic arenas for gay men. Yet, paradoxically, it has been considered somewhat of a safer space for lesbians. To understand why this is, it is important to understand that sports was founded largely in Western culture based on the early twentieth-century idea of preventing male youths from becoming effeminized or from 'becoming' homosexual. Sport was used to engender a form of masculinity that valued risk-taking and physical aggression, and it quickly became the leading institution for socializing boys into a homophobic and misogynistic form of masculinity. Traditionally, gay men were presumed too 'woman-like' to exist within the sporting arena, and women were formally banned from sport. But with feminist gains during the 1970s, women began to play sport in increasing numbers.

In contemporary culture, sport remains characterized as a highly masculinized terrain; therefore, when women began to play sport they were heavily stigmatized as 'mannish' and were suspected of being lesbian. This stereotype, ironically, actually drew lesbian women to sport; lesbians continue to use sport as a way to meet and socialize with other lesbian women. Unfortunately this has created tension between lesbian and heterosexual women since heterosexual female athletes often resent the purported stereotype by which they are identified. Thus, homophobia within women's sports has created a highly contested and nuanced space regarding gender for both heterosexual and lesbian athletes.

For men, sport has generally remained an extremely homophobic institution since its history is couched in a long-standing tradition of hypermasculinization and because the homosocial nature of sport allows for physical contact and emotional intimacy between ostensibly heterosexual male players. Sport (for both men and women) is also an extremely homoerotic activity because it displays highly fit, culturally esteemed and sexually desired bodies. Homophobia presents itself within men's sports as a way to mitigate the homoeroticism of fraternal bonding associated with athletics.

Relatively speaking, there have been very few gay male athletes to come out of the closet (at any level) (see **Closet**; **Coming out**). There have, for example, been only two major team-sport athletes to come out while still playing sports and only two who have come out after retiring. However, research shows that the athletic culture is not immune to change on issues of homosexuality as it occurs in the dominant culture. Youth are increasingly inclined to accept gay males in the larger culture and this has had an affect on the degree to which homophobia takes shape in sport. For example, heterosexual male athletes are more willing to accept gay athletes as long as they adopt other aspects of dominant forms of masculinity and are

valuable to the overarching mantra of sport – victory. Heterosexual male athletes more readily agree that 'The sexual orientation of a teammate does not matter as long as he can play ball'. Athletes are also willing to accept gay men as long as they do not act 'effeminate' or 'don't make an issue out of it'.

Similarly, gay male athletes appear eager to adopt all other attributes of hetero-masculinity, except for their sexuality. When gay male athletes play for 'heterosexual' teams, they manage their identities by performing as 'straight' while frequently denouncing their less-masculine brethren as 'queens' or 'flamers'. They keep pace with the construct of being masculine by acting tough, competing well and (often) partaking in sexist and homophobic discourse alongside their heterosexual teammates. In return, heterosexual athletes are willing to accept gay athletes as part of the team. In this manner gay and heterosexual athletes are begrudgingly working together for the slow but progressive assimilation of only one type of gay male into mainstream sporting culture.

Interestingly, when not playing within mainstream sports, gay and lesbian athletes sometimes 'queer' the structure of sport. For example, some gay and lesbian clubs, leagues and organizations attempt to downplay the competitiveness and masculinity of sport and, instead, stress cooperative teamwork, while other organizations integrate gays and lesbians into the same teams. The **Gay Games**, for example, permits all athletes, regardless of ability, to play.

See also: Coaching and homophobia

ERIC ANDERSON

SPRINGFIELD, DUSTY

b. 1939; d. 1999

singer

Hailed as one of Britain's greatest female vocalists, Dusty Springfield (born Mary

Isobel Catherine Bernadette O'Brien) is also a gay icon, her status earned through memorable torch song performances and her trademark blonde bouffant hair, 'panda eye' makeup and turbulent struggles with bisexuality and alcoholism. As a teenager she and her brothers formed pop/folk band The Springfields, scoring success with the single 'Silver Threads and Golden Needles' (1962). She had international solo hits with 'I Only Wanna Be With You' (1964) and 'You Don't Have to Say You Love Me' (1966). Disillusioned with the British music industry, she worked extensively in America's burgeoning soul and Motown music scenes in the late 1960s. After alluding to her bisexuality in a British newspaper interview in 1975, she relocated to Los Angeles, struggling with a career slump and alcohol and drug abuse problems. Her collaboration with the **Pet Shop Boys** (notably 'What Have I Done To Deserve This?' [1987]) marked an impressive comeback.

JOHN FORDE

SPRINKLE, ANNIE

b. 1956

performance artist, sex educator, porn star, writer, filmmaker

Born Ellen Steinburg in Philadelphia, Pennsylvania, Annie Sprinkle graduated from the School of Visual Arts in New York City with a BA in Fine Arts. Self-proclaimed 'multimedia whore', Sprinkle worked in the sex trade for 20 years before working as a sex-trade workers' advocate, performance artist, sexologist and theorist. Famous for showing her cervix on stage (she claims to have shown her cervix to 25,000 people), Sprinkle's work integrates feminist sexual politics with queer practices. Annie co-directed the first female-to-male transsexual docu-drama love story, *Linda/Les & Annie* (1989). More recent work includes *Annie Sprinkle: Post-Porn Modernist* (1993), *Hardcore from the Heart: The Plea-*

sures, Profits and Politics of Sex in Performance (2001) and the performance piece, *Annie Sprinkle's Herstory of Porn: Reel to Real*. In 2002 she received her PhD at the Institute for Advanced Study of Human Sexuality in San Francisco.

JEAN BOBBY NOBLE

STABANE

Stabane is a common Zulu and Ndebele term for a homosexual that originally suggested 'hermaphrodite'. It remains highly pejorative in popular usage but is often co-opted by gays and lesbians in a positive way.

MARC EPPRECHT

STADLER, MATTHEW

b. 1959

writer

Novelist Matthew Stadler's first novel, *Landscape: Memory* (1990), tells the coming-of-age story of a boy in San Francisco at the beginning of the twentieth century. This work and his second novel, *The Dissolution of Nicholas Dee* (1993), were very well received critically for their lyrical blending of memory and reality. He followed these novels with *The Sex Offender* (1994), the story of a teacher undergoing an experimental form of rehabilitation being convicted of having had an affair with a 12-year-old student. The complex and extravagant story manages to satirize both the psychological profession and the state, with which it is complicit. His fourth novel, *Allan Stein* (1999), is the story of another teacher, again in the wake of a sex scandal, who passes himself off as a friend and goes to research the strange case of the nephew of Gertrude Stein in Paris. Stadler also works as an editor for art and architecture journals.

DANIEL HENDRICKSON

STAJANO, GIÒ

b. 1931

writer, personality

Born into a prominent fascist family, Giò Stajano was one of the first out homosexuals in postwar Italy. As one of the prime movers of *la dolce vita* he inspired a character in Fellini's film. In 1959 he published *Roma capovolta* (*Rome Turned Upside Down*), an account of his gay affairs. His first novels sparked off huge scandals and were banned on charges of immorality. Subsequent novels were *Le signore sirene* (*The Mermaid Ladies*) and *Il letto stretto* (The Narrow Bed). He provided gossip stories for the popular press and in 1971 became editor-in-chief of soft-core magazine *Men*, where he ran the first gay columns in the Italian press.

In 1981 Stajano underwent a sex change (he was also one of the first Italian transsexuals). In 1992, after turning to religion, she wrote her memoirs, *La mia vita scandalosa* (*My Scandalous Life*).

MARCO PUSTIANAZ

STAR, DARREN

b. 1961

TV producer

Creator of the glossy sex-and-celebrity-filled dramas *Beverly Hills 90210*, *Melrose Place* and *Sex and the City*. Star has also written scripts for TV sitcom *Charles In Charge* (1984–90), and teen movies, including *If Looks Could Kill* (1991). His skill at creating youth-friendly programmes landed him the position of creative director for the teen drama *Beverly Hills 90210* produced by TV mogul Aaron Spelling. The series was an instant success and developed a dedicated gay following, bolstered by the sex appeal of male leads Jason Priestley and Luke Perry. Star's spin-off project, *Melrose Place*, followed the careers and sex lives of a group of affluent gay and straight Los Angelinos. He then moved to CBS to cre-

ate *Central Park West* (1995), which was cancelled following disappointing ratings. His New York-based comedy series for HBO, *Sex and the City* (1998–2004), gained massive popularity for its witty dialogue and sexual frankness, and was a notable success among gay audiences. Star's recent projects include *The $treet* and *Grosse Pointe* (2000).

JOHN FORDE

STEINER, ADIR

b. 1966

activist

Steiner was the same-sex partner of Colonel Doron Meisel, a senior officer in the Medical Corps of the Israeli army. In the 1990s, following Meisel's death, he was involved in litigation seeking recognition as Meisel's spouse under the military service pension laws and a law providing special payments for families of deceased soldiers. After winning the pension-rights case, but losing the special-payments case, Steiner and the army reached a settlement granting Steiner a significant proportion of the payments for which he sued. Following further litigation, the army agreed to recognize Steiner as Meisel's 'family member' for the purposes of memorial ceremonies. The Steiner litigation drew attention to the issue of gays in high-ranking military positions in the Israeli army and to the civil rights of same-sex couples in Israel generally. Later, Steiner went on to become a consultant to the mayor of Tel-Aviv on glbt issues. In 2004 he won another victory for gay rights, when the Israeli tax authorities agreed to recognize his current same-sex partner as his spouse for tax purposes.

AEYAL GROSS

STEPS FOR THE FUTURE

Steps for the Future is an international collaboration of filmmakers working on an

HIV and AIDS campaign for southern Africa. It brings together broadcasters from around the world and AIDS organizations based in southern Africa, to produce professional films that reflect life in the region for local and international audiences. The films examine a wide range of subjects, including sexuality. One of the 40 films produced by Steps for the Future was *Simon and I* (2002), which tells the story of two prominent figures within South Africa's gay and lesbian social movement – Simon **Nkoli** and the filmmaker herself, Beverley **Ditsie**. The film combines personal testimony and political history through the filmmaker's narration and the mixed format of interviews and archival footage. It is a moving personal testimony to anti-apartheid and gay activist Nkoli, culminating in his untimely death from AIDS-related causes in 1998.

GRAEME REID

STICKY RICE QUEEN

An Asian man who dates only Asian men.

TRAVIS KONG

STIPE, MICHAEL

b. 1960

singer

One of contemporary music's most charismatic figures, Michael Stipe rose to fame as the lead singer of internationally renowned rock band REM. Formed in 1980, the band scored their first hit with the single, 'Radio Free Europe'. Their album *Automatic For The People* (1992) was an international success, featuring 'Monty Get Your Gun', Stipe's tribute to tortured gay actor Montgomery Clift, and 'Man On the Moon', a tribute to comedian Andy Kaufman. Tall, lanky and soft-spoken, Stipe's dramatic performance style and androgynous appearance added much to the band's popularity, enjoying crossover appeal with rock and folk fans alike. Famously non-committal about his sexual orientation through most of the 1990s, he once described himself as an 'equal opportunity lech', before coming out as a 'queer artist' in 2001 and revealing a three-year gay relationship. He has also worked as executive producer on glam-rock biopic *Velvet Goldmine* (1998) and *Being John Malkovich* (1999).

JOHN FORDE

STONE, SANDY

performance artist

Allucquére Rosanne (Sandy) Stone is Associate Professor at the University of Texas, Austin, where she is head of the Advanced Communication Technologies Laboratory (ACTLab) and the Convergent Media programme. An eclectic male-to-female transsexual, Stone has come up with interesting results not only as a cultural theorist but also as a filmmaker, neurologist, social scientist, rock 'n' roll music engineer and performer. Her research activity focuses on body, desire, technological prosthetics, gender and sexuality, transgender studies, media and performance. Notable among her theoretical contributions are *The Empire Strikes Back: A Posttranssexual Manifesto* (1991), analysing gender and transsexualism in late capitalism, and *The War of Desire and Technology at the Close of the Mechanical Age* (1995), one of her best-known books internationally, in which she examines the ways that computer-mediated communication – through phone sex, role games, MUDs and MOOs and chat lines – is positively challenging traditional notions of gender identity.

MONICA BARONI

STONEWALL

gay rights organization

England's leading gay rights advocacy group, Stonewall, named after the gay rights **Stonewall Riots** in New York in 1969, works to achieve legal equality and social justice for lesbians, gay men and bisexual people in Great Britain. It was formed in 1988 to protest the conservative Thatcher government's introduction of the homophobic **Section 28** laws and to lobby for the lowering of the age of homosexual consent (then set at 21, as opposed to 16 for heterosexual sex). With the support of celebrity members such as actor Ian McKellen, it successfully lobbied to equalize the age of consent in 2002, and for the repeal of Section 28 in 2003. Stonewall continues to work on gay rights and anti-discrimination initiatives, including the decriminalization of all consenting adult same-sex activity and the legal recognition of same-sex relationships. It provides information, policy analysis and support to government, business and community organizations on gay rights issues.

JOHN FORDE

STONEWALL RIOTS

The Stonewall Riots were a six-night series of demonstrations and violent resistance by a crowd of mostly gay men against the police that erupted during a raid on the Stonewall Inn, a gay club in New York City's Greenwich Village, beginning on the night of 27 June and ending on 2 July 1969. The raids are considered a watershed because they were the first sustained uprising by gay people. They are, however, more significant historically because the militancy displayed by rioters inspired the creation of the **Gay Liberation Front (GLF)** and shortly thereafter of the Gay Activists Alliance (GAA). The GLF and GAA began the gay liberation movement, which transformed the previous homosexual political movement (the **homophile movement**) into a larger and more militant mass movement that continues to spread worldwide. Because of their symbolic and historic importance, these riots are commemorated annually with Gay Pride celebrations.

The history of the Stonewall Inn can only be understood in the context of the era's laws, especially those concerning alcohol. New York's State Liquor Authority (SLA), created when Prohibition ended, was granted broad powers to interpret laws concerning liquor licenses. Businesses that received such licenses were not supposed to be dissolute or disorderly, and the SLA saw the mere presence of homosexuals as evidence of a bar being dissolute. Dancing between persons of the same sex was thus not allowed in bars. As SLA policies and restrictions made it impossible for honest businesspersons to operate gay bars, the Mafia opened gay clubs and paid off the police.

When the Stonewall Inn opened in 1967, it became New York's most popular gay club because it offered the best venue for dancing for gay people at a time when gay men were generally not allowed to dance, even in Mafia clubs. At the Stonewall, patrons were allowed to dance freely. The club attracted a cross-section of the gay male community, as well as the occasional lesbian and some transgender patrons. Its most loyal clientele were gay homeless youths, a group of men who, having been disowned by their families for being effeminate, found a sanctuary there.

Because it could not obtain a license from the SLA, the Stonewall Inn operated under the fiction of being a private 'bottle club', a legal establishment where dues-paying club members could bring and store their own bottles of alcoholic beverages. In reality the Stonewall Inn served anyone they chose to admit who appeared to be homosexual. The club seems sometimes to have operated by membership and routinely

538

had customers sign in upon entering as part of the pretence of being a bottle club. Apparently the information gained through membership applications and through seduction of some customers by the Stonewall's staff was used to blackmail patrons, particularly those who worked on Wall Street. Ed Murphy, one of Stonewall's managers, had previously been arrested for running a nationwide blackmail ring that had victimized thousands of gay men.

According to Deputy Inspector Seymour Pine, who (along with Charles Smythe) headed the First Division of the Public Morals police, his commanding officer informed him of a scheme by which bonds had been stolen from depository houses by blackmailing their homosexual employees. Pine says he was told that the Stonewall seemed to be connected with this extortion scheme and that he was ordered to shut it down. When Pine raided the Stonewall Inn towards the end of June, one of the bar's Mafia managers taunted him by saying that the club would reopen the following day. Pine then decided to apply extra pressure to the club by raiding it a second time that week and by searching for evidence of additional violations of city and federal ordinances to try to put the club out of business.

The carefully planned raid began on Friday, 27 June, with Pine sending four plainclothes agents inside the club to gather evidence of illegal activity. The raid began to go wrong almost as soon as it began when two of the undercover agents, both women, never exited the club as they were supposed to by prearranged plan. Pine, fearing for their safety, began the raid without their having exited.

Pine had planned only to arrest Mafia personnel and to let the club's patrons leave. However, and according to Pine, soon after the raid began he ran into resistance from some of the transvestites and transsexuals inside the club and this began to complicate the situation. Other witnesses talk about a general attitude of resistance among club patrons. When the customers were released, instead of dispersing they gathered in the street and waited. There they discussed the raid on the Stonewall earlier in the week as well as raids on other popular bars.

At first the gay men gathered outside cheered the exiting patrons, some of whom camped it up as they departed. Eventually however the mood became angrier, especially when arrested bar personnel, transvestites and transsexuals were placed in a patrol wagon. The mood of the crowd definitively changed when a lesbian exited, fighting with the police. The very masculine-appearing lesbian, dressed in male attire, had apparently been clubbed by a policeman. She fought fiercely as the police forced her into a patrol car. She then escaped the car twice and fought her way back to the Stonewall Inn. The third time she was picked up and bodily thrown into the car, causing the throng to go wild.

The crowd, having grown in size as Village residents and others had joined it, began to throw objects at the police and tried to overturn a patrol wagon. As the crowd became angrier, one policeman was hit in the eye. After the patrol wagon and police cars departed with the arrested parties, Pine, Smythe and the other police officers barricaded themselves in the Stonewall along with a *Village Voice* reporter.

A full-scale attack on the Stonewall Inn was undertaken by the crowd, who threw bricks, cobblestones, garbage, bottles and dustbins at the club. A parking meter was uprooted and used as a battering ram on the club's entrance and the wooden subwalls in the club's windows. There were also attempts by the crowd to set fire to the club, although witnesses disagree about whether the use of fire was symbolic or serious.

The *Village Voice* account of the police trapped inside the Stonewall depicts the terror they felt at the tremendous rage gay people were expressing. Pine, who had written the manual the US Army used for hand-to-hand combat in the Second World War, underlines the fearsomeness of that anger when he said: 'There was never any time that I felt more scared than I felt that night'. Beyond fear for his own life and the lives of his officers, Pine was worried that his officers would panic and fire on the rioters, causing a massacre. Just as the crowd had succeeded in battering open one of the subwalls and hurling a flaming dustbin inside, fire engines arrived. Riot police soon followed.

With the police rescued from the building, riot police were deployed to clear the streets. Greenwich Village is famous for its erratic streets, but the Village's geography is especially confusing in the immediate area surrounding the Stonewall Inn. This gave an advantage to the protesters – many of whom lived or socialized in the Village. The police repeatedly chased the protesters down one street only to turn around and find them coming at them from behind: the rioters had simply run down one street and circled back on another. Those on the front lines sometimes threw their arms around each other and kick danced, Rockettes-style, in a parody of the phalanx style of the police formations. As they danced they sang self-affirming lyrics, such as: 'We are the Stonewall Girls, / We wear our hair in curls, / We wear no underwear, / We show our pubic hairs'.

Finally, and in spite of persistent resistance by the gay populace, the police succeeded in clearing the streets early on Saturday morning.

Which person or groups should be credited with starting the riots? Witnesses and other evidence shows that it was gay homeless street youth who were on the front lines of action when general violence broke out early on Saturday morning. These same youths were the main fighters throughout the riots, the ones taunting the police and physically engaging them. Beyond the gay street youth, Marsha Johnson, a black transvestite prostitute, was also among the first to attack the police. Pine says the first to resist inside, albeit verbally, were transgen-

dered men. There is good evidence that throughout the riots, and probably especially on the first night, the contribution of transgendered men to the fighting was significant. Finally, the masculine appearance of the lesbian who fought the police and whose resistance precipitated the outbreak of the rioting is noteworthy. While we do not know how she regarded herself, she violated many gender-role expectations in her appearance, dress and behaviour. While the majority of those who fought the police were homeless or transgendered, the most prevalent characteristic among those who fought the hardest (with the exception of a few blue-collar men) is that they were gender-nonconformist.

After the first night of riots, five nights of street violence followed. Word spread rapidly of the revolt and crowds of gay men and women came to the Village on Saturday night both to see what had happened and to protest the police raid. Huge crowds filled the Village for blocks around the Stonewall Inn.

On Sunday night the crowds were much smaller and the riot police were deployed early in an attempt to preempt more protests. The **Mattachine Society** also encouraged gay people not to use violence. The police managed to keep the streets open and there was less violence than on the previous nights. Poet Allen Ginsberg visited the Stonewall Inn on Sunday. Noticing the joyful air among the gay men there he said, 'You know, the guys there were so beautiful. They've lost that wounded look that fags all had 10 years ago.' Although Monday and Tuesday saw only sporadic action, the riots came back in full force on Wednesday after gay people were angered by the tone of the *Village Voice*'s reporting on the riots.

With the end of the rioting, some individuals realized that the protests had created a unique opportunity for change. These persons organized a series of meetings out of which the GLF was born at the end of July.

There were many factors – political, geographical, historical, social and others –

that came together to cause the riots. Perhaps the most important causes were geographical: the Stonewall Inn was located at a transportation nexus (among various major avenues, subway lines and an intra-state train line), in a neighbourhood with an irregular street plan yet with many open spaces, and set out in a pattern that made it easy for rioters to enter and leave the area and difficult for the police to seal it off. The ending of entrapment by the New York City Police Department under John Lindsay's administration in 1966 as the result of a campaign by the Mattachine Society of New York no doubt raised the expectations of the homosexual populace. Raids on several gay clubs, including the Stonewall Inn, led many gay people to believe they were seeing a return to the old pattern of oppression.

Because of their symbolism, the Stonewall Riots have often been depicted in novels about homosexuality and have been celebrated in plays, songs, films, poetry, paintings and at least one sculpture. The word Stonewall has itself become symbolic both as signifying gay resistance to homophobia and oppression but also as a historic dividing line, commonly used to describe the world before gay issues were widely acknowledged (being 'in the closet') and after (being 'out' and 'proud'), so that phrases such as 'pre-Stonewall' and 'post-Stonewall' are common markers in literature about glbt life.

The Stonewall Historic District includes both the site of the former Stonewall Inn as well as the surrounding area where the actual resistance to the police took place. In 1999 it became the first site placed on the National Register of Historic Places by the United States because of its significance for glbt history.

Further reading

Carter, David (2004) *Stonewall: The Riots That Sparked the Gay Revolution*, New York: St Martin's Press.

DAVID CARTER

STRAYHORN, BILLY

b. 1915; d. 1967

composer, musician

Openly gay African-American jazz musician and composer, best known for his 30-year-long musical collaboration with Duke Ellington. William Thomas (Billy) Strayhorn was born in Dayton, Ohio. A talented classical pianist, he studied at the Pittsburgh Musical Institute. In 1939 he joined Ellington's jazz band as a pianist. The two musicians soon became an inseparable team, absorbing each others' musical technique and working together on composition and musical arrangement. Strayhorn composed many of Ellington's signature pieces, including 'Take the A Train', 'Lotus Blossom' and 'Clementine', and he worked with Ellington on 'The Deep South Suite', 'Such Sweet Thunder' and two suites based on African-American history, 'Jump For Joy' and 'My People'. Although he went largely unrecognized during his own lifetime, he is now seen as the creative power behind Ellington.

JOHN FORDE

STREB, ELIZABETH

b. 1950

dancer, choreographer, artistic director

Born on 23 February 1950 in Rochester, New York, Streb studied dance at SUNY Brockport before she danced with Margaret Jenkins in San Francisco. She moved to New York City during the early 1980s and began to experiment with choreography, including use of trampolines, harnesses and constructed walls that allowed dancers to engage gravity fully in body slams, collisions and rebounding off immobile surfaces; her work would later be termed 'pop action'. Eschewing music, the aesthetics of grace or specialized treatment of gender, Streb pits her male and female dancers against gravity and spatial force to explore the drama of movement itself, with action as the subject of dance. Her work engages a queer butch aesthetic unconcerned with artifice. In *Little Ease* (1985) she trapped herself in a constrictive box, with one side open to the audience, and manoeuvred, with palpable difficulty, within its confines. In *Breakthru* (1997) she dove through a pane of glass, exemplifying her approach to performance as a negotiation of fear and physical possibility through dance theatre. In 2003 she opened the Streb Laboratory for Action Mechanics in Brooklyn, New York, a performance garage that includes a flying trapeze apparatus. She is artistic director of STREB USA.

THOMAS F. DEFRANTZ

STREISAND, BARBRA

b. 1942

actor, singer, director

One of the defining icons of postwar American showbusiness, Streisand's combination of unconventional beauty, torch-song singer charisma and well-publicized personal insecurities have endeared her to generations of gay audiences. She dazzled 1960s Broadway with her performance as Ziegfeld Follies star Fanny Brice in *Funny Girl*, filmed in 1968 by William Wyler. The role seemed tailor-made for her ascending career – both were self-described 'ugly ducklings' who achieved success through their self-deprecating wit, talent and determination – winning her a Tony and an Oscar. She played variations on her trademark Jewish princess persona in hits including *The Owl and the Pussycat* (1970), *The Way We Were* (1973) and *A Star Is Born* (1976), alongside a hugely successful music career. She scored success as an actor-director in *Yentl* (1983), in which she played a cross-dressing female rabbi, and with *The Prince of Tides* (1991)

and *The Mirror Has Two Faces* (1996). Her son is the openly gay actor-director Jason Gould.

JOHN FORDE

STRYKER, JEFF

b. 1962

porn star

Born Charles Casper Peyton in Carmi, Illinois, this former military school graduate is undoubtedly the 'biggest' icon in the history of gay pornography. Stryker's legendary career began in the mid-1980s when, while attending a real estate course, he was persuaded by a friend to try out for a modelling advertisement in a local paper. His photos drew the attention of gay porn producer John Travis, who persuaded the young and apparently heterosexual Stryker to fly to Los Angeles where he became the prototypical role model for the industry's ongoing fascination with straight men in 'gay-for-pay' erotica in such films as *The Switch Is On* (1985), *Powertool* (1986) and *Stryker Force* (1987). Remaining persistently evasive about his sexuality, despite appearing in both straight and bisexual films, Stryker quickly rose to fame as one of the most successful male performers in the Adult industry, garnering a number of awards and even attaining some crossover success in B-movie horror *After Death* (1988), and more recently appearing in cult German queer filmmaker Rosa von Praunheim's comedy short film *Can I Be Your Bratwurst, Please?* (1999).

ROBIN GRIFFITHS

STUDIO 54

nightclub

A short-lived but legendary New York nightclub, which became the spiritual home of the hedonistic queer-friendly 1970s and 1980s party scene. Opened by

Steve Rubell and Ian Schrager in 1977, it became as famous for its drug use and polymorphous sexual activity as for its celebrity guests, who included Andy Warhol, Calvin Klein, Bianca Jagger, Liza Minnelli, Diana Ross, Elizabeth Taylor, Truman Capote, Madonna and Elton John. Its iconic status was cemented by Bianca Jagger's birthday party, during which she rode onto the dancefloor on a white horse. The club was closed in 1980 after Rubell and Schrager were imprisoned for tax evasion, but reopened in 1981. However, it failed to regain its former popularity, closing again in 1986. Rubell's life and the Studio 54 party scene were portrayed in the film *54* (1998).

JOHN FORDE

SUEDE

pop group

Suede were a key band on the British 1990s neo-glam pop scene. Controversial declarations by singer Brett Anderson (b. 1967, Haywards Heath, England) regarding his own uncertain sexual identity ('I feel like a bisexual who's never had a homosexual experience') boosted the sensation created by his androgynous image (accompanied by a significant cover for their first album, released in 1993, showing two sexually indeterminate figures kissing) and by the unique, outlandish, timbral character of Anderson's high-pitched voice. An overstylized image, music and voice, along with a constant winking and referencing, in their lyrics, to the gay lowlife of drugs and promiscuity, made Suede, along with **Blur**, one of the foremost Britpop bands and a protagonist of the queer 1990s. While after 1996 they lost their momentum, their stylish decadence harked back to early Bowie personae and the androgyny and transvestite playfulness of 1970s **glam rock**.

FABIO CLETO

SULLIVAN, ANDREW

b. 1963

writer

British-born, Harvard-educated (PhD) Andrew Sullivan became the iconoclastic, Catholic, anti-abortion, pro-Israel editor of *The New Republic* at age 28. Five years later, in 1996, he resigned, acknowledged his HIV status, but also declared victory over AIDS in *The New York Times Magazine*. A fierce critic of gay promiscuity and of Bill Clinton's sexual indiscretions, Sullivan drew fire for his 2001 Internet solicitation of unsafe sex (barebacking), but held onto powerful friends in journalism including the *Washington Post*'s Howard Kurtz. He split publicly and bitterly with the *Times* in 2002, while post-9/11, his Web blog vigorously promoted George Bush's war on terror. Sullivan later broke with Clinton over his stance on gay marriage.

PAUL SCHINDLER

SUMMER, DONNA

b. 1948

singer

An African-American pop singer and songwriter, Donna Summer achieved international fame and gay cult status during the 1970s as the 'Queen of Disco'. After singing as the lead vocalist with a number of nondescript bands in her hometown of Boston, Summer moved to Europe, where she teamed up with producer Giorgio Moroder for her breakthrough 1975 hit, 'Love to Love You Baby'. Featuring 16 minutes of erotic groans set to a hypnotic synth-beat, the song become a runaway smash and catapulted Summer into the international limelight. A series of best-selling albums followed, with hits such as 'I Feel Love', 'Last Dance' and 'Down Deep Inside' consolidating Summer's image as a sensual queen of the dance floor.

Summer's relationship to gay male cultures has been an integral component of her career. During her heyday, Summer performed widely at gay venues and, with its combination of overt sexuality and diva iconography, her image and music made strategic appeals to gay consumers. The relationship soured, however, in 1984 when allegations surfaced that Summer, who had recently become a born-again Christian, referred to AIDS as a form of divine punishment. Despite repeated denials from Summer and her management that she had ever made the remarks, the gay press called for a popular boycott of the artist; she would spend the better part of the next two decades trying to rebuild bridges with her gay fan base. Founded or otherwise, the controversy highlights the growing influence of the gay consumer market in contemporary entertainment industries.

BRETT FARMER

SUPERMODELS

A term describing a cluster of 1990s models, notably Nadja Auermann, Naomi Campbell, Linda Evangelista, Kate Moss, Christy Turlington, Cindy Crawford and Claudia Schiffer, whose personal profiles became as celebrated as the designer couture they modelled. Coinciding with a rejection of grunge culture and a return to consumerist glamour, supermodels became favourites of the tabloids, who gave frequent coverage to partying, drug and alcohol abuse and disposable boyfriends, a lifestyle epitomized in Evangelista's much-quoted maxim: 'I don't get out of bed for less than $10,000 a day'.

JOHN FORDE

SUTHERLAND, JOAN

b. 1926

opera singer (coloratura soprano)

Born on 7 November 1926 in Point Piper, Sydney, Australia to a successful tailor and a teacher, Sutherland grew up mimicking the voice of her mother, a gifted mezzo soprano. Her mother's coaching laid down solid technical foundations, and after only three years of formal training she made her debut in Sydney, aged 21, in Purcell's *Dido and Aeneas*. Several major awards followed, and she moved to London in 1951 to study at the Royal College of Music with Clive Carey, making her first Covent Garden appearance the following year, as the First of the Three Ladies in Mozart's *Magic Flute*.

Sutherland forged a remarkable creative partnership with the pianist Richard Bonynge, whom she married on 16 October 1954. Detecting a potentially fine *bel canto* soprano in Sutherland, Bonynge began to coax the voice upwards out of its mezzo range, transposing familiar arias beyond what his wife believed she was capable of singing. His musical judgement proved sound: her 1959 Covent Garden performance as the doomed heroine of Donizetti's *Lucia di Lammermoor* drew immense critical acclaim, launching an international career that would span over four decades and more than 1,800 performances. She played Lucia again in debuts at La Scala and the New York Metropolitan Opera in 1961, and for many opera queens her heartrending performance of Lucia's 'mad scene' has become iconic.

Sutherland's reputation rests on purity and clarity of tone, and brilliant execution of coloratura (richly ornamented, virtuosic music that exploits the upper reaches of the voice). What Maria Callas was to fire and passion, Sutherland was to vocal dexterity, warmth and flexibility, as can be heard in her two-disc compilation *The Art of the Prima Donna* (1960). As a leading figure in the *bel canto* revival of the 1950s and 1960s, she helped to revive majestic, romantic roles from the early nineteenth century – e.g. Bellini's Norma and Amina, Rossini's Semiramide and Donizetti's Mary Stuart, Lucrezia Borgia and Anne Boleyn – her towering physical presence and long red hair adding greatly to their impact on stage. She made her Italian and American debuts as Handel's malevolent sorceress Alcina, earning the soubriquet 'La stupenda', and was a particularly impressive Cleopatra in his *Giulio Cesare*. But she also worked with contemporary composers, creating the role of Jenifer in *A Midsummer Marriage* for Michael Tippett, the openly gay British composer, in 1955.

Sutherland's modesty, warmth and professionalism has endeared her to many – qualities at variance with the temperamental behaviour normally associated with the opera diva. She became a Dame of the British Empire in 1979, and gave her farewell performance in Sydney in 1990 as Marguerite de Valois in Meyerbeer's *Les Huguenots*.

See also: Diva; Opera

Further reading

Major, N. (1987) *Joan Sutherland*, with an introduction by Dame Joan Sutherland, London: Macdonald/Queen Anne.

RACHEL COWGILL

SWIMMING

Swimming occupies a different position than that of several other sports in relationship to glbt culture and the degree to which homophobia occurs within the sport. Unlike football (in which male athletes are presumed heterosexual) or figure skating (in which male athletes are presumed homosexual), swimmers (of both genders) generally escape social assumptions about their sexuality. Although swimmers are subject to the heterosexism of society at large, a more nuanced understanding of sexuality occurs within the sport when compared to many other sports that both make assumptions about the heterosexuality or homosexuality of those who play and exhibit higher degrees of homophobia. Because of this social tolerance, the creation of a safer space for many gay and lesbian athletes has taken root. This safer space, combined with

the sheer homoeroticism of athletic bodies clad in revealing swimwear, has made the sport somewhat of a haven for gay athletes. There also exists a large queer culture via community-level swimming clubs.

There have been a number of openly gay Olympic-calibre swimmers, such as Greg **Louganis**. There are also a relatively large number of openly gay male high school and collegiate swimmers who have come out to their teams while actively participating in the sport.

ERIC ANDERSON

SWINTON, TILDA

b. 1961

actor

British actor Tilda Swinton, best known for her association with filmmaker Derek **Jarman**, made her film debut in 1986 in his *Caravaggio* and has been involved in all his subsequent films. She won Best Actress at the Venice Film Festival for her role as Queen Isabella in his *Edward II* (1991). With a few exceptions (notably *The Beach* [2000]), Swinton has eschewed the mainstream and has often chosen gender-bending roles. In *Man to Man* (1992) she plays a working-class woman impersonating her dead husband during the Second World War. Also in 1992 she appeared as the titular character in Sally Potter's *Orlando*, based on Virginia Woolf's novel of the same name. Orlando is an Elizabethan nobleman who lives for 400 years, changing sex along the way. This role, along with her work for Jarman, has won Swinton a following among art-house film fans and those interested in gender issues within cinema.

CHANTAL STOUGHTON

SYDNEY

The state capital of New South Wales, Australia, Sydney was founded as part of

Britain's penal colonies and is now considered to be Australia's gay capital. Oxford Street in Darlinghurst hosts the annual Gay and Lesbian Mardi Gras parade and marks Sydney's oldest and largest gay precinct. While this area caters primarily to a gay male clientele, queer women in Sydney tend to gravitate to the suburb Newton, the city's second significant gay ghetto.

KELLIE BURNS

SYLVESTER

b. 1947; d. 1988

singer

Born in Los Angeles, as a young man Sylvester moved to San Francisco, where his gospel music background brought a new dimension to the radical gay troupe The Cockettes. After working with Hot Band, Sylvester began a solo career under the direction of music scout Harvey Fuqua. Disco classics such as 'Dance' (1978) followed, and soon Sylvester's piercing falsetto voice and gender-bending appearance came to embody black, gay disco, an iconic status easily verified by his most famous song, 'You Make Me Feel (Mighty Real)' (1978). The record won numerous awards and is still prized for its affirmation of realness, a feeling of pride with regard to African-American culture and a full range of gay sexual identities. Backing singers, Martha Wash and Izora Redman, originally called Two Tons of Fun and later dubbed the Weather Girls, were integral to the sound of Sylvester at the height of his career, which was cut short by AIDS.

GABRIEL GOMEZ

SYNAGOGUES, GAY

The phenomenon of gay synagogues emerged in 1972 in Los Angeles (Beth Chayim Chadashim [House of New Life]) and New York (CBST/Congregation Beth Simchat Torah [House of Joy in the Torah]). Since then the gay-Jewish movement has grown to more than 20 institutions in metropolitan centres across North America, ranging in size from a few dozen to nearly a thousand members. The congregations began as lay-led associations staffed by volunteers who managed all committees, performed in leading ritual and supported administrative roles. Later, congregations hired professionals to serve in major roles.

The ritual and liturgical style of the synagogues is close to the Reform, the Reconstructionist or the Conservative American-Jewish denominations. A few congregations are officially affiliated with the Reform movement in particular. The gay synagogues are fully identified with the major cultural and political activities of the gay scene in North America and cooperate with all other gay religious movements.

MOSHE SHOKEID

T

TAIPEI

Taipei's most celebrated queer location is New Park, home to a gay cruising and sex-work subculture since the 1940s and a rich site of collective memory for gay communities today. The first gay bars opened in the 1960s in the Zhongshan North Road area, in the red-light precinct catering to American GIs during the Vietnam War. Lesbian bars followed in the 1980s. The Gongguan district, near Taiwan University, houses Gin Gin's, Taiwan's first queer bookshop.

FRAN MARTIN

TAIWAN, FILMMAKING IN

Taiwan's earliest gay-themed film was Yu Kan-ping's little-known *The Outcasts* (*Nie zi*, 1986), an adaptation of Pai Hsien-yung's novel *Nie-zi* (*Crystal Boys*, 1983). More familiar to international audiences, however, is Ang Lee's now-classic *The Wedding Banquet* (*Hsi yen*, 1993), a tragic-comic melodrama about the repercussions of a gay Taiwanese-American's fake wedding. Lee's film is one of the most successful locally made films in Taiwan to this day.

Art-house director Tsai Ming-liang, who was born in Malaysia but lived for many years in Taiwan, has directed a film-cycle that is a cinematic rumination on urban alienation and solitary queer yearning. From *Rebels of the Neon God* (*Qingshaonian Nuozha*, 1992) through *Vive L'Amour* (*Aiqing wansui*, 1994) to *The River* (*Heliu*, 1996), Tsai's films follow the life of the young man Hsiao Kang, who becomes sexually attracted to a series of men he notices in his wanderings through the city. Finally, in *The River*'s audacious climax, Hsiao Kang finds himself being masturbated by his own father in a gay sauna. Tsai's most recent film, *What Time is it There?* (*Ni nabian jidian?*, 2001), includes a lesbian scene in which a young Taiwanese woman shares a bed with a Hong Kong woman while holidaying in Paris. Although Tsai's overall outlook seems bleak, nonetheless the moments of queer longing in his films are treated with immense tenderness.

Independent videomaker Mickey Chen has directed two documentaries: *Not Simply a Wedding Banquet* (*Bu zhi shi xi yan*, 1996, co-directed with Ming-hsiu Chen), about the same-sex wedding between author Hsu Yoshen and his partner Gray Harriman, and *Boys for Beauty* (*Meili shaonian*, 1998), about the family lives of three gay Taiwanese teenagers. The latter obtained theatrical release and was a surprise hit with local audiences.

Two lesbian dramas were released during the early 1990s: female director Huang Yu-shan's Taiwanese–Hong Kong co-production *Twin Bracelets* (*Shuang zhuo*, 1990), on the loving bond between two women in rural eastern China; and Zheng Shengfu's *The Silent Thrush* (*Shisheng huamei*, 1992), on the homoerotic world of the all-female Taiwanese opera (based on Ling Yan's novel).

Recent lesbian-themed productions include Lin Cheng-sheng's *Murmur of Youth* (*Meili zai changge*, 1997), newcomer Hung Hung's *The Love of Three Oranges* (*San ju zhi lian*, 1998) and lesbian director Chen Jo-fei's *Incidental Journey* (*Haijiao Tianya*, 2001). *Murmur* is a faintly magic-realist drama about two young women who share the same name but are of different social classes, and who fall in love while working together in a cinema ticket booth. Hung's quirky film tells the story of a love triangle that develops between a young lesbian couple and an ex-boyfriend of one of the women; the overall impression is of an interchangeability of sexual roles, where romantic attachments develop almost regardless of gender. Chen's film is a poetic tale about a woman who chances to meet another woman when her car runs out of gas in the mountains; the women spend a few idyllic days together and appear to be falling in love, but ultimately they go their separate ways.

Yee Chih-yen's bigger budget Taiwanese–French co-production, *Blue Gate Crossing* (*Lanse da men*, 2002), is a gentle, nostalgic coming-of-age tale centring on a love triangle between three classmates. The film could also be interpreted as a lesbian coming-out narrative of sorts.

One video that created a sensation in local lesbian subcultures was first-time director Li Xiangru's low-budget *2, 1* (1999), a documentary about a young lesbian couple who were planning a wedding ceremony but who, during the course of filming, instead broke up. Through a series of interviews with the women themselves, as well as their friends and family members, Li's film offers a fascinating insight into local lesbian life.

Further reading

Berry, Chris (2000) 'Asian Values, Family Values: Film, Video and Lesbian and Gay

Identities', *The Journal of Homosexuality* 40, 3/4: 211–32.

Lim, Song Hwee (2002) 'Contesting Celluloid Closets: Representing Male Homosexuality in Chinese Cinemas', *Tamkang Review* XXXIII, 2 (Winter): 55–75.

Martin, Fran (2003) 'Globally Chinese at *The Wedding Banquet*' and 'Perverse Utopia: Reading *The River*', in *Situating Sexualities: Queer Representation in Taiwanese Fiction, Film and Public Culture*, Hong Kong: Hong Kong University Press, pp. 141–61 and 163–84.

FRAN MARTIN

TAIWAN, LITERATURE

One of the most exciting developments on Taiwan's literary scene during the 1990s was the rise of a new wave of lesbian, gay, queer and transgender-themed writing. Such fiction was written by both established authors and a new generation of young writers, and received high praise from the literary establishment and a lively response from readers. Indeed, this small island has now emerged as the world's foremost producer of glbt fiction in Chinese – or **tongzhi** fiction, as it is called in Mandarin. Taiwanese *tongzhi* writing reaches readers worldwide, from Southeast Asia to the Chinese diaspora in the West, as well as mainland China, where Taiwanese books are often lesbian and gay people's first point of contact with queer writing.

The 'new *tongzhi* literary wave' of the 1990s was not without precedent. Two popular novels set in lesbian subcultures were published during the 1970s: Xuan Xiaofo's *Outside the Perfect Circle* (*Yuan zhi wai*, 1976) and Guo Lianghui's *Beyond Two Kinds* (*Liangzhong yiwaide*, 1978; republished as *The Third Sex* [*Disan xing*, 1987]). Another 1970s work on love between women was 'Waves Scour the Sands' ('Lang tao sha', 1976), written by Chu T'ien-hsin when she was just 18. 'Waves' describes the emotional turmoil of a teenage girl in love with her tomboy best friend and has attained the status of classic among

Taiwan's lesbian readerships. The best-known pre-1990s gay-themed work is without doubt Pai Hsien-yung's *Crystal Boys* (*Nie zi*), published in 1983. Set during the socially repressive years of the 1970s, *Crystal Boys* follows the careers of a community of young male sex workers and their lovers and patrons, whose social life orbits around Taipei's famous gay cruising spot, New Park. *Crystal Boys'* style and theme are echoed in Pai's story, 'A Sky Full of Bright, Twinkling Stars' ('Mantianli liangjingjingde xingxing', 1983).

The 1990s marked a watershed in Taiwanese glbt writing. The appearance of a distinct *tongzhi* fiction paralleled the rise of *tongzhi* activism following the lifting of martial law in 1987. Several *tongzhi*-themed works were published early in the decade by sisters Chu T'ien-wen and Chu T'ien-hsin, by then both well-established authors. Chu T'ien-wen's novel, *Notes of a Desolate Man* (*Huangren shouji*, 1994), winner of the China Times Novel Prize, is a postmodernist chronicle of the mental life of a gay Taiwanese intellectual, Xiao Shao, as he grieves the recent death of a close friend as a result of AIDS. Chu T'ien-hsin, meanwhile, wrote 'A Story of Spring Butterflies' ('Chunfeng hudie zhi shi', 1992), in which a male narrator reluctantly reveals his knowledge of his wife's undying love for a female ex-schoolmate. In 1991 Ling Yan's *The Silent Thrush* (*Shisheng huamei*, 1990) won the Independence Times Novel Prize. Ling's novel is set in the world of the all-female Taiwanese opera, *goa-a-hi*, and focuses on sexual relationships that form between actresses. Another influential lesbian work published the same year is Tsao Li-chuan's 'The Maidens' Dance' ('Tongnü zhi wu'), a romance between adolescent schoolgirls. Tsao's later story, 'Regarding Her White Hair and Other Matters' ('Guanyu tade baifa ji qita', 1996), narrates the life stories of an older lesbian and her circle of friends. In 1996 Du Xiulan's lesbian coming-of-age novel *Rebel Daughter* (*Ninü*) won the

Crown Popular Novel Prize. Popular gay-themed fiction, meanwhile, was written by prolific author Hsu Yoshen, who in 1996 held a public wedding ceremony in Taipei with his male partner – a milestone in Taiwan's *tongzhi* history.

A remarkable literary talent who emerged during the 1990s was Qiu Miaojin, now Taiwan's best-known lesbian author. Qiu is most remembered for her novel, *The Crocodile's Journal* (*Eyu shouji*, 1994), which was awarded the China Times Honorary Novel Prize in 1995, following Qiu's suicide that same year while studying in Paris. *Crocodile* weaves together a first-person narrative about a lesbian university student with a second narrative about a cartoon-like crocodile mercilessly hounded by the popular press and a voyeuristic public. The crocodile story is often read as an allegory for a homophobic society's treatment of lesbians. Qiu's second novel, *Montmartre Testament* (*Mengmate yishu*, 1996), published posthumously, presents an autobiographical narrative of Qiu's life in France leading up to her suicide. Qiu's writing, although painful, continues to hold immense significance for lesbian readers within Taiwan and beyond.

In its stylistic innovation, anti-homophobic critique and authorship by a young, out author, Qiu's writing is exemplary of a distinct subcategory of 1990s *tongzhi* fiction referred to as 'queer literature' (*ku'er wenxue*). Other major writers in this category are Chi Ta-wei, Hong Ling and Chen Xue. Gay author Chi Ta-wei and lesbian writer Hong Ling both write experimental-style queer fiction informed by Euro-American queer theory. Their writing is generically eclectic, as can be judged from Hong Ling's series of gothic lesbian vampire narratives and Chi's prize-winning queer science-fiction novella 'The Membranes' ('Mo', 1996). Chen Xue, meanwhile, writes in a psychological-realist style about women's sexuality, including narratives on lesbianism, bisexuality and incest (her 'Searching for the Lost Wings of the Angel', ['Xunzhao tianshi yishide chibang', 1995] combines all three elements). All three of the young *ku'er* writers maintained a high media profile and made an important contribution to 1990s *tongzhi* culture in their role as queer public intellectuals.

Transgender-themed fiction also began to appear late in the decade. Dong Qizhang's prize-winning novel *Doubleself* (*Shuangshen*, 1997) and Wu Jiwen's *Galaxies in Ecstasies* (1998) both centre on male-to-female transgender journeys.

Tongzhi writing is also often published outside the traditional book format, including popular fiction in *tongzhi* magazines and on the Internet. Indeed, post-1990s *tongzhi* Internet fiction is an increasingly significant phenomenon, as a new generation of young authors begins to emerge from this medium. For example, lesbian writer AD, who writes humorous, slice-of-life tales with lesbian characters, became known to readers via the Internet before publishing her first story collection *Hand in Hand* (*Wo shou*, 2002). With its accessibility and cheapness, Internet fiction is widely and enthusiastically consumed both within Taiwan and abroad and seems certain to play a key role in the future of Taiwanese queer writing.

Further reading

Chi Ta-wei (1998) 'The Scent of HIV' and 'I'm Not Stupid', trans. Fran Martin, *antiTHESIS* 9 (University of Melbourne): 141–51.

Chu T'ien-wen (1999) *Notes of a Desolate Man*, trans. Howard Goldblatt and Sylvia Li-Chun Lin, New York: Columbia University Press.

Hong Ling (2001) 'Fever', trans. Paola Zamperini, in Patricia Sieber (ed.) *Red is Not the Only Color: Contemporary Chinese Fiction on Love and Sex Between Women*, Lanham: Rowman & Littlefield, pp. 149–51.

Martin, Fran (ed. and trans.) (2003) *Angelwings: Contemporary Queer Ficiton from Taiwan*, Honolulu: University of Hawaii Press.

Pai Hsien-yung (1995) *Crystal Boys*, trans. Howard Goldblatt, San Francisco: Gay Sunshine Press.

—— (2000) 'A Sky Full of Bright, Twinkling Stars', trans. Pai Hsien-yung and Patia Yasin, in George Kao (ed.) *Wandering in the Garden, Waking from a Dream: Tales of Taipei Characters*, Chinese-English Bilingual Edition, Hong Kong: Chinese University Press, pp. 311–25.

Tsao Li-chuan (2002) 'Dance of a Maiden', trans. Shou-Fang Hu-Moore, *The Chinese Pen* 30, 1 (Spring): 71–102.

FRAN MARTIN

TAKAHASHI, MUTSUO

b. 1937

writer

Mutsuo Takahashi is a Japanese poet, novelist and autobiographer who was an early protégé of novelist Yukio Mishima. His work is characterized by both a Buddhist and Catholic-inspired mysticism and a recurring homoeroticism. His 1971 *Homeuta* (Ode) is a massive Whitmanesque catalogue of his fascination with the male body and contains many startling images describing male genitalia. Takahashi has written over two dozen volumes of poetry and his work has received several important literary prizes in Japan. Many of his homoerotic poems were gathered together and translated into English in 1975 as *Poems of a Penisist*.

MARK McLELLAND

TARTARUGA, LA

publishing company

The Italian feminist publishing house La Tartaruga began operations in Milan in 1975. Virginia Woolf's *The Three Guineas* (*Le tre ghinee*, 1975) was the first book to be published, works by both major and new authors, Italian and foreign followed. Alongside the series of novels and poetry, which included texts by Gertrude Stein, George Sand, Marina Cvetaeva and Anna Banti, La Tartaruga also published the 'Saggi', a series of essays inaugurated with *Il pensiero della differenza sessuale* by the Italian Diotima philosophical community, featuring texts by Luce **Irigaray**. In 1990 the publisher Mondadori bought the majority of the company's shares, while leaving complete editorial freedom in place. Effectively, La Tartaruga has translated a great deal of feminist literature and lesbian texts, almost all from English yet practically unknown in Italy. Importantly, the publisher has remained committed to seeking out new Italian writers. La Tartaruga has consistently addressed the investigation of the female condition and the multiple facets that occur in the search for self- and gender identity. It also publishes texts of historic documentation, which has led to a revival of a female cultural tradition.

MONIA ANDREANI

TASMANIAN LAW REFORM

Tasmania was the last federal state of Australia to repeal the laws against homosexuality. Sections 122 and 123 of the Tasmanian Criminal Code of 1924 (inherited from British colonial law) criminalized all sexual activity between men, even that between consenting adults. In 1988 activist Rodney Croome formed the Tasmanian Gay and Lesbian Rights Group (TGLRG) to lobby for law reform. Later that year the TGLRG protested at a Hobart City market stall, leading to the arrest of 130 protesters. In 1992 TGLRG member Nicholas Toonen took a case to the United Nations Human Rights Committee, arguing that the Criminal Code breached his rights of equality and privacy under the International Covenant on Civil and Political Rights 1966, to which Australia was a signatory. In 1994 the Committee ruled that the Criminal Code breached Toonen's privacy rights, and ordered its repeal. The Tasmanian legislature refused to comply with the Human Rights Committee's rul-

ing. The Australian Federal government passed a new privacy law overriding the Tasmanian law, but again the Tasmanian legislature rejected another attempt at law reform. In 1996 the dispute went to the High Court of Australia. Before the Court made its decision on the case, the Tasmanian legislature repealed the Criminal Code in May 1997.

JOHN FORDE

TATCHELL, PETER

b. 1952

activist, writer

A radical gay and human rights activist, Australian-born Peter Tatchell is also a theorist and author dedicated to non-violence and direct action through such groups as the Gay Liberation Front (1972), ACT UP (1989) and OutRage! (1990). Tatchell is famous for speaking out, variously at meetings of anti-gay psychiatrists in 1972, after seizing the pulpit at Canterbury Cathedral in 1998 and after challenging the anti-gay bigotry of Archbishop George Carey. He promotes gay rights, especially the equality of 'age-of-consent' laws in Britain and throughout Europe by working through Europe-wide institutions. Tatchell lobbied the African National Congress to renounce anti-gay discrimination in 1987, leading to South Africa being the first country in the world to include sexual orientation protections in its constitution.

In 1999, in London, Tatchell attempted a citizen's arrest of Zimbabwean President Robert Mugabe for human rights abuses. His activism includes publicly shaming closeted public officials who worked against gay rights; his actions have subjected him to hundreds of personal assaults.

See also: ACT UP; Gay Liberation Front (GLF); OutRage!

ANDY HUMM

TATTOO

Body art made by breaking the skin's surface and drawing with ink in stylized patterns/imagery. The word is Polynesian: 'tatu' meaning 'to mark something', or 'tatao', 'to tap'. In recorded history, the earliest tattoos were done in ancient Egypt. Modern Western culture associated tattoos with bikers and delinquents and had little tolerance until the latter part of the twentieth century, and its growth among countercultural movements. Tribal tattoos were reclaimed in the 1980s by rebellious punks, gays and lesbians. Some used tattoos and piercings to make a statement about alienation from society, while others chose symbols to formalize and make recognizable membership of a subculture.

MICHAEL PINFOLD

TAVEL, RONALD

b. 1941

writer

Although known primarily as a playwright, Ronald Tavel began his writing career with the novel *Street of Stairs* (1962). He met Andy **Warhol** and became resident screenwriter at the artist's Factory. Between 1964 and 1966 Tavel wrote and otherwise worked on several Warhol productions, most notably *The Life of Juanita Castro*, *Screentest #2* and *Vinyl*. Elements of drag and sexual ambiguity are frequently featured in his scripts. After the period working with Warhol, Tavel worked mostly in the theatre, first with the Play House of the Ridiculous in the late 1960s and then in other Off-Off-Broadway productions. His plays are some of the prime examples of the Theater of the Ridiculous (see **Ludlam**, Charles), marked by playful double-entendres, sexual innuendoes and frequent references to Hollywood cinema. They include *Shower* (1965), *The Life of Lady Godiva* (1966), *Gorilla Queen* (1967) and

Boy on the Straight-Back Chair (1969), for which he won an Obie Award. Tavel currently lives and works in Bangkok.

DANIEL HENDRICKSON

TAYLOR, ELIZABETH

b. 1932

actor

As a child star at MGM during the 1940s, Elizabeth Taylor appeared as a jockey in *National Velvet* (1945), a horse film beloved by lesbians. After a series of films as a dull ingenue, Taylor moved into her Oscar-bait 'neurotic period' playing highly strung women in intense melodramas. There are the fabulously campy *Butterfield 8* (1960) and *Reflections in a Golden Eye* (1967); and the adaptations of Tennessee Williams' *Cat on a Hot Tin Roof* (1958), *Suddenly, Last Summer* (1959), *Boom!* (aka, *The Milk Train Doesn't Stop Here Anymore*, 1968) and *Sweet Bird of Youth* (1989). Her finest hours are as Martha in Edward Albee's *Who's Afraid of Virginia Woolf?* (1966) and in *Cleopatra* (1963), the film that changed the makeup style of drag queens around the world. Taylor's queer credentials also include being the best gal pal of Rock **Hudson**, Montgomery **Clift** and James **Dean**, her heroic AIDS education and fund-raising efforts and that strange friendship with Michael Jackson.

ALEX DOTY

TCHELITCHEV, PAVEL

b. 1898; d. 1957

artist

When Pavel Tchelitchev (alternative spellings: Tchelitchew or Tchelitcheiff) was a young boy, his father warned him against his interests in 'effeminate' activities such as ballet and painting. His father suggested he study for work in the sciences, but Tchelitchev would have none of it. Born in

Kaluga, outside Moscow, and raised in a bourgeois Russian family, Tchelitchev was granted access to the arts and homosexual culture, which proved central to his development as a queer artist. Once the Bolshevik Revolution occurred, however, the 'white' Tchelitchev family was stripped of both their financial and cultural resources. The young painter subsequently left for Constantinople (today Istanbul) in 1919.

Tchelitchev spent time in Berlin and Paris where he worked with, among others, the queer impresario Sergei Diaghilev and the beautifully obsessive, heterosexual choreographer George Balanchine. During the 1920s Tchelitchev's interest in forging multimedia experiences drew together painting, cinema and dance, especially in Diaghilev's production of *Ode* (1928). Significantly, his use of these different media was engaged to evoke his particular vision of the visceral body. Throughout his work (from painting to theatre), Tchelitchev explored the interiority of the body as it might reveal the perverse and beautiful 'freaks' (to borrow the term Parker Tyler often used to describe his work) who made up the artist's cultural milieu.

In 1934 Tchelitchev moved to New York with his lover, Charles Henri **Ford**. There he continued to work with Balanchine and met his greatest champion and patron, Lincoln **Kirstein**. By 1938 he had completed what many consider his greatest work, *Phenomena* which, like his later 'Interior Landscapes' series, fully realized his view of what Kirstein called 'simultaneity' or 'metamorphosis'. That is, Tchelitchev's vision of interior corporeality commingled with the exterior world where it was revealed in the work of art. The more macho American artists and critics of the period, such as Clement Greenberg and Thomas Hart Benton, aligned Tchelitchev's work with Surrealism and Neo-Romanticism (categories Tchelitchev himself denied) and, by extension, homosexuality. Greenberg, most notably, championed painters such as Jackson Pol-

lock over Tchelitchev in the pages of *Partisan Review* while Ford, Tyler and Kirstein took up Tchelitchev's cause in the pages of the more queer-inflected art journal, *View*.

With Ford, Tchelitchev travelled between New York and Italy where, after years of stomach ailments and other painful illnesses, he died in 1957.

DAVID A. GERSTNER

TE AWEKOTUKU, NGAHUIA

b. 1949

writer, curator, academic, activist

Ngahuia Te Awekotuku was born in Rotorua, Aotearoa/New Zealand of Te Arawa, Waikato and Tuhoe descent (tribal identities of the indigenous Maori people). A significant Maori, lesbian and feminist activist during the 1970s and 1980s, Te Awekotuku contributed to the establishment of the Gay Liberation Front in Auckland in 1972 (later, the Gay Liberation Auckland Inc.). She is the author of a number of books, including *Tahuri and Other Stories* (1989), a work of fiction drawing upon Te Awekotuku's experiences as a Maori lesbian in a traditional village environment (among other subjects). *Mana Wahine Maori: Selected Writings* collects together her political writings and speeches made between 1970 and 1990. She is particularly noteworthy for her rewriting of Maori mythology, which functions to reconstruct a tradition that honours the presence of lesbian and gays within Maori history, a presence denoted by the term *takataapui* (intimate companion of the same sex).

JO SMITH

TEA ROOMS

Places men meet to engage in sexual activity. The term originated in nineteenth-century England where same-sex relationships were illegal. A man would invite another man to his study under the pretext of 'taking tea'. Some of the men who engaged in these activities publicly led heterosexual lives.

MICHAEL PINFOLD

TÉCHINÉ, ANDRÉ

b. 1943

director

Openly gay French screenwriter and director, André Téchiné has gained critical acclaim and popularity for his evocatively personal brand of filmmaking and rich sense of visual composition. A dedicated cinephile, Téchiné started his career as a film reviewer and screenwriter before launching out as a director with a series of highly artistic, if slightly arcane, films in the 1970s. More accessible fare in the 1980s, such as *Hôtel des Amériques* (1981), saw him emerge as an influential cineaste, noted in particular for his sensitive work with leading female actors such as Catherine Deneuve. International success came in 1994 with *Les Roseaux sauvages* (*Wild Reeds*), a poignant coming-of-age story centred around a group of youths, one of whom, loosely based on Téchiné himself, struggles with his emerging homosexuality. Although few of Téchiné's other films are explicitly gay, they frequently deal with queer-resonant issues and are often tinged with homoerotic subtexts.

BRETT FARMER

TEENA, BRANDON

b. 1972; d. 1993

Born in Lincoln, Nebraska, Teena Renae Brandon, biological female, began passing as a male during adolescence, having affairs with women as Brandon Teena. Arrested for forging cheques on various occasions, Brandon decided to move to Falls City in southern Nebraska. As a male she began an affair with Lana Tisdel, but upon arresting her for forging cheques the police found out Teena's identity and the news hit the local press. Lana took the news well enough but her friends, John Lotter and Tom Nissen, who had become friends with Brandon, were shocked and began to vent their rage, first humiliating Teena, then raping her. Teena reported the rape to the police but the two went free, and on New Year's Eve, 1993, they shot Teena. The story became a nationwide issue, raising the problem of homophobic violence. Teena's story has been recorded in documentaries and films the world over. The 1999 film about Brandon Teena, *Boys Don't Cry*, earned an Academy Award for Best Actress for Hilary Swank, who played Teena.

MONICA BARONI

TELEDILDONICS

Teledildonics is a term referring to the possibility of two people having sex at a distance in a computer-simulated virtual reality (VR). The idea of Teledildonics originated in the United States in the 1980s, in a cultural climate characterized by the spread of Internet and technological experimentation such as VR and changes came in models of sexuality following the AIDS-generated panic. Actually, the original idea behind Teledildonics is not as yet practicable, but there do exist sex toys able to produce sensorial and sexual stimulation with impulses controlled by a computer programme.

MONICA BARONI

TELETUBBIES

children's TV programme

This British TV show, written for a preschool audience and featuring four portly and kindly aliens with TV sets on their bellies who speak in gibberish, gained added notoriety in 1999 when one character caught the attention of Reverend Jerry

Falwell. He accused the fun-loving, purple Tinky Winky of being gay and recruiting children to the homosexual lifestyle – after all, he had a triangular antennae hat, and sometimes accessorized his outfit with a red handbag. In fact, Tinky Winky had gained a following from mature gay viewers even before Falwell served to publicize the character. The show, which first aired in 1997, has survived the Reverend's tirade.

ED MILLER

TELEVISION, GAY

Television portrayals of homosexuals are becoming increasingly frequent in TV serials, movies and sitcoms on US major broadcast networks and cable TV. In contrast with the first occasional appearances of queer characters in TV sitcoms and serials in the late 1970s, relying mainly on traditional stereotypes, the 1990s saw producers and scriptwriters setting out to offer a more complex picture of the characters, as well as bringing them to 'normalization'. The success of series such as *Ellen*, **Will & Grace**, **Queer as Folk**, **Six Feet Under**, **Buffy The Vampire Slayer**, **Queer Eye for the Straight Guy** and **The L Word**, broadcast in early 2004, evidences a new social and media perception of glbtq issues. Moreover, the now widespread idea of queers as constituting an interesting, lucrative market target has opened up investment by major companies, as in the case of Viacom, the conglomerate that owns MTV, Showtime, CBS and other media outlets, which has now decided to launch a new cable channel dedicated a gay, lesbian, bisexual and transgender audience.

See also: DeGeneres, Ellen

MONICA BARONI

TELEVISION TALK SHOWS

Throughout their history, TV talk shows have provided a forum for gay, lesbian, bisexual and transgendered people to express and discuss their identity, and have contributed to greater public visibility and acceptance of homosexuality in Western culture. Talk shows have also been guilty of stereotyping and marginalizing homosexuality, or exploiting gay people as freakish entertainment. The first American talk show to feature gay and lesbian subjects was David Susskind's *Open End*, aka *The David Susskind Show* (1958–87). In a 1967 episode, Susskind featured Dick Leitsch, president of the New York Mattachine Society, facing off with anti-gay psychiatrist Lawrence Hatterer. Ohio-based TV host Phil Donahue is credited with developing the modern talk show format. In *The Phil Donahue Show* (1970–96), he encouraged audience participation and adopted a progressive, non-judgemental viewpoint towards his guests. He featured regular discussions about homosexuality and women's rights and helped to 'normalize' homosexuality for audiences. He interviewed sex researchers William Masters and Virginia Johnson about their book *Homosexuality in Perspective* and was one of the first hosts to focus attention on the AIDS epidemic. Although Donahue occasionally resorted to sensationalism – such as an episode about cross-dressing where he appeared wearing a skirt – his work promoted tolerance towards homosexuality and a commitment to destroying sexual stereotyping. Donahue's style spawned a number of imitators, notably *The Sally Jesse Raphael Show* (1985–2002), *The Oprah Winfrey Show* (later *Oprah*, 1986–), *The Ricki Lake Show* (1993–) and *The Geraldo Rivera Show* (1987–98). Winfrey continued Donahue's liberal ethos, albeit with a greater emphasis on guests confessing their problems and receiving therapeutic advice, regularly interviewing gay and lesbian people and facilitating coming-out processes with families.

Elsewhere, talk shows in the 1980s moved towards prurience or sensationalism.

The popularity of conservative host Morton Downey's talk show, in which he encouraged audiences to criticize his unorthodox guests, encouraged other programmes to adopt a sensationalist, combative format. *The Jerry Springer Show* (1991–) epitomized the genre as freak show. Episodes typically focus around a guest making a spectacle of their own perversity or revealing a controversial secret to partners or family members, degenerating into abuse and fighting between guests and audience members. In 1995 *The Jenny Jones Show* featured a gay guest, Jonathan Amedure, revealing his secret sexual attraction to a heterosexual friend Jonathan Schmitz. Three days after the episode was broadcast, Schmitz shot Amedure dead, claiming that the show's producer lied to him about the sex of his secret admirer and that he had been publicly humiliated. Schmitz's lawyers successfully sued the producers of the show for $25 million, leading to the show's cancellation and to other talk shows reducing their focus on homosexual subjects and 'ambush' interviewing.

The 1990s saw a number of shows hosted by gay and lesbian interviewers, including *The Jim J. and Tammy Faye Show* (1996) with gay actor Jim J. Bullock and former TV evangelist Tammy Faye Bakker, and *The Ru Paul Show* (1996–8) with drag performer Ru Paul. Actor and comedian Rosie **O'Donnell** hosted an extremely popular show (1996–2002), using her profile to come out publicly as a lesbian. Comedian Ellen **DeGeneres**, who used Oprah Winfrey's show to come out in 1997, scored a success with her own talk show (2003–) although she largely downplays her lesbianism and any discussion of sexuality issues.

JOHN FORDE

THAILAND, FILMMAKING

Although the Thai movie industry dates from the silent era of the 1920s, the 1950s and 1960s was its 'golden era', when local companies produced up to 100 movies a year, mostly B-grade action dramas, romances, slapstick comedies and horror movies. After falling into deep decline in the mid-1990s, when less than a dozen films a year were made, Thai cinema has enjoyed a minor renaissance since the beginning of this decade.

Queer characters were largely absent from early Thai cinema. Camp and/or cross-dressing men, known as *kathoeys*, first began appearing regularly in minor comedy roles in the 1970s, a period of tremendous cultural efflorescence in Thailand when the restrictions of decades of military rule ended after the student-led people's revolution of October 1973. However, it was only in the mid-1980s that queer characters assumed leading roles. Phisarn Akharaseni's 1985 tragi-comedy phleng *sut-thai* (The Final Song) recounted the fated affair between a *kathoey* cabaret star and a handsome mechanic. When the mechanic abandons his transsexual lover for a 'real woman', the cabaret performer commits suicide on stage at the end of her signature number. Although often called Thailand's first 'gay movie', *The Final Song* in fact included a diverse cast of gay men, lesbians and transsexuals, and for the first time revealed the full diversity of Thailand's modern queer cultures to local audiences. The film was so popular that in 1986 Phisarn produced a sequel, *rak thoraman* (Tormented Love) in which the surviving characters of the previous film avenge the death of the jilted cabaret singer. In 1987, M.L. Phanthewanop Thewakun directed 'But Darling, I'm a Man' (*chan phu-chai na ya*), the film version of Dr Seri Wongmontha's Thai adaptation of Mart Crowley's *Boys in the Band*.

No queer-themed movies were produced in the 1990s, but recent years have seen a mini-explosion of Thai queer cinema. In 2000 Phot Anon directed *kohok plin-plom kalorn tor-lae* (Go Six), a dramatic comedy about two women who compete for a young businessman's affections. While one woman finally succeeds in wedding the eligible bachelor, she is revealed to be a transsexual *kathoey* when her husband, desperate to become a father, chances upon her medical records. In 2001 Yongyuth Thorngkornthun produced the internationally successful comedy, *satri lek* (*Iron Ladies*), based on the true story of a team of *kathoey* and gay volleyball players who, in 1996, won the Thai men's national sporting competition. The following year saw the release of the intriguing dramatic comedy *Sayiw* (Enraptured). Directed by Khongdet Jaturunrasmi and Kiat Songsanan and set in early 1980s Bangkok, *Sayiw* follows the adventures of a sexually inexperienced teenage tomboy who draws on her still-to-be-realized sexual fantasies of women to write heterosexual erotic stories for an under-the-counter personal experiences magazine.

The box office success of *Sayiw* has incited a succession of *kathoey*-themed comedies that do little more than lampoon transsexuals. In 2002 Yongyuth Thorngkornthun produced *Iron Ladies II*, a poorly conceived prequel to *Iron Ladies*. Dechai Srimata directed *phrang chomphoo kathoey prajanban* (Saving Private Tootsie) in which homophobic Thai army commandos rescue a band of *kathoeys* from insurgents after their plane crashes in the jungle of the Thailand–Burma border. Although marketed as a movie with a queer-positive message, *Saving Private Tootsie* merely reproduced stereotypes of *kathoeys* as sex-obsessed drama queens more concerned about their mascara than their survival. In 2003 Phot Anon released another queer-themed movie, *wai beum, chia kraheum lok* (*I'm Lady* [sic]), a superficial teen comedy about a clash between all-girl and all-*kathoey* cheer squads for competing university rugby teams. In *wai krit: meu-prap sai-phan mai* (X-Generation Cop), directed by Nusorn Phanangkhasiri, a homophobic

cop must cross-dress and compete in a *kathoey* beauty contest to track down a murderer. The most recent Thai 'kathoey-exploitation' flick is Phot Anon's 2004 offering, *plon na ya* (Spicy Queen in Bangkok), a one-joke movie styled as 'Priscilla Queen of the Desert goes to Bangkok'. In this egregious toilet humour comedy a group of ageing *kathoey*-misfits rob a bank to pay off their debts to an underworld loan shark who is threatening to kneecap them and close down their beauty parlour.

Of much higher quality and greater merit is Ekachai Uekrongtham's poignant 2003 movie *Beautiful Boxer*, which was promoted with the catchphrase, 'He fought like a man to become a woman', and which recounts the true-life story a young *kathoey* Thai kickboxer, known as Norng Tum. During the late 1990s Norng Tum, who makes a cameo appearance in the movie, won a series of national boxing matches, subsequently using his winnings to pay for a sex-change operation and realize his dream of becoming a woman. Thailand has a nascent independent film sector, with some queer-themed short movies being shown at local festivals. The best known of these is the hilarious *Iron Pussy* series by American-educated performance artist Michael Shoawanansai, in which the director himself plays Thai gay superhero, Iron Pussy, who saves Thai queers and sex workers from the evil clutches of an array of Asian and Western sex tourists.

In 2003 Thai producers began making movies for immediate sale on DVD rather than for cinematic release. This innovation for the local industry has permitted the production of several movies oriented to local queer audiences. *Chan rak nai phu-chai mi ong* (Miss Queen Thailand), directed by Japanese expatriate, Tomoko Eruyo, is a bitchy comedy in which rival *kathoey* gangs compete for the crown of the Miss Queen Thailand transsexual beauty contest. In *patibatkan tomboy commando* (Tomboy Commando, director not named on the

557

DVD packaging), the members of a tomboy girl band are helped by the ghost of a nineteenth-century Thai tomboy to fight a gang of hoodlums for a magical amulet, which the tomboys use to realize the wish of having a penis and becoming real men. An underground hit amongst Bangkok gay audiences was Yutthana Khunkhongsathian's *Thang rak si-rung* (Rainbow), in which the tomboy host of a radio talkback show gets into trouble with station management for advising gay, lesbian and *kathoey* callers to be proud of their sexuality and stop fooling themselves and the world that they are straight.

See also: Indigenous queer identities; Wongmontha, Seri

PETER A. JACKSON

THAILAND, LITERATURE

Thai classical literature includes only occasional references to queer sexualities and genders. The hero of the eponymous early nineteenth-century epic poem, *Inao*, by King Rama II, engages in amorous liaisons with both men and women. The famed nineteenth-century poet Sunthorn Phu includes a number of dismissive references to female homoeroticism in his works. The extended satirical poem *Morm Pet Sawan* (Lady Heavenly Duck, *c.*1841–2), attributed to the female poet Khun Suwan, which pokes fun at the love affair between two ladies in waiting in the court of King Rama III, was the first Thai literary work to place same-sex eroticism at the centre of the narrative. In 1913 the homosexual King Vajiravudh (Rama VI, r. 1910–26) commissioned court poet Phraya Srisunthornwohan to compose a classically styled narrative poem, *Ilarat Kham-chan*, which recounts a section of the classical Hindu epic the Ramayana in which King Ilarat changes sex to a woman at the behest of the god Shiva, becoming the lover of the deity Phra Phut (Mercury) and bearing that god a son.

Modern Thai literature only began dealing with queer themes in the post-Second World War period, when P. Intharapalit, the prolific author of satirical paperback novellas, penned several stories about *kathoey* (male transvestites), including *Lakkaphet* (The Drag Queen, *c.*1947), *Nang Kathoey* (Miss Kathoey *c.*1950), *Kathoey Sao* (The Young Kathoey *c.*1955) and *Chao Gay* (Gay People, *c.*1968). To maximize their income, many modern Thai novelists serialize their works in magazines, with the more popular serialized novels subsequently being published in book form. Kritsana Asoksin, a highly popular female author of women's romances, was the first prominent Thai writer to publish novels specifically on gay, lesbian and transgender themes, *Balang Yai Bua* (The Throne of Lotus Threads, first serialized 1971–2), *Pratu Thi Pit Tai* (The Locked Door, first serialized 1974–5) and *Rup Thorng* (The Golden Body, first serialized 1987–8). However, her treatment of gay issues is rarely sympathetic, with her most famous 'gay' novel, *The Locked Door*, exploring a wife's lament at her abandonment by her gay husband. Occasional collections of short stories that appeared during the late 1970s, such as *Gay 79* (1979, edited by Jarit Maya) and *Thi-sut Kheu Khwam-wang-plao* (And the End is Emptiness, 1990, edited by Khajorn Raksa), were the first modern literary forms written by self-identified gay authors for a gay readership. Autobiographies of gay men and *kathoeys* also first appeared in the early 1980s.

Well-known Bangkok socialite and hairdresser, the late Pan Bunnak (d. 1993), was the first openly gay man to publish autobiographical anecdotes in *Het-chanai Theung Torng Pen Gay* (Why Must You be Gay?, *c.*1980), while Kirati Chana was the first Thai male-to-female transsexual to write about her life in the acclaimed *Thang sai thisam* (The Third Path, first serialized 1980–1). Natee Teerarojjanapongs, founder of Thailand's first gay non-governmental organization, the White Line HIV/AIDS education group, published the first Thai coming-out autobiography in 1990, *Kwa-ja Kao Kham Sen Si-Khao* (Before I Stepped Across the White Line). Since the early 1990s a small but steady stream of novels by openly gay authors has continued to be published, with the most successful of this younger generation of Thai gay authors being Wirat Kanokanukhroh, who in addition to publishing several science-fiction novels has become well known for his gay novels *Sak Dork-mai* (Dying Flowers, first serialized 1995–6) and *Dai si-muang* (The Purple Thread, 2002).

See also: Indigenous queer identities

PETER A. JACKSON

THAILAND, POPULAR MUSIC

Thailand has a thriving popular music industry drawing upon diverse influences including Western rock, folk and hip-hop, Chinese Canto-pop and Mandarin pop, Japanese J-pop, and the Thai country-and-western-styled *luk-thung* ('child of the rice fields') genre.

Queer themes first emerged in Thai pop during the 1980s when the tomboy style of soft rock songstress Anchalee Jongkhadikit made her Thailand's first lesbian pop icon. However, Anchalee's popularity among Thai lesbians collapsed after she converted from Buddhism to Christianity and announced that she now believed homosexuality to be a sin.

The deliberately ambiguous, ever-youthful and never-married Thongchai McIntyre, known by his nickname Bird, first achieved fame in the 1980s for his saccharine love songs. Now in his forties, Bird remains as popular as ever by style-surfing and a David Bowie-like capacity for constant self-reinvention.

During the mid-1980s crooner Jae (Danuphon Kaewkan) released the first song to portray *kathoey* positively. His haunting ballad 'Sida' recounted the true-life tragedy of the suicide of a famous 1960s *kathoey* performer of classical Thai dance. Thailand's first openly queer singer was the male-to-female transsexual Jern-jern Bunsungnern. Singing a blend of Thai *luk-thung* and Canto-pop, the beautiful post-op Jern-jern released three popular albums in the early 1990s, *chan kor pen phu-ying khon neung* (I am (Kind of) a Woman, 1993); *kha kheu khon Thai* (I am Thai, 1993) and *phi-seu ratri* (Butterfly of the Night, 1995).

The year 1994, however, saw the release of Thailand's first explicitly homophobic song, 'Kliat Tut' (I Hate Faggots), by the all-male heavy metal band Sepia. Sepia's crude and violent lyrics meant their songs were never broadcast, but their eponymous album *Kliat Tut* nonetheless became a benchmark for Thailand's anti-establishment heavy metal scene. Unlike the anti-gay sentiment of Western heavy metal, the invective of 'I Hate Faggots' was directed against *kathoeys* who, it was claimed, both arouse and frustrate male desires with their fake feminine beauty. This theme was repeated in Thai Thanawut's 1999 soft rock song 'Pratheuang'. This humorous number describes a man's arousal at seeing a beautiful woman but ends with the would-be Romeo's shock discovery that the 'woman' is his school buddy, Pratheuang, who has had a sex-change operation. This song was so popular that 'Pratheuang', a Thai male name, quickly became a new slang word for *kathoey*. Issues of gender confusion came to the fore in Thailand's pop industry in early 2004 when popular husky-voiced *luk-thung* songstress, Siriphorn Amphaiphong, appeared on national television to deny rumours that she is a *kathoey*. Brandishing identity documents to prove the genuineness of her womanhood, Siriphorn confronted a TV panel of prominent *kathoeys* who concurred that in their 'professional opinion' Siriphorn is not a transsexual.

Queer-themed songs and albums have continued to appear in recent years: 2003 saw the release of *Rainbow Collection*, an album of ten songs performed by a chorus of seven openly gay and transgender artists and inspired by memories of Thailand's first gay movie, *phleng sut-thai* (The Final Song, 1985).

See also: Indigenous queer identities

PETER A. JACKSON

THAILAND, TELEVISION

Television is the most influential and also the most stringently controlled cultural medium in contemporary Thailand, with five of the country's six free-to-air stations owned by state agencies. While standard fare (Hollywood movies), dubbed or subtitled in Thai, dominate the cinema box office, American programmes are largely absent from Thai television. Because the majority of programmes are produced locally, television often reflects Thai cultural sensibilities more than the Western-dominated cinema and, despite the stringency of state controls, queer images of transgender and transsexual *kathoeys* now abound. While gay men and lesbians remain relatively rare figures on the television, making only occasional appearances in behind-the-news public issues programmes, the vast profusion of *kathoeys* in comedies, soap operas, game shows and TV talk shows means that even a simple listing of *kathoey* appearances in the history of Thai television would be a task of encyclopedic proportions.

Kathoeys have not always been staple characters on Thai television. Before the 1970s even mentioning transgenderism, let alone permitting *kathoeys* to speak on their own behalf, was largely a taboo area. In the mid-1960s, a prominent psychologist working in sex education was criticized for 'obscenity' when he talked about transsexual *kathoeys* during a TV interview. However, in the following decade the traditional reticence of talking publicly about homo-

sexuality and transgenderism rapidly began to disappear, to such an extent that in 1980 the late Pan Bunnak, a prominent beautician, gay activist and journalist, wrote that *kathoeys* so fascinated Thai people that '[i]t seems that every TV soap opera has to have a *kathoey* story line'.

The 'boom' in the imaging of *kathoeys* on television has been paralleled by public debates about whether they provide bad role models for children who, it is sometimes argued, may be influenced to experiment with cross-dressing and perhaps become a *kathoey*. These debates peaked in 1999, when an anti-*kathoey* email campaign led then Prime Minister Chuan Leekpai to try to ban cross-dressing actors from all TV programmes. However, the press lampooned the government's attempt at censorship, pointing out that the 1997 pro-democratic constitution placed public broadcasting in the hands of an independent body specifically to prevent state interference. TV station managers also opposed the ban since *kathoey* characters are tremendously popular and help 'sell' large numbers of programmes. The brief '*kathoey* ban' was dropped with negligible impact on programming.

Since 1999 the presence of *kathoeys* on television has become even more common and they have begun to move beyond stereotypical comedy roles. In 2002 a *kathoey* Thai language teacher known as Khru Lilly (Teacher Lilly) hosted her own daily advice programme on correct language usage. The popularity of Teacher Lilly, who has also published her autobiography and appeared in 'language is fun' stage shows, suggests that at the beginning of the twenty-first century the majority of the Thai public appears to be at ease with the idea of *kathoeys* appearing on national television in the culturally respected role of teachers.

See also: Indigenous queer identities

PETER A. JACKSON

THEORY AND THEORISTS, QUEER

Queer theory refers to work on sexuality which emerged from the start of the 1990s and which adopts a poststructural approach to knowledge. Its intellectual heritage includes feminist theory as well as the work of Michel Foucault, but it was originally associated with the writings of Judith **Butler**, Teresa **De Lauretis** and Eve Kosofsky **Sedgwick**. This entry reviews their writings as well as considering some of the main tendencies of queer theory.

In a 1991 special edition of the journal *differences*, De Lauretis argued that Lesbian and Gay Studies elides specifically lesbian feminist concerns and encourages the mere adding in of race, ethnicity, gender or disability to an otherwise dominant approach to questions of sexuality (De Lauretis 1991). Instead, De Lauretis proposed the term 'queer' because she wanted to ask how heterosexuality maintains a normative position against which homosexuality is defined as marginal. In addition, she moved away from the tendency within lesbian and gay studies to regard homosexuality as natural but merely different to heterosexuality. Finally, she asked questions about the identity-based or 'ethnic model' of sexuality so prevalent during the 1980s.

In 1990 two other texts strongly associated with queer theory were published. Eve Kosofsky Sedgwick's *Epistemology of the Close It* (1990) argued that all knowledge is reliant upon an assumed hetero-/homosexual binary, in which heterosexuality subordinates, but also depends upon an exclusion of, homosexuality. Sedgwick's anti-homophobic study examined the place of this binary division within various texts, and she argued that post-Romantic literature displays a constant presence and simultaneous denial of homosexuality – what she termed 'male homosexual panic'. Sedgwick stated that her aims were to break the silence about, and foreground questions of, sexuality in the study of literature and cultural ideas, and to challenge the search for the origins of homosexuality that she saw as betraying the desire to eradicate it.

Judith Butler's *Gender Trouble* (1990) problematized identity-based theories of gender and sexuality, arguing that these are instead a set of regulatory regimes designed to maintain a uniform or compulsory gender and heterosexuality. This set of practices Butler saw as performative, in that they must be constantly repeated and asserted in order to maintain the illusion that heterosexuality and traditional genders are 'natural'. Parodies of gender performativity, such as drag, have the potential to expose the imitative structure of gender, Butler argued. In addition, she suggested that there is no 'original' that is simply being copied. Rather, gender is a 'stylized repetition of acts' for everyone at all times (Butler 1990: 140).

Following the publication of these works, other texts now associated with queer theory appeared during the 1990s (Halperin 1995; Jagose 1996; Warner 1993). Queer theory, however, does not refer to an agreed or definite set of ideas, since there is much debate among these queer theorists. Nevertheless, it is possible to discern a number of tendencies within queer theory.

Most queer theorists adopt a poststructuralist concern with issues of language and signification (Belsey 2002), in which ideas about sexuality are not descriptive of how things really are, but rather are specific claims situated within a system of knowledge that actually sanctions some views over others. This is also influenced by Foucault's work on discourse and his view of sexuality as a system of thought that both constrains and enables our sexual choices. Queer theory therefore asks how discourse makes certain ideas or questions about sexuality possible, but rules out others.

This challenges identity-based models of sexuality on a number of levels. First, queer theorists, following Foucault, tend not to consider the individual as the source of sexual knowledge, but instead ask how individuals are made subjects through discourse. Second, they find that identity-based models cannot adequately account for the multiple differences that exist amongst those who call themselves lesbian or gay. Finally, queer theorists argue that all such sexuality categories are disciplinary in that they are part of a system of knowledge that frames our ideas within moral and political hierarchies. An example of this would be David M. Halperin's suggestion that to 'come out' does not free one from the web of power relations, since one then enters into a new set of sexual meanings (Halperin, 1995).

Queer theory turns a deliberate spotlight on what it calls 'heteronormativity' (Warner, 1993), asking how heterosexuality has both a privileged and taken-for-granted status within mainstream societies. Finally, queer theory rejects assimilationist or liberal equality rights agendas, suggesting that these will result only in the accommodation of lesbians and gay men into an otherwise unchanged and heteronormative organization of society. This version of queer theory is concerned with activism and direct challenges to heterosexual superiority, and has been represented by the groups **Queer Nation** in the United States and **OutRage!** in the United Kingdom.

There have been problems with, and critiques of, queer theory. In 1994, De Lauretis said that 'queer' had mutated away from her original concerns to become just 'a conceptually vacuous creature of the publishing industry' (De Lauretis, 1994: 297). In addition, others have argued that queer theory is ignorant of race and gender issues, or that it is obsessed with the cultural and refuses to engage with political agendas (Edwards, 1998). Finally, queer theory has a tendency to display some historical amnesia about the lesbian feminist, interactionist and ethnomethodological theorists who prefigured many of the ideas that now circulate under its banner.

However, the idea that queer theory is apolitical is disputed, and many queer the-

orists work from feminist, postcolonial and anti-racist positions. Queer theory has had a major impact upon the humanities and, to a lesser extent, the social sciences. It is a highly influential body of work that demonstrates a shift away from a focus upon lesbian and gay identities towards an analysis of cultural, social and institutional practices, and discourses that are productive of sexual knowledges and subjects.

Bibliography

Belsey, C. (2002) *Poststructuralism: A Very Short Introduction*, Oxford: Oxford University Press.

Butler, J. (1990) *Gender Trouble: Feminism and the Subversion of Identity*, New York: Routledge.

De Lauretis, T. (1991) 'Queer Theory, Lesbian and Gay Studies: An Introduction', *differences: A Journal of Feminist Cultural Studies* 3, 2: iii–xviii.

– (1994) 'Habit Changes', *differences: A Journal of Feminist Cultural Studies*, 6, 2–3: 296–313.

Edwards, T. (1998) 'Queer Fears: Against the Cultural Turn', *Sexualities*, 1, 4: 471–84.

Halperin, D.M. (1995) *St Foucault: Towards a Gay Hagiography*, New York: Oxford University Press.

Jagose, A. (1996) *Queer Theory*, Melbourne: Melbourne University Press.

Sedgwick, E.K. (1990) *Epistemology of the Closet*, Berkeley: University of California Press.

Warner, M. (1993) 'Introduction', in M. Warner (ed.) *Fear of a Queer Planet: Queer Politics and Social Theory*, Minneapolis: University of Minnesota Press.

Further reading

Turner, W.B. (2000) *A Genealogy of Queer Theory*, Philadelphia: Temple University Press.

STEPHEN HICKS

THOMPSON, SCOTT

b. 1959

actor

Canadian actor and comedian Scott Thompson grew up in Ontario and studied drama at York University before joining the comedy group, 'Kids in the Hall', in 1984. Starting in 1989, the group broadcast its own TV series and Thompson quickly became famous for his recurring roles, most notably that of Buddy Cole, the lisping, bitchy, gay bar owner. Thompson has also appeared in many feature films, including the Kids in the Hall's own *Brain Candy* (1996) and Bruce La Bruce's *Super-8 1/2* (1993). After *The Kids in the Hall* went off the air and the group disbanded, Thompson played in the TV series *The Larry Sanders Show*. In 1998 he returned to his old TV character Buddy Cole when he co-wrote *The Autobiography of Buddy Cole* with Paul Bellini.

DANIEL HENDRICKSON

TILLEY, BRIAN

filmmaker

Openly gay filmmaker, whose documentaries profile political and social outsiders in his native South Africa. He is best known for the award-winning documentary *Ma vie en plus* (It's My Life, 2001), featuring Zackie **Achmat**, an HIV+ South African activist who protested the unavailability of AIDS treatment for African countries by refusing to take his own medication. His other films include *Lucky Day* (2000), about the plight of black day workers, and *Joburg Stories* (1997), co-directed with Oliver Schmitz, a mosaic of life in the town of Gauteng. He collaborated with Schmitz for the documentary *In a Time of Violence* (1994), an unflinching look at urban violence in Soweto and Johannesburg in the final months of South Africa's apartheid regime, igniting national controversy after its TV broadcast. His recent work includes the TV drama series *Behind the Badge* (2002).

JOHN FORDE

TILMANS, WOLFGANG

b. 1968

photographer

German photographer Wolfgang Tilmans first moved to London in the late 1980s and began working as a photographer for the magazines *i-D* and *The Face*. He studied at Bournemouth and Poole College of Art and Design, then moved back to London. He came to the attention of the art world with raw, snapshot-style photographs of a hip young generation, a group of people who had not been the subjects of serious photography before. He furthermore challenged the norms of the art world by simply tacking up or taping his photographs to the wall. He lived in New York during the mid-1990s and it was here he met painter Jochen **Hick**, who was his lover until Hick's death from AIDS in 1997. Tilmans has exhibited in galleries and museums all over the world and won the Tate's prestigious Turner Prize in 2000.

DANIEL HENDRICKSON

TIPPING THE VELVET

TV programme

Adapted by Andrew Davies from the 2002 Sarah **Water**'s novel, this TV drama reflects an increasingly celebratory depiction of queer culture on British mainstream television. Set in 1890s London, the main character, Nan (Rachael Stirling), gains a sexual and emotional education as she progresses through the world of the music hall, male impersonation and 'male' prostitution. She lives as the sexual toy of a rich woman and finally finds real love with the socialist Florence (Jodhi May). Lesbianism is portrayed positively. The drama concludes with Nan at the centre of a stable but unconventional 'family'.

KYM MARTINDALE

TOGO, KEN

b. 1932

activist

Ken Togo is one of Japan's earliest and most high-profile queer activists and community leaders. In 1971 he founded the Miscellaneous People's Party (Zatsumin To) whose membership included a variety of sexual minorities as well as other individuals discriminated against in Japan, such as children born out of wedlock and unmarried couples. Togo ran for office in national elections to the Diet, Japan's parliament, throughout the 1970s, but his effeminate mannerisms and extremely vocal antipathy to the Emperor system meant that he was an unelectable, albeit conspicuous, figure. During this time he founded and edited the gay magazine *The Gay*, which was unusual among Japanese gay publications for its emphasis upon activist issues and its illustrations, which often flaunt obscenity laws (forbidding the exposure of genitalia). Togo remains a vocal critic of censorship, fighting for freedom of expression in the courts.

MARK McLELLAND

TOKYO

In Tokyo homosexual and transgender practice long revolved around kabuki theatre but, since the Second World War, cabaret-style 'gay bars' have proliferated, proving hospitable for the development of both male and female transgender entertainers, many now with mainstream careers. Tokyo caters to over 200 bars for gay men but only a handful for lesbians. In recent years Tokyo has become a site for queer activism. Japan's first lesbian and gay parade took place in 1994; it is now an annual event.

MARK McLELLAND

TOM OF FINLAND

b. 1920; d. 1991

artist

One of the twentieth century's most recognizable and controversial gay artists, Tom of Finland's sexually explicit images of muscle-bound gay men became the definitive images of gay leather culture for generations of gay communities worldwide.

Born Touko Laaksonen, 8 May 1920, in Kaarina, a small village on the south coast of Finland, to schoolteacher parents, Tom showed an early interest in art and music – and, by his own account, an equally passionate interest in the muscular farmers and loggers who worked in the neighbouring farmlands. In 1939 he moved to art school in Helsinki and first began to sketch erotic pictures of the construction workers, policemen and sailors he encountered there. Following Stalin's invasion of Finland in the Second World War, he was conscripted into the army, giving him free rein to live out his erotic fantasies of sex with uniformed soldiers and his fascination with military costume and ritual. After the war, he worked in advertising and joined the Helsinki bohemian community, but felt uncomfortable associating with the dilettentish gay subculture. In 1953, he met Veli, who became his long-term partner (they were together for 28 years).

At the encouragement of a friend, Tim submitted some of his erotic sketches to the American bodybuilding magazine *Physique Pictorial* in 1956, signing them simply 'Tom'. The editor was delighted with the work and featured Laaksonen's drawing of a laughing lumberjack on the cover of the magazine's Spring 1957 issue, credited to 'Tom of Finland' – and his career was born.

At a time when erotic art was heavily censored and pornographers risked imprisonment, Tom's work was unusually bold and explicit in its sexual content, and demonstrated a radical break with prevailing stereotypes of gay men as effeminate asexual Wildean dandies. Inspired by his erotic fantasies of military men and the burgeoning gay leather subculture, his work featured square-jawed muscle-bound men with broad shoulders and narrow waists, frequently sporting handlebar moustaches, tattoos and chest hair, with tight-cut jeans or leather trousers accentuating their throbbing erections and tightly muscled buttocks.

His technique combined photorealistic detail of the minutiae of male anatomy and musculature with the fetishistic hypersexualization of pornography. His work shone a light on an all-male enclave of hidden but passionate sex, set in prisons, parks, forests, gay bars and locker rooms. This suggestion of a secret world of uninhibited desires adds to the significant sexual charge of his work – Tom's men smile and wink at the viewer, inviting them to enjoy the taboo pleasures on display. Tom's work provides a playful but insightful view of the psychology of leather culture – the worship of the hypermasculine body and the gleeful fetishizing of military codes of discipline and domination that enflame sexual desire.

Remarkably, his gay characters were happy and unashamed of their sexuality, suggesting a gay sensibility which defiantly rejects the invisibility, homophobia and victimization of pre-liberation homosexuality. His men broke established assumptions about 'active' and 'passive' sexual roles, showing men enjoying both giving and receiving anal and oral sex.

Tom worked in advertising until the mid-1970s, when he was finally able to support himself solely through his art. His work was first exhibited in 1973, in a gallery in Hamburg, Germany, but this proved to be a negative experience when all but one of the drawings were stolen. Tom reluctantly agreed to an exhibition in Los Angeles in 1978, and made his first visit to America, where he was enthusiastically embraced by the leather scene and developed a friendship with the photographer Robert **Mapplethorpe**.

With the growing popularity of his work, and the liberalization of gay culture, his work progressed to depict nudity, fully erect penises, and bondage and sadomasochistic scenes. His images became a staple of erotic fantasy and pornography, and his 'leatherman' look was enthusiastically and ritualistically adopted by generations of gay men. His critics were appalled at the aggressiveness and apparent violence of his sexual couplings, arguing that his work marginalized gay male sexuality as a brutal and unnatural subculture. Others praised the confidence and unprecedented honesty in presenting gay male sexuality, and hailed Tom for reclaiming gay masculinity.

The influence of Tom's work can be seen in a range of cultural imagery, most notably in the works of filmmakers Kenneth **Anger** and Bruce **La Bruce** and of fashion designer Jean-Paul **Gaultier**. His legacy can be seen most clearly in the work of Robert Mapplethorpe, whose carefully composed and sexually explicit photographs of male nudes, gay sex and sadomasochistic sexual practices recall Tom's frankness and air of menace.

Tom of Finland died on 7 November 1991 in Helsinki, Finland.

JOHN FORDE

TOMBOY (SOUTHEAST ASIA)

Can globalization transform identities not only at the local and national levels, but at regional and global levels also? One indication involves the possibility of a 'tomboy' female-to-male transgendered identity that stretches across Southeast Asia (and is possibly linked to similar identities beyond Southeast Asia). Southeast Asia is known as a region where male-to-female transgenders are visible in public life, including *waria* (Indonesia), *kathoey* (Thailand), *bantut* (southern Philippines) and *pondan* (Malaysia).

Female-to-male transgenders in Southeast Asia, however, are typically known by terms such as *tomboi* (Indonesia), *tom* (Thailand), or *tomboy* (Philippines). Even though 'tomboys' rarely know there are similar persons in neighbouring countries, they share many characteristics. For instance, while 'gay' Southeast Asians usually see a clear distinction between their identities and identities such as *waria* and *kathoey*, 'lesbian' Southeast Asians usually see 'tomboys' as ideal partners. This appears to illustrate how globalization is shaped by particularities including gender, ethnicity, class and religion.

See also: Female-to-male (FTM) transsexual; Indigenous queer identities; Male-to-female (MTF) transsexual

TOM BOELLSTORFF

TONGZHI

A Cantonese term for comrade, appropriated as a synonym for gays and lesbians in the 1990s. It is a very popular term used by both straight and gay Chinese people.

KEN WONG

TONGZHI FORUM (1997)

The 1997 Tongzhi Forum (formerly called the 1997 Lesbigay Forum) began life in the 64 Bar in Hong Kong's Central district in 1992, but gradually faded out in during the late 1990s. It was a gathering of anyone who was interested in discussing gay-related issues. Responding to the overemphasis upon consumption and leisure within the gay and lesbian community, Xiaomingxiong (or Samshasha), the organizer, hoped that gay and related social issues would be discussed in the forum in a serious but open manner. In particular, the forum acted as a platform from which to discuss the social, cultural and political implications for gays and lesbians living in

Hong Kong under the uncertainties of 1997, the year of Hong Kong's handover from British to mainland Chinese rule. The Forum could be seen as an embryo form of Chinese Tongzhi Conference but on a much smaller scale.

TRAVIS KONG

TOP

Sexual partner or partners playing the penetrative/insertive role to the **bottom** in anal sex. Almost exclusively used in gay male circles.

MICHAEL PINFOLD

TOURETTE, PUSSY

musician

San Francisco-based drag performer Pussy Tourette worked as a go-go dancer in Bay Area queer clubs, where she performed and sang her own compositions. She quickly became one of the hottest acts in the city, popular with both gay men and lesbians. After recording her first CD, *Pussy Tourette in Hi-Fi* (1994), she toured nationally, including a performance at the national March on Washington for Gay and Lesbian Rights. Her raunchy, blues-style songs mix humour with a sophisticated take on sex and gender. She followed up her successful debut CD with *Who Does She Think She Is?* in 1996.

DANIEL HENDRICKSON

TOURNIER, MICHEL

b. 1924

writer

French novelist Michel Tournier was born in Paris. His parents were both students of German, and Tournier learned to speak the language quite early. After working for French radio, television and publishing, in

1967 he published his first novel at the age of 43. The novel, *Friday; or The Other Island* (1969), is a retelling of the Robinson Crusoe story, but with an extra philosophical turn. This, and his next novel, *The Ogre* (1972), set during the Second World War, both won prestigious literary prizes, sealing Tournier's fame. They and most of his other books are reworkings of myths and legends, but always with an eye to contemporary philosophical or political debates. He has written novels and short stories that speak to current gender relations as well as to the question of racism against North Africans in France.

DANIEL HENDRICKSON

TRANSFORMISTA

Euphemism used among Bolivian drag queens, especially female impersonators and occasional cross-dressers, who wish to differentiate themselves from the medical connotations associated with the term transvestite.

PEDRO ALBORNOZ

TRANSGENDERISM

Transgenderism, a modern term, refers to individuals who consider themselves somewhere between the two defined male or female sexes, or feel they are the opposite sex from their birth sex. The term also includes those who are born with dual or near dual genitalia, i.e. who possess both male and female genitalia. Sometimes the term is used more narrowly as a synonym for the word *transsexual*, but increasingly it is used as a more general term for those who identify themselves along some area of the gender continuum other than conventionally male and female. Generally speaking, the term transgender is best seen as an umbrella term that allows for the variances of all these different historical and cultural descriptions of individuals not easily defined into either accepted male or female gender roles.

Through historical research, we know this aspect of the human condition has existed as long as there has been historical documentation. Social acceptance and the status of transgender individuals has varied widely throughout history and from culture to culture.

Terminology

Many world cultures refer to transgender individuals through the use of a variety of terminology. Historically, perspectives have differed between the observer cultures and their description of these individuals, as opposed to how these individuals described themselves and how their own culture may have described them.

One such example is the French explorers travelling through the North American continent in the sixteenth and seventeenth centuries, who referred to individuals they found within the native population as *berdache* (from the French term *bardache*) which described them as sexual oddities, lumping transgender people together with homosexuality. The native people had their own terms for their transgender and homosexual members, which changed from nation to nation but collectively defined these people as full genders between the recognized male and female genders. Often one term was used for the male-to-female (MTF) transgender 'gender' and another for the female-to-male (FTM) transgender gender. Still another term was used to refer to the homosexual female gender, and another term referred to the homosexual male gender, creating categories for six different genders.

The term '*berdache*', which specifically means 'kept boy' or 'male prostitute', is usually considered offensive by native people. The term 'two spirit', which means the spirit of a man and the spirit of a woman living together in the same body, is more often used as the general term for people who define themselves as one of the four additional genders beyond simply male or female. Other traditional Native American terms for people in the gay, lesbian, and transgender communities include *winkte* (Lakota), *kwidó* (Tewa) and *nádleeh* (Navajo).

Other terms referring to specific aspects of transgenderism have gone in and out of use for a variety of reasons. Some terms derive from medical observations, some from cultural misunderstandings and others have originated with transgender individuals themselves. *Cross-dresser* and *transvestite* both describe the practice of dressing in clothing associated with the opposite of one's birth gender, i.e. a man wearing clothing society would expect only to be worn by a woman, or a woman wearing clothing society would expect only to be worn by a man. Both terms describe the practice, but the term *transvestite*, being older and associated with the medical community's negative view of the practice, has come to be seen as a derogatory term. The term *cross-dresser*, in contrast, having come from the transgender community itself, is a term seen as not possessing these negative connotations.

Transsexual is a medical term that refers to an individual who must undergo hormonal and surgical procedures to appear as the opposite from their birth gender. This term is used to describe both males and females. The terms *transsexual male* and *transsexual female* are more specific terms and acknowledge the transgender aspect of the individual's condition. A transsexual male is someone who appears male but whose birth gender is female; a transsexual female is someone who appears female but whose birth gender is male. Transsexual males may also be known as F-to-M, T-men or trans men, and transsexual females may also be known as M-to-F or trans women.

A variety of derogatory terms are still used to describe any aspect of the trans-

gender condition. These terms for the most part come from non-medical observers.

Terminology also becomes an issue with regard to pronouns. Some members of the transgender community have encouraged developing gender neutral pronouns, such as s/he or h/ir. This is acknowledged as somewhat impractical in common conversation, and so usually transgender individuals appreciate being referred to by pronouns in synch with how they are dressed. When in doubt, one may ask politely how the person wishes to be referred to. However, not all transgender individuals see themselves as completely crossing into the opposite gender, preferring to remain between genders, and therefore may reject the conventional pronoun categories of 'he' and 'she'.

Medical issues

The transgender individual from any world cultural background may face many medical issues. Cultural acceptance or non-acceptance of these individuals contributes to the extent or impact these medical issues may have on the individual. If the transgender individual is only concerned with hormonal treatments to alter his or her physical appearance, the availability of these hormones, and the monitoring of health while on these hormones, may or may not be easily obtained. Financial concerns may also come into play even if a person's cultural status as a transgender individual is accepted. Socio-economic status comes into play throughout the transgender community once the need for medical care of the individual is involved.

The medical aspect of transgenderism sets it apart from the larger queer culture. The transgender community is often dependent on the medical community to address the issue of body modification.

The most common path of body modification is sexual reassignment surgery (SRS). MTF gender reassignment typically involves hormone replacement therapy (i.e. oestrogen), the transition into living full-time as a member of the opposite sex, and surgery involving orchidectomy (removal of the testes), penectomy (removal of the penis), vaginoplasty and breast enhancement. FTM gender reassignment typically involves hormone replacement therapy (i.e. testosterone), transitioning into living full-time as a member of the opposite sex and surgery involving mastectomy and hysterectomy. At the time of writing (2005), penis construction is still in its experimental stages and many FTM transsexuals do not opt for penis construction. It should also be noted that not all transsexuals go through surgery, for either financial or personal reasons.

The first documented MTF sexual reassignment surgery occurred in Germany in 1930. The recipient was Lili Elbe. Christine Jorgensen is perhaps the most famous person to undergo sexual reassignment surgery, in Denmark in 1952. One of the best-known persons in the field of sexual reassignment is Dr Harry Benjamin, whose International Gender Dysphoria Association pioneered standards of care for people with gender identity issues.

However, the medical community is not always accessible to transgender people wishing to modify their bodies. This has made the growth of underground access to medical needs a flourishing worldwide business, with questionable standards of safety. Many sham products and procedures are bought and sold to the transgender community without regulation or concern for the risks this brings to the transgender community's health. For example, 'natural' plant source hormones are sometimes sold as equivalent to prescription hormones; they are not. Similarly, hormone creams are not the same as hormones given by prescription. There is also the risk of hormonal overdose, leading to chronic hepatitis and even death, with unregulated medications taken without a physician's care. Even more alarming are unregulated surgical procedures and programmes that flourish at the expense of transgender individuals who find no other resource.

Social and cultural issues

The social acceptance or non-acceptance of transgender people, worldwide, has moulded the ways in which each member of the transgender community may see him or herself.

At the time of writing, few world cultures accept the transgender individual as a full member of their society. In Western cultures the dualistic view of only two genders has forced the transgender community to 'make a choice' of gender, rather than be seen as a full gender aside from the two accepted genders.

Because most societies have only two accepted categories for gender, it is often seen as important for transgender people to 'pass' as a particular gender. Visually, it is often easier for FTM transgender people to pass as male than for MTF transgender people to pass as female. One reason for this is that testosterone, taken by male transsexuals, gives one facial hair and lowers the voice. Conversely, oestrogen, taken by female transsexuals, does not affect the biological male voice. The female transsexual still needs to alter her male voice through either vocal training or vocal surgery, neither of which is very successful at creating a passable female voice.

The unequal nature of passing also sometimes leads to the perception that there are more MTF transgender people than FTM transgender people, but in fact this is incorrect. There are relatively equal numbers of male and female transgender people.

For those transgender individuals who find themselves physically in-between male and female, the simple act of having to choose which public toilet to use presents a real danger. This simple decision can result in violence towards the transgender individual or legal consequences, which may include arrest.

Transgenderism can also affect one's economic opportunities. Worldwide, many careers and jobs are often unavailable to transgender individuals because of the lack of social acceptance of transgenderism in their community. This has resulted in whole transgender cultures in various countries finding their only means of employment is in the underground, often within the sex industry. Or transgender individuals may find themselves completely dependent upon a culture's tradition of taking care of persons outside of their normal society, or dependent upon a defined role within a family structure that would provide for their welfare.

The varying resources available to the transgender individual greatly influence whether that individual can or cannot become a financially and socially independent member of the greater society. These varying resources also exercise great influence on how individuals view themselves and their roles within that specific larger culture.

Sexuality

Sexual attraction does not necessarily correspond to one's gender – either birth gender or transgender. For example, one can be a biological male, attracted to women, go through gender reassignment, be legally a woman, yet still be attracted to women. That said, sexual attractiveness can also be seen as an area of validation that one is passing successfully as the opposite of one's birth gender.

Hormones will affect a person's emotions, physical reactions and sensations to varying degrees. A MTF transgender person, without surgery, may still get an erection. Oestrogen alone reduces testosterone to a certain extent but does not eliminate its production. Testosterone suppressants will make it more difficult to maintain an erection. For FTM transsexuals, testosterone can enlarge the clitoris, causing increased sexual interest and sensation. In addition, anti-depressants are frequently prescribed to transgender people and can have side effects with regard to sexual function.

Legal issues

The movement for legal rights for transgender people has been linked with legal rights for the gay and lesbian community at least since the 1969 Stonewall Riots, when people could be arrested for not wearing, or dancing with someone not wearing, at least three items of clothing associated with their gender. In the last few decades, various states have passed human rights amendments reiterating basic rights for members of the gay and lesbian community, and sometimes, but not always, transgender people have been included in these rights bills.

Transgender people can petition to have their gender legally changed but it does not necessarily guarantee one's status in the legal system in all locales. Some states recognize gender by genitalia, not by legal status; i.e. a transsexual female described as female on her driver's license but not having undergone sexual reassignment surgery might still be considered a male and placed with men in jail and prison.

Even for individuals who have gone through sexual reassignment surgery and had their gender legally changed, some states and countries do not recognize the change. This can affect whether one can be legally married or claim other spousal benefits.

While sexual reassignment and the desire to pass as the opposite of one's birth gender can make it attractive for members of the transgender community to remain closeted, there is a movement in the community to come out as transgender and work for legal and social acceptance beyond traditional male and female roles.

LYNETTE REINI-GRANDELL
VENUS

TRANSSEXUAL MENACE

advocacy group

High-profile American transgendered advocacy group, formed by activist Ricki Ann **Wilchins** following the closure of Transgender Nation, to advocate for equal rights for transgendered people and to provide a public outlet for her community's outrage over the brutal murder of transgendered teenager Brandon **Teena** in Nebraska in 1993. In 1994 the group protested the exclusion of transgendered people from Stonewall 25, the anniversary parade in New York and successfully agitated for inclusion in the festivities. In the same year, the group protested the Michigan Womyn's Music Festival's 'womyn-born womyn' policy which excluded transgendered people from entering. Wilchins and her group set up Camp Trans just outside the festival site to establish visibility and distribute information on transgendered rights issues, but were unable to lift the ban.

JOHN FORDE

TRAVEL AND TOURISM, GAY

In order to understand the birth of gay travel in the United States, one must take into account the growth of visible gay communities in its major urban centres. Troop mobilization for the Second World War meant that millions of men and women from the interior of the country had to pass through two key ports: **New York** and San Francisco. Already by this time, small pockets of what would come to be known as gay and lesbian life had developed in both of these cities, particularly in the bohemian enclave of Greenwich Village in New York. Having seen at first hand the possibilities, when it came time to return to the United States, many gay and lesbian troops and personnel made a decision to remain. The numbers overall were small,

but this contributed to the rise of both of these cities as important gay centres (Wright 2000; Kissack, 2000).

Further social changes after the Second World War, particularly de-industrialization and car culture, led to an abandonment of the urban inner core, contributing indirectly to the growth of these communities. During this period, large numbers of African-Americans also moved to northern cities in search of jobs. Racial tensions increased and the concurrent flight of whites depopulated entire neighbourhoods. Many of these spaces were filled by artists and creative people. Gays and lesbians were among them, seeking safety from a conservative world. Such under-utilized housing has been associated with the creation of gay neighbourhoods (Bailey, 1999) (see **Ghetto, gay**).

There was ample evidence of the activity of homosexual subcultures in New York, Los Angeles and San Francisco as early as the 1950s and 1960s. This included the publication of *Physique Pictorial, One* and *The Advocate* (still published today), all in Los Angeles alone. The 1964 protest by the New York League for Sexual Freedom might even have been the first public gay and lesbian rights demonstration in the United States and predates Stonewall (Romesburg, 2001). With such activity, these cities were becoming major gay destinations even before Stonewall brought the gay rights movement to public attention. These destinations began to embed themselves into the psyche of gays and lesbians throughout the world. The desire to see them, and perhaps taste freedom, if only briefly, became important to the concept of knowing that one was homosexual.

A few areas stand out as important gay neighbourhoods and travel destinations: Greenwich Village in New York, San Francisco's Castro, Los Angeles, West Hollywood in Miami and eventually Miami's South Beach. There were also several beach resorts with year-round gay populations, difficult to get to but within a few hours' drive of major cities. Provincetown in Massachusetts, Key West, Florida and **Fire Island**, New York, were the most important of these locations.

The concept of gay travel was segregated in a sense, shunted into these few destinations. Many gay travellers were simply people who lived in these areas and who travelled from one such place to another. For gays and lesbians who lived outside of these major centres, a trip to these cities and resorts was often the only time they could be in completely gay environments. The very existence of such spaces was important to gay and lesbian identity, even for those who could never travel to them, and they became the settings for books and other literature with gay themes.

Looking at the earliest gay guidebooks gives some indication of the importance of these destinations. Two guidebooks were created during this time and still continue to be basic building blocks of gay travel information. Bob Damron, a San Francisco gay bar owner and avid traveller, created his eponymous book *Damron's* in 1964 and 1965. At first, and according to Gina Gatta, the current president of the company, Damron listed venues only in the largest US cities. But two books predate even this one: the 1954 text produced by the **Mattachine Society**; and the 1953 guidebook *Lavender Baedeker*, printed by Damron's business partner and lover Hal Call for the Mattachine Society (Gatta, 2001). The German publication *Spartacus* was first published in the late 1960s, with listings from around the world (Bedford and Rauch, 2000).

These books indicate that gay travel was developing along formal lines, its main function being how to connect with other gay people when visiting other cities. The first true gay travel company was started in 1972 by Hanns Ebensten, a New York travel agent (Ebensten, 2001). Yet even this company operated somewhat clandestinely.

Without using the term gay, but by instead indicating that tours were all-male, Ebensten was able to develop a client list, often on referral from straight clients with whom he worked. Most clients were from the largest US cities, but many came from small towns; this was both their gateway to an openly gay travel experience and the only time they could be in all-gay groups. Details of Ebensten's early gay trips appear in his memoir *Volleyball with the Cuna Indians* (Ebensten, 1993).

Ebensten's company offered a range of diverse locations, including Chile's Easter Island, but in general most holiday destinations were limited to a handful of places. This was important for gay identity, as it helped to create a cohesive gay culture (White, 1980; Hughes, 1997). Unfortunately the concentration of men within only a few cities facilitated the spread of the as-yet unknown HIV, the virus that causes AIDS. Gay travel became linked to the spread of the disease. Some discussions of this time period blame a single person, a French Canadian flight attendant, as key to the spread of the infection in Los Angeles, New York and San Francisco, an accusation based on his patterns of travel (Schilts, 1987; Rotello, 1997). This man, Gaeten Dugas, has since become known as Patient Zero.

Throughout the 1980s, gay travel maintained the pattern of being separate from mainstream travel. It consisted of holidays based exclusively in the major gay centres and resorts and resources such as hotels that in general catered only to men. The IGLTA, or International Gay and Lesbian Travel Association, then known as the International Gay Travel Association, was created by a group of friends in a Hollywood bar in 1983. By 1986, RSVP, an exclusively gay cruise company, had come into being. In 1990 Olivia cruises began operating women-only lesbian cruises, although the company had roots stretching as far back as 1973 when it was a lesbian travel company servicing rock music events. The company has since expanded to land-based itineraries also.

By the 1990s, there would however be a remarkable change in how gay travel would be defined and viewed by the general public. Changes both economic and social would create a greater awareness of the gay market, and mainstream companies would begin to specifically target it. One of the most basic reasons for this was that the gay rights movement became one of the most important social forces of this decade, which some likened to the African-American civil rights movement of the 1960s. MTV's *Real World,* with its openly gay character Pedro **Zamora**, also showed San Francisco's gay environments to a young audience of millions. The idea of visiting them, even for straights, was no longer out of the question.

Gay and lesbian rights demonstrations became highly visible but, more importantly, lucrative tourist attractions for the cities in which they occurred (although not necessarily for their sponsors, who in many cases lost money). The 1993 March on Washington and New York's Stonewall 25 and Gay Games in 1994, which all received generally favourable mainstream press, exemplify this trend. Much discussion at the time focused on the economic impact of these events. The mainstream corporate world took notice of the buying power that could be associated with the movement of gay people. The recession of the early 1990s had also caused some businesses to actively seek out alternative sources of income. With the notion of the '**pink dollar**' (or pink pound / pink whatever currency), gays and lesbians seemed to be 'recession-proof' market niches (Holcomb and Luongo, 1996). By the decade's end, various cities, including London, began to actively promote themselves as gay destinations. Companies have been created to aid destinations in this effort, including Community Marketing and Witeck-Combs.

Commercialization and the interest of mainstream companies made possible gay travel magazines, supported by advertisers. In 1989 *Our World* became the world's first gay travel magazine. *Out & About* was first published in 1992, and became a monthly publication. This also helped to reify the notion of gay travel and identity, with accounts of gay communities around the world. While the gay community had created its own guidebooks nearly 30 years before, mainstream publishers began to seek out this market at this time. Andrew Collins' *Fodor's Gay Guide to the USA,* published in 1996, was the first gay guidebook by a mainstream US publisher. Other companies began to do similar projects, namely *Frommer's Gay & Lesbian Europe* by David Andrusia. The Internet has changed much of the way that gays and lesbians gathered travel information however, in the same way that it did for mainstream travel. *Our World* went out of business in 2003, and in 2005 *Out & About* made a decision to no longer be in print. Bought out by the *PlanetOut.com* web site, it became an online and downloadable source of information and guides to various locales. Yet at the same time, new publications were born, such as *Passport* magazine in 2001 and *Out Traveler* in 2004.

A new phenomenon also developed in gay travel in the 1990s – the circuit party. These were huge dance parties, with the original intent of raising funds for AIDS organizations. While situated in locations already established as gay destinations, they helped to draw concentrated attention to the city in which they occurred, spurring tourism. In his 1997 book *Life Outside*, Michelangelo Signorile discusses how one man he interviewed about The White Party credits it with making Miami an important gay destination: 'If you go back a few years ago to the beginning of the Vizcaya [mansion holding the White Party] event, that was the beginning of the scene in Miami' (1997: 98). Cities as diverse as

Philadelphia, Washington and Phoenix use these parties to stimulate attention. Even people who would not come to the parties gained increasing awareness of the cities in which they were held and the resources that would be available to them in terms of bars and other gay cultural venues.

By 2005 the number of vacation spots welcoming the gay and lesbian market was nearly impossible to count. Using companies such as Coda Travel, gay groups now travel to far-flung destinations such as Egypt, Libya, Eastern Europe and many others never previously on the gay radar. This is an astounding change from only 20 years ago, when gay and lesbian vacationers rarely travelled as openly gay to all but a handful of urban districts and shore resorts. This trend has come about partly because of marketing interest as tourism boards and travel agencies seek to increase profitability, as well as because of civil rights advances throughout the world. Even traditionally conservative Latin societies such as Spain and Argentina have enacted liberal civil unions laws that bring awareness of their strong gay communities and the comfort with which gays and lesbians from around the world can travel to them. Gay and lesbian equality is a major component of the European Union's agenda, and nations in Eastern Europe, even Turkey, have had to look again at their policies towards these communities, further creating awareness to travellers from other countries. At the same time, the Internet has allowed any destination or travel company to market itself to a broader audience. Many city and national tourism web sites even advertise directly to the gay market on their home pages, or have rainbow buttons that code gay material without letting their mainstream clients know of the simultaneous marketing. Still, in spite of this increasing openness within what were once societies that shunned gay life, other countries, such as Cuba, experienced increasing amounts of gay tourism while still oppressing local gays and lesbians. In some ways the furtive nature of such travel, so different from the welcome in other locations, created a sense of a clandestine step into the past no longer available in countries now officially welcoming gays.

The social movements within the gay community in the United States during the early 2000s have also helped to spur gay tourism. A continuation of the 1990s movement, when gays in the military were the hot topic, civil unions and marriage became the key issue. States that granted such privileges, such as Vermont, became key centres for tourism, and many gays and lesbians would tie in holidays with tying the knot. Post-legislation, both *Our World* magazine and *Out & About* featured cover articles on Vermont on how to do this. In 2004 images of San Francisco's City Hall and its gay community were broadcast all over the world when gay marriage certificates (briefly) were allowed. Following broadcasts on CNN and BBC, these images were discussed by politicians in such diverse areas as Afghanistan and Zimbabwe, forcing the topic in places where ordinarily it would never have been on the agenda. With increasing conservatism and anti-gay legislation under the conservative Bush administration, it remains to be seen how this situation will impact on. However, areas such as Canada and Europe have already used their liberality and civil unions laws as a draw to encourage tourism.

Gay travel historically has been associated with the reification of gay identity, but this is changing as increasingly it becomes part of the mainstream. There may once have been a secret thrill to travelling to distant places – to the small all-gay hotel on the last island of the Florida Keys, or hidden on the backstreets of an emerging gay neighbourhood in Philadelphia. Yet now, with so many companies vying for gay money, two men can request a single bed in even most luxurious five-star hotel on a remote Polynesian island with little concern about discrimination. With increasing attention being paid to the pink dollar, and its relationship to the ongoing gay and lesbian civil rights movement, if gays and lesbians become equal with the United States and other countries, the idea of gay travel as separate from mainstream travel may even cease to exist.

Bibliography

Andrusia, David (1997) *Frommer's Gay & Lesbian Europe*, New York: Frommer

Bailey, Robert W. (1999) *Gay Politics, Urban Politics: Identity and Economics in the Urban Setting*, New York: Columbia University Press.

Bedford, Briand and Rauch, Robin (2000) *Spartacus*, Berlin: Bruno Gmunder Verlag GMBH.

Collins, Andrew (1996) *Fodor's Gay Guide to the USA*, New York: Fodor.

Ebensten, Hanns (1993) *Volleyball with the Cuna Indians: And Other Gay Travel Adventures*, New York: Penguin.

—— (2001) Former Owner of Hanns Ebensten Travel Company, personal communication.

Gatta, Gina (2001) Damron Company Editor and Publisher, personal communication.

Holcomb, B. and Luongo, M. (1996) 'Gay Tourism in the United States', *Annals of Tourism Research* 23, 2: 711–13.

Hughes, Howard (1997) 'Holidays and Homosexual Identity', *Tourism Management* 18, 1: 3–7.

Kissack, Terrence (2000) 'New York City', in George Haggerty (ed.) *Gay Histories and Cultures: An Encyclopedia*; New York: Garland Publishing.

Romesburg, D. (2001) 'Innovation Through the Ages', *The Advocate*, August 14.

Rotello, Gabriel (1997) *Sexual Ecology: AIDS and the Destiny of Gay Men*, New York: Penguin.

Shilts, Randy (1987) *And The Band Played On: Politics, People and the AIDS Epidemic*, New York: St Martin's Press.

Signorile, Michelangelo (1997) *Life Outside*, New York: HarperPerennial.

White, Edmund (1980) *States of Desire: Travels in Gay America*, New York: Dutton.

Wright, Les (2000) 'San Francisco', in George Haggerty (ed.) *Gay Histories and Cultures: An Encyclopedia*; New York: Garland Publishing.

Further reading

Angelo, Eli and Bain, Joseph (1999) *Odysseus: The International Gay Travel Planner*, Port Washington (New York): Odysseus Enterprises Ltd.

MICHAEL T. LUONGO

TREMBLAY, MICHEL

b. 1942

writer

The French Canadian playwright and novelist Michael Tremblay began writing for the stage during the late 1960s and quickly became one of the most successful French Canadian writers, a result both of his extraordinarily prolific output and of the local specificity of his work. Virtually all of his work is set in Montreal's east end and is written in *joual* (the French language of the working-class Québécois). His initial successes as a playwright with, among others, *Les Belles-Soeurs* (The Sisters-in-Law, 1968) and *Hosanna* (1974), have been followed by an enormous output in a range of formats, including screenplays, short stories, novels and memoirs. His novel, *Le Coeur decouvert* (1987), about a middle-aged gay French professor and his relationship with a younger actor, was made first into a successful film and later into Canada's first gay-themed TV series.

DANIEL HENDRICKSON

TREUT, MONIKA

b. 1954

filmmaker

Monika Treut is screenwriter, director and producer of independent features and documentaries screened at film festivals throughout the world. Born in Germany, she began her video work in the mid-1990s. Her first, controversial film, co-directed with Elfi Mikesch, is *Verführung; die grausame Frau* (Seduction: The Cruel

Woman, 1985), where she addresses the psychological aspects of sadomasochism through the character of a German lesbian dominatrix. In all her films and documentaries Treut offers an innovative, challenging view of sexuality – especially lesbian and female sexuality – and queer issues at large. Particularly important here is the documentary *Gendernauts* (1999), shot in San Francisco, which offers a traversal of 'cyborg' people, gender mixers, male-to-female and FTM transsexuals and transgender who modify their bodies with new technologies and hormone treatments, shaking up the gender borderlines. Since 1990 Treut has also been teaching and lecturing at colleges, art institutes and universities within the United States.

MONICA BARONI

TROCHE, ROSE

b. 1964

filmmaker

American independent filmmaker, born in Chicago, Troche is identified with New Queer Cinema. Her major film, *Go Fish* (1994), is a 16-mm romantic comedy that portrays the lesbian subculture of Chicago's Wicker Park. The female protagonist looks for love, experiences failed relationships and develops a romance with an older woman. In an important initiation scene, the lover gets her hair cut short. This act is shot from different angles, symbolizing her emancipation into and adoption of a different lifestyle. Troche's *Bedroom and Hallways* (UK, 1998) is a more mainstream romantic comedy, set in London and featuring various gay characters. The male protagonist is initially attracted to a handsome straight Irishman, but finally falls in love with his former high-school girlfriend. Troche recently directed *The Safety of Objects* (2001), the story of four suburban American families who suffer from various psycho-cultural maladies.

See also: New Queer Cinema, International

GILAD PADVA

TROPICANA, CARMELITA

performance artist, writer

Alina Troyano (Carmelita Tropicana) is a Cuban-American lesbian performance artist and writer based in New York. In 1999 she received an Obie Award for Sustained Excellence of Performance and, in 2003, the Plumed Warrior writing award from Llego, a national, Latin, gay, lesbian, bisexual and transgender organization. Her book, *I, Carmelita Tropicana: Performing Between Cultures* (2000) was a nominee for a Lambda Award for theatre. The text includes some of Troyano's most famous works, including the script from her celebrated 1995 film, *Your Kunst is Your Waffen* (written with her sister, film director Ela Troyano). The film won Best Short Film at the Berlin Film Festival and the audience award at the Eighteenth International Gay and Lesbian Film Festival. Troyano's theatre has been presented throughout the United States as well as internationally. Her theatre pieces and essays have been published in various anthologies. In collaboration with Latina lesbian comedian Marga **Gómez**, Troyano recently co-wrote and starred in *Single Wet Female* in 2002. That production was nominated for a GLAAD Award for Outstanding New York Theatre: Off-Off-Broadway.

See also: Gómez, Marga

MELISSA FITCH

TSIOLKAS, CHRISTOS

b. 1965

writer

One of Australia's most talented and controversial young writers, Christos Tsiolkas' novels and short stories explore the conflicting ties of cultural and sexual identity. Born into a working-class Greek-Australian family, he studied at Melbourne University, where he formed an enduring interest in socialist politics. He made an explosive literary debut with his first novel *Loaded* (1995), a nihilistic, sex- and drug-fuelled portrait of a young Greek Australian man struggling to reconcile his conservative family upbringing with his homosexuality. Widely praised for its honest and confrontational portrayal of homophobia and racism in contemporary Australia, *Loaded* was successfully filmed as *Head On* (1998). His second novel, *The Jesus Man* (1999), explores similar conflicts between ethnicity, religion and sexuality. He co-authored *Jump Cuts* (1996), an autobiography of Australian socialist campaigner Sasha Soldatow, and co-edited *Complex Entanglements* (2003), a collection of essays about globalization and multiculturalism in Australia.

JOHN FORDE

TUAN HSIU (THE CUT SLEEVE)

Emperor Ai (6 BC–AD 1) of China's Han dynasty was said to have cut his sleeve so as not to awake his sleeping male favourite, who was lying on it. An alternative story is that Ai ordered his favourite male to wear a short-cut sleeve and members of the royal court followed suit. The cut sleeve (*tuan hsiu*) became a euphemism in Chinese literature for male homosexuality.

TRAVIS KONG

TURKEY, FILMMAKING

Speaking in terms of contemporary cultural and critical studies, Turkey can be regarded as one of the countries overwhelmed by the hybridity of national, religious, ethnic and sexual identities, because of its geopolitically permeable position. Thus, the issue of visually narrative representations of identities subject to the identificatory regimes and politics provides Turkish artists with an arena very rich in contextual quality. Turkish cinema and contemporary visual art has also been influenced by debates during the 1980s and 1990s on cultural politics, especially in regard to subjectivity, representation, performative identities and power of knowledge; as a result, visual textuality, its texualized sexuality, its being as commodities-on-display have also been studied and criticized. If queer is to be regarded as a term of non-normativity, immanent critique of discourses on genders in general, then the history of Turkish cinema, especially after 1980, comprises many examples which enable such a perspective to operate. The examples below are the most outstanding ones, their common success of which comes from their regard to gender identity not as an independently singular cultural determinant but as a summation of repetitive acts hybridly constituted with other cultural factors, e.g., nationality, religion, ethnicity.

The film *Donersen Islik Cal* (*Whistle, If You Come Back*, 1993), directed by Orhan Oguz, narrates the queer friendship between a dwarf and a transvestite in the dangerous and dark streets of Istanbul, stressing and investigating visually gender–body–space relations in an urban context. Ferzan Özpetek's film *Le Fate ignoranti* (*Cahil Periler* [*His Secret Life*], 2001) is about the relationship between a gay man and a woman whose dead husband had an affair with the gay man. Özpetek, by creating a love story between these two characters, lovers of the same man, blurs the identification–desire relations in his imagery. Even though there are similar representative examples for Turkish queer cinema, Kutlug Ataman could be regarded as the most distinguished artist/director, writing his unique visual contemporary queer theory by criticizing the issues of gaze, representation, sexualization versus textualization.

577

Kutlug Ataman, in his film *Lola + Bilidikid* (1999), problematizes transcultural sexual identities by narrating the lives of Turkish transvestites and gay men living in Germany. By parodying femininity, transvestism in the film critically highlights the constructed nature of gender; moreover, the relation to national identity in this gendered construction – the mimability, subvertability and reiterability of gendered acts – necessarily depends upon the national values as cultural determinants for performative effects on the body. The relationship between Lola (transvestite) and Bilidikid (a macho gay man) in the film represents the relation of compulsory heterosexuality within the marginal sexualities, that is, the heterosexist discourse restructures and reiterates the gender norms leading Bilidikid to force Lola to have an operation in order to become a woman so that they can marry. The film focuses also on genders as transcultural identities (German-Turk transvestites and gays), by presenting the constituted-ness of gender and nationality as the fear both of loss of the phallus and the belonging to a nation, respectively. Ataman exposes immanently the hypocritical illusion of national heterosexuality, 'the mechanism by which a core national culture can be imagined as a sanitized space of sentimental feeling and immaculate behaviour, a space of pure citizenship' (Berlant and Warner, 2003: 171), by reminding the spectator that identity is constructed melancholically (Freud, 1991) through the fear of loss of belonging, where the loss is always already a lack.

Ataman's video installation *Women Who Wear Wigs* (2001) comprises interviews with four Turkish women who have different reasons for wearing wigs: as a political disguise and closure (Leyla), as a feminine attribute hiding the effects of cancer treatment (Nevval Sevindi), as an approval of the heterosexist dependence upon vision in order to make the passing of a transgender less depressing (Demet

Demir) and as a tool for a politically resisting de-sexualization of the body to allow a Turkish Muslim university student (The Voice) to be able to study in the university, not with a headscarf but a wig. Ataman underlines through his imagery that the fetishistic/scopophilic symbolic gaze leads identities to operate through a power/resistance dialectics. Gender is constructed and discursively acted, further, the subject displays his/her body and expresses its sexuality by using symbolic codes of visuality and by queering the image's textuality. However, by means of his unique interview technique with the four women, Ataman also puzzles over the debate that visual textuality comprises a convergence of Marxist/Freudian fetishisms on the screen by both being a commodity and putting commodities on display (Mulvey, 1996: 8).

In the video *Never My Soul* (2003), Ataman manipulates and simultaneously frees his drag hero(ine) Ceyhan Firat, and the spectator becomes confused because s/he cannot distinguish fiction from reality, performance from 'not-acted', which is a similar experience for the subject to construct an identity through the reiteration of norms/discourses, which can be regarded as Foucauldian subjective experiences. 'I came here for a long-lasting film project. Ceyhan Firat whose life I will act will get married in this film' says Ceyhan Firat, confusing the spectator at the very beginning. Through the film, Ceyhan plays a parody where s/he teases all stereotypical images of gender and Turkish 'national' understanding thereof, especially women's sexuality. The repetitive act, constituent for gender construction is not only sexual, as also previously narrated in Ataman's films; one also repeats/reiterates national, ethnic, religious norms to develop a sense of belonging to a gendered category. To criticize heterosexual melancholy with a parody, thus leads to the criticism of nationality, i.e. the imagined nature of both gender and nation.

Bibliography

Berlant, Lauren and Warner, Michael (2003) 'Sex in Public', in Robert J. Corber and Stephen Valocchi (eds) *Queer Studies: An Interdisciplinary Reader*, London: Blackwell Publishing.

Freud, Sigmund (1991) *On Metapsychology*, Harmondsworth: Penguin.

Mulvey, Laura (1996) *Fetishism and Curiosity*, Bloomington: University of Indiana Press.

CÜNEYT ÇAKIRLAR

TURNBULL, COLIN M.

b. 1924; d. 1994

anthropologist

English–American anthropologist Colin M. Turnbull's research among the Ba'Mbuti Pygmies of eastern Congo (*The Forest People*, 1961) and the Ik people of Uganda (*The Mountain People*, 1972) are among the classics of African studies. Where the first portrays a marginal people who maintain their dignity and cultural integrity, the second is a searing account of the devastation a once-proud hunting culture experienced through 'development'. Turnbull is also renowned as a pioneer in the struggle for civil rights in the United States and for Tibetan freedom. From 1960, when he and his African-American partner, John Towles, first took wedding vows, until 1988 when Towles died of AIDS–related illness, the couple lived as an openly gay, interracial couple. Turnbull himself died of AIDS after leaving his entire estate to the United Negro Fund for the advancement of African-American rights.

MARC EPPRECHT

28'S NINEVITES

The 28's Ninevites is a criminal gang dating from the 1890s. Originating in Johannesburg mine compounds and prisons, the gang remains notorious for its extreme violence and hierarchical system of homosexual 'marriage'.

MARC EPPRECHT

TYLER, PARKER

b. 1904; d. 1974

poet, novelist, film critic

Parker Tyler's life and work represent an ideal bridge between early twentieth-century queer writing and later, post-Stonewall cultural critique; between the upper-class camp of intellectual Greenwich Village cafes and parties, and the serially produced camp of Andy Warhol's Factory, peopled by drag queens, poor little rich girls, and hyped and trashed starlets, and the gay activism that would follow. A poet and writer, he co-authored with fellow poet Charles Henri **Ford**, *The Young and Evil* (1933), possibly the first novel to deal with gay characters without apology or derision. Tyler established himself as a major film critic in the 1940s, with two books (*The Hollywood Hallucination*, 1944; *Magic and Myth of the Movies*, 1947) that made his familiarity with Surrealism a splendid tool for framing cinema as an occasion for poetic, imaginative, ironic readings. During the 1950s and 1960s he moved from mainstream Hollywood cinema to the underground, exploring the experimental art of the New York scene: he became a regular contributor to art magazines, and in 1969 he authored *Underground Film*, the first critical history on the subject. While his style lost the ebullient, high camp character of earlier years, in this book and in *Sexing the Screen* (1972), the first lengthy study ever to address the highly coded cinematic representation of homosexuality, Tyler offered a signpost pointing to the definition of a politically committed gay film criticism, preceding and announcing Vito Russo's landmark book, *The Celluloid Closet* (1981).

FABIO CLETO

U

UNITED KINGDOM, FILMMAKING

Perhaps more than any other national cinema, British films have approached homosexuality with an open mind, especially when compared to those made in Hollywood. Many landmark films in queer cinema were produced in the United Kingdom, beginning with Basil Dearden's *Victim* (1961), one of the first movies to plead tolerance for homosexuals and the first in which the words 'homosexual' and 'homosexuality' were uttered. Dirk Bogarde plays Melville Farr, a married, gay, highly virtuous barrister who stands up to a blackmailer. In his memoir *Snakes and Ladders*, Bogarde writes that taking the role of Farr 'was the wisest decision I ever made in my cinematic life'.

Another milestone British film from the 1960s is Robert Aldrich's *The Killing of Sister George* (1968), the third instalment of the director's 'Stardom' trilogy (which also includes *What Ever Happened to Baby Jane?* [1962] and *The Legend of Lylah Clare* [1968]). Based on the play by Frank Marcus, *Sister George* centres on the relationship between butch June 'George' Buckridge (Beryl Reid) and her younger femme lover, Childie (Susannah York), who ultimately leaves George for Mercy Croft (Coral Browne). Although Aldrich's film is often accused of perpetuating negative stereotypes about lesbians, the X-rated *Sister George* was one of the boldest – and one of

the most sympathetic – films on the subject. One scene in the film was shot at the Gateways Club, an actual London lesbian bar, using regular patrons as extras. Aldrich included a 119-second scene, considered shocking at the time, of Mercy Croft's seduction of Childie. And although she is certainly not without foibles, George is by far the most complex and humane character in the film.

Other important queer UK films from the 1960s include those by British directors Lindsay Anderson and Ken **Russell**. Although his filmic output was not large, Anderson has a prominent place in British cinema history as one of the founders of the Free Cinema movement of the late 1950s and early 1960s, a collective of directors committed to making films about the travails of the working class and the significance of everyday life. Anderson's greatest contribution to queer British cinema is *If…*(1968). Inspired by Jean Vigo's 1933 short film *Zéro de Conduite* (Zero for Conduct), *If…*depicts the lives of young men in a repressive boarding school who ultimately lead a full-scale revolution. Anderson's anti-establishment film is distinguished by a calm, casual depiction of homosexuality and male friendship.

Many of Russell's most notable films, particularly his literary adaptations and biopics, contain a feverish, queer sensibility. His adaptation of D.H. Lawrence's *Women in Love* (1969), with a screenplay by Larry

Kramer, features a famous nude wrestling match between Oliver Reed and Alan **Bates**. The following year Russell filmed *The Music Lovers* (1970), his take on the life of Tchaikovsky, starring Richard **Chamberlain** as the composer and Christopher Gable as his boyfriend. Almost 20 years later Russell adapted another Lawrence novel, *The Rainbow* (1988), with a notable performance by Amanda Donohoe as Winifred, a bohemian lesbian. Russell also paid homage to Oscar Wilde in *Salome's Last Dance* (1988), a fanciful interpretation not only of Wilde's play *Salome*, itself a delirious vision of the biblical meeting between Salome, the daughter of King Herod, and John the Baptist, but also of the life of Wilde himself. Russell's amalgam of biography and literary adaptation depicts Wilde (played by Nickolas Grace) and his real-life lover Lord Alfred 'Bosie' Douglas (Douglas Hodge) visiting a male brothel where *Salome* is performed; as Wilde watches the play, he fondles a gold-painted pageboy.

Queer filmmaking in the United Kingdom during the 1970s was marked by three different types of cinematic milestone: *Sunday, Bloody Sunday* (1971), by John **Schlesinger** marked the first time that two men kissed on the lips in a major studio release; Jim Sharman's *The Rocky Horror Picture Show* (1975), the gender bending cult-movie classic; and Ron Peck and Paul Hallam's *Nighthawks* (1978), Britain's first independent gay-themed film. The openly gay Schlesinger made *Sunday* (the script was written by *New Yorker* film critic Penelope Gilliatt) after the enormous success of the Hollywood-produced *Midnight Cowboy* (1969), the tale of a male hustler and a tubercular derelict living in New York City. Set in London, *Sunday* centres around the lives of two men and a woman in a love triangle: gay Dr Daniel Hirsh (Peter Finch) and straight employment counsellor Alex Greville (Glenda Jackson) are both in love with younger bisexual artist Bob Elkin (Murray Head). Although the passionate kiss between Finch and Head certainly made *Sunday* quite daring for its time, Schlesinger's film is just as remarkable for its rich, nuanced – and non-judgemental – portrayal of not only homosexuality and bisexuality, but the messy, complicated emotional lives of adults.

Based on the British stage musical, *The Rocky Horror Picture Show* (1975) is more than non-judgemental – it actually celebrates homosexuality, bisexuality and transvestism. This campy science-fiction spoof-cum-rock musical exhorts its viewers, in one song, to 'give yourself over to absolute pleasure'. Starring Tim Curry as the alien, bisexual, transvestite scientist Dr Frank N. Furter, *Rocky Horror* is infused with the libertine flamboyance of the glam-rock era, which reached its peak in the United Kingdom during the early 1970s. The film's high-natured sexual anarchy has proven so popular that it is still a fixture on the midnight film circuit. *Rocky Horror*'s most ardent fans dress up as characters from the movie and act out scenes in front of the screen, frequently encouraging audience participation.

A far more sober but nonetheless provocative film, *Nighthawks* (1978), explores the life of Jim (Ken Robertson), a closeted geography teacher popular with his middle-school students who spends his nights as an habitué of London's gay bars and discos. Filmed in black-and-white using mostly non-professional actors, Peck and Hallam's film is deliberately paced, privileging long takes of 'cruising', or the act of looking – and being looked at. Jim's closeted life ends when one of his students asks if he's gay; he answers truthfully, then stalwartly responds to other questions from his pupils.

The 1970s also marked the emergence of one of Great Britain's most important queer – and independent – filmmakers, Derek **Jarman**, whose extremely personal, artistically innovative, non-traditional-narrative films have marked him as a progenitor of New

Queer Cinema. Jarman's first feature film, *Sebastiane* (1976), is a highly homoerotic telling, complete with graphic scenes of sex and torture, of the legend of St Sebastian and is filmed entirely in Latin. Defying all expectations, *Sebastiane* enjoyed a successful one-year run in London and played in major cities in the United States. *Sebastiane* was the first in a series of Jarman films that examined – with the director's trademark stylistic flourishes – the lives of queer historical figures. *Caravaggio* (1986), Jarman's take on the life of the bisexual Italian Renaissance painter (played by Nigel Terry), marks the screen debut of Tilda Swinton (who would star in several other films by Jarman) as Lena, the painter's mistress who comes between him and his male lover, Ranuccio (Sean Bean). A radical reworking of Christopher Marlowe's play, *Edward II* reconfigures the fourteenth-century monarch as a gay rights martyr. Featuring lots of queer sex, *Edward II* is also distinguished by Jarman's use of anachronism, such as scenes of protesting members of the AIDS activist group OutRage!. Jarman's queer biography series concluded with *Wittgenstein* (1993), a lushly austere, black-and-white exploration of the life of the gay philosopher.

In addition to his gay biography series, Jarman's work in the AIDS film genre also constitutes a substantial contribution to the history of queer filmmaking in the United Kingdom. Jarman, who discovered that he was HIV+ in 1986, made *The Garden* in 1990 as an allegory for AIDS. Featuring opulent, dreamlike images of male love and beauty contrasted with nightmarish visions of persecution and death, *The Garden* is Jarman's quietly poetic plea for tolerance and understanding. Jarman's last work, *Blue* (1993), made a year before his death in 1994, would be his most stylistically radical – and most personal – film. Reflecting Jarman's own greatly impaired eyesight, *Blue* consists of a completely blue screen for all 76 minutes of its duration. With the voices

of, among others, Nigel Terry, Tilda Swinton and Jarman himself reading from the director's diaries, *Blue* recounts Jarman's resigned, yet never maudlin, thoughts on his deteriorating health, the deaths of loved ones and his steadfast dedication to art.

While Jarman was crafting his singular, often introspective films, other British directors were making landmark works that examined race, class and sexuality. One of the first of these films was *My Beautiful Laundrette* (1985), directed by Stephen **Frears** and written by the Anglo-Pakistani Hanif **Kureishi**. The story of two friends – Omar (Gordon Warnecke), an English-born Pakistani, and Johnny (Daniel Day-Lewis), a white street punk – who become lovers and co-operators of the titular laundry facility, Frears' film candidly depicts not only the physical intimacy between Omar and Johnny but also the racism and classism of Thatcherite England. Frears next directed *Prick Up Your Ears* (1987), which was adapted from John Lahr's 1978 biography of Joe Orton, the gay playwright whose scathing farces were a vital part of British theatre during the 1960s.

Overlapping somewhat with Jarman's work in terms of its experimental structure and creative approach to queer biography, *Looking for Langston* (1989), a short film by Isaac **Julien**, celebrates the life of the gay Harlem Renaissance poet Langston **Hughes**. Combining the poetry of Essex Hemphill, archival footage of Hughes and Harlem during the 1920s, original footage of two tuxedoed male lovers, and house music, *Looking for Langston* is an anachronistic reflection on race and sexuality in America. Julien's feature-film debut, *Young Soul Rebels* (1991), is another period piece. Set in 1977, the year of Queen Elizabeth II's Silver Jubilee, *Rebels* centres around two black DJs – one gay, one straight – punk and funk music and the murder of a closeted gay man.

Not as trenchant in its observations about race and sexuality as Julien's work but one of the most talked-about films of its day, Neil Jordan's *The Crying Game* (1992) is both a conventional thriller and an unconventional romance. The film's love story revolves around Fergus, a white IRA operative (Stephen Rea), and Dil, his black hairdresser girlfriend (Jaye Davidson). Miramax Films, the distributor of *The Crying Game*, begged critics not to give away the film's 'secret': that Dil is actually a biological man, which is revealed to both Fergus and the audience when Dil lets her/his kimono fall open.

Queer British films since the mid-1990s have fallen into a range of genres. Biopics such as Brian Gilbert's *Wilde* (1997), starring Stephen Fry as the Irish writer; and John Maybury's *Love Is the Devil* (1998), featuring Derek Jacobi as the British painter Francis Bacon, take their subjects' homosexuality as a point of departure. Boy-meets-boy films such as Hettie MacDonald's *Beautiful Thing* (1996) explore the difficulties – and joys – of being a gay teen. Of a more *sui generis* nature are Michael Winterbottom's *Butterfly Kiss* (1995), a lesbian psychodrama-cum-road movie; Will Gould's gay werewolf tale, *The Wolves of Kromer* (1998); and Duncan Roy's *AKA* (2002), the story of a young man's desperate climb to the upper echelons of gay society told using three simultaneous frames. These are all notable contributions to a national cinema that has a distinguished queer filmmaking lineage.

See also: United Kingdom, filmmaking, independent and documentary

Further reading

Bourne, S. (1999) *Brief Encounters: Lesbians and Gays in British Cinema, 1930–1977*, London: Cassell Academic.

Howes, K. (1994) *Broadcasting It: An Encyclopedia of Homosexuality on Film, Radio and TV in the UK, 1923–1993*, London: Cassell Academic.

Murray, R. (1994) *Images in the Dark: An Encyclopedia of Gay and Lesbian Film and Video*, Philadelphia: TLA Publications, Inc.

Russo, V. (1987) *The Celluloid Closet: Homsexuality in the Movies*, New York: Harper & Row.

MELISSA ANDERSON

UNITED KINGDOM, FILMMAKING, INDEPENDENT AND DOCUMENTARY

As recent studies testify, it is difficult in any account of the inconsistent and fragmented nature of funding in British cinema to label its industry as anything but 'independent'. This is especially pertinent, however, with 'minority' filmmaking, whose marginal status places it more than any other at odds with the limited funding resources and strategic commercial agendas of the British film 'industry' – lesbian and gay filmmaking in particular.

The history of gay British independent narrative and documentary filmmaking can be traced, albeit contentiously, to the formative films of the Free Cinema and New Wave 'kitchen sink' era of the 1950s and 1960s. Woodfall Films, a company set up in 1958 by two bisexual men, director Tony Richardson and playwright John Osborne, was one of the first truly independent film companies in postwar British cinema, and exhibited a quite distinctive fascination with alienated masculine identity and sexuality. The same can also be said of the earlier documentary films of Richardson's Free Cinema Movement collaborations with Karel Reisz and Lindsay Anderson, whose films such as *We Are The Lambeth Boys* (1959), cast a decidedly appreciative middle-class queer eye on the working-class teenage subjects under exploration. Although in no way an openly lesbian and gay or bisexual film company – something that would have been impossible to conceive of in any case because of the illegality of homosexuality in Britain until 1967 – Woodfall was one of the first independently financed companies to produce a film that sympathetically addressed the subject of homosexuality. In *A Taste of Honey* (1961),

583

based upon the stage play of the same name, Richardson broke new ground with his portrayal of a young gay man on the brink of social acceptance. And despite stereotypically adhering to the 'Sad Young Man' stereotype defined by British gay film historian Richard Dyer, an allusion to homosexuality, predominantly in implicit terms, permeated a number of social realist independent films of the 1960s, from the lonely queers of *The L-Shaped Room* (1962), to the clone-like motorcycle enthusiast in *The Leather Boys* (1963) or the unashamed 'poofs' of Swinging London in *Darling* (1965), directed by gay director John **Schlesinger**. The films of the 1960s 'New Wave' therefore paved the way forward for the more direct and visible representation of gays in film, and the development of gay filmmaking, that emerged in the more liberated climate of the 1970s.

However, despite these early tokenistic attempts at representation, the first 'official' independent gay film was undoubtedly *Sebastiane* (1976), the first feature-length film by queer auteur Derek **Jarman**. Co-directed by Paul Humfress, *Sebastiane* was unique not only because it was an explicitly homoerotic exploration of the legend of gay martyr St Sebastian, but also because it attained worldwide critical and financial success, establishing Jarman as a leading visionary in independent queer filmmaking in the UK throughout the 1980s and 1990s, until his untimely death from AIDS in 1994. Yet, despite this success, a number of gay critics at the time were less than satisfied with the rather avant-garde preoccupation of Jarman's oeuvre which, in their view, was decidedly detached from the everyday real experiences of lesbians and gay men living in Britain during the 1970s and 1980s. It was therefore independent directors Ron Peck and Paul Hallam, whose debut feature *Nighthawks* (1978) was the first uncompromisingly honest attempt to reflect the realities of the burgeoning gay lifestyle in London during the late 1970s. A complex documentary-style portrait of the nocturnal adventures of an 'out' young schoolteacher as he cruises the thriving London gay scene in search of sexual and emotional fulfilment, the film was a landmark in British cinema.

The rise of Thatcherism in Britain during the 1980s, with its renewed right wing extremism and institutionalized homophobia, subsequently provided new difficulties for any real attempt at lesbian and gay filmmaking in the UK. The resulting onslaught of tabloid-fuelled AIDS hysteria and the increase of artistic censorship and funding cuts that dominated the decade made it impossible for lesbian and gay filmmakers really to produce any significant work beyond the margins of the short film and video festival circuit. With the exception of the Channel Four funded mainstream hit *My Beautiful Laundrette* (Stephen Frears, 1986), in which homosexuality appears as a mere incidental dimension to a relationship whose narrative focus is more concerned with the racial and class tensions produced by such an 'unconventional' coupling, and the brief showcase for documentaries and short films provided by the short-lived *Out on Tuesday* TV series on Channel Four (1989–90), it was Jarman who was once again placed at the forefront of independent gay filmmaking in the UK. However, the highly personal and surreal nature of such poetic works as *The Angelic Conversation* (1985) and *The Last of England* (1988), some critics have argued, did little to address the oppressive political climate of Britain in any effective sense because of their rather elitist status as art-house pseudo-political self-indulgence. And hence it seemed Jarman's work posed little threat to the Thatcherite government or mainstream perceptions of homosexuality in the hostile lead up to the imposed ban on positive representations of lesbian and gay identity in the arts that followed the introduction of Clause 28 in 1988.

In a similar vein to the rise of New Queer Cinema as a post–AIDS 'indie' movement in the United States at the end of the 1980s, a number of notable lesbian and gay filmmakers emerged from the short film and video scene in the UK with a similarly renewed political impetus to represent queer identity and sexuality in the final decade of the millennium. Films such as Richard Kwietniowski's camp documentary *Alfalfa* (1987) and romantic *Flames of Passion* (1989), or Isaac Julien's *Looking for Langston* (1989), *Young Soul Rebels* (1991) and *The Attendant/Caught Looking* (1992) to Pratibha Parmar's radical documentaries *ReFraming AIDS* (1988) and *Khush* (1991), were ground-breaking celebrations and reassessments of the diverse political, racial and historical configurations of homosexual identity in British culture and society during the twentieth century. And the death of conservatism in 1990s Britain that gave way to the 'cool Britannia' cultural diversity espoused by Blairite New Labour has led to a small but significant rise in independently produced lesbian and gay filmmaking in the UK in recent years. Most notably, the international success of such films as Hettie Mcdonald's *Beautiful Thing* (1996), Paul Oremland's *Like It Is* (1998), John Maybury's *Remembrance of Things Fast* (1993) and *Love Is The Devil* (1998) and Lisa Gornick's *Do I Love You?* (2003), have made very real attempts to optimistically reimagine the future for lesbian, gay and queer desire and representation in British independent film in the new millennium.

See also: New Queer Cinema, International; United Kingdom, filmmaking, independent and documentary

Further reading

Dyer, R. (2002), *Now You See It: Studies on Lesbian and Gay Film*, 2nd edn, London: Routledge.
Gever, M., Greyson, J. and Parmar, P. (eds) (1993) *Queer Looks: Perspectives on Lesbian and Gay Film and Video*, London: Routledge.
Griffiths, R. (ed.) (2005) *British Queer Cinema*, London: Routledge.

ROBIN GRIFFITHS

UNITED KINGDOM, LITERATURE

The appearance of glbtq characters and the writing of glbtq literature in the United Kingdom have been conditioned by legal proscription and censorship. With the gradual emergence of a glbtq subculture, after the publication of the government's **Wolfenden Report** in 1958, and the ensuing Sexual Offences Act (1967), there has been increased opportunity both to reflect upon gay-oriented literature of the past and to catalogue that which is now emerging. Any historical overview has to note that texts were deliberately altered to remove references to homosexual practices, and that only recently has this been addressed, if at all. Devout medieval monks literally defaced with tar innumerable manuscripts containing early gay drinking songs, *The Killing of Abel* (c.1460–75), a vernacular mystery play, was recorded by John Quincy Adams in his *Chief Pre-Shakespearean Drama* (1924) with asterisks blocking out what were deemed obscene homosexual references, and the homoerotic poetry of Richard Barnfield (1574–1627) was not included in anthologies such as Hyder Rollins' *The Renaissance in England* (1954) after being deemed unsavoury. It is true to say that homosexual literature written before 1900 is still generally unavailable, the effect of which is to deprive the gay community of any sense of continuity or self-appreciative history. In contrast, scholars do not have to dig deep to uncover gay awareness even in mainstream literary output, and there has been a growing awareness of the emergence of both gay-themed and gay-peopled literature ever since.

There is a clear poetic lineage to the recording of homosexual desire stretching back to the Gawain poet's work *Cleanness* (late fourteenth century, also known as *Purity*), which specifies sodomitic practices, and Geoffrey Chaucer (*c.*1343–1400), where the figure of the Pardoner is described as 'a gelding or a mare', beardless and therefore effeminized, in *The Canterbury Tales* (the Parson also mentions 'thilke abhomynable sinne...openly reherced in holy writ' as an aside). The court of Elizabeth I gave full reign to open sonneteering about gay love, blatantly by Barnfield as noted above, more contentiously by Sir Francis Bacon (1561–1626), who endured gossip levelled at his relationships with young men (most notably Henry Percy) and whose poem *Of Beauty* includes only references to men, and most explosively by Shakespeare himself. The 'Bard's' sonnets were written in the mid-1590s and the first 126 of them (from a total of 154) were addressed to a young man, 'Mr. W.H.' (variously identified as William Herbert, Earl of Pembroke, Henry Wriothesley, Earl of Southampton and the commoner Willy Hewes). They were first printed in 1609, but by 1640 their editor (John Benson) had replaced 'he' and 'him' with 'she' and 'her' to disguise the object of affection; it was not until Oscar Wilde undertook research into them that their truths were more widely publicized. Sonnet 20 has become the most notorious, where Shakespeare rails at Nature about the uses of his lover:

> By adding one thing to my purpose nothing.
> But since she prick'd thee out for women's pleasure,
> Mine be thy love, and thy love's use their treasure.

Critics and commentators have revealed more about themselves in the arguments and interpretations that have ensued through the centuries than Shakespeare definitively did about himself, and an air of mystery persists around the meaning. Needless to say the fluidity of sexual relationships of the era seem obvious. That poetic tradition has continued ever since, with masters of English poetry revealing homosexual inclinations through the lines they have written.

Close friendships have been elegized by Edmund Spenser (1552–99) for Sir Philip Sydney (1554–86) in *Astrophel* (*c.*1590), John Milton (1608–74) for Edward King (1612–37) in *Lycidas* (1638), Thomas Grey (1716–71) for Richard West in *Elegy Written In A Country Church Yard* (1751), Percy Shelly (1792–1822) for John Keats (1795–1821) in *Adonais* (1821), Alfred Tennyson (1809–92) for Arthur Hallam in *In Memoriam* (1850) (which contains the most sentimental of lines: 'Tis better to have loved and lost / Than never to have loved at all'), Matthew Arnold (1822–88) for Arthur Clough in *Thyrsis* (1866) and T.S. Eliot (1888–1965) for Jean Verdenal in *The Waste Land* (1922). A.E Housman's (1859–1936) unrequited love for A.J. Jackson contributed to the restrained sorrow of his poetry; First World War poets Wilfred Owen (1893–1918) and Siegfried Sassoon (1886–1967) were both gay and the transatlantic influence of the American poet Walt Whitman (1819–92) on John Addington Symonds (1840–93) and Edward Carpenter (1844–1929) effectively started the homophile movement in Britain, and was the forerunner of gay liberation as we understand it.

More recent gay poetry is unequivocally tied to the times in which it has been written; W.H. Auden's (1907–73) *The Platonic Bow* (or *A Day For A Lay*) sparked controversy with its emergence in 1958, describing 'a spring day, a day, a day for a lay, when the air / Smelled like a locker-room, a day to blow or get blown...', while Adam Johnson's (1965–93) *The Playground Bell* (1994), in a later and differently historically contingent era, memorializes its author's battle with AIDS. Poetry, it has been argued, may not have the impact of drama or the novel in English literature, but it is lasting, poignant, transcends literary fashion and continues to be the marker for the evolution of language in its written form.

The dramatic tradition has had to encounter a heterosexually dominated audience and so deals with homosexuality only peripherally. Boys did play female roles in early English drama, so that morals in the theatre were always questionable; much early drama relied upon what is now understood as gender performativity for its action. The plays of Shakespeare, Webster and Jonson all engage with the juggling of gender and sexuality, but obvious gay characters are absent until John Vanbrugh's play *The Relapse* (first performed in 1696), which features Coupler, the arranger of marriages. Christopher Marlowe (1564–93) offers the only gay drama of the era with *Edward II* (printed in 1594), where Gaveston is presented as an over-indulged gilded youth and where the king meets his end at the hands and the infamously phallic and punishing red-hot poker of the seductive Lightborn.

The gay playwrights of later generations have been compromised in their output by the overwhelmingly heterosexual obsessions of the theatre-going public; the nearest Oscar Wilde (1854–1900) comes to presenting homosexual desire is in *Salome* (1893), in the pageboy Herodias' love for the Syrian guardsman, and allusions to the living of double lives in *The Importance of Being Earnest* (first published in 1899) and blackmail in *An Ideal Husband* (published 1899). Joe **Orton** (1933–67) presents an imposed bisexuality in *Entertaining Mr Sloane* (1964) and in *What The Butler Saw* (1969) sexual partnerships proliferate to the amusing exclusion of the father and mother, the husband and wife – nevertheless these are not the much less well known gay dramas that emerged from the London-based acting and theatre company **Gay Sweatshop** between 1975 and 1997, nor most recently, in more enlightened

times, from Mark Ravenhill with *Shopping and Fucking* (1996).

Prose dealing with gay themes has managed to find its own audience, and in line with a developing liberalization and relaxation of attitudes to homosexuality there has been a considerable emergence of new texts and an ongoing critical tradition of rereading the old. *Sodom: or, The Quintessence of Debauchery,* attributed to John Wilmot, Earl of Rochester (1647–80), was published in Antwerp in 1684 and was the first literary work to be censored in England on the grounds of obscenity; as homosexual Restoration erotica it was not republished until 1966, when it found an eager readership. It was really the efforts of publishers overseeing the actual production of books that secured recognition for a gay literary canon; from the 1930s onwards, the Fortune Press (run by Reginald Ashley Caton from 1924 to 1971) published novels about homosexuality and promoted the first works of Philip Larkin (1922–85) and Kingsley Amis (1922–95), looked back to the anonymous Don Leon (reputed to Lord Byron [1788–1824]) and listed contemporary novels on gay themes such as Terrence Greenidge's *The Magnificent* (1933), Richard Rumbold's *Little Victims* (1933) and Reginald Underwood's *Bachelor's Hall* (1934), *Flame of Freedom* (1936) and *Hidden Lights* (1937), as well as all 12 undated volumes of *The 'Boy' Diaries* by Aubrey Fowkes/Esmond Quinterley. A gay sensibility can be traced prior to this, weaving through the literary output of the masters of the novelistic genre, but an exclusively gay thematic is rarely present. It does not become noteworthy until it is obvious in society, with the passing of the LaBouchere Amendment in 1885, which led to the trial of the author of the novella *The Picture of Dorian Gray* (published 1891), Oscar Wilde. The extreme castigation that he suffered, indeed his virtual martyrdom, has in turn led to the backlash of a proliferation of homosexually themed literature, which makes its presence felt to this day and which goes some way to recoup the indignities that he and other gay authors have had to endure through the times in which they lived.

The twentieth century reveals a host of gay authors dealing either implicitly or explicitly with gay themes, both from the male homosexual's viewpoint and, not insignificantly, from a lesbian perspective. Radclyffe Hall's *The Well of Loneliness* (1928) portrayed the first lesbian-themed narrative based upon the life story of the central character Stephen Gordon, a masculine-named heroine; Virginia **Woolf**, in *Orlando* (1928), disturbed gender certainties by presenting a character who crossed from masculinity to femininity; Lytton Strachey's sister Dorothy Bussy presented a gay milieu in *Olivia* (1930). The more recent era, in part through the popularization of lesbian themes in TV transcriptions of fictional works, has witnessed the emergence of works such as Jeanette Winterson's *Oranges Are Not The Only Fruit* (1985), *Sexing the Cherry* (1990) and *The Passion* (1997), and Sarah Waters' *Tipping The Velvet* (2000).

Many of the great names of UK English literature have increasingly been identified as gay or bisexual and their texts act as testament to the emergence of what would now be recognized as gay liberation. D.H. Lawrence, Christopher **Isherwood**, Lawrence Durrell, E.M. **Forster** (his famous gay romance, *Maurice* [1913–4] was published posthumously in 1971), Evelyn Waugh, Angus **Wilson** (whose prolific postwar oeuvre forms a canon of gay literature in itself, with *Hemlock And After* [1952], *The Middle Age of Mrs. Eliot* [1958], *Late Call* [1964] and *No Laughing Matter* [1967] to mention but a few), James Purdy (*Eustace Chisholm And The Works*, 1967; *Narrow Rooms*, 1978) have laid positive foundations for contemporary gay fiction writers. What they have also encouraged is an encounter with the fluidity of sexual possibilities in more straight-identified authors. Hanif Kureishi's ground-breaking *The Buddha of Suburbia* (1990) portrayed a bisexual Asian young man, reflecting more accurately the cultural mix that was emerging within Great Britain. J.G. Ballard's *Crash* (1995) introduced the kinkier aspects of disabled and differently orgasmic sex, while the celebrity novel, such as Rupert Everett's *Hello Darling, Are You Working?* (1998) internationalized the British gay and bisexual experience. What has ensued is a host of recognizably gay authors in effect standing shoulder to shoulder with their straight counterparts. Timothy Ireland's first novel, *Who Lies Within* (1984), established his career, David Leavitt's *While England Sleeps* (1993) and Patrick Gale's *The Facts of Life* (1995) have charted on best-seller lists, while Neil Bartlett's *Ready To Catch Him Should He Fall* (1990) is deemed a modern classic, as is the less well-known Michael Arditti's *The Celibate* (1993). Alan Hollinghurst's Booker prize-nominated *The Swimming Pool Library* (1988) and Man Booker Prize-winning *The Line of Beauty* (2004) have emerged from a rich and hard-fought-for tradition to be rated alongside the best fiction of their era.

See also: Auden, W.H.; Hollinghurst, Alan; Waters, Sarah; Winterson, Jeanette

Further reading

Anderson, Patrick and Sutherland, Alistair (eds) (1963) *Eros: An Anthology of Male Friendship*, Citadel: New York.

Jones, Sonya L. (ed.) (1998) *Gay and Lesbian Literature Since World War II: History and Memory*, New York: Harrington Park Press.

Reade, Brian (ed.) (1970) *Sexual Heretics: Male Homosexuality in English Literature from 1850 to 1900*, London: Routledge and Kegan Paul.

Toibin, Colm (2002) *Love In A Dark Time: And Other Explorations of Gay Lives and Literature*, New York: Scribners.

Woods, Gregory (1998) *A History of Gay Literature: The Male Tradition*, New Haven and London: Yale University Press.

MICHAEL PINFOLD

UNITED STATES, LITERATURE

The literature of the United States since 1945 has been intimately linked to radically changing queer cultural dialectics. Therefore, to better understand American literature, it is important to situate its writings within their cultural contexts. Since 1945 queer culture has engaged in what Michael Warner (2002) terms a dialectic of publics and counter-publics – that is, it has both created queer subcultures largely invisible to the mainstream and appropriated more conventional mainstream discourses. Accommodationist and radical political strategies exist in tension, as do coalitions between gay men and lesbians, and larger 'queer' political coalitions. These tensions suggest that queer culture, whatever its setbacks and challenges, is more varied, vibrant and visible than ever before in American culture.

The 1950s to early 1960s

The stereotype of queer culture during the 1950s and early 1960s is one of repression, invisibility and violence. While these were key components of gay life, the era also developed the institutions that would become the backbone of later visibility and activism: bars, identified urban neighbourhoods, sports leagues and other civic institutions. One of the most striking aspects of these queer counter-publics was, and is, their role as a meeting place for the marginal. Drag queens, sex workers and the transgendered mingled with butches and femmes, tops and bottoms, in gay bars, providing a tenuous community that was always at risk of violent repression by the police.

Queer political activism also began during this period. Early activist organizations included the **Mattachine Society**, formed in 1950 in Los Angeles; the **Daughters of Bilitis**, formed in San Francisco; and the Homophile League of New York, the first mixed homosexual activist group, formed in the 1960s. Alfred Kinsey's work on sexuality exposed a liberated underside to perceived 1950s conformity, including a shocking percentage of men who had had same-sex encounters.

In literary culture, queer culture was present in both open and coded ways – and usually associated with other forms of marginality and rebellion. The Beats challenged the conformity of the 1950s, thinking beyond the suburban nuclear family to other, freer choices. Sexual non-conformity was a recurring theme in their writing, both implicitly (Jack Kerouac and Neal Cassady's relationship bubbled up in the margins of their prose) and explicitly, with Allen Ginsberg's *Howl* (1956) bravely proclaiming homosexual desire. Gore **Vidal**, later known for his historical and political novels of America, wrote openly, and non-tragically, of gay relationships and desire in his 1948 novel, *The Pillar and the Salt* (1948).

Southern expatriates, meanwhile, negotiated the 'open secret' of gay identity in their writing and lives. Truman **Capote**, best known for *Breakfast at Tiffany's* (1958) and *In Cold Blood* (1966), wrote about gay themes in *Other Voices, Other Rooms* (1948). As important, however, was his public persona of eccentric, fey dandy, a coded gay icon. Carson McCullers, a close friend of Capote's, wrote of unconventional relationships in her first novel, *The Heart is a Lonely Hunter* (1940), even as she negotiated affairs with both men and women. Tennessee **Williams** became one of America's most honoured playwrights; *The Glass Menagerie* (1944), *Cat on a Hot Tin Roof* (1955) and *A Streetcar Named Desire* (1947) feature primitive violence and suppressed desires seething under the surface of modern life. Although rarely addressed explicitly, homosexual desire also seeps through in his drama, challenging 1950s conventional facades.

James **Baldwin** epitomizes the possibilities and contradictions of gay writers during the

1950s. Baldwin was one of the most honoured and provocative writers of the 1950s and 1960s. He became the most visible voice of black America during the rising foment of the civil rights movement, electrifying readers with works such as *Notes of a Native Son* (1955), *Nobody Knows My Name* (1961) and *The Fire Next Time* (1963). Baldwin's homosexuality became another influence in his work, from the white narrator of *Giovanni's Room* (1956), whose denial and self-hatred leads to his lover's demise, to the complex sexual and racial identities in *Another Country* (1962). For Baldwin, sexual identity was less important than the racial realities of Jim Crow America, and yet it was a crucial part of himself that he refused to gloss over. His honesty won him snubs from mainstream civil rights activists, who disparagingly referred to him as 'Martin Luther Queen', and radicals such as Eldridge Cleaver who attacked his 'perfumed prose' in graphic homophobic language.

Gay and lesbian pulp fiction provided dramatic stereotypes of queer life that were meant to titillate and repel, entertaining commuters with exotic, sensational stories of vice while punishing homosexuals in the last chapter. Gays and lesbians used these mainstream creations to their advantage, often skipping the final retaliatory chapter while retaining the scenes of liberated debauchery for their own purposes. And some writers, both famous and obscure, challenged the obligatory tragic ending. In a well-known example, Patricia **Highsmith** wrote a happy ending to *The Price of Salt* (aka *Carol*, 1952) under a pseudonym. But, as John Howard notes in *Men Like That* (1999), even obscure pulp fiction writers such as Mississippi's Carl Corley resisted, writing under their own names and allowing endings other than the homosexual suicide/homicide myth. These 'queer' readings of mainstream culture often included rewritings of popular culture; Captain Kirk/Spock erotica circulated in gay circles

during the early 1960s, leading to the gay and lesbian fan fiction of the 1990s. More public expressions of gay culture were left to writers such as Ginsberg, Baldwin and Vidal until gay activism burst on the scene at the end of the 1960s.

The late 1960s to the 1970s

Queer activism during the 1970s has been characterized by a single word: Stonewall. Certainly, the events at the Stonewall Inn in Greenwich Village – in which gay patrons resisted a customary police raid on the day of Judy Garland's funeral, forcing the police inside the bar, setting it on fire and starting three days of riots in the Village – galvanized a generation of gay and lesbian activists to become more visible and more demanding than ever before. Inspired by the political radicalism of the 1960s, and specifically the Black Power movement, activists created multiple queer publics that interacted with, and sometimes antagonized, more mainstream publics. Many institutions that had existed tenuously, such as gay bars, became more visible and more protected, and other markers of gay culture were created during this period, including Gay Pride marches and gay and lesbian bookstores. Drawing on the Black Power phrase, 'Black is Beautiful', activists rallied under the slogan 'Gay is Good'.

The most sensational of these public displays involved expressions of sexuality that lay outside of heterosexual monogamy. The stereotype of the promiscuous 'homosexual lifestyle' crystallized during the sexual liberation of the 1970s. **New York** and San Francisco were the two anchors for a national gay culture that promised sexual freedom and facilitated anonymous sexual encounters in semi-public places such as bars, parks and **bathhouses**. *Tales of the City* (1978), a series of novels by Armistead **Maupin**, captures the ethos of this ideal. San Francisco is a Mecca not only for gay men but for iconoclasts of all sorts, including

Midwestern farm girls, transgendered men and women, 1960s radicals and cult leaders – in other words, transgressors of cultural, racial, gender and sexual boundaries. *Tales of the City*'s publication in the *San Francisco Chronicle* marked the increasingly mixed audience for gay fiction. In New York City, another group of gay writers emphasized a starker view of urban gay life. John **Rechy** shocked audiences with his autobiographical description of the life of a hustler in *City of Night* (1963); Felice Picano's *The Lure* (1979) was a dark thriller that took New York gay culture as the site for violence and murder; Andrew Holleran's *The Dancer From the Dance* (1978) explored a young man's search for love through the varied, and sometimes perverse, gay sites of New York.

While queer transgression defined gay culture during the 1970s, lesbian culture embraced a more political and gender-specific notion of queer identity. Rather than emphasizing inversion and **butch/femme** relationships, lesbian feminism theorized lesbianism as the ultimate expression of female identity. As Eve Kosofsky Sedgwick (1990: 36) argues about lesbian feminism: 'women who loved women were seen as *more* female'. The most famous articulation of this appeared in *Compulsory Heterosexuality and Lesbian Existence* by Adrienne **Rich**, in which she coined the term 'lesbian continuum' to describe the different kinds of women's relationships, from friendship to sexual expression. Lesbian feminism built feminist coalitions extremely well, but many of its assumptions based around lesbian identity and sexuality would be severely challenged by queer activists.

Feminist novels featured many lesbian writers, from popular works to experimental. The most famous lesbian novel of the 1970s is *Rubyfruit Jungle* (1973) by Rita Mae **Brown**, a picaresque coming-of-age novel that rejects self-loathing for confident sexual adventuring. Bertha Harris explored lesbian desire in her experimental *Lover*,

featuring what Harris terms 'the sexually subversive elite', an evocative celebration of women's sexual pleasure. Joanna Russ reformed the often phallocentric genre of science-fiction in *The Female Man* (1975), with complex pairings of four women who challenge gender and sexual boundaries. Isabel Miller even appropriated romance in her historical novel *Patience and Sarah* (1972). The 1977 novel *The Color Purple* by Alice **Walker** featured rural Southern black life and broken linguistic, cultural and sexual boundaries; at its centre is a romantic love triangle in which the two women, Celie and Shug, end up together. Although the lesbian content has often been subsumed by its racial import, *The Color Purple* explored both simultaneously, much as Baldwin did in his fiction and elegant prose.

The 1980s to the present day

Queer culture changed profoundly with the outbreak of AIDS during the 1980s. The sexual liberation of the late 1960s and 1970s had provided the means for the tragically efficient transmission of the disease. The conservative backlash against glbt culture that began with Ronald Reagan's election in 1980 withheld both crucial research funds and sympathy, using the 'gay disease' as evidence of God's punishment and the superiority of heterosexual monogamy. AIDS made gay culture both visible and toxic to mainstream America, which figured queer sexuality as inherently deadly even as hundreds of thousands of gay men died, unmourned and neglected outside the gay community.

The societal and governmental neglect of people with AIDS led to a new militancy in queer culture. Groups such as ACT UP and **Queer Nation** staged public protests in government buildings, restaurants and neighbourhoods to challenge middle-class respectability and hypocrisy. One consequence of AIDS activism is that gays and lesbians were more likely to see themselves as allies, unlike during the 1970s, when many lesbians saw their primary allegiance as being to other women rather than to gay men, while gay men often ignored lesbians. Queer activists and academics, by contrast, assumed that gay men and lesbians shared a common experience by being defined as 'queer' in mainstream culture. Tony Kushner's Pulitzer Prize-winning *Angels in America* (1993), which brought AIDS and AIDS activism to Broadway, writes gay identity into the mainstream of American politics, religion and culture, and insists upon the visibility of gays as citizens. In addition, famous radical activists such as Angela **Davis** came out in the 1990s, further queering radical activism.

Gay and lesbian writers inhabit the broadest cultural spectrum imaginable. Postmodern writer Kathy **Acker** continues the tradition of Bertha Harris, weaving lesbian desire into complicated literary experiments. David Leavitt, a *New Yorker*-published writer while still in college, writes social novels in which the voice of the gay narrator dominates. Sarah Schulman's New York novels combine gritty urban realism with political activism, promoting an uncompromising denunciation of middle-class America. Michael Cunningham's haunting family dramas found critical acclaim in his homage to Virginia Woolf, *The Hours* (1998). Carol Anshaw, with novels such as *Seven Moves* (1997) and *Lucky in the Corner* (2003), writes complex investigations of desire, commitment and relationships that rework simpler, liberating, coming-out narratives.

Popular culture has also continued to accommodate gay and lesbian writers. E. Lynn **Harris**, whose autobiographical fiction began with *Invisible Life* (1991), has taken his stories of black gay life to the very highest levels of the best-seller list. His is the most well-known of a score of auto-biographical **coming-out novels** that continue to appeal to gay and lesbian readers.

The genre has expanded to explore other 'queer' identities, notably transgendered identity, with *Stone Butch Blues* (1993) by Leslie **Feinberg**, a devastating portrait of coming of age, and into male identification, in working-class Buffalo, New York State.

Genre fiction is another productive site for gay and lesbian writers. Samuel **Delany**, an African-American writer, began exploring queer sexualities during the 1960s with *Babel-17* (1966) and has continued challenging science-fiction readers with novels such as *Dhalgren* (1974) and trenchant essays of queer sexuality and race. Nicola Griffith began her science-fiction career with the women-only *Ammonite* (1993) and has moved to hard-boiled crime in *The Blue Place* (1999). Lesbian detective fiction continues to be a vibrant category of genre fiction, evolving into queer identities such as Barbara Wilson's *Gaudi Afternoon* (1990).

The tensions between older and newer definitions of 'queer culture', among multiple and sometimes contradictory publics, continue into the new millennium. Such competing visions of gay and lesbian identity are a sign of gay and lesbian literature's successful engagement with American public life.

See also: Acker, Kathy; ACT UP; Black glbtq literature; Cunningham, Michael; Homophile movement; Kinsey, Alfred; Kushner, Tony; Schulman, Sarah

Bibliography

Sedgwick, Eve Kosovsky (1990) *Epistemology of the Closet*, Berkeley: University of California Press.

Warner, Michael (2002) *Publics and Counterpublics*, New York: Zone Books, 2002.

Further reading

Farwell, Marilyn (1996) *Heterosexual Plots and Lesbian Narratives*, New York and London: New York University Press.

Haggerty, George and Zimmerman, Bonnie (eds) (1995) *Professions of Desire: Gay and*

Lesbian Studies in Literature, New York: Modern Language Association.

Summers, Claude J. (ed.) (1995) *The Gay and Lesbian Literary Heritage: A Reader's Companion to the Writers and their Works, from Antiquity to the Present*, New York: Henry Holt.

Woods, Gregory (1999) *A History of Gay Literature: The Male Tradition*, New Haven: Yale University Press.

Zimmerman, Bonnie (1990) *The Safe Sea of Women: Lesbian Fiction, 1969–1989*, Boston: Beacon Press.

JAIME HARKER

URBAN BUSH WOMEN

modern dance company

Urban Bush Women is an all-women's modern dance company founded by Jawole Willa Jo Zollar (b. 1950). After studying dance at Florida State University, Zollar worked with Dianne McIntyre and her company, Sounds in Motion. Zollar formed Urban Bush Women in 1984, and critics immediately hailed her work for its dynamic presentation of the poetic and harsh realities facing African-American women. The company's postmodern approach mixes modern and jazz choreography with vocal production, autobiographical storytelling, and Caribbean and African rhythms. Based in Brooklyn, the company also conducts workshops on making dance theatre from women's experience at Florida State University, where Zollar is a Professor of Dance. Their feminist work includes *Bones and Ash: A Gilda Story* (1995), which explores relationships among lesbian vampires across a century of American history, and *Shelter* (1988), which offers an account of life on the street for homeless women.

THOMAS F. DEFRANTZ

URBAN CENTRES

Urban centres are the material sites where articulated sexual cultures, categories, identities and politics were all invented, and crucial material sites where these phenomena continue to be (re)produced and struggled over.

The very categories 'homosexual' and 'heterosexual' were inventions of the nineteenth-century industrial city, made possible by the rise of wage labour, mass production and commodity consumption. Wage labour and mass production displaced the family from its position as a unit of production, materially freeing individuals from traditional kinship bonds and formation; it became conceivable to live outside the bonds of marriage and family in industrialized cities (Adam 1996; D'Emilio 1983a). The concomitant growth of a consumer culture, stimulated by a new mass media and advertising, entailed the creation of newly desiring subjects and the promise of pleasure in the form of commodity consumption. This valorization of pleasure, self-gratification and personal satisfaction made it possible to conceive of sexuality in terms of object choice – heterosexual v. homosexual – rather than in terms of prior gender-defined roles (Hennessy, 2000).

All of this played out in an urban context where it was possible to socialize, oftentimes in public and commercial spaces, outside the purview of the family. In these contexts people fashioned same-sex or otherwise queer sexual and social networks, sexual identities, sexual subcultures and sexual politics. To the extent that these spaces became visible to the dominant culture, they attracted ever more people, including people who would migrate to them from rural areas (Boyd, 2003; Chauncey, 1994; D'Emilio, 1983b; Laumann *et al.*, 2004).

See also: Ghetto, gay

Bibliography

Adam, Barry D. (1996) 'Structural Foundations of the Gay World', in Steven Seidman (ed.) *Queer Theory/Sociology*, London: Blackwell.

Boyd, Nan Alamilla (2003) *Wide Open Town: A History of Queer San Francisco to 1965*, Berkeley: University of California Press.

Chauncey, George (1994) *Gay New York: Gender, Urban Culture, and the Making of the Gay Male World 1890–1940*, New York: Basic Books.

D'Emilio, John (1983a). 'Capitalism and Gay Identity', in Ann Snitow, Christine Stansell and Sharon Thompson (eds) *Powers of Desire: The Politics of Sexuality*, New York: Monthly Review Press.

—— (1983b) *Sexual Politics, Sexual Communities: The Making of a Homosexual Minority in the United States, 1940–1970*, Chicago: University of Chicago Press.

Hennessy, Rosemary (2000) 'Cultural Study, Commodity Logic, Sexual Subjects', in *Profit and Pleasure: Sexual Identities in Late Capitalism*, London: Routledge.

Laumann, Edward O., Ellingson, Stephen, Mahay, Jenna, Paik, Anthony and Youm, Yoosik (2004) *The Sexual Organization of the City*, Chicago: University of Chicago Press.

Further reading

Bell, David and Valentine, Gill (eds) (1995) *Mapping Desire: Geographies of Sexualities*, London: Routledge.

Bech, Henning (1997) *When Men Meet: Homosexuality and Modernity*, trans. Teresa Mesquit and Tim Davies, Chicago: University of Chicago Press.

Faderman, Lilian (1991) *Odd Girls Out and Twilight Lovers: A History of Lesbian Life in Twentieth-Century America*, New York: Columbia University Press.

Ingram, Gordon Brent, Bouthillette, Anne-Marie and Retter Yolanda (eds) (1997) *Queers in Space – Communities, Public Places, Sites of Resistance*, Seattle: Bay Press.

Kennedy, Elizabeth and Davis, Madeline D. (1993) *Boots of Leather, Slippers of Gold: The History of a Lesbian Community*, New York: Routledge.

JEFFREY EDWARDS

V

VACCARO, JOHN

performance artist

John Vaccaro was born to Italian parents in a small town in Ohio. He studied at Ohio State University and became involved in the arts there before moving to New York City. He began working as an actor with the American Poets' Theater Company and appeared in underground films, including *Normal Love* (1964) by Jack Smith. In 1966 he teamed up with Ronald **Tavel** to direct two of Tavel's plays, *Shower* and *The Life of Juanita Castro*. The sets for the production were done by Smith. Although the exact history of this period is clouded by subsequent disagreements among all the parties involved and by rival claims to fame, it seems clear that out of this collaboration was born the Theater of the Ridiculous (see **Ludlam**, Charles), one of the most important developments in American theatre in the 1960s and 1970s. Vaccaro went on to direct and act in many productions on the New York off-Broadway scene, including several plays by Kenneth Bernard.

DANIEL HENDRICKSON

VACHON, CHRISTINE

b. 1962

film producer

A key figure in American independent filmmaking, Vachon has produced some of contemporary cinema's leading gay and lesbian-themed features, particularly within the 1990s New Queer Cinema movement. Openly lesbian, her projects typically address gay, lesbian, and transgender themes, frequently inciting controversy. Her first major producing success was Todd Haynes' homoerotic triptych *Poison* (1991), which won the Sundance Grand Jury Prize and attracted criticism from the American Family Association. Vachon continued to work with Haynes, producing *Safe* (1995), *Velvet Goldmine* (1998) and *Far From Heaven* (2002). Vachon's other notable projects include Tom Kalin's *Swoon* (1992), Rose Troche's *Go Fish* (1994), Nigel Finch's *Stonewall* (1995), Mary Harron's *I Shot Andy Warhol* (1996), Todd Solondz's *Happiness* (1998), Kimberly Peirce's *Boys Don't Cry* (1999), an Oscar-winning biopic about murdered transsexual Brandon Teena, John Cameron Mitchell's *Hedwig and the Angry Inch* (2001), Todd Graff's *Camp* (2003) and World of Wonder's Fenton Bailey and Randy Barbato's *Party Monster* (2003).

See also: Finch, Nigel; Haynes, Todd; Kalin, Tom; Mitchell, John Cameron; New Queer Cinema, International; Solondz, Todd; Troche, Rose

JOHN FORDE

VAID, URVASHI

b. 1958

activist, writer

Urvashi Vaid was born in India and moved to the United States with her family at the

age of eight. A long-time community organizer and grassroots activist, Vaid has been
involved in the progressive, glbtq and feminist movements since the early 1980s. Her
most prominent position was as executive
director of the **National Gay and Lesbian
Task Force** (NGLTF), one of the nation's
oldest and most influential gay rights organizations. She served as executive director
of the NGLTF for three years, from 1989
to 1992. Then in 1992 she resigned her
position to work on a book, *Virtual Equality*, which was published in 1995. In 1997
she returned to NGLTF as Director of its
Policy Institute, a position she held until
2001 when she left to become a programme office at the Ford Foundation.
Vaid has not limited her community service
to glbtq rights. She is a former staff attorney
with the **American Civil Liberties Union**
(ACLU), where she worked on behalf of
prisoners as part of the ACLU's National
Prison Project.

SURINA KHAN

VALCÁRCEL, ROBERTO

b. 1951

multimedia artist

The contemporary multimedia artist
Roberto Valcárcel is deliberately cryptic
about his oeuvre and private life; he prefers
to let the audience interpret his life and
work with as little information directly
provided by the artist as possible. Deliberately overriding any labels, Valcárcel stylistically recreates himself continually. While
mainstream art critics and scholars consciously omit a discussion of homoerotic
and gay cultural references in his work, the
knowing eye views Valcárcel's work as in
keeping with a camp aesthetic that blatantly
plays with and subverts heterocentrist gender and sexual expectations. His refusal to
offer a total interpretation of his work
allows it to obtain mainstream recognition
in a homophobic third-world Bolivia, but

also allows for appropriation from its
underground gay subculture. The most
well-known example of his work is his
exhibit *Gayshas*, in which he painted geishas who, upon closer inspection, turned
out to be men in drag. All the paintings
were sold and currently reside in homes of
respected and public figures who ignore the
queer subtext.

PEDRO ALBORNOZ

VALENTINO

b. 1932

fashion designer

Among the most famous of Italy's fashion
designers, Valentino Clemente Ludovico
Garavani was born in Voghera, north of
Milan. He opened his first atelier on Via
Condotti, Rome, at the beginning of the
1960s during the so-called *dolce vita* era. His
worldwide success came in 1962 when his
first show in Florence was welcomed as a
sign of genius and quickly celebrated by the
international press. In 1967 the famous 'V'
first appeared, soon becoming a global
symbol of elegance and luxury. In 1990,
aided by his friend Elizabeth Taylor,
Valentino founded the association, LIFE, to
assist HIV+ people.

ALBERTO EMILETTI

VALK, MAPS

b. 1917

writer

Maps Valk wrote an intriguing lesbian
novel, *Mijn vriendin Jacoba* (My Friend
Jacoba, 1960), which describes a close
friendship between an adolescent girl and
her formidable English teacher in the context of a boarding school. Jacoba is both
feared and admired by the older girls, one
of whom, each year, is singled out as
'favourite'. Sporting mannish looks, Jacoba
excels as a teacher of modern literature and

is a devoted intellectual, working on her dissertation. The first-person narrator describes Jacoba as similar to her father. When the narrator 'sees' Jacoba with another woman, she suddenly becomes aware of her lesbianism, and is deeply shocked. In an interesting literary turn, she distances herself from the teacher in a very cruel way, pretending to have slept with a boy and asking Jacoba to cover up for her. Although the story appears to be written from a heterosexual perspective, and the lesbian threat is ostensibly warded off, the subtext shows the narrator's profound attachment to Jacoba and her desire to follow in her footsteps in more ways than one. The feelings of guilt resulting from her betrayal of Jacoba keep nagging her long after their separation. In the novel's final sentence, the narrator retrospectively refers to Jacoba as her 'lover'.

MAAIKE MEIJER

VAN SANT, GUS
b. 1952
film director, screenwriter

One of the leading figures of the New Queer Cinema movement, Van Sant's portraits of alienation and sexual ambivalence have won him a dedicated gay fan base. Born in Louisville, Kentucky, he rose to fame with *Drugstore Cowboy* (1989), a gritty story about drug addicts. *My Own Private Idaho* (1991) starred River Phoenix and Keanu Reeves as young gay hustlers in a doomed love affair. After abandoning a project about gay politician Harvey Milk, Van Sant made the lesbian-themed *Even Cowgirls Get The Blues* (1993). In *Good Will Hunting* (1997), he teased out the homoerotic subtext in a story of heterosexual male friendship, winning a Best Director Academy Award nomination. His shot-for-shot remake of Hitchcock's *Psycho* (1998) included outing the Lila Crane character as a lesbian. *Elephant* (2003), a drama inspired by the Columbine shootings, won the Palme d'Or

prize at Cannes. He has also published a novel, *Pink* (1997), music albums and collaborated on projects with William S. Burroughs.

See also: New Queer Cinema, International

JOHN FORDE

VANILLA SEX

An expression used, often satirically or derogatorily, to describe sex between gay or heterosexual partners which is gentle and conventional, and which does not feature sexual practices such as role play, domination, bondage, **sadomasochism**, **leather** or **water sports**.

JOHN FORDE

VEBER, FRANCIS
b. 1937
director

A prolific French screenwriter and director, Francis Veber has been the force behind some of the most popular comedy films of contemporary French cinema. After honing his writing skills with comic scripts for radio and TV, Veber earned enormous success as a screenwriter of major film hits of the 1970s such as *Le Grand blond avec une chaussure noire* (*The Tall Blond Man With One Black Shoe*) and the international smash *La Cage aux folles*. The latter's combination of high farce, queerness and sexual confusion became a recurrent theme of Veber's work, revisited in subsequent efforts such as *Partners* (1982) and *Le Placard* (*The Closet*, 2001). While criticized by some for his use of broad gay stereotypes, Veber is championed by others for unsettling sexual hierarchies through farcical inversion. Since the 1990s, Veber has been actively involved in remaking many of his French hits for US audiences, for example *The Birdcage* (1996), a remake of *La Cage aux folles*.

BRETT FARMER

VELVET UNDERGROUND

See: Reed, Lou and the Velvet Underground

VERHOEVEN, PAUL

b. 1938

film director

Born in Amsterdam during the early years of the Second World War, Paul Verhoeven has emerged as one of the most provocative, controversial and misunderstood directors working in Hollywood today. His interest in film began while working as a documentary filmmaker for the Royal Dutch Navy's Marine Film Service in the 1960s, and he is credited with directing some of the most successful Dutch films ever made. However, he is more widely known for such notorious headline-grabbing shockers as *Spetters* (1980), with its graphic male rape scene, and gay psychological thriller *The Fourth Man* (*De Vierde Man*, 1983). An obsession with 'deviant' sexuality permeates most of Verhoeven's oeuvre and, after re-locating to Hollywood in the mid-1980s, accusations of homophobia that had dogged his earlier Dutch films reached crisis point with the 1992 release of his psychotic lesbian thriller *Basic Instinct*. Although later reclaimed for its political subversiveness by queer film academics, the film was initially greeted with violent protest throughout the US from gay activist group the **Gay and Lesbian Alliance Against Defamation** (GLAAD), and subsequently became the most commercially successful film of the year. Controversy followed again with his next film *Showgirls* (1995), featuring yet another pathological and predatory lesbian, but this time it was met with universal derision, and is still unanimously regarded as one of the worst films ever made.

ROBIN GRIFFITHS

VERSACE, GIANNI

b. 1946; d. 1997

fashion designer

Born in Reggio di Calabria, Italy, Versace started his career as a fashion designer in 1972 and presented his first signed collection in 1978. During the 1980s, Versace began a fortuitous cooperation with photographers such as Richard Avedon and artist Maurice Bejart. Versace became an active costume designer for the Teatro alla Scala of Milan and many other important theatres. These collaborations highlight the attention Versace gave to the arts, media and new technologies in relation to his fashion design. Through the years, numerous articles, books and awards have celebrated the genius of a creator who successfully merged fashion and art, producing a unique style. Versace never hid his homosexuality and lived openly with his lover of many years, Antonio D'Amico. In July 1997 he was gunned down in Miami, Florida. Some weeks later the man suspected of his killing, Andrew Cunanan, was found dead, an evident suicide.

ALBERTO EMILETTI

VERSTRATEN, PAUL

actor, director

Dutch-born actor and director who with his partner Eric De Kuyper has made a number of homoerotically themed films. Verstraten starred in *Naughty Boys* (1983), which won the 1984 Netherlands Film Festival's Jury Prize. This was followed by *Casta Diva* (1983), a silent film following the erotically charged choreography of Verstraten and other actors dressing, undressing and dancing. Verstraten and De Kuyper co-directed *A Strange Love Affair* (1985), a gay love story between an American film teacher and a young Dutch athlete. Evocatively shot in black and white, the film pays homage to Hollywood melodrama, including camp classic *Johnny Guitar* (1954) starring Joan **Crawford**.

JOHN FORDE

VIDAL, GORE

b. 1925

writer

A prolific novelist, playwright, screen-writer and essayist, Gore Vidal is one of America's most distinguished writers. His grandfather was a co-founder and first Senator of the state of Oklahoma and he is related by marriage to both the late Jacqueline Kennedy and former vice-president Al Gore.

After a private school education and military service abroad, he wrote *The City and the Pillar* (1948), a dark, semi-autobiographical novel that takes place in Hollywood and concerns a young gay man's love for a school friend. Shocking critics on its release, the novel became an international best seller. Other novels include *Messiah* (1955), *Julian* (1964) and *Myra Breckinridge* (1968), a satiric comedy parodying the cult of Hollywood film stardom, featuring a movie-obsessed female-to-male transsexual intent on seducing and destroying mankind (1970).

During the 1950s Vidal wrote plays for live television and film screenplays for MGM. His adaptation of Tennessee Williams' play, *Suddenly Last Summer* (1959), retained a compelling queer sensibility, despite heavy censorship of its homosexual themes. Vidal claims he persuaded director William Wyler to insert a gay subtext into *Ben-Hur* (1959), instructing actor Stephen Boyd to act as if Messala was in love with Charlton Heston's unwitting Ben-Hur. An accomplished essayist, Vidal won the 1993 National Book Award for his collection *United States: Essays, 1952–1992*. His memoir, *Palimpsest*, was published in 1995.

A writer of immense intelligence, poise and wit, Vidal's work eloquently defends individual rights, questions cultural assumptions about gender, reproduction and population control, and displays both a contempt for and fascination with popular culture.

JOHN FORDE

VILANCH, BRUCE

b. 1948

writer, actor, comedian

Born in New York City and raised in Patterson, New Jersey, this one-time child model wrote on entertainment for the *Chicago Tribune* until 1970 when, after his review of Bette Midler, she was so impressed that she asked Vilanch to write for her. Soon after, Vilanch moved to Los Angeles, where he worked with other comedians (Richard Pryor, Lily Tomlin, Joan Rivers, Whoopi Goldberg and Billy Crystal). As a comedy writer, Vilanch gained even more acclaim, writing for the Academy Awards. But in 1993 the jokes he penned for Ted Danson's widely criticized appearance in blackface at a Friars Club roast of Whoopi Goldberg cast a temporary shadow over his career. Finally, in 1998, Vilanch became a full-time TV personality with regular appearances on *Hollywood Squares*. In 2000 he appeared Off-Broadway in *Bruce Vilanch: Almost Famous*, a title that may well describe his celebrity status until he found fame as 'Edna Turnblad' in the touring production of the John Waters' creation *Hairspray* (2003).

GABRIEL GOMEZ

VILLAGE PEOPLE

pop group

American **disco** group noted for its camp imagery and satirical songs. One of the music industry's most audacious marketing ploys, the Village People were created by entrepreneur Jacques Morali in a bid to exploit the sizeable gay audience for disco music in the 1970s. After successfully pitching his idea for a 'gay disco group' to Casablanca Records in 1977, Morali set about refining and realizing his vision. He named the group after Greenwich Village, the predominantly gay neighbourhood of New York City, and styled its six members upon caricatured figures of gay erotic iconography such as the cowboy, biker, soldier, policeman and construction worker. This sense of playful camp parody further extended to the group's musical material. Songwriters Phil Hurtt and Peter Whitehead were contracted to compose material with thinly veiled gay subtexts and allusions. The result was songs such as 'San Francisco', 'Macho Man', 'In the Navy' and 'YMCA' that not only proved popular with gay audiences but achieved major crossover success, climbing to the top of mainstream pop charts around the world. Whether the teenyboppers and suburban radio listeners who consumed their music in the millions fully gleaned its homoerotic significance is debatable but, for much of the late 1970s, the Village People were an iconic part of the general pop culture. Although the group's fortunes took a downward turn with the demise of disco in the early 1980s, they have continued to perform, albeit with variant line-ups, trading on their 1970s popularity and repertoire.

BRETT FARMER

VIRGIN OF GUADALUPE

The traditional image of the Virgin of Guadalupe has been revised by many Chicana artists and feminists to inspire social change, especially with regards to gender roles (see **López**, Yolanda).

DANIEL ENRIQUE PÉREZ

VISCONTI, LUCHINO
b. 1906; d. 1976
theatre, opera and film director

Luchino Visconti was one of the most prominent Italian filmmakers; he is also considered a quintessential figure of gay aestheticism. Born in Milan into a long-standing aristocratic family from France, he became familiar with the Marxist intelligentsia. When he moved to Rome he directed his masterpiece of Italian neo-realism, *Ossessione* (Obsession, 1943). This film, based on James Cain's American novel, *The Postman Always Rings Twice* (1934), did not lack in gay nuance and was banned by fascist censors. Even in post-fascist Italy Visconti was frequently censored by the Christian Democratic Government on moralistic and political grounds.

As a theatre director he alternated innovative productions of classics with contemporary, controversial authors (Tennessee **Williams**, Jean **Cocteau**, Arthur Miller). Focused on expressionistic theatricality, his opera productions, together with the gay icon Maria **Callas**, had a revolutionary impact. Following other neo-realistic movies (among them *Rocco e i suoi fratelli* (*Rocco and His Brothers*) [1960], a Dostoevskyan story about immigration packed with gay undertones), he directed the films, *Senso* (*Livia*, 1954) and *Il Gattopardo* (*The Leopard*, 1963) in which he explored death and decadence with morbid and melodramatic overtones. Visconti's trend in melodrama and decadence reached its climax with his German trilogy *La caduta degli dei* (*The Damned*, 1969), centring on the beginning of the Nazi period and featuring an openly gay character; *Morte a Venezia* (*Death in Venice*, 1971), taken from Thomas Mann's novel on paederastic love; and *Ludwig* (1972), the telling of the Bavarian arch-camp crazy and scandalous gay prince. Famous for his manic reconstructions, the core of his work rests in his obsessions with queer culture: melodrama, excessive passions and empathy for a pompous past defeated by history.

MASSIMO FUSILLO

VLEUGEL, GUUS

b. 1932; d. 1998

playwright, composer

Guus Vleugel was born on 29 April 1932 in Goes, the Netherlands. He earned his fame writing for the theatre. Vleugel was a merciless observer of the rapid developments in society during his time. He was also a songwriter, his lyrics combining humour with poignant commentary.

Vleugel studied Dutch and French literature. He published poetry under the pseudonym Guus Valleide. In 1962 he wrote for the radical cabaret group Lurelei, attacking traditional ideas concerning religion, royalty and social behaviour. Although Vleugel himself made no secret of his homosexuality throughout his career, Lurelei never specifically stressed homosexual topics, but rather dealt critically with sexual hypocrisy in general.

Vleugel received a literary award in 1973 (C.W.van der Hoogt prijs). After taking time off following a serious mental breakdown, he returned to the spotlight in 1982 with a number of novels, as well as controversial plays, co-written with his new partner Ton Vorstenbosch. One of the latter focused on the influence of Islam on feminism and gay rights. He died of lung cancer on 12 August 1998.

WARD SCHRIJVER

VNS MATRIX

VNS Matrix is a group of cyberfeminist artists and activists formed in Adelaide, Australia, in 1991, by Josephine Starrs, Julianne Pierce, Francesca da Rimini and Virginia Barratt. With creative use of digital technologies and cyberspace the work of

VNS Matrix can be seen as the epitome of cyberfeminist philosophy – as a positive but also critical and ironical attitude to the ever-more problematic relations between gender, body, technology and power.

MONICA BARONI

VOGUING

A cultural practice raising issues of race, sex, authenticity, the mainstream and the subculture, 'voguing balls' were the rage in 1980s Harlem among gay black and Latino men. Voguing balls were drag competitions that campily appropriated the style of glamorous fashion shows and magazines so as to reward the best costume and pose struck on the improvised runways. Rooted in the New York black drag balls of the 1960s and the 1970s gay disco club communities, by the end of the 1980s voguing had moved beyond the enclosed circle of gay **New York**. While Jennie Livingston's reportage, *Paris is Burning* (filmed in 1987–8, aired in 1990), first exposed a wider audience to voguing, Madonna's pop song 'Vogue' (1991), with its highly stylized video featuring men doing just that, introduced the sensational, alluring poses of gay voguers to the MTV audience. The remarkable success of both video and song – an immediate dance floor hymn – made it an extremely popular, albeit faddish, dance style all over the world.

See also: Madonna

FABIO CLETO

VOLCANO, DEL LAGRACE

b. 1957

photographer

Born in California as Debra Dianne Wood, Volcano lives in London, where she was well known as lesbian photographer Della Grace until the mid-1990s. She then

601

became **intersex** and took the name Del LaGrace Volcano, defining herself as a 'gender terrorist', as someone who 'consistently and intentionally subverts, destabilizes and challenges the binary gender system'. In her process of metamorphosis Volcano embodies the same changes occurring within the queer community and the more general historical-cultural transformations around and within sexuality as the twentieth century came to a close. Her photos bear witness to this process of personal and cultural mutation, showing the changes in her body after taking hormones and enacting gender performance – in particular of masculinity – while documenting glbtq demonstrations, scenes from queer bars, female-to-male cross-dressing, butch dykes and drag king contests in San Francisco, London, New York, Berlin and Paris.

MONICA BARONI

W

WADDELL, TOM

b. 1937; d. 1987

athlete, activist

Tom Waddell is remembered for his out-standing contributions to sport, medicine and gay and lesbian activism. Born to Elmer and Marion Flubacher of Paterson, New Jersey, Tom took the family name of mentors Gene and Hazel Waddell, who inspired him to pursue his love of dance and gymnastics. Tom became a seasoned athlete and earned a place on the 1968 US Olympic Decathlon team. His belief that sport could transform personal lives and facilitate social and political change provided impetus for his role as founder of the **Gay Games**. Through his involvement with the Games, Tom met Sara Lewinstein, a lesbian activist who shared his desire to have a family. Tom and Sara were married and soon after gave birth to their daughter Jessica. Before he died of AIDS–related pneumonia in July 1987, Tom recorded a message for his daughter in the form of a diary.

KELLIE BURNS

WADIA, RIYAD

b. 1967; d. 2003

filmmaker

Riyad Vinci Wadia is considered India's first gay filmmaker. He began his career with the documentary *Fearless: The Hunter-wali Story* (1993) about India's legendary stunt actor Mary Evans Wadia (popularly known as Nadia), who dominated the film industry from 1935 to 1959. The adventures of the whip-cracking Nadia on horseback in films such as *Diamond Queen* (1940), *Lady Robinhood* (1946) and *Jungle Goddess* have gained iconic status for feminists and glbt cinephiles. After *Fearless*, Riyad 'came out' more explicitly with *BomGay* in 1996, a stylized avant-garde film structured around six poems by the gay poet R. Raj Rao. The film circulated widely in glbt circles and at over 50 International Film Festivals. His next film, *A Mermaid Called Aida* (1996) was a feature-length documentary on well-known transsexual Aida Banaji. Working from Mumbai and New York, Riyad remained a prolific writer, traveller and polemicist until his unexpected and premature death.

SHOHINI GHOSH

WAINWRIGHT, RUFUS

b. 1973

singer

Singer and songwriter whose baroque vocals, rich melodic compositions and witty lyrics have won him comparisons with Cole Porter, George Gershwin and Elton John. Wainwright was born on 22 July 1973 in Rhinebeck, New York. The son of folk singers Loudon Wainwright III and Kate McGarrigle, by his early teens he was performing music in the McGarrigle Sisters & Family band. He wrote a song for the children's film *Tommy Tricker and the Stamp Traveller* (1988) and publicly declared his homosexuality at age 14. Signed to Dreamworks Records in 1986, his debut, self-titled album (1988) and follow-up *Poses* (2001) were immediate successes. He made musical contributions to the films *Moulin Rouge* (2001; a melancholy torch song set to lyrics by Jean Cocteau) and *Shrek* (2001). After seeking treatment for his alcohol and drug addiction, he scored a career best with the twin albums *Want One* (2003) and *Want Two* (2004), developing his signature operatic compositions and ironic torch-song performance style. He had a cameo singing appearance in the film *The Aviator* (2004).

JOHN FORDE

WALKER, ALICE

b. 1944

writer, activist

Alice Walker's career as a scholar, writer and activist includes poetry, novels, essays and film. She is acknowledged as a founding mother of contemporary black women's studies and particularly for reclaiming Zora Neale Hurston from obscurity and developing 'womanism' as a theoretical framework.

Walker's consciousness-raising method of writing and her vernacular style have allowed her to use her life experiences as a critical lens through which she interprets such diverse issues as female genital mutilation, civil rights and lived-sexual realities. This has been a source of liberation for many readers both inside and outside academia.

Walker has also received criticism for treating black male characters too harshly. Her depiction of a same-sex relationship between black women in *The Color Purple* (1982) won her the National Book Award. Her non-fiction works include *Warrior*

Marks (1993) with Pratibha **Parmar** and *In Search of Our Mothers' Gardens* (1983) in which she developed the concept of womanism.

MICHAEL QUIETO

WALSCHAP, CARLA

b. 1932

writer

Carla Walschap, daughter of the Flemish writer Gerard Walschap, wrote the lesbian story 'Femmes Damnées' (1959), in answer to Baudelaire's famous poem with the same title. On a boat trip, the first-person narrator is seduced by a beautiful Italian woman.

Walschap's third novel, entitled *De Eskimo en de roos* (The Eskimo and the Rose, 1963) focuses on the gradual development of a lesbian relationship between the 25-year-old masseuse Claire and the fascinating Greek woman Madeleine, whose impotent husband does not mind his wife's lesbian preferences. Warm and exuberant Madeleine ('the rose' of the title), who is 10 years older than Claire ('the eskimo'), teases the latter and helps her to overcome her standoffishness and inhibitions. Despite its controversial theme, the novel was received quite favourably, and frequently compared to Simon Vestdijks' *Alpenroman* (1961) – an influential Dutch literary model of the lesbian love story at the time. What makes Walschap's contributions to lesbian literature so memorable are both the truly joyful and unproblematic presentation of lesbian desire and the fact that she succeeds in shedding all associations with the mythic mannish lesbian.

MAAIKE MEIJER

WARHOL, ANDY

b. 1928; d. 1987

artist

Born Andrew Warhola, 6 August 1928, in Pittsburgh, Pennsylvania to Czech immigrant parents, Andy Warhol would go on to become one of the most famous artists of the twentieth century, as much based upon the celebrity personae that he created for himself as for the work that he produced as a painter, photographer, film-maker, music producer and publisher.

After graduating from Carnegie Tech in 1949, Warhol moved to New York where he worked as a commercial artist, quickly becoming one of the best-known and highest paid illustrators and window dres-sers. Through his work in the fashion and design industries, he met and became friends with a host of other young gay men, who often served as models for his highly homoerotic figure drawings of male nudes. By 1960 he was gaining recognition as an artist, and from that point until the end of his life, he returned continuously to the subject of the male nude body, treating it in the most erotic and sexual of ways, and often inspired by the gay male pornography that increasingly was being produced at the time. This is most evident in the work he produced during the 1960s, especially in films such as *Sleep* (1963), *Haircut* (1963), *Blow Job* (1964), *13 Most Beautiful Boys* (1964), *Bike Boy* (1967), *Lonesome Cowboys* (1968) and *Flesh* (1968). Late-night screen-ings were attended by members of the downtown New York art and gay scenes and were an important part of a gay male **American underground cinema** in the years just prior to the gay liberation move-ment of the early 1970s.

Always surrounded by the most beautiful young men that Manhattan had to offer, Warhol documented their visits to his stu-dio by asking them point-blank to drop their pants so that he could draw pictures of their genitals in his sketchbooks, or take Polaroid photographs of them (again, often nude). The latter eventually served as the basis for the series of silk-screens *Torso* (1977) and *Sex Parts* (1978). For Warhol, sex, art and work were all various forms of trade, no one more elevated or denigrated

than any other. In blurring the moral and ideological lines that are so often drawn between art and pornography, Warhol instilled in his audience a sense that both endeavours necessarily involved the exchange of money, desire, beauty and bodies, and therefore, in the end, were really no different from each other.

In the midst of all of this attention paid to the young nude male body, Warhol crafted a personal affect that was often read, per-haps somewhat mistakenly, as asexual and cold; it might be more accurate to char-acterize it as a depersonalized erotic rapport with other bodies, situations and things, best summed up by Warhol himself when he stated that 'sex is so abstract'. Yet War-hol's abstraction, whether sexual or aes-thetic or, more importantly, both at once, was rigorously superficial in the sense of being attuned to and capable of capturing the immediate qualities and effects of the most mediated and simulated aspects of late twentieth-century society: Coca-Cola bot-tles and Campbell's Soup cans; race riots and auto wrecks; and tabloid pictures of Hollywood celebrities. For Warhol, this openness extended to include being the most 'out' visual artist, exhibiting in public a social-sexual sensibility that was at once camp, affectless and seemingly without depth.

In a certain sense it might be argued that Warhol's archive was almost exclusively located in the well-stocked aisles and checkout lines of the modern American supermarket, a place that in the 1960s was still very much a female-gendered public place and extension of the domestic sphere, in particular of the kitchen and pantry as the site of women's work within the home. By locating himself so far from male-dominated spaces of labour and production, he not only transported everyday mer-chandise into the realm of serious art, but also insinuated a decidedly anti-macho dimension into post-Second World War artistic practice, troubling the masculinist rhetoric that defined artistic discourse at the time, and confusing gender codes and identifications. It is, then, particularly ironic that he would name his large, collaborative art, music and film studio space, The Factory.

An interest in the blurring of gender and sexual identities is also evidenced in Warhol's many works that refer to and depict **drag queens** and the world of cross-dressing. From the many drag queens that he cast in his films, to his series of silk-screened portraits of black queens bearing the dual-gendered, introductory title of *Ladies and Gentleman*, to his image of *Diamond Dust Shoes*, Warhol regularly turned to, and relied upon, subjects who questioned the notion of coherent and stable identities. One might even extend this drag performance to Warhol's signature platinum blond wigs, always so obviously and deliberately fake, and the hundreds of studio photographs taken by Chris Makos of Warhol dressed in wigs and makeup and in feminine poses.

Attracted to the glamour and spectacle of celebrity culture, Warhol courted and pursued friendships with some of the most well-known Hollywood, literary and fashion stars of the era, and in the process gained a celebrity status that was equal to, if not at times greater than, theirs. Many of them were already icons in gay culture (Elizabeth **Taylor**, Liza **Minnelli**, Truman **Capote**), and Warhol's large, boldly coloured, silk-screen portraits only further enshrined their iconic status. In fact one might argue that many of these celebrity personalities continue to be known and recognized in and as Warhol's portrayal of them. Each of these stars has become a Warhol, through a serially repetitive artistic process that might be understood, somewhat ironically, as a cloning of the artist in the guise of various others.

The notion of a repeatedly disguised self-presentation that at the same time does not hide anything behind or underneath its surface, so characteristic of Warhol's entire oeuvre, was perhaps most explicitly rendered in a late series of large photographic self-portraits in which his entire head and face are covered, and variously coloured, with a camouflage print design.

Only since the 1990s have scholars, critics and curators begun to consider seriously Warhol's life and work in terms of sexual and gender issues, and to redress what was, up until then, a rather consistently homophobic reception and assessment. Informed by the new academic disciplines of gay and lesbian studies and queer theory, these practitioners insist that a queer sensibility informs nearly all aspects of Warhol's life and work, and a recognition of its centrality is necessary for any proper understanding of the value and importance of his work.

Further reading

Doyle, D., Flatley, J. and Esteban Muñoz, J. (eds) (1996) *Pop Out: Queer Warhol*, Durham and London: Duke University Press.

Koch, K. (1985) *Stargazer: Andy Warhol's World and His Films*, New York: Marion Boyars.

Meyer, R. (2002) *Outlaw Representation: Censorship and Homosexuality in Twentieth-Century American Art*, London: Oxford University Press.

Silver, K.E. (1993) 'Modes of Disclosure: The Construction of Gay Identity and the Rise of Pop Art', in R. Ferguson (ed.) *Hand-painted Pop: American Art in Transition, 1955–62*, New York: Rizzoli.

Warhol, A. and Hackett, P. (1980) *POPism: The Warhol '60s*, New York: Harcourt Brace Jovanovich.

JOHN PAUL RICCO

WARING, MARILYN

b. 1952

writer, educator, political economist

In 1975 Waring became the youngest female MP in the New Zealand Parliament. In 1984 she opposed her party's position on nuclear ships visiting New Zealand ports, a position that contributed to a snap election during which her party (the National Party) was ousted from government. In 1985, after leaving politics, and in an environment where the New Zealand Homosexual Law Reform Act was being hotly debated, Waring came out as a lesbian. Shortly after, she wrote her first book, *Women, Politics and Power* (1985), which documents a male-dominated era of New Zealand political life. Her critique of economic rationalism, the undervalued labour of women and the global world order are also articulated in *Counting for Nothing: What Men Value and What Women Are Worth* (1988) and *The Three Masquerades: Equality, Work and Human Rights* (1996). Waring is a farmer, an Associate Professor in Politics and an international development consultant.

JO SMITH

WARNER, DEBORAH

b. 1959

director

Born on 12 May 1959 in Oxfordshire, England, Deborah Warner is an acclaimed stage and film director, best known for her innovative reinterpretations of Shakespeare, Beckett and Brecht, mostly in collaboration with her long-time leading lady and partner, actor Fiona **Shaw**. She started her own theatre troupe, Kick, during her twenties, winning a London Critics' Circle Theatre Award in 1985. At 28, she was one of the first women directors invited to join the Royal Shakespeare Company, winning acclaim and awards for her production of Shakespeare's *Titus Andronicus* in 1987. She aroused controversy with her productions of *Footfalls* (1994) and *Richard III* (1995), both starring Shaw as the male leads. She made her American directing debut in 1996 with an award-winning production based on T.S. Eliot's poem 'The Waste Land' starring Shaw (filmed for television in 1995). Other stage productions include *Hedda Gabler* (1991, filmed 1993), *Medea*

(2001 UK, 2003 USA) and *Julius Caesar* (2004). Her film direction includes *The Last September* (1999).

JOHN FORDE

WARNER, MICHAEL

writer, activist

Academic, author and activist who, as a spokesperson for queer activist group **Sex Panic!**, argues against the 'normalization' of gay culture. In his book *The Trouble With Normal: Sex, Politics, and the Ethics of Queer Life* (1999), he controversially took issue with activists and authors Michelangelo **Signorile**, Gabriel Rotello and Andrew **Sullivan**, arguing that they advocated a neo-conservative and sexually restrictive gay culture. He critiqued the same-sex marriage debate as a misguided attempt to sanitize queer sexuality and assimilate homosexuality into a cultural mainstream, arguing that marriage confers unfair privileges on its participants which in turn marginalizes and excludes other sexual subcultures. A staunch supporter of sexual freedom, Warner protested against the closing of sex clubs in New York and other urban centres and has written explicit accounts about the pleasures of anonymous gay sex. He has also edited *Fear of a Queer Planet: Queer Politics and Social Theory* (1993).

JOHN FORDE

WATER SPORTS

A term used as a collective expression for any sexual activity involving urination. The most common practice involves urinating on the face, body or in the mouth of one's partner, also known as a 'golden shower'. Water sports are popular in **leather**, S&M (**sadomasochism**) and fetish subcultures within both gay and straight communities.

JOHN FORDE

WATERS, JOHN

b. 1946

filmmaker

John Waters always felt that growing up gay in middle-class, 1950s Baltimore was all he needed to make the shocking 'gross out' comedy-melodramas for which he is best known. From his earliest Warhol-esque experimental short *Hag in a Black Leather Jacket* (1964), Baltimore has provided the atmospheric backdrop for his films. Populated by defiant, sometimes crazed, outsider figures and smug, sometimes crazed, bourgeois characters, Waters' films create worlds that throw together the middle class he grew up in with the counter-culture into which he fled – with very queer results. As von Sternberg had Dietrich, Waters had **Divine** (Glenn Milstead), a plus-sized actor who played major female roles in six Waters feature films: *Mondo Trasho* (1969), *Multiple Maniacs* (1970), *Pink Flamingos* (1972), *Female Trouble* (1974), *Polyester* (1981) and *Hairspray* (1988). Around Divine, Waters built up a stock company of actors which included Mink Stole, David Lochary, Edith Massey, Cookie Muller and Mary Vivian Pearce. While *Pink Flamingos*, wherein Divine and her trailer trash clan vie for the title of 'Filthiest Person Alive' with suburban baby black marketeers Connie and Raymond Marble, is perhaps the most notorious of the Divine–Waters films, most queer fans prefer *Female Trouble* – with Divine as Dawn Davenport, a juvenile delinquent who ends up in the electric chair for acting out the ideal 'Crime is Beauty' – or *Hairspray,* a relatively benign musical comedy with Divine as Edna Turnblad, the lower-middle-class mother of a teenage girl who becomes the star of a local dance show and a civil rights activist.

For all the anarchic queerness in his films, it is troubling that much of the gross-out humour in Waters' work comes from representations of queerly 'heterosexual' or lesbian sex. Waters has never shown gay sex and, indeed, rarely features a gay character in his films. The most prominent gay character in a Waters film appears in *Female Trouble* as a blind date for one character's nephew, who she is afraid will turn out to be straight. This set up elicits one of the great lines of all Waters' films, as Aunt Edie warns her nephew, who is resisting the date: 'The world of the heterosexual is a sick and boring life.' To be fair, Waters seems to find sex itself, in any form, a rather grotesque and laughable affair. His approach to most of his characters, no matter what they are doing, is one that combines affection and revulsion. The wry, sardonic and outrageous sense of humour of Waters' films is also apparent in *Crack Pot* (1986), a collection of essays on subjects ranging from exploitation film showmanship to mass murderers and 'The Pia Zadora Story' to *National Enquirer,* and *Shock Value* (1981), an autobiographical volume tracing his early life and struggle to make the films that would help define the notion of 'cult films' and 'midnight movies' during the 1970s and 1980s. A hit Broadway musical of his film *Hairspray* opened in 2002.

ALEX DOTY

WATERS, SARAH

b. 1966

novelist

Academic and prize-winning British novelist Sarah Waters researched the history of Victorian lesbian and gay writing for her PhD, which inspired her three novels published between 1998 and 2002: *Tipping the Velvet* (1998), *Affinity* (2001) and *Fingersmith* (2002). As Waters herself admits, she appropriates nineteenth-century fiction for a lesbian agenda. If there is a progression in Waters' fiction, it is in her exploration of the darker, more uncomfortable aspects of power shifts in relationships across class and gender. Her work also shows a light-hearted yet rigorous interest in perception and different realities, the supremacy of the image, and presentation of self. Given this, it is unsurprising that madness, the subcultures of spirituality, cross-dressing and the Victorian underworld all feature variously in the novels. Importantly for modern gay readers, Waters unflinchingly depicts queer sexualities as complex and brutal, as well as sensual and affirming.

KYM MARTINDALE

WEAVER, LOIS

See: Shaw, Peggy and Lois Weaver

WEBER, BRUCE

b. 1946

photographer

Born in Greensburg, Pennsylvania, Bruce Weber attributes his passion for photography to his father's habit of taking pictures on Sundays, and his style to the all-American aesthetics of his pastoral childhood. At New York University in the 1960s he studied film, and photography under Lisette Model, heavily influenced by his friend, Diane Arbus. Commercial work for Calvin **Klein**, Ralph Lauren and **Abercrombie & Fitch** reveals images of chiselled masculinity, charged with homoeroticism and denying the reality of homosexuality proper. His own work pictures male youth as nostalgic, white and flawless, for instance *The Andy Book* in 1987, devoted to the high-school boxer Andy Minsker, or *Bear Pond* (1991), featuring young boys skinny-dipping. Film work is also celebrated; his 1989 documentary focusing on jazz trumpeter Chet Baker, *Let's Get Lost*, was nominated for an Academy Award, while his feature, *Chop Suey* (2001), is in part an autobiographical record of his own career.

See also: Abercrombie & Fitch

MICHAEL PINFOLD

WEEKS, JEFFREY

b. 1945

scholar

Educated at University College London and the University of Kent at Canterbury, Weeks early on became engaged in gay politics; he was a founding member of the Gay Left Collective. In London during the early 1970s, the Gay Left Collective carried Mary McIntosh's argument to its logical conclusions: namely, that sexual identity was itself historical. Jeffrey Weeks granted that same-sex desires may indeed be innate, but that such a thing was not knowable given that desires were only intelligible in social contexts. In 1977, Weeks published his book-length work *Coming Out: Homosexual Politics in Britain from the Nineteenth Century to the Present* wherein he drew the first cogent distinction between what he saw as homosexual acts and homosexual identity. In 1994 he became professor of sociology at South Bank University. He has published widely editing anthologies and writing such books as *Sex, Politics, and Society* (1981) and *Invented Moralities* (1997).

See also: McIntosh, Mary

J. TODD ORMSBEE

WELBON, YVONNE

b. 1962

filmmaker

Yvonne Welbon was born and raised in Chicago, then attended Vassar College. In 1984 she moved to Taipei, Taiwan, where she taught English, learned Mandarin, and founded the arts magazine *Bang,* which she published for five years. Back in the United States, Welbon earned a Masters degree at the School of the Arts Institute of Chicago (1994) and a PhD in Radio/TV/Film at Northwestern University (2001). In the widely screened *Remembering Wei Yi-Fang, Remembering Myself* (1996), Welbon examines her experiences abroad as an African-American lesbian filmmaker invigorated by a chance to escape racist cultural expectations in the US. Her other films, and her efforts with a variety of African-American or queer filmmakers such as Zeinabu Irene Davis, Cheryl **Dunye**, Thomas Allen Harris and Catherine Crouch continue her exploration of possibilities. Her film, *Sisters in Cinema* (2003), reclaims a history of possibility in the work of overlooked African-American women filmmakers from throughout the twentieth century.

GABRIEL GOMEZ

WELLS, PETER

b. 1950

film director, writer

New Zealand's first openly gay novelist and filmmaker, Wells started making short films with his then partner, Stewart **Main**, notably *Foolish Things* (1980), a poignant gay love story, and *Jewel's Darl* (1985), a drama about two transvestites. His TV drama *A Death in the Family* (1986), a passionate, angry drama about gay men caring for a dying HIV+ friend and contending with his conservative family, was inspired by the death of Wells' brother from AIDS. His first feature, *Desperate Remedies* (1993), co-scripted and directed with Main, was a flamboyant historical melodrama of lesbian love and homoerotic desire. He co-directed *Georgie Girl* (2001), a documentary about New Zealand transsexual politician Georgina **Beyer**. Also an award-winning author, Wells' writings include short-story collections *Dangerous Desires* (1991) and *Duration of A Kiss* (1994), a novel, *Boy Overboard* (1997), and a memoir, *Long Loop Home* (2001). He co-edited (with Rex Pilgrim) *Best Mates: Gay Writing in Aotearoa, New Zealand* (1997).

JOHN FORDE

WEST, MAE

b. 1893; d. 1980

actor

Having started a vaudeville career at age 5, Mae West was, by age 14, being billed as 'The Baby Vamp'. Soon afterwards she wrote the plays *Sex* (1926), which landed her in jail on obscenity charges, *Drag* (1927), about homosexuality, and *Diamond Lil* (1928), a Broadway hit that showcased her wry, bawdy and self-confident persona and gained her international fame. Her starring-role performance in *I'm No Angel* (1933) hastened the reinforcement of Hollywood self-censorship via the Production Code. West's characters appeal, to gay men in particular because of their healthy sexual appetites, lusty appraisal of man flesh and self-consciously camp sense of humour. West kept these attributes in her club acts throughout the 1950s and 1960s as she moaned her way through blues songs, dripped double entendres and made sex objects of her musclemen chorus boys. Her final starring roles in *Myra Breckinridge* (1970) and *Sextette* (1978) did not live up to the witty and refreshing humour of her earlier films.

See also: Production Code, the (Hollywood)

ALEX DOTY

WHALE, JAMES

b. 1889; d. 1957

film director

A gifted filmmaker, known for his macabre classics *Frankenstein* (1931), *The Old Dark House* (1932), *The Invisible Man* (1933) and *Bride of Frankenstein* (1935), James Whale was one of classic Hollywood's most openly gay figures, and his life and work enjoyed a renaissance during the 1990s. A First World War veteran who turned to stage acting, design and direction, Whale came to

Hollywood to film his stage success of male bonding in the Great War trenches, *Journey's End*. He became Universal Studios' ace, helming successful films across many genres. His horror films are treasured for their vivid, expressionistic visuals, rich characterizations and combination of camp gallows humour with sympathy for monstrous outsiders. Other films, including melodramas (*Waterloo Bridge*, 1930; *One More River*, 1934), a musical (the best version of *Show Boat*, 1936) and comedy (*By Candlelight,* 1933), display a similar theatrical virtuosity, gender play and a critique of heterosexual norms.

Whale lived with producer David Lewis, but his career declined when bankers seized Universal; several box-office failures meant that studios would not hire a high-priced, gay freelancer. Whale took up painting but committed suicide when his health declined. He was a cult figure until Christopher Bram's novel *Father of Frankenstein* (1995) fictionalized his final days, garnering him a broader audience. Later attention came from the film version *Gods and Monsters* (1998), several biographies and academic gay studies.

DAVID M. LUGOWSKI

WHITE, EDMUND

b. 1940

writer

Raised in the Midwest and educated at the University of Michigan (where he studied Chinese), White moved to New York City in the 1960s, where he became a founding member of the gay writers' group the Violet Quill. He gained renown as a chronicler of 1970s gay life with his two groundbreaking books, the illustrated sex manual *The Joy of Gay Sex* (co-authored with Dr Charles Silverstein, 1977) and his 1980 travelogue *States of Desire*. As a novelist he is most known for his autobiographical trilogy (*A Boy's Own Story* [1982], *The Beautiful Room is Empty* [1988] and *The Farewell*

Symphony [1997]), which spans from the years before Stonewall to the height of the AIDS epidemic. White was one of the first American writers to publicly declare his HIV+ status and has written frequently on the epidemic. His work includes a major biography of Jean Genet and a shorter study of Marcel Proust.

DAVID KURNICK

WHITE, PATRICK

b. 1912; d. 1990

writer

Patrick Victor Martindale White was born into Australian farming wealth but turned against his bourgeois background, becoming a writer. Starting in London, where Francis **Bacon** was one of his lovers, then in Australia, White set about creating a monumental literature in novels, stories, plays, and a memoir. Prickly outsiders – explorers, lunatics, artists – were often the core characters of his fiction, perhaps a metaphor for his own homosexuality. In a late novel, *The Twyborn Affair* (1980), White made a homosexual character central for the first time. He was a believer in advanced causes, from Aboriginal rights to republicanism, but he shied away from gay liberation. When awarded the Nobel Prize in 1973, White only attended the ceremony after the invitation to his partner, Manoly Lascaris, was hurriedly changed from 'secretary' to 'family'.

PETER WELLS

WHITEHOUSE, MARY

b. 1910; d. 2001

moral crusader

Mary Whitehouse was a pioneering campaigner against sex and violence in the British media. The National Viewers' and Listeners' Association, which she founded in 1964, vocally opposed 'the propaganda of disbelief, doubt and dirt that the BBC projects into millions of homes through the television screens'. Homosexual representation caused her particular concern. In 1977 she successfully charged blasphemous libel against the editor of the UK's *Gay News* for publishing James Kirkup's poem insinuating that Jesus was gay. Later, she campaigned against the inclusion of a homosexual relationship in the popular British TV drama *Eastenders*. Often a figure of ridicule, her anti-sex rhetoric proved popular with conservatives and Prime Minister Margaret Thatcher commended her work. Her indefatigable efforts in alerting the British public to the dangers of watching TV sex scenes were acknowledged by the Queen in 1980 when she was awarded a CBE.

MARK McLELLAND

WICCA

This earth-based neo-pagan religion is particularly suited to queer peoples because it lacks any canonical dogma to prescribe an acceptable sexuality. Without any transcendent truths, Wicca allows for individual paths to knowledge. Otherwise known as The Craft of the Wise, or witchcraft, Wiccans 'do as they will and harm no-one' in a magical practice that draws upon pre-Christian traditions to express an ecological respect for the living planet. For some it is a polytheistic religion that worships gods and goddesses of various sexualities. However, others adopt an atheistic approach towards divinities, seeing them as humanly created symbols rather than actual beings.

WREN SIDHE

WILCHINS, RICKI ANN

activist

Transsexual activist who has founded a number of transgendered support and advocacy groups. She first became involved with advocacy group Transgender Nation. After the group folded in 1994, she formed **Transsexual Menace** to advocate for equal rights for transgendered people and to provide an outlet for her community's outrage over the brutal murder of transgendered teenager Brandon **Teena** in Nebraska in 1993. She went on to found GenderPAC (**Gender Public Advocacy Coalition**) in 1996, the United States' largest national organization committed to ending discrimination against gender diversity. In 2001 *Time* Magazine named her one of its '100 Civic Innovators for the 21st Century'.

JOHN FORDE

WILL & GRACE

TV programme

Will & Grace premiered in 1998 as a sitcom about a gay lawyer and a straight, female interior designer who are friends and, initially, roommates in New York. While Will Truman (Eric McCormack) and Grace Adler (Debra Messing) are the title characters, secondary characters Karen Walker (Megan Mullally) and Jack McFarland (Sean Hayes) have significant screen time, not least because they are the most ostensibly queer characters in their habits. Socialite Karen has become more and more bisexual as the show has continued, while Will's friend Jack remains a sexually ravenous mantrap. Will and Grace themselves were scripted to act as a straight married couple in the first few seasons, although Grace eventually married Leo (Harry Connick Jr), only to eventually suffer marital problems and divorce. Throughout the first five seasons, Will had only two- or three-episode-long romances and a very quick kiss with someone other than Jack. Gay and queer fans lived in constant hope that Will might have a bed scene, a long-term relationship or at least a hot, prolonged kiss before the series ended. In its sixth and seventh seasons, Will finally became involved in a relationship with Vince, a police officer.

ALEX DOTY

WILLIAMS, CECIL

b. 1909; d. 1979

producer, activist

Cecil Williams, a British-born, South African theatre producer, was a Communist activist and a founder of the Springbok Legion (the first and only mass organization of whites to oppose discrimination against non-whites under apartheid). A homosexual, Williams' radical politics stemmed in part from his desire to be free from the homophobia dominating white South African society from the late 1940s onwards. After he directed the anti-apartheid play *Kimberly Train* (1959), he became the object of state surveillance. In 1962 he was arrested while driving Nelson Mandela, then on the run from the police for organizing an underground military wing of the African National Congress. ANC leaders have credited Williams with sensitizing black African leadership in the anti-apartheid movement to the need for gay rights. His story is told in *The Man Who Drove With Mandela*, written by Mark Gevisser (dir. Greta Schiller, 1998). He died in exile in London.

MARC EPPRECHT

WILLIAMS, KENNETH

b. 1926; d. 1988

actor

A camp, sharp-tongued comic actor, Kenneth Williams became one of Britain's most popular entertainers. He is best known for his appearances in the **Carry On** films, including most famously *Carry On Sergeant* (1958) and *Carry on Nurse* (1959). Williams'

comic persona played on the unspoken but obvious fact of his homosexuality – inferred through sexual innuendo, bitchy humour and his edgily displayed effeminacy. He wrote and starred in radio comedies *Round the Horne* (1965–8) and *The Secret Life of Kenneth Williams*, was a frequent guest on celebrity radio game show *Just A Minute* (1967–87) and hosted *The Kenneth Williams Show* (1970) for television. A long-time friend of playwright Joe **Orton**, Williams acted in Orton's play *Loot* in 1965. His meticulously chronicled diaries and letters, published after his death in 1994–5, revealed his struggles with clinical depression and self-loathing over his homosexuality. He died of a (possibly suicidal) drug overdose in 1988.

See also: Julian and Sandy

JOHN FORDE

WILLIAMS, ROBBIE

b. 1974

pop singer

One of the most successful British recording artists of the 1990s, Williams began his career in boy band Take That, leaving in 1995 to launch a solo career. His combination of catchy pop tunes and a carefully crafted, sexually ambiguous stage persona won him iconic status as the epitome of 1990s 'New Lad' culture. Shrewdly playing to both gay and straight audiences, Williams successfully combined the hairy-chested sexual bravado of 1960s British crooner Tom Jones, alongside camp onstage theatrics, provocative displays of nakedness in his music videos (notably for 'Rock DJ' [2000]) and teasing references to gay sex in his song lyrics. He has subsequently denied being gay. Despite massive commercial success in Britain, Williams has been unable to find success in the American music market, although he achieved moderate acclaim with *Swing When You're*

Winning (2000), a Sinatra-esque tribute album of big band covers.

JOHN FORDE

WILLIAMS, TENNESSEE

b. 1911; d. 1983

dramatist

One of the twentieth century's most brilliant and celebrated playwrights, Williams' writing revolutionized American theatre, combining intense lyrical beauty with a fearless exploration of tortured sexuality and a sympathetic identification with society's outsiders.

Born Thomas Lanier Williams on 26 March 1911 in Columbus, Mississippi, he spent most of his childhood living with his mother and disabled older sister in the home of his maternal grandfather, an Episcopalian minister. He studied at the University of Missouri, but left after having a nervous breakdown and went to work in a shoe factory. He continued to suffer from mental illness for most of his life, as well as alcoholism and an addiction to painkillers. Like many gay men of his generation, he had an ambivalent attitude towards his own homosexuality, and his guilt and anxiety informs much of his work.

Williams' first major theatrical success, *The Glass Menagerie* (1945), was a lyrical (and heavily autobiographical) drama of Tom, a factory worker with literary aspirations who struggles against the suffocating responsibilities of providing for his overbearing mother and his crippled sister. Although Tom's sexuality is never explicitly defined, his final monologue eloquently sketches the emotional pain of a generation of exiled, isolated gay men. Williams reputedly gave his mother a share of the royalties after she complained that he had simply quoted her verbatim in the script.

He followed this with the electrifying *A Streetcar Named Desire* (1947), a feverish melodrama set in New Orleans in which the fragile, flirtatious Blanche DuBois goes to war with her brother-in-law Stanley Kowalski, whose aggressive sexual energy both attracts and repels her. The first Broadway production, directed by Elia Kazan, created a sensation, elevating its star Marlon Brando to overnight stardom. The play's emotional and sexual violence (including Blanche's rape and eventual madness) shocked audiences and ushered in a new wave of frankness and honesty in American playwriting. Williams wrote the screenplay for Kazan's successful film version (1951), starring Brando and Vivien Leigh.

Along with his contemporary Edward **Albee**, Williams provided a compelling emotional trajectory of the pains of closeted homosexuality and the sexual hypocrisy of American society. Although always sympathetic to his protagonists, Williams refused to provide them with happy endings. His protagonists are invariably victims whose artistic aspirations and dreams of refinement become traps that destroy them.

Williams seldom depicted homosexual characters onstage, although the spectre of homosexuality is ever-present as a guilty secret or a destructive force. In *Streetcar*, Blanche is haunted by the memories of her first husband, who shot himself when she confronted him in bed with another man. The Freudian drama *Cat on a Hot Tin Roof* (1955) takes place on a plantation once owned by a gay couple, and Maggie and Brick's failing marriage is disrupted by Brick's sexually ambiguous friendship with the dead Skipper. In *Suddenly Last Summer* (1958), Mrs Venables attempts to lobotomize her niece Catherine to hide the ugly truth about her dead son Sebastian, who was killed and eaten by the Mexican boys whose sexual favours he sought.

Critics have argued that Williams coded a deeper gay subtext into much of his work. Like Albee's warring married couple in *Who's Afraid of Virginia Woolf?* (1962),

Blanche may be read as a gay man who eroticizes the brutal dominance of Stanley, who is himself a gay fantasy of an unattainable hypermasculine ideal. Williams arguably wrote Blanche as a gay surrogate, through which he expressed the passions of gay men that would otherwise be unspeakable on stage. Half a century after its first performance, *Streetcar* still retains an enduring appeal for gay audiences, and Blanche's final words – 'I have always depended on the kindness of strangers' – has become a catchphrase for the bittersweet pleasures of gay sex – and an oft-quoted line of repartee for drag queens.

Similarly, his play *The Milk Train Doesn't Stop Here Anymore* (1950) and the novella *The Roman Spring of Mrs Stone* (1950), which both feature middle-aged women who commence doomed relationships with younger men, can be read as Williams' lament for the loneliness of middle-aged gay life. Williams reversed the formula in *Sweet Bird of Youth* (1959), in which the older woman abandons her gigolo, who submits to castration as punishment for his corruption of a young woman.

As well as *Streetcar*, film adaptations of his plays were great successes, with the actor Elizabeth Taylor proving a ideally spirited heroine for Maggie in *Cat On a Hot Tin Roof* (filmed 1958) and *Suddenly Last Summer* (filmed 1959). *The Milk Train Doesn't Stop Here Anymore* was given a bizarre, kitschy treatment by Joseph Losey in his film *Boom!* (1968), starring Taylor, Richard Burton and Noël Coward as the Witch of Capri. Despite being a critical and commercial flop, *Boom!* has since been adopted as a camp classic by gay audiences.

Williams' tragic vision was ameliorated somewhat by the influence of his long-term lover Frank Merlo. They met in 1947 and stayed together until Merlo's death in 1961. Inspired by a holiday they took to Merlo's ancestral homeland in Sicily, Williams wrote the comic drama *The Rose Tattoo* (1948), his only major play with a happy ending. After Merlo's death, Williams fell into a deep 10-year depression. His output waned in the 1970s, although he published his *Memoirs* (1975), displaying his customary ambivalence about discussing his sexuality. He died on 24 February 1983, after choking on a bottle cap, apparently as a result of an alcoholic binge, at the Hotel Elysée in New York City.

JOHN FORDE

WILSON, ANGUS
b. 1913; d. 1991
writer

One of England's first openly gay writers, Angus Wilson was born in Bexhill, East Sussex. During the Second World War he was a code-breaker at Bletchley Park and started to write after advice from his psychotherapist following a nervous breakdown, caused by paranoid fears (as a gay man he was a target for gossip and for blackmail, as homosexuality was illegal at that time). His first novel was *Hemlock and After* (1952), drawing upon his gay experiences. At this time he met Tony Garrett, 16 years his junior; they settled in Suffolk and Wilson spent the remainder of his life with him. *Anglo-Saxon Attitudes* (1956) and *The Old Men at the Zoo* (1961) criticized middle-class double standards but gave rise to little debate as the 'angry young men' – John Osborne, Alan Sillitoe – dominated the literary scene. Through 1966–78 he lectured in English at the University of East Anglia. He was knighted in 1980.

MICHAEL PINFOLD

WILSON, LANFORD
b. 1937
playwright

Lanford Wilson's involvement with New York theatre began during the early 1960s when he relocated from Chicago and became involved with the nascent Off-Off-Broadway experimental movement at Café Cino. His first play, *So Long at the Fair* (1963), was produced there. His next play, *Home Free* (1964), dealt with the taboo subject of incest. In 1965 he wrote *Balm in Gilead* (1965), which was critically acclaimed for its unorthodox structure and its huge cast of 56 characters. He also won the Vernon Rice Award for *The Rimers of Edlritch,* both *Balm* and *Rimers* dealt with his recurring themes of alienation, isolation and the struggle to accept reality. Wilson was one of the founders of Circle Repertory Company in 1969 whose first major hit was Wilson's *Hot L Baltimore* (1973), which ran for more than 1,000 performances before moving to Broadway. In 1977 his *Fifth of July* introduced a central gay character in its discussion of war.

CHRIS BYRNE

WINGS, MARY

b. 1949

writer

Born in Chicago, Illinois, Mary Wings now lives in San Francisco, California, the setting for all but one of her popular Emma Victor mysteries. The brash and sensible-shoe-wearing lesbian detective arrived on the scene in 1986 in Wings' first novel, *She Came Too Late*, published by The Women's Press. Four more books follow in the series: *She Came In A Flash* (1988), *She Came By The Book* (1996), *She Came To The Castro* (1997) and *She Came In Drag* (1999). Wings' Emma Victor novels offer readers the quintessential 1980s lesbian detective: sarcastic, self-consciously hard-boiled and perpetually unlucky in love. Taking a break from the subgenre in 1993, Wings published *Divine Victim*, a modern reworking of the female gothic tale. Wings is also the author of several

short works and her reviews and articles have appeared in *New Statesman*, *Out* and *The Advocate*.

ALIDA M. MOORE

WINTERSON, JEANETTE

b. 1959

writer

British novelist, short-story writer, essayist and journalist, best known for her first novel *Oranges Are Not the Only Fruit* (1985), which was published to great acclaim. A painful and humorous portrait of the artist as a young lesbian growing up in a fundamentalist religious community, *Oranges* was later dramatized for television (1990), bringing the fictional representation of lesbianism into the mainstream and making Winterson a significant figure for women coming to lesbianism for the first time. In Winterson's subsequent writings lesbian desire continues to subvert conventional heterosexual narratives, but her fifth novel, *Written on the Body* (1990), ignited controversy among lesbian critics over its apparent retreat from lesbianism and politics as perceived in its genderless narrator and postmodernist literary preoccupations. Subversion remains Winterson's method nevertheless, in this and in later work, placing her within a new generation of writers engaged in queering 'high art' and culture.

See also: *Oranges Are Not the Only Fruit*

CATHERINE CLAY

WITTIG, MONIQUE

b. 1935; d. 2003

novelist, poet, social theorist

Born in France, Monique Wittig's work has had a fundamental impact upon feminist theory and lesbian and gay theory worldwide. Her work has been translated into a dozen languages, including Italian, German, Dutch, Finnish, Japanese and Spanish. Within the framework of a critique of thought oriented by a materialist lesbian approach, Wittig is concerned with laying bare the mechanisms of knowledge and power of heteronormative thought, both in texts of a theoretical character, such as *The Straight Mind* (1992), and in texts of a literary sort, including *Le Corps Lesbien* (*The Lesbian Body*, 1975).

Wittig observes how, despite the movements for the liberation of women, lesbians and homosexuals, critical thought has scarcely touched on the mechanisms of power through which the dominant heterosexual culture still focuses the theoretical gaze in relation to concepts such as man and woman. These latter persist as nuclei of resistance in the culturalist critique within the category of nature and are utilized as if they were primitive and natural. According to Wittig, these concepts must be discussed, retracing within them the brand of social stratification. For this reason Wittig declares that lesbians are not women, in the sense that they do not respond to the link through which the female has been culturally bound to the male by a rigid mechanism of a binary type, necessary both for the definition of female and for its identification.

For Wittig, literary work must be like a Trojan Horse, a war machine which presents itself within the cultural scene as extraneous, and which in reality conceals within its peculiarity the power of demolishing the old forms of expression and their conventional rules. This is the sense in which we can interpret the novel *The Lesbian Body* in which, behind the narration of the love story, there emerges the materialist and desecrating proposition of the reappropriation of the lesbian body. Effectively, the novel presents a fragmentation of the body of the loved–lover woman that occurs as the story evolves. Here, the body sets itself in the foreground in all its

organic complexity, in all its solidity. The body transcends simple identification with a single entity. It is the 'you' of the loved one, on the one hand, yet, on the other hand, overflows into a collective 'you/us' which is proper to the lesbian body while extraneous to the dynamics of social utilization of the female body. And so, in *The Lesbian Body*, Wittig plays at reversing the meaning imposed by the male world upon the female body, a persuasive bodily image made to measure for male desire, a woman's body that is ethereal, angelic and virginal or dedicated to sexual consumption and delineated exclusively by its sexual attributes.

MONIA ANDREANI

WOJNAROWICZ, DAVID
b. 1954; d. 1992
artist

David Wojnarowicz was born in New Jersey into an extremely unstable family. He started living on the streets in New York while he was still in high school, working as a hustler to support himself. In his early twenties he travelled extensively throughout the United States, mostly hitchhiking and freight-hopping. During this time he developed an acute awareness of the inequities in American society, and began attending demonstrations by the Black Panthers and other political groups. He saw Jean **Genet**'s film, *Un Chant d'amour* (1950), which he credits with giving him a new perspective on homosexuality. He began reading, Genet again, but also William **Burroughs**, and made his first attempts at writing himself. In the late 1970s he lived for a year in France, where he continued writing and drawing. Back in New York, he held his first exhibitions. He worked in film, photography, painting and performance in addition to writing.

In 1987 his friend the photographer Peter Hujar died from AIDS and Wojnarowicz himself was diagnosed HIV+. From then on his work would become fiercely political, decrying injustice and the indifference of political and medical authorities to the crisis. His vitriolic attacks on conservative politicians, coupled with his blatantly homoerotic work, made him a favoured target in the right-wing attack on gay and lesbian artists in the late 1980s. In 1991 he published *Close to the Knives: A Memoir of Disintegration*, a collection of autobiographical essays on queer and AIDS politics in the US. He remained extremely active, both artistically and politically, until his death in 1992.

DANIEL HENDRICKSON

WOLFENDON REPORT, THE

A 1957 British government study, officially entitled The Report of the Committee on Homosexual Offences and Prostitution, chaired by Sir John Wolfenden, which controversially recommended the decriminalization of homosexual behaviour between consenting adults in private. After a number of high-profile prosecutions for homosexual behaviour (including the arrest of actor Sir John Gielgud), the 13-person committee was formed in 1953 to investigate Britain's sex laws, which prohibited male homosexuality (lesbianism was never a criminal offence). Over a three-year period, the committee interviewed gay people, policemen, psychiatrists, social workers and religious leaders, during which Sir John Wolfenden discovered that his son Jeremy was homosexual. The resulting report condemned homosexuality as immoral and destructive, but recommended by 12 votes to 1 that consenting homosexual acts between adults over the age of 21, carried out in private, should be decriminalized. The committee's findings provoked a national debate about homosexuality, and the recommended reforms of Britain's sex

laws were stalled for a decade before being enacted in 1967.

JOHN FORDE

WOMAN–WOMAN MARRIAGE

Woman–woman marriage is a custom found in dozens of cultures throughout Africa, from the Fon of Benin (former Dahomey) to the Lovedu of South Africa. Senior women pay 'bride price' in the same manner as a man would in order to marry. The senior woman, often a widow but in other cases a figure of ritual importance or a 'king', becomes a husband to the young wife, who may then become pregnant through an invited male lover. The offspring would belong to the female husband, providing a means for elite women to acquire wealth independently of men. Previously it was assumed (and at times vehemently asserted) that there was no sexual relationship in such marriages, but research since the 1950s has suggested that lesbian-like intimacy was in fact likely.

MARC EPPRECHT

WOMEN'S LIBERATION MOVEMENT

The women's liberation movement that began in the 1960s aimed to eliminate gender-based oppression and to liberate women from their 'second-class' status in the world. It went beyond the concerns of traditional politics to define sexuality as a major site of struggle. In addition to equal pay and equal opportunities for education and employment, the objectives of women's liberation include free contraception and abortion, an end to discrimination against lesbians, the right to self-defined sexuality, and an end to domestic and sexual violence. The movement created new political organizations such as small anti-hierarchical women-only groups organized for consciousness-raising and exploring alternative living patterns. Construction of new and resistant identities, or cultural politics in general, is a key dimension of the movement. Through publishing feminist academic works, developing women's studies programmes and setting up women's presses and bookstores, the movement sought to control the means of cultural production and distribution.

DAY WONG

WONG, ANTHONY

b. 1962

pop musician

Anthony Wong Yiu-ming was born on 16 June 1962. He made his debut performance as the lead singer of Tat Ming Pair, one of the most popular Hong Kong alternative bands of the 1980s. He embarked on his career as a solo artist in 1991 and has earned numerous music awards not only for his unique, airy, new romantic style but also for their underlying meanings. His songs cleverly and subtly portray social and political issues in Hong Kong, such as homosexuality ('Wang Ji Ta Shi Ta', 'Hou Chuang', and 'Jin Se'), AIDS ('Ai Zai Wen Yi Wan Yan Shi'); the immigration wave before the 1997 handover to China ('Jin Tian Ying Gai Hen Gao Xing'); and political themes ('Shi Ge Jiu Huo De Shao Nian', 'Mei You Zhang Yang De Ming An', and 'Da Ya Wan Zhi Lian').

KEN WONG
STEPHANIE LEE

WONG, PAUL

b. 1955

performance artist

Canadian interdisciplinary video and performance artist, curator and anti-censorship advocate. Known as the 'Chinese Canadian Warhol' and Vancouver's prolific video pioneer, Wong has played off queer and Asian identities against both West Coast cultural politics and the international high art conceptual scene for almost three decades. Wong's 1976 *60 Unit Bruise*, made in collaboration with artistic partner and erstwhile 'boyfriend' Ken Fletcher (1954–78), is a minimalist video performance showing an injection of the white, blond Fletcher's blood spreading across Wong's back. Wong nurtured his interest in sexual identities and lifestyles, and his video installation work *Confused: Sexual Views* (1984), 9 hours of 27 people 'yakking' about sexuality, became the decade's most celebrated censorship scandal when the Vancouver Art Gallery pulled out at the last minute. The courageous and persistent artist sued, then lost the courtroom battle, but ultimately won the war, receiving the Bell Canada Award in Video Art in 1992 for his sustained commitment to the convergence of aesthetic innovation and identity exploration.

THOMAS WAUGH

WONGMONTHA, SERI

b. 1949

playwright

Gay playwrights, performers and directors have played a central role in Thai live theatre and cinema since the 1980s. The most prominent of these is Dr Seri Wongmontha, the openly gay former Dean of the Faculty of Mass Communications at Bangkok's Thammasat University. In 1986 Wongmontha translated and adapted Mart Crowley's *The Boys in the Band* for the Thai stage. Retitled, *chan phu-chai na ya* ('But Darling, I'm a Man'), this production took Bangkok by storm, receiving rave press reviews and performing to packed houses. Wongmontha himself played a role, and the programme notes included a dictionary of the Thai gay slang terms that peppered the characters' bitchy conversations. Wongmontha also acted in a successful film version of the play, which was released in 1987. Seri's acclaimed stage adaptation is widely regarded as having provided the impetus to resuscitate modern Thai theatre, which had languished for decades after the disruptions of the Second World War years.

Since the late 1980s, university and amateur dramatic troupes have staged numerous locally written plays dealing with gay, lesbian and transgender themes, with the Thai theatre becoming the country's most queer-friendly cultural medium and the venue for the most realistic and thoughtful representations of Thai queer people's lives today. Wongmontha's play and film have also had a lasting impression on mainstream discourses about homosexuality. The Thai title *chan phu-chai na ya* playfully reflects the bitchy language of Thai drag queens, and the two words *na ya* are now generally understood as code words for gay men and *kathoeys* and continue to be used in the Thai press and electronic media. In 1989 Seri translated and adapted Larry Kramer's *The Normal Heart* for the Thai stage under the title, *hua-jai mai pen AIDS* (My Heart Doesn't Have AIDS).

See also: Thailand, filmmaking

PETER A. JACKSON

WOOD, ED

b. 1924; d. 1978

film director

Known largely as a B-movie director, Edward Davis Wood was born in Poughkeepsie, New York in 1924. He served in the US Marine Corps during the Second World War, surviving Tarawa. After his front teeth were knocked out in combat and a machine gun wound developed gangrene, he was honourably discharged in 1944, receiving the Silver and Bronze Stars, two Purple Hearts and the Sharpshooter's Medal.

After the Second World War, he attended Northwestern University in Chicago, then joined a travelling carnival sideshow, starring as 'Half Man, Half Woman'.

Inspired by the Christine Jorgensen sexchange story, Wood wrote and directed the 1953 film *Glen or Glenda*. He is also known for the 1958 film *Plan 9 from Outer Space*. In addition to film work, Wood wrote pulp fiction with transgender themes, including *Death of a Transvestite* (1967) and *Killer in Drag* (1965).

His 1955 marriage to Norma McCarthy was annulled after six months due to his cross-dressing, but a second marriage in 1957 to Kathy Wood lasted until his death in 1978.

LYNETTE REINI-GRANDELL
VENUS

WOOD, ROBIN

b. 1931

film scholar

Born in England, Robin Wood was educated at Cambridge. He is currently Professor Emeritus and Senior Scholar at York University in Toronto, Canada. Wood's earliest books were a series of critical studies written during the height of auteur theory: *Antonioni* (co-authored, 1968), *Howard Hawks* (1968), *Ingmar Bergman* (1969), *Claude Chabrol* (co-authored, 1970) and *Arthur Penn* (1970). The most famous and influential of these studies is *Hitchcock's Films* (1969), which was expanded with new essays for *Hitchcock's Films Revisited* (1991). Changes in Wood's personal and ideological outlook during the 1970s moved him to write criticism informed by feminism, Marxism, gay and lesbian perspectives, and the work of F.R. Leavis. The result has been a series of books that are models of personally invested, philosophically complex and politically committed film studies: *Personal Views: Explorations in Film* (1976), *Hollywood from Vietnam to Reagan* (1986/2003), and *Sexual Politics and Narrative Film: Hollywood and Beyond* (1998).

ALEX DOTY

WOODS, GREGORY

b. 1947

poet, critic

British academic who spent his childhood in Africa after being born in Cairo,
Woods is a highly regarded historian of
gay literature and culture. He is the author
of a ground-breaking book on male
homoeroticism in poetry (*Articulate Flesh*,
1987) and an acclaimed volume on the
male tradition in gay writing (*A History of
Gay Literature,* 1997). He also penned a
number of highly regarded books of poetry,
making him a leading figure in contemporary British gay poetry. He was
named Professor of Lesbian and Gay Studies at Nottingham Trent University in
1998, the first such post in Britain. The
appointment divided the press, provoked
the indignation of various Members of
Parliament and overjoyed gay campaigning
groups.

FABIO CLETO

WOOLF, VIRGINIA

b. 1882; d. 1941

writer

A prolific novelist, essayist, diarist and
critic, whose experiments in literary narrative and insightful feminist critiques established her as one of twentieth-century
literature's leading talents. Woolf was born
on 25 January 1882 in London. With her
sister, the painter Vanessa Bell, she formed
the Bloomsbury Group, a radical group of
artists and philosophers. She married Leonard Woolf in 1912, with whom she
established the Hogarth Press. Her novels
broke with conventional literary narrative,
developing the 'stream of consciousness'
technique of recording the uninterrupted
flow of her characters' thoughts. Her writings focus on the lives of women, frequently exploring bisexual and lesbian
identity, notably in *Mrs Dalloway* (1925)

and *To The Lighthouse* (1927). She had a
number of intense relationships with
women and a love affair with Vita Sackville-
West, who inspired the historical satire
Orlando (1928), in which the 400-year-old
hero/-ine changes sex. In her essays 'A
Room Of One's Own' (1928) and 'Three
Guineas' (1936), she critiqued patriarchal
power systems that denied women's
economic and artistic independence and
posited a connection between bisexual
identity and creativity. Her influence on
other artists has been extraordinary, and
includes Michael Cunningham's Pulitzer
Prize-winning novel *The Hours* (1998),
which posits a queer reading of *Mrs
Dalloway*.

Woolf died on 28 March 1941 in Sussex,
England.

See also: Cunningham, Michael

JOHN FORDE

WORLD CONGRESS OF GAY AND LESBIAN JEWISH ORGANIZATIONS

Founded in 1975, the World Congress of
Gay and Lesbian Jewish Organizations
grew out of an ad hoc meeting held by
lesbian and gay Jewish activists following
the United Nations' decision to equate
Zionism with racism. The World Congress of GLBT Jews – Keshet Ga'avah
(Rainbow Pride) consists today of some
65 synagogues, political organizations and
social groups around the world (Mexico,
Israel, Argentina, Munich, San Francisco).
The work of the Congress includes working within the wider Jewish community
to combat homophobia as well as participating in significant gay rights battles in
the United States, Israel and other countries. During its early years, it worked to
combat anti-Semitism in the wider glbt
community.

LEE WALZER

WORLD HEALTH ORGANIZATION (WHO)

WHO, established in 1948, is the United Nations agency for health, governed by 192 member states through the World Health Assembly. The executive board is made up of 32 members, all qualified in the field of health. The philosophy underpinning the WHO is that health is a fundamental human right regardless of race, religion, political belief or economic or social condition, and the overall objective of the WHO is the attainment of an optimum level of health for all people. The WHO's current definition of health has moved beyond biological causes to view health more holistically and in its social context. The WHO defines health as 'a state of complete physical, social and mental well-being, not merely an absence of disease, illness and infirmity' (1948). The Ottawa Charter of 1986 extended this definition to emphasize personal resources and the realization of aspirations as health-enhancing factors. The key idea behind the Ottawa Charter was the instigation of the process of enabling people to increase control over, and to improve, their own health (the underpinning philosophy of much-promoting activity in global communities).

WHO maintains that all policy and practice should give full attention to:

- Equity (the equal right to healthcare);
- Community participation (the involvement of people in the planning and implementation of decisions involving their health);
- Recognition of the role of different agencies working together.

This philosophy is reflected in the 'Health for All' strategy outlined in the Alma Ata declaration of 1977 that committed all member countries to its principles. The initiative was a reorientation away from treatment and cure towards prevention and protection, setting a target for the year 2000. Sexual health has subsequently figured highly in governments' priorities and has had particular consequences for glbt communities. In relation to HIV/AIDS campaigns, during the 1980s and 1990s there was a general resistance to undertaking any public education campaign that addressed forms of sexual relationships that might be perceived as undermining 'traditional family values'. As a consequence, international HIV/AIDS health education and health promotion strategies have been criticized as being implicitly racist, homophobic and erotophobic. There was a general failure to emphasize all sexual behaviour over the identity of a particular group or individual (i.e. the targeting 'high-risk' groups such as gay men). This resulted in popular misconceptions of HIV/AIDS as a 'Gay Plague' and the relative complacency of the heterosexually defined population. In general terms, the focus on prevention strategies has been criticized as giving way to a burgeoning of strategies of surveillance through which the areas of life and health monitored by health-promoting agencies has increased rapidly. Other critics have challenged the idea of 'absolute' health enshrined in WHO's definitions as a utopian ideal that relies on particular definitions of 'health' and 'illness'.

WHO addresses glbt issues in relation to specific areas of health promotion and research, for example adolescent health and reproduction.

KATHERINE WATSON

WORLD PRIDE 2000

Taking place in Rome, Italy, World Pride was the first global event ever organized to celebrate the **Stonewall Riots**. Over 500,000 people participated in the parade, although the Vatican asked the Italian government not to permit the demonstration to be held during the Jubilee.

ALBERTO EMILETTI

WOWEREIT, KLAUS

b. 1953

politician

Klaus Wowereit was born and raised in Berlin (the Western part) and was politically active from an early age. He joined the Social Democratic Party (SPD) in 1972. After studying law, he continued his involvement in local politics, quickly rising through the ranks of the party. In 1999 he was elected leader of the local party faction. After the split in the so-called Grand Coalition between the SPD and the conservative Christian Democrats (CDU), he was named Mayor of Berlin. During the following elections, and in an effort to stave off the attacks of his CDU opponent and the conservative tabloids, Wowereit took the offensive on the topic of his homosexuality, unapologetically outing himself publicly by saying 'I'm gay, and that's good'. He won the election easily over his admittedly incompetent opponent. Since his coming out, he has maintained an active presence in Berlin's gay scene, appearing officially and unofficially at many gay functions.

DANIEL HENDRICKSON

WRESTLING

Olympic wrestling, also known as Greco-Roman wrestling, originated with military training for Greek soldiers and dates back 5,000 years. The ancient Greeks are also credited with developing the activity into a spectator sport. Wrestling was an important part of Greek culture; it was considered vital for male youths to learn how to wrestle. The sport sees two fit male bodies in full, intertwined contact, struggling, mostly horizontally, as each attempts to gain leverage over the other, so that he may pin his opponent to the floor for victory. Although the original Olympic wrestlers lathered their bodies in oil and wrestled nude in order to avoid giving their opponent something to take hold of, today's wrestlers wear skin-tight uniforms in order to prevent opponents from gaining leverage. These uniforms highlight the well-defined muscles of the highly trim bodies characteristic of Greco-Roman wrestlers. All of this, combined with the vocalizations of grunts and moans as athletes struggle in locked arms, nearly perfectly resembles sexual activity between two men. While this was not problematic for the Greeks, the sheer homoeroticism of the sport does not escape the attention of those who play and/or watch the sport in contemporary society. The salience of homoeroticism within wrestling is therefore met with an equal degree of homophobia, presumably in an attempt to mitigate the homoeroticism of their chosen activity. Wrestling has therefore remained steadfast in its reproduction of homophobia in contemporary culture, forcing its gay members into the closet.

ERIC ANDERSON

WRIGHT, DOUGLAS

b. 1956

dancer, choreographer

In a country where a choreographer is expected to create and present a new work in seven weeks (versus the European tradition of 6–12 months), Wright remains one of New Zealand's most esteemed contemporary dance choreographers. Wright began his dance career in 1980 with New Zealand dance company Limbs. He trained with the Paul Taylor Dance Company of New York between 1983 and 1987, then returned to New Zealand. In 1988 he performed his first full-length dance, *Now Is*

The Hour, a work that gained national notoriety for its nudity and transvestite themes. In 1989 he formed the Douglas Wright Dance Company and produced works such as *How on Earth* (1989), *Gloria* (1990), *Forever* (1993) and *Buried Venus* (1996). Diagnosed with HIV in 1990, subsequent performances initially attracted 'disaster tourists', curious to see the spectacle of Wright performing as an HIV+ artist. The film *Haunting Douglas* (2003) documents his life and work.

JO SMITH

X

XENA, WARRIOR PRINCESS

TV series

By its final episode in 2000, the campy action-adventure series *Xena, Warrior Princess,* was a celebrated, if problematic, addition to television's queer corpus. From (a loosely rendered) ancient Greece, Xena (Lucy Lawless) and her companion Gabrielle (Renee O'Connor) travelled the globe battling evil. From the opening episode in 1995, many fans of the show saw more to the duo's relationship than that of platonic hero/sidekick. Because of this the show developed a strong lesbian following. In response, *Xena*'s producers and screen-writers, along with Lawless and O'Connor, deliberately 'played up' what became known as the show's (lesbian) 'subtext', although the exact nature of the pair's relationship was never precisely revealed. Thus, over the show's six seasons, fans were both delighted and infuriated by (at times barely ambiguous) proclamations of love, sapphic references, on-screen kisses, naked bathing laden with innuendo, implied liaisons with Amazonian tribeswomen and numerous other decidedly queer nuances, the significance of which are examined and debated on Internet fan sites.

In addition to an extensive Internet presence that includes an online journal and novel-length **slash fiction**, Xena has appeared at Pride parades, in the gay media and is referenced as a queer cultural icon in numerous media texts. Her status as queer icon is not without dissent however. The show's deliberate ambiguity has been critiqued as courting the mainstream at the expense of affirmative gay representation.

ANITA BRADY

XIAOMINGXIONG

b. early 1950s

writer

Xiaomingxiong, also known as Samshasha, was Hong Kong's first gay activist. Born of mainland-Chinese parents in Hong Kong, he received his university education in the United States. He encountered the gay rights movement during his American sojourn and returned to Hong Kong in 1979 at a time when homosexual contact between men was illegal. In 1980, after a series of homosexual scandals, the colonial government attempted to introduce law reform but was thwarted by sectors within the Chinese community which insisted that homosexuality was a Western vice. To counter this, Xiaomingxiong wrote about gay issues in a minority rights column in *City Magazine*. He also published gay liberation texts in Chinese including *A Chinese Gay's Manifesto* (1980), the first such booklet published in Hong Kong, and *Pink Triangle* (1981), Hong Kong's first underground gay newsletter. In 1984 he published *The History of Homosexuality in China* (in Chinese), which remains the most comprehensive account of the topic.

MARK McLELLAND

Y

'YAN DAUDA

A Hausa (Nigerian) word for effeminate male homosexual or transvestite. In traditional Muslim society, where overt homosexuality was strongly disparaged, this accepted gender role allowed men to have sex with other men without identifying themselves as gay or bisexual.

MARC EPPRECHT

YANG, WILLIAM

b. 1943

photographer, performance artist

A third-generation Chinese-Australian, William Yang's photography and performance work explores marginalized sexual and ethnic identities in Australian society.

Yang trained as an architect, moving to Sydney in 1969 where he worked as a playwright for an experimental theatre group. His first, highly acclaimed, solo exhibition, 'Sydneyphiles' (1977) was a frank depiction of the Sydney gay party scene. He has also won critical acclaim for his stage performances, combining slide projections of his photographs with autobiographical monologues and live music, starting with *The Face of Buddha* (1989), and including *The North* (1996), *Friends of Dorothy* (1998), a personalized history of Sydney's gay community, and *Blood Links* (2001). He achieved international success with *Sadness* (1992), an elegy to his mother and to gay friends and lovers who had died of AIDS, and which was filmed by gay Australian filmmaker Tony **Ayres** in 1999. In *Shadows* (2002), Yang examines the Australian government's mistreatment of ethnic minorities.

JOHN FORDE

YAU, CHING

b. 1966

multimedia artist, educator

Born in Hong Kong, Yau Ching received her BA in Comparative Literature and Philosophy in Hong Kong, her MA in Media Studies in New York and her PhD in Media Arts in London. A filmmaker, multimedia installation artist, writer and educator, Yau has produced a large number of feminist and queer writings, which focus primarily on issues of marginality, cultural identity, gender and sexuality in both literary and visual forms.

Yau's works – short films, videos and installations – have received awards at festivals worldwide. They include: *Is There Anything Specific You Want Me To Tell You About?* (1990), *Flow* (1993), *The Ideal/ Na(rra)tion* (1993), *Video Letters 1–3* (1993), *Diasporama: Dead Air* (1997), *June 30, 1997* (aka, *Celebrate What?*) (1997), *I'm Starving* (1999) and *Suet-sin's Sisters* (1999). In 2002 Yau made her feature debut with *Ho Yuk: Let's Love Hong Kong*, which tells the story of three lesbians in Hong Kong whose lives magically intersect with one another.

TRAVIS KONG

YONFAN

b. 1947

photographer, filmmaker

Noted for his aesthetic portrayals of beautiful women and men, Yonfan is one of the most distinguished Hong Kong directors and photographers. Born in mainland China and educated in both Hong Kong and Taiwan, Yonfan later studied arts and performance in the United States where he also worked as an actor in Hollywood productions during the late 1960s.

In 1973 Yonfan returned to Hong Kong and found Far Sun Film Company Limited which distributed French New Wave films such as *Les Parapluies de Cherbourg* (The Umbrellas of Cherbourg, 1964). Working primarily as a professional photographer, he also produced entertainment TV shows. Since his directorial debut, *A Certain Romance* in 1984, he has made a series of films, and he has been recognized for his delicate touches of romance. His first international hit, *Bugis Street* (1995), features a community of drag queens who work in the famous red light district in 1970s Singapore. Later, in 1998, Yonfan wrote and directed *Bishonen*, which poses policemen in concert with a number of call boys. In *Peony Pavilion* (2001), his signature aesthetic was revived by integrating Kunqu opera with a dubious relationship between two women and a man in 1930s Suzhou. Yonfan has also published photographic works including *Tibet: A Distant Horizon*.

KEN WONG

YU TAO (THE REMAINING PEACH)

A Chinese legend has it that Duke Ling of Wei (534–493 BC) had a favourite male who tasted a piece of sweet peach and gave the rest to Wei. 'The Remaining Peach' (*Yu tao*) became a euphemism for male homosexuality in Chinese literature.

TRAVIS KONG

YU, LI

b. 1973

filmmaker

A well-known TV host in China, the Beijing-based Li Yu ventured into feature production in 2001, making her directorial debut with *Fish and Elephant*, the first lesbian-themed mainland film. Filmed on 16 mm and cast entirely with non-professional actors, the film features two single women in Beijing. An elephant keeper at the Beijing Zoo, Xiaoqun goes on various blind dates set up by her mother, which constitute some of the funniest moments in the film. Some of these 'dates' were recruited by personal ads placed by the director. Their partially improvised conversations with Xiaoqun take unexpected turns when she reveals her sexual preference for women. A chance meeting brings together Xaioqun and a street clothing vendor Xiaoling who is trying to avoid her ex-boyfriend. The two soon share an apartment and bed together. The film was screened at the 2002 Inside Out Toronto Lesbian and Gay Film and Video Festival.

CUI ZI'EN
YING ZHU

627

Z

ZAMORA, PEDRO

b. 1972; d. 1994

AIDS educator

Pedro Zamora was infected with HIV while in high school and became an AIDS educator immediately after graduation, advocating AIDS-prevention policies that addressed in frank terms the sexual lives of gay teens. In 1994 he became a celebrity when he featured as part of the MTV reality show, *The Real World*. However, despite the exposure, Zamora's appraisals of public AIDS-prevention policies and his frank articulation of gay sexuality never made it on the show. He died just as the season's last episode was broadcast and remains a prominent 'face of AIDS'.

Zamora's brushes with life-threatening infections provided viewers with a partial view of what it meant to be young, Latino, gay and uninsured with AIDS in the United States.

YASMIN NAIR

ZAMUDIO, ADELA

b. 1854; d. 1928

poet, educator

Bolivian feminist, poet and educator Adela Zamudio published under the pseudonym Soledad. The numerous biographies written about her excuse her great devotion to young women as a sort of 'moral mother-hood'. These writers portray Zamudio (extremely beautiful in her youth) as a virginal and sexless woman surrounded by a tight circle of non-sexual girlfriends. Biographers refuse to read further into the matter. Her most famous poem, 'Nacer Hombre', fiercely denounces male privilege, exposing the marginalization of female participation in the fields of education and politics. Her legacy – assimilated and domesticated – remains influential for Bolivian culture and education.

PEDRO ALBORNOZ

ZANE, ARNIE

see: Jones, Bill T. and Arnie Zane

ZAZIE DE PARIS

performer

The French diva Zazie de Paris was born in Paris to Jewish parents from Poland and Bessarabia. Now one of the most renowned figures in Berlin theatre and club culture, the transsexual chanteuse was initially trained as a classical dancer. Aged 18 she went to Japan, where she performed for the first time as a woman in a transvestite show. Back in Paris she began working as a choreographer and continued to explore her relationship to her gender. After making the decision to live as a woman, she left Paris for Germany. She arrived in the thriving club and cabaret scene of West Berlin and quickly made a name for herself. After some difficult years running her own clubs and working in other parts of Europe, her career took a new direction during the 1980s. She began working as a serious actor on the German stage in Berlin, Hamburg, and other cities.

DANIEL HENDRICKSON

ZHOU HUASHAN

b. 1962

scholar

Born in Hong Kong and a graduate of the University of Hong Kong, Zhou Huashan (Chou Wah Shan) completed his PhD in sociology at University of York (UK) in 1996. His early works focused on film and women's studies. In the mid-1990s, in collaboration with others, Zhou wrote extensively on gay and lesbian issues. Texts include *Tongzhi shenxue* (Tongzhi Theology, 1994); *Tongzhi lun* (Tongzhi Theory, 1995); *Yigui xing shi: Xianggang ji Ying Mei tongzhi yundong* (The Closet Sexual History: Gay Movements in Hong Kong and Britain/USA, 1995); *Hou zhimin tongzhi* (Postcolonial Tongzhi, 1997); and *Tongzhi: Politics of Same-Sex Eroticism in Chinese Societies* (2000). Zhou was not the first to appropriate the term *tongzhi* (comrade), but he popularized its use in gay and lesbian studies when he compared the significance of *tongzhi* with that of queer. He later devoted himself to studying the Mosuo community (Yunnan, China), where people practice a marriage system called Axia (visiting-marriage).

TRAVIS KONG

ZI'EN, CUI

b. 1958

filmmaker, author

Frequently referred to as a 'queer auteur', Cui Zi'en is a Beijing-based novelist, literary and film scholar, screenwriter and an outspoken queer activist. A prolific writer, Cui has published many novels and short stories dealing with bisexuality and homosexuality in China, one of which, *Uncle's Past*, won him the 2001 Radio Literature Award in Germany. He also publishes books on film and literary criticism and writes columns for a number of Chinese art magazines, advocating independent art films. Cui began to make digital video (DV) adaptations of his own novels in 2001 and has so far made seven, including *Enter the Clown* (2001) and *Feeding Boys, Ayaya* (2003). Made on a shoestring, Cui's *Enter The Clowns* unfolds as a serendipitous succession of episodes from a disturbing confrontation between a young man and his gender-bending parent to a series of sketches involving gay desire. Stylistically, the film is a deliberate assortment of long takes, mundane action and non-professional acting. Cui is unyielding in his radical and provocative approach, both in terms of subject matter and style, and is considered the most avant-garde DV maker in China. In 2002 he received a Felipa Award from the International Gay and Lesbian Human Rights Commission.

YING ZHU

ZOO PARIS

activist organization

Zoo Paris is a French queer activist organization set up in the mid-1990s. It is a loose grouping of people from various politico-sexual minorities, many of whom come from arts or academic backgrounds. The political positions of the group are highly influenced by the work of Michel **Foucault**, queer theory and politics in the United States. Zoo has organized seminars, film screenings and other cultural events, published articles and journals and militated for curricular changes within the French university system.

DANIEL HENDRICKSON

appendix a
archives of glbt research materials (international)

An archive can be defined as a place in which public records or historical documents are preserved. There are numerous archives worldwide devoted to collecting and disseminating information about glbt culture and history. Some are affiliated with major libraries and universities while others belong to community groups and small organizations. The existence of these archives serves not only as a testament to the presence and contributions of glbt individuals and groups, but as an important vehicle for research and education. The following is a geographical directory of major glbt archives open to researchers and the general public. The information supplied includes the name of the archive, location and/or mailing address, a brief description of holdings, access availability, a contact phone number and the Internet URL.

AUSTRALIA

Australian Lesbian and Gay Archives, 6 Claremont St, South Yarra, Melbourne. Mailing address: PO Box 124, Parkville, VIC 3052. Founded in 1978 at the Fourth National Homosexual Conference in Sidney, the ALGA actively collects, preserves and makes available glbt materials from across the country. Materials, drawn from the works of writers, artists, performers, political leaders and community organizations, include 694 periodical titles, radio broadcasts, posters, theses, clippings, court transcripts and ephemera. Working in conjunction with the Victoria AIDS Council, the Archives sponsor educational programmes, publish online databases and are open to the public on Thursday evenings or by appointment.
Contact: (03) 83-44-6865;
http//home.vicnet.net.au/~alga/welcome.htm

BELGIUM

Fonds Suzan Daniel, Daniel vzw, PO Box 569, Gent 1, B-9000. Funded by membership and volunteers, Fonds Suzan Daniel organizes and catalogues all information on glbt history, especially from Belgium, and places it at the disposal of interested parties. Over 300 metres of post-Second World War documentation is distributed among established professional archives, guided by the belief that the history of the gay/lesbian movement is a part of social history in general. Materials include anything written,

printed, sung, photographed or created that might be preserved. Locations and hours of operation vary.
Contact: (0)9-223-6374;
http//www.fondssuzandaniel.be

RoSa Documentation Center and Archives on Feminism, Equal Opportunities, and Women's Studies, Koningsstr. 136, Brussels, 1000. RoSa – an abbreviation for '*rol en samenleving*' meaning 'gender role and society', is devoted to education on a broad range of gender-related subjects. Founded in 1978, the Center contains 2,500 reports on women's issues in the European Union as well as a substantial lending book collection. Online resources include fact sheets, timelines, news articles, bibliographies and posters. Open Monday–Thursday and Friday by request, RoSa is closed the last week of December.
Contact: (0)2-209-3410;
http//www.rosadoc.be/site/nieuw/start.htm

CANADA

Nova Scotia

Public Archives of Nova Scotia, 6016 University Ave., Halifax, Nova Scotia, B3H 1W4. Established by Provincial statute in 1989, the Public Archives collection focuses on Nova Scotia history from 1970 to the present day and contains considerable documentation on the Gay Alliance for Equality (GAE), Gay and Lesbian Alliance (GALA) and Gaiezette Newspaper. Open to the public seven days a week, they offer research space, photocopying, audiovisual facilities, exhibitions and reference assistance.
Contact: 902-424-6060;
http//www.gov.ns.ca/nsarm/

Ontario

Canadian Lesbian and Gay Archives, 56 Temperance St, #201, Toronto, Ontario. Mailing address: PO Box 639, Station A, Toronto, Ontario, M5W 1G2. Dedicated to the preservation of lesbian and gay history in Canada and beyond, this growing collection focuses upon people, organizations, issues and events. The James Fraser Library of 13,000 books and periodicals is supplemented by an archive of vertical files, photographs, sound recordings, artwork and other artefacts. The Archives offer a searchable online catalogue and are open to the public on Tuesday, Wednesday, Thursday evenings, and by appointment.
Contact: 416-777-2755;
http//www.clag.ca

Quebec

Archives Gaies du Quebec, 4067 Boul. St-Laurent, bureau 202, Montreal, Quebec, H2W 1Y7. International in scope, Archives Gaies houses documentation and materials of interest in the field of glbt history, including 40,000 photographs, 1,000 periodical titles, 200 sound recordings, 50 AIDS reports and other government documents. The organization offers full information and referral services, sponsors conferences and colloquia, conducts book sales and publishes an online bulletin. The collections are open to the public on Thursday evenings or by appointment.
Contact: 514-287-9987;
http//www.agq.qc.ca

Saskatchewan

Saskatchewan Archives Board, Murray Building, #91, University of Saskatchewan, 3 Campus Dr., Saskatoon, Saskatchewan, S7N 5A4. As the official archives of the Province of Saskatchewan, the Board collects all materials that have historical

significance pertaining to glbt people in Saskatchewan from 1964 to the present day. Materials include manuscripts, organizational records, vertical files, media and ephemera, with early gay rights activity documented in the papers of Doug Wilson and Neil Richards. The Board offers research space, photocopying, reference assistance, borrowing privileges and is open to the public Monday–Friday with access restriction on individual collections.
Contact: 306-933-5832;
http//www.gov. sk.ca/govt/archives

DENMARK

LBK, National Association for Gays and Lesbians, Teglgårdstr. 13, Copenhagen. Mailing address: PO Box 1023, Copenhagen, K1007. LBK, one of Europe's first gay political organizations, was founded in 1948 and since then has functioned as a community resource and archive for Denmark and beyond. The free library and reading room maintains a 10,000-volume, multi-language collection of gay fiction, non-fiction, newspaper clippings, travel guides, comics, magazines and poetry. A separate archive contains organizational records, personal files and memorabilia relating to 100 individuals and organizations. The Association offers membership, borrowing privileges, referral service and exhibits. The Library is open seven days a week and the Archive is available by appointment.
Contact: 33-13-1948;
http://www.lbl.dk

FRANCE

Archives Recherches Cultures Lesbiennes, Maison des Femmes, 163 rue de Charenton, Paris. Mailing address: PO Box 362, Paris, F75526. Founded in 1984, ARCL brings together contemporary and historical archives and a lending library focusing on the documentation of French lesbian, feminist and co-gender homosexual move-

ments. The collection includes 50 organizational records and personal papers, 3,000 books, 25 periodical titles, 200 photos, 650 audiovisual materials and is open to researchers on Fridays.
Contact: (0)14-628-5494;
http//arcl.free.fr/

Centre National d'Etudes de Recherches et de Documentation sur les Sexualités Plurielles, 38 bis rue Royale, Lille, 59800. Affiliated with the non-profit association Gai-Kitsch-Camp, Centre National is dedicated to the study, research and documentation of sexual diversity and maintains an archive that focuses on French glbt history and current events. Important collections include the records of French gay press Editions Question de Genre and the Lille Gay and Lesbian Film Festival. The organization offers membership, a lending library, meeting space, information and referral services and is open Monday–Saturday.
Contact: (0)32-006-3391;
http//www.gaykitschcamp.com/sommaire.html

Conservatoire des Archives et des Mémoires Homosexuelles de l'Académie Gay et Lesbienne, PO Box 28, Vitry sur Seine cedex, 94402. Collecting documents and artefacts since 1976, the Archives' mission is to celebrate the cultural diversity of glbt persons and groups. Holdings include 20,000 personal and organizational records, 500 periodical titles, 1,000 objects of ephemera and 15 AIDS reports. The organization offers membership, accepts donations, publishes online guides, limits photocopying and is open to all individuals by appointment.
Contact: (0)69-832-8120;
http//www.archiveshomo.info

GERMANY

Centrum Schwule Geschichte, Vogelsanger Str. 61, Cologne, 50823. CSG was founded

in 1984 with the mission of collecting and disseminating information on the history of gay men in order to support the struggle to achieve homosexual equality. The Center's archive, library and exhibition areas contain materials that document 100 years of gay life in the Rhineland and holdings include 5,000 books, 100 periodicals, 50 organizational records, manuscripts, clippings, photographs and oral histories. The reference-only collection is open by appointment.
Contact: (0)22-152-9295;
http//www.csgkoeln.de/

Ida Archiv der deutschen Frauenbewegung, Gottschalkstr. 57, Kassel, 34127. Ida is a consortium of 42 women's/lesbian libraries, archives and documentation centres from Germany, Austria, Switzerland and Luxembourg. Founded in 1984, this umbrella organization is dedicated to collecting literature that cannot be found in general libraries, offering rare documents for study and research and serving as suppliers of women's information to a larger public. In addition to documenting the women's movement in German-speaking Europe, Ida's goals are networking and the exchange of knowledge and ideas.
Contact: (0)561-989-3670;
http//www.ida-dachverband.de

Magnus-Hirschfeld-Archiv für Sexual wissenschaft, Humboldt-Universität zu Berlin, Prenzlauer Promenade 149-152, Berlin, D-13189. Founded in 1994 as a sub-unit of the federal Robert Koch Institute, the mission of the Archives is to promote, protect and preserve sexual health by collecting and disseminating scientific information. Holdings include extensive publications and manuscripts dealing with the history of homosexuality, among them letters written by gay rights pioneer Dr Magnus Hirschfeld. The Archive sponsors activities, maintains a database of international sexological institutions, organizations, resource centres and training programmes, and offers online access to scientific journals, papers and books. Admission is free and open to the general public Monday–Friday.
Contact: (0)30-479-7198;
http//www2.hu-berlin.de/sexology/index.html

Schwules Museum, Archives and Library, Mehringdamm 61, Berlin, 10961. Opened in 1985 the Museum mounts regularly changing displays that provide an overview of the gay history of Germany, with a special focus on Berlin from 1790 to the present. A permanent exhibit of 1,000 works of art is supplemented by books, biographies, manuscripts, autographs, clippings, photographs, costumes and audiovisual materials. Admission prices and hours of operation vary.
Contact: (0)30-693-1172;
http//www.schwulesmuseum.de

ITALY

Archivio Massimo Consoli, Piazzale degli Archivi 27, Roma, 00144. Established in 1959 around the personal collection of gay activist Massimo Consoli, the Archive's mission is to document the history and culture of the Italian glbt community. Holdings include 100 manuscripts, 2,000 monographs, 200 periodical titles, 3,000 articles, 1,500 postcards, 5,000 photographs, 100 audiovisual recordings and 800 AIDS manifestos. Open to all individuals by advance appointment, services include bibliographies, online catalogues, finding aids and fact sheets.
Contact: (0)65-454-8521;
http//www.cybercore.com/consoli/archivio.htm

Fondazione Sandro Penna, Via Santa Chiara 1, Torino, 10123. Founded in 1980 by the FUORI activist group, the Foundation's aim is to gather and disseminate historical and cultural studies about homosexuality and lesbianism. The collection's focus is the country of Italy from 1971 to the present and includes 20 national and local organizational records, 30 personal papers and manuscripts, books, pamphlets and audiovisual materials. The Foundation sponsors outreach programmes, publishes a newsletter and is open to the public by appointment.

Contact: 11-521-2033; http//www.arpnet.it/fsp/

MEXICO

Centro de Documentación y Archivo Histórico Lésbico de México, América Latina y el Caribe, Nancy Cárdenas, Prolongación Lucas Alaman 11, Parque Delegación Venustiano Carranza, Ciudad de México. CDAHL was formed in 1995 with the mission of centralizing the great dispersion of libraries and archives relating to the lesbian movement in Latin America. Named after lesbian activist Nancy Cárdenas, the Centre's collection includes 221 organizational and manuscripts files, 1,135 books, 431 periodical titles, 724 pamphlets, 215 leaflets, 382 articles, 86 oral histories and 6 videos. Services include borrowing privileges, interlibrary loan, reference, referral and outreach. Hours of operation are Monday–Friday.

Contact: 57-64-2367; http//www.laneta.apc.org/cdahl

THE NETHERLANDS

Internationaal Homo/Lesbisch Informatiecentrum en Archief: Homodok-Lesbisch Archief, Nieuwpoortkade 2A, Amsterdam, 1055RX; Anna Blaman Huis, Noordvliet 11, Leeuwarden, 8901EB. IHLIA is a glbt archive, library and information centre with branches in Amsterdam and Leeuwarden. International in scope, the organization also serves as a national repository for the records of Dutch gay and lesbian persons and groups. The diverse collections include a searchable catalogue of 20,000

books, 4,800 monographs, 4,100 periodicals titles, 6,500 articles, 10,000 press clippings, 2,000 video recordings, posters, artwork and ephemera. Both branches are open to visitors Monday through Friday with additional Saturday hours at Anna Blaman Huis.

Contact: Homodok-Lesbisch Archief, (0)20-606-0712; Anna Blaman Huis, (0)58-212-1829; http://www.homodok.nl

Internationaal Informatiecentrum en Archief voor de Vrouwenbeweging, Obiplein 4, Amsterdam, 1094RB. Since 1935 the IIAV has collected, stored and documented information about the social position of women, emancipation and feminism. International in scope, the collection contains 78,000 monographs, 1,000 metres of periodicals, 6,800 biographies, 65 metres of clippings, 825 metres of organizational records and personal papers and 24,500 photographs and posters. The Centre maintains an online catalogue, address database and diary of events. Hours and access vary.

Contact: (0)20-665-0820; http//www.iiav.nl

NEW ZEALAND

Lesbian and Gay Archives of New Zealand, Alexander Turnbull Library, 58–78 Molesworth St, Wellington. Mailing address: PO Box 11-695, Manners St, Wellington. LAGANZ is dedicated to the active collection, preservation and making available for creative use of the historical and cultural records of lesbians and gay men. Holdings of material from national organizations, individuals and community groups include 5,000 monographs, 1,600 periodical titles, 450 organizational records, 500 manuscripts, posters, photographs, clippings and theses. Much of the catalogue is available through the National Library and

there is an online serials list. Use is by advance appointment and hours of operation vary.
Contact: 644-474-3000;
http//www.laganz.org.nz/

SOUTH AFRICA

Gay and Lesbian Archives of South Africa, William Cullen Library, University of Witwatersrand, 1 Jan Smuts Ave., Braamfontein, Johannesburg. Mailing address: PO Box 31719, Braamfontein, Johannesburg, 2107. Established in 1997 GALA provides a permanent institutional home for historical and archival material relating to the gay and lesbian experience in South Africa. The collection includes 160 archival subject files, a lending library of 1,200 books, 250 videos, oral histories, exhibits and documentary films. The Archives offer an online catalogue and are open to the public Monday–Friday and Saturday by appointment.
Contact: 27-11-717-4239;
http//www.wits.ac.za/gala

SWITZERLAND

Schweizerisches Schwulenarchiv, Stadelhoferstr. 21, Zürich. Mailing address: PO Box CH-8023, Zürich, 8001. National in scope, the Swiss Gay Archives were established in 1993 to collect, preserve and make available documents relating to the emergence and evolution of the Swiss gay movement. The 100 archival collections include diaries, journals, photographs, personal legacies, and audio and video recordings from gay associations and individuals. Working in conjunction with the Swiss Social Archives, the Schwulenarchiv sponsors events, supports research and offers training for archival preservation. It is open to the public by appointment.
Contact: 41-43-268-8740;
http//www. schwulenarchiv.ch

UNITED KINGDOM

Glasgow Women's Library (GWL), 109 Trongate, Glasgow, G1 5HD, Scotland. Established in London in 1984 as the Lesbian Archive and Resource Centre, GWL is the only women's lending library in the United Kingdom. With 1,300 members, the Library offers research consultancy, a monthly cuttings service and a jobs database, and publishes a newsletter. The collection is open to women Tuesday–Saturday and to men by special appointment.
Contact: (0)141-552-8345;
http//www. womens-library.org.uk

Hall-Carpenter Archives, BM Archives, London, WC1N 3XX, England. Originally set up in the mid-1970s as the Campaign for Homosexual Equality, the Archives actively champion lesbian and gay rights by using national media monitoring as a means of collecting evidence concerning discrimination and police arrests. The core collection includes 80,000 press clippings housed at Middlesex University as well as 25 organizational records, photographs and serials donated to the London School of Economics. Permission is required to use the collection and days of operation vary during the academic year.
Contact: (0)207-955-7223;
http//www.adpa.mdx.ac.uk/services/ilrs/hca/hca.htm

UNITED STATES

California

AIDS History Project, University of California, San Francisco Library and Center for Knowledge Management, 530 Parnassus Ave., San Francisco, CA 94123-0840. The AHP is a collaboration of historians, archivists and AIDS activists with a mission to preserve the history of the AIDS epidemic in the San Francisco Bay Area from 1981–94. Holdings include 132.5 cubic ft of

archival records for more than 50 individuals and organizations. AHP offers reference services, indices, finding aids, photocopying and loan agreements for exhibits with restrictions and fees for certain items. They are open to the public Tuesday and Wednesday, and by appointment.
Contact: 415-476-8112;
http//www.library.ucsf.edu/sc/index.html

The Bisexual Archives, c/o Gay and Lesbian Historical Society of San Diego, PO Box 40389, San Diego, CA 92164. Founded by Fritz Klein and Regina Reinhardt in 1996, the Bisexual Archives is housed and mentored by the Lesbian and Gay Historical Society of San Diego. Focusing on all aspects of bisexuality of any period or region, the collection includes 12 ft of archival manuscripts, organizational records, clippings, and subject files. There is unrestricted access to the public and they are open Sundays, except holiday weekends, and by appointment.
Contact: 619-260-1522;
http//www-rohan.sdsu.edu/~clgoyne/lghssd/bisexualarch.html

California State University, Northridge, Human Sexuality Collection, University Library, 18111 Nordhoff St, Northridge, CA 91330-8326. Established in 1973, the Human Sexuality Collection supports the research and instructional interests of students, faculty and the activities of the Center for Sex Research. Glbt materials include 500 books, manuscripts and periodicals from the 1960s onwards. They offer reference assistance, interlibrary loan and exhibitions and are open to all researchers Monday–Friday.
Contact: 818-677-2597;
http://library.csun.edu/spcoll/bullough.html

Lesbian and Gay Historical Society of San Diego, University Heights, San Diego, CA. Mailing address: PO Box 40389, San Diego, CA 92164. Founded by Jess Jessop

in 1987, this independent organization documents the history of gay and lesbian individuals and groups based in the San Diego region from the 1940s to the present day. Included in the collection are 55 ft of manuscripts, 37 ft of organizational records, 100 ft of printed material, 12 ft of vertical files, thousands of ephemeral items, 16 ft of video, 13 ft of audio and 14 ft of photographs as well as books and periodicals. The Society offers a limited reference service and photocopying, mounts exhibits, publishes a newsletter and is open to the public on Sunday (except holiday weekends) and by appointment.
Contact: 619-260-1522;
http//www-rohan.sdsu.edu/~clgoyne/lghssd/ homepage.html

Gender Equity Resource Center, 202 Cesar Chavez Center, University of California, Berkeley, CA 94720-2440. Formerly known as the Women's Resource Center, the GERC Library has maintained information about the entire glbt community since its inception in 1972. Strong in early lesbian history and literature, the collection includes 500 books, 6 ft of pamphlet files, as well as organizational newsletters, journal articles, bibliographies and grassroots women's newspapers of the 1970s. The Center offers a full range of reference and referral services with borrowing privileges limited to Berkeley students, staff and faculty. Any individual may access the resources Monday–Friday during the academic year.
Contact: 510-642-4786;
http//students.berkeley.edu/sas/geneq

GLBT Historical Society, 657 Mission St, #300, San Francisco, CA 94105. The Society's purpose is to document the tremendous diversity of glbt history and focuses on sexual, social, political, economic, cultural and religious aspects. The 400 archival collections include manuscripts, periodicals, oral histories and ephemera that detail the

637

lives of people, as well as the workings of informal groups and organizations. The Society is open to the public by advance appointment and limited photocopying is available on a fee basis.
Contact: 415-777-5455;
http//www.glbthistory.org

James C. Hormel Gay and Lesbian Center, San Francisco Public Library, 100 Larkin St, San Francisco, CA 94102. The Hormel Center is devoted to collecting, preserving and providing access to material on all aspects of the glbt experience. International in scope, its holdings include 30,000 books, 900 periodical titles, 41 archival manu-scripts, media, ephemera, and children's and young adult collections. The centre is open to the public seven days a week, offers meeting rooms, mounts exhibits and sponsors programmes with community organizations.
Contact: 415-557-4499;
http://sfpl.org/librarylocations/main/glc/glc.htm

June L. Mazer Lesbian Archives, 626 North Robertson Blvd, West Hollywood, CA. Mailing address: PO Box 491389, Los Angeles, CA 90049. The Mazer Archives was created for the purpose of sharing with other lesbians the excitement of redis-covering the lives and struggles of the women who came before them. Holdings include 2,300 book titles and 550 period-icals as well as unpublished papers, photos, artwork, scrapbooks, games and audiovisual recordings. The Archives publishes a newsletter, hosts events and is open to the public the first Sunday of each month, every Thursday and by appointment.
Contact: 310-659-2478;
http//mazerlesbianarchives. org/

Oakland Museum of California, 1000 Oak St, Oakland, CA 94607-4892. The Oak-land Museum provides unique collections, exhibitions and educational opportunities designed to generate a broader and deeper understanding of and interest in California's environment, history, art and people. A growing collection of glbt archives include books, audiovisual materials, photographs, posters, comic books and ephemera including garments and accessories from drag performances. The Museum is open Wednesday–Sunday, is closed on holidays and admission rates vary.
Contact: 510-238-3842;
http//www.museumca.org

ONE Institute and Archives, 909 West Adams Blvd, Los Angeles, CA 90007. With 43,000 holdings, ONE houses the world's largest research library on glbt heritage and concerns. Affiliated with the University of Southern California, the Institute's mission is to foster acceptance of sexual and gender diversity by supporting worldwide educa-tion and research. The library is open to the public Monday–Saturday, offers tele-phone reference and maintains an online catalogue.
Contact: 213-741-0094;
http//www.oneinstitute.org

Stanford University, Cecil H. Green Library, Department of Special Collections, Stanford, CA 94305-6004. The Depart-ment is devoted to gay and lesbian history of Stanford University and alumni from 1972 to the present. Major archival hold-ings include Kerrigan Black Papers 1963–93, Gerard Koskovich AIDS Activism publications, and Newton 'Bud' Flounders' 3,000 volume collection of gay literature. The Library offers reference services, find-ing aids and an online catalogue, and is open to scholars and researchers with insti-tutional affiliation from Monday–Friday.
Contact: 415-752-1022;
http//www-sul.stanford.edu/depts/spc/spc.html

University of California, Los Angeles, University Research Library, Department of Special Collections, #A1713, Box

951575, Los Angeles, CA 90095-1575. Founded in 1946, the Department has been amassing glbt materials in support of its long-standing collection areas of local imprints, literature, culture and psychology. Archival documents pertaining to over 300 hundred prominent individuals include 500 ft of manuscripts, 7,500 books, 20 ft of clippings, 200 objects of ephemera, 250 audiovisual recordings and 5,000 photographs. Users must present photo identification and there are fees for telephone and mail requests by researchers not affiliated with the university. Hours of operation are Monday–Saturday during the academic year.
Contact: 310-825-4988;
http//www.library.ucla.edu/libraries/special/scweb

Colorado

Colorado Historical Society and Museum, 1300 Broadway, Denver, CO 80203. A state governmental agency since 1879, the Society Library contains materials relating to Colorado State from its inception onwards. Significant glbt archival collections include *Evans* v. *Romer* (US Supreme Court, 1996), Metropolitan Church of the Rockies, and AIDS in Colorado. Other materials include 16 manuscripts files, Denver TV news broadcasts since 1958, photos, clippings, newspapers, oral histories and ephemera. The reference-only collection is open to the public Tuesday–Saturday.
Contact: 303-866-4603;
http//www.coloradohistory.org

Connecticut

Gender Equity Archives, Elihu Burritt Library, 1615 Stanley St, New Britain, CT 06050. Working in conjunction with the Central Connecticut State University, the Archives' mission is to acquire, preserve and disseminate materials relating to the glbt communities in Connecticut. Dating

from 1963 to the present, the 1,000 archival files of personal papers, organizational records and gay rehabilitation materials are supplemented with 3,500 books, 825 periodical titles, oral histories, videos and ephemera. Open to the public seven days a week during the academic year, the Archives sponsor research, has an online catalogue, offers interlibrary loan and publishes a newsletter.
Contact: 860-832-2055;
http//library.ccsu.edu/lib/archives/equity

Florida

Stonewall Library and Archives, 1717 North Andrews Ave., Fort Lauderdale, FL 33311. Dedicated to preserving glbt culture since 1973, Stonewall Library has the largest collection of lesbian and gay books, periodicals and archival materials in the southeast United States. Holdings include 10,000 books, 1,000 periodical titles, a multimedia collection and archives of political, historical and social documents relevant to the glbt community. Stonewall is open to documented researchers only, Monday–Friday, and offers limited photocopying on a fee basis.
Contact: 954-763-8565;
http//www.stonewall-library.org

Georgia

Atlanta History Center, 130 W. Paces Ferry Rd NW, Atlanta, GA 30305. Founded in 1991, the Center actively collects and preserves any material that documents the history of the glbt community of Atlanta from 1957 to the present. The 50-cubic-ft archive includes gay and lesbian publications from throughout the southeast, organizational papers pertaining to gay rights and AIDS, as well as personal papers of gay and lesbian activists in Georgia. The Center is open Monday through Saturday and users

with identification are required to complete a patron form.
Contact: 404-814-4000;
http//www.atlhist.org

Illinois

Charles Deering McCormick Library of Special Collections, Northwestern University, 1935 Sheridan Road, Evanston, IL 60208-2355. McCormick Library focuses upon documenting the women's movement worldwide from the 1960s to the present day. The collection contains published lesbian books, journals and ephemera as well as male material relating to the gay liberation movement. There are in-house guides for ephemera and journal files, an online catalogue and electronic resources for over 100 journals. The Library publishes a newsletter, mounts exhibits, offers phone reference and is open Monday–Friday with no special requirements for admission.
Contact: 847-491-2895;
http://www.library.northwestern.edu/spec/

Gerber/Hart Library, 1127 West Granville Ave., Chicago, IL 60660. Founded in 1981 as a depository for the records of glbt individuals and organizations, Gerber/Hart is a circulating library of over 14,000 volumes, 800 periodical titles and 100 archival collections. The Library hosts programmes and events that support the belief that knowledge is critical to fostering pride and self-confidence. The collection is open to researchers by appointment and offers photocopying and interlibrary loan.
Contact: 773-381-8030;
http//www.gerberhart.org

Leather Archives and Museum, 6418 North Greenview Ave., Chicago, IL 60626. Serving the leather communities of the world, the LAAM collects stories, artefacts and information from generations of leather men and women for the purpose of revealing the traditions and truths of those who live leather, S&M and fetish lives. The Archives contain books, manuscripts, periodicals, photographs, club colours, pins, boots, posters, toys and devices, and the Museum features an exhibition gallery, 164-seat auditorium and gift shop. Admission is free and the Museum is open to the public Thursday, Saturday, Sunday and by appointment.
Contact: 773-761-9200;
http//www.leatherarchives.org

Indiana

Chris Gonzalez Library and Archives, Diversity Center, 1112 Southeastern Ave., Indianapolis, IN. Mailing address: PO Box 441473, Indianapolis, IN 46202. The growing Library began as Michael Bohr's private collection and moved to the Diversity Center in 1995. The collection focuses on glbt life in central Indiana and materials include 2,250 books, 30 videotapes, 50 photographs of local female impersonators, original artwork and complete runs of Indianapolis gay and lesbian publications. The Library accepts new acquisitions, offers research space, photocopying, reference assistance, limited borrowing privileges and is open to the public Tuesday and Saturday.
Contact: 317-639-4297;
http//www.gayindy.org

Kinsey Institute for Research in Sex, Gender, and Reproduction, Library and Archives, Morrison Hall, # 313, Indiana University, Bloomington, IN 47405. Founded in 1947 by Dr. Alfred Kinsey, the Institute Library's mission is to acquire information about sexual behaviours, attitudes and lifestyles. A portion of the materials documents glbt history and the photography collection includes works by Wilhelm von Gloeden, George Platt Lynes

and Pavel Tchelitchev. Use is restricted to qualified researchers, by appointment only, Monday–Friday.
Contact: 812-855-7686;
http//kinseyinstitute.org/library

Kentucky

Williams-Nichols Archive and Library for GLBT Studies, William F. Ekstrom Library, Belknap Campus, University of Louisville, Louisville, KY. Mailing address: PO Box 4264, Louisville, KY 40204. Originally begun by David Williams in 1982, the expanding collection is housed within the University of Louisville library system. Post-1950s materials focus on glbt individuals and groups from the Kentucky, Indiana, Ohio and Tennessee regions. Holdings include 1,000 books, 305 periodical titles, 60 ft of clippings, 12 ft of archival records, 300 photographs, 300 video and sound recordings, 200 objects of ephemera, posters, banners and autographs. The Library offers telephone and online reference, publishes acquisitions lists and is open to anyone by appointment only.
Contact: 502-852-6762;
http//library.louisville.edu/ekstrom

Maryland

National Library of Medicine, History of Medicine Division, 8600 Rockville Pike, Bethesda, MD 20894. The NLM's expansive collection of books, manuscripts, journals, pamphlets, dissertations and other materials provides the general public with a comprehensive survey of the world's history of medicine. Particularly of interest is information and posters on AIDS as well as the Surgeon-General's Office catalogue, which has various subheadings under the subject 'sexual instinct'. In addition, some of the many databases available online include CATLINE, SERLINE, AVLINE and MEDLARS. Open to the public Monday through Friday, the Library offers

research space, photocopying, telephone and online reference assistance.
Contact: 800-272-4787;
http//www.nlm.nih.gov/pubs/factsheets/hmd.html

Massachusetts

Amherst College Library, Marshall Bloom Collection, Amherst College, #2256, Box 5000, Amherst, MA 01002-5000. Named after the founder of the Liberation News Service, the Bloom Collection has been a nationwide repository of underground newspapers since 1966. In addition, the Library contains 2,100 monographs, 130 periodical titles, 50 videos, 20 sound recordings and 6 theses. Services include limited photocopying, restricted circulation of book materials, exhibitions, telephone and online reference. Access is from Monday–Friday, with offsite materials requiring 24-hour advance notice.
Contact: 413-542-2068;
http//www.amherst.edu/~library

The History Project, Cambridge Women's Center, 46 Pleasant St, Cambridge, MA 02139. Founded in 1980, the History Project's mission is to collect, preserve and disseminate information concerning glbt persons and groups of the greater Boston area from the 1940s to the present. Materials include 22 ft of organizational records, 250 reference books, 1,000 objects of ephemera, 6 ft of photographs, as well as slides, clippings and oral histories. Open by appointment only, the Project offers research space, conducts telephone reference, loans exhibits and publishes finding aids and a newsletter.
Contact: 617-557-1082;
http//www.historyproject.org

Northeastern University Library, Archives and Special Collections Department, 92 Snell Library, Boston, MA 02115. As part of the larger Northeastern University Library system, the growing Special Collections

Department houses archival records of 25 significant glbt organizations and groups from the 1970s onwards. Materials include corporate documents, minutes, clippings, media, photographs and ephemera. Some access restrictions are set by donors and the collection is open by appointment only.
Contact: 617-373-2351;
http//www.lib.neu.edu/archives

Schlesinger Library on the History of Women in America, Radcliffe College, 10 Garden Street, Cambridge, MA 02138. Originally founded in 1943 as the Women's Archives and renamed in 1967 to honour historians Arthur and Elizabeth Schlesinger, the library collects all material of relevance to American women from the 1800s onward. Materials include 50,000 books, 500 periodical titles and 180 ft of glbt-related manuscripts, photographs and microfilm. There is an online catalogue and the non-circulating collection is open to the public with proper identification from Monday to Friday and by appointment.
Contact: 617-495-8647;
http//www.radcliffe.edu/schles

Smith College Archives and Sophia Smith Collection, William Allen Nielson Library, Smith College, Northampton, MA 01063. Begun in 1908 as a college history collection, the Archives contains administrative records and college publications that document policies, practices and public relations concerning glbt student issues. The Sophia Smith Collection was founded in 1942 and documents the lives and activities of all women, especially lesbians. Materials include 200 ft archival records, 100 student letters and journals, 51 ft of subject files and 50 ft of women's liberation items. The Library offers an online catalogue with finding aids, publishes an annual report and newsletter, limited photocopying and is open to anyone with photo identification. Hours of operation vary.
Contact: 413-585-2970;
http//www.smith.edu/libraries/ca/home.htm

Women's Movement Archives, Cambridge Women's Center, 46 Pleasant St, Cambridge, MA 02139. Since 1981 the Women's Movement Archives have been preserving the records of grassroots Boston-area feminist organizations and groups. Materials from 1960 through the present include 25 organizational records, 3,000 monographs, 15 ft of vertical files, 500 objects of ephemera, 25 videos, 400 sound recordings and 4 ft of photographs and slides. Access is by appointment only and copying facilities and audiovisual equipment are limited.
Contact: 617-354-8807;
http//www.cambridgewomenscenter.org

Michigan

Michigan State's University Libraries, Special Collections, East Lansing, MI 48823. The Library began collecting glbt items in 1971 as part of the American Radicalism Collection. International in scope and dating from the 1950s onward, materials include 1,500 books, 350 journal titles, 200 ft of archival records, 37 ft of clippings, 100 comic books, and 30 recordings. The Library offers telephone and online reference, limited photocopy services, interlibrary loan, and is open to the public Monday–Friday.
Contact: 517-355-3770;
http//specialcollections.lib.msu.edu/

Minnesota

Minnesota Historical Society, 345 West Kellogg Blvd, St Paul, MN 55102-1906. The Society was chartered in 1849 as the second act of the Territorial Legislature, its mission to document the human history of Minnesota. Since 1971 it has functioned as a repository of statewide glbt materials and includes archival records from the State Department of Human Rights and the Minneapolis Department of Civil Rights as well as manuscripts, photographs, newspapers, artwork and oral histories dating from 1940. The museum galleries and research library are open without charge to the public, Monday and Wednesday–Saturday. *Contact:* 651-296-2143; http://www.mnhs.org/library/about/index. html

Nevada

James L. Dickinson Library, Special Collections, University of Nevada, PO Box 457010, Las Vegas, NV 89154-7010. Founded in 1965 to combine rare books, Nevada and gaming collections, the Library acquired the Lesbian and Gay Archives in 1986. Statewide material from 1955 to the present includes 51 ft of manuscripts and organizational records, 18 ft of periodicals and 20 objects of ephemera. Open Monday–Friday to anyone, the Library offers research space, audiovisual facilities, reference service, finding aids and mounts exhibits. *Contact:* 702-895-3954; http//www.library.nevada.edu/speccol/index.html

New Jersey

Rutgers Special Collections and University Archives, Rutgers University, New Brunswick, NJ 08903. A manuscript and rare books repository since the 1940s, the division for Rutgers University Records expanded its collection in 1962 to include all of statewide New Jersey. Over 17 ft of archival materials document the Rutgers University Lesbian and Gay Alliance, New Jersey Lesbian and Gay Coalition and other papers of New Jersey glbt individuals and organizations. Anyone can access the collection Monday–Saturday during the academic year and reference assistance, photocopying and interlibrary loan are available. *Contact:* 908-932-7006; http://www.libraries.rutgers.edu/rulib/spcol/spcol htm

New York

Human Sexuality Collection, Carl. A. Kroch Library, #2B, Cornell University, Ithaca, NY 13853. The actively expanding Collection seeks to preserve and make accessible primary sources that document historical shifts in the social construction of sexuality, with a focus on American glbt history and the politics of pornography. Materials include personal papers, oral histories, rare books, 156 archival manuscripts and 1,750 periodical titles. The Library offers reference assistance, conducts tours, publishes an online catalogue, permits limited photocopying and is open seven days a week during the academic year. *Contact:* 607-255-3530; http//rmc.library.cornell. edu/HSC

International Gay Information Center, New York Public Library, 42nd St and Fifth Ave., #316, New York, NY 10018. Begun in 1982 as a community-based repository of the History Committee of the Gay/Lesbian Activists Alliance, the Center acquired organizational records, personal papers and other materials from a wide range of sources. The collection includes 4,000 books, 2,000 periodical titles, 300 audiovisual recordings, 40 collections of archival manuscripts, and ephemera. Users with traceable identification can apply for an admission card to access the collection Tuesday through Saturday and advance orders can be placed by phone. *Contact:* 212-930-0801; http//www.nypl.org/research/chss/spe/rbk/igic.html

Lesbian, Gay, Bisexual and Transgender Community Center, The National Archive of Lesbian, Gay Bisexual and Transgender History, 208 West 13th Street, New York, NY 10011. Rich Wandel founded the Archive in 1988 at the request of the Center's Board of Directors and since then its mission has been to collect glbt materials

from across all time periods and places. In addition to the Center's lending library of books, archival holdings include 100 ft of manuscripts, 50 ft of organizational records, 150 ft of periodicals, 30 ft of subject files, 10 ft of ephemera, 12 ft of audiovisual materials and 12 ft of photographs. The Archive is open to everyone, Monday, Thursday or by appointment, and offers lectures, walking tours, finding aids and a newsletter.
Contact: 212-620-7310;
http//www.gaycenter.org/resources/archive/

Lesbian Herstory Archives, 484 14th St, Brooklyn, NY. Mailing address: PO Box 1258, New York, NY 10116. Dedicated to collecting and printing information on the lives of all lesbians, Herstory strives to break the elitism of traditional archives by being housed within the community and being involved in political struggles against gender bias and barriers to women. The collection includes 20,000 volumes, 1,600 periodical titles, 12,000 photographs, 300 special collections, 1,300 subject files, art, media and ephemera. The Archives publishes a calendar of events and is open to the public by advance appointment.
Contact: 718-768-DYKE (3953);
http//www.lesbianherstoryarchives.org

Leslie/Lohman Gay Art Foundation, 127-B Prince Street, New York, NY 10012-3154. The Foundation was established in 1990 by Charles Leslie and J. Frederic Lohman to preserve and protect glbt art from endangerment by censorship, prejudice or misunderstanding. The museum and archive contain 250 works of twentieth-century art, biographical information about artists, 3 ft of organizational records, 21 ft of subject files, videos and photographs. Galleries are open Tuesday–Saturday with archival material available by appointment only.
Contact: 212-673-7007;
http//www.leslielohman.org

New York Public Library for the Performing Arts, 40 Lincoln Center Plaza, New York, NY 10023-7498. The Performing Arts Library at Lincoln Center exhaustively collects all formats of materials related to theatrical performance from all time periods and geographical areas. Materials in the Dance, Music, Theatre and Recorded Sound Divisions provide a historical view of the works and opinions of glbt performing artists, tracking them as they have become more outspoken about their sexuality and how it affects their creativity. The collections are made up of 10,000 folders of clippings, 5,200 film and videotapes, 700 reels of microfilm, 650 hours of performance videotapes and oral history recordings, 20,200 programmes, and 800 posters, transcripts and photographs. Holdings also include numerous works with gay themes and characters as well as 7,500 books, 130 ft of manuscripts and 40 ft of organizational records documenting individual glbt artists. Users with traceable identification can apply for an admission card to access the collection, Tuesday–Saturday, and advance orders can be placed by phone.
Contact: 212-870-1630;
http//nypl.org/research/lpa/lpa.html

Schomburg Center for Research in Black Culture, New York Public Library, 515 Malcolm X Blvd, New York, NY 10037-1801. As part of a larger collection documenting African-American culture, the Schomburg Center actively collects all formats of material relating to Black glbt life from any time period and geographical area. Holdings include 34 ft of manuscripts and organizational records, 100 monographs, 3 ft of subject files, 2,400 photographs and 6 microfiche. Open Tuesday–Saturday to anyone with photo identification, the Center offers research space, audiovisual facilities, exhibitions, telephone reference, loan agreements for exhibits and fee-based photocopying.
Contact: 212-491-2225;
http//nypl.org/research/sc/sc.html

North Carolina

Duke University, Rare Book, Manuscript and Special Collections Library, Box 90185, Durham, NC 27708-0185. Originally founded in 1931, the Library has been collecting material relating to glbt activism in the southeastern United States since 1989. Major holdings include a lesbian pulp novel collection, 33,750 periodicals and 45,000 archival items from the Atlanta Feminist Alliance, North Carolina Lesbian and Gay Health Project and other regional individuals and groups. The Library publishes an online catalogue, guide to collections, newsletter and offers unrestricted access to individuals with identification from Monday through Saturday during the academic year.
Contact: 919-660-5822;
http//odyssey.lib.duke.edu

Ohio

Browne Popular Culture Library, University Libraries, Bowling Green State University, Bowling Green, OH 43403. Created in 1969 to support Bowling Green State's programmes in cultural studies, the Library's 1,250 book and periodical titles include westerns, erotic stories, science-fiction, underground comics, alternative press publications and other glbt materials from nineteenth- and twentieth-century America. The collection is open to anyone with photographic identification, seven days a week during the academic year. Research space, photocopying and telephone reference are available.
Contact: 419-372-2450;
http//www.bgsu.edu/colleges/library/pcl/pcl.html

Northeast Ohio Lesbian/Gay Archives, 10825 East Blvd, Cleveland, OH 44106. Working in collaboration with the Western Reserve Historical Society, this programme documents the achievements of glbt individuals living in the Western Reserve area prior to 1970. The collection of 5,000,000 items includes 233,000 books, 25,000 volumes of newspapers, 600,000 photographic prints and negatives, and 3,000 archival manuscripts. Open Tuesday–Saturday, admission is free to members, with a nominal fee for the general public.
Contact: 212-721-5722;
http//www.lgcsc.org/archives.html

Ohio Lesbian Archives, Cincinnati Women's Building, #304, 4039 Hamilton Ave., Cincinnati, OH 45223. Begun in 1978 by the staff of DINAH, a local lesbian newsletter, the collection moved in 1989 to its permanent home in the Cincinnati Women's Building. The Archives focus is on post-Second World War lesbian material relating to the Ohio, Kentucky, and Indiana regions. Holdings include 20 manuscript collections of women's papers, 4 ft of organizational records, 120 ft of monographs and periodicals, 17 ft of clipping files, 500 objects of ephemera, 9 ft of audio/video recordings and 250 photographs. All collections are open Tuesday and Thursday evenings and by appointment, with borrowing privileges for individuals.
Contact: 513- 541-1917;
http//www-lib.usc.edu/~retter/ohiomain.html

Pennsylvania

Andy Warhol Museum and Archive, 117 Sandusky Street, Pittsburgh, PA 15212-5890. Celebrating the life and work of artist Andy Warhol, the Museum opened its doors in 1994 as one of the Carnegie Museums of Pittsburgh. Part of the collection includes a separate Archive containing 1,500 ft of manuscripts, 100 ft monographs, 50 scrapbooks, 4,000 audiovisual recordings and 10,000 photographs. Galleries are open Tuesday–Sunday at variable admission prices. The Archives, free to the public by

appointment only, offers research space, telephone and online reference, as well as loan agreements for exhibits.
Contact: 412-237-8300;
http//www.warhol.org

University of Pennsylvania, Archives and Records Center, North Arcade, Franklin Field, Philadelphia, PA 19104-6320. The Archives and Records Center was established in 1940 as a repository of University documents. Materials include the papers of Samuel Hadden, a psychotherapist who practised homosexual 'cures', as well as 16 ft of manuscripts and 51 ft of organizational records of various glbt individuals and campus groups. The Center offer research assistance, finding aids, interlibrary loan and is open to all, at variable hours, Monday–Friday. Registration and identification are required.
Contact: 215-898-7024;
http//www.upenn.edu/AR/

Rhode Island

Brown University Special Collections Department, John Hay Library, 20 Prospect St, Box A, Providence, RI 02912. As part of a larger collection devoted to twentieth-century American history and literature, the Special Collections Department houses an 83-cubic-ft glbt archive of manuscripts, organizational records, photographs and ephemera, including a complete run of John Preston's *On Our Backs* magazine. The Library is open Monday–Friday at variable hours, offers telephone and online reference, an online catalogue, research aids and interlibrary loan.
Contact: 401-863-1512;
http//www.brown.edu/Facilities/
University_Library/libs/hay/

Texas

Archives of the Episcopal Church, 606 Ratherview Pl., Austin, TX. Mailing address: PO Box 2247, Austin, TX 78768. The Archives' mission since 1993 has been to collect and preserve records created by and about the Episcopal Church, related Anglican bodies and individual Episcopalians. Glbt materials include 32-cubic-ft of material related to Integrity, Inc., National Steering Committee for Human Sexuality Dialogues, and records of the National AIDS Memorial. The collection is open Monday–Friday by appointment only and some restrictions apply.
Contact: 512-472-6816;
http//episcopalarchives.org/index.html

Phil Johnson Historic Archives and Research Library, 2701 Reagan St, Dallas, TX. Mailing address: PO Box 190869, Dallas, TX 75219-0869. Housed within the Dallas Gay and Lesbian Community Center since 1994, this regional collection celebrates the post-Second World War history of glbt individuals and groups of the Dallas area and beyond. Holdings include 2,000 books, 10 complete journal titles, 200 photographs, 40 objects of ephemera, 50 audiovisual recordings, 1 ft of organizational records and 5 Masters theses. It is open to any individual seven days a week, with limited material available for borrowing.
Contact: 214-528-9254;
http//www.rcdallas.org/glcc.html

University of Texas at San Antonio, Archives for Research on Women and Gender, 801 South Bowie St, San Antonio, TX 78205-3296. The Archives for Research on Women and Gender was founded in 1992 to collect, preserve and make available primary source materials documenting the diversity of the South Texas region. Focusing on education about, and civil rights for, glbt persons, over 10 cubic ft of archival documents include material from the International Conference on Transgender Law and Employment Policy, transgender activists Cynthia and Linda Phillips papers, and the

Texas Lesbian Conference. Services include interlibrary loan, online catalogue and reference assistance. Researchers with identification may use the collection by appointment only Monday–Friday.
Contact: 210-458-2385;
http//www.lib. utsa.edu

Women's Collection, Blagg Huey Library, Texas Woman's University, Bell Ave., Denton, TX. Mailing address: PO Box 425528, Denton, TX 76204-5528. The Woman's Collection was established in 1932 and has grown into one of the nation's major collections on the history of women. With its focus on Texas women and Texas women's organizations of the twentieth century, holdings include 300 books, 73 journal titles, 14 ft of manuscripts, 15 ft of organizational records and 5 ft of subject files. The Collection is open to researchers Monday–Friday and offers interlibrary loan, telephone and online reference, borrowing privileges and loan agreements for exhibits.
Contact: 817-898-3751;
http//venus.twu.edu/www/twu/ library

Washington

University of Washington Libraries, Manuscripts and Archives Division, Allen Library South, Box 352900, Seattle, WA 98195. Associated with the Northwest Lesbian and Gay History Museum Project, the Division has been collecting glbt material since 1993. The collection is devoted to documenting the history of sexual minorities in Greater Seattle and western Washington and includes 30 cubic ft of manuscripts, organizational records, subject files, audiovisual recordings, photographs and oral histories. Open Monday–Friday with quarterly breaks, access varies depending on donor instructions.
Contact: 206-543-1879;
http//www.lib. washington.edu/

Wisconsin

Wisconsin Historical Society, 816 State St, Madison, WI 53706. As part of a larger collection documenting the history of Wisconsin state, the Society houses 70 cubic ft of material relating to glbt issues and activism. Holdings include manuscripts, organizational records, clippings and audiovisual materials for the Madison Committee for Gay Rights, Madison Gay Men and Lesbians United, National Coalition of Gay Sexually Transmitted Disease Services and other individuals and groups. The Society is open to anyone Monday–Saturday and offers research space, photocopying facilities and telephone reference.
Contact: 608-264-6460;
http//www.shsw.wisc.edu/archives

CATHERINE R. BURKE

appendix b
sex laws (international)

For up-to-date information, please visit http://www.sodomylaws.org/

AFGHANISTAN

Islamic Shari'a law, which forbids homosexual relations for both men and women, applies in Afghanistan. The chaotic state of the country is reflected in the way in which justice is applied. Amnesty International has received reports of five men convicted of sodomy by an Afghan Shari'a in 1998 who were executed by having a wall of dried mud collapsed on top of them.

ALBANIA

Before 1995 homosexuality was a criminal offence under Article 137 of the Penal Code, which specified punishments of up to 10 years' imprisonment. Lesbianism has never been a criminal offence. The law was repealed in 1995, and under Article 116 of the Criminal Code, the age of consent for same-sex sexual acts is 18 years. The age of consent for heterosexual sex is 14 years.

ALGERIA

Article 388 of the Algerian Penal Code 1966 makes 'sodomy' punishable by imprisonment from 2 months to 2 years and a fine. When one of the partners is under 18 years of age, the punishment for the older person can be raised to 3 years and a fine. In 1984 a 'Code de Famille', based upon Islamic principles, was passed, which punishes sodomy with imprisonment from 2 months to 2 years. Article 333 of the Code also criminalizes 'acts against nature' with a member of the same sex (presumably covering lesbianism), for which the penalty can be imprisonment from 6 months to 3 years, and a fine.

ANDORRA

The age of consent for all sexual activity is 16 years.

ANGOLA

Homosexual acts are illegal, described as offences against public morality.

ANTIGUA AND BARBUDA

The laws of the United Kingdom apply, with a higher age of consent for homosexual acts at 18 years.

ARGENTINA

The minimum age limit for gay sex is 16 years. The 'corruption' of minors (under the age of 18) is a criminal offence. A civil partnerships act for same-sex couples was passed in 2003.

ARMENIA

Until 2003, Article 116 of the Armenian Penal Code 1934 criminalized anal intercourse between men with a maximum penalty of 5 years' imprisonment, in line with the corresponding Section 121 of the former Soviet Union's Penal Code. Armenian legislation did not explicitly criminalize non-penetrative homosexual sex between consenting adults, or lesbian sex. In 2000 the Parliamentary Assembly of the Council of Europe made the repeal of Article 116 a condition of membership of the Council of Europe. In 2003 the Armenian National Assembly approved a new Criminal Code, which repealed article 116. The age of consent for all consenting sexual activity is now 16 years.

ARUBA

The laws of Netherlands Antilles apply, which specify an age of consent of 16 years for all sexual activity.

AUSTRALIA

Australia is a federal government comprising six states and two territories, each with its own independent legislatures and sex laws.

Australian Capital Territory

Homosexuality was decriminalized in 1976. The age of sexual consent is 16 years for heterosexual and gay sex. Lesbianism has never been a criminal offence. The ACT Discrimination Act 1991 prohibits discrimination on the basis of sexuality, which is defined as 'heterosexuality, homosexuality (including lesbianism) or bisexuality' and transsexuality. The Act covers discrimination in employment, education, access to premises,

goods, services and facilities, accommodation, clubs and requests for information.

New South Wales

In 1984 homosexuality was decriminalized and the age of sexual consent set at 18 years. The age of consent for heterosexual sex is 16 years. Lesbianism has never been criminalized. The Anti-Discrimination Act 1977 prohibits discrimination on the grounds of sexual orientation in employment, accommodation, education, the provision of goods and services, and club membership or benefits. In 1996 the Act was amended to prohibit discrimination against transsexuals. In 1994 the government passed laws prohibiting vilification of individuals on the grounds of sexuality, transsexuality and HIV/AIDS status.

Northern Territory

Male homosexuality was decriminalized in 1983. The age of consent for male homosexuality is 18 years, compared to 16 for heterosexual and lesbian sex. The Northern Territory Anti-Discrimination Act 1992 prohibits discrimination on the grounds of sexuality, which is defined as meaning heterosexuality, homosexuality, bisexuality or transsexuality, and covers employment, education, accommodation and the provision of goods and services. Section 37 allows a person to discriminate on the grounds of sexuality where work with children is involved.

Queensland

Male homosexuality was decriminalized in 1982. The age of consent for anal sex between men is 18 years, and 16 for all other consenting heterosexual and homosexual activity. Public decency laws still exist, containing a preamble that includes a passage condemning homosexuality. Lesbianism has never been a criminal offence. The Anti-Discrimination Act 1991 protects lesbians and gay men from discrimination on the limited ground of their 'lawful sexual activity'. The Act allows exemptions where people are working with children.

South Australia

Homosexuality was decriminalized in 1972. The age of consent for gay sex is 17 years. Lesbianism has never been a criminal offence.

Tasmania

In 1997 male homosexuality was decriminalized. The age of consent for all sexual activity is 17 years. Lesbianism has never been a criminal offence. In 1998 legislation was passed prohibiting discrimination on the basis of sexuality.

Victoria

Male homosexuality was decriminalized in 1980 with the reform of the Crimes (Sexual Offences) Act 1980. Lesbianism has never been a criminal offence. The age of consent for all sexual activity is 16 years. The Victorian Equal Opportunity Act 1995 prohibits discrimination on the basis of 'lawful sexual activity' rather than 'sexual orientation', which excludes transgendered people. Exemptions allow discrimination in employment involving children or to allow compliance with religious beliefs.

Western Australia

Homosexuality was decriminalized in 1990. The age of consent for all sexual activity is 16 years.

AUSTRIA

Homosexuality was decriminalized in 1971. Article 209 of the Penal Code stipulated an age of consent of 18 for gay male sex, compared to heterosexual and lesbian sex. The age of

consent for gay male sex was raised to 19 years in 1988, but was repealed in 2002. The age of consent is now 14 years for all consenting sexual activity. In 1997 Articles 220 and 221 of the Code, which banned positive information about homosexuality and on gay and lesbian associations, were repealed.

AZERBAIJAN

Before 1988 Article 113 of the Penal Code criminalized anal intercourse between men, with a penalty of between 5 and up to 7 years' imprisonment, followed the corresponding Section 121 from the former Soviet Union's Penal Code. Lesbian and non-penetrative gay sex between consenting adults was never a criminal offence. In 1988 homosexuality was decriminalized, with a common age of consent for all sexual activity of 16 years.

BAHAMAS

The Sexual Offences and Domestic Violence Act 1991 legalizes homosexuality, with an age of consent of 18 years, compared to 16 for heterosexuals.

BAHRAIN

Homosexuality is illegal. The Indian Penal Code, implemented by the British, was applied until 1956. Under Article 377 of the Code, sodomy was punished by deportation for 20 years, imprisonment for up to 10 years, or a fine. The new Penal Code introduced in 1956 made 'unnatural sexual offences' punishable by imprisonment not exceeding 10 years, with or without corporal punishment. This Code remained in force after Bahrain gained independence from Great Britain.

BANGLADESH

Section 377 of the Penal Code states that anyone who voluntarily has 'carnal intercourse against the order of nature with any man, woman or animal' shall be punished with life imprisonment and a fine, or deportation if the participants are non-nationals.

BARBADOS

Homosexuality is illegal. The age of consent for heterosexual acts is 16 years.

BELARUS

Until 1994 Article 119(1) of the Criminal Code criminalized male anal intercourse with a penalty of up to 5 years' imprisonment, following the equivalent legislation from the former Soviet Union. In 1994 male homosexuality was decriminalized, with an age of consent of 18 years. The age of consent for all sexual activity is now 16 years.

BELGIUM

Homosexuality was decriminalized in 1792. The age of consent for all sexual activity is 16 years. In 2003 marriage laws were amended to allow same-sex couples to marry, excluding the right to adopt children.

BELIZE

Homosexuality was decriminalized in 1998, with a common age of consent for all sexual activity of 16 years.

BENIN

Article 88 of the Penal Code 1996 states that anyone who commits 'an indecent act or an act against nature' with an individual of the same sex will be punished with 1 to 3 years' imprisonment and a fine.

BERMUDA

Until 1994 Section 175 of the Penal Code prohibited male homosexuality with a penalty of up to 10 years' imprisonment. Attempted homosexual contacts were punishable by up to 5 years' imprisonment. In 1994 the Bermudan legislature legalized sex between men over age 18. The age of consent for lesbian and heterosexual relationships is assumed to be 16 years, in line with the laws of the United Kingdom.

BHUTAN

Male homosexuality is illegal, punishable by a maximum prison sentence of life imprisonment.

BOLIVIA

The Penal Code does not explicitly mention homosexuality. Amnesty International has received reports of regular intimidation and arrests of homosexuals by police. The age of sexual consent is 17 years.

BOSNIA-HERZOGOVINA

As part of the former Yugoslavia, male homosexual acts were illegal under the Penal Code 1959. In 1977 the power over penal legislation was devolved from the Federal Republic to the eight states and provinces. Bosnia-Herzegovina chose to retain the ban, with Section 93(2) of the Criminal Code punishing male homosexual acts ('unnatural debauchery') with a penalty of up to 1 year's imprisonment. Lesbianism was never a criminal offence. In 1998, the Criminal Code was amended and homosexuality was decriminalized. The age of consent is 16 for all sexual activity. A Gender Equality Law was adopted in 2003, prohibiting discrimination based upon sexual orientation.

BOTSWANA

Chapter 8.01, Sections 164–7 of the Penal Code state that any person who 'has carnal knowledge of any person against the order of nature' or permits a male person 'to have carnal knowledge of him or her against the order of nature' is guilty of an offence and can be imprisoned for up to 7 years, or 5 years for attempts. Section 167 outlaws 'acts of gross indecency' between men, whether in public or private.

BRAZIL

Brazil decriminalized most homosexual acts in 1823. The age of consent is 14 for all forms of sexual activity. It is a criminal offence to 'corrupt' minors (those under 18) by sexual acts. Amnesty International has received reports of the police using laws relating to the 'safeguarding of morality and public decency' and 'preventing outrageous behaviour' to stop, arrest and bring gay men to trial. Brazil now recognizes same-sex relationships.

BRUNEI

Sections 292, 294 and 377 of the Criminal Code criminalize homosexuality, with a penalty of up to 10 years' imprisonment or a fine.

BULGARIA

The age of consent for male anal intercourse is 18 years, and 14 years for heterosexual and non-penetrative homosexual activity. Article 157 of the Penal Code prohibits 'scandalous homosexuality', homosexuality in public and activities that may 'lead to perversion' with a punishment of up to 5 years' imprisonment.

BURKINA FASO

Under Section 331 of the Penal Code, the age of consent for homosexual acts is 21 years, compared to 13 for heterosexuality.

BURMA/MYANMAR

Male homosexuality is illegal under the Penal Code 1882.

BURUNDI

Homosexuality is punishable as an 'immoral act'.

CAMBODIA/KAMPUCHEA

There are no laws prohibiting homosexuality. The age of consent for all consenting sexual activity is 16 years.

CAMEROON

Article 347 of the Penal Code criminalizes sexual activity between members of the same sex with a penalty of 6 months to 5 years' imprisonment and a fine. More severe sentencing is imposed if one of the persons involved is aged between 16 and 21 years.

CANADA

Homosexuality was decriminalized in 1969, with an age of consent for homosexual acts of 21 years. In 1988 this was lowered to 18. There is now a common age of consent for all sexual activity of 14 years. Discrimination on the basis of sexual orientation is prohibited and same-sex relationships are recognized in most states. In 2005 the state of Ontario legalized same-sex marriage and it is expected that a similar nationwide law will be passed.

CAPE VERDE

As a former Portuguese territory, the 1886 Portuguese Penal Code was imposed and stayed in force after Cape Verde gained independence. Sections 390 and 391 of the Code criminalize homosexual sex as 'acts against nature' and 'assaults on public or personal decency'.

CAYMAN ISLANDS

Article 142 of the Penal Code criminalizes male homosexual conduct.

CENTRAL AFRICAN REPUBLIC

Homosexuality is legal, although not explicitly mentioned in the criminal law.

CHAD

Homosexuality is legal, although not explicitly mentioned in the criminal law.

CHILE

Until 1998 Article 365 of the Chilean Criminal Code prohibited homosexuality with punishments of up to 5 years' imprisonment. In 1998 homosexuality was decriminalized, with an age of consent of 18 years, compared to 12 for heterosexuality. Lesbianism has never been a criminal offence.

CHINA, PEOPLE'S REPUBLIC OF

China's criminal law does not explicitly mention homosexuality, but a common age of consent for all sexual activity is set at 14 years.

COLUMBIA

Homosexuality was decriminalized in 1980, with a common age of consent for all sexual activities of 14 years. The 1991 Constitution prohibits the death penalty, forced disappearances, torture and cruel, inhuman and degrading treatment, and guarantees equal protection of the law, the right to 'personal and family intimacy', rights to free expression, assembly and association, and the right to 'the free development of one's personality'.

COOK ISLANDS

Although a territory of New Zealand, where homosexuality is legal, Section 155 of the Cook Islands' Criminal Code prohibits male anal intercourse with a penalty of up to 7 years' imprisonment, and Section 154 pro-hibits 'indecent acts' between males with a punishment of up to 5 years' imprisonment.

COMOROS

No reliable information is available, although as Comoros is an Islamic republic, homosexuality is assumed to be illegal.

CONGO, DEMOCRATIC REPUBLIC OF

Homosexuality is not explicitly mentioned in the criminal law, but Articles 168–70 and 172 of the Criminal Code, which punish 'crimes against family life', are frequently used to persecute gay men.

COSTA RICA

Consensual homosexual acts between adults are legal and the age of consent for all forms of sexual activity for both males and females is 15.

CROATIA

As part of the former Yugoslavia, sex between men was illegal under the 1959 Penal Code. During the 1970s the power over penal legislation was devolved from the Federal Republic to the eight states and provinces. In 1977 Croatia decriminalized male homosexuality, setting the age of consent for gay sex at 18 years, compared to 14 for heterosexuals. In 1998 the new Penal Code of 1997 equalized the age of consent for all sexual activities at 14 years. Lesbianism was never a criminal offence. Discrimination on the basis of sexual orientation is prohibited.

CUBA

Article 303A of the Penal Code 1988 punishes 'publicly manifested' homosexuality with between 3 months and 1 year's imprisonment, or a fine for people 'persistently bothering others with homosexual amorous advances'.

CYPRUS

Until 1998 Article 171 of the Criminal Code completely prohibited male homosexual acts between consenting adults, with a sentence of 2 to 14 years' imprisonment, or 3 years' imprisonment for attempts. In 1993 the European Court of Human Rights held that the Cypriot law constituted a violation of Article 8 of the European Convention of Human Rights. In 1998 homosexuality was decriminalized and the age of consent for homosexuality set at 18 years, compared to 16 for heterosexuality. In 2000 the Cyprus Parliament enacted legislation removing all pejorative descriptions of gay sex in the law. When Cyprus joined the European Community, in 2004, a common age of consent for all sexual activities was set at 17 years. Lesbianism has never been a criminal offence.

CZECH REPUBLIC

Homosexuality was decriminalized in 1961. The age of consent for all sexual activity is 15 years.

DARUSSALAM

No information.

DENMARK

Male homosexuality was decriminalized in 1930. Lesbianism was never a criminal offence. In 1976 the age of consent was equalized at 15 for all consenting sexual activities. Article 225 of the Criminal Code makes it an offence to 'induce' a person under 18 to sexual acts 'by gravely abusing superior age or experience'. In 1987, discrimination and vilification on the basis of sexual orientation was prohibited. In 1989 Denmark became the first country in the world to introduce a registered partnerships law for same-sex couples, with the same rights and responsibilities as heterosexual married couples. Same-sex couples may only adopt their partner's children.

DJIBOUTI

Homosexuality is illegal and the Criminal Code is thought to apply to both women and men.

DOMINICAN REPUBLIC

The age of consent for all sexual activity is 18 years. Article 330 of the Penal Code, which penalizes 'every violation of decorum and good behaviour on public streets' with up to 2 years' imprisonment, is frequently used to persecute gay men.

ECUADOR

Until 1997 Article 516 of the Penal Code prohibited male homosexuality, with punishments of 4 to 8 years' imprisonment. The law was repealed in 1997. Article 23 of the Constitution prohibits discrimination on the basis of sexual orientation.

EGYPT

Homosexuality is not explicitly mentioned in the law. However, Article 9C of the Law on the Combat of Prostitution 1961, which prohibits 'habitual debauchery', is regularly used to arrest, prosecute and imprison gay men.

EQUATORIAL GUINEA

No information is available.

EL SALVADOR

The criminal law does not explicitly refer to homosexuality and sets a common age of consent for all sexual activity of 18 years. Laws relating to 'moral behaviour and good habits' have been used to persecute gay men.

ERITREA

The age of consent for all sexual activities is 18 years.

ESTONIA

Until 1992 Article 118 of the Penal Code followed the corresponding Section 121 from the former Soviet Union, which criminalized 'buggery' (anal intercourse between men). Lesbian and non-penetrative gay sex between consenting adults was not explicitly mentioned in the law. In 1992 male homosexuality was decriminalized and a common age of consent for all sexual activities set at 18 (or 14–17 with parental consent).

ETHIOPIA

Sections 600 and 601 of the Penal Code prohibit male and female homosexuality, with a penalty of 10 days to 3 years' imprisonment. This penalty may be increased by 5 or more years when the offender 'makes a profession of such activities' or exploits a dependency relation in order to exercise influence over the other person. The maximum sentence of 10 years' imprisonment can be applied when one partner transmits a venereal disease to the other, when fully aware of being infected; or when distress, shame or despair drives the other partner to commit suicide. The age of consent for heterosexual sex is 15 years.

FALKLAND ISLANDS (MALVINAS)

The age of consent for male homosexual acts is 18 years, compared to 16 for heterosexual and lesbian acts.

FAROE ISLANDS

Article 225(2) of the Criminal Code sets an age of consent for male homosexual acts of 18 years, compared to 15 for heterosexuals.

Article 225(3) of the Penal Code criminalizes homosexual 'seduction' of persons under the age 21, compared to an age limit of 18 for heterosexuals. 'Seduction', in the case of heterosexual relations, is set as 'inducement by gravely abusing superior age or experience', while for homosexual relations the abuse need not to be 'grave'.

FIJI

Section 175 criminalizes male anal intercourse (defined as 'carnal knowledge against the order of nature') with a punishment of imprisonment for up to 14 years. Section 177 states that other 'indecent practices between males' are punishable by imprisonment of up to 5 years. Despite its prohibition upon male homosexuality, Fiji became only the second country in the world to include sexual orientation in its Constitution's anti-discrimination clause in 1998.

FINLAND

Homosexuality was decriminalized in 1971, with an age of consent of 16 years, compared to 15 for heterosexuals. In 1998 the age of consent was equalized at 16 years for all sexual activity, and Article 20.9.2 of the Penal Code, banning the 'public encouragement or incitement of inchastity between members of the same sex', was repealed. Discrimination on the basis of sexual orientation is prohibited and in 2002 a civil partnerships scheme for same-sex couples was introduced.

FRANCE

The French Revolution decriminalized all consenting sexual activity in 1791. The Napoleonic Code of 1810 accordingly made no reference to sodomy or same-sex relations. Homosexuality has remained legal in France ever since, but the age of consent was not equalized with heterosexuality (15 years) until 1982. Since 1985 discrimination on the basis of sexual orientation is prohibited, including within the armed forces. In 1990 the Pact of Civil Solidarity was introduced, providing legal recognition of same-sex partnerships.

FRENCH GUYANA

The laws of France apply, which specify an age of consent for all sexual activity of 15 years.

FRENCH POLYNESIA/TAHITI

The laws of France apply, which specify an age of consent for all sexual activity of 15 years.

GABON

The age of consent for heterosexuality is 15 years, and is thought to be 21 for homosexuality.

GAMBIA, THE

Article 144 of the Criminal Code 1965 states that any person who 'has carnal knowledge of any person against the order of nature' or who permits any male person to have carnal knowledge of him or her 'against the order of nature' is guilty of a felony and is liable to imprisonment for a term of 14 years.

GEORGIA

Until 2000 the Georgian Penal Code followed the corresponding Section 121 from the former Soviet Union, which criminalized 'buggery' (anal intercourse between men). Lesbian and non-penetrative gay sex between consenting adults was not explicitly mentioned in the law. In 2000 male homosexuality was decriminalized, with a common age of consent for all sexual activities of 16 years.

GERMANY

Homosexuality was decriminalized in West Germany in 1969, setting an age of consent of 21 years, which was later reduced to 18. In 1989 the East German parliament equalized the age of consent for homosexuality to 14 years, in line with heterosexuality. In 1994 the unified German Parliament introduced a common age of consent for all sexual activities of 14 years. In 2004 the Parliament introduced laws extending some legal protection to same-sex partnerships.

GHANA

Article 105 of the Penal Code 1960 states that 'unnatural carnal knowledge' with any person is a misdemeanour, even if consent is given. It is assumed that this law is used to punish homosexual activities.

GIBRALTAR

The age of consent for homosexuality is 18 years.

GREECE

Homosexuality was decriminalized in 1951. Until 1987 the age of consent for heterosexuals and lesbians was 16 years, and 17 years for gay men. The age of consent for all consenting sexual activity is now 15 years.

GREENLAND

Greenland is a self-governing dependency of Denmark and has a common age of consent for all sexual activity of 15 years. When Denmark became the first country to introduce a partnership law in 1989, Greenland declined to adopt the law. The Greenland Parliament eventually adopted the Danish law in 1996.

GRENADA

Male homosexuality is illegal. There is no mention of lesbianism in the criminal law. The age of consent for heterosexuality is 17 years.

GUADELOUPE

The laws of France apply, which specifies an age of consent for all sexual activity of 15 years.

GUAM

The age of consent for all sexual activity is 16 years.

GUATEMALA

The age of consent for all consenting sexual activity is 14 years. There is a law against the corruption of minors (persons under 18 years) that may be applied if one of the partners is over 18 years of age. However this law can be or is only applied in cases where the complaint is brought before the authorities by the parents or guardians of the minor.

GUINEA

Article 325 of the Penal Code states that 'any indecent act or act against nature' committed with an individual of the same sex will be punished by a maximum 3-year prison sentence and a fine. If the act is committed with a minor (a person under 21 years), the maximum penalty is imposed. Articles 327 and 362, which punish 'public acts of indecency', are also used to persecute gay men. The age of consent for heterosexuality is 15 years.

GUINEA BISSAU

A military code of law applies, which makes no reference to homosexuality.

GUYANA

Section 351 of the Criminal Law Offences Act prohibits acts or attempted acts of 'gross indecency' in private or public, with a penalty of up to 2 years' imprisonment. Section 352 criminalizes 'buggery' with a punishment of life imprisonment or up to 10 years for attempts.

HAITI

The age of consent for heterosexuality is 18 years. It is unclear whether this also applies to homosexuality.

HONDURAS

The age of consent for all sexual activity is 18 years. Police frequently charge, or threaten to charge, gay men, transvestites, prostitutes and lesbians with offending 'morality and public decency' if seen expressing physical affection in public. Transvestites and prostitutes are often charged with 'public scandal' merely for cross-dressing or appearing in public.

HONG KONG

As a former British colony, male homosexuality was illegal until 1991, when an age of consent of 21 was set, compared to an age of 16 for heterosexual and lesbian sex. In 2000 Hong Kong reverted to Chinese rule. Homosexuality continues to be widely accepted in Hong Kong.

HUNGARY

Homosexuality was decriminalized in 1961, with an age of consent of 20 years, reduced to 18 years in 1978. In 2002 the age of consent was equalized with heterosexuality at 14 years and the country introduced a domestic partnership scheme for same-sex couples.

ICELAND

In 1992 a common age of consent for all consenting sexual activities was set at 14 years. Discrimination on the basis of sexual orientation is prohibited and a registered partnership scheme confers the same rights as for married couples upon same-sex couples, including the right to adopt a partner's child.

INDIA

Section 377 of the Penal Code criminalizes anal and oral intercourse ('carnal intercourse against the order of nature') with any man or woman, punishable by life imprisonment or with imprisonment of either description for a term that may extend to 10 years, and shall also be liable to a fine. Section 294 of the Code, which penalizes any kind of 'obscene behaviour in public', is also used against gay men.

INDONESIA

There is no explicit reference to homosexuality in the criminal law. The age of consent is 18 years.

IRAN

Iran has adopted Islamic Shari'a law, under which male and female homosexuality is illegal. Article 110 of the Islamic Penal Code 1991 states that sodomy is a crime, punishable by death if the participants are consenting adults. A non-adult who engages in consensual sodomy is subject to a punishment of 74 lashes. Articles 121 and 122 state that 'tafhiz' (frottage) committed by two men is punishable by 100 lashes, or death on the fourth occasion. Articles 123 and 124 state that if two men 'stand naked under one cover without any necessity', both are punished with up to 99 lashes. Article 155 prohibits a man 'kissing another with lust', with a punishment of 60 lashes.

Articles 127–30 state that the punishment for lesbianism involving persons who are mature, of sound mind and consenting is 100 lashes, or death on the fourth occasion. Article 134 states that women who 'stand naked under one cover without necessity' and are not relatives are punished by up to 100 lashes.

IRAQ

Article 395 of the Penal Code 1969 sets an age of consent for male homosexuality at 18 years. Where one of the partners is between 15 and 18 years old, the adult may be punished with imprisonment of up to 7 years. Where the minor is 14 years or younger, the adult may be punished with a maximum of 10 years' imprisonment.

IRELAND, REPUBLIC OF

Until 1993 male homosexuality was criminalized by two statutes inherited from the British colonial era: the Offences against the Person Act of 1861, which criminalized anal intercourse, and the Criminal Law Amendment Act of 1885, criminalizing all other sexual acts between men as 'gross indecency'. The 1982 case *Norris* v. *Attorney-General* challenged the legality of the anti-sodomy laws. On appeal to the European Court of Human Rights in 1989 the Commission ruled that the laws breached Article 8 of the European Convention of Human Rights and recommended their repeal. The laws were eventually repealed in 1993, with an age of consent for male homosexuality of 17 years. The age limit for lesbian relations and for heterosexual relations (except for vaginal and anal intercourse) is set at 15.

ISRAEL

Until 1988 male homosexuality was punishable under Section 351 of the Penal Code with up to 10 years' imprisonment, although there was already a policy of non-prosecution. In 1988 the law was repealed, with an age of consent for all sexual activity of 16 years.

ITALY

The age of consent for all consenting sexual activity is 14 years.

IVORY COAST

The criminal law makes no explicit reference to homosexuality.

JAMAICA

Sections 76–9 of the Penal Code prohibit male homosexuality with a penalty of up to 10 years' imprisonment and hard labour. Attempts to commit homosexual acts or 'indecent assaults' on another male incur up 7 years' imprisonment, with or without hard labour.

JAPAN

The law defines sexual conduct as that which occurs between partners of different sexes and does not characterize same-sex activity as true 'sexual conduct'. The Japanese phrase for homosexuality is therefore '*seikou-ruiji-koui*', meaning conduct that is similar to sexual conduct. The age of consent for all sexual activities is 13 years. The Youth Protection Law prohibits adults (over 18 years) from having sex with persons under the age of 17 years.

JORDAN

Homosexuality is illegal. The age of consent for heterosexuals is 16 years.

KAZAKHSTAN

Before 1997 Article 104 of the Penal Code criminalized 'buggery', following the corresponding Section 121 from the former Soviet Union, which criminalized anal intercourse between men. In 1997 the law was repealed and replaced with a common age of consent for all sexual activity of 16 years. Lesbianism was never a criminal offence.

KENYA

Sections 162–165 of the Penal Code criminalize male homosexuality, called 'carnal knowledge against the order of nature', which incurs a penalty of 5–14 years' imprisonment. Lesbianism is not mentioned in the law.

KIRIBATI (FORMERLY GILBERT ISLES)

Sections 153 and 154 of the Penal Code criminalize 'buggery' with a penalty of up to 14 years' imprisonment, and attempts with up to 7 years' imprisonment. Section 155 criminalizes acts of 'gross indecency' in private or public with a penalty of up to 5 years' imprisonment.

KOREA, NORTH

The Criminal Code makes no explicit reference to homosexuality, but violations of 'the rules of the collective socialistic life', punishable by 2 years' imprisonment, can be used to persecute gay men.

KOREA, SOUTH

Homosexuality is legal, with a common age of consent for all sexual activity set at 13 years.

KUWAIT

Article 193 of the Penal Code punishes sexual intercourse between men over 21 years of age with imprisonment of up of to 7 years. Islamic Shari'a law, which forbids homosexual relations for both men and women, also applies.

KYRGYZSTAN

Before 1998 male homosexuality was an offence under Article 112 of the Penal Code, in line with the old Section 121 from the former Soviet Union. In 1998 male homosexuality was decriminalized. Lesbianism and non-penetrative gay sex between consenting adults was never criminalized.

LAOS

Homosexuality is not a criminal offence but is considered an offence against local manners and customs.

LATVIA

Until 1992 Paragraph 124(1) of the Criminal Code criminalized male homosexuality, following Section 121 from the former Soviet Union, which specifically criminalized 'anal intercourse between men', punishable by up to 5 years imprisonment. In 1992 the law was repealed, with an age of consent set at 18 years, compared to 16 for heterosexuals. There is a common age of consent for all sexual activity of 16 years. Lesbianism was never a criminal offence.

LEBANON

Article 534 of the 1943 Penal Code criminalizes homosexuality, which is punishable by imprisonment not exceeding 1 year. The definition of homosexuality is thought to also include lesbianism, but is seldom prosecuted.

LESOTHO

Homosexuality is legal but is not explicitly mentioned in the criminal law.

LIBERIA

Section 14(74) of the penal law provides that a person who engages in 'deviate sexual intercourse' or 'voluntary sodomy' has committed a punishable offence.

LIBYA

In 1953 Libya enacted a Penal Code, based upon the Egyptian model (based upon the Italian Code, which dates back to the Napoleonic Code), in which homosexuality was legal. After the 1969 coup, which brought Colonel Gaddafi to power, the criminal law was revised. Section 407(4) of the Code criminalizes homosexuality with 3–5 years' imprisonment. Article 408 punishes 'indecent acts' between men.

LIECHTENSTEIN

In 1989 Section 129 of the 1852 Penal Code was repealed, decriminalizing male homosexuality and setting an age of consent of 18 years, compared to 16 for heterosexuals and lesbians. There is a common age of consent for all consenting sexual activity of 14 years. A so-called 'protection clause' for under-18-year-olds exists: when one of the partners is under 18 years, the age difference between the partners must not be more than 3 years.

LITHUANIA

Until 1993 male homosexuality was criminalized, following the corresponding Section 121 from the former Soviet Union which criminalized 'anal intercourse between men'. Lesbian and non-penetrative gay sex was never criminalized. In 1993 the law was repealed, setting the age of consent at 18 for male homosexuality. Lesbian and non-penetrative gay sex was never criminalized. In 2002 the age of consent was equalized at 16 for all consenting sexual activity. In 2005 an act was passed prohibiting discrimination on the basis of sexual orientation.

LUXEMBOURG

Homosexuality was decriminalized in 1792. In 1992 the Penal Code was reformed, setting an age of consent for all consenting sexual activity of 16 years. In 2004 a civil partnership law for same-sex couples was introduced.

MACAO

As a Portuguese territory, the laws of Portugal applied until 2000, when Macao reverted to a Chinese territory, where homosexuality is not explicitly mentioned in the criminal law.

MACEDONIA

Until 1977 the Penal Code 1959 criminalized male homosexual activity in all of the former Yugoslavia. During the 1970s the power over penal legislation was devolved from the Federal Republic to the eight states and provinces. Macedonia chose to retain the ban. From 1977 Section 101(2) of the Criminal Code criminalized male homosexual acts ('unnatural debauchery') and punishable by up to 1 year's imprisonment. Lesbianism was never illegal. In 1995 Macedonia was admitted to the Council of Europe and the government undertook to reform the Penal Code and decriminalize homosexuality.

MADAGASCAR

Homosexuality is legal, with an age of consent of 21 years.

MALAWI

Section 153 of the Penal Code, which prohibits 'unnatural offences', and Section 156 concerning 'public decency', are used to punish homosexual acts. Non-nationals who commit homosexual acts with Malawians can be prosecuted under Article 156 and deported as 'undesirable aliens'.

MALAYSIA

Section 377(A) of the Penal Code punishes 'carnal intercourse against the order of nature', (defined as male anal or oral intercourse), punishable by up to 20 years' imprisonment or a public whipping. The revised text makes it clear that the law does not apply to lesbians. The state's Religious Affairs Department has a new law imposing a fine, six beatings with a rotan cane and/or 3 years' imprisonment for sexual 'offences' including prostitution, heterosexual adultery, lesbianism and anal intercourse.

MALDIVES, REPUBLIC OF

The laws of India apply, stating that homosexuality is illegal.

MALI

Homosexuality is legal, but Article 179 of the Penal Code, which prohibits 'public indecency', carries a punishment of from 3 months to 2 years' imprisonment and a fine.

MALTA

In 1973 Section 220 of the Penal Code, which criminalized anal intercourse ('unnatural carnal connection'), was repealed. The common age of consent for all sexual activity is 12 years.

MARSHALL ISLANDS

Part XXV, Section 53, of the Penal Code defines 'sodomy' as an 'abominable and detestable crime against nature' and is subject to 10 years' imprisonment.

MARTINIQUE

The laws of France apply, which specifies an age of consent for all sexual activity of 15 years.

MAURITANIA

Subarticle 331(3) of the 1947 Penal Code of the Federation of French West Africa, of which Mauritania was part before gaining independence in 1960, set an age of consent for homosexual activities of 21 years. This law is thought to have been superseded by Islamic Shari'a law, which prohibits homosexuality.

MAURITIUS

Section 250 of the Penal Code criminalizes acts of 'sodomy', with a maximum punishment of 5 years' imprisonment. Behaviour that 'excites, encourages or facilitates the debauchery or corruption of youth [under the age of 18 years]' is punishable by 1 year's imprisonment and a fine.

MEXICO

Homosexuality is legal, with a common age of consent for all sexual activities of 18 years. Mexico's Constitution protects individual freedom in relation to sexual orientation.

MICRONESIA

The criminal law does not explicitly refer to homosexuality.

MOLDOVA

Until 1995 Article 106 of the Penal Code criminalized male homosexuality, following the corresponding Section 121 from the former Soviet Union, which criminalized male anal intercourse. In 1995 the law was repealed and an age of consent for male anal intercourse was set at 18 years, compared to 16 years for heterosexual and non-penetrative homosexual sex. Lesbianism was never a criminal offence. There is now a common age of consent for all sexual activity of 14 years.

MONACO

The common age of consent for all sexual activity is 16 years. Sex between an adult and a young person between the ages of 12 and 16 is legal if the young person consents. A prosecution may only be made based upon a complaint from the young person or the young person's parents.

MONGOLIA

Section 113 of the Penal Code, which prohibits 'immoral gratification of sexual desires', can be used to prosecute gay men.

MOROCCO

Section 489 of the Penal Code 1962 criminalizes 'lewd or unnatural acts with an individual of the same sex', with a penalty of between 6 months and 3 years' imprisonment and a fine.

MOZAMBIQUE

Sections 70 and 71 of the Penal Code criminalize male homosexuality with a penalty of up to 3 years' imprisonment in a 're-education institution' where hard labour is used to alter the prisoners' 'aberrant behaviour'.

NAMIBIA

Male homosexuality is illegal, based upon the common-law offence of committing 'an unnatural sex crime'. It is not clear whether lesbian acts are an offence. The age of consent for heterosexual sex is 16 years.

NAURU

Homosexuality is illegal.

NEPAL

Paragraph 4(16) of Nepal's civil code punishes any kind of 'unnatural sex' with up to

1 year's imprisonment. Non-nationals can be deported for committing homosexual acts.

NETHERLANDS, THE

Homosexuality was decriminalized in 1811. The common age of consent for all sexual activities is 16. Sex between an adult and a young person between the ages of 12 and 16 is legal, as long as the young person consents, and may only be prosecuted by complaint from the young person or the young person's parents. Article 1 of the Constitution prohibits discrimination on the basis of sexual orientation. In 2001 the Netherlands became the first country in the world to extend its marriage and adoption laws to same-sex couples.

NETHERLANDS, ANTILLES

The age of consent for all sexual activities is 16 years.

NEW CALEDONIA

The laws of France apply, which specify an age of consent for all sexual activity of 15 years.

NEW ZEALAND

Male homosexuality was decriminalized in 1986, with the age of consent set at 16 for heterosexual and homosexual activities. Lesbianism was never a criminal offence. In 1994 discrimination on the basis of sexual orientation was prohibited. In 1999 the De Facto (Relationships) Property Act granted same-sex couples inheritance and property-sharing rights equivalent to married couples. In 2005 the Civil Unions Act allowed formal registration of same-sex relationships with the equivalent rights of married couples.

NICARAGUA

Article 204 of the Penal Code criminalizes 'sodomy', defined as 'the cohabitation between individuals of the same sex', imposing a punishment of up to 4 years' imprisonment. The Code also provides that anyone who 'induces, promotes, propagandises or practises in scandalous form sexual intercourse between persons of the same sex' commits the crime of sodomy, punishable by one to 3 years' imprisonment.

NIGER

Article 282 of the Penal Code 1993 sets the age of consent for same-sex activity at 21 years. Article 275 of the Code defines 'public indecency' as 'any material act that affronts public decency committed under conditions that a third party likely to be offended by it has witnessed or may have witnessed' and carries a punishment of up to 3 years' imprisonment and a fine.

NIGERIA

Articles 214 and 215 of the Penal Code punish any person who 'has carnal knowledge of any person against the order of nature or permits a male person to have carnal knowledge of him or her against the order of nature' with up to 14 years' imprisonment or 7 years for attempts. This law is generally interpreted to mean male anal intercourse. All other same-sex activity ('gross indecency') is criminalized under Article 217 and punishable by up to 3 years' imprisonment. Lesbian sexual activity is not mentioned in the law.

NIUE

Section 170 of the Penal Code prohibits 'buggery', with a penalty of up to 10 years' imprisonment. 'Attempted buggery' and 'indecent assaults on men' are punishable by penalties of up to 5 years' imprisonment.

NORWAY

Male homosexuality was decriminalized in 1972. Lesbianism has never been a criminal offence. The age of consent for all sexual activity is 16 years. In 1981 discrimination on the basis of sexual orientation was prohibited and public threats or hate speech about homosexuality were also prohibited. In 1993 same-sex partnership legislation was introduced, granting same-sex couples the same rights as married couples, excluding the right to adopt children.

OMAN

Articles 32 and 33 of the Penal Code make acts of sodomy and 'sahq' (lesbianism) punishable by imprisonment from 6 months to 3 years.

PAKISTAN

Section 377 of the Penal Code criminalizes 'carnal knowledge of any man against the order of nature' with a penalty of 2 years up to life imprisonment and corporal punishment of a 100 lashes. Islamic Shari'a law was reintroduced in 1990, which punishes male and female homosexuality with whipping or death by stoning.

PALESTINE

No information available.

PANAMA

Homosexuality is legal, although the age of consent is unclear. Article 39 of the Constitution, which prohibits forming companies, associations or foundations that are 'contrary to moral and legal order', has been used to prevent formation of gay and lesbian organisations.

PAPUA NEW GUINEA

Anal intercourse is punishable by imprisonment of up to 14 years, regardless of the sex of the partners. Non-penetrative male homosexuality is punishable by up to 5 years. Lesbianism is not a criminal offence. The age of consent for heterosexuals is 16 years.

PARAGUAY

Homosexuality is not explicitly mentioned in the Criminal Code. The age of consent for all sexual activities is 16 years, although charges of 'corruption of minors' and 'offences against morals' are often used to prosecute gay men.

PERU

Homosexuality is not explicitly referred to in the criminal law. The age of consent for all sexual activities is 14 years, although laws punishing 'public immorality' are often used to prosecute gays and lesbians.

PHILIPPINES

Homosexuality is not explicitly referred to in the criminal law. The age of consent for homosexuality and penetrative heterosexual sex is 18 years, compared to 12 years for non-penetrative heterosexual activities.

POLAND

Homosexuality was decriminalized in 1932, establishing an equal age of consent for all sexual activities of 15 years.

PORTUGAL

Homosexuality was first decriminalized in 1852, but the ban was reintroduced in 1912. In 1945 Portugal decriminalized homosexuality, with an age of consent of 16 years. In 1995 the government lowered the age of consent for heterosexual sex to 14, but maintained the unequal age of consent for homosexuality. In 2001 a same-sex partnership scheme was introduced.

PUERTO RICO

Puerto Rico is neither a state of the United States, nor an independent nation. Its citizens have US citizenship, but are not entitled to vote in US elections. Article 103 of the Penal Code criminalizes male and female homosexuality, and marriage is defined exclusively as being between a man and a woman. The age of consent for heterosexual sex is 14.

QATAR

Article 201 of the Penal Code 1971 punishes anal intercourse with up to 5 years' imprisonment, regardless of the sex of the partners. Islamic Shari'a law is applied, which also punishes homosexuality with whipping or death.

REUNION

The laws of France apply, which specifies an age of consent for all sexual activity of 15 years.

ROMANIA

Section 200 of the Penal Code, which criminalized homosexuality, was repealed in 1986 but replaced with restrictive laws prohibiting homosexual acts causing a 'public scandal', which were used to prosecute gay men. In 2000 Section 200 was repealed and a common age of consent for all sexual activities set at 18 years.

RUSSIA

Until 1993 Article 121(1) of the Russian Federation Criminal Code criminalized male anal intercourse, punishable by up to 5 years' imprisonment. Lesbianism was never a criminal offence. The law was repealed in 1993 and the 1997 Criminal Code makes no mention of consenting homosexuality. The age of consent for all sexual activities is 16 years.

RWANDA

The age of consent for all sexual activity is 18 years.

ST KITTS AND NEVIS

The age of consent for all sexual activity is 16 years.

ST LUCIA

Homosexuality is illegal.

SAN MARINO

Homosexuality was partially decriminalized in 1864. In 1974 the Parliament adopted a new Penal Code, containing Article 274, which punished men engaging in homosexual acts 'habitually', thereby causing 'public scandal', with 3 months' to 1 year's imprisonment. These laws were later repealed and the age of consent for all sexual activity set at 14 years.

SAUDI ARABIA

A very conservative form of Shari'a law is followed in Saudi Arabia. Accordingly, homosexual acts are illegal and subject to whipping (usually for unmarried persons) or a maximum penalty of death by stoning or beheading. A non-Muslim who has anal intercourse with a Muslim may be punished with death by stoning.

SENEGAL

Article 319(3) of the Penal Code criminalizes homosexuality ('improper or unnatural act with a person of the same sex') with a punishment of 1 and 5 years' imprisonment and a fine. If one of the partners is under 21 years, the maximum sentence is applied.

SERBIA

As part of the former Yugoslavia, male homosexuality was illegal under the Penal Code 1959. In 1977 the power over penal legislation was devolved from the Federal Republic to the eight states and provinces. Serbia chose to retain the ban, with Section 110(3) of the Penal Code, criminalizing male homosexuality ('indecent acts against nature') and punishable by up to 1 year's imprisonment. Lesbianism was never a criminal offence. In 1994 male homosexuality was decriminalized and the age of consent set at 14 years.

SEYCHELLES

Homosexuality is illegal.

SIERRA LEONE

Male homosexuality is illegal and described as 'an unnatural act'. There is no reference in the criminal law to lesbianism.

SINGAPORE

Section 377 of the Criminal Code criminalizes anal intercourse ('carnal intercourse against the order of nature with any man, woman or animal'), punishable by between 10 years and life imprisonment plus a fine. Section 377A also punishes all other male homosexual activity ('gross indecency with another male person') with up to 2 years' imprisonment. The laws are no longer actively prosecuted and tolerance towards homosexuality is widespread. Lesbianism is punishable under Section 20 of the Miscellaneous Offences (Public Order and Nuisance) Act, which refers to 'riotous, disorderly or indecent behaviour' in a public setting, punishable by 1 month's

imprisonment or a fine, but there are no cases of prosecution under this law.

SLOVAKIA

Male homosexuality was decriminalized in the former Czechoslovakia in 1961, with an age of consent set at 15 years. Slovakia retained these laws upon gaining political independence.

SLOVENIA

Under the Penal Code 1959, male homosexuality was criminalized in all of the former Yugoslavia. During the first half of the 1970s the power over penal legislation was devolved from the Federal Republic to the eight states and provinces. Slovenia chose not to retain the old law and decriminalized homosexuality in 1977. Lesbianism was never a criminal offence. In 1995 a common age of consent for all sexual activity was set at 14 years.

SOLOMON ISLANDS

Section 153 of the Penal Code criminalizes male anal intercourse ('buggery') with a penalty of up to 14 years' imprisonment. Section 154 prohibits 'attempts to buggery and indecent assaults' with a penalty of up to 7 years' imprisonment. Section 155 punishes acts of 'gross indecency', in private or public, with up to 5 years' imprisonment, and was amended in 1989 to include females as well as males.

SOMALIA

The Indian Penal Code was applied in British Somalia from 1925 to 1973, and prohibited male homosexuality. In 1973 a Somali Penal Code was adopted. Article 409 of the Somali Code criminalizes sexual intercourse with a person of the same sex, with punishments of 3 months' to 3 years' imprisonment. All other homosexual activities ('an act of lust different from sexual intercourse') are punishable by 2 months' to 2 years' imprisonment. Under Article 410 a police surveillance measure may be added to a sentence for homosexual acts, to guarantee that the person convicted does not engage in these activities again. The laws are not thought to apply to lesbianism.

SOUTH AFRICA

Section 20A of the Offences Act, based upon Roman-Dutch law, prohibited male homosexuality, named 'sodomy' and 'unnatural sexual offences'. In 1988 Section 19 was amended making it an offence for any woman to commit 'an immoral or indecent act' with a girl under 19. In 1998 the Johannesburg High Court declared the laws unconstitutional. The age of consent for homosexual activities is 19, compared to 16 for heterosexuals. In 1996 South Africa became the first country in the world to enshrine lesbian and gay rights in its new Constitution. Clause 9(3) provides that the state may not 'unfairly discriminate directly or indirectly against anyone' on grounds including sexual orientation.

SPAIN

Homosexuality was decriminalized in 1822, with the exception of the offence of 'habitual homosexual acts' in the years 1928–32. The common age of consent for all sexual activity is 13 years. In 1995 discrimination on the basis of sexual orientation was prohibited. In 2005 the government extended marriage laws to include same-sex couples.

SRI LANKA

Section 365A of the Penal Code criminalizes all sexual activity between men, punishable by up to 10 years' imprisonment.

SUDAN

The Penal Code 1983, which is based upon Islamic Shari'a law, criminalizes 'zina' (fornication), defined as 'penetration with the penis into the vagina or the anus of a person other than a married partner'. Article 316 of the Code prescribes capital punishment for a 'muhsan' (married man) and whipping for a 'gair muhsan' (unmarried man).

SURINAM

The age of consent for homosexuality is 18 years, compared to 16 for heterosexuals.

SWAZILAND

The common-law criminal offence of sodomy applies to both males and females and prohibits persons of the same sex engaging in a sexual relationship. The possible penalty is imprisonment or a fine. The last offence was tried in 1983 (IOC/1995).

SYRIA

Article 520 of the Penal Code 1949 criminalizes anal intercourse ('carnal knowledge against the order of nature'), regardless of the sex of the partners, with a punishment of up to 1 year's imprisonment.

SWEDEN

Homosexuality was decriminalized in 1944. Since 1978 the age of consent for all sexual activity has been equalized at 15 years. In 1987 discrimination on the basis of sexual orientation, including hate speech, was made a criminal offence. In 1999 the office of the Ombudsman Against Discrimination on the Basis of Sexual Orientation was established. There is a registered partnerships scheme for same-sex couples.

TAIWAN

Homosexuality is not explicitly mentioned in the criminal law, but the Criminal Code sets the age of consent for all sexual activities at 16 years.

TAJIKISTAN

Before 1998 Section 125(1) of the Criminal Code followed the corresponding Section 121 from the former Soviet Union, which criminalized male anal intercourse. Lesbian and non-penetrative gay sex was never a criminal offence. In 1998 homosexuality was decriminalized.

TANZANIA

Section 154 to 157 of the Penal Code criminalizes male homosexuality, with a penalty of up to 14 years' imprisonment.

THAILAND

Homosexuality is legal and the age of consent for all sexual activity is 15.

TOGO

Homosexual acts are illegal and are often prosecuted as rape or assault, punishable by fines and up to 3 years' imprisonment.

TOKELAU

Section 170 of the Criminal Code criminalizes sodomy ('buggery'), punishable by up to 10 years' imprisonment. Section 171 criminalizes non-penetrative sexual acts between men ('indecent assault on a male') with punishment of up to 5 years' imprisonment.

TONGA

Sections 136–9 of the Criminal Code punish male anal intercourse ('the abominable crime of sodomy') with up to 10 years' imprisonment. Section 138 prohibits 'indecent assaults' between men, which covers non-penetrative sexual acts.

TRINIDAD AND TOBAGO

Section 13 of the Sexual Offences Act 1986 criminalizes anal intercourse ('buggery'), punishable by up to 10 years' imprisonment. Section 16, relating to 'serious indecency', provides a penalty of up to 20 years' imprisonment for homosexual acts between men and between women. The age of consent is 18.

TUNISIA

Article 230 of the Penal Code 1913 (revised 1964) criminalizes anal intercourse ('sodomy'), punishable by imprisonment of up to 3 years. Lesbianism is not mentioned in the criminal law.

TURKEY

The age of consent for all sexual activity is 18 years. There are no articles on homosexuality in the law although it contains vague references to public morals and public order. Articles 419, 547 and 576 of the Turkish Criminal Code, which relate to public indecency, are frequently used to persecute gay and lesbian people.

TURKMENISTAN

Article 135 of the Criminal Code criminalizes male homosexuality with punishments of up to 5 years' imprisonment. Non-nationals can be deported for breaches of this law. Lesbianism is not mentioned in the criminal law.

TURKS AND CAICOS ISLANDS

Section 41 of the Offences Against the Person Ordinance 1877 criminalizes male homosexuality with a maximum punishment of life imprisonment. The age of consent for heterosexuals is 16 years. Lesbianism is not mentioned in the criminal law.

TUVALU

Sections 153 and 154 of the Penal Code criminalize male anal intercourse ('buggery') with a penalty of up to 14 years' imprisonment and 'attempts to buggery and indecent assaults' with up to 7 years' imprisonment. Section 155 punishes non-penetrative homosexual acts ('gross indecency'), in private or public, with up to 5 years' imprisonment. Lesbianism is not mentioned in the criminal law.

UGANDA

Sections 140 and 141 of the Penal Code criminalize male anal intercourse ('carnal knowledge against the order of nature') with a maximum penalty of life imprisonment or up to 7 years' imprisonment for attempts. Section 143 criminalizes non-penetrative homosexual acts ('gross indecency') with punishment of up to 5 years' imprisonment. Lesbianism is not mentioned in the criminal law.

UKRAINE

Until 1991 Article 122 of the Penal Code criminalized male homosexuality, following the corresponding Section 121 from the former Soviet Union which punished male anal intercourse with up to 5 years' imprisonment. Lesbianism was never a criminal offence. The law was repealed in 1991 and a common age of consent set at 16 years.

UNITED ARAB EMIRATES

As well as a federal criminal statute, there are Penal Codes in four of the seven emirates: Dubai, Abu Dhabi, Ras al-Haima and Sarga. Article 354 of the Federal Penal Code 1988 criminalizes male anal intercourse, which is punishable by death. The Federal Code also allows constituent states to charge a defendant under the Islamic Shari'a law, which punishes male sodomy with whipping or death by stoning. Article 80 of the Abu Dhabi Penal Code criminalizes male anal intercourse, punishable by imprisonment of up to 14 years. Article 177 of the Penal Code of Dubai punishes male anal intercourse with imprisonment for up to 10 years.

UNITED KINGDOM

Homosexuality was decriminalized in 1967 in England, Scotland and Wales, with an age of consent of 21, compared to the heterosexual age of consent of 18. The age of consent for all sexual activities is now equalized at 16 years. In 2003 the English Parliament repealed Section 28 of the Local Government Act, which prohibited the 'promotion' of homosexuality to young people. In 2005 the Civil Unions Act will allow same-sex couples to register their relationships and receive the equivalent rights and responsibilities of married couples.

In Northern Ireland, homosexuality was not decriminalized until 1982, after an appeal to the European Court of Human Rights in *Dudgeon* v. *United Kingdom* (1991). The Court upheld Dudgeon's argument that Northern Ireland's anti-sodomy laws violated his rights to privacy guaranteed in Article 8 of the European Convention of Human Rights. The age of consent for all sexual activities is 17 years.

UNITED STATES OF AMERICA

The United States is composed of a federal government (the Senate) with a Constitution, and 52 constituent states, each with its own legislature and Penal Code. All state laws must be consistent with the Constitution, which is interpreted by the Supreme

Court. Homosexuality was illegal in all states until 1961, when Illinois first legalized male homosexuality. In the 1986 case of *Bowers* v. *Hardwick*, the Supreme Court upheld the anti-sodomy laws in the state of Texas, declaring that there was no constitutional right to privacy in relation to homosexual activity, even if conducted in private between consenting adults. The position was reversed in the 2003 case *Lawrence* v. *Texas*, which declared Texas's anti-sodomy laws unconstitutional, subsequently invalidating all American state laws prohibiting consensual adult homosexuality. To date many states have not repealed their anti-gay legislation; in these cases, the age of consent for homosexual activity is assumed to be the same as that for heterosexuals.

Alabama

Section 13(A)-6-65 criminalized 'deviate sexual intercourse', punishable by up to 1 year's imprisonment. The law was declared unconstitutional in 2003 under *Lawrence* v. *Texas* but has not yet been repealed. The age of consent for heterosexuals is 18 years.

Alaska

The law relating to oral sex was repealed in 1971 and the sodomy law in 1980. The common age of consent for all sexual activity is 16 years.

Arizona

Section 13–1411 of the Penal Code criminalized 'infamous crimes against nature' and 13–412 criminalized 'any lewd or lascivious act upon or with the body or any part or member thereof of a male or female adult, with the intent of arousing, appealing to or gratifying the lust, passion or sexual desires', both punishable by up to 1 month's imprisonment. The laws were repealed in 2001. The age of consent is 18 years.

Arkansas

Section 5-14-122 of the Penal Code criminalized 'sodomy', with a punishment of up to 1 year's imprisonment. The law was declared unconstitutional in 2002 in *Picado* v. *Jegley*. The age of consent is 16 years.

California

Sodomy laws repealed in 1976 under the Consenting Adults Act. The age of consent for all sexual activity is 18 years.

Colorado

Sodomy laws repealed in 1972. The age of consent for non-penetrative heterosexual sex is 15 years and 17 years for penetrative heterosexual sex and homosexuality.

Connecticut

Sodomy laws repealed in 1971. The age of consent for all sexual activity is 16 years.

Delaware

The sodomy laws were repealed in 1973. The age of consent for non-penetrative heterosexual sex is 16 years and 18 years for penetrative heterosexual sex and homosexuality.

District of Columbia

Section 22–3502 punishes any person who 'takes into his or her mouth or anus the sexual organ of any other person or animal, or who shall be convicted of placing his or her sexual organ in the mouth or anus of any other person or animal, or who shall be convicted of having carnal copulation in an opening of the body except sexual parts with another person', punishable by up to 10 years' imprisonment. The law was repealed in 1995. The age of consent is 16 years.

Florida

Section 800.02 of the Penal Code criminalized 'unnatural and lascivious acts', punishable by up to 60 days' imprisonment. The law was declared unconstitutional in 2003 under *Lawrence v. Texas* but has yet to be repealed. The age of consent for non-penetrative heterosexual sex is 16 years and 18 years for penetrative heterosexual sex.

Georgia

Section 16-6-2 of the Penal Code criminalized sodomy, defined as 'when a man or woman performs or submits to any sexual act involving the sex organs of one person and the mouth or anus of another', punishable by up to 20 years' imprisonment. The law was repealed in 1998 in *Powell* v. *State*. The age of consent for all sexual activity is 16 years.

Hawaii

The sodomy laws were repealed in 1973. The age of consent for all sexual activity is 16 years.

Idaho

Section 18–6605 criminalized sodomy, called 'crimes against nature', punishable by 4 years up to life imprisonment. The law was declared unconstitutional in 2003 under *Lawrence* v. *Texas* but has not yet been repealed. The age of consent for non-penetrative heterosexual sex is 16 years and 18 years for penetrative heterosexual sex.

Illinois

In 1961 Illinois adopted the American Law Institute's Model Penal Code, which decriminalized homosexual acts between consenting adults in private. The age of consent for all sexual activity is 17 years.

Indiana

The sodomy law was repealed in 1977. The age of consent for all sexual activity is 16 years.

Iowa

The sodomy law was repealed in 1978. The age of consent for non-penetrative heterosexual sex is 14 years and 16 years for penetrative heterosexual sex and homosexuality.

Kansas

Section 21–3505 of the Penal Code criminalized 'criminal sodomy', defined as 'persons who are 16 or more years of age and members of the same sex' and punishable by up to 6 months' imprisonment. It was declared unconstitutional in 2003 under *Lawrence* v. *Texas* but has not yet been repealed. The age of consent for heterosexuals is 16 years.

Kentucky

The sodomy law was declared unconstitutional in 1992 in *Commonwealth* v. *Wasson*. The age of consent for all sexual activity is 16 years. Louisiana Section 14.89 of the Penal Code criminalized 'crimes against nature' as 'unnatural carnal copulation by a human being with another of the same or opposite sex', providing an exception for anal intercourse within marriage and punishable by up to 5 years' imprisonment. The law was declared unconstitutional in 2003 under *Lawrence* v. *Texas*, but has not yet been repealed. The age of consent for heterosexual sex is 17 years.

Maine

The sodomy laws were repealed in 1976. The age of consent for all sexual activity is 16 years.

Massachusetts

Chapter 272 Chapter 34 of the Penal Code criminalized anal intercourse, defined as 'crimes against nature' and punishable by up to 20 years' imprisonment. Section 272–35 criminalized oral sex, defined as 'unnatural and lascivious acts', punishable by up to 5 years' imprisonment. In 1974 the Massachusetts Supreme Judicial County declared in *Balthazar* v. *Commonwealth* that private consensual sexual activity was constitutionally protected in the state. This was confirmed in 2002 in *Doe* v. *Reilly*. The age of consent is 16 years.

Maryland

Section 27–553 criminalized anal intercourse ('sodomy') and Section 27–554 criminalized oral sex ('unnatural or perverted sexual practices'), except within marriage, both punishable by up to 10 years' imprisonment. In 1990 the case *Schochet* v. *State* declared that the 'unnatural or perverted sexual practices' was not constitutional when applied to non-commercial, heterosexual activity in private. In 1998 *Williams* v. *Glendening* held that the Schochet verdict applied equally to homosexual acts. In 1999 the sodomy law was found to be unconstitutional in a settlement with the American Civil Liberties Union which argued *Williams* v. *Glendening*. The age of consent is 16 years.

Michigan

Section 750.158 criminalized anal intercourse ('the abominable and detestable crime against nature'), punishable by up to 15 years' imprisonment. The law was declared unconstitutional in 2003 under *Lawrence* v. *Texas* but has not yet been repealed. The age of consent for heterosexuals is 16 years.

Minnesota

Section 609.293 of the Penal Code criminalizes 'sodomy', defined as 'carnally knowing any person by the anus or by or with the mouth' and punishable by up to 1 year's imprisonment. In 2001 the Hennepin County District Court ruled in *Doe, et al.* v. *Jesse Ventura, et al.* that the sodomy laws were unconstitutional. The age of consent is 16 years.

Mississippi

Section 97-29-59 of the Penal Code criminalized 'unnatural intercourse', defined as 'the detestable and abominable crime against nature committed with mankind' and punishable by up to 10 years' imprisonment. The law was declared unconstitutional in 2003 under *Lawrence* v. *Texas* but has not yet been repealed. The age of consent for heterosexuals is 16 years.

Missouri

Section 566.090 of the Penal Code criminalized 'sexual misconduct', defined as 'deviate sexual intercourse with another person of the same sex' and punishable by 1 year's imprisonment. In 1999 the Missouri Court of Appeal held that a revision of the law had, in effect, decriminalized consensual sodomy in the state. The 2003 case *Lawrence* v. *Texas* confirmed that the law was unconstitutional. The law has not yet been repealed. The age of consent for heterosexuals is 14 years for non-penetrative heterosexual acts and 17 for penetrative heterosexual sex.

Montana

Section 45-5-505 of the Penal Code criminalized 'deviate sexual conduct', punishable by up to 10 years' imprisonment. In 1997 the sodomy law was declared unconstitutional in *Gryczan* v. *State*. The age of consent is 18 years.

Nebraska

The sodomy law was repealed in 1978. The age of consent is 17 years.

Nevada

The sodomy law was repealed in 2003. The age of consent for homosexuality is 18 years, compared to 16 years for heterosexuals.

New Hampshire

The sodomy law was repealed in 1975. The age of consent for homosexuality is 18 years, compared to 16 years for heterosexuals.

New Jersey

The sodomy law was repealed in 1979. The age of consent for all sexual activity is 16 years.

New Mexico

The sodomy law was repealed in 1975. The age of consent for all sexual activity is 17 years.

New York

Section 130.38 of the Penal Code criminalized 'consensual sodomy', defined as 'deviate sexual intercourse', defined further in Section 130.00 as 'sexual conduct between persons not married to each other consisting of contact between the penis and the anus, the mouth and penis, or the mouth and the vulva'. In 1980 the law was declared unconstitutional in *People* v. *Onofre*, and the law was repealed in 2000. The age of consent for all sexual activity is 17 years.

North Carolina

Section 14–177 criminalized sodomy ('crime against nature'). The law was declared unconstitutional in 2003 under *Lawrence* v.

Texas but has yet to be repealed. The age of consent for heterosexuals is 16 years.

North Dakota

The sodomy law was repealed in 1975. The age of consent is 18 years.

Ohio

The sodomy law was repealed in 1974. The age of consent is 16 years. Oklahoma Section 21–886 of the Penal Code criminalized 'the detestable and abominable crime against nature', punishable by up to 10 years' imprisonment. The law was declared unconstitutional in 2003 under *Lawrence* v. *Texas* but has yet to be repealed. The age of consent for heterosexuals is 16 years.

Oregon

The sodomy laws criminalized 'sodomy or the crime against nature, or any act or practice of sexual perversity', punishable by between 1 and 15 years' imprisonment or sterilization of those 'addicted' to sodomy. The law was repealed in 1972. The age of consent for all sexual activity is 18 years.

Pennsylvania

The sodomy law was ruled unconstitutional in 1980 in *Commonwealth* v. *Bonadio* and repealed in 1995. The age of consent for all sexual activity is 16 years.

Rhode Island

Section 11-10-1 of the Penal Code criminalized sodomy, defined as 'the abominable and detestable crime against nature' and punishable by between 7 and 20 years' imprisonment. The law was repealed in 1998. The age of consent is 16 years.

South Dakota

The sodomy law was repealed in 1977. The age of consent is 16 years.

South Carolina

Section 16-15-120 of the Penal Code criminalizes sodomy, defined as 'the abominable crime of buggery', punishable by up to 5 years' imprisonment. The law was declared unconstitutional in 2003 under *Lawrence* v. *Texas* but has yet to be repealed. The age of consent for heterosexuals is 16 years.

Tennessee

The Homosexual Practices Act, which refers to 'crimes against nature' and also refers to sodomy and buggery, was declared unconstitutional by the Tennessee Appeals Court in 1996 under *Campbell* v. *Sundquist*. The age of consent is 18 years.

Texas

Section 21.01 of the Penal Code criminalized 'deviate sexual intercourse', defined as 'any contact between any part of the genitals of one person and the mouth or anus of another person, or the penetration of the genitals or the anus of another person with an object' and punishable by a fine. The law was declared unconstitutional in 2003 under *Lawrence* v. *Texas* but has yet to be repealed. The age of consent for heterosexuals is 17 years.

Utah

Section 76-5-403 of the Penal Code criminalizes sodomy, defined as 'any sexual act with a person who is 14 years of age or older involving the genitals of one person and mouth or anus of another person, regardless of the sex of either participant' and punishable by up to 6 months'

imprisonment. The law was declared unconstitutional in 2003 under *Lawrence v. Texas* but has yet to be repealed. The age of consent for heterosexuals is 18 years.

Vermont

The sodomy law was repealed in 1977. The age of consent is 16 years.

Virginia

Chapter 18.2–361 of the Penal Code criminalizes 'crimes against nature', defined as 'carnally knowledge of any male or female person by the anus or by or with the mouth' and punishable by up to 5 years' imprisonment. The law was declared unconstitutional in 2003 under *Lawrence v. Texas*. Virginia continues to arrest and prosecute under this law. The age of consent for heterosexuals is 18 years.

Washington

The sodomy law was repealed in 1976. The age of consent is 18 years.

West Virginia

The sodomy law was repealed in 1976. The age of consent for homosexuality is 18 years, compared to 16 years for heterosexual sex.

Wisconsin

The sodomy law was repealed in 1983. The age of consent for all sexual activity is 18 years.

Wyoming

The sodomy law was repealed in 1977. The age of consent is 18 years.

American Samoa

The sodomy laws were repealed in 1979.

Guam

Sodomy became a criminal offence in 1933 under the Naval Criminal Code. The law was repealed in 1976.

Northern Mariana Islands

Sodomy was outlawed in 1952 by Executive Order of the Commissioner of the trusteeship set up by the United Nations. The law was repealed in 1983.

Virgin Islands, American

The sodomy laws were repealed in 1984.

URUGUAY

The age of consent for all sexual activities is 18 years. In 2003 a law was passed protecting sexual minorities from 'physical and printed homophobic abuse'. Laws prohibiting public indecency can still be used to prosecute gay and lesbian people for public displays of affection.

UZBEKISTAN

Of all the states of the former Soviet Union, Uzbekistan is the only state to continue to criminalize male homosexuality. Article 120 of the Penal Code 1995 criminalizes male anal intercourse ('*besakalbazlyk*', loosely translated as 'buggery') with a punishment of up to 3 years' imprisonment. This follows Section 121 of the old Soviet Union Criminal Code. Non-penetrative gay sex and lesbianism was never a criminal offence.

VANUATU/NEW HEBRIDES

The age of consent for all sexual activity is 18 years.

VATICAN CITY

The Vatican is an ecclesiastic state, governed by the Roman Catholic Church. Homosexuality is not explicitly referred to in the law, but is *de facto* illegal, based upon the Church's objections to homosexuality.

VENEZUELA

The age of consent for all sexual activity is 18 years.

VIETNAM

There is no explicit reference to homosexuality in the law. Homosexuality is considered a 'social evil' and laws relating to 'undermining public morality' can be used to prosecute homosexual conduct in public.

VOJVODINA

Under the Penal Code 1959, male homosexuality was illegal in all of the former Yugoslavia. During the 1970s the power over penal legislation was devolved from the Federal Republic to the eight states and provinces. Vojvodina's government decriminalized homosexuality, but set an age of consent of 18 years, compared to 14 for heterosexuals. Lesbianism was never a criminal offence.

WESTERN SAMOA

Section 58E of the Crimes Ordinance 1961 criminalizes male anal intercourse ('sodomy') and non-penetrative sexual acts between men ('indecency between males'), both punishable by up to 5 years' impri-

675

sonment. The age of consent for hetero-sexual and lesbian sex is 16 years.

YEMEN

Homosexuality is illegal, and punishable by death.

ZAIRE

Homosexuality is not explicitly referred to in the criminal law, but can be punish-able under Sections 168–72. Section 168 criminalizes assault with a punishment of 6 months to 5 years' imprisonment. Section 170 criminalizes rape, with a penalty of 5–40 years' imprisonment.

ZAMBIA

Chapter 87 of Zambia's Penal Code describes homosexuality as an 'offence against morality'. Section 155 criminalizes male anal intercourse ('carnal knowledge of any person against the order of nature'), punishable by up to 14 years' imprison-ment.

ZIMBABWE

Zimbabwean law (which is based upon Roman-Dutch common law, as amended by Zimbabwean legislation) recognizes three classes of 'unnatural offences' – anal intercourse ('sodomy'), bestiality and a residual group of sexual acts referred to generally as 'unnatural offences', punishable by harsh sentences of imprisonment. There have been no prosecutions of lesbian beha-viour under these laws.

JOHN FORDE

appendix c
international political and
community organizations

ALITT (ASOCIACIÓN DE LUCHA POR LA IDENTIDAD TRAVESTI–TRANSEXUAL)

A transvestite-transsexual organization that has been active in Argentina since 1997. Works to promote and defend the human rights of transvestite and transsexual people in Argentina.

SURINA KHAN

ALLIANCE RIGHTS NIGERIA

The first national gay rights association in Africa's most populous country. Established in 2001, it held its first national conference in 2003. Much of ARN's advocacy work avoids direct confrontation with popular prejudices by focusing upon HIV and AIDS education.

MARC EPPRECHT

ARCIGAY

Arcigay is Italy's major organization defending the rights of homosexual people. Founded in 1985, Arcigay has its headquarters in Bologna at Il Cassero, with many affiliated circles throughout the country. The organization takes up the cudgels in the political and cultural battle against homophobia, heterosexism, prejudice and anti-homosexual discrimination, and to assert equal dignity and opportunity among individuals regardless of sexual orientation. To this end Arcigay also organizes projects in collaboration with political parties and the unions. It is fighting for the legal recognition of gay couples and is active in the fields of culture and information, offering training and refresher courses to social-health workers and teachers, and carrying out information and prevention campaigns against AIDS through training courses, self-managed consulting rooms, helplines, street units and research work. In 2001 Arcigay's honorary president Franco Grillini and Arcilesbica president Titti de Simone were elected as members of the Italian parliament.

MONICA BARONI

ARCILESBICA

ArciLesbica is a national association, founded in 1996, that recognizes the significance of gender difference within the glbtq community. It defines itself as feminist, laical, pacifist, non-party, anti-fascist, anti-racist and anti-prohibitionist. It pursues political and cultural aims, working to combat every form of violence, prejudice and discrimination against lesbians, and to this end submits proposals at political and legislative level to institutions, parties and labour unions demanding the recognition and full enjoyment of civil rights for lesbians.

MONIA ANDREANI

ASSOCIATION OF PARENTS, RELATIVES AND FRIENDS OF HOMOSEXUALS (AGEDO) (ASSOCIAZIONE DI GENITORI, PARENTI E AMICI DI OMOSESSUALI)

The 'association of parents, relatives and friends of gays and lesbians' was founded in 1992 by Paola Dall'Orto, mother of Giovanni Dall'Orto. It aims to reach other parents and bring about a culture of 'coming out' in Italy. The association has promoted educational campaigns in schools (producing the video *Nessuno uguale*) and lobbied political and religious institutions. It has chapters in 22 Italian cities.

MARCO PUSTIANAZ

BELAH DO'EGET

Organization dedicated to furthering AIDS awareness within the glbt community in Israel. Established in 1994, it organizes educational campaigns and Wigstock, an annual fund-raising event.

AMIT KAMA

CASSERO, IL (BOLOGNA)

Il Cassero in Bologna, Italy (former headquarters of the 'Circolo 28 giugno', thereafter of Arcigay) made history when, in 1982, it became the first building to be assigned by a local (left-wing) council to a gay association. It came to house the largest gay and lesbian centre in Italy, where political meetings, disco nights, cultural events,

AIDS activism and helpline services all took place, as well as hosting the largest Italian glbtq documentation centre.

MARCO PUSTIANAZ

CHI HENG FOUNDATION

A Hong-Kong based charitable organization that promotes AIDS prevention and holds fund-raising activities to fight discrimination against groups such as sexual minorities and AIDS orphans in China. Founded in 1999.

TRAVIS KONG

CIVIL RIGHTS FOR SEXUAL DIVERSITIES

A Hong-Kong-based non-governmental organization that seeks to end prejudice against people based upon their sexual orientation and HIV+ status. Founded in 2000.

TRAVIS KONG

CLAF (COMMUNITY OF LESBIAN FEMINISTS)

A political and social organization based in Israel (established 1987), led by and for feminist lesbians. The all-women organization publishes *Pandora*, a lesbian journal, and runs a community centre.

AMIT KAMA

CLI (COLLEGAMENTO FRA LE LESBICHE ITALIANE)

A separatist association of the Italian lesbian movement which has been operating in Rome since 1981. Since 1984 it has published a monthly bulletin called *Bollettina del CLI*.

MONICA ANDREANI

COMPANIONS ON A JOURNEY

Founded in 1995 in Sri Lanka, this organization works for social justice and human rights issues for people with alternative sexualities living in Sri Lanka.

SURINA KHAN

ENTRE AMIGOS

An organization that works for the rights of lesbian, gay, bisexuals and transgender people in El Salvador, where it has encountered severe threats of violence over the years.

SURINA KHAN

EQUAL OPPORTUNITIES COMMISSION (HONG KONG)

With the passing of the Anti-Discrimination Laws in 1995, the Equal Opportunities Commission (EOC) was set up the following year as a statutory body in Hong Kong to implement the Sex Discrimination Ordinance (SDO), the Disability Discrimination Ordinance (DDO) and the Family Status Discrimination Ordinance (FSDO). It is the only governmental organization to deal with cases of sex, marital status, pregnancy, disability and family-status discrimination. Complaints lodged under the above-mentioned Ordinances will be investigated by the Commission. Legal proceedings would be brought to the court if the disputed parties in the case fail to reach conciliation. The EOC also organizes different public educational programmes to advocate equal opportunities and create a better understanding of discrimination and inequality in Hong Kong.

SANDRA YIM

FEDERATION OF GAY GAMES

An organization that selects teams to host each of the Gay Games. Non-profit-based and governed by an Executive Director and large international volunteer Board of Directors, it offers advice and resources for establishing local gay and lesbian sporting organizations.

KELLIE BURNS

FREEMAN (XIAO YAO PAI)

A Hong-Kong-registered non-profit social group that organizes cultural and recreational activities solely for gay men. Originally based in Isvara. Founded in 1996.

TRAVIS KONG

FTM INTERNATIONAL (FTMI)

Based in San Francisco and founded in 1986, FTMI is the largest and longest-running educational organization serving female-to-male (FTM) transgendered people and transsexual men. Since its founding, it has held support and information meetings as well as published a quarterly newsletter. An international network, FTMI has members in more than 17 countries; it changed its name to include 'international' in 1994. FTMI produces an annual resource guide that lists available resources including professionals and clinics for gender dysphoria as well as other groups and publications of interest to the FTM community. Its web site details a range of resources including links to other organizations, annotated bibliographies, a glossary of terms and other useful information.

SURINA KHAN

FUORI (FRONTE UNITARIO OMOSESSUALE RIVOLUZIONARIO ITALIANO)

FUORI (1971–82) was the first gay liberation group to be set up in Italy. Founded in Turin, it was inspired by the American gay liberation movement and, specifically, the Gay Liberation Front. On 5 April 1972 members of FUORI first came out to disrupt a conference on 'sexual deviancy' in San Remo, while 1973 saw the alliance with the Radical Party, a non-Marxist, liberal organization then campaigning successfully for civil rights. Several revolutionary collectives abandoned FUORI when the political climate became more radical in 1976–7. FUORI broke up as a national organization in 1982, after its eighth Conference.

MARCO PUSTIANAZ

GALZ (GAYS AND LESBIANS OF ZIMBABWE)

Gays and Lesbians of Zimbabwe (GALZ), a membership association formed in 1990, provides services to glbt people and campaigns for the removal of all homophobic legislation. The organization has confronted many social and political challenges. In 1994, for example, GALZ attempted to advertise its counselling services in the state-controlled media but the advertisement was rejected. After two appearances on radio, GALZ was unofficially banned from the airwaves. Despite official assurances to the contrary, the government, in January 1995, launched an anti-gay campaign referring to homosexuality as 'a white man's disease', contradictory to biblical teachings and as being 'against Zimbabwean culture'. In response, GALZ applied for participation in the annual Zimbabwe International Book Fair (ZIBF), the theme of which was 'Human Rights and Justice'. Ultimately, ZIBF refused GALZ's application, under pressure from the government, even though the organization gathered support from many quarters for its inclusion. In his opening speech to the ZIBF that year, Robert Mugabe launched the first of a series of vitriolic attacks on glbt people. In 1996, when GALZ again applied to ZIBF, the government instituted a ban. GALZ, however, took the government to court and won its right to exhibit.

In 1998, during the Eighth Assembly of World Councils of Churches in Harare, GALZ campaigned for the acceptance of glbt people into the church. Additionally, GALZ has lobbied for the inclusion of sexual orientation both in the government-led Constitutional Commission and the civic-based National Constitutional Assembly. GALZ operates openly from its Harare offices, providing services to around 500 members. It has done much to normalize glbt issues in Zimbabwe and now supports similar groups throughout Africa. Its most important campaign relates to HIV and AIDS.

KEITH GODDARD

GAY ACTIVISTS ALLIANCE

The Gay Activists Alliance (GAA) was the organization most responsible for the success of the gay liberation movement, the new glbt movement that emerged from the Stonewall Riots and transformed the previous small homophile movement into a mass movement that began successfully to challenge anti-gay laws and policies. Organized in New York City in 1969, this militant group with New Left values effectively challenged the media, the political establishment and private organizations. One of the reasons for the group's rapid growth and nationwide spread was the 'zap' – carefully planned protests that combined elements of humour with militancy in order to win media coverage. Through its centre, the Firehouse, GAA helped foster a nascent gay culture by, for example, holding dances and discussions of gay themes in films screened at the Firehouse.

DAVID CARTER

GAY AND LESBIANS ALLIANCE, UGANDA

Uganda's first gay rights association, established in 2001. Following high-level homophobic statements and the caning to death of a schoolgirl accused of lesbianism in 2003, chair S.W.I. Lule adopted a bold public profile, including the threat to launch a gay political party.

MARC EPPRECHT

GAY AND LESBIAN RIGHTS LOBBY (NSW)

During the early 1980s a group of gay men from Sydney formed the Gay Rights Lobby (GRL) in an effort to convince the acting Labour government to decriminalize male homosexuality in the state of New South Wales (NSW); this was achieved in 1984. In 1988 the GRL was renamed the Gay and Lesbian Rights Lobby (GLRL) in an effort to broaden its agenda to include the interests and concerns of lesbian women, previously working independently in feminist organizations around the country. The decade that followed found the GLRL speaking on a number of significant political and social issues pertaining to age of consent laws, violence against lesbians and gay men, youth education and support, same-sex partnership rights, the rights of Australians living with HIV/AIDS, gays and lesbians in the military and the rights of transgendered people.

KELLIE BURNS

GE'UT

A glbt caucus within the left-wing Israeli political party Meretz. The caucus successfully promoted several gay and lesbian candidates, among them Member of Parliament Uzi Even.

AMIT KAMA

HOMOSEXUELLENINITIATIVE BERLIN

The Homosexuelleninitiative Berlin, founded in 1973, was the first gay and lesbian organization in the former Eastern bloc.

The group organized discussions in private homes, trips to the region around Berlin and, under the guise of birthday parties, rented club rooms and restaurants for dance events. This became impossible after their discovery by the authorities in 1975. Charlotte von Mahlsdorf then made the basement of her private Gründerzeit Museum available to them. Along with lectures and discussions, the group also organized satirical cabaret performances under the name *Hibaré*; the act achieved notoriety through the German Democratic Republic.

One of the group's goals was to set up an advice and communication centre. In 1975 Michael Eggert was delegated to approach the East German authorities on behalf of the group to demand a public meeting place for homosexuals. After years of negotiations, in 1979 their demand was finally and officially denied. Despite a ban on a lesbian meeting to be held in the Gründerzeit Museum in 1978 and on the group's activities in general, several members continued to pursue the group's goals. In 1986 another organization, the Mittzwanziger-Klub declared itself prepared to organize gay and lesbian events. After a successful beginning, the club was closed within a year. The group reverted to the older strategy of organizing events in restaurants, this time under the term *Sonntags im Club* (Sundays at the Club). Since 1990 the Sonntags-Club has been officially recognized and remains one of the most significant gay, lesbian and transgender community centres in Berlin.

DANIEL HENDRICKSON

HUMSAFAR TRUST

Based in Mumbai, India. Focuses on issues concerning gender, sexuality and sexual minorities. Its mission is to 'strive to educate and empower society to seek informed safer practices for better sexual health'.

SURINA KHAN

681

IGLHRC (INTERNATIONAL GAY AND LESBIAN HUMAN RIGHTS COMMISSION)

Founded in 1991, the mission of IGLHRC is 'to secure the full enjoyment of the human rights of all people and communities subject to discrimination or abuse on the basis of sexual orientation or expression, gender identity or expression, and/or HIV status'. A US-based non-profit, non-governmental organization (NGO), IGLHRC effects this mission through advocacy, documentation, coalition-building, public education and technical assistance. IGLHRC responds to human rights violations on the basis of actual or perceived sexual orientation or expression, gender identity or expression, and/or HIV and AIDS status. It documents cases and patterns of discrimination and abuse and mobilizes communities to bring to bear pressure and scrutiny in order to end discriminatory and abusive laws, policies and practices, as well as being an advocate for progressive changes in laws, policies and practices by states and non-state actors. It provides assistance to individuals seeking asylum on the basis of their sexual orientation or expression, gender identity or expression and/or HIV/AIDS status. IGLHRC has focused much of its resources in the policy realm, in particular within the United Nations, where it has been instrumental in moving sexual rights advocacy forward. After years of advocacy by IGLHRC staff, in 2001 six UN Independent Experts issued a public call for information about human rights violations against glbtq people, marking an important victory in making abuses against people with alternative sexualities and forms of gender expression visible to major human rights monitors.

SURINA KHAN

ILGA (INTERNATIONAL LESBIAN AND GAY ASSOCIATION)

ILGA is an international federation of national and local groups dedicated to achieving equal rights for lesbians, gay men, bisexuals and transgender people around the world. Founded in 1978, it has more than 400 member organizations, including members from every continent and approximately 90 countries. ILGA member groups range from small collectives to national groups and, in some cases, entire cities. ILGA focuses public and government attention upon cases of discrimination against glbtq people by supporting programmes and protest actions, asserting diplomatic pressure, providing information and working with international organizations and the international media. The hallmark of the organization is its world conferences, held in different parts of the world every one to two years, which bring together hundreds of activists from many countries and play an important role in networking international glbtq activists and organizations. The ILGA World Conference is the highest decision-making body of the organization regarding legislation, approval of new members and internal and external priorities. Each member organization expresses its opinions and concerns and votes on conference matters. The ILGA Executive Board consists of two Secretaries General (one female and one male); a Women's Secretariat and two representatives (one female and one male) from each of the six ILGA regions: Africa; Asia; Australia, New Zealand and the Pacific Islands; Europe; Latin America and the Caribbean; and North America. In the 1990s ILGA was embroiled in controversy when it applied for consultative status with the United Nations and Jesse Helms, then a right-wing Senator from North Carolina, opposed ILGA's application to the UN by attacking the organization for including the US-based National Man/Boy Love Association (NAMBLA) as a member.

SURINA KHAN

ILGCN (POLAND)

Polish division of the International Lesbian and Gay Cultural Network and organizers of the Equality Parade and Queer Culture Days (Warsaw).

DANIEL HENDRICKSON

JAMAICA FORUM OF LESBIANS, ALL-SEXUALS AND GAYS (J-FLAG)

Founded in December 1998. The first human rights organization in Jamaica's history intended to serve the needs of lesbians, gays and 'all-sexuals', a term used to indicate that all-sexual behaviour is part of a sexual continuum in which classifications such as 'gay', 'lesbian' and 'bisexual' often cannot be rigidly applied.

SURINA KHAN

JERUSALEM OPEN HOUSE

An independent organization located in Israel that runs a community centre and whose goal is to create a tolerant and pluralistic Jerusalem in which sexual and other minorities can live equally and openly.

AMIT KAMA

KHULI ZABAN

Meaning 'open tongue' in Hindi and Urdu, this is a Chicago-based organization of South Asian and West Asian lesbian, bisexual, questioning and transgender women.

SURINA KHAN

KHUSH

An email discussion list for gay, lesbian, bisexual and transgender South Asians and their friends to discuss culture, experiences, issues and to provide social and support networks.

SURINA KHAN

LAGABLAB (PHILIPPINES) (LESBIAN AND GAY LEGISLATIVE ADVOCACY NETWORK).

The largest network of glbtq groups in the Philippines. It was instrumental in advocating for the passage of a comprehensive anti-discrimination bill on the basis of sexual orientation and gender identity; the bill was approved by the House of Representatives in 2003.

SURINA KHAN

LAVENDER HILL MOB

A group formed in 1986 primarily to oppose government inaction in finding treatments for people with AIDS. Co-founders and former Gay Activists Alliance (GAA) members Marty Robinson and Bill Bahlman brought the 'zap' – a media-savvy political confrontation Robinson had perfected in GAA – and civil disobedience tactics to this new organization, whose activism eventually led to the creation of ACT UP, which was co-founded by members of the Mob.

DAVID CARTER

LEGATRA

Lesbian, Gays and Transsexuals of Zambia. The first, short-lived gay rights association in Zambia. Founded in 1998 by 26-year-old agriculture student Francis Yabe Chisambisha, LEGATRA created an unprecedented homophobic uproar in the press. After the formation of a vigilante group to oppose it, LEGATRA closed down in 1999 and Chisambisha sought political asylum in South Africa.

MARC EPPRECHT

LESBIANS, GAYS AND BISEXUALS OF BOTSWANA

Established in 1998 as Botswana's first gay rights lobby and counselling association.

MARC EPPRECHT

LILA (LEGA ITALIANA PER LA LOTTA CONTRO L'AIDS)

An Italian nationwide association formed to fight AIDS and to assist HIV+ people.

ALBERTO EMILETTI

MASALA (MASSACHUSETTS AREA SOUTH ASIAN LAMBDA ASSOCIATION)

Based in Boston, Massachusetts. Works to provide a safe and supportive social environment for gay, lesbian, bisexual, transgender and questioning New England-based South Asians.

SURINA KHAN

MOVIMENTO LESBICO SEPARATISTA

A feminist lesbian and separatist movement set up during the 1970s. Lesbians began to measure themselves politically, taking the problems of their own lived experience as a starting point for political action.

MONIA ANDREANI

NATIONAL CENTER FOR LESBIAN RIGHTS (NCLR)

A US-based national legal centre with a primary commitment to advancing the rights and safety of lesbians and their families through litigation, public policy advocacy, legal advice and counselling, and public education. Also provides representation and resources for gay men and bisexual and transgender individuals on key issues that also advance lesbian rights.

SURINA KHAN

NATIONAL COALITION FOR GAY AND LESBIAN EQUALITY (NCGLE)

Established in 1994 as an umbrella body of South African lesbian and gay organizations. Successfully spearheaded a lobbying campaign to ensure that 'sexual orientation'

was included in the Bill of Rights of South Africa's Constitution.

GRAEME REID

OCCUR

OCCUR is the English name used by Japan's most prominent lesbian and gay movement (Ugoku Gei to Rezubian no Kai) which broke away from the Japan branch of the International Lesbian and Gay Association (JILGA) in 1986 due to disagreements over the latter's authoritarian management style. OCCUR has waged a number of successful campaigns, such as the reform of Japanese dictionary definitions of homosexuality so as to remove derogatory nuances and, in 1994, it launched and won a court case against the Tokyo Metropolitan Government, which had denied the group access to overnight youth facilities. However, OCCUR has also been criticized for its narrow politics. Lesbian author and activist Sarah Schulman, for instance, was accused of 'serious crimes' by members of the organization during a trip to Tokyo in 1992 for supporting a lesbian and gay film festival of which sponsors OCCUR disapproved.

MARK McLELLAND

OLAVA (ORGANIZED LESBIAN ALLIANCE FOR VISIBILITY AND ACCEPTANCE)

Formed in 1999 in response to vandalism following the release of Deepa Mehta's film *Fire*, OLAVA became the first group for lesbian, bisexual and transgendered women in Pune, India.

SURINA KHAN

PROGAY PHILIPPINES (PROGRESSIVE ORGANIZATION OF GAYS IN THE PHILIPPINES)

Founded in 1993 to advocate for the full recognition of economic, social and political rights of all sexual minorities. Among its numerous accomplishments, it led the first Gay March in Asia in June 1994.

SURINA KHAN

RAINBOW PROJECT, THE

Namibia's first gay rights association, established in 1997, this quickly became an outspoken critic of authoritarian rule and a leading voice in the pro-democracy, Non-Government Organizations Forum.

MARC EPPRECHT

SALGA (SOUTH ASIAN LESBIAN AND GAY ASSOCIATION)

A New York City-based social, political and support group for lesbian, gay, bisexual and transgender people of South Asian descent.

SURINA KHAN

SANGAMA

Based in Bangalore, India. Opposes discrimination based upon sexual orientation and gender identity by lobbying for changes to existing discriminatory laws, changing public discourse and advocating for the rights of sex workers and people living with HIV and AIDS.

SURINA KHAN

SANGINI

Based in New Delhi, India. Founded in 1997 to support lesbians in India. The organization provides information, counselling, support, help and advice, through a telephone helpline, for lesbians and women exploring their sexuality.

SURINA KHAN

SATSANGA

Founded in 1994. Means 'soul mates' in Sanskrit. A Hong Kong-based non-profit organization that promotes psychosocial health for lesbians and gay men.

TRAVIS KONG

SOCIETY FOR THE PROTECTION OF PERSONAL RIGHTS

An Israeli political and social umbrella organization (established 1975), also known as 'Agudah', it runs several community centres around Israel and publishes a monthly magazine, *Zman Varod* (Pink Time).

AMIT KAMA

TALLER LÉSBICO CREATIVO

Focusing upon rural areas of Puerto Rico, uses popular theatre and workshops to promote discussion amongst lesbian and bisexual women and the glbtq community in Puerto Rico.

SURINA KHAN

TEN PERCENT CLUB

Founded in 1986. The first non-governmental gay and lesbian organization in Hong Kong.

TRAVIS KONG

TRAVESCHILE

The national transgender organization of Chile. Based in Santiago, it has representation in several Chilean cities and advocates for the rights of transgender people.

SURINA KHAN

TREATMENT ACTION CAMPAIGN (TAC)

A grassroots South African political lobby group and development education organization established in 1998. TAC pioneered the worldwide campaign for affordable anti-retroviral drugs in the developing world, including successful court challenges to the multinational pharmaceutical companies and against a recalcitrant South African government. In 2004 its founder and chairperson, Zackie Achmat, was nominated for the Nobel Peace Prize.

MARC EPPRECHT

TRIKONE

Founded in 1986 in the San Francisco Bay Area. Works for glbtq people of South Asian descent through social and political activities. Also publishes a quarterly magazine.

SURINA KHAN

VISIBILIA

A separatist lesbian cultural association formed in Bologna, Italy, in 1989. Since 1993 it has organized Immaginaria, the International Lesbian Film Festival.

MONICA BARONI

WOMEN'S SUPPORT GROUP (WSG)

Founded in 1999. The only organization in Sri Lanka working to support and advance the rights of lesbian, bisexual and transgender women.

SURINA KHAN

XX GATHERING

Founded in 1993–4 to hold regular meetings for lesbians and bisexual women, and hosted by different women groups. XX Gathering later became a function of Queer Sisters. The name is derived from the fact that the presence of two X chromosomes denotes a female foetus.

TRAVIS KONG

index

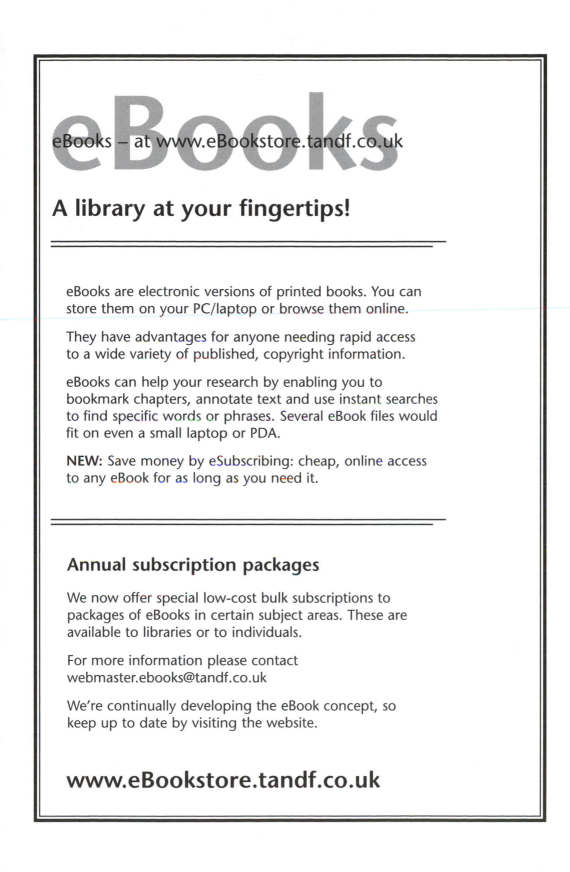